Faith in Public Debate

On Freedom of Expression, Hate Speech and Religion in France & the Netherlands

School of Human Rights Research Series, Volume 68

The titles published in this series are listed at the end of this volume.

Faith in Public Debate

On Freedom of Expression, Hate Speech and Religion in France & the Netherlands

Esther Janssen

intersentia
Cambridge – Antwerp – Portland

Intersentia Publishing Ltd
Sheraton House | Castle Park
Cambridge | CB3 0AX | United Kingdom
Tel.: +44 1223 370 170 | mail@intersentia.co.uk

Esther Janssen
Faith in Public Debate. On Freedom of Expression, Hate Speech and Religion in France & the Netherlands
www.estherjanssen.nl | www.faithinpublicdebate.com

ISBN 978-1-78068-309-6
D/2015/7849/41
NUR 828

Cover image: © Simon Rogers/TwitterData.
Twitter Heatmap showing the #jesuischarlie hashtag being tweeted at its height. The hashtag has become one of the most popular in the history of Twitter as people around the world showed their solidarity with the victims of the Paris massacre at the offices of the French satirical magazine Charlie Hebdo where 12 people were slaughtered when Islamist terrorists stormed their offences in Paris on 7 January 2015 sparking a series of attacks lasting three days. At its height the hashtag was tweeted at a rate of 6500 times a minute and featured in 3.4 million tweets in just one 24-hour period.

British Library Cataloguing in Publication Data. A catalogue record for this book is available from the British Library.

'This study contains a thorough and detailed description, comparison and analysis of Dutch and French legislation and case law concerning hate speech. It focuses on the most sensitive issues of freedom of expression and its limitations: hate speech related to race and religion. The book highlights the differences in the Dutch and French approach, takes into account the jurisprudence of the European Court of Human Rights, criticizes the inconsistencies in the case law, and formulates concepts and proposals with regard to the scope and boundaries of the freedom of expression. It is a comprehensive source of information and provides insight for all who deal with these issues in practice and in theoretical studies.'
Ben Vermeulen, Member of the Council of State, Professor of Law, Radboud University Nijmegen

'Esther Janssen has written an impressive book, which is as thorough as it is captivating. Its publication is very timely because hate speech has become a pressing issue in so many jurisdictions. Including France, rather than the U.S or the UK, in the comparison is both fortunate and refreshing.'
Tom Zwart, Professor of Human Rights, Utrecht University and Director of the Netherlands School of Human Rights Research

'Hate speech and blasphemy have long been topical issues, but they are even more so in the aftermath of what happened to Charlie Hebdo. If only for that reason, a book like this one, which objectively and neutrally analyses the consistency of legal rules and case-law in this difficult area, should be warmly welcomed. This book is all the more valuable because of the author's choice to provide a comprehensive comparison of the legal responses in France and the Netherlands – two national systems with very different traditions of regulation and different attitudes towards freedom of expression. Esther Janssen thus provides a sound and comprehensive overview of the history and functioning of both systems, as well as of the European Court of Human Rights, which makes this book a good read for anyone interested in blasphemy and hate speech in modern-day Western European legal systems.'
Janneke Gerards, Professor of European Law, Radboud University Nijmegen

'Giant steps are what you take
Walking on the moon
I hope my legs don't break
Walking on the moon
We could walk forever
Walking on the moon
We could live together
Walking on, walking on the moon'
...

Roseaux featuring Aloe Blacc / Original 'Walking on the Moon' by Sting

Acknowledgements

First and foremost, I would like to thank my advisor, Nico van Eijk, for giving me the opportunity to do this research, for his flexibility and constructive approach. Secondly, I would like to thank my daily supervisor, Aernout Nieuwenhuis, for his time, dedication, expert guidance, and feedback. I am very grateful to him for teaching me the craft of scientific research and for his critical input on written texts, which has undeniably enhanced their quality.

In addition, I have benefited enormously from the expertise of and inspiring discussions with Egbert Dommering. I would like to thank him for so generously sharing his world of ideas, for his interest and confidence in mine and for stimulating me to work from a concept of justice. I am also particularly grateful to Committee member Janneke Gerards for her thorough and sharp commentary on my manuscript, which has enabled me to improve its overall scientific quality.

Furthermore, I would like to thank Annabel Brody and Matthijs Janssen for their tremendous editing job, which makes this study look so much smarter, and Tarlach McGonagle for his kind support and, generally, for caring. On this note, I would also like to thank Janne Nijman and Bernt Hugenholtz for making time for me and for lending their ears on crucial moments. I probably could not have finished this project without their professional advice.

I want to thank Frederik Borgesius and Catherine Jasserand for being such great roommates and Bart van der Sloot for being the perfect neighbour-colleague during the years covering this research; for their talks over coffee, useful legal discussions as well as providing comic relief. In this respect, other (ex-) colleagues from the University of Amsterdam and beyond that I would especially like to thank are: Christina Angelopoulous, David Korteweg, Gerard Mom, Hana van Ooijen, Martine Beijerman, Uladzislau Belavusau and Wolfgang Sakulin.

I am very grateful to have met so many knowledgeable people with whom I was able to share information and ideas: Ben Vermeulen, Birgit van Roessel, Els Lucas, Françoise Tulkens, Gerard Spong, Jeroen Temperman, Marloes van Noorloos, Paul Velleman, Rick Lawson, Theo Rosier and Ties Prakken. During my time at the Sorbonne, Paris I was fortunate enough to meet many experts in the field. I have greatly relied on the expertise of and have received immensely valuable input from: Anne de Fontette (district attorney Paris prosecution office), Anne-Marie Sauteraud (judge Paris District Court press chamber), Bernard Schmid (MRAP), Prof. Emmanuelle Dreyer, Macha Pariente (LICRA), drs. Nathalie Droin, Nicolas Tavieaux Moro (barrister), Prof. Véronique Champeil-Desplats. Thank you very much.

It has been a true privilege to have spent the past few years studying the interesting topic of hate speech; I have enjoyed every second. But there have also been some difficult moments during the completion of this PhD project and I want to thank all who have eased those moments with their warm friendship, starting with my two Para nymphs Adriaan Dokter, for dancing the tango and endlessly discussing life in the Engelbewaarder with me, and Nienke van der Meulen, for all her encouragement, comfort and conviviality, Caitilin McGivern, Janine Dortmundt, Joost Overdijkink, Martin van Harten, Melchior Bussink, Myrddin van Westendorp, Robert Pieters, Roos Kraanen, Sanne van Ruitenbeek, Sarah Lindenboom, Stef LeFevre and Tanja de Vette.

Finally, I would like to thank my family: my parents Harry and Gusta and my brother Matthijs, Olesja, Diana and Margje for their patience, unconditional love and support. Our side-projects such as renovating my apartment and creating Amsterdam's most beautiful garden (& shed), the drinks and couch surfing in Bilthoven and the dinners and movie nights in The Hague have provided the necessary distraction to eventually realize this project.

Amsterdam, June 2014

This thesis was conducted at the Institute for Information Law (IVIR), Law Faculty of the University of Amsterdam.

The research for this thesis was officially completed in January 2014; only the most necessary updates were made after this date.

Contents

CHAPTER 1
GENERAL INTRODUCTION

Faith in Public Debate forms an inquiry into the relationship between freedom of expression and hate speech pertaining to religion and race in France, the Netherlands and international and European law. This chapter gives a brief introduction into the research topic (1.1). Subsequently, it explains the aim of the research (1.2) and determines the research question (1.3). Furthermore, it reveals the outline of this study and elaborates on the chosen methodology (1.4). The chapter concludes with a demarcation of the scope of the research; it also considers the relevance of the study in the light of the already existing literature on the topic (1.5).

1.1. Introduction

Should a politician be free to fiercely attack the religion of a sector of the population? Should he be allowed to strongly reject the culture of a particular minority group? Should religious adherents be allowed to advocate the transition from a democratic to a theocratic state? Should a pastor or imam be able to compare homosexuality with criminality or a disease? Should citizens be free to vituperate a particular religious or racial group on the Internet? These sort of questions concern 'the place of faith in public debate' and continue to dominate public discussion that has been fuelled by a series of events, including the terrorist attacks in New York, Madrid and London (2001, 2004 and 2005); the public statements and assassination of Dutch politician and Islam critic Pim Fortuyn (2002); the assassination of Dutch film director Theo van Gogh (*Submission*) by Islamic fundamentalist Mohammed Bouyeri (2004); the affair of the Danish Cartoons (2006); the prosecution of Dutch politician Geert Wilders for his film *Fitna* (2009); the worldwide demonstrations and violent protests against the film *Innocence of Muslims* by Nakoula (2012); and the massacre in Paris where 12 people were slaughtered when Islamist terrorists stormed the offices of French satirical magazine *Charlie Hebdo* sparking a series of attacks lasting three days and the "republican march" from Place de la République to Place de la Nation via boulevard Voltaire, attended by 1–2 million people and held in defiance of terror and in defence of free speech (2015).

The overarching question triggered by these events concerns the relationship between freedom of expression and the regulation of 'hate speech'; which forms of hate speech should the state prohibit, on what grounds and by which means? Notably, the restriction of hate speech uttered in the context of the public debate about multiculturalism, immigration, integration and Islam, and of religious fundamentalism has become a topic of lively discussion.[1] Some advocate the 'right to offend', which would leave little room for criminal speech offences and would question existing hate speech bans. In the Netherlands, several proposals have been made to abolish the offences of blasphemy, group insult, and incitement to hatred or discrimination. Others invoke the 'right not to be offended' in one's feelings and question the permissibility of gross utterances. Certain Dutch proposals are therefore precisely aimed at the extension of the offence of group insult or the creation of an offence of Holocaust denial.

Hate speech bans undeniably constitute restrictions to the right to freedom of expression. However, the precise boundary between controversial contributions to public debate and punishable utterances is not certain. The question of how restrictions to hate speech must be balanced with the right to freedom of expression has led to strong differences of opinion within the European Court of Human Rights (ECtHR). In the exemplary case of *Féret v. Belgium*,[2] the ECtHR found, by a thin majority of 4:3, the conviction of Belgium politician Daniel Féret for inciting hatred against Muslims through statements such as 'Attacks in USA: it is the couscous clan' to be a permissible restriction to the right of freedom of expression. According to the dissenters, however, Féret's remarks lacked a racist purport. Such differences of opinion raise the question as to whether restrictions to hate speech can be interpreted, applied or reviewed in an unambiguous and consistent manner.

In fact, it is difficult to establish when exactly offensive utterances become prohibited forms of defamation or insult. It is also difficult to draw the boundary between strong criticism of government policy and punishable forms of incitement to hatred and discrimination. This ambiguity also emerges, in particular, in cases where the religion of the target group of expression plays a role. Differences of opinion may exist in relation to the interpretation and valuation of utterances. When an utterance is interpreted as a formulation of honest concern about immigration and Islam, freedom of expression probably weighs more heavily than when it is understood as a demagogue's deceit of the public. When one prioritizes the feelings of minorities, an utterance about the prophet or the Koran might affect them more than an utterance about Muslims as a group.

Differences of opinion may thus furthermore exist in relation to the rationales of existing hate speech bans and the particular interests they aim to protect: the feelings, good name or dignity of a group, the tenets of a religion, the remembrance of a historical event, the public order or safety, the functioning of democracy or the values of the constitutional state. If hate speech bans are primarily directed against possible disturbances of the public order, the protection of social peace or the political order, their scope may be confined to utterances that unequivocally incite others to violent actions, but understood broadly could be used to temper

1 Dommering, E.J., De Teddybeer Mohammed, gesluierde homo's en het lawaai van Wilders: Over de stand van de vrijheid van meningsuiting anno 2008, *Nederlands Juristenblad*, 2008–7, p. 376–382.

2 ECtHR 16 July 2009, no. 15615/07 (Féret v. Belgium).

oppositional political views that are too vehement. If hate speech bans, however, form part of the broader anti-discrimination policy that primarily looks to the protection of minorities to enhance their social functioning, the scope of the bans may extend to utterances that affect the dignity of minorities through invectives, abuse and negative imaging or that are aimed at affecting the rights of minorities.

In the famous case against Geert Wilders,[3] leader of the populist Dutch Freedom Party (PVV), the judicial authorities disagreed on all of these points, i.e. the rationale and scope of the Dutch hate speech bans, the application of the bans to Wilders' statements and the interpretation of Wilders' statements. While the court that had ordered Wilders' prosecution considered his statements such as 'Stop the tsunami of islamization' to be punishable forms of hate speech against Muslims, the prosecution, who had initially refused to prosecute Wilders, and the court found it to be permissible criticism of Islam and the Government's failing immigration and integration policy. In the Netherlands, more than before, public and political debate is hard lined.[4] Social conceptions on the criminality of insulting and offensive utterances appear to have changed, which is reflected in case law; the acquittal of Wilders forms a perfect example of this. The case raised the question of the desirability of existing hate speech bans, but also of the feasibility of their enforcement. The public prosecution has announced that they will prosecute Wilders, following the thousands of complaints that were filed against him for promising that he would arrange for there to be 'fewer Moroccans' in the Netherlands to his chanting supporters ('fewer, fewer, fewer') at a local election night.[5] It is striking that Dutch politicians generally tend not to take a public stand against the excessiveness of certain expression; they rather attempt to ignore it.

This raises curiosity about how restrictions to hate speech are determined in other countries. In France the political discourse on the immigration and integration of Muslims is also hard lined and notably conducted by the far-right Front National (FN);[6] its leader Marine Le Pen, who is also a member of the European Parliament, has even expressed party's ambition to pair up with Wilders during the European parliamentary elections.[7] Contrary to the *Wilders* case, the French prosecutors precisely requested that the European parliament lift the parliamentary immunity of Marine Le Pen, so she could be prosecuted for incitement to hatred for having

---

3 Amsterdam District Court 23 May 2011, *LJN* BQ5561.

4 ECRI Report on The Netherlands (fourth monitoring cycle), adopted 20 June 2013, section III, Climate of opinion and racism in public discourse, p. 35 *et seq.*, section VI, Vulnerable/target groups, Muslim community, p. 43.

5 E.H. Janssen, Wilders, waardigheid en de grenzen van het politiek debat, *Nederlands Juristenblad* 2014–24, p. 1814–1820.

6 ECRI Report on France (fourth monitoring cycle), adopted 29 April 2010, section IV, Racism in public discourse, p. 26 *et seq.*, section V, Muslim communities, p. 29–30.

7 'Marine Le Pen wil Wilders helpen bij campagne Europese verkiezingen', *NRC Handelsblad* 14 September 2013.

compared street prayer by Muslims with the Nazi occupation.[8] Earlier, FN's former leader and French politician Jean-Marie Le Pen had been convicted on charges of incitement to hatred, discrimination and violence for having depicted Muslims as a danger to French society,[9] which according to the ECtHR did not constitute a violation of freedom of expression.[10] Furthermore, the French public prosecution also prosecuted the extreme right magazine *Minute* for public insult on the basis of race with regard to a photo of the French Minister of Justice Christiane Taubira under the headline 'Maligne comme un singe, Taubira retrouve la banane' on the cover of its issue of November 2013. The cover referred to a series of insults previously uttered against Taubira. French politicians unanimously condemned the publication and several French anti-racism associations, including *SOS Racisme*, *LICRA* and *MRAP*, and filed complaints to the police. The prosecution took action on the basis of the complaint of the French Prime Minister himself. The Paris District Court considered that the Minister's comparison with a monkey was a clear racist stereotype that aimed at her origin or race rather than a criticism of her government policy. The publication overstepped the limits to humorous expression and the director of publication was convicted to a fine of 10.000 euros.[11]

In sum, the increasing confusion and difference of opinion about the scope of existing hate speech bans, their underlying rationales, and their relationship with freedom of expression, calls for a reassessment of the relationship between freedom of expression and so-called hate speech. To this end, a comparison between national approaches to hate speech can be of value.

1.2. Aim of research

The aim of this research is to develop new insights in relation to what extent – that is whether, and if so how – restrictions to hate speech, notably on the basis of religion and uttered in the context of a public debate, can be determined in a consistent manner. To this end, this research compares Dutch law with French law that is relevant to the issue of hate speech. The research discusses the background

---

8 'Marine Le Pen compare les 'prières de rue' des musulmans à une 'occupation', *Le Monde* 11 December 2010; ''Incitation à la haine raciale': que risque vraiment Marine Le Pen?', *Le Monde* 2 July 2013.

9 French Supreme Court, crim. Ch., 3 February 2009, n°06–83063 08–82402, *Bull. Crim.* 2009, n°25.

10 ECtHR 20 April 2010, no. 18788/09 (Le Pen v. France).

11 TGI de Paris, 30 October 2014, *Légipresse* n° 321 – November 2014, p. 588. The series of insults included the event that a little girl had shouted at Taubira, during her visit to Angers, 'C'est pour qui la banane? C'est pour la guenon' and the event that a candidate of the FN had recently been removed from the municipal elections for having compared Taubira with a monkey. The same court found another magazine not guilty of racial insult with regard to a cartoon mocking the Taubira affair by depicting a weeping monkey next to a laywer saying: 'My client files complaint for being hatefully characterized as Madam Taubira!'. TGI de Paris, 30 October 2014, *Légipresse* n° 321 – November 2014, p. 588–589.

of the national hate speech bans and the reason for their introduction by the legislator. This analysis aims to reveal the exact interests the legislator has aimed to protect with the speech offences and how they relate to freedom of expression. Furthermore, this research analyses the application and interpretation of the hate speech bans by the judge and the weight given to freedom of expression in individual cases. The analysis is principally confined to the discriminatory grounds of 'religion' and 'race', due to the fact that a certain interaction and overlap exist between these two discriminatory grounds.

National restrictions to hate speech are to a significant extent influenced by historically developed traditions of constitutional thought about fundamental rights, in particular freedom of expression, and must be placed against the background of the characteristics of the constitutional state. This research therefore examines the protection of freedom of expression in Dutch and French law more generally: the demarcation of its scope and the possible grounds for restrictions as they result from its limitation clause and its interrelationship with other fundamental rights, values and interests incorporated into the Constitution. It focuses on the criminalization of hate speech by the state, but it also examines the relationship between criminal and civil restrictions to freedom of expression. Furthermore, the restrictions to hate speech on grounds of race and religion cannot be understood without placing them against the background of national conceptions on minorities and state and religion relationships.

The practical enforcement of hate speech bans is determined, on the one hand, by the competence of the public prosecution and its prosecution policy and, on the other hand, by the possibilities of victims or anti-racism and minority associations to bring complaints against particular utterances. Overall, restrictions to hate speech are determined by the interplay of different actors: the legislator, the public prosecution, the judge, and victims or anti-racism and minority associations. In their respective functions and positions, all balance the interests served by the restriction of hate speech with the right to freedom of expression. The interrelationship of these actors differs per country and can be comprehended as arising from the characteristics of the constitutional state. As these actors and their interrelationship influence the consistency of national restrictions to hate speech, they play an important role in the comparative study. The comparative study provides insight as to how national legal cultures influence national restrictions to hate speech, but also evaluates French and Dutch law in order to draw inspiration from the different legal frameworks.

There is a presumption that a solid balancing act must be made between the right to freedom of expression and the interests served in restrictions to the right. This presumption is confirmed by international law. National restrictions to hate speech are partly determined by international and European human rights law. For the purposes of this study, five international and European instruments, that are particularly relevant to the regulation of hate speech in Europe, have been selected and analysed. The right to freedom of expression is incorporated in several conventions, including the International Covenant on Civil and Political Rights (ICCPR) and the European Convention on Human Rights (ECHR). These do not concern unlimited rights to freedom of expression. In fact, certain international norms oblige state parties to criminalize forms of hate speech; an important example is the International Convention on the Elimination of All Forms of Racial Discrimination (ICERD). Both the Netherlands and France are state parties to these treaties.

Furthermore, as member states of the European Union (EU), both states are also bound by the EU Council Framework Decision on combating certain forms and expressions of racism and xenophobia by means of criminal law. These norms are thus directly relevant to this research, which aims to analyse how the obligations must be interpreted and how they relate to freedom of expression. In addition, within different sections of the Council of Europe, non-binding standards with regard to the regulation of hate speech have been developed in the form of resolutions and recommendations, as well as an Additional Protocol to the Convention on cybercrime, concerning the criminalization of acts of a racist and xenophobic nature committed through computer systems. Most attention is, however, paid to Article 10 ECHR, which protects the right to freedom of expression and the Article 10 case law of the ECtHR, which occupies centre stage of European law. The impact of Article 10 ECHR on national law and the extent to which the judge attaches importance to the ECtHR's case law when applying national speech offences may, however, differ from country to country.

This research is not confined to a description of the positive law. In reaction to the previously mentioned series of events, many new publications have supplemented the already existing wealth of scientific literature on this topic.[12] From the discussion in literature, four substantive factors are distilled that notably form the subject of controversies and therefore can be assumed to be particularly relevant for the consistent determination of restrictions to hate speech. Furthermore, theories on freedom of expression are advanced to the extent that they are relevant to the regulation of hate speech. The four factors are analysed and presented as opposite pairs: the performance of physical *actions* versus the expression of *opinions*; contributions to *public debate* versus *other* types of expression, such as utterances that can be qualified as 'private speech' that is directly directed at a particular individual or an abuse of rights and therefore do not form contributions to a public debate; imputations of specific *facts* versus the expression of *value judgments*; and utterances about *race* versus utterances about *religion*. These factors regroup the more traditional presentation in literature of, on the one hand, the justifications for the right to freedom of expression and, on the other hand, the

12 Important recent collective works comprise: Hare, I. & Weinstein, J. (Eds.), *Extreme Speech and Democracy*, Oxford: Oxford University Press 2009; Herz, M., & Molnar, P. (Eds.), *The Content and Context of Hate Speech: Rethinking Regulation and Responses*, Cambridge: Cambridge University Press 2012; Maitra, I., & McGowan, M. K., *Speech & Harm: Controversies over Free Speech*, Oxford: Oxford University Press 2012.

harms in hate speech that justify restrictions to this right. Together the factors form an analytical framework for the analysis of the positive law.

To conclude, this research explores whether, and if so how, French law, Dutch law and international and European law make consistent choices as far as these factors/opposite pairs are concerned for the determination of restrictions to hate speech. After all, the fact that the discussion notably revolves around these factors is a result of the examined international literature about hate speech. The subject of investigation is not whether the different legal systems are consistent with one another, but whether they are consistent themselves. The systems are, however, certainly compared in order to evaluate how restrictions can be drawn in a consistent manner and which role the different actors can play therein. It would, for example, be inconsistent for the judge to consider in one case that no principle distinction exists between statements about a particular race and statements about a particular religion for the determination of their criminality, and to consider this distinction paramount in a comparable case. It would also be inconsistent for the legislator to envision hate speech bans to protect particular interests and to have a certain scope, and for the judge to then attribute a different rationale to the bans and to interpret and apply them either more strictly or more broadly. For example, when the legislator has justified the criminalization of hate speech amongst others by reference to the effect such speech has on the public order in relation to the social climate, it would be wrong for the judge to order a requirement of proof of any direct effect on the public order in relation to a breach of the peace as an extra criteria for liability under the hate speech bans. In the context of hate speech, the term public order can thus be interpreted and used differently, which can lead to inconsistencies.

Consistency forms an important value where the setting of restrictions to hate speech is concerned, which is precisely why this value has been chosen as a point of comparison for this research. In fact, consistency in the setting of restrictions to hate speech assures a fundamental basic principle of law: legal certainty. In accordance with the principle of legal certainty, the law must be sufficiently clear and accessible for the citizens to whom it is addressed. If legal norms are imprecise or ambiguous, rights are not assured. After all, uncertain rules are susceptible to unequal application. They also breach individual freedom by not precisely determining restrictions and therefore can have a chilling effect. Hence, legal certainty relating to restrictions to hate speech guarantee the rights and interests those restrictions aim to protect, as well as the exercise of the fundamental right to freedom of expression. These considerations also underlie the principle of legality, from which results the necessity for the legislator to define criminal offences, i.e. hate speech bans, in sufficiently clear and precise terms. The principles of legal certainty and legality also form the basis of the requirement for the judge to, in his application of hate speech bans in concrete cases, give a clear, robust motivation of his decisions. This ensures that, despite changing contextual circumstances, a consistent line arises from the body of case law that can form a basis for citizens to attune their behaviour. On a more fundamental level, a problem underlying possible inconsistencies in restrictions to hate speech may form a difference of opinion about the exact interests restrictions to hate speech aim to protect and how their rationales must be translated into concrete requirements of statutory offences that determine their scope. The question of consistency in restrictions to hate speech thus cannot be addressed separately from the more substantive issue of how the conflicting rights and interests must be balanced and whether the law reflects the outcome of that balancing-test in a sufficiently clear and precise manner.

So far this general introduction has used the terms 'hate speech' and 'hate speech bans' as if they were self-evident. The contrary is true. Despite the frequent use of the term in international literature, there is no universally accepted definition of 'hate speech'.[13] The precise concept of 'hate speech' thus remains vague. One problematic aspect is that the notion of 'hate speech' is used both in a descriptive and a normative manner in international literature and legal documents; sometimes 'hate speech' simply refers to a social phenomenon, sometimes it refers to a category of speech that – in the eyes of the author – should be prohibited by law. This research does not provide its own definition of hate speech. The exact meaning of the term shall depend on and become apparent from the context in which it is used.

Hare & Weinstein regard hate speech as a specific category of the broader category 'extreme' speech, i.e. 'speech that many believe poses an unacceptable threat to essential values in modern multicultural democracies, or in some cases to democracy itself'. Hate speech in particular consists of 'expression which articulates hatred for another individual or group, usually based on a characteristic (such as race) which is perceived to be shared by members of the target group'.[14] Many scholars share this idea that hate speech consists of expression, which is necessarily directed against a person or particular group of persons.[15] From this perspective 'hate speech' must be distinguished from other categories of 'extreme' speech possibly motivated by hatred, such as speech directed against the state, public authorities and officials, 'subversive' speech that incites to overthrow the existing form of government, speech that incites to lawless action, glorifies or incites to terrorism.

In its Recommendation 97(20) on 'hate speech', the Committee of Ministers of the Council of Europe defined the term 'hate speech' as 'covering all forms of expression which spread, incite, promote or justify racial hatred, xenophobia, anti-

13 Weber, A., *Manual on hate speech,* Council of Europe, Leiden: Martinus Nijhoff Publishers 2009, p. 3; Molnar, P & Post, R., Interview with Robert Post, in: Herz & Molnar 2012, p. 31.

14 Weinstein, J. & Hare, I., General introduction: free speech, democracy, and the suppression of extreme speech past and present, in: Hare & Weinstein 2009, p. 4.

15 For example Parekh, B., Is There a Case for Banning Hate Speech?, in: Herz & Molnar 2012, p. 40.

Semitism or other forms of hatred based on intolerance, including: intolerance expressed by aggressive nationalism and ethnocentrism, discrimination and hostility against minorities, migrants and people of immigrant origin'.[16] Although most European states have adopted national legislation prohibiting expressions that amount to 'hate speech' thus broadly defined, definitions in national 'hate speech bans' differ when determining what exactly is being prohibited. A glance at national hate speech bans brings Waldron to conclude that 'all of them are concerned with the use of words that are deliberately abusive and/or insulting and/or threatening and/or demeaning directed at members of vulnerable minorities, calculated to stir up hatred against them'.[17]

Under the umbrella term of 'hate speech', this research analyses national prohibitions of 'group defamation', 'group insult', and 'incitement to hatred, discrimination or violence', as well as relevant jurisprudence relating to these prohibitions. It also examines the demarcation of the term with 'blasphemy' and its relation to 'Holocaust denial'. Precisely in order to further delineate the notion of hate speech, certain attention is necessarily paid to sedition laws and case law on forms of extreme or subversive speech.

1.3. Research question

Against this background, this research aims to answer the following research question:

> *'To which extent can restrictions to hate speech on the ground of religion be determined in a consistent manner?'*

To answer this central research question, this research examines a number of sub-questions. A first question is what are the restrictions to hate speech – on the ground of religion – in French law, Dutch law and international, and European human rights law *(Q1)*. The next question is how the four factors, i.e. *actions* versus *opinions*; *public debate* versus *other* types of expression; *facts* versus *value judgments*; and *race* versus *religion*, influence the determination of restrictions to hate speech in the examined legal systems *(Q2)*. Subsequently, the question arises as to what extent the restrictions in the examined legal systems are drawn in a consistent manner *(Q3)*. The final question considers on what basis this research can provide for a further elaboration of consistent restrictions to hate speech *(Q4)*.

16 Recommendation No. R 97(20) of the Committee of Ministers of the Council of Europe on 'hate speech'.

17 Waldron, J., *The Harm in Hate Speech*, Cambridge: Harvard University Press 2012, p. 8–9.

1.4. Outline and methodology

To answer these questions, this research uses the following outline and method. *Chapter 2* presents the analytical framework and discusses the relevance of the factors that determine restrictions to hate speech. Four factors are analysed and theories about freedom of expression are advanced to the extent that they are relevant to the regulation of hate speech, using legal theory, that sometimes is influenced by and overlaps with language theory, philosophy and social science as sources. Where relevant, reference is made to examples from positive law. The chapter critically examines the relevant literature, but does not value the theories discussed. The main aim of the chapter is to highlight and examine where problems of consistency occur with the four factors.

Chapter 3 discusses international and European law, using as selected sources international treaties, their drafting histories, case law, annotations, soft law instruments, and international legal literature, including scientific articles, dissertations and manuals *(Q1–2)*. It discusses the different legal instruments separately; only the non-binding standards of the different sections of the Council of Europe are discussed together, thus highlighting the diverging approaches within this broader legal system. A specific synthesis of the ECHR is reserved for the final conclusion of this research. Chapter 3 concludes with a more general synthesis of the obligations concerning hate speech arising from international and European human rights law.

Chapters 4 and *5* together comprise the most significant part of this research and consist of the comparative study on French respectively Dutch law *(Q1–2)*. These chapters analyse the content and scope of the existing national hate speech bans, their underlying rationales, and their relationship with freedom of expression. Furthermore, particular attention is paid to the interplay between the different actors in the determination of the restrictions to hate speech. The chapters already provide the reference points for the synthesis of the comparative study – on the basis of the four factors of the analytical framework – in Chapter 6. The study uses as sources: national legislation, its drafting history, case law, annotations, policy and other legal documents, national legal literature, including scientific articles, dissertations, monographs and manuals.

The comparative study has a distinctive structure. Both chapters are divided into three parts. This three-partition is based on the devise of the French Republic '*Freedom, Equality, Brotherhood*' that inspires French public law and is also understood to reflect three pillars of the democratic constitutional state.[18] Elaborating on the signification of these notions in the comparative study, the chosen structure thereby enables to discuss the relationship between freedom of

[18] Borgetto, M., *La devise "Liberté, Égalité, Fraternité"*, Que sais-je?, n° 3196, Paris: Presses Universitaires de France 1997; Gonthier, C.D., Liberty, Equality, Fraternity: The Forgotten Leg of the Trilogy, or Fraternity: The Unspoken Third Pillar of Democracy, *Mc Gill Law Journal* 2000, vol. 45, p. 567.

expression and restrictions to hate speech in national law against the background of the national conception of democracy.

Chapter 6 formulates the conclusion of the research (*central research question)* and is divided into two parts. The first part provides a synthesis of the comparative study in Chapters 4 and 5 *(Q3)*. This synthesis is presented separately from the comparative study itself, because it is not confined to an overview of the similarities and differences between French and Dutch law, but is followed by a comparison with the approach under the ECHR. It includes a further analysis of the consistency of restrictions to hate speech in these legal systems on the basis of the four factors. This joint analysis forms the basis for the concluding observations made in the second part. The second part advances, on the basis of the entire research, a number of observations in order to determine restrictions to hate speech on the ground of religion uttered in public debate in a consistent manner *(Q4)*.

This research mainly uses comparative constitutional law and is largely descriptive in nature. The latter applies, in any event, to the analysis of international and European law and to the comparative study in Chapters 3–4. The analytical framework in Chapter 2 may not be normative in itself; it does function as the standard for the evaluative conclusions drawn and observations made in Chapter 6. The analytical framework builds on all relevant international literature, in which American free speech/ hate speech doctrine and jurisprudence appears to be most dominant. References to American doctrine and jurisprudence are not intended to provide a detailed legal comparison with the European approach towards hate speech. They form 'illustrations' in the general, abstract discussion of aspects that are relevant for the setting of restrictions to hate speech in Chapter 2.

The choice of the Netherlands for the comparative study was fixed in advance and that of France was easily made. As previously mentioned, in France a comparable discourse on Islam and immigration exists that has resulted in a number of hate speech cases, in which the consistency of restrictions also forms a pivotal question. Furthermore, historically, since the Enlightenment, French Republicanism has stressed the importance of 'civic virtues' and the 'common good', whereas liberalism was based on individualism. It was therefore expected that, more than in dominant free speech doctrine, freedom of expression is embedded in the French Constitution and the values contained therein. In France, formal legislation can be tested against the Constitution. This is not the case in the Netherlands, where the Constitution has less normative force and a more open character. This is why this study aims to compare these two national approaches to hate speech and the influence of European law and free speech doctrine on national law.

1.5. Scope and relevance

This research does not discuss all aspects of freedom of expression. As a result of technological developments, hate speech can be disseminated widely and in large quantities, for example through 'hate sites' on the Internet. This raises practical questions about the enforcement of hate speech bans, about transnational jurisdiction and questions about the liability of intermediaries on the Internet.[19] These questions fall outside the scope of this research. Although the regulation of media necessarily influences the distribution and publication of hate speech, it does not fundamentally question restrictions on hate speech based on content. An in-depth empirical investigation of the effect and effectiveness of hate speech bans also falls outside the scope of this primarily legal research. Nevertheless sometimes reference is made to social science research.

Many strategies can be implemented, and are developed that contribute to counter or prevent the existence and use of hate speech, such as policies that aim to enhance awareness about intolerance through school education or aim to stimulate the reflection of a diversity of speakers and opinions in the media and the training of media professionals.[20] However, this research focuses on what the law can and cannot do as far as the setting of restrictions to hate speech is concerned. To this end, this research compares the legal prohibition of hate speech in two civil law countries. Therefore, the outcome of the comparative study can form a source of inspiration for the discussion on the legal prohibition of hate speech in, next to the countries concerned, i.e. other civil law countries. However, it may be informative for the discussion in common law systems too.

Dutch comparative studies on freedom of expression focus on America, as well as Germany and the United Kingdom.[21] Practically no knowledge of freedom of expression in France exists in the Netherlands. Although in international scientific literature considerable attention is paid to the French criminalization of Holocaust denial,[22] no international comprehensive studies of French law on freedom of expression and hate speech exist. This research constitutes the first international study that provides a profound analysis of freedom of expression and the regulation of hate speech in France and the Netherlands from a constitutional law perspective.

Hence, this research contributes to the existing international scientific literature on hate speech. It also makes reference to the most recent international hate speech literature and discusses its key issues. Its added value lies in its evaluation of the

---

19 McGonagle, T., *The Council of Europe against online hate speech: Conundrums and challenges*, Expert paper, doc.no. MCM 2013(005), the Council of Europe Conference of Ministers responsible for Media and Information Society, 'Freedom of Expression and Democracy in the Digital Age: Opportunities, Rights, Responsibilities', Belgrade, 7–8 November 2013.

20 McGonagle, T.E., *Minority rights, freedom of expression and of the media: dynamics and dilemmas*, Cambridge: Intersentia 2011.

21 Nieuwenhuis, A.J., *Over de grens van de vrijheid van meningsuiting*, Nijmegen: Ars Aequi Libri 2011; Peters, J.A. *Het primaat van de vrijheid van meningsuiting* (diss.), Nijmegen: Ars Aequi Libri 1981; Rosier, T.E., *Vrijheid van meningsuiting en discriminatie in Nederland en Amerika* (diss.), Nijmegen: Ars Aequi 1998. Van Noorloos, M., *Hate Speech Revisited, A comparative and historical perspective on hate speech law in the Netherlands and England & Wales* (diss.), Antwerpen: Intersentia 2011.

22 See for example several contributions to: Hennebel, L. & Hochmann, T. (eds.), *Genocide denials and the law*, Oxford: Oxford University Press, 2011.

consistency of considerations regarding restrictions on hate speech rather than presenting yet another ultimate answer to the question of what those restrictions should be. This research can, thereby, form a source of inspiration for anyone interested or involved in the regulation of hate speech: interested citizens; politicians; scientists; legislators; judges; prosecutors; and involved NGO's. Hopefully, it can contribute to enhancing the quality of scientific, political and public discussion about the regulation of hate speech; and eventually contribute to the 'faith in public debate', by elucidating its possible boundaries.

CHAPTER 2
ANALYTICAL FRAMEWORK

INTRODUCTION

This chapter discusses the relevant international scientific literature on freedom of expression and the regulation of hate speech on the basis of four factors that are presented as opposite pairs: Actions versus Opinions; Public Debate versus Other Types of Expression; Facts versus Value judgments; and Race versus Religion. It is precisely *these* factors that can be assumed to be particularly relevant for the consistent determination of restrictions to hate speech on the ground of religion uttered in public debate, due to the fact that they form the core subject of controversies in literature. In fact, the factors regroup the more traditional presentation in literature of, on the one hand, the justifications of the right to freedom of expression and, on the other hand, the harms in hate speech that justify restrictions to this right. Therefore a certain interaction and overlap exist in the discussion of the factors. This applies in particular to the first two factors.

The first factor concerns the distinction between the performance of physical *actions* and the expression of *opinions*.[23] It discusses different visions about what possible effects of the expression of opinions may justify a restriction to freedom of expression. More specifically, it discusses different notions of harm and perspectives on the harmful effects of hate speech that may result in different requirements for criminal liability for hate speech (para. 1). These different perspectives on harm and criminal liability for hate speech are inextricably linked to the value or function that is attributed to the free public debate in a democracy. Therefore, they are continued in the second factor that examines the distinction between contributions to public debate and other types of expression,[24] such as 'private speech', which is directly directed at a particular individual or utterances that can be qualified as an abuse of rights (para. 2).

Subsequently, the third factor concerns the distinction between imputations of specific *facts* versus the expression of *value judgments*.[25] In principle, false statements of fact about a particular person are not protected by freedom of expression. This does not apply – to the same extent – to negative value judgments about a person; in principle ample room must exist for such opinions. Difference of opinion exists to the extent this distinction may be relevant for demarcating free critical contributions to public debate from prohibited hate speech (para. 3). Finally,

---

23 Schauer, F., *Free speech a philosophical enquiry*, Cambridge: Cambridge University Press 1982.

24 Post, R., The Constitutional Concept of Public Discourse: Outrageous Opinion, Democratic Deliberation, and Hustler Magazine v. Falwell, *Harvard Law Review*, 1990, vol. 103, no. 3, p. 601–686.

25 Sadurski, W., *Freedom of Speech and its Limits*, Dordrecht: Kluwer Academic Publishers 1999.

the fourth factor examines the role therein of the distinction between negative utterances about *race* versus negative utterances about *religion*.[26] Some consider that the two are equally harmful and therefore the same legal restrictions must apply to both types of speech. Others make a stricter distinction between 'classic racist hate speech' and other forms of intolerant speech that, in their eyes, do not have a racist purport and are therefore less reprehensible (para. 4).

Although particular types of hate speech or hate speech bans may be discussed under one specific factor, *all* factors are relevant for the evaluation of consistency in restrictions to these types of hate speech and in the application of these hate speech bans. The paragraphs always conclude with a synthesis that defines the factors for the purpose of further analysis in this study. The chapter concludes with a synthesis of the factors thus defined that explain the interrelationship and meaning of the factors for the evaluation of consistency in restrictions to hate speech uttered in public debate (para. 5). Together the factors form an analytical framework for the analysis of the positive law. Following chapters will explore whether, and if so how, French law, Dutch law and international and European law make consistent choices as far as these factors/opposite pairs are concerned for the determination of restrictions to hate speech pertaining to religion uttered in public debate.

1. Actions versus Opinions

Free speech theories aim to determine what should be the extent of freedom of expression in a democratic society. The question arises as to which consequences of the expression of an opinion may be sufficient to justify a restriction to freedom of expression. Subsequently, the question is what are the consequences of hate speech? Also, what interests do restrictions to hate speech precisely protect? A final question then is how can the rationales behind restrictions of hate speech be translated into concrete legal requirements for criminal liability/statutory offences; how can utterances be qualified under those offences?

Generally a distinction could be made between the expression of *opinions* and conduct consisting of the performance of physical *actions*. Traditionally, the prohibition of the expression of opinions has been proposed due to a strict *connection* with contingent subsequent actions by third parties (1.1). A contra position may however propose to prohibit the expression of opinions that amount to hate speech even though they do not have a (strict) connection with subsequent actions, because of the *intrinsic* properties of hate speech and how it affects the members of a specific target group. This argument may, however, differ little from the argument of what negative effects hate speech may have in the mid-term on its victims; third parties and society at large (1.2). Some may even envision expressions

26 Barendt, E., Religious Hatred Laws: Protecting Groups or Belief?, *Res Publica* 2011, vol. 17, p. 41–53.

that amount to hate speech as forms of 'actions' and propose to prohibit it on that basis (1.3).

The first approach still underlies the requirement in American free speech doctrine that (hate) speech may only be prohibited if it poses a 'clear and present danger' or when it is 'directed to inciting or producing imminent lawless action and is likely to incite or produce such action' (1.4). European hate speech bans are, on the other hand, generally grounded in the second approach and therefore normally require a less strict connection with subsequent actions for criminal liability for hate speech (1.5). The paragraph concludes with a synthesis that defines the factor 'Actions versus Opinions' for the purpose of the further analysis in this study (1.6).

1.1. The distinction between actions and opinions and a strict connection between opinions and subsequent actions

The free expression of opinions is generally regarded as varying from the general freedom to act, with regard to its value, function, nature and effect. According to the traditional Millian speech and harm-principle, only an expression that very likely causes direct harmful conduct may therefore be prohibited. This principle has formed the rationale for the creation of offences of seditious libel and incitement to crimes.

1.1.1. The general freedom to act, the free expression of opinions and autonomy

In order to determine what the extent of freedom of expression in a democratic society should be, free speech theories generally strictly distinguish the expression of *opinions* from conduct consisting of the performance of physical *actions*. The expression of opinions is, like the exercise of all rights, not by definition free from consequences and therefore cannot be absolute.[27] However, it has been argued that a '*free speech principle*' implies that for the restriction of free speech a *greater justification* is required than for the restriction of other conduct, even when the consequences of speech are just as great as that of other conduct.[28] The specific protection by the law of the right to freedom of expression, whether relative or compared to the general freedom to act, is grounded in the particular justifications that apply to the right to freedom of expression in specific. The three arguments that are generally considered to justify the right of freedom of expression in specific are: 'the argument from truth' (para. 3.1 *infra*), 'the argument from autonomy' (*infra*), and 'the argument from democracy' (para. 2.1 *infra*).

27 Fish, S. & Olson, G.A., *There's no such thing as free speech and it's a good thing, too*, New York: Oxford University Press 1994. Cf. Berlin, I., *Two concepts of liberty*, Oxford: Clarendon Press 1958.

28 Schauer, F., *Free speech a philosophical enquiry*, Cambridge: Cambridge University Press 1982, p. 3–14.

In this respect, *autonomy* essentially appears to be an argument for a general freedom to act. It primarily relates to human agency and the capacity to control one's own destiny and make one's own choices.[29] Autonomous action is a condition of self-expression and self-fulfilment.[30] Free expression and communication can be regarded as essential components of autonomy. This primarily applies to the autonomy of the *speaker*. When a person speaks he discloses his views and values to the world and thus chooses how to present himself to others. This is how a person defines himself and takes an autonomous place in society.[31]

Furthermore, free expression and communication may also be regarded as an essential component to the autonomy of the *receiver*. If the state does not allow people to receive speech that may influence their beliefs, the state fails to respect people's autonomy. A person can only be autonomous if he is as fully informed as possible and free to weigh the arguments for or against certain conduct.[32, 33]

1.1.2. The Millian speech and harm-principle and the concept of the 'délit d'opinion'

A premise of liberalism is thus that freedom may only be prohibited on certain limited grounds. In *On Liberty*, first published in 1859, John Stuart Mill explained his harm principle, stating that: 'the only purpose for which power can be rightfully exercised over any member of a civilized community, against his will, is to prevent harm to others.'[34] Mill's speech theory subsequently holds that only expression that is very likely to cause direct harmful conduct, such as the incitement to violence, justifies state coercion. This theory cannot be understood separately from Mill's view on the need for state neutrality towards the content of expression in light of the special value attributed by him to the free expression of opinions, true or false, in (scientific) discussion (para. 3.1 *infra*). Mill had much faith in the intellectual exchange of thoughts. This does not signify that for Mill the expression of thoughts would be, contrary to other conduct, harmless to others, but that free discussion must be allowed – *despite* its possibly harmful effects –, because it leads to ultimate goods such as truth. In order for its restriction to be allowed, the opinion thus does not have to be followed by effect, but nevertheless a very strict probable connection

29 Raz, J., *The morality of freedom*, Oxford: Clarendon Press 1988, p. 369.

30 Sadurski, W., *Freedom of Speech and its Limits*, Dordrecht: Kluwer Academic Publishers 1999, p. 17.

31 Baker, C. E., Hate Speech, in: Herz, M., & Molnar, P. (Eds.), *The Content and Context of Hate Speech: Rethinking Regulation and Responses*, Cambridge: Cambridge University Press 2012, p. 63. See also: Baker, C.E., *Human Liberty and Freedom of Speech*, New York: Oxford University Press 1989.

32 Scanlon, T., A Theory of Freedom of Expression, *Philosophy & public affairs* 1972, vol. 1, no. 2, p. 204.

33 Scanlon 1972, p. 204–226.

34 Mill, J.S., *On Liberty*, Fourth ed., London: Watts & Co. Ltd., 1936, p. 11.

must exist between an opinion and subsequent contingent harmful conduct.[35] Mill's harm principle can therefore be closely linked to the interest in the protection of the public order and the prevention of public disturbances of the peace through violent conflicts.

Likewise, the French 1789 Declaration of the rights of Men and the Citizen cites that 'La liberté consiste à pouvoir faire tout ce qui ne nuit pas à autrui'. With regard to freedom of expression, in the nineteenth century, Benjamin Constant expounded an idea similar to that of Mill, according to which the state may not prohibit the expression of an opinion as long as it does not support a criminal or punishable act. If expression produces such actions, it merges with them and must be prohibited on this ground. But the opinion that is separate from the action must remain free.[36] By these words Constant articulated the French classical concept of the *'délit d'opinion'*. This concept of the *'délit d'opinion'* thus strictly distinguishes actions from opinions where purposes of the law are concerned. It equally requires a very strict probable connection with subsequent contingent harmful conduct for the restriction of an opinion to be allowed and it thus equally appears to start from a narrow conception of harm to others limited to physical actions that also affect public order.

1.1.3. Seditious libel and public order

In former times, harm to public order has formed a ground for the creation of offences of seditious libel that prohibit violent, revolting speech uttered by persons or groups directed against state authorities and offences penalizing for example the 'incitement to crimes'. On the one hand, the view that the prohibition of such expression is legitimate in order to prevent harm to others is understandable. After all, one could argue that a primary task of the state is to preserve security and stability, because public order is necessary to ensure people's rights.

On the other hand, the public order argument might afford the state large appreciation to restrict all kinds of speech that criticizes the government and is considered to be disturbing. It has been argued that the old offences of seditious libel could be justified, because at the time of their creation the power of the government was so weak that it had to be protected against public contempt in order to prevent its subversion. However, the prosecution for seditious libel became inappropriate when the government became better organized and its power increased.[37]

Former offences of seditious libel have been characterized as the oldest form of 'hate speech' laws. However, this subsumption/assimilation may be criticized. While the former concerned speech directed against the government, the latter concerned speech directed against racial and religious minorities. One could argue that – other than the state – the position of minorities in society is not so well

---

35 Mill 1936, p. 67–68.

36 See further Chapter 4.

37 Waldron, J., *The Harm in Hate Speech*, Cambridge: Harvard University Press 2012, p. 30.

assured that they are no longer in need of protection against racist attacks.[38] Moreover, to the extent that the offences of seditious libel covered criticism of the government by the opposition, this is not appropriate in a democracy. This is different with regard to vehement criticism of certain minority groups in society that may sooner be considered as harmful to them.

Some therefore argue that, as far as restrictions to freedom of expression are concerned, the 19th century conception of harm as envisioned by Mill is outdated and has nowadays been superseded by the concept of immaterial harm, such as psychological harm, harm to human dignity, (para. 1.4 *infra*) and speech act theory (para. 1.5 *infra*).[39] However, the prevention of imminent harm to others as envisioned by Mill has not entirely lost its importance, because it still forms a ground for existing offences criminalizing sedition and the incitement to crimes. But it is true that the prevention of imminent harm in the Millian sense does not form the rationale underlying existing hate speech bans. According to the current conception of harm as defined by Feinberg, *harm* is a setback of one's interest as the result of a previous wrongful act. Therefore it is a *wrong* in the sense that it *violates* one's *rights*.[40] For Feinberg, the prevention of harm to others thus defined is appealing as a justification for restrictions to freedom through criminal law due to its objectiveness.[41] The questions thus arise: What is the legally relevant notion of harm in hate speech? How does hate speech violate the rights of others?

1.2. Contra position: the *intrinsic* properties of opinions

Next to Free Speech theories based on the Mill inspired traditional distinction between actions and opinions, certain more recent theories have been developed that make a less strict distinction between actions and opinions and rather start from the *intrinsic* properties of opinions. It is then proposed to prohibit hate speech due to its – racist – *message* alleged to harm the *human dignity* and *equality* of its victims. This argument may, however, differ little from the argument of what negative effects hate speech may have in the mid-term; on the victims, third parties and society at large.

---

38 Waldron 2012, p. 22; 26; 30.

39 Dommering, E.J., Féret en daarna, in: Turner, C.J. *et al* (eds.), *25 jaar Mediaforum, Een voorblik door de achteruitkijkspiegel*, Amsterdam: Otto Cramwinckel Uitgever 2013, p. 165.

40 Feinberg, J., *The moral limits of the criminal law, vol. 1 Harm to Others*, New York: Oxford University Press 1984, p. 36; 216.

41 From a liberal perspective, restrictions based on the protection against moral decline (moral *legal paternalism*) or the enforcement of public morality (*legal moralism*) are however not valid. Although *offence* may form a justification of a restriction to freedom under certain conditions. See: Feinberg, J., *The moral limits of the criminal law, vol. 4 Harmless wrongdoing*, New York: Oxford University Press 1990; Feinberg, J., *The moral limits of the criminal law, vol. 2 Offense to Others*, New York: Oxford University Press 1985.

1.2.1. Human dignity

The term *human dignity* figures in the preambles of several human rights treaties and constitutions as a ground for fundamental rights and freedoms.[42, 43] Dignity, thereby, underpins a so-called 'legal humanism'.[44] Dignity is a desirable state, an aspiration, rather than a right as such. The law can at best provide a circumscribing circle of rights, which in some of their effects help to preserve the field for a dignified life.

Different concepts of dignity can however be discerned.[45] One concept focuses on *autonomy*. Dignity then concerns the intrinsic worth each individual has simply by virtue of being human. It does not confer any social status or social standing to a person but refers to the minimum dignity that belongs to every human being qua human and which is equal for all humans.[46] It relates to human agency and can be associated with negative liberty and freedom from interference.[47]

Indeed, the notion of human dignity is often regarded as underpinning freedom of expression. For example, Dworkin argues that a large freedom of expression follows from recognition of the dignity of speakers.[48] Likewise, the U.S. Supreme Court has considered that a large free public debate 'will ultimately produce a more capable citizenry and more perfect polity and in the belief that no other approach would comport with the premise of *individual dignity* and choice upon which our political system rests.'[49] This concept of dignity as autonomy thus does not appear

---

42 The first phrase of the preamble of the Universal Declaration of Human Rights of 1948 reads 'Whereas recognition of the inherent dignity and of the equal and inalienable rights of all members of the human family is the foundation of freedom, justice and peace in the world' and Article 1 reads 'All human beings are born free and equal in *dignity* and rights. They are endowed with reason and conscience and should act towards one another in a *spirit of brotherhood*'.

43 McCrudden, C., Human Dignity and Judicial Interpretation of Human Rights, *European Journal of International Law* 2008, vol. 19, no. 4, p. 655–724. McCrudden analyses the historical development of human dignity as a legal concept. It became internationally recognized as such, when it was inserted into the preamble and first article of the Universal Declaration of Human Rights adopted by the UN after WWII in 1948. However, the term owed its success precisely to its neutral character. In fact, the delegates of the different countries could not agree on a theoretical basis for the human rights that the Declaration would list: religion, natural rights, liberal individualism or communitarian ideals. Under the heading of dignity all participants could abide by their own foundations and thus agree on the term without agreeing on its meaning.

44 Feldman, D., Human Dignity as a legal value: Part 1, *Public Law* 1999, Winter, p. 682; 687. See also: Feldman, D., Human Dignity as a legal value: Part 2, *Public Law* 2000, Spring, p. 61–76.

45 Rao, N., Three concepts of dignity in constitutional law, *Notre Dame Law Review* 2011, vol. 86, p. 183–271. The third concept not further discussed here concerns substantive conceptions of dignity that promote substantive judgments about the good life and can for example be connected to positive social and economic goods for a minimum standard of living.

46 Rao 2011, p. 196.

47 Rao 2011, p. 200; 203.

48 Dworkin, R.M., *Taking rights seriously*, Cambridge, MA, Harvard University Press 1979, p. 272.

49 *Cohen v. California*, 403 U.S. 15 (1971) at 24.

to be the most appropriate argument for the regulation of hate speech. Although, the concept might underlie the later discussed idea that hate speech causes the 'silencing' of its victims and prevents them from using their free speech rights.

Another concept, however, focuses on dignity as *recognition*. This concept depends upon a conception of the person as an essential part of the community. One can have dignity and a sense of self only through recognition by the broader society.[50] Individuals must receive respect and recognition both from other individuals, who must recognize each other as citizens and community members, and also from the state, as embodiment of the community's legal and social norms. The state must require and enforce 'interpersonal *respect*' between citizens, for example through hate speech bans.[51] Although hate speech might result in discrimination or violence against members of targeted groups, the primary concern is thus how hate speech can damage a person's sense of dignity by undermining membership within the community for the targeted individuals and groups.[52]

Based on natural rights law, Heyman argues 'Recognition is the most fundamental right that individuals have, a right that lies at the basis of all their other rights. At the same time, mutual recognition is the bond that constitutes the political community. For these reasons, individuals have a duty to recognize one another as human beings and citizens. Hate speech violates this duty in a way that profoundly affects both the targets themselves and the society as a whole.'[53] Heyman considers hate speech to inflict serious injury precisely because of its content.[54] Such speech is wrongful, because it constitutes a form of *aggression* against others. Therefore it may be regarded as a breach of the peace in and of itself. It signals a condition of mutual hostility and animosity, a condition in which the parties intend to treat one another as enemies. The right to be free from aggression must be regarded as an aspect of personal *security*.[55]

From a similar strand of thought, Waldron holds that hate speech expresses the idea that members of another group are unworthy of *equal citizenship*.[56] It undermines their *basic social standing*, the *basics of their reputation* by associating ascriptive characteristics like ethnicity, race or religion with conduct or attributes that should disqualify someone from being treated as a member of society in good standing. Hate speech is a calculated affront to the dignity of vulnerable members of society and a calculated assault on the *public good* of inclusiveness.[57]

---

50 Rao 2011, p. 244.

51 Rao 2011, p. 249.

52 Rao 2011, p. 252; see also: Tsesis, A., Dignity and Speech: The Regulation of Hate Speech in a Democracy, *Wake Forest Law Review*, 2009, vol. 44, p.497–532.

53 Heyman, S., *Free Speech and Human Dignity*, New Haven, Conn: Yale University Press 2008, p. 171; Heyman, S., Hate Speech, Public Discourse and the First Amendment, in: Hare & Weinstein 2009, p. 158–181.

54 Heyman 2008, ch. 6.

55 Heyman 2008, p. 142–145.

56 Waldron 2012, p. 5; 39.

57 Waldron 2012, p. 5; 39.

The argument that hate speech must be prohibited, because it *violates* human dignity as a public good may be criticized for being just as paternalistic and moralistic as the argument that blasphemy or pornography must be prohibited, because it *violates* public morality. A distinct argument would be that hate speech must be prohibited, because it *affects* the human dignity of its victims. However this latter argument may differ little from the rationale of the prevention of harm in the sense of the mid-term effects of hate speech.

The notion of human dignity thus may be criticized for being rather vague.[58] This vagueness could possibly constitute a danger to freedom of expression. On the other hand, one could argue that human dignity may not have an independent significance, but rather be an additional condition for the restriction of expression that amounts to hate speech.[59]

1.2.2. Equality

The notion of equality is closely related to human dignity and often also regarded as underpinning freedom of expression. For example, Dworkin argues that the government must treat people with equal respect and concern and must not constrain liberty on the ground that one person's conception of the good life is nobler or superior to another's.[60] In the context of freedom of expression, equality has been referred to as the '*equal opportunity to speak and be heard*'.[61] A state may adopt positive measures to realize the equal access for minorities to mass media in order to assure the equal distribution of their ideas and viewpoints next to those of dominant groups.[62]

The notion of equality might also form a ground to limit freedom of expression. Hate speech bans then could be regarded as a form of '*affirmative action*'.[63] The question however arises whether and how hate speech could violate the equality of the victims it targets. Proponents of hate speech bans argue that by allowing racists to express opinions that amount to hate speech, the victims of such speech are prevented from exercising their equal free speech rights. There are two ways in which an unlimited existence of hate speech in society might cause the '*silencing*' of its victims.[64]

---

58 McCrudden 2008.

59 Then it appears to solve several famous paradoxes; to which extent a liberal democracy should permit illiberal opinions; to which extent it should tolerate intolerant opinions.

60 Dworkin 1979, p. 272.

61 Sadurski 1999, p. 74.

62 McGonagle, T.E., *Minority rights, freedom of expression and of the media: dynamics and dilemmas*, Cambridge: Intersentia 2011.

63 Sadurski 1999, p. 100.

64 See several contributions to Post, R.C., *Censorship and silencing, practices of cultural regulation*, Los Angeles: Getty Research Institute for the History of Art and the Humanities 1998, Part III, p. 247 *et seq.*

Firstly, hate speech may be very intimidating and it may cause victims to refrain from publicly expressing their views out of fear of receiving racist responses. Assaultive speech may have far reaching consequences for the victims of that type of speech, such as serious psychological and physical harms including fear, stress, withdrawal from society, damaged self-image, lower aspiration and depression, and economic harms including reduced opportunities in life through low performance in employment settings.[65] One may argue that, even though hate speech may have such negative effects on its victims, its racist message does not actually *prevent* them from speaking.

Secondly, hate speech may have a negative effect on the public, who might experience the points of views of the targeted minorities as of less value, because they are stigmatized and denigrated by such speech. One may argue that hate speech does not necessarily have such negative effects on the entire public, but if so a racist speaker may only have tried to persuade the public to adopt his ideas and should not be responsible for the actions of the public. Moreover, the taking into account of the latter would bring us back to the rationale of the prevention of harm in the sense of the mid-term effects of hate speech. This does not alter the fact that hate speech may undeniably cause a hardening of public debate and also cause a distortion of relations within a community and the dissolution of the norms for mutual respect (dignity).

1.3. Opinions as 'discriminatory actions'

A particular position is taken by those who advocate hate speech bans, because such expression would *constitute* discriminatory *actions* in and of themselves. The vision that hate speech should be prohibited because of its performative power has notably been advanced since the 1990s by the *Critical Race Theorists* (CRT). Their *Theory of Discursive Violence* considers the perspective of the victims of assaultive speech and argues that the identity of individuals is defined in terms of ethnic and cultural bonds, while the life choices and deliberative capabilities of individuals are formed through contact with others.[66] According to the theory, hate speech does not describe a racial social reality, but rather creates one and maintains racial hierarchy. It teaches minorities 'their place'. Such racial categorization serves the interests of the dominant group.[67]

The theory builds on the language philosophy called *Speech Act Theory*. In his language philosophy, Austin distinguishes *locutions* from *illocutions* and

---

65 Delgado, R. & Stefancic, J., *Understanding words that wound*, Boulder, CO: Westview Press 2004, p. 12–15.

66 For a clear introduction: Douglas, L., The Force of Words: Fish, Matsuda, MacKinnon, and the Theory of Discursive Violence, *Law & society review* 1995, vol. 29, no. 1, p. 169 *et seq.*

67 Delgado & Stefancic 2004, p. 32.

perlocutions.[68] Locution is the content of an utterance. Perlocution is the effect of an utterance that consists of its causal consequences. Illocution is an action performed by saying something. An example of the latter is: 'Muslims are not allowed in this bar'. This speech act constitutes discrimination, not because it causes the hearer to think in a certain way (perlocution), but because as actual conduct it constitutes unequal treatment. Words being illocutions can do many things, including subordinating others.[69]

For CRT, racist speech in general consists of the structural subordination of a group based on an idea of racial inferiority.[70] Racist speech acts can subordinate members of a group as follows: it ranks target groups as having inferior worth; it legitimates discriminatory behaviour of others; and it deprives target groups of some important powers.[71] Therefore, three criteria can be formulated to determine whether speech should be prohibited: when the message is of racial inferiority; when the speech is directed against a historically oppressed group; and where the speech is persecutory, hateful and degrading.[72]

The viewpoint that hate speech *literally* constitutes acts of discrimination is controversial. Firstly, a requirement in speech-act theory is that for a speech act to be effective, it has to be performed by someone who is in a position of authority. A historical example of an illocution that subordinates blacks is as follows: 'Blacks are not permitted to vote', which was expressed as an enactment of apartheid law.[73] But this speech act expressed by the average racist speaker who is has no authority on the matter is bound to fail or 'misfire'.

Secondly, CRT base their argument on the premise that hate speech can constitute a prohibited form of conduct on the negative *effects* it has on the victims (severe psychological harms) and on the public who will regard and treat the victims as inferior. One may argue that there is no empirical evidence that the message of racial inferiority causes this kind of 'silencing'. Moreover, CRT seems to use perlocutionary explanations to draw conclusions in illocutionary terms.[74] Then again we are back to the rationale of the prevention of harm in the sense of the mid-term effects of hate speech.

---

68 Austin, J.L., *How to do things with words*, Oxford: Oxford University Press 1976. Actual founder of speech act theory is Jonathan Searle: Searle, J., *Speech Acts: An Essay in the Philosophy of Language,* Cambridge: Cambridge University Press 1969.

69 See several contributions to Maitra, I. & McGowan, M.K., *Speech & Harm: Controveries over Free Speech*, Oxford: Oxford University Press 2012.

70 Matsuda, M., Public Responses to racist Speech: Considering the Victim's Story, *Michigan Law Review*, 1989, vol. 87, p. 2358.

71 Langton, R., Speech Acts and Unspeakable Acts, *Philosophy & public affairs* 1993, vol. 22, no. 4, p. 293–330.

72 Matsuda 1989, p. 2357–2358.

73 Langton, R., Subordination, Silence, and Pornography's Authority, in: Post (ed.) 1998, p. 262.

74 Sadurski, W., 'On seeing speech through an equality lens': a critique of egalitarian arguments for suppression of hate speech and pornography, *Oxford journal of legal studies* 1996, vol. 16, no. 4, p. 713–724.

On the one hand, using the *metaphor* of hate speech as discriminatory actions nevertheless appears to be a way to bring to the fore just how severely hate speech can actually affect the members of a particular group in society, who may experience such speech as acts of discrimination, and why, according to the CRT, it may be prohibited. Based on the relevant literature, the negative impact of hate speech may not be underestimated. Although the harm in hate speech may not reach the same level as facts that, for example, constitute a violation of one's physical integrity, the harm inflicted by racist speech may be real and far from trivial.[75] On the other hand, speech act theory has also articulated the opposite argument that minorities can better resist their verbal subjugation by others by contradicting them in public debate and thereby change the meaning of such words, their force and thereby, their social position. As the (discriminatory) force of words is determined by their social, historical context,[76] the state should not be afforded the authority to *a priori* criminalize hate speech *in abstracto*.[77] This cultural analysis and external perspective thus disregards the distinction that – from an internal legal perspective – can be made between, on the one hand the creation of hate speech bans by the state as such, and on the other hand, the application of hate speech bans in concrete cases and the qualification of a specific utterance under a particular hate speech ban by the judge on the basis of a number of contextual factors.

1.4. The 'clear and present danger' and 'imminent lawlessness' tests in American free speech doctrine

In certain legal systems the Millian speech and harm principle form the basis for the establishment of factual causation in criminal liability for expressions, as well as those that amount to hate speech. This can be illustrated by the American Free Speech doctrine that generally requires a strict connection between speech and subsequent conduct. A standard test used by American courts requires that speech may only be prohibited if it poses a *'clear and present danger'*.[78, 79] The U.S.

75 Vrielink, J., *Van Haat Gesproken? Een rechtsantropologisch onderzoek naar de bestrijding van rasgerelateerde uitingsdelicten in België*, Antwerpen-Apeldoorn: Maklu-Uitgevers 2010, p. 404–405.

76 Words – such as 'nigger' – would have no universal, fixed meaning.

77 Butler, J., *Excitable speech a politics of the performative*, New York, NY: Routledge 1997.

78 In *Schenck v. United States*, 249 *U.S.* 47 (*1919*) Justice Oliver Wendell Holmes wrote 'Words which, ordinarily and in many places, would be within the freedom of speech protected by the First Amendment may become subject to prohibition when of such a nature and used in such circumstances a to create a clear and present danger that they will bring about the substantive evils which Congress has a right to prevent. The character of every act depends upon the circumstances in which it is done.' P. 249 U.S. 51.

79 Geenawalt, K., 'Clear and Present Danger' and Criminal Speech, in: Bollinger, L.C. & Stone, G.R. (Eds.), *Eternally vigilant, Free Speech in the Modern Era*, Chicago: The University of Chicago Press 2002, p. 96–119.

Supreme Court has even considered that advocacy of violence or lawlessness is constitutionally protected '*except where such advocacy is directed to inciting or producing imminent lawless action and is likely to incite or produce such action*'.[80] In fact, this standard may be compared with the incitement to crimes. According to the Supreme Court this is not easily the case. Others opine that the evaluation of the imminence and likelihood of such action is a highly contextual matter.[81] These strict tests are said to have been developed in reaction to the '*bad tendency*' test used for example during WWI, which allowed the state to suppress expression of all kinds of anti-war sentiments as forms of sedition and incitement to violence against state authorities, because it had the '*tendency*' to cause '*future*' illegal conduct.[82]

The stricter tests result from the basic principle that it takes a 'compelling interest', i.e. an extremely strong governmental interest, to permit restrictions to freedom of expression protected in the First Amendment. This may already be suggested by the text of the First Amendment itself that formulates the freedom as seemingly absolute and does not list the circumstances in which it may be restricted: 'Congress shall make no law (…) abridging the freedom of speech, or of the press'.[83] The standards of the threat of a clear and present danger or of imminent lawlessness cannot be understood separately from the special value American Free Speech Doctrine attributes to the free expression of opinions in the public debate that must function as a 'marketplace of ideas', which legitimizes state authority (the law), thus underpinning democracy. These high standards do not apply outside the context of a public debate; racist epithets when addressed to a citizen and likely to provoke his violent reaction, so called 'fighting words', can be prohibited (para. 2.1–2.2 and 3.1 *infra*).

In fact, the stricter tests express a strong preference for the *individual liberty* or freedom from state interference of the speaker and receiver. As a result, the state must afford a large freedom of expression and allow much 'uncivil' speech even when it violates values of equality or important community values. The criminalization of hate speech not likely to produce imminent lawlessness would be contrary to the First Amendment.[84] America has, therefore, not created specific hate speech bans. It has been argued that such expression might be reprehensible, but that freedom of expression should precisely afford the 'freedom for the thought we hate'.[85] As a general principle, the expression of opinions may not rashly be prohibited on account of its content, meaning or message.[86]

---

80 *Brandenburg v. Ohio,* 395 U.S. 444, 447 (1969).

81 Molnar, P., Responding to 'Hate Speech' with Art, Education, and the Imminent Danger Test, in: Herz & Molnar 2012, p. 193;195.

82 Molnar, P & Post, R., Interview with Robert Post, in: Herz & Molnar 2012, p. 29–30.

83 Schauer, F., The Exceptional First Amendment, in: Ignatieff, M. (Ed.), *American Exceptionalism and Human Rights*, Princeton: Princeton University Press 2005, p. 29 *et seq.*

84 Schauer 2005.

85 Lewis, A., *Freedom for the thought we hate*, New York, NY: Basic Books 2009.

86 For a clear explanation in the American context see: Stone, G.R., Free Speech in the Twenty-First Century: Ten Lessons from the Twentieth Century, *Pepperdine Law Review* 2009, vol.36, p. 273–300.

American free speech doctrine is thus based on a strong *distrust* against government control over the content of expression.[87] Content-based restrictions to freedom of expression may not entirely be prohibited, but they call for the strictest scrutiny. Moreover, the government must remain *neutral* with regard to *different* contents. It cannot restrict certain viewpoints, while allowing others; this would amount to 'viewpoint discrimination'.[88] The strict tests appear to be very neutral; prohibitions of speech are not based on content but on the consequences consisting of violent or illegal conduct thus 'objective harms'. It can be argued that one cannot strictly distinguish such conduct from the message or ideas conveyed by the speech; the former may be provoked by the latter.[89]

For example, the U.S. Supreme Court has considered that public cross burning in the front yard of a black family by white people can signal a threat of violence against those black people, due to the history of cross burning by the KKK. It can thus constitute a '*true threat*' and therefore, lack the protection of the First Amendment. Contrarily, cross burning during KKK gatherings is allowed as 'potent symbols of shared group identity and ideology'; to ban such a gathering is contrary to the First Amendment.[90]

The U.S. Supreme Court has even found a march of neo-Nazis carrying swastikas through a predominantly Jewish neighbourhood permissible, despite the hostility of its Jewish residents, including Holocaust survivors, to their racist ideas.[91] In this case, the demonstrators, however, might have also wanted to provoke an angry reaction of the victims.[92] In other circumstances, such violent conduct may be performed by *third parties* who are incited to assault victims of hate speech. It has been argued that such harm results from the fact that speech is 'mentally mediated' by listeners. The latter should be solely responsible for their responses or reactions to certain speech.[93] The state, therefore, should only interfere with the conduct that follows speech and never the speech that precedes conduct.[94]

The requirement of a strict connection between opinions and subsequent actions can be related to the concept of the '*heckler's veto*', according to which the hostility of an 'uncaptive' audience against certain ideas cannot justify the suppression of speech. The audience must impose self-restraint or even avoid being confronted

---

87 Schauer, F., Media Law, Media Content, and American Exceptionalism, in: IRIS *Special*, Political Debate and the Role of the Media, the Fragility of Free Speech, European Audiovisual Observatory, Strasbourg 2004, p. 61–70.

88 Stone 2009; Schauer 2005.

89 Noorloos, M., Hate Speech Revisited, A comparative and historical perspective on hate speech law in the Netherlands and England & Wales, Cambridge: Intersentia 2011, p. 41.

90 *Virginia v. Black*, 538 U.S. 343 (2003). See also: *R.A.V. v. St Paul*, 505 U.S. 377 (1992).

91 *National Socialist Party of America v. Village of Skokie*, 432 U.S. 43 (1977).

92 Sadurski 1999, p. 197;199–200.

93 Baker 2012, p. 63; Baker 1989.

94 Scanlon 1972, p. 204–226. Later he changed this radical view: Scanlon, T., Freedom of expression and categories of expression, *University of Pittsburg Law Review* 1979, vol. 40, no. 3, p. 519–550.

with, in their opinion, offensive speech. It has been argued that even in extreme cases the speaker must be protected against an intolerant audience, not the other way around, because promoting tolerance against the speaker enhances the capacity for general tolerance in society.[95]

1.5. European hate speech bans

In European countries, the law generally requires a less strict connection between speech and subsequent conduct than American doctrine, in order to justify restrictions to speech.[96] This will become apparent in the discussion of French and Dutch hate speech laws. Then, the criminalization of speech of a particular racist content or purpose is not regarded as fundamentally wrong. The offences are the outcome of a balancing act by the legislator of the interest of freedom of expression with other rights, interests and values, such as the respect for the equal human dignity, which have been for example, incorporated into the Constitution. National constitutional provisions protecting freedom of expression – and Article 10 of the European Convention of Human Rights (ECHR) – generally provide for such a balancing act by listing the interests for which the freedom might be curtailed. Freedom of expression then is not regarded as a right that is deserving of 'exceptional' treatment, but as one of several constitutional, fundamental rights.

The criminalization of hate speech is partly required by international treaties, such as the International Convention on the Elimination of all forms of Racial Discrimination (ICERD), or certain European conventions. However, international and European institutions may not use the exact same standards. This also applies to different European countries that may criminalize hate speech to varying degrees based on its connection with subsequent acts of discrimination and violence. An important question, therefore, is whether expression may be prohibited as hate speech, because it may lead to intolerance, discriminatory views and possible future discrimination or violence; or whether a clearer connection must exist between speech and subsequent – prohibited – acts of discrimination and violence.

One could imagine a sliding scale of types of speech offences that criminalize particular expressions according to their more or less strict connection with subsequent actions. From the American perspective, with such bans legislators and

---

95 Bollinger, L.C., *The tolerant society,* New York: Oxford University Press 1986, p. 182; Bollinger, L.C., 'The tolerant society': a response to critics, *Columbia Law Review* 1990, vol. 90, no. 4, p. 979–1003.

96 Rosenfeld, M., Hate Speech in Constitutional Jurisprudence, A Comparative Analysis, in: Herz & Molnar 2012, p. 242–289 (published earlier in: *Cardozo Law Review*, 2003, vol. 24, p.1523–1567; see several contributions to the theme issue 'Symposium: An Ocean Apart – Freedom of Expression in Europe and the United States', *Indiana Law Journal* 2009, vol. 84, no. 3, p. 809 *et seq.* An exception forms Hungary, see: Molnar, P., Towards an improved law and policy on 'Hate Speech' – The clear and present danger test in Hungary, in: Hare, I. & Weinstein, J. (Eds.), *Extreme Speech and Democracy*, Oxford: Oxford University Press 2009, p. 237–264.

judges find themselves on a 'slippery slope' that may result in censorship of unpopular speech.[97] Indeed, a consistent norm must mark a spot somewhere on this gradual scale.

In fact, group defamations and insults and 'incitements to hatred, discrimination, or violence' may have the *potential* or are *likely* to *eventually* lead to illegal or violent actions. Therefore, they may be regarded as not directly harmful – in the sense of the Millian-harm principle. Group defamation and hate speech also have a more indirect effect. Such speech may cause a poisoned or even threatening atmosphere, set groups against each other and thereby affect social cohesion.

This notably applies to group defamation and insult laws. These generally aim to protect groups against racial epithets, insults and allegations that violate reputation, good name, honour or dignity based on race or religion and so on. They thereby primarily seem to protect the members of the group against mental distress and psychological harm or against devaluation in the eyes of others, rather than to protect against a provoking others to actions that disturb the public order. However, the law may elevate the threshold for liability by requiring that group defamations and insults are uttered with the aim to incite others to hatred against the victims. For example, in England, group insults are only punishable when they consist of 'abusive, threatening or insulting words intended to stir up racial hatred and the racial hatred is likely to be stirred up thereby'.[98]

Incitements to hatred, discrimination, or violence may by their very nature be causally closer related to certain actions by others that affect public order than group defamations and insults. However hatred forms a particular attitude, also defined as an 'extreme form of dislike'[99] and 'discrimination' forms a controversial political concept, not particular illegal actions.[100] The question, therefore, is whether the expression is capable, likely or probable to provoke others to commit acts of discrimination or violence and whether hatred and disorder must actually occur. The public order argument may elevate the threshold for liability under hate speech bans.

However, in the context of hate speech uttered by one citizen or group and directed against another citizen or group, thus between citizens, the notion of public order might take on a different meaning than it does in the context of sedition and incitement to crimes uttered by one citizen or group and directed against state authorities. Public order might have a more substantial significance and refer to the preservation of the social order, an orderly democratic society free from discrimination. It could be argued that if no direct harm is required, then the public

---

97 Schauer, F., Slippery Slopes, *Harvard Law Review,* 1985, vol. 99, p. 361–383; Rosenfeld 2012, p. 286.

98 Noorloos 2011, p. 253 *et seq.*

99 Post, R., Hate speech, in: Hare & Weinstein 2009, p. 123.

100 According to Malik, 'Hate speech restriction is a means of rebranding certain, often obnoxious, ideas or arguments as immoral, a way of making certain ideas illegitimate without bothering politically to challenge them, which is dangerous.' Molnar, P., & Malik, K., Interview with Kenan Malik, in: Herz & Molnar 2012, p. 81;86.

order arguments might merge into paternalistic and moral considerations. Another possibility is, however, that the mid-term effects of hate speech are already considered as harmful to society. This therefore concerns a different value conflict and a different notion of harm.

Another question is what kind of utterances may fall under hate speech bans. Must expression, in order to be punishable, explicitly, according to its exact wording, defame a group or incite to particular acts of discrimination or violence against a group or can more disguised forms of defamation and hate speech already be punishable. On the one hand, phrases of a direct and unambiguous discriminatory purport and goal, such as: 'I urge all café owners to deny Muslims access to their bars' seem more reprehensible than vague phrases, such as: 'Stop the Islamization, Islam out of the country' and: 'Muslims have a backward culture'. On the other hand, it might be more effective and successful for encouraging others to racial discrimination and violence to plant a seed in the mind of others through negative imaging and vague allegations. Therefore, more indirect, disguised forms of hate speech can, given the specific context in which they are uttered, amount to a prohibited form of group defamation or incitement to hatred and discrimination against a particular group.

1.6. Synthesis Actions versus Opinions

There are good reasons for the state to prohibit hate speech by law. Hate speech may be prohibited because of the effect it has on the members of its target group, on third parties and due to the effect it has on society at large. Yet, the primary reason to prohibit hate speech is always the prevention of harm to persons and the protection of their rights. Restrictions to hate speech are, however, not grounded on the classical concept of harm by Mill. In fact, the perceived harm in hate speech is not the direct physical harm resulting from the imminent violent and lawless actions, which such speech – regardless of its content – can produce. This speech must also directly threaten public order.

Rather, hate speech can be considered harmful, because it can cause a poisonous atmosphere, set groups against each other, affect the social climate and form a breeding ground for future acts of discrimination and violence; it is therefore prohibited on account of its mid- and long term effects. Hate speech may then be prohibited precisely because of the racist message or ideas it conveys that are likely to cause such harmful effects. When hate speech is prohibited according to its more or less strict connection with subsequent acts of discrimination or violence, a consistent norm must mark a spot somewhere on this gradual scale.

Hate speech can also be considered harmful, because it affects the dignity of the members of its target group, it is therefore prohibited based on the direct effect it has on its victims (not via actions of third parties against them). The perceived harm in hate speech is that it undermines people's basic social standing by associating characteristics such as race, ethnicity or religion with attributes that should disqualify someone from being treated as a member of society in good standing. Hate speech may then be prohibited precisely because of the racist message or ideas it conveys that express the idea that members of another group are unworthy of equal citizenship. When hate speech is prohibited because its affects the dignity of its victims, a consistent norm must clarify that 'dignity' must not be understood as a 'public moral' separate from its harm to persons.

In fact, hate speech that affects the dignity of its victims can have far-reaching consequences for them, such as psychological harms, including fear, stress, low self-esteem, and low esteem by the public and can thereby cause their 'silencing'. Such hate speech also causes a hardening of public debate and the dissolution of norms for mutual respect. The argument that hate speech may be prohibited to prevent the harm it causes to people's dignity thus underlies, on a more fundamental legal level, the rationale of the prevention of harm in the sense of the mid-term effects of hate speech. Although these identified types of harm in hate speech must not be underestimated, hate speech does not literally constitute acts of discrimination in and of itself; the law cannot prohibit hate speech on that basis.

2. Contributions to Public Debate versus Other Types of Expression

An important justification for freedom of expression and the free political and public debate is its particular value or function in a democracy (2.1). Scholars, however, disagree on how to define free 'public discourse' and to what extent the government may delimit it, because the existence of free public discourse legitimizes state authority and the laws of the state. Whether scholars think hate speech should be either prohibited or allowed in public discourse is, in the end dependent upon their different conceptions of harm and perspectives on the harmful effects of hate speech (2.2). The question arises as to whether an ultimate limit may be reached when contributions to public debate amount to an abuse of the right to freedom of expression (2.3). Subsequently, one may question whether politicians and the media have either a particular freedom to or a particular responsibility in the exercise of the right and whether one can distinguish between different typologies of hate speech offenders (2.4). The paragraph concludes with a synthesis that defines the factor 'Public Debate versus Other Types of Expression' for the purpose of the further analysis in this study (2.5).

2.1. Democracy; popular sovereignty and political participation

Freedom of expression is generally regarded as having a particular value or function in a democracy. Freedom of speech is *a sine qua non* for a democracy, a tool for democratic decision-making by means of public and political debate.[101] However, the notion of democracy may be interpreted in different ways. One component of democracy is *popular sovereignty*, i.e. the *procedure* of decision making that results in the control of a majority of the people over the government.[102] The commitment to popular sovereignty creates a strong right to freedom of expression. If the people

---

101 Schauer 1982, p. 35 *et seq.*; Barendt 2005, p. 18.

102 Meiklejohn's procedural definition of self-governance in which the people are ultimately responsible for government decisions by means of their direct or indirect decision-making comes close to the term *majoritarianism*. See: Meiklejohn, A., *Political freedom the constitutional powers of the people,* Westport, Conn.: Greenwood Press 1979.

are the ultimate source of political authority, they must be able to speak to each other about all matters within the scope of this authority.[103]

This protects the interests of the audience as well. Citizens must be exposed to a wide range of views and be provided with enough information to hold government accountable. The commitment to popular sovereignty thus creates a rather narrow right to freedom of expression that is limited to *political* speech. From this perspective, the right to freedom of expression merely serves – the maintenance of – democracy. One could argue that extreme speech, such as hate speech or the advocacy to overthrow the government, lacks this purpose.

The people may thus, in the exercise of their sovereignty, adopt legislation that restricts such extreme speech. They may freely decide to no longer tolerate certain speech in the future. This may be regarded as undemocratic and illiberal. Moreover, they may even – through a democratic process – abolish the democratic government system, if no mechanisms are put in place to ensure its preservation.

To counter majoritarian tendencies, theorists of democracy often argue that minorities in society should be protected against the 'tyranny of the majority' by putting in place mechanisms that ensure equal participation of minorities in the deliberative political process and that legitimize the rules adopted by the majority. Another component of democracy therefore is the *individual right to equal political participation*, including not only the right to vote but also the right to participate in the discussion by which public opinion is formed.[104]

This right prevents governments from using their power to exclude speakers from this discussion, just because they disagree with their views. One could argue that extreme speech, such as hate speech and speech challenging the government, must be tolerated in public debate, because the state may not determine the boundaries of that public debate. From this perspective, democracy does not form a foundation for free speech, but the equal right to political participation through the exercise of free speech underpins democracy.[105] One could object that hate speech then must still be prohibited in public debate, precisely because it affects this equal right to political participation of its victims.

2.2. Public discourse

Democracy, characterized by popular sovereignty and the right of political participation, is connected with the notion of self-determination of people that forms the basis for *self-governance*.[106] Every citizen has the right to participate in public debate by which the people govern themselves through the formation of

103 Weinstein, J., Extreme Speech, Public Order, and Democracy: Lessons from *The Masses*, in: Hare & Weinstein 2009, p. 26.

104 Weinstein 2009, p. 27.

105 Barendt 2005, p. 20.

106 Post, R., Religion and Freedom of Speech, Portraits of Muhammed, *Constellations: an international journal of critical and democratic theory*, 2007, vol. 14, no. 1, p. 72–90.

public opinion. Another term for this process of public opinion forming is *'public discourse'*.[107] The question arises as to how to determine whether expression forms part of public discourse. One way would be by focusing on the content of speech. It is generally argued that public discourse is not limited to political speech in the narrow sense of holding government accountable. It includes all 'speech concerning the organization and culture of society'[108] or 'all matters of public concern' – as opposed to 'matters of purely private concern'.[109] However, the term 'matters of public concern' is open to different interpretations. It could relate to speech about matters that ought to be relevant to democratic self-governance. Criticism of the government, its officials and of public figures falls under this category. But it could also relate to speech about matters that interest large numbers of people, for example speech about celebrities. Interpretations of the term thus risk being either under or over inclusive.[110]

Another way would be by focusing on whether speech is distributed 'publicly' through 'democratic forums', such as public places and meetings and the media, including newspapers, literature, film, television, the Internet. Such dissemination then supposes that a speaker has intended to contribute to public debate and that his speech reaches a relatively large audience.[111] Speech distributed through media that form part of the 'structural skeleton' necessary for democratic self-governance, might be considered part of public discourse, regardless of its content.[112] However, overtly political speech distributed through such media might be regarded as forming part of 'core' public discourse.[113] This may include political criticism of public officials or the government's immigration and integration policy. Contrarily, speech about celebrities, the advertising of products or the proclaiming of a religion and proselytism may not be regarded as core public discourse.

The U.S. Supreme Court combines these approaches. The Court has considered that 'expression on public issues has always rested on the highest rung of the hierarchy of First Amendment values'[114] and that speech on matters of 'public concern' is 'entitled to special protection'.[115] Contrarily, commercial speech and indecent speech are afforded less protection. Even less protection is afforded to private, face-to-face, speech consisting of so-called *'fighting words'*, defined by the Court as 'personally abusive epithets which, when addressed to the ordinary citizen, are, as a matter of common knowledge, inherently likely to provoke violent

---

107 Post, R., The Constitutional Concept of Public Discourse: Outrageous Opinion, Democratic Deliberation, and Hustler Magazine v. Falwell, *Harvard Law Review*, 1990, vol. 103, no. 3, p. 626.

108 Weinstein 2009, p. 29; Barendt 2005, p. 189.

109 Post 1990, p. 667.

110 Post 1990, p. 667–674.

111 Post 1990, p. 675–676.

112 Weinstein 2009, p.30.

113 Weinstein 2009, p.30.

114 *Carey v. Brown*, 447 U.S. 455, 467 (1980).

115 *Snyder v. Phelps*, 131 S. Ct. 1207 (2011).

reactions'.[116] Such speech may be categorized as 'low value speech' that does not further the core of the First Amendment values.[117] The contours of public discourse may however run straight through the categorization often made by courts in artistic, humoristic, commercial, religious and political speech. It is generally accepted that some of these domains of speech are more valuable than others.[118] Political speech is generally regarded as having the strongest claim to be free from regulation. One could, however, argue that the state must afford equal protection to speech in all of these domains. The distinction between these categories of speech appears difficult, precisely because the government may not delimit the contours of public discourse.[119] Moreover, categories might partly overlap.[120] One could think of politically engaged art and humour or religious advertisements.

Expression that qualifies as hate speech could take any of these forms. For example, a humoristic cartoon depicting the terrorist attack on the WTC in New York with the text 'everybody has dreamt about it, Hamas did it' published right after on 9/11; a novel or poems that glorify the Holocaust; a political pamphlet with the text 'Blacks out of the country, white people first'; the advertisement of Nazi memorabilia; or the religiously motivated proclamation that homosexuality is a sin that must be exterminated may all incite to hatred, discrimination or violence. A different question is whether expression must form a qualitative contribution to a public debate. This appears central to the highly debated question of whether hate speech should be prohibited or allowed in public discourse. Scholars answer this question not only according to what in their view hate speech is and does, but also how they interpret the individual right to equal political participation in the light of their conception of the state as a political entity.

Post strictly distinguishes the domain of *community*, i.e. the social life governed by shared mores and norms, from the domain of *democracy*, i.e. the political domain where citizens come to identify with the actions and decisions of their government through (potential) participation in public discourse (collective self-determination).[121] In the former domain, the state may prohibit hate speech, because it may conflict with community standards of *civility* and *respect*. In the latter

---

116 *Cohen v. California*, 403 U.S. 15 (1971). In 1942 the U.S. Supreme Court more broadly defined fighting words as 'those which by their very utterance inflict injury or tend to incite an immediate breach of the peace' in: *Chaplinsky v. New Hampshire*, 315 U.S. 568 (1942).

117 Stone 2009, p. 283. Over the years the U.S. Supreme Court has characterized other categories of *low value speech*, including express incitement of unlawful conduct, threats, fighting words, false statements of fact, obscenity, and commercial advertising.

118 In the American context, a well-known method to evaluate restrictions to speech is the use of different 'levels of scrutiny' depending on social value of the speech in question. Then, 'low value speech' calls for a 'lenient scrutiny', while 'high level speech' calls for a 'strict scrutiny'. Restrictions to the latter will sooner constitute a violation of freedom of expression than restrictions to the former.

119 Post 1990.

120 Randall, M.H., Commercial Speech under the European Convention on Human Rights: Subordinate or Equal?, *Human Rights Law Review*, 2006, vol. 6, no. 1, p. 53–86.

121 Post 1990, p. 601–686.

domain, the state, itself consisting of different communities, must, however, remain neutral to competing civility rules and the 'marketplace of communities'. As public discourse must be open to the opinions of all, *within* public discourse hate speech must be immune from regulation. The 'paradox of public discourse' is, however, that public discourse requires *rational deliberation*, which itself appears to depend on the observance of the civility rules it negates.[122]

According to Post, hate speech must thus be allowed in public debate, not only because public debate is indispensable for democratic decision-making and legitimizes state authority (the law), but also because for Post hate speech merely violates certain personal moral standards, the compliance of which ought to be a purely private matter. Even though hate speech might affect the dignity of its victims or lead to acts of discrimination in the mid- and long term, the wrongfulness of such speech is to be decided in the public debate itself that underpins a democracy. Post's theory, in the end, rests on a vision of the state as a political entity strictly separate from civil society and a strong public/private divide.

One could argue that a society cannot be strictly divided into different domains. It is contended that the right to freedom of expression, because of its inherent individuality, carries sources of tension that, in the course of exercising the right – which inevitably takes place in the community and before the community – erupt almost unavoidably. A harmonious balance must be created between the exercise of the individual right and the interest of the community. Therefore, freedom of expression is an ideal, an 'unreachable mirage' that we are striving to reach, while taking into account certain community considerations.[123] In the natural rights tradition, the state is envisioned as a 'social contract' through which individuals establish a community for the mutual preservation of their rights. This conception of the state still underpins the French Republic (Chapter 3, para. 1.5 *infra*). *Within* the state, citizens, therefore, still have the duty to respect each other's natural rights. They must view and recognize each other as free, equal, rational persons. Such mutual recognition, therefore, may also form a precondition and an integral aspect of public discourse itself; as hate speech denies such *recognition*, it must be banned within public discourse.[124]

The same conclusion may be drawn from Habermas' theory of the 'Deliberative Democracy'.[125] Habermas argues that the democratic decision-making process consists of an on-going cooperative, rational communication between citizens that is focused on *consensus* on elementary moral values.[126] One could argue that hate speech does not form rational communication aimed at consensus, but is aimed at

---

122 Post 1990, p. 643.

123 Koltay, A., *Freedom of speech: the unreachable mirage*, Budapest: Complex 2013.

124 Cf. Heyman 2008, p. 171–172.

125 Habermas, J. & Rehg, W., *Between facts and norms, contributions to a discourse theory of law and democracy*, Cambridge, Mass.: The MIT Press 1996.

126 Only then will citizens experience the process and its results as responsive to their ideas and values and will democracies be stable and legitimate.

subordinating others.[127] Therefore, it may not comply with the presuppositions for the deliberative process, being that no one capable of making a relevant contribution has been excluded; participants have an equal voice; they are free to speak their honest opinion; and the process is free from coercion.[128] Other than Post, these perspectives thus presume that hate speech does not merely contravene morals, but causes actual harm to its victims and violates their rights. The regulation of hate speech in public debate thus is not merely grounded in 'community standards of civility and respect'. Hate speech then must be prohibited in public debate due to its direct consequential effects and effects in the mid- and long term; by denying the recognition of the equal dignity of the victims, it affects their position in society and also affects their equal participation in public debate ('silencing'). Such equal participation is indispensable for democratic decision-making focussed on reaching consensus about the law.

However, Mouffe objects that there are limits to consensus in a democracy, because many disagreements exist that cannot be resolved through deliberation and discourse. By attempting to build consensus, democracies precisely oppress differing opinions, races, classes and worldviews. A 'radical democracy' must, however, not let particular power relations in society suppress conflicts, but must accept and channel *difference* and *dissent*.[129] This is the precise basis for the allowance of extreme speech in public debate to a great extent. The political debate may indeed be considered as characterized by framing, stereotyping and hostility against political opponents and this may indeed even be considered necessary to bring colour to democracy. One may therefore accept these means in order to consolidate or change particular power relations in society. However, one could argue that this still does not justify the use of hate speech in public discourse that causes harm to minorities, for example, through their stigmatization.[130] In the main, scholars seem to agree that freedom of expression and the existence of a free, lively, inclusive public discourse is of fundamental importance to the proper functioning of democracy, but in the end their different conceptions of harm and perspectives on the harmful effects of hate speech appear to determine whether they think hate speech should be prohibited or allowed in public debate.

2.3. Abuse of rights

One can nevertheless discern two ways in which freedom of expression and democracy may interrelate. Firstly, citizens have the right to freedom of expression and its free exercise underpins democracy. From this perspective, the prohibition on

---

127 Cf. Heyman 2008, p. 178–179.

128 Habermas & Rehg 1996.

129 Laclau, E. & Mouffe, C., *Hegemony and Socialist Strategy, Towards a Radical Democratic Politics*, 2nd ed., London: Verso 2001.

130 Dommering, E.J., Féret en daarna, in: Turner, C.J. *et al* (eds.), *25 jaar Mediaforum, Een voorblik door de achteruitkijkspiegel*, Amsterdam: Otto Cramwinckel Uitgever 2013, p. 164.

the utterance of hate speech in public debate may be regarded as 'undemocratic'. Secondly, freedom of expression exists within democracy. From this perspective, the prohibition on uttering hate speech in public debate may be regarded as necessary to prevent excesses of unlimited democracy.[131] The extent of the freedom to express hateful speech in public debate then, in the end, depends on the particular conception of the constitutional state.

For example, according to the German concept of the '*wehrhafte* or *streitbare Demokratie*', the constitutional state has extensive powers and duties to defend the liberal democratic order against those who violate its basic constitutional principles or want to abolish it.[132] In Germany, freedom of expression is coloured by the constitutional basic value of the inviolability of human dignity.[133] Different versions of the '*militant democracy*' are however imaginable.[134] One important common tool may form the prohibition of the abuse of rights, i.e. the use of rights aimed at the destruction of the fundamental rights and freedoms of others.

Hate speech might, under certain circumstances, constitute an abuse of the right to freedom of expression. Hate speech bans may be used, when democracy is at stake. This might be considered the case, for example, when gross criticism on particular minorities uttered in public debate in the course of elections by a populist party, that strives to decrease the rights of such groups, finds acceptance with the public and the party tends to obtain a political majority in a country.

The question is, however, to what extent one can distinguish hate speech directed against minorities from speech directed against the government. Insult or hatred against a politician may be interpreted as criticism of the government, when the insult or hatred concerns his public function. Likewise, the insult or hatred against minorities might also be interpreted as criticism of the government, when the insult or hatred concerns, for example, the failure of the government's minority or immigration policy. Both may be considered part of a free debate on matters of public concern.

Yet, there is a distinction between the two. Some politicians are political officials who bear responsibility for the political acts of the government, whereas other politicians strive to obtain political power. Therefore, harsh criticism on the actions of such politicians must be possible. But the limits to legitimate criticism on the

---

131 Greene, J., Hate Speech and the Demos, in: Herz & Molnar 2012, p. 92.

132 The concept of the Militant Democracy was, however, already developped in: Loewenstein, K., Militant Democracy and Fundamental rights I, *The American Political Science Review*, 1937, Vol. 31, No. 3, p. 417–432; Loewenstein, K., Militant Democracy and Fundamental rights II, *The American Political Science Review*, 1937, Vol. 31, No. 4, p. 638–658.

133 Grundgesetz [GG] Article 1. Furthermore, the right to freedom of expression must be balanced with the right to personal honor, a constitutional right protected in Article 5(2) of the German Constitution.

134 For different versions of the concept, see: Sajó, A. (ed.), *Militant democracy*, Utrecht: Eleven International Publishing 2004; Thiel, M. (ed.), *The 'Militant Democracy' Principle in Modern Democracies*, Farnham, Surrey: Ashgate 2009.

government via gross comments about minorities that are at their expense may be reached earlier.

The question arises as to where to draw the line with regard to far-reaching political and legislative proposals in the context of a vehement political debate on immigration and integration issues that, if they were effectuated, could violate an existing prohibition of discrimination. An example could be the proposal to expel Muslims from the country, purely based on their adherence to Islam. One could argue that democracy requires the allowance of such proposals in political debate, because they may only be realized after a political party that advocates such a proposal has – in a democratic manner – gained enough political power and support. After all, such proposals do not directly incite third parties to commit concrete described acts of discrimination themselves.

Such discriminatory proposals inevitably have a negative effect on the members of the target group. However, a state may assume that free public and political debate is of such vital importance that the harmful effects such discriminatory proposals may have on its victims – the effect on their dignity and on their possibilities to participate in public debate or of being discriminated – must be taken for granted and that the protection of the public debate prevails. Then the question is: what is the ultimate standard for determining if such proposals *are* excessive?

One could require a strict connection between a political proposal and possible disturbances of the public order by the risk of direct, subsequent acts of discrimination by third parties or violent conflicts between groups in society – which result in imminent lawlessness. Then the state might only take a seemingly neutral position as regards the discriminatory content of expression, because the establishment of such a link might precisely require an evaluation of the content of the proposal concerned and how its purport may be received by the public given the particular social context, in which discrimination and violence against the particular group exists to a certain extent. Moreover, the state – that in first instance may have restricted hate speech to prevent harm to dignity and harms in the mid- and long term – would fall back on a more narrow conception of harm through direct actions in the Millian sense that does not underlie the regulation of hate speech.

A more appropriate, transparent, substantive standard for excessiveness could, therefore, be whether expression constitutes an abuse of rights. This clearly requires an evaluation of the discriminatory content of a proposal, i.e. whether its aim is the destruction of the fundamental rights of others, which the constitutional state guarantees without distinction based on race or religion. This standard would leave ample room for many far-reaching proposals as a solution for existing problems in society, but the outer line is drawn with the violation of people's equal fundamental rights. Such expression endangers the 'public order' in the sense that it endangers the interest in an orderly democratic society free from discrimination. This, therefore, concerns a different value conflict and a different notion of harm; as may be the case in the previous example of the proposal to expel members of a particular minority group from a country.

It has, however, been argued that discriminatory hate speech must be permitted in public debate in order to *legitimize* the existence of anti-discrimination laws. Opponents of discrimination laws must not only have the opportunity to *vote*, but also to *voice* against them.[135] Through discriminatory hate speech they can express their dissent and 'blow off steam', but at the same time respect the anti-discriminations laws, with which they disagree.[136] Generally criticism uttered in the context of a vehement political debate on immigration and integration issues takes a less concrete form than criticism of discrimination laws. It may rather consist of suggestive language through all kinds of negative associations and 'framing', for example utterances that connect 'islamization' and Muslim-immigration with increased crime rates or economic decline. Such forms of stigmatization harm the dignity of the minorities concerned, while they do not formulate any solutions to the indicated problems. In such cases, should the public debate argument honestly prevail?

2.4. The special position of politicians, the media and a typology of offenders

In principle, the possible special protection of contributions to public debate may apply equally to the contributions of all citizens participating in the debate. The question arises as to whether a distinction may be made between different participants *within* public debate. It has been argued that hate speech regulation has largely been a reaction to WWII and the hate speech perpetrated in Nazi Germany by the *government* as part of its official ideology and policy, but that nowadays hate speech is primarily used by *opponents* of the government and members of marginalized groups that hope to achieve political power.[137]

One could argue that notably a politician – of the opposition – must have the opportunity to partake in public debate and criticize the government. This forms the core of a democratic society. Political criticism uttered by a politician pre-eminently qualifies for the protection of freedom of expression, also in the context of immigration and integration issues. One could argue that a politician has a bigger responsibility to weigh his words and to avoid inciting to religious intolerance, hatred, discrimination or violence. Therefore, restrictions on his political speech may be sooner justified. In fact, politicians strive to obtain the support of citizens

---

135 Dworkin, R.M., Foreword, in: Hare & Weinstein 2009, vii.

136 For a criticism of the argument and a response, see: Waldron, J., Hate Speech and Political Legitimacy, in: Herz & Molnar 2012, p. 329–340; Dworkin, R., Reply to Jeremy Waldron, in: Herz & Molnar 2012, p. 341–344.

137 Despite the general increase of hate speech among mainstream political and social actors in the aftermath of the 9/11 attacks. Furthermore, hate speech may be used by members of groups long victimized by racist policies and rhetoric (blacks) against their perceived racist oppressors (whites). See: Rosenfeld 2012, p. 244.

for their ideas. This is precisely why they may be aware of the effect of their speech. Furthermore, they may be considered to take into account the principles of a democracy, precisely because they strive to obtain political power. The relationship between the special freedom and the special responsibilities of politicians is thus a complex one.

To a certain extent this special protection also applies to journalists or the media in general. They too are regarded as indispensable in a democracy, because of their specific role. On the one hand, they may be entitled to a large freedom of expression, because they provide access to information and thereby ensure that citizens can hold government accountable. On the other hand, they may have a bigger responsibility, because they may influence the shaping of public opinion, the placing of issues on the political agenda and the success of politicians and political parties. A prohibition of the 'dissemination' or 'spreading' of racist propaganda and all ideas based on hatred may in particular concern the media.

From an anthropological perspective, speakers who use hate speech in public debate could be categorized in different types of offenders. One could for example differentiate between 'ideologists', 'instrumentalists/ activists' and 'incidentalists'.[138] Ideologists consciously – and often structurally – violate hate speech bans, out of pure conviction. The same applies to instrumentalists/activists, who are more calculative; they generally aim to use their criminal prosecutions for their own political purposes. Finally, incidentalists do not, in their own experience, consciously violate the law. They do not form part of radical political parties or groupings and their utterances are less extreme.[139] For the application of hate speech bans, these types of offenders may not be translatable into particular responsibilities, but may be translated into criteria for the determination of the intent of the speaker, the qualification of utterances and the severity of the sanction.

138 Vrielink 2010, p. 466 *et seq.* This categorization is, however, not confined to contributions to public debate as referred to in this study.

139 Vrielink 2010, p. 467.

2.5. Synthesis Public Debate versus Other Types of Expression

The existence of a free, lively and inclusive political and public debate is of fundamental importance to the proper functioning of democracy and for the legitimization of state authority (the law). Therefore, the state must set the contours of the political and public debate broadly; it may include speech on all matters of public concern and/or speech distributed publicly through all kinds of democratic forums. Overtly political speech, such as criticism of public officials or government policies, distributed through mass media forms part of 'core' public discourse. Given their special value, such contributions to public debate are entitled to a higher level of protection than speech that does not have this purpose.

In principle, many extreme and unpopular political opinions must therefore be allowed in public debate that may be characterized by a certain vehemence and hostility against political opponents and views. Such expression should not be prohibited, merely because it would contravene personal standards of morality, civility or respect. Contrarily, in principle, utterances that amount to hate speech against particular minorities in society do have a special position in public debate and may therefore be prohibited, precisely because of the harm it inflicts on its victims and the social climate, including the effect on the possibilities of its victims to participate on an equal basis in public debate; hence their right to equal political participation.

A state can nevertheless consider that in certain cases free public and political debate is of such vital importance that the harmful effects a particular form of hate speech may have on its victims – the effect on their dignity, on their possibilities to participate in public debate or of being discriminated – must be taken for granted and that the protection of the public debate prevails. This notably applies to discriminatory political proposals by politicians that do not directly incite citizens to commit concrete described acts of discrimination themselves, but if effectuated might violate an existing anti-discrimination law. A consistent norm must then clarify its ultimate standard for determining when such proposals are excessive.

In light of the foregoing, it would be inconsistent to set the outer limits of political proposals with the direct risk of disturbance of the 'public order' through violent conflicts between groups in society, thus imminent lawlessness. Then the state would fall back on a conception of harm through direct actions in the Millian sense that does not underlie the regulation of hate speech. A more appropriate standard can be that public debate must leave ample room for far reaching proposals as a solution to existing problems in society. The outer line is drawn, however, when political proposals constitute an abuse of rights, because they violate people's equal fundamental rights. Such expression endangers the 'public order' in that it negatively impacts on the interest in an orderly democratic society free from discrimination. This thereby concerns a different value conflict and a different notion of harm.

3. Allegation of Facts versus Value Judgments

An important justification for free discussion without state interference is the search of truth. The political and public debate is, therefore, also envisioned as the 'marketplace of ideas' (3.1). As far as the setting of restrictions to public debate is concerned, free speech doctrine, however, generally distinguishes the expression of value judgments from statements of fact. The distinction between facts and value judgments is notably relevant in the context of defamation law (3.2). The question arises as to whether this distinction may be relevant for determining liability for hate speech uttered in public debate, notably when it consists of *group* defamation, and if so, whether the distinction is consistently made in the application of hate speech bans (3.3). This also applies in particular to one form of hate speech; Holocaust denial (3.4). If hate speech is prohibited, the question arises whether hate speech bans may be of a criminal and/ or civil nature (3.5). The paragraph concludes with a synthesis that defines the factor 'Allegation of Facts versus Value judgments' for the purpose of the further analysis in this study (3.6).

3.1. Truth and the marketplace of ideas

Freedom of expression of opinion is generally regarded to be indispensable for the search for truth.[140] The search for truth is a way to further knowledge, but also a way for individuals to develop their talents and to reach their potential, that is self-realization. For these reasons, in *On Liberty* (1859) John Stuart Mill argued that the authorities should not suppress opinions based on their alleged falsity, because silenced opinion may be true. The authorities may deny its truth, but we can never know for certain whether an opinion is true or false. To deny this is to assume our own infallibility.[141]

It is through the public exchange of different views that truth can be discovered and justified. In a free and open discussion truth-claims can be tested and the truth eventually will prevail.[142] Even when accepted opinions are in fact true, Mill says it

140 For criticism on the justification of truth see: Barendt 2005, p. 8 *et seq.*
141 Mill 1936, p. 20.
142 Mill 1936, p. 42.

is still good to continuously challenge such opinions because those opinions will only be held stronger. Moreover, accepted opinions will often only be partially true and rejected opinions will only be partially false. Therefore, knowledge will increase if we allow opinions accepted to be true to be refined by opinions accepted to be false.[143]

Mill's speech theory has been criticized for failing to adequately consider the possibility to suppress opinions for reasons other than their alleged falsity – except for the prevention of violence. Mill regards the increase in knowledge as a value that has priority over almost any other good. However, restrictions to speech are often motivated not by epistemic goals, but for other reasons. One could argue that even if a suppressed view were true, losing that truth may be considered a price well worth paying to achieve these other goals.[144]

For example, it has been argued that even if there were racial correlated differences in human intelligence, allowing such discourse might be considered undesirable, because it may increase racial discrimination. As we have seen, hate speech bans may aim to protect people's equal dignity, create a comfortable living environment or lessen the degree of religious or racial tension and discrimination. Hence, there could be a social value in the suppression of a view that would be largely or entirely independent of the truth or falsity of the view.[145] The question is whether Mill's theory is applicable outside the context of a purely scientific discussion?

Nevertheless, a famous metaphor for the search for truth in the political domain is the concept of the 'marketplace of ideas', formulated in American free speech doctrine by U.S. Supreme Court judge Holmes as: 'the best test of truth is the power of the thought to get itself accepted in the competition of the market'.[146] In other words, truth, or at least the best idea, will emerge out of the competition of ideas in a free public discussion.[147] The concept of the marketplace of ideas is based on an analogy to the economic concept of a free market and does not – like Mill does – start from a coherent, objective notion of truth that can actually be discovered, but from a relative, subjective one: truth is the mere *outcome* of the process of discussion. Therefore, according to American free speech doctrine, in principle even the most extreme or hateful ideas can be allowed in the marketplace of ideas and can legitimately become a 'political truth' when a majority opts for them.

One could, however, question whether the market place of ideas will always produce the truth or the best idea. The concept may be criticized for overestimating the capacity of individuals to use their own reasoning to distinguish between right

143 Mill 1936, p. 55; summary of the argument on p. 63–64.

144 Schauer, F., Social Epistemology, Holocaust Denial, and the Post-Millian Calculus, in: Herz & Molnar 2012, p. 132.

145 Cf. Schauer 2012, p. 132.

146 *Abrams v. US*, 250 U.S. 616 (1919).

147 Alexander, L., *Is there a right of freedom of expression?*, Cambridge: Cambridge University Press 2005, p. 128–129.

and wrong.[148] For example, the question is whether racist ideologies are susceptible to argument? Moreover, 'public opinion' may form a power factor that hinders the critical opinion forming of individuals.[149] In the end not the best idea, but the most popular idea may survive. In fact, which ideas the marketplace of ideas will advance may depend on many social factors, including whether minorities have equal access to and equal opportunities to express their views in the media.

It has been argued that one may prohibit hateful racist views in public or political debate, because the falsity of racial doctrines would no longer be a live issue and an open question in politics, but could be regarded as more or less settled. Therefore, allowing a robust debate about the truth of such views would outweigh the cost of hate speech, i.e. attacks on the dignity of minority groups.[150] However, even if one agrees that the benefits of allowing hate speech do not outweigh the disadvantages, some might nevertheless still oppose that – because to them hate speech merely concerns *moral* truth claims, i.e. the existence of *objective* moral truths is controversial and that *consensus* on moral issues appears nearly impossible.[151] Then it is thought that hate speech may affect people's dignity, affect the social climate and lead to discrimination in the mid term, but is not wrongful in the sense that it violates people's rights, because it is not directly harmful in the Millian sense.

Hence, whether one thinks hate speech should be prohibited or allowed in public debate in the end still depends on one's conception of harm and perspective on the harmful effects of hate speech, as well as one's perspective on the interrelationship between freedom of expression (public debate) and democracy. Again it can be said that precisely because the public and political debate constitutes a market place of ideas that does not concern universal truth finding, but the formation of power and the laws of the state, political opinions that amount to hate speech against minorities in society do have a special position in public debate and, therefore, may be prohibited if they affect the equal human dignity and are intended to destroy the fundamental rights of the members of the target group (para. 2.2 *supra*).

3.2. The fact/opinion-distinction and defamation laws

Where Mill's argument from truth may be applied to both factual and moral propositions equally, the law generally clearly distinguishes statements of fact from statements of opinion for purposes of restricting an expression. This distinction is understandable. Opinions convey value judgments that contain personal evaluations. They are subjective in the sense that they may vary from person to

---

148 However, Milton argued that individuals should have unlimited access to the ideas of others in a free and open encounter precisely to properly exercise their reason. See: Milton, J., *Areopagitica and other political writings of John Milton*, Indianapolis: Liberty Fund 1999.

149 Nieuwenhuis, A.J., *Over de grens van de vrijheid van meningsuiting*, Nijmegen: Ars Aequi Libri 2011, p. 31.

150 Waldron 2012, p. 195–197.

151 Cf. Laclau & Mouffe 2001.

person and are relative in the sense that they might depend on their context. By their very nature, opinions cannot 'be proved true or false'.[152] As the U.S. Supreme Court has stated, 'Under the First Amendment, there is no such thing as a false idea'.[153] Therefore, the State may not determine whether value judgments are true or false and suppress them based on of their alleged falsity.

In this respect, statements of fact differ from opinions. They are objective in the sense that a fact does not depend on who believes it or who presents it. By their very nature, facts can 'be proved true or false'. As the U.S. Supreme Court has stated, 'there is no constitutional value in false statements of fact.'[154] Therefore, the state may take into account the alleged falsity, when suppressing speech considered harmful. This notably also includes false statements of fact that violate an individual's reputation, i.e. 'the esteem in which an individual is generally held within a particular community',[155] which generally forms the object of defamation laws.

It is outside the scope of this study to deeply delve into the particular differences between defamation law in common law and civil law countries.[156] Generally, defamation laws distinguish *defamation*, i.e. the imputation or allegation of a specific fact to a particular person, from *insult*, i.e. speech about a particular person not concerning a specific fact. It is generally accepted that in defamation cases, a defendant must have the possibility to prove the truth of his factual statement. Other than for insult, the proof of truth would remove liability for defamation. However, strong negative value judgments, such as calling someone a 'Nazi', may require a sufficient factual basis in order to escape liability for insult.

The fact/opinion distinction thus may not be razor sharp. Therefore, courts may find difficulty in drawing a consistent distinction between constitutionally protected statements of opinion and prohibited false statements of fact. For example, does calling someone a 'liar' or a 'criminal' constitute a factual assertion or an opinion? To answer this question several factors may be considered relevant, including the precision or ambiguity of the statement, its verifiability, the literary context and the broader context in which the statement occurred.[157] An opinion could then be defined as a statement that 'does not contain a factual connotation, which could be proved to be false or cannot reasonably be interpreted as stating actual facts given all the circumstances, including the language used (such as rhetoric, hyperbole, satire or jest)'.[158]

---

152 Post 1990, p. 655.

153 *Gertz v. Robert Welch, Inc.*, 418 U.S. 323 (1974).

154 *Gertz v. Robert Welch, Inc.*, 418 U.S. 323 (1974).

155 Defining Defamation, Principles of Freedom of Expression and Protection of Reputation, Article 19, July 2000, p.1, available at: www.article19.org.

156 In common law countries, defamation largely forms the object of tort law. In civil law countries, defamation may form the object of specific statutory criminal and or civil prohibitions. Furthermore, defamation may be regulated under the civil norm of the 'wrongful act'.

157 *Ollman v. Evans*, 750 F.2d 970 (D.C. Cir. 1984) (en banc), *cert. denied,* 471 U.S. 1127 (1985).

158 Defining Defamation, Principles of Freedom of Expression and Protection of Reputation, Article 19, July 2000, p. 12.

Defamatory statements of fact that contain falsities may however be made in order to comment on matters of public interest and may, as such, nevertheless be justified. Therefore, in most countries, a defendant or suspect in a defamation case may evoke the defence of 'reasonable publication' or an analogous defence based on 'fair comment',[159] 'due diligence' or 'good faith', which could remove liability for his defamatory statement, if the defendant could demonstrate that he had observed certain standards (fair hearing, absence of animosity, moderate language, aim to inform the public). This right to *inform* the public on public or political issues 'in good faith' is, however, much narrower than the previously discussed right to enter into a free public debate on matters of public concern.[160] The question arises as to how these two justifications interrelate.

It can be said that over time the notion of the interest of a free political and public debate in society has increased and therefore has superseded the narrower right to inform the public as a justifying ground in defamation cases. Nowadays vehement criticism on conduct, views or government policies of political figures by means of strong allegations can be regarded as forming an integral or even necessary part of the democratic debate, not only in its ability to consolidate or change particular power relations but also to expose forms of power (democratic control). However, this does not signify that minorities in society may be attacked in public debate with the same level of vehemence; direct stigmatizing attacks against minorities in society have very little connection with any of these functions of democratic debate.

3.3. Group defamation

In order to be defamatory, a factual statement must violate a persons' 'reputation'. One can distinguish three different concepts of 'reputation' that the law of defamation attempts to protect.[161] Firstly, reputation as *property* is akin to goodwill, a private interest and the fruit of an individual's effort and labour in the market society. Secondly, reputation as *honour* is a persons' personal reflection of the status which society ascribes to his social position; a public good in the deference society. Thirdly, reputation as *dignity* is the respect that arises from full membership in society, maintained by – from Post's perspective – 'rules of civility' in both the individual and public interest.[162] In order to be defamatory, statements

159 In common law countries, the fact/opinion-distinction underlies the traditional privilege of 'fair comment', a defence in defamation cases that guarantees 'the freedom of the press to express statements on matters of public interest, as long as the statements are not made with ill will, spite, or with the intent to harm the plaintiff.' Nowadays – at least in America – the 'fair comment'-privilege has largely been replaced by the requirement that statements of fact only amount to defamation when they are made with 'actual malice'.

160 Cf. Post 1990, p. 661 *et seq.*

161 Post, R.C., The Social Foundations of Defamation law: Reputation and the Constitution, *California Law Review* 1986, vol. 74, p. 691–742; Milo 2008, p. 26 *et seq.*

162 Post 1986.

of fact must thus violate one of these three values that underlie the concept of reputation.

Furthermore, defamation laws can only protect individuals or entities against harm to a reputation, which they have or merit. One could argue that objects, such as state- or religious symbols, flags or national insignia, and the state or nation as such do not have a 'reputation' and therefore cannot be protected by defamation laws.[163] Likewise, one could question whether racial and religious groups can have a 'reputation' and can be protected by defamation laws. Individual defamation and hate speech consisting of group defamation may, however, be thought of as two forms of injuring people's reputation that raise distinct problems.

Defamation laws can be said to protect the particularity or intricate detail of each individual's personalized reputation (reputation as property or honour). In this case there must be defamation of a particular identifiable person, or of a group so confined that the allegation descends to particulars. Group defamation laws on the other hand prohibit generalizations that all members of a large group allegedly possess a certain discrediting characteristic.[164] These laws can be said to protect the broad foundations of each person's reputation or civic dignity. They protect large numbers of people, thought of as a group, against attacks on the fundamental reputation of all persons of that kind.[165]

However, it seems impossible to impute an entire group of having committed *one specific* fact. As a group cannot have a common reputation based on one specific fact, it seems questionable to prohibit group defamation. But one could also argue that as one cannot impute one specific fact to an entire group, group defamation must be prohibited. For example, it is very hard to sustain that "The Muslims' killed Dutch anti-Islam filmmaker Theo Van Gogh'. Therefore, such an expression can evidently be qualified as group defamation. Group defamations may however often consist of vague allegations and generalizations, such as 'Muslims are a danger to our society', and racist epithets, such as 'Muslims are goat-fuckers' that are more on the opinion rather than on the fact side. Therefore, group defamation laws may not necessarily distinguish between defamation and insult of – thus facts and opinions about – a group, but could be formulated more broadly and comprise both.

One may argue that in the end group defamation laws do not protect the dignity of the group as such, that is a specific *group dignity*, but protect *individuals* when defamatory imputations are associated with shared characteristics such as race, ethnicity, religion, gender, sexuality and national origin.[166] There is no real group involved, because such characteristics should not be used to undermine *individual dignity*. However, a racist forms certain prejudices by viewing, for example, Arabs

163 Cf. Defining Defamation, Principles of Freedom of Expression and Protection of Reputation, Article 19, July 2000, p. 5.

164 Sadurski 1999, p. 194; 216.

165 Waldron 2012, p. 52–53.

166 Waldron 2012, p. 56–57; 60.

or Africans as objectionable groups or communities. As prejudice is contempt of one group for another, it must be countered at that level too: by insisting on the equal dignity of groups as a positive response to the denigration of individuals based on their race.[167]

The question of whether group defamation laws protect groups *qua group* or the individual persons belonging to a group, as an aggregate of individuals, is important, because it may determine *who* may invoke the prohibitions in relation to *what* kind of utterances. Criminal group defamation laws often do not formulate mere aggravating circumstances to generic offences of defamation and insult, but constitute independent offences that – according to their wording – protect 'groups', not individual persons belonging to a group. These offences may therefore cover phrases such as: 'Muslims are criminals', but not phrases such as: 'Ali is a criminal Muslim'. It seems unlikely that generic defamation and insult laws could provide sufficient protection against gross generalizations regarding non-further specified groups.

However, it is sometimes argued that specific group defamation bans are unnecessary, precisely because the law already prohibits or criminalizes defamation and insult of an individual person. Such generic laws would suffice for the protection of individual persons. Indeed, one could argue that the *arguments* for restricting group defamation are connected with arguments for restricting a larger category such as defamation or insult not necessarily limited to race, religion and so on. The same might be said of incitement to hatred, discrimination or violence in relation to the incitement to illegality. In this sense, hate speech is not an entirely unique category and its alleged harms have potential counter parts apart from this particular domain.[168]

On the other hand, the *harms* of group defamation may not necessarily be considered to be the same as those of generic defamation or insult. It is argued that by its very nature group defamation may cause greater aggregated harm than defamation of an individual in general; it inflicts a deeper injury to a person qua member of a group than qua individual personally, hurts a greater number of people[169] and can even cause tensions between groups in society.

Contrarily, others opine that group defamation would be less severe, because the nexus between the defamation and the victim is less certain than in the case of individual libel. This is precisely the reason that, for example, in America a member of a defamed group may not recover unless the defamatory statement can be reasonably understood to refer specifically to that individual.[170] Another example is

---

167 Waldron, J., The Dignity of Groups, in: Barnard-Naudé, J. *et al.* (Eds.), *Acta Juridica 2008: Dignity, Freedom and the Post-Apartheid Legal Order*, South Africa, Juta Law 2008, p.81;-82;84.

168 Schauer 2012, p. 142–143.

169 Sadurski 1999, p. 216. See also: Lerner, N., Group Libel Revisited, *Israel Yearbook on Human Rights* 1987, 17, p. 189.

170 Stern, N., The certainty principle as justificiation for the group defamation rule, *Arizona State Law Journal*, 2008, vol. 40, p. 951–1001; Polelle, M.J., Racial and ethnic group defamation: a speech-friendly proposal, *Boston College Third World Law Journal* 2003, vol. 23, p. 213–273.

that of Germany, where German courts generally regard religious groups such as Protestants, Catholics or Christians to be insufficiently demarcated to be protected by defamation laws. Contrarily, defamation of Jews in general is a defamation of all individual Jews because of the special history of Germany.[171]

Given the particularity of group defamation bans, the question arises as to whether a defendant or suspect of group defamation must be allowed to prove the truth of his statement.[172] This seems unlikely both in the event that group defamation is prohibited because racist imputations are regarded as necessarily false and in the event that group defamation is prohibited for reasons that are independent of the truth or falsity of the racist view. But will the extent to which an allegation is true never play a role for the determination of an author's liability for statements about a group of people in public debate? Imagine that, for example, a politician makes the following statement in the media in the context of the immigration and integration problematics in a country: 'Moroccans are overrepresented in crime rates; such criminal behaviour is inherent in their religion and culture'. Does this statement constitute a free contribution to the public debate on problems related to immigration and integration or a prohibited form of hate speech against Moroccans based on their religion and ethnic background? What standard can be used to answer that question?

The statement that people of Moroccan descent are overrepresented in crime rates might be true but does this form a sufficient factual basis for the general negative conclusion that such behaviour is inherent to, and thus caused by their religion or culture and that all members of the group are necessarily guilty of such behaviour? In principle, there appears to be nothing wrong with serious research into the question of to what extent a person's religion may play a role in certain reprehensible conduct. However, to simply hold that all Muslims per definition display such behaviour is a different issue, especially when this is followed by the conclusion that the only way to resolve immigration and integration problematics is that they must all be expelled from the country. Then, a person's affiliation with a particular religion or race is presented as a ground to discriminate against them, which violates one's equal basic dignity. The latter equally applies to hate speech consisting of racist epithets, invectives, and terms of abuse. One could argue that such expression is of little value in public debate, because it does not convey ideas that are actually susceptible to discussion.

In order to consistently distinguish free critical contributions to public debate from prohibited hate speech, a norm must accurately differentiate between factual statements and value judgments, hence different types of utterances. The limit of public debate may be reached with, next to pertinent untrue statements, strong value judgments that lack a sufficient factual basis or in any event are 'gratuitously

---

171 Mahlmann, M., Free Speech and the Rights of Religion, in: Sajó, A. (Ed.), *Censorial sensitivities: free speech and religion in a fundamentalist world*, Utrecht: Eleven International Publishing 2007, p. 47.

172 It is less disputed that the proof of the truth is irrelevant with regard to the allegation of having incited to racial hatred, discrimination or violence.

offensive'. The question arises as to whether the latter standard concerns the form of expression or style in which it is presented and/ or the substance of expression. It might be difficult to strictly separate the form of expression from its substance; the form may precisely give an utterance its particular – racist – meaning or, vice versa, the substance of an utterance may precisely determine its form.[173] Hence, there is a distinction between the assertions that 'Muslims are criminal and violent by nature' and 'Muslims are overrepresented in crime rates'. The depiction of Muslims as rats or cockroaches or merely calling them silly can also be evaluated differently. The same applies to the imputation 'The Jews have invented the Holocaust for their own financial gain and the creation of the state of Israel' and the plea that 'Historians must be able to freely discuss the events of the Holocaust'.

3.4. Holocaust denial

A particular form of hate speech is the denial of the Holocaust. Holocaust denial generally consists of the negation, trivialization or minimization of historical facts and crimes, which have evidently occurred during the Nazi-regime. In Germany, where there is a special historical connection with World War II, the Holocaust may remain a highly sensitive issue. Therefore, it is understandable that the 'Auschwitzlüge' is criminalized in specific offences in the German Criminal Code.[174]

However, specific Holocaust denial laws exist in many other countries.[175] In certain countries, the existence of such laws may be explained as a firm symbolic act of the state to distance itself from relatively recent atrocities committed by the Nazis, in which they may have collaborated. From this perspective, such laws may rather be of a declarative nature than having a practical effect and express the commitment of the state to denounce racism.[176] This may equally explain the existence of other genocide denial laws that, for example, prohibit the negation of the Armenian genocide.

In other countries, such 'memorial laws' may be regarded as unconstitutional, because the state and the judge, by criminalizing the negation of genocides, establish and proclaim an official fixed historical truth, i.e. 'government declared truth'. This is contrary to free historical scientific research and opinion on, and

---

173 Rosier, T., *Vrijheid van meningsuiting en discriminatie in Nederland en Amerika*, Nijmegen: Ars Aequi Libri 1997, p. 20 *et seq.*

174 Section 130(3); 130 (4) of the German Criminal Code. See also: Pech, L., The Law of Holocaust Denial in Europe, in: Hennebel, L. & Hochmann, T. (Eds.), *Genocide Denials and the Law*, Oxford: Oxford University Press 2011, p. 191 *et seq.*; Grimm, D., The Holocaust Denial Decision of the Federal Constitutional Court of Germany, in: Hare & Weinstein 2009, p. 557–561.

175 See: Hennebel & Hochmann 2011.

176 Weil, P., The Politics of Memory: Bans and Commemorations, in: Hare & Weinstein 2009, p. 562–579; Suk, J.C., Denying Experience: Holocaust Denial and the Free-Speech Theory of the State, in: Herz & Molnar 2012, p. 144–163.

interpretation of historical events. The idea of punishing an idea due to its falsity goes to the very heart of the principle of freedom of speech.[177]

However, the question arises as to whether the statutory wording of specific Holocaust and genocide denial laws correctly reflects their underlying aim. Often revisionist theories and pseudo-scientific research conceal the author's intention to defame or spread hatred against a particular group. For example, through the minimization of the number of victims of the Holocaust, an author may aim to legitimize and spread Nazi ideology. Holocaust denial laws may aim to counter not the negation as such, but rather its racist purport and intention. They may aim to protect Jews against false allegations and to prevent the spreading of Anti-Semitism or racist ideologies and their adoption by others.

The question arises whether in order to counter such more disguised forms of racist defamation and hatred there is a need for such specific Holocaust and genocide denial laws or whether existing hate speech bans, such as offences of group defamation and incitement to hatred, discrimination or violence, suffice. On the one hand, the latter offences seem to better reflect the core of what is criminalized and why. On the other hand, if one starts to bring such more disguised forms of defamation and hatred under these offences there is a danger that their scope can be stretched endlessly. For example, why would they not include anti-Islam speech that may conceal the author's intention to defame or spread hatred against Muslims (para. 4 *infra*)?

3.5. Criminal and/ or civil law

When forms of hate speech are prohibited, the legislator is faced with a choice in relation to the nature of the limitations to freedom of expression that will be implemented, i.e. the creation of specific criminal offences and/or limitations in civil law. More controversy exists in relation to the criminalization of group defamation than, for example, 'incitements', such as incitement to violence. Different institutions advocate the abolishment of criminal defamation laws and, where necessary, their replacement with appropriate civil defamation laws. The protection of one's reputation is regarded primarily as a private interest and criminalizing defamatory statements would be unnecessary for the adequate protection of reputation. Furthermore, in certain countries criminal defamation laws are abused by the authorities to limit criticism of government and to stifle public debate, in an effort to maintain public order or to protect public interests other than the right to reputation. It is argued that, at the very minimum, prison sentences or excessive fines should not be available as a sanction for defamation laws.[178]

---

177 Schauer 2012, p. 130.

178 Defining Defamation, Principles of Freedom of Expression and Protection of Reputation, Article 19, July 2000, p.7, available at: www.article19.org; Resolution 1577 (2007) of the

The call for decriminalization in any event concerns defamation of individual persons and state officials.[179] Likewise, the question arises as to why the legislator would *criminalize group* defamation. As discussed previously (para. 3.3 *supra*), some may regard group defamation as verbal assaults by one person or group to another group, thus between citizens, and therefore form a purely private issue. After all, there seems to be no *public issue* in relation to the matter that such expression violates the public order by carrying a direct threat of disorder or violence or that it violates public morality, comparable with 'incitement' of third parties to action, sedition, obscenity or blasphemy. Therefore, the maxim 'criminal law forms an *ultimum remedium*' is often used as an argument against criminalization.

However, as previously discussed, group defamation can indeed be regarded as a public issue, because such expression violates people's basic human dignity and human dignity can be considered a *public good*,[180] which may be derived from the fact that it forms a core value in the Constitution. From this perspective, keeping the peace is only one dimension of public order that might comprise an interest in maintaining a proper sense of the basic dignity of citizens and the mutual recognition of their equal citizenship.[181] Then the protection of the public order takes on a different meaning in the sense that it maintains an orderly democratic society free from discrimination. This thus concerns a different value conflict and a different notion of harm.

Furthermore, there may be another reason behind the criminalization of group defamation. It can be argued that in a constitutional state based on the separation of powers, a primary task of the legislator is to assure *legal certainty* for its citizens by creating clearly defined, demarcated norms. The prohibition of group defamation directly interferes with the core of the right to freedom of expression. Creating specific criminal offences may be considered the appropriate means to clearly demarcate such substantive limitations and thereby guarantee freedom of expression.

One could object that the legislator could also create specific civil prohibitions of group defamation. This does not, however, seem to fit in with the system in certain civil law countries, where civil limitations to freedom of expression are determined through the general prohibition of the wrongful act. Even though existing criminal speech offences could function as a guideline for determining civil liability considerations, other factors may play a role that would, in principle, be irrelevant for determining criminal liability, such as: the subjective intentions of the author of expression, due diligence norms, and the protection against the offence

---

Parliamentary Assembly of the Council of Europe, *Towards decriminalization of defamation*.

179 Furthermore, it is advocated to entirely abolish defamation laws that protect individuals or entities that do not have or merit a reputation, such as State- or religious symbols, flags or national insignia, and the State or nation as such. See further para. 3.3 *supra*.

180 Cf. Waldron 2012.

181 Waldron 2012, p. 46.

of feelings. Such criteria may blur the exact limitations to freedom of expression. In light of legal certainty, it can be argued that expression may only be considered unlawful when it is punishable under a specific speech offence.

The choice for the creation of criminal and/or civil restrictions to hate speech also influences the role of different actors in the practical enforcement of restrictions to hate speech. Although it is primarily the legislator who creates the statutory restrictions to freedom of expression, it is the judge who is confronted with a series of complicated questions in their application. It appears inevitable that the judge, in one way or another, attaches importance to freedom of expression. In principle, with criminal restrictions, primacy is given to the legislator and less room is afforded for judicial interpretation and balancing than with civil restrictions. The question arises as to how the legislator can provide a framework that facilitates consistent judicial adjudication.

Another question is how can the state assure the effective enforcement of hate speech bans? The prosecution of criminal hate speech bans is a task – and often an exclusive right – of the public prosecution. Generally, individual victims and anti-racism associations can initiate civil proceedings against hate speech themselves or join a criminal case initiated by public prosecution as a civil party. It is not common that the law affords civil parties the right to *set in motion* public prosecutions of hate speech and to make them a *prosecuting party* to the *criminal* case. However, collective actions of anti-racism associations may be an important instrument to fight certain types of structural forms of hate speech against vulnerable minority groups.

3.6. Synthesis Facts versus Value Judgments

The search for truth forms an important justification for freedom of expression. The premise is that the state should not prohibit opinions based on their alleged falsity. Rather, the truth or falsity of opinions should be tested in a free and open (scientific) discussion and as a result the universal truth will prevail. However, the political and public debate rather constitutes a 'marketplace of ideas' that concerns the formation of power and the laws of the state. Political opinions that amount to hate speech do have a special position in public debate and can therefore be prohibited. The suppression of hate speech in public debate is not motivated by epistemic goals, but by the social value in the protection of people's equal dignity and the prevention of discrimination.

In order to consistently distinguish free critical contributions to public debate from prohibited hate speech, a norm must, however, accurately differentiate between factual statements and value judgments, i.e. different types of utterances. Hate speech can consist of racist epithets, invectives and terms of abuse, but also of vague allegations and generalizations that associate certain actual or supposed behaviour or practices with people's race or religion (including forms of Holocaust denial) and subsequently present them as a ground to discriminate against the people concerned. An ultimate limit of public debate may be reached when hate speech consists of pertinent untrue statements and value judgments that lack a sufficient factual basis or are, in any event, gratuitously offensive.

The forms of hate speech described above can have both a defamatory/insulting and an 'inciting' character. As far as the creation of specific hate speech bans is concerned, the state can however prohibit, next to 'incitement to hatred, discrimination or violence'. It can also prohibit 'group defamation/insult'. After all, defamatory false statements of fact or insulting value judgments about a group associated with its shared characteristics such as race or religion can already harm the individual dignity of the group members. Given the public good in the protection of people's equal human dignity, group defamation/insult can be prohibited by criminal law offences. Clearly defined statutory offences can afford legal certainty in relation to the rights and interests they protect as well as the extent of freedom of expression.

4. Race versus Religion

As far as the setting of restrictions to hate speech in public debate is concerned, a distinction is generally made between utterances about people's race and utterances about people's religion. Hate speech bans are almost by definition directed and used against racist speech (4.1). Less frequently, they also cover hate speech based on religion (4.2). Over the past decade there has been an increase of anti-Islam and anti-Muslim expression. This has brought to the fore the question of whether the same legal restrictions should apply to hate speech on the ground of religion as to hate speech on the ground of race (4.3)? Moreover, a central issue that has been highlighted is how one must consistently distinguish hate speech against people on the ground of their religion from blasphemous expression and the defamation of a religion as such (4.4). Finally, the question is, in which other categories, in addition to race and religion, hate speech bans must be included (4.5)? The paragraph concludes with a synthesis that defines the factor Race versus Religion for the purpose of the further analysis in this study (4.6).

4.1. Race

There exist different notions of 'race' as a discriminatory ground. One can discern a narrow definition of race as a biological characteristic from a broader definition that includes ethnicity, nationality and other criteria of 'otherness'.

4.1.1. Race as a biological characteristic

It can be argued that – other than religious beliefs – race or skin colour are fixed biological and physical characteristics that a person cannot change. Even though the *actual* existence of different races is disputed and it is objected that race as an unchangeable characteristic only exists in the eyes of the racist, this does not alter the fact that discrimination and hate speech on the basis of unchangeable facts seems particularly unfair.[182] A narrow definition of *racism* would accordingly be confined to race as a biological characteristic and would consist of views and practices reflecting the belief that human populations are divided into separate races that share certain attributes, which makes certain races, due to their unchangeable, negative characteristics, inferior to others and their differential treatment (discrimination) justified.[183] Many 19th century scientists subscribed to such essentialist ideas of racial superiority. During the 20th century, such ideas have politically and ideologically underpinned racial segregation in the US, European

---

182 Sadurski 1999, p. 212.

183 Cf. 'racism' Oxford online dictionaries; Merriam-Webster online dictionary. Retrieved 12 April 2013.

colonization, Apartheid in South Africa and the genocide of the Holocaust executed by the Nazi regime.

The International Convention for the Elimination of all forms of Racial Discrimination (ICERD), drafted by the United Nations after World War II, obliged state parties to criminalize the spreading of ideas based on racial superiority. This naturally refers to the spreading of National Socialism as an ideology *known* to be racist and aimed at the destruction of Jews. More generally, this includes the expression of negative ideas about a particular race, such as: 'the black race is inferior to the white race', because such ideas are considered to *per definition* contain negative conclusions about the people belonging to that race, simply because they cannot abandon this biological characteristic. Hence, no fundamental distinction exists between hateful expression about a particular *race* and hateful expression about *individuals* belonging to that race.

4.1.2. Ethnicity

ICERD, however, uses a broad notion of 'race': its scope is not limited to discrimination on the grounds of biological characteristics such as race and skin colour, but includes other discriminatory grounds, such as *national* and *ethnic descent*. *Ethnicity* is often assumed to be the *cultural identity* of a group in a nation state[184] and can include a common ancestry, language or religion. This inclusion in ICERD can be explained by the fact that, like racism and discrimination based on race, racism and discrimination based on ethnicity often also starts from essentialist thinking of the superiority of one culture over another. On the one hand, there seems nothing wrong with the different valuation of cultures. After all, cultures are value systems in themselves and susceptible to change. On the other hand, one must distinguish *cultural practices* from a person's *descent*. People cannot renounce or change their descent, i.e. their personal cultural background and history.

Maybe an author who speaks of the superiority of one culture over another has the same intention as an author who speaks of the superiority of one race over another. To the extent that, for an author of expression, having a different culture is an unchangeable, negative characteristic, expression of negative ideas about a particular culture necessarily contains negative conclusions about the people who share this culture. When this vision leads to an exclusion of the target group and a violation of their fundamental rights, then hate speech based on ethnicity does not necessarily have to differ from hate speech based on race. Moreover, the distinction between race and ethnicity is generally regarded as problematic in itself; it is argued that, as race is rather a social and cultural construct than a biological characteristic, racism always has a cultural component to it.[185]

---

184 Cf. 'ethnicity' Oxford online dictionaries. Retrieved 12 April 2013.

185 Haney Lopez, I.F., The Social Construction of Race, *Harvard Civil Rights – Civil Liberties Law Review*, 1994, vol. 29, p. 1–62; Smedley, A. & Smedley, B.D., Race as biology is fiction, racism as a social problem is real: anthropological and historical perspectives on the social construction

4.1.3. *Nationality and xenophobia*

A similar reasoning can be applied to people's *nationality*. If speech combines views on race with views on culture and national territory, it may take the form of *ethnic nationalism*; the nation state is then defined as a shared heritage, including a common ancestry, language, religion and culture.[186] In the eyes of a nationalist, his own national culture is superior to foreign cultures and must therefore be exclusively preserved within the nation state, even when this violates the fundamental rights of foreign inhabitants of the nation state.

The desire to deny certain rights to persons with a foreign nationality will, however, not always constitute a form of racism. One must distinguish nationality in relation to *national descent* from nationality in relation to *citizenship*. National citizenship as a basis for the attribution of certain rights and duties is not in itself discriminatory. One can think of the eligibility to vote or the right to stand for election as a member of parliament. On the other hand, an example of a *practice* amounting to the making of an unjustified distinction is that of favouring national citizens over people with a foreign nationality in job applications. One could however argue that it must be possible to freely discuss the desirability of such a practice.

Particular forms of racism can manifest themselves through all kind of assumptions, negative stereotyping or prejudice against people based on their race, ethnicity and nationality. The common trait seems to be a general fear, hatred or intolerance against '*Otherness*'.[187] Racist hate speech can therefore be connected with the broader notion of '*xenophobia*', i.e. expression of an intense and irrational dislike or fear of anything or anyone who is different, strange or foreign.[188] As discussed previously and further on (para. 1.5 *supra*; Chapter 3), international and European institutions disagree on whether hate speech laws must be so broad that they counter any advocating of fear, hatred and intolerance against people based on all kinds of differences.[189]

---

of race, *The American Psychologist*, 2005, Vol. 60, no. 1), p.16 – 26; McGeever, B.F. & Ashe, S.D., Marxism, racism and the construction of 'race' as a social and political relation: an interview with professor Robert Miles, *Ethnic and Racial Studies*, 2011, Vol. 34, no. 12, p. 2009–2026.

186 Muller, J.Z., Us and them: the enduring power of ethnic nationalism, *Foreign Affairs*, March-April, 2008, Vol. 87, no. 2, p. 18 – 35.

187 Kyriakides, C., Virdee, S. & Modood, T., Racism, Muslims and the National Imagination, *Journal of Ethnic and Migration Studies*, 2009, Vol. 35, no. 2, p. 289–308.

188 Cf. 'xenophobia' Oxford online dictionaries; Merriam-Webster online dictionary. Retrieved 12 April 2013.

189 An affirmative answer seems to follow from the broad definition of hate speech in CM CE recommendation 97 (20): 'the term "hate speech" shall be understood as covering all forms of expression which spread, incite, promote or justify racial hatred, xenophobia, anti- Semitism or other forms of hatred based on intolerance, including: intolerance expressed by aggressive nationalism and ethnocentrism, discrimination and hostility against minorities, migrants and people of immigrant origin.'

4.2. Religion

The notion of religion as a discriminatory ground poses a number of specific problems. It is notably difficult to demarcate a religious group and to make a consistent distinction between the convictions and practices of a religion and persons adhering to a religion. This issue is brought to the fore by an emerging religious intolerance, the phenomena of 'Islamophobia' and 'Defamation of religions'.

4.2.1. Religion as a discriminatory ground

In international law race and religion are equated as discriminatory grounds to a certain extent. For example, Article 20 sub 2 of the International Covenant on Civil and Political Rights (ICCPR) obliges state parties to prohibit by law any advocacy of national, racial or religious hatred that constitutes incitement to discrimination, hostility or violence. But the question arises as to how far the analogy between religion and race can go? A religion or belief consists of doctrines and religious rules that its religious adherents assume to be true. A religion therefore forms a guideline for, and partly determines the behaviour of its religious adherents. Furthermore, religion often forms the basis for people's position on all kinds of social and political issues. Hence, one can criticize people for adhering to a particular religion, but not for belonging to a particular race.

It is therefore understandable why religion as a discriminatory ground was deliberately excluded from the scope of ICERD. It is less imaginable that an international convention would oblige state parties to criminalize the spreading of ideas based on the superiority of a particular religion. After all, the proclamation of the superiority of a particular religion is inherent in many religions and should not be considered punishable but a free exercise of a religion. In fact, such expression can also aim to convert adherents of another religion. One could even imagine a free market place of religions,[190] although the idea of a level playing field for religions may be controversial. To a certain extent a religion thus may be compared with political ideologies such as communism, capitalism or colonialism.[191]

From the perspective of freedom of expression, one must also be free to openly criticize and express disagreement with the tenets, dogmas, doctrines, practices, rituals, offices and institutions of a religion. Such criticism of a particular religion does not necessarily constitute criticism of its religious adherents and does not necessarily contain negative conclusions about the people adhering to that religion.[192] After all, a religion is not an immutable characteristic and a person can

---

190 Weinstein, J., Overlapping Consensus or Marketplace of Religions? Rawls and Smith, *Philosophia*, 2012, Vol. 40, no. 2, p. 223–236.

191 Cf. Rosenfeld 2012, p. 277.

192 Contrarily: Barendt, E., Religious Hatred Laws: Protecting Groups or Belief?, *Res Publica* 2011, vol. 17, p. 41–53.

change his religion or renounce his beliefs.[193] In principle, a distinction thus can be made between expression about a particular *religion* and expression about *individuals* adhering to that religion.

This latter distinction can be diffuse and is notably difficult to make when the criticism concerns the behaviour of and practices exercised by religious adherents. Just as with nationality, ethnicity and culture, having a different religion can also be regarded as an unchangeable, negative characteristic. For an author of expression, all kinds of undesirable, criminal or violent supposed or actual behaviour of persons belonging to a particular religion can be necessarily associated with and caused by their religion and inherent in all members of that group. Gross criticism that at first sight merely targets a religion, such as: 'Islam is a violent and dangerous religion that must be conquered', might conceal the intent to defame or spread hatred against the people adhering to that religion. The question, therefore, is whether or not it is unfair to use the argument of personal choice against protection of religious groups against such religious hatred; it is argued that this would amount to imposing a penalty upon people who do not renounce their particular conduct, values, or set of beliefs.[194]

Religion could also be regarded as a central component of ethnic group identity and therefore play an important role in xenophobia, racism, and group hatred.[195] Religious minorities tend to be of a different ethnic and national origin than the majority. For example, in a predominantly Christian European country with an Arab minority that is in large part Muslim, anti-Arab and anti- Muslim hate speech may overlap.[196] Precisely because of the nexus between race and religion, it has been suggested to extend the scope of ICERD to the mixed form of 'aggravated discrimination', that is, discrimination on the grounds of race *and* religion.[197]

Generally, however, religions are not principally connected to a particular people. This applies, for example, to Buddhism, Christianity and Islam. This implies that anti-Buddhism, anti-Christianity and anti-Islam speech must be distinguished from racism. Contrarily, Judaism is often regarded as a religion that is inextricably connected with the Jewish people. Historically, Anti-Semitism has therefore been grounded on both race and religion.[198] A primary reason to insert the discriminatory ground of religion into hate speech bans might precisely have

---

193 Cf. Haarscher, G., Are religious sensitivities above the Constitution? Reflections on the collective defamation of religious people, in: Sajó, A. (Ed.), *Is there something above/behind the Constitution?*, Kluwer 2009.

194 Sadurski 1999, p. 213.

195 Lerner, N., The Nature and Minimum Standards of Freedom of Religion or Belief, *Brigham Young University Law Review* 2000, p. 905–932.

196 Rosenfeld 2012, p. 276–277.

197 Keane, D., Addressing the aggravated meeting point of race and religion, *University of Maryland Law Journal of Race, Religion, Gender & Class* 2006, p. 367–406; Lindgren Alves, J.A., Race and Religion in the United Nations Committee on the Elimination of Racial Discrimination, *University of San Francisco Law Review* 2008, vol. 42, p. 941–982.

198 Rosenfeld 2012, p. 276.

been to deprive authors of Anti-Semitic speech from the defence that their hate speech against Jews is not race-, but religion-based.

4.2.2. Demarcating a religious group

The insertion of religion as a distinct discriminatory ground in hate speech bans is controversial. First of all, defining and demarcating a religion or belief for purposes of law is highly complex.[199] Generally, a religion or belief is required to consist of a fundamental and coherent set of convictions about the meaning of existence. This does not comprise political convictions.[200] But it is argued that due to the process of secularization in the Western European world, people's religion nowadays constitutes a very limited part of their identity. Gross criticism based on their religion, therefore, does not say anything about their appreciation as a person.

Furthermore, one could argue that due to the individualization of beliefs, religious groups nowadays are too heterogeneous to be protected against vilifications or insults on the basis of a *collective identity*. Some scholars argue that in order for a religious group to have the moral standing for a claim, it is not required to have a specific identity based on religion as a shared objective feature. A claim can be made if there is a strong intra-group solidarity where individuals feel themselves strongly bound together as members of the group with which they identify and have a shared interest, for example, in protection against hatred or defamation on the basis of their religion. They therefore reject the *corporate* conception of a group that has moral standing *qua* group and instead advance a *collective* conception of a group as an aggregate of individuals.[201] But this appears to be an idea that more generally underlies prohibitions that protect the dignity of individuals against defamatory imputations associated with all kinds of shared characteristics such as race, ethnicity, gender, sexuality, and national origin (para. 3.3 *supra*). An additional complication connected with *religion* remains, of course, that a religion is also a set of ideas about the meaning of existence that can be separated from the religious adherents.

---

199 Evans distinguishes three approaches for a definition of religion based on content, function or analogy with generally accepted world religions. See: Evans, C., *Freedom of religion under the European Convention on Human Rights*, Oxford: Oxford University Press 2001, p. 51–66. See also: Gunn, T.J., The Complexity of Religion and the Definition of 'Religion' in International Law, *Harvard Human Rights Journal*, 2003, vol. 16, p.189–215; Greenawalt, K., Religion as a concept in constitutional law, *California law review*, 1984, vol. 72, no. 5, p. 753–815; Sadurski, W., On Legal Definitions of Religion, *The Australian law journal*, 1989, vol. 63, p. 834 *et seq.*

200 Greenawalt 1984.

201 Galenkamp, E.M., Individualism versus collectivism, the concept of collective rights, Arnhem: Gouda Quint 1998; McDonald, M., Should communities have rights? Reflections on liberal individualism, *Canadian Journal of Law and Jurisprudence*, 1991, Vol. 4, no. 2, p. 217–217. Cf. Jones, P., Human Rights, Group Rights and Peoples' Rights, *Human Rights Quarterly: a comparative and international journal of the social sciences, philosophy and law*, 1999, vol. 21, no. 1, p. 80–107.

Nevertheless, this functional approach to religious group rights fits in particularly well with the idea that religions have regained their function as '*imagined communities*'.[202] For a long time religions functioned as cultural systems and religious institutions as 'community cults'. When the modern nation state took over this function, religions became embedded in territory. Now globalization has led to both the deterritorization and a revival of old civilizations and world religions.[203, 204] At least it can be argued that in modern European multi-cultural and multi-religious societies the protection of religious 'identities' has not entirely lost its importance.

4.2.3. Religious intolerance, 'Islamophobia' and 'Defamation of Religions'

Since 9/11, expressions and acts of religious intolerance and 'Islamophobia' have emerged worldwide and notably also in Europe.[205] Although there is not one widely accepted definition of the term, the phenomenon of Islamophobia has become a concept used in social sciences for comparative objectives. One author has defined Islamophobia as 'indiscriminate negative attitudes or emotions directed at Islam or Muslims'.[206] For purposes of the law, this definition is problematic, because it conflates criticism of Islam with hatred and discrimination against Muslims. 'Islamophobia' is indeed a highly contested and politicized concept and, therefore, not an official legal concept under international law. Nevertheless, the term has featured in many policy instruments and reports of international organizations, including the United Nations (UN). The same is true of the notion of 'defamation of religions'.

Since 1999, on the initiative of the Organization of the Islamic Conference (OIC),[207] a group of Islamic countries within the UN, the Human Rights Council[208]

---

202 Casanova, J., Articles – 2000 Presidential Address – Religion, the New Millennium and Globalization, *Sociology of religion: a quarterly review*, 2001, vol. 62, no. 4, p. 415–441.

203 Huntington's famous thesis of a 'clash of civilizations' may be criticized for its essentialism. According to Huntington global conflicts will run along civilizational fault lines: western European highly developed Christian civilizations versus eastern less developed Islamic civilizations. This thesis demonstrates a west-centric hegemonic vision that pictures cultures and religions as unchangeable entities and civilizations as territorial units akin to nation states. This analysis denies the fact that globalization implies the deterritorialization of all cultural systems, including religion. Huntington, S.P., *The clash of civilizations and the remaking of world order*, New York: Simon & Schuster 1996.

204 Casanova 2001.

205 Pew Research Center, *Unfavorable Views of Jews and Muslims on the Increase in Europe*, Report, September 17, 2008; EUCH, *Summary Report on Islamophobia in the EU after 11 September 2001*, Vienna, May 2002.

206 Bleich, E., What is Islamophobia and How Much Is There? Theorizing and Measuring an Emerging Comparative Concept, *American Bahavioral Scientist* 2011, 55, p. 1581–1600.

207 The official website of the OIC is www.oic-oci.org.

208 HRC Resolution 4/9 of 30 March 2007 *Combating defamation of religions*; HRC Resolution 4/10 of 30 March 2007 *Elimination of all forms of intolerance and of discrimination based on religion or belief*; Resolution 6/37 of 14 December 2007; HRC Resolution 7/19 of 27 March 2008 *Combating defamation of religions.*

(HRC, formerly the Commission on Human Rights,[209] CHR) and the General Assembly[210] have adopted several resolutions combatting the 'Defamation of religions'. For a considerable time, the OIC had protested against the discrimination of Muslims in Europe and the rest of the world and the negative portrayals of Muslims and their faith in the media.[211] In short, in these resolutions the 'defamation of religions' and the 'negative stereotyping of religions' are regarded as causes of social disharmony and leading to violations of human rights of the adherents of the target religion. Freedom of speech is regarded as subject to limitations as necessary for the 'respect for religions and beliefs'. After the Danish Cartoons affair in 2005,[212] the OIC focused its combat on the support of blasphemy laws and the proposal to criminalize the defamation of religions on the basis of Article 20(2) ICCPR.[213]

The resolutions initially obtained wide support, also from Western countries. Until 2008, in several reports by the UN Special Rapporteur on contemporary forms of racism, racial discrimination, xenophobia and related intolerance[214], the UN Special Rapporteur on freedom of religion and belief[215], the UN High Commissioner for Human Rights[216] and the UN Secretary General[217], 'defamation of religions' is also still considered as a form of incitement to religious and racial hatred and regarded as a new form of racism that demands repression comparable to Anti-Semitism. However, international developments, such as the events of 9–11, the resurgence of

---

209 CHR Resolution 1999/82 of 30 April 1999 *Defamation of religions*; Resolution 2000/84 of 26 April 2000; Resolution 2001/4 of 18 April 2001; Resolution 2002/9 of 15 April 2002; Resolution 2003/4 of 14 April 2003; Resolution 2004/6 of 13 April 2004; Resolution 2005/3 of 12 April 2005.

210 General Assembly Resolution 60/150 of 16 December 2005 *Combating defamation of religions;* Resolution 61/164 of 19 December 2006; Resolution 62/154 of 18 December 2007; Resolution 63/171 of 18 December 2008.

211 The OIC was established 25 September 1969. According to its present Charter the OIC aims – amongst others – to "Protect and defend the true image of Islam, to combat defamation of Islam and encourage dialogue among civilizations and religions".

212 Keane, D., Cartoon Violence and Freedom of Expression, *Human Rights Quarterly* 2008, 30, p. 845–875.

213 For some critical accounts see: Leo, L.A., Gaer, F.D. & Cassidy, E.K., Protecting Religions from 'Defamation': A Threat to Universal Human Rights Standards, *Harvard Journal of Law & Public Policy* 2011, 34, p. 769–784; Belnap, A.G., Defamation of Religions: A Vague and Overbroad Theory that Threatens Basic Human Rights, *Brigham Young University Law Review* 2010, p. 635–685; Parmar, S., The Challenge of 'Defamation of Religions' to Freedom of Expression and the International Human Rights, *European Human Rights Law Review* 2009, 3, p. 353–375; Temperman, J., Blasphemy, Defamation of Religions and Human Rights Law, *Netherlands Quarterly of Human Rights* 2008, 26/4, p. 517–545.

214 E/CN.4/2003/23 of 3 January 2003; E/CN.4/2005/19 of 23 December 2004; E/CN.4/2005/18/Add.4 of 3 January 2005; E/CN.4/2006/17 of 13 February 2006; A/HRC/2/3 of 20 September 2006; A/HRC/4/19 of 12 January 2007; A/HRC/6/6 of 21 August 2007.

215 A/HRC/6/5 of 20 July 2007.

216 A/HRC/4/50 of 1 March 2007; A/HRC/6/4 of 4 September 2007; A/HRC/9/25 of 5 September 2008; A/HRC/9/7 of 12 September 2008.

217 A/63/365 of 19 September 2008; A/64/209 of 31 July 2009.

the Israel-Palestine conflict and the American intervention in Afghanistan and Iraq, turned Western and Islamic countries into opposite blocks within the UN.[218]

Since 2008, the UN rapporteurs[219] have increasingly stressed the importance of freedom of expression and the legitimacy of criticism of religions. Their recommendations include a shift away from the sociological concept of defamation of *religions* towards the legal norm of non-incitement to national, racial and religious hatred against *persons* of Article 20(2) ICCPR. Subsequently, in the outcome document of the Durban Review Conference, a UN World Conference against Racism[220] in 2009, the concept of defamation of religions was no longer mentioned. Instead reference is made to 'the global rise and number of incidents of racial or religious intolerance and violence, including Islamophobia, anti-Semitism, Christianophobia and anti-Arabism manifested in particular by the derogatory stereotyping and stigmatization of *persons* based on their religion or belief'.[221] Likewise, since then, in its resolutions, the HRC has shifted from referring to the negative 'stereotyping of religions' towards the 'stereotyping of vulnerable individuals or groups of individuals'.[222]

4.3. Relevance of the distinction for specific hate speech bans

The relevance of the distinction between race and religion as discriminatory grounds can vary depending on the particular form of hate speech, hence per specific hate speech offence. Offences of group defamation or group insult primarily aim to protect the dignity of the members of particular groups. It is a problem to consistently determine whether defamatory or insulting expression concerning people's religion falls under this scope. In principle, defamatory and insulting expression about a religion or its religious figures may fall outside of this scope and only expression about the religious adherents may fulfil the statutory elements of the offences. This is, in any event, the case when expression explicitly names a religious group (ex. 'Muslims'). But the question arises as to whether people can never be indirectly insulted or defamed via insulting or defamatory statements about their religion (ex. 'Islam'). For example, sentences such as 'Protestantism promotes violence' or 'Catholicism leads to paedophilia'

218 Parmar 2009.

219 A/HRC/9/12 of 2 September 2008; A/HRC/12/38 of 1 July 2009; Joint statement by Mr. Githu Muigai, Special Rapporteur on contemporary forms of racism, racial discrimination, xenophobia and related intolerance; Ms. Asma Jahangir, Special Rapporteur on freedom of religion or belief; and Mr. Frank La Rue, Special Rapporteur on the promotion and protection of the right to freedom of opinion and expression, OHCHR side event during the Durban Review Conference, Geneva, 22 April 2009, *"Freedom of expression and incitement to racial or religious hatred"*.

220 In 2009 the Durban Conference Review, Durban II, was held as a follow up to the World Conference against Racism, Racial Discrimination, Xenophobia and Related Intolerance in Durban, South Afrika, in 2001.

221 Outcome document of the Durban Review Conference 2009, para. 12.

222 A/HRC/12/L.14/Rev.1 of 30 September 2009.

may seem to imply or to be just another way of saying that 'Protestants are violent' or 'Catholics are paedophiles'. This shows the particular difficulty with demarcating lawful from unlawful criticism concerning practices associated with a religion.

The question arises as to whether requiring expression to explicitly name the religious adherents as a group must be the primary determinant factor for liability under religious group defamation and insult laws. In order to consistently demarcate free criticism of religion from prohibited religious group defamation, in principle the criterion that expression must designate a particular group may be a simple helpful tool. In fact, utterances about a religion shall sooner constitute a free value judgment, while utterances about religious adherents shall sooner require a factual basis. This is different with race. But then a norm must clarify whether this signifies that an utterance must explicitly name a group, whether the group must have a certain degree of homogeneity in the sense of a collective identity or whether a negative quality is in fact attributed to all members of the group (*supra*). With regard to the latter, another criterion may be whether an utterance treats the actual or supposed practices associated with a religion as a central component of people's ethnic or national descent and identity, thus as an unchangeable characteristic. This may be the case in the following statement: 'Morroccans are overrepresented in crime rates, because Islam is a violent religion and the problems are inherent in the community itself'.

However, with regard to expression that does not explicitly refer to a particular group, negative utterances about a race may sooner fulfil the statutory elements of offences of group defamation and group insult than such expression about a religion. The dignity of people can sooner be harmed and people can more easily be indirectly insulted or defamed via insulting or defamatory statements about their race than their religion. For example, the statements: 'the black race is backward and had better be rejected', and: 'Islam is backward and had better be rejected', have very different purports. Expression that minimizes or denies the Holocaust may take a special position in the sense that it generally has a racist purport given the context in which it is often uttered and therefore amounts to a form of indirect racial defamation or insult or hatred, even though it does not explicitly name Jews as a group or the Jewish race.

The distinction between race and religion may also be relevant to the offence of incitement to hatred, discrimination or violence. In principle, other than for race, it seems possible to distinguish statements that express certain hatred for a particular religion from expression of hatred towards individuals. On the other hand, it seems implausible to comprehend, for example, an incitement to discrimination or violence against Islam as a religion as merely directed against the body of thoughts and not also against the persons who will be the victims of the effectuation of such an incitement. While it is imaginable that gross insults about a religion can at the same time respect the dignity of its adherents, the 'incitement to discrimination or violence' against a religion by its very nature seems to be necessarily, also or precisely, directed against its adherents.[223] Nevertheless, expressing the desire to abolish the multi-religious society or to stop the 'islamization' of society has a very different purport than expressing the desire to abolish the multi-racial society or to stop the 'blackening' of society. The former does not necessarily aim at religious discrimination or violence. It can also be interpreted as criticism on existing religion-state relationships and the place or influence of religions in the public domain.

Forms of hate speech as described above can, depending on the context in which it is uttered, have both a defamatory/insulting and an 'inciting' character, and thus fall under both the offence of group defamation/insult and the offence of incitement to hatred, discrimination or violence. A way in which to evaluate the possible racist, essentialist purport of expression and to determine liability under a specific hate speech ban, establishing the intent of the author may play an important role. The difficulty remains, however, that an author's intent must be objectified to a certain extent and primarily be derived from the expression itself. It was stated previously that in order to consistently distinguish free critical contributions to public debate from prohibited hate speech, a norm must accurately differentiate between factual statements and value judgments, i.e., different types of utterances (para. 3.6 *supra*); one can differentiate between minor insults, particular gross generalizing vilifications that are unmistakably untrue, insults that lack any factual basis and the denigration of a group by using strong epithets, invectives, abusive or threatening words at their address. For the assessment of liability for expression on the basis of this standard the fact that expression concerns either people's race or religion therefore plays a role.

4.4. Demarcation of hate speech from blasphemy

An issue closely related to the demarcation of hate speech based on race from hate speech based on religion forms the demarcation of blasphemy from hate speech on the ground of religion. A distinction between the latter two is that prohibitions of blasphemy are generally based on the protection of religious feelings from offence, while prohibitions on hate speech are generally grounded on the protection of the dignity of persons. Both blasphemy and hate speech on account of religion raise the larger question of the interrelationship of the rights of freedom of religion and freedom of expression.

---

223 Vermeulen, B., 'Strafbare belediging van God, godsdienst, godsdienstigen', in: P.H.P.H.M.C. van Kempen e.a. (red.), *Levend strafrecht, strafrechtelijke vernieuwingen in een maatschappelijke context, Liber amicorum Ybo Buruma*, Deventer: Kluwer 2011, p. 663–664.

4.4.1. The offence of Blasphemy

Offences of blasphemy generally prohibit the gross defamation or insult of God's person. As the idea that God or a religion can truly be protected is, however, contestable, the offence may rather be seen as protecting religious adherents against the intended insult of their sensitivities and feelings. Indeed, the prohibition of blasphemy used to protect the official religion of the Christian majority in a country, because the Christian religion served as a guideline for the moral views of citizens. Historically, the prohibition can be explained by the entanglement of religion and the state. Another rationale of the offence therefore may be the preservation of public morality. Due to the processes of secularism and secularization, in many Western European countries the offence of blasphemy has been abolished. There may be several additional reasons for this development.

Firstly, religious feelings and sensibilities are very subjective. If the state protects people in personal convictions, representations and ideas that they hold to be sacred, it may lose its neutrality towards competing claims about religious truths; it may take a certain side in a religious debate.[224] Secondly, as the offence is tailored to the monotheistic Christian faith, in modern European multi-cultural and religious societies the offence may be unegalitarian in effect. To the extent that the offence of blasphemy is expected to protect religious truths, in theory a state could try to defend all religious creeds, but in practice this seems impossible because one religious truth often necessarily denies another. Thirdly, a state may find the preservation of the offence of blasphemy as a religious relic useful to at some point control excrescences of public debate on religious topics (often related to Islam) to maintain public order. This could, however, set false expectations to religious groups about their rights.

4.4.2. Offence versus dignity

In fact, a primary reason to prohibit blasphemous expression seems to be the protection of people from *offence*. It may be said that the argument of offence protects citizens from unsuspected confrontation with displeasing views.[225] The fact that certain opinions are contrary to personal moral convictions and therefore cause emotional problems, i.e., 'mental harm', to the hearer may be considered as an insufficient ground for the suppression of speech.[226] According to Feinberg, other than harm, offence is an unpleasant temporary experience and does not constitute a wrong in the sense that it impedes on a person's interests and violates his rights.[227] Although profound offence can form a ground to limit freedom

224 Cf. Barendt, E., Free Speech and Religion: Secular and Religious Perspectives on Truth, in: Sajó 2007, p. 25.

225 Feinberg I 1984, p. 46–49.

226 Feinberg I 1984, p. 46–49.

227 Feinberg I 1984, p. 46–49.

through criminal law, in his eyes, offence through blasphemous expression is not serious enough.[228]

The prohibition of blasphemy can also be connected to both *legal moralism* and *legal paternalism*. If blasphemy is assumed not to harm persons, but to target a religion, a state that nevertheless prohibits it then could consider blasphemy to be immoral, a wrong in itself.[229] From a liberal perspective, this may not constitute a valid reason to restrict the freedom of individuals. In the context of blasphemy and 'defamation of religion', some scholars therefore emphasize the distinction between offence and *dignity*. However, the argument that severe cases of 'defamation of a religion' can cause *profound* offence to religious adherents may differ little from the argument that the dignity of religious adherents can be affected by serious insulting remarks about their religion and religious practices (para. 4.3 *supra*). Nevertheless, it can be argued that a denial of a person's convictions or beliefs does not necessarily signify a denial of his dignity as a person.[230] Here the distinction between race and religion re-emerges. For example, it seems more plausible that the denial of the Holocaust implies the denial of the dignity of Jews, as a part of the particular history of the Jewish people (para. 3.3–3.4 *supra*).

4.4.3. Freedom of religion and freedom of expression

It is sometimes argued that blasphemous and other offensive expression about a religion must be prohibited, because it forms a direct violation of the freedom of religion of its religious adherents. This is, however, difficult to imagine. Even though blasphemous speech might indirectly cause some negative effects such as offence, it does not evidently prevent believers from holding religious beliefs or exercising their religious freedom by wearing a headscarf, going to church or enjoying religious education. It could influence their beliefs, but here we see benefits from freedom of religion: the outcome of the 'free market place of religions' is that religious adherents either hold their thoughts more actively and strongly or they change their beliefs, which would be more difficult when beliefs are not exposed to opposite beliefs or criticism.

For similar reasons, it is also difficult to imagine how group defamations or insults and incitements to hatred, discrimination or violence against a religious group can come into direct conflict with the right to freedom of thought and religion of religious adherents. Although an imminent threat of particular acts of discrimination and violence might refrain believers from freely exercising their

---

228 Feinberg II 1985, p.53–54. The seriousness of an offense is determined by: the magnitude of the offence (in intensity; duration; extent); the standard of reasonable avoidability; the Volenti maxim (the extent to which the offence is voluntarily incurred); the discounting of abnormal susceptibilities. See: p. 35.

229 Cf. Feinberg II, 1985, p. 68.

230 Rosier, T.E., *Vrijheid van meningsuiting en discriminatie in Nederland en Amerika* (diss.), Nijmegen: Ars Aequi 1998, p. 61 *et seq.*

religion or induce them to go underground. However, these prohibitions are primarily justified by general principles of equality and non-discrimination. The possible effect on freedom of religion and other fundamental rights may therefore only play an indirect role.[231]

Nevertheless, the European Court of Human Rights (ECtHR) does not principally oppose the existence of offences of blasphemy grounded in national morals and has even considered that freedom of religion comprises the right to respect of religious feelings.[232] From this perspective, offensive expression about a particular religion can constitute a direct violation of freedom of religion. This right of respect of religious feelings as an integral part of religious freedom is controversial. It seems to be inspired by the concept of religious toleration that can, however, be considered as underpinning both freedom of religion and freedom of expression. It can be argued that religious toleration relates to the peaceful coexistence of different religious thoughts and practices, but not to the peaceful coexistence of opinions on religious matters; these must clash in an open and free debate, provided that participants are respected as equal persons.[233, 234]

Freedom of religion and freedom of expression have a common origin; the inter- and intra-religious wars of the 16th and 17th century and the power struggle between the church and the state. The freedoms could be imagined as 'twins separated at birth' and subsequently brought up in the religious domain, respectively the worldly, political domain. A religion can, however, also inspire people's position on all kinds of social and political issues. Therefore, freedom of religion and freedom of expression can converge.

For example, believers may not only preach and proclaim that homosexuality is a sin, but can also oppose the legalization of gay marriage. They may not only

---

231 Samkalden, Ch., Een woord een woord: godsdienst en beperkingen van de uitingsvrijheid, in: Nieuwenhuis, A.J. & Zoethout, C.M. (Eds.), *Rechtsstaat en religie*, Nijmegen: Wolf Legal Publishers 2009, p. 163–188.

232 Martínez-Torrón, J., Freedom of Expression versus Freedom of Religion in the European Court of Human Rights, in: Sajó 2007, p. 233–269; Tulkens, F., Conflicts between fundamental rights: contrasting views on Articles 9 and 10 of the European Convention on Human Rights, in: *Blasphemy, insult and hatred, Finding answers in a democratic society*, Science and technique of democracy, No. 47, Venice Commission, Strasbourg: Council of Europe Publishing 2010, p. 121–131.

233 The latter presupposition seems to solve the famous paradox of the limits to toleration. As toleration is a matter of reciprocity, 'the intolerant cannot be tolerated'. However, the characterization of certain groups and views as intolerant seems to be an arbitrary, one-sided and intolerant act. This is precisely the manner in which in the past toleration of for instance, atheists, heretics or Catholics has been denied. For example Mill, Locke.

234 Forst therefore suggests to distinguish between the intolerance of those who exceed the limits of toleration because they deny toleration as a norm in the first place, and the lack of tolerance of those who do not want to tolerate a denial of the norm. Only the first type of intolerance cannot be tolerated, because such views and practices violate the principle of justification of toleration itself. Forst 2003, p. 71–85.

condemn sex before marriage and contraception, but also oppose the legalization of abortion. These appear to be possibly rejectable, but nevertheless permissible contributions to political debate on matters of public concern. In political philosophy, however, disagreement exists whether, and to what extent, believing citizens have the duty to translate their religiously based political views into secular or at least reasonably comprehensible and generally acceptable arguments in order to reach consensus on regulatory matters in public debate.[235]

The question arises as to whether more extreme religiously motivated speech, such as: 'homosexuals and procurers of abortion are criminals', deserves special protection on the basis of its convergence with freedom of religion. On the one hand, one may consider such special protection to be justifiable by the sincerity or innocence of a suspect's motive. On the other hand, in light of the principles of equality and state neutrality it seems incomprehensible why religious convictions uttered in public debate must be afforded a higher level of protection than secular political opinions. This also seems to apply to religious fundamentalist speech that advocates the overthrowing of the existing democratic form of government to impose a religious regime, with or without the use of violence.[236]

4.5. Hate speech based on other discriminatory grounds: handicap, gender and sexual orientation

Hate speech bans generally protect, in addition to race and religion, other categories, such as handicap, gender and hetero- and homosexual orientation. With regard to the latter, again a distinction can be made between criticism of the *sexual praxis* and criticism of *individuals*. More generally, the relative importance of freedom of expression seems to vary per discriminatory ground. For example, the statement: 'blacks should not be allowed in the army', may be assessed differently than if the statement concerned seriously disabled persons.

The protection of these groups triggers the question as to whether hate speech bans are not discriminatory in themselves. After all, the laws protect a limitative enumeration of specific groups based on their common characteristic (race, religion, handicap, gender, hetero-or homosexual orientation), but not other groups who are possibly in need of protection.[237] It has been argued that 'once you start group libel laws, every influential body of men will urge that it has an equal claim to be

---

235 Audi, R., *Religion in the public square, the place of religious convictions in political debate*, Lanham, MD: Rowman & Littlefield 1997; Nagel, T., Moral Conflict and Political Legitimacy, *Philosophy & public affairs*, 1987, vol. 16, no. 3, p. 213 *et seq.*; Rawls, J., *Political liberalism*, New York: Colombia University Press 1993; Habermas, J., Religion in the public shere, *European journal of philosophy*, 2006, vol. 14, no. 1, p. 1–25.

236 Alexander, L., Liberalism, Religion, and the Unity of Epistemology, *San Diego law review*, 1993, vol. 30, no. 4, p. 763–798.

237 Heinze, E., Cumulative Jurisprudence and Hate Speech: Sexual Orientation and Analogies to Disability, Age and Obesity, in: Hare & Weinstein 2006, p. 265–285.

protected by such legislation'.[238] But 'because groups are constantly evolving, the meaning of group identity is ambiguous, and hence there is no natural brake to claims for group protection'.[239]

Would it then be better to criminalize hate speech against persons in general, on any ground whatsoever? On the one hand, a limitative enumeration of the most vulnerable groups or historically oppressed communities seems a welcome demarcation of the offences. On the other hand, apart from defamation and insult, there appears to be no general offence in national laws for individuals to fall back on who are victims of incitement to hatred, discrimination or violence, for example, if they are overweight. Nevertheless, they too can form a vulnerable group.

This raises another question: should hate speech bans only protect minorities or should it also protect majorities? The answer seems to depend on whether one sees hate speech bans primarily as part of a broader minority and non-discrimination policy aimed at assuring people's dignity and equal enjoyment of fundamental rights or as an ultimate means of tempering heated public debates in an effort to preserve the public order. These different rationales may result in the protection of very different groups. From a minority perspective, one could argue that religious majorities, women or heterosexuals are not in need of such protection because they have the ability to handle strong verbal attacks.

On the other hand, a strong reaction by such groups to verbal attacks based on their religion, gender or orientation can have a high impact on the public order, precisely because of the considerable size of the group. But if one would subsequently only counter hate speech against majorities uttered in public debate in the event of a risk of direct violent conflicts between groups in society, thus imminent lawlessness, then one would fall back on a conception of harm through direct actions in the Millian sense that does not underlie the regulation of hate speech. In contrast, one can say that hateful speech against a majority group may be, given its solid position in society, less likely harm the dignity of its group members, affect the social climate or lead to discrimination against them than if it concerned hateful speech against minorities. But this concerns a different value conflict and a different notion of harm (para. 1.6 *supra*).

---

238 Chafee, Z., *Government and Mass Communications*, Cambridge: Cambridge University Press 1948, p. 125.

239 Post, R., Cultural Heterogeneity and Law: Pornography, Blasphemy and the First Amendment, *California Law Review,* 1988, vol. 76, no. 2, p. 332.

4.6. Synthesis Race versus Religion

Free criticism of the convictions and practices of a particular religion in public debate must be allowed. Blasphemous and other religiously offensive expression cannot be prohibited merely because it would violate the feelings of religious adherents. A right to respect of religious feelings does not form an integral part of religious freedom. Religious toleration may relate to the peaceful coexistence of different religious thoughts and practices, but not to the peaceful co-existence of opinions on religious matters; these must clash in an open and free debate, provided that participants are respected as equal persons. One aspect is that religiously motivated and secular opinions uttered in public debate are afforded an equal level of protection.

Another aspect is that when vehement criticism of the convictions and practices of a particular religion amounts to hate speech against its adherents, it can be prohibited in public debate. Criticism of a particular race may, however, sooner amount to a prohibited form of hate speech than criticism of a religion. Other than race, religion is not an immutable characteristic and a person can change his religion or renounce his beliefs. Moreover, a person's conduct may in fact be inspired by his/her religion and may be criticized on that basis too. Religious criticism can also concern existing religion-state relationships and the place of religion in the public domain. In principle, a distinction can thus be made between expression about a religion and expression about religious adherents.

In order to consistently demarcate free contributions to public debate about religion from prohibited hate speech on the basis of religion, in principle the criterion that expression must designate a particular religious group can be a simple, helpful tool. In fact, utterances about a religion shall sooner constitute a free value judgment, while utterances about religious adherents shall sooner require a factual basis. But then a norm must clarify whether this signifies that an utterance must explicitly name a group, whether the group must have a certain degree of homogeneity in the sense of a collective identity; or whether a negative quality is in fact attributed to all members of the group. A speaker may find that actual or supposed behaviour of persons belonging to a particular religion can be necessarily associated with and caused by their religion and inherent to all members of that group.

In this respect, another criterion to consistently demarcate free contributions to public debate about religion from prohibited hate speech based on religion can be whether an utterance treats the actual or supposed practices associated with a religion as a central component of people's ethnic or national descent and identity. The essential question remains as to whether an utterance harms people's equal dignity or is likely to lead to discrimination, which may be sooner the case with hateful speech against the religion of minorities than with majorities. In order to answer this question consistently, it is not only important to differentiate between factual statements and value judgments; proper weight must also be given to whether the expression concerns either people's race and/ or religion.

5. Conclusion

This chapter analysed the difference of opinion in literature about the relationship between freedom of expression and the regulation of hate speech – on the basis of religion – using four factors: *actions* versus *opinions*; *public debate* versus *other types* of expression; *facts* versus *value judgments*; and *race* versus *religion*. Every paragraph resulted in a synthesis that provided a description of the factor concerned for further analysis in this study. The analysis showed that a certain overlap and interaction exists in the discussion of the factors. Taken together, the factors thus defined, may result in a final conclusion about the types of problems involved when trying to consistently determine the restrictions to hate speech based on religion uttered in public debate.

Hate speech consists of all kinds of utterances that stigmatize a particular group in society, from literal incitements to commit concrete acts of discrimination and discriminatory political proposals to racist epithets; invectives and terms of abuse; and vague allegations and generalizations that associate certain actual or supposed behaviour or practices with people's race or religion, including forms of holocaust denial or attacks on a religion, and are subsequently presented as a ground to discriminate against a particular group. Such speech may not produce imminent violent and lawless actions that cause direct physical harm and affect the public order; it harms the dignity of the members of the target group, lead to discrimination against them and affect the social climate.

As far as the creation of specific hate speech bans is concerned, it must be clear what interests such restrictions aim to protect; one may question whether a norm that does not clarify which consecutive effects of hate speech form the ground for its prohibition can be consistently applied. Subsequently, rationales behind restrictions of hate speech must be translated into concrete legal requirements for criminal liability/statutory offences that determine their scope. Clearly defined statutory offences should afford legal certainty about the rights and interests they protect as well as the extent of freedom of expression. Finally, for the application of the hate speech bans in concrete cases it must be clear how utterances should be qualified under those offences and what weight is to be given therein to the interest of a free public debate.

Hate speech may be prohibited because its racist message or ideas can lead to hatred, discrimination and violence against its victims in the mid- or long term; a consistent norm then must mark a spot somewhere on this gradual scale. Hate speech may also be prohibited because its racist message or ideas affect the dignity of its victims; a consistent norm then must clarify that 'dignity' must not be understood as a 'public moral' separate from its harm to persons. Then hate speech that violates human dignity is not prohibited because it contravenes certain standards of 'morality, civility or respect', but because the assault on the dignity of victims of hate speech becomes a concrete problem for them (psychic harm, devaluation in the eyes of others). Given the public good in the prevention of discrimination and the protection of people's equal human dignity, a state can prohibit the 'incitement to hatred, discrimination or violence' as well as 'group defamation/insult' as such by criminal law offences.

Whether or not hate speech bans must also be applied to contributions to public debate appears to depend primarily on what the perspectives on the harmful effects of hate speech are and which notion of harm is used in light of the importance that is afforded to that debate to legitimize democracy. The existence of a free, lively, inclusive public discourse is of fundamental importance to the proper functioning of democracy and, therefore, ample room must exist for a free political and public debate; it may include many extreme and unpopular political opinions, also about people's religion in the context of religion-state relationships or problems related to immigration and integration. Such discussions can, however, culminate in hate speech against a group on account of their religion. It must be borne in mind that the public and political debate is not directed at universal truth finding, but concerns the formation of power and the laws of the state; this is precisely why contributions to public debate that amount to hate speech have a special position and may be prohibited. One can nevertheless consider that the free public and political debate is of such vital importance that the harmful effects of these forms of hate speech must be taken for granted and that the protection of the public debate prevails. Then it must still be clear when hate speech does overstep the outer boundaries of public debate. One may question whether a norm that does not clarify wherein the excessiveness of hate speech uttered in public debate resides, can be consistently applied.

In order to consistently distinguish free critical contributions to public debate from prohibited hate speech, one must accurately differentiate between factual statements and value judgments, hence different types of utterances. In fact, a problem with the demarcation of free critical remarks from racist hate speech is that somewhat inconsistent argumentations are being used that do not clarify to what extent a negative utterance about a group must be substantiated by a sufficient factual basis. The limit to public debate can be reached when hate speech affects people's dignity because it consists of pertinent untrue statements and value judgments that lack a sufficient factual basis and are gratuitously offensive.

This may sooner be the case with criticism of a particular race than criticism of a particular religion. After all, other than race, certain practices and behaviour can actually be grounded in religious prescriptions or motivations that may be freely discussed. This may lead to somewhat inconsistent argumentations that do not clarify how to 'demarcate a religious group' in the context of hate speech. One aspect is that it must be observed whether a religion is, or is not treated as a central component of people's ethnic or national descent and identity.

A norm must also clearly distinguish criticism of government policies from political proposals targeting the fundamental rights of certain minorities. Then hate speech can constitute an abuse of rights, because it aims at the destruction of people's equal fundamental rights. Such expression endangers the 'public order' in relation to the interest in an orderly democratic society free from discrimination. This concerns a different value conflict and a different notion of harm than disorder through violent actions.

Hence, in order to be able to determine the boundaries of public debate, restrictions to hate speech must appropriately be embedded in a broader conception of the constitutional state. A constitutional provision that declares the respect of the equal human dignity and the equal enjoyment of fundamental rights can function as a compass and a reference point for the setting of clear and well motivated restrictions to hate speech uttered in public debate by the legislator and the judge; this notably applies when the rationales of hate speech bans, the concrete requirements of the statutory offences and the case law on hate speech are itself unclear. Such a constitutional guideline can assure that the substantive balancing act of opposing rights and interests in setting restrictions to hate speech remains within the same value conflict.

Chapter 3
European and International Law

Introduction

The previous chapter discussed the relevant international scientific literature on the relationship between freedom of expression and the regulation of hate speech – on the basis of religion, using four factors: *actions* versus *opinions*; *public debate* versus *other types* of expression; *facts* versus *value judgments*; and *race* versus *religion*. The chapter provided a definition of these factors and taken together they formed an analytical framework for the analysis of the positive law. This chapter analyses the international and European law on the restriction of hate speech. Five international and European instruments are selected that are particularly relevant to the regulation of hate speech in Europe. As both France and the Netherlands are state parties to the selected instruments, these are directly relevant to the comparative study in the following chapters. The aim of this chapter is twofold. Firstly, it aims to determine what, according to the selected legal instruments, the state obligations with regard to the restriction of hate speech are. Secondly, it aims to evaluate the consistency thereof in the light of the factors of the analytical framework.

The chapter begins with a detailed analysis of the case law of the European Court of Human Rights (ECtHR) on Article 10 of the European Convention of Human Rights (ECHR). After all, decisions of the ECtHR are *binding* and whatever norms on hate speech arise from the Court's case law have effect on national law (para. 1). In the following two paragraphs a number of non-binding standards with regard to the regulation of hate speech of different sections of the Council of Europe are discussed, subdivided into a selection of Resolutions and Recommendations of institutions of the Council of Europe (para. 2) and the Additional Protocol to the Convention on cybercrime, concerning the criminalization of acts of a racist and xenophobic nature committed through computer systems (para. 3). These are followed by an examination of the obligations arising from Council Framework Decision on combating certain forms and expressions of racism and xenophobia by means of criminal law of the European Union (para. 4).

Then the attention is shifted to international law. Paragraph five analyses the obligation for states to prohibit by law 'any advocacy of national, racial or religious hatred that constitutes incitement to discrimination, hostility or violence' of Article 20(2) of the International Covenant on Civil and Political Rights (ICCPR) and its relationship with the right to freedom of expression protected in Article 19 ICCPR (para. 5). Subsequently, paragraph six discusses the obligation for states to criminalize forms of racial hate speech of Article 4a of the International Convention on the Elimination of All Forms of Racial Discrimination (ICERD) and its relationship with the 'due regard' clause of Article 5 ICERD. Unlike with the ECHR, the focus is more on the interpretation of the norms themselves than on the case law of the monitoring bodies of the ICCPR and ICERD; after all, other than the ECtHR, the latter issue *non-binding* communications in cases of individual complaints.

The chapter concludes with a brief summary of the state obligations with regard to the restriction of hate speech as they arise from the selected instruments and the consistency thereof in the light of the factors from the analytic framework (para. 7).

1. The European Convention on Human Rights (ECHR)

The European Convention on Human Rights (ECHR) was adopted in 1950 and entered into force in 1953. The European Court of Human Rights (ECtHR) ensures the enforcement and the implementation of the Convention by the member states and deals with individual complaints about alleged violations of the Convention articles. Its decisions are binding on the member states. The ECtHR has in its case law developed a number of general standards for the interpretation and application of the right to freedom of expression as protected in Article 10 ECHR (1.1). Subsequently, the Court's case law sets clear and strict requirements with regard to the restriction of speech directed against the government that amounts to incitement to violence (1.2). The standards for restrictions to hate speech are, however, less clear (1.3). The same applies to the demarcation of hate speech from blasphemy and religious offence (1.4). The Court treats Holocaust denial as a particularly condemnable form of hate speech (1.5). Although speech that amounts to hate speech may be prohibited, the ECtHR appears reluctant to develop any positive state obligations with regard to its criminalization and prosecution (1.6). The paragraph concludes with a synthesis of the state obligations with regard to the restriction of hate speech under the ECHR and the consistency thereof in the light of the factors from the analytic framework (1.7).

1.1. The general framework of Article 10 ECHR

1.1.1. Scope of freedom of expression under Article 10(1) ECHR

Freedom of expression is protected in Article 10(1) ECHR that reads 'Everyone has the right to freedom of expression. This right shall include freedom to hold opinions and to receive and impart information and ideas without interference by public authority and regardless of frontiers. This article shall not prevent States from requiring the licensing of broadcasting, television or cinema enterprises.'[240] The ECtHR is generally said to interpret the scope of freedom of expression broadly.[241]

This primarily applies to the *substance* of expression. The ECtHR has considered that 'freedom of expression is applicable not only to 'information' or 'ideas' that are favourably received or regarded as inoffensive or as a matter of indifference, but also to those that *offend, shock or disturb* the State or any sector of the population'.[242] This phrase has become standard case law, which the ECtHR has reiterated on many occasions.[243]

Furthermore, the ECtHR has emphasized that 'Article 10 protects not only the substance of the ideas and information expressed, but also the *form* in which they are conveyed'.[244] Article 10 is not restricted to 'certain categories of information, ideas or forms of expression'.[245] Finally, the ECtHR has stated that 'Article 10 applies not only to the content of information, but also to the *means* of transmission or reception since any restriction to the means necessarily interferes with the right to receive and impart information'.[246]

Hence, in principle Article 10(1) protects freedom of expression of ideas and information regardless of their substance or nature and regardless of the medium or distribution channel used.[247] Subsequently, the broad protection of Article 10(1) has been afforded to a wide range of expressions, including offensive or insulting speech, defamatory statements, political criticism in a polemic and aggressive tone, advertisements, artistic expression, interviews and statements in books, articles, magazines, newspapers, on the radio or television, pamphlets, cartoons, public speeches and many more.[248]

Next to oral and written speech, Article 10 also covers conduct consisting of *physical actions*. The ECtHR has considered that protests, although in the form of physically impeding the activities of which the protesters disapproved, nonetheless

240 Article 10 ECHR does not explicitly guarantee the freedom to *seek* information and ideas. However, the refusal by public bodies to provide access to documents holding information needed for public debate is a violation of Article 10. See: ECtHR 14 April 2009, *no. 37374/05 (Társaság a Szabadságjogokért v. Hungary), para. 35–39).* See also: ECtHR (Grand Chamber) 3 April 2012, no. 41723/06 (Gillberg v. Sweden).

241 Vande Lanotte, J. & Haeck, Y., Handboek EVRM, Antwerpen: Intersentia 2004, p. 901; Van Dijk, P., Van Hoof, F., Van Rijn, A. & Zwaak, L., Theory and Practice of the European Convention on Human Rights, Antwerpen: Intersentia 2006, p. 779; Harris, D.J., O'Boyle, M. & Warbrick, C., Law of the European Convention on Human Rights, Oxford: Oxford University Press 2009, p. 444.

242 ECtHR 7 December 1976, no. 5493/72 (Handyside v. United Kingdom), para. 49.

243 ECtHR 24 May 1985, no. 10737/84 (Muller v. Switzerland), para. 33; ECtHR (Grand Chamber) 23 September 1994, no. 15890/89 (Jersild v. Denmark), para. 37.

244 ECtHR (Grand Chamber) 23 September 1994, no. 15890/89 (Jersild v. Denmark), para 31; ECtHR 23 May 1991, no. 11662/85 (Oberschlick v. Austria), para. 57.

245 ECtHR 16 December 1992, no. 12945/87 (Hadjianastassiou v. Greece), para. 39.

246 ECtHR 22 May 1990, no. 12726/87 (Autronic v. Switzerland), para. 47.

247 Vande Lanotte & Haeck 2004, p. 900.

248 Vande Lanotte & Haeck 2004, p. 901–911.

constituted expressions of opinion within the meaning of Article 10.[249] Likewise, with regard to symbolic speech, the ECtHR has considered that a person's decision to wear a red star in public must be regarded as his way of expressing his political views and that the display of vestimentary symbols falls within the ambit of Article 10.[250] However, not all physical actions are afforded protection under 10 ECHR, only 'expressive' conduct that communicates information or ideas.

Freedom to express opinion can be closely connected to the exercise of other fundamental rights protected in the ECHR, notably freedom of thought, conscience and religion (9 ECHR) and freedom of assembly and association (11 ECHR). The latter freedoms could be regarded as *leges speciales* to Article 10. One could argue that Article 9 ECHR protects the freedom to express opinions that reflect an author's conviction.[251] In situations where several persons jointly express a given opinion, for example during a demonstration, Article 11 ECHR may apply next to Article 10.[252] The delimitation of the articles and their application may vary according to the particular circumstances of the case (*infra*).

Not every measure by the state that in some way affects a person's freedom of expression however constitutes a matter falling within the scope of Article 10, only when a measure is, for example, *primarily* based on a person's political opinion. According to the Court, this was the case with regard to the dismissal of a civil servant by virtue of her association with the German Communist Party[253] and with regard to the decision not to promote a police officer on the ground of his membership of an extreme-right winged party.[254]

Although the scope of freedom of expression under Article 10(1) is thus quite broad – it includes all kind of conduct as long as it communicates information or ideas – not all measures that may affect freedom of expression form an Article 10 issue, but measures based on such information or ideas do.

1.1.2. Limitations to freedom of expression under 10(2) ECHR

Freedom of expression as protected under Article 10(1) ECHR is not absolute, but may be restricted under the conditions set in 10(2).[255] Article 10(2) stipulates that

---

249 ECtHR 23 September 1998, no. 24838/94 (Steel and Others v. The United Kingdom), para. 92.

250 ECtHR 8 July 2008, no. 33629/06 (Vajnai v. Hungary), para 47.

251 Van Dijk, Van Hoof, Van Rijn & Zwaak 2006, p. 791.

252 Van Dijk, Van Hoof, Van Rijn & Zwaak 2006, p. 791.

253 ECtHR (Grand Chamber) 26 September 1995, no. 17851/91 (Vogt v. Germany).

254 ECtHR 24 November 2005, no. 27574/02 (Otto v. Germany).

255 Article 10 (2) reads 'The exercise of these freedoms, since it carries with it duties and responsibilities, may be subject to such formalities, conditions, restrictions or penalties as are prescribed by law and are necessary in a democratic society, in the interests of national security, territorial integrity or public safety, for the prevention of disorder or crime, for the protection of health or morals, for the protection of the reputation or rights of others, for preventing the disclosure of information received in confidence, or for maintaining the authority and impartiality of the judiciary.'

the exercise of freedom of expression carries with it *duties and responsibilities*. Such reference is absent with regard to the exercise of other freedoms listed in the Convention. During the drafting of the ECHR, it was maintained that freedom of expression was a precious heritage as well as a dangerous instrument and, in view of the powerful influence the modern media of expression had on individuals and on national and international affairs, that these 'duties and responsibilities' should be specially emphasized. This would offer State parties an express tool to counter abuse of power by the modern mass media.[256]

The reference could suggest that there are *inherent* or *implied* limitations to freedom of expression. As a general rule, the reference is, however, not to be interpreted as such.[257] In its case law, the ECtHR rather seems to refer to the duties and responsibilities of a speaker as an additional argument in case the Court has come to the conclusion that a restriction to a particular statement was justified, which is notably the case with regard to speech uttered by political figures (para. 1.3 *infra*).

Under 10(2) the ECtHR primarily determines whether a measure by the State constitutes an *interference* with an applicant's freedom of expression or opinion in the form of 'formalities, conditions, restrictions or penalties'. Preventive measures are not prohibited as such.[258] Subsequently, the ECtHR determines whether a measure by the State constitutes a *violation* of an applicant's freedom of expression or opinion by reviewing whether a restriction is a) *prescribed by law*; pursues b) *a legitimate aim*; and is c) *necessary in a democratic society*. Given the broad scope of Article 10(1), the onus is on the State to demonstrate that its interference is justified under 10(2).

ECtHR has further elaborated these requirements. A norm must be 'accessible' to a citizen in order for him to have an adequate indication of the legal rules applicable to a given case and 'foreseeable', i.e. formulated with 'sufficient precision' to enable a citizen to foresee the consequences which a given action may entail.[259] It has been established that even though the general prohibition of the wrongful act in a country's civil law code might produce problems of interpretation, such a provision is not too vague and insufficiently precise to form a legal basis for restrictions to freedom of expression, if the norm is further elaborated in the case law of the Supreme Court.[260] However, in the chapters on France and the Netherlands it will become apparent that the national law of European countries may strongly differ on this point.

The limitative enumeration of grounds on which a state may impose restrictions does not concern the *content* of expression, but a listing of permissible *purposes* for interference. It includes 'the interests of national security, territorial integrity or

256 Council of Europe, European Commission of Human Rights Preparatory work on Article 10 of the European Convention on Human Rights, DH (56) 15.

257 Harris, O'Boyle & Warbrick 2009, p. 493.

258 Although, –temporary- prohibitions on press publications call for 'particularly close scrutiny', because they can annul their news value. See: ECtHR 26 April 1979, no. 6538/74 (Sunday Times v. The United Kingdom), para. 63.

259 ECtHR 26 April 1979, no. 6538/74 (Sunday Times v. The United Kingdom), para. 49.

260 ECmHR, 21 October 1998, *Mediaforum* 1999–1, nr. 3.

public safety, for the prevention of disorder or crime, for the protection of health or morals, for the protection of the reputation or rights of others, for preventing the disclosure of information received in confidence, or for maintaining the authority and impartiality of the judiciary'. These grounds must be interpreted restrictively and 'within the meaning of the Convention'.[261]

Most relevant to this study are the limitation grounds of morals, the reputation or rights of others, national security, public safety and the prevention of disorder. With the term 'disorder' the drafters of the ECHR aimed to avoid the uncertainty that was connected to the broader term of the protection of the 'public order' used in other human rights instruments.[262] The English non-legal term 'public order' was generally used to mean the absence of disorder. Contrarily, the French legal term 'l'ordre public' was best translated as 'public policy' and would allow for far-reaching restrictions that could completely undermine freedom of expression.[263]

In the evaluation of restrictions by the ECtHR, the emphasis is often on the necessity-test. The Court has explained the test as follows: in order for a restriction to be necessary there must be a *pressing social need* for the restriction; the restriction must be *proportional* to the legitimate aim pursued; and the reasons for the restriction must be *relevant and sufficient*.[264, 265] Furthermore, the necessity of a restriction must be *convincingly established*.[266] It is generally assumed that the ECtHR *balances* the interest in freedom of expression of the applicant against the countervailing interest of the state and/or other persons protected by the restriction in the light of all the circumstances of the case. Important factors in the balancing-test include the content and context of expression, the person of the speaker, his intention, the medium used, the possible impact of expression on the public and the nature (proportionality) of the restriction.

The ECtHR, however, has a different function than national courts and does not constitute a court of 'fourth instance'. It therefore affords state parties a certain margin of appreciation for determining whether a restriction is necessary, because 'by reason of their direct and continuous contact with the vital forces of their countries, State authorities are in principle in a better position to judge the necessity of a particular restriction'. Nevertheless, the ECtHR stipulates that the domestic margin of appreciation 'goes hand in hand with a European supervision', which is not limited to a due diligence review and ascertaining whether a respondent State exercised its discretion 'reasonably, carefully and in good faith'.[267]

---

261 ECtHR 26 April 1979, no. 6538/74 (Sunday Times v. The United Kingdom), para. 55.

262 Article 19 ICCPR.

263 Council of Europe, European Commission of Human Rights Preparatory work on Article 10 of the European Convention on Human Rights, DH (56) 15, p. 25.

264 ECtHR 7 December 1976, no. 5493/72 (Handyside v. The United Kingdom), para. 48–50; ECtHR 26 April 1979, no. 6538/74 (Sunday Times v. The United Kingdom), para. 62.

265 Fenwick & Phillipson speak of a '*3-fold-test*'. See: Fenwick, H. & Phillipson, G., *Media Freedom under the Human Rights Act*, Oxford: Oxford University Press 2006, p. 93.

266 ECtHR (Grand Chamber) 6 May 2003, no. 48898/99 (Perna v. Italy), para. 39.

267 ECtHR 26 April 1979, no. 6538/74 (Sunday Times v. The United Kingdom), para. 59.

In fact, the extent of the margin of appreciation depends on the particular nature of expression and the particular limitation ground in question. With regard to limitation grounds concerning 'objective notions' and speech for which there exists a 'European common ground', the ECtHR affords states a small margin. Examples are restrictions on the press and political speech and for the protection of national security or the prevention of disorder. In such cases, the ECtHR generally exercises an *integral* review and independently evaluates the arguments of the opposing parties.

Contrarily, as morals and religion concern 'subjective notions' for which no such 'European common ground' exists, in these fields the ECtHR affords states a large margin. In such cases, the ECtHR generally exercises a more distanced, restraint or *marginal* review. The application of a marginal review by the ECtHR is criticized for sometimes amounting to balancing *in abstracto* the interest of the expression itself against the interest of the purpose of the restriction – so-called '*speech/harm balancing*' – instead of starting from the right to freedom of expression that is subjected to a limitative number of restrictions that are to be interpreted restrictively.[268]

It is argued that such an abstract test runs the risk of merely rationalizing legal preferences and disregarding the context of the case.[269] Moreover, the ECtHR is criticized for sometimes starting from a 'presumption in favour of the State' and shifting the onus to the side of the plaintiff, who then must demonstrate the unreasonableness of the measure.[270] One may question whether in such cases the Court performs an actual balancing-test. When the ECtHR affords states a large margin, it generally determines whether or not a State could have reasonably come to its decision. This may come down to a mere due diligence review after all.

It is argued that the ECtHR's use of the margin of appreciation doctrine as an instrument to deal with the need to reconcile European standard setting and national diversity must be improved;[271] especially the legal certainty created by proper application of the doctrine in a predictable and well-structured fashion is of great value in a highly case-based system. Moreover, it is argued that the application of the doctrine must be embedded more into the ECtHR's practice of '*incrementalism*' and the gradual creation of general principles through case-based decision-making that are applicable in following cases.[272]

---

268 Fenwick & Phillipson 2006, p. 101–102.

269 Fenwick & Phillipson 2006, p. 101–102.

270 Schokkenbroek, J.G.C., *Toetsing aan de vrijheidsrechten van het Europees Verdrag tot bescherming van de rechten van de mens: een onderzoek naar de toetsing aan de beperkingsclausules bij de Europese vrijheidsrechten in de Europese en in de Nederlandse rechtspraak*, Zwolle: W.E.J. Tjeenk Willink 1996, p. 82–83.

271 For suggestions see: Gerards, J.H., Pluralism, Deference and the Margin of Appreciation Doctrine, *European Law Journal* 2010, vol.17, issue 1., p. 80–120.

272 Gerards, J.H., Diverging Fundamental Rights Standards and the Role of the European Court of Human Rights, To be published in: M. Claes and M. De Visser (eds), *Constructing European Constitutional Law*, Oxford: Hart 2014.

It is notably in the field of freedom of expression that the ECtHR has created such general principles, which will be discussed in following sections. But a consistent application of these principles is precisely complicated by the ECtHR's use of the margin of appreciation. Why would the ECtHR not exercise a stringent review of restrictions on hate speech uttered in a political discussion on a country's immigration problems, like it normally does with regard to political speech? And why would the ECtHR not apply the distinction between facts and value judgments, which it uses to evaluate convictions for defamation, to hate speech that generally consists of factual imputations against or strong value judgments about a particular group? These questions will be elaborated on later (para. 1.3 *infra*).

The evaluation system of restrictions to freedom of expression as used by the ECtHR results in a complex body of Article 10 case law. Deriving a consistent line therein is complicated, on the one hand by the manner in which the doctrine of margin of appreciation and general principles are applied and on the other hand, by the (laudably) high contextualization of 'stringent review' cases. Moreover, the ECtHR is often strongly divided and in such cases the final judgment of the Court is counterbalanced by the dissenting opinions that may reflect a diametrically opposite view. This also notably applies in cases concerning forms of hate speech (para. 1.3 *infra*).

1.1.3. Categorization of expression

For the evaluation of restrictions to freedom of expression the ECtHR generally distinguishes between different categories of speech. Hate speech may fall under any of these categories. Depending on the nature of the speech at issue, the ECtHR uses a different standard of review, which must be seen in the broader context of the doctrine of the 'margin of appreciation' granted to the national authorities to determine the necessity of a restriction to a particular expression (*supra*). The ECtHR affords the highest level of protection to political speech, for which it uses a stringent standard of review (*supra*).

The ECtHR has furthermore brought artistic expression under the scope of Article 10, considering that it 'affords the opportunity to take part in the public exchange of cultural, political and social information and ideas of all kinds (...) Those who create, perform, distribute or exhibit works of art contribute to the exchange of ideas and opinions which is essential for a democratic society. Hence the obligation on the State not to encroach unduly on their freedom of expression.'[273] An important aspect of artistic expression is the freedom to receive it.[274]

---

273 ECtHR 24 May 1988, no. 10737/84 (Muller and Others v. Switzerland), para. 27 and 33.

274 ECtHR 16 February 2010, no. 41056/04 (Akdas v. Turkey), para. 30. In this case concerning the criminal conviction for the publication of a Turkish translation of the French erotic novel 'Les onze mille verges' of Appolinaire, the ECtHR stressed the importance of having access to European literary heritage.

Artistic expression is nevertheless accorded a less privileged position than political expression. This may be explained by the fact that in cases before the ECtHR concerning artistic expression the expression concerned often questions existing public morals or religious convictions in a provocative manner. As morals or religious convictions may vary from one society to another, the ECtHR gives states more leeway to restrict speech concerning these issues. The ECtHR's case law concerning artistic expression thus reflects a certain relativism regarding morals.[275]

In certain cases, this results in allowing the state to prohibit harsh criticism of a minority in order to protect the sensitivities and feelings of a religious majority.[276] However, the norm that expression may 'offend, shock and disturb' is especially important to artistic expression, because of the 'inherently subversive nature of the artistic impulse'.[277] Moreover, the role of avant-gardes that artists play is essential for a pluralistic democracy.

Finally, commercial expression, which may be defined as 'the expression of information and ideas for the promotion of an economic activity and the right to receive it',[278] falls under the scope of Article 10. Such commercial expression is afforded even less protection than political or artistic expression. The ECtHR justifies its lax standard of review of restrictions to commercial expression by referring to the values underlying freedom of expression that would primarily purport to protect political ideas, to the need to protect consumers from misleading advertising and to the need to restrict unfair competition practices.[279]

The ECtHR seemingly treats political, artistic and commercial speech as mutually exclusive categories and may be criticized for not acknowledging more explicitly the possibility of category-crossovers. It is exactly the existence of mixed categories that entails the risk of mis-categorization.[280] In cases that held the ECtHR strongly divided, a pivotal question was often whether or not the artistic or commercial expression entered into a political or public debate and consequently which standard of review was to be used.[281] In some cases, the ECtHR decided that gratuitously offensive expression could not form part of public debate.[282]

This markedly applies in the field of religion. The ECtHR has not developed a particular category of 'religious expression' under 10 ECHR. On the one hand,

---

275 See further para. 1.4.

276 Notably: ECtHR 20 September 1994, no. 13470/87 (Otto Preminger Institute v. Austria). See further para. 1.4.

277 Harris, O'Boyle & Warbrick 2009, p. 474, f. 114.

278 Cf. Harris, O'Boyle & Warbrick 2009, p. 461.

279 Randall, M.H., Commercial Speech under the European Convention on Human Rights: Subordinate or Equal?, *Human Rights Law Review*, 2006, vol. 6, no. 1, p. 53–86.

280 Randall 2006, p. 75–76.

281 See notably: ECtHR 29 March 2005, no. 40287/98 (Alinak v. Turkey); ECtHR 8 July 1999, no. 23168/94 (Karakaş v. Turkey); ECtHR 25 January 2007, no. 68354/01 (Vereinigung Bildender Künstler v. Austria).

282 ECtHR 20 September 1994, no. 13470/87 (Otto Preminger Institute v. Austria).

religiously motivated expression directed against secular values fall under the broader category of anti-democratic speech (para. 1.3 *infra*).[283] On the other hand, whether or not criticism of religious convictions forms part of public debate, notably depends on the form or media used (para. 1.4 *infra*).[284]

1.1.4. Facts or value judgments

Another form of 'categorization' of expression used by the ECtHR for the evaluation of restrictions to freedom of expression is the distinction that the ECtHR makes between statements of fact and the expression of value judgments. In principle, the protection of the reputation and honour of individuals through the prohibition of defamatory expression in criminal or civil law is a legitimate aim. Such an interference with freedom of expression is allowed under Article 10(2) in order to protect 'the rights of others'. It falls outside the scope of this study to give a detailed account of the rich case law, in which the ECtHR examined the proportionality of national measures against alleged defamatory speech.[285] From this case law a number of general principles can however be derived.

The Court primarily emphasizes that 'a careful distinction needs to be made between facts and value judgments. The existence of facts can be demonstrated, whereas the truth of value judgments is not susceptible of proof.'[286] The ECtHR considered the accusation of the Austrian Prime Minister of 'the basest opportunism' and acting in an 'immoral' and 'undignified' manner to constitute a value judgment on a matter of political concern for which the state could not require the proof of truth. Therefore, the conviction for defamation by lack of proof was disproportionate.[287]

Likewise, the ECtHR found the conviction for defamation with regard to a description of the leader of the Austrian Freedom Party (FPO), Jörg Haider, as an 'idiot' to violate freedom of expression. According to the Court, the term did not constitute 'a gratuitous personal attack', but an opinion in a polemic tone. It formed part of a political discussion provoked by a speech of Haider that was itself provocative.[288]

The ECtHR thus generally thoroughly examines whether the expression at issue must be classified as either a factual assertion or a value judgment and does not leave states a wide margin in this area. The ECtHR does not examine statements in isolation, but may conclude on the basis of their overall context that they constitute

---

283 ECtHR (Grand Chamber), 13 February 2003, no. 41340/98 41342/98 41343/98 41344/98 (Refah Partisi and others v. Turkey).

284 Notably: ECtHR 24 May 1988, no. 10737/84 (Muller and Others v. Switzerland); ECtHR 20 September 1994, no. 13470/87 (Otto Preminger Institute v. Austria). See further para. 1.4.

285 For a thorough analysis, see: Harris, O'Boyle & Warbrick 2009, p. 479–482; 496–511.

286 ECtHR 8 July 1986, no. 9815/82 (Lingens v. Austria), para. 46; ECtHR 24 February 1997, no. 19983/92 (De Haes and Gijsels v. Belgium), para. 42.

287 ECtHR 8 July 1986, no. 9815/82 (Lingens v. Austria), para. 42–43.

288 ECtHR 1 July 1997, no. 20834/92 (Oberschlick v. Austria no. 2), para. 33.

'value judgments for which no proof of truth is possible'.[289] Furthermore, the ECtHR uses a broad meaning of the notion of value judgment. In this manner it affords a high level of protection to freedom of expression.

For example, a politician had been convicted for defamation with regard to his remark that sects have as a common feature a totalitarian character and show fascist tendencies. The national court considered this to be a statement of fact not proven to be true. Contrarily, the ECtHR considered the remark to be a value judgment and a fair comment on matters of public interest.[290] Likewise, the ECtHR found the comparison by a Jehovah's Witness of the method of 'deprogramming' offered by an organization that aided victims of religious sects with the Soviet method of psychological internment of dissidents to constitute a value judgment, not a statement of fact.[291]

However, the ECtHR considers that *strong* value judgments must be grounded in at least some objective data and therefore examines whether such value judgments have a 'sufficient factual basis'.[292] The Court found the remark '*But these are Nazis, these are Nazi methods',* made in the course of a local discussion about the creation of a foster home for mentally ill persons in reaction to an opponent of the plan who argued that the value of houses would be lowered in the neighbourhood, to be particularly offensive given the special stigma attached to Nazism. Therefore the applicant had exceeded the limits of acceptable criticism.[293]

Yet, the distinction between facts and value judgments is less important with regard to political speech than in other contexts. In one case, the ECtHR considered that 'the distinction between statements of fact and value judgments is of less significance in a case such as the present, where the impugned statement is made in the course of a lively political debate at local level and where elected officials and journalists should enjoy a wide freedom to criticize the actions of a local authority, even where the statements made may lack a clear basis in fact.'[294]

With regard to statements made in a novel, an artistic, literary work based on real political events and figures, the making of a consistent distinction between facts and value judgments and the proof of a factual basis becomes particularly difficult. The ECtHR found a criminal conviction for defamation with regard to the comparison of an 'ex-leader of an extreme right political party' with a 'chief of a gang of killers' and the allegation against him of having 'advocated' the murder of

289 ECtHR 28 August 1992, no. 13704/88 (Schwabe v. Austria), para. 34.

290 ECtHR 27 February 2001, no. 26958/95 (Jerusalem v. Austria), para. 44.

291 ECtHR 22 December 2005, no. 54968/00 (Paturel v. France).

292 ECtHR 26 February 2002, no. 28525/95 (Unabhängige Initiative Informationsvielfalt v. Austria), para. 39–40; ECtHR (Grand Chamber) 17 December 2004, no. 49017/99 (Pedersen and Baadsgaard v. Denmark, para. 76.

293 ECtHR 17 November 2005, no. 56720/00 (Metzger v. Germany).

294 ECtHR 24 April 2007, no. 7333/06 (Lombardo v. Malta), para. 60.

an immigrant in the novel 'Jean-Marie Le Pen on Trial' not to violate Article 10. This equally applied to a reproduction of the statements in the press.[295]

The ECtHR considered that 'there is no need to make this distinction (fact/opinion – EHJ) when dealing with extracts from a novel', but that it does become fully pertinent where 'the impugned work is not one of pure fiction but introduces real characters or facts'. The applicants had failed to make a 'basic verification' for their factual assertions that were formed in particularly virulent words.[296] The dissenters objected that 'a reality novel largely remains a novel, just as docu-fiction remains, for the most part, fiction.' The distinction becomes 'partly pertinent when the novel and the reality coincide.'[297]

In the press, factual accusations, contrary to value judgments, cannot be expressed rashly. Journalists must act 'in good faith to provide accurate and reliable information in accordance with the ethics of journalism.'[298] In a way, this 'duty and responsibility' counterbalances their right to include 'a certain degree of exaggeration and provocation'.[299] The ECtHR thus reviews whether journalistic research has been carefully conducted, notably with regard to serious accusations, such as the imputation of criminal facts.[300] However, journalists who report in the press may rely on authoritative sources, such as a government report concerning the malpractices in seal-hunting.[301] Then the press does not have to check all relevant facts for itself.[302]

When a defendant is criminally convicted for defamation based on the falsity of his statement, he must have had the opportunity to prove the truth of his allegation. In a case concerning a conviction for the allegation that the police was responsible for the murder of Basque activists and that the Government was responsible for the impunity of the perpetrators, the ECtHR found the fact that the defence of truth was not allowed in respect of insults directed at the state institutions to violate freedom of expression.[303] Another case concerned a conviction for the allegation that the Moroccan Royal family had a direct responsibility in international drug trafficking. Likewise, the ECtHR considered the inadmissibility of the proof of truth for the charge of the offence of insulting a foreign head of state disproportionate.[304]

---

295 It was legitimate to try to ensure 'a minimum degree of moderation and propriety, especially as the reputation of a politician, even a controversial one, must benefit from the protection afforded by the Convention.' ECtHR (Grand Chamber) 22 October 2007, no. 21279/02 36448/02 (Lindon, Otchakovsky-Laurens and July v. France), para. 57.

296 *Ibid.*, para. 37.

297 *Ibid.*, Joint partly dissenting opinion of judges Rozakis, Bratza, Tulkens and Šikuta, para. 5.

298 ECtHR (Grand Chamber) 20 May 1999, no. 21980/93 (Bladet Tromsø and Stensaas v. Norway), para. 65.

299 ECtHR 30 March 2004, no. 53984/00 (Radio France and others v. France), para. 38.

300 ECtHR 10 July 2012, no. 46443/09 (Björk Eiðsdóttir v. Iceland).

301 ECtHR (Grand Chamber) 20 May 1999, no. 21980/93 (Bladet Tromsø and Stensaas v. Norway), para. 68.

302 ECtHR 25 June 2002, no. 51279/99 (Colombani and others v. France), para. 65.

303 ECtHR 24 April 1992, no. 11798/85 (Castells v. Spain), para. 48–50.

304 ECtHR 25 June 2002, no. 51279/99 (Colombani and others v. France), para. 66.

Sometimes the ECtHR notably evaluates an interference with freedom of expression as disproportionate on the basis of the severity of the sanction. The ECtHR considers that 'a criminal sentence or an award of damages for defamation must bear a reasonable relationship of proportionality to the injury to reputation suffered.'[305] This is not the case in relation to the award of excessive damages[306] or far reaching injunctions such as a total ban on the distribution of expression.[307] The absence of legal aid for a defendant in a defamation case may amount to an inequality of arms, thus unfair proceedings that have a chilling effect on freedom of expression.[308]

The question arises as to whether the general principles the ECtHR has developed for the distinction between facts and value judgments in its case law concerning defamation about individuals and public figures are also relevant for the Court's evaluation of restrictions to hate speech that generally consists of imputations against or strong value judgments about a particular group and, if so, whether these principles are consistently applied by the Court (para. 1.3 *infra*). From the foregoing it is clear that the distinction between facts and value judgments is relevant in particular with regard to statements made in the press and the media.

1.1.5. Public debate and the media

According to the ECtHR, the *press* plays the vital role of a 'public watchdog' in a democracy.[309] It is the task of the press and journalism to impart information and ideas on matters of public interest, including political issues, which the public has the right to receive. On the one hand, the press places policy decisions and government actions and omissions under the scrutiny of the public opinion. On the other hand, the press facilitates citizens to participate in the decision making process.[310] Moreover, a free press affords the public one of the best means of discovering and forming an opinion of the ideas and attitudes of political leaders.[311]

The press is thus an important means to shape an informed public opinion and stimulate critical debate that extends to all matters of general public interest.[312] Given its vital role in democracy, the ECtHR has afforded a large scope of press freedom that may include a certain degree of exaggeration and provocation.[313] Restrictions on press freedom call for strict scrutiny by the ECtHR and criminal

---

305 ECtHR 13 July 1995, no. 18139/91 (Tolstoy Miloslavsky v. The United Kingdom), para. 49.

306 *Ibid.*

307 ECtHR 18 May 2004, no. 58148/00 (Editions Plon v. France), para. 53–55.

308 ECtHR 15 February no. 68416/01, (Steel and Morris v. The United Kingdom), para. 72; 95.

309 ECtHR 26 November 1991, no. 13166/87 (Sunday Times 2 v. The United Kingdom), para. 50 (b).

310 ECtHR 23 April 1992, no. 11798/85 (Castells v. Spain), para. 43.

311 ECtHR 8 July 1986, no. 9815/82 (Lingens v. Austria), para. 42.

312 ECtHR (Grand Chamber) 17 December 2004, no. 33348/96 (Cumpana v. Romania), para. 93.

313 ECtHR 30 March 2004, no. 53984/00 (Radio France and Others v. France), para. 37.

sanctions in the form of prison sentences and high penalties or the prohibition to exercise one's profession may have an unacceptable chilling effect.[314]

Furthermore, the ECtHR has brought freedom of expression through television and radio broadcasts[315] and the Internet,[316] under the scope of Article 10. A state may regulate its national broadcasting through a licensing system or even through a public monopoly in order to ensure objective and impartial reporting and the existence of a diversity of opinions or to preserve cultural diversity through a balanced and diverse program content. Such measures may not, however, have discriminatory results.[317]

The press and the media could, just as politicians and political parties (*infra*), be seen as 'actors' in political and public debate and the ECtHR has also set boundaries to their use of freedom of expression. The Court has considered that the suspension of a radio-broadcasting license for a year for having broadcasted songs during a radio program that incited to violence, terrorism, racial discrimination and feelings of hatred did not violate Article 10.[318] Contrarily, the ECtHR found that the criminal conviction of a journalist for 'aiding and abetting' the racist statements of a particular youth group by broadcasting them in a television interview did violate Article 10. The item did not have as its *purpose* the propagation of racist views and ideas, but was aimed at informing the public and animating public discussion about the existence of the racist views of the group. As well as this, the journalist had distanced himself from and rebutted the racist statements.[319] Statements made by interviewed persons thus cannot simply be attributed to the interviewing journalist (para. 1.3 *infra*). The media has a special role in the fulfilling of the function of freedom of expression in a democracy.

1.1.6. Public debate and democracy

In its preamble, the ECHR establishes a clear connection between the Convention and democracy in general by stating that the maintenance and further realization of human rights and fundamental freedoms are best ensured by an effective political democracy. The ECtHR has pointed out that democracy is a fundamental feature of the European public order[320] and that the Convention was designed to maintain and promote the ideals and values of a democratic society.[321] Furthermore, from the fact

---

314 ECtHR (Grand Chamber) 17 December 2004, no. 33348/96 (Cumpana v. Romania), para. 114.

315 ECtHR 10 July 2003, no. 44179/98 (Murphy v. Ireland).

316 ECtHR 18 October 2005, no. 5446/03 (Perrin v. The United Kingdom); ECtHR 10 March 2009, no. 3002/03 23676/03 (Times Newspapers LTD v. United Kingdom no. 1 and 2).

317 ECtHR 7 November 2000, no. 44802/98 (United Christian Broadcasters Ltd. V. The United Kingdom).

318 ECtHR 14 November 2006, no. 32842/02 (Medya FM Reha Radyo ve İletişim Hizmetleri A.Ş. v. Turkey).

319 ECtHR (Grand Chamber) 23 September 1994, no. 15890/89 (Jersild v. Denmark), para. 33–36.

320 ECtHR (Grand Chamber) 23 March 1995, no. 15318/89 (Loizidou v. Turkey), para. 75.

321 ECtHR 7 December 1976, no. 5095/71 5920/72 5926/72 (Kjeldsen, Busk Madsen and Pedersen v. Denmark), para. 53.

that restrictions to Articles 8–11 ECHR must be 'necessary in a democratic society', the ECtHR has deduced that 'democracy appears to be the only political model contemplated by the Convention and, accordingly, the only one compatible with it'.[322]

Freedom of expression, as protected by Article 10 ECHR has a special position within the ECHR. This is mainly due to its capability to support the assurance of other fundamental rights; through free expression the public can be informed about the development of the democratic state and the status of human rights.[323] On many occasions, the ECtHR has taken as a starting point that freedom of expression 'constitutes one of the essential foundations of a democratic society and one of the basic conditions for its progress and each individual's self-fulfilment.' Ideas and information may offend, shock or disturb, because 'such are the demands of that pluralism, tolerance and broadmindedness without which there is no 'democratic society''.[324]

One of the principal characteristics of democracy is 'the possibility it offers of resolving a country's problems through dialogue, without recourse to violence, even when they are irksome. Democracy thrives on freedom of expression'.[325] Freedom of expression thus has special relevance, when its aim is to contribute to the development of vulnerable 'newly established democracies'.[326] In the end, it is the government who is the 'ultimate guarantor of the principle of pluralism'.[327] Hence, the state has the obligation to ensure the existence of a plurality of opinions.

The state must therefore afford ample room to political and public debate. The ECtHR has emphasized that 'freedom of political debate constitutes a particular aspect of freedom of expression. Indeed, freedom of political debate is at the very core of the concept of a democratic society'.[328] In other words, 'freedom of political debate and free elections form the bedrock of any democratic system'.[329] Therefore, the ECtHR considers that 'there is little scope under 10(2) of the Convention for restrictions on political speech or on matters of public interest'.[330] Restrictions on political expression call for stringent review by the Court and 'must however be construed strictly and the need for any restrictions must be established

---

322 ECtHR (Grand Chamber) 30 January 1998, no. 19392/92 (United Communist Party of Turkey and Others v. Turkey), para. 45.

323 Vande Lanotte & Haeck 2004, p. 854.

324 ECtHR 24 May 1985, no. 10737/84 (Muller v. Switzerland), para. 33; ECtHR (Grand Chamber) 23 September 1994, no. 15890/89 (Jersild v. Denmark), para. 37.

325 ECtHR (Grand Chamber) 30 January 1998, no. 19392/92 (United Communist Party of Turkey and Others v. Turkey), para. 57.

326 ECtHR 19 April 2001, no. 32686/96 (Maronek v. Slovakia), para. 56; ECtHR 12 July 2001, no. 29032/95 (Feldek v. Slovakia), para. 80–84.

327 ECtHR 24 January 1993, no. 13914/88 15041/89 15717/89 15779/89 17207/90 (Lentia and Others v. Austria), para. 38.

328 ECtHR 20 May 1999, no. 25390/94 (Rekvényi v. Hungary), para. 26.

329 ECtHR (Grand Chamber)19 February 1998, no. 24839/94 (Bowman v. The United Kingdom), para. 42.

330 ECtHR 25 November 1996, no. 17419/90 (Wingrove v. The United Kingdom), para. 58.

convincingly'.[331] In order to *effectively* guarantee freedom of political expression, the ECtHR reviews, amongst others, whether a restriction has a 'chilling effect' or whether there was a 'less restrictive alternative'.[332] The ECtHR thereby pays attention to the speaker as a particular actor in public debate.

1.1.7. Public debate, politicians and political parties or groupings

The ECtHR has highlighted freedom of expression of certain actors *within* political and public debate. Next to the press and the media (*supra*), the freedom of expression of parliamentarians and *politicians* must particularly be safeguarded. The ECtHR has recalled that 'while freedom of expression is important for everybody, it is especially so for an elected representative of the people. He represents his electorate, draws attention to their preoccupations and defends their interests. Accordingly, interferences with the freedom of expression of an opposition Member of Parliament, like the applicant, call for the closest scrutiny on the part of the Court'.[333] Moreover, immunity may even be afforded to political speech uttered during the parliamentary debates in parliament in order to protect the interest of the entire parliament.[334]

The question is whether a politician's greater freedom is accompanied by a greater responsibility in the context of hate speech (para. 1.3 *infra*). One can ascribe an exemplary role to politicians, whose words inevitably have a larger impact on society. To a certain extent, the duties and responsibilities of politicians can be compared with those of teachers, who, according to the ECtHR, form a symbol of authority for their students and therefore must act with reserve and tolerance, even in their activities outside the school.[335]

The other side of the coin (of political freedom) is that members of government and political figures must tolerate a higher degree of criticism than private persons, when such criticism concerns their political function. As the ECtHR has considered: '[u]nlike the latter, the former inevitably and knowingly lays himself open to close scrutiny of his every word and deed by both journalists and the public at large, and he must consequently display a greater degree of tolerance'.[336] This notably applies when a politician has made himself a public statement that is susceptible to criticism. The same applies to individuals or associations that voluntarily enter the arena of public debate.[337] Although the reporting of aspects of the private lives of

331 ECtHR 8 June 2001, no. 24699/94 (VGT Verein gegen Tierfabriken v. Switzerland), para. 66.
332 Harris, O'Boyle & Warbrick 2009, p. 455.
333 ECtHR 23 April 1992, no. 11798/85 (Castells v. Spain), para. 42; ECtHR 27 February 2001, no. 26958/95 (Jerusalem v. Austria), para. 36.
334 ECtHR 17 December 2002, no. 35373/97 (A. v. The United Kingdom).
335 ECtHR 18 May 2004, no. 57383/00 (Seurot v. France); ECtHR 7 June 2011, no. 48135/08 (Gollnisch v. France).
336 ECtHR 8 July 1986, no. 9815/82 (Lingens v. Austria), para. 42.
337 ECtHR 27 February 2001, no. 26958/95 (Jerusalem v. Austria), para. 38.

political figures may serve the public interest,[338] this does not include details on the private lives of public figures that are irrelevant to their public function.[339]

Furthermore, the ECtHR has considered that *political parties* have 'an essential role in ensuring pluralism and the proper functioning of democracy' and that '[i] nasmuch as their activities form part of a collective exercise of the freedom of expression, political parties are also entitled to seek the protection of Article 10 of the Convention'.[340] However, the ECtHR has set boundaries to the use of this freedom by political parties in order to incite to violence and aim to destroy the democratic system or the rights of others.[341] To a certain extent, the ECtHR thus seems to advocate the concept of the 'militant democracy'.

However, the ECtHR has also stressed that 'measures of a preventive nature to suppress freedom of assembly and expression other than in cases of incitement to violence or rejection of democratic principles – however shocking and unacceptable certain views or words used may appear to the authorities, and however illegitimate the demands made may be – do a disservice to democracy and often even endanger it'.[342] The question thus is in which situations political parties constitute such a danger to democracy that their speech may be curtailed or they may even be dissolved.

In *Refah Partisi v. Turkey*, the ECtHR considered that the dissolution of a political party can be justified depending on (i) the proof that 'the risk to democracy' was 'sufficiently imminent'; (ii) whether the acts and speeches of the leaders and members of the political party concerned were imputable to the party as a whole; and (iii) whether the acts and speeches imputable to the political party formed a whole which gave a clear picture of a model of society conceived and advocated by the party which was incompatible with the concept of a 'democratic society'.[343]

The ECtHR finally found the dissolution of Refah Partisi, the Welfare Party, by the Turkish Constitutional Court acceptable under 11(2), because its long-term political policy to set up a regime based on the Sharia was contrary to the concept of a democratic society and also because its leaders did not exclude the recourse to violence to force the implementation of this policy.[344] The Court considered that a

---

338 ECtHR 18 May 2004, no. 58148/00 (Plon v. France).

339 ECtHR 24 June 2004, no. 59320/00 (Hannover v. Germany), para. 62–64.

340 ECtHR (Grand Chamber) 30 January 1998, no. 19392/92 (United Communist Party of Turkey and Others v. Turkey), para. 43.

341 ECtHR (Grand Chamber), 13 February 2003, no. 41340/98 41342/98 41343/98 41344/98 (Refah Partisi and others v. Turkey), para. 98, 110.

342 ECtHR 2 October 2001, no. 29221/95 29225/95 (Stankov and the United Macedonian Organization Ilinden v. Bulgaria), para. 97.

343 ECtHR (Grand Chamber) 13 February 2003, no. 41340/98; 41342/98; 41343/98 and 41344/98 (Refah Partisi and Others v. Turkey), para. 104.

344 *Ibid.*, para. 132. Contrarily, in *Erbakan v. Turkey*, the ECtHR considered the conviction of the leader of the Welfare Party for the public incitement to religious hatred and hostility to constitute a violation of Article 10, precisely because his political discourse during an election campaign did not generate 'an actual risk' and 'imminent danger' for society. See: ECtHR 6 July 2006, no. 59405/00 (Erbakan v. Turkey). An important factor did form the large time lap between the moment on which the expression was uttered and the prosecution of its author.

state cannot be required to wait, before intervening, until a political party has seized power and begun to take concrete steps to implement a policy incompatible with the standards of the Convention and democracy, when the danger of that policy for democracy is sufficiently established and imminent.[345]

This was the case and a pressing social need existed for the dissolution, because the opinion polls bore witness to a considerable rise in Refah's influence as a political party and its chances of coming in to power alone. The ECtHR accordingly considered that at the time of its dissolution, Refah had the real potential to seize political power without being restricted by the compromises inherent in a coalition. If Refah had proposed a programme contrary to democratic principles, its monopoly of political power would have enabled it to establish the model of society envisaged in that programme.[346]

The strict 'imminent risk' standard for anti-democratic speech appears somewhat tailored to the far-reaching measure of the *dissolution* of political parties. This signifies that, in principle, the dissolution of a – relatively small – political party due to its anti-democratic ideas and policies is not likely to be found acceptable by the ECtHR, when it only has little political support and few seats in Parliament. The ECtHR has been criticized for affording political parties a larger freedom to contribute to public and political debate under Article 11 than individuals have under Article 10, while anti-democratic ideas expounded by political parties form a greater threat to democracy the more they reach the centre of power.[347]

But an important decisive factor appears to be whether the ECtHR interprets a statement either as speech that is primarily directed against the democratic system or as hate speech primarily directed against particular groups in society. For example, in *Gündüz v. Turkey*, the ECtHR found a conviction of the leader of an Islamic sect for the public defence of the Sharia in a television show without the call to establish such a system by using violence to constitute a violation of Article 10.[348] Contrarily, the dissenters considered the restriction to freedom of expression justified, because the notion of hate speech equally comprised the incitement to hatred on account of religion and other forms of hatred based on religious intolerance. In fact, the ECtHR considers that such speech that targets a particular group in society may be restricted sooner, because minorities are in need of such protection (para. 1.3 *infra*).

For precisely the latter reason, the ECtHR has laid particular emphasis on the rights of *minorities* to form associations and to express their views. On several occasions the ECtHR has considered that 'Although individual interests must on

345 *Ibid.*, para. 102.
346 *Ibid.*, para. 107.
347 Sottiaux, S. & Rummens, S., Concentric democracy: Resolving the incoherence in the European Court of Human rights' case law on freedom of expression and freedom of association, *I•CON* 2012, vol. 10, no. 1, p. 106–126.
348 ECtHR 4 December 2003, no. 35071/97 (Gündüz/Turkey).

occasion be subordinated to those of a group, democracy does not simply mean that the views of a majority must always prevail: a balance must be achieved which ensures the fair and proper treatment of minorities and avoids any abuse of a dominant position'.[349] Hence, the ECtHR at least adheres to a concept of democracy that aims to counter majoritarian tendencies. For example it must be possible to freely express controversial opinions during organized demonstrations.

The ECtHR has considered that, when a demonstration is organized against, and held nearby an anti-racism demonstration, a state should find the least restrictive means to prevent a disturbance of the peace and the occurrence of violence that would, in principle, enable both demonstrations to take place.[350] The ECtHR found that the sanctioning of the act of silently holding the *Árpád* striped flag, a symbol of the Hungarian Nazi (Arrow Cross) Regime, in such a context purely on the basis of its provocative character, to constitute a violation of Article 10. Ill feelings and sentiments of outrage or uneasiness cannot alone, in the absence of intimidation, set the limits to freedom of expression; otherwise, the latter freedom is subjected to the '*heckler's veto*'.[351]

In *Vona v. Hungary*, the ECtHR, however, found the dissolution of the Hungarian Guard Movement acceptable under 11(2), because the movement had held a series of paramilitary parades organized to keep 'Gipsy criminality' at bay, amongst others in villages with a large Roma population. The parades were reminiscent of the Arrow Cross movement, which was the backbone of the regime that was responsible for the mass extermination of Roma in Hungary. According to the ECtHR, such a paramilitary march goes beyond the mere expression of a disturbing or offensive idea, but amounts to *intimidation* and a *true threat* – its message is accompanied by the physical presence of a threatening group of organized activists – and is capable of implementing a policy of racial segregation.[352]

The ECtHR thus considers that a democratic society can restrict the freedom of politicians, political parties or groupings to express their opinions under 10(2) or 11(2), if their speech amounts to the expounding of doctrines contrary to democratic principles, incitement to violence or intimidation. Moreover, the ECtHR can consider that such speech even falls outside the scope of the right to freedom of expression, because it would constitute an abuse of the right in the sense of Article 17 ECHR.

---

349 ECtHR 13 August 1981, no. 7601/76 7806/77 (Young, James and Webster v. the United Kingdom), para. 63; ECtHR (Grand Chamber) 29 April 1999, no. 25088/94 28331/95 28443/95 (Chassagnou v. France), para. 112; ECtHR (Grand Chamber) 10 November 2005, no. 44774/98 (Leyla Sahin v. Turkey), para. 108.

350 Cf. ECtHR 29 June 2006, no. 76900/01 (Öllinger v. Austria).

351 ECtHR 24 July 2012, no. 40721/08 (Fáber v. Hungary), para. 57.

352 ECtHR 9 July 2013, no. 35943/10 (Vona v. Hungary), para. 63–69. The intimidating effect of the marches was increased by the fact that they were backed up by an officially registered political association, the Hungarian Guard Association, with which the Movement had an organizational link.

1.1.8. Article 17 ECHR in the light of Article 10

Early drafts of the ECHR did not contain the abuse of rights clause of Article 17. Its final insertion into the ECHR can be explained by reference to the political climate in Europe at the time of the elaboration of the ECHR and the general intention of its drafters to provide for an institutional framework based on liberal democratic values to overcome the Nazism and Fascism as recently experienced by European states and as a counterbalance against the emerging threat of Communism at the time.[353] The Parliamentary Assembly of the Council of Europe adopted the provision without much debate.

On the necessity to include the Article, the Greek representative stated that: '[h] uman freedom just because it is sacred must not become an armory in which the enemies of freedom can find weapons which they can later use unhindered to destroy this freedom.' 'Every right implies as an indispensable, inseparable, irrefutable corollary, a corresponding duty which is inherent in law.' The ECHR had to be drafted 'not only against the tyrannical acts of those who misuse power, but also against those who misuse freedom.'[354]

This motivation is clearly reflected in the wording of Article 17 ECHR, which reads: '[n]othing in this Convention may be interpreted as implying for any state, group or person any right to engage in any activity or perform any act aimed at the destruction of any of the rights and freedoms set forth herein or at their limitation to a greater extent than is provided for in the Convention'. Article 17 ECHR can thus be regarded as an instrument of a 'militant human rights concept'. It applies to those cases where fundamental rights and democracy are threatened, but when one cannot speak of a state of emergency threatening the nation that would justify the entire derogation from certain Convention rights for the purposes of Article 15 ECHR.[355]

A particular feature of Article 17 is that it is addressed at both individuals and the state and thus can be invoked by an individual against a state interference with a particular Convention right and by the state to justify such an interference. Furthermore, Article 17 cannot be invoked independently, but only together with a Convention right or freedom alleged to be abused. The ECmHR has considered that Article 17 covers 'essentially those rights which will facilitate the attempt to derive therefrom a right to engage personally in activities aimed at the destruction of any of the rights and freedoms set forth in the Convention'. In particular, the Commission has found that the freedom of expression enshrined in Article 10 of the Convention may not be invoked in a sense contrary to Article 17.[356]

---

353 Council of Europe, European Commission of Human Rights Preparatory work on Article 17 of the European Convention on Human Rights, DH (57) 4, CDH (75) 7, p. 10.

354 *Ibid.*, p. 2–3.

355 Harris, O'Boyle & Warbrick 2009, p. 650.

356 ECmHR 28 May 1986, no. 12194/86 (Kuhnen v. Germany).

Indeed, most Article 17 cases concern the abuse of the right to freedom of expression and/ or freedom of association. The question arises in relation to when the mere expression of an opinion can be qualified as an activity or act aimed at destroying or limiting the rights of others[357] On many occasions the ECmHR and ECtHR have recalled that 'the general purpose of Article 17 is to prevent totalitarian groups from exploiting in their own interests the principles enunciated by the Convention.'[358] The ECmHR and ECtHR thus have applied Article 17 primarily with regard to political parties and movements or its members that formed a threat to the democratic system and institutions by expounding totalitarian doctrines or engaging in activities inspired by National-Socialism.

For example, the ECmHR allowed the ban of the Communist Party by Germany, because the party proclaimed the aim of the proletarian revolution and the dictatorship of the proletarian. The recourse to a dictatorship for the establishment of a regime is incompatible with the Convention, inasmuch as it includes the destruction of many of the rights or freedoms enshrined therein.[359] In another case, the ECmHR considered that the publications of a leader of an organization aiming to reinstitute the NSDAP in Germany, by advocating National-Socialism, aimed at impairing the basic order of freedom and democracy. The applicant sought to use the freedom of information as a basis for activities, which were 'contrary to the text and spirit of the Convention'.[360]

In subsequent cases, the ECtHR has broadened the scope of Article 17 to situations outside of the context of totalitarian groups and thus to other activities deemed as 'contrary to the text and spirit of the Convention'. The ECtHR has considered that the negation or revision of 'clearly established historical facts' (Holocaust denial) 'undermines the Convention's underlying values that support the fight against racism and anti-Semitism'[361] and is 'removed from protection of Article 10 by Article 17'.[362] Furthermore, the ECtHR has applied Article 17 in cases concerning anti-Semitic expression and incitement to hatred against Jews unrelated to Holocaust denial.[363] On one occasion, the ECtHR has even considered that Islamophobic expression constituted 'such a general, vehement attack against a religious group, linking the group as a whole with a grave act of terrorism, is incompatible with the values proclaimed and guaranteed by the Convention, notably tolerance, social peace and non-discrimination.'[364]

---

357 Council of Europe, European Commission of Human Rights Preparatory work on Article 17 of the European Convention on Human Rights, DH (57) 4, CDH (75) 7, p. 20.

358 For example: ECtHR 1 July 1961, no. 332/57 (Lawless v. Ireland no. 3), para. 6; ECtHR 2 September 2004, no. 42264/98 (W.P. and Others v. Poland).

359 ECmHR 20 July 1957, no. 250/57 (Kommunistische Partei Deuthschlands v. Germany).

360 ECmHR 12 May 1988, no. 12194/86 (Kuhnen v. Germany).

361 ECtHR 24 June 2003, no. 12194/86 (Garaudy v. France).

362 ECtHR 23 September 1998, no. 24662/94 (Lehideux and Isorni v. France), para. 47.

363 ECtHR 2 September 2004, no. 42264/98 (W.P. and others v. Poland); ECtHR 20 February 2007, no. 35222/04 (Ivanov v. Russia).

364 ECtHR 16 November 2004, no. 23131/03 (Norwood v. The United Kingdom).

Finally, the ECtHR has applied Article 17 with regard to cases concerning incitement to violence. The ECtHR allowed the ban in Germany of *Hizb Ut-Tahrir*, an Islamic organization that advocates the overthrow of governments throughout the Muslim world and their replacement by an Islamic State in the form of a recreated Caliphate. In several publications it had called to *Jihad,* aimed at the violent destruction of the State of Israel, as a solution to the Israeli-Palestinian conflict and the killing of Jews. Such ends were 'clearly contrary to the values of the Convention, notably the commitment to the peaceful settlement of international conflicts and to the sanctity of human life.'[365] Here, the ECtHR seemed to connect the Convention values more with the consequential effects of the speech in question.

The broadening of the scope of Article 17 to all these forms of extreme speech is highly criticized, notably because of its radical function as a 'guillotine provision'.[366] When the ECtHR qualifies a particular expression as an abuse of rights, the ECtHR declares the complaint of a violation of freedom of expression inadmissible and does not have to review a restriction under 10(2). Through this *direct* application of Article 17, the ECtHR excludes certain categories of expression from the protection of Article 10(1) in the admissibility-phase by reference to broad Convention values. As a negative effect, such admissibility decisions are *prima facie* based on the content of expression, do not place the expression in its broader context, balance opposing interests and thoroughly review the necessity and proportionality of the state measure as a review under 10(2) would demand, but instead strongly rely on the argumentation of the state that invoked Article 17.[367]

The ECtHR, however, increasingly applies Article 17 in an *indirect* manner, as an interpretative tool, when it examines the necessity of a restriction on expression in a democratic society under 10(2) in the case on the merits. This notably also applies to cases concerning hate speech (para. 1.3 *infra*). Some authors welcome this development, because it prevents an abusive recourse by states to Article 17 or the adoption of implied limitations; Article 10(1) should cover all types of speech, however appalling, but limitations to them may be justified and must be reviewed under 10(2).[368] Others consider any application of Article 17 undesirable, because of the aforementioned negative effects and the idea that the goal of Article 17 to protect the democratic system and human rights could be achieved under the framework of Article 10 just as well.[369]

From the increasingly indirect application by the ECtHR, one may deduce that there is a general preference of the ECtHR to review *all* restrictions to freedom of

365 ECtHR 12 June 2012, no. 31098/08 (Hizb Ut-Tahrir v. Germany).

366 Keane, D., Attacking hate speech under Article 17 of the European convention on human rights, *Netherlands Quarterly of Human Rights*, 2007, vol. 25, no. 4, p. 642–663; Cannie, H. & Voorhoof, D., The abuse clause and freedom of expression in the European human rights convention: an added value for democracy and human rights protection?, *Netherlands Quarterly of Human Rights*, 2011, vol. 29, no. 1, p. 54–83.

367 Cannie & Voorhoof 2011, p. 58.

368 Harris, O'Boyle & Warbrick 2009, p. 450.

369 Cannie & Voorhoof 2011, p. 73.

expression, including those justifiable under Article 17, under Article 10(2)/ 11(2) or at least that they comply with the limitation clauses. But when the ECtHR joins Article 17 in the case on the merits, it often does not explicitly refer to Article 17 in its explanation for its decision under 10(2)/ 11(2). An example is the *Refah Partisi* case, in which the ECtHR found the dissolution of Refah acceptable under 11(2) on the ground of its 'imminent risk to democracy' (*supra*).

However, the added value of Article 17 appears notably to be that it could explicitly ground the development of such a test and form an additional argument in the Court's reasoning to justify the far-reaching measures of the *prohibition* or *dissolution* of larger groupings and political parties that abuse their freedom of expression for anti-democratic designs, measures that might not easily pass the test in accordance with Article 10(2)/ 11(2). Furthermore, Article 17 could play a role in the development of positive obligations; it seems reasonable that expression that can be qualified as an abuse of rights must at least be prohibited by law or even criminalized and prosecuted by the state. This in principle does not only apply to political parties, but also to individual politicians or citizens (para. 1.6 *infra*).

The main criticism in relation to the direct application of Article 17 by the ECtHR remains, however, that so many different types of extreme speech are *prima facie* excluded from the protection of Article 10(1) if their aims are deemed contrary to broad Convention values or 'intentions' rather than on the basis of their 'real or expected consequences'.[370] Although, in cases of incitement to violence the ECtHR seems to interlink these two grounds (*supra*). In the categorical approach the Court does not thoroughly weigh the interest in preventing the harmful effects of speech against the interest of public debate nor does it thereby distinguish between factual statements and value judgments or between racial remarks and speech about religion. However, when the ECtHR evaluates restrictions to extreme speech under 10(2) these considerations can equally dissolve in the large margin of appreciation as sometimes used by the ECtHR. In this respect, it again appears decisive whether the ECtHR qualifies expression as hate speech primarily directed against particular groups in society (para. 1.3 *infra*) or as incitement to violence against state authorities.

1.2. Incitement to violence

Much of the ECtHR's criteria for 'incitement to violence' can be derived from the hundreds of cases against Turkey concerning complaints about a violation of freedom of political expression and press freedom starting in the mid and late

370 Buyse, A., Contested Contours, the limits of freedom of expression from an abuse of rights perspective – Article 10 and 17 ECHR, in: Brems, E., & Gerards, J. (eds.), *Shaping Rights in the ECHR, the Role of the European Court of Human Rights in Determining the Scope of Human Rights,* Cambridge: Cambridge University Press 2014, p. 183–208.

1990s, and particularly in a series of decisions by the Grand Chamber in 1999.[371] Since 1991, Turkey has had an Anti-Terrorism Act prohibiting propaganda against 'the territorial integrity of the Republic of Turkey' or 'the indivisible union of the nation'. The Act has formed the basis for many convictions concerning expression about the Armenian or Kurdish question and criticism on the Turkish unitary state. In the majority of these cases, the ECtHR found a violation of freedom of expression. On several occasions, the Court has summarized its general principles as follows:

> 'The Court reiterates that there is little scope under Article 10 §2 of the Convention for restrictions on political speech or on debate on matters of public interest.
> Furthermore, the limits of permissible criticism are wider with regard to the government than in relation to a private citizen or even a politician. In a democratic system the actions or omissions of the government must be subject to the close scrutiny not only of the legislative and judicial authorities but also of public opinion. Moreover, the dominant position, which the government occupies, makes it necessary for it to display restraint in resorting to criminal proceedings, particularly where other means are available for replying to the unjustified attacks and criticisms of its adversaries. Nevertheless, it certainly remains open to the competent State authorities to adopt, in their capacity as guarantors of public order, measures, even of a criminal-law nature, intended to react appropriately and without excess to such remarks.
> Finally, where such remarks incite to violence against an individual, a public official or a sector of the population, the national authorities enjoy a wider margin of appreciation, when examining the need for an interference with the exercise of freedom of expression.'[372]

In the early case *Zana v. Turkey,* the ECtHR found no violation of Article 10.[373] The case concerned the conviction of a former mayor of an important Turkish city for having 'publicly praised or defended a serious crime' with regard to the statement in an interview published in a national newspaper: 'I support the PKK national liberation movement; on the other hand, I am not in favor of massacres. Anyone can make mistakes, and the PKK kill women and children by mistake.' The Court found the interference justified in order to maintain national security and public safety 'at a time when serious disturbances were raging in south-east Turkey'.

The interference was also proportionate. Although the statements contained contradictions and ambiguities, they were uttered by a former mayor in a daily newspaper, 'coincided with murderous attacks carried out by the PKK on civilians in south-east Turkey' and in that special context were 'likely to exacerbate an

---

371 Voorhoof, D. 'Het Europese First Amendment'. De Straatsburgse jurisprudentie over artikel 10 EVRM (1996-juli 1999), *Mediaforum* 1999, no. 10, p. 269.

372 ECtHR (Grand Chamber) 8 July 1999, no. 23556/94 (Ceylan v. Turkey), para. 34; ECtHR 28 September 1999, no. 22479/93 (Öztürk v. Turkey), para. 66.

373 ECtHR (Grand Chamber) 25 November 1997, no. 18954/91 (Zana v. Turkey).

already explosive situation in that region'.[374] This emphasis on the particular context of the case, the authority of the speaker and the 'likelihood of the danger' has been compared with the American 'clear-and-present-danger'-test.[375]

The ECtHR's approach to incitement to violence however clearly differs from American doctrine. This can be illustrated by *Sürek no. 1 v. Turkey*, in which the ECtHR equally found no breach of freedom of expression.[376] The applicant had been convicted for dissemination of separatist propaganda by publishing two letters in a weekly review that vehemently condemned the military actions of the Turkish authorities in South-East Turkey, but did not explicitly call for violent resistance. According to the Court, the expression had 'a clear intention to stigmatize the other side to the conflict' by the use of labels such as 'the fascist Turkish army', 'the TC murder gang' and 'the hired killers of imperialism' and references to 'massacres', 'brutalities' and 'slaughter'.

According to their content, the letters 'amounted to an appeal to bloody revenge by stirring up base emotions and hardening already embedded prejudices, which have manifested themselves in deadly violence'. Given the security situation in South-East Turkey, 'the content of the letters must be seen as capable of inciting to further violence (...) the message which is communicated to the reader is that recourse to violence is a necessary and justified measure of self defence in the face of the aggressor.'[377]

The dissenters precisely criticized the Court's focus on the content and tone of the expression rather than its likely impact considering the general context. Palm objected that the applicant had been convicted for his political message. According to Palm, his harsh language constituted mere 'fighting words' that were protected by Article 10, because there was not 'a real or genuine risk' of his speech inciting to hatred or to violence. Tulkens, Casadevall and Greve held that freedom of expression might only be curtailed when there is 'direct provocation to commit serious criminal offences'.[378]

Bonello advocated the 'clear-and-present-danger'-test and considered 'When the invitation to the use of force is intellectualized, abstract, and removed in time and space from the foci of actual or impending violence, then the fundamental right to freedom of expression should generally prevail.'[379] Furthermore he opined that 'only the advocacy of violence that is directed to incite or produce imminent lawlessness and is likely to excite or produce such action may be proscribed'.[380]

---

374 ECtHR (Grand Chamber) 25 November 1997, no. 18954/91 (Zana v. Turkey), para. 60.

375 Sottiaux, S., The 'Clear and Present Danger' Test in the Case Law of the European Court of Human Rights, *Zeitschrift für ausländisches öffentliches Recht und Völkerrecht* 2003, vol. 64, nr. 3, p. 670–671.

376 ECtHR (Grand Chamber) 8 July 1999, no. 26682/95 (Sürek no. 1 v. Turkey).

377 *Ibid.*, para. 62.

378 *Ibid.*, Partly dissenting opinion of Judge Palm.

379 *Ibid.*, Joint partly dissenting opinion of Judges Tulkens, Casadevall and Greve.

380 *Ibid.*, Partly dissenting opinion of Judge Bonello.

In many other cases the ECtHR considered that the Turkish Government had to tolerate severe criticism on its policy and the actions of the Turkish army in South East Turkey, the public support for the PKK (Workers Party of Kurdistan) and the claim to independence of the Kurdish people or the call to find a peaceful resolution of the Kurdish question. The Court often considered the high pecuniary penalties and convictions to imprisonment and preventive measures such as the confiscation of publications to be disproportionate.[381]

On one occasion, the ECtHR considered that even against the background of serious disturbances in South East Turkey the support of the idea of a separate Kurdish entity could not be regarded as 'inevitably exacerbating the situation'. Therefore, the criticism of the authorities and the security forces even 'in colorful and derogatory terms' could not be regarded as advocating or inciting the use of violence.[382] In another case, the ECtHR considered that it was 'naturally aware of the concern of the authorities about words or deeds which have the potential to exacerbate the security situation in the region', but that 'the views expressed in the interview cannot be read as an incitement to violence; nor could they be construed as *liable* to incite to violence'.[383]

The ECtHR thus does attach importance to the probable harmful effect of the expression and for that purpose takes into account the form/ medium used. Expression disseminated through mass media, given its wide audience, has a possibly large impact on the general public. Therefore the ECtHR stresses that 'the duties and responsibilities (...) of media professionals assume special significance in situations of conflict and tension. Particular caution is called for when consideration is being given to the publication of the views of representatives of organizations which resort to violence against the State lest the media become a vehicle for the dissemination of hate speech and the promotion of violence.'[384]

Contrarily, the Court considered a work of poems that through the frequent use of pathos and metaphors called for self-sacrifice for 'Kurdistan' and included some particularly aggressive passages directed at the Turkish authorities to be protected by freedom of expression; although 'taken literally, the poems might be construed as inciting readers to hatred, revolt and the use of violence', 'the medium used by the applicant was poetry, a form of artistic expression that appeals to only a minority of readers'.[385]

Likewise, the ECtHR found a conviction with regard to an academic work that alleged that 'the 'racist policy of denial' *vis-à-vis* the Kurds had been instrumental in the development of the 'fascist movement', to be disproportionate. As the

---

381 Examples of cases where the ECtHR found a violation of Article 10 form Incal, eleven of thirteen decisions of 8 July 1999, Zarakolu and C.S.Y.

382 ECtHR 16 March 2000, no. 23144/93 (Özgür Gündem v. Turkey), para. 70.

383 ECtHR (Grand Chamber) 8 July 1999, no. 25067/94 25068/94 (Erdoğdu and İnce v. Turkey), para. 52.

384 *Ibid.*, para. 54.

385 ECtHR (Grand Chamber) 8 July 1999, no. 23168/94 (Karataş v. Turkey), para. 49.

statements 'featured in an academic study on the socio-economic evolution of Turkey in a historical perspective and of the prevailing political ideology in that country', the authorities had 'failed to have sufficient regard to the freedom of academic expression and to the public's right to be informed of a different perspective on the situation in south-east Turkey, irrespective of how unpalatable that perspective may be for them.'[386]

The latter also formed a primary consideration of the ECtHR in a case concerning the conviction for incitement to violence with regard to the publication and distribution of the statement of a leading member of the PKK: '[t]he war will go on until there is only one single individual left on our side' made during an interview with a weekly review. The conviction constituted a breach of freedom of expression, because 'the interviews had a newsworthy content which allowed the public both to have an insight into the psychology of those who are the driving force behind the opposition to official policy in south-east Turkey and to assess the stakes involved in the conflict.'[387]

This reasoning may be contrasted with other case law. In *Zana*, the ECtHR found the conviction proportionate, amongst others because the author of the expression was a person with some political standing – a former mayor and activist for the Kurdish cause. Contrarily in *Incal v. Turkey*, the ECtHR found the conviction of a member of the Turkey's People Party for distributing a pamphlet that criticized the 'state terror against Turkish and Kurdish proletarians' disproportionate, amongst others because nothing indicated that the author 'was in any way responsible for the problems of terrorism in Turkey'.[388]

Particularly striking is the fact that the ECtHR in all these cases deals with restrictions to alleged incitements to violence under the general framework of 10(2). As – even – Holocaust denial generally engages Article 17 (para. 1.5 *infra*), one could question why the incitement to violence or terrorism against the state or individuals is not also suitable to engage Article 17.[389] The ECtHR, however, consistently exercised an integral review and conducted a detailed contextual analysis under 10(2), in which it evaluated the content and tone of expression, the person of the speaker, his intent, the medium used, the impact of expression and the nature of the sanction.

The Court thereby set relatively clear and strict criteria for 'incitement' and the likelihood of its impact. Although, whether these criteria are met might in the end depend on the interpretation by the majority of the ECtHR of the particular words used given the particular context. The ECtHR did not require any 'imminent' threat of violence, but afforded the state a large margin – only – for the assessment of the national security situation.

---

386 ECtHR (Grand Chamber) 8 July 1999, no. 23536/94 24408/94 (Başkaya and Okçuoğlu v. Turkey), para. 64–65.

387 ECtHR (Grand Chamber) 8 July 1999, no. 23927/94 24277/94 (Sürek and Özdemir v. Turkey), para. 61.

388 ECtHR (Grand Chamber) 9 June 1998, no. 22678/93 (Incal v. Turkey), para. 58.

389 Cannie & Voorhoof 2011, p. 74.

The interpretation of the expression by the Court is, however, open for debate. For example, what to think of *Le Roy v. France*, in which the ECtHR unanimously found the conviction for glorification of terrorism with regard to the publication of a cartoon of the attacks of 9/11 with the slogan 'We have all dreamt about it ... Hamas did it.' – a parody of the advertisement 'We have all dreamt about it ... Sony did it.' – in a Basque weekly acceptable under 10(2). According to the ECtHR, the cartoon did not criticize American imperialism, but supported and glorified its violent destruction. It thereby violated the dignity of the victims of the attacks and its publication in a politically sensitive area and right after the terrorist attacks could attract violence.[390]

In its 'Turkish case law' the ECtHR generally qualified alleged incitements to violent and terrorist action as political criticism directed against the *government*, restrictions on which call for the strictest scrutiny by the Court. The Court's case law concerning incitement to violence appears to diverge from its case law concerning hate speech and Holocaust denial particularly on the point of the margin of appreciation.

1.3. Hate speech

1.3.1. The notion of hate speech in the ECtHR's case law

The ECHR does not have a specific prohibition of hate speech comparable with Article 20(2) ICCPR. Although the ECtHR in its case law often uses the notion of hate speech, it has never given a precise definition of the term.[391] The ECtHR generally describes hate speech as 'all forms of expression which spread, incite, promote or justify hatred based on intolerance (including religious intolerance)'.[392] But the term is not evidently clear and we will see that it does not in itself form a solution to the disagreement within the Court about its exact criteria.

This broad conception of hate speech is inspired by Recommendation no. R (97) 20 on 'hate speech' of the Committee of Ministers of the Council of Europe that defines hate speech as 'all forms of expression which spread, incite, promote or justify racial hatred, xenophobia, anti-Semitism or other forms of hatred based on intolerance, including: intolerance expressed by aggressive nationalism and ethnocentrism, discrimination and hostility against minorities, migrants and people of immigrant origin'.[393]

The ECtHR often refers to the Recommendation, as well as other non-binding international human rights instruments, such as ECRI's General Policy

---

[390] ECtHR 2 October 2008, no. 36109/03 (Le Roy v. France), para. 43–45.

[391] Weber, A., *Manual on Hate Speech*, Strasbourg: Council of Europe Publishing 2009, p. 3.

[392] ECtHR 4 December 2003, no. 35071/97 (Gündüz v. Turkey), para. 40.

[393] Recommendation No. R (97) 20 on "hate speech" adopted by the Committee of Ministers of the Council of Europe on 30 October 1997.

Recommendation no. 7 on national legislation to combat racism and racial discrimination, when dealing with hate speech.[394] However, the ECtHR uses an autonomous interpretation of the term; it does not consider itself bound by definitions used in these instruments, nor in national laws or by national jurisdictions. It has been argued that the Court prefers to proceed on a case-by-case basis and avoid being constrained by definitions, which could limit its power of action in subsequent cases.[395]

Therefore, the 'hate speech'-case law of the Court comprises cases concerning convictions based on a large variety of national prohibitions, including incitement to hatred, discrimination or violence, Holocaust denial and group defamation. In fact, the ECtHR even referred to the term in *Sürek no. 1 v. Turkey*, next to the glorification of violence.[396] Even subversive speech and incitement to violence and terrorism may thus be considered as a form of hate speech, when it is directed against particular persons or groups.[397] Based on the ECtHR's case law convictions for hate speech on the ground of such national prohibitions will normally not constitute a violation of Article 10 ECHR as long as criminal sanctions remain proportionate.

Furthermore, as a result of the case law the ECtHR's notion of hate speech does not only include utterances that target people on the basis of their race or religion, but also utterances that target people on the basis of their sexual orientation. In *Vejdeland and Others v. Sweden,* the ECtHR found the conviction for the agitation against homosexuals with regard to the distribution of leaflets in a secondary school to constitute no violation of Article 10.[398] According to the ECtHR, although the statements did not directly recommend individuals to commit hateful acts, they were serious and prejudicial allegations. The Court thereby stressed that discrimination based on sexual orientation is as serious as discrimination based on 'race, origin or colour'.[399] The Court thus does not principally distinguish between racist hate speech and hate speech on other discriminatory grounds and implies that all are equally reprehensible.

Finally, as a result of the case law, the prohibition of hate speech under the ECHR is thus primarily informed by its underlying values of equal human dignity

---

394 General Policy Recommendation no. 7 of the Council of Europe's European Commission against Racism and Intolerance (ECRI) on national legislation to combat racism and racial discrimination adopted on 13 December 2002.

395 Oetheimer, M., Protecting freedom of expression: the challenge of hate speech in the European Court of Human Rights case law, *Cardozo Journal of International and Comparative Law* 2009, vol. 17, p. 428–429.

396 ECtHR (Grand Chamber) 8 July 1999, no. 26682/95 (Sürek no. 1 v. Turkey), para. 62.

397 See also the ECtHR's Factsheet on Hate speech of July 2013, available at: www.echr.coe.int/Documents/FS_Hate_speech_ENG.pdf.

398 ECtHR 9 February 2012, no. 1813/07 (Vejdeland and Others v. Sweden). The leaflets described homosexuality as 'a deviant sexual proclivity' that had 'a morally destructive effect on the substance of society' and as one of the main reasons why HIV and AIDS gained foothold and alleged that the 'homosexual lobby' tried to play down paedophilia.

399 *Ibid.*, para. 54–56. An important factor did form the fact that the leaflets were left in the pupils' lockers and thereby imposed on them on a sensitive age.

and non-discrimination.[400] According to the ECtHR, it may be considered necessary in certain democratic societies to sanction or even prevent hate speech, because 'tolerance and respect for the equal dignity of all human beings constitutes the foundations of a democratic, pluralistic society'.[401] General, vehement attacks against a particular group are 'incompatible with the values proclaimed and guaranteed by the Convention, notably tolerance, social peace and non-discrimination'.[402] More generally, the Convention's underlying values 'support the fight against racism and anti-Semitism'.[403]

The ECtHR therefore interprets Article 10 in line with international human rights instruments to that effect, notably the international Convention on the Elimination of all forms of Racial Discrimination (Art. 4 ICERD). In one case, the ECtHR considered that 'the object and purpose pursued by the UN Convention are of great weight in determining whether the applicant's conviction, which – as the Government have stressed – was based on a provision enacted in order to ensure Denmark's compliance with the UN Convention, was 'necessary' within the meaning of Article 10 para. 2 (...) Denmark's obligations under Article 10 must be interpreted, to the extent possible, so as to be reconcilable with its obligations under the UN Convention.'[404]

However, between the judges of the ECtHR large disagreement exists not only in relation to the exact definition of hate speech, but also about the interpretation of the relevant international instruments, how to balance prohibitions of hate speech with freedom of expression under Article 10(2) and/ or the application of Article 17. In relation to hate speech the ECtHR, therefore, has not developed clear standards and precise criteria of review comparable with those for incitement to violence. Important considerations – about the specific harmful effects of speech in question weighed against the interest of public debate or about the place of the distinction between factual statements and value judgments or between racial remarks and speech about religion therein – are often dissolved in the large margin of appreciation the ECtHR affords states to set restrictions to hate speech under 10(2) or in the categorical approach under 17.

1.3.2. Hate speech on the basis of race under Article 17

An early case concerning racial hate speech under Article 17 was *Glimmerveen and Hagenbeek v. the Netherlands.*[405] The case concerned the conviction of two

400 See also: Tulkens, F., When to say is to do, Freedom of expression and hate speech in the case law of the European Court of Human Rights, in: Freedom of Expression, Essays in honour of Nicolas Bratza, President of the European Court of Human Rights, Oisterwijk: Wolf Legal Publishers 2012, p. 279–297.

401 ECtHR 4 December 2003, no. 35071/97 (Gündüz v. Turkey), para. 40.

402 ECtHR 16 November 2004, no. 23131/03 (Norwood v. The United Kingdom).

403 ECtHR 24 June 2003, no. 12194/86 (Garaudy v. France).

404 ECtHR (Grand Chamber) 23 September 1994, no. 15890/89 (Jersild v. Denmark), para. 30.

405 ECmHR 11 October 1979, no. 8348/78 8406/78 (Glimmerveen and Hagenbeek v. the Netherlands).

members of a Dutch extreme right political party, the 'Nederlandse Volks Unie' (NVU), for possessing leaflets found to be inciting to racial discrimination. The basic principles of the NVU were 'a world conception which grants each nation a proper state, as well as the belief that the general interest of a state is best served by an ethnical homogeneous population and not by racial mixing'.

The leaflets, addressed to the 'white Dutch people', contained statements such as 'the major part of our population since a long time has had enough of the presence in our country of hundreds of thousands Surinamers, Turks and other so-called guest workers' and '[a]s soon as the NVU will have gained political power in our country, it will put order into business and to begin with: 1) remove Surinamers, Turks and other so-called guest workers from the Netherlands'.

The ECmHR appeared insusceptible to the argument made by the applicants during the national proceedings that they had aimed to reach their goal merely through lawful means; the Commission considered that 'the policy advocated by the applicants is inspired by the overall aim to remove all non-white people from the Netherlands' territory, in complete disregard of their nationality, time of residence, family ties, as well as social, economic, humanitarian or other considerations' and 'this policy is clearly containing elements of racial discrimination, which is prohibited under the Convention'. The ECmHR underscored the seriousness of – the aim of – racial discrimination, amongst others, by pointing out that 'discrimination based on race could, in certain circumstances, of itself amount to degrading treatment within the meaning of Article 3 of the Convention'.

The ECmHR was of the opinion that the duties and responsibilities that accompany the exercise of the right to freedom of expression 'find an even stronger expression in a more general provision, namely Article 17' and that Article 17 does not permit the use of Article 10 to spread ideas, which are racially discriminatory. According to the ECmHR, 'the expression of the political ideas of the applicants clearly constitutes an activity within the meaning of Article 17'. Therefore, the applicants could not rely on Article 10. The NVU leaflets thus fell outside of the scope of Article 10 on the basis that their aims were deemed to be contrary to the Convention rather than on the basis of their harmful effects.

Another case concerning racial hate speech under Article 17 is that of *Pavel Ivanov v. Russia.*[406] The case concerned a conviction for public incitement to ethnic, racial and religious hatred through the use of the mass media with regard to a series of publications in a newspaper portraying the Jews as the source of evil in Russia. The ECtHR opined that in the articles the applicant accused an entire ethnic group of plotting a conspiracy against the Russian people and ascribed Fascist ideology to the Jewish leadership. Both in his publications and during the national proceedings, he consistently denied the Jews the right to national dignity, claiming that they did not form a nation.

406 ECtHR 20 February 2007, no. 35222/04 (Pavel Ivanov v. Russia).

The ECtHR therefore found the complaint of violation of Article 10 manifestly ill founded by reason of Article 17 considering that '[t]he Court has no doubt as to the markedly anti-Semitic tenor of the applicant's views and it agrees with the assessment made by the domestic courts that he sought through his publications to incite hatred towards the Jewish people. Such a general and vehement attack on one ethnic group is in contradiction with the Convention's underlying values, notably tolerance, social peace and non-discrimination'. This direct application of Article 17 by the ECtHR reflects the Court's desire to underscore its firm rejection of speech that is incompatible with fundamental democratic values.[407]

The publications thus fell outside the scope of Article 10 on the basis of their aims, which were deemed contrary to Convention values rather than on the basis of their harmful effects. The underlying reason why the ECtHR found the statements to constitute a prohibited attack on Jews appears to be that they constituted 'false factual allegations or strong negative value judgments that lacked a sufficient factual basis' about them. But the ECtHR did not explicitly refer to these principles.

1.3.3. Hate speech on the basis of race under Article 10(2)

The ECtHR dealt with racial hate speech for the first time on the merits under Article 10(2) in *Jersild v. Denmark*.[408] It set criteria for racial hate speech in the sense that it results from this case that the racist statements concerned lacked the protection of Article 10. Prior to *Jersild*, complaints of violation of freedom of expression with regard to convictions for racist speech had all been declared inadmissible (*supra*). As the dissenters in the case pointed out: '[t]his is the first time that the Court has been concerned with a case of dissemination of racist remarks which deny to a large group of persons the quality of 'human beings'. In earlier decisions the Court has – in our view, rightly – underlined the great importance of the freedom of the press and the media in general for a democratic society, but it has never had to consider a situation in which 'the reputation or rights of others' (Article 10–2) were endangered to such an extent as here.'[409]

The dissenters disagreed with the ECtHR's finding of a violation of freedom of expression by 12:7 votes. The case concerned the criminal conviction of Jersild, a journalist, for having broadcasted a television interview, in which three members of the youth group called the 'Greenjackets' made racist statements such as the comparison of blacks with animals, gorillas and drug dealers. Jersild was found guilty of 'aiding and abetting' the public 'statement or other communication by which a group of persons are threatened, insulted or degraded on the basis of their race, color, national or ethnic origin'.

The ECmHR considered that taken in isolation the statements of the Greenjackets were highly insulting, but the reputation or rights of others were not

---

407 Cf. Cannie & Voorhoof 2011, p. 83.

408 ECtHR (Grand Chamber) 23 September 1994, no. 15890/89 (Jersild v. Denmark).

409 *Ibid.*, Joint dissenting opinion of judges Ryssdal, Benhardt, Spielmann and Loizou, para. 1.

significantly affected and, as legitimate aims for restricting the freedom of expression, carried little weight; the remarks were made by members of an insignificant group of persons and rather had the effect of ridiculing their authors. Moreover, the program drew attention to racism, intolerance and simplemindedness and the final message, which was conveyed, was that of anti-racism. The program thus touched upon an issue of great public concern. The ECmHR found the interference disproportionate to the legitimate aim pursued and not 'necessary in a democratic society'.[410]

The dissenters in the Commission found, on the other hand, that although there was no evidence that the statements in question *provoked any acts of racist persecution*, they were, nevertheless, *outrageous* and *likely to insult* and *hurt the feelings* of people belonging to certain minority groups in Denmark. The assumption that the sole effect of the program was to ridicule the persons behind the propaganda was purely theoretical; the program was seen by a wide public, comprising people who may not necessarily have a critical mind, and whose living conditions may render more receptive to racist propaganda.[411]

The dissenters notably grounded their opinion in ICERD considering that '[i]t was the view of the Danish courts that such statements could only be justified if balanced by opposing considerations which could have outweighed the wrongfulness of the statements. This is very much in line with the interpretation indicated in the preparatory work of the Convention on the Elimination of All Forms of Racial Discrimination and of the following amendments of the Danish Penal Code which clearly were not intended to restrict scientific or otherwise serious discussion of problems of public concern.'[412]

Before the ECtHR the question of how Article 10 ECHR should interrelate with Article 4 ICERD became a pivotal issue between the parties. According to Denmark, Article 10 could not be interpreted in such a way as to limit, derogate from or destroy the right to protection against racial discrimination under ICERD. Contrarily, Jersild referred to the due regard clause of Article 4 ICERD to underline the need to strike a balance between freedom of expression and the rights of others. After stressing the importance of ICERD to the interpretation of Article 10 (*supra*), the ECtHR considered: '[h]owever, it is not for the ECtHR to interpret the 'due regard' clause in Article 4 of the UN Convention, which is open to various constructions. Nonetheless the ECtHR found its interpretation of Article 10 in the present case to be compatible with Denmark's obligations under the UN Convention.'[413]

Subsequently, the ECtHR summed up the factors for its assessment of the necessity of Jersild's conviction: the *manner* in which the Greenjackets feature was prepared, its *contents*, the *context* in which it was broadcast and the *purpose of the*

410 Report of the ECmHR adopted 8 July 1993, no. 15890/89 (Jersild v. Denmark), para. 42–45.

411 *Ibid.*, Dissenting opinion of mr. Gaukur Jörundsson, joined by Sir Basil Hall and mr. Jean-Claude Geus.

412 *Ibid.*

413 ECtHR (Grand Chamber) 23 September 1994, no. 15890/89 (Jersild v. Denmark), para. 27–28; 30.

program and, given the obligations under ICERD, whether the item appeared from an objective point of view to have had *as its purpose the propagation of racist views and ideas*.[414] The ECtHR considered: '[t]here can be no doubt that the remarks in respect of which the Greenjackets were convicted were more than insulting to members of the targeted groups and did not enjoy the protection of Article 10'. This consideration has given rise to the question whether the ECtHR conceived the remarks as an abuse of rights by the *Greenjackets* in the sense of Article 17. However, according to the Court, the item of the *journalist* did not have as its *purpose* the propagation of racist views and ideas, but aimed to inform the public and animate public discussion about the existence of the racist views of the group. It was part of a serious Danish news program and was intended for a well-informed audience.[415]

In the Court's view, the journalist had sufficiently distanced himself from and rebutted the racist statements. Most importantly, the ECtHR considered that news reporting based on interviews constitutes one of the most important means whereby the press is able to play its vital role of 'public watchdog'. The punishment of a journalist for statements made by another person in an interview would seriously hamper the contribution of the press to discussion of matters of public interest and could only be justified by particularly strong reasons. The fact that Jersild was sanctioned with a limited fine was irrelevant; what mattered was that the journalist was convicted.[416]

The dissenters of the ECtHR objected that Jersild should have added at least a clear statement of disapproval, because certain parts of the public could find in the television spot support for their racist prejudices. ICERD also supported the opinion that the media too can be obliged to take a clear stand in the area of racial discrimination and hatred. The protection of racial minorities couldn't have less weight than the right to impart information and the ECtHR should not have substituted its own balancing of the conflicting interests for that of the Danish Supreme Court that had a margin of appreciation in deciding in this sensitive issue.[417]

The stringent review that the ECtHR applied in this landmark case seems notably grounded in the importance of press freedom and the role of journalists and can be contrasted by the Court's approach in another case concerning racial hate speech, *Balsyte-Lideikiene v. Lithuania* in which the ECtHR unanimously found no violation of freedom of expression.[418]

The case concerned the publication of the annual Lithuanian calendar in 2000, which portrayed the Poles as the executioners of the Lithuanians and the Jews as

---

414 *Ibid.*, para. 31.
415 *Ibid.*, para. 33–34.
416 *Ibid.*, para. 35.
417 *Ibid.*, Joint dissenting opinion of judges Ryssdal, Benhardt, Spielmann and Loizou, para. 3; 5.
418 ECtHR 4 November 2008, no. 72596/01 (Balsyte-Lideikiene v. Lithuania).

accomplices of the Russian occupants and referred to them as perpetrators of war crimes and genocide against the Lithuanians. Moreover, the back cover of the calendar contained a map of the Republic of Lithuania, on which the neighbouring territories of Poland, Russia and Belarus were marked as 'ethnic Lithuanian lands under temporary occupation'. Before the national court, the publisher of the calendar was sanctioned with an administrative penalty in the form of a warning for the 'production, storage and distribution of information materials promoting ethnic, racial or religious hatred' and the unsold copies of the calendar and the production means were confiscated.

The ECtHR's assessment of the case focused on the necessity-test and afforded a large margin to Lithuania in determining the pressing social need of the measures. The ECtHR took into account 'the Government's explanation as to the context of the case that after the re-establishment of the independence of the Republic of Lithuania on 11 March 1990 the questions of territorial integrity and national minorities were sensitive'. As the calendar had caused negative reactions from diplomatic representations of Poland, Belarus and Russia, the ECtHR pointed to Lithuania's obligations under international law.[419]

Subsequently, the ECtHR qualified the language used in the calendar as 'aggressive nationalism and ethnocentrism' and the statements as 'inciting hatred against the Poles and the Jews'. The Court adopted the analysis of the expert report used in the national proceedings that, although the calendar did not directly incite violence against the Jewish population, nor did it advocate implementing discriminatory policy against this ethnic group, 'a one-sided portrayal of relations among nations hindered the consolidation of civil society and promoted national hatred'.[420]

In relation to the proportionality of the measures, the ECtHR found that the confiscation could be considered relatively serious, but the warning was the mildest administrative punishment available. Overall, the measures thus could 'reasonably be considered necessary in a democratic society to protect the reputation or rights of others'.[421] The underlying reason why the ECtHR found the statements to constitute a prohibited hatred against the Poles and the Jews appears to be that they constituted 'false factual allegations or strong negative value judgments that lacked a sufficient factual basis'. But again, the ECtHR did not explicitly refer to these principles.

A case before the ECtHR concerning the *direct* incitement to discrimination is that of *Willem v. France*.[422] Strictly speaking, the case concerned discrimination based

---

419 *Ibid.*, para. 78. On the particular national context, see: Belavusau, U., A *Dernier Cri* from Strasbourg: An Ever Formidable Challenge of Hate Speech (*Soulas & Others v. France, Leroy v. France, Balsyte-Lideikiene v. Lithuania*), *European Public Law* 2010, vol. 16, no. 3, p. 378–379.

420 *Ibid.*, para. 16; 28; 79–80.

421 *Ibid.*, para. 84–85.

422 ECtHR 16 July 2009, no. 10883/05 (Willem v. France).

on *nationality* and not *race*. However, the ECtHR upheld a conviction and would certainly do the same with regard to the incitement to racial discrimination. The case concerned the conviction of Willem, mayor of the small French town of Seclin, for incitement to discrimination based on ethnic background, nation, race or religion with regard to his announcement, in which he requested his catering services to boycott Israeli products as a protest against the politics of Sharon against the Palestinian people uttered during a City council meeting and published in an open letter on the city's website. By 6:1 votes, the ECtHR, strongly relying on the argumentation of the state, found no violation of freedom of expression.

According to the ECtHR, the mayor was not convicted for his political opinions, but his appeal on the catering services to a positive act of discrimination and an explicit refusal to enter into commercial relations with producers with an Israeli nationality.[423] The diffusion of the message on the Internet in polemic terms aggravated its discriminatory character.[424] A mayor had the duty and responsibility to conserve certain neutrality and reserve and could not act as the Government in ordering boycotts.[425]

However, even such literal incitements to concrete action are open to different interpretations and therefore the judges of the Court can disagree whether they must be interpreted as having a discriminatory racist purport. Dissenting judge Jungwiert objected that the ECtHR had disregarded the intention of the mayor; the expression rather reflected an opinion or political position of an elected official in the context of an escalation of violence in the Israeli-Palestinian conflict.[426] In the context of a public debate of general interest, certain exaggeration and provocation was permitted. Moreover, the proposal was quite vague as to its effectuation; its impact was limited as it concerned the catering services of a small community and finally, its *concrete effects* and *practical consequences* had not been demonstrated. The decision thus lacked sufficient reasoning on the necessity of the measure.

1.3.4. Hate speech on the basis of religion under Article 17

Although the case law of the ECtHR does suggest that racist expression and anti-Semitism, notably in the form of Holocaust denial, qualifies sooner as an abuse of rights, the ECtHR has also found extreme speech about religion to fall outside the scope of Article 10 by reference to Article 17. The ECtHR dealt with Islamophobic speech under Article 17 for the first time in *Norwood v. United Kingdom*.[427] The case concerned the conviction of Norwood, a regional organizer for the extreme right British National Party (BNP), for displaying in the window of his flat a BNP poster with a photograph of the Twin Towers in flames, the words 'Islam out of

423 *Ibid.*, para. 35.
424 *Ibid.*, para. 36.
425 *Ibid.*, para. 37; 39.
426 *Ibid.*, dissenting opinion of judge Jungwiert.
427 ECtHR 16 November 2004, no. 23131/03 (Norwood v. The United Kingdom).

Britain – Protect the British people' and a symbol of a crescent and star in a prohibition sign. Norwood was fined GBP 300 for 'displaying, motivated by hostility towards a racial or religious group, any writing, sign or other visible representation which is threatening, abusive or insulting, within the sight of a person likely to be caused harassment, alarm or distress by it'.

The applicant held that his poster referred to Islamic extremism and was not abusive or insulting. He submitted that criticism of a religion was not to be equated with an attack upon its followers. In any event, he lived in a rural area not greatly afflicted by racial or religious tension and there was no evidence that a single Muslim had seen the poster. Remarkably, the ECtHR unanimously declared the complaint inadmissible by reference – on its own initiative – to Article 17. The Court adopted the vision of the national courts that the words and images on the poster amounted to a public attack on all Muslims in the UK and concluded that: '[s]uch a general, vehement attack against a religious group, linking the group as a whole with a grave act of terrorism, is incompatible with the values proclaimed and guaranteed by the Convention, notably tolerance, social peace and non-discrimination.'

Again, although the ECtHR did not explicitly refer to these principles, the underlying reason why the ECtHR found the poster to constitute a prohibited attack against Muslims appears to be that it constituted a 'false factual allegation or strong negative value judgment that lacked a sufficient factual basis' about them. In any event, under certain circumstances strong allegations about Islam that do not explicitly name Muslims as a group thus may be interpreted as an (indirect) urge to readers that all Muslims should be removed from the country and as a warning that the presence of Muslims in the country constitutes a threat or danger to the people.

1.3.5. Hate speech on the basis of religion under Article 10(2)

The ECtHR generally deals with religious hate speech under 10(2). The Court's approach to religious hate speech can be explained on the basis of three relatively recent cases, being *Soulas and others v. France*, *Féret v. Belgium* and *Le Pen v. France.*[428] In all cases, the ECtHR upheld a criminal conviction and found no violation of freedom of expression. In *Soulas* and *Le Pen*, the ECtHR unanimously reached its decision, but the ECtHR decided with only a slight majority of 4:3 in *Féret*. As a result of this case law, expression that amounts to 'hate speech' may be prohibited, but the term is not evidently clear and does not in itself form a solution to the disagreement within the Court about its exact criteria.

In relation to hate speech the ECtHR, therefore, has not developed clear standards and precise criteria of review comparable with those for incitement to violence. Important considerations – about the specific harmful effects of speech in

[428] ECtHR 10 July 2008, no. 15948/03 (Soulas and others v. France); ECtHR 16 July 2009, no. 15615/07 (Féret v. Belgium); ECtHR 20 April 2010, no. 18788/09 (Le Pen v. France).

question weighed against the interest of public debate or about the place of the distinction between factual statements and value judgments or between racial remarks and speech about religion therein – are often dissolved in the large margin of appreciation the ECtHR affords states to set restrictions to hate speech.

Soulas and others v. France concerned the conviction of the publisher and the author of the book entitled 'The colonization of Europe' and subtitled 'True discourse about the immigration and the Islam' that notably claimed the incompatibility between the European and Islamic civilizations within one geographic area and proclaimed the necessity of a violent conflict between native inhabitants and immigrants. The applicants were fined with € 7622.45 and had to pay the symbolic amount of € 0.15 in damages to the civil parties for 'incitement to hatred, discrimination and violence on the ground of race, nation, ethnic background or religion'.

The ECtHR primarily considered that the book addressed a topic of general interest, because the problems related to the installation and integration of immigrants formed the object of heated debates in European societies, both in politics as in the media. This applied, in particular, to France, who had accommodated a large number of immigrants, whose integration process was long, laborious and difficult and therefore had already resulted in violent clashes between the police and some radical elements of the population. However the ECtHR opined that, as the problems related to immigration and integration varies from country to country, states could set the limitations to the public debate about this topic differently. The ECtHR thus afforded the state a large margin of appreciation in the matter, while this is unusual with regard to restrictions on contributions to political debate (para. 1.1 *supra*).[429]

This approach thus appears inconsistent and also questionable. Firstly, immigration and integration are highly political – European – issues and the ECtHR generally exercises a stringent review of restrictions on political speech, regardless of its specific topic. The fact that member states may adopt different solutions to counter political problems generally does not alter this. Secondly, the exercise of a stringent review of restrictions on political speech need not necessarily result in the conclusion that Article 10 ECHR has been violated. The two should not be equated. The ECtHR could also arrive at the conclusion that a measure is justified because a particular form of hate speech is not acceptable in political debate. The ECtHR, however, essentially seems to be reluctant to set criteria for hate speech in the politically sensitive context of immigration and integration.

Another remarkable point is that the ECtHR considered the book to address a large public due to its accessible style, while it generally considers the impact of books rather limited. As to its content, the ECtHR found the style polemic and several passages to present a negative image of the targeted groups and the effects of immigration as catastrophic.[430] The ECtHR dealt with the appeal to Article 17

429 ECtHR 10 July 2008, no. 15948/03 (Soulas and others v. France), para. 36–38.

430 *Ibid.*, para. 39; 41.

made by France in the case on the merits, but explicitly stated that the passages concerned were not sufficiently serious to constitute an abuse of rights.[431]

Based on the motivation of the national courts that 'the words in the book were intended to provoke in the reader a sense of rejection and antagonism – increased by the use of military language – against targeted communities identified as the main enemy, and to induce him to share the solution advocated by the author, that of a war of ethnic conquest.' and the fact that no prison sentence was imposed, the ECtHR did find the restriction necessary in a democratic society under 10(2).[432]

An important factor thus was that, according to the ECtHR, the book did not enter into a free discussion about the place of Islam in society as a result of immigration, but concerned the attribution of negative qualities or behaviour to immigrants, foreigners, or a particular ethnic group on account of their religion, as it were their inherited biological characteristics. If the ECtHR found the restriction in this case acceptable, because a religion was in fact treated as the hallmark of people's racial and ethnic identity, it had better more explicitly explain why.

The *Soulas* case formed an important precedent for *Féret v. Belgium*. The case concerned the conviction of Daniel Féret, president of the extreme right political party Front National and representative in Parliament at the time of the national proceedings, as the author and editor of a series of posters and leaflets distributed and published on the Internet during the election campaigns. The publications comprised statements against the immigration of freeloaders and the 'islamization' of Belgium and slogans such as 'Priority for the Belgians and the Europeans' and 'Attacks in USA: it is the couscous clan'.

After the public prosecution had obtained the waiver of his parliamentary immunity, Féret was prosecuted for 'incitement to discrimination, segregation, hatred or violence against a group, community or its members on account of race, colour, nation or ethnic background' and he was convicted to 250 hours of employment in the sector of the integration of foreigners and prohibited to exercise the right of eligibility for ten years.

The ECtHR again joined the exception of Article 17 evoked by Belgium in the case on the merits, but finally found that the content of the publications could not justify the application of Article 17.[433] The restriction was however admissible under 10(2), because 'the publications presented immigrant communities as criminal and interested in exploiting the advantages of residing in Belgium and aimed to mock them. Such a discourse inevitably evoked with the public, especially among the least informed, feelings of disdain, rejection or, even with some, hatred against foreigners.'[434]

---

431 *Ibid.*, para. 23; 48.

432 *Ibid.*, para. 43; 46.

433 ECtHR 16 July 2009, no. 15615/07 (Féret v. Belgium), para. 52; 82.

434 *Ibid.*, para. 69.

According to the ECtHR, the language used clearly incited to racial hatred and discrimination. With regard to the tract 'Attacks in USA: it is the couscous clan', the ECtHR adopted the vision of the national courts that 'such an oversimplified representation that equated all Muslims with terrorists was an incitement to hatred against all members of this group, without distinction, and translated the desire of its authors to recur to this hatred.'[435]

The Court's main concern was that in order for a restriction to be acceptable 'the incitement to hatred does not necessarily require this or that act of violence or another punishable act. The injury of persons by insulting, ridiculing or defaming certain parts of the population and specific groups or the incitement to discrimination, as in the present case, suffices in order for the authorities to privilege the fight against racist discourse facing a freedom of expression that is irresponsible and violates the dignity or even the security of these parties or groups of the population. Political discourses that incite to hatred founded on religious, ethnic or cultural prejudices represent a danger for the social peace and political stability in the democratic States.'[436]

The ECtHR interpreted Féret's statements thus as an incitement to hatred against Muslims rather than political criticism of the Government's immigration policy. Another point stressed by the ECtHR thus concerned the duties and responsibilities of politicians: 'it is of crucial importance that politicians, in their public discourses, avoid to diffuse remarks susceptible to nourish intolerance.' 'Politicians should be particular attentive to the defence of democracy and its principles, because their ultimate objective is the seizure of power itself.' The ECtHR found the waiver of Féret's parliamentary immunity justified, because 'the incitement to exclusion of foreigners constitutes a fundamental violation of the rights of individuals'.[437]

The ECtHR acknowledged that political discourse required a high level of protection and that political parties had a broad freedom of expression in order to convince their electors and propose solutions for problems related to immigration. However, in the context of an electoral campaign that aimed to reach the electorate at large, thus the entire population, racist and xenophobic discourse had a larger and more harmful impact on the public order and the cohesion of the social group. 'Such behaviour risks to evoke with the public reactions incompatible with a serene social climate and to undermine the confidence in the democratic institutions.'[438] As Belgium, despite the length of the ineligibility, had testified for restraint in the recourse to criminal law, the restriction was necessary in a democratic society.

The ECtHR did not develop clear standards and precise criteria for review comparable with incitement to violence, such as the expression of actual 'incitement', the intention of the speaker to stigmatize others and the likelihood of

435 *Ibid.*, para. 71.
436 *Ibid.*, para. 73.
437 *Ibid.*, para. 75.
438 *Ibid.*, para. 76–77.

subsequent violent action as a probable effect of the expression. Nor did the ECtHR require any demonstration of *how* hate speech consisting of group defamation affects the dignity or security of the target group, for example, by reference to its psychological effects. The ECtHR's approach towards hate speech has therefore been compared with the American 'bad tendency test' and criticized on this account: the nature of the act – incitement – and the intention of the author are deduced from the 'tendency' of the words to persuade others to adopt hateful or discriminatory attitudes.[439]

The underlying reason why the ECtHR found the statements to constitute a prohibited incitement to hatred against Muslims appears to be, however, that they constituted 'false factual allegations or strong negative value judgments that lacked a sufficient factual basis' about them. An important factor therein appeared to be that, according to the ECtHR, Islam as a religion was in fact treated as the hallmark of people's racial and ethnic identity (that of immigrants/foreigners). But again, the ECtHR did not explicitly refer to these principles in its reasoning. In fact, the ECtHR left the national authorities a certain margin to interpret and apply its national provisions prohibiting specific forms of hate speech.

The dissenters took a diametrical opposite view on freedom of expression and the criminal restrictions that are allowed in a democratic society.[440] Firstly, they acknowledged that the long-term impact of xenophobic propaganda constitutes a major problem for democratic societies. However, they objected to the regulation of a discourse on the basis that its mere content was deemed incompatible 'with the spirit of the Convention', because a 'spirit' does not offer a clear standard and opens the door for abuse.

Moreover, the dissenters opined that human beings tend to qualify as inadmissible, opinions that are inconvenient to them. However, when remarks are considered to be of little value in the search for truth, this was to be demonstrated undeniably in the light of the circumstances of the specific case concerned. The protection of political opinions was precisely grounded on the idea that human beings are sufficiently rational to make informed choices; the controllers of political powers were not to establish a catalogue of false or inacceptable ideas. This apparently also applied to defamatory statements and negative value judgments about an entire group in society, without distinction, such as those of Féret.

According to the dissenters, expressions that form part of public debate could only be sanctioned if they incited particular acts or forms of discrimination. This would, for example, be the case if expression called the public to boycott, refuse services to or avoid migrants – such as in *Willem v. France*. It was incumbent upon the State to demonstrate the *direct effect* of such speech; a *potential* impact on the rights of others did not suffice for the restriction of a human right. For the criteria

---

439 Sottiaux, S., 'Bad Tendencies' in the ECtHR's Hate Speech' Jurisprudence, *European Constitutional Law* 2011, vol. 7, no. 1, p. 53.

440 *Ibid.*, Dissenting opinion of judge Sajó, Zagrebelsky and Tsotsoria.

for 'incitement' to discrimination, the dissenters based themselves on the case *Sürek no. 1* concerning incitement to violence and considered that 'expressions must be susceptible to favour discrimination by instilling a profound and irrational hatred against those who were presented as responsible for the alleged atrocities. Discrimination, like violence, implies action.'

This signified, in the eyes of the dissenters, that in order for a restriction on discourse to be acceptable the demonstration of the existence of a punishable illegal act that directly resulted from the discourse or was at least significantly and truly favoured by it was required. Another crime had to be committed or had to be susceptible to be committed and that's when prevention intervenes. Incitement constituted 'a strong, or even decisive, psychological exhortation supposed to give birth to another punishable offence.' The simple intolerance, the sentiment without action or at least without the manifest tendency to action could not constitute an offence; its criminalization would constitute a 'délit d'opinion', i.e. a thought crime.

Féret's expression did not meet the dissenters' high thresholds. His remarks had to be interpreted neither in isolation nor in combination with other randomly chosen remarks, but in the context of the entire publication. The remarks had to be qualified as political criticism directed against the *Government*, the political parties and their politics favourable to migrants and vague political proposals addressed to the Government that did not call on actions on the part of the population. Neither did Féret incite them to violence against a part of the population, in which case the state would have had a larger margin of appreciation.

The dissenters admitted that ambiguity of expression could contribute to the formation of a xenophobic mentality that could lead to discriminatory or violent behaviour and could also result in the support of political parties with anti-democratic aims. However, this was a problem of the 'militant democracy', whose norms applied rather to *political parties* than to *individuals* – like Féret. Apparently, the dissenters opined that individuals are entitled to a larger freedom of expression. The dissenters criticized the fact that the ECtHR had used the broad definition of hate speech in Recommendation n° R (97) 20, because this instrument aimed at prohibiting the *media* such as radio and television stations from distributing a 'discourse of hatred' and thus did not apply in this case. We will see later on that this argument is incorrect, because the recommendation is not specifically limited to the media (para. 2 *infra*).

The dissenters also strictly distinguished *racism* from other forms of discrimination. Féret's remarks were not racist in themselves, because they neither referred to the superiority or inferiority of a race nor attributed inherited biological characteristics to an identifiable group. ICERD, to which the ECtHR had referred, included discrimination on other grounds, but not between *citizens and non-citizens*. It also did not include the incitement to *religious and cultural prejudices*.

According to the dissenters, the ECtHR had thus rapidly extended the list of acceptable prohibitions on political opinions on the simple ground of constituting 'dangerous discourse' without further precision, while in a democracy elections did not constitute a source of danger requiring special restrictions on discourse. Finally, the dissenters found the severity of Féret's penalty to be comparable with that of a war criminal for the offence of collaboration and hence disproportionate. Given the voting weights in the case, this dissenting opinion could be considered as an important counter balance to the ECtHR's majority opinion.

To recapitulate, to a majority of the ECtHR the bad influence of hatred based on prejudices on the political stability and serene social climate (mid/ long term effects) and the violation of people's dignity is sufficient in order to justify its restriction. The Court does not, however, differentiate between types of hate speech (incitement, insult, defamation, intolerance) and does not set clear criteria for 'incitement' or require any demonstration of *how* hate speech harms people's dignity. An underlying consideration often appears to be that speech in question may be prohibited, because it constitutes 'false factual allegations or strong negative value judgments that lacked a sufficient factual basis' about a group and treat people's religion as the hallmark of their racial and ethnic identity.

The minority within the ECtHR requires a stricter connection between the content of expression (actual incitement) and subsequent concrete forms of discrimination and violence by others in order to justify a restriction. It also makes a stricter distinction between classic racist speech and other forms of intolerance. Criticism of government policy can consist of factual allegations and negative value judgments about a group, the wrongfulness of which must be determined by public debate itself.

The approach of the dissenters in the *Féret* case was, however, not adopted in the subsequent inadmissible decision of the ECtHR in *Le Pen v. France*.[441] Le Pen, at the time president of the extreme right political party Front National, was sanctioned with a fine of € 10,000 for 'provocation to discrimination, hatred or violence' with regard to his statement in an interview with the newspaper *Le Monde* 'On the day that France will count no longer 5 million but 25 million of Muslims, they will be in command. The French will clean the streets and walk the sidewalks with their eyes facing down. If they don't, they will be told: 'Why are you looking at me like that? Are you looking to fight?' And if then you don't run, you'll get punched.'

The ECtHR dealt with the case under 10(2) and made no reference to Article 17. It primarily noted that the statements made by Le Pen formed part of a debate of general interest about the problems relating to the immigration and integration of foreigners. However, the ECtHR subsequently recalled, referring to the *Soulas* case, that states had a large margin to determine the necessity of restrictions to the debate on immigration and integration. The ECtHR cited the analysis of the national courts, i.e. that Le Pen's words were susceptible to give a negative, and even alarming, image of the 'Muslim community' as a whole and instilled in the mind of

441 ECtHR 20 April 2010, no. 18788/09 (Le Pen v. France).

the public the conviction that the security of the French would proceed with the rejection of Muslims and that the anxiety and fear caused by their presence in France would stop if they would decrease in numbers and disappear. In this manner, the ECtHR concluded that Le Pen set the French against a community explicitly designated on the basis of its religion and presented as a menace to the dignity and security of the French. His words were susceptible to evoke a feeling of rejection and hostility towards the targeted community.

Importantly, for the first time the ECtHR gave explicit consideration to the distinction between facts and value judgments in the context of hate speech, just as the dissenters in *Féret* had referred to the 'catalogue of false ideas'. But here the ECtHR precisely rejected Le Pen's reference to news facts that were supposed to support his assertions; these did not constitute 'a sufficient factual basis' for his value judgments, but in reality challenged the appreciation of the national courts. The question arises as to what according to the ECtHR would have constituted a sufficient factual basis for Le Pen's assertions. However, the ECtHR neither discussed the content of these news facts nor did it provide any further explanation of this point. Therefore, the decision does not shed much light on the requirement of a 'sufficient factual basis' for allegations in hate speech cases. As Le Pen in principle was liable for a prison sentence, his conviction of a fine was not disproportionate and Article 10 was not violated.

1.4. Demarcation with blasphemy and religious offence

1.4.1. The right to respect for religious feelings in accordance with 9 ECHR

The ECtHR's case law concerning *blasphemy* and religious offence must be distinguished from the previously discussed case law concerning religious *hate speech.* Unlike the latter, the ECtHR generally conceives the former issue as a direct conflict between freedom of expression and freedom of religion that subsequently – oddly enough – does not engage Article 17. The starting point of the ECtHR's established case law concerning blasphemy were the cases of *Otto Preminger Institute v. Austria* and *Wingrove v. United Kingdom.*[442] In both cases the ECtHR upheld the measures and found no violation of freedom of expression by 6:3, and 7:2 votes respectively.

The *Otto Preminger* case concerned the film 'Das Liebeskonzil', the plot of which was based on a play by playwright Panizza, in which God appears as a senile old man, Jesus is mentally defective and God, Jesus and the Virgin Mary agree with the devil to punish immorality by infecting the world with syphilis.[443] The Otto Preminger Institute in Innsbruck (Tyrol) had announced the screening of the film in

442 ECtHR 20 September 1994, no. 13470/87 (Otto Preminger Institute v. Austria); ECtHR 25 November 1996, no. 17419/90 (Wingrove v. The United Kingdom).

443 ECtHR 20 September 1994, no. 13470/87 (Otto Preminger Institute v. Austria), para. 20–22.

its bulletin, in several display windows and in a local newspaper. Before it was shown, the film was seized and confiscated for constituting blasphemy, prohibited by Austrian criminal law.

The ECtHR found that the measure pursued the legitimate aim of protecting the rights of others, more specifically the right to respect one's religious feelings and considered this to be an integral part of the right to freedom of religion as protected in Article 9 ECHR. The ECtHR recalled that freedom of religion 'is, in its religious dimension, one of the most vital elements that go to make up the identity of believers and their conception of life.'[444]

Although religious believers could not 'reasonably expect to be exempt from all criticism', 'in extreme cases the effect of particular methods of opposing or denying religious beliefs can be such as to inhibit those who hold such beliefs from exercising their freedom to hold and express them.' The respect for the religious feelings of believers could already be violated 'by provocative portrayals of objects of religious veneration; and such portrayals can be regarded as malicious violation of the spirit of tolerance, which must also be a feature of democratic society.'[445]

The ECtHR continued that amongst the 'duties and responsibilities' connected with the exercise of freedom of expression – in the context of religious opinions and beliefs – may legitimately be included 'an obligation to avoid as far as possible expressions that are gratuitously offensive to others and thus an infringement of their rights, and which therefore do not contribute to any form of public debate capable of furthering progress in human affairs'. 'This being so, as a matter of principle it may be considered necessary in certain democratic societies to sanction or even prevent improper attacks on objects of religious veneration.'[446]

However, the ECtHR observed that it was 'not possible to discern throughout Europe a uniform conception of the significance of religion in society'. Therefore, it was 'not possible to arrive at a comprehensive definition of what constitutes a permissible interference with the exercise of the right to freedom of expression where such expression is directed against the religious feelings of others.'[447] Finally, the ECtHR thus afforded the state a large margin of appreciation to determine the necessity of restrictions on such speech.

The ECtHR subsequently quite uncritically adopted the arguments put forward by the state. It considered that, although the access to the film was subjected to an admission fee and an age limit, the film was widely advertised and therefore sufficiently 'public' to cause offence. Moreover, the film constituted an abusive attack on the Roman Catholic religion according to the conception of the Tyrolean public. As this was the religion of 'the overwhelming majority of Tyroleans', Austria acted 'to ensure religious peace in that region and to prevent that some

[444] *Ibid.*, para. 47.
[445] *Ibid.*, para. 47.
[446] *Ibid.*, para. 49.
[447] *Ibid.*, para. 50.

people should feel the object of attacks on their religious beliefs in an unwarranted and offensive manner'.[448]

The ECtHR's marginal review resulted in the conclusion that Austria had not overstepped its margin of appreciation. The Court neither balanced the opposing interests for itself in the light of the full context of the case, nor assessed the existence of a pressing social need for the restriction, its proportionality and whether its reasons were relevant and sufficient. It thereby placed a very high burden on the applicant to prove a violation of freedom of expression and placed a very low burden on the state to prove the legitimacy of its measures.

The ECtHR's approach was very similar in *Wingrove v. The United Kingdom*. The case concerned the video *Visions of Ecstacy*, for which the British Board of Film Classifications (BBFC) refused to accord a 'classification certificate' and thereby obstructed its distribution in England. The video depicted the visions of the sixteenth century nun Saint Theresa of Avila as erotic ecstasies for which she was assisted by Christ and a woman symbolizing her spirit.[449] According to the BBFC, the video was blasphemous and therefore violated English criminal law.

Importantly, the Court rejected the arguments of the applicant that the offence of blasphemy was too vague and found the interference prescribed by law, considering that: 'the offence of blasphemy cannot by its very nature lend itself to precise legal definition. National authorities must therefore be afforded a degree of flexibility in assessing whether the facts of a particular case fall within the accepted definition of the offence.'[450]

The ECtHR found that the state's aim of affording protection against the presentation of a religious subject in a contemptuous, reviling, insulting, scurrilous or ludicrous tone, style or spirit calculated to outrage religious believers or sympathizers to correspond with the protection of the 'rights of others' in Article 10(2) and also fully consonant with the aim of the protections afforded by Article 9 to freedom of religion.[451] Despite this initial reference to Article 9, the Court subsequently laid less emphasis on freedom of religion than it had done in *Otto Preminger*. It concluded that the refusal of a distribution certificate was intended to 'provide protection against seriously offensive attacks on matters regarded as sacred by Christians', but did not explicitly qualify such protection as an integral part of the right to freedom of religion.[452]

Finally, the ECtHR affirmed the large margin of appreciation for states to determine the extent and necessity of measures against attacks on religious convictions stating: '[w]hat is likely to cause substantial offence to persons of a particular religious persuasion will vary significantly from time to time and from

448 *Ibid.*, para. 56.
449 ECtHR 25 November 1996, no. 17419/90 (Wingrove v. The United Kingdom), para. 9.
450 *Ibid.*, para. 42.
451 *Ibid.*, para. 48.
452 *Ibid.*, para. 57.

place to place, especially in an era characterized by an ever growing array of faiths and denominations.'[453]

Again the ECtHR applied a rather marginal review and accepted the vision of the state that the work focussed 'less on the erotic feelings of the character than on those of the audience, which is the primary function of pornography' and engaged the viewer in a 'voyeuristic erotic experience' and therefore could outrage and insult the feelings of believing Christians.[454] The fact that the measure amounted to a total distribution ban was not unreasonable, because once videos become available on the market they can, in practice, easily escape from control. Other measures such as restricting the distribution to licensed sex shops or using a case with a warning about the content would therefore only have had a limited effect.[455]

The decisions in *Otto Preminger* and *Wingrove* have been highly criticized by both the dissenters and commentators. The dissenters in *Otto Preminger* stressed that 'it should not be open to the authorities of the State to decide whether a particular statement is capable of 'contributing to any form of public debate capable of furthering progress in human affairs'; such a decision cannot but be tainted by the authorities' idea of 'progress'. They also pointed out that 'The Convention does not, in terms, guarantee a right to protection of religious feelings. More particularly, such a right cannot be derived from the right to freedom of religion, which in effect includes a right to express views critical of the religious opinions of others.' In the end, the advertisement of the film enabled the religiously sensitive to make an informed decision to stay away and made it unlikely that anyone would be confronted with the material unwittingly.[456]

Commentators have also notably criticized the presentation of the issue of religious offence as a conflict between freedom of expression and freedom of religion.[457] It has been argued that the freedom of religion of others certainly constitutes a legitimate ground for limiting free speech, but should not be equated with a right not to be insulted in one's religious feelings. It cannot be advanced as a ground for limitation on speech by a state without at least some proof and concrete indication that religious rights are at stake. This threshold is much higher than the likelihood of a group being insulted.[458] Moreover, the ECtHR's argument that an

453 *Ibid.*, para. 58.

454 *Ibid.*, para. 61.

455 *Ibid.*, para. 62–63.

456 Joint dissenting opinion of judges Palm, Pekkanen and Makarczyk, para. 3; 6; 9 at: ECtHR 20 September 1994, no. 13470/87 (Otto Preminger Institute v. Austria).

457 Evans, M., The Freedom of Religion or Belief and the Freedom of Expression, *Religion and Human Rights*, Vol. 4, No. 2–3, September 2009, p. 197–235; Haarscher, G., Are Religious Sensitivities above the Constitution? Reflections on the Collective Defamation of Religious People, in: Sajo, A, & Uitz, R., *Constitutional Topography: Values and Constitutions*, Issues in Constitutional law, no. 6, The Hague: Eleven Publishing 2010, p. 367–384.

458 Temperman, J., Freedom of expression and religious sensitivities in pluralist societies: facing the challenge of extreme speech, *Brigham Young University Law Review* 2011, p. 734.

overwhelming majority of the population adhered to Catholicism could also be turned around; it was quite unlikely that an extreme view of a minority could effectively undermine anyone's religious rights. This would be more plausible if the targeted group was a vulnerable minority or if the group according to statistics indeed suffered from hate crimes or persecution.[459]

The dissenters in *Wingrove* questioned the necessity of the measure in a democratic, pluralistic society on the basis of the discriminatory nature of the offence of blasphemy that solely protected the Christian faith.[460] The ECtHR should at least have expressed its reasoning in terms of both religious beliefs and philosophical convictions; the rights of others under 10(2) could not be restricted solely to protect of the rights of others in a single category of religious believers or philosophers or a majority of them.[461]

Despite this harsh criticism the ECtHR continued its line of reasoning in *I.A. v. Turkey*,[462] concerning the conviction for blasphemy against 'God, the Religion, the Prophet and the Holy Book' with regard to the publication of a novel by Abdullah Riza Ergüven entitled 'Yasak Tümceler' (The forbidden phrases) that included the passage: 'Look at the triangle of fear, inequality and inconsistency in the Koran; it reminds me of an earthworm. God says that all the words are those of his messenger. Some of these words, moreover, were inspired in a surge of exultation, in Aisha's arms… God's messenger broke his fast through sexual intercourse, after dinner and before prayer. Muhammad did not forbid sexual relations with a dead person or a live animal.'

By a narrow majority of 4:3, the ECtHR found no violation of freedom of expression. It considered that '[t]he issue before the Court therefore involves weighing up the conflicting interests of the exercise of two fundamental freedoms, namely the right of the applicant to impart to the public his views on religious doctrine on the one hand and the right of others to respect for their freedom of thought, conscience and religion on the other hand'.[463] The Court has been lauded for no longer referring to the right not to be insulted in one's religious feelings under Article 9.[464]

However, again the ECtHR did not explain in which manner the expression that did not deny Muslims the free exercise of any aspect of their faith could have interfered with and violated their freedom of religion. The ECtHR simply found the novel to constitute 'an abusive attack on the Prophet of Islam' and the measure

459 Temperman 2011, p. 735.

460 Dissenting opinions of judges Meyer & Lohmus at: ECtHR 25 November 1996, no. 17419/90 (Wingrove v. The United Lingdom).

461 Dissenting opinion judge Pettiti at: *ibid.*

462 ECtHR 13 September 2005, no. 42571/98 (I.A. v. Turkey).

463 *Ibid.*, para.27.

464 Temperman 2011, p. 734.

against it intended to provide protection against 'offensive attacks on matters regarded as sacred by Muslims'[465] and reasonable as it concerned a limited fine.

The dissenters objected that any criminal conviction has a 'chilling effect' and that the *limited practical impact* of the novel on society was not taken into account. They called the ECtHR to revise all of its case law that placed too much emphasis on conformism or uniformity of thought.[466] Indeed, in theory every critical opinion on religious affairs that does not presume their sacredness devaluates the character of such affairs and could therefore be considered as gratuitously offensive, even when conveyed in neutral terms.

Starting in 2006, the ECtHR changed course and increasingly began to distinguish unprotected attacks on people on the basis of their religion from protected criticism on religious dogmas. It has been argued that the ECtHR did so in reaction to international developments at the time such as the affair of the Danish Cartoons and the UN 'defamation of religions' resolutions.[467] Subsequently, the following case *Tatlav v. Turkey* sharply contrasted with the ECtHR's previous case law.[468]

In this case, the ECtHR unanimously found a conviction for the profanation of 'one of the Religions' with regard to the publication of a book entitled 'İslamiyet Gerçeği' (the Reality of Islam), which formed a critical commentary of the Koran to constitute a violation of freedom of expression.[469] According to the ECtHR, the issue again 'implied a balancing act between the right to communicate one's ideas on a religious doctrine to the public and the right of others to respect for their freedom of thought, conscience and religion'.[470]

However, the ECtHR found the assertion in the book that the effect of religion was to legitimize social injustice by presenting it as the 'Will of God' to form 'a critical point of view of a non-believer regarding religion in the socio-political domain'. Contrary to the *I.A.* case, the book did not have an insulting tone directed at the person of believers, nor did it constitute a harmful attack on sacred symbols, notably of Muslims, even though they certainly could feel offended by this sharp comment on their religion.[471] Now the ECtHR concluded that 'a criminal conviction could deter authors and editors from publishing opinions not conformist to religion

---

465 ECtHR 13 September 2005, no. 42571/98 (I.A. v. Turkey), para. 30.

466 *Ibid.*, Joint dissenting opinion of judges Costa, Cabral Barreto and Jungwiert, para. 2;6; 8.

467 Chelini-Pont, B., La mobilisation de l'Organisation de la Conférence Islamique Mondiale contre la diffamation de l'Islam (1999–2009) et ses conséquences en Europe, *Droit et Religions* 2009–2010, vol. 4, p. 525–552.

468 ECtHR 26 May 2006, no. 50692/99 (Aydin Tatlav v. Turkey).

469 The book proclaimed that Islam had the tendency to repress criticism and freedom of thought and constituted an ideology based on cruel sanctions, because of a lack of self-confidence. In fact, God did not exist but was created by the mind of the illiterate and the Koran was a primitive, superficial book filled with repetitions. See: *Ibid.*, para. 12.

470 *Ibid.*, para. 26.

471 *Ibid.*, para. 28.

and forms an obstacle in the protection of pluralism, which is indispensable for the healthy evolution of a democratic society.'[472]

1.4.2. Group defamation on the basis of religion

The ECtHR's case law concerning *blasphemy* can be contrasted with the Court's case law concerning national convictions for *group defamation* on the basis of religion. In the former, the ECtHR conceived offensive criticism of religious dogmas as an indirect insult of religious adherents and therefore found restrictions to such speech acceptable. Contrarily, it results from the latter that criticism on the conduct of particular religious institutions or officials cannot be considered as an indirect defamation of the entire group of adherents on account of their religion and/ or a violation of their freedom of religion per se. According to the ECtHR, such speech rather forms a contribution to public debate and, when it is not gratuitously offensive, its restriction violates freedom of expression.

A famous example is the case of *Giniewski v. France*.[473] In reaction to the publication of the papal encyclical 'Veritatis Splendor', Giniewski had published an article in a French newspaper, in which he criticized the Catholic Church and the position of the Pope and alleged that '[m]any Christians have acknowledged that anti-Judaism and the doctrine of the 'fulfilment' of the Old Covenant in the New lead to anti-Semitism and prepared the ground on which the idea and implementation of Auschwitz took seed.'[474]

The ECtHR unanimously found the civil conviction for defamation of the Christian community on the basis of their religion to violate Article 10. The interference did have the legitimate aim of protecting 'the reputation or rights of others' and was also fully consonant with the aims of Article 9.[475] This reference to freedom of religion is striking. Generally, the ECtHR regards reputation rights as forming part of the right to privacy protected in Article 8 ECHR. Now it seemingly connected the protection of the reputation of religious groups with freedom of religion.

The ECtHR, however, continued stating that: '[b]y considering the detrimental effects of a particular doctrine, the article in question contributed to discussion of the various possible reasons behind the extermination of the Jews in Europe, a question of indisputable public interest in a democratic society.' Although the issue concerned 'a doctrine upheld by the Catholic Church, and hence a religious matter,' the article did not 'contain attacks on religious beliefs as such, but a view which the applicant wishes to express as a journalist and historian.' It was 'essential in a democratic society that a debate on the causes of acts of particular gravity amounting to crimes against humanity should be able to take place freely.'[476]

---

472 *Ibid.*, para. 30.
473 ECtHR 31 January 2006, no. 64016/00 (Giniewski v. France).
474 *Ibid.*, para. 14.
475 *Ibid.*, para. 40.
476 *Ibid.*, para. 51.

The state had argued that the article did not convey an opinion or a value judgment but referred to an (untrue) fact; it charged the Catholic Church, and therefore its members, with responsibility for the extermination of the Jews by the Nazi regime. Contrarily, the ECtHR considered that the article did not 'cast doubt in any way on clearly established historical facts' and 'it is an integral part of freedom of expression to seek historical truth', and that 'it is not its role to arbitrate' the underlying historical issues. Finally, the article was not gratuitously offensive, because it was not intentionally insulting or defamatory, nor did it incite hatred or disrespect.[477]

The ECtHR confirmed its approach in *Klein v. Slovakia*, where it again unanimously found a violation of Article 10.[478] The case concerned an article published in a weekly that sharply criticized a Catholic Archbishop for calling to withdraw the film 'The People versus Larry Flynt' and its advertisement on the basis of its blasphemous character. The article questioned why decent Catholics do not leave the organization, which is headed by such an 'ogre'. Two religious organizations complained that the defamatory statement about the highest representative of the Catholic Church in Slovakia had offended the religious feelings of their members. Subsequently, the author of the article was prosecuted and convicted of religious group defamation.[479]

According to the ECtHR however, the article neither unduly interfered with the right of believers to express and exercise their religion, nor did it denigrate the content of their religious faith. Furthermore, the strongly worded pejorative opinion related exclusively to the Archbishop and the statements did not discredit and disparage a sector of the population on the basis of their Catholic faith. The fact that the statements could have offended some members of the Catholic Church did not alter this.[480] Therefore, the conviction of the criminal offence of defamation of other persons' belief was in itself inappropriate in the particular circumstances of the case.[481]

Interestingly, the ECtHR started by pointing out that the issue 'does not require the examination of whether a sufficient factual basis existed for the impugned statements directed at the person of the Archbishop', but did not further explain this point.[482] Therefore, it remains unclear whether, according to the Court, this requirement in principle does not apply to (religious) group defamation, or whether *in casu* it was irrelevant, because the article exclusively criticized the Archbishop and thus did *not* constitute group defamation. Also, the Archbishop had withdrawn from the criminal proceedings as an injured party and publicly pardoned the applicant.

---

477 *Ibid.*, para. 51–52.
478 ECtHR 31 October 2006, no. 72208/01 (Klein v. Slovakia).
479 More specifically, the offence of public defamation of 'a group of inhabitants of the republic for their political belief, faith or because they have no religion'.
480 *Ibid.*, para. 51–52.
481 *Ibid.*, para. 53.
482 *Ibid.*, para. 49.

In this respect, the case conflicted with *Albert Engelmann v. Austria*.[483] The latter concerned a conviction for *individual* defamation in a civil case initiated by the Vicar General of the Archdiocese of Salzburg, Paarhammer, with regard to a publication in a Catholic newspaper that suggested that he was a 'rebel' and reproached him for having publicly criticized and disparaged the Pope in an extremely offensive manner.[484] The ECtHR did, however, find a violation of Article 10.

Firstly, the ECtHR stressed that the statements 'related to a religious debate, which was of considerable interest to the concerned religious community at the time of the events.'[485] Furthermore, contrary to the national courts that qualified the statements as statements of fact that lacked sufficient factual basis, the ECtHR considered that they had to be understood as permissible value judgments. Their sufficient factual basis consisted in the proof of Paarhammer's public criticism against the Holy See. They did not constitute a 'gratuitous personal attack on his person'.[486]

1.5. Holocaust denial as a particular form of hate speech

Holocaust denial can be regarded as a particular form a hate speech in the ECtHR's case law. The ECtHR affords a special protection against revisionist speech and Holocaust denial and has gradually treated it as a particular category of expression that is excluded from the protection of Article 10 by Article 17. In certain early cases concerning publications suggesting that the gas chambers in the concentration camps during the Nazi regime had never existed, the former ECmHR held that such publications 'ran counter to one of the basic ideas of the Convention, as expressed in its preamble, namely justice and peace, and further reflect racial and religious discrimination.'[487] The ECmHR considered the criminal convictions of an editor and a publisher for incitement to hatred and race hatred for false propaganda to constitute measures that were necessary in a democratic society and justified under 10(2) for the prevention of disorder and crime and the protection of the reputation and rights of others. On these grounds, the ECmHR found the applications manifestly ill-founded and inadmissible and only indirectly referred to Article 17.[488]

In a number of cases, notably against France, the ECtHR further elaborated the application of Article 17 in the context of Holocaust denial and revisionist speech.

483 ECtHR 19 January 2006, no. 46389/99 (Albert-Engelmann-Gesellschaft MBH v Austria).

484 Subsequently, Paarhammer was recalled from his function and appointed elsewhere. Dissenting judges Steiner & Kovler therefore objected that the quite severe allegations (of fact) had positively damaged Paarhammer's reputation and found no violation of Article 10.

485 *Ibid.*, para. 30.

486 *Ibid.*, para. 32–33.

487 ECmHR 6 September 1995, no. 25096/94 (Otto E.F.A. Remer v. Germany); ECmHR 18 October 1995, no. 25062/94 (Honsik v. Austria).

488 See also: ECmHR 24 June 1996, no. 31159/96 (Marais v. France).

Lehideux and Isorni v. France concerned the criminal conviction for the publication of an advertisement in the French journal *Le Monde* that sought the rehabilitation of Marshal Pétain, French Head of State during the Vichy Regime, on the ground of publicly defending the crimes of collaboration with the enemy.[489]

According to the ECtHR, the publication by describing Pétain's policy as 'supremely skilful' rather supported the 'double game theory' (according to which Vichy aimed to protect France from the excesses of Nazism and secretly engaged with the Allies waiting for the right time to switch sides). The ECtHR considered 'it is not its task to settle this point, which is part of an ongoing debate among historians about the events in question and their interpretation. As such, it does not belong to the category of clearly established historical facts – such as the Holocaust – whose negation or revision would be removed from the protection of Article 10 by Article 17.'[490, 491]

The categorical approach to Holocaust denial by the ECtHR can be explained by the direct historical context, in which the ECHR was drafted, and can be contrasted with the ECtHR's approach to other forms of hate speech that are generally dealt with on the merits under 10(2) (para. 1.3 *supra*). *Garaudy v. France* illustrates this point well.[492] The case concerned the controversial book *The founding Myths of Israeli Politics* by French philosopher, writer and former politician Garaudy. Garaudy had been convicted on the one hand for denial of crimes against humanity by denying the attempt of the Nazis to exterminate the Jews and on the other hand for racial defamation and incitement to racial hatred by strongly criticizing the political actions of the State of Israel and the Jewish community. The ECtHR separated these two issues. It dealt with the conviction for denial of crimes against humanity under Article 17 and considered that Garaudy questioned the reality, extent and seriousness of the historical events relating to the Second World War that are not the subject of debate between historians, but – on the contrary – are clearly established;

'There can be no doubt that denying the reality of clearly established historical facts, such as the Holocaust, as the applicant does in his book, does not constitute historical research akin to a quest for the truth. The aim and the result of that approach are completely different, the real purpose being to rehabilitate the

489 On the one hand, the publication 'tried to justify Pétain's decisions by endeavoring to give them a different meaning' and on the other hand, it 'omitted to mention historical facts which were a matter of common knowledge and inescapable and essential for any objective account of the policy concerned' ECtHR 23 September 1998, no. 24662/94 (Lehideux and Isorni v. France), para. 46.

490 ECtHR 23 September 1998, no. 24662/94 (Lehideux and Isorni v. France), para. 47.

491 The ECtHR finally found a violation of freedom of expression. Certain dissenters objected that the issue arose out of particular French historical circumstances and fell into the *moral* domain. France therefore should have a large margin to decide whether the publication constituted an implicit support of the Regime and whether such racism and Anti-Semitism could be condoned. See: Joint dissenting opinion of judges Foighel, Loizou and Sir John Freeland at: ECtHR 23 September 1998, no. 24662/94 (Lehideux and Isorni v. France).

492 ECtHR 24 June 2003, no. 65831/01 (Garaudy v. France).

National-Socialist regime and, as a consequence, accuse the victims themselves of falsifying history. Denying crimes against humanity is therefore one of the most serious forms of racial defamation of Jews and of incitement to hatred of them. The denial or rewriting of this type of historical fact undermines the values on which the fight against racism and anti-Semitism are based and constitutes a serious threat to public order. Such acts are incompatible with democracy and human rights because they infringe the rights of others. Their proponents indisputably have designs that fall into the category of aims prohibited by Article 17 of the Convention.'[493]

Contrarily, the ECtHR dealt with the convictions for racial defamation and incitement to racial hatred under 10(2). The Court expressed serious doubts about whether Garaudy's opinions could be protected by Article 10, given the generally revisionist tenor of the book. Although political criticism of a State indisputably fell under the Article, Garaudy had not limited himself to such criticism, but pursued a proven racist aim. Unanimously, the ECtHR found the application manifestly ill-founded and declared it inadmissible.

In subsequent cases, the ECtHR has continued to distinguish free serious historical research from prohibited denial of clearly established historical facts with a racist aim. In one clear case of Holocaust denial, the ECtHR considered that 'the requirements of protecting the interests of the victims of the Nazi regime, outweigh, in a democratic society the applicant's freedom to impart views denying the existence of gas chambers and mass murder therein'.[494]

Contrarily with regard to a critical book about of the possible involvement of certain members of the French Resistance in the arrest of their leaders by the Nazi Regime, the Court considered: 'it is an integral part of freedom of expression to seek historical truth and it is not the Court's role to arbitrate the underlying historical issues, which are part of a continuing debate between historians that shapes opinion as to the events which took place and their interpretation.'[495]

Likewise with regard to a television programme that critically examined the role of Switzerland during the Second World War, the ECtHR considered it unreasonable to require the journalist who made the programme 'to make it any clearer that the programme reflected his own 'subjective' views and not the 'sole historical truth' – which, in any event, does not exist in relation to historical debate'.[496] Hence, the aim of authorities to ensure objective accounts of historical truth must not result in protecting a 'government declared truth'.

The ECtHR is very clear in its rejection of Holocaust denial and revisionist speech. Nevertheless, the case law raises a number of questions. Firstly, it seems to be inconsistent of the ECtHR to treat Holocaust denial under Article 17, precisely because it *qualifies* Holocaust denial as a form of 'racial defamation and incitement

---

493 ECtHR 24 June 2003, no. 65831/01 (Garaudy v. France).

494 ECtHR 20 April 1999, no. 41448/98, (Witschz v. Germany).

495 ECtHR 29 September 2004, no. 64915/01 (Chauvy v. France), para. 69.

496 ECtHR 21 December 2006, no. 73604/01 (Monnat v. Switzerland), para. 68.

to hatred', with which it generally deals under 10(2). Moreover, as the ECtHR gives an autonomous qualification of expression, Holocaust denial cases before the ECtHR may very well originate in national convictions for racial defamation, insult or hatred.

Secondly, the ECtHR qualifies Holocaust denial as a 'reflection of racial and religious discrimination', but does not require that in order for such an *opinion* to constitute an abuse that it is directly accompanied by or is likely to induce others to *actions* aimed at destroying or limiting the rights of others. In fact, the ECtHR is silent about the imminence of the threat that such expression poses. It is sufficient that it 'undermines the values on which the fight against racism and anti-Semitism are based' and that an author uses his freedom of expression 'for ends which are contrary to the text and spirit of the Convention. *Such ends, if admitted, would contribute* to the destruction of the rights and freedoms guaranteed by the Convention.'[497] This reasoning is highly hypothetical.

Thirdly, the latter can notably be considered worrisome, because the ECtHR has brought not only the flat denial but also the *minimization or trivialization* of 'clearly established historical facts' under Article 17. Critical or negative remarks about such a sensitive issue as the Holocaust may easily be interpreted as minimizing or trivializing it. For example, the ECtHR found a disciplinary measure for the statement '[a]s to the existence of the gas chambers, this is up to historians to discuss and determine.' acceptable on the basis of its ambiguous nature and *eventual* contribution to revisionist theories and possible subsequent disorder.[498] Another point is whether the category of revisionist speech equally includes historical facts other than the Holocaust. The difficulty is that it may be undisputed that certain atrocities historically have taken place, but that it is highly disputed whether they could be qualified in law as a crime against humanity.[499]

Unlike other categories of speech, the ECtHR continues to treat holocaust denial and the proclaiming of revisionist theories under Article 17. The question is whether it would also be preferable to evaluate this category of speech under 10(2). Then the ECtHR could perform a more contextual analysis to determine the possible racist aim and purport of such speech and the actual threat it poses to the rights of others and the democratic system.

1.6. Positive state obligations and access to the ECtHR

1.6.1. Hate speech

Freedom of expression under Article 10 ECHR is essentially a negative right against state interference. In first instance, the ECtHR therefore determines not which

497 ECtHR 24 June 2003, no. 65831/01 (Garaudy v. France).

498 ECtHR 7 June 2011, no. 48135/08 (Gollnisch v. France).

499 Cf. Harris, O'Boyle & Warbrick 2009, p. 452.

restrictions are prescribed but only which restrictions are in violation with Article 10 and which not. The ECtHR thus does not oblige states to criminalize forms of hate speech, but does leave this possibility for states open. The ECtHR does not principally favour the use of civil law to counter hate speech. Based on the ECtHR's case law concerning hate speech one could argue that national convictions for utterances that amount to hate speech will not evidently constitute a violation of Article 10 as long as criminal sanctions remain proportionate and for example do not consist of long prison sentences.

But the question arises as to whether member states also have any *positive obligations* under the Convention to prosecute and convict utterances that amount to hate speech, thus to restrict and sanction such use of freedom of expression. A subsequent question is whether victims of hate speech can complain before the ECtHR, when a state refuses to prosecute or to convict in a particular case of hate speech. Given the large margin of appreciation that the ECtHR affords states to determine the necessity of restrictions to hate speech, no such obligations can be derived from the ECtHR's case law, even as regards the abuse of rights. However, Article 17 could play a role in the development of positive obligations; it seems reasonable that expression that can be qualified as an abuse of rights must at least be prohibited by law or even criminalized and prosecuted by the state (para. 1.1 *supra*).

In a relatively recent decision by the Grand Chamber, the ECtHR did consider that Article 8 ECHR can comprise a positive obligation for states to take measures to prevent the stigmatization of a person on the ground of his ethnic identity to effectively ensure his private life.[500] According to the ECtHR, 'any negative stereotyping of a group, when it reaches a certain level, is capable of impacting on the group's sense of identity and the feelings of self-worth and self-confidence of members of the group. It is in this sense that it can be seen as affecting the private life of members of the group.'[501] However, the ECtHR found that *in casu* the state did not violate Article 8 by allowing the expression concerned.

The case concerned the book 'The Gypsies of Turkey' published by the Ministry for Culture that referred to the biased portrayal of the Roma in order to demonstrate the perception of the Roma community by the public. It also concerned two dictionaries – one entitled 'Dictionary for pupils' – published by the Turkish Language Association and part-financed by the Ministry of Culture that was comprised of entries concerning the word Gypsy that explained their 'metaphorical use', i.e. significance in common parlance. 'Becoming a Gypsy' was for example defined as 'displaying miserly behaviour'.

In national proceedings the applicant requested the confiscation of the book and a ban on its distribution for being insulting towards the Roma/Gypsy community, and requested the removal of the dictionary entries alleged to be discriminatory to Gypsies. Furthermore, he requested damages, because the publications would

---

500 ECtHR (Grand Chamber) 15 March 2012, nos. 4149/04 and 41029/04 (Aksu v. Turkey).

501 *Ibid.*, para. 58–59.

constitute an attack on his identity as a Roma/Gypsy. After the national courts rejected the claims, the applicant complained of a violation of Article 8 and 14 ECHR before the ECtHR.

The ECtHR found that the book, examined as a whole, was neither insulting nor did it have a racist intention. Although the author pointed to certain illegal activities on the part of some members of the Roma community living in particular areas, nowhere in the book did he make negative remarks about the Roma population in general or claim that all members of the Roma community were engaged in illegal activities. The book had to be considered as a serious academic work.[502] As for the dictionary entries, the ECtHR observed that a dictionary is a source of information, which reflects the language used by society. In a dictionary aimed at pupils, more diligence is required when giving the definitions of daily language. Therefore, it was preferable to label such expressions as 'pejorative' or 'insulting', rather than merely 'metaphorical'. However, the dictionary was not a school textbook, was not distributed to schools, nor was it recommended by the Ministry for Education.[503]

For these reasons, in the end, the State could 'reasonably have come to its conclusions' and in doing so had 'not overstepped its margin of appreciation'.[504] An important factor also was that the applicant was provided with an effective means of redress.[505] The ECtHR thus appeared quite reluctant to further develop any concrete positive obligations under Article 8 to prevent the stigmatization on account of ethnic identity – even for government-funded speech directed at pupils. It did stress that the Roma formed a vulnerable minority that required special protection and agreed with the conclusions of reports by ECRI that the Turkish Government should pursue their efforts to combat negative stereotyping of the Roma, notably through education.[506]

Dissenting judge Gyulumyan disagreed with the conclusion of the majority that 'the applicant has not succeeded in producing *prima facie* evidence that the impugned publications had a discriminatory intent or effect' and objected: 'Alternatively [the Court] should, in my view, hold that when a member of a disadvantaged minority group suffers harm in an environment where racial tensions are high and impunity of State offenders epidemic, the burden to prove that the event was not ethnically induced shifts to the Government'.[507]

Another important point is that the case concerned the complaint concerning a violation of Article 8 filed by an *individual* about being *personally insulted* by the publications.[508] The state contested the applicant's victim status, because he had not

502 *Ibid.*, para. 70–72.

503 *Ibid.*, para. 84–86.

504 *Ibid.*, para. 76; 88.

505 *Ibid.*, para. 73; 87.

506 *Ibid.*, para. 75; 85.

507 *Ibid.*, Dissenting opinion of judge Gyulumyan, para. 1.

508 The ECtHR has found acquittals for *individual* defamation with regard to publications that accused persons *mentioned by name* of specific facts to violate the positive state obligation under Article 8 to protect their reputation in: ECtHR 14 October 2008, no. 78060/01 (Petrina v. Romania); ECtHR 30 March 2010, no. 20928/05 (Petrenco v. Moldova).

been *directly affected* by the expressions, and qualified his complaint as an *actio popularis* that the Convention did not permit. Contrarily, the ECtHR stressed 'the need to apply the criteria governing victim status in a flexible manner' and found that although the applicant was not personally targeted by the passages, he could have felt offended by the remarks concerning the ethnic group *to which he belonged.* Furthermore, the applicant's standing in the national proceedings had not been in dispute.[509]

It has been argued that the ECtHR should also develop positive obligations to counter hate speech against particular *groups* and afford them standing under Article 8 and/ or Article 9 ECHR. This would remove the inequality of access to the ECtHR between speakers who can complain about violations of their freedom of expression and addressees who cannot complain about violations of their dignity, reputation or safety.[510] It seems unlikely that such a development could be hindered by problems related to the standing and victim status of the minorities targeted by the hate speech.[511] In practice, it seems likely that the Court will consider groups of individual victims, anti-racism and minority organizations that were an undisputed party in national proceedings and which members belong to the target group to be directly affected by the (absence of a) measure. In principle, however, organizations may only defend their own rights before the ECtHR and not those of its members, unless they have obtained their explicit mandate.[512]

Another important admissibility criterion may be whether the national remedies have truly been exhausted. This may depend on the precise relationship between criminal and civil law in the national system concerned. For example, when the victims of certain hate speech joined a criminal prosecution for this speech as a civil party and the case resulted in an acquittal and a rejection of their civil claims, the question arises as to whether the civil parties could appeal this latter decision or subsequently initiate a civil case and whether they actually did so. In the end, however, the further materialization by the ECtHR of concrete obligations for member states to counter hate speech may be rather hindered by the Court's broad understanding of the term and margin of appreciation in this field.

In this respect, it is a pity that the ECtHR found the complaint of a violation of Article 9 with regard to the acquittal of Dutch politician Geert Wilders from group insult and incitement to hatred, discrimination and violence on the basis of religion with regard to his statements about Islam and Muslims inadmissible.[513] The case

509 *Ibid.*, para. 46; 53.

510 Lawson, R.A., Schuifelend langs de muur, Het Hof markeert de grenzen van de vrijheid van meningsuiting voor politici, *NTM/NJCM-bulletin* 2010, vol. 35 no. 5, p. 539–540.

511 Article 34 ECHR determines that 'The Court may receive applications from *any person, non-governmental organization or group of individuals* claiming to be the victim of a violation by one of the High Contracting Parties of the rights set forth in the Convention or the Protocols thereto.'

512 Van Dijk, Van Hoof, Van Rijn & Zwaak 2006, p. 509.

513 The complaint was denied by letter of 11 October 2012 sent to the applicant (unpublished). Therefore, one can only speculate about the ECtHR's motivation. One reason could be that the

could have further clarified the positive obligations to prevent religious hate speech that can be located somewhere in between those in the 'light' cases of religious offence and those in the 'severe' case of religious violence.

1.6.2. Blasphemy, religious offence and religious violence

If the ECtHR envisions the issue of blasphemy and religious offence as a direct conflict between freedom of expression and freedom of religion, one could imagine that the Court would declare complaints about the refusal of states to prevent such speech admissible and, in certain situations, would find such omissions to constitute a violation of Article 9. So far, the ECtHR however notably established a possible positive obligation of the state to ensure the rights flowing from Article 9 in very general terms – in Otto Preminger.[514]

On the one hand, this did not *oblige* states on the ground of Article 9 to prevent certain expression about a particular religion, by some experienced as insulting, in specific cases. In *Choudhury v. United Kingdom*, the ECmHR found the complaint of a violation of Article 9 and 14 with regard to the refusal to prosecute the publishers of *The Satanic Verses* by Salman Rushdie on the ground of blasphemy, because this common law offence did not extend to religions other than Christianity, inadmissible.[515] The refusal to prosecute did not *directly* interfere in the applicant's freedom to *manifest* his religion or belief. Furthermore, Article 9 did not extend to guarantee a right to bring any specific form of proceedings against those who offend the sensitivities of an individual or of a group of individuals. Therefore, there also was no issue of discrimination in the enjoyment of Article 9. One could object that although the Convention does not require states to prohibit blasphemy in order

---

applicant, the As-Soennah mosque in Rotterdam, lacked victim status and standing. On the one hand, the mosque did obtain an explicit mandate of its members to represent their interests before the ECtHR. On the other hand, although the Mosque had obtained the court order that ordered the public prosecution to prosecute Wilders, it did not form a joint civil party to the criminal case on the merits. Another reason could be that the national remedies were not exhausted. In fact, under Dutch law, speech that is not punishable may nevertheless be prohibited under civil law on the ground of due diligence norms. As the mosque could have started a civil case, the national *civil* remedies appeared not to be exhausted. A final reason could be the motivation of the complaint. The applicant argued that Wilders' offensive statements about *Islam* and the *Koran* affected the 'peaceful enjoyment' by its members of their freedom of religion (Application of 12 August 2011 filed by the As-Soennah mosque, unpublished). The applicant might have had more success, if it had complained of 1) a violation of Article 9 on the ground that Wilders' political proposals were discriminatory towards Muslims and formed an actual threat to the equal exercise of their religion or b) a violation of Article 8, on the ground that notably Wilders' attribution of an inherent criminal nature to Muslims on account of their religion and culture formed 'a negative stereotyping of the group, capable of impacting on the group's sense of identity and the feelings of self-worth and self-confidence of members of the group, thus affecting the private life of members of the group' (Aksu). See further Chapter 5 on The Netherlands.

514 ECtHR 20 September 1994, no. 13470/87 (Otto Preminger Institute v. Austria), para. 47.

515 ECmHR 5 March 1991, no. 17439/90 (Choudhury v. United Kingdom).

to protect freedom of religion, it does allow states to do so and, in that case, they may not apply their laws in a discriminatory manner.

Furthermore, a right to have criminal proceedings instituted against a third person can also not be derived from Article 6 ECHR, which guarantees the right to a fair trial and more specifically the right of access to a court.[516] Hence, in *Dubowska and Skup v. Poland*, the ECmHR rejected such a claim with regard to the decision of the public prosecution to discontinue the criminal investigations on the suspicion of publicly insulting religious feelings with regard to the image of Madonna and Child covered with gasmasks on the cover of a weekly with the headline 'Death in the air – norms exceeded by 120%'.[517] The ECmHR also considered that the applicants were not inhibited from exercising their freedom to hold and express their belief and the fact that the authorities, after careful research, found no violation of an offence did not in itself amount to a violation of Article 9.

Finally, the decision of the Danish public prosecution not to prosecute the Danish newspaper *Jyllands-Posten* for publishing the Danish cartoons, despite the many complaints of Muslim organizations filed with the police about their blasphemous and insulting nature, has equally been challenged before the ECtHR on the ground of Article 9.[518] It may be considered a pity that the ECtHR had to declare itself incompetent to decide in this famous case, since there was no jurisdictional link between the applicants, a Moroccan national and two associations based in Morocco, and Denmark.

On the other hand, when a state does not afford individuals any protection against religiously inspired violence and does not take any steps to investigate the discriminatory motives of such violence, that state violates a positive obligation on the ground of Articles 3 *juncto* 9 *juncto* 14 ECHR. This results from *97 members of the Gldani congregation of Jehovah's witnesses and 4 others v. Georgia* that concerned the refusal of the police to promptly intervene in the physical attacks and intimidation of members of the Congregation of the Jehovah's Witnesses during a religious meeting by a group of Orthodox extremists and the subsequent refusal of the authorities to investigate the criminal offences.[519] With regard to Article 9, the ECtHR considered that 'through their inactivity, the relevant authorities failed in their duty to take the necessary measures to ensure that the group of Orthodox extremists led by Father Basil tolerated the existence of the applicants' religious community and enabled them to exercise freely their rights to freedom of religion.'[520]

---

516 This right of access to a court under Article 6 rather affords a *suspect* the right to be tried on the charge in a court.

517 ECmHR 18 April 1997, no. 33490/96 (Dubowska and Skup v. Poland).

518 ECtHR 11 December 2006, no. 5853/06 (Ben El Mahi and others v. Denmark).

519 ECtHR 3 May 2007, no. 71156/01 (97 members of the Gldani congregation of Jehovah's witnesses and 4 others v. Georgia).

520 *Ibid.*, para. 134.

1.7. Synthesis ECHR

The ECtHR describes hate speech broadly as 'all forms of expression which spread, incite, promote or justify hatred based on intolerance (including religious intolerance)'. The prohibition of hate speech thus described under the ECHR is primarily informed by its underlying values of equal human dignity and non-discrimination. According to the case law of the ECtHR, expression may be prohibited as hate speech for the reason that it is insulting, ridiculing or defamatory of a group and violates their dignity and security and because it can lead to intolerance and feelings of distrust, rejection or hatred towards foreigners or other groups.

The negative influence of hatred based on prejudices on the political stability and serene social climate is thus sufficient in order to justify a restriction. The ECtHR has, therefore, not developed clear standards and precise criteria of review comparable with incitement to violence, such as the expression of actual 'incitement', the intention of the speaker to stigmatize others and the likelihood of subsequent violent action as a probable effect of the expression. Nor does the ECtHR require any demonstration of *how* hate speech consisting of defamatory and insulting remarks affects the dignity or security of the target group, for example by reference to its psychological effects. In fact, the ECtHR does not principally distinguish between different types of hate speech.

An implicit consideration of why the ECtHR finds restrictions to statements about a group acceptable, however, often appears to be that they consist of 'false factual allegations or strong negative value judgments that lacked a sufficient factual basis' about them. As for speech concerning people's religion, an important factor therein appears to be that, according to the ECtHR, a religion is in fact treated as the hallmark of people's racial and ethnic identity (that of immigrants/foreigners). But the ECtHR does not explicitly refer to these principles in its reasoning. Important considerations – about the specific harmful effects of speech in question weighed against the interest of public debate or about the place of the distinction between factual statements and value judgments or between racial remarks and speech about religion therein – are often dissolved in the broad notion of hate speech used by the ECtHR and the large margin afforded to states in determining the restrictions to the immigration and the integration debate under 10(2).

The latter appears to be inconsistent with the ECtHR's general strict review of restrictions to political speech. If the ECtHR would start using a stricter review of restrictions to the highly sensitive immigration debate as well, it could differentiate more between different types of hate speech and develop clear and consistent standards for their restriction and for distinguishing free critical remarks from prohibited hate speech, just as it has increasingly done with regard to the distinction between free criticism of religion and religious group defamation and free historical debate and Holocaust denial. Possible inconsistencies in the ECtHR's case law might, however, continue to flow from difficulties in interpreting expression.

In the end, the ECtHR leaves national authorities a certain margin to interpret and apply its national provisions prohibiting specific types of hate speech. This has consequences for the effect of the ECtHR's case law on national law on hate speech. This would only be different, if clearly defined obligations to make the act in question a criminal offence followed from this case law, and at the moment this is not the case, even as regards the abuse of rights. The ECtHR applies Article 17 also inconsistently. Its added value appears to be that it could form an additional argument in the Court's reasoning to justify far-reaching measures against speech that constitutes an imminent risk to democracy under Article 10(2)/ 11(2). Moreover, it could play a role in the development of positive obligations for the criminalization and prosecution of forms of hate speech by the state.

2. Selection of Resolutions and Recommendations of institutions of the Council of Europe

At the Summit of Heads of State and Government of the Council of Europe member states, held in Vienna from 8–9 October 1993, a Declaration and Plan of Action on combating racism, xenophobia, anti-Semitism and intolerance was adopted that set out a range of measures in order to effectively counter the resurgence of these phenomena.[521] It notably also stressed the relevance of the media in the fight against racism and intolerance.[522] Subsequently, the Council of Europe has developed a number of strategies to counter hate speech.[523]

Recommendation No. R (97)20 of the Committee of Ministers to member states on 'hate speech' was adopted on 30 October 1997. Its definition of hate speech makes it clear that the recommendation applies to hate speech generally and does not seek to create special legal obligations for the media. The recommendation puts particular emphasis on hate speech disseminated via the media, because of its greater and more damaging impact, notably in situations of tension or armed conflict. Public institutions and officials must refrain from hate speech in the media. The freedom of the media to report on racism and other forms of intolerance must, however, be protected.[524]

---

521 Vienna Declaration, 9 October 1993, Vienna.

522 Given the importance of media freedom and editorial independence, it was decided to prepare two recommendations: one on 'hate speech' in general addressed to member states that calls for legal measures and another one addressed at the media that rather calls for measures of encouragement. See: *Recommendation No. R (97)21 of the Committee of Ministers to member states on 'the media and the promotion of a culture of tolerance'*, adopted on 30 October 1997.

523 For a comprehensive analysis, see: McGonagle, T., A Survey and Critical Analysis of Council of Europe Strategies for Countering 'Hate Speech', in: Herz & Molnar 2012, p. 456–498.

524 Recommendation No. R (97)20 on 'hate speech', Principles 1; 6;7. Explanatory Memorandum to Recommendation No. R (97)20 on 'hate speech', para. 20–21.

The recommendation's broad notion of hate speech that includes 'all forms of intolerance' must be understood against the background of the Vienna Declaration; it thus focuses on combatting racism, xenophobia and anti-Semitism. Although 'intolerance', in principle, covers a very wide range of attitudes and opinions relating to a wide range of discriminatory grounds, the grounds of sex, sexual orientation, age, handicap etc. were expressly excluded.[525]

According to the recommendation, member states 'should establish or maintain a sound legal framework consisting of civil, criminal and administrative law provisions on hate speech, which enable administrative and judicial authorities to reconcile in each case respect for freedom of expression with respect for human dignity and the protection of the reputation or the rights of others'.[526] Interferences with freedom of expression must however be narrowly circumscribed and meet the standards of Article 10(2) ECHR.[527]

With regard to criminal law, the recommendation stresses that prosecution authorities must be allowed to give special attention to, but must also be particular cautious in dealing with hate speech cases.[528] Given the difficulties in obtaining sufficient evidence, 'it might be advisable to concentrate efforts on strong cases where prosecution is likely to result in a conviction. In the area of hate speech, there is a real danger that suspects present themselves to the public as 'martyrs' or 'victims' or, in the event of an acquittal, that they present the outcome of the case as a victory for their views'. Therefore it is recommended that a coordinated prosecution policy in this field should be established. Prison sentences for hate speech should remain the exception.[529]

It was however thought that criminal law may not always be suited to deal with particular cases of hate speech and that civil law generally offers greater flexibility.[530] Therefore, the recommendation suggests the examination of means to 'enhance the possibilities of combating hate speech through civil law, for example by allowing interested non-governmental organizations to bring civil law actions, providing for compensation for victims of hate speech and providing for the possibility of court orders allowing victims a right of reply or ordering retraction'.[531]

The *European Commission against Racism and Intolerance (ECRI)* forms the Council of Europe's monitoring body, specialized in combating racism, xenophobia, anti-Semitism and intolerance in Europe.[532] ECRI has made several general policy recommendations in the field. Worth mentioning is *ECRI General Policy*

---

525 Explanatory Memorandum, para. 22.
526 Principle 2.
527 Principle 3; Explanatory Memorandum, para. 27–30.
528 Principle 5.
529 Explanatory Memorandum, para. 37.
530 *Ibid.*, para. 34.
531 Principle 2.
532 ECRI was established as part of the Vienna Declaration of 1993.

Recommendation No. 7 on National legislation to combat racism and racial discrimination, adopted on 13 December 2002. It recommends, amongst others, the criminalization of five forms of hate speech, committed intentionally: a) public incitement to violence, hatred or discrimination; b) public insults and defamation; c) threats; d) the public expression of a racist ideology; and e) the public denial of grave crimes.[533] Furthermore, it recommends the criminalization of the 'public dissemination or distribution' and the 'instigating, aiding, abetting or attempting to commit' thereof.[534]

These offences are defined quite broadly. '*Public*' includes words pronounced during meetings of neo-Nazi organizations or exchanged in a discussion forum on the Internet and 'dissemination' includes dissemination through the Internet. All offences in (a-c) must be committed 'against a person or a grouping of persons on the grounds of their race, colour, language, religion, nationality, or national or ethnic origin'. '*Groupings*' is not limited to a specific group, but includes larger groupings such as asylum seekers or foreigners.[535] The offence in (d) includes 'any ideology which claims the *superiority* of or which *depreciates* or *denigrates*' such a grouping on such grounds. The offence in (e) includes the '*denial, trivialization, justification* or *condoning* of crimes of genocide, crimes against humanity or war crimes' as defined in international law.[536] Both offences in (d-e) must however be committed 'with a racist aim'.

In the specific field of blasphemy and religious hatred, the *Parliamentary Assembly* of the Council of Europe has established several non-binding principles. *Resolution 1510 (2006) on Freedom of expression and respect for religious beliefs* was adopted on 28 June 2006, after the affair of the Danish Cartoons. It takes the position that freedom of expression should not be further reduced to meet increasing sensitivities of certain religious groups.[537] Attacks on individuals on the ground of their religion or race cannot be permitted, but blasphemy laws should not be used to curtail freedom of expression and thought. At the same time, the Assembly emphasizes that hate speech against any religious group is not compatible with the ECHR and the case law of the ECtHR. Finally, it invites media to discuss media ethics and encourages 'intercultural and interreligious dialogue'.[538]

The following *Recommendation 1805 (2007) on Blasphemy, religious insults and hate speech against persons on grounds of their religion*, adopted on 29 June 2007, takes it a step further. It assumes that a distinction should be drawn between

---

533 General Policy Recommendation No. 7, para. 18 a-e.

534 *Ibid.*, para. 18 f; 20.

535 Explanatory Memorandum to General Policy Recommendation No. 7, para. 38–40; 42.

536 *Ibid*, para. 41. That is, the Convention for the Prevention and Punishment of the Crime of Genocide (Art. II); the Statute of the International Criminal Court (Art.6); and the Statute of the International Criminal Court (Art. 7–8).

537 Explanatory Memorandum to Resolution 1510 (2006), Doc. 10970, 24 June 2006.

538 Resolution 1510 (2006), para. 3;12; 15–16.

condemning insults (religious or other) and related acts and criminalizing them.[539] It recommends that the Committee of Ministers ensures that national law and practice a) are reviewed in order to decriminalize blasphemy as an insult to a religion; and only criminalize expressions that b) call for a person or group to be subjected to hatred, discrimination or violence on account of religion as on any other ground and c) intentionally and severely disturb the public order and call for public violence by reference to religious matters.[540]

The Recommendation is in line with the conclusions of a report adopted on 17–18 October 2008 by the Council of Europe's *European Commission for Democracy through Law* (the Venice Commission) that was requested to compile the national legislation of member states in this field.[541, 542] It recommended that a) incitement to religious hatred should be punishable and the offence should contain an explicit requirement of intention or recklessness; b) it is neither necessary nor desirable to create an offence of religious insult (that is, insult to religious feelings) *simpliciter*, without the element of incitement to hatred as an essential component; and c) the offence of blasphemy should be abolished.[543]

The approach in these recommendations thus differs from the approach of the ECtHR towards religious offence and certainly from the UN 'defamation of religions' resolutions adopted at the time. They rather match the current interpretation of the relationship between Articles 19 and 20(2) ICCPR (para. 5.3 *infra*).

3. Additional Protocol to the Convention on Cybercrime, concerning the criminalization of acts of a racist and xenophobic nature committed through computer systems

The Convention on Cybercrime, adopted on 8 November 2001 by the Committee of Ministers of the Council of Europe,[544] is principally aimed at harmonizing domestic criminal offences committed by means of computer-systems, providing for domestic criminal procedural law powers and setting up a fast and effective regime of international co-operation in the area of 'cybercrime'.[545] During its drafting, the possible inclusion of the offence of the distribution of racist propaganda through computer systems was discussed, but no consensus could be reached on the

---

539 Explanatory Memorandum to Recommendation 1805 (2007), Doc. 11296, 8 June 2007.

540 Recommendation 1805 (2007), para. 4;12; 13; 15; 17.2.2–17.2.4.

541 *The relationship between freedom of expression and freedom of religion: the issue of regulation and prosecution of blasphemy, religious insult and incitement to religious hatred*, Report of the Venice Commission, Study no. 406 2006, Strasbourg, 23 October 2008, CDL-AD(2008)026.

542 The report and other CoE documents are included in: *Blasphemy, insult and hatred, Finding answers in a democratic society*, Science and technique of democracy, No. 47, Venice Commission, Strasbourg: Council of Europe Publishing 2010.

543 Report of the Venice Commission 2008, para. 89 a-c.

544 Convention on Cybercrime, CETS No. 185.

545 Explanatory report to the Convention on Cybercrime, para. 16.

criminalization of such conduct. Therefore, it was decided to draw up an additional Protocol to the Convention, a binding legal instrument open to the signature and ratification of the Convention parties.[546] The Additional Protocol entered into force on 1 March 2006 and has been signed by 17 states and ratified by 20 states, including France and the Netherlands.[547]

It was thought that 'the emergence of international communication networks like the Internet provide certain persons with modern and powerful means to support racism and xenophobia and enables them to disseminate easily and widely expressions containing such ideas'. The purpose of the Protocol therefore is 'firstly, harmonizing substantive criminal law in the fight against racism and xenophobia on the Internet and, secondly, improving international co-operation in this area'.[548] For this purpose, the Protocol obliges states parties to criminalize four acts of a racist and xenophobic nature committed through computer systems, being: dissemination of *racist and xenophobic material* through computer systems (Art. 3); racist and xenophobic motivated *threat* (Art. 4); racist and xenophobic motivated *insult* (Art. 5); and *denial*, gross minimization, approval or justification of genocide or crimes against humanity (Art. 6). Furthermore, it obliges the criminalization of the 'aiding and abetting' of these offences (Art.7).[549]

To satisfy these obligations, state parties not only must enact appropriate legislation, but must also to ensure that it is effectively enforced.[550] The Protocol, however, explicitly allows state parties to make certain reservations to these offences. It thereby allows states to require a relatively strict connection between expression and resulting actions compared to the non-binding standards of the Council of Europe and the notion of hate speech employed by the ECtHR. The question thus arises of whether the Protocol will meet its objective of harmonization. The Explanatory Report to the Protocol gives detailed definitions of the terms used in these offences that facilitate their interpretation and application.[551] With regard to certain elements of the offences, it precisely determines that they may be interpreted according to domestic criminal law.

All offences require that the conduct involved be done 'without right'. This signifies that the conduct described is not punishable *per se*, but may be justified by

546 Additional Protocol to the Convention on cybercrime, concerning the criminalization of acts of a racist and xenophobic nature committed through computer systems, ETS No. 189, Explanatory report, para. 4.

547 In France, the Additional Protocol entered into force on 1 May 2006. In the Netherlands, the Additional Protocol entered into force on 1 November 2010.

548 Explanatory report, para. 3.

549 'Aiding and abetting' includes the intent that the crime be committed. Without such intent, a service provider cannot be held criminally liable under the provisions for serving as a conduit or host of a website containing material that amounts to one of the offences. To avoid criminal liability, a service provider thus does not have to actively monitor content. *Ibid.*, para. 45.

550 Explanatory report, para. 9.

551 It however does not constitute an instrument providing an authoritative interpretation of the Protocol.

principles or interests that lead to the exclusion of criminal liability, such as for law enforcement, academic or research purposes, but are not covered by established legal defences. States are free to determine how such exemptions are implemented within their domestic legal system.[552] Furthermore, all offences must be committed 'intentionally', the meaning of which is left to national interpretation (and thus may vary from specific intent to mere recklessness).[553]

Finally, the 'insult', 'threat' or 'advocacy, promotion, or incitement to hatred, discrimination or violence' must be directed against a person or group distinguished by 'race, colour, descent or national or ethnic origin, as well as *religion, if used as a pretext* for any of these factors'.[554] According to the Explanatory report, 'religion' is to be interpreted in this strict sense. Although the term 'religion' refers to 'conviction and beliefs', its insertion as such would carry the risk of going beyond the ambit of the Protocol.[555] This implies that, strictly speaking, the Additional Protocol only obliges member states to criminalize cases of an 'intersectionality' between race and religion and 'multiple' or 'aggravated' racism. States however remain free to criminalize the offences on account of religion more broadly.

In relation to the dissemination of 'racist and xenophobic material' (Art. 3(1)), the latter is defined as 'any written material, any image or any other representation of *ideas or theories, which advocates, promotes or incites hatred, discrimination or violence*'. The definition refers to conduct to which the content of the material may lead, rather than to the expression of feelings/belief/aversion as contained in the material concerned. Hence, the dissemination of mere 'ideas as such' is not punishable, but those that constitute 'advocacy, promotion or incitement' are.[556] States may however reserve the right *not* to criminalize conduct that advocates, promotes or incites discrimination that is *not* associated with hatred or violence, provided that other effective remedies are available (Art. 3(2)). Moreover, they may reserve the right not to apply the offence at all to those cases of discrimination for which they cannot provide such remedies in the light of freedom of expression (Art. 3(3)).

As for racist and xenophobic motivated 'insult' (Art. 5(1)), the latter refers to 'any offensive, contemptuous or invective expression, which prejudices the honour

---

552 Explanatory report, para. 24.

553 For example, without the required intent under domestic law, a service provider cannot be held criminally liable under the provisions for serving as a conduit or host of a website containing material that amounts to one of the offences. *Ibid.*, para. 25.

554 'Descent' refers to groups or persons, who descend from persons identifiable by certain characteristics that not necessarily still exist. 'National origin' refers to the nationality or origin of one's ancestors or people's own national belonging. See: para. 18; 20.

555 *Ibid.*, para. 21.

556 'Advocates' refers to 'a plea in favor of', while 'promotes' to 'an encouragement to or advancing'; and 'incites' to 'urging others to' hatred discrimination or violence. 'Violence' refers to 'the unlawful use of force', while 'hatred' to 'intense dislike or enmity' and 'discrimination' to 'a different unjustified treatment given to persons or to a group of persons on the basis of certain characteristics'. Whether treatment is discriminatory or not must be considered 'in the light of the specific circumstance of the case'. See: para. 13–16.

or dignity of a person'. It should be clear from the expression itself that the insult is directly connected with the insulted person's belonging to the group.[557] States may however require that the insult has the effect that the person or the group is actually exposed to hatred, contempt or ridicule (Art. 5(2)).

With regard to the dissemination of the denial of grave crimes (Art. 6(1)), it was thought that such expressions 'have inspired, stimulated and encouraged racist and xenophobic groups in their action', insult the – memory of – the victims of such evil and their relatives and 'threatens the dignity of the human community'.[558] The offence extends to the denial of grave crimes as defined by international law and recognized as such by final and binding decisions of international courts. States may however require that the denial is committed 'with the intent to incite to hatred, discrimination of violence' (Art. 6(2)). For example, the Netherlands has made a reservation to that effect.[559]

With regard to the offences of insult and the denial of grave crimes, states are even allowed to reserve the right not to apply the paragraph in the whole. Contrarily, the offence of 'racist and xenophobic threat' (Art. 4) offers no possibility for any reservation. It concerns the threatening with the commission of a 'serious criminal offence', the interpretation of which is left to states.[560] The article also covers threats 'by private communications', while the other offences are limited to the 'public' insult and the distribution or otherwise making available 'to the public' of material that is racist or xenophobic or denies grave crimes.

The Additional Protocol thus specifically takes into account the interest in freedom of expression by offering states the possibility to make reservations as to the scope of the offences and by limiting them to public communication.[561]

4. EU Council Framework Decision on combating certain forms and expressions of racism and xenophobia by means of criminal law

The Framework Decision on combating certain forms and expressions of racism and xenophobia by means of criminal law, adopted on 28 November 2008 by the

---

557 *Ibid.*, para. 36.

558 *Ibid.*, para. 39.

559 The reservation reads 'The Kingdom of the Netherlands will comply with the obligation to criminalize the denial, gross minimization, approval or justification of genocide or crimes against humanity laid down in Article 6, paragraph 1, of the Protocol where such conduct incites hatred, discrimination or violence on the grounds of race or religion.'

560 *Ibid.*, para. 34–35.

561 In addition, Article 15 of the Convention itself determines that the establishment, implementation and application of criminal procedural law powers for these offences must comply with the state obligations under the ECHR and ICCPR and must 'incorporate the principle of proportionality'.

Council of the European Union,[562] obliges member states to criminalize the incitement to hatred or violence and the denial of grave crimes. The Framework Decision replaced the non-binding Council Joint Action concerning action to combat racism and xenophobia, adopted on 15 July 1996,[563] whose main objective was to ensure effective legal cooperation between member states in combating racism and xenophobia.[564] However, it left member states the choice of incriminating the forms of conduct concerned.[565] According to the evaluation of the Joint Action, some difficulties were still experienced regarding judicial cooperation and therefore, there was a need for further approximation of member states' criminal law.[566]

The Framework Decision acknowledges that combating racism and xenophobia requires various kinds of measures and may not be limited to criminal matters.[567] Nevertheless, its objective is 'namely ensuring that racist and xenophobic offences are sanctioned in all member states by at least a minimum level of effective, proportionate and dissuasive criminal penalties'.[568] States may have more far-reaching offences. Although it was necessary to define a common criminal law approach in the EU to racism and xenophobia, given the member states' different cultural and legal traditions, full harmonization of criminal laws was not possible.[569] Therefore, the Framework Decision is limited to particularly serious forms of 'racism and xenophobia', terms that are contrary to an earlier draft,[570] not defined. The Decision is binding upon member states in relation to the result to be achieved, but leaves them the choice of the form and methods of implementation.[571]

Article 1(1) cites the offences concerning racism and xenophobia that member states must criminalize.[572] Only *intentional* conduct is punishable. The offences require a relatively strict connection between expression and resulting actions compared to the non-binding standards of the Council of Europe and the notion of hate speech employed by the ECtHR. Articles 1(1) a) and b) are limited to the public

---

562 Council Framework Decision 2008/913/JHA of 28 November 2008, OJ L 328/55, 6 December 2008.

563 Council Joint Action 96/443/JHA of 15 July 1996, OJ L 185, 24 July 1996, p. 5.

564 It was adopted to avoid so-called 'forum-shopping'.

565 Proposal for a Council Framework Decision on combating racism and xenophobia, 28 November 2001, COM(2001) 664 final, Explanatory Memorandum, p. 6.

566 Council Framework Decision, preamble, para. 4. In fact, the various reports of racism in Europe by the EUMC and ECRI were grounds for concern. See: COM(2001) 664 final, Explanatory Memorandum, p. 2–3.

567 *Ibid.*, para. 6.

568 *Ibid.*, para. 13.

569 *Ibid.*, para. 5–6.

570 'racism and xenophobia' were defined as 'the belief in race, colour, descent, religion or belief, national or ethnic origin as a factor determining aversion to individuals or groups'. See: COM(2001) 664 final, Explanatory Memorandum, p. 8.

571 COM(2001) 664 final, Explanatory Memorandum, p. 7; Article 34(2)(b) TEU.

572 Article 2 obliges member states to criminalize the 'instigation, aiding and abetting' of the conduct referred to in Article 1.

incitement to violence and hatred and the dissemination thereof. Articles 1(1) c) and d) are limited to the public condoning, denying or grossly trivialising crimes of genocide, crimes against humanity and war crimes that are *likely to incite to violence or hatred.* It concerns the grave crimes as defined in the Statute of the International Criminal Court (Art. 6–8) and the Charter of the International Military Tribunal (Art. 6). Member states have the choice to only criminalize the denial of these crimes, when they have been *established by a final decision* of a national and/or international court.[573] Furthermore, member states may prohibit the denial of crimes against a group defined by, for example, social status and political convictions.[574]

As for the implementation of the offences of Article 1(1), member states may 'choose to only punish conduct which is either carried out in a manner *likely to disturb public order* or which is *threatening, abusive or insulting*'.[575] This option may be interpreted as a possibility for member states, for example the UK, to ensure the criminalization of the conduct in Article 1(1) under (the terminology of) existing national offences that set higher requirements with regard to the effect expression must have on either third parties and society at large or the members of the group it targets. In fact, an earlier draft included more far-reaching offences, such as 'public incitement to racist or xenophobic behaviour which may cause substantial damage to individuals or groups concerned; public insults or threats towards individuals or groups for a racist or xenophobic purpose; and public dissemination or distribution of material containing expressions of racism and xenophobia'.[576] On these offences no consensus could be reached.

The current offences criminalize incitement, dissemination thereof and denial of crimes directed against a group or person defined by reference to '*race, colour, religion, descent or national or ethnic origin*'.[577] 'Religion' must be understood 'as broadly referring to persons defined by reference to their religious convictions or beliefs'.[578] However, it is provided that the reference to 'religion' is intended to cover, *at least*, conduct which is a *pretext* for directing acts against a group or person defined by reference to 'race, colour, descent, or national or ethnic origin'.[579] This implies again that, strictly speaking, the Framework Decision only obliges member states to criminalize cases of an 'intersectionality' between race and religion and 'multiple' or 'aggravated' racism. States, however, remain free to criminalize the offences on the basis of religion more broadly.

---

573 Article 1 (4).

574 Council Framework Decision, preamble, para. 10.

575 Article 1 (2).

576 COM(2001) 664 final, Explanatory Memorandum, p. 17.

577 'Descent' refers to groups or persons, who descend from persons identifiable by certain characteristics that not necessarily still exist. See: Council Framework Decision, preamble, para. 7.

578 *Ibid.*, para. 8.

579 Article 1 (3).

According to the Framework Decision, the offences must be punishable by criminal penalties of a maximum of at least between 1 and 3 years of imprisonment.[580] Furthermore, it determines that the investigation into or prosecution of the offences shall not be dependent on a report or an accusation made by a victim.[581] Finally, for other offences, member states must ensure that racist and xenophobic motivation is considered to be an aggravating circumstance or that such motivation may be taken into consideration by the courts in the determination of the penalties.[582]

The Framework Decision explicitly states that it shall not have the effect of modifying the obligation to respect freedom of expression and association.[583] Moreover, it shall not have the effect of requiring the adoption of measures contrary to the freedom of the press and other media and the rules governing their liability.[584] In other words, member states must always balance the enforcement of offences that implement Article 1 in a particular case with the fundamental rights of freedom of expression and association and must not abridge the freedom of the media to disseminate expression.

5. The International Covenant on Civil and Political Rights (ICCPR)

The International Covenant on Civil and Political Rights (ICCPR) was adopted by the National Assembly of the United Nations in 1966.[585] The UN Human Rights Committee (HRC) monitors the implementation of the Covenant articles, amongst others, by dealing with individual complaints of alleged violations of the articles. Its 'communications' are non-binding. The HRC publishes its interpretation of the Covenant articles in the form of General Comments that are considered to constitute authoritative legal analysis based on the HRC's practice. Therefore, the general comment to the right to freedom of expression protected in the ICCPR can be regarded as an important source for the interpretation of the right. Freedom of opinion and expression is protected in Articles 19 (1–2) ICCPR (5.1), while Article 19(3) determines the possible restrictions to this right (5.2). The obligation for states to prohibit by law 'any advocacy of national, racial or religious hatred that constitutes incitement to discrimination, hostility or violence' of Article 20(2) is compatible with and complements 19(3) (5.3).). The paragraph concludes with a

580 Article 3 (2).

581 Article 8.

582 Article 4.

583 Article 7 (1). Similarly, an earlier draft mentioned that the exercise of these freedoms as secured by Articles 10 and 11 ECHR must be balanced with the prevention of disorder or crime and the protection of the reputation or rights of others. See: COM(2001) 664 final, Explanatory Memorandum, p. 7.

584 Article 7 (2).

585 Adopted by the UN General Assembly, 16 December 1966, entered into force on 23 March 1976.

synthesis of the state obligations with regard to the restriction of hate speech under the ICCPR in the light of the factors from the analytic framework (5.4).

5.1. Articles 19(1–2) ICCPR: freedom of opinion and expression

Freedom of expression and information was considered to be the 'touchstone of all the freedoms to which the United Nations is consecrated'.[586] Therefore, consensus existed within the UN[587] on the inclusion of the right in the ICCPR.[588] Freedom of opinion and expression is protected under Article 19 ICCPR.

Article 19(1) protects 'the right to hold opinions without interference'. This is an absolute right, to which the Convention permits no exception or restriction.[589] Although 19(1) initially included both freedom of opinion and expression, – other than for 10 ECHR– it was decided to separate these rights, because of their different characters; freedom of opinion was closely related to freedom of thought and formed a right without qualifiers.[590]

New General Comment no. 34 on Article 19 (GC 34), adopted in 2011,[591] notes that it includes the right to change one's opinion, to be free from coercion of holding or not holding any opinion and from any impairment of rights under the Covenant on the basis of one's actual, perceived or supposed opinions. Furthermore, 19(1) protects all forms of opinion, including political, scientific, historic, moral or religious opinions; the criminalization of holding an opinion is incompatible with 19(1).[592]

Article 19(2) protects the right to freedom of expression as the 'freedom to seek receive and impart information and ideas of all kinds, regardless of frontiers, either orally, in writing or in print, in the form of art, or through any other media of his choice'. The words 'of all kinds' are not to be found in Article 10 ECHR. They are

586 UN General Assembly Resolution 59 (1), 14 December 1946.

587 E/CN.4/SR.37, 120, 170, 171.

588 In 1948, The United Nations Conference on Freedom of Information met in Geneva and prepared several draft conventions. Initially, a specific draft convention on freedom of information was prepared. Therefore, the question raised whether the ICCPR should include an article on freedom of expression and information at all. This draft convention was, however, never adopted.
See: Final Act, United Nations Conference on Freedom of Information, Geneva, Switzerland, 23 March – 21 April 1948. E/Conf.6/79.

589 New General Comment no. 34 on Article 19 notes in para. 5 that it can never become necessary to derogate from freedom of opinion during a state of emergency, even though the right is not listed as a non-derogatory right in Article 4 ICCPR.

590 Bossuyt, M.J., *Guide to the 'Travaux Préparatoires' of the International Covenant on Civil and Political Rights*, Dordrecht: Martinus Nijhoff Publishers 1987, p. 378.

591 HRC, Summary Record of the 2820th meeting, 21 July 2011, CCPR/C/SR.2820, para. 86. It replaces General Comment no. 10 that dates back to 1983. See: HRC, General Comment no. 10: Freedom of Expression (art. 19), 29 June 1983, HRI/GEN/1/Rev. 9 (Vol. 1), at 181;1–2 IHRR 9 (1994).

592 General Comment no. 34, para. 9–10.

taken to signify that 19(2) includes the expression and receipt of communications of every form of idea and opinion capable of transmission to others; political discourse, commentary on public affairs, discussion of human rights, journalism, cultural and artistic expression, religious discourse and commercial advertising. It even embraces expression that is regarded as 'deeply offensive'.[593]

Furthermore, it equally protects all forms of expression and the means of their dissemination, including spoken, written and sign language and non-verbal expression such as images and objects of art, books, newspapers, posters, banners, pamphlets, dress and all audio-visual, electronic and internet-based modes of expression.[594] Unlike 10 ECHR, Article 19 lacks a reference to the protection of the right 'without interference by public authority'. This has been explained as an emphasis on the horizontal application of the right and has been connected with the need to prevent control of all media, including modern mass media, in both the public and private sectors.[595]

GC 34 stresses that a free, uncensored and unhindered press or other media is one of the cornerstones of a democratic society and essential in any society to ensure freedom of opinion and expression and the participation in public affairs.[596] Article 19(2) therefore embraces – unlike in 10 ECHR – a general right of access to information held by public bodies, including a right whereby the media has access to information on public affairs and the right of the general public to receive media output.[597]

5.2. Article 19(3): restrictions on freedom of expression

Other than freedom of opinion, freedom of expression is not absolute, but may be restricted under the conditions set in Article 19(3). Article 19(3) stipulates that the exercise of freedom of expression carries with it '*special* duties and responsibilities'. The addition of the word 'special' in the ICCPR and not in the ECHR does not appear to be of particular importance. As in 10 ECHR, this reference does not constitute an inherent or implied restriction.[598]

Restrictions may only be imposed when they are 1) provided by law; and are 2) necessary; for a limited list of purposes of interference, being 3a) for respect of the rights or reputation of others; and 3b) for the protection of national security or of

593 *Ibid,*, para. 11.

594 *Ibid,* para. 12.

595 O'Flaherty, M., Freedom of Expression: Article 19 of the International Covenant on Civil and Political Rights and the Human Rights Committee's General Comment No 34, *Human Rights Law Review* 2012, vol. 4, p. 637.

596 General Comment no. 34, para. 13–17; 20.

597 *Ibid.,* para. 18–19. Furthermore, individuals must be able to acertain which public authorties, private individuals or bodies control or may control their files containing personal data.

598 Nowak, M., *U.N. Covenant on Civil and Political Rights: CCPR commentary*, Kehl: N.P. Engel 2005, p. 457.

public order (*ordre public*), or of public health or morals. To a certain extent, the restriction-system under 19(3) is comparable to that under 10(2) ECHR, but it also differs from it in several respects.

Strictly speaking, unlike 10(2), 19(3) does not require restrictions to be necessary 'in a democratic society'. However, in practice the HRC often invokes the role freedom of expression plays in ensuring a democratic society.[599] Furthermore, 19(3) cites a much more limited list of purposes of interference than 10(2) ECHR that also mentions the grounds of the interests of territorial integrity or public safety, for the prevention of crime, for preventing the disclosure of information received in confidence and for maintaining the authority and impartiality of the judiciary.

In relation to the ground of the rights of others, 'rights' includes – but is not limited to – human rights and 'others' relates to other persons individually or as members of a community and thus may refer to individual members of a community defined by its religious faith or ethnicity.[600] Unlike 10(2) ECHR, which uses the narrow term of the prevention of 'disorder', 19(3) uses the broader term of the protection of the 'public order'. On the basis on the maintenance of public order, it may be permitted to restrict speech in particular public spaces or expression that amounts to contempt of court.[601]

Importantly, the protection of 'morals' forms the only ground for which GC 34 elaborates a definition; 'the concept of morals derives from many social, philosophical and religious traditions; consequently, limitations… for the purpose of protecting morals must be based on principles not deriving exclusively from a single tradition. Any such limitations must be understood in the light of universality of human rights and the principle of non-discrimination.'[602] It thereby appears to aim to ensure the existence of a plurality of opinions, including in particular minority views.

In order to be deemed necessary, restrictions to freedom of expression must be proportional; they must be appropriate to achieve their protective function; the least intrusive instrument amongst those, which might achieve their protective function; and proportionate to the interest to be protected. GC 34 sets a particularly high threshold for restrictions and the burden to prove their necessity and proportionality is on the state, which must demonstrate the precise nature of the threat, and the necessity and proportionality of the specific action taken, 'in particular by establishing a direct and immediate connection between the expression and the threat' to the invoked restriction ground.[603]

Unlike the ECtHR, the HRC, which has explicitly refused to categorize forms of expression and subject any form of expression to varying degrees of limitation with

599 O'Flaherty 2012, p. 639.

600 General Comment no. 34, para. 28.

601 *Ibid.*, para. 31.

602 *Ibid.*, para. 32.

603 *Ibid.*, para. 34–35.

the result that some forms of expression, may suffer broader restrictions than others.[604] It has adopted the method of 'ad hoc balancing', i.e. presumptively treating all categories of expression the same and balancing the different interests at stake in an *ad hoc* fashion.

Nevertheless, a primary area, in which only a limited scope of restrictions on freedom of expression exists under the ICCPR, is political discourse. GC 34 states, for example, 'the value placed by the Covenant upon uninhibited expression is particularly high in the circumstances of public debate in a democratic society concerning figures in the public and political domain'. It expresses concern regarding laws such as defamation of the head of state and public officials and the prohibition of criticism of institutions.[605] Other than the ECtHR, it advocates 'the decriminalization of defamation' in general.[606]

Strikingly, GC 34 stresses that for the determination of the necessity of restrictions in a particular situation by the HRC, the scope of this freedom is not to be assessed by reference to a 'margin of appreciation'.[607] In an early communication concerning a ban by a broadcaster of those parts of a program discussing homosexuality, the HRC still considered that the non-interference by the State did not violate 19(3), because 'public morals differ widely. There is no universally applicable common standard. Consequently, in this respect, a certain margin of appreciation must be accorded to the responsible national authorities'.[608] This can be regarded as the ICCPR-counterpart of the margin of appreciation doctrine applied by the ECtHR that however appears to have been abandoned.

On the basis of GC 34, under the ICCPR the evaluation of restrictions to expression in the 'subjective' fields of morals and religion, such as alleged blasphemy and other religiously offensive speech, differs from that under the ECHR. In fact, GC 34 explicitly states: 'Prohibitions of displays of lack of respect for a religion or other belief system, including blasphemy laws, are incompatible with the Covenant', except when they meet the requirements of Article 20(2), and such laws may not 'discriminate in favour of or against one or certain religions or belief systems, or their adherents over another, or religious believers over non-believers' nor 'be used to prevent or punish criticism of religious leaders or commentary on religious doctrine and tenets of faith'.[609]

Likewise, 'Laws that criminalize the expression of opinions about historical facts' are deemed incompatible with the Covenant that 'does not permit general prohibition of expressions of an erroneous opinion or an incorrect interpretation of past events'.[610] It is argued that GC 34 hereby 'overrules' *Faurisson v. France*, in

---

604 *John Ballantyne, Davidson and McIntyre v. Canada,* (359/1989) and (385/1989) CCPR/C/47/D/359/1989 and 385/1989/Rev.1 (1993), para. 11.3.

605 General Comment no. 34, para. 38.

606 *Ibid.,* para. 47.

607 *Ibid.,* para. 36.

608 *Herzberg v. Finland,* (61/1979), CCPR/C/15/D/61/1979 (1982), para. 10.3.

609 General Comment no. 34, para. 48.

610 *Ibid.,* para. 49.

which the HRC found the criminal conviction of Faurisson for having denied the Holocaust not to violate 19(3), because Holocaust denial formed 'the principal vehicle for anti-Semitism'. In that case, the HRC, however, did consider that the application of the 'Gayssot Act' under different conditions may lead to decisions or measures incompatible with the Covenant.[611] On the basis of GC 34, the evaluation of restrictions to Holocaust denial under the ICCPR defers from that under the ECHR.

Overall, it can be said that Article 19, interpreted as in GC 34, aims to offer a robust protection of freedom of expression by affording the right a broad scope in 19(2) and laying down strict conditions for its restriction in 19(3). However, it has been pointed out that GC 34 sets standards (for blasphemy, Holocaust denial and defamation laws) to which many state parties do not comply and that are not necessarily grounded in the practice of the HRC – yet.[612]

5.3. Article 20(2): the prohibition of hate speech and relationship with Article 19

Article 20(2) obliges state parties to prohibit by law 'any advocacy of national, racial or religious hatred that constitutes incitement to discrimination, hostility or violence'. The Article was drafted in response to the Nazi racial hatred campaigns; its rationale was to combat fascism, racism and National Socialism at their roots and to prevent the public incitement of racial hatred and violence within a state or against other states and peoples.[613]

Its adoption was quite controversial; most Western States voted against it, arguing that Article 19(3) was sufficient to prevent incitement to racial hatred and that provisions going beyond this would endanger freedom of expression. The Soviet representative held on the other hand that the experiences with manipulative power of modern propaganda called for far-reaching criminal prohibitions. The final Article reflects a middle course; it obliges a prohibition *by law*, but does not require a prohibition by *criminal* law, nor does it authorize prior censorship.[614]

General Comment 11 on Article 20 (GC 20) stresses its mandatory character.[615] Many states however made reservations to the Article. For example, The United Kingdom declared that Article 20 must be interpreted in conformity with the rights of political liberty in Articles 19–22 ICCPR and reserved the right not to enact any prohibitions going beyond the existing legislation.[616]

It has been argued that Article 20 can be understood as placing a special duty on the state to ensure the rights to life, non-discrimination and equality guaranteed in

611 *Faurisson v. France*, (550/1993), CCPR/C/58/D/550/1993, para. 9.3; 9.6–9.7.
612 O'Flaherty 2012, p. 653.
613 Nowak 2005, p. 475.
614 Nowak 2005, p. 470.
615 UN Human Rights Committee, General Comment No. 11, adopted 29 July 1983.
616 Nowak 2005, p. 479.

Articles 6, 2(1) and 26 ICCPR. To combat the systematic violation of these central articles, it was decided to create preventive prohibitions in the area of formation of public opinion. Thereby the prohibition of discrimination would be given a certain priority over the rights of political liberty.[617]

Although the Article equally applies to other rights in the ICCPR, it has a close nexus to freedom of expression. On the interrelationship between Articles 19 and 20, GC 34 states not only that they 'are compatible with and complement each other', but also that 'a limitation that is justified on the basis of Article 20 must also comply with Article 19(3)'. The distinction between the specific forms of expression indicated in Article 20 and other acts that may be subject to restriction under 19(3) is that only with regard to the former are state parties obliged to have legal prohibitions. However, all restrictions to freedom of expression must be justifiable in strict conformity with Article 19.[618]

This appears to settle a certain ambiguity in the approach by the HRC towards Articles 19 – 20. In fact, the HRC has only dealt with violations of Article 19 on the merits, not with Article 20(2). In an early case concerning anti-Semitic expression, the HRC declared the complaint of a violation of Article 19 inadmissible by reference to 20(2).[619] In a case concerning hate speech against Roma's, the HRC found the complaint of a violation of Article 20(2) inadmissible, because the authors had insufficiently substantiated the facts. Thereby it avoided the question whether individuals may invoke Article 20 under the Optional Protocol.[620] In *Faurission v. France*, the HRC ignored Article 20 and dealt with the case on the merits under 19(3).[621] In another case concerning anti-Semitic expression, *Ross v. Canada*, the HRC adopted a middle course by using Article 20 as an additional argument in the interpretation of Article 19(3).[622]

This latter approach resembles the increasingly indirect application by the ECtHR of the prohibition of the abuse of rights in Article 17 ECHR. Although, under the ECHR it has not been established with so many words that a limitation that is justified on the basis of Article 17 must also comply with Article 10(2) – yet. The ICCPR also has a prohibition of the abuse of rights in Article 5 ICCPR. However, GC 34 rather stresses that the function of this article as a tool to prevent excessive restrictions than as a justification for restrictions. It recalls the provision

617 Nowak 2005, p. 471.

618 General Comment no. 34, para. 50–52.

619 The complainant complained of a violation of Article 19, because he was prevented from disseminating anti-Semitic messages through the post and telephone system. His complaint was declared inadmissible, because the State had the obligation to prevent such advocacy of racial and religious hatred. *J.R.T. and the W.G. Party v. Canada*, 104/1981, CCPR/C/OP/2 (1984), para. 8 (b).

620 By doing so the HRC avoided the question as to whether the expressions constituted prohibited hate speech. According to dissenting judge Anor, the HRC should have applied 20 and discussed this matter on the merits. *Vassilari et al. v. Greece*, 1570/2007, CCPR/C/95/D/1570/2007 (2009).

621 *Faurisson v. France*, 550/1993, CCPR/C/58/D/550/1993.

622 *Ross v. Canada*, 736/1997, CCPR/C/70/D/736/1997.

directly after stressing that restrictions on freedom of expression may not jeopardize the right itself and that the relation between right and restriction and between norm and exception must not be reversed.[623] This supports the broad scope of Article 19. Other than the ECtHR, the HRC thus appears to object to the categorical exclusion of any expression, including Holocaust denial, from it on the basis of either Article 20(2) and/ or 5.[624]

Article 20(2) only prohibits the 'advocacy of hatred' that constitutes 'incitement to discrimination, hostility or violence'. During the drafting of Article 20(2), it was pointed out that 'incitement to violence' was a legally valid concept, while 'incitement to discrimination' or 'incitement to hostility' was not. On the other hand, it was argued that to prohibit only incitement to violence would not represent progress in international legislation. Often it was hostility or discrimination that led to violence.[625] Strictly speaking, the article requires a stricter connection between the expression (incitement) and subsequent actions (discrimination, violence) than the ECtHR, whose notion of hate speech extends to 'spreading and justifying hatred based on (religious) intolerance', and ICERD that prohibits the 'dissemination of ideas' and the 'incitement to hatred' separate from discrimination or violence.

Some argue that Articles 19–20 ICCPR provide precise and coherent standards for prohibitions on hate speech. Although the question could be asked whether there is any scope under 19(3) for restrictions which go beyond the requirements of 20(2), there would be very little scope for this.[626] Others stress that the exact interpretation of the terms in Article 20(2) remains uncertain.[627] Between 2008 and 2012, the Office of the High Commissioner for Human Rights (OHCHR) has held a series of expert seminars on Articles 19 and 20 ICCPR with regard to freedom of expression and incitement to hatred to clarify the scope of state obligations under 20 ICCPR. The outcome document, the Rabat Plan of Action, proposed a high threshold for the criminal prohibition of incitement to hatred.[628] It was suggested that the domestic legal framework on incitement should be guided by express reference to Article 20 of the ICCPR and should consider including robust definitions of key terms like hatred, discrimination, violence, hostility, etc.[629]

For the determination of criminal liability for incitement to hatred, a six part threshold test was proposed based on the factors: context; speaker; intent; content

---

623 General Comment no. 34, para. 21.

624 *Faurisson v. France*, 550/1993, CCPR/C/58/D/550/1993.

625 Bossuyt 1987, p. 405; 408.

626 Mendel, T., Does International Law Provide for Consistent Rules on Hate Speech?, Herz & Molnar 2012, p. 417–429.

627 O'Flaherty 2012.

628 Rabat Plan of Action on the prohibition of advocacy of national, racial or religious hatred that constitutes incitement to discrimination, hostility or violence, Conclusions and recommendations emanating from the four regional expert workshops organized by OHCHR, in 2011, and adopted by experts in Rabat, Morocco on 5 October 2012.

629 Legislation could draw, inter alia, from the guidance and definitions provided in the Camden Principles, Principle 12.

or form; extent of the speech; and likelihood, including imminence. The test provides clear but broad parameters that could form a guideline for a more consistent interpretation and application of national incitement offences by national judges. A similar but slightly adapted test has been proposed in the context of ICERD (para. 6.2 *infra*). According to the test, Article 20(2) ICCPR requires 'advocacy' and 'incitement' rather than mere distribution or circulation, thus 'intent' and not mere negligence and recklessness. As for the identification of the degree of risk of resulting harm, the courts must determine that there was 'a reasonable probability that the speech would succeed in inciting actual action against the target group, recognizing that such causation should be rather direct', thus a 'likelihood, including imminence'.[630]

Restrictions to expression that has such a direct connection with subsequent actions of discrimination or violence are certainly permissible under 19(3). For example, in *Ross v. Canada* the HRC found the removal of a teacher from his teaching position for having expressed anti-Semitic views in out-of-school activities permissible under Article 19(3); although there was no direct evidence that the author's off-duty conduct had impacted on the school district, it was reasonable to anticipate that there was a causal link between the expressions and the 'poisoned school environment' experienced by Jewish children in the School district through the 'repeated and continual harassment in the form of derogatory name calling of Jewish students, carving of swastikas into desks of Jewish children, drawing of swastikas on blackboards and general intimidation of Jewish students'. The restriction was necessary to protect their right and freedom to have a school system 'free from bias, prejudice and intolerance'.[631]

Unlike the ICERD, Article 20(2) ICCPR includes religion as a discriminatory ground. A highly controversial issue in the past has been the relationship between Articles 19 and 20 with regard to attacks on a particular religion and its distinction from attacks on religious adherents.[632] Therefore, it will be interesting to see the communication of the HRC on the complaint of violation of Article 20(2) ICCPR with regard to the acquittal of Dutch politician Geert Wilders with regard to his statements about Islam and Muslims in the context of the public debate on immigration and integration, filed by a group of Dutch-Moroccan Muslims.[633] Firstly, it is not certain that the HRC will decide that individuals may invoke Article 20 under the Optional Protocol, but if so, it might for the first time directly deal with a case on the merits on the ground of Article 20(2).

The question is whether the HRC will then address the question that was underexposed before the national court; whether Wilders' critical statements about

630 Outcome document, para. 22, p. 6.

631 *Ross v. Canada*, 736/1997, CCPR/C/70/D/736/1997, para. 4.3; 11.6.

632 Temperman, J., Blasphemy, Defamation of Religions and Human Rights Law, *Netherlands Quarterly of Human Rights* 2008, 26/4, p. 517–545.

633 Communication of 15 November 2011, available at: www.prakkendoliveira.nl/user/file/complaint-ep-geanonimiseerde-s60bw-111111712190.pdf.

Islam and Muslims could not be regarded as mere criticism of a religion, because the statements, according to their context, could be interpreted as being directed against Arabs and immigrants on the basis of both their religion and national, ethnic background (see further *para.* 6.4). Even if the HRC assumes that this is the case, on the basis of the strict requirements developed for 'incitement' under Article 20(2) during the previously discussed expert seminars, it is not certain that the HRC will decide that the acquittal in the *Wilders* case amounts to a violation of that article. This does not signify that, if Wilders would have been convicted and had filed a complaint of a violation of freedom of expression, his conviction could not be considered permissible under Article 19(3).

5.4. Synthesis ICCPR

Article 20(2) ICCPR obliges states to prohibit by law 'advocacy of hatred' only when it constitutes 'incitement to discrimination, hostility or violence', but not necessarily by *criminal* law. To date, the HRC has not directly dealt with cases concerning a violation of article 20(2) ICCPR. Whether individuals may invoke 20(2) ICCPR under the Optional Protocol remains undecided. Recent research into the state obligations to prohibit 'hate speech' under 20(2) proposes high thresholds for the criminal prohibition of 'incitement', including: 'intent' and a 'likelihood, including imminence' that the speech would succeed in inciting actual action against the target group. This does not signify that article 20(2) would be limited to literal incitements to concrete acts. But, on the basis of the proposed requirements, national acquittals or the refusal of a state to prosecute for a particular case of hate speech are not likely to amount to a violation of 20(2) ICCPR. At the same time, convictions for these cases of hate speech may very well be permissible under Article 19(3). Hence, under the ICCPR a certain margin of appreciation exists for states to counter 'hate speech', which has consequences for its effect on national law.

In any event, restrictions to hate speech must comply with 19(3). For *criminal* restrictions, the HRC strictly holds on to the threshold of 'incitement'; criminal offences of blasphemy, defamation or holocaust denial are incompatible with the ICCPR. This does not signify that in certain contexts extreme speech about a religion, defamatory statements about a particular group or the denial of the Holocaust cannot constitute an 'incitement', the restriction of which cannot be permissible under 19(3) or even be required under 20(2). It is uncertain to which extent 19(3) would allow for civil prohibitions of statements about a group that directly harm the dignity of the group members, separate from its possible effect on third parties or the public order. It appears that for a consistent determination of restrictions to hate speech under 20(2) and 19(3) ICCPR the distinction between factual statements and value judgments or between racial remarks and speech about religion could form important factors when weighing the specific harmful effects of speech in question against the interest of public debate.

6. The International Convention on the Elimination of All Forms of Racial Discrimination (ICERD)

The International Convention on the Elimination of All Forms of Racial Discrimination (ICERD) was adopted by the National Assembly of the United Nations in 1965.[634] The Committee on the Elimination of All Forms of Racial Discrimination (CERD) monitors the implementation of the Convention articles, amongst others, by dealing with individual complaints of alleged violations of the articles. Its 'communications' are non-binding. ICERD prohibits all forms of racial discrimination (6.1). More specifically, Article 4a ICERD obliges member states to criminalize certain forms of hate speech on the basis of *race* (6.2), albeit with due regard to the fundamental rights enumerated in Article 5 ICERD, notably freedom of expression (6.3). The possible 'intersectionality of race and religion' raised the question of whether under ICERD additional standards must be developed for discrimination and hate speech on account of religion (6.4).

6.1. The prohibition of all forms of racial discrimination in ICERD

The ICERD is the primary binding international instrument that specifically prohibits racial discrimination.[635] It was adopted after the establishment of a – non-binding – Declaration on racial discrimination in 1963.[636] Parallel to the Declaration and Convention on *racial discrimination*, a Draft Declaration and Convention on *religious intolerance and discrimination* was prepared.[637] The two sets were conceived as 'twin' declarations and conventions; both rooted in an outbreak of anti-Semitic incidents around 1959 and 1960.[638]

The decision to split the instruments of racial and religious discrimination was a compromise solution to overcome the opposition of mainly Arab countries eager to displace the issue of anti-Semitism and Communist representatives who did not consider religious discrimination to be an important matter.[639] Consensus on the creation of norms in the field of religion, notably on definitions, proved particularly difficult and a binding Convention on Religious Intolerance did not come into

634 General Assembly Resolution 2106 (XX), 21 December 1965.

635 Schwelb, E., The International Convention on the Elimination of All Forms of Racial Discrimination, *The International and Comparative Law Quarterly* 1966, vol. 15, no. 4, p. 996–1068.

636 Proclaimed by UN General Assembly Resolution 1904 (XVIII), 20 November 1963.

637 Lerner, N., The Nature and Minimum Standards of Freedom of Religion or Belief, *Brigham Young University Law Review* 2000, p. 905–932; Sullivan, D.J., Advancing the Freedom of Religion or Belief Through the UN Declaration on the Elimination of Religious Intolerance and discrimination, *The American Journal of International Law* 1988, vol. 82, no. 3, p. 487–520.

638 Lerner, N., *The U.N. Convention on the Elimination of all Forms of Racial Discrimination*, Alphen aan den Rijn: Sijthoff & Noordhoff 1980, p. 8.

639 Lerner 1980, p. 2.

being. After long deliberation, the non-binding Declaration on the Elimination of All Forms of Intolerance and of Discrimination Based on Religion or Belief was adopted in 1981.[640] It is therefore said that there are parallel unequal regimes for the elimination of racial and religious discrimination in international human rights law.[641]

ICERD reasons from the premise underlying human rights law that human beings are born with a distinctive inheritance consisting of genetic and other characteristics that may not form a ground for discrimination. The Preamble of the Convention stresses the conviction that 'any doctrine of superiority based on racial differentiation is scientifically false, morally condemnable, socially unjust and dangerous, and that there is no justification for racial discrimination, in theory or in practice, anywhere'. State parties to the Convention therefore resolved 'to adopt all necessary measures for speedily eliminating racial discrimination in all its forms and manifestations'.

Racial discrimination is defined in Article 1(1) as 'any distinction, exclusion, restriction or preference based on race, colour, descent, or national or ethnic origin which has the purpose or effect of nullifying or impairing the recognition, enjoyment or exercise, on an equal footing, of human rights and fundamental freedoms in the political, economic, social, cultural or any other field of public life'. Its prohibition in Article 2 is thus not confined to *intentional* discrimination, but comprises discrimination in *effect*, which is sometimes equated with *indirect* discrimination.[642]

The umbrella term for ICERD is not 'race' but 'racial discrimination'.[643] The scope of ICERD is broader than discrimination due to its biological characteristics and encompasses other aspects that make people different.[644] Article 1 mentions five discriminatory grounds being 'race, colour, descent, or national or ethnic origin'. The notion of racial discrimination is, however, more complex because the article excludes 'distinctions, exclusions, restrictions or preferences between *citizens and non-citizens*' and 'special measures' of positive discrimination.

Religion was deliberately excluded from the catalogue of discriminatory grounds and discrimination on the basis of religion therefore does not fall under the ambit of ICERD. Some authors, however, stress the impossibility of disentangling racial or ethnic characteristics from religious characteristics. Religion is often a central component of ethnic group identity and interwoven in the political, cultural

640 Proclaimed by UN General Assembly Resolution 36/55, 25 November 1981.

641 Keane, D., Addressing the aggravated meeting point of race and religion, *University of Maryland Law Journal of Race, Religion, Gender & Class* 2006, p. 367.

642 General Recommendation no. 32, 6 October 2009, CERD/C/GC/32, para. 7. On these definitions, see also: Vandenhole, W., *Non-Discrimination and Equality in the View of the UN Human Rights Treaty Bodies*, Antwerpen: Intersentia 2005, p. 35–36; 40–42.

643 Thornberry, P., Forms of Hate Speech and the Convention on the Elimination of all Forms of Racial Discrimination (ICERD), *Religion & Human Rights* 2010, vol. 5, p. 102.

644 Lindgren Alves, J.A., Race and Religion in the United Nations Committee on the Elimination of Racial Discrimination, *University of San Francisco Law Review* 2008, vol. 42, p. 952.

and socio-economic life of the community. Religion thus might play a weighty role in xenophobia, racism and group hatred.[645]

In fact, the Convention prohibits *racial* discrimination in the enjoyment of rights enumerated in its Article 5, including freedom of *religion*. Therefore, it has been argued that so-called 'aggravated discrimination', that is when racial discrimination is aggravated by religious discrimination, should fall under the scope of ICERD.[646] The Committee on the Elimination of All Forms of Racial Discrimination (CERD) has explicitly recognized the 'intersection between racial and religious discrimination'.[647] CERD has notably also explored the overlap between race, ethnicity and religion in cases concerning hate speech.

6.2. Article 4 ICERD: the prohibition of hate speech

Article 4 ICERD obliges member states to criminalize forms of hate speech and reads:

> States Parties condemn all propaganda and all organizations which are based on ideas or theories of superiority of one race or group of persons of one colour or ethnic origin, or which attempt to justify or promote racial hatred and discrimination in any form, and undertake to adopt immediate and positive measures designed to eradicate all incitement to, or acts of, such discrimination and, to this end, with due regard to the principles embodied in the Universal Declaration of Human Rights and the rights expressly set forth in article 5 of this Convention, inter alia:
>
> (a) Shall declare an offence punishable by law all dissemination of ideas based on racial superiority or hatred, incitement to racial discrimination, as well as all acts of violence or incitement to such acts against any race or group of persons of another colour or ethnic origin, and also the provision of any assistance to racist activities, including the financing thereof;
> (b) Shall declare illegal and prohibit organizations, and also organized and all other propaganda activities, which promote and incite racial discrimination, and shall recognize participation in such organizations or activities as an offence punishable by law;
> (c) Shall not permit public authorities or public institutions, national or local, to promote or incite racial discrimination.

Its drafters regarded Article 4 as central to the struggle against racial discrimination. At the time, there was a widespread fear of the revival of authoritarian ideologies.[648]

645 Sullivan 1988, p. 508; Lerner 2000.
646 Keane 2006.
647 General Recommendation no. 32, 6 October 2009, CERD/C/GC/32, para. 7.
648 General Recommendation no. 15, 23 March 1993, CERD/A/48/18, para. 1.

Nevertheless, the article evoked lively debates. This notably also applied to Article 4 (a) that cites four categories of offences:[649]

1) Dissemination of ideas based on racial superiority or hatred;
2) Incitement to racial hatred;
3) All acts of violence against any race or group of persons of another colour or ethnic origin;
4) Incitement to such acts.

The proposal to prohibit incitement to violence met little opposition. Less consensus existed about the other categories.[650] Many emphasized the connection between the propagation of racial hatred and the incitement to discrimination; 'the fact of creating an atmosphere of racial hatred would inevitably lead indirectly to racial discrimination'.[651] Others considered that states could not intervene before acts of violence are committed, or are likely to be committed. The criminalization of advocacy to racial discrimination and hatred would amount to punishing intentions or feelings. On the other hand, states could not wait until the unlimited right of expression and association reaches a stage of imminent violence against sectors of the population.[652]

Strictly speaking, Article 4 (a) only obliges the criminalization of incitement to discrimination, but it may be read as including incitement to racial hatred. After all, the heading of Article 4 combines the promotion of 'racial hatred and discrimination'. Moreover, the obligation to criminalize the 'dissemination of ideas based on racial hatred' appears to be even more far-reaching. It covers a variety of racist expressions that would not meet the threshold of Article 20(2) ICCPR that prohibits any advocacy of national, racial or religious hatred that constitutes incitement to discrimination, hostility or violence.

Although the preamble of the Convention rejects any doctrine of racial superiority, the actual prohibition of the 'dissemination of ideas' met strong opposition; the Convention should not be read as objecting to the dissemination of scientific ideas that deal with questions concerning race. The proposal not to prohibit the dissemination of racist theories at all, because in a democracy such opinions must be countered with the use of arguments and not by criminal law,[653] was however rejected. CERD has continued to stress the compatibility of the prohibition with the right to freedom of opinion and expression.[654]

---

649 *Ibid.* para. 3.

650 Mahalic, D. & Mahalic, J., The Limitation Provisions of the ICERD, *Human Rights Quarterly* 1987, p. 94.

651 Lerner 1980, p. 52.

652 Cf. Meron, T., The Meaning and Reach of the ICERD, *The American Journal of International Law* 1985, vol. 79, no. 2, p. 296–298; Lerner 1980, p. 51.

653 Lerner 1980, p. 46–47.

654 For example in: General Recommendation 15 (1993) UN Doc. A/48/18, para. 4.

In fact, in its general recommendation no. 35 on combatting racist hate speech, CERD considers that the prohibitions on dissemination of ideas of racial superiority are an important complement to the provisions on incitement. Whereas the provisions on dissemination of ideas attempt to discourage the flow of racist ideas 'upstream', those on incitement address their 'downstream' effects.[655] As Article 4 is not self-executing, States parties must adopt legislation to combat legislation that falls within its scope. CERD has recommended States parties to declare and effectively sanction as offences punishable by law:

(a) All dissemination of ideas based on racial or ethnic superiority or hatred, by what ever means;
(b) Incitement to hatred, contempt or discrimination against members of a group on grounds of their race, colour, descent or national or ethnic origin;
(c) Threats or incitement to violence against persons or groups on the grounds in (b) above;
(d) Expression of insults, ridicule or slander of persons or groups or justification of hatred, contempt or discrimination on the grounds in (b) above, when it clearly amounts to incitement to hatred or discrimination;
(e) Participation in organizations and activities which promote and incite racial discrimination.[656]

Furthermore, CERD has recommended that state parties declare as offences punishable by law 'public denials or attempts to justify crimes of genocide and crimes against humanity, as defined by international law, provided that they clearly constitute incitement to racial violence or hatred.' Contrarily, 'the expression of opinions about historical facts' should not be prohibited or punished.[657]

To a certain extent, the interpretation of Article 4 (a) by CERD matches the interpretation of 20(2) ICCPR by the HRC in GC no. 34, to which CERD refers several times in recommendation no. 35. For the qualification of 'dissemination' and 'incitement' as offences punishable by law, CERD takes into account a number of contextual factors that are inspired by the six part threshold test developed for the determination of criminal liability for 'incitement' under 20(2) ICCPR (para. 5.3 *supra*).[658] The factors concern: the content and form of the speech; the economic, social and political climate; the speaker; the reach of the speech; the objectives of the speech. These factors again provide clear but broad parameters that could form a guideline for a more consistent interpretation and application of national hate speech bans by national judges.

CERD specifies that '[r]acist hate speech can take many forms and is not confined to explicitly racial remarks. (...) speech attacking particular racial or

655 General Recommendation no. 35, 26 September 2013, CERD/C/GC/35, para.11; 30.
656 *Ibid.*, para. 13.
657 *Ibid.*, para. 14.
658 *Ibid.*, para. 15.

ethnic groups may employ indirect language in order to disguise its targets and objectives.' It emphasizes 'the role of politicians and other public opinion-formers in contributing to the creation of a negative climate towards groups protected by the Convention' and the extent of communication; 'in particular when repetition suggests the existence of a deliberate strategy to engender hostility towards ethnic and racial groups'.

A distinction with the ICCPR remains, however, that it is only with regard to the incitement offences that, according to CERD, state parties should take into account as important elements the *intention* of the speaker and the *imminent risk or likelihood* that the conduct desired or intended by the speaker will result from the speech in question. In principle this does not apply to the offence of dissemination of ideas based on racial superiority or hatred, the threshold of which may thus be exceeded earlier.[659]

6.3. Articles 4 and 5 ICERD: relationship between hate speech and freedom of expression

During the drafting, the 'due regard clause' was inserted into Article 4 ICERD, which requires that measures to eliminate incitement and discrimination must be made with due regard to the principles of the Universal Declaration of Human Rights (UDHR) and the rights enumerated in Article 5 ICERD, including freedom of expression: 'In particular, this clause was intended to protect against overly broad limitations on the freedom of expression and association.'[660] The due regard clause can be interpreted in different ways.[661] It can signify firstly, that states are not allowed to take action that would impair the 'freedoms'; secondly, that a balance must be struck between the freedoms and the duties under the Convention; and thirdly, that states may not invoke the protection of civil rights in order to avoid implementation of the Convention.

Many states, however, made reservations, declarations or interpretations to the Convention to the effect that they are only willing to adopt measures of implementation that are compatible with freedom of expression and association. For example, America made the following declaration: 'The Constitution of the United States contains provisions for the protection of individual rights, such as the right of

---

659 CERD has once stated that the mere acts of 'dissemination' and 'incitement' are criminalized, despite the lack of intention to commit an offence and irrespective of the consequences of such dissemination or incitement. However, it has been argued that, precisely given the non-self-executing nature of Article 4, state parties have a margin of appreciation in its application, which covers the *actus reus* and *mens rea* for the offence. See: CERD Study of 1983, para. 83; 96, UN Doc. A/CONF.119/10; Thornberry 2010, p. 109–110.

660 Lerner 1980, p. 48; Mahalic & Mahalic 1987, p. 89.

661 Partsch, K.J., Racial speech and human rights: Article 4 of the Convention on the Elimination of All Forms of Racial Discrimination, in: Coliver, S., (ed.), *Striking a Balance: Hate Speech, Freedom of Expression and Non-Discrimination*, London: Article 19 1992, p. 21–28. Cited by: Thornberry 2010, p. 111.

free speech, and nothing in the Convention shall be deemed to require or to authorize legislation or other action by the United States of America incompatible with the provisions of the Constitution of the United States of America.'[662]

Nevertheless, CERD opines that during the drafting of the Convention the balance with the principle of freedom of expression has already been made;[663] 'it could not have been the intention of the drafters of the Convention to enable State parties to construe the phrase safeguarding the human rights in question as cancelling the obligations relating to the prohibition of the racist activities concerned'.[664] With regard to the scope of national provisions implementing Article 4 (a), CERD has expressed its disapproval of the insertion of extra elements to the offences, such as the requirement that expression generates a disturbance of the public order or the risk of violence.[665, 666]

CERD considers, on the other hand, that the due regard clause does imply that, in the creation and application of offences, the principles of the UDHR and the rights in Article 5 ICERD, particularly freedom of expression, must be given appropriate weight in decision-making processes. For example, the expression of ideas and opinions made in the context of academic debates, political engagement or similar activity, and without incitement to hatred, contempt, violence or discrimination, should be regarded as legitimate exercises of the right to freedom of expression, even when such ideas are controversial.[667]

The right to freedom of opinion and expression also has a positive role in combating racial hatred. CERD stipulates that the protection of persons from racist hate speech is not simply one of opposition between the right to freedom of expression and its restriction for the benefit of protected groups; the latter also enjoy the right to freedom of expression. However, 'racist hate speech potentially silences the free speech of its victims'. States parties should therefore adopt policies empowering all groups within the purview of ICERD to exercise their right to freedom of expression.[668]

6.4. Additional standards for discrimination and hate speech on the ground of religion?

CERD uses an extensive interpretation of the 'grounds' of discrimination in practice by addressing situations of 'double' or 'multiple' discrimination;[669] when an element of 'intersectionality' between racial and religious discrimination can be

662 UN Doc. ST/LEG/SER.D/11, p. 98.
663 Report CERD 1987, p. 69 *et seq.* Cf. Mahalic & Mahalic 1987, p. 91.
664 UN Doc. A/33/18 (1978), 112, cited by Meron 1985, p. 300–301.
665 Mahalic & Mahalic 1987, p. 98.
666 With the implementation of national legislation, however, many states have made their own further balance with freedom of expression. *Ibid.*, p. 93.
667 General Recommendation no. 35, para. 19; 25.
668 *Ibid.*, para. 27–29. Cf. Rabat Plan of Action, para. 25.
669 On these definitions, see also: Vandenhole 2005, p. 36; 42–43.

established, CERD considers itself competent to deal with individual complaints.[670] Contrarily, when the alleged discrimination or hate speech targets a particular religion or religious group alone, CERD considers itself not competent.

Hence, in an early case CERD found the conviction for the circulation of leaflets vilifying Islamic immigrants, Islam and the Norwegian immigration policy for Islamic foreign workers, to be in line with ICERD, because the leaflets 'had treated the religious beliefs of the immigrants as the hallmark of their racial and ethnic identity and had explicitly invoked racial categories and racist attitudes'.[671]

Contrarily, in another case CERD declared a complaint concerning public statements of a politician against immigration and Muslims inadmissible, because 'the impugned statements specifically referred to the Koran, to Islam and to Muslims in general without any reference whatsoever to race, colour, descent, or national or ethnic origin.' Therefore 'no specific national or ethnic groups were directly targeted as such'. According to CERD, 'Muslims currently living in the State party are of heterogeneous origin' and 'Islam is not a religion practiced solely by a particular group'.[672]

For similar reasons, CERD declared a complaint concerning statements about Muslims in a political debate about the prohibition of corporal punishment to be inadmissible. In both cases, CERD recognized 'the importance of the interface between race and religion' and its competence to consider a claim of 'double' discrimination. However, the *Travaux Préparatoires* of the Convention unquestionably revealed that 'discrimination based exclusively on religious grounds was not intended to fall within the purview of the Convention'.[673]

The approach of CERD in individual complaints can be contrasted with its consideration of state reports, where it has stressed its concern about increasing 'Islamophobia' in certain countries,[674] for example in the Netherlands.[675] An examination on the elaboration of complementary standards to combat racism and discrimination within the UN, however, resulted in the conclusion, not that ICERD should be extended to cover discrimination and hate speech on the basis of religion, but that CERD adopts a General Recommendation on methodologies for multiple or aggravated discrimination.[676]

---

670 General Recommendation no. 32, 6 October 2009, CERD/C/GC/32, para. 7.

671 Communication No. 134 B/1981, CERD/C/107/Add.4 (1984), para. 14. Cited by Sullivan 1988, p. 508–509.

672 *P.S.N. v. Denmark*, Communication No. 36/2006, A/62/18, para. 6.2–6.3.

673 *A.W.R.A.P. v. Denmark*, Communication No. 37/2006, A/62/18, para. 6.3.

674 Berry, S.E., Bringing Muslim Minorities within the International Convention on the Elimination of All Forms of Racial Discrimination – Square Peg in a Round Hole?, *Human Rights Law Review* 2011, vol. 11, no. 3, p. 431.

675 Concluding Observations regarding The Netherlands, 1 April 2010, CERD/C/NLD/CO/17–18, para. 14.

676 Human Rights Council, Complementary International Standards, Conclusions and Recommendations, 18 February 2008, A/HRC/AC.1/1/CRP.4; Report, 27 August 2007, A/HRC/4/WG.3/6.

It has been suggested that CERD should put more emphasis on the concepts of 'discrimination in effect' or 'indirect discrimination', because '[c]ases can arise where the hate speech discourse is careful to avoid direct racial or ethnic insult, and may have 'switched' its language from the racial/ethnic to the religious in relation to the same targeted community'.[677] Furthermore, it has been argued that not only perpetrators of discrimination, but also Muslim immigrant communities identify themselves along both ethnic and religious lines. Discrimination against Muslims may thus disproportionately affect those belonging to an ethnic group and racism does not need to be aimed at one homogeneous ethnic group alone in order to constitute racism.[678]

Controversy has equally arisen over the question of whether ICERD should cover attacks against a religion *as such*. After the affair of the Danish cartoons, despite the pressure of Islamic states, CERD has refused to adopt a general recommendation for state parties to prohibit blasphemy or 'defamation of religions'.[679] It is generally accepted that the Convention protects – vulnerable – groups and individuals rather than – religious – norms and practices.[680]

It would be interesting to compare the success rates of a possible complaint about the acquittal of Dutch politician Geert Wilders on the grounds of group defamation and incitement to hatred and discrimination with regard to his statements about Islam and Muslims before the monitoring bodies of the three different international instruments: the ECtHR/ ECHR (para. 1.6 *supra*), the HRC/ ICCPR (para. 5.3 *supra*) and CERD/ ICERD. Paradoxically, the success rate may be the highest before CERD, even though ICERD is strictly speaking limited to racial discrimination and hate speech.[681]

6.5. Synthesis ICERD

Article 4a ICERD obliges states to prohibit by *criminal* law not only the 'incitement to hatred, discrimination or violence' on grounds of race, but also the much broader

---

677 Thornberry 2010, p. 104.

678 Berry 2011, p. 446–447.

679 Lindgren Alves 2008, p. 953.

680 Cf. Thornberry 2010, p. 115–116; Berry 2011, p. 438.

681 After all, out of all three treaties, the ICERD is the only treaty that actually obliges its member states to *criminalize* the dissemination of ideas based on hatred and the incitement to hatred and discrimination and to effectively enforce offences that criminalize such expression. In fact, the national offences on the basis of which Wilders was prosecuted were introduced in order to implement the ICERD into Dutch law. Furthermore, Wilders' statements about Islam and Muslims in the context of a public debate on immigration and integration may form a pre-eminent case of an 'intersectionality between race and religion'. Finally, in principle and generally speaking, under 4 (a) ICERD the required degree of probability that the speech would succeed in inciting actual action against the target group is in principle less strict than under 20 ICCPR. Therefore, the threshold for criminal liability for hate speech under the ICERD may be reached earlier. See further: Chapter 5 on The Netherlands.

'dissemination of ideas based on racial or ethnic superiority or hatred'. Unlike the ECHR and the ICCPR, the ICERD thus actually obliges its member states to *criminalize* these forms of hate speech and to effectively enforce the prohibitions. In principle, these obligations for states are binding on them as to the result to be achieved, but they do not prescribe the implementation of exact uniform provisions. Hence, even under the ICERD a certain margin of appreciation exists for states to counter 'hate speech'.

Nevertheless, member states may be expected to interpret and apply national hate speech bans intended to implement ICERD in conformity with the obligations arising from its article 4a, including CERD's recommendations with respect thereto. With regard to the qualification of 'incitement', CERD has recommended that states take into account the *intention* of the speaker and the *imminent risk or likelihood* that the conduct desired or intended by the speaker will result from the speech in question. This does not apply to the qualification of 'dissemination', which covers a variety of racist opinions that would not meet the thresholds of the ICCPR ('incitement'). This does not signify that the prohibition of 'incitement' would be limited to literal incitements to concrete acts. In fact, article 4a constitutes a multiform prohibition.

Furthermore, although ICERD concerns hate speech on grounds of race, in practice it extends to cases of 'intersectionality between race and religion'. In certain contexts and under certain conditions extreme speech about a religion, defamatory statements about a particular racial group that are related to their religion or the denial of the Holocaust thus can all constitute a form of 'incitement' prohibited under ICERD. For a consistent determination of restrictions to hate speech under 4a ICERD the distinction between factual statements and value judgments and between racist remarks and speech about religion could then form important factors when weighing the specific harmful effects of speech in question against the interest of public debate.

7. Conclusion

This chapter analysed the obligations with regard to the restriction of hate speech in five selected international and European law instruments and how these must be interpreted. The analysis has shown that international and European human rights law provides a patchwork of standards on so-called hate speech. Not only do the different international and European legal instruments use different notions of hate speech, the systems also have different normative force in national legal orders. For this reason alone, international and European human rights law hardly functions as a coherent and consistent framework for setting restrictions to hate speech. Furthermore, obligations for states to prohibit by law specific forms of hate speech are binding on them in relation to the result to be achieved, but they do not prescribe the implementation of exact uniform provisions. Moreover, states are left a certain margin to imbed them in the principles of their national legal systems. This even applies to the instruments aimed at European harmonization of criminal law. The six-part threshold test for the determination of criminal liability for incitement offences in the Rabat Plan of Action may, however, develop into a standard guideline for a more consistent interpretation and application of national hate speech bans by national judges.

On the whole, complete consensus only appears to exist in relation to the prohibition of the actual incitement of third parties to undesirable or prohibited actions directed against an identifiable group or its members, thus expression that has a strict connection to subsequent actions. This requires 'the activation of a triangular relationship between the object and subject of the speech as well as the audience'. The outer limit is constituted by the *incitement to hatred/hostility or violence.* Such expression may be prohibited under the ECHR and must be prohibited by law under the ICCPR, but not necessarily by criminal law. The criminalization of incitement to hatred or violence is required by ICERD, under the Additional Protocol to the Cybercrime Convention and by the EU Council Framework Decision that however allows for the insertion of the requirement of the likelihood of a disturbance of the public order. The criminalization of *incitement to discrimination* separate from incitement to violence or hatred or the requirement of a likelihood of a disturbance of the public order is more controversial and actually only required by ICERD. The ICCPR does require its prohibition by law.

Up to now the HRC has not, however, dealt with cases about a violation of a positive state obligation to prevent incitement to hatred, discrimination or violence under 20(2) ICCPR. The ECtHR has drawn the line with the failure of the state to take measures against actual violence. In fact, with regard to prohibitions of 'incitement', no uniform standard appears to exist for the determination of the probability that the expression would succeed in inciting actual action against the target group and/or produces broader effects on society at large. In first instance it remains up to national legislation and courts to determine the degree of risk of resulting harm and the likelihood, imminence or directness of such causation. The international and European instruments generally do demand that criminal offences of forms of hate speech are limited to public expression and require the intent of the author to incite. The exact meaning of 'intent' is, however, generally left to national interpretation and thus may vary from specific intent to mere recklessness.

The criminalization of the *'dissemination of ideas based on racial hatred'* without any intent requirement or reference to the undesirable or prohibited effects of such dissemination, as is required by ICERD and recommended by ECRI, is thus controversial. This offence covers a variety of expressions of racist opinions that would not meet the thresholds of the ICCPR ('incitement'). Likewise, the Additional Protocol to the Cybercrime Convention and the EU Council Framework Decision only require the criminalization of dissemination of expression that constitutes an 'incitement'. The criminalization of the 'dissemination of racist ideas' is on the other hand certainly permitted by the ECtHR, whose broad notion of hate speech includes any 'spreading, incitement, promotion or justification of hatred based on intolerance'.

However, no single binding instrument obliges states to prohibit by law, let alone by criminal law, racist expression on the basis of its possible direct negative effects on the members of the target group, such as psychological harm, offence, or infringement of their dignity through invectives, abuse or negative imaging, separate from its possible effect on third parties or the public order. For example, the Additional Protocol to the Cybercrime Convention allows the insertion of the requirement of '*exposure to hatred, contempt or ridicule*' for the offence of *insult* or *defamation* of a particular group or its members. The ECtHR permits both civil and criminal prohibitions of group defamation and insult, but states will only violate a positive obligation to take measures against such speech, when the negative stereotyping of a group takes a serious level. The HRC particularly objects to the criminalization of any form of defamation of individuals.

The regimes under the ECHR and the ICCPR differ on more points. Other than the ECtHR, the HRC has taken position against certain laws *in abstracto*. For criminal restrictions on expression, the HRC strictly holds on the threshold of 'incitement'. Hence, the HRC considers laws that criminalize opinions about historical facts to be incompatible with the ICCPR. Likewise, the Additional Protocol to the Cybercrime Convention and the EU Council Framework Decision only require the criminalization of the denial of grave crimes committed with the intent to or that is likely to incite to violence or hatred. Contrarily, the ECtHR generally considers criminal restrictions to *Holocaust denial* not to be in violation of freedom of expression, because it assumes that the denial as such constitutes not an opinion, but a false statement with a racist purport, thus a form of group defamation or incitement to hatred, discrimination or violence against Jews in itself and therefore an abuse of rights that is categorically excluded from the protection of Article 10 ECHR.

The ECtHR's position on *blasphemy* is also exceptional. The ECtHR does not principally reject the criminalization of blasphemy and continues to regard the issue of religious offence as a direct conflict between freedom of expression and freedom of religion that would include the right of respect of religious feelings of others. The ECtHR increasingly distinguishes between attacks on a religion and attacks on religious adherents. States are allowed to prosecute expression that amounts to blasphemy and religious offence but have no duty to do so. The HRC on the other hand again considers laws penalizing blasphemy without the requirement of 'incitement' to be incompatible with the ICCPR. Likewise, different institutions of the Council of Europe have recommended the decriminalization of blasphemy, because such offences restrict opinions about religious matters and are discriminatory between religions and the confinement of criminal law to incitement to hatred, discrimination and violence on the basis of religion.

For the appreciation of the criminality of the different legal categories – group insult, defamation, ideas based on racial hatred, Holocaust denial and blasphemy – by the international and European instruments, the distinction between facts and value judgments appears to implicitly play an important role. The criminality of these legal categories appears to lie in fact that they are considered to constitute either false statements of fact or value judgments that lack a sufficient factual basis and not mere offensive but free opinions. For this reason, the legal categories are then considered to be prohibited either in themselves; because they aim to or are likely to incite to violence or hatred; or because they constitute a form of incitement hatred. The distinction between facts and value judgments is valued differently with regard to hate speech on the basis of race than with regard to hate speech on the basis of religion.

In international and European human rights law, the regimes for hate speech on the basis of *religion* and hate speech on the basis of *race* appear to differ. Religion does figure alongside race as a discriminatory ground in 20(2) ICCPR. Likewise, restrictions to discourses that incite to hatred founded on religious prejudices are just as acceptable under the ECHR as restrictions to hatred founded on racist prejudices. Contrarily, ICERD in principle concerns hate speech on the basis of race, although in practice it extends to cases of 'intersectionality between race and religion'. Likewise, the Additional Protocol to the Cybercrime Convention and the EU Council Framework Decision only require the criminalization of forms of hate speech on the basis of religion, if religion is used as a pretext for the factors race, colour, and national or ethnic origin. States are, however, free to create offences of hate speech on the basis of religion as an independent discriminatory ground.

ICERD, the Additional Protocol to the Cybercrime Convention and the EU Council Framework Decision that oblige states parties to criminalize particular forms of hate speech all refer to freedom of expression. This signifies that restrictions must be strictly construed and in their enforcement in concrete cases states must have due regard to freedom of expression. The HRC and the ECtHR also balance the interest of particular restrictions with the interest of freedom of expression in the specific contexts of cases. The ECtHR affords states a strikingly large margin to determine the restrictions to hate speech against a particular religious or ethnic group in the context of a public debate on their immigration and integration. On the whole, international and European human rights law appears to set broad frameworks, within which states have the option to set a variety of restrictions to hate speech. Such restrictions are therefore still first and foremost determined by national law and can be best comprehended against the background of the constitutional traditions of the respective national legal systems.

CHAPTER 4
FRANCE

ABBREVIATIONS

AGRIF	L'Alliance Générale contre le Racisme et pour le respect de l'Identité Française et chrétienne
Bull	Bulletin of judgments of the French Supreme Court
Bull Crim	Bulletin of judgments of the criminal chamber of the French Supreme Court
Cons. Con.	Constitutional Council
CA	Court of Appeal
CESDIP	Centre de recherche sociologique sur le droit et les institutions pénales
civ.ch.	Civil chamber
CJFI	Courrier Juridique des Finances et de l'Industrie
CNCDH	Commission nationale consultative des droits de l'homme
CNRS	Centre national de la recherche scientifique
CCE	Communication Commerce électronique
crim.ch.	Criminal chamber
D	Recueil Dalloz
Dr. pén.	Droit pénal (éditions techniques)
GP	Gazette du Palais
JCP G	Juris-Classeur périodique, La Semaine Juridique, Édition Générale
JO	Journal official – French law gazette
JORF	Journal official de la République Française – French law gazette
JP	Jurisprudence
LDH	Ligue des Droits de l'Homme
LICRA	Ligue Internationale Contre le Racisme et l'Antisémitisme
LPA	Les petites affiches
MRAP	Mouvement contre le racisme et pour l'amitié entre les peuples
RLDI	Revue Lamy droit de l'immatériel
RSC	Revue de sciences criminelles et de droit pénal comparé
RTDH	Revue trimestrielle des droits de l'homme
RUDH	Revue universelle des droits de l'homme
TGI	Tribunal de Grande Instance
Trib. Corr.	Tribunal correctionnel

INTRODUCTION

This chapter gives an in-depth examination of the relationship between freedom of expression and restrictions to hate speech at national level in France. The chapter provides an analysis of the content and scope of the existing French hate speech bans, their underlying rationales and their relationship with freedom of expression on the basis of their drafting history, their application by the judge, their embedding in French law, and on the basis of primarily French literature. Furthermore, particular attention is paid to the interplay between the different actors in the determination of the restrictions to hate speech: the French legislator, the public prosecution, the judge and the victims of hate speech and anti-racism and other civil society associations. The chapter provides the reference points for the comparison with Dutch law and the approach under the European Convention of Human Rights (ECHR) which is assessed in Chapter 6 – on the basis of the four factors of the analytical framework of Chapter 2, i.e., Actions versus Opinions; Public Debate versus Other Types of Expression; Facts versus Value judgments; and Race versus Religion.

The current chapter has a distinctive structure and is divided into three parts. This three-partition is based on the devise of the French Republic *'Liberté, Égalité, Fraternité'* ('Freedom, Equality, Brotherhood') that inspires French public law[682] and is also understood to reflect three pillars of the democratic constitutional state.[683] The chosen structure thereby enables the discussion of French law in relation to hate speech against the background of the French conception of democracy. In fact, the French hate speech laws may be regarded as a corollary of the French devise; the French legislator frequently invoked the devise, notably the principle of brotherhood, to justify the adoption of the Pleven Act of 1 July 1972 concerning the fight against racism that created the main French hate speech laws. It was stated: 'From 1789, France has launched into the world its message of brotherhood (…) Those who raise their voice to insult, defame and humiliate men, women or even children on account of their race or religion risk to strike a mortal blow to the prestige of our country (…) We want a France faithful to its devise of freedom and brotherhood'.[684]

For a good comprehension of the French law on hate speech, it is thus essential to firstly understand the origin, historical evolution and the legal implications of the French Republican devise. From the beginning of the French Revolution in 1789, the triad *Freedom, Equality, Brotherhood* played an important role in the emergence of the French Republic. Although the triad figures amongst numerous invoked

---

682 Borgetto, M., *La devise "Liberté, Égalité, Fraternité"*, Que sais-je?, n° 3196, Paris: Presses Universitaires de France 1997.

683 Gonthier, C.D., Liberty, Equality, Fraternity: The Forgotten Leg of the Trilogy, or Fraternity: The Unspoken Third Pillar of Democracy, *Mc Gill Law Journal* 2000, vol. 45, p. 567.

684 Assemblée Nationale, débats parlementaires, séance du 7 Juin 1972, Lutte contre le racisme, Discussion des conclusions d'un rapport, *JO* 8 Juin 1972, p. 2285.

slogans, many revolutionists adopted it as a reference to democratic principles and a symbol to advance their Republican ideal. During the course of the nineteenth century the triad, developed from being a 'principle' of the Second Republic referred to in the preamble of the Constitution of 1848 to *the* official devise of the Fourth Republic referred to in the Constitution of 1946. Subsequently, the current Constitution of 1958 – of the current Fifth Republic – proclaims the triad as the Republic's official devise in Article 2. This suggests that the three terms are consubstantial to the democratic Republic and, taken together, inspire its laws.[685]

The influence of the thoughts of Jean-Jacques Rousseau on the conceptualization of the Republican devise cannot be neglected. Rousseau attributed no other goal to the legislator than the accession of the two ideas of *freedom* and *equality* into political society. Rousseau established an indissoluble link between *freedom* and *equality* by making freedom the first and fundamental good to conquer and equality the instrument conditional to its existence; in his eyes, freedom can only be acquired and maintained if all associates are equal, because then no one can be submitted by the will of others, nor can anyone submit the will of others to his own.[686] In addition, Rousseau at least enables the adjunction of the idea of *brotherhood* with these two terms by attributing an eminent place to the idea of '*Patrie*' or *Homeland*, the laws of which guarantee the common liberty of citizens who learn to cherish each another as brothers.[687] The bond of brotherhood can thus be considered to be a political one founded on belonging to the same political collectivity.[688] The Republic then may be designated as the privileged space of freedom, equality and brotherhood in the sense that it *postulates* the first two and *implies* the third.[689]

The constitutional principles of freedom, equality and brotherhood can thus be considered to be interdependent and interrelated in the sense that one cannot be acquired or maintained without the others. In order for the principles to have legal force, they must, however, be translated into concrete legislation. It is generally accepted that the principles of freedom and equality can each form a direct ground for rights and obligations susceptible of sanction under the law that protects individual and public liberties, respectively assuring equality before the law. Contrarily, it can be argued that 'brotherhood' cannot, in itself, be enforced by the

685 Borgetto 1997, p. 65–66.

686 Rousseau, J.-J., *Du contrat social* (1762), book II, chap. XI.

687 Rousseau, J.-J., *Discours sur l'economie politique* (1755), sec. II. Furthermore, the freemasons are also said to have a certain role in the development of the devise and the movement of 1789 on account of the new sociability they pursue. In fact, the notion of brotherhood occupies a central place with the freemasons, indicating both their institution or Order (a Brotherhood) and its members (who are all brothers). It is argued that the freemasons have contributed to the introduction of the notion of brotherhood, associated with religious discourse (we are all brothers because we are all children from one God), into the strictly political discourse. See: Borgetto 1997, p. 14–17.

688 Borgetto 1997, p. 26.

689 Borgetto 1997, p. 20–27.

law and directly ground certain legal norms to that effect. However, brotherhood can be said to obtain a legal significance in connection with freedom and or equality. It has often been suggested that the term 'brotherhood' should be replaced with the term *solidarity*, because 'brotherhood' would have too much of a religious connotation. The French legislator has frequently invoked brotherhood/ solidarity as a justification for the adoption of legislation aimed at eliminating inequalities in the social domain.[690]

As an idea of solidarity, the principle of brotherhood also has a particular vocation in the fight against forms of racism, xenophobia and intolerance. In fact, former republicans understood freedom and brotherhood to consist of an *active participation* in civil and political rights and collective power rather than a peaceful enjoyment of individual independence.[691] The particular role that the French legislator has afforded to French anti-racism and other civil society associations in the enforcement of the hate speech bans may be placed in this light. Brotherhood in the sense of solidarity can more in general be said to ground the actions of certain French anti-racism associations themselves, such as *SOS-Racisme* that operates under the slogan '*touche pas à mon pote*';[692] *LICRA*, which advanced '*50 propositions pour une France plus fraternelle*' during the presidential elections in 2012;[693] or *MRAP*, which stands for '*Mouvement contre le Racisme et pour l'Amitié entre les Peuples*'.[694]

Against this background, *Part One on Freedom* discusses the central characteristics of the protection of freedom of expression of opinion in French law. *Part Two on Equality* discusses the hate speech bans as restrictions to freedom of expression of opinion in French law. *Part Three on Brotherhood* discusses the shared role of the French government, anti-racism, and civil society associations in the enforcement of the hate speech bans in French law. While the first and third part of the chapter forms an introduction, which is respectively complementary to the second part, the latter forms the body of the chapter and consists of several paragraphs. The paragraphs are always completed with a conclusion. This differs from the layout of the chapter as a whole, which does not culminate in a final conclusion. To avoid unnecessary repetitions, chapter 6, the last chapter of this study, provides in a joint further analysis and synthesis of the consistency of restrictions to hate speech in French and Dutch law, followed by a comparison with the approach under the ECHR, on the basis of the four factors of the analytical framework (Chapter 6, para. 1 *infra*).

---

690 Borgetto, M., *La notion de fraternité en droit public français*, Titre II La solidarité comme principe inspirateur du droit public actuel, Paris: L.G.D.J. 1993, p. 509 *et seq.*

691 Antoine, G., *Liberté, Égalité, Fraternité ou les fluctuations d'une devise*, Paris: Presses Universitaires de France 1981, p. 160.

692 Www.sos-racisme.org/.

693 Www.licra.org/fr/50-propositions-pour-france-plus-fraternelle. It included several propositions in the field of racism and discrimination, such as the creation of an independent national observatory of hate speech on the Internet with the capacity to act in court.

694 Www.mrap.fr/.

I. LIBERTÉ: FREE EXPRESSION OF OPINION IN FRENCH LAW

'Les individus doivent jouir d'une liberté d'opinion soit intérieure, soit manifestée, aussi longtemps que cette liberté ne produit pas des actions nuisibles. Lorsqu'elle en produit, elle se confond avec ses actions et doit être à ce titre réprimée et punie. Mais l'opinion séparée de l'action doit rester libre. La seule fonction de l'autorité est de la renfermer dans son domaine propre, la spéculation et la théorie.'

Benjamin Constant, *Principes de politique applicables à tous les gouvernements*[695, 696]

1. History and fundaments: free expression of opinion or abuse by punishable acts

In France, the right to the free expression of an opinion is constitutionally protected (1.1). The restrictions to this right based on the content of expression are determined on the basis of the concept of the 'délit d'opinion' (1.2) and are incorporated in a specific law; the 1881 Press Act (1.3). The determination of the restrictions to freedom of expression is to a significant extent influenced by the primacy in French law of the legislator in relation to the judge (1.4) and can be understood in light of the French conception of rights as rights *through* the state (1.5). These particular characteristics explain the somewhat strenuous relation of the French law with the international law, notably the case law of the European Court of Human Rights (ECHR) (1.6). The analysis results in a general conclusion about the free expression of opinion in France law (1.7).

695 Constant, B., *Principes de politique applicables à tous les gouvernements,* Hofmann, E. (ed.), *Tome II, Livre XVII: Des vrais principes de la liberté, ch. 1 De l'impossibilité d'abuser jamais des vrais principes de la liberté*, Genève: Librairie Droz S.A. 1980, p. 459–460. Also cited by P. Rolland, Du délit d'opinion dans la démocratie française, in: *Pouvoir et Liberté, Études offertes à Jacques Mourgeon*, Brussels: Bruylant 1998, p.668.

696 For an English translation see: Constant, B., *Principles of politics applicable to all governments*, Hofmann, E. (ed.), O'keeffe, D. (trans.), *Book XVII: On the True Principles of Freedom, ch. 1 On the inviolability of the true principles of freedom*, Indianapolis, Indiana: Liberty Fund 2003, p. 383, available at: http://files.libertyfund.org/files/861/0452_LFeBk.pdf. 'Individuals must enjoy complete freedom of opinion either private or public, as long as that freedom does not produce harmful actions. When it does produce such, it becomes identified with them, and under this heading it must be repressed and punished. Opinion separated from action, however, must remain free. The only function [460] of the government is to confine it to its proper domain, speculation and theory.'

1.1. Constitutional protection of the free expression of an opinion

The French Constitution itself contains no human rights catalogue. In France, human rights do, however, have constitutional value and are protected through the Déclaration des droits de l'homme et du citoyen of 1789 (DDHC); the Constitution's preamble contains a reference to human rights as enshrined in the Declaration and to the preamble to the Constitution of the Fourth Republic (1946–1958) of 1946 that refers to the human rights and principles as enshrined in the Declaration. The preamble to the Constitution of 1946 further declares that 'tout être humain, sans distinction de race, de religion, ni de croyance, possède des droits inaliénables et sacrés'. The preamble to the Constitution of 1958 declares that 'Le peuple français proclame solennellement son attachement aux droits de l'homme et aux principes de la souveraineté nationale tels qu'ils ont été définis par la Déclaration de 1789, confirmée et complétée par le préambule de la Constitution de 1946'. The Constitutional Council has established that the preamble to the Constitution of 1958 has constitutional value[697] and that the Declaration of 1789 forms part of French positive law and the entire body of French constitutional provisions, which are collectively also called 'le bloc de constitutionalité'.

Article 1 of the 1789 Declaration declares: 'Les hommes naissent et demeurent libres et égaux en droits'. Subsequently, Article 4 defines a general principle of liberty that is not absolute, but relative: 'La liberté consiste à pouvoir faire tout ce qui ne nuit pas à autrui: ainsi l'exercice des droits naturels de chaque homme n'a de bornes que celles qui assurent aux autres membres de la société la jouissance de ces mêmes droits. Ces bornes ne peuvent être déterminées que par la loi.' This liberty is thus inspired by the classic maxim 'one person's freedom ends where another person's freedom begins'. Between the dispositions of the Declaration of 1789 and the preambles of the Constitutions of 1946 and 1958 no hierarchy exists: they all have the same constitutional value.[698] When one norm competes with another, a French judge must not introduce a certain hierarchy between the norms, but must instead try to conciliate them.[699] In other words, the liberties are not absolute and can be restricted by law in the interest of the protection of another liberty, i.e., the general interest or the public order.[700] The restrictions imposed by the French legislator must not result in the complete negation of the liberty in question or the interdiction of its exercise, which would violate Article 5 of the Declaration of 1789, which requires that the law can only interdict 'actions nuisibles'. The Declaration of 1789 thus holds a concept of limited 'liberté individuelle', which is also denominated as 'liberté personnelle'.[701]

---

697 DC 71–44, L. Favoreau and L. Philip, *Les grandes décisions du Conseil constitutionnel*, Dalloz, 10thedition, 1999, n° 19.

698 *Code constitutionnel et des droits fondamentaux commenté*, 1st edition, Paris: Éditions Dalloz 2012, p.4.

699 Code constitutionnel commenté 2012, p.11.

700 Code constitutionnel commenté 2012, p.11.

701 Code constitutionnel commenté 2012, p.11.

Freedom of opinion is protected in Article 10, which reads: 'Nul ne doit être inquiété pour ses opinions, mêmes religieuses, pourvu que leur manifestation ne trouble pas l'ordre public établi par la loi.' The article connects the freedom of opinion with the freedom of conscience, but does not clearly define these freedoms. Rivero defines freedom of conscience as 'la possibilité pour l'homme de choisir ou d'élaborer lui-même les réponses qu'il entend donner à toutes les questions qui lui pose la conduite de sa vie personnelle et sociale, de conformer à ces réponses ses attitudes et ses actes et de communiquer aux autres ce qu'il tient pour vrai.'[702] Defined as such, freedom of conscience appears to be the sum of a series of liberties, being freedom of opinion, freedom of religion, freedom of communication, and freedom of education.[703] Indeed, although freedom of conscience is essentially linked in the constitutional provisions with religion[704], the French Constitutional judge has afforded freedom of conscience a much broader meaning by detaching it from the texts that afford rights and liberties without distinction on the ground of religion and declaring it to be a fundamental principle recognized by the laws of the French Republic.[705]

Freedom of opinion, as defined by Rivero, signifies 'la possibilité donnée à chaque homme de déterminer par lui-même ce qu'il croit vrai dans quelques domaines que ce soit'.[706] Freedom of opinion and freedom of conscience as protected in Article 10 are essentially internal, but form an indispensable condition to all expression of thoughts and opinions. Article 10 must be understood to recall that the opinion and conscience of an individual cannot be used against him as long as he exercises his freedom in respect of public order.[707]

Freedom of opinion and conscience can be combined with the 'laïque' character of the French Republic, the neutrality of the State towards religion. The parliamentary debates about the 1789 Declaration essentially concerned religious questions. Had the Declaration been placed under the invocation of God or the Supreme legislator of the Universe? Finally, in the Declaration reference was made to the Supreme Being, an expression that would not shock persons who did not adhere to any religion. More importantly, the Declaration did not recognize Catholicism as the official religion of the State. These parliamentary debates are reflected in the redaction of Article 10, the aim of which appears to be to limit the

---

702 Rivero, J., *Libertés publiques,* Tome 2, 7th edition, Paris: Presses universitaires de France 2003, p.126.

703 Rivero 2003, p.127.

704 Such as in paragraph 5 of the preamble to the Constitution of 1946 that declares that no person can be violated in his a work or job on the ground of his opinions or beliefs and; in paragraph 16 of the preamble to the Constitution of 1946 that envisions France and the French overseas departments as a union based on equal rights and duties without distinction on the ground of religion; and in Article 1 of the Constitution of 1958 that assures the equality of all citizens before the law without distinction on the ground of religion and the respect by the State of all beliefs.

705 Code constitutionnel commenté 2012, p.148.

706 Rivero 2003, p.129.

707 Code constitutionnel commenté 2012, p.148.

religious question to opinions 'même religieuses'.[708] Hence, the manifestation of religious opinions falls under the freedom of opinion that protects religious and non-religious opinions on equal footing. Although the freedom of conscience forms an aspect of freedom of religion, the Declaration of 1789 thus does not protect this latter freedom in a separate article. In French law, the 'libertés des cultes', being the freedom to practice a religion individually and collectively, is essentially regulated in the Act of 1905 (para.2.5 *infra*).

Freedom of opinion and conscience in Article 10 are intrinsically linked to the following article; Article 11 protects the free communication of thoughts and opinions and reads: 'La libre communication des pensées et des opinions est un des droits les plus précieux de l'homme; tout citoyen peut donc parler, écrire, imprimer librement, sauf à répondre de *l'abus de cette liberté* dans les cas déterminés par la loi' [curs. EHJ]. Read together, Articles 10 and 11 protect the manifestation and communication of all kinds of opinions – philosophical, ideological, religious and non-religious – on equal footing.

Thus, French law does not refer to the freedom of expression, but to the freedom of communication. Nevertheless, the Article subsequently only cites acts of expression and not activities to receive such acts. While in 1789 communication meant to speak, write and print, the scope of Article 11 has nowadays been extended to all modern forms of communication, comprising audio-visual and electronic communication, as well as the press. On several occasions the Constitutional Council has defined the purport of the freedom, being a fundamental freedom: 'd'autant plus précieuse que son exercice est une condition de la démocratie et l'une des garanties essentielles du respect des autres droits et libertés'.[709] With regard to all forms of communication, the French Constitutional Council considers the principle of pluralism to be a common, indispensable element in order to effectively exercise this freedom. In order to assure the free choice of the receiver of communication in receiving trends in thoughts and opinions, the State must respect, next to pluralism of communication organs (journals or channels), the existence of different contents.[710] These objects of constitutional value are protected in Article 34 of the Constitution of 1958 that regulates 'la liberté, le pluralisme et l'indépendance des médias' and Article 4, which guarantees pluralist expression of political opinion and equitable participation of political parties at the democratic life of the French nation.

The French vision on free expression of opinion has a long tradition, which originates in articles 10 and 11 of the 1789 Declaration. The French legislator has protected the freedom of opinion in a negative form by the suppression in criminal law of all '*délits d'opinion*'. In the vision of the French legislator, the public manifestation of an opinion alone cannot be criminally repressed and considered as

---

708 Code constitutionnel commenté 2012, p.6.

709 Cons. Con. 20 May 2011, n°2011–131 QPC; Cons. Con. 28 February 2012, n°2012–647 DC. See also: Rivero 2003, p.168.

710 Code constitutionnel commenté 2012, pp.153–154.

an offence. The criminalization of an opinion as such would constitute a 'délit d'opinion'. For this reason, in the vision of the French legislator, present French criminal law does not comprise any 'délits d'opinion'. Nevertheless, what do exist in present French law are offences penalizing the *abuses* of the freedom to manifest and communicate an opinion.[711] The Constitutional Council has indicated that two objectives of constitutional value must be conciliated with the freedom of communication: on the one hand the protection of the rights of others, and on the other hand the public order.[712] In 1994, the Constitutional Council elevated the respect of human dignity to a principle of constitutional value (para.9.4 *infra*).[713] When determining the abuses of the free expression of an opinion, the French legislator can be inspired by the desire to protect either the rights of others, human dignity or the public order.

With regard to freedom of expression, the Constitutional Council has more so generally considered that 'les atteintes portées à l'exercice de cette liberté doivent être nécessaires, adaptées et proportionnées à l'objectif poursuivis',[714] a consideration that suggests a certain influence of the European law.[715] However, confronted with a question about the constitutionality of a particular speech offence, neither the Constitutional Council nor the French Supreme Court have applied this proportionality test, but have instead reviewed whether the offence complied with the principle of criminal legality or of the normativity of the law.[716] This will be discussed later in this chapter (Part II, para. 9.4 and 9.7 *infra*).

1.2. The concept of the 'délit d'opinion'

1.2.1. Definition of a 'délit d'opinion' in French legal doctrine

In French legal doctrine no coherent and unambiguous definition of a 'délit d'opinion' exists. French legal scholars firstly disagree on the question as to what constitutes a 'délit d'opinion', subsequently, on the question as to whether French law contains or has in the past contained 'délits d'opinion', and finally, on the question as to which existing press offences must be suppressed and which should not.

---

711 Vgl. Rivero 2003, p.130.

712 Cons. Con. 27 July 1982, n° 82–141 DC §5, Cited in: Code constitutionnel commenté 2012, p.155.

713 Cons. Con. 27 July 1994, n°94–343/344 DC.

714 Cons. Con. 20 May 2011, n°2011–131 QPC; Cons. Con. 28 February 2012, n°2012–647 DC.

715 See in general: Burgorgue-Larsen, L.,The impact of European fundamental rights on the French Constitutional Court, in: Patricia Popelier, P., Van de Heyning, C. & Van Nuffel, P. (Eds.), *Human Rights Protection in the European Legal Order: the Interaction between the European and the National Courts*, Cambridge: Intersentia 2011, p. 211–236.

716 De Lamy, B., La Constitution et la liberté de la presse, *Les Nouveaux Cahiers du Conseil Consitutionnel, Dossier La liberté d'expression et de communication, Dalloz* n°36–2012, p. 19–29; Carcassonne, G., Les interdits et la liberté d'expression, *Ibid.*, p. 55–65.

Hauriou distinguishes a general 'délit d'opinion' that is inadmissible in light of the principle of freedom from more specific offences, which are sufficiently described and circumscribed by law and are perfectly admissible.[717] A justification for such 'délits d'opinion' can be found in the possibility, from a philosophical and moral perspective, to distinguish between good and evil. However, as positive law is unable to precisely define such offences, an absolute freedom of opinion is preferable in the hope that the press is capable of moralizing itself.

For Fauvel, it is equally its imprecision that discerns a 'délit d'opinion' from a press offence.[718] The ordinary press offences are those offences that amount to the impairment of a right. They leave no room for any arbitrary interpretation. Contrarily, the former 'délit de tendance' and 'délit d'opinion' that existed in former French law do not criminalize a precise harmful act committed through the press, but a series of articles or an article that contains an attack of established institutions without impairing any particular right, any determined interest. They thus leave more room for arbitrary criminalization.

From 1810 onwards, Benjamin Constant enounced the principle, according to which: 'Les individus doivent jouir d'une liberté d'opinion soit intérieure, soit manifestée, aussi longtemps que cette liberté ne produit pas des actions nuisibles. Lorsqu'elle en produit, elle se confond avec ses actions et doit être à ce titre réprimée et punie. Mais l'opinion séparée de l'action doit rester libre. La seule fonction de l'autorité est de la renfermer dans son domaine propre, la spéculation et la théorie.'[719]

Rolland provides a definition of a 'délit d'opinion' that closely resembles the principle of Constant and the vision of the French legislator of 1881 (para.1.3.2 *infra*): 'interdire l'expression d'une opinion sans autre circonstance que le fait d'être jugée mauvaise par les pouvoirs publics ou le juge'.[720] He strictly excludes from the definition the opinion considered as dangerous. As a democracy is constituted by the free expression of opinion, to interfere with an opinion that is either good or bad, is to interfere with the fundament of democracy itself. In order to protect it, without violating the freedom of opinion, a precise and fine distinction must be made between actions and opinions. The key question thus becomes: what is the nature of the link between the expression of an idea and a following reprehensible act?[721]

Droin derives three characteristics of the 'délit d'opinion' from the discussion in French legal doctrine.[722] Firstly, contrary to the press offences, the 'délit d'opinion' does not form the object of a precise qualification by the French legislator. Secondly,

---

717 Hauriou, M., *Précis de droit constitutionnel*, Paris: Sirey 1929, p.662.

718 Fauvel, L, *Le délit de tendance et le délit d'opinion dans les lois sur la presse,* (diss.) Paris: Librairie nouvelle de droit et de jurisprudence 1912, p.29.

719 Constant, B., *Principes de politique applicables à tous les gouvernements*, Book V, Ch. 3 'De la manifestation de la pensée', p.130. Cited in: Rolland 1998, p.668.

720 Rolland 1998, p.649.

721 Rolland 1998, p.657.

722 Droin, N., *Les limitations à la liberté d'expression dans la loi sur la presse du 29 juillet 1881, Disparition, permanence et résurgence du délit d'opinion*, (diss.) Paris: L.G.D.J. 2009, p.20.

it does not determine the specific right or interest with which it interferes: it criminalizes a simple opinion, and not the support of a criminal or punishable act. Thirdly, its arbitrary prosecution and sanction constitutes a danger to the free expression of an opinion.

1.2.2. Le délit d'outrage à la morale publique et religieuse

An example 'par excellence' of an offence that is generally regarded as a délit d'opinion in French legal doctrine forms the former 'délit d'outrage à la morale publique et religieuse', created by the Act of 17 May 1819 and abolished by the 1881 Press Act (para.1.3.2 *infra*), which marked the end of the criminalization of religious offences in France.

From early on, next to canon law, ancient French law had sanctioned the offence of blasphemy, which was often punished with the death penalty. Pursuant to a declaration of 16 April 1757, authors and editors who were responsible for a publication that was aimed at attacking a religion were decapitated.[723] During the Ancien Régime (15th -18th Century), next to the offence of blasphemy, the offence of sacrilege was created in case law that aimed to sanction writings that attacked and therefore constituted a danger to the public religious order.[724] The philosophers of the Enlightenment denounced the public religious morality of the eighteenth century and the sanctioning of blasphemy in civil laws. During the French Revolution, in 1791, the offences of blasphemy and sacrilege were abolished. It was during the Restoration, in 1825, that Charles X and the 'ultra-royalistes' reintroduced a certain form of blasphemy into civil law. The Act of 20 April 1825 sanctioned the sacrilege with the death penalty. The Act was, however, not applied and was abolished during the July Revolution, on 11 October 1830.[725]

In 1819, le Comte de Serre, Minister of Justice at the time, deposed a draft Act concerning the repression of offences committed through the press, comprising of its Article 8 'tout outrage à la morale publique ou aux bonnes mœurs par l'un des moyens énoncés en l'article 1er, sera puni d'un emprisonnement d'un mois à un an et d'une amende de 16 francs à 500 francs'. With this offence, De Serre aimed to re-establish moral principles.[726] In order to protect religion against the excesses of freedom of expression, an amendment added to the words 'morale publique' the words 'et religieuse'.[727] In its final version, the adopted article 8 thus sanctioned the 'outrage à la morale publique', the 'outrage à la morale religieuse', and also the 'outrage aux bonnes mœurs', which was already provided for in the Penal Code of 1810.

---

723 Droin 2009, p.431.

724 *Ibid.*

725 Boulègue, J., *Le Blasphème en procès 1984–2009, l'église et la mosquée contre les libertés*, Paris: Nova Éditions 2010, pp.18–19.

726 Droin 2009, p.432.

727 *Parliamentary archives*, XXIII, assembly of 17 April 1819, House of Representatives, p.668; p.676.

The Act of 25 May 1822 extended this offence to the 'outrage à la religion'. Article 1 read 'quiconque par l'un des moyens énoncés en l'article 1er de la loi du 17 mai 1819 aura outragé ou tourné en dérision la religion de l'Etat, sera puni d'un emprisonnement de 3 à 5 ans et d'une amende de 300 à 6000 francs'. The same sanctions applied in relation to other religions that were officially recognized in France. Compared to article 8 of the Act of 1819, the penalties of this article 1 were much more severe.

The Acts of 1819 and 1822 thus strongly reinforced the legislation protecting religious convictions. Due to their redaction, the scope of the two offences was particularly broad, as per the intention of the legislator. Obscene publications, publications that contested certain truths as established by the religions recognized by the State, and public manifestations of atheism were all condemned on the grounds of the articles.[728]

Under the Second Republic (1848–1852) and the Second French Empire (1852–1870), the offence of 'outrage à la morale publique et religieuse' was excessively applied.[729] It formed the ground for many prosecutions of authors whose literary works form part of the literary movement of Realism that shocked the existing morals. Flaubert was prosecuted on the ground of article 8 of the Act of 1819 for his novel *Madame Bovary*. The novel tells the story of Madame Bovary, the wife of a doctor in the French countryside, who dreams of a life in the city, seeks refugee in the reading of romantic novels to escape from boredom and commits adultery. On 7 February 1857, the criminal tribunal of the Seine acquitted Flaubert. According to the tribunal, the prosecuted passages were in bad taste, but it nevertheless concerned a serious novel that did not aim to incite to debauchery.[730]

In the same year, Baudelaire, who formed part of the literary movement of Symbolism, was also prosecuted on the ground of article 8 of the Act of 1819 for his volume of poetry *Les Fleurs du Mal*. The themes of these poems related to decadence and eroticism. In contrast to Flaubert's acquittal, Baudelaire was condemned. However, in its decision of 20 August 1857, the criminal tribunal of the Seine distinguished between the 'outrage à la morale publique' and the 'outrage à la morale religieuse'. While the latter offence was not established, the judge considered that the poems necessarily incited the senses through their gross realism that offended the chastity and therefore constituted an 'atteinte à la morale publique et aux bonne mœurs'.[731] Subsequently, for many years, this important classic volume of poems in French literature could not be published, until the French Supreme Court, in a decision of 31 May 1949, revised the condemnation and rehabilitated *Les Fleurs du Mal*.[732]

---

728 Generally see: Gaultier, J., *Un délit d'opinion: le délit d'outrage à la morale publique et religieuse*, 1819–1881, (diss.) Caen, 1924.

729 *Ibid.*

730 Tribunal corr. de la Seine, 7 February 1857, *La Gazette des tribunaux*, 9 February 1857.

731 Tribunal corr. de la Seine, 20 August 1857, *La Gazette des tribunaux*, 21 August 1857.

732 French Supreme Court, 31 May 1949, *D.* 1949, I, pp.348–349. The Act of 25 September 1946 permitted the revision of a condemnation on the ground of the 'outrage aux bonnes mœurs par la voie du livre'.

The 'outrage à la morale religieuse' was particularly enforced.[733] In 1858, Proudhon was prosecuted for his work *De la Justice dans la Révolution et dans l'Eglise*. In this work, he declared God useless and qualified religion as an immoral mission. On 2 June 1858, the criminal tribunal of the Seine condemned Proudhon to an imprisonment of three years on the ground that his expressions offended in the most hurtful manner the religious convictions for which the law commanded respect.[734] The suspects prosecuted on the ground of article 8 of the Act of 1819 varied from pamphleteers, to priests and magistrates.[735] Due to the many condemnations, the suppression of article 8 of the Act of 1819 had been requested within the legislative bodies during the end of the Second Empire and the beginning of the Third Republic (1870–1940). However, one had to wait for the new Press Act of 1881 in order for the article to be truly suppressed.

The 1881 Press Act (para.1.3 *infra*) abandoned all offences of religion. Reporter of the draft in the House of Representatives, Eugène Lisbonne, affirmed that the 'outrage à la morale publique et religieuse' could no longer be preserved: 'Délits d'opinion s'il en fut, délits insaisissables au point de vue de l'intention, délits stériles au point de vue l'effet qu'ils peuvent produire'.[736] As the offence had been principally applied to sanction those who had offended God himself, Lisbonne considered 'c'est une étrange manie que celle des hommes qui prétendent se constituer les vengeurs de la divinité. Les anciens qui n'avaient pas le Bonheur de connaître le vrai dieu, avaient dans leur philosophie mondaine une maxime plus large [...]: il faut laisser aux dieux le soin de se venger eux-mêmes'.[737] While the House of Representatives accepted the suppression of the offence, in the Senate a reintroduction of the 'outrage à la morale religieuse' was proposed. This amendment was considered to revive the 'délit d'opinion' and for this reason was finally rejected by the Senate.[738] And so, the 'délit d'outrage à la morale publique et religieuse' was suppressed from French law. What remained was the existence of 'le délit d'outrage aux bonnes mœurs' in the French Penal Code of 1810. Due to the press freedom afforded by the new 1881 Press Act, during the Third Republic (1870–1940), much anticlerical and anti-religious expression in the form of violent cartoons was published in anticlerical magazines such as *La Calotte*, *L'Assiette au beurre*, *Les Corbeaux*.[739]

733 Droin 2009, p.435.
734 Tribunal corr. de la Seine, 2 June 1858, *La Gazette des tribunaux*, 5 June 1858.
735 Droin 2009, p.435.
736 Report of Eugène Lisbonne, 5 July 1880, *JO* 18 July 1880, House of Representatives, Annex, n° 2865, p.8297.
737 *Ibid.*
738 *JO*, Parliamentary debates, 12 July 1881, the Senate, p.1008; p.1106.
739 Boulègue 2010, pp.18–19.

1.3. The 1881 Press Act

1.3.1. The liberal aim of the 1881 Press Act

The freedom of expression and communication of thoughts and opinions constitutionally protected in Articles 10 and 11 DDHC are further regulated in the French Press Act of 29 July 1881 that broadly regulates the freedom of the press. In France, the history of the regulation of freedom of opinion is intrinsically connected with the history of the regulation of freedom of the press.[740] The fight for freedom of the press by the Liberals in the Eighteen-century was directed against the political power; against the strict regulation of the occupations of the printing press and bookshops, and especially against the royal censorship exercised on literary or scientific works, which was accompanied with severe criminal sanctions.[741] Between 1789 and 1881, with the succession of different regimes, a strict authority with regard to the press was sometimes alternated by relative liberalism and a liberal conception of the regulation of the press evolved. The legislator of the Third Republic (1870–1940) desired a complete reform of all articles that regulated the press and were spread out over more than twenty different texts. A special commission designed a draft of a complete new Press Act that was proposed to the parliament by Member of Parliament Eugène Lisbonne on 5 July 1880. The central idea of the Press Act was to form a privileged legal regime favourable to the Press.

Firstly, the aim of the Press Act was to repress every preventive regime and to provide for freedom of the occupations of the printing press and bookshops, which entailed the suppression of censorship, the requirements of preliminary authorization and deposit. Article 1 therefore declares 'l'imprimerie et la librairie sont libres'. Article 5 further specifies: 'Tout journal ou écrit périodique peut être publié, sans autorization préalable et sans dépôt de cautionnement, après la déclaration prescrite par l'article 7.' The Act comprises further norms concerning 'l'imprimerie et la librairie'; 'la presse périodique' and 'l'affichage'.

Secondly, the aim of the Press Act was to suppress all 'délits d'opinion' and to incorporate into the act only the abuses of the manifestation of an opinion on strictly circumscribed terms in specific press offences. The Press Act lists all press offences in Chapter IV concerning 'crimes et délits commis par la voie de la de presse ou par tout autre moyen de publication'.

Thirdly, the aim of the Press Act was to precisely determine the persons criminally responsible for the violation of the press offences. The Act (article 42 *et seq.*) distinguishes between the responsibility of the primary author and the responsibility of an accomplice. As primary author, the 'directeur de publication' or 'éditeur' (chief editor or editor) is responsible. In his absence, the 'auteur' (author of the publication) is prosecuted as a primary author. If the latter two escape from prosecution, the

740 Beignier, B., De Lamy, B., Dreyer, E., *Traité de droit de la presse et des médias*, Paris: LexisNexis SA Litec 2009, Chapter 1.

741 Rivero 2003, p.171.

'imprimeur' (printer) is principally responsible, and in last instance, the 'vendeur', 'distributeur' and 'afficheur' (salesman, distributor and displayer) is held to be responsible. This system is called the 'responsabilité en cascade'. When the 'directeur de publication' is prosecuted, the author and salesman or distributor can be prosecuted as an accomplice, while the printer cannot. A safe harbour has been created in 2009 for the 'directeur de publication' for User Created Content (UCC) published online.[742]

Fourthly, the aim of the Press Act was to create a specific regime for the prosecution and repression of the press offences, comprising of strict procedural rules that derogated from the French code of criminal procedure. The prosecuting party must comply with these strict procedural rules, often under penalty of nullity. Examples of this can be found in Articles 65, 53 and 50 of the Press Act. The prescriptive period of three months in accordance with Article 65 has always been considered as one of the essential elements of the regulation of freedom of expression. Pursuant to Article 65, formal charges against an offender of the provisions of the 1881 Press Act have to be pursued within 3 months (as opposed to 3 years for ordinary crimes), under penalty of nullity. However, the prescriptive period applicable to the criminal prosecution for press offences related to racism (24–8; 24*bis*; 32–2; 33–3) has been extended to one year pursuant to Article 65–3. The Constitutional Council has ruled that Article 65–3 is in conformity with the Constitution, because the difference of treatment that results from it depending on the nature of the offence is not disproportionate in relation to the pursued objective.[743] However, since 2011, a legislative proposal is being prepared to align the prescriptive period of the offences of defamation, insult and provocation on the grounds of sex, sexual orientation or handicap with that of the offences of defamation, insult and provocation based on race etc.[744]

Article 53 requires that the content of the summons uses the correct legal definition of the acts, that is, the exact qualification of the criminal act and the applicable article, under penalty of nullity. If the indictment is incorrect, the prosecution is invalid and the court cannot find the existence of a different offence, as it may in ordinary criminal cases. As a consequence, the prosecuting party must make a clear choice as to the ground of the prosecution. Article 50 requires that if the public prosecution makes a request for information, it must use in its requestor the correct legal definition of the acts, that is, the exact qualification of the criminal act and the applicable article, under penalty of nullity.

---

742 See further: Dreyer, E., *Responsabilités civile et pénale des médias*, Paris: LexisNexis 2011, p. 245 and more generally p.238–246.

743 Cons. Con. 12 April 2013, n°2013–302 QPC, *Légipresse* n°306 June 2013, p. 350–352, annotation B. Ader.

744 Proposition de loi n°3794, *relative à la suppression de la discrimination dans les délais de prescription prévus par la loi sur la liberté de la presse du 29 juillet 1881*, deposé le 5 Décembre 2011. For the status of the legislative procedure see: www.senat.fr/dossier-legislatif/ppl11–122.html#block-timeline. See also Proposition de loi n° 265, visant à *porter* de *trois mois* à *un an* le *délai* de *prescription* des *propos injurieux* ou *diffamatoires* à *caractère homophobe*, *transphobe*, *sexiste* ou à raison du *handicap,* deposé le 16 Janvier 2013 au Sénat.

1.3.2. The press offences of the 1881 Press Act

The offences that existed before the adoption of the 1881 Press Act and that of the legislator of 1881 considered as 'délits d'opinion' comprised amongst others 'l'outrage aux religions reconnues par l'Etat', 'le délit d'attaque contre la liberté des cultes' and 'le délit à troubler la paix publique en excitant le mépris ou la haine des citoyens les uns contre les autres'.[745] The parliamentary debates about the adoption of the 1881 Press Act formed a fundamental discussion about the distinction between the new press offences and offences penalizing an opinion.[746] The drafters of the Act held that the press offences in reality constituted punishable acts. Lisbonne, reporter of the draft, considered 'la nouvelle loi [...] supprime tous les délits d'opinion, tous les délits de doctrine, tous les délits de tendance. Elle ne retient que ce qui constitue des actes criminels ou délictueux, des actes portant atteinte à la sécurité publique ou à la liberté d'autrui'[747] and 'La répression [...] ne s'attache qu'aux actes que le rédacteur de l'exposé des motifs de la loi du 17 mai 1819 considérait comme des délits de droit commun. Ce sont les actes inspirés par l'intention de troubler l'ordre social, c'est à dire de nuire à la sécurité de la collectivité des citoyens, de porter atteinte à l'intérêt privé, actes que le droit commun incrimine, abstraction faite des moyens à l'aide desquels leur auteur a pu les accomplir. Le projet laisse par conséquent libre carrière aux opinions. Il ne donne asile, dans ses dispositions nouvelles, à aucun délit de doctrine, de tendance, à aucun délit purement politique...'.[748] In the vision of the French legislator, the Press Act thus criminalizes acts and not opinions. The justification of the creation of the press offences formed the link between the expression of an idea and the reprehensible act.

Chapter IV of the Press Act, which concerns 'felonies and misdemeanours committed through the press or any other means of publication', is subdivided into five paragraphs, penalizing the 'provocation to felonies and misdemeanours'; 'misdemeanours against the public cause'; 'misdemeanours against persons';

---

745 The complete list, as cited in Droin 2009, pp.11–12, is: 'l'outrage aux religions reconnues par l'Etat; le délit d'attaque contre la liberté des cultes; le délit d'attaque à la Constitution, au principe de la souveraineté du peuple et du suffrage universel; le délit d'excitation à la haine et au mépris du gouvernement; le délit à troubler la paix publique en excitant le mépris ou la haine des citoyens les uns contre les autres; le délit d'attaque contre le respect dû aux lois et à l'inviolabilité des droits qu'elles ont consacrés; le délit d'apologie de faits qualifies de crimes ou de délits par la loi; le délit d'enlèvement ou de dégradation des signes publics de l'autorité opéré en haine ou au mépris de cette autorité; le délit d'exposition, dans les lieux ou réunions publics, de distribution ou de mise en vente de tous signes ou symboles propres à propager l'esprit de rébellion ou à troubler la paix publique; le délit de port public de tous les signes extérieurs de ralliement non autorisés par la loi ou par des règlements de police'.

746 For a thorough analysis see: Droin 2009, p.19 *et seq.* More generally see: Blin, H.; Chavanne, A.; Drago, R., *Traité du droit de la presse*, Paris: Librairies techniques 1969.

747 Parliamentary debates, *JO* 25 January 1881, French national assembly, p.34.

748 Report of Eugène Lisbonne of 5 July 1880, *JO* 18 July 1880, French national assembly, annex n° 2865.

'misdemeanours against the Head of State and foreign diplomatic agents'; and 'prohibited publications and immunities of defence'. In these five paragraphs in Chapter IV, the Press Act cites general press offences that can be aggravated by particular grounds, when so stipulated in the sub-paragraphs of the relevant article. A determinant criterion of all press offences is the publicity of the expression. According to the famous maxim of Barbier, 'C'est la publication qui fait l'acte'.[749] Subsequently, Article 23 describes the means of publication by which the press offences can be committed, being 'des discours, cris ou menaces proférés dans des lieux ou réunions publics, soit par des écrits, imprimés, dessins, gravures, peintures, emblèmes, images ou tout autre support de l'écrit, de la parole ou de l'image vendus ou distribués, mis en vente ou exposés dans des lieux ou réunions publics, soit par des placards ou des affiches exposés au regard du public, soit par tout moyen de communication au public par voie électronique'. In fact, the press offences of the 1881 Press Act constitute all public speech offences in French law, either committed in the printed press, the audiovisual media or on the Internet. In this study, I will, however, use the terminology of the French legislator and speak of press offences, not public speech offences.

The basic liberal principle of the Press Act of 29 July 1881, according to which an opinion is only punishable on the ground of its link with a following reprehensible act, brought the French legislator of 1881 to include in the paragraph concerning 'provocations' only *direct* provocations to felonies and misdemeanors. It was this link that also formed an argument to preserve many existing speech offences, such as the 'provocations *non suivi d'effet*' or the 'cris et chants séditieux proférés dans des lieux ou reunion publics', while the opposition in parliament argued that this constituted offences that criminalized an opinion.[750] Over time, the French legislator has introduced many new prohibitions of the manifestation of an opinion, both within and outside of the framework of the 1881 Press Act.[751] Since 1881, the Press Act has thus been modified and supplemented by many new press offences or new sub-paragraphs. The French legislator has introduced into the paragraph concerning 'provocations' the 'apologies of felonies and misdemeanors', as *indirect* forms of provocations. The Act of 1 July 1972 created the offences of racial defamation; racial insult and racial provocation; the Act of 13 July 1990 created the offence of Holocaust denial; the Act of 30 December 2004 enlarged the scope of the offences of group defamation, insult and provocation to the discriminatory grounds of sex, sexual preference and handicap. These press offences have not, during their drafting, been submitted to the Constitutional

---

749 Barbier, G., *Code expliqué de la presse*, Paris: Éditions Marchal et Billard 1911, vol.1, spéc. n° 243.

750 Parliamentary debates, *JO* 1 February 1881, French national assembly, p. 98; Parliamentary debates, *JO* 2 February 1881, French national assembly, p.116.

751 For an overview: Mathieu, B., La liberté d'expression en France: de la protection constitutionnelle aux menaces legislatives, *RDP* 2007, pp.321 *et seq.*; De Bellescize, D., Délits d'opinion et liberté d'expression, *D.* 2006, p.1476.

Council for a constitutional review except for the draft act that sought to create the offence of the denial of genocides (para.9.7 *infra*).

Despite the basic liberal principle of the 1881 Press Act, its contemporary evolution incontestably tends towards an increasing restriction of freedom of expression. The requirement of a link between the expression of an idea and the reprehensible act as a justification for the creation of a press offence seems to be diluted; could it be either replaced or supplemented by other rationales? Mathieu and De Bellescize point out that since the Third Republic (1870–1940) and the creation of the 1881 Press Act, the limitations to freedom of expression have been aimed at the protection of the public interest through the protection of the regime and the authorities, but that they have been followed by limitations that aim to protect individuals considered in their differences and singularities and even limitations stemming from an ideology or Communautarism.[752] De Bellescize concludes that the definition of a 'délit d'opinion' has evolved over time. But an opposite effect thereof is also that the legislator has recently removed certain offences from the Press Act and inserted them into the general Penal Code. Act n° 2014–1353 of 13 November 2014 *strengthening provisions on the fight against terrorism* transferred the penalisation of 'provocation and glorification of terrorism' from Article 24–6 of the Press Act to new Article 421–2–5 of the French Penal Code. It was argued that these forms of provocation and glorification do not concern *abuses of freedom of expression*, but *facts that are directly at the basis of terrorist acts*. Article 421–2–5 has, however, been criticized, because it no longer distinguishes provocation followed by effect from provocation not followed by effect and therefore has a potentially very broad scope. Moreover, with the transfer, the strict procedural rules applicable to the press offences are circumvented, in order to facilitate the prosecution. The question of the compatibility of the article with freedom of expression thus might nevertheless be brought before the Constitutional Council.[753]

1.3.3. The primacy of the 1881 Press Act

The relationship between French press law and civil responsibility remains ambiguous.[754] For a long period, the French case law has resisted the tendency of the intrusion of the civil responsibility of the wrongful act – of Article 1382 of the Civil Code[755] – in the field of press law. Whenever a wrongful act disguised an

---

752 *Ibid.*

753 De Bellescize, D.; Francescini, L., *Droit de la communication*, Paris: PUF 2005, p.376. Lazerges, C., La lute contre le terrorisme peut-elle mettre en danger la liberté d'expression, *Légipresse* n° 321, November 2014, p. 579–581; Derieux, E., Lutte contre le terrorisme et droit de la communication, *Légipresse* n° 322, December 2014, p. 686–691.

754 See generally: Lécuyer, G., *Liberté d'expression et responsabilité, Étude de droit privé*, (diss.) Paris: Dalloz 2006.

755 Article 1382 CC provides that 'Tout fait quelconque de l'homme, qui cause à autrui un dommage, oblige celui par la faute duquel il est arrivé à le réparer'.

offence provided and repressed by the 1881 Press Act, such as defamation or insult, the tribunals requalified the prosecuted facts and applied the short prescriptive period of Article 65 (para.1.3.1 *supra*). The introduction of Article 1382 CC was not intended to permit the circumvention of this procedural rule of the 1881 Press Act. Contrarily, Article 1382 CC could be applied outside this closed legal world. Multiple wrongful acts have thus been developed parallel to the 1881 Press Act in order to limit the violation of concurring interests suffered as a result of the exercise of freedom of expression, such as the infringement of religious beliefs (para.5.4.1 *infra*).[756] As the boundary between the press offences and the principle of civil responsibility was increasingly blurred, the French Supreme Court has specified the criteria for application of 1382 CC in press law cases.

In its four famous decisions of 12 July 2000, the plenary assembly of the French Supreme Court considered that 'les abus de liberté d'expression prévus et réprimés par la loi du 29 juillet 1881 ne peuvent être *réparés* sur le fondement de l'article 1382 du Code civil.' [curs. EHJ][757] As a result of this judgment, Article 1382 CC can be applied in the event that an expression cannot be qualified as a violation of the 1881 Press Act. A second step can be seen in a decision of 29 March 2001, in which the French Supreme Court further specified that 'les abus de la liberté d'expression prévus et réprimés par la loi du 29 juillet 1881 ne peuvent être *poursuivis* sur le fondement de l'article 1382 du Code Civil'[curs. EHJ].[758] Here, the Court does not only refuse to repair any action instituted on the grounds of one of the press offences in accordance with article 1382 CC, but actually prohibits the institution of a proceeding on the ground of article 1382 CC, if the conduct can be qualified as a violation of the Press Act. In a decision of 25 September 2005, the French Supreme Court went even further and considered with regard to 1382 CC: 'les abus de la liberté d'expression envers les personnes ne peuvent être poursuivis sur le fondement de ce texte.'[759] Here, the French Supreme Court completely excludes the application of Article 1382 CC to any abuse of freedom of expression. Only precisely contoured penal or civil provisions could limit freedom of expression.

After this latter radical and criticized solution, the French Supreme Court has applied more moderate formula. In a decision of 29 November 2005, the Court

---

756 Lécuyer, G., Responsabilité civile et droit de la presse: le tumulte permanent, annotation at: French Supreme Court, civ.ch. I, 6 October 2011, n°10–18142, *Bull.* 2011 I, *Légipresse* n°290, January 2012, p.31.

757 French Supreme Court, plenary assembly, 12 July 2000, n°98–10160, *Bull.* 2000 A. P., n° 8 p.13; *Légipresse*, October 2000, III, p.153, conclusions L. Joinet, RTD Civ 2000, p. 842, observation P. Jourdain.

758 French Supreme Court, civ.ch. II, 29 March 2001, n°99–10332, *Bull.* 2001 II, n° 67 p.44; French Supreme Court, civ.ch. II, 10 March 2004, n°00–16934, *Bull.* 2004 II, n° 114 p.94.

759 French Supreme Court, civ.ch., 27 September 2005, n°03–13622, *Bull.* 2005 I, n° 348 p. 289; annotation F. Watrin 'Les abus de la liberté d'expression envers les personnes ne peuvent être poursuivis sur le fondement de l'article 1382 du Code Civil', *Légipresse*, n° 230, April 2006, p.57. The judgment has been confirmed by: French Supreme Court, civ.ch. I, 19 March 2009, n°07–19667, *Légipresse* n°262–1, p.83.

considered 'les abus de la liberté d'expression *prévus et réprimés* par la loi du 29 juillet 1881, tels que l'injure, ne peuvent être *réparés* sur le fondement de l'article 1382 de Code civil' [curs. EHJ].[760] Contrarily, in a decision of 6 October 2011, the French Supreme Court adopted its most radical solution and considered 'les abus de la liberté d'expression ne peuvent être réprimés que par la loi du 29 juillet 1881.'[761] The Supreme Court no longer affirms the prevalence of the 1881 Press Act where there is a concurrence of qualifications, but seemingly consecrates an absolute monopoly of the 1881 Press Act to sanction the abuses of freedom of expression. It remains unclear as to whether and if so to what extent the French Supreme Court has aimed to leave any residual domain to Article 1382 CC.[762] In a decision of 10 April 2013, the French Supreme Court even found a civil condemnation on the basis of Article 1382 CC with regard to certain publications on the Internet that violate Article 10 of the European Convention of Human Rights, because even though they were lies they did not fall under any specific restriction determined by the law.[763] The Supreme Court, therefore, apparently considers Article 1382 CC to be neither a restriction to freedom of expression as *prescribed by law* or necessary for the protection of the reputation or rights of others in accordance with article 10(2) ECHR. Contrarily, the ECtHR has itself on several occassions decided that the identical equivalents of Article 1382 CC in Belgium and Luxembourg complied with the requirements of foreseeability pursuant to Article 10(2) ECHR. It is also contended that the French Supreme Court has taken this case law into account and allows the application of Article 1382 CC in freedom of expression cases as long as the procedural rules of the Press Act are not circumvented.[764]

Despite these ambiguities, settled case law of the French Supreme Court has shown that in French press law, criminal and civil law is unified to a high extent.[765] Originally, the 1881 Press Act has in essence been an act of penal nature, but it has

---

760 French Supreme Court, civ.ch. I, 29 November 2005, n° 04–16.508, *Bull.* 2005 I, n° 453 p. 380. See even: French Supreme Court, civ.ch. I, 30 October 2008, n°07–19223, *Bull.* 2008 I, n°244, annotation E. Dreyer, *Légipresse* n°258-I, p.12.

761 French Supreme Court, civ.ch. I, 6 October 2011, n°10–18142, *Bull.* 2011 I, annotation G. Lécuyer, Responsabilité civile et droit de la presse: le tumulte permanent, *Légipresse* n°290, January 2012, p.31. In the same sense: French Supreme Court, civ.ch. I, 6 May 2010, n° 09–67.624, *Bull.* 2010 I, n° 103.

762 Lécuyer, G., Responsabilité civile et droit de la presse: le tumulte permanent, annotation at: French Supreme Court, civ.ch. I, 6 October 2011, n°10–18142, *Bull.* 2011 I, *Légipresse* n°290, January 2012, p.33 *et seq.*

763 French Supreme Court, civ. Ch., 10 April 2013, n° 12–10177, *Bull.* 2013, I, n° 67, *Légipresse* n°307 July/August 2013, p. 425–429, annotation N. Verly.

764 ECtHR 29 March 2001, n°38432/97, *Thoma v. Luxembourg*; ECtHR 24 February 1997, n°19983/92, *De Haes and Gijsels v. Belgium*. Latil, A., Les fautes d'expression, Ou la renaissance de l'article 1382 du Code civil en matière de liberté d'expression, *Légipresse* n° 318, July-August 2014, p. 409–412.

765 See further: Dreyer, E., *Responsabilités civile et pénale des médias*, 3rd edition, Paris: LexisNexis 2011, p. 3–24.

developed into a hybrid act that also applies in civil cases. In a number of judgments, the French Supreme Court gradually established that in press law cases the norms of the 1881 Press Act take priority over the general norms in civil law. Civil proceedings concerning expression that can be qualified as one of the offences of the 1881 Press Act cannot be based on Article 1382 CC, which prohibits wrongful acts or Article 809 Code of Civil Procedure[766], but must be based on the press offences of the 1881 Press Act. The articles do not thus form a guideline in civil proceedings based on Article 1382 CC, but form independent legal grounds. The strict procedural rules of the 1881 Press Act equally apply in civil proceedings. For example, the French Supreme Court has ruled that Article 53 of the Press Act must also be applied in civil cases[767] and the Constitutional Council has decided that this does not violate the right to an effective judicial remedy.[768] The primacy of the 1881 Press Act guarantees that the specific solutions adopted in the Act in order to protect freedom of expression have a comprehensive effect.

1.4. Relation between the legislator and the judge

The previously discussed central characteristics of freedom of expression of opinion in French law[769] can be understood in light of the general principles anchored in the constitutional texts that express the objective of the law to protect the rights of citizens and the democratic principle on which *in fine* the French constitutional order is founded; the normativity of the law and the separation of powers.

Article 16 DDHC affirms that the rights of citizens are guaranteed by the French State. From this article, the principle of legal certainty is created, in accordance with which the law must be sufficiently clear and accessible for citizens to whom it is addressed.[770] Rights are not assured if legal norms are imprecise or ambiguous, as in the case of the délit d'opinion. A law that edicts an uncertain rule is not only susceptible of unequal application, but also breaches individual freedom by not

---

766 Article 809 CCP affords the summary judge a special competence, according to which 'Le président peut toujours, même en présence d'une contestation sérieuse, prescrire en référé les mesures conservatoires ou de remise en état qui s'imposent, soit pour prévenir un dommage imminent, soit pour faire cesser un trouble manifestement illicite'.

767 French Supreme Court, Plenary Assembly, 15 February 2013, n° 11–14637, *Légipresse* n° 303 March 2013, p. 152–164, annotation P. Guerder.

768 Cons. Con. 17 May 2013, n°2013–311 QPC, *Légipresse* n°307 July/August 2013, p. 415–417, annotation G. Lécuyer. For a critical analysis of the conformity of the application of the procedural rules in civil cases with Article 6 ECHR see: Dreyer, E., L'accès au juge civil en matière de presse, *Légipresse* n°291, February 2012, pp.83–89.

769 Being the strict distinction between free opinions and punishable acts made by the French legislator, the rationale of the existence of a link between an opinion and a following reprehensible act for the creation of specific and precise press offences in order to avoid the creation of a 'délit d'opinion' and the primacy of the 1881 Press Act over general civil norms and of the press offences over Article 1382 CC in civil press law cases.

770 Code constitutionnel commenté 2012, p.192.

precisely determining the restrictions that can be posed to this freedom. Hence, legal certainty thus guarantees the exercise of fundamental rights[771], *in casu* freedom of expression of opinion.

This is equally true of the principle of the normativity of the law that is created as a result of Article 6 DDHC, which reads: 'la loi est l'expression de la volonté générale'. As a result of this article, the law has the vocation to create rules and therefore must have a normative character. According to the Constitutional Council 'vouloir n'est pas expliquer, souhaiter, considérer, désirer, estimer ou constater'.[772] We will see that certain legislation concerning the denial of genocides is at odds with this principle (para.9.7 *infra*). Before the Fifth Republic (1958-present), the French legislator was, however, competent to deliberate on any subject and to create rules of any character and in any field. The 1958 Constitution limited the power of the National Assembly by determining in its Article 34 the fields of competence of the National Assembly. The definition of the law is no longer merely formal, but also substantial. The law is not determined by the legislator, but by the Constitution. The Constitutional Council, created by the 1958 Constitution, supervises the French legislator to ensure that it does not create laws that fall outside the competences assigned to it by the Constitution. It follows that 'La loi n'étant l'expression de la volonté générale que dans le respect de la Constitution.'[773]

The French Constitution can said to be 'rigid' in the sense that it can only be amended following a special procedure and there are certain substantive limitations to its revision.[774] Article 89–4 of the Constitution prohibits any proposal to abandon the republican form of government. The article can, however, be interpreted in different ways. If this prohibition merely signifies the interdiction to re-establish the Monarchy or the Empire, the limitation it poses on the Constituent power to revise the Constitution is small because the risk of such a re-establishment can itself be regarded as small. If this prohibition signifies, on the other hand, the obligation to respect the values and principles that shape a regime's 'republican form', for example 'la laïcité, l'égalité, la fraternité, la dignité humaine', the feedom of the Constituent power is strongly reduced.[775] The efficacy of these limitations is highly problematic, because it is always possible to amend the revision clause of the Constitution itself.[776] Moreover, although the Constitution poses the limitations to its revision, the control of the respect thereof is not assured; in 2003, the Constitutional Council decided that it lacked jurisdiction to review constitutional amendments.[777]

---

771 Mathieu, B., *Cahiers du Conseil constitutionnel* n° 21 (Dossier: la normativité) – January 2007.

772 Cons. Con. 29 July 2004, n° 2004–500 DC.

773 Mathieu 2007-II.

774 Bermann, G.A. & Picard, E., *Introduction to French law*, Alphen aan den Rijn: Kluwer Law International 2008, p.11.

775 Rousseau, D., La revision de la Constitution sous la Vème République, *La Constitution en 20 questions: question n°20 La Constitution peut-elle être modifiée?*, available at: www.conseil-constitutionnel.fr.

776 Bermann & Picard 2008, p. 12.

777 Cons. Con. 26 March 2003 n° 2003–469 DC.

The principle of the normativity of the law is closely connected to the separation of powers between the legislature, the executive and the judiciary, guaranteed in Article 16 DDHC. According to the traditional case law of the Constitutional Council, uncertain or ambiguous legislation would 'reporter sur des autorités administratives ou juridictionnelles le soin de fixer des règles dont la détermination n'a été confiée par la Constitution qu'à la loi'.[778] This perspective, which takes into account the risk of free judicial interpretation subscribes to the classic vision of the function of the juge as the 'bouche de la loi'. It is the task of the legislator to seek the general interest by passing laws and it is the task of the judge to ensure compliance with the laws thus adopted. The principle of the separation of powers places the judge in second position relative to the legislator.[779] This explains why the French judge, as we will see (para.1.6.1 and part II *infra*), treats press offences as 'closed entities' and is reluctant to, in their strict application, accommodate or 'import' the Article 10 case law of the ECtHR that sets standards concerning the general interest of a public debate.

The principles as mentioned above underlie the principle of the legality of criminal offences and sanctions guaranteed by Article 8 DDHC. The article primarily ensures that the judiciary do not create laws, but that they strictly interprets criminal law, which is also provided in Article 111–4 of the French Penal Code that reads 'La loi pénale est d'interprétation stricte'. It interdicts the penal judge to give an analoguous interpretation, because he is not allowed to bridge eventual lacunae in the law. It does not, however, impose a literary interpretation nor does it interdict a teleological interpretation in order to produce the full effect of a provision.[780] Finally, as a result of the article, it is necessary for the legislator to define the criminal offences in sufficiently clear and precise terms.[781]

The ensemble of these principles explains why the French judge has given priority to the 1881 Press Act over the general civil norms and why, as we will see (part II *infra*), the French legislator is reluctant to abrogate the press offences to the benefit of the open, civil norm of the wrongful act (1382 CC).

1.5. Rights through the state and not against the state

The previously discussed central characteristics of the free expression of opinion in French law and of the French Press Act can furthermore be understood in light of the particular conception of rights in French legal culture as defined by French scholars as rights *through* the state and not as rights *against* the state.[782] The idea that rights are primarily against the state can be connected to a particular form of liberalism. According to this view, the guarantee of rights lies in a strict limitation

778 Mathieu 2007-II.
779 Mathieu 2007-II.
780 Code constitutionnel commenté 2012, p.107.
781 Code constitutionnel commenté 2012, p.107.
782 Bermann & Picard 2008, p. 16.

of the power of the State and of the lawmaker. This view is, however, said to have never been part of French legal culture. Contrarily, the State has primarily been perceived not as a threat, but as a protector of rights.[783] This might in itself already explain the somewhat paternalistic conception of freedom of expression in France.[784]

This conception of the nature of rights and the state goes back to the French Revolution. The National Assembly that adopted the Declaration of Rights of Man and Citizen of 1789 did not consider the need to *create* rights, but instead merely *declared* the 'natural, unalienable, and sacred rights of man' that were supposed to have pre-existed both the state and society. Men had entered society in order to have these rights protected against any authority or person that might threaten them. According to Article 2 DDHC, the purpose of society is therefore the 'preservation' of these rights. The latter can, however, not be absolute, because then they will conflict with the rights of others.[785] It is only because statutes define the *limits* to the *exercise* of the natural rights that the rights can be preserved (Articles 4 and 5 DDHC). These limitations can then be considered to define at the same time both the rights they restrict and the rights of others, thus the rights of citizens against other citizens.[786] These rights are thus not rights against the legislative power, but rather they are rights *through* statutes, i.e. the legislative power, defined *erga omnes*, i.e. against the executive and against other individuals.[787] This is particularly clear in the case of freedom of expression; Article 11 DDHC defines this freedom as the right to be punished only according to the law, thus as the right to do what the law permits. It is argued that this does not signify that statutes may limit freedom of the press, but rather that there is no freedom of the press that can be conceived outside of statutes.[788]

Furthermore, the concept of a state as a public entity endowed with legal personality, separate from civil society and limited by way of rights is said to be absent from French legal culture. The purpose of the Revolution was precisely to abandon this concept, which was present in the Ancien Régime by abolishing the separation between citizens and the state or between the state and society. Articles 16 and 6 DDHC therefore express the sacred right of man to live in a *society* where there is a separation of powers and where the law, i.e. statutory law, expresses the *general will.* From this perspective, the relation between state and citizens is not hierarchical but horizontal. And legislation is the only genuine source of law. The convergence of criminal and civil law in French Press law and the

[783] Troper, M., Who Needs a Third Party Effect Doctrine? – The Case of France, in: Sajó, A. & Uitz, R. (Eds.), *The Constitution in Private Relations: Expanding Constitutionalism*, The Hague: Eleven International Publishing 2005, p. 119.

[784] Mbongo, B., Hate speech, extreme speech and collective defamation in French law, in: Hare & Weinstein 2009, p. 221–236.

[785] Bermann & Picard 2008, p. 16.

[786] Troper 2005, p. 120.

[787] Troper 2005, p. 121.

[788] *Ibid.*

hybrid nature of the French press offences that form the legal ground in both criminal and civil cases can be placed in this light. In fact, as we will see, the law permits civil parties to set in motion both criminal and civil cases on the basis of the hate speech bans of the French Press Act (para. 10 *infra*). One could therefore even imagine the French hate speech bans as 'subjective rights' distributed by the French legislator to citizens in political society against other citizens.

Finally, the French conception of rights as rights *through* the state *erga omnes* and not as rights *against* the state also explains why French legal doctrine lacks a 'third party effect', 'horizontal effect' or 'indirect effect' doctrine of fundamental rights. After all, pursuant to the above, the French Constitution recognizes rights that are indistinctly vertical and horizontal and empowers the legislature to define and institute them.[789] One may argue that this distinction vanishes precisely when statutory law restricts fundamental rights in their core. This is notably also the case with the press offences, which restrict the right to freedom of expression at its core. The fact that an appeal for freedom of expression against the application of the press offences by the judge is not referred to as a 'horizontal effect' of the right does, however, not signify that the right cannot *de facto* function as such or that freedom of expression is necessarily less protected. The latter could, on the other hand, be a possible consequence of too rigid an application of the press offences by the judiciary as a result of the strict separation of powers.

1.6. Relation to international law: 'l'exception française'

1.6.1. A 'nationalistic' defence-reflex towards international law

Relevant treaties and conventions comprising norms concerning freedom of expression that France has signed and ratified are the ECHR and the ICCPR. France has a monist system. Pursuant to Article 55 of the French Constitution, treaty law takes precedence over national statutes, both earlier and subsequent. The ECHR can therefore directly be relied upon before all French courts.[790]

In conformity with the requirements of the case law of the ECtHR, the French courts must assure case-by-case that any restriction imposed on freedom of expression is strictly 'necessary'. However, the judgments by the French Supreme Court or lower courts often contain stereotypical motivations. Generally put, the French courts confine themselves to affirm that the restriction to the freedom of expression in question, being either the press offence itself or its application, has the objective to guarantee one of the interests mentioned in Article 10(2) ECHR and that its necessity is therefore incontestable. For example, the Douai Court of Appeal considered in one single phrase that the Act that criminalized the insult on the ground of sexual orientation was necessary to protect homosexuals and that 'les

789 Troper 2005, p. 123.
790 Code constitutionnel commenté 2012, p.742.

articles 24, alinéa 3 et 6, 24 bis et 33, alinéa 4 de la loi du 29 juillet 1881, entrent dans les exceptions prévues à l'alinéa 2 de l'article 10 de la Convention européenne des droits de l'Homme et des libertés fondamentales et *dès lors* ne sont pas contraires à l'alinéa 1er du même article [curs. EHJ].'[791]

According to Beignier, De Lamy & Dreyer, this superficial motivation seems to dissimulate a 'nationalistic' defence-reflex of the French laws.[792] With regard to the French Supreme Court, Dreyer notes 'le premier réflexe de la Cour de cassation a été de considérer que la loi du 29 juillet 1881 réalisait en elle-même un équilibre suffisant entre liberté d'expression, garantie à l'article 10(1) de la Convention, et intérêts protégés en vertu du paragraphe 2 du même texte.'[793] With regard to the *three-step-test* of Article 10(2) ECHR, Dreyer notes that often only the first two steps – the control of the legality of the norm that interferes with the right, and of the legitimacy of the aim pursued by the norm – appear in the motivation of decisions by the French courts. The courts omit to take into account the predominant question of whether or not the measure is necessary. The proportionality of a measure is deduced from the legitimacy of the legal text that is applied. Often French courts thereby determine *in abstracto* whether a requested sanction does not constitute an excessive infringement of freedom of expression.[794]

Hence, due to the very legalistic, even rigid French legal system, in which expression constitutes either a free opinion or a punishable act and in which the French legislator must *a priori* determine the abuses of freedom in strict circumscribed terms, the French courts have for long time refrained from effectively balancing the conflicting norms in every case. In reality, the courts do not perform an act of conciliation *in concreto* between the right to freedom of expression and the rights and interests that oppose its free exercise, as required by the ECtHR for the examination of the necessity of every restriction.[795] Conte explains 'la jurisprudence européenne déplace l'argumentation juridique du terrain de la légalité à celui de l'opportunité (...) là où notre tradition juridique nous conduit à vérifier si les composantes d'une qualification sont réunies dans les conditions que fixe la loi, les juges de Strasbourg s'interrogent sur l'opportunité d'une décision, ce qui relève d'une autre culture juridique.'[796] As a result, France has in the past been condemned many times by the ECtHR for violations of Article 10 ECHR.

---

791 Cited in: Beignier, De Lamy & Dreyer 2009, p.127.

792 Beignier, De Lamy & Dreyer 2009, p.127.

793 Dreyer, E., *Voies de recours. Contrôle exercé par la Cour de cassation: JCL. Communication*, Fasc. 3100, n° 59.

794 Dreyer, E., *Responsabilités civile et pénale des médias*, 3rd edition, Paris: LexisNexis 2011, p. 40–41 and more generally p. 24–52.

795 Beignier, De Lamy & Dreyer 2009, p.128.

796 French Supreme Court, crim.ch., 11 March 2008, *Dr. pén.* 2008/4, p.871, annotation Ph. Conte. Cited in: Monfort, J.-Y., L'apparition en jurisprudence du critère du '*débat d'intérêt général*' dans le droit de la diffamation, *Légipresse* n°290 January 2012, p.21.

1.6.2. France before the ECtHR

Between 1959 and 2014, France has been condemned 31 times by the ECtHR for violations of Article 10. It has the third highest score with regard to violations of Article 10 amongst all member states; Turkey currently leads with 248 violations followed by Austria with 34 violations.[797] Many of these cases concern the 1881 Press Act. These cases can be divided into cases in which the ECtHR a) criticized the *existence* of a particular press offence *as such* and b) criticized the *application* of one of the press offences of the 1881 Press Act by the French judge.[798]

The cases *Ekin v. France*[799, 800] and *Colombani v. France*[801, 802] are two noteworthy historical cases, in which the nature of the article of the Press Act itself, respectively Article 14 that gave the French Minister of Interior powers to impose general and absolute bans throughout France on the circulation, distribution or sale of any document written in a foreign language or of foreign origin and Article 36 that criminalized the 'offense à chef d'état étranger', was up for discussion rather

797 Statistics by States and table of violations accessible on: www.echr.coe.int.

798 For an analysis of cases since the nineties, see: De Bellescize, D., La France et l'article 10 de la Convention européenne de sauvegarde des droits de l'homme, *RTDH* 61 2005, pp.225–259.

799 ECtHR 17 July 2001, n° 39288/98, *Association Ekin/France*. On the basis of Article 14, the Minister had interdicted the work *Euskadi en guerre* written with the participation of several Basque universities, for its alleged encouragement to separatism. The ECtHR considered the interference with freedom of expression unnecessary in a democratic society, underlining the lacunae of the text of the article that did not state the circumstances in which the power may be used and gave no definition of the concept of "foreign origin" nor any indication of the grounds on which a publication deemed to be foreign may be banned.

800 Although those gaps had gradually been filled by the administrative courts' case-law, the application of those rules had, in certain cases, produced results that are at best surprising and in some cases verge on the arbitrary, depending on the language of publication or the place of origin. See: ECtHR 17 July 2001, n° 39288/98, *Association Ekin/France*, para. 60. Such legislation appeared to be in direct conflict with the actual wording of paragraph 1 of Article 10 of the Convention, which provides that the rights set forth in that Article are secured "regardless of frontiers". See: ECtHR 17 July 2001, n° 39288/98, *Association Ekin/France*, para. 62.

801 ECtHR 25 June 2002, n° 51279/99, *Colombani and others/France*. On the basis of Article 36, the French journal *Le Monde* and Colombani, its director of publication, had been condemned in relation to two articles, in which were at issue Maroc as the first export country of cannabis in the world and the first supplier of cannabis on the European market and the involvement of the authorities around the Moroccan King Hassan II therein, despite their statements to take measures against drugs trafficking. The article was based on a confidential report drafted by the European Union. The ECtHR criticized the fact that the applicants were not able to rely on a defence of justification – that is to say proving the truth of the allegation – to escape criminal liability on the charge of insulting a foreign head of State. The inability for a suspect to plead for a justification was a measure that went beyond what was required to protect a person's reputation and rights, even when that person was a head of State or government. See: para. 66.

802 According to the Court, the effect of Article 36 was to confer a special legal status on heads of State, shielding them from criticism solely on account of their function or status, irrespective of whether the criticism was warranted. That amounted to conferring on foreign heads of State a special privilege that could not be reconciled with modern practice and political conceptions. Such a privilege exceeded what was necessary for that objective to be attained. See: para. 68.

than its application in the given circumstances and in which France was severely and unanimously condemned by seven judges of the ECtHR. Although the ECtHR did not openly request France to abrogate the articles in question, the decisions amounted in practice to the annihilation of any possibility to apply them. Under the influence of the decisions of the ECtHR the French legislator reluctantly abrogated Articles 14[803] and 36[804] of the 1881 Press Act for being contrary to freedom of expression.[805]

The second type of cases are, however, of more interest to this study due to the fact that they notably concerned a suspect's right to prove the truth of his or her statement or good faith in defamation cases, which is why I will discuss them in the paragraph concerning defamation (para.4.4.3 *infra*). However, the case Eon/ France[806] is a noteworthy recent case, in which the ECtHR decided with 6:1 votes that the application of Article 26 of the Press Act that criminalizes the 'offense au Président de la République' amounted to a violation of freedom of expression. The case concerned the conviction of Eon for waving a small placard reading 'casse-toi, pov'con' (get lost, you sad prick) during a visit to Laval by the President of France as the President's party was about to pass by. Eon was thereby making an allusion to a phrase, which the President himself had uttered in response to a farmer, who refused to shake his hand, an event that had been largely diffused by the media.

The ECtHR considered 'criminal penalties for conduct such as that of the applicant in the present case are likely to have a chilling effect on satirical forms of expression relating to topical issues. Such forms of expression can themselves play a very important role in open discussion of matters of public concern, an indispensable feature of a democratic society'.[807] Dreyer questions whether the ECtHR thereby does not step into the same pitfall as the French jurisdictions. In fact, the Court reproaches the latter of having a too theoretical appreciation of the concerned interests, and thus to disregard the circumstances of the case. But in this case the Court itself seemed to legitimize a type of discourse rather than to look at the actual words concerned.[808] This comment fits into the general criticism of French scholars on the case law of the ECtHR. Hereunder follows a brief sketch of the reaction of French legal scholars to this European case law in order to underscore the French vision on freedom of expression.[809]

---

803 Decree n° 2064–1044 of 4 October 2004 abrogating Decree-law of 6 May 1939 concerning the control of foreign press.

804 Act of 9 March 2004 concerning the adaptation of justice to evolutions of criminality, 'Loi Perben 2'.

805 De Bellescize 2005, pp.243–259.

806 ECtHR 14 March 2013, n°26118/10, *Eon v. France, Légipresse* n°305 May 2013, 304–13, annotation E. Dreyer.

807 *Ibid,*,para. 61.

808 Annotation E. Dreyer at: ECtHR 14 March 2013, n°26118/10, *Eon v. France, Légipresse* n°305 May 2013, p. 293.

809 For comprehensive comparative studies on the right to freedom of expression in France and America see: Pech, L., *La liberté d' expression et sa limitation: les enseignements de*

In French legal doctrine, condemnations of France by the ECtHR have been variously received. For some scholars, the condemnations show that the French traditional conception of freedom of expression is too restrictive. Beignier, De Lamy & Dreyer opine that the French supreme jurisdictions, from a fear of installing a 'gouvernement des juges', have systematically refused to fundamentally reflect on the necessity of the numerous restrictions posed to freedom of expression since the vote of the 'grande loi libérale de 1881' that can, without doubt, be historically justified, but pose real problems to freedom of expression.[810] In their view, for a long time, the French case law has, in a systematic manner, given priority to the right of reputation and the right to privacy over freedom of expression and has severely determined the limits to political debate without taking into account whether or not the expression in question formed a matter of public interest. Beignier, De Lamy & Dreyer therefore welcome an increasing influence of the case law of the ECtHR on French case law.[811] Bellescize argues that, while the ECtHR has sometimes overstepped the margin of appreciation of French judges by imposing an interpretation of texts that is susceptible to criticism and the Court has censured certain provisions of the 1881 Press Act, the ECtHR has implicitly or explicitly recognized the compatibility of most of its provisions.[812] According to Bellescize, *in fine*, if the European judge obliges the Press Act to adapt and to correct its imperfections, freedom of expression will benefit from it.[813]

For many scholars, however, the ECtHR holds an excessively liberal conception of freedom of expression that does not match the French legal tradition to search for a conciliation or balance between rights that appear to oppose each other. Derieux & Granchet state that the case law of the ECtHR concerning Article 10 ECHR ('qu'elle interprète à sa façon!') generally appears to be very favourable to freedom of expression and seems to give it a value superior to all other freedoms, considering the fact that interferences, restrictions or limitations, despite being provided for in Article 10(2), can rarely be justified.[814] For scholars Flauss[815] and Cohen-Jonathan,[816] the ECtHR is inspired too much by the Constitution of the United

l'expériences européennes (Allemagne, France et Convention européenne des droits de l' homme), diss., Clermont-Ferrand: Presses Universitaires de la Faculté de droit de Clermont-Ferrand 2003; Robitaille-Froidure, A., *La liberté d'expression face au racisme, Étude de droit comparé franco-américain*, Paris: L'Harmattan 2011.

810 Beignier, De Lamy & Dreyer 2009, p.132.

811 Beignier, De Lamy & Dreyer 2009, p.132.

812 The court recognized the compatibility of the regime of defamation implicitly in the *Colombani* case, and explicitly in the cases *Radio France* and *Chauvy et autres*, and the compatibility of the offence of Holocaust denial with Article 10 ECHR in the cases *Lehideux et Isorni* and *Chauvy et autres*.

813 De Bellescize 2005, pp.258–259.

814 Derieux, E. & Granchet, A., *Droits des médias, droit français, européen et international*, 6th edition, Paris: L.G.D.J. 2010, p.854.

815 Flauss, J.F., La présence de la jurisprudence de la Cour suprême des Etats-Unis d'Amérique dans le contentieux européen des droits de l'homme, *RTDH* 2005, p.313.

816 Cohen-Jonathan, G., Débats. Rapport Favoreu, *RUDH* 1995, p.361.

States and the case law of the American Supreme Court, and does not sufficiently takes into account the constitutional traditions of the member states. Morange regrets that certain solutions in French law are revised by case law of the ECtHR that is too uniform, casuistic and often poorly motivated and that manifestly neglects the balance that the drafters of Article 10 ECHR intended to strike.[817]

1.7. Conclusion

In French law, Articles 10 and 11 of the 1789 Declaration constitutionally protect the manifestation and communication of all kinds of opinions – philosophical, ideological, religious, and non-religious – on equal footing. The existence of plurality of thoughts and opinions forms an object of constitutional value. In order to conciliate the free expression of opinion with the rights of others, human dignity or the interest in the protection of the public order, the French legislator must determine the abuses of the freedom. According to the principle that the manifestation of an opinion as such cannot be criminalized, in the vision of the French legislator, present French criminal law does not comprise any 'délits d'opinion'.

Although no one single, clear definition of the 'délit d'opinion' exists in French legal doctrine, Droin points out three common characteristics [Droin 2009]. Firstly, contrary to the press offences, the 'délit d'opinion' does not form the object of a precise qualification by the French legislator. Secondly, it does not determine the specific right or interest with which it interferes: it criminalizes a simple opinion, and not the support of a criminal or punishable act. Thirdly, its arbitrary prosecution and sanction constitutes a danger to the free expression of an opinion. An example 'par excellence' of an offence that is generally regarded as a délit d'opinion in French legal doctrine is the former 'délit d'outrage à la morale publique et religieuse', as created by the Act of 17 May 1819 and abolished by the 1881 Press Act, which marked the end of the criminalization of religious offences in France.

In French law, the freedom of expression of opinion is essentially regulated by the French Press Act of 29 July 1881, the rationale of which was to establish a liberal regime for the printed press. The Act suppressed all preventive regimes and censorship and established norms for the printing press and bookshops, journals, and placards. It replaced all 'délits d'opinion' with specific press offences and determined the persons criminally responsible through a 'responsabilité en cascade'. Finally, the principle of freedom of expression is assured by the establishment of very strict procedural rules for the prosecution of the press offences that derogate from the French code of criminal procedure.

---

817 Morange, J., *La conception française de la liberté d'expression*, in: Zoller, E. (ed.) *La liberté d'expression aux Etats-Unis et en Europe*, Paris: Dalloz 2008, p.172.

In its Chapter IV concerning 'felonies and misdemeanours committed through the press or any other means of publication', the 1881 Press Act cites all public speech offences in French law. In the vision of the French legislator, the offences merely criminalize the abuses of the freedom of opinion, not opinions as such. For the French legislator of 1881, the justification for criminalization formed the link between the expression of an idea and the following reprehensible act. The new press offences, created by the 1881 Press Act, increasingly protect, individuals considered in their differences and singularities and not the authorities; the requirement of the existence of a link between the expression and the reprehensible act seems to be diluted.

Originally, the 1881 Press Act has in essence been an act of penal nature, but has developed into a hybrid act that also applies in civil cases. In press law cases the norms of the 1881 Press Act take priority over the general norms in civil law. This primacy of the 1881 Press Act guarantees that the specific solutions adopted in the Act in order to protect freedom of expression have a comprehensive effect and equally apply in civil cases.

The central characteristics of freedom of expression of opinion in French law can be understood in light of the general principles anchored in the constitutional texts that in order to protect the rights of citizens guarantee the normativity of the law and the separation of powers. According to these principles, the legislator determines the general interest by voting laws that contain precise and unambiguous norms and the judge occupies second place relative to the legislator; he functions as the 'bouche de la loi' and must, in his application of the law, give a strict interpretation.

The French legalistic legal system poses real problems for the accommodation or 'importation' of the Article 10 case law of the ECtHR that sets standards concerning the general interest of a public debate. The priority lies with the French legislator who *a priori* has to determine the abuses of freedom of expression. The French courts have for long time refrained from effectively balancing the conflicting norms in every case and have not performed an act of conciliation *in concreto* between the right to freedom of expression and the rights and interests that oppose its free exercise. Due to the condemnations of France by the ECtHR, France has reluctantly abrogated provisions or adapted regimes in the 1881 Press Act in order to offer greater protection to freedom of expression. According to many French legal scholars, however, the liberal conception of freedom of expression of the ECtHR does not match the French legal tradition to conciliate or balance conflicting rights.

II. EGALITÉ: HATE SPEECH BANS IN ACCORDANCE WITH THE FRENCH PRESS ACT

'(...) Une liberté aussi fondamentale que la liberté de la presse s'exerce très naturellement dans le cadre de la loi qui l'organise. (...) Au raciste, la loi refuse la liberté de provoquer à la discrimination raciale. C'est qu'en réalité, exprimer une opinion est une chose, provoquer à la discrimination en est une autre (...).'[818]

'Mais je me refuse à nommer opinion une doctrine qui vise expressément des personnes particulières et qui tend à supprimer leurs droits ou à les exterminer. (...) L'antisémitisme ne rentre pas dans la catégorie de pensées que protège le droit de libre opinion.'

J.-P. Sartre, *Réflexions sur la question juive*[819]

This section begins with a characterization of the French notion of equality as it has developed from relevant French law and policies (2). Against this setting, the background and purport of the Pleven Act of 1 July 1972, which introduced the main hate speech bans into French law, are examined (3). Subsequently, the three following paragraphs analyse the main French hate speech bans and their application by the French judge, respectively the offences of 'racial defamation' (4); 'racial insult' (5); and 'racial provocation' (6). The French Supreme Court uses these terms to refer to the offences in their entirety. French legal doctrine further distinguishes between *racial* defamation; insult or provocation, i.e. on the basis of a person's origin and membership or non-membership of an ethnic group, nation or race, and *religious* defamation; insult or provocation, i.e. on the ground of religion. This chapter adopts these approaches. The three paragraphs are followed by a discussion of the modifications of the Pleven Act since its adoption (7). The attention then shifts to the background and purport of the Gayssot Act of 13 July 1990, which introduced the offence of Holocaust denial into French law (8). The section ends with an analysis of the offence of Holocaust denial and its application by the French judiciary (9).

2. THE FRENCH NOTION OF EQUALITY

The notion of equality forms a central characteristic of the French Republic (2.1). The strict or abstract understanding of the notion explains the non-recognition of minorities under French law (2.2) and also influences the French immigration and integration policy (2.3), but does not prevent the existence of a lively practice of

818 J. Foulon-Piganiol, annotation at: Paris 17 June 1974, *Recueil Dalloz*, 1975.J.468. cited by E. Derieux, Lutte contre le racisme et liberté d'expression, *Légipresse* n° 94, September 1992/7, p. 81.

819 Sartre, J.P., *Réflexions sur la question juive*, Paris: Gallimard 1954, p. 10.

consultation between the French government and religious and anti-racism associations representing minority interests (2.4). However, the accommodation of religious practices in the public domain runs counter to *la laïcité,* French State neutrality, which can be regarded as a subset of freedom and equality (2.5). The analysis results in a general conclusion about the French notion of equality (2.6).

2.1. Equality as a central characteristic of the French Republic

The principle of equality is mentioned in several reprises in the Constitution of 1958 and in the texts it refers to in its preamble. Equality is a recurrent principle that has been affirmed since 1789. In the 1789 Declaration the term is used in Article 1, which affirms the equality of men in general. Article 6 provides for equality before the law, from which results the equal access to public occupations: 'La loi est l'expression de la volonté générale. Tous les citoyens ont droits de concourir personnellement, ou par leurs représentants, à sa formation. Elle doit être la même pour tous, soit qu'elle protège, soit qu'elle punisse. Tous les citoyens étant égaux à ses yeux sont également admissibles à toutes dignités, places et emplois publics, selon leurs capacité; et sans autre distinction que celle de leurs vertus et de leurs talents.' Article 13 provides for the equal distribution of public charges.

The first paragraph of the preamble of the 1946 Constitution affirms the principle of non-discrimination by referring to the absence of distinction on the grounds of *race, religion or belief.* Article 1 of the Constitution of 1958 refines the principle of non-discrimination specifying that equality before the law comprises the absence of a distinction on the ground of *origin* and provides 'La France est une République indivisible, laïque, démocratique et sociale. Elle assure l'égalité devant la loi de tous les citoyens sans distinction d'origine, de race ou de religion. Elle respecte toutes les croyances …'. Article 2 of the 1958 Constitution uses the term in the devise of the Republic: 'La devise de la République est "Liberté, Égalité, Fraternité"'. Equality thus forms a central characteristic of the French Republic. The rather abstract ideal of equality influences the French approach towards minorities.

2.2. Non-recognition of minorities under French law

The French approach to minorities is strongly influenced by the ideology of French Republicanism. According to the traditional French Jacobin understanding of the state, the mission of the state is to guarantee the general interest above all other interests of individuals and groups and forms the sole representative of the people in order to act in the name of the collective will for the collective good. The spirit of the French Revolution was to suppress all intermediary bodies between the citizens and the state, fearing the development of factions that would distort the general will.[820] Individuals must thus be regarded as citizens, who have a direct link to the state. The development of groups defined by race, religion, ethnicity, culture or any other common characteristic would constitute 'communautarisme'. France opposes any creation of what can be regarded as a 'nation within a nation'.[821] This would undermine the constitutional principles of the indivisibility of the French Republic, the equality before the law and the unicity of the French people. The French Republic is founded on a social pact, which precisely transcends all differences; and to which every individual can willingly adhere, regardless of his or her biological characteristics or personal convictions. The affirmation of one's identity is a personal choice, not one based on criteria that can, a priori, be used to define a particular group.[822]

According to the case law of the Constitutional Council, it follows from the constitutional principle of equality before the law without distinction of origin, race or religion, that the recognition of national 'minorities' is not possible in the French constitutional order. The constitutional principle is opposed to affording any group defined by a common origin, culture, language or belief, collective rights on the grounds of its common characteristics.[823] France has therefore made an exemption to the only legally binding text of a universal nature, which refers specifically to minorities, Article 27 ICCPR. Article 27 provides: "In those States in which ethnic, religious or linguistic minorities exist, persons belonging to such minorities shall not be denied the right, in community with the other members of their group, to enjoy their own culture, to profess and practice their own religion, or to use their own language." In its initial and second periodic report submitted to the Human Rights Committee (HRC) under Article 40 of the ICCPR, France explained: "Since the basic principles of public law prohibit distinctions between citizens on grounds of origin, race or religion, France is a country in which there are no minorities and, as stated in the declaration made by France, Article 27 is not applicable as far as the Republic is concerned."[824]

Likewise, France has not ratified the European Charter for Regional or Minority Languages that recognizes the right to use a regional language both in the private and public sphere.[825] The Constitutional Council has confirmed the position of the French Government, i.e. that ratification of the charter is contrary to Article 2 of the

820 Mény, Y., 'La légitimation des groupes d'intérêts par l'administration Française', *Revue Française de l'Administration Publique*, 1986, 39, p. 483–94.

821 Brubaker, B., *Citizenship and nationhood in France and Germany*, London: Harvard University Press 1992, p. 106.

822 See generally the contributions by various authors in: Fenet, A.; Soulier, G. (ed.), *Les minorités et leur droits depuis 1789*, Paris: L'Harmattan 1989.

823 Cons. Con. 15 June 1999, n°99–412 DC.

824 *Consideration of Reports Submitted by States Parties Under Article 40 of the Covenant: France*, U.N. GAOR, HRC, 26 August 1987, 540, U.N. Doc. CCPR/C/46/Add.2 (1987); *Consideration of Reports Submitted by States Parties Under Article 40 of the Covenant: France*, U.N. GAOR, HRC, 10 May 1982, U.N. Doc. CCPR/C/22/Add.2 (1982).

825 Code constitutionnel commenté 2012, p.353.

1958 Constitution, which provides 'La langue de la République est le français', considering that a linguistic unity appears to be an indispensable corrolaire of the constitutional principle of the unity of the French people of Article 1 of the 1958 Constitution.[826] The constitutional reform of 2008 inserted into the 1958 Constitution Article 75–1, which provides 'Les langues regionales appartiennent au patrimoine de la France'.[827] This reform aimed to meet France's international obligations, but it does not seem to alter the fact that, for the first time, France, which has nevertheless signed the charter, cannot ratify it for being contrary to the Constitution.[828]

On the ground that the French Constitution merely acknowledges the French people, composed of all French citizens without distinction of origin, race or religion, the Constitutional Council equally found the reference by the French legislator in the Act on the statute of the territorial unit of Corsica – concerning the legal status of Corse – to the 'peuple corse, composante du peuple français', thus to the specific characteristic of French citizens being Corse, to be unconstitutional.[829]

The abstract ideal of equality explains why since 2002 several legislative proposals have been made to suppress the term 'race' from the French Constitution and or French legislation.[830] These proposals have been motivated by the allegedly profound legal ambiguity of the term 'race'. Historically, the term has served as a ground for racial discrimination; in the 17th century it implicitly underlay the 'code noir' of the French colonial legislation and during the Vichy-Regime it formed an explicit legal category in the French anti-Semitic legislation. It is thought that its presence in current French legislation, even to prohibit discrimination, would also amount to implicitly admitting the existence of races as far as the law is concerned. However, the proposals have always been rejected by a majority of the National Assembly, because the term would be an indispensable legal instrument for an effective fight against racism.[831]

During the presidential campaign in 2012, the ambition to suppress the term 'race' in the French Constitution was once again expressed by Hollande, who stated 'il n'y a pas de place dans la République pour la race'. Subsequently, on 16 May 2013, the National Assembly adopted in its first reading, a legislative proposal '*tendant à la suppression du mot 'race' de notre législation*'.[832] It was

826 Cons. Con. 15 June 1999, n°99–412 DC.

827 Code constitutionnel commenté 2012, p.1049.

828 Code constitutionnel commenté 2012, p.353.

829 Cons. Con. 9 May 1991, n°91–290 DC.

830 For an overview see: Rapport n°989 fait au nom de la commission des lois constitutionnelles sur la proposition de loi n°218 '*tendant à la suppression du mot 'race' de notre législation*', Assemblée Nationale, 24 avril 2013, p. 13–14.

831 *Ibid.*

832 Proposition de loi '*tendant à la suppression du mot 'race' de notre législation*', texte adopté n°139, Assemblée Nationale, 16 mai 2013. For the discussion in Parlement see: www.assemblee-nationale.fr/14/cri/2012–2013/20130240.asp.

considered to be unnecessary and inopportune to first omit the term 'race' from Article 1 of the 1958 Constitution. After certain amendments to the initial proposal,[833] the proposal now envisions the omission of the term 'race' and certain derivatives of 'race', such as 'racial', from French legislation entirely and to replace these terms with 'legally neutral' terms. In the hate speech bans of the French Press Act, the words 'une race' are replaced by 'ou pour des raisons racistes'.[834]

Given the fact that the proposal by no means aims to alter the substance of the legal provisions containing the term 'race', it can be understood to primarily have a political symbolical significance; indeed Article 1 of the proposal states 'La République française condamne le racisme, l'antisémitisme et la xénophobie. Elle ne reconnaît l'existence d'aucune prétendue race'. The aim of the amendments is precisely to prevent the existence of legal gaps, which would reduce the effectiveness of the fight agaist racism, and to assure the compatibility of the proposal with international and European law.[835] French legal scholars, however, disagree on whether the new legally neutral terms 'ou pour des raisons racistes' in the French hate speech bans will have the negative effect of requiring a more subjective appreciation by the French judge for the determination of the offence.[836] This would not benefit legal certainty.

The prevailing conception of equality is indissolubly linked to the image of the French Republic as a social, unitary, uniform, and homogenous body; differences are not only prohibited or denied, but also repressed in case they pose a threat to the unity of the nation.[837] This equally explains the fact that French law does not permit the census to count those who are defined as 'minorities' as well as the French reticence towards any politics of quota, even as a means of fighting discrimination.[838] The use of statistics based on categories of ethnicity and race would be based on an ethno-racial analysis of society, which would contribute to

833 Proposition de loi n°218 '*tendant à la suppression du mot 'race' de notre législation*', Assemblée Nationale, 26 septembre 2012; Proposition de loi n°218 '*tendant à la suppression du mot 'race' de notre législation*', texte de la Commission, Assemblée Nationale, 24 avril 2013.

834 In French law, the term race or its derivatives appear in 9 legal codes and 13 non-codified laws; in total it concerns 59 articles.

835 Rapport n°989, p. 15–20.

836 Derieux, B., Des incidences de la suppression du mot "*race*" sur l'efficacité de la legislation reprimant les comportements racistes, *Légipresse* n°306 June 2013, p. 327; Jouanneau, B., Oui, on peut supprimer le mot "*race*" de la loi, sans dommage!, *Légipresse* n°307 July/August 2013, p. 387.

837 Lochak, D., 'Les minorités et le droit public français: du refus des différences à la gestion des différences', in: Fenet, A. and Soulier, G. (ed.), *Les minorités et leur droits depuis 1789*, Paris: L'Harmattan 1989, p. 125–128.

838 In 2012, the CNCDH advised not to permit in order to fight discriminations the gathering of data based on ethnicity, but only data based on 'origine', i.e. nationality, 'notamment en matière de logement, d'accès aux biens et services et d'accès aux soins.' See: CNCDH, *Avis sur les statistiques 'ethniques'*, 22 March 2012.

the actual construction of 'races' and 'ethnicities' as political actors against the ensemble of the republican principles.[839]

Hence, in 2007 the Constitutional Council found the provision designed to allow processing of personal data 'indicating, directly or indirectly, the racial or ethnic origins' of persons for the carrying out of studies of diversity of origin, discrimination and integration in the law concerning the control of immigration, integration and asylum to be unconstitutional. Such studies may only be conducted on the ground of 'objective data'.[840] In its annual report *La lutte contre le racisme et la xénophobie*, the French National Human Rights Consultative Commission (*la Commission Nationale Consultative des Droits de l'Homme* – CNCDH) publishes the annual statistics on the prosecution of offences penalizing acts of discrimination, including the French hate speech bans as created by the Pleven Act of 1 July 1972.[841] These statistics are confined to the three categories of racism, anti-religion and anti-semitism and thus lack the category of 'ethnicity'.

Precisely because of the non-recognition of ethnic minorities under French law, the French State does not officially engage in 'affirmative action' or 'positive discrimination' in order to advance the fortunes of groups to remedy past discrimination. In France, the principle of equality is interpreted as 'egalité des chances' thus the focus is on equality of opportunities rather than equality of end results. The principle of equality is notably assured by repressive criminal laws penalizing forms of discrimination and labour laws (para. 3.3.3 *infra*).[842, 843] Individuals belonging *de facto* to a certain minority group are thus protected against discrimination on the ground of their specific common characteristics. French law, however, protects *individuals 'minoritaires'* and not *groups 'minorités'* and does not afford individuals the right to be different, but rather protects the right of indifference towards an individual's specific characteristics.[844] The French hate speech bans can be understood as an elaboration of the French ideal of abstract equality and a means of social integration; in the French Republic individual and equal citizens are not to be addressed on the basis of their specific characteristics. However, the difficult position of *de facto* existing minorities in French society was one of the rationales of the act (para.3.3.1 *infra*).

---

839 Haut Conseil à l'Intégration, *La France sait-elle encore intégrer les immigrés? Les élus issus de l'immigration dans les conseils régionaux (2004–2010)*, Paris: la Documentation Française 2011, p. 98.

840 Cons. Con. 15 November 2007, n° 2007–557 DC.

841 Lochak, D., Les références à la "race" dans le droit français, in: Decaux, E. (ed.), *Le droit face au racisme*, Paris: Éditions A. Pedone 1999, p. 37 *et seq*. The Pleven Act 1 July 1972 was the first Act that introduced provisions prohibiting and penalizing racial discrimination into French law. See: Lochak 1989, p. 116.

842 Schain, M.A., *The politics of immigration in France, Britain and the United States, a comparative study*, 2nd edition, New York: Palgrave Macmillan 2012, p. 13.

843 Lochak 1989, p. 113–119.

844 *Koubi*, G., *Droit, droit* à la *différence, droit* à l'*indifférence*, en *France*, *RTDH* 1993, 4, 14, p. 243 *et seq*; Wallon, E., Entre globe et le groupe: le paradoxe français, in: Decaux, E. (ed.), *Le droit face au racisme*, Paris: Éditions A. Pedone 1999, p. 17–23; Lochak 1999, p. 28.

The failure to include specific rights of minority groups in French law appears to be an after-effect of the individualistic conception of rights and human rights dominant at the age of the French Revolution.[845] However, international human rights bodies such as CERD and ECRI have put growing pressure on the French authorities to communicate their statistics based on ethnic origin in order to monitor the existence of discrimination in France. In response to this pressure, the French authorities aim to find a formula that will enable the State to develop ethnic and racial categories to gather statistics, pursue studies, and recommend legislation. The new term that is often used is 'visible minorities'.[846] In order to promote the equality of opportunities and to fight discrimination, the different sections of society, notably the workplace, the media,[847] and politics, must give an adequate reflection of the 'diversity' of the French population that can be pursued on the basis of economic and social criteria or people's nationality or the birthplace of one's parents.[848] Furthermore, affirmative action has equally been developed on the basis of 'objective criteria', for example, by targeting spatial concentrations for education policy (ZEP's) or by designating sensible urban districts (ZUS), but not by targeting specific ethnic groups.[849]

2.3. Immigration and integration policy

French Republicanism thus influences French immigration and integration policy. France is the epitome of a nation-state: unitarian, universalist and egalitarian. Citizenship is regarded as the best means to integrate into French society. Social cohesion can be best preserved by underlining national identity and not personal characteristics.[850] The French model of integration is based on the assimilation of individuals who have made a political choice to become citizens; assimilation forms a basis for equality.[851] The expectation of public institutions is that immigrants will conform to French cultural and legal norms and that there is an acceptance of a common public space that is separate from religious faith and expression, where the principle of 'raison publique' reigns.[852] Immigrants can obtain French citizenship

---

845 Lochak 1989, p.112.

846 Schain 2012, p. 87.

847 Haut Conseil à l'Intégration, *Le bilan de la politique d'intégration 2002–2005*, Paris: La Documentation Française 2005, p. 49–81.

848 Haut Conseil à l'Intégration 2011, p. 98–99.

849 Schain 2012, p. 82.

850 Van Ooijen, H., *Religious Symbols in Public Functions, A comparative analysis of Dutch, English and French justifications for limiting the freedom of public officials to display religious symbols*, Antwerpen: Intersentia 2012, p. 170.

851 Kastoryano, R., French secularism and the headscarf affair, in: Modood, T., Triandafyllidou, A., Zapata-Barrero, R. (eds), *Multiculturalism, Muslims and Citizenship, A European Approach*, London: Routledge 2006, p. 62.

852 Schain 2012, p.15.

on the basis of *jus soli*, territorial birth.[853] Those who are born on French soil to parents born outside France have a right to French citizenship.[854] Since 1945, the French Civil Code (Articles 21–24) determines that no one can be naturalized without demonstrating his 'assimilation to the French community' through knowledge of the French language. The French Government has the power to refuse French citizenship to a person by fault of assimilation.[855]

Historically, France has been a country of immigration and has generally welcomed immigrants as being necessary for the labour market. In the twentieth century, France experienced four waves of immigration; first Italian and Belgian immigration, followed by Polish and Algerian immigration during WWI, after WWII immigration from Spain and Portugal. Since the 1960s, there has been notable Muslim immigration from the former French colonies of North Africa (the *Maghreb*) and sub-Saharan Africa, such as Algeria, Morocco and Tunisia, but also from Turkey.[856] The war of Independence of Algeria[857] in the 1950s had left a very negative connotation with Islam; the bloody acts of terrorism by the Algerian terrorist group Front de libération nationale (FLN) were partly inspired by Islam. After Algeria's victory in 1962, many traumatized *pied-noirs*, French colonists, and *harkis*, allied soldiers of Algerian origin in the French army, fled to France.[858]

Originally, Muslim labour immigrants did not intend to stay and commuted between their countries of origin and France. Because of their temporary stay in France, they did not openly practice Islam; they instead did so in improvised facilities.[859] However, in 1974, in reaction to the oil crisis and mass unemployment, France suspended labour immigration from non-European countries and terminated its generally open policy. Subsequently, Muslim immigrants decided to stay out of France for fear of losing their residency status. By the 1980s the largest component of immigration thus became family reunion. This raised the question of their integration and the accommodation of their religious practices in a predominantly Catholic France.[860]

---

853 See generally: Weil, P., *How to be French, Nationality in the Making since 1789,* London: Duke University Press 2008.

854 Schain 2012, p. 77.

855 Since 1998, young people can claim French citizenship starting at age 16. If they fail to do so, French nationality is attributed to them at age 18, provided that they do not explicitly decline it. This emphasis on an active request for citizenship has resulted in an increased number of declarations of and claims to French citizenship.

856 Schain 2012, p.39.

857 Algeria was conquered by France in 1830 and became independent on 5 July 1962.

858 Fetzer, J.S. & Soper, J.C., *Muslims and the State in Britain, France and Germany,* New York: Cambridge University Press 2005, p. 64.

859 This became known as 'cellar Islam'.

860 Fetzer & Soper 2005, p. 65. For an analysis of the development of a – divers- Muslim community and practice in France see generally: Kepel, G., *Les banlieues de l'Islam: Naissance d'une religion en France*, Paris: Éditions du Seuil 1987; Kepel, G., *La diversité de l'islam en France – Quatre vingt treize*, Paris: Gallimard 2012.

Subsequently, the French Government has tightened the requirements for family reunification, naturalization and citizenship and has facilitated expulsions of undocumented immigrants.[861] Since 2003, immigrants must demonstrate their knowledge of the rights and duties of French citizens. Immigrants must sign The Reception and Integration Contract (CAI), a document that offers them free language courses and civic education. Since 2007, adherence to this contract is a condition for obtaining a long-term visa. Moreover, the CAI is required for all family unification and the evaluation of 'language competence and knowledge of the values of the Republic' takes place before permission is granted to enter France.[862] However, in 2006, Minister of Internal Affairs, Nicolas Sarkozy proposed a politics of 'immigration choisie' that focuses on acceptable forms of immigration, such as the attraction of highly qualified manpower to France, instead of 'immigration subie' that focuses on the termination of immigration.[863] In its report *La France sait-elle encore intégrer les immigrés?*, which was published in 2011, the Haut Conseil à l'Intégration advised the continuation of the Republican model of 'une ardente obligation d'intégration'.[864] In a previous report in 2005, the conseil rejected the notions of assimilation or communautarisme and advanced the republican tradition of *political* integration, which did not entail *ethnic* integration.[865]

The increasingly strict immigration and integration policy can be partly explained by the politicization of the issue by the extreme right winged political party National Front (le Front National – FN) since the 1980s. Public opinion has always been more negative about Muslim immigrants from the Maghreb, notably Algeria, who are seen by many Frenchmen as fundamentally 'unassimilable', in relation to European immigrants.[866] According to an ethno-centric reading of French Republicanism, Muslims could never become true French citizens, because all authentic French people are (Catholic) Christians.[867] However, immigration did not form an electoral issue. After its electoral breakthrough in 1983, the FN reframed the issue of immigration from a need for manpower to a concern for ethnic balance and a danger for French identity. In 2002, former leader of the FN Jean-Marie Le Pen received 18 percentage of the French votes. In reaction to the popularity of Le Pen, established political parties used a strict immigration policy as a tool to undermine the ability of the FN to frame and define the issue.[868]

---

861 Schain 2012, p. 40–41.

862 Schain 2012, p. 86.

863 Haut Conseil à l'Intégration, *La France sait-elle encore intégrer les immigrés?*, Paris: La Documentation Française 2011, p. 42.

864 Haut Conseil à l'Intégration 2011, p. 115–116.

865 Haut Conseil à l'Intégration, *Le bilan de la politique d'intégration 2002–2005*, Paris: La Documentation Française 2005, p. 24.

866 Fetzer & Soper 2005, p. 67; Schain 2012, p. 73.

867 Fetzer & Soper 2005, p. 95.

868 Schain 2012, p. 103.

The polarization of the debate on immigration re-emerged in 2012, most notably during the campaigns of the presidential elections, in which current leader of the FN Marine Le Pen also received approximately 18 percentage of the French votes. In its 2012 annual report, *La lutte contre le racisme, l'antisémitisme et la xénophobie*, the CNCDH observes that, in line with the tendencies of the political discourse, in public opinion the fear of a loss of French identity, the fear of religious fundamentalism, the perception that integration has failed, the sentiment that there are too many immigrants in France, criticism of Islamic and Muslim practices increased significantly; the extremely negative image of Roma migrants even more so.[869] According to the statistics of the Ministry of Interior Affairs, the Ministry of Justice, as well as the contributions from several anti-racism associations published in the report, the acts of violence and discrimination and expressions of hate speech against Muslims also increased significantly.[870] This development is said to have been fuelled by several events, including the 'Affaire Merah' and demonstrations held by Muslims against the publication of the Mohammed cartoons by the magazine *Charlie Hebdo* and the film *Innocence of Muslims*.[871]

Schain points out, however, that social research shows that the idea that Muslims do integrate well is actually more strongly held in France than in other European countries. French Muslims themselves are by far the most integrative in their orientation and the least conflicted between their Muslim and national identities. They are the most positively oriented toward 'national customs', as well as the most accepting of Christians and Jews in their societies. On the other hand, the idea of 'national customs' and citizenship is certainly the strongest in France.[872] Schain cites Lamont, who analyses:

> 'French social scientists often argue that the French political culture of republicanism produces a low level of racism because it delegitimizes the salience of ascribed characteristics in public life, hence facilitating integration of racial minorities. In contrast, my analysis suggests that republicanism has a contradictory impact: it delegitimizes one form of racism, but also strengthens another by drawing a clear distinction between those who share this universalistic culture (citizens) and those who do not (immigrants). This boundary is reinforced by traditional anti-Muslim feelings found in Christian France, by a lasting historical construction of French culture as superior and by a caste-like relationship of the French with members of their former colonies.'[873]

---

869 CNCDH, *La lutte contre le racisme, l'antisémitisme et la xénophobie 2012*, Chapter 1 Perceptions du racisme, de l'antisémitisme et de la xénophobie, p. 13–48, available at: www.cncdh.fr/fr/publications/la-lutte-contre-le-racisme-lantisemitisme-et-la-xenophobie-annee-2012.

870 CNCDH report 2012, p. 95 *et seq*; 241 *et seq*; 385 *et seq.*

871 CNCDH report 2012, p. 129. In the Merah affair Mohammed Merah, an Islamic terrorist, killed several persons with a gun in the streets of Toulouse and Montauban while driving a scooter.

872 Schain 2012, p. 18.

873 Lamont, M., *The Dignity of Working Men: Morality and the Boundaries of Race, Class, and Immigration,* Cambridge MA: Harvard University Press 2000, p. 212–213.

2.4. Representation through and consultation with religious and anti-racism associations

Before WWII the most powerful instruments to integrate minority groups into French society were through 'universal' organizations such as trade unions and the Communist party. In 1958, the Fonds d'Action Sociale (FAS) was created to finance associations that could defend the rights of immigrants, notably North Africans.[874] The activism of French anti-racism associations, such as MRAP and LICRA, can be traced back to the associational boom of the 1970's, in the wake of 'new socialist movements'. The anti-racism associations aimed to defend human and fundamental social rights and the rights of immigrants; the 'sans', such as the 'sans-emploi, sans-logis, sans-papiers'.[875] In 1981, the prohibition on foreigners to form associations was abrogated in French law.[876] Since 1980s, the French Government became increasingly involved in the development of ethnic organization. This was related to the problem of urban riots and violence in the suburbs of large cities such as Paris and Lyon between the local youth and French law officials, which started after the death of two young men of North African origin who were pursued by the police. This unrest continued for more than two decades.[877] State authorities were desperately searching for – local – interlocutors for the 'second generation'.[878] In 1984, one year after the first national anti-racism manifestation 'la marche des beurs'[879] in France in 1983, the association *SOS Racisme* was created with the devise 'Touche pas à mon pote', which symbolized its advocacy of 'fraternité', 'multiculturalisme' and the 'integration' rather than 'assimilation' of immigrants.[880]

The French State has established very strong and solid relationships with associations in areas where it is difficult to differentiate between public and private interests. The State does not reject their inclusion in policy-making as long as they are defined as representative and act in consultation, due to the fact that any form of protestation or mobilization goes against republican values. Such practice seems to conflict with the traditional Jacobin understanding of the State (para.2.5 *supra*). The inclusion of anti-racism associations by the French State could, however, be interpreted as an attempt to reinforce its hold on civil society (top down) rather than a characteristic of France as a 'participatory and associative democracy' (bottom

---

874 Haut Conseil à l'Intégration, *Investir dans les associations pour réussir l'intégration*, Paris: La Docuimantation Française 2012, p. 6.

875 Barthélemy, M., *Associations: un nouvel âge de la participation?*, Paris: Presses de Sciences Po 2002.

876 Loi n° 81–909 abrogated Title IV 'Des associations étrangères' from the Loi du 1er juillet 1901, relative au contrat d'association.

877 Wihtol de Wenden, C., Urban riots in France, SAIS Review 2006, 26.2, p. 47–53; Body-Gandrot, S., Urban 'Riots' or Urban Violence in France?, Policing 2007, 1 (4), p. 416–427.

878 Schain 2012, p. 81.

879 'Beur' is French slang for 'Arab'.

880 Www.sos-racisme.org/.

up).[881] As a follow up to its 2011 report in its report *Investir dans les associations pour réussir l'intégration* of 2012, the Haut Conseil à l'Intégration advised the State to invest in less numerous and more professional associations, to financially support them and to conclude partnerships with them to assist immigrants towards 'citizenship', notably in the context of the CAI.[882]

In fact, the historical process of the legitimization of associations in France since 1901 can be characterized as one of canalization, domestication and control – notably of religious congregations.[883] It is precisely because of the rich history of tensions between religion and the State that France has a well-established approach to dealing with organized religion. Moreover, French Republicanism recognizes people's religious identity rather than their ethnic identity, deals with integration through rules and regulations on religion rather than on ethnicity and has a tradition of dealing with ethnic groups through religious interlocutors.[884] Hence, Islamic immigrants from Turkey or the Maghreb are seen as one Muslim group regardless of their ethnic background, while they might not see themselves as such.[885]

In 2003, the *Conseil Français du Culte Musulman* (CFCM) was created as a representative body of the Muslim community, parallel to comparable organizations of Catholics, Protestants and Jews, as a contact point for the French Government.[886] Such institutionalized consultation was initiated in order to help undermine the rise of Islamic fundamentalism and the construction of a moderate French Islam. Prior to this, many other Muslim associations already existed that were represented by the *Union des Organisations Islamiques de France* (UOIF).[887] On 17 June 2010, the Minister of Internal Affairs signed a framework convention with CFCM, in which parties agreed to exchange statistics on hate crimes ('actions') and hate speech ('menaces') against Muslims in order to better measure intolerance against the Muslim community in France and to effectively fight this phenomenon. Pursuant to the framework convention, parties meet and supply information once every trimestre and evaluate the data annually.[888] To that effect, CFCM has created

881 Barthélemy 2002.

882 Haut Conseil à l'Intégration, *Investir dans les associations pour réussir l'intégration*, Paris: La Docuimantation Française 2012.

883 For a long time, France has been considered as a 'civic desert'. The legal recognition for associations was only to arrive in 1901. The law of 1901 defines associations broadly as the contract by which two or more people put together their knowledge or their activity, for 'another purpose than profit'. See: Saurugger, S., Democratic 'Misfit'? Conceptions of Civil Society Participation in France and the European Union, *Political Studies,* 2007, vol. 55, p. 390.

884 Schain 2012, p. 86.

885 Van Ooijen 2012, p. 171; Wieviorka, M., Race, Culture and Society: The French Experience with Muslims, in: AlSayyad, N. and Castells, M. (eds.), *Muslim Europe or Euro-Islam, Politics, Culture and Citizenship in the Age of Globalization*, Lanham: Lexington Books 2002, p. 133; Michalak, L. and Saeed, A., The Continental Divide: Islam and Muslim Identities in France, in: AlSayyad & Castells 2002, p. 151–152.

886 Www.lecfcm.fr/.

887 Www.uoif-online.com/v3/.

888 Www.lecfcm.fr/wp-content/uploads/2010/06/2010-06-18-convention.pdf.

L'Observatoire National contre L'Islamophobie.[889] The statistics are published in the annual reports of the CNCDH, which observes a significant increase of 'actions et menaces antimusulmanes' in 2012 compared to previous years.[890] This evolution is confirmed by the reports of *Collectif Contre l'Islamophobie en France* (CCIF).[891]

The limited political influence of Muslim minorities on other Islam related policies has been ascribed, not to a lack of representative associations or the French assimilationist model of integration, but to the incompatibility of religious accommodations with the particular French notion of 'Laïcité'.[892]

2.5. 'Laïcité' as a subset of freedom and equality

The unitarian, universalist and egalitarian ideal can be connected with another characteristic of the French Republic; la laïcité, the French State neutrality and indifference of the French State towards religions and cults.[893] This principle is without doubt the most particular characteristic of the French Republic. Of all Western states only the French Constitution refers to the principle that is said to be untranslatable in any other language. For these reasons 'la laïcité' is also called 'une exception française', although this idea is controversial.[894] The principle appeared for the first time in the Constitution of 1946 and features in Article 1 of the 1958 Constitution. Numerous previously discussed constitutional provisions specify the purport of 'la laïcité républicaine'; while Article 1 of the 1958 Constitution provides that the French Republic assures the equality before the law of all citizens without distinction of religion and the respect of all beliefs, other provisions protect citizens against discrimination on the ground of religion. Hence, 'la laïcité républicaine' can be understood in terms of equality and religious freedom.[895]

The process of 'laïcisation' dates back to 1789. For a long time, the Catholic faith functioned as the official religion of France, until the Revolution of 1789 caused a schism. During the Revolution, freedom of religion was laid down in the Declaration of the Rights of the Man and Citizens. Although the Concordat concluded by Napoleon and the Catholic Church in 1801 acknowledged that 'the Catholic faith is the faith of the majority of the French population', it assumed at the same time a certain religious pluralism and a separation of civil regulations and religious prescriptions (for example the notion of the civil state). The Restoration

---

889 Www.lecfcm.fr/?page_id=3517.

890 CNCDH report 2012, p. 129–131.

891 CCIF was created in 2003 and in 2011 became a consultative member of ECOSOC (UN). www.islamophobie.net/rapport-annuel.

892 Fetzer & Soper 2005, p. 95; 126.

893 For analysis of the genealogy of the concept see: Mély, B., *De la séparation des Eglises et de l'Ecole. Mise en perspective historique. Allemagne, France, Grande-Bretagne, Italie,* (diss.) Lausanne: Editions Page deux, collection 'Cahiers libres', 2004; Report of the French Council of State, 2004, general considerations: *Un siècle de laïcité*, Paris: La Documentation Française, 2004.

894 Report of the French Council of State 2004, p.7, p.121.

895 Code constitutionnel commenté 2012, p.334.

did not reinstate the Catholic faith as the official religion of France. During the course of the nineteenth century, the battle between the church and the state focused in particular on education. 'La Loi de Jules Ferry' of 28 March 1882 introduced obligatory free public education. Following this 'laïcisation' of education other social institutions, such as hospitals, were soon 'laïcised'. One speaks of 'les grandes lois de laïcisation des années 1880'.[896]

These developments resulted in the Act of 1905 that forms the key to 'la laïcité'[897] and is still central to the relation between the church and the state in France. Article 1 regulates freedom of religion and reads: 'La République assure la liberté de conscience. Elle garantit le libre exercice des cultes sous les seules restrictions édictées ci-après dans l'intérêt de l'ordre public.' Article 2 regulates the separation of the church and the state and reads: 'La République ne reconnaît, ne salarie ni ne subventionne aucun culte.' The Act of 1905 subsequently cites offences that specifically protect freedom of conscience and freedom of religion. Article 31 criminalizes the coercion of a person to exercise or abstain from exercising a cult. Article 32 criminalizes the obstruction, delay, or interruption of the exercise of a cult, i.e. every religious act performed by a clergyman in the interest of his congregation.

The principle of laïcité thus expresses the neutrality of the state, which is seen as a pre-condition for freedom of religion that has a place in the private sphere and the public sphere, but not in the domain of public institutions. According to the Council of State, it is a fundamental principle recognized by the laws of the Republic and it results from the constitutional texts that the laic character of the State applies to the ensemble of public services;[898] Community services are therefore prohibited from directly subsidizing any religious association, even with regard to interreligious manifestations, or to indirectly subsidize a religious association by putting, at its free disposal, a presbytery belonging to the community.[899]

The principle of laïcité is of particular importance in the field of public education. The Preamble of the 1946 Constitution provides 'l'organisation de l'enseignement public et gratuit et laïque à tous les degrés est un devoir de l'État'. However, this does not prevent the existence of private education, or even the granting of state support in private education under the conditions defined by the law.[900] In 2004, the French legislator reinforced the principle of laïcité in public education by amending the French Code of education and prohibiting the conspicuous wearing of religious symbols and dress – comprising the headscarf – in French public primary and secondary schools.[901]

---

896 Report of the French Council of State 2004, p.16.

897 Report of the French Council of State 2004, p.20.

898 CE 6 April 2001; CE 9 October 1992. Cited in: Code constitutionnel commenté 2012, p.349.

899 Code constitutionnel commenté 2012, p.349.

900 Cons. Con. 23 November 1977, n°77–87 DC. Cited in: Code constitutionnel commenté 2012, p.345.

901 Act n° 2004–228 of 15 March 2004 'encadrant, en application du principe de laïcité, le port de signes ou de tenues manifestant une appartenance religieuse dans les écoles, collèges et lycées publics', *JORF* n° 65 of 17 March 2004, p.5190.

'La laïcité' can thus be considered as the underlying principle to all laws that regulate the position of religion in the French public sphere. However, certain areas of the French Republic, i.e. the Alsace and Moselle departments, have remained under the regime of the Concordat of 1801. In these territories the Act of 1905 concerning the separation of the church and the state does not apply; priests, pastors, and rabbis are state officials, religious education is obligatory in primary and secondary schools and a community service can give a financial contribution to the functioning of a cult in order to satisfy a general interest objective.[902]

The constitutional requirement of 'laïcité' is not a fixed concept and has been the subject of further interpretation and elaboration since 1905.[903] It is the subject matter of a continuous discussion that nowadays obviously focuses on the accommodation of practices of Islamic faith.[904] In its 2000 report, *L'islam dans la République*, the Haut Conseil à l'Intégration concluded that the introduction of Islam in France gives occasion to redefine and contribute to the enrichment of the principle of 'laïcité', but that Muslims must assume the requirements that result from it.[905] In 2010, the French Penal Code was amended in order to prohibit the covering of the face, which included the wearing of the burqa and the niqab in public areas, defined as the public road and places open to the public or intended for public services.[906, 907] Furthermore, legislative proposals are being prepared concerning the respect of religious neutrality in enterprises and associations in general[908] and in private organizations charged with childcare in particular.[909] The traditional, dominant, political conception of 'laïcité' that focuses on state neutrality is, however, criticized for completely banning religion

902 Code constitutionnel commenté 2012, p.344.

903 On 29 April 2008, the MP for the UMP, Jacques Myard, deposed at the parliament a bill (n° 843) of constitutional reform 'visant à interdire à un parti politique de se réclamer d'une religion ou d'une ethnie', because Article 4 of the French Constitution enumerates as sole limitations to the values or ideologies political parties may refer to, 'the respect of the principles of national sovereignty and democracy'. The proposal is under examination of the 'commission des lois constitutionnel'.

904 In September 2011, a ban came into effect on the public worship in the streets practised in Paris, Nice and Marseille by French Muslims unable to find space in mosques. See: Interview Guéant: 'Les prières dans la rue doivent cesser', *Le Figaro* 14 September 2011; Le gouvernement déterminé à faire cesser les prières de rue, *Agence France Presse*, 16 September 2011.

905 Haut Conseil de l'Intégration, *L'islam dans la République*, Paris: La Documentation Française 2000, p. 81.

906 Act n° 2010–1192 of 11 October 2010 'interdisant la dissimulation du visage dans l'espace public', *JORF* n° 0237 of 12 October 2010, p.18344. The Act came into effect on 11 April 2011.

907 For a critical analysis of the law, see: Prélot, P-H., Religious symbols and the law of 1905: reflections on the prohibition of the full veil in light of the French law on religious practices, *Société, Droit et Religion* n°2, 2011.

908 Proposition de loi n° 998 *relative au respect de la neutralité religieuse dans les entreprises et les associations*, deposed at the National Assembly 24 April 2013.

909 Proposition de loi n° 61 *visant à étendre l'obligation de neutralité aux structures privées en charge de la petite enfance et à assurer le respect du principe de laïcité*, deposed at the National Assembly 2 July 2012.

from the public sphere, replacing religion by a 'civil religion' and constituting 'republican fundamentalism'.[910] Bauberot elaborates a more social conception of 'laïcité' that permits a more flexible relation between the state, religions and individuals.[911]

From the principle of laïcité, the freedom to manifest and express religious convictions also emerges.[912] Although the absence of an offence of blasphemy in French law is not a feature exclusive to the French laic Republic, the abrogation of the 'délit d'outrage à la morale publique et religieuse' by the French legislator of 1881 can be understood in light of the ongoing process of 'laïcisation' at that time. Such an offence does not fit into the laic principle that resulted in the Act of 1905. As the repression of blasphemy supposes the recognition of the existence of God, laic states that primarily France cannot provide for such a criminalization.[913] It constitutes an unequal treatment by the laic State of religious and other philosophical convictions and violates freedom of conscience, expression and religion (para.5.4.1 *infra*; para.1.2.2 *supra*). In the Alsace and Moselle departments, where the Act of 1905 does not apply, a regional legislation has survived from the German period of 1871 to 1918 that criminalizes 'le blasphème public contre Dieu'. This particular legislation is based on the German criminal code of 1871 and has been validated by the Act of 17 October 1919 and the Decree of 25 November 1919. Article 166 reads 'Celui qui aura causé un scandale en blasphémant publiquement contre Dieu par des propos outrageants, ou aura publiquement outragé un des cultes chrétiens ou un communauté religieuse [...] ou les institutions et cérémonies de ces cultes [...] sera puni d'un emprisonnement de trois ans au plus'. However, as a single conviction on the ground of this offence cannot be found in the national judicial database, the offence can be considered as a local relic from the past without practical effect.[914]

2.6. Conclusion

The principle of equality is mentioned at several reprises in the Constitution of 1958 and in the texts it refers to in its preamble. Equality is a recurrent principle

---

910 Boulègue 2010, pp.20–23.

911 Baubérot, J. *et al.*, Déclaration internationale sur la laïcité au XXIe siècle, 2005, available at: www.aidh.org/txtref/2005/Images/declaration_bauberot.pdf. See further: Baubérot, J., *L'intégrisme républicain contre la laïcité*, Paris: Aube ed. 2006; Baubérot, J., *La laïcité expliquée à Nicolas Sarkozy et à ceux qui écrivent ses discours*, Paris: Albin Michel 2008.

912 CE, advice, 27 November 1989, n°346–893, *RFDA* 1990, 1, annotation Rivero. Cited in: Code constitutionnel commenté 2012, p.349.

913 Beignier, B., *L'honneur et le droit*, (diss.) Paris: L.G.D.J. 1995, p.339.

914 *Report on the relationship between freedom of expression and freedom of religion: the issue of regulation and prosecution of blasphemy, religious insult and incitement to hatred*, European Commission for Democracy through Law, study no.406/2006, Strasbourg: Council of Europe, 23 October 2008, Annex II, pp. 37–38.

that has been affirmed since 1789 and forms a central characteristic of the French Republic.

The prevailing conception of equality is indissolubly linked to the image of the French Republic as a social, unitary, uniform and homogenous body. It follows that it is not possible in the French constitutional order to afford any group defined by a common origin, culture, language or belief collective rights on the grounds of its common characteristics. This does not signify that French law does not protect individuals belonging *de facto* to a certain minority group on the grounds of their specific characteristics. To the contrary, the Pleven Act of 1972 that created the French hate speech bans can be understood as an elaboration of the French ideal of strict equality and a means of social integration; in the French Republic individual and equal citizens are not to be addressed on the grounds of their specific characteristics.

The French ideal of strict equality can be connected with another characteristic of the French Republic; la laïcité, the strict separation of the church and the state and the indifference of the French State towards religions and cults. The Act of 1905, that regulates 'la liberté des cultes', forms the key to 'la laïcité' and is still central to the relation between the church and the state in France. 'La laïcité' can, however, be considered as the underlying principle to all laws that regulate the position of religion in the French public sphere. Numerous constitutional provisions, such as the principle of respect for all beliefs and the prohibition of religious discrimination, specify the purport of 'la laïcité républicaine' that can thus be understood in terms of equality and religious freedom. From the principle of laïcité equally springs the freedom to manifest and express religious convictions. Although the absence of an offence of blasphemy in French law is not a feature exclusive to the French Republic, such an offence does not fit into its laic principle and constitutes an unequal treatment by the State of religious and other philosophical convictions and violates freedom of conscience, expression and religion. The abrogation of the 'délit d'outrage à la morale publique et religieuse' by the French legislator of 1881 can be understood in this context.

3. The Pleven Act of 1 July 1972

With the adoption of the Pleven Act of 1 July 1972, France implemented the International Convention on the Elimination of all forms of Racial Discrimination (ICERD) (3.1). Before the adoption of the Pleven Act, hate speech was regulated by the Decree-law Marchandeau of 1939 (3.2). The Pleven Act introduced a number of new prohibitions of forms of hate speech and discrimination and provisions about their prosecution (3.3). The analysis results in a general conclusion about the background and purport of the Pleven Act (3.4).

3.1. Adhesions and reservations made to ICERD

France adhered to ICERD on 28 July 1971[915] and implemented this convention by adopting the Pleven Act of 1 July 1972, concerning the fight against racism.[916] The French Government was of the opinion that French law already largely complied with the Convention and therefore made four reservations.[917, 918] With regard to Article 4 ICERD, France declared: 'En ce qui concerne l'article 4, la France tient à préciser qu'elle interprète la référence qui y est faite aux principes de la Déclaration Universelle des Droits de l'Homme ainsi qu'aux droits énoncés dans l'article 5 de la même Convention comme déliant les Etats parties de l'obligation d'édicter des dispositions répressives qui ne soient pas compatibles avec les libertés d'opinion et d'expression, de réunion et d'association pacifique qui sont garanties par ces textes'.[919] The declaration does not take the form of an explicit reservation, but has been interpreted as such.[920] However, in reaction to a question of the General Secretary of the United Nations, the French Government has further clarified 'l'intention du Gouvernement français n'est pas de réduire la portée des obligations prévues (...) mais seulement de consigner son interprétation dudit article'.[921]

Initially the French Government held that French law was largely compliant with the ICERD and that as such no new legislative measures were necessary for the application of the Convention.[922] This was contradicted by the Reporter of la Commission des lois constitutionnelles in Parliament, Terrenoire, and many representatives, namely of the Communist and the Socialist groups, during the

---

915 The official publication of the adhesion formed part of: the Decree of 2 November 1971, Journal official, 10 novembre 1982, p.3553.

916 Foulon-Piganiol, J., La lutte contre le racisme, Commentaire de la loi du 1er juillet 1972, D 1972, Chronique XL, pp.261 et seq.

917 Assemblée Nationale, séance du 15 avril 1971, Convention international sur l'élimination de la discrimination raciale, *JO*, 16 avril 1971, para. 6, p.1116.

918 The reservations comprised a reservation made to article 6 ICERD concerning the access to court. The French Government declared to regulate the matter under norms of general law. Furthermore, France did not sign the facultative declaration of article14 ICERD that empowered the CERD- committee to receive and examine communications by individuals complaining of a violation of ICERD by the Member State. According to the French government, French law afforded sufficient guaranties to protect individuals. The system of communications was therefore super fluent and could form a pretext to abusively interfere with internal affairs. Finally, France did not assent to article 15 ICERD that referred to the Declaration on the granting of independence to colonial countries and peoples by the General Assembly of the United Nations (G.A. res. 1514 (XV), 15 U.N. GAOR Supp. (No. 16) at 66, U.N. Doc. A/4684 (1961). According to the French Government, the UN was not to intervene with the conduct of non-autonomous territories in respect of the principle of non-interference with internal affairs.

919 Cited in: Korman, C., Le délit de diffusion d'idées racistes, JCP, G, 1989, n° 30, I, 3404.

920 Korman 1989, 3404.

921 JO, 10 November 1971, p.11100 *et.seq.*, cited in: Korman 1989, 3404.

922 Assemblée Nationale, séance du 15 avril 1971, Convention international sur l'élimination de la discrimination raciale, *JO*, 16 avril 1971, para. 6, p.1116–1117.

parliamentary debates.[923] They argued that, at the time of the adoption of the Pleven Act, racist manifestations existed and threatened to poison public opinion; the French government had allowed the public gatherings of the fascists movement 'Ordre Nouveau' – a forerunner of the extreme right French political party le Front National[924] – and had not taken any measures against the hate campaigns conducted by the weekly *Minute*. Immigrant workers coming from North Africa and the French Overseas Departments, as well as Jews and Gipsies suffered from violent attacks and discrimination. These racist manifestations could not be countered, because of the lacunae existent in French law. The National Assembly, notably the Communist group had therefore submitted many proposals to reinforce anti-racism and discrimination laws since 1959.

3.2. The situation prior to the adoption of the Pleven Act: the Decree-law Marchandeau

The original 1881 Press Act did not comprise of any press offences with a racial character. The first act that had provided an offence of collective defamation was the Act of 25 March 1822 that punished in accordance with Article 10 whoever 'aura cherché à troubler la paix publique en excitant le mépris ou la haine des citoyens contre une ou plusieurs classes de citoyens'. The term 'classe' signified: 'toutes personnes prises collectivement, soit qu'on les désigne par le lieu de leur origine, la religion qu'elles professent, les opinions qu'on leur attribue, le rang qu'elles occupent dans la société, les fonctions qu'elles remplissent, la profession qu'elles exercent ou de toute autre manière.' As a result, everyone was free to form classes, including noble men, priests, journalists and bakers.[925] The Act of 9 September 1835 sanctioned the 'provocation à la haine entre les diverses classes' and the Decree of 11 August 1848 repressed writings seeking 'à troubler la paix publique en excitant le mépris ou la haine des citoyens les uns contre les autres.'[926] These provisions were, however, barely used in an age of ardent individual liberalism.[927] The Press Act of 1881 thus abandoned all protection of the honour of a collectivity. The absence of such an offence was beyond discussion; the draft project did not include it, nor did any amendment seek its insertion.[928]

It was the Decree-law of 21 April 1939, known as 'Decree-law Marchandeau', that finally inserted, in the general offences of defamation (Article 32) and insult (Article 33), a paragraph that criminalized defamation and insult 'envers les

923 Assemblée Nationale, séance du 15 avril 1971, Convention international sur l'élimination de la discrimination raciale, *JO*, 16 avril 1971, para. 6, p.1118.

924 Shields, J.G., *The Extreme Right in France: from Pétain to Le Pen*, London: Routledge 2007.

925 Beignier 1995, p.249.

926 Blin, H., Chavanne, A. & Drago, R., *Traité du droit de la presse*, Paris: Librairies techniques 1969, p.334.

927 Beignier 1995, p.250.

928 *Ibid.*

personnes qui appartiennent par leur origine à une race ou à une religion déterminée… lorsqu' elles auront eu pour but d'exciter à la haine entre les citoyens ou habitants'.[929] The Decree-law Marchandeau had been created under the pressure of menaces of war, manifestations of anti-Semitism and Nazi-propaganda. Its aim was the reinforcement of the national unity. With the insertion of Articles 32–2 and 33–3, the French government intended to counter the racist and mostly anti-Semitic activities that troubled the public order, infringed national unity and were contrary to French traditions and the principles of liberty, tolerance and fraternity, inscribed in the Declaration of Human Rights of men and citizens.[930] Without doubt, this context explains why the terms are more restrictive than those of the 1848 Act. The offence resembles the offences of provocation of Article 23 and following articles of the 1881 Press Act, but these texts were considered as insufficient to permit the repression of a racism that had become contagious.[931] The reporter of the Decree explained: 'En l'état de la jurisprudence, il est donc permis de dire que l'excitation publique à la division entre les citoyen ou la diffamation accomplie dans ce but contre un groupe de personnes, peuvent être difficilement poursuivies (…) mais ce n'est pas proprement leur intérêt qui est en jeu sous ce rapport, c'est bien plutôt celui de la collectivité nationale. Tout ce qui la divise l'affaiblit. Tout ce qui favorise son union la rend plus forte. Elle est donc directement engagée à voir réprimer toute tentative de dissociation et de discorde, toute excitation à la haine entre Français.'[932]

The Decree-law Marchandeau was abrogated by Pétain during the Vichy regime, but reinstalled during the Liberation. Moreover, the offences of the Decree-law Marchandeau appeared to be very difficult to apply, because of the several conditions that had to be met in practice.[933] In order to preserve freedom of opinion, the offences have been applied with prudence in case law. Firstly, proof of the existence of defamation as defined by law was required. Hence, the Paris Court of Appeal refused to apply Article 32–2 to a publication that showed certain distrust against Jews, opposed to the prosecution of this form of racism and advocated an 'antisémitisme raisonnable'.[934] According to Blin, freedom of the press signified that the thresholds for the repression of speech should be very high, and that the publication of immoral and dangerous texts should be allowed.[935]

What is more, it was required to prove that the author of the expression had had the desire to incite to hatred. This requirement of malicious intent was impossible

---

929 Racial and religious defamation was sanctioned with an imprisonment of one month to one year and a fine of 300 to 300.000 Francs. Racial or religious insult was sanctioned with an imprisonment of five days to six months and a fine of 150 to 150.000 Francs or only one of these two penalties. Blin, Chavanne & Drago 1969, p.336.

930 De Lamy, B. de, *La liberté d'opinion et le droit penal*, (diss.) Paris: L.G.D.J. 2000, p.315.

931 Blin, Chavanne & Drago 1969, p.335.

932 Cited in: Beignier 1995, p.250.

933 Foulon-Piganiol, J., Réflexions sur la diffamation raciale, Eléments constitutifs du délit et imperfections du texte actuel, D 1970, Chronique XXIX, pp. 133–136.

934 CA Paris 26 March 1952, *D.* 1953, J, 342. Cited in: Blin, Chavanne & Drago 1969, p.335.

935 Blin, Chavanne & Drago 1969, p.335.

to prove; it gave way to too much subjectivity. The Paris Court of Appeal went as far as to exclude the application of the article in the event that the author of a defamation had not incited violence, because the offence no longer comprised 'le mépris, le détournement de clientèle, ni l'antipathie, ni l'aversion, mais l'excitation à la haine, c'est-à-dire le soulèvement de passions, génératrices de troubles, de désordres sociaux et raciaux et d'agitations, en un mot de violences'.[936] However, the French Supreme Court recalled a strict interpretation of the Decree by considering that hatred did not necessarily require violence. Hatred can generate violence, but does not constitute violence. An incitement to hatred was therefore sufficient.[937]

Finally, the Decree-law only protected the group against defamation or insult on the ground of his or her race or religion, and not certain members of the group individually. The French Supreme Court decided that an incitement to hatred, which was grounded neither on race or religion, but on nationality or profession, did not fall under the scope of the article. Hence, the Court refused to apply the article to a publication that aimed to rouse the Africans from Dakar against the Lebanese and Syrian bakers and merchants in this city.[938] Likewise, nationalism did not fall under the scope of the offence. Furthermore, the defamation had to be committed against a group and not an individual, who disposed of Articles 31 and 32–1 of the 1881 Press Act for protection. Article 32–2 afforded a collective protection under the condition of the existence of personal and direct prejudice. Incitements to racial or religious hatred could nevertheless be committed through defamation against one single person.[939] According to the French Supreme Court, this was, however, not the case when Minister Pierre Mendès was insulted because he was Jewish; then the ordinary offences of the 1881 Press Act, which protect members of the Government, applied.[940]

Before its creation by the Pleven Act of 1 July 1972, the offence of provocation to racial discrimination, hatred or violence did not exist. Several proposals to create a similar offence had been made.[941] Notably, in 1959, a draft act seeking to 'assurer la répression de la provocation à la haine ou à la violence en raison de la race ou de la religion' remained without effect.[942] Subsequently, in 1968, the draft act of Robert Ballanger, representative of the communist party, 'tendant à réprimer la provocation à la haine raciste et à rendre plus efficace la législation sur la répression

936 CA Paris 9 April 1951, *GP* 1951, I, 417. Cited in: Blin, Chavanne & Drago 1969, p.335.

937 French Supreme Court, crim.ch., 26 June 1952, *D.* 1952, J, 641. Cited in: Blin, Chavanne & Drago 1969, p.336.

938 French Supreme Court, crim.ch., 12 January 1956, *Bull. Crim.* 1956, n°52. Cited in: Blin, Chavanne & Drago 1969, p.336.

939 Blin, Chavanne & Drago 1969, p.336.

940 French Supreme Court, crim.ch., 17 October 1956, *Bull. Crim.* 1956, n°650. Cited in: Beignier 1995, p.251.

941 Foulon-Piganiol, J., Nouvelles réflexions sur la diffamation raciale, Critique des propositions de loi en instance devant le Parlement, D 1970, Chronique XXXV, p. 163.

942 Draft Act deposed on 9 November 1959, National Assembly I, parliamentary documents, n°358.

des menées racistes et antisémites'[943] and the draft act of representative Edouard Charret, 'tendant à la répression des discriminations raciales et de la provocation à la haine raciste'.[944] The latter envisioned the creation of the offence of provocation to racial hatred, which would comprise of an attempt to provoke racial hatred and at the same time the suppression of the offence of racial defamation.[945] The substitution of the offence of racial defamation was desired, because it was considered to be insufficient in the fight against racial discrimination. The proposals, however, remained without effect.[946]

Article 48 of the 1881 Press Act explicitly provided that public prosecution on the ground of the French hate speech bans could be set in motion at the request of the affected party, who subsequently constituted a civil party, even when the public prosecutor had not taken the initiative to prosecute. However, the dominant interpretation of the Decree-law Marchandeau rendered the article void; as the Decree-law Marchandeau concerned anti-discrimnatory press offences only against a group of people on the ground of their race or religion, the case law had generally concluded that an individual person, even when he or she belonged to the group, had to be declared inadmissible. Only a group that was very restricted in number was admissible, because only then the honour of every individual person belonging to that group could be violated. For an anti-racism association, the situation was not much better if it could not demonstrate a sufficient link with the target group it claimed to represent. In practice, only the public prosecutor could initiate criminal proceedings and only the anti-racism associations that were directly affected by a publication could set in motion public prosecutions and constitute as a civil party. As governmental orders were not issued, the public prosecutors remained inactive and the request for public prosecutions by anti-racism associations and their constitution as a civil party was systematically declared inadmissible for not having been – personally – attacked in the publication in question.[947]

Due to these difficulties, the Decree-law Marchandeau in practice entailed the anti-racism association Le mouvement contre le racisme, l'antisémitisme et pour la paix (MRAP). MRAP had tried to convince the French Government of the necessity of the drafting of new anti-racism laws since 1957 and had begun to prepare a draft. The proposals made by MRAP were adopted in the previously discussed draft acts. In addition, MRAP tried to demonstrate the inactivity of the public prosecution by persisting in the engagement of prosecutions in the knowledge that they would be

943 National Assembly, IV n°313, annex to P.V. of the séance of 3 October 1968.

944 National Assembly, IV n°293, annex to P.V. of the séance of 3 October 1968.

945 The offence reads: 'Ceux qui, par l'un des moyens énoncés dans les art. 23 et 28, auront provoqué ou tenté de provoquer à la haine ou à la violence à l'égard de citoyens ou habitants considérés, soit individuellement, soit collectivement, comme se rattachant par leur origine à une race ou religion déterminée, seront punis d'un emprisonnement d'un mois à un an et de 500 F à 10.000 F d'amende ou de l'une de ces deux peines seulement'.

946 Foulon-Piganiol, 1970-II.

947 Foulon-Piganiol 1970-I, p.32.

declared inadmissible. The possibility to take legal action in order to defend the collective interests they aimed to defend was at stake.[948]

3.3. The merit of the Pleven Act

3.3.1. Rationale of the Pleven Act of 1 July 1972

The Pleven Act of 1 July 1972 was adopted unanimously by the General Assembly and the Senate.[949] As a result of the drafting history and the debates in the National Assembly and the Senate, large consensus existed in relation to the question as to what was the central rationale of the Pleven Act; the protection of the human dignity and the equality of French inhabitants. As these notions formed central characteristics of the French Republic, the Act aimed to assure, at the same time, the Republican values and social peace in and the unity of the French nation itself. As one member of Parliament stated: 'Nous aurions voulu que la France, où le racisme apparait comme une insulte à sa culture, à son humanisme, s'associât plus réellement à ce combat international pour la dignité de tous les hommes.'[950] Before the Senate, the reporter of la commission des lois constitutionelles, Mailhe, described the Pleven Act as a result of the fight against 'ce qu'il y a de plus abominable dans les rapports humains: la négation du concept de dignité et l'absence de tout élan fraternel.'[951]

The French Minister of Justice at the time, Pleven, considered '... rien n'est plus étranger à l'authentique tradition française et aux sentiments profonds de notre peuple que le racisme ou la xénophobie.' (...) 'cette tradition, qui est aussi celle du peuple français, vous a toujours fait donner en toutes choses la priorité au respect de la personne humaine.'[952] According to Pleven, the danger of racism lied in its contagiousness, ignorance, irrationality and intolerance: 'Car le racisme est une lèpre sans cesse renaissante et très vite contagieuse. Les préjugés raciaux, parce qu'ils trouvent leur source dans les profondeurs de l'inconscient, parce qu'ils se nourrissent de l'ignorance, de la crainte, de l'envie, parce qu'ils ne cèdent ni devant le raisonnement ni devant l'évidence des faits, parce qu'ils sont une manifestation de ce que comporte d'animalité la nature humaine, sont particulièrement

---

948 Secondi-Nix, M., *Lutte contre le racisme et justice pénale, Rôle des associations*, CNRS, CESDIP, October 1996, p. 34.

949 Assemblée Nationale, débats parlementaires, séance du 7 Juin 1972, Lutte contre le racisme, Discussion des conclusions d'un rapport, *JO* 8 Juin 1972, p.2295; Senat, séance du 22 Juin 1972, Lutte contre le racisme, Adoption d'une proposition de loi, *JO* 23 Juin 1972, para. 5, p.1181.

950 Assemblée Nationale, débats parlementaires, séance du 7 Juin 1972, Lutte contre le racisme, Discussion des conclusions d'un rapport, *JO* 8 Juin 1972, p.2284.

951 Senat, séance du 22 Juin 1972, Lutte contre le racisme, Adoption d'une proposition de loi, *JO* 23 Juin 1972, para. 5, p.1172.

952 Senat, séance du 22 Juin 1972, Lutte contre le racisme, Adoption d'une proposition de loi, *JO* 23 Juin 1972, para. 5, p.1180.

redoutables.' 'N'être pas raciste, ce n'est pas seulement respecter un texte de loi ou même un code de conduite; c'est un état d'esprit, un état d'esprit que nous dicte le cœur mais aussi la raison. L'intolérance est le poison dont meurt une société; le racisme est la forme la plus pernicieuse de cette intolérance.'[953]

The protection of the public order in relation to the prevention of immediate violence between different groups in society did not form an explicit rationale of the Pleven Act – exclusive of the general rationale to prevent a repetition of the horrors of the Second World War. During the drafting, Pleven held on to the Government's position, i.e. that French law was largely compliant with the ICERD and sufficient to counter racism, because in France racist acts did not frequently occur and, if they did, the public prosecutors did engage in proceedings. However, Pleven agreed that France was a nation with considerable immigration figures, in which ethnic or national minorities lived that could in particular be victims of racism. Therefore, 'il n'est pas inutile de prévoir à l'encontre de ces agissements une répression plus ferme et de caractère plus spécifique, afin de se prémunir par avance contre tout danger de contagion raciste, quand bien même un tel danger n'apparait pas immédiat.'[954]

3.3.2. The hate speech bans

The Pleven Act of 1 July 1972 did not create, for the implementation of article 4 ICERD, an independent offence that criminalized the 'diffusion of ideas based on racial superiority or hatred'. Korman concludes that the French legislator has not implemented Article 4 ICERD completely and must therefore create an independent 'délit de propagande raciste, le fait de justifier ou d'encourager toute forme de haine et de discrimination raciales'.[955] However, it can be argued that it results from the traditional French conception on freedom of opinion that the criminalization of the manifestation (diffusion) of 'ideas based on racial superiority or hatred' would signify the criminalization of an opinion that seeks its adoption by others merely on the basis of its reprehensible content (an opinion) and not for reasons of its direct

953 Assemblée Nationale, débats parlementaires, séance du 7 Juin 1972, Lutte contre le racisme, Discussion des conclusions d'un rapport, *JO* 8 Juin 1972, p.2291.

954 Assemblée Nationale, débats parlementaires, séance du 7 Juin 1972, Lutte contre le racisme, Discussion des conclusions d'un rapport, *JO* 8 Juin 1972, p.2291. Before the Senate, Pleven recapitulated: 'Pour construire une société plus juste et plus humaine, pour avancer dans la voie d'une nouvelle société, il s'efforce de lutter contre les injustices ou les inégalités matérielles qui subsistent dans notre pays; il cherche à donner à chacun de nos concitoyens sa chance d'épanouissement humain et professionnel; mais il veut aussi donner à chaque Français, à chaque habitant de notre pays, le sentiment de sa dignité, l'assurance qu'elle est protégée et qu'il est lui-même pleinement intégré à la communauté nationale ou accueilli sans réticence dans notre pays. La loi que vous allez voter apportera à la construction de cette société nouvelle une contribution importante et marquera, au-delà de la solidarité matérielle ou financière de la nation, une solidarité plus importante encore: la solidarité de cœur et d'esprit entre tous les habitants de notre patrie.' Senat, séance du 22 Juin 1972, Lutte contre le racisme, Adoption d'une proposition de loi, *JO* 23 Juin 1972, para. 5, p.1180.

955 Korman 1989, 3404.

link with a reprehensible act. From this strand of thought, Droin concludes that the French legislator has rightly avoided the creation of a 'délit d'opinion'.[956] The declaration made by the French government with regard to article 4 ICERD can be interpreted in this light.

The Pleven Act of 1 July 1972 did create three distinct press offences of a racial character, being 'diffamation raciale', 'injure raciale' and 'provocation à la discrimination, à la haine ou à la violence'.[957] The French legislator thought that defamation and insult were not the only means through which the public order could be violated by inciting hatred between citizens. Expressions that lacked a defamatory element could still have an offensive character. It therefore convened to maintain the offences of racial defamation and insult and to create a new offence that would be better adapted to the multiple faces of racism that fell outside the scope of the offence of defamation, which was regarded as too narrow and outdated.[958]

The Pleven Act of 1 July 1972 amended the existing offences of racial defamation and racial insult. It removed all references 'au but d'excitation à la haine entre les citoyens et les habitants'. The case law had laid much emphasis on the imperative character of this condition. The rationale of the former offences was more to establish harmony between citizens than to protect their honour or reputation. Contrarily, the Act of 1 July 1972 created the offences of racial defamation and racial insult *as such*.[959] Furthermore, the Act of 1 July 1972 enlarged the application of the existing articles; it added the discriminatory grounds of origin, and the membership or non-membership of an ethnic group and nation, and allowed for the protection of, next to a group of persons, a single person. The fact that the ICERD concerned racial discrimination and that Article 4 ICERD did not require the insertion of the category of religion that already existed since the Decree-law Marchandeau did not raise any discussion during the drafting as to what extent criticism on a certain religion or religious behaviour or practices would fall in or outside the scope of the offences.

During the lecture of the article 'provocation à la discrimination, à la haine ou à la violence' in Parliament, the question was addressed as to whether the article would apply to the multiple disqualifications in the press of French citizens coming from the island Corsica – and French citizens from the Over Seas Departments, or whether, next to the categories of ethnic and national origin, the category of

956 Droin 2009, p.147.

957 For an evaluation of their application the last fourty years see: Les apports de la loi de 1972 en matière de droit de la presse, Actes de colloque, *Légipresse* n° 300 December 2012, p. 686–699.

958 Assemblée Nationale, séance du 15 avril 1971, Convention international sur l'élimination de la discrimination raciale, *JO*, 16 avril 1971, para. 6, p.1117; Assemblée Nationale, débats parlementaires, séance du 7 Juin 1972, Lutte contre le racisme, Discussion des conclusions d'un rapport, *JO* 8 Juin 1972, p.2282–2283.

959 Foulon-Piganiol 1972.

provincial origin needed to be inserted. The Minister of Justice opined that, although the matter was to be decided by case law, the article certainly permitted the sanctioning of such expression, as the term 'ethnic origin' had a different signification than the term 'race'.[960]

La Commission des lois constitutionnelles had initially proposed the use of both verbs of 'provoquer' and 'inciter' in the offence of 'provocation raciale', because the latter verb would have a supplementary meaning to the first. During the parliamentary debates, it was argued that the verbs were synonyms and the Government decided to delete the verb 'inciter'. According to the Minister of Justice, instead of using the term 'provocation directe', a term that was commonly used in the Press Act of 29 July 1881, the Government would use the term 'provocation' without using 'direct' or 'indirecte', and hence 'le Gouvernement donne au mot 'provoquer' son sens plein lequel couvre certainement l'acception du verbe 'inciter''.[961] The verb 'provoke' in the offence of provocation raciale is therefore neither larger nor smaller in scope than the verb 'incite' used in Article 4 ICERD.

The offences of racial defamation and racial insult were inserted into the second and third subparagraphs (Articles 32–2 and 33–3) of the general offences of defamation (Article 32) and insult (Article 33) in the third paragraph of Chapter IV concerning 'misdemeanours against persons'. The offence of racial provocation was inserted into the sixth subparagraph of Article 24 as one of the forms of provocation to felonies and misdemeanours not followed by effect in the fourth paragraph of Chapter IV concerning 'provocation to felonies and misdemeanours'.[962] De Lamy raises the question as to why the anti-racism offences have not been classified under the paragraph concerning the infractions 'contre la chose publique', considering the danger of racism for society, although this was not an influence in their regime.[963] According to Mathieu, the rationale of offences is rather the protection of the values

[960] Assemblée Nationale, débats parlementaires, séance du 7 Juin 1972, Lutte contre le racisme, Discussion des conclusions d'un rapport, *JO* 8 Juin 1972, p.2292.

[961] Parliamentary Debates, National Assembly, séance of 7 June 1972, *JO* 8 June 1972, p.2293.

[962] The others are: willful injury against life, willful offences against the physical integrity of the person, and sexual aggressions defined in Book II of the Penal Code; theft, extortion and destruction, defacement and damage dangerous to persons defined by Book III of the Penal Code; violations to the fundamental interests of the nation defined in Title I, Book IV of the Penal Code; defending the felonies of willful injury against life, willful offences against the physical integrity of the person, and sexual aggressions defined in Book II of the Penal Code, war crimes, crimes against humanity and the crimes of collaboration with the enemy; acts of terrorism prescribed by Title II, Book IV Penal Code or defending such crimes.

[963] De Lamy 2000, p.328. Paragraph 2 concerning 'Délits contre la chose publique' comprises article 26 that sanctions 'L'offense au Président de la République' and article 27 that sanctions 'La publication, la diffusion ou la reproduction, par quelque moyen que ce soit, de nouvelles fausses, de pièces fabriquées, falsifiées ou mensongèrement attribuées à des tiers lorsque, faite de mauvaise foi, elle aura troublé la paix publique, ou aura été susceptible de la troubler,' and 'la publication, la diffusion ou la reproduction faite de mauvaise foi sera de nature à ébranler la discipline ou le moral des armées ou à entraver l'effort de guerre de la Nation'.

– existent or supposed – of the French Republic, than the protection of public order.[964] Indeed, the drafting history shows that the offences principally aimed at the protection of human dignity and equality of French citizens that form inherent characteristics of the French Republic and not the protection of the public order in relation to the public authorities or the prevention of immediate disturbances of the peace.

3.3.3. The criminalization of discrimination

The Pleven Act of 1 July 1972 created two articles that repressed racial discrimination; Article 187–1 of the French Penal Code that criminalized discrimination on the ground of origin, and the membership or non-membership of a determined ethnic group, nation, race or religion by public officials and citizens charged with public services and Article 416 of the French Penal Code that criminalized discrimination on those grounds in the field of employment and the supply of goods and services. The articles have been renumbered and supplemented with new discriminatory categories. The current French Penal Code defines discrimination in Article 225–1, inserted in section I of Chapter V concerning 'offences against the dignity of persons', as 'any distinction applied between natural persons by reason of their origin, sex, family situation, physical appearance or patronymic, state of health, handicap, genetic characteristics, sexual morals or orientation, age, political opinions, union activities, or their membership or non-membership, true or supposed, of a given ethnic group, nation, race or religion. (...)'.[965] The article does not have an independent significance and does not criminalize discrimination in general, but explains the criminalization of the acts of discrimination in Article 225–2, consisting of the refusal to supply goods or services; obstructing the normal exercise of any given economic activity; the refusal to hire, to sanction or to dismiss a person; subjecting the supply of goods or services to a condition based on one of the factors referred to under article 225–1; subjecting an offer of employment, an application for a course or a training period to a condition based on one of the factors referred to under article 225–1; refusing to accept a person onto one of the courses referred to under 2° of article L.412–8 of the Social Security Code.

Article 225–3 gives evidence of the relative weight of the different grounds of discrimination; it excludes the application of Article 225–2 to discrimination based on one's state of health, when it consists of operations aimed at the prevention and coverage of the risk of death, of risks for the physical integrity of the person, or the

---

964 Mathieu 2007-I, p.321 *et seq.*

965 The article continues: 'Discrimination also comprises any distinction applied between legal persons by reason of the origin, sex, family situation, physical appearance or patronymic, state of health, handicap, genetic characteristics, sexual morals or orientation, age, political opinions, union activities, membership or non-membership, true or supposed, of a given ethnic group, nation, race or religion of one or more members of these legal persons.'

risk of incapacity to work or invalidity; discrimination based on a person's state of health or handicap, if it consists of a refusal to hire or dismiss based on a medically established incapacity; and recruitment discrimination based on gender when the fact of being male or female constitutes the determining factor in the exercise of an employment or professional activity. No such exclusions exist in relation to discrimination based on ethnic group, nation, race or religion.

Complementary to the two offences penalizing acts of discrimination, the Pleven Act of 1 July 1972 furthermore inserted into the Act of 10 January 1936 concerning combat and vigilant groups, an article that permitted the pronouncement of the dissolution by decree of any association that 'soit provoqueraient à la discrimination, à la haine ou à la violence envers une personne ou un groupe de personnes à raison de leur origine ou de leur appartenance ou de leur non-appartenance à une ethnie, une nation, une race ou une religion déterminée, soit propageraient des idées ou théories tendant à justifier ou encourager cette discrimination, cette haine ou cette violence.'[966] During the parliamentary debates, it was argued that associations and groupings could openly be constituted with the aim to propagate racist myths and that their existence was perfectly legal as long as they did not attack the republican order. This was considered to be a lacuna in French law, because 'Peut-on être sûr que l'ordre républicain serait considéré comme menacé si ces milices prônaient le racisme? L'attitude du Gouvernement à l'égard de certains groupes de combat d'extrême droite permet d'en douter.'[967] While the French Government did not thus create an independent press offence penalizing every 'propagande raciste, le fait de justifier ou d'encourager toute forme de haine et de discrimination raciales', such 'opinions' were repressed if they formed part of a larger discriminatory practice or 'act'.[968]

Furthermore, the French Penal Code has been amended in order to create so-called 'hate crimes' by making a racist motive an aggravating factor in specific common criminal offences. In 2003, the *Loi Lellouche* created Article 132–76, which mandates more severe penalties for crimes of violence committed on the basis of the victim's actual or supposed membership or non-membership of a particular ethnic group, nation, race or religion. Criteria for the determination of the motivation of the offence include the use of 'spoken or written words, images, items, or acts of any kind that are injurious to the honor or esteem of the victim, or group of persons including the victim, by virtue of their actual or supposed membership or non-membership of a particular ethnic group, nation, race or religion'.[969] Subsequently, a new Article 132–77 was added that extends the

966 Senat, séance du 22 Juin 1972, Lutte contre le racisme, Adoption d'une proposition de loi, *JO* 23 Juin 1972, para. 5, p.1181.

967 Assemblée Nationale, séance du 15 avril 1971, Convention international sur l'élimination de la discrimination raciale, *JO*, 16 avril 1971, para. 6, p.1119.

968 Korman 1989, 3404.

969 Law 2003–88 of 3 February 2003.

provisions on aggravating circumstances to include bias on the basis of sexual orientation.[970] These two articles apply, amongst others, to the offences of wilful homicide, torture and barbarous acts, violence inadvertently resulting in death, violence resulting in permanent disfigurement or disability, violence entailing nine or more days of sick leave from work, violence entailing up to eight or fewer days of sick leave or no sick leave, damage to private property and damage to private property caused by dangerous means. Since 2004, these articles equally apply to the criminal offences of threats, thefts and extortion. The specific common criminal offences stipulate specific aggravated penalties for racist and homophobic bias.[971]

3.3.4. The right of anti-racism associations to set in motion public prosecutions

The Pleven Act of 1 July 1972 inserted a first paragraph into Article 48 of the 1881 Press Act (Article 48–1) that expressly authorized associations that according to their statutes have the objective of combatting racism to exercise, in the field of racial defamation, racial insult, and racial provocation, the rights afforded to the civil, affected party in his or her place. The Act also inserted a first paragraph into Article 2 of the French Code of Criminal Procedure (Article 2–1 CCP), which expressly authorized associations that have the objective of combatting racism to exercise according to their statutes, in the field of acts of racial discrimination, the rights afforded to the civil, affected party in his or her place. The Pleven Act thus allowed for the public prosecution of the French hate speech bans to be set in motion at the request of anti-racism associations that subsequently constituted as a civil party, even when the public prosecutor had not taken the initiative to prosecute (para.10.3.1 *infra*). These articles were the most debated and innovating provisions of the new legislative text.

Pleven stipulated that in order to afford an association that has not directly suffered harm from a violation of the law, but according to its statutes has the objective of combatting racism, the right to intervene before the court signified a derogation from the fundamental rules in French law.[972] La Commission des lois constitutionnelles had therefore at first advised limiting the capacity to intervene before a court to associations that had been afforded a recognition of public utility by the French authorities, which would be in conformity with the Decree-law Marchandeau. It was, however, argued both in the National Assembly and in the Senate, that such a requirement would undermine the importance of the role that existing anti-racism associations lacking such a recognition played in the fight

970 Law 2003–239 of 18 March 2003.

971 Law 2004–204 of 9 March 2004. For example, the aggravated penalties for both racist and homophobic crimes include life imprisonment instead of 30 years for murder, and fifteen rather than ten years of imprisonment for violent attacks leading to permanent disability. See: Articles 221–4 and 222–10 of the French Penal Code.

972 Assemblée Nationale, débats parlementaires, séance du 7 Juin 1972, Lutte contre le racisme, Discussion des conclusions d'un rapport, *JO* 8 Juin 1972, p.2291.

against racism, such as MRAP and La Ligue internationale contre l'antisémitisme (LICA), which would become La Ligue internationale contre le racisme et l'antisémitisme (LICRA) in 1979.[973] In fact, it was notably these two anti-discrimination associations that played a determinant role in the creation of the Act of 1 July 1972, as well as the possibility to exercise the rights of the affected party with regard to the press offences with a racist character; the Act is inspired for a large part on their suggestions and years of preparatory work.[974]

During the parliamentary debates it was argued that affording these rights to anti-racism associations 'Cela permettra à des hommes, qui ne se rendent pas toujours exactement compte du sort qui leur est fait ... d'être défendus, même lorsqu'ils ne connaissent pas l'étendue de leurs droits dans notre pays de liberté et d'égalité des citoyens par des associations qui, partageant ces responsabilités avec nous, avec le Gouvernement, avec le Parlement, sachent rendre leurs droits à chacun de ces hommes, nos égaux.'[975] And 'Il est important d'encourager toutes les associations qui tendent à resserrer les liens de fraternité entre les individus vivant dans une même société.'[976] And 'La justice est encore couteuse; la solliciter c'est aller au-devant de soucis, de dérangements. Aussi suis-je persuadé que les associations ayant mission de défendre les victimes du racisme ne se multiplieront pas dans le seul but d'aller devant le juge. Celles qui existent n'agissent qu'à bon escient. Les associations à venir feront de même. Elles auront conscience qu'agir sans discernement, abuser du droit d'action serait une manière de fortifier le camp des racistes (...) Oui, dans notre lutte antiraciste les associations sont nos alliés naturels.'[977]

It was, however, also feared that anti-racism associations would become too powerful in the field of instituting proceedings. One representative remarked: 'chacun a ses racismes et ses anti-racismes, que l'opinion se saisit de manière très sélective des problèmes qu'elle juge urgents et de ceux qu'elle néglige. Il est vrai aussi que les combattants de la lutte antiraciste, quelque infatigables qu'ils soient, se sont parfois un peu spécialisés et ont pu oublier quelques problèmes nouveaux.'[978] As a compromise, the requirement of recognition of a public utility

---

973 Assemblée Nationale, débats parlementaires, séance du 7 Juin 1972, Lutte contre le racisme, Discussion des conclusions d'un rapport, *JO* 8 Juin 1972, p. 2290; Senat, séance du 22 Juin 1972, Lutte contre le racisme, Adoption d'une proposition de loi, *JO* 23 Juin 1972, para. 5, p.1173 and 1175.

974 Assemblée Nationale, débats parlementaires, séance du 7 Juin 1972, Lutte contre le racisme, Discussion des conclusions d'un rapport, *JO* 8 Juin 1972, p.2281. Secondi-Nix, M., *Lutte contre le racisme et justice pénale, Rôle des associations*, CNRS, CESDIP, October 1996, p.34.

975 Assemblée Nationale, débats parlementaires, séance du 7 Juin 1972, Lutte contre le racisme, Discussion des conclusions d'un rapport, *JO* 8 Juin 1972, p.2281.

976 Assemblée Nationale, débats parlementaires, séance du 7 Juin 1972, Lutte contre le racisme, Discussion des conclusions d'un rapport, *JO* 8 Juin 1972, p.2288.

977 Assemblée Nationale, débats parlementaires, séance du 7 Juin 1972, Lutte contre le racisme, Discussion des conclusions d'un rapport, *JO* 8 Juin 1972, p.2290.

978 Assemblée Nationale, débats parlementaires, séance du 7 Juin 1972, Lutte contre le racisme, Discussion des conclusions d'un rapport, *JO* 8 Juin 1972, p.2290.

was replaced by the insertion of several other requirements.[979] Firstly, associations, that according to their statutes combat racism, have to be regularly declared at least five years before the occurrence of the criminal offence. This would prevent 'associations circonstancielles' from being created after a violation of a specific hate speech ban, with the mere aim of engaging a prosecution. Another fear was that a divergence of opinion could exist between the association and the victim. Article 48 was therefore completed with a second paragraph 48–2 that requires the association to obtain the consent of an individual person in order to engage a proceeding, if the hate speech offence is committed against that particular person considered individually.

3.4. Conclusion

France has implemented ICERD by the adoption of the Pleven Act of 1 July 1972 concerning the fight against racism. France made a declaration to Article 4 ICERD that can be interpreted as expressing the position of the French Government, i.e. that the criminalization of the diffusion of 'ideas based on racial superiority or hatred' would be contrary to the French traditional conception of freedom of opinion. The Pleven Act signified a reinforcement of the anti-racism and discrimination laws in order to more effectively protect primarily the human dignity and equality of French citizens as a central characteristic of the French Republic, not the protection of the public order and the prevention of disturbances of the peace. The merit of the Pleven Act was threefold: the creation of next to the offences of racial defamation and insult *as such*, the creation of the new offence of racial provocation; the criminalization of acts of discrimination; and the right of anti-racism associations to set in motion public prosecutions on the grounds of these offences and constitute as a civil party. The anti-racism associations le MRAP and LICRA have played a determinant role in the creation of the Pleven Act. In the vision of the French legislator such associations share a responsibility with the French Government to protect the fraternity between French citizens and are indispensable actors for an effective fight against racism and discrimination.

4. Racial defamation

The offence of racial defamation is characterized by a number of elements, being defamation (4.1), intent thereto (4.2) and the designation of a group on the basis of race or religion (4.3). The justifications for the offence of racial defamation allowed by the law are limited to the proof of good faith (4.4). However, in the application of the offence, the French judge does – to a certain extent – take into account the

979 Senat, séance du 22 Juin 1972, Lutte contre le racisme, Adoption d'une proposition de loi, *JO* 23 Juin 1972, para. 5, p.1175.

context of expression (4.5). The analysis results in a general conclusion about the offence of racial defamation in French law (4.6).

4.1. The criminalization of defamation

In 2008, the report of the 'Commission Guinchard' recommended 'la dépénalisation de la diffamation à l'exception des diffamations présentant un caractère discriminant (raciste, sexiste ...). Ainsi seule le voie civile ... sera possible', and suggested the decriminalization of defamation – and insult – against individuals to the benefit of civil law and civil responsibility as an only recourse.[980] The report has been variously received by French legal scholars. Most scholars have criticized the proposition for taking away the fine balance that the 1881 Press Act, with its specific press offences and procedural law, aims to strike between freedom ofthe press and the rights of victims of defamation and insult.[981] For example, Malaurie cites Carbonnier, according to whom 'Dans la théorie pénale de la diffamation et de l'injure, elle [la jurisprudence] trouvait une philosophie toute élaborée, le produit de réflexions séculaires sur les bienfaits et les méfaits de la langue des hommes, sur les aveuglements respectifs de l'envie et de l'amour-propre, etc., tandis que l'article 1382 ne pouvait lui offrir qu'un schéma sec, dépouillé (...)'.[982]

Decriminalization would signify the disappearance of 'un droit de délits spéciaux et un monde judiciaire clos' and the offences of defamation and insult would fall under 'l'obscure clarté qui tombe de l'article 1382'.[983] Derieux is more favourable to the proposal for two main reasons. Firstly, with right the proposal is inspired in particular to circumvent the strict procedural rules of the 1881 Press Act that form a real obstacle for victims of defamation in the prosecution; while these procedural particularities might have been justified in 1881 in order to assure press freedom, in the context of today they do not have the same raisons d'être.[984] Secondly, the proposal would solve certain difficulties related to the offence of defamation itself. While the criminalization of *racial* defamation is justified, because it notably aims to protect society against elements causing social disorder, this does not hold true to the same extent for the criminalization of defamation

---

980 Proposal n° 12–1 of the Report of la Commission sur la répartition des contentieux présidée par Serge Guinchard, *L'ambition raisonnée d'une justice apaisée,* Paris: La documentation française, coll. 'Rapports officiels' 2008, available at: http://lesrapports.ladocumentationfrançaise.fr.

981 Bigot, C., Contentieux de la presse: les errements de la commission Guinchard, *Légipresse*, September 2008, n° 254, I, pp.109–110; Jouanneau, B., A propos de la dépénalisation de la diffamation, *Légipresse*, January-February 2009, n° 258, I, p.2; De Lamy, B., Vers une dépénalisation de la diffamation et de l'injure, *JCP G* 2008, I, p.209.

982 Carbonnier, J., Le silence et la gloire, *D.* 1951, chron., p.119.

983 Malaurie, P., Ne dépénalisons pas la diffamation et l'injure. – Contre la proposition n° 12, alinéa 1 du rapport Guinchard, *JCP G* n° 39, 24 September 2008, act.566.

984 Derieux, E., Dépénalisation de la diffamation. Contribution à la réflexion, in: *Philosophie juridique du journalisme, La liberté d'expression journalistique en Europe et en Amérique du Nord*, Mbongo, P. (ed.), Paris: Éditions Mare & Martin, 2011, p.84.

against individuals that is rather based on the protection of personal interests than on the prevention of social disorder.[985] Other motives in favour of the decriminalization of defamation concern problems related to its definition and – with regard to its possible justifications – the compatibility of the French notion of a suspect's good faith with the European notion of a free public debate on a matter of general interest; later on these issues will be discussed in more detail to the extent that they are relevant in the context of 'racial defamation'. The recommendation of the Commission Guinchard has, however, not been implemented.[986]

Ancient French law did not distinguish between defamation and insult, but made a distinction between oral insults, the 'outrage par paroles', and written insults, the 'libelle diffamatoire'. The French Penal Code of 1810 introduced the distinction between 'la calomnie' and 'l'injure'. Article 367 of the Penal Code defined the calomnie as the imputation against an individual of facts that '*s'il existaient*, exposeraient celui contre lequel ils sont articulés à des poursuites criminelles ou correctionnelles ou même l'exposeraient seulement au mépris ou à la haine des citoyens' [curs. EHJ].[987] In literature, la calomnie has also been described as expression 'qui suppose ce qui n'est pas', as opposed to 'la médisance, qui objecte ce qui est',[988] which was not repressed in the Penal Code of 1810. The Act of 17 May 1819 abrogated the offence of calomnie of Article 367. The offence was thought to be of no importance whether or not the posed facts existed and were true. Instead, the Act introduced an offence of defamation that did not make such a distinction and comprised la médisance. The 1881 Press Act abrogated the Act of 17 May 1819,[989] but adopted its definition of defamation in Article 29 that reads 'Toute allégation ou imputation d'un fait qui porte atteinte à l'honneur ou à la considération de la personne ou du corps auquel le fait est imputé est une diffamation.' While Article 32–1 of the 1881 Press Act sanctions the public defamation of private individuals (also called the 'diffamation simple'),[990] Article 32–2 sanctions the defamation of a person or a group of persons on the ground of their origin, membership or non-membership of an ethnic group, nation, race or religion with a fine of up to € 45.000, or imprisonment of up to one year.[991] In the absence of

---

985 Derieux 2011, pp.75–76.

986 Dreyer, E., *Responsabilités civile et pénale des médias*, Paris: LexisNexis 2011, p. 5.

987 Cited in: Beignier, De Lamy & Dreyer 2009, pp.441–442. The Code equally contained, under the prevention of 'outrages' in Articles 222–227 French Penal Code, provisions penalizing certain oral defamations or insults against persons holding public functions.

988 Cited in: Beignier, De Lamy & Dreyer 2009, p.445.

989 The 1881 Press Act also abrogated the Act of 22 March 1822 that had created other offences of public 'outrages' against citizens, 'outrages diffamatoires ou injurieux'. Contrarily, Articles 222–227 of the French Penal Code have been preserved.

990 With a fine of up to € 12.000,-.

991 According to the last paragraph of Article 32, the tribunal can order the public display or dissemination of the decision taken in accordance with Article 131–35 of the French Penal Code.

publicity, racial defamation of a person or a group is a petty offence criminalized in Article R. 624–3 of the Penal Code.[992]

Defamation supposes, as a constituent element of the offence, an allegation or an imputation of a specific fact. In literature, the allegation has been defined as 'l'énonciation d'un fait, sur la foi d'autrui, ou l'assertion qui se produit sous l'ombre du doute', while the imputation has been defined as 'l'affirmation personnelle de celui qui parle ou écrit'.[993] This distinction remains purely theoretical, as both terms are used interchangeably in case law.[994] After giving a definition of defamation, Article 29 continues: 'La publication directe ou par voie de reproduction de cette allégation ou de cette imputation est punissable, même si elle est faite sous forme dubitative ou si elle vise une personne ou un corps non expressément nommés, mais dont l'identification est rendue possible par les termes des discours, cris, menaces, écrits ou imprimés, placards ou affiches incriminés.' Subsequently, the French Supreme Court has on several occasions established that defamation 'sous une forme déguisée, ou dubitative ou par voie d'insinuation' can equally constitute the offence.[995]

The French Supreme Court has furthermore established that 'pour être diffamatoire, une allégation ou une imputation doit se présenter sous la forme d'une articulation précise de faits de nature à être, sans difficulté, l'objet d'une preuve et d'un débat contradictoire.'[996] When the allegation or imputation does not thus concern a specific fact that is susceptible of proof and the object of a contradictory debate, it can only be deemed as constituting the offence of insult, which is sanctioned less severely. The French judiciary must interpret expression according to its nature and not according to the motive of the suspect: 'le caractère légal des accusations diffamatoires s'apprécie non d'après le mobile qui les a dictés mais selon la nature du fait sur lequel elles portent.'[997] What is more, the judiciary can take into account, next to the direct context of the publication, 'des éléments extrinsèques de nature à donner à l'expression incriminée son véritable sens et à caractériser l'infraction poursuivie'. The broader context of an expression outside the publication can even render a simple interrogation punishable.[998]

---

992 Article R.624–3 reads: La diffamation non publique commise envers une personne ou un groupe de personnes à raison de leur origine ou de leur appartenance ou de leur non-appartenance, vraie ou supposée, à une ethnie, une nation, une race ou une religion déterminée est punie de l'amende prévue pour les contraventions de la 4e classe; Est punie de la même peine la diffamation non publique commise envers une personne ou un groupe de personnes à raison de leur sexe, de leur orientation sexuelle ou de leur handicap.

993 Cited in: Beignier, De Lamy & Dreyer 2009, p.443.

994 Cohen, F., *La difficile insertion de la legislation penale sur la lutte contre le racisme dans la loi sur la presse*, (diss.) Paris I 2003, pp.192–193.

995 French Supreme Court, crim.ch., 2 January 1980, n° 78–92224, *Bull. Crim.* 1980, n° 3; Bigot 2004, p.60.

996 French Supreme Court, crim.ch., 17 February 1981, n° 79–92748, *Bull. Crim.* 1981, n° 64.

997 French Supreme Court, crim.ch., 15 March 1983, n° 82–90533, *Bull. Crim.* 1983, n° 82.

998 Bigot, C., *Connaître la loi de 1881 sur la presse*, Guide Légipresse, Paris: Victoires-Éditions 2004, p.61.

Defamation furthermore supposes, as a constituent element of the offence, the violation of a person's honour or consideration. During the drafting of the offence of defamation, a distinction between the two notions was made: the consideration 'se rattache à l'idée que les autres ont de vous', while the honour 'se rattache davantage à l'idée que vous tenez à en conserver vous-même'.[999] However, the notions have never been defined in case law. According to Bigot, a person's honour is violated when expression constitutes an accusation of a violation of the law, such as the commitment of a crime or lesser offences, or even conduct contrary to 'moral duties', while a person's consideration is violated when the expression violates a person's good name or damages his or her reputation.[1000] The French Supreme Court has established that for the interpretation of the notions neither the subjective opinion of the person concerned nor the public opinion is determinant; the judge must objectify the notions: 'pour déterminer si l'allégation ou l'imputation faite porte atteinte à l'honneur ou à la considération de la personne à laquelle le fait est imputé, les juges n'ont pas à rechercher quelles peuvent être les conceptions personnelles et subjectives de celle-ci concernant la notion de l'honneur et de la considération; qu'ils n'ont pas, non plus, à tenir compte à cet égard, de l'opinion que le public a de cette personne, que les lois qui prohibent et punissent la diffamation protègent tous les individus, sans prévoir aucun cas d'exclusion fondé sur de tels éléments.'[1001]

4.2. Intent and the presumption of bad faith

Being an 'infraction intentionelle', the intention of the author to defame forms a constituent element of the offence of defamation. The author must thus have the intention to defame. This 'intention coupable' is characterized by the *dol generalis* and consists of 'la volonté ou la conscience de porter atteinte à l'honneur et à la considération d'autrui'.[1002] In case law, sometimes reference is made to the authors 'intention de nuire' that is characterized by the *dol specialis*.[1003] As the intention to harm is not required by law, it would form a supplementary condition to the offence of defamation. According to Dreyer, this supplementary condition has no practical effect, because in order for the offence of defamation to be constituted the intention of the author does not have to be proven.[1004] Indeed, the French Supreme Court has established that, as the author of defamation is necessarily conscientious of the fact that his expression violates the honour or the consideration of the person he targets, the existence of the author's intention must be presumed.[1005] In other words, from

999 Beignier, De Lamy, Dreyer 2009, p.449.

1000 Bigot 2004, p.67.

1001 French Supreme Court, crim.ch., 2 July 1975, n° 74–91717, *Bull. Crim.* 1975, n° 174.

1002 Beignier, De Lamy & Dreyer 2009, p.457.

1003 French Supreme Court, crim.ch., 16 March 1993, *Bull. Crim.* 1993, n° 115.

1004 Dreyer, E., *Droit de l'information, responsabilité pénale des médias*, Paris: Litec 2002, n° 110.

1005 French Supreme Court, crim.ch., 30 June 1893, *DP* 1897, I, 341. Cited in Beignier, De Lamy & Dreyer 2009: p.458.

the moment the judge has established the defamatory character of the expression, he does not have to demonstrate explicitly the authors 'bad faith'. This 'presumption of bad faith' is of great influence to a suspect's position of defence, because it shifts the burden of proof towards the suspect. A suspect cannot, however, counter this 'presumption of bad faith' by proving the absence of his intention to defame. The French Supreme Court has established that the presumption of bad faith can only be countered by presenting justifying facts that are sufficient to admit the suspects 'good faith' (para.4.4.2 *infra*).[1006] The 1881 Press Act explicitly refers to the notion of bad faith in Article 35 *bis* that reads 'toute reproduction d'une imputation qui a été jugée diffamatoire sera réputé faite de mauvaise foi, sauf preuve contraire par son auteur' and aims to prevent the re-publication of defamatory statements in journals with a large public readership that have originally been published in magazines with a small audience, which is why a condemnation would be useless.

4.3. The designation of a group

4.3.1. Racial groups

Article 29 specifies that the offence of defamation is constituted even if a person is 'non expressément nommée mais dont l'identification est rendue possible'. The French Supreme Court has established that it is his task to 'contrôler le sens et la portée des écrits incriminées' and 'l'identification de la victime de l'infraction'.[1007] With regard to racial defamation, the courts have for a long time considered it necessary for the defamatory expression to be aimed at the group in its entirety. For example, in early 1991, the Paris Court of Appeal considered the imputation that young 'beurs' – slang for 'arabes' – are arrogant, benefit from impunity and privileges, and had behaved violently during a manifestation not to aim at 'les jeunes d'origine maghrébine dans leur globalité: les prévenus ont donc en l'espèce, été relaxés du chef de diffamation envers un groupe de personnes en raison de leur appartenance à une race.'.[1008] Nowadays, this is no longer required. According to established case law, it suffices, in order for the offence of racial defamation to be constituted, that the expression is aimed at a group of people, regardless of its size, on the ground of its membership of one of the protected grounds. Hence, in 2004, the French Supreme Court considered the imputation 'de jouer du tam-tam toute la nuit et de vivre de prestations sociales' against 'Africains d'Afrique noire' in France and not to the African people in their totality to constitute a racial defamation.[1009]

1006 French Supreme Court, crim.ch., 18 May 1954, *Bull. Crim.* 1954, n° 186. Cited in Beignier, De Lamy & Dreyer 2009: p.458.

1007 French Supreme Court, crim.ch., 7 December 1993, n° 92–81094, *Bull. Crim.* 1993, n° 373, p. 931.

1008 CA Paris, 30 January 1991, *JCP* 1991, IV, p.207.

1009 French Supreme Court, crim.ch., 6 January 2004, n° 02–87803, *unpublished.*

Contrary to the offence of racial provocation (para.6.3 *infra*), the French Supreme Court has given a restrictive interpretation of the discriminatory grounds of origin, nation or ethnic background with regard to the offence of defamation. According to the French Supreme Court, defamatory expression concerning'étrangers' is too vague to refer to a category of people on the ground of their membership of a nation.[1010] Likewise, the French Supreme Court has considered that the Corsican community, as a community within the French territories, does not form a group of people on the grounds of origin or ethnic background that is protected by Article 32–2.[1011] Contrarily, during the drafting of the Pleven Act of 1972 the French legislator considered the Corsican community to constitute a group in the sense of Article 24–8.

In any event, an imputation or an allegation must be made against a group exclusively on the ground of their origin, membership or non-membership of an ethnic group, nation, race or religion, and not for other reasons. Hence, in 2009, the French Supreme Court considered that the qualification of the 'Harkis' – persons of North African origin that have served in the French army in Algeria from 1954 until 1962 – and their descendants as 'traitres à la patrie', because of their political choice during the Algerian war, did not constitute the offence of defamation on the ground of ethnic background, nation or religion. And, as the 'Harkis' do not constitute a group for the purposes of Article 32–2, the prosecuting associations could not act in their defence on the ground of Article 48–1 and had to be declared inadmissible, even though Article 5 of the Act of 24 February 2005[1012] interdicts any insult or defamation against a person or a group on the ground of the actual or supposed qualification as harki and declares that the State must assure the respect of this principle in the context of the laws in force.[1013] Derieux rightly criticizes the judgment, arguing that even though this latter provision is not equipped with any sanction, the rights it affords to the Harkis should not be deprived of all significance.[1014]

4.3.2. Religious groups

With regard to religious defamation, the French Supreme Court has, on several occasions, demarcated the punishable imputation of a specific fact against a designated religious group from the free opinion concerning religious practices. In 1998, the French Supreme Court found a publication under the title 'Pèlerinage

---

[1010] French Supreme Court, crim.ch. 6 May 1986, *Bull. Crim.* 1986, n° 153.

[1011] French Supreme Court, crim.ch., 3 December 2002, n° 01–86088, *Bull. Crim.* 2002, n° 218.

[1012] Act of 23 February 2005, n° 2005–158, portant reconnaissance de la Nation et contribution nationale en faveur des Français rapatriés: *JO* 24 February 2005.

[1013] French Supreme Court, crim.ch., 31 March 2009, n° 07–86.892, n° 07–88.021, *Bull. Crim.* 2009, n° 61, n° 62.

[1014] Derieux, E., Diffamation et injure envers les Harkis: une infraction non réprimée, *JCP G*, n° 16, 15 April 2009, act.207.

intégriste Chartres-Paris ... 100 kilomètres à pied, ça use les fumiers' of drawings and legends, in which the march made by Catholic pilgrims at the occasion of Pentecost was compared to a military parade made by the Nazis and Catholic pilgrims were qualified as 'nazis en culottes courtes' and 'nazillon polonais', not to constitute a defamation, because it did not impute any specific fact and the terms 'nazis' or 'nazillon' constituted mere insults.[1015]

Equally in 1998, the French Supreme Court evidently found the expression 'secte abominable' used to define the Christian community very pejorative, but the equation of this community to a sect could not, in itself, constitute a defamation, 'en raison de l'imprécision du concept de secte qui n'a jamais été défini de manière précise... L'absence de législation spécifique pour lutter contre les sectes a permis aux juges de justifier leur décision en considérant que l'expression incriminée ne comporte pas l'imputation d'un fait déterminée.'[1016] Likewise, in 1999, the Douai Court of Appeal had found the qualification of the religious movement of the Jehovah witnesses as a sect and its equation to an 'association de malfaiteurs' made by a father during a television interview concerning his book that narrated the drama experienced by his family since his daughter had become a Jehovah witness to be pejorative, but to constitute an opinion on the movement of the Jehovah witnesses, which had been recognized as a sect in a parliamentary report, in the context of a debate on the harmful consequences of sects. In 2002, however, the French Supreme Court annulled this judgment considering that the expression constituted a punishable defamation, because it was susceptible of proof and a contradictory debate.[1017]

The question as to the demarcation of a group appears to be extremely sensible with regard to the discriminatory ground of religion. The case law of the French Supreme Court concerning the distinction between expression concerning a religion and expression concerning a religious group might cause some confusion in relation to how to interpret the following example in relation to the previously discussed case. In 1999, the French Supreme Court considered the qualification of the religious movement of Jehovah witnesses as 'une secte, l'une des plus dangereuses, qui a, à son bilan, un grand nombre de suicides', because of its methods of indoctrination and rupture with family and original background and abstention from any participation in public life, did not constitute a determined religious group on the group of its religion, because the expression was not aimed at the common belief that united the members of the organization, but brought up for discussion the manner in which the group, of which these individuals formed part of, functioned.[1018]

1015 French Supreme Court, crim.ch., 29 January 1998, n° 95–83763, *unpublished.*

1016 French Supreme Court, crim.ch., 28 April 1998, n° 96–81655, *unpublished.*

1017 French Supreme Court, civ.ch. II, 14 March 2002, n° 99–19238, *Bull.* 2002 II, n° 46, p.39.

1018 French Supreme Court, crim.ch., 14 December 1999, n° 98–87529, *Bull. Crim.* 1999, n° 305, p.943.

In any event, it will suffice, as with the offence of racial defamation in order for the offence of religious defamation to be constituted, that the expression is aimed at a religious group, regardless of its size. Hence, in late 1991, the French Supreme Court considered the imputation against *American* Jews to exploit 'the legend of the Holocaust' to constitute a punishable defamation of a group of people on the ground of their religion.[1019]

Two cases from 1993 show that not only the question of the demarcation of a group but also whether an association can act on behalf of a group on the ground of Article 48–1 are particularly relevant factors with regard to *religious* groups (para.10.3.1 *infra*). In the first case, the French Supreme Court found the imputation against 'les églises catholiques de l'Est' to often be racist or anti-Semitic, and as such constituted a defamation against Christians on the ground of their religion, because these defamatory imputations aimed at '...les communautés chrétiennes des pays de l'Est, accessoirement à leur localité géographique, en raison de leur obédience catholique et du comportement prête à leurs membres'. The Court annulled the decision of the Court of Appeal, which had considered that the statements 'ne visaient pas l'église catholique dans son université mais des entités religieuses des pays de l'Est désignées comme institutions géographiquement localisées et non pas à l'ensemble de la communauté catholique ... qu'aucun groupe de personnes pris à raison de son appartenance à une religion n'est visé, mais seulement les groupements que constituent les Eglises de l'Est'.[1020] In the second case, the French Supreme Court found a 'jeu de mots' concerning the installation of the Carmel of Auschwitz that associated Catholic adherents with both the war crimes committed by French war criminal Paul Touvier during the Nazi regime and the drug crimes committed by French war criminal Klaus Barbie as part of the Colombian 'cartel of Medellin'[1021] to constitute a punishable imputation of criminal behaviour against not only the congregation of Auschwitz as a legal personality, but also its individual members and even all religious adherents that are susceptible of being associated with this behaviour, on the ground of their adherence to a religion.[1022] In both cases, the anti-racism association AGRIF could act in the name of religious adherents, even though it had not received the explicit consent thereto of 'les églises catholiques de l'Est', respectively the Carmel of Auschwitz.

1019 French Supreme Court, crim.ch., 8 October 1991, n° 90–83336, *Bull. Crim.* 1991, n° 334.

1020 French Supreme Court, crim.ch., 2 March 1993, n° 91–84653, *Bull. Crim.* 1993, n° 94, *Légipresse* n° 110, p.44.

1021 The article entitled 'Ce qu'il faut jeter d'ici l'an 2000' and 'A vos poubelles' comprised the phrases 'En priorité, je jette le cartel de Medellin, et le carmel d'Auschwitz. A moins que ce ne soit le contraire: le cartel d'Auschwitz et le carmel de Medellin! Souvenons-nous, Klaus... était en Colombie, il s'est occupé de la drogue, alors que Touvier, son adjoint, était planqué dans un couvent!'

1022 French Supreme Court, crim.ch., 7 December 1993, n° 92–81094, *Bull. Crim.* 1993, n° 373, p.931.

4.4. Justifications

4.4.1. The exception of truth and the excuse of provocation: exclusion in the field of racial defamation

Pursuant to Article 35 of the 1881 Press Act, truth is a defence to an allegation of defamatory. It allows for a person charged with defamation to prove the truth of his or her defamatory statements and cites the situations in which such proof is not possible.[1023] In case law this possibility to prove the truth of defamatory expression has always been excluded with regard to the offence of defamation of a person or a group of persons on the grounds of origin, membership or non-membership of an ethnic group, nation, race or religion. In 1972, the French Supreme Court considered 'Lorsque la diffamation entre dans les prévisions de l'article 32 alinéa 2, de la loi du 29 juillet 1881, la preuve de la vérité des imputations diffamatoires ne serait être admise.'[1024] The possibility to deliver the truth of imputations or allegations that attribute facts to people exclusively on the ground of their race or other characteristics does seem to be contrary to the core of anti-discriminations laws. This was certainly the opinion of the Paris Court of Appeal that considered in 1995: '... pour être exonératoire, le fait justificatif de la vérité du fait diffamatoire invoqué par les prévenus devrait établir non seulement que des jeunes maghrébins ont commis des actes de vandalisme et de violence etc., mais aussi que c'est en raison de leur appartenance à la communauté des immigrés maghrébins qu'ils ont eu ce comportement. Un tel débat se révélerait à l'évidence contraire au but poursuivi par le législateur de 1972: lutter contre toutes les sortes de discriminations et notamment contre les préjugés raciaux et apparaitrait contraire à l'ordre public, en excitant 'la haine entre les citoyens'.'[1025]

1023 Article 35 cites the following situations: a) Lorsque l'imputation concerne la vie privée de la personne; b) (Abrogé); c) Lorsque l'imputation se réfère à un fait constituant une infraction amnistiée ou prescrite, ou qui a donné lieu à une condamnation effacée par la réhabilitation ou la révision. The French Constitutional Council has however declared the unconstitutionality of Article 35c, because it 'vise sans distinction, dès lors qu'ils se réfèrent à un fait constituant une infraction amnistiée ou prescrite, ou qui a donné lieu à une condamnation effacée par la réhabilitation ou la révision, tous les propos ou écrits résultant de travaux historiques ou scientifiques ainsi que les imputations se référant à des événements dont le rappel ou le commentaire s'inscrivent dans un débat public d'intérêt général; que, par son caractère général et absolu, cette interdiction porte à la liberté d'expression une atteinte qui n'est pas proportionnée au but poursuivi; qu'ainsi, elle méconnaît l'article 11 de la Déclaration de 1789.' Cons. Con. 7 June 2013 n° 2013–319, QPC, para. 9. Furthermore, the French Constitutional Council has also declared the unconstitutionality of Article 35–5 that excludes the proof of the truth for statements made more than ten years previously. Cons. Con. 20 May 2011, n° 2011–131, QPC. See also: Mallet-Poujol, N., Diffamation et amnistie: l'étrange sacrifice du filter de la bonne foi, *Légipresse* n° 309 October 2013, p. 531–537.

1024 French Supreme Court, crim.ch., 11 July 1972, n° 70–93211, *Bull. Crim.* 1972, n° 236, p.618.

1025 CA Paris, 28 September 1995, final judgment, *Légipresse* 1995, n° 129, p.19. cited in: Cohen 2003, p.205.

Furthermore, 'l'excuse de provocation', the excuse that a suspect has been provoked to defame a person or a group by a defamation previously committed against his own person, which is permitted as a justifying fact in the field of insult (para.5.3 *infra*), is excluded in the entire field of defamation, including racial defamation. According to the French Supreme Court, the excuse of provocation 'ne supprime pas l'intention coupable, en matière de diffamation et n'empêche pas les poursuites.'[1026]

4.4.2. The demonstration of good faith

The 'presumption of bad faith' (para.4.2 *supra*) is of great significance in relation to the possible defence of a suspect of defamation. In fact, it shifts the burden of proof towards the suspect. Although the exception of truth and the excuse of provocation are excluded in the field of racial defamation, a suspect of a racial defamation can prove that he or she has acted in good faith, 'sa bonne foi'. The demonstration of a suspect's good faith is not evidence that a suspect did not have the intention to defame, i.e. the proof of an absence of intention, but forms a justification with regard to the fact that a suspect has uttered defamatory statements. In other words, a suspect who willingly and consciously imputes or alleges a specific fact against a person that violates his honour or consideration can, as a justifying fact, demonstrate his good faith.

This demonstration of good faith is not required by any provision and its criteria are developed in case law. The French Supreme Court discerns four elements, being: 'le but légitime d'informer le public, l'existence d'une enquête sérieuse, la prudence et l'objectivité du propos, l'absence d'animosité personnelle'.[1027] According to the Court, these elements are cumulative, which signifies that 'l'absence de l'un de ces éléments conduit le juge à exclure le prévenu du bénéfice de ce fait justificatif.'[1028] The subjective opinion of the suspect with regard to the existence of these criteria is irrelevant and the suspect's good faith thus cannot result from his personal belief in the accuracy of his expression.[1029]

De Lamy argues that, just like the exception of truth, the demonstration of a suspects good faith should not be permitted in the field of racial defamation, because 'il ne peut y avoir un bon raciste'.[1030] Indeed, the suspect's good faith as a justifying fact is often rejected in French case law concerning racial defamation. In essence, French judges attach importance to the right to freedom of expression, when they qualify expression either as the imputation of a fact, or as an opinion or value judgment, thus at the level of the statutory elements of the offence and not after they have qualified expression as a punishable imputation as a possible means

[1026] French Supreme Court, crim.ch., 23 February 1950, *Bull. Crim.* 1950, n° 69, *D.* 1951, 217.

[1027] Bigot 2004, p.83.

[1028] French Supreme Court, crim.ch., 27 February 2001, n° 00–82557, *unpublished.*

[1029] Beignier, De Lamy & Dreyer 2009, p.487.

[1030] De Lamy 2000, p.193.

to justify defamatory expression.[1031] French judges have, however, had difficulties with making the correct distinction between facts and opinions or value judgements and France has been condemned several times by the ECtHR for violation of Article 10 ECHR, because it had not drawn the correct line between, on the one hand, punishable defamations and, on the other hand, a free debate of ideas or the right to freely criticize.

4.4.3. The influence of the case law of the ECtHR on the notion of good faith

The notion of good faith, as it has been interpreted by the French jurisdictions, has proved to be too strict to meet the European standards of freedom of expression.[1032] On several occasions, the ECtHR has criticized the particular rigour with which the French jurisdictions interpret expression, which is difficult to reconcile with the right to respect of freedom of expression.[1033] Confronted with an interference of freedom of expression, the ECtHR has exercised control over the application by the French jurisdictions of the four criteria of good faith. With regard to the criteria of the prudence and objectivity of the expression, the ECtHR has challenged the rejection of good faith by the French judge exclusively on the ground that the expression lacked a moderation in the words used, because in a public debate of a general interest a certain exaggeration or provocation must be allowed.[1034] With regard to the criteria of the existence of a serious research and a verification of sources, the ECtHR has found that information originating from a serious context does not have to be verified before it can be further distributed or used.[1035] With regard to the criteria of the absence of personal hostility, the ECtHR has considered that criticism of the behaviour of politicians does not have to be devoid of all personal hostility and that this is especially the case if both parties have shown a certain personal hostility in their expression.[1036] When interpreting the proportionality of the interference with freedom of expression, the ECtHR has consistently advanced the criterion of the legitimate aim to inform the public of matters of a general interest, which is imperative to 'transcend' the French criteria of the good faith.[1037]

Previously in this chapter, a certain resistance in French doctrine against the influence of European case law on French press law and the difficulties for French courts to integrate this European case law into their decisions has been discussed (para. 1.6 *supra*). However, in light of the case law of the ECtHR, the French

[1031] Cf. Ader, B., Quelles limites à la polémique politique?, *Légipresse* n° 294 May 2012, p. 292–296.

[1032] Wachsmann, P., Le délit d'offense envers un chef d'Etat étranger à l'épreuve de la Convention européenne des droits de l'homme, *RTDH* 2003, n° 55, p.996.

[1033] Beignier, De Lamy & Dreyer 2009, p.491.

[1034] ECtHR 7 November 2006, n° 12697/03, *Mamère/France*.

[1035] ECtHR 30 March 2004, n° 53984/00, *Radio France/France*.

[1036] ECtHR 22 December 2005, n° 54968/00, *Paturel/France*; ECtHR 14 February 2008, n° 20893/03, *July/France*.

[1037] Beignier, De Lamy & Dreyer 2009, p.491.

Supreme Court has revaluated the notion of good faith. According to Wachsmann, the French Supreme Court grants a certain priority to the criterion to inform the public of a matter of public interest over the other criteria of good faith.[1038] According to Monfort's analysis, the criterion of the 'subject of general interest' is appreciated in the field of good faith, but does not remove the defamatory character of the expression, which is analyzed in an autonomous manner at a previous stage. The exact purport for reference to the general interest of the treated subject and its articulation with the traditional criteria of good faith, remain unclear.[1039] In the words of Ader, the French Supreme Court has introduced a proportionality test in relation to the weighing of the criteria of good faith by the French judiciary.[1040] According to Bigot, this proportionality test enables the judge to better adapt the juridical response to the sociological reality and in doing so, assure justice. One must however be careful not to turn the general interest, being an eminently subjective or even ideological concept, into a purely moral notion aimed at judicially defining what constitutes good press as opposed to bad press. The contours of 'information of general interest' must be defined, because 'il ne faut pas se cacher que le juge se trouve devant une montagne.'[1041]

One case in which the French Supreme Court required the right to freedom of expression to be balanced more *in concreto* with the reputation or the rights of others concerned the allegation against the politician Le Pen of committing acts of torturing during the Algerian war. In a decision of 24 November 2000, the French Supreme Court considered that the protection of the reputation of the politician Le Pen had to be reconciled with the free discussion on his suitability for his political functions. According to the Court, as the allegations concerned le Pen's public activities and did not form an attack on his private life and were expressed in the context of a political debate, they were justified by the author's good faith.[1042] In another case concerning a conviction for defamation with regard to the imputation against a French general as being an accomplice in the genocide of Rwanda in 1994, the French Supreme Court, however, decided that the benefit of good faith could not be accorded to the applicant without examining whether the alleged imputation, even if it concerned a subject of general interest, relied on a sufficient factual basis.[1043] The interpretation of the notion of good faith by the French jurisdictions also appears to vary according to the specific context of the expression. De Lamy discerns a strict interpretation made by judges with regard to racist expression or

1038 Wachsmann, P.: *JCl. Libertés, V° Liberté d'expression*, Fasc. 800, n° 89, 2008.

1039 Monfort 2012, pp.24–25.

1040 French Supreme Court, 11 March 2008, n° 06–84712, *Légipresse* 2008, n° 253, III, 130, annotation B. Ader.

1041 Bigot, C., La portée de la rénovation de la théorie de la bonne foi sous l'emprise de l'intérêt general, *Légipresse* n°290, January 2012, pp.29–30.

1042 French Supreme Court, mixed ch., 24 November 2000, n° 97–81554, *Bull. Ch. M.* 2000, n° 4, p.5.

1043 French Supreme Court, crim. Ch., 13 March 2012, n° 11–85580, *Légipresse* n° 297 September 2012, p. 510.

expression in the context of a historical debate from a broader interpretation made by judges with regard to expression in a political context or in a humoristic context.[1044] This equally follows from an analysis of the case law concerning racial and religious defamation.

4.5. Racial or religious defamation in context

4.5.1. The imputation of a specific fact on the ground of race or a value judgment in the context of a political debate: the ***Edgar Morin*** *case*

In the field of racial defamation, the *Edgar Morin* case forms an excellent example of the difficulties French jurisdictions have in distinguishing the punishable imputation of a specific fact on the ground of race from a free opinion or value judgment in the context of a political debate. The case concerned the publication of an article entitled 'Israel-Palestine: Le Cancer' in *Le Monde* of 4 June 2002 by the famous sociologist Edgar Morin and two co-authors, the writer Danièle Sallenave and European parliamentarian Sami Nair. The article imputed the Jews of Israel and Jews in general of humiliating, despising and persecuting the Palestinians, just as the Jews themselves had been treated by the Nazis.[1045] Two associations assigned the authors, the editor of the journal and the director of the publication before the civil judge. While the TGI de Nanterre rejected the demand against each defendant to pay € 15,000 in damages, the defendants were condemned by the Versailles Court of Appeal on the ground of racial defamation to pay one euro in damages. According to the Court, the passages 'par l'imputation outrancière des faits précis rappelés se distinguent du reste de l'article qui renferme l'expression des convictions personnelles des auteurs dans le cadre d'un débat politique dont le caractère grandement polémique se justifie par la nature même du conflit [Israel-Palestine, EHJ]'. The Court rejected the defendant's good faith, because the defamatory passages could not be justified by the necessity to inform the readers and considered: (the passages) 'ne contiennent pas la critique virulente de la politique israélienne, ne trouvent pas de justification dans le paradoxe invoqué de la mise en

[1044] De Lamy 2000, pp.192–216.

[1045] The article comprised the passage: 'On a peine à imaginer qu'une nation de fugitifs, issus du peuple le plus longtemps persécuté dans l'histoire de l'humanité, ayant subi les pires humiliations et le pire mépris, soit capable de se transformer en deux générations en peuple dominateur et sûr de lui et à l'exception d'une admirable minorité, en peuple méprisant ayant satisfaction à humilier; Les Juifs d'Israël, descendants des victimes d'un apartheid nommé ghetto, ghettoïsent les Palestiniens. Les Juifs qui furent humiliés, méprisés, persécutés, humilient, méprisent, persécutent les Palestiniens. Les Juifs qui furent victimes d'un ordre impitoyable imposent leur ordre impitoyable aux Palestiniens. Les Juifs, victimes de l'inhumanité montrent une terrible inhumanité. Les Juifs, boucs émissaires de tous les maux, "boucs émissarisent" B... et l'Autorité palestinienne, rendus responsables d'attentats, qu'on les empêche d'empêcher'.

comparaison des comportements subis par les juifs et des comportements qui leur sont imputés', but they constituted 'un constat péremptoire de la nation juive'.[1046]

In its decision of 12 July 2006, the French Supreme Court annulled this judgment, because contrary to the Court of Appeal, it opined that the passages did not constitute an imputation of a specific fact, and were not, therefore, a punishable defamation, but a free opinion. The Court considered: 'les propos poursuivis, isolés au sein d'un article critiquant la politique menée par le gouvernement d'Israël à l'égard des palestiniens, n'imputent aucun fait précis de nature à porter atteinte à l'honneur ou à la considération de la communauté juive dans son ensemble en raison de son appartenance à une nation ou à une religion, mais sont l'expression d'une opinion qui relève du seul débat d'idées'.[1047]

The desire of the Supreme Court in this case has without doubt been to preserve freedom of expression, which has been approved by French legal scholars. Its motivation has, however, received strong criticism. Firstly, Tillement points out that, as good faith as a justifying fact is generally rejected in the field of racial defamation, the judge can only rely on the constituent elements of the offence, in order to demonstrate the impunity of defamatory expression. According to Tillement, in the field of racial defamation it is, however, impossible to require the same precision of a specific fact that is susceptible of proof as in the field of defamation against an individual, because the accusations often spring from 'l'imaginaire raciste le plus délirant'.[1048] Indeed, in the Morin-case, the specific facts imputed against the Jews of Israel seem sufficiently precise to qualify as defamation: to humiliate, despise and persecute the Palestinians, especially if we compare them to imputations that have been found punishable in previously discussed cases: the imputation against American Jews to 'exploit the legends of the Holocaust' and the imputation against North Africans to 'live on social security benefits and play the drums all night' (para.4.3.1 *supra*).

Tillement concludes that the rejection of good faith as a justifying fact has resulted in an incoherent case law concerning the constituent elements of the offence of racial defamation: the distinction between imputations of specific facts and free opinions.[1049] Droin regards the notion of good faith as interpreted by the French courts as the root of the problem.[1050] Both scholars argue that judges should more explicitly consider the context of the debate of a matter of general interest by referring to Article 10 ECHR, instead of dissimulating the importance they attach

---

1046 Cited by: French Supreme Court, civ.ch. I, 16 July 2006, n° 05–17704, *Bull.* 2006 I, n° 395 p.340, *Légipresse* n° 237, December 2006, annotation G. Tillement, pp.223–228.

1047 French Supreme Court, civ.ch. I, 16 July 2006, n° 05–17704, *Bull.* 2006 I, n° 395 p. 340, *Légipresse* n° 237, December 2006, annotation G. Tillement, pp.223–228.

1048 Tillement, G., Diffamation raciale et critique de la politique Israélienne, annotation at: French Supreme Court, civ.ch. I, 16 July 2006, n° 05–17704, *Bull.* 2006 I, n° 395 p. 340, *Légipresse* n° 237, December 2006, p.224.

1049 Tillement 2006, p.225.

1050 Droin 2009, p.495.

to freedom of expression when qualifying expression under the offence.[1051] However, the admission of a justifying ground in the interest of freedom of expression for expression that in first instance can be qualified as defamation seems to be difficult to introduce into a French system that strictly distinguishes free opinions from punishable acts. The reference to Article 10 ECHR by the courts is often limited to the consideration that freedom of expression, as guaranteed by Article 10–1 ECHR, can be submitted to certain restrictions in the interests enumerated in Article 10–2 ECHR and that 'tel est l'object de l'article 32 alinéa 2, de la loi susvisée, dont il a été fait application en l'espèce'.[1052]

*4.5.2. The imputation of a specific fact on the ground of religion or a value judgment in the context of a historical debate: the **Paul Giniewski** case*

In the field of religious defamation, the *Paul Giniewski* case is a famous example of the difficulties French jurisdictions have in distinguishing the punishable imputation of a specific fact on the ground of religion from a free opinion or value judgment concerning a religion that might hurt religious sensitivities in the context of a historical debate. The case concerned the publication in *Le quotidien de Paris* of 4 January 1994 of the article 'L'obscurité de l'erreur' by journalist, sociologist and historian Paul Giniewski, which was a reaction to the publication of the papal encyclical 'Veritatis Splendor'. In the article, Giniewski criticized the position of the Pope and held that certain principles of the Catholic religion tend towards anti-Semitism and have favoured the Holocaust.[1053] The association AGRIF considered the article defamatory of Catholics and initiated judicial proceedings. The criminal tribunal of Paris condemned Giniewski to a fine of 6000 francs and 1 euro in damages, because Giniewski had imputed the Catholic Church or even Catholics themselves of being partly responsible for the atrocities carried out by the Nazis. The tribunal rejected Giniewski's good faith, because by using outrageous terms he had shown a personal hostility towards the Christian community. Contrarily, the Paris Court of Appeal considered that the article contributed to the ongoing theological and historical debate on the origins of the Holocaust. According to the Court, the thesis held by Giniewski exclusively entered into a doctrinal debate and did not constitute an imputation of a specific fact that was possible of defamation.[1054] On 28 April 1998, the French Supreme Court annulled this decision, because the

---

1051 Tillement 2006, pp.226–228; Droin 2009, p.495.

1052 French Supreme Court, crim.ch., 7 December 1993, n° 92–81094, *Bull. Crim.* 1993, n° 373, p.931.

1053 The article contained the following passage: 'The Catholic Church sets itself up as the sole keeper of divine truth… It proclaims clearly the fulfillment of the Old Covenant in the New, and the superiority of the latter. Many Christians have acknowledged that anti-Judaism and the doctrine of the "fulfillment". of the Old Covenant in the New lead to anti- Semitism and prepared the ground in which the idea and implementation. of Auschwitz took seed'.

1054 TGI Paris, 8 March 1995; CA Paris, 9 November 1995, cited in: ECtHR 31 January 2006, n° 64016/00, *Giniewski/France*.

expressions 'imputaient à la communauté catholique une incitation à l'antisémitisme et la responsabilité des massacres commis à Auschwitz'.[1055] After referral, the Orléans Court of Appeal confirmed the judgment of the Supreme Court. It considered Giniewski's expression as constituting a defamatory imputation of a specific fact and, as the tribunal had done, rejected the good faith of Giniewski, because of the virulent general tone of the article and the use of terms like 'doctrine de l'accomplissement' et 'l'accomplissement d'Auschwitz'.[1056] Giniewski was ordered to pay the symbolic amount of one franc in damages and the costs for the publication of the verdict in a newspaper. On 14 June 2000, The French Supreme Court rejected a new appeal, considering that the court had rightly rejected Giniewski's good faith.[1057]

Giniewski filed a complaint with the ECtHR that unanimously decided that the measures constituted a violation of Giniewski's freedom of expression, thus Article 10 ECHR. The ECtHR considered that by considering the detrimental effects of a particular doctrine, the article contributed to the discussion of the various possible reasons behind the extermination of the Jews in Europe, which the Court considered to be a question of indisputable public interest in a democratic society. According to the Court, the article did not contain attacks on religious beliefs as such, but a view that Giniewski wished to express as a journalist and historian. It was essential in a democratic society that a debate on the causes of acts of particular gravity amounting to crimes against humanity should be able to take place freely and it formed an integral part of freedom of expression to seek historical truth'.[1058] The article was not gratuitously offensive and did not overstep a limit, because it was not intentionally insulting or defamatory, nor did it incite to hatred or disrespect. Contrarily, it entered into a free historical debate on a matter of public interest, which is essential in a democracy, and the conviction to publish the verdict in a newspaper was therefore disproportional.

The judgment of the ECtHR has been variously received by French legal scholars. Derieux finds the appreciation by the ECtHR that the expression was not gratuitously offensive and did not incite to irrespect or hatred very subjective and even contestable. According to him, the expression did form an imputation of a specific fact, but Giniewski lacked good faith.[1059] According to Docquir, the ECtHR rightly qualified Giniewski's expression not as an attack of religious convictions as

1055 French Supreme Court, crim.ch., 28 April 1998, n° 95–85958, *unpublished.*

1056 CA Orléans, 14 December 1998, cited in: ECtHR 31 January 2006, n° 64016/00, *Giniewski/ France.*

1057 French Supreme Court, crim.ch., 14 June 2000, n° 99–80043, *unpublished.*

1058 ECtHR 31 January 2006, n° 64016/00, *Giniewski/France*, §51.

1059 Derieux, E., Contestation de la doctrine Catholique et bonne foi, annotation at ECtHR 31 January 2006, n° 64016/00, *Giniewski/France, Légipresse* n° 230, April 2006, p.49.

such,[1060] but Dreyer disagreed with the ECtHR that Giniewski's expression entered into a purely historical debate, rightly because it formed a reaction to the recently published papal encyclical.[1061] In my view, the ECtHR has rightly corrected the French jurisdictions that had interpreted an opinion or value judgment as an imputation of a specific fact – the criticism of a religious doctrine as a defamation against the entire Catholic community – and the ECtHR has rightly given priority to a purely historical debate of a general interest, whereas the French jurisdictions had narrowly applied Giniewski's good faith as a justifying fact.

4.5.3. The imputation of a specific fact on the ground of religion or criticizing a religion in a humoristic context: ***Charlie Hebdo***

The French judges have on several occasions afforded a right to ridicule a religion in order to criticize its institutions and considered that the ridiculing of a religion forms part of a free debate of opinions. Because of the strict criteria of the offence of religious defamation, many cases concerning the ridiculing of a religion have, however, been dealt under the offences of religious insult in Article 33–3 and provocation to religious hatred or discrimination in Article 24–8 (para.5.2.2; 5.4 and 6.5.1 *infra*). In cases initiated on the ground of religious defamation, the motivation is centred – again – around the question in relation to the qualification pursuant to the offence and not around the question as to whether a suspect has proven his good faith or whether the interest in a free debate of opinions can form a *justification* of the expression: such expression simply lacks the allegation of a specific fact against a determined religious group. Hence, in a case concerning an article ridiculing the Pope published in the famous French openly anticlerical and grossly satirical journal *Charlie Hebdo*,[1062] the French Supreme Court endorsed the decision of the Court of Appeal that had considered: 'ces propos ne sont pas révélateurs de la diffamation poursuivie en l'absence d'allégations de faits précis pouvant être imputés à un groupe religieux déterminé et de nature à porter atteinte à l'honneur et à la réputation de celui-ci, qu'il s'agit

1060 Docquir, P.-F., La Cour européen des droits de l'homme sacrifie-t-elle la liberté d'expression pour protéger les sensibilités religieuses?, annotation at ECtHR 31 January 2006, n° 64016/00, *Giniewski/France*, *RTDH* n° 68, 2006, p.839.

1061 Dreyer, E., Les infractions de septembre 2005-novembre 2006, *Légipresse* 2007, 239-II, p.35.

1062 Passages of the article read:'Viens inverser le cours du temps qui passe, à coups… de messages d'amour imprégnés comme des éponges du sang des hommes de la liberté"… "Tu es l'allié de tous ceux qui voient dans la misère des uns la bonne affaire des autres. Depuis deux mille ans…", "Débarque avec ton barda: tissus de non-sens sanctifiés, miracles pour handicapés mentaux, fables pour paumés, répression de la joie de vivre, haine du plaisir, censure de la connaissance, passion du pouvoir, déguisements de carnaval, ordre soi-disant moral pour maintenir les consciences dans un sous-développement propice à l'acceptation de l'asservissement, antisémitisme sournoisement doctrinal"; "Tu as fait cause commune avec les intégristes musulmans. Vous êtes d'accord sur l'essentiel du programme: mort à la liberté, mort à l'émancipation, mort à la connaissance, mort à la culture, mort à l'égalité'.

non d'attaques contre les fidèles d'une religion mais de critiques dont la virulence ne peut être appréciée qu'au regard du caractère ouvertement anticlérical et grossièrement satirique du journal Charlie hebdo, et qui, portant sur le rôle et les positions à travers l'histoire de l'Eglise catholique, en tant qu'institution représentée par le pape, relèvent d'un débat d'opinions qu'il n'appartient pas aux tribunaux d'arbitrer'.[1063]

4.6. Conclusion

In French legal doctrine, the criminalization of *racial* defamation and insult is beyond discussion, because its aim is to protect a society against elements causing social disorder and the rights of others. Racial defamation consists of willingly and consciously imputing or alleging a specific fact, susceptible of proof and a contradictory debate, against a person or a group *exclusively* on the grounds of their origin, membership or non-membership of an ethnic group, nation, race or religion. On the one hand, the discriminatory grounds are restrictively interpreted; a group must be precisely designated and foreigners, Corsicans or Harkis do not form a group for the purposes of Article 32–2. On the other hand, expression does not have to be aimed at a group in its entirety; a group is designated regardless of its size. A suspect's intention to defame does not have to be proven, but is presumed. A suspect can only counter this presumption of his bad faith by demonstrating his good faith as a justifying fact; the justifying facts consisting of the exception of truth and the excuse of provocation are excluded in the field of racial defamation.

As the French notion of good faith has proven to be too strict to meet the European standards of freedom of expression, the French Supreme Court has revaluated it in light of the case law of the ECtHR and requires that judges balance freedom of expression more *in concreto* with the reputation or rights of others. In the field of racial defamation, the suspect's good faith is however often rejected. Judges rather attach importance to a suspect's right to freedom of expression by strictly discerning an imputation of a fact from a free opinion or value judgment, when qualifying expression under the offence, than seeing it as a justification for defamatory expression, which has resulted in an incoherent case law concerning the distinction between imputations of specific facts and free opinions. Legal scholars have suggested that French judges should refer more explicitly to freedom of expression as a justifying fact. However, this practice matches the French traditional vision on freedom of opinion that strictly distinguishes free opinions from punishable acts. As a result of the case law concerning racial and religious defamation, French jurisdictions do take into account the context in which the expression is uttered, whether political, historical, or humoristic.

1063 French Supreme Court, civ.ch. II, 26 April 2001, n° 99–10490, *Légipresse,* 2001, n° 183–35.

5. Racial insult

The offence of racial insult is characterized by a number of elements, being insult and intent thereto (5.1) and the designation of a group on account of race or religion (5.2). The justifications for the offence of racial insult allowed by the law are limited to the excuse of provocation (5.3). In a special series of case law, the French judiciary has clearly demarcated religious insult from the offence of religious feelings (5.4). In the application of the offence, the French judge takes – to a certain extent – into account the context of expression (5.5). The analysis results in a general conclusion about the offence of racial insult in French law (5.6).

5.1. Insult and intent

Article 375 of the French Penal Code of 1810 criminalized 'expressions outrageantes' that consisted of 'l'imputation d'aucun fait écrit mais celle d'une vice déterminé'. The Act of 17 May 1819 reorganized the repression of l'injure and distinguished between the imputation of a vice, ordinary public insults and non-public insults.[1064] The 1881 Press Act suppressed all distinction between an ordinary insult and the imputation of a vice, but adopted the definition of the insult of the Act of 1819 in Article 29–2 that reads 'Toute expression outrageante, termes de mépris ou invective qui ne renferme l'imputation d'aucun fait est une injure' and admitted 'l'excuse de provocation'. While Article 33–2 of the 1881 Press Act sanctions the public insult of private individuals, if it has not been preceded by provocations (also called the 'injure simple'),[1065] Article 33–3 sanctions, under the same conditions, the insult of a person or a group of persons on the grounds of their origin, membership or non-membership of an ethnic group, nation, race or religion fine of up to € 22.500, or imprisonment up to 6 months.[1066] In the absence of publicity, racial insult of a person or a group is a petty offence criminalized in accordance with Article R. 624–4 of the Penal Code.[1067]

Insult supposes as a constituent element of the offence an outrageous expression, a term of contempt or an invective, terms that can serve as a useful guideline for the French judge when qualifying expression as an insult. In case law, an outrageous

1064 Beignier, De Lamy & Dreyer 2009, p.492.

1065 With a fine of up to € 12.000,-.

1066 According to the last paragraph of Article 33, the tribunal can order the public display or dissemination of the decision taken in accordance with Article 131–35 of the French Penal Code.

1067 Article R.624–4 reads: L'injure non publique commise envers une personne ou un groupe de personnes à raison de leur origine ou de leur appartenance ou de leur non-appartenance, vraie ou supposée, à une ethnie, une nation, une race ou une religion déterminée est punie de l'amende prévue pour les contraventions de la 4e classe; Est punie de la même peine l'injure non publique commise envers une personne ou un groupe de personnes à raison de leur sexe, de leur orientation sexuelle ou de leur handicap.

expression has been defined as 'tout propos qui, sans contenir l'imputation d'un fait précis, est de nature à porter atteinte à l'honneur ou à la délicatesse de celui auquel il s'adresse', while a term of contempt has been defined as 'un terme ne respectant pas la dignité de celui auquel s'adresse en le rabaissant publiquement'.[1068] This distinction remains pure theoretical, because all three categories of insult are used in case law and have the common characteristic to constitute excessive language that constitutes a deliberate aggression of the person.[1069] It falls outside the scope of this research to give a comprehensive overview of expression that has been found to constitute a punishable insult against individuals.[1070] Examples comprise the terms 'voleur',[1071] 'dangereux salaud',[1072] 'manipulateur, menteur, bonimenteur'[1073] and terms associating a person with the war crimes committed by the Nazis, such as the epithet 'crematoire' to designate a Minister,[1074] or the statement that a political person or his political party is surrounded by a perfume of 'Zyklon B'.[1075]

Insult is defined negatively in relation to defamation, thus in relation to an imputation of a specific fact that is susceptible of proof and the object of a contradictory debate. The French Supreme Court generally holds that if expression lacks such qualities 'il ne peut s'agir que d'une injure'.[1076] For example, the French Supreme Court found the term 'neo-nazi notoire' to constitute the expression of an opinion that could not have the effect as to 'donner à un propos injurieux un caractère diffamatoire'.[1077] The relevance of the distinction between the two offences lies in the fact that the offence of insult is sanctioned less severely and the offence of defamation cannot, contrary to the offence of insult, be justified by the excuse of provocation. Dreyer, however, questions the opportunity of the distinction between racial defamation and racial insult, because in the field of racial defamation the exception of truth is excluded, which could justify the creation of one single broader offence of 'offense raciale', which in turn would diminish the risks of mistakes in the qualification of the offence.[1078]

Pursuant to Article 53 of the 1881 Press Act, one unique fact cannot be prosecuted at the same time on the ground of defamation and insult. In order for the suspect to know exactly what he is accused of and to prepare his defence, the prosecuting party must uniquely and definitively qualify the facts in the summons from the

1068 Cohen 2003, p.182.
1069 Bigot 2004, p.106.
1070 For an overview, see: Beignier, De Lamy & Dreyer 2009, p.493–494.
1071 French Supreme Court, crim.ch., 8 February 1972, n° 71–91102, *Bull. Crim.* 1972, n° 48.
1072 French Supreme Court, crim.ch., 10 May 2006, n° 05–82971, *unpublished.*
1073 French Supreme Court, crim.ch., 30 March 2005, n° 04–85709, *Bull. Crim.* 2005, n° 110.
1074 French Supreme Court, crim.ch., 20 October 1992, n° 91–84253, *Bull. Crim.* 1992, n° 329.
1075 French Supreme Court, crim.ch., 19 June 2001, n° 00–86167, *unpublished.*
1076 French Supreme Court, crim.ch., 17 February 1981, n° 79–92748, *Bull. Crim.* 1981, n° 64.
1077 French Supreme Court, crim.ch., 14 February 2006, n° 05–82475, *Bull. Crim.* 2006, n° 40.
1078 Dreyer, E., Le fondement de la prohibition des discours racistes en France, *Légipresse* n° 199, March 2003, p.21.

beginning (para.1.3.1 *supra*). A cumulative qualification would create uncertainty with the suspect as to the object of the prosecution. Hence, the French Supreme Court has established that when certain expression constitutes defamation, but at the same time consists of insulting comments of the impugned facts, those insulting terms are indivisibly and directly linked to the defamatory facts and are therefore dependent on them. In the event of such an 'indivisibilité entre l'injure et la diffamation', the insult is absorbed by the defamation and the expression must be qualified as defamation. The French Supreme Court has considered: 'lorsque les expressions outrageantes ou appréciations injurieuses se rattachent directement à une imputation diffamatoire, le délit d'injure s'absorbe dans celui de diffamation et ne peut être relevé seule.'[1079] A certain text can, however, also contain multiple allegations that contain both defamatory words and insulting words that do not refer to the impugned fact constituting defamation. In such an event, an accumulation of qualifications remains possible and a suspect can be declared punishable on the grounds of both defamation and insult.[1080]

A prosecution and condemnation solely on the ground of insult remains possible, however, if the insult refers to expression lacking a defamatory character. In a decision of 24 November 2009, the French Supreme Court rejected an appeal against the condemnation of the famous French television host Arthur on the ground of insult with regard to his qualification of the humourist Dieudonné famous for his anti-Semitic statements as 'la dernière des pourritures' and the statement that 'même les mecs du Front National ont honte que Dieudonné soit venu les voir' during a radio interview. As this latter statement could not be considered as a defamatory allegation of anti-Semitism, the Court of Appeal had rightly qualified the expression as an insult that was not absorbed by defamation.[1081]

Choosing the wrong qualification has the far-reaching consequence that the French judge must annul the entire prosecution and acquit a suspect, because it is not permitted for the French judge to requalify the facts under another offence – again in order to assure a suspect's possibilities of defence. Tillement, however, advocates the introduction of the possibility for the French judge to requalify the facts under the offence of racial insult. With regard to a prosecution on the ground of *racial* defamation, for which neither the exception of truth or a justification of good faith exists, contrary to the prosecution on the ground of defamation of an individual – such requalification will not put the rights of the defendant in danger.[1082] The Morin-case (para.4.5.1 *supra*) perfectly shows how difficult it can be to rightly qualify expression either as an imputation of a specific fact, or as an opinion or value judgment that might constitute an insult if it is deliberately uttered in excessive terms.

1079 French Supreme Court, crim.ch., 24 January 1995, n° 93–84701, *Bull. Crim.* 1995, n° 33.

1080 French Supreme Court, crim.ch., 22 February 1966, n° 65–90518, *Bull. Crim.* 1966, n° 62.

1081 French Supreme Court, crim.ch., 24 November 2009, n° 09–83256, *Bull. Crim.* 2009, n° 193.

1082 Tillement, G., Diffamation raciale et critique de la politique Israélienne, annotation at: French Supreme Court, civ.ch. I, 16 July 2006, n° 05–17704, *Bull.* 2006 I, n° 395 p.340, *Légipresse* n° 237, December 2006, p.228.

Like the offence of defamation, the offence of insult is an 'infraction intentionelle.' The author of an insult must have the intention to insult, the existence of his intention must be presumed and the judge does not explicitly have to establish a suspect's intention. According to the French Supreme Court, 'les expressions outrageantes, termes de mépris ou invectives sont réputés de droit prononcés avec une intention coupable' and 'seule l'excuse de provocation est de nature à leur ôter leur caractère punissable.'[1083] Thus, contrary to the offence of defamation, in order to counter this presumption of bad faith, the author of an insult cannot prove his good faith, because with regard to the offence of insult only the excuse of provocation is allowed as a justifying act (para.5.3 *infra*). The French Supreme Court exercises strict control over the qualification of the expression by the lower judges under the elements of the offence that they extract from the expression itself and the context in which it is uttered.[1084] Thus, in the words of Dreyer, the French judiciary takes the intention of the author of an insult into account, not to establish its presence or absence, but to determine the actual sense and purport of the expression.[1085] The French judge notably considers the use of strong racist terms of contempt, invectives and outrageous expression to constitute an intentional insult. In 2011, the famous designer John Galliano was convicted of racial insult due to his remarks 'fucking ugly jewish bitch'; 'fucking Asian bastard'; and 'dirty jewish face' uttered to several persons, while sitting on a terrace of a Parisian café. Although Galliano was drunk and could not remember the event, his intent was established because he was conscious of the effect of his addictions.[1086]

5.2. Designation of a group

5.2.1. Racial groups

Like the offence of racial defamation, a racial insult must be made against a group exclusively on the grounds of their origin, membership or non-membership of an ethnic group, nation, race or religion, and not for other reasons. The French Supreme Court has given a restrictive interpretation of the discriminatory grounds. Hence, in 2000, the French Supreme Court considered that the qualification of the 'Harkis' and their descendants as 'traitres à la patrie', because of their political choice during the Algerian war, did not constitute the offence of insult on the grounds of ethnic background, nation or religion.[1087] Agostinelli argues that the fact that the element of the racial group could not be constituted does not remove the insulting character of the expression. However, as the expression was not aim at

1083 French Supreme Court, crim.ch., 10 May 2006, n° 05–82971, *unpublished.*

1084 French Supreme Court, crim.ch., 20 October 1992, n° 91–84253, *Bull. Crim.* 1992, n° 329.

1085 Dreyer 2002, n° 329.

1086 TGI de Paris 17e Ch. 8 September 2011, *Légipresse* n° 287 October 2011, 287–14, p. 529.

1087 French Supreme Court, crim.ch., 12 September 2000, n° 99–82281, *unpublished.*

one particular person, the expression could not be prosecuted on the ground of the offence of insult against an individual. Agostinelli therefore questions the added value of the offence of racial insult, when interpreted as such.[1088] As with the offence of racial defamation, the French judciary seems to rather attach importance to a suspect's right to freedom of expression, when qualifying expression under the offence, this time by strictly interpreting the notion of a group on the ground of origin, than seeing it as a justification for insulting expression concerning a specific group. One could, however, argue that although the Harkis do form a determined, designated group, the judge simply desired to preserve freedom of expression on this particular topic.

Contrarily, an example of a case in which the judge seems to have simply thought the expression to overstep the limits of freedom of expression, but in which the designation of the group seems questionable, forms a condemnation of the humourist Dieudonné by the tribunal correctionnel de Paris and the Paris Court of Appeal with regard to a performance at the Zénith stadium in Paris in 2008. During the performance, Dieudonné had declared his desire to surpass the accusation made by Bernard-Henri Lévy and the media in general that Dieudonné organized anti-Semitic meetings and for this purpose had invited former professor and notorious revisionist Robert Faurisson on stage. After Faurisson appeared on stage, a technician disguised as a deported Jew, with a yellow star on his chest awarded Faurisson a prize of insolence: a grotesque chandelier covered with fruit. Subsequently, Dieudonné and Faurisson presented themselves as victims of the memorial laws and accused the 'affirmationnistes' of mistaking revisionism for negationism.

The courts considered that although the expression was not formally aimed at a determined group, the elements of the performance had given the expression its true sense: the mentioning of the word 'Juif' on the yellow star, the chandelier caricaturizing the menorah and the sole presence of a notorious negationist were sufficient to conclude that Dieudonné aimed at the Jewish community on the ground of their origin or religion.[1089] Moreover, Dieudonné had invited his audience to participate '*à une oeuvre collective de glissage de quenelle*'. 'Glisser un quenelle', an expression invented by Dieudonné, consists of stretching out one arm and hand towards below and placing the other hand on one's shoulder, by some interpreted as a symbol of fisting the system and notably the media, by others interpreted as a reversed Nazi Salute and an anti-Semitic geste.[1090] Given the context of the rest of his show, Dieudonné had clearly aimed to 'glisser une quenelle' at Jews as a group and not the system or the media.[1091]

1088 Agostinelli, X., Provocation à la discrimination, diffamation et injure raciales, *Légicom* 2002/3, n° 28, pp.54–55.

1089 CA Paris, 17 March 2011, annotation D. Lefranc, Dieudonné ou la subversion par l'ambiguïté, *Légipresse* n° 285, July/August 2011, p.430.

1090 Www.metronews.fr/info/photo-polemique-de-mamadou-sakho-qu-est-ce-que-la-quenelle-de-dieudonne/mmik!PldbRjwCs8Jo6/.

1091 CA Paris, 17 March 2011, annotation D. Lefranc, Dieudonné ou la subversion par l'ambiguïté, *Légipresse* n° 285, July/August 2011, p.430–431.

With regard to Dieudonné's freedom of expression, the Court of Appeal considered that in this case the respect for human dignity prevailed over the freedom of artistic and humorous expression, because the sketch could be characterized as a political meeting rather than a performance.[1092] According to annotator Lefranc, the performance could only be considered as a political meeting, if the audience was aware in advance of its political nature, but this was uncertain. The judgment wrongly afforded a larger scope of freedom of expression in an artistic context than in a political context, because artists and politicians have in common in addressing sensible issues. If Dieudonné, who was also known for having actual political aspirations, could not appeal on the basis of his freedom of expression, it was simply because he had clearly overstepped its limits.[1093]

Indeed, in subsequent cases the French judge considered that the right to humorous expression finds its limit in the violation of the respect for people's human dignity and in personal attacks, both in the event that the expression was uttered in an artistic context and a professional context. In 2012, the former president of the French parfum company Guerlain was convicted of racial insult with regard to his joke 'Pour une fois, je me suis mis à travailler comme un nègre. Je ne sais pas si les nègres ont toujours tellement travaillé, mais enfin ...' during a television interview about his profession.[1094] Later that year Dieudonné was again convicted of racial insult for having mocked the deportation and extermination of Jews by the Nazis in WWII in a satirical video placed on the Internet. The video showed Dieudonné, dressed up as a jewish deportee with a pineapple in his hands, singing 'Shoah ananas tu me prends par la Shoah je te prends par l'ananas' and 'Shoah ananas Allez on bouge le cul', a parodie of the song 'Chaud Cacao' by Annie Cordy. The conviction was confirmed in appeal.[1095] After numerous convictions, in January 2014, the French government even decided to ban Dieudonné's recent theatre show 'Le Mur' (The Wall) after it was held in the Théâtre de la Main d'Or in Paris for being anti-Semitic (para. 9.4 *infra*).[1096]

1092 Lefranc, D., Dieudonné ou la subversion par l'ambiguïté, annotation at CA Paris, 17 March 2011, *Légipresse* n° 285, July/August 2011, p.431.

1093 Lefranc 2011, p.432.

1094 TGI de Paris 17e Ch. 29 March 2012, *Légipresse* n° 294 May 2012, 294–12, p. 284, annotation J-M Delas at p. 316.

1095 TGI de Paris 17e Ch. 27 November 2012, *Légipresse* n° 303 March 2013, 303–21, p. 142–143. CA Paris, 28 November 2013, *Légipresse* n° 315 April 2014, 315–16, p. 205.

1096 The show included a sketch, in which the humorist mimed urinating against a wall. He then revealed that it was the Wailing Wall in Jerusalem. He also uttered salvos of abuse at prominent French Jewish performers, including radio presenter Patrick Cohen, concluding: 'Gas chambers ... a shame.' On 12 February 2014, the TGI de Paris ordered the withdrawal of certain passages of *le Mur* in an online video of Diedonné for constituting provocation to racial hatred and negationism. TGI de Paris, 12 February 2014, *Légipresse* n° 314 March 2014, 314–18, p. 140–141.

5.2.2. *Religious groups*

It is exactly the requirement established by the French Supreme Court of the designation of a group, however, that distinguishes the punishable insult of a religious group from free opinion concerning a religion that might hurt religious feelings, which can be demonstrated by another famous Dieudonné-case (see further para.5.4 *infra*). In its issue n°360 of 23–29 January 2002, the journal *Lyon Capitale* published an interview with the famous French humourist Dieudonné who at that time ran as a candidate for the presidential elections. In response to the question posed by a journalist 'que pensez-vous de la montée de l'antisémitisme parmi certains jeunes beurs?', Dieudonné had answered: 'Le racisme a été inventé par Abraham. Le peuple élu c'est le début du racisme. Les musulmans aujourd'hui renvoient la réponse du berger à la bergère. Juifs et musulmans pour moi ça n'existe pas. Ce sont deux notions aussi stupides l'une que l'autre. Personne n'est juif ou alors tout le monde. Je ne comprends rien à cette histoire. Pour moi les juifs c'est une secte, une escroquerie. C'est une des plus graves parce que la première. Certains musulmans prennent la même voie en remaniant des concepts comme la guerre sainte etc ...'. Pursuant to a complaint by the association l'Union des étudiants juifs de France (UEFJ), the public prosecutor prosecuted Dieudonné on the grounds of racial insult and racial provocation with regard to the phrase 'Pour moi les juifs c'est une secte, une escroquerie. C'est une des plus graves parce que la première' and four associations – UEFJ, LICRA, le Consistoire central and l'Union des Communautés Juives de France – constituted as a civil party.

The tribunal correctionnel de Paris acquitted Dieudonné and rejected the demands of the civil parties.[1097] In appeal, the Paris Court of Appeal confirmed this judgment, considering that the terms 'secte et escroquerie' taken in isolation are very shocking, but placed in the context of the article, Dieudonné appeared to reject the idea of Communautarism and promoted the universality of man and by criticizing other religions, notably the Catholic and Muslim faith, in equally vivid terms he had merely manifested 'son hostilité au principe même du fait religieux et que ces invectives ne s'adressaient pas à la communauté juive en tant que telle'.[1098] On 15 March 2005, the French Supreme Court annulled this decision with regard to the offence of racial insult, because 'alors que les propos litigieux mettaient spécialement en cause la communauté juive, présentée comme 'une des plus graves escroqueries' parce que 'la première de toutes', les juges n'ont pas tiré les conséquences légales de leurs propres constatations.'[1099] After referral, however, another section of the Paris Court of Appeal persisted in the interpretation made by

[1097] Tribunal correctionnel de Paris, 9 November 2003, cited in: Report of M. Gueudet, reporting judge, at French Supreme Court, plenary assembly, 16 February 2007, n° 06–81785, *Bull. Crim.* 2007, n° 1, p.1, available at: www.courdecassation.fr.

[1098] CA Paris, 30 June 2004, cited in: French Supreme Court, crim.ch., 15 March 2005, n° 04–84463, *Bull. Crim.* 2005, n° 90, p.321.

[1099] French Supreme Court, crim.ch., 15 March 2005, n° 04–84463, *Bull. Crim.* 2005, n° 90, p.321.

the tribunal and the Court of Appeal and confirmed their judgments considering that the terms 'les juifs c'est une secte, une escroquerie' replaced in their context 'relèvent d'un débat théorique sur l'influence des religions et ne constituent pas une attaque dirigée contre la communauté juive en tant que communauté humaine'.[1100] Against this decision, the associations Le Consistoire central and Union des communautés juives de France filed a request in cassation, which was submitted to the plenary assembly of the French Supreme Court.

According to the Advocate-General in the Supreme Court Mouton, Dieudonné had designated the Jewish community as a group of people on the ground of their origin by using the words '*les* juifs'. Subsequently, he had qualified this community, not a religion as such but as a 'secte' and a 'escroquerie', which are terms of an undisputable downgrading, outrageous and insulting character. What is more, Dieudonné had associated Jews with fraudulent money, which over decades has often been done by anti-Semites. The A-G attached importance to the fact that Dieudonné had previously been condemned several times for having uttered racist expression; it did not concern an isolated case. Despite his profession as a humourist, Dieudonné had not made his statement in a humorous context, which could have removed the insulting character of the expression, but in his capacity as an election candidate. This political context did not remove the insulting character of the expression, because Dieudonné had not uttered it in an electoral polemic, a situation of debate or direct confrontation, which might elicit ill-considered expression. As the French Supreme Court had established: 'la circonstance qu'une injure s'est produite dans un contexte électorale ne saurait en modifier le caractère'.[1101] In fine, Mouton considered the expression to be gratuitously offensive and a condemnation on the ground of racial insult in conformity with Article 10 ECHR. On 16 February 2007, the plenary assembly of the French Supreme Court endorsed this advice and again annulled the decision of the Paris Court of Appeal, considering that the phrase 'ne relève pas de la libre critique du fait religieux, participant d'un débat d'intérêt général mais constitue une injure visant un groupe de personnes en raison de son origine, dont la répression est une restriction nécessaire à la liberté d'expression dans une société démocratique.'[1102] In 2013, Dieudonné was convicted for insult, defamation and provocation to violence against Jews for having affirmed in another interview diffused on the Internet: 'les gros escrocs de la planète, ce sont des Juifs'.[1103]

1100 CA Paris, 9 February 2006, cited in: French Supreme Court, plenary assembly, 16 February 2007, n° 06–81785, *Bull. Crim.* 2007, n° 1, p.1.

1101 French Supreme Court, crim.ch., 20 October 1992, n° 91–84253, *Bull. Crim.* 1992, n° 329; French Supreme Court, crim.ch. 30 March 2005, n° 04–85709, *Bull. Crim.* 2005, n° 110.

1102 Advice of Advocate – General M. Mouton at French Supreme Court, pleneray assembly, 16 February 2007, n° 06–81785, *Bull. Crim.* 2007, n° 1, p.1, available at: www.courdecassation.fr. French Supreme Court, plenary assembly, 16 February 2007, n° 06–81785, *Bull. Crim.* 2007, n° 1, p.1.

1103 CA Paris, 28 November 2013, *Légipresse* n°315 April 2014, p. 204–205.

5.3. Justifications: the excuse of provocation

Pursuant to Article 33–2, an insult is not punishable, if it is preceded by provocations: one is entitled to insult a person as a counter attack against an insult previously committed against one's own person coming from that same person. The excuse of provocation has an absolute character in the sense that it exempts a suspect from a penalty, but it does not 'neutralize' his criminal responsibility like a justifying fact would do – such as the demonstration of good faith by the suspect of defamation.[1104] The French Supreme Court has adopted a restrictive notion of the excuse of provocation by considering that a provocation can only result from 'de propos, d'écrits injurieux, et de toutes autres actes de nature à atteindre l'auteur de l'infraction, soit dans son honneur ou sa considération, soit dans ses intérêts pécuniaires ou moraux.'[1105] Furthermore, there must be a 'relation directe entre provocation et l'injure'.[1106] What is more, such a direct link must concern the content of the insult and supposes that the insult is uttered within a reasonable time after the provocation and is proportionate to the tenor of the provocation.[1107]

These criteria can be clarified by the decision of 13 April 1999 of the French Supreme Court, in which the Court rejected an appeal against a condemnation of Le Pen on the ground of racial insult for having called the president of the anti-racism association SOS Racisme a 'Gros zebu fou' during a press conference. The Court of Appeal had ecarted the appeal made by Le Pen on the excuse of provocation due to the fact that the day before the president had publicly imputed Le Pen of having 'du sang sur les mains'. The Supreme Court endorsed the motivation of the court that had considered 'd'une part, qu'eu égard à la teneur et au caractère racial de l'injure incriminée, il n'y a pas de proportionnalité entre l'attaque et la riposte, et d'autre part, que cette injure, proférée lors d'une conférence de presse organisée par le prévenu, sur un sujet précis, n'est pas une riposte immédiate et irréfléchie aux propos diffamatoires du protagoniste.'[1108]

5.4. The special case of the protection of religious feelings

5.4.1. The development of the right to respect for religious feelings pursuant 1382 CC and 809 CCP

With the abolishment of le délit d'outrage à la morale publique et religieuse, the 1881 Press Act erased the last traces of the offence of blasphemy in French law. According to the French legislator of 1881 and the overall consensus in French legal

---

1104 Beignier, De Lamy & Dreyer 2009, p.504.
1105 French Supreme Court, crim.ch., 10 May 2006, n° 05–82971, *unpublished*.
1106 French Supreme Court, crim.ch., 16 April 1985, n° 83–94866, *Bull. Crim.* 1985, n° 140.
1107 French Supreme Court, crim.ch., 13 April 1999, n° 98–81625, *Bull. Crim.* 1999, n° 77.
1108 French Supreme Court, crim.ch., 13 April 1999, n° 98–81625, *Bull. Crim.* 1999, n° 77.

doctrine, such an offence constitutes a délit d'opinion and is contrary to the concept of laïcité (para.1.2.2 and 2.5 *supra*). However, in the eighties and nineties of the previous century associations that defended religious interests increasingly sought recourse to the civil judge in legal actions against expression alleged to have hurt religious feelings.[1109] In these civil cases grounded on Articles 1382 CC and 809 CCP, the French judiary have developed a right to respect for religious feelings, by referring to the fundamental principle enounced in Article 1 of the 1958 Constitution, according to which the French Republic respects all beliefs. The French civil judge, who has tried to conciliate the right to free criticism of a religion with the principle of respect of beliefs, is highly criticized in French legal doctrine, most notably for having reintroduced a prohibition of blasphemy into French law.

The first 'blasphemy' case was the *Ave Maria* case in 1984. The Catholic association La Fraternité Saint-Pie-X and several other Catholic associations[1110] requested the prohibition of the big billboards of the film *Ave Maria* by Jacques Richard in summary proceedings before the TGI de Paris. The film tells the story of a young woman in a village, who is persecuted by its pious inhabitants who formed part of a religious sect. The poster in question showed the actress Isabelle Pasco, covered only with a blouse around the hips, with her arms and feet tied to a cross. The judge prohibited the poster; he considered that the representation of the cross in a provocative advertisement campaign that was forced on the public in a space of public passage constituted an aggressive and gratuitously offensive infringement of the deepest intimate convictions of those who freely use the public highway and do not search for any contact with a certain work, but who are necessarily unwillingly confronted with disputable, misleading and commercial advertising.[1111] The commercial and public nature of the expression and its forced cognition by the public formed important factors of what in essence constituted a manifest unlawful disturbance on the ground of 809 CCP; the infringement of the deepest intimate convictions of religious adherents. The judge thus decided to protect a religious community in their religious feelings and did not distinguish between criticism of a religion that might offend religious feelings and the insult of a group of people on the ground of their religion.

In the two following cases *Je vous salue Marie* and *La Dernière Tentation du Christ,* which were both grounded on Article 809 CCP, the French Supreme Court seemingly adopted a more liberal attitude by endorsing the refusal of the lower

---

1109 See generally: Boulègue, J., *Le Blasphème en procès 1984–2009, l'église et la mosquée contre les libertés*, Paris: Nova Éditions 2010; Fourest, C.; Venner, F., *Tirs croisés, La laïcité à l'épreuve des intégrismes juif, chrétien et musulman*, Paris: Le livre de Poche, Calmann-Lévy 2003.

1110 Including: Les Associations de la Sainte-Croix, de defence de l'École catholique, Notre-Dame-du-Pointet, Saint-François-Régis, Saint-Grégoire-des-Minimes, Saint-Léon-IX, Credo, "Femme Liberté".

1111 TGI de Paris, 23 October 1984, *GP* 1984, p.722; *D.* 1985, p.31, annotation R. Lindon.

jurisdictions to prohibit expression alleged to hurt religious feelings. Again, an important factor in these cases was the degree of publicity of the expression. Contrary to the *Ave Maria* case, the expression in question was not of a public nature and not forced on the public. However, the French Supreme Court either implicitly or explicitly affirmed the existence of the right to respect for religious feelings and left room for a possible prohibition of the expression, if uttered more publicly.

In 1985, AGRIF and la Confédération nationale des associations familiales catholiques requested the prohibition not of the poster, but of the running of the film *Je vous salue Marie* by Jean-Luc Godard in the French cinema and subsidiarily, the suppression of certain passages of the film that offended religious feelings of Catholics before the TGI de Paris. The film is a modern narration of the birth of Christ, in which Joseph is a taxi driver and Maria an employee of a gas station who loves to play basketball. What is more, in search of a way to unify her body and spirit, Maria actively explores her sexuality. Not surprisingly, the film was highly controversial, caused global protests and even caused blockades of cinemas by opponents of the film.

In three instances, the request by the associations was denied. While the associations argued before the lower courts that the film infringed the right to respect for the religious feelings of the faithful they represented, the lower courts considered that, while certain aspects of the film could shock the religious sensitivities of the adherents of the associations, the film was not reprobated unanimously by all Catholics and that the effect of the film was attenuated and could be avoided as the film was merely distributed in cinemas. The infringement to religious feelings made by the offensive aspects of the film was limited to those spectators that had taken the initiative to go to the cinema.[1112]

The associations filed an appeal against the decision of the court of appeal, arguing that it had wrongly required that the expression caused a manifestly unlawful disturbance 'to a certain degree' and had wrongly founded its judgment on the advice of the religious French journal La croix and certain religious representatives of the Catholic Church, while the expression caused an 'objective' manifestly unlawful disturbance against the Catholic community in its entirety. In 1990, the French Supreme Court rejected the appeal, considering that 'la cour d'appel, qui n'a pas dit que le trouble devait dépasser un certain degré d'ampleur pour pouvoir donner lieu aux mesures sollicitées, a relevé que, si certains aspects du film pouvaient choquer la sensibilité religieuse des adhérents des associations appelantes ou intervenantes, il n'en résultait pas pour autant l'existence d'un trouble manifestement illicite, seul de nature à limiter la liberté d'expression, dès lors que la réprobation n'était pas unanime chez les catholiques pour une œuvre qui, de compréhension difficile et achevant sa carrière dans l'indifférence, n'avait eu qu'un impact très limité.'[1113]

1112 TGI de Paris, 28 January 1985, *D.* 1985, p.129, annotation R. Lindon; CA Paris, 13 May 1985, *GP* 1985, p.344.

1113 French Supreme Court, civ.ch. I, 10 January 1990, n°88–14235, *Bull.* 1990 I, n°11, p.9.

In 1988, AGRIF and several other associations requested a prohibition, again not of the film poster, but of the running of the film *The Last Temptation of the Christ* by Martin Scorsese in French cinemas. The film tells the story of Christ who tries to resist the temptations of life on earth, including the sin of lust. The love scene between Maria Magdalena and Christ provoked a lot of protest and even arson attacks in cinemas. Many Christians had difficulties with the tone of the film: the face of Christ was too human and Christ was in too much doubt as to whether to choose between his earthly life and his divine vocation. The violent protest against the running of the film moved the cardinals and archbishops of Lyon and Paris to issue a statement against the running of the film emphasizing that anyone's freedom is based on the respect of others.

In three instances, the request of the associations, who argued that the film infringed the sensitivity of Christians and presented a misconceived image of their religion, was rejected. Instead, the courts demanded that the defence circulate a *communiqué* that informed the spectator about the objections of the associations and to insert at the beginning of the film and on the film poster a warning clarifying that the film was not an adaptation of the gospel, so as to prevent anyone from being offended in his deepest convictions when unexpectedly confronted with certain scenes, due to insufficient information as to the content of the film.[1114]

In 1990, the French Supreme Court rejected an appeal, according to which the manifestly unlawful disturbance was constituted by the ridiculing and misrepresentation of a religion as such and the violation of religious feelings resided not only in the running of the film in cinema, but also in the publicity surrounding the film in the media; the 'objective' disturbance of the catholic community in its entirety had to be taken as a starting point, not the subjective personal disturbance of the individual spectator. The Supreme Court considered that 'le principe de la liberté d'expression, notamment en matière de création artistique, d'une part, comme, d'autre part, celui du respect dû aux croyances et le droit de pratiquer sa religion étant d'égale valeur, il appartenait aux juges du fait de décider des mesures appropriées à faire respecter ce nécessaire équilibre'. The Paris Court of Appeal could have struck a balance between these two interests as it did, using the avoidance of infringement of deepest convictions and the unexpected confrontation in a public space as a guiding criterion.[1115] Despite the favorable outcome for freedom of expression, the Supreme Court thus explicitly affirmed that the respect for beliefs formed a legitimate restriction to freedom of expression, while it is not prescribed by the 1881 Press Act or any other law.

By placing emphasis on the degree of publicity of the expression the civil judge, however, often circumvents to explicitly decide on the core question as to whether expression about a religion that hurts the religious feelings of religious adherents,

---

1114 TGI de Paris, 22 September 1988; CA Paris, 27 September 1988, Cited in: TGI de Paris, 20 February 1997, *Légipresse* April 1997, pp.50–51, annotation M-N. Louvet, *Liberté d'expression et respect des croyances.*

1115 French Supreme Court, civ.ch. I, 29 October 1990, n°88–19366, *Bull.* 1990 I, n°226, p.161.

who experience such expression as an insult to them as a religious group, constitutes an unlawful indirect insult of a religious community on the ground of their religion. For example in 1989, the Paris tribunal decided against the party that requested the prohibition of *The satanic verses*, the famous controversial novel by Salman Rushdie ruling that 'personne ne se trouve contraint de lire un livre'.[1116]

In the *VSD* case in 1993, the balance between the right to freedom of expression and the right to respect for religious feelings of religious adherents was explicitly found in favour of the latter interest. The association AGRIF initiated a civil case on the ground of 1382 CC with regard to a cover of the magazine *VSD* that represented a naked women crucified on a cross entitled 'Pourquoi Dieu n'aime pas les femmes'. In two instances the judges considered that the expression did not form defamation or provocation to hatred, but did constitute a wrongful act in accordance with 1382 CC; although the question as to the place of women in religions formed part of a free debate of ideas in which VSD was free to participate, because of its incongruous and slutty presence the image of a naked women associated with the symbol of the crucifix offended the religious feelings of a certain number of religious adherents.[1117]

In the *Larry Flint* case in 1997, the French jurisdictions continued to base their reasoning from the premise of the existence of a right of respect of religious feelings, as it had been affirmed by the French Supreme Court. The case concerned the poster of the film *The people vs Larry Flint* by Milos Forman, over which people from all over the world cried shame. The poster depicted Woody Harrelson, the actor who played the role of porn tycoon Larry Flint, in the position of the crucified Christ covered only with a loincloth of the American flag against the background of the lap of a woman in bikini bottoms. In France, in Paris the original poster was placed on the walls of a building at the beginning of the Christian holidays. AGRIF requested the removal of the poster in summary proceedings. In appeal, AGRIF was joined by the episcopate. As a result of this, the American film company decided to replace the poster with a less offensive version.

In two instances, the judge decided that, considering the current status of social development, the poster did not constitute an obvious insult to the religious feelings of AGRIF. Because of the American flag and the cheerful expression of the actor, the poster did not remind one of a traditional depiction of Christ. The image did not even show a real cross! The poster could certainly be considered as intentionally provocative and a sign of bad taste, but that did not make it an attack on a religion or its adherents. The poster was not prohibited. Again, despite the favorable outcome for freedom of expression, the judge merely decided that the expression

---

1116 TGI de Paris, 29 July 1989. Cited in: Pierrat, E., *Le droit du livre*, Paris: Éditions du cercle de la librairie 2005, p.138.

1117 TGI de Paris, 15 December 1993; CA Paris, 3 July 1995, *JCP G* 1996, II, 22601, annotation C. Duvert.

did not constitute an unlawful attack on a religion or its adherents. It results *a contrario* that if the poster did insult religious feelings, it could have been unlawful. What is more, the judge attached much importance to the fact that the Catholic Church hierarchy had not considered it necessary to take the matter to court.[1118] Leclerc notes that the judge thus used the opinion of the church hierarchy as the starting point for his decision, although, the French Republic does not acknowledge the hierarchy of any service.[1119]

In order to be able to insult a religious group in its convictions, an expression must therefore constitute an obvious abuse of the traditional iconography. An expression may not be gratuitously offensive. According to the ensemble of case law developed since the *Ave Maria* case, an expression will be gratuitously offensive when the expression has a commercial character and when the public is forced to take note of the expression. Unexpected confrontation in a public space should be distinguished from the conscious choice for a closed medium. While intrusive billboards in public places increase the offensive effect, the closed cinema reduces it. The same goes for books, as these are also held to be a closed medium by the judiciary. The case law shows that by emphasizing these criteria and not explicitly referring to the offences of the 1881 Press law and their constitutive elements, the judge does not always explicitly decide on the core question as to whether offensive criticism of a religion can constitute an unlawful indirect insult of a religious community on the ground of their religion.

Massis concludes that the ensemble of case law developed since the *Ave Maria* case has rightly derived from the constitutional principle of respect for beliefs that figures alongside the principle of human dignity in the 1958 Constitution an autonomous and fundamental personality right of respect of religious feelings, which would 'resulte de la combinaison du principe de liberté de conscience, d'une part, et d'autre part, de la liberté d'aller et de venir sans risqué d'agression et d'outrage.'[1120]

According to Beignier, the French judiciary has, however, not aimed to protect God, but to protect its religious adherents and has wisely tried to conciliate conflicting interests by safeguarding free expression in religious domains by avoiding general and absolute interdictions and only prohibiting aggressions against a religion, blasphemeous expression or sacrileges in the public sphere; 'L'incroyant doit respecter le croyant, et le croyant, l'incroyant.'[1121] The case law is evident of

1118 TGI de Paris, 20 February 1997, *Légipresse* April 1997, p.49, annotation *Liberté d'expression et respect des croyances.*

1119 Leclerc, H., *Vinci et le code*, annotation at: CA Paris, 8 April 2005, *Légipresse* n° 223 July/ August, p.145.

1120 Massis, Th., Respect des croyances, dignité et loi du 29 juillet 1881, *Légipresse* 197, December 2002, p.173.

1121 Beignier 1995, p.335.

great wisdom and is inspired by a true spirit of equity, being equality in rights.[1122] While the protection of religious feelings has no legal sanction in France, the case law effectively assures it.[1123]

However, prohibiting blasphemous expression from the moment it becomes public on the ground of the civil offence of religious feelings created by the French civil judge in case law pursuant to 1382 CC or 809 CCP that has no equivalent in the 1881 Press Act has without doubt a chilling effect on the free debate concerning religion and approaches what the French legislator of 1881 itself considered to constitute a délit d'opinion. The value of the free expression of opinion does not merely reside in the freedom to express and to receive opinions in a publicly accessible place but also in a private place.

5.4.2. The right to respect for religious feelings weakened by the priority of the press offences

The civil prohibition of offence of religious feelings and the right to respect for beliefs created by the civil judge has been weakened by the principles established by the French Supreme Court in its decisions of 12 July 2000. According to these principles, in the field of the press, the 1881 Press Act has priority over general civil norms and Article 1382 CC cannot be used if the facts constitute one of the press offences of the 1881 Press Act and a legal action cannot be repaired on the ground of Article 1382 CC if the facts do not constitute one of the press offences of the 1881 Press Act (para.1.3.3 *supra*). In a 2001 decision, the French Supreme Court applied these principles in a civil case initated by AGRIF against expression ridiculing the Pope on the ground of Article 24–8 of the Press Act, subsidiarily Article 1382 CC (para.6.5.1 *infra*). The French Supreme Court rejected an appeal against the decision of the Court of Appeal that had rejected the demands of AGRIF. The Supreme Court considered that due to the fact that the expression did not constitute an incitement to discrimination, hatred or violence in acoordance with Article 24–8, no wrongful act on the ground of 1382 CC could be retained. In other words, in the absence of a provocation in accordance with Article 24–8, the French Supreme Court refused to sanction the offence to a religion or religious feelings on the ground of Article 1382 CC.[1124]

In the *Amen* case in 2002, the summary judge applied these principles and in doing so revised the case law and weakened the right to respect for beliefs that had been developed since the *Ave Maria* case. AGRIF requested the prohibition of the poster of the film *Amen* by Costa-Gavras on the ground of 809 CCP and explicitly referred to the definition of defamation in Article 29 and the offence of religious defamation

1122 Beignier 1995, p.336.
1123 Beignier 1995, p.339.
1124 In the same sense: Droin 2009, p.443.

in Article 32–2 of the 1881 Press Act. The poster depicted the Christian cross prolonged by the swastika, a catholic clergyman and a Nazi officer. While AGRIF considered the poster to be defamatory of the catholic population, because it would wrongly suggest that Catholics had approved of Nazism, the defence argued that the film poster concerned a debate on the Holocaust that had taken place in the ignorance or even with the approval of those represented by AGRIF today. The French judge considered 'le principe de légalité exige que toute restriction apportée à la liberté d'expression soit inscrite dans le droit positif; seule l'existence d'une diffamation au sens de la loi sur la presse serait susceptible de caractériser le trouble allégué.'[1125] Hence, in casu, if the expression offended a religion or religious feelings, it could only be condemned on the ground of the offence of defamation and if the facts of the case did not constitute the elements of the offence, the same facts could not be condemned on any other ground of civil responsibility.[1126]

According to the French judge, the poster did not constitute defamation and was held it to be permissible. The poster did not represent the Catholic cross extended by the swastika. By no means was the mix obvious: whatever the intention of the author had been, strictly speaking, the swastika was not a real swastika, because it looked incomplete and one arm had been unfolded downwards. The judge thus rejected the interpretation of both parties and assessed the poster himself in light of the film and the history that the film evoked: the judge set his 'lecture ouverte' against the interpretation of AGRIF that showed a 'lecture fermé'. With this open reading of the poster one could see the intention to replace the connotation of the swastika as a symbol of totalitarianism with a humane connotation.

According to Tricoire, the motivation of the judge is too far-reaching and dangerous. A judge should refrain from giving a value judgment, as well as from founding his decision on subjective criteria. According to Tricoire, the poster should have been considered to be 'l'œuvre d'un auteur', a fictive representation subject to multiple interpretations.[1127] What is more, the judge attached much importance to the fact that l'Église de France had admitted that the silence that the bishops had kept in relation to the atrocities of the Nazis had been wrong and that l'Église de France had failed in her mission to educate consciences. Leclerc notes that, again, the judge relied in his decision on a position taken by the Church.[1128]

Massis denounces this revision of case law for not respecting the fundamental right of respect for beliefs. According to Massis, the specific character of the Press Act

[1125] TGI de Paris, 21 February 2002, *JCP G* n°17 – 23 April 2003, annotation P. Malaurie, *Légipresse* n° 192 June 2002, pp.105–106, annotation A. Tricoire, *Interprétation du sens de l'affiche d' un film par le juge*.

[1126] In the same sense: Droin 2009, p.444.

[1127] Tricoire, A., *Interprétation du sens de l'affiche d' un film par le juge*, annotation at: TGI de Paris, 21 February 2002, *Légipresse* n° 192 June 2002, p.108.

[1128] Leclerc, H., *Vinci et le code*, annotation at: CA Paris, 8 April 2005, *Légipresse* n° 223 July/August, p.146.

must not override this right of constitutional value that protects the human person. For Massis 'la faute civile est caractérisée par l'offense aux sentiments religieux. Ainsi par une voie détournée, il a été mis à l'écart un droit fondamental à valeur constitutionnelle. Il y a là un appauvrissement de notre droit.'[1129] However, the position of the French Supreme Court and the lower judges seems to rather be in conformity with the aim of the French legislator of 1881, who abrogated all délits d'opinion, comprising the 'délit d'outrage à la morale publique et religieuse'. By applying the principle of the primacy of the Press Act, the French Supreme Court and the lower judges thus merely seem to refuse to reintroduce into French law a délit d'opinion consisting of the offence to religious feelings on the ground of civil responsibility. From this strand of thought, Mallet-Poujol stipulates that while the ridiculing of one of the officially recognized religions in France used to be condemned on the ground of the 'délit d'outrage à la morale publique et religieuse' or the 'outrage aux religions reconnues par l'Etat', 'la faute civile ne saurait alors les rétablir et l'article 1382 CC ne saurait être instrumentalisé en 'cheval de Troie' pour la défense d'un certain ordre moral.'[1130]

5.4.3. *The distinction between a religion and its adherents safeguarded by the French Supreme Court: the cases of* ***Girbaud*** *and* ***Sainte Capote***

After the solution offered in the *Amen* case in 2002 based on the case law of the French Supreme Court, the French judge has nevertheless in several proceedings on the merits condemned criticism of a religion that offended the religious feelings of its adherents on the ground of the offence of insult of a group of people on the ground of their religion criminalized in Article 33–3. Examples can be seen in the cases of *Sainte Capote* and *Girbaud*, in which the lower judges equated an insulting expression of a religion with the insult of a group of people on the ground of their religion and thereby seemed to disregard the aim of the French legislator of 1881 to suppress the 'délit d'outrage à la morale publique et religieuse' and the rationale of the Pleven Act of 1972 to protect people against discrimination and not religious beliefs.[1131] However, in both cases the distinction between a religion and its adherents was safeguarded by the French Supreme Court who annulled the condemnations by the courts of appeal.

The *Sainte Capote* case concerned a prospectus that had been handed out by the organization *Aides Haute-Garonne* in order to announce an informative evening about the prevention of HIV entitled 'La nuit de la Sainte-Capote' (the night of the Holy Condom). The prospectus contained an image of the bosom of a religious

---

1129 Massis 2002, p.174. And: Massis, T., La liberté d'expression et le droit au respect des croyances, *Légipresse* n° 298 October 2012, p. 531–532.

1130 Mallet-Poujol, N., De la "cohabitation" entre la loi du 29 juillet 1881 sur la liberté de la presse et l'article 1382 du Code civil, *Légipresse* n° 234, September 2006, p.95.

1131 In the same sense: Droin 2009, p.463.

woman wearing heavy pink make-up who – apart from a headscarf and a necklace with a cross – was naked. On her right there are two pink condoms. The picture was accompanied by the text 'Sainte Capote protège-nous'. In the case initiated by AGRIF the Toulouse Court of Appeal considered that the expression constituted a provocative amalgam of bad taste and created the idea of a certain anticlericalism; this image could legitimately have been experienced by at least certain Catholics as an offence of them on the ground of their beliefs and practices.[1132]

In 2006, the French Supreme Court annulled the decision of the Court of Appeal, considering 'si le tract litigieux a pu heurter la sensibilité de certains catholiques, son contenu ne dépasse pas les limites admissibles de la liberté d'expression.'[1133] Firstly, the image was possibly provocative, definitely in bad taste and probably offensive to the Catholic community, but did not overstep the limits to freedom of speech. The 'jugement de gout' issued by the lower judges was contrary to the principle of a strict interpretation of criminal law. Subsequently, the Supreme Court considered that 'L'injure devant être objectivement établie à l'égard d'un groupe précis et déterminé, l'excès de sensibilité d'une fraction de croyants ne saurait rendre indisponible dans l'espace public la représentation d'une religieuse associée à la lutte contre le sida sous le vocable 'Sainte Capote protège-nous'[1134] and thereby seemed to refer to the objective of AGRIF, i.e. to defend the case of religious extremists or fundamentalists. The sensitivity of such a fraction of the faithful should not manifest itself in the French neutral public space. Finally, the organization was humoristic and had good intentions. Even within the Catholic Church, different opinions exist as to the question of whether or not the use of condoms is allowed. The representation thus entered into a free political discussion.

In 2005, the famous *Girbaud* case attracted a lot of media attention in France. The subject of argument was a billboard of Marithé François Girbaud, a brand of women's clothing. The billboard, which was 40 meters long by 11 meters wide, was placed on a building on the Avenue Charles-de-Gaulle in Neuilly-sur-Seine in March 2005. The poster depicted a parody of the Last Supper by Leonardo da Vinci, in which the apostles and Christ were replaced by women wearing clothes by Marithé and the only man of the group was the person on Christ's right side. A hand holding a dove, the traditional symbols of the Father and the Holy Ghost, figured between the women's legs. The poster was a wink to the novel *The Da Vinci Code* by Dan Brown that expounds the theory that on the painting the person on Christ's right side is Mary Magdalene. *La Conférence des évêques de France* considered the

1132 CA Toulouse, 12 January 2005, *Légipresse* 2005 n°222–1, p.17.

1133 French Supreme Court, crim.ch., 14 February 2006, n°05–81932, *Bull. Crim.* 2006, n°42, p.165, *Légipresse* n° 232 – June 2006, p.116, annotation A. Tricoire, *Unjure envers la communauté catholique: contrôle de la cour de cassation.*

1134 French Supreme Court, crim.ch., 14 February 2006, n°05–81932, *Bull. Crim.* 2006, n°42, p.165, *Légipresse* n° 232 – June 2006, p.116, annotation A. Tricoire, *Unjure envers la communauté catholique: contrôle de la cour de cassation.*

poster to be a gross insult to religious feelings and the Catholic faith and its public display to constitute a manifestly unlawful disturbance and therefore requested – in the capacity of *L'Association Croyances et Libertés* – the prohibition of the poster in summary proceedings on the ground of 809 CCP together with 29–2 j 33–3 of the 1881 Press Act.

The judge's reasoning is almost identical to the reasoning in the *Ave Maria* case that contrarily was merely grounded on Article 809 CCP. According to the judge, the poster constituted an insult to Catholics that was disproportionate to its commercial nature. It was beyond discussion that the poster was 'une oeuvre de création', but 'because of its nature – merely intended to promote the selling of clothes – the poster did not, like a literary or cinematographic work would do, form part of a debate of ideas, was gratuitously offensive and thus insulting.' The judge thereby applied the 1881 Press Act in light of the *Otto Preminger* case, in which the ECtHR had adopted the right to respect for religious feelings as a legitimate restriction to freedom of expression, and more importantly, in light of Article 1 of the French Constitution and considered that the poster infringed the respect for religious beliefs; its placement was prohibited in all public spaces.[1135]

The decision was upheld in appeal. The judge placed the application of the 1881 Press Act in light of the laic character of the French Republic and the Act of 1905, considering that the separation of the church and the state did not obstruct the application of the law when a religion is insulted, because the 1881 Press Act criminalizes the insult of a group of people on the ground of their religion. As in first instance, the judge equated an insulting expression of a religion with the insult of a group of people on the ground of their religion and gave a particularly large interpretation of religious group insult criminalized in Article 33–3. Again, the commercial nature and the forced cognizance of the expression formed important criteria. In addition, according the judge, the choice to publish the poster just a week before Easter increased its insulting character.[1136]

Pierrat argues that in the *Girbaud* case, the judge has reintroduced the offence of blasphemy and, therefore, in the future even publishers of literary books should be on alert.[1137] Contrarily, Rolland agrees with Beignier (para.5.4.1 *supra*) and is of the opinion that an offence of blasphemy would only have been reintroduced if the judge had prohibited all means of distribution of the poster: from a religious point of view, blasphemy exists regardless of the public nature of the expression, but, from a legal point of view, what makes blasphemy an offence is its publicity. He approves the restriction brought to mere commercial expression in the spirit of tolerance towards religious adherents.[1138] Tricoire takes a completely opposite position, opining that the right to criticize a religion results from freedom of expression and

---

1135 TGI de Paris, 10 March 2005, *D.* n° 20 2005, pp.1326–1327, annotation P. Rolland.

1136 CA Paris, 8 April 2005, *D.* n° 20 2005, pp.1327–1328, annotation P. Rolland.

1137 Pierrat, E., *Le droit du livre*, Paris: Éditions du cercle de la librairie 2005, p.138.

1138 Rolland, P., *La critique, l'outrage et le blasphéme*, annotation at: TGI de Paris, 10 March 2005 and CA Paris, 8 April 2005, *D.* n° 20 2005, pp.1328–1331.

the only restriction to this freedom should be the attack of persons.[1139] Indeed, the solution in the *Girbaud* case seems to be contrary to the rationale of the Pleven Act of 1 July 1972, i.e. to protect people against discrimination on the ground of religion, and not religious convictions, dogmas, rituals or other sacred matters. Leclerc clearly articulates the false premises from which the judges reasoned; contrary to the vision of Massis (para.5.4.1 *supra*), Article 1 of the French Constitution does not contain a right to respect, but a characteristic of the French laic Republic that concerns both the freedom to believe and the freedom not to believe. He reproaches the judges for a lack of tolerance.[1140] According to Leclerc, the starting point for the assessment of offensive expression is the nature of the words, not the feelings of the victim or the opinion of religious authorities. The decisions, however, show that on this subject it is not easy to preserve the serene neutrality that the judiciary of the Republic is required to exhibit.[1141]

In 2006, the French Supreme Court annulled the condemnation by the Court of Appeal, considering 'les articles 29 alinéa 2 et 33 alinéa 3 de la loi du 29 juillet 1881 ne répriment pas l' impiété ou l'outrage à la religion dont les fidèles sont les victimes indirectes, mais les expressions outrageantes pour la considération de chacun lorsqu'elles sont exprimées directement contre la personne d'hommes ou de femmes afin d'en faire publiquement un sujet d'aversion de mépris à raison de leur obédience religieuse, ce qui doit être apprécié d'après le contenu effectif et non équivoque de la publication; qu'en retenant que l'utilisation d'un thème sacré à des fins de publicité constituait une injure au sens des articles précités dès lors que 'c'est la religion qui est outragée' et qu'elle ferait outrage à la foi des catholiques, la cour d'appel a violé les textes susvisés.'[1142] According to the Supreme Court, the parody merely represented the Last Supper in a different form and was not intended to insult Catholics or offend their honor. The poster did not constitute an insult, because it was not a personal and direct attack on a group of people on the ground of their religion. In this decision, the French Supreme Court thus clearly established that the insult of a religion cannot constitute an indirect insult of a religious group and thereby put a definitive end to the development of the right to respect for religious feelings in case law.

In 2007, the French Supreme Court confirmed its position in the *Christ en Gloire* case. The case concerned the publication in the daily newspaper *Libération* of a cartoon by the famous cartoonist Willem. The cartoon depicted a naked Christ

---

1139 Tricoire, A., De l'ordre moral à l'ordre religieux. Les juges condamnent une image pour blasphème, *Hommes & Libertés,* n°130, April-May-June 2005, pp.22–25.

1140 Leclerc, H., *Vinci et le code*, annotation at: CA Paris, 8 April 2005, *Légipresse* n° 223 July/August, p.149.

1141 Leclerc, H., *Vinci et le code*, annotation at: CA Paris, 8 April 2005, *Légipresse* n° 223 July/August, p.147.

1142 French Supreme Court, civ.ch. I, 14 November 2006, n°05–15822 05–16001, *Bull.* 2006 I, n°485, p.417, *Légipresse* n° 238 January/February 2007, p.11.

wearing a condom, who is observed by a group of bishops, amongst whom a white bishop says to a black bishop: 'Lui-même aurait sans doute utilisé un préservatif!' AGRIF filed a complaint considering that the cartoon insulted the Catholic population, but in three instances drew a blank. The French Supreme Court ruled that the court of appeal had rightly decided that the drawing may have shocked the sensitivity of some Christians or Catholics, but it illustrated the debate amongst cardinals about the necessity to protect against HIV and was aimed at calling the attention of the reader to the HIV plague in Africa; the cartoon therefore did not overstep the limits of freedom of speech.[1143]

5.4.4. *Affirmation of the free criticism of a religion:* ***Charlie Hebdo*** *and the* ***Mohammed cartoons*** *case*

It was just one month before the decision by the tribunal in the famous French Mohammed cartoon case that the plenary assembly of the French Supreme Court rejected an appeal against the condemnation in the *Dieudonné* case (para.5.2.2 *supra*). The French Supreme Court ecarted Dieudonné's appeal to a free debate of religions in a laic and democratic society and to the absence of a délit d'outrage à la moral religieuse in French law, because his particularly gross insult of Jews on the ground of their religion and origin even constituted the strict interpretation of the offence of religious group insult. The *Mohammed cartoons* affair shows more resemblances with the case brought against the French author Michel Houllebecq in 2002 by four Muslims associations[1144] on the ground of Articles 24–8 and 33–3 of the 1881 Press Act with regard to, amongst others,[1145] his expression during an interview about his new novel *Platforme* published in the French magazine *Lire*,

1143 French Supreme Court, crim.ch., 2 May 2007, n°06–84710, *Bull. Crim.* 2007, n°115, *Légipresse* n° 244 – September 2007, p.122.

1144 *La Mosquée de Paris*, in the capacity of the French Muslim association *La société des habous et des lieux saints de l'Islam, l'Association rituelle de la Grande Mosquée de Lyon, la Fédération nationale des musulmans de France, la Ligue islamique mondiale.*

1145 With regard to the two remarks equally made by Houellebecq 'Oui, oui, on peut parler de haine' and 'La lecture du Coran est une chose dégoûtante. Dès que l'islam naît, il se signale par sa volonté de soumettre le monde. C'est une religion bellique, intolérante, qui rend les gens malheureux.', the tribunal considered 'M. Houellebecq exprime dans cet extrait non plus un sentiment intime mais des opinions personnelles présentées comme relevant successivement des domaines de l'analyse littéraire, historique et théologique. Ces jugements peuvent bien évidemment être désapprouvés, discutés ou refutes. Il est aisément comprehensible que ces propos aient pu heurter les musulmans, compte tenu, notamment, de l'adjectif "dégoûtant" pour qualifier la lecture du Coran. Ces propos ne sont cependant accompagnés d'aucun appel à en tirer des conséquences discriminatoires à l'égard de quiconque. Les personnes se réclamant de l'islam sont au contraire présentées comme les victims de la religion à laquelle elles appartiennent et font l'objet d'une commiseration qui n'apparaît teintée ni d'ironie ni de mépris. L'expression de ces jugements de valeur portés sur une religion au travers de son texte saint, de son développement historique et de ses caractéristiques doctrinales, ne renferme ainsi aucune incitation à la haine, à la violence ou à la discrimination envers le groupe des fidèles musulmans eux-mêmes.' Cited in: Boulègue 2010, pp.82–83.

'La religion la plus con, c'est quand même l'islam. Quand on lit le Coran, on est effondré.' The tribunal acquitted the author, considering 'l'utilisation du superlative...démontre cependant qu'aux yeux du prévenu, toutes les religions... méritent d'être affublées de ce qualificatif, mais à des degrés différents. L'appréciation ainsi portée concerne donc uniquement une religion considérée comme système de pensée et comparée à d'autres. Dans ces conditions, écrire que 'L'islam est la religion la plus con' ne revient nullement à affirmer ni à sous-entendre que tous les musulmans devraient être ainsi qualifiés. Ce propos ne renferme aucune volonté d'invective, de mépris ou d'outrage envers le groupe de personnes composé des adeptes de la religion considérée.'[1146] It is exactly this development in case law in favor of free criticism of a religion, as affirmed by the French Supreme Court in the cases *Girbaud* and *Sainte Capote* that was upheld by the lower judge in the affair of the *Mohammed cartoons.*

In September 2005, the Danish newspaper *Jyllands-Posten* published twelve satirical cartoons about Islam.[1147] One of the cartoons depicted the prophet Mohammed carrying a bomb in his turban. Another cartoon showed Mohammed standing on a cloud trying to stop terrorists with the words 'Stop, stop, we ran out of virgins!' The cartoons caused a scandal, as they offended many Muslims around the world. The decision in Denmark not to prosecute the newspaper for the publication of the cartoons was followed by demonstrations and boycotts of Danish products in Arabic countries. In western countries, several newspapers and magazines supported the Danish newspaper by republishing the cartoons.

Similarly, in France the managing director of *France soir* had published the cartoons in his newspaper of 1 February 2006, a choice that cost him his job. In solidarity, the French satirical weekly *Charlie Hebdo* released a special issue, in which, apart from the Danish cartoons, many French cartoons about Islam were published. The front cover of the magazine with the heading 'Mohammed débordé par les intégristes' showed a cartoon by the famous French cartoonist Cabu depicting the prophet Mohammed covering his eyes with his hands and roaring 'C'est dur d'être aimé par les cons'.[1148] After a request for seizure of the edition in summary proceedings had failed, *La Mosquée de Paris* – in the capacity of the French Muslim association *La société des habous et des lieux saints de l'Islam* – initiated a legal action against Philipe Val, chief-editor of *Charlie Hebdo*, on the ground of Article 33–3 and was joined by several other Muslim associations.[1149] The associations restricted their complaint to the two previously mentioned Danish cartoons and the cartoon on the front cover by Cabu.

1146 TGI de Paris, 22 October 2002, *unpublished.* Cited in: Boulègue 2010, pp.82–83. See also: *Le Monde* Thursday 24 October 2002, p.12.

1147 The Danish cartoons are available at: http://img220.imageshack.us/img220/3415/52na.jpg.

1148 The cartoons in *Charlie Hebdo* are available at: www.parijsblog.nl.

1149 Amongst others the associations *L'Union des organisations islamiques de France* and *la Ligue islamique mondiale.*

In March 2007, the tribunal acquitted the chief-editor and rejected the demands of the civil parties.[1150] Primarily the judge recalled the fundamental principles according to which: 'en France, société laïque et pluraliste, le respect de toutes les croyances va de pair avec la liberté de critique les religions quelles qu'elles soient et avec celle de représenter des sujets ou des objets de vénérations religieuses; que le blasphème, qui outrage la divinité ou la religion, n'y est pas réprimé, à la différence de l'injure dès lors qu'elle constitue une attaque personnelle et directe contre une personne ou un groupe de personnes à raison de leur appartenance.' With regard to the function of caricatures, the tribunal considered 'toute caricature s'analyse en un portrait qui s'affranchit du bon gout pour remplir une fonction parodique, que ce soit sur le mode burlesque ou grotesque; que l'exagération fonctionne alors à la manière du mot d'esprit qui permet de contourner la censure, d'utiliser l'ironie comme instrument de critique sociale et politique, en faisant appel au jugement et au débat;'.[1151] The tribunal affirmed that the caricature as a literary genre falls under the scope of freedom of expression of opinion and one must take into account 'de l'exagération et de la subjectivité inhérentes à ce mode d'expression pour analyser le sens et la portée des dessins litigieux, le droit à la critique et à l'humour n'étant cependant pas dépourvu de limites.'[1152]

Starting from these principles, the tribunal analyzed the three cartoons separately. The tribunal considered the image of Mohammed on a cloud and the image of Mohammed on the front cover not to be insulting to Muslims, because in these images only the fundamentalists were ridiculed and not Islam or the entire group of its adherents. These cartoons, therefore, did not constitute a personal and direct attack on Muslims as a whole. Contrarily, the tribunal considered that the cartoon showing Mohammed with a bomb in his turban insinuated that terrorist violence is inherent in the Muslim community. The cartoon, if examined in isolation, therefore formed an insult to the entire Muslim community. However, the context of the publication of the cartoon removed Charlie Hebdo's intention to insult; the affair of the Danish cartoons had evoked a political and public debate and *Charlie Hebdo* had published the cartoon in a critical manner.[1153] The tribunal concluded 'en dépit du caractère choquant, voire blessant de cette caricature pour la sensibilité des musulmans, le contexte et les circonstances de sa publication dans le journal Charlie Hebdo apparaissent exclusifs de toute volonté délibérée d'offenser directement et gratuitement l'ensemble des musulmans; que les limites admissibles de la liberté d'expression n'ont donc pas été dépassées, le dessin litigieux participant du débat public d'intérêt général né au sujet des dérives des musulmans qui

[1150] TGI de Paris, 22 March 2007, *Légipresse* n° 242 – June 2007, p.123 *et seq.*, annotation H. Leclerc, *Caricatures, blasphème et défi.*

[1151] TGI de Paris, 22 March 2007, *Légipresse* n° 242 – June 2007, p.123 *et seq.*, annotation H. Leclerc, *Caricatures, blasphème et défi.*

[1152] TGI de Paris, 22 March 2007, *Légipresse* n° 242 – June 2007, p.123 *et seq.*, annotation H. Leclerc, *Caricatures, blasphème et défi.*

[1153] TGI de Paris, 22 March 2007, *Légipresse* n° 242 – June 2007, p.125, annotation H. Leclerc, *Caricatures, blasphème et défi.*

commettent des agissements criminels en se revendiquant de cette religion et en prétendant qu'elle pourrait régir la sphère politique.'[1154] According to Droin, by referring to a 'volonté délibérée d'offenser' the judge required the proof of a *dol specialis*, while the chief-editor without doubt had consciously taken the risk to offend Muslims, which should have been sufficient to establish the *dol generalis*.[1155]

The association *L'Union des organisations islamiques de France* filed an appeal, arguing that the cartoon of Mohammed with a bomb in his turban constituted an insult to Muslims, because it assimilated their prophet with terrorism. While in March 2008 the Court of Appeal confirmed the judgment of the tribunal, with regard to this latter cartoon it took a different approach, considering 'La troisième caricature, si elle peut choquer et susciter l'émoi comme en ont témoigné plusieurs personnes…ne peut être comprise qu'à la lumière de l'ensemble du contenu du journal qui porte un regard critique non pas sur la communauté musulmane mais sur certains de ses membres.'[1156] Hence, even the cartoon showing Mohammed with a bomb in his turban referred to a fraction of all Muslims, being the fundamentalists, and not to the Muslim community as a whole. In the vision of the court, no confusion could exist about the fact that all cartoons formed a legitimate contribution to the public debate on terrorists and fundamentalists and did not express any opinion on Islam or the Muslim community.[1157]

On the one hand, the *Mohammed cartoons* case clearly reflects the development in French case law in favor of free criticism of a religion, according to which, in order for expression to constitute a religious group insult it must constitute a personal and direct attack against a group on the ground of their religion. On the other hand, the *Mohammed cartoons* case clearly reflects the influence of the case law of the ECtHR on the decisions of the French judges, according to which, in the core the cartoons critical of Islam form part of the public debate of a general interest.

After the acquittal in the *Mohammed cartoons* case Charlie Hebdo has continued to publish satirical cartoons ridiculing and criticizing religion. On 2 November 2011, the magazine's offices in Paris were fire-bombed and entirely destroyed, an attack presumed to be linked with the special 'Charia Hebdo' issue launched that same day as a response to the introduction of sharia law in Libya and the victory of the Islamist party in Tunisia. The cover listed prophet Muhammad as the 'editor in chief' and featured a cartoon of him saying '100 coups de fouet, si vous n'êtes pas morts de rire!' (100 lashes with the whip if you don't die laughing). On 19 September 2012, Charlie Hebdo again published a series of satirical cartoons of Muhammad,

---

1154 TGI de Paris, 22 March 2007, *Légipresse* n° 242 – June 2007, p.125, annotation H. Leclerc, *Caricatures, blasphème et défi.*

1155 Droin 2009, p.475.

1156 CA Paris, 12 March 2008, *Légipresse* n° 252 – June 2008, pp. 107–110, annotation H. Leclerc, *Les caricatures de Mahomet, suite.*

1157 CA Paris, 12 March 2008, *Légipresse* n° 252 – June 2008, p. 107–110, annotation H. Leclerc, *Les caricatures de Mahomet, suite.*

including a nude caricature, which prompted the French government to shut embassies and school in twenty countries. On 2 January 2013, Charlie Hebdo released a 65-page special edition illustrated biography of the Muslim prophet.

Increased security measures at Charlie Hebdo's new headquarters could not prevent the attack on 7 January 2015 where two Islamist terrorists, Chérif and Saïd Kouachi, stormed the magazine's offices and killed 12 people, including staff cartoonists Charb, Cabu, Honoré, Tignous and Wolinkski, with guns while shouting 'Allahu akbar' (God is great) and 'The Prophet is avenged'. The cover of the Charlie Hebdo issue published just before the attack did not mock the Prophet but did show a grotesque caricature of French novelist Michel Houellebecq under the headline 'The Predictions of Wizard Houellebecq', 'In 2015, I lose my teeth', 'In 2022, I do Ramadan', in reference to his new novel *Submission*, which imagines France falling under sharia law. The attack sparked a series of attacks lasting three days whereby Islamist terrorist Amedy Coulibaly killed a policewoman during a traffic stop and another four people when hostages were held in a Jewish supermarket in Paris. The police killed all three terrorists.

On 11 January 2015 a 'republican march' took place from Place de la République via boulevard Voltaire to Place de la Nation, attended by 1–2 million people and held in defiance of terror and in defense of free speech. Many participants held placards with the words *Je suis Charlie*, a slogan first used on Twitter but which rapidly spread over the Internet becoming a worldwide symbol in favor of free speech. After having participated in the mass march, controversial French comedian Dieudonné was, however, arrested for 'glorifying terrorism' for posting a mocking statement '*Je me sens Charlie Coulibaly*' on his facebook page – on the basis of a circular of 12 January 2015 (2015/0213/A13) issued in response to the attacks in Paris by the Minister of Justice to reinforce the prosecution of racism and discrimination. In its first issue since the Paris attack, the *Charlie Hebdo* magazine itself reacted with a cover that features a weeping Mohammad holding a *Je suis Charlie* sign under the headline 'Tout est pardonné' (All is forgiven), which has been subject to different interpretations. Five million copies of this 'survivors' issue were sold globally.

5.5. Conclusion

Racial insult consists of uttering an outrageous expression, a term of contempt or an invective that does not constitute an imputation of a specific fact that is susceptible of proof and the object of a contradictory debate about a person or a group of persons *exclusively* on the ground of their origin, membership or non-membership of an ethnic group, nation, race or religion. Like the offence of racial defamation, a suspect's intention to insult must be presumed, but, contrary to racial defamation, the author of a racial insult cannot prove his good faith, because with regard to the offence of racial insult only the excuse of provocation is allowed as a justifying fact, if a direct link exists between the content of the insult and its previous provocation and if the insult is uttered within a reasonable time after the provocation and is proportionate to the tenor of the provocation. In order for the suspect to know exactly what he is accused of and to prepare his defence, one unique fact cannot be prosecuted at the same time on the ground of racial defamation and racial insult. In the event of indivisibility between a racial insult and a racial defamation, the racial insult is absorbed by the racial defamation and the expression must be qualified as racial defamation. The relevance of the distinction between the two offences lies in the fact that the racial insult is sanctioned less severely and the offence of racial defamation cannot be justified by the excuse of provocation. However, the actual distinction between the offences of racial defamation and racial insult is relative, because in the field of racial defamation the exception of truth is excluded and an author's good faith is often rejected. This could justify the creation of one single broader offence of 'offense raciale' or the possibility for the judge to requalify the facts.

As with the offence of racial defamation, the French judge attaches importance to a suspect's right to freedom of expression, when qualifying expression under the offence of racial insult, and does not regard it as a justification for insulting expression, this time notably by interpreting the discriminatory grounds restrictively. On the one hand, expression does not have to be aimed at a group in its entirety; a group is designated regardless of its size. On the other hand, a group must be precisely designated and Harkis do not form a group in the sense of Article 33–3. The French judge has been criticized for creating an incoherent case law concerning the requirement of the designation of a group, dependant on the question as to whether or not he desires the preservation of freedom of expression concerning a specific topic. It is, however, exactly this requirement that has enabled the judge to distinguish the punishable insult consisting of a direct and personal attack of a religious group from a free opinion concerning a religion that might hurt religious feelings.

6. Racial provocation

The offence of racial provocation is characterized by a number of elements, being provocation and intent thereto (6.1), discrimination, hatred or violence (6.2) and the designation of a group (6.3). The law allows no justifications for the offence of racial provocation (6.4). In the application of the offence, the French judge takes into account – to a certain extent – the context of expression (6.5). The analysis results in a general conclusion about the offence of racial provocation in French law (6.6).

6.1. Provocation and intent

The Pleven Act of 1 July 1972 inserted the current Article 24–8 into the 1881 Press Act that sanctions (ceux qui) 'par l'un des moyens énoncés à l'article 23, auront provoqué à la discrimination, à la haine ou à la violence à l'égard d'une personne ou d'un groupe de personnes à raison de leur origine ou de leur appartenance ou non appartenance à une ethnie, une nation, une race ou une religion déterminée' with a fine of up to € 45.000 and or imprisonment of up to one year.[1158] As the redaction of Article 24 with regard to the numbering of the paragraphs is unclear and new paragraphs have been inserted, over time the offence is confusingly referred to in case law as Article 24–5, 24–6 or Article 24–8. The general secretary of the French Government therefore issued a circular that provided for a re-enumeration and brought the offence under Article 24–8.[1159] In the absence of publicity the provocation to discrimination, hatred or violence against a person or a group constitutes a petty offence criminalized in Article R.625–7 of the French Penal Code.[1160]

The statutory elements of the offence of racial provocation derogate in several respects from the offence of direct provocation to felonies and misdemeanours followed by effect in Article 23 of the 1881 Press Act and the offences of direct provocation to felonies and misdemeanours not followed by effect in Articles 24–1 – 24–4 and 24–6 of the 1881 Press Act.

Firstly, the wording of the offence of racial provocation does not, like articles 23 and 24–1 - 24–4 and 24–6, explicitly require that the provocation must be direct. With regard to these latter offences of direct provocation, the French judge must demonstrate that the expression contains a precise, explicit call to commit a determined fact.[1161] According to traditional case law concerning the direct provocations of articles 23 and 24–1, 24–4 and 24–6: 'Attendu que les articles 23 et 24 précités exigent, pour qu'il y ait lieu à répression pénale, qu'il y ait eu provocation directe à commettre les délits et crimes spécifiés, c'est-à-dire qu'il y ait une relation incontestable entre le fait de la provocation et les crimes ou délits auxquels elle se rattache par un lien étroit.'[1162] And 'la provocation non suivie d'effet doit être une

1158 The tribunal can order the public display or dissemination of the decision taken in accordance with Article 131–35 of the French Penal Code and can deprive the offender of his right to be elected and his right to hold a judicial office, or to give an expert opinion before a court, or to represent or assist a party before a court of law for a maximum period of five years (Article 131–26 para. 2 and 3 French Penal Code).

1159 Dreyer, E., *Responsabilité civile et pénale des medias*, Paris: Litec 2008, n° 924.

1160 Article R.625–7 of the French Penal Code reads: La provocation non publique à la discrimination, à la haine ou à la violence à l'égard d'une personne ou d'un groupe de personnes à raison de leur origine ou de leur appartenance ou de leur non-appartenance, vraie ou supposée, à une ethnie, une nation, une race ou une religion déterminée est punie de l'amende prévue pour les contraventions de la 5e classe. Est punie de la même peine la provocation non publique à la haine ou à la violence à l'égard d'une personne ou d'un groupe de personnes à raison de leur sexe, de leur orientation sexuelle ou de leur handicap, ainsi que la provocation non publique, à l'égard de ces mêmes personnes, aux discriminations prévues par les articles 225–2 et 432–7.

1161 Beignier, De Lamy & Dreyer 2009, p.510.

1162 French Supreme Court, 5 January 1883, *DP* 1883, jurispr. P.95. Cited in: Beignier, De Lamy & Dreyer 2009, p.511.

incitation directe, non seulement par son esprit, mais par ses termes, à commettre des faits matériellement déterminés, eux-mêmes constitutifs d'un crime ou d'un délit'.[1163] Doctrines and opinions therefore fall outside the scope of the articles.

The same holds true for an expression that merely evokes in the public a feeling of excitement or a passion.[1164] In 1954, the French Supreme Court considered that the distribution of tracts calling the French and Algerian population to show their solidarity with the Tunisian population with regard to their accession to independence did not constitute a direct provocation to subtract the authority of France from part of its territories, because the tracts simply were aimed at evoking 'un mouvement d'opinion, ce mouvement devant susciter un état d'esprit, lequel à son tour serait propre à permettre la naissance de cette entreprise'.[1165] Likewise, in 2005, the Versailles Court of Appeal considered that the response of actress Ophélie Winter 'non, je pense qu'il faut tuer Raël' to the question, during an interview, as to whether human cloning is the future, did not constitute a direct provocation to commit such a crime against her colleague actor mister Vorilhon, because this humorous metaphor aimed rather at the project of human cloning, in which Vorilhon was engaged under the pseudonym 'Räel', than to his person.[1166]

The French legislator deleted the term 'direct' in Article 24–8, in order to bring the 'incitement' under the scope of the offence of racial provocation (para.3.3.2 *supra*). The offence is generally referred to by legal scholars as the 'indirect provocation'.[1167] Indeed, the wording of the offence of racial provocation does not exclude the possibility that discriminatory discourse consisting of ambiguous and insidious expression that does not constitute an explicit call to act, but creates an ambiance, a context, that favours the passage to the act, can fall under its scope.[1168] The French judge has further specified in case law that the racial provocation must take the form of 'non pas forcément une exhortation, mais un acte positif d'incitation manifeste à la haine, à la discrimination, ou à la violence, ce qui n'exige pas un appel explicite à la commission d'un fait précis tendant à susciter un sentiment d'hostilité ou de rejet'.[1169]

This signifies that, in order to be punishable, racial provocations do not always have to be that clear, but can also take more implicit or disguised forms. One tribunal considered that the offence constituted, because the suspects 'se sont laissés entraîner dans la voie d'un racisme latent, quotidien, en fin de compte plus

1163 CA Versailles, 30 June 2005, *Légipresse* n°228, January/February 2006, annotation B. Ader, pp.19–20.

1164 Beignier, De Lamy & Dreyer 2009, p.510.

1165 French Supreme Court, crim.ch., 25 February 1954, *Bull. Crim.*, 1954, n°89. Cited in: Beignier, De Lamy & Dreyer 2009, p.510.

1166 CA Versailles, 30 June 2005, *Légipresse* n°228, January/February 2006, annotation B. Ader, pp.19–20.

1167 Beignier, De Lamy & Dreyer 2009, p.515 *et seq.*

1168 Agostinelli 2002/2003, p.56.

1169 TGI de Paris, 18 February 2011, *Légipresse* n°282, p.240, annotation E. Derieux.

dangereux, car plus insidieux, qu'un racisme déclaré'.[1170] Beyond the literal sense of the expression, the aim of the author then may become a determinant factor that can be deduced from the humoristic or artistic context. It is argued that this evolution of the notion of provocation compensates the absence of the offence of blasphemy in French law by influencing the criminalization of the provocation to hatred on the ground of religion (para. 6.5.1–6.5.2 *infra*). It is said to assure, in any event, that French law complies with the obligations of ICERD, even though it does not formally criminalize the 'diffusion of racist ideas'.[1171]

Secondly, the offence of racial provocation does not explicitly require that the expression provokes others to commit a determined, punishable act under French law (para.6.2 *infra*). Contrarily, Articles 24–1 to 24–3 of the 1881 Press Act sanction the direct provocation not followed by effect to a limitative list of infractions.[1172] These infractions comprise 'les atteintes volontaires à la vie, les atteintes volontaires à l'intégrité de la personne et les agressions sexuelles, définies par le livre II du Code pénal' and 'les vols, les extorsions et les destructions, dégradations et détériorations volontaires dangereuses pour les personnes, définies par le livre III du Code pénal'. Article 24–4 adds to this list the direct provocation to 'crimes et délits portant atteinte aux intérêts fondamentaux de la nation prévus par le titre Ier du livre IV du Code pénal'. Article 24–6 criminalizes the direct provocation to 'actes de terrorisme prévus par titre II du livre IV du Code pénal'.

Thirdly, Article 121–7 of the French Penal Code considers the provocation to a felony or a misdemeanour by means of a gift, promise, threat, order, or an abuse of authority or powers as a form of complicity to that felony or misdemeanour. Likewise, Article 23 of the 1881 Press Act criminalizes as accomplices to a felony or misdemeanour those who, through certain means of publicity, shall have directly provoked the perpetrator(s) to commit the punishable action, if the provocation has been followed by effect. Pursuant to the second paragraph, the same applies if the provocation is merely followed by an attempt to commit a felony. Judges must therefore equally demonstrate that a felony, an attempt thereto, or a misdemeanour, has been committed. Subsequently, they must demonstrate that a causal link exists between the object of the expression and the infraction committed.

Contrarily, the offence of racial provocation and the offences of direct provocation of Article 24 do not require that the provocation is followed by effect. The offences do not concern provocations that have reached their goal, but concern provocations that 'merely' put others in danger.[1173] The judge can therefore only demonstrate the punishable character of these provocations by assessing the

---

1170 TGI Grenoble 18 December 1973, *D.* 1975, p. 489, annotation J. Foulon-Piganiol.

1171 Dreyer 2011, p. 151.

1172 With a fine of up to 45.000 Euros or an imprisonment of up to five years. Article 61 provides for a supplementary penalty, being the confiscation of the published expression and the suppression or destruction of all exemplars that are for sale, have been distributed or are exposed to the public. This penalty is however not applicable to the provocations to the 'crimes et délits portant atteinte aux intérêts fondamentaux de la nation' and to the 'actes de terrorisme'.

1173 Beignier, De Lamy & Dreyer 2009, p.508.

expression. The difficulty in qualifying the provocation to discrimination, hatred and violence consists of the characterization of the causal link between the expression and acts of discrimination or violence or the existence of hatred as a following effect. The French Supreme Court exercises a strict control over the question as to whether or not 'tant par son sens que par sa portée, le texte incriminé tend à inciter le public à la discrimination, à la haine ou à la violence', thus whether or not the expression charged can be qualified under Article 24–8, and can take into account the full context in which the expression is uttered, being 'tous les éléments, même extrinsèques aux dessins ou au propos incriminés, lui permettant d'en apprécier le sens et la portée'.[1174]

According to Cohen, since the creation of the offence by the Act of 1 July 1972 the French Supreme Court has shifted from the requirement of a direct link between the expression and its following effect that is determined on the basis of a literal, textual interpretation to admitting a less strong link that is determined on the basis of a broader context outside the mere literal, textual context, which has enabled French courts to bring under the scope of the offence and criminalize more disguised forms of racist and discriminatory expression.[1175] The French Supreme Court has decided that in order to establish this link, the French judge must demonstrate, not that the expression is capable, but merely that it is likely to provoke others to discrimination, hatred or violence.[1176]

Contrary to the offences of racial defamation and racial insult, where the bad faith of the author is presumed, in the field of racial provocation the intention of the author must be demonstrated by the prosecuting party.[1177] The subjective intention of the author is, however, of limited importance; the objective intention must be derived from the expression itself that must leave no doubt about the authors' intention. It is argued that this approach permits to put aside the reproach sometimes made that the offence of racial provocation reintroduces the 'délit d'opinion' into French law; the provocation to dangerous behaviour is criminalized rather than an author's motives.[1178] In 1997, the French Supreme Court endorsed the condemnation by the Court of Appeal of humorist Patrick Sébastien, who during an emission on television had intended to caricaturize the extreme right winged politician Jean Marie Le Pen with regard to his anti-immigration opinions. Disguised as the politician, Sébastien had sung 'Casser du noir', a parody of 'Casser la voix', a song by Patrick Bruel, containing the phrases 'Casser du noir' and 'Allumez les briquets, on va leur foutre le feu!'. According to the Court of Appeal, the text taken literally constituted a call to hatred against a group of people on the ground of their race or

1174 French Supreme Court, crim.ch., 24 October 1995, n° 94–83666, *D.* 1996.

1175 Cohen 2003.

1176 French Supreme Court, crim.ch., 3 February 2009, n°06–83.063 08–82.402, *Bull. Crim.* 2009, n° 25.

1177 TGI de Paris, 15 October 2002, *Légipresse* n°197, I, p.155.

1178 Dreyer 2011, p. 159.

ethnic background. Nothing had been done in order for the viewer to have any other interpretation.[1179] Therefore, the author could not rely on his good faith and the justification of constituting humour was excluded.

Likewise, in 2013, the TGI de Bobigny, in summary proceedings initiated by association LICRA, announced the interdiction of the re-publication by Alain Soral of five books, for containing passages that incited hatred against the Jewish community, were insulting and defaming to them, or constituted negationism. It concerned the re-publication of *The controversity of Zion* by Douglas Reed (1985); *le Salut par les Juifs* by Léon Bloy (1892); *La France juive* by Edouard Drumont (1886); *The international Jew* by Henri Ford (1920); and *Anthologie des propos contre les Juifs, le judaïsme et le sionisme* by Paul Eric Blanrue (2007). According to Ader, it was crystal clear that the publisher did not want to publish these books because of their historical value, but to diffuse pre-war anti-Semitic propaganda, which is why LICRA did not merely request that the re-editions be accompanied with a warning, as it had done with regard to the re-publication of *Mein Kampf* in the 1970s. Indeed, the court found that, according to the introductory text on the cover, the editor 'non seulement ne prend aucune distance avec te texte don't il propose la réédition, mais bien au contraire en accrédite les thèses antisémistes, dont il souligne l'actualité; et par consequent l'argument de la valeur historique du texte en cause, est, dans ce context, inopérant.'[1180]

In order for an expression to constitute a racial provocation punishable on the ground of Article 24–8, it must constitute a message addressed to the public that incites the latter, thus others and third parties, to discriminate, use violence, or to hatred against a person or a group. In 1995, the French Supreme Court overruled the condemnation by the court of appeal of an airplane official for having said 'Si je vous avais connue il y a 60 ans à Vichy je vous aurais cramée' towards a security post at the airport. The Court of Appeal considered that the presentation of a person as a person to be physically eliminated on the ground of race or religion constitutes the offence of incitement to racial hatred. The expression was uttered in public and overheard by several persons. The Supreme Court considered 'Qu'en prononçant ainsi, par des motifs qui n'établissent pas que le propos tendait, tant par son sens que par sa portée, à provoquer *autrui* à la discrimination, à la haine ou à la violence, la cour d'appel a fait une fausse application de l'article 24, alinéa 8, de la loi du 29 juillet 1881.'[1181] [curs. EHJ]

1179 A passage of the song reads: 'J'peux plus voir les étrangers même en peinture. J'suis pas là pour leur fabriquer un pays, m'en veux pas si ce soir j'ai envie d'casser du noir; les bronzes, les marrons qu'on tolère et qui restent, qui vous prennent pour des cons et puis qui vous détestent; les magasins brûlés à la moindre colère… et les journaux qui traînent dans la boue mes amis, ça m'goût tellement la haine que ça m'réveille la nuit. Casser du noir. Casser du noir… Allumez les briquets, on va leur foutre le feu!' Cited in: Cohen 2003, p.125. French Supreme Court, crim.ch., 4 November 1997, n° 96–84338, *Dr. pén.*, 1998, annotation M. Veron.

1180 CA Paris, 11 July 1979, GP 1979 (Mein Kampf); TGI de Bobigny (ord. réf.), 13 November 2013, LICRA c/ Alain Soral, *Légipresse* n° 313, February 2014, p. 107–114, annotation Ader.

1181 French Supreme Court, crim.ch., 29 January 2008, n°07–83695, *Bull. Crim.* 2008, n°25, p.98.

Contrary to the offences of racial defamation and racial insult, (para.4.1 and 5.1 *supra*), one fact can be prosecuted at the same time on the ground of racial defamation or racial insult and racial provocation. When expression does not meet the strict criteria of the offence of racial defamation and thus cannot be qualified as such, this does not hinder its qualification as racial provocation.[1182] In a final decision of 18 February 2011, the Paris TGI condemned journalist Eric Zemmour, who during a television debate had uttered 'la plupart des trafiquants sont noirs et arabes, c'est comme ça, c'est un fait', on the ground of the offence of provocation to racial discrimination, but acquitted him on the ground of racial defamation. The racial defamation was not established, because the expression neither affirmed nor supposed the existence of a causal link between the origin or the skin colour of the groups and their alleged overrepresentation among the drugs travellers; Zemmour had confined himself to present his assertion as an acquired fact. Contrarily, the provocation to racial discrimination was established, because 'En justifiant de la sorte des contrôles discriminatoires, le propos d'Eric Zemmour, tant par son sens que par sa portée, incite clairement à la discrimination à l'égard d'un groupe de personnes, défini comme les noirs et les Arabes en général, et ce à raison de leur origine ou de leur appartenance à une 'race' au sens de la loi, seuls critères de choix sur lesquels les contrôles en cause se pratiquent.'[1183] Derieux questions whether the distinction between the two offences is so obvious that the decision is justified or whether the judge merely aimed at satisfying both parties; on the one hand the suspect and on the other hand the anti-racism associations constituted as a civil party.[1184]

Likewise, when expression cannot be qualified as a racial provocation, this does not hinder its qualification as racial insult. In the *Dieudonné* case (para.5.2.2 *supra*), the French Supreme Court considered that the humorous context did not remove the insulting character of the expression '(…) les juifs, c'est une secte, une escroquerie (…)'. The Court, however, did confirm the acquittal on the ground of 24–8 by the Court of Appeal that considered 'que ces propos ne sont assortis d'aucune exhortation ou incitation adressée à des tiers en vue d'en tirer des conséquences discriminatoires ou de violence'.[1185]

6.2. Discrimination, hatred or violence

French doctrine generally holds that the desire of the French legislator was to criminalize in Article 24–8 the provocation to *punishable* acts of discrimination in accordance with Article 225–2 and Article 432–7 of the French Penal Code that

---

1182 Tillement 2006, p.224.

1183 TGI de Paris, 18 February 2011, *Légipresse* n°282, April 2011, pp.240–243, annotation E. Derieux.

1184 *Affaire Zemmour: distinction entre diffamation et provocation à la discrimination raciales*, annotation E. Derieux at: TGI de Paris, 18 February 2011, *Légipresse* n°282, April 2011, p.243.

1185 French Supreme Court, crim.ch., 15 March 2005, n°04–84.463, *Bull. Crim.* 2005 n°90, p.321

criminalizes a public authority or public service official, who, in the exercise of his or her function, refuses the benefit of a right conferred by the law or hinders the normal exercise of any given economic activity to a natural or legal person, although Article 24–8 itself does not explicitly refer to these articles.[1186] In 1976, the French Supreme Court indeed considered that the provocation to racial discrimination implies the provocation to facts defined and criminalized in the French Penal Code.[1187] This considerably limits the scope of the offence.

When the French legislator extended the scope of the offence of provocation to discrimination, hatred or violence to the discriminatory grounds of sex, sexual orientation, or handicap, he inserted in the new paragraph – current Article 24–9 – after the term discrimination the words 'provided in Articles 225–2 and 432–7 of the Penal Code', in order to prevent the existence of any argument on this point.[1188] In order to be punishable, the fact that expression has a 'sexist or homophobic' character thus does not suffice. A link must instead be established between the expression and such forms of discrimination (para. 7.2 *infra*). It is argued that if the French Supreme Court does not align the regime of Article 24–8 with that of 24–9, in order to be punishable, provocations on the ground of race may be indirect, but must be direct when on the ground of sex or sexual orientation.[1189]

The scope of the offence of provocation of discrimination is, however, much more limited than the scope of the definition of discrimination itself; Article 225–1 cites several other discriminatory grounds, being 'la situation de famille; la grossesse, l'apparence physique, le patronyme, l'état de santé, les caractéristiques, les mœurs, l'âge, les opinions politiques, l'activité syndicale'.

The term 'violence' equally refers to acts of violence that are criminalized in French law[1190] and signifies 'toute atteinte volontaire à la vie ou à la l'intégrité physique'.[1191] A certain overlap therefore exists between Article 24–8 and Article 24–2 that criminalizes, amongst others, the direct provocation to infractions of 'atteintes volontaires à l'intégrité de la personne' in the sense that they both criminalize provocations to acts of violence.[1192] It is argued that 'la provocation à la violence ne constitue qu'un supérieur dans la provocation à la haine'.[1193] However, incitement to hatred can exist without any call to violence.

1186 Beignier, De Lamy & Dreyer 2009, p.521; Droin 2009, p.167.

1187 French Supreme Court, crim.ch., 12 April 1976, n° 74–92515, *Bull. Crim.* 1976, n° 112, p.273.

1188 Article 24–9 reads: Seront punis des peines prévues à l'alinéa précédent ceux qui, par ces mêmes moyens, auront provoqué à la haine ou à la violence à l'égard d'une personne ou d'un groupe de personnes à raison de leur sexe, de leur orientation sexuelle ou de leur handicap ou auront provoqué, à l'égard des mêmes personnes, aux discriminations prévues par les articles 225–2 et 432–7 du code pénal.

1189 Dreyer 2011, p.154.

1190 For example: Articles 222–7 – 222–12–2 and Articles R.624–1 and R.625–1 of the French Penal Code.

1191 Beignier, De Lamy & Dreyer 2009, p.516.

1192 Droin 2009, p.168.

1193 Foulon-Piganiol, J., La lutte contre le racisme, *D* 1972, p. 272.

Contrary to the terms 'discrimination' and 'violence', the French Penal Code neither defines nor criminalizes the term 'hatred'. The French judge regards hatred rather as a sentiment than a determined act and has equated the term hatred with 'un sentiment d'hostilité ou de rejet'.[1194] It is argued that 'la haine n'est pas reprehensible en tant que telle', because criminal law 'ne peut obliger les gens à s'aimer', but 'le droit répressif peut empêcher les paroles ou les écrits qui entendent faire naître ces sentiments d'hostilité'.[1195] The provocation to hatred can thus be considered as an 'illicit incitement to a licit fact'. According to Mémeteau, the incitement to licit acts is repressed when such acts are considered as reprehensible on the basis of their immorality or lack of responsibility and because their multiplication wouldviolate the public order or morals.[1196] Indeed, during the drafting of the article much emphasis was placed on the danger of the contagiousness of racism.

Article 24–8 thus does not require that the expression provokes an act that is precisely defined by an infraction, but merely requires that it provokes discriminatory behaviour, violent conduct or a manifestation of hatred. Nevertheless, the French Supreme Court has considered that Article 24–8 is defined in clear and precise terms and, therefore, is not incompatible with Article 7 ECHR, which incorporates the legal principle of *nullum crimen, nulla poena, sine lege.* Furthermore, the French Supreme Court has rejected to transmit a QPC about the compatibility of Article 24–8 and 24–9 of the French Press Act with Articles 8 and 11 of the DDHC. According to the Supreme Court, Articles 24–8 and 24–9 violated neither the principle of precision of criminal law nor the right to freedom of expression.[1197] An analysis of the case law concerning article 24–8 shows that the imprecision of the offence, however, brings the French judge to criminalize and qualify expression rather as a provocation 'à la discrimination, à la haine ou à la violence' than as a provocation 'à la discrimination' or 'à la haine' or 'à la violence' and does not require expression to explicitly contain a description of a precise, determined act of discrimination, violence or a manifestation of hatred to which it seeks to provoke others to commit.

Hence, in cases from lower courts, a regional representative of the Front National has been convicted for incitement to racial hatred and violence for a post on his Facebook in which Muslims were assimilated to '*dealers et prostitués*' and '*racailles qui vendent de la drogue toute la journée*'; a deputy of the French political party UMP has been convicted for inciting racial discrimination in a tweet in

1194 CA Paris, 16 December 1998, *Légipresse* 1999, n° 159-III, p.30.

1195 De Lamy 2000, p. 317.

1196 For a critical analysis of such prohibitions: Mémeteau, G., L'incitation illicite à des faits licites ou: les remords du legislateur, *JCP, G,* 1976, I, 2781.

1197 Droin 2009, p.169. French Supreme Court, crim.ch., 13 June 1995, n° 93–82144, *Bull. Crim.*1995, n° 217, p.591; French Supreme Court, crim. Ch., 16 April 2013, n° 13–90008/ 13–90010, *Légipresse* n° 306 June 2013, p. 337–338.

reaction to violent acts that occurred during a French football match saying '*Les casseurs sont sûrement des descendants d'esclaves ils ont des excuses. Taubira va leur donner une compensation!*'; a man has been convicted for inciting racial hatred for posting a series of articles on the Internet which contained repetitive calls to hatred against Jews, Muslims, and Gipsies accompanied with photos of Adolf Hitler and a soldier of the Waffen SS; and a weekly magazine has been convicted for inciting racial violence for an article entitled '*Cannes: le festival de l'impureté*' that stigmatized Jews by associating them with impurity, pornography, sexual crimes, immorality, greed and arrogance of the wealth.[1198]

The French Supreme Court categorically confirms condemnations on the ground of provocation to feelings of fear and hostility, thus hatred, against the Jewish community, with regard to clearly anti-Semitic expression, even when such expression does not explicitly call others to act or feel in a certain manner and does not explicitly refer to the Jewish community. Examples can be found in an article reproducing two stickers with the text 'Rapport Leuchter, fini les chambres à gaz?' and 'les coupeurs de verge à la grande vergue' that imputed the Jewish community to lie about the existence of gaz chambers;[1199] an article entitled 'Souvenez-vous de l'Internationale juive' that suggested that the Jewish community maintained an international lobby for world domination;[1200] an article entitled 'Refusons le bâillon', 'Contre l'inquisition cosmopolite, contre l'oppression, contre l'imposture', in which the Jewish community was presented as 'mafia cosmopolite' and 'une association de malfaiteurs' that aimed to dominate the French;[1201] or the publication on the Internet of the phrase 'France Culture est une radio qui appartient pratiquement à la communauté juive et qui diffuse en permanence sur la Bretagne sa propagande à la gloire des juifs et pour le remplacement physique des Européens (...)'.[1202]

Furthermore, the French Supreme Court has on several occasions endorsed condemnations on the ground of Article 24–8 with regard to criticism of the politics of the State of Israel that the lower courts considered as a disguised form of provocation to discrimination or hatred against Israeli or the Jewish community as a whole. An example of this is a drawing of an Israeli soldier and officer who shouted towards a group of Palestinian citizens 'les hommes à Gaza, les femmes à Jéricho' that imputed the Jewish community to practice in Israel a politics of

---

1198 Trib. Corr. de Nîmes, 28 February 2013, *Légipresse* n° 305 May 2013, p. 270; TGI de Paris, 19 September 2014, *Légipresse* n° 320 October 2014, p. 526; TGI de Paris, 8 July 2014, *Légipresse* n° 319 September 2014, p. 461; and TGI de Paris, 26 September 2014, *Légipresse* n° 321 November 2014, p. 591–592.

1199 French Supreme Court, crim.ch., 16 July 1992, n° 91–86.156, *Bull. Crim.* 1992, n° 273, p.740.

1200 French Supreme Court, crim.ch., 29 January 1998, n° 96–84851, *GP* 1998, I, p.75, annotation J.P. Doucet.

1201 French Supreme Court, crim.ch., 13 June 1995, *JCP*, 1995, IV, 2350.

1202 French Supreme Court, crim.ch., 22 June 2010, n°10–82337, *unpublished.*

deportation identical to the one the Nazis had practiced against themselves.[1203] Another example is the reproduction on the Internet of the expression of a mayor, who had indicated during a meeting, to have requested the restaurant to boycott products of Israel in protest against the politics of the Sharon government towards the Palestinians. The mayor had incited the restaurant to take into account the origin of the products and thereby had hindered the economic activity of Israeli producers.[1204] Whether such political criticism on the State of Israel via the call to boycott Israelian products constitutes a punishable provocation to discrimination may be contestable. In 2011, the French Supreme Court, however, refused to transmit a 'Question Prioritaire de Constitutionalité' (QPC) concerning the application of Article 24–8 to the call to boycott Israelian products to the Constitutional Council, because the request evidently aimed at contesting the qualification of the expression, which is not the goal of the QPC (see further para. 9.4 *infra*).[1205]

The French Supreme Court has clarified, to a certain extent, the limitations to the free political and public debate concerning the problems related to the immigration and integration of foreigners. Criticism of certain undesirable behaviour or practices of immigrants or foreigners, apart from their race or origin, does not fall under the scope of Article 24–8. In 1980, the French Supreme Court rejected an appeal against an acquittal with regard to an article criticizing in strong language the presence of many door-to-door salesmen of African origin in a city, because of the sales methods they used. Such criticism did not constitute a punishable provocation to discrimination, hatred or violence against the Senegalese salesmen on the ground of their race or nationality.[1206]

The Court draws a line when the criticism attributes undesirable behaviour or practices to immigrants or foreigners, precisely because of their race or nationality, portrays them exclusively as harmful to French society and seeks to convince the reader to reject their presence in France and favour their departure. In 2001, the French Supreme Court rejected an appeal against a condemnation concerning a tract criticizing the behaviour of immigrants, because 'les juges retiennent, par motifs propres et adoptés, que le tract en cause présente les immigrés sous un jour exclusivement nuisible, en les rendant responsables de l'insécurité, du chômage et de l'accroissement de la charge fiscale; qu'ils ajoutent que l'écrit instille, dans l'esprit du lecteur, la conviction que la sécurité passé par le rejet des immigres et que l'inquiétude et la peur, liées à leur présence en France, cesseront à leur départ.'[1207]

1203 French Supreme Court, crim.ch., 24 October 1995, n° 94–83.666, *unpublished.*

1204 French Supreme Court, crim.ch., 28 September 2004, n°03–87450, *unpublished.*

1205 French Supreme Court, crim.ch., 7 June 2011, n°10–88315, *Crim. Bull.* 2011, *published.*

1206 French Supreme Court, crim.ch., 3 March 1980, n° 78–91949, *Bull. Crim.* 1980, n° 74.

1207 French Supreme Court, crim.ch., 13 November 2001, n°01–80510, *unpublished.*

The French Supreme Court generally considers expression that attributes criminal behaviour to a certain group on the ground of its race, ethnic background or national origin, to constitute a punishable provocation to hatred. In 1995, the French Supreme Court found punishable the publication of an article which included a drawing that showed young black and North African people brandishing knives and clubs, with the caption 'L'insécurité est souvent le fait des bandes ethniques', because 'le but recherché est de créer un lien entre les communautés noires et maghrébines et la criminalité; que cette association, compte tenu de la puissance émotive du dessin, est de nature à susciter des réactions d'hostilité et de rejet vis-à-vis de ces communautés'.[1208]

Likewise, in 1996, the French Supreme Court considered an article that cited the President of the French Republic as having said that 'la nation française ressent profondément l'utilité de la présence d'immigrés chez nous' to constitute the offence, because the article subsequently ascribed various incidents involving foreigners from North and black Africa and the gypsy community to their membership of a particular ethnic group, race or religion. Such juxtaposition had given the text a particular force and 'a été de nature à susciter immédiatement chez le lecteur, contre les personnes visées comme le auteurs de tels agissements et 'les vecteurs principaux des formes les plus répréhensibles de la délinquance', des réactions de rejet, voire de haine et de violence'.[1209]

However, in a recent decision of 7 June 2011, the French Supreme Court established that severe problems related to the integration of a particular group can form a matter of public interest that can even justify the denomination of that group as criminal. The Court annulled a conviction of a former foreign service officer for his harsh criticism of the Roma community during a political television talk show entitled 'Délinquance, la route des Roms' dedicated to the integration of the Roma population into French society. The Court of Appeal had considered that the officer 's'est livré, par des affirmations péremptoires et des constats lapidaires et non étayés, à une dénonciation sans appel ni réserve de la communauté rom qu'il a désignée comme particulièrement criminogène et donc dangereuse, pratiquement inassimilable et finalement susceptible de déferler en masse sur le territoire français; (...) que le sujet de l'émission exigeait, à tout le moins, qu'il fasse prévue d'un pessimisme raisonné et argumenté;' Contrarily, the French Supreme Court held that the difficulties with regard to the integration of the Roma community concerned a question of public interest; the expression, therefore, did not overstep the admissible limits to freedom of expression.[1210]

1208 French Supreme Court, crim.ch., 7 September 1995, *Dr. pén.* 1995, 280, annotation M. Véron.

1209 French Supreme Court, crim.ch., 21 May 1996, n° 94–83365, *Bull.Crim.* 1996, n° 210, p.593, annotation Ph. Delmas-Saint-Hilaire.

1210 Without referral, the French Supreme Court acquitted the officer. French Supreme Court, crim. ch., 7 June 2011, n° 10–85179, *Légipresse* n°287, October 2011, pp.550–554, annotation N. Verly.

6.3. The designation of a group

French doctrine generally holds that it is not required that the group being the victim of a racial provocation is identified with the same precision that is required with regard to the offences of racial defamation and racial insult.[1211] However, to preserve the principle of freedom of expression, the French Supreme Court has traditionally held onto the requirement that in order for expression to constitute a provocation to discrimination, hatred or violence 'against a group on the ground of their origin, ethnic background, nation, race or religion' the expression must undisputedly have a racist and discriminatory purport in the sense that it expresses an absolute rejection of a determined group for reasons exclusively of their belonging to a specific origin, ethnic background, nation, race or religion.[1212] The French Supreme Court found a rap comprising the phrases 'La France est une garce, n'oublie pas de la baiser' and 'La France est une de ces putes de mères qui t'a enfanté' not to stigmatize any particular group of the French nation, but rather to be deliberately and uniquely aimed at the French State. It therefore did not incite to hatred against the French as a whole.[1213]

For a long time, the French Supreme Court opined that expression about immigrants or foreigners can not constitute a provocation to racial discrimination punishable under Article 24–8, because immigrants and foreigners do not constitute any of the determined categories of origin, ethnic background, nation, race or religion. According to the French Supreme Court, 'la seule crainte du racisme ne saurait priver les citoyens de la liberté de pensée et d'expression, dans la mesure où le débat se déroule de bonne foi et sans but de discrimination au sens de l'article 24 de la loi du 29 juillet 1881'.[1214] This consideration of the Court is often cited as a defence by suspects prosecuted on the ground of Article 24–8.[1215]

In 1994, the French Supreme Court upheld an acquittal concerning a tract denouncing the high concentration of immigrants in the northern quarters of Colombes, considering 'que le texte et le dessin ne font que refléter une réalité locale résultant de la politique de la municipalité et ne tendant qu'à protester précisément contre la discrimination dont feraient l'objet les Français de souche; qu'on ne peut tenir sans abus d'interprétation que ce tract serait dirigé contre une race ou une ethnie particulière, cependant que le dessin, aux dires mêmes des parties civiles, vise des ressortissants étrangers de plusieurs races ou ethnies manifestement pris en leur qualité d'immigrés et non en leur appartenance raciale ou ethnique étant observé que c'est le problème de l'immigration qui est en question

---

1211 Robert, J-H., *JCI Communication*, 'Apologies et provocations de crimes et délits', n°22.

1212 Beignier, De Lamy & Dreyer 2009, p.517.

1213 French Supreme Court, crim.ch., 3 February 2009, n°08–85220, *unpublished.*

1214 French Supreme Court, crim.ch., 17 May 1994, n° 91–82129, *Dr. pén.* 1994, 258.

1215 French Supreme Court, crim.ch., 3 February 2009, n°06–83.063 08–82.402, *Bull. Crim.* 2009, n° 25.

et que les immigrés ne constituent aucune catégorie ethnique, ni raciale, ni confessionnelle'.[1216]

In a decision of 24 June 1997, the French Supreme Court altered this case law and extended the notion of a group. The Court rejected an appeal against the condemnation of a French local politician for an election pamphlet making a commitment to fight immigration fiercely, calling for the 'envahisseurs' to be driven out immediately, denouncing French officials as accomplices or collaborators with the 'occupants de notre sol', and demanding the expulsion of 'des étrangers irrespectueux et nuisibles'. According to the Court of Appeal, these accusations 'induisent une notion d'agression, et tendent à susciter un sentiment de haine ou des actes de discrimination envers les immigrés, considérés comme un groupe de personnes, et visés à raison de leur non-appartenance à la communauté française'. The French Supreme Court confirmed 'Qu'en effet, les étrangers résidant en France, lorsqu' ils sont vises *en raison de leur non-appartenance à la nation française*, forment un groupe de personnes au sens de l'article 24 alinéa 6 de la loi du 29 juillet 1881'.[1217] [curs. EHJ] The French Supreme Court has further considered the 'commerçants extra-européens' to constitute a group for the purposes of Article 24–8.[1218]

It is argued that this approach permits the repression of expression that is the most dangerous to public order, but also that it may deprive the notion of a 'group' from its relevance. The boundary between criticism of non-individualized persons and the free discussion of abstract ideas becomes minimal. The offence then less concerns the protection of particular communities than the dignity of the human person, the status of which must not depend on any personal characteristic. This may entail the risk of repressing simple opinions.[1219]

6.4. No justifications

The perpetrator of a provocation to discrimination, hatred or violence cannot benefit from a justifying fact. The excuse of provocation, the possibility for a suspect to demonstrate that he or she has been provoked to utter his or her expression by a previous attack that is admitted in the field of insult, cannot justify a provocation to discrimination, hatred or violence. The same holds true for the exception of truth, i.e. the possibility for a suspect to prove the truth of his statement that is permitted in the field of defamation. The possibility for a suspect to demonstrate his good faith as a justifying fact that is generally admitted in the field of provocations not followed by effect is equally excluded in the field of provocation

1216 French Supreme Court, crim.ch., 18 January 1994, n°91–86228, *unpublished.*
1217 French Supreme Court, crim.ch., 24 June 1997, n° 95–81187, *Bull.Crim.* 1997, n°253, p.864.
1218 French Supreme Court, crim.ch., 14 May 2002, n°01–85482, *unpublished.*
1219 Dreyer 2011, p. 157.

to discrimination, hatred or violence.[1220] Veron however criticizes the decision by the French Supreme Court concerning the ridiculing of Le Pen with the song 'Casser du noir' notably for completely interdicting an author to prove his good faith, which would go far beyond the presumption of bad faith that 'merely' shifts the burden of proof of his intention towards the suspect and which would be contrary to Article 121–3 of the French Penal Code that reads 'il n'y a point de délit sans intention de le commettre'.[1221]

Freedom of expression or the interest of a public debate can also not form a general *justification* for the offence of racial provocation. The French Supreme Court has on several occasions declared the offence of provocation to discrimination, hatred or violence compatible with Article 10 ECHR. In one case the Court considered 'que, d'autre part, le texte précité entrant dans les restrictions prévues au paragraphe 2 de l'article 10 de la Convention européenne des droits de l'homme, la méconnaissance du principe de la liberté d'expression affirme par le paragraphe 1er dudit article ne saurait être invoquée'.[1222] And in another case the Court considered that according to the second paragraph of Article 10 ECHR freedom of expression 'peut être soumis à certaines formalités, conditions, restrictions ou sanctions, prévues par la loi, qui constituent, dans une société démocratique, des mesures nécessaires notamment à la protection de la morale et des droits d'autrui; que tel est l'objet des articles susvisés de la loi du 29 juillet 1881'.[1223]

The case law concerning Article 24–8 shows that the French judge attaches importance to the interest of freedom of expression by narrowly interpreting and strictly circumscribing the statutory elements of the offence of racial provocation ('incitation manifeste' and 'groupe parfaitement designé'). However, once the French judge has established that an expression constitutes a punishable provocation to discrimination, hatred or violence in the sense of Article 24–8, it is impossible for him/her to make any further act of balancing with the freedom of expression.

6.5. Provocative expression concerning a religion in a humoristic or political context

6.5.1. The ridiculing of the Catholic faith

The French Supreme Court has established in several judgments that in order for expression to constitute a punishable provocation to discrimination, hatred or violence, it must not merely evoke negative feelings with third parties towards the

1220 French Supreme Court, crim.ch., 16 July 1992, n°91–86156, *Bull. Crim.* 1992, n°273, p.740; French Supreme Court, crim.ch., 4 November 1997, n° 96–84338, *Dr. pén.,* 1998, annotation M. Véron.

1221 French Supreme Court, crim.ch., 4 November 1997, n° 96–84338, *Dr. pén.,* 1998, annotation M. Véron.

1222 French Supreme Court, crim.ch., 14 May 2002, n°01–85482, *unpublished.*

1223 French Supreme Court, crim.ch., 20 June 2006, n°05–86690, *Bull. Crim.* 2006, n°187, p.667.

targeted religious person or group or merely hurt the feelings of the targeted religious person himself or group itself. As a general rule, the Court endorses acquittals concerning expression that ridicules the Christian or Catholic religion, its convictions, symbols, rites and practices and therefore hurts the sensibility and religious feelings of Christians or Catholics, but, considering its humorous context, does not constitute a 'incitation manifeste' against a 'groupe parfaitement designé'.

In 1993, the French Supreme Court rejected an appeal against an acquittal with regard to an article entitled 'Confessions en direct: déguisés en curés, nous avons recueilli vos péchés' published in a monthly magazine. The article narrated the adventures of two reporters who – dressed as a priest and a religious woman – had approached passengers on the street and asked them to take confession in a car bus equipped with a big cross, which had been converted into a confessional box. The article was accompanied by two photos and comprised the phrase: 'Au top 50 des péchés avoués celui de l'adultère est numéro un. Comble de la rigolade pour nos deux reporters qui, entre les traditionnels Pater, durent conseiller à plusieurs reprises les préservatifs...'[1224] The Paris Court of Appeal had considered that '... s'il tendait à tourner en dérision la confession en usage dans l'Eglise catholique, l'article incriminé ne suscitait aucun sentiment d'hostilité envers les adeptes de cette religion (.), ledit article n'est pas de nature à inciter à la haine, à la violence ou à la discrimination envers des citoyens de religion catholique'.[1225]

Again in 1993, the French Supreme Court confirmed an acquittal concerning the caricature 'Christ en croix gonflé' published on the cover of the December 1989 issue of the magazine *Fluide glacial.* It depicted a religious woman standing in front of a Christmas tree surrounded by Christmas presents, busy inflating her Christmas present with a bicycle pump: an inflatable crucified Christ. The Court considered 'Attendu qu'après avoir admis que le symbole religieux utilisé en page de couverture, ainsi que les images et propos de la bande dessinée, tendaient incontestablement à tourner en dérision les religieuses représentées sous des traits grotesques, et étaient de nature à heurter la sensibilité des catholiques, comme le respect qu'ils portent aux religieuses, l'arrêt énonce, pour relaxer le prévenu et débouter la partie civile, que ces faits ne constituent cependant pas le délit prévu par l'article 24, alinéa 6, de la loi du 29 juillet 1881, et que ce texte 'suppose une provocation délibérée à la discrimination, à la haine ou à la violence à l'égard de personnes à raison de leur appartenance ou non-appartenance à une religion déterminée, ce qui n'est pas le cas en l'espèce, faute d'incitation manifeste, d'instigation ou d'exhortation à ces sentiments'.'[1226]

1224 Other phrases were: 'Bien, va en paix, tu mentiras moins et réciteras 87 Pater et 54 Ave...'; 'Peine extrêmement sévère. Mais facile à purger, ce pécheur connaissait ses Pater et ses Ave sur le bout de ses doigts impurs...'; 'Terriblement excité par la cornette de notre consœur, un noir splendide succombe à la tentation du confessionnal...'; 'Un client raconte sa vie, prenant le confessionnal pour le cabinet d'un psy...'

1225 French Supreme Court, crim.ch., 7 December 1993, n°92–84.439, *Bull. Crim.*1993 n°374, p.935.

1226 French Supreme Court, crim.ch., 7 December 1993, n°92–81.091, *Bull. Crim.* 1993 n°374, p.935.

Likewise, in 2001, the civil chamber of the French Supreme Court considered several caricatures and texts ridiculing the Catholic faith – comprising a picture of a bedridden patient with the text '… – Nouveau spectacle – Je suce était son nom –…' concerning the theatre play 'Jésus était son nom'; a picture of the Pope being sodomized by a transvestite with the title 'Le pape chez les travelos'; a drawing entitled 'Les Kgbistes recyclés en prêtres' picturing a priest plunking a child in a baptism shell and declaring 'On a les moyens de te faire parler, sale gosse' – as mere parodies and therefore rejected an appeal against an acquittal. The Court considered 'que tous les dessins en cause tournent en dérision la religion catholique, les croyances, les symboles et les rites de la pratique religieuse, mais n'ont pas pour finalité de susciter un état d'esprit de nature à provoquer à la discrimination, la haine ou la violence, et ne caractérisent pas l'infraction prévue par l'article 24, alinéa 6, de la loi du 29 juillet 1881.'[1227]

6.5.2. The political and public debate about Islam, 'islamization', and Muslim-immigration

The French Supreme Court has on several occasions judged the criminality of criticism of Islam, the 'islamisation' of French society or the financing of mosques by the French State on the ground of the offence of provocation to discrimination, hatred, or violence. According to the Court, such expression generally enters into a free political or public debate about the place of Islam in French society, in which the laic character of the French Republic plays an important role.

In 1992, the French Supreme Court rejected an appeal against an acquittal concerning the distribution of a pamphlet by the extreme right winged political party Le Front National entitled 'Non à l'islamisation de Saint-Nazaire' during a council meeting of Saint-Nazaire, containing the phrases 'Dans vingt ans c'est sûr la France sera une République islamique' and 'Le refus de s'intégrer: L'organisation en France de communautés étrangères soumises à la loi islamique (la 'charria') incompatible avec nos mœurs et nos traditions'.[1228] The Court of Appeal considered

---

1227 French Supreme Court, civ.ch. II, 8 March 2001, n°98–17.574, *Bull.* 2001 II n°47, p.32. In the same sense, concerning several publications in issues of the satirical magazine *Charlie Hebdo*: French Supreme Court, crim.ch., 8 June 1999, n°98–83.461, *unpublished* (drawings and texts that denounced the actions taken by anti-abortion commandos and invited the reader to create 'commandos anti bon dieu') and French Supreme Court, crim.ch., 15 March 2011, n°10–82.809, *unpublished* (the qualification of the Gospel of Saint Marcus as a pornographic work that demonstrated that Christ was a gross pig and a paedophile and the phrase 'on redonne les chrétiens à bouffer aux lions!'). See also: TGI de Paris, 26 September 2014, *Légipresse* n° 321, November 2014, p. 591. The court acquitted the publishers of a cartoon by Plantu of pope Benoît XVI sodomising a child, as it did not incite hatred, discrimination or violence against members of the Catholique community.

1228 The full passages read: 'Dans vingt ans c'est sûr la France sera une République islamique (Hussein Moussawi chef Hezbollah 11 septembre 1986); 1989; un centre culturel islamique s'édifie au Cœur de votre ville (passage Paul-Perrin près de la gare); 1999: le centre est devenu mosquée. Les nazairiens vivent à l'ombre du minaret, au rythme des appels du muezzin; 2009:

'si les expressions employées et les images volontairement forcées pourrait engendrer un sentiment de peur, de crainte, voire même de refus d'une situation décrite comme alarmante, force est de constater qu'aucun des termes employés, si déplaisants puissent-ils être estimés, ne comporte une exhortation ou une provocation caractérisée à la discrimination, à la haine ou à la violence à l'égard de la communauté islamique'.[1229]

Likewise, in 2007, the French Supreme Court rejected an appeal against an acquittal concerning the distribution by two regional politicians of Le Front National of a pamphlet entitled 'Pas de cathédrale à la Mecque, pas de mosquée à Strasbourg' denouncing the financing of the construction of a Mosque in Strasbourg and appealing to the public to protest against it. The Court of Appeal considered '(...) qu'il ne critique pas la religion musulmane en elle-même ni ceux qui la pratiquent; que le dessin qui l'assortit relève de la dérision; qu'il peut choquer les membres de la communauté musulmane mais n'incite pas à leur égard à la discrimination, à la haine ou à la violence; (...) que la critique porte sur la décision de financer un lieu de culte mais n'a pas pour objet de stigmatiser ceux qui pratiquent ce culte, de manière à les exposer à la haine d'autrui; (...).' and had thereby justified its decision, as the expression did not exceed the limitations admissible to freedom of expression for the purposes of Article 10 ECHR.[1230]

However, when such criticism of Islam, the 'islamisation' of French society or the financing of mosques is coupled with an explicit disqualification of Muslims by placing them opposite to French native citizens and portraying them as a danger to the French society, the French Supreme Court generally found that the offence of provocation to discrimination, hatred, or violence was constituted. Such was the case in relation to a pamphlet entitled 'Stop à l'immigration (...) trop d'immigrés, la France aux Français (...)' that suggested that Muslims imposed their laws, customs, religions, and morality, abused social security and governmental financial support to the disadvantage of French native citizens and caused an augmentation in diseases and delinquency.[1231] publications on the Internet site *Riposte laique* containing the phrase 'Occupation – Bien sûr que les prières dans la rue, les violes,

---

les nazairiennes portent le tchador, l'alcool est prohibé, le Coran fait loi; La France est devenue une République islamique; Est-ce cela que vous voulez? Pour vous, pour vos enfants? Non! Le refus de s'intégrer: L'organisation en France de communautés étrangères soumises à la loi islamique (la "charria") incompatible avec nos mœurs et nos traditions; La transformation du quartier: Boutiques, école islamique, reconnaissance d'un clergé dont les pouvoirs iront croissant. Demain il sera trop tard. Pour défendre vos intérêts, les intérêts du peuple français soutenez le Front National avec Jean-Marie Le Pen.'.

1229 French Supreme Court, crim.ch., 28 January 1992, n° 91–81778, *Dr. pén.* 1992, 223, annotation M. Véron.

1230 French Supreme Court, crim.ch., 30 May 2007, n°06–84.328, *Bull. Crim.* 2007 n°140. In the same sense: French Supreme Court, crim.ch., 17 May 1994, n°91–82.129, *unpublished.*

1231 French Supreme Court, crim.ch., 30 January 1990, n°88–86.549, *unpublished.*

le halal, et les mosquées sont des symboles d'occupation et de conquête!';[1232] a pamphlet depicting the Mayor of the city of Menton as a Calife and his wife as Shéhérazade (mille et une nuit), the city of Menton as an oriental city, and the city's church as a mosque in order to oppose to the plan of the Mayor to place in the old hospice of the city an institute of political science destined to Arab and Muslim students;[1233] an article in an informative magazine distributed to the students of a secondary school and their parents that warned for the 'debarkation of hordes of Muslims unable to assimilate';[1234, 1235] and a communiqué denouncing in harsh terms the 'slaughtering' of the French identity by the exercise of religious practices by Muslims in France, such as ritual slaughtering ('On égorge femmes, enfants, nos moines, nos fonctionnaires, nos touristes et nos moutons, on nous égorgera un jour et nous l'aurons bien mérité. La France musulmane avec une Marianne maghrébine pourquoi pas, au point où on en est').[1236]

The context of a political debate concerning the place of Islam in French society is sometimes regarded by lower courts as a particular context that permits expression that would otherwise constitute a punishable provocation on the ground of Article 24–8. Based on this reasoning, in 2011, the criminal tribunal of Nanterre acquitted the extreme right winged politician Le Pen, who had distributed a campaign poster entitled 'Non à l'islamisme' depicting a woman in burqa next to a map of France covered by an Algerian flag plus several minarets in the form of rockets, during regional elections in February 2010 and on the Internet.[1237]

1232 TGI de Paris (17e ch.), 23 March 2012, Ministère public c/P.Cassen et a., *Légipresse* n°295 June 2012, p. 346.

1233 French Supreme Court, crim.ch., 11 September 2007, n°07–80783, *unpublished.*

1234 The article comprised the passage: 'les illusionnistes n'avaient pas prévu qu'en échange de la fuite éperdue de ces maudits français d'Afrique du Nord, des hordes musulmanes inassimilables débarqueraient et investiraient les plus reculés de nos cantons; ils sont aujourd'hui cinq millions, construisent partout des mosquées et quand ils parlent de mettre les voiles… ne vous réjouissez pas trop, ce n'est qu'à leurs sales gamines arrogantes'.

1235 French Supreme Court, crim.ch., 7 September 1999, n°98–85177, *unpublished.*

1236 French Supreme Court, crim.ch., 25 January 2000, n°98–87278, *unpublished.* Recently the TGI de Paris found the author Roland Camus guilty of incitement to racial hatred with regard to his statements made during a public gathering entitled 'Assises internationals sur l' islamisation de nos pays', in which Muslims were presented as 'voyous', 'soldats', the authors of 'vols', 'rackets au sein des écoles' and 'colonisateurs'. TGI de Paris, 10 April 2014, *Légipresse* n° 318, July-August 2014, p. 398–399.

1237 TGI de Nanterre, 5 April 2011, *Légipresse* n°286, September 2011, p.465. The tribunal considered: 'l'affiche en cause a été diffusée dans le cadre d'une campagne électorale, et qu'il s'agit par conséquence d'un contexte particulier dans lequel des propos qui ne seraient pas tolérés autrement sont proférés sur un mode d'exagération, voire caricatural, et s'inscrivent dans un débat qui peut être passionné. Celui-ci énonce que, de plus, la place de l'islam dans la société française prend place actuellement dans le débat politique français. (…) l'affiche, même si elle procède d'un amalgame entre l'islamisme et l'Algérie, n'incite pas directement à la haine contre la communauté algérienne résidant en France, mais plutôt au rejet d'une pratique extrême de la religion musulmane. Celui-ci en déduit qu'on ne peut retenir que l'affiche

The French Supreme Court has, however, established that within the context of a political debate concerning a matter of public interest, the freedom of expression of a representative has the same scope as the freedom of expression of any other citizen. In 2002, the Court endorsed a condemnation by the Court of Appeal on the ground of provocation to religious hatred and violence with regard to the expression 'le peuple colonisé par 80% de musulmans est devenu une terre d'Islam!, les 20% de yougoslaves sont martyrisés sur leur sol, il est demandé aux habitants de Villefontaine de méditer sur cet exemple pour éradiquer la ghettoïsation, lorsqu'ils auront changé de maire'. The Court of Appeal considered: 'un élu a la possibilité de s'exprimer sur les sujets de sociétés et notamment sur l'insécurité, il n'en demeure pas moins, aux termes de la loi et d'une jurisprudence constante, que ce droit de libre expression reconnu à tout citoyen (*l'élu étant un citoyen comme les autres*) comporte des limites imposées par la loi, qu'elle soit nationale ou européenne, et que 'l'article 10 de la Convention européenne des droits de l'homme prévoit expressément dans son second paragraphe, que *l'exercice de la liberté d'expression comportant des devoirs et des responsabilités*, peut être soumis à certaines conditions, restrictions ou sanctions prévues par la loi, qui constituent des mesures nécessaires dans une société démocratique, notamment dans la protection des droits d'autrui, ce qui est l'objet de l'article 24, alinéa 6, de la loi du 29 juillet 1881'.[1238] [curs. EHJ]

As a result of the case law of the French Supreme Court, political proposals can constitute a punishable provocation to religious discrimination, when it remains unclear whether the politician aims to directly provoke voters, the public, third parties to *themselves* discriminate against – certain – Muslims or whether a politician aims to gain political power in order to install such discriminatory measures *himself*. For example, the Court rejected an appeal against a condemnation on the ground of provocation to religious discrimination of a cantonal election candidate for having diffused among the voters a tract entitled 'Islamistes dehors, remettons de l'ordre en France'.[1239]

6.5.3. *Jean-Marie Le Pen and Le Front National*

The extreme right winged politician Jean-Marie Le Pen and (members of) his extreme right winged political party le Front National have been convicted for their political discourse with an anti-Semitic or racist purport on the ground of racial defamation, racial insult or provocation to racial discrimination, hatred or violence in two dozen cases, several of which have been discussed in previous paragraphs. On 14 July 2014, the Cayenne District Court condemned Anne-Sophie Leclère, a

incriminée incite à la discrimination ou à la haine mais exprime plutôt un refus des opinions et pratiques engendrées par une vision minoritaire de l'islam qui s'inscrit dans le débat démocratique.'

1238 French Supreme Court, crim.ch., 14 May 2002, n°01–85482, *unpublished.*

1239 French Supreme Court, crim.ch., 2 March 2004, n°03–82549, *unpublished.*

candidate of the FN for the municipal elections, for insult and provocation to hatred based on race, after she had placed a photo collage on her website that compared a photo of French Minister of Justice, Christiane Taubira, to a photo of a monkey. The Court imposed a prison sentence of nine months and deprived her of the right of eligibility for five years. The Cayenne District Court considered: '*Le fait d'assimiler une personne humaine, quelle qu'elle soit à un animal, constitue une injure faite à l'humanité entière'*, but emphasized the gravity of this case as it concerned persons from a territory '*marqué par l'esclavage, caractérisé par l'assimilation par le Code noir des "Nègres" à des biens meubles ou à du bétail'*. (see further: Introduction *supra*).[1240]

For their part, Le Pen and le Front National have initiated several defamation cases against allegations of racism and anti-Semitism, in several of which the French judge has acknowledged the racist character of their expression. On one occasion, with regard to the accusation that Le Pen's expression constituted a permanent 'incitation au racisme, avec pour résultat très clair une élévation moyenne du niveau de racisme dans le pays', the Court of Appeal considered that an objective correlation between expressions by Le Pen and adherents of le Front National and an recrudescence of racist sentiments in public opinion was sufficiently established.'[1241]

A famous case against Le Pen that has been brought before the ECtHR concerned a statement made by him: 'd'autant que quand je dis qu'avec 25 millions de musulmans chez nous, les français raseront les murs, des gens dans la salle me disent non sans raison: 'mais monsieur Le Pen, c'est déjà le cas maintenant'', which he uttered during an interview published in the journal *Rivarol*. In this case, the Paris Court of Appeal that condemned Le Pen eloquently summarized the criteria for Article 24–8 as they have been established in French case law. In 2009, the French Supreme Court rejected an appeal by Le Pen against the judgment of the Court that had considered:

> 'qu'à travers les propos poursuivis, Jean-Marie X..., qui ne conteste pas en être l'auteur, explique sans détour qu'alors qu'il se contente lui-même, en sa qualité de président du Front national, de faire valoir aux "gens" qu'une forte croissance de la communauté musulmane constitue une menace pour les français qui seront dominés, humiliés et victimes de violences, ceux-ci, qui, au-delà de ses électeurs et du lectorat de Rivarol, forment le peuple français, lui disent que, d'ores et déjà, en présence de musulmans, ils doivent se tenir à distance d'eux et faire preuve de soumission à leur égard; que ce faisant, *le prévenu oppose les "français" aux "musulmans", les "gens" de France*, dont les réactions vont bien plus loin que ses propres propos condamnés, à une communauté étrangère présentée comme une multitude envahissante, et *tend à susciter*, par le sens et la portée qu'il donne à son message, et à celui des "gens", qu'il

---

1240 Charrière-Bournazel, C., La liberté d'opinion, le racisme et l'histoire, Les neuf mois ferme de Cayenne, *Légipresse* n°319, September 2014, p. 451–452.

1241 *Ibid.* Cases cited in: Taguieff, P.-A., Mobilisation national-populiste en France. Vote xénophobe et nouvel antisémitisme politique, *Lignes* n° 9, March 1990, annex; Cohen 2003, p.132.

fait finalement sien, *un sentiment de rejet et d'hostilité* envers la communauté musulmane; que *son propos instille dans l'esprit du public la conviction que la sécurité des français passe par le rejet des musulmans et que l'inquiétude et la peur, liées à leur présence croissante en France, cesseront si leur nombre décroît et s'ils disparaissent*;
qu'une fois caractérisé, le délit prévu et réprimé par l'article 24, alinéa 6, de la loi du 29 juillet 1881 ne peut constituer une violation de la liberté d'expression protégée par l'article 10 de la Convention européenne de droits de l'homme, dès lors que ce texte a réservé la possibilité de restrictions légales, telle la protection des droits et libertés d'autrui, lorsqu'elles constituent des mesures nécessaires dans une société démocratique; qu'en l'occurrence, s'il était légitime, dans le cadre du débat politique, pour Jean-Marie X..., leader d'opinion, de faire connaître son point de vue sur la question de l'immigration ou celle de la place des religions, *sa liberté d'expression ne peut justifier des propos comportant une provocation à la discrimination, à la haine ou à la violence envers un groupe de personnes*";'[1242] [curs. EHJ]

6.6. Conclusion

In order for expression to constitute the offence of provocation to racial discrimination, hatred or violence, it must take the form, not necessarily of an exhortation, but of a positive act of manifest incitement to discrimination, hatred or violence, which does not require an explicit call to commit a precise determined fact that is punishable under French law. The expression must not be capable, but merely likely to provoke others to discrimination, hatred or violence. The objective intention of the author to provoke must be derived from the expression itself. The expression must undisputedly have a racist and discriminatory purport in the sense that it expresses an absolute rejection of a specific designated group for reasons exclusively of their belonging to a specific origin, ethnic background, nation, race or religion, or of their not belonging to the French nation (immigrants). Both the textual and broader context of the expression can be taken into account in order to assess its punishable character. No justifications exist for the provocation to discrimination, hatred or violence. The French judge attaches importance to the interest of freedom of expression by narrowly interpreting and strictly circumscribing the statutory elements of the offence of racial provocation, but once he has established that an expression constitutes a punishable provocation to discrimination, hatred or violence for the purposes of Article 24–8, no further act of balancing with freedom of expression can be made. On the basis of these principles, the French Supreme Court has established that expression that merely hurts religious feelings of a particular religious group, such as the ridiculing of the Catholic faith, does not constitute a punishable provocation to discrimination, hatred or violence against that group. The same applies to the political and public

---

1242 French Supreme Court, crim.ch., 3 February 2009, n°06–83063 08–82402, *Bull. Crim.* 2009, n° 25.

debate about the place of Islam in French society, the islamization of France or Muslim-immigration, in which the preservation of the laic character of the French Republic plays an important role and in which the scope of freedom of expression of a representative is equal to the freedom of any other citizen. The interest in a free political debate on a matter of public interest can, however, not remove the punishable character of expression that disqualifies in harsh terms a determined group by depicting it as criminal or dangerous for French society exclusively on the ground of their race or religion and therefore constitutes an offence pursuant to Article 24–8.

7. Modifications of the Pleven Act

After the adoption of the Pleven Act in 1972, several draft proposals to criminalize racist propaganda and the diffusion of racist ideas have failed (7.1), while the hate speech bans have successfully been extended to the discriminatory grounds of sex, sexual preference and handicap (7.2). The analysis results in a general conclusion about the evolution of the Pleven Act of 1972 and the criminalization of hate speech in French law (7.3).

7.1. Draft proposals to modify the Pleven Act in order to criminalize racist propaganda or the diffusion of racist and xenophobic ideas

It results from the French vision of freedom of expression of opinion that racist propaganda or the diffusion of racist and xenophobic ideas *as such* that do not exhibit any link to an act of racial discrimination against a specific designated group do not fall under the scope of the French hate speech bans. In 1989, the TGI Paris considered that the simple manifestation of a preference for ideologies that refuse 'the mixing of races' without manifestly inciting to commit one of the acts criminalized by law did not constitute a provocation to discrimination in the sense of Article 24–8.[1243] In order to – more effectively – fight such racist propaganda or diffusion of racist and xenophobic ideas, several draft proposals to modify the Pleven Act have been made.

In 1993, a draft proposal sought the insertion of an offence penalizing racist propaganda, defined as 'the effort to promote racism as such' into the French Penal Code that would complement the 1881 Press Act in order to tackle the problem in a more permanent manner and to circumvent the strict procedural rules of the 1881 Press Act. The proposal was inspired by the suggestions made by LICRA.[1244] According to La direction des Affaires criminelles et des Grâces, however, the

[1243] TGI de Paris, 12 July 1989, *Légipresse,* 1989, n°66-I, p.69.

[1244] Secondi-Nix, M., *Lutte contre le racisme et justice pénale, Rôle des associations,* CNRS, CESDIP, October 1996, pp.60–61.

offence was unclearly demarcated and would overlap with the offences of racial defamation and insult in the 1881 Press Act. It therefore preferred a fusion of the offences of racial defamation and insult into one single and broader offence that would be inserted into the Press Act.[1245]

Subsequently, in 1994, a draft proposal concerning 'la lutte contre la diffusion d'idées racistes ou xénophobes' proposed to fuse the offences of racial defamation and insult into one offence and sought the insertion of an Article 25 into the 1881 Press Act penalizing 'la diffusion d'idées racistes ou xénophobes', for which derogatory procedural rules would apply.[1246] The *Commission nationale consultative des droits de l'homme* (CNCDH), however, advised changing the title of the proposal in 'la lutte contre la propagation du racisme et de la xénophobie' and to maintain the two distinct infractions of the Pleven Act.[1247] After this text, no further legislative action was taken.

In 1996, the expression by Le Pen 'Je crois à l'inégalité des races' during a summer university of the extreme right winged political party Le Front National caused a scandal and revived the debate concerning the necessity of law reform. The Minister of Justice, Jacques Toubon,[1248] proposed a draft proposal 'renforçant la répression de la diffusion de messages racistes ou xénophobes'. The draft proposal proposed the replacement of the offences of racial defamation, racial insult and provocation to racial discrimination, hatred or violence with a new offence penalizing 'le fait de diffuser, par quelque moyen que ce soit, un message portant atteinte à la dignité, l'honneur, ou la considération d'une personne ou d'un ou plusieurs groupes de personnes en raison de leur appartenance ou non-appartenance, vraie ou supposée, à une ethnie, une nation, une race ou une religion, qu'elle soit ou non déterminée ou non déterminée'.[1249] As the new offence enabled the prosecution of expression that was merely offensive according to its tenor and no longer required that expression to be defamatory, insulting or provocative and directly addressing a person or a group, this offence encompassed most racial and anti-religious expression. The draft was more far-reaching than previous proposals in the sense that it envisioned a complete removal of the offences with a racial character from the 1881 Press Act and the insertion of the new offence in the French Penal Code. In so doing, the prosecution of all racist expression would no longer be bound by the strict procedural rules of the 1881 Press Act.

The associations LICRA, MRAP and SOS Racisme declared that they were in favour of such reform in light of an effective prosecution, while the association la Ligue des Droits de l'Homme (LDH) advocated the preservation of the press

---

1245 Secondi-Nix, M., *Lutte contre le racisme et justice pénale, Rôle des associations*, CNRS, CESDIP, October 1996, p.60 *et seq.*

1246 De Lamy 2000, p.326.

1247 Avis concernant un avant-projet de loi relative à la 'lutte contre la diffusion d'idées racistes ou xénophobes', *CNCDH* 3 November 1994, accessible at: www.cncdh.fr.

1248 Member of the political party RPR (Le Rassemblement pour la République) that merged into the UMP in 2002.

1249 Cited in: Derieux, E., Lutte contre le racisme, *Légipresse* n° 135, October 1996, p.122.

offences and the mere amendment of their procedural rules.[1250] The CNCDH, however, advised that the legal arsenal against racism within the framework of the 1881 Press Act be maintained and that a new Article 25 that criminalizing the 'atteinte à la dignité à caractere raciale' should be introduced.[1251] As the CNCDH feared that the draft proposal would be too general and would establish a moral regime, it excluded all reference to a religion.[1252] Derieux has criticized the draft proposal, arguing that it would be better to revise the strict procedural rules of the 1881 Press Act altogether.[1253] The proposal received considerable media attention, where it has notably been criticized for being prompted by the circumstances and uniquely directed against the expression of Le Pen.[1254] The project has finally been abandoned and was never discussed before Parliament. In 1998, the Aix-en-Provence Court of Appeal acquitted Le Pen considering that the expression 'Je crois à l'inégalité des races' merely constituted an opinion and not a provocation to racial hatred.[1255]

7.2. The Act of 30 December 2004: extension of the scope of the Pleven Act to the discriminatory grounds of sex, sexual preference and handicap

The Act of 30 December 2004 concerning 'la Haute autorité de lutte contre les discriminations et pour l'égalité', primarily created an independent administrative authority for the fight against discriminations (la HALDE),[1256] that has since been brought under *le Défenseur des droits*, the French Ombudsman, created by the Act of 23 July 2008 concerning the modernization of the institutions of the Fifth

1250 Secondi-Nix, M., *Lutte contre le racisme et justice pénale, Rôle des associations*, CNRS, CESDIP, October 1996, pp.62–63.

1251 Avis portant sur un projet de loi renforcant la repression de la diffusion de messages racistes ou xenophobes, *CNCDH* 26 September 1996, accessible at: www.cncdh.fr; Bernard, P., La commission consultative veut une réécriture du projet Toubon; Elle en approuve le principe, estimant la législation antiraciste inadaptée, *Le Monde* 28 September 1996.

1252 Boulègue 2010, pp.73–74.

1253 Derieux 1996, p.122.

1254 Mazeaud, P., La bêtise doit-elle tomber sous le coup de la loi?, *Le Monde* 21 September 1996; Gaubert, P., Le Pen raciste: légiférer enfin, *Le Monde* 21 September 1996; Bernard, P., L'avant-projet de loi antiraciste élargit le champ de la répression; Visant explicitement l'extrême droite, le texte élaboré par Jacques Toubon fait du racisme un délit de droit commun et sanctionne la diffusion de messages racistes ou xénophobes. Les associations approuvent cette démarche, qui suscite des réserves au sein du RPR, *Le Monde* 23 September 1996; Chemin, A., Le projet de loi contre le racisme va punir la diffusion de messages racistes; Selon M. Toubon, des propos anti-français pourront être poursuivis, *Le Monde* 17 October 1996; Montvalon, J.-B. de, Les députés RPR et UDF récusent le projet antiraciste de M. Toubon, *Le Monde* 18 October 1996; Chombeau, C., L'extrême droite mène campagne contre le projet de loi sur le racisme, *Le Monde* 23 October 1996.

1255 CA Aix-en-Provence 9 March 1998, *JCP* 1999, IV, n°2764.

1256 Loi n° 2004–1486 du 30 Decembre 2004 portant sur la creation de la Haute autorité de lutte contre les discriminations et pour l'égalité, *JO* 31 December 2004.

Republic (1958-present).[1257] Furthermore, the Act of 30 December 2004 modified the 1881 Press Act and extended the scope of the Pleven Act by inserting into the 1881 Press Act offences penalizing sexist and homophobic expression. While the Act of 15 June 2000 suppressed the penalty of imprisonment from the press offences that they had provided for until then,[1258] the penalty of imprisonment had been preserved with regard to the press offences of a racist and discriminatory nature, being the offences of racial defamation, racial insult, racial provocation, and the offence of Holocaust denial in accordance with Article 24*bis* (para.9 *infra*). The legislator of 2004 adopted the same approach with regard to the repression of sexist and homophobic expression.

The modifications that the Act of 30 December 2004 brought to the 1881 Press Act were threefold. Firstly, the Act created the offences of defamation and insult on the ground of sex, sexual orientation or handicap that resemble the offences of racial defamation and racial insult. It inserted Articles 32–3 and 33–4 into the Press Act that sanction defamation and insult against a person or a group 'à raison de leur sexe, de leur orientation sexuelle ou de leur handicap', with a year imprisonment and a fine of € 45,000 and six months imprisonment and a fine of € 22,500 respectively (both with the supplementary sanction of the publication of the decision).

Secondly, the Act created the offence of provocation on the ground of sex, sexual orientation or handicap that differs from the offence of racial provocation. It inserted Article 24–9 into the Press Act that sanctions the provocation to discrimination '*prévues par les articles 225–2 et 432–7 du Code pénal*', hatred and violence against a person or a group 'à raison de leur sexe, de leur orientation sexuelle ou de leur handicap' with a year imprisonment and a fine of € 45,000. Contrary to Article 24–8, Article 24–9 thus specifies that expression must provoke discrimination consisting of the refusal to supply goods or services; obstructing the normal exercise of any given economic activity; the refusal to hire, to sanction or to dismiss a person; subjecting the supply of goods or services to a condition; subjecting an offer of employment, an application for a course or a training period to a condition; or the refusal of the benefit of a right conferred by the law or hindering the normal exercise of any given economic activity to a natural or legal person the public authority or public service official. On this point the offence is thus more restrictive.[1259]

Thirdly, with regard to these press offences of a sexist or homophobic character, the Act created rules for the engagement of proceedings by the Public Prosecution

---

[1257] Article 71–1 of the La loi constitutionnelle n° 2008–724 du 23 juillet 2008 de modernisation des institutions de la Ve République.

[1258] Loi n° 2000–516 du 15 juin 2000 renforçant la protection de la présomption d'innocence et les droits des victimes.

[1259] Monfort, J-Y, Les nouvelles incriminations de la loi du 30 décembre 2004 au regard de la liberté d'expression et des droits de l'homme, *GP* 17 December 2005, n°351, p.2 *et seq.*

and associations that resemble those in the field of racial discrimination. In Article 48, sub-paragraph 6, it extended the possibility for the Public Prosecution to take the initiative to prosecute in the field of defamation and insult of a sexist or homophobic character against a group of persons, without the need to request the consent of the victim thereto. Contrarily, when sexist or homophobic expression concerns one person individually, a prosecution cannot be engaged without the victim's consent thereto. With regard to these French hate speech bans on the grounds of sex, sexual orientation and handicap, in Articles 48–4 – 48–6, it conferred on associations the rights afforded to the civil parties and permitted associations to set in motion the public prosecution, in the event that the Public Prosecution remained inactive. This right to institute legal proceedings can only be exercised by associations that have been declared five years before the occurrence of the facts and that according to their statutes have the objective of combatting violence and discrimination based on sex, sexual orientation and handicap. What is more, when sexist or homophobic expression concerns one person individually, the complaint of an association is only admissible if it has obtained the victim's consent thereto. However, the Act did not amend Article 65–3, which provides for a prescriptive period of one year with regard to the press offences with a racial character. Consequently, press offences with a sexist or homophobic character are subject to a prescriptive period of three months. However, since 2011, a legislative proposal is being prepared in order to align the prescriptive period with that of the press offences with a racial character (para. 1.3.1 *supra*).[1260]

The initial proposal of law reform provoked a lively debate between its advocates and opponents in the public opinion.[1261] The criticism concerned both the opportunity of the legislation and its conformity with the French Constitution and the ECHR, more generally its compatibility with the right to freedom of expression. On 18 November 2004, the CNCDH adopted the advice to withdraw the proposal.[1262] The CNCDH strongly rejected this multiplication of categories of persons in need of a specific protection, because it constituted a segmentation of human rights that violated their universality and indivisibility; such Communitarainism was contrary to the French traditions and legal principles, notably the right to freedom of expression. The CNCDH considered: 'Parce que c'est l'être humain en tant que tel, et non en raison de certains traits de sa personne,

1260 Proposition de loi n°3794, *relative à la suppression de la discrimination dans les délais de prescription prévus par la loi sur la liberté de la presse du 29 juillet 1881*, deposé le 5 Décembre 2011. For the status of the legislative procedure see: www.senat.fr/dossier-legislatif/ppl11–122.html#block-timeline. See also Proposition de loi n° 265, visant à *porter* de *trois mois* à *un an* le *délai* de *prescription* des *propos injurieux* ou *diffamatoires* à *caractère homophobe, transphobe, sexiste* ou à raison du *handicap*, deposé le 16 Janvier 2013 au Sénat.

1261 Padova, Y., Liberté d'expression versus repression du sexisme et de l' homophobie, À propos de la loi du 30 décembre 2004, *GP* 17 March 2005, n° 76, p.2 *et seq.*

1262 Avis sur le projet de loi relative à la lutte contre les propos discriminatoires à caractère sexiste ou homophobe, *CNCDH* 18 November 2004, available at: www.cncdh.fr.

qui doit être respecté et protégé, la CNCDH émet des réserves sur la multiplication des catégories de personnes nécessitant une protection spécifique. Cette segmentation de la protection des droits de l'homme remet en cause leur universalité et leur indivisibilité. Légiférer afin de protéger une catégorie de personnes risque de se faire au détriment des autres, et, à terme, de porter atteinte à l'égalité des droits (…) qu'il n'était pas démontré que l'orientation sexuelle d'une personne ou d'un groupe de personnes génère une vulnérabilité nécessitant une protection spécifique de l'État. (…) C'est par la libre communication des pensées et des opinions (…) et non par la répression que la société française a progressé et continuera à progresser vers l'acceptation des différences et le respect de la dignité de chaque être humain.'[1263]

Subsequently, the Government abandoned its initial project for several months and amended its provisions into less controversial provisions.[1264] The initial proposal envisioned the creation of the offences of defamation and insult merely of a homophobic character and not also on the ground of sex. The Government has endorsed the criticism made by the associations defending the rights of women that the fact that the law would consider defamation or insult of women less reprehensible than defamation or insult of homosexuals.[1265] Associations defending the rights of homosexuals, for their part, criticized the imprecision of the discriminatory ground 'orientation sexuelle' that merely signifies a person's sexual preference; transsexuals could therefore fall outside its scope. Padova argues that the same should apply to pedophiles, because legal sexual practices deserve protection.[1266] The scope of the discriminatory ground is to be determined in case law.

The initial proposal furthermore envisioned the creation of the offence of provocation to discrimination without further specifying the notion of discrimination. As the definition of discrimination in Article 225–1 concerned *every distinction* between persons on the ground of – amongst others – their sexual orientation, the effect of a broad interpretation of the notion could be that the offence would comprise of the provocation to legal discriminations.[1267] An example of a legal form of discrimination on the ground of sexual orientation under French law is the *former* impossibility of same sex marriage. Based on this reasoning, certain representatives of the monotheistic religions especially from the Catholic Church, such as Cardinal Lustiger, raised their concern – as part of the advice of the CNCDH – that the effect of the act was to prohibit religious texts that strongly condemn homosexuality, the possibility for religious adherents to publicly proclame personal religious convictions based on such texts or to oppose on the ground of

1263 Avis sur le projet de loi relative à la lutte contre les propos discriminatoires à caractère sexiste ou homophobe, *CNCDH* 18 November 2004, available at: www.cncdh.fr.

1264 Monfort 2005, p.2 et seq.

1265 Padova 2005, p.2 *et seq.*

1266 Padova 2005, p.2 *et seq.*

1267 Padova 2005, p.2 *et seq.*

their religious convictions proposals of law reform that seek, for example, the legalization of gay marriage. Under the initial proposal such latter expression would constitute provocation to discrimination against homosexuals, merely because it pleads in favour of the preservation of the legal regime that was existent at the time, which differed on the ground of a person's sexual orientation.[1268] Bigot reduces this discussion to the core principles of the French traditional conception of freedom of opinion and stipulates that 'la répression de l'action ne doit pas être confondue avec la répression de l'opinion, surtout lorsqu'il s'agit de s'appuyer sur des critères communautaristes. Nemélangeons pas les actes et les propos.' While in French law certain sexist and homophobic acts are repressed in several offences where the sexual orientation of the victim forms an aggravating circumstance, such as Article 221–4 sub-paragraph 7 of the French penal Code penalizing 'le meurtre à raison de l'orientation sexuelle de la victime', contrarily, French law should not criminalize opinions that might hurt certain feelings.[1269]

The Government has endorsed the criticism made by the CNCDH and religious representatives by specifying that in order for expression to be punishable on the ground of Article 24–9, it must provoke discrimination *'prévues par les articles 225–2 et 432–7 du Code pénal'*. The French legislator has thus signified that the offence of provocation to discrimination on the ground of sex, sexual orientation or handicap is not constituted, if expression provokes discrimination that is not criminalized under French law. Padova argues that the French legislator had better chosen to repress 'les provocations aux discriminations 'illegales''. The criminalization of provocation to illegal discrimination would assure that a debate concerning legal discriminations on the ground of sexual orientation, such as the impossibility of gay marriage – at that time –, would remain possible and has the advantage that it does not have to enumerate all illegal acts of discrimination on the ground of sex, orientation and handicap.[1270] From this strand of thought, Veron criticizes the decision made by the French legislator for creating new problems; homosexuals are not merely the victim of provocation to acts of discrimination enumerated in Articles 225–2 et 432–7 of the French Criminal Code.[1271]

It is stipulated that in 2012, leading up to the approval by the French National Assembly of a bill to allow same sex marriage and adoption, large protests against the bill were held by notably religious, conservative groupings and a significant increase of acts of violence and hate speech, particularly on the Internet, against homosexuals was recorded.[1272] The 'marriage for all' law was finally passed on

1268 Position du Cardinal Jean-Marie Lustiger, annex to: Avis sur le projet de loi relative à la lutte contre les propos discriminatoires à caractère sexiste ou homophobe, *CNCDH* 18 November 2004, available at: www.cncdh.fr.

1269 Bigot, C., Sexisme, homophobie et liberté d'expression, *Légipresse* n° 209, March 2004, pp.35–36.

1270 Padova 2005, p.2 *et seq.*

1271 Veron, M., La lutte contre le sexisme et l'homophobie, *Dr. pén.* n° 12, December 2004, p.3.

1272 Www.sos-homophobie.org/rapport-annuel-2013.

17 May 2013[1273] after the Constitutional Council declared it compatible with the French Constitution.[1274] Before, the speech offences of a sexist and homophobic character have, however, generally not frequently been applied. The French Supreme Court has had the opportunity to set out the criteria of the offence of insult on the ground of sexual orientation in its decision of 12 November 2008. The Court annulled the condemnation of the Douai Court of Appeal with regard to the statement made by a representative in an interview in the magazine 'La Voix du Nord' that homosexuality was morally inferior to heterosexuality and constituted certain behavior performed by individuals, but not a characteristic of the identity of a group or a community comparable to race or ethnic background. The Court of Appeal had considered that people's sexual orientation does not merely refer to their behaviour, but also defines their identity and homophobic insults, therefore, violate their human dignity. According to the Court the statements were 'offensants et contraires à la dignité des personnes visées en ce qu'ils tendaient à souligner l'infériorité morale de l'homosexualité alors que les fondements philosophiques de ce jugement de valeur ne s'inscrivaient pas dans un débat de pensée'.[1275] Contrarily, the Supreme Court found that 'les propos litigieux, qui avaient été tenus dans la suite des débats et du vote de la loi du 30 décembre 2004, ont pu heurter la sensibilité de certaines personnes homosexuelles, leur contenu ne dépasse pas les limites de la liberté d'expression.'[1276] The mere moral rejection of homosexual behavior or practices that might hurt the feelings of homosexuals does not thus fall under the scope of the offence.

7.3. Conclusion

The French legislator has envisioned several modifications of the 1972 Plevent Act that all saw at the enlargement of its scope in order to – more effectively – fight against racism and discrimination. The proposals that sought the criminalization of racist propaganda or the diffusion of racist and xenophobic ideas *as such* that do not exhibit any link to an act of racial discrimination against a specific designated group have been abandoned and since these texts, no further legislative action has been taken. The proposals seem to be at odds with the traditional requirements that the press offences must criminalize, in strictly circumscribed terms, the abuses of freedom of expression of opinion, which have a clear link with a reprehensible act so as not to constitute délits d'opinion. According to their wording, the proposals were rather aimed at the protection of people against opinions that violate their human dignity.

1273 LOI n° 2013–404 du 17 mai 2013, *ouvrant le mariage aux couples de personnes de même sexe, JORF* n° 114 du 18 mai 2013 p. 8253, texte n° 3.

1274 Cons. Con. 17 May 2013, n° 2013–669 DC.

1275 CA Douai 25 January 2007, annotation B. Ader 'Injure à raison de l'orientation sexuelle: les limites de la liberté d''opinion'', *Légipresse* 2007, n° 242-III, p.139.

1276 French Supreme Court, crim.ch., 12 November 2008, n° 07–83398, *Bull. Crim.* 2008, n° 229.

The Act of 30 December 2004 that extended the scope of the offences of racial defamation, insult and provocation to the discriminatory grounds of sex, sexual orientation or handicap seems to comply with the traditional requirements. The Government has even specified that in order for expression to be punishable on the ground of Article 24–9, it must provoke to discriminations *'prévues par les articles 225–2 et 432–7 du Code pénal'*, thus punishable forms of discrimination. It thereby seems to have endorsed the criticism that the Act would criminalize mere opinions on homosexual behavior or practices that might hurt the feelings of homosexuals and would therefore introduce délits d'opinion. This is prevented by a strict interpretation of the offences in case law.

8. The Gayssot Act of 13 July 1990

With the adoption of the Gayssot Act of 13 July 1990 the French legislator aimed to create an adequate legal response to the increase of negationistic discourse and anti-Semitic acts in the eighties and nineties of the former century that appeared difficult to qualify under the existing hate speech bans (8.1). The Gayssot Act notably introduced the offence of Holocaust denial into French law, but also brought a number of changes with regard to the existing hate speech bans (8.2). The analysis results in a general conclusion about the background and purport of the Gayssot Act (8.3).

8.1. The situation prior to the adoption of the Gayssot Act of 13 July 1990

Before the creation of the Gayssot Act of 13 July 1990, revisionist expression, consisting of expression that puts up for discussion the history of the Second World War and tends to deny or minimize the genocide of the Jews by the Nazis,[1277] could only be prosecuted on the ground of the French hate speech bans of racial defamation, racial insult, racial provocation or offences of apology, such as the apology of crimes against humanity in Article 24–3 of the Press Act. The absence of a specific offence penalizing revisionist or negationist discourse, however, entailed several problems related to the qualification of the facts.

In 1954, the French Supreme Court confirmed a condemnation of the author Maurice Bardèche with regard to his book *Nuremberg ou la terre promise* on the ground of article 24–1 penalizing the apology of the crime of murder. The decision was motivated rather by the fact that Bardèche had manifested his anti-Semitism and Nazi sympathies than by the fact that he had actually made an apology of a crime of murder.[1278] In that same year, the French Supreme Court declared an association inadmissible in its prosecution of the author Paul Rassiner on the ground of the offences of insult and defamation with regard to his book *Le*

1277 Le Petit Larousse illustré, dictionnaire encyclopédique, édition 1997, Paris: Larousse 1997.

1278 French Supreme Court, crim.ch., 11 February 1954, *Bull. Crim.* 1954, n°71.

mensonge d'Ulysse, a study on the living conditions in concentration camps based on his own experiences, in which he contested the existence of gas chambers in Buchenwald, and acquitted the author.[1279]

According to Droin, negationist discourse was most often successfully repressed on the ground of the offence of racial defamation.[1280] The difficulty of retaining the offence of racial provocation lay in the requirement to prove the intention of the author to provoke, because the expression was often presented as a – pseudo – historical or scientific work. For example, in 1983, the French Supreme Court endorsed the condemnation by the Court of Appeal of Robert Faurisson on the ground of racial defamation, but also endorsed its acquittal on the ground of provocation to racial hatred with regard to his expressions 'Le prétendu génocide des juifs'; 'mensonge historique'; 'la gigantesque escroquerie politico-financière dont bénéficièrent et l'état d'Israël et le sionisme international et les juifs de la diaspora'.[1281]

Because of the difficulties victims of negationist expression met when trying to obtain a condemnation on the ground of the press offences, they increasingly turned to the civil judge seeking a condemnation on the ground of Article 1382 of the Civil Code.[1282] The civil judges who lacked the guidance of precise statutory elements of the press offences were thus confronted with the task of giving judgments in historical questions. Droin analyses how the civil judges, in order to avoid having to judge historical truths, focussed on the scientific method that the authors of negationist expression used, but by doing so could not escape from mixing in the free practice of historical research.[1283]

One famous case based on the ground of Article 1382 CC is the affair of 'le point de détail'. In May 1990, Le Pen was condemned on the ground of 1382 CC for having stated in a radio interview that the use of gas chambers in order to exterminate the Jews was a 'point de détail' in the history of the Second World War. This decision was confirmed in appeal. In 1995, the French Supreme Court rejected an appeal. The Court considered that the victims could act on the ground of 1382 CC, because the expression did not constitute any of the press offences of the Act of 1 July 1972. The Court endorsed the consideration of the Court of Appeal that the expression did not constitute the offence of racial provocation, but was nevertheless shocking and intolerable and 'rendait moins spécifiquement dramatiques les persécutions et les souffrances infligées'. For this reason the expression constituted a wrongful act in accordance with 1382 CC.[1284]

It was the particular difficulties in qualifying negationist expression as one of the French hate speech bans which, in the eighties and nineties of the twentieth

1279 French Supreme Court, crim.ch., 16 December 1954, *Bull. Crim.* 1954, n°410.
1280 Droin 2009, p.216.
1281 French Supreme Court, crim.ch., 28 June 1983, *Bull. Crim.* 1983, n°202.
1282 Droin 2009, p.216 *et seq.*
1283 Droin 2009, p.217.
1284 French Supreme Court, civ.ch. II, 18 December 1995, n°91–14785, *Bull.* 1995 II, n°314, p.184.

century, prevented an adequate legal response to the increase of negationistic discourse and anti-Semitic acts. In May 1990 the profanation of over thirty Jewish graves in a cemetery in Carpentras shocked the country. In response, many manifestations against racism and anti-Semitism were organized.[1285] In this political context, the French legislator decided that legislative reform was necessary.

8.2. The merit of the Gayssot Act

8.2.1. Rationale of the Gayssot Act of 13 July 1990

In 1990 Jean-Claude Gayssot, representative of the Communist group in the National Assembly deposed at the National Assembly a draft act seeking to reinforce the existing anti-racism and discrimination legislation created by the Pleven Act of 1 July 1972 in order to more effectively fight against racism. The proposal aimed at several modifications of the 1881 Press Act, but notably proposed the creation of the offence of denial of crimes against humanity committed by the Nazi regime in Article 9. During the parliamentary debates, the insufficiency of existent anti-racism and discrimination laws as a direct cause or rationale of the proposal was clearly articulated by Gayssot and Pierre Arpaillange, the Minister of Justice representing the Government that was in favour of the proposal. Gayssot considered 'la multiplication des crimes racistes montre jusqu'à quelle extrémité peut conduire le poison du racisme. Le Parlement français se doit de participer au combat avec la plus grande vigueur face à cette dérive dangereuse pour la démocratie et les droits de l'homme. Un sursaut est nécessaire.'[1286] And 'Malgré l'existence de la loi de 1972, les délits racistes restent trop souvent impunis ou insuffisamment réprimés, et des théories racistes, des incitations au crime tendent à être assimilées à des idées comme les autres, et leurs auteurs traités comme des interlocuteurs ordinaires, sinon privilégiés. Il est donc nécessaire de renforcer les moyens légaux et juridiques de lutte contre le racisme, qui compléteraient de manière significative les textes existants.'[1287]

Arpaillange explained 'Certes, les écrits qui contestent la réalité de l'holocauste contiennent en général, pour le soutien de leur argumentation, des allégations telles qu'elles caractérisent des infractions soit de diffamation raciale, soit de provocation à la haine, à la discrimination ou à la violence raciale. Et les auteurs sont à ce titre poursuivis. Mais j'ai constaté aussi que ces auteurs, qui, sans doute, ont fait l'apprentissage de la loi sur la presse, sont de plus en plus prudents et s'entendent parfaitement à donner à leur écrits une résonance raciste que les incriminations pénales existantes ne permettent pas d'appréhender totalement.'[1288]

1285 'Grandes affaires criminelles 28 – 1990. La profanation de Carpentras. Des tombes juives vandalisées', in: *Le Monde* 11 August 2006.
1286 Parliamentary debates, *JO* 2 May 1990, French national assembly, p.917.
1287 Parliamentary debates, *JO* 2 May 1990, French national assembly, p.919.
1288 Parliamentary debates, *JO* 2 May 1990, French national assembly, p.905.

In the vision of its proponents, the aim of the Act was also to protect the French Republic itself, because the banalization of acts of racism not only violated humanity, but also the central characteristics or values of the French Republic. One representative considered 'Qu'entendons-nous en face, sinon un discours idéologique qui tend à banaliser ce qui est une infraction majeure contre notre Constitution, contre les principes qui fondent notre démocratie et notre République? Oui, c'est en répondant par les lois de la République, c'est-à-dire l'égalité, la liberté, la fraternité, la laïcité, c'est en répondant sur le plan idéologique que nous combattrons le racisme et que nous éviterons la banalisation exécrable de ces crimes non pas seulement contre l'humanité mais aussi contre notre nation, contre notre patrie.'[1289] Another representative exclaimed 'c'est fondamentalement un texte de défense de la République.'[1290]

Contrary to the Pleven Act of 1 July 1972 that had been adopted unanimously by the National Assembly and the Senate, the proposal met severe criticism during the drafting in both the National Assembly and the Senate. The criticism primarily concerned Article 9, because the offence of denial of crimes against humanity would be contrary to the right to freedom of expression of opinion and free historical research. The Act thus formed the object of a sharp-tongued debate between its proponents, who consisted of representatives of the socialist and communist groups, and its opponents, representatives of the conservative and right winged parties Rassemblement pour la République (RPR), Union pour la démocratie française (UDF) and the Front National.

Opponents of the Act argued that the existent anti-racism and discrimination laws were sufficient in order to counter racist expression. Phillippe de Villiers, representative of UDF, stated 'Ce texte cherche à accréditer l'idée que la France serait devenue un pays raciste! (.) la France est le pays au monde le moins raciste qui soit. Nous ne pouvons pas tolérer d'entendre dire que la France est un pays raciste.'[1291] and thus seemed to deny the existence of acts of racism in France in order to honour the French democratic ideal that in France only equal citizens existed. One of the most ardent opponents of the Act was Marie-France Stirbois, the only representative of the Front National in Parliament. Stirbois expressed the fear that the ever expanding French anti-racism and discrimination laws rendered any criticism concerning immigration and foreigners impossible and cited famous Greek philosophers of democracy who refused to equate citizens and foreigners in order to protect a democratic society from foreign dangers.[1292] This argument was, however, severely contradicted by the other representatives who argued amongst others 'il y a bien longtemps que notre société est bâtie sur d'autres bases que celles des philosophes grecs, même si l'on peut avoir le plus grand respect pour Platon et

1289 Parliamentary debates, *JO* 2 May 1990, French national assembly, p.912.
1290 Parliamentary debates, *JO* 2 May 1990, French national assembly, p.929.
1291 Parliamentary debates, *JO* 2 May 1990, French national assembly, p.907.
1292 Parliamentary debates, *JO* 2 May 1990, French national assembly, p.909.

ses disciples. La société divisée en classes ou en ordres, avec des esclaves ou des serfs, des guerriers, des maîtres ou des seigneurs, elle a disparu en 1789!'[1293]

The lively parliamentary debates caused the Minister of Justice to sigh: 'J'aurais souhaité retrouver l'unanimité de 1972. A l'époque, le Parlement avait oublié ses querelles partisans pour s'engager de manière résolue dans la lutte contre le racisme.'[1294] The National Assembly finally adopted the Act by a majority of 307 against 265 votes.[1295] However, the Senate adopted a motion by a majority of 216 votes against 92 that signified the rejection of the proposal, primarily because it considered the offence of denial of crimes against humanities to constitute a 'délit d'opinion'.[1296] The National Assembly disregarded the position of the Senate and nevertheless adopted the final text of the Act on 30 June 1990 on the request of the Government.[1297]

8.2.2. The criminalization of revisionism

The Gayssot Act of 13 July 1990 primarily created in Article 9 of the Act the new offence of denial of crimes against humanities committed by the Nazi regime, also referred to as the offence of Holocaust denial. The main accusation of the opponents was that this offence formed a délit d'opinion. According to Stirbois, the offence of provocation to racial hatred and violence introduced by the French legislator in 1972 already constituted a délit d'opinion, because the terms hatred and violence did not constitute punishable acts but merely a sentiment, respectively an attitude and because it was not required that the provocation was direct. Likewise, Article 9 criminalized the expression of an opinion and not the support of a criminal act by repressing the denial of a history established by the Tribunal of Nuremberg. The Gayssot Act formed a memorial law; it signified the establishment of an official history, thus government declared truth, and altered judges into historians.[1298] According to Stirbois, however, the criminalization of racism was to be strictly defined and the independence of the judges was to be assured.[1299] Jacques Toubon, representative of RPR, equally argued that judges already found difficulties in the application of the Pleven Act of 1972 and often risked the violation of freedom of expression by sanctioning opinions and thus approaching the délit d'opinion. It was therefore better not to add a new offence that would cause even more delicate problems for judges and not to 'laisse le soin aux juges de faire le boulot!'[1300]

1293 Parliamentary debates, *JO* 2 May 1990, French national assembly, p.912.
1294 Parliamentary debates, *JO* 28 June 1990, French national assembly, p.3196.
1295 Parliamentary debates, *JO* 2 May 1990, French national assembly, p.962.
1296 Parliamentary debates, *JO* 11 June 1990, French Senate, p.1464.
1297 Parliamentary debates, *JO* 28 June 1990, French national assembly, p. 3103 *et seq.*
1298 Parliamentary debates, *JO* 2 May 1990, French national assembly, p.933.
1299 Parliamentary debates, *JO* 2 May 1990, French national assembly, p.914.
1300 Parliamentary debates, *JO* 2 May 1990, French national assembly, p.956.

Furthermore, the opponents criticized the Communist origin of the proposal and stipulated the danger for the state to intervene in history by viciously recalling the massacre of over 2000 Polish people in Katyn in 1940. It had been the USSR – thus Communists themselves – that had tried to falsify history during the Nuremberg trials by imputing the Nazis of these crimes that had been actually committed by the Russian police on orders from Stalin, which the Communist group had refused to acknowledge for a long time.[1301] The opponents opposed the introduction of a special protection of the Jewish community with regard to the Holocaust, where other communities and genocides lacked such protection; such a 'loi d'exception' was contrary to the spirit of the republican legislator who had the task of creating texts of a general application.[1302] The opponents also contradicted the effectiveness of the law. The law would be counter-productive; the criminalization of the denial of crimes committed by the Nazis, more specifically of the Holocaust, signified the acknowledgement of the idea that one cannot doubt the reality of the Holocaust. Hence, the offence would turn negationnists into martyrs and their prosecution before a tribunal would offer them a stage to expound their racist propaganda.[1303] More generally, they regretted the repressive nature of the Act and advocated a more preventative approach through the continuous education of morality and tolerance.[1304]

The opponents found the Senate on their side that declared in its motion: 'Considérant que la création d'un délit de contestation de l'existence des crimes contre l'humanité conduirait à instituer une vérité historique officielle et instaurerait ainsi un délit d'opinion, que la falsification historique opérée par les auteurs d'écrits révisionnistes doit être démontrée et non condamnée pénalement sauf, comme le permet le droit actuel, lorsqu'elle s'accompagne de provocation à la discrimination, à la haine ou à la violence raciale, ou de diffamation ou d'injure à caractère raciste, et qu'enfin il appartient aux autorités disciplinaires de prendre les mesures éventuellement nécessaires à l'encontre d'enseignants qui diffuseraient les thèses révisionnistes auprès de leurs élèves.'[1305]

During the parliamentary debates, the Minister for Justice argued that the opponents of the Act overlooked the core starting point that Holocaust denial formed an expression of racism and the principle vector of anti-Semitism: 'la négation de l'holocauste n'est qu'une expression du racisme et le principal vecteur contemporain de l'antisémitisme. Avec ces pseudo-historiens, on revient un siècle en arrière, à Gobineau, à tous ces esprits égarés qui ont voulu donner une tournure scientifique à la peur, une justification à l'agression. C'est pourquoi, à mon sens, pour combattre

1301 Parliamentary debates, *JO* 2 May 1990, French national assembly, p.933.
1302 Parliamentary debates, *JO* 2 May 1990, French national assembly, p.934.
1303 Parliamentary debates, *JO* 2 May 1990, French national assembly, p.921.
1304 Parliamentary debates, *JO* 2 May 1990, French national assembly, p.907; p.926.
1305 Parliamentary debates, *JO* 11 June 1990, French Senate, p.1461.

ceux qui nient l'holocauste, il est vain de démontrer une fois encore la vérité de l'histoire. Ce n'est pas la question de la vérité qui est en jeu pour eux!'[1306]

The vision that racism did not constitute an opinion, but an offence, was expounded by most proponents of the Act: 'Le racisme, ce n'est pas une opinion, c'est un délit.'[1307] One représentative replied to Stirbois 'Madame, vous avez cité Platon et Aristote. Vous me permettrez de vous citer une réflexion de Jean Paul Sartre. (…) Jean Paul Sartre disait: 'Je me refuse à nommer opinion une doctrine qui vise expressément des personnes particulières et qui tend à supprimer leurs droits ou à les exterminer.'[1308]

The Minister for Justice even argued that racism constituted an aggression and for this reason wondered whether it would be better if the racist offences were inserted into the Penal Code: 'Le racisme n'est pas une opinion, c'est une agression! Chaque fois que le racisme parvient à s'exprimer, l'ordre public est immédiatement et gravement compromis.'[1309] 'Dès lors, la question n'est pas celle de la liberté d'expression ou de la liberté de la presse. Il n'y a pas de liberté qui tienne si cette liberté vise à agresser. C'est pour cela que j'ai posé la question de savoir si les délits racistes ne devraient pas être "sortis" de la loi sur la presse pour être inscrits dans le code pénal.'[1310] Toubon criticized the Minister of Justice's inconsistency in distinguishing between an opinion and an agression: 'Vous avez soutenu que le racisme n'était pas une opinion, mais une agression. Redoutable distinction! A partir de quand l'expression d'une idée cesse-t-elle d'être une opinion pour devenir une agression, pour qui, quand, comment, sur quel sujet? Distinction si redoutable que je vous invite à exclure d'urgence toutes ces infractions de la loi sur la presse. Sinon, sur ce terrain glissant, nous allons peu à peu embarquer la liberté d'expression et la liberté de la presse. Par conséquent, si vous voulez être cohérent avec vous-même, maintenez ces infractions et ces peines dans le code pénal mais sortez-les de la loi sur la presse!'[1311] The French legislator did not follow this advice. However, in order to avoid the creation of a délit d'opinion, he has provided for a most precise circumscription of the statutory elements of the offence (para.9.1–9.3 *infra*).[1312]

8.2.3. An aggravation of the sanctions of the hate speech bans

The Gayssot Act of 13 July 1990 further aggravated the sanctions of the existing – and new – French hate speech bans by offering the judge the possibility to

---

1306 Parliamentary debates, *JO* 2 May 1990, French national assembly, p.905.

1307 Parliamentary debates, *JO* 2 May 1990, French national assembly, p.909; p.912; p.918; p 919; p.929; p.930.

1308 Parliamentary debates, *JO* 2 May 1990, French national assembly, p.916.

1309 Parliamentary debates, *JO* 2 May 1990, French national assembly, p.902.

1310 Parliamentary debates, *JO* 2 May 1990, French national assembly, p.930.

1311 Parliamentary debates, *JO* 2 May 1990, French national assembly, p.952.

1312 Derieux, E., Répression du racisme de l'antisémitisme et de la xénophobie. Commentaire de la loi du 13 juillet 1990, *Légipresse* n° 75, October 1990, p.56.

pronounce supplementary penalties, such as the display and publication of the decision and the deprivation of certain civil rights, such as the right of eligibility and access to public functions. It was for this reason that the opponents of the Act, primarily Stirbois, accused the Communist group of creating a law that was prompted by the circumstances and solely aimed at Le Pen and the Front National, thus constituting a law *ad hominem*. The reporter of la commission des lois, Francois Asensi, had, however, explicitly recognized this aim of the Act in his report by considering 'Nous ne sommes plus en 1972 ou l'extrême-droite représentait au plus 2 p. 100 du corps électoral.'[1313] With regard to Le Pen and the Front National one representative remarked: 'dont nous ne partageons ni les valeurs ni le discours: mais nous ne vous permettrons pas aujourd'hui de faire une loi *ad hominem*![1314] The opponents accused the Act of constituting a 'loi scélérate', thereby referring to a series of laws created during the Third Republic (1870–1940) that aimed to repress the anarchistic movement.[1315]

The argument did not affect the Minister for Justice who replied 'le chef du parti de Mme Stirbois se sent visé et c'est quand même un bien étrange discours que de dire en même temps: je ne suis pas raciste, mais si vous faites de l'expression raciste un délit, je serai condamné. A ce dilemme, je propose à Mme Stirbois une solution: changer totalement de discours.'[1316]

8.2.4. *A reinforcement of the rights of anti-racism associations*

Finally, the Gayssot Act of 13 July 1990 reinforced the rights of anti-racism associations. Contrary to the Pleven Act of 1972, no associations were however involved at the drafting of the Gayssot Act. On the one hand, given the political climate, the government kept the associations away from the drafting debates under the pretexte of urgency. On the other hand, the associations did not desire to participate in the drafting debates, rightly because they considered it to be a political manoeuvre. The LDH opposed the creation of the offence of denial of crimes against humanity, while MRAP merely opposed its motivation; censoring the Front National.[1317]

Nevertheless, the Gayssot Act inserted Article 48–2 into the Press Act, which affords associations that according to their statutes defend 'les interest moraux et l'honneur de la Résistence ou des déportés' the right to set in motion a public prosecution on the ground of the new offence of denial of crimes against humanity, but also on the ground of the offences of 'apologie des crimes de guerre, des crimes contre l'humanité ou des crimes ou délits de collaboration avec l'ennemi' in

1313 Parliamentary debates, *JO* 2 May 1990, French national assembly, p.909.
1314 Parliamentary debates, *JO* 2 May 1990, French national assembly, p.906.
1315 Parliamentary debates, *JO* 2 May 1990, French national assembly, p.907; p.922.
1316 Parliamentary debates, *JO* 2 May 1990, French national assembly, p.931.
1317 Secondi-Nix, M., *Lutte contre le racisme et justice pénale, Rôle des associations*, CNRS, CESDIP, October 1996, pp.55–56.

Article 24–3 and constitute as a civil party. The Act also inserted a new Article 13–1 into the Press Act that afforded anti-racism associations the right of reply in the written and audiovisual press 'lors qu'une personne ou un groupe de personnes auront, dans un journal ou écrit périodique, fait l'objet d'imputations susceptibles de porter atteinte à leur honneur ou à leur réputation à raison de leur origine ou de leur appartenance ou de leur non-appartenance à une ethnie, une nation, une race ou une religion déterminée'. Article 13 already afforded such a right of reply to any person, comprising natural persons and corporate bodies, who has been personally affected. The extension was justified by the fact that victims of racial defamation are often not aware of their rights, do not dare to complain or demand that the media insert a response to the racist expression in question.[1318]

During the parliamentary debates the proposal to afford associations a right of reply in the media was severely contested on the ground of being counterproductive; every time an anti-racism association would use its right of reply in order to counter racist expression in the media, it would raise a discussion concerning racism.[1319] What is more, associations called into suspicion the – racist – nature of the media in question. The fact that during the drafting of the article no consultation with the professional media had taken place was therefore highly criticized.[1320] In order to prevent any abuse of the right of reply by associations the Act brought two restrictions. Firstly, with regard to racist expression that targets an individual person, an association can only exercise the right of reply when it has obtained the consent of the victim thereto. Secondly, if one association has exercised its right of reply 'aucune association ne pourra requérir l'insertion d'une réponse'.[1321]

8.3. Conclusion

The French legislator adopted the Gayssot Act of 13 July 1990 in order to more effectively fight against racism and discrimination. Its aim was to provide for an adequate legal response to the increase of negationistic discourse, which often could not be qualified under the existing French hate speech bans created by the Pleven Act of 1972, of anti-Semitic acts and of the rise of the political influence of the extreme right in the eighties and nineties of the previous century. As such manifestations of racism violated the central characteristics and values of the French Republic, the Actwas regarded as fundamentally defending the Republic. The merit of the Gayssot Act was threefold: the creation of the offence of denial of crimes against humanity; the aggravation of the sanctions of the French hate speech bans; and a reinforcement of the rights of anti-racism associations, consisting of the right to set in motion public prosecutions on the grounds of the offences of 24*bis*

1318 Véron, M., Le renforcement du dispositif répressif contre la discrimination et le racisme. Présentation des lois des 12 et 13 juillet 1990, *Dr. pén.* October 1990, p.3.

1319 Parliamentary debates, *JO* 2 May 1990, French national assembly, p.927.

1320 Parliamentary debates, *JO* 2 May 1990, French national assembly, p.949.

1321 Véron 1990, p.3.

and 24–3, constitute as a civil party and the right of reply in the media with regard to expression punishable on the ground of the French hate speech bans. Contrary to the Pleven Act of 1972 that had been adopted unanimously, the Gayssot Act met severe criticism during its drafting. The criticism primarily concerned the creation of the offence of denial of crimes against humanity; it would notably signify the establishment by the French legislator of an official history with regard to the Holocaust and thus constitute a 'délit d'opinion'. Contrarily, in the vision of the French legislator, pseudo-scientific negationistic discourse formed an expression of racism and the principle contemporary vector of anti-Semitism. Racism did not constitute an opinion, but a punishable act, an aggression that seriously violated the public order.

9. Holocaust denial

The offence of Holocaust denial is characterized by a number of elements, being denial (9.1), intent (9.2) and crimes against humanity (9.3). The constitutionality of the offence is a subject of controversy in French legal doctrine and is either claimed by reference to the value of human dignity or disputed on the basis that it constitutes a 'délit d'opinion' (9.4). The compatibility of the offence with international law comes as a result of international case law (9.5), which inspires French legal doctrine to consider revisionism punishable as an abuse of rights (9.6). The offence of Holocaust denial can be distinguished from the development of several 'memorial laws' since 1990 (9.7). The analysis results in a general conclusion about the offence of Holocaust denial in French law (9.8).

9.1. Denial

The Gayssot Act of 13 July 1990 inserted Article *24bis* into the 1881 Press Act that sanctions 'ceux qui auront contesté, par un des moyens énoncés à l'article 23, l'existence d'un ou plusieurs crimes contre l'humanité tels qu'ils sont définis par l'article 6 du statut du Tribunal militaire international annexé à l'accord de Londres du 8 août 1945 et qui ont été commis soit par les membres d'une organisation criminelle en application de l'article 9 dudit statut, soit par une personne reconnue coupable de tels crimes par une juridiction français ou internationale' with a fine of up to € 45.000 and or imprisonment of up to one year.[1322] Contrary to the non-public racial defamation and racial insult, the French legislator has not criminalized the non-public denial of crimes against humanity as a petty offence.

[1322] The tribunal can order the public display or dissemination of the decision taken in accordance with Article 131–35 of the French Penal Code and can deprive the offender of his right to be elected and his right to hold a judicial office, or to give an expert opinion before a court, or to represent or assist a party before a court of law for a maximum period of five years (Article 131–26 para. 2 and 3 French Penal Code).

The French legislator has criminalized not only the 'negation', but the 'contestation', the denial of crimes against humanity. The term permits to bring under its scope not only the total negation of a crime against humanity, but also the partial, nuanced, conditional or interrogative denial of such a crime.[1323] Although the question as to whether the term should be broadly or restrictively interpreted has divided legal scholars; the legislator seems to have brought under the scope of the offence all expression that puts up for discussion the exact reality of the crimes against humanity.[1324] The French Supreme Court has confirmed this by specifying that the offence of Article 24*bis* is even constituted, if the denial is presented 'sous une forme déguisée, dubitative ou par voie d'insinuation.'[1325] Expressions such as 'prétendu holocauste' or 'prétendues chambres à gaz' are therefore punishable on the ground of Article 24*bis*.[1326]

In principle, however, the minimization of the number of victims of the Holocaust as such does not fall under the scope of Article 24*bis*. This is only the case if the expression is excessive or exaggerated and has a clear revisionist intention and thus is clearly made in bad faith. In 1997, the French Supreme Court annulled an acquittal by the Court of Appeal with regard to the phrase 'Auschwitz 125,000 morts!' published in the November issue of the magazine *Révision* in 1992, considering: 'si la contestation du nombre des victimes de la politique d'extermination dans un camp de concentration déterminé n'entre pas dans les prévisions de l'article *24bis* de la loi du 29 juillet 1881, la minoration *outrancière* de ce nombre caractérise le délit de contestation de crimes contre l'humanité prévu et puni par ledit article, *lorsqu'elle est faite de mauvaise foi*.'[1327] As a result of this decision, historical research of the number of victims of the Holocaust and the method of extermination of Jews as practised by the Nazis is permitted as long as such research does not trivialize their war crimes.

The evoking of controversies about the legitimacy of the grounds of the Gayssot Act is also not prohibited; contesting the law is not necessarily the same as contesting the existence of a crime against humanity. Furthermore, although the law permits the sanctioning of the 'contestation through insinuation', it does not allow the condemnation of expression solely because it is uttered by men, who are part of a particular political movement known for its acquaintance with revisionist theories.[1328] In 2012, the French Supreme Court overruled and annulled – without referral – the conviction by the Court of Appeal of Bruno Gollnisch, a French

---

1323 Veron 1990, p.1.

1324 Veron 1990, p.1.

1325 French Supreme Court, crim.ch., 29 January 1998, n°96–82731, *GP* 24/26 May 1998, p.32.

1326 Beignier, De Lamy, Dreyer 2009, p.531.

1327 French Supreme Court, crim.ch., 17 June 1997, n°94–85126, *Bull. Crim.* 1997, n°236 p.786, *D.* 1998, p.51, annotation J.P. Feldman.

1328 Ader, B., L'état de la jurisprudence sur la notion de négation depuis la loi Gayssot, *Légipresse* n° 293, April 2012, p. 236.

academic and politician and member of the Front National (FN) and the European Parliament, with regard to his statements 'l'existence des chambres à gaz, c'est aux historiens d'en discuter (.) je ne nie pas les chambres à gaz homicides, mais la discussion doit rester libre' during a press conference held by the FN at the Lyon III University.[1329]

The Court of Appeal had considered that this appeal for a debate between historians had the objective of doubting the reality of the massive use of gas chambers and even testified of a 'parti pris personnel en donnant de ces historiens hétérodoxes ou négationnistes, une presentation complaisante'. Contrarily, the Supreme Court held that the statements 'qui renferment des énonciations contradictoires, ne permettent pas de caractériser (.) le délit (.). The Court of Appeal had therefore misunderstood Article 24 bis. Derieux questions whether the Supreme Court refrained from referring the case for a new appreciation on the merits out of fear of an eventual condemnation by the ECtHR.[1330] However, in 2011, the ECtHR found the disciplinary measure imposed by the Lyon III University on Gollnisch with regard to his teaching position as a Professor at the University for the same expression acceptable due to its ambiguous nature and *eventual* contribution to revisionist theories and possible subsequent disorder (Chapter 3, para. 1.5 *supra*).[1331]

The possibly large scope of the offence of 'contestation' of crimes against humanity brings up the question as to how Article 24*bis* relates to the other French hate speech bans that have formed a legal ground for the condemnation of a variety of anti-Semitic expression that could be understood to signify the denial, trivialization or apology for the crimes committed by the Nazi regime, notably the Holocaust, such as imputations against Jews to exploit the legends of the Holocaust, to lie about the existence of the gas chambers, to lobby for world domination or to compare practices of Israeli with practices of the Nazis (para. 4.5.2 and 6.2 *supra*). The French Supreme Court has ruled that the offence of revisionism and the offence of apology for crimes against humanity in Article 24–3 cannot be applied at the same time, because these offences protect the same values.[1332] Contrarily, the French Supreme Court has ruled that one fact can be prosecuted on the ground of Article 24*bis* and the offence of racial defamation, because they protect interests of a different nature and for this reason, 'lorsqu'elles sont en concours ne sauraient constituer un cumul idéal d'infractions'.[1333]

1329 French Supreme Court, crim. Ch., 23 June 2009, *Légipresse* n° 269, February 2010, III 269–19, annotation E. Derieux.

1330 Annotation E. Derieux at: French Supreme Court, crim. Ch., 23 June 2009, *Légipresse* n° 269, February 2010, III 269–19, p. 38.

1331 ECtHR 7 June 2011, no. 48135/08 (Gollnisch v. France).

1332 French Supreme Court, crim.ch., 26 April 2000, n°98–87633, *Bull. Crim.* 2000, n°167, p.486.

1333 French Supreme Court, crim.ch., 12 September 2000, n°98–88201, *unpublished.*

9.2. Intent and the presumption of bad faith

Article 24*bis* supposes, like most press offences, the existence of a *dol generalis*. The prosecuting party does not explicitly have to prove the author's intention; his intention is implied and is a result of the tenor of the expression and his bad faith is presumed.[1334] A suspect thus has the difficult task of proving his good faith.[1335] Article 24*bis* thus requires that the author consciously publicly contests the existence of crimes against humanity committed by the Nazi regime. This intention is twofold: the author must have the intention to contest and the intention to do so publicly.

In its decision of 17 June 1997, the French Supreme Court insisted on the requirement of the author's bad faith (para.9.1 *supra*). On the one hand, the Court required that the expression constituted a 'minoration *outrancière*', which implies an author's bad faith. On the other hand, the Court stipulated the requirement of the author's bad faith. In its annotation, Feldman argues that the aim of the French Supreme Court has rightly been to prevent a too extensive interpretation of the offence that the term 'contestation' might entail. According to Feldman, however, the Court's reference to the author's bad faith is redundant, because it is difficult to imagine a 'minoration *outrancière*' made in good faith.[1336] Contrarily, De Lamy criticizes the emphasis on the author's bad faith, because the terms of the expressionitself must be sufficiently explicit in order to derive the intention of the author. More generally, revisionists should not have the possibility of proving their good faith.[1337]

With regard to the intention to *publicly* contest crimes against humanity, in 2002 the French Supreme Court endorsed the condemnation by the Court of Appeal of a person who had posted on a website, which had the objective of fighting against revisionism, a message in which he denied the existence of the gas chambers. The Court had rightly rejected the suspect's defence of having supposed that the website concerned a – private – discussion forum, because the suspect could not ignore the fact that his messages would be publicly diffused.[1338]

9.3. Crimes against humanity

Article 24*bis* only criminalizes the denial of crimes against humanity committed during the Second World War. The text of the Article refers to 'l'existence d'un ou plusieurs crimes contre l'humanité tels qu'ils sont définis par l'article 6 du statut du Tribunal militaire international annexé à l'accord de Londres du 8 août 1945'.

1334 Beignier, De Lamy & Dreyer 2009, p.533.

1335 Veron 1990, p.2.

1336 French Supreme Court, crim.ch., 17 June 1997, n°94–85126, *Bull. Crim.* 1997, n°236 p. 786, *D.* 1998, p.51, annotation J.P. Feldman.

1337 De Lamy 2000, p.370; p.369.

1338 French Supreme Court, crim.ch., 5 November 2002, n°01–88461, *Bull. Crim.* 2002, n°200, p.745.

Article 6 of the Statute of the tribunal of Nuremberg defines crimes against humanity as 'murder, extermination, enslavement, deportation, and other inhumane acts committed against any civilian population, before or during the war, or persecutions on political, racial or religious grounds in execution of or in connection with any crime within the jurisdiction of the Tribunal, whether or not it is in violation of the domestic law of the country where the act is perpetrated.' Article 6 further indicates that the Nuremberg tribunal is only competent to judge persons who have acted 'in the interests of the European Axis countries'. Likewise, Article 24*bis* specifies that the crimes against humanity must have been committed 'soit par les membres d'une organisation criminelle en application de l'article 9 dudit statut, soit par une personne reconnue coupable de tels crimes par une juridiction français ou internationale'. The Nuremberg tribunal has declared as criminal the chefs of the Nazi party, the SD the SS and the Gestapo.[1339] Hence, Article 24*bis* criminalizes the denial of crimes against humanity for the purposes of Article 6 of the Statute of Nuremberg, committed by the members of such organizations or a person found guilty of such crimes by a French or international jurisdiction. In the latter case it is not a requirement that a person is a member of one of these organizations.

It was in order to avoid the creation of a délit d'opinion that the National Assembly adopted the proposal of the Government to provide for a most precise circumscription of the statutory elements of the offence by referring to Article 6 of the statute of the tribunal of Nuremberg.[1340] By doing so, the French legislator thought not to itself declare or create an official history, but merely to assume, take as a starting point a historical reality as established by French and international jurisdictions, in other words the authority of legal judgments. From this perspective, the offence of denial of crimes against humanities did not constitute a memorial law in senso strictu.

In case law, the 'Union des Tsiganes et voyageurs de France' has been found admissible in its complaint and constitution as a civil party on the ground of 24*bis* with regard to expression concerning *all* groups of people being the victim of the concentration camps.[1341] Case law has thus acknowledged the criticism that the offence of denial of crimes against humanity would merely protect the Jewish community from offence.

French case law has always refused to apply the offence of the denial of crimes against humanity committed in other periods. For example in 1994, the Tribunal Correctionnel of Paris acquitted Bernard Lewis, expressed the idea that the reality of the Armenian genocide only existed in the imagination of the Armenian population on the ground of 24*bis*. The Court considered that the double reference in Article 24*bis* to Articles 6 and 9 of the Statute of the International Military

1339 Beignier, De Lamy & Dreyer 2009, p.533.

1340 Parliamentary debates, *JO* 2 May 1990, French national assembly, pp.956–957.

1341 French Supreme Court, crim.ch., 20 December 1994, n°93–80267, *Bull. Crim.* 1994, n°424, p.1031.

Tribunal 'a pour effet d'exclure de la protection contre la contestation, instituée par la loi, tous les autres crimes contre l'humanité, comme, en l'espèce, ceux dont a été victime le peuple arménien en 1915.'[1342]

In 1994, the French Supreme Court rejected two arguments often used by suspects of the offence of denial of crimes against humanity in their defence.[1343] Firstly, suspects argue that they are not familiar with judgments – condemnations on the ground of crimes against humanity – by the Nuremberg tribunal, because they have not been published in the French law gazette (Journal Officiel). For this reason, the judgments cannot be used against them. In casu, the Court rejected the argument considering that, on the one hand the authority of legal decisions are a result of their pronouncement and definitive character, independently from their publication, and on the other hand the judgment of the Nuremberg tribunal had been officially translated into French.[1344]

Secondly, suspects argue that Article 24*bis* violates their presumption of innocence as protected in Article 6 ECHR, because Article 24*bis* imposes judgments – condemnation on the ground of crimes against humanity – by the Nuremberg tribunal on the French judge, which is why the suspects cannot prove the truth of their statements and the French judge is not impartial. The Court rejected the argument, because the suspect is not prosecuted on the ground of the offence of crimes against humanity itself, but on the ground of the offence of *denial* of crimes against humanity. The suspect's presumption of innocence thus concerns his expression, his denial, and not the act, i.e. the war crime itself. The French judge thus decides as to whether expression can be qualified under the legal definition of the offence of *denial* of crimes against humanity, not whether the act can be qualified as a crime against humanity. However, it is precisely because of its reference to the Statute of the Nuremberg tribunal that the offence of denial of crimes against humanity is highly controversial in French legal doctrine.

9.4. Constitutionality and the value of human dignity: the *Dieudonné* case

Despite its difficult drafting history, the Gayssot Act was not submitted to the Constitutional Council – it is said for political reasons. The question arises as to whether the Constitutional Council, when confronted with such a question, would consider the offence of denial of crimes against humanity to be in conformity with the French Constitution or, on the contrary, incompatible with the freedom of communication of an opinion as protected in Articles 10 jo 11 DDHC. The question does not remain purely theoretical, but is of practical importance. Since the

1342 Cited in: CNCDH 1994, p.61.

1343 French Supreme Court, crim.ch., 20 December 1994, n°93–80267, *Bull. Crim.* 1994, n°424, p.1031.

1344 In the same sense: French Supreme Court, crim.ch., 13 March 2001, n°00–85102, *unpublished.*

constitutional reform of 2008, which came into force on 1 March 2010, a citizen can dispute the constitutionality of a statutory provision during an on-going proceeding before a court. When it is argued that a certain statutory provision violates the rights and freedoms guaranteed by the Constitution, the Constitutional Council can be seized – on remand of the Council of State or the French Supreme Court – in order to ask a 'Question Prioritaire de Constitutionalité' (QPC).[1345] As a result of the case law of the Constitutional Council, freedom of expression must be conciliated with the protection of the public order, the rights of others and the respect for human dignity (para.1.1 *supra*). Does Article 24*bis* meet these objectives? According to Mbongo, if any provision in the 1881 Press Act is regarded as unconstitutional in French legal doctrine, it is the criminalization of revisionism in Article 24*bis*.[1346] The question as to the constitutionality of the article keeps French legal scholars highly divided. Their pros and cons resemble those put to the fore during the parliamentary debates.

Rolland considers negationistic discourse as constituting opinions or value judgments on historic events. He recalls that opinions can only be criminalized, because of their link with a following reprehensible or punishable act. However, the precise problem with negationistic expression was the fact that it could not be condemned on the ground of racial provocation, because no manifest link existed between such expression and a reprehensible act. According to Rolland, the offence thus constitutes a délit d'opinion and for this reason must be abrogated.[1347]

Mathieu sums up as to why the Gayssot Act and memorial laws in general would be unconstitutional: they would constitute government declared truth and the State would install an official History; they would be contrary to the principle of equality, because they would protect the memory of one historic event and of one specific group – not other genocides of other groups – and would thus be inspired by Communautarism; they would lack the precision that the principle of legality of offences and sanctions and legal certainty requires; and they would violate free historical research.[1348] Mathieu therefore advocates the abrogation of Article 24*bis* and with regard to revisionist expression to permit recourse only before the civil judge, on the ground of Article 1382 CC. According to Mathieu, Article 24*bis* adds to the development of the multiplication of press offences and a regime of criminal

---

1345 La loi constitutionnelle n° 2008–724 du 23 juillet 2008 de modernisation des institutions de la Ve République inserted Article 61–1 into the French Constitution of 1958 that provides: Lorsque, à l'occasion d'une instance en cours devant une juridiction, il est soutenu qu'une disposition législative porte atteinte aux droits et libertés que la Constitution garantit, le Conseil constitutionnel peut être saisi de cette question sur renvoi du Conseil d'État ou de la Cour de cassation qui se prononce dans un délai déterminé.

1346 Mbongo, P., Droit des medias et question prioritaire de constitutionnalité, *Légipresse* n° 283, May 2011, p.284.

1347 Rolland 1998, p.651 *et seq.*

1348 Mathieu, B., Les lois mémorielles ou la violation de la constitution par consensus, *D.* 2006, p.3001, *LPA* 15 December 2006, n°250, p.7.

responsibility disconnected from an author's intention and the existence of actual prejudice. What is more, Article 24*bis* would open up a Pandora's box for the legislator to interfere with historical research. Contrarily, Article 1382 CC would permit the civil judge to apply the traditional rules of civil responsibility and to determine the actual abuse of the right of freedom of expression that harms the rights of others or the public order by focussing on the non-respect of scientific methods, which could indicate an author's racist intention.[1349] It is recalled that such recourse before the civil judge is impossible, since the French Supreme Court decided in 2000 that 'les abus de la liberté d'expression prévus et réprimés par la loi du 29 juillet 1881 ne peuvent être réparés sur le fondement de l'article 1382' (para.1.3.3 *supra*).[1350]

These arguments do not convince the proponents of the offence. Beignier highly objects to the qualification of the offence as a délit d'opinion. He strictly discerns opinions or value judgments from *facts*: 'c'est une opinion d'estimer que le roi Louis XVI était innocent et ne devait pas être condamné par la Convention, ou le contraire. Ce n'est pas une opinion que de constater qu'il fut décapité le 21 janvier 1793 et ce ne serait pas non plus une opinion que de prétendre qu'il ne le fut pas. Nul n'a à avoir de sentiment sur le constat d'un fait.'[1351] Negationism does not form a vision on history or a thesis, but an affirmation concerning facts, a factual declaration that the Holocaust has not taken place or the gas chambers have not existed.[1352] Although Beignier considers the criticism that the offence is too imprecise to be correct, it is partly countered by the fact that in case law, the offence is interpreted restrictively and the free serious historical research is preserved through the emphasis on an author's bad faith. According to Beignier, the law on revisionism must, however, be revised in order to permit other genocides, such as the Armenian genocide, to fall within its scope.[1353] Likewise, Dreyer argues that all denial of the existence of crimes against humanity should be treated equally and therefore advocates an extension of the scope of Article 24*bis* by creating one single offence penalizing the denial of the existence of crimes against humanity as they are recognized by law.[1354]

1349 Mathieu 2007-I, p.321 *et seq.*

1350 French Supreme Court, plenary assembly, 12 July 2000, n°98–10160, *Bull.* 2000 A. P., n° 8 p.13; *Légipresse*, October 2000, III, p.153, conclusions L. Joinet, RTD Civ 2000, p. 842, observation P. Jourdain.

1351 Beignier, B., "De la langue perfide, délivre moi…", Réflexions sur la loi du 13 juillet 1990 dite "Loi Gayssot", in: *Pouvoir et Liberté, Études offertes à Jacques Mourgeon*, Brussels: Bruylant 1998, p.509. Earlier, Beignier considered however that 'Il y a même quelque chose de tragique dans cette interdiction, une sorte de desespoir de ne pouvoir faire triompher la vérité contre le mesonge.' in: Beignier 1995, p.256.

1352 In the same sense: Droin 2009, p.282.

1353 Beignier 1998, p.525; p.533.

1354 Dreyer 2003, p.25.

The argument most used in favour of the offence is, however, the special nature of negationistic discourse; its anti-Semitic nature and its disguised political aim to rehabilitate National Socialism. Wachsmann explains that negationistic discourse consists of a factual allegation of which the false character and the intention to harm the victims of the facts in question is certain.[1355] Troper argues, therefore, that negationistic discourse must be criminalized, because it constitutes a threat to the rights and liberties of others and an impairment of the democratic regime itself. The negation of the Armenian genocide is of a very different character.[1356] Beignier equally considers that where the rationale of freedom of expression is to support democracy, negationism is grounded on an ideology contrary to democracy.[1357]

De Lamy opines that if the offence would have been submitted to the Constitutional Council, it could have referred to the principle of human dignity as enshrined in the preamble of the Constitution of 1946.[1358] In a famous decision in 1994 concerning the so-called 'bioethics Act', the Constitutional Council considered that it resulted from the preamble of the 1946 Constitution that the dignity of the human person against all forms of enslavement and degradation is a constitutional principle. Therefore, the freedoms garantueed in Articles 1, 2 and 4 of the DDHC must be conciliated with the constitutional principle of human dignity.[1359] In this context, human dignity is considered to be an integral part of the inalienable rights of personality.

According to Mathieu, the constitutional principle of human dignity can be regarded as expressing 'la volonté républicaine d'integration': it assures the unity and indivisibility of the French Republic. Like the respect for all beliefs, the respect for human dignity is thus inscribed in the 'pacte républican'. The dignity concerned here must, however, be considered as a value and not as a right: it signifies the interdiction to injure the human dignity of a person and is therefore an objective right rather than a subjective right. These values can be considered as essential values of the French Republic, i.e the fundamental principles of the French legal order. They form limitations to freedom of expression that protect values rather than rights and have the aim of respecting fundamental principles rather than preventing disturbances.[1360]

1355 Wachsmann, P., Liberté d'expression et négationnisme, *RTDH* 2001, p.591.

1356 Troper, M., Droit et négationnisme: la loi Gayssot et la Constitution, *Annales Histoire Sciences Sociales* 1999, n°6, p.1239 *et seq.*

1357 Beignier 1998, p.497 *et seq.*

1358 De Lamy 2000, p.373.

1359 Cons. Con. 27 July 1994, n°94–343/344 DC. The Constitutional Council declared the Bioethics Act that regulates various issues related to 'medically assisted reproduction' such as embryo selection and paternity to be constitutional. (in full: Respect for Human Body Act and Donation and Use of Parts and Products of the Human Body, Medically Assisted Reproduction and Prenatal Diagnosis Act).

1360 Mathieu 2007-I, pp.321 *et seq.*

The latter can be illustrated by the famous *Dieudonné* case. In a decision of 9 January 2014, the French Council of State agreed with the decision of the prefect of the Loire-Atlantique to prohibit the theatre show 'Le Mur' (The Wall) of humourist Dieudonné scheduled at Saint-Herblain, Nantes for being anti-Semitic.[1361] The show had previously been held in the Théâtre de la Main d'Or in Paris. It included a sketch, in which the humorist mimed urinating against a wall. He then revealed that it was the Wailing Wall in Jerusalem. He also uttered salvos of abuse at prominent French Jewish performers, including radio presenter Patrick Cohen, concluding: 'Gas chambers … a shame.' The Administrative Court of Nantes, seized by the humorist's lawyers in summary proceedings, had annulled the order of the prefect of the Loire-Atlantique prohibiting the show. According to the Administrative Court, a *perceived risk* to public order could not be used to 'justify as radical a measure as banning the show'.

But the Council of State considered that 'the reality and gravity of the risk of trouble to public order' was 'established'; 'pour interdire la représentation à Saint-Herblain du spectacle "Le Mur", précédemment interprété au théâtre de la Main d'Or à Paris, le préfet de la Loire-Atlantique a relevé que ce spectacle, tel qu'il est conçu, contient des propos de caractère antisémite, qui incitent à la haine raciale, et font, en méconnaissance de la dignité de la personne humaine, l'apologie des discriminations, persécutions et exterminations perpétrées au cours de la Seconde Guerre mondiale; que l'arrêté contesté du préfet rappelle que M. Dieudonné M'Bala M'Bala a fait l'objet de neuf condamnations pénales, dont sept sont définitives, pour des propos de même nature; qu'il indique enfin que les réactions à la tenue du spectacle du 9 janvier font apparaître, dans un climat de vive tension, des risques sérieux de troubles à l'ordre public qu'il serait très difficile aux forces de police de maîtriser;'[1362]

The Council of State, therefore, overturned the decision, finding 'Les allégations selon lesquelles les propos pénalement répréhensibles et de nature à mettre en cause la cohésion nationale relevés lors des séances du spectacle Le Mur tenues à Paris ne seraient pas repris à Nantes ne suffisaient pas pour écarter le risque sérieux que soient de nouveau portées de graves atteintes au respect des valeurs et principes, notamment de dignité de la personne humaine, consacrés par la Déclaration des droits de l'homme et du citoyen et par la tradition républicaine; qu'il appartient en outre à l'autorité administrative de prendre les mesures de nature à éviter que des infractions pénales soient commises;'[1363] In subsequent decisions, the Council of State has validated the decisions of the mayors of Tours and Orléans to prohibit the show in their cities.[1364]

1361 'Dieudonné: le Conseil d'Etat maintient l'interdiction du spectacle à Nantes' *Le Monde* 9 January 2014.

1362 CE Ordonnance of 9 January 2014, n°374508, para.5.

1363 CE Ordonnance of 9 January 2014, n°374508, para.6.

1364 CE Ordonnance of 10 January 2014, n°374528; CE Ordonnance of 11 January 2014, n°374552.

The decision of the Council of State has been lauded as a 'victory of the Republic', but has also been criticized as a 'defeat of democracy'. It is argued that, with the interdiction of the spectacle, the Council reversed the organization of the legal system that gives priority to the repressive regime over the preventive regime. Given the severity of the measure, it has even been suggested that this 'Jurisprudence Dieudonné' could be brought before the ECtHR. Furthermore, the argument that the performance could endanger the 'national cohesion' was considered very unfortunate. Discriminatory expression aimed at cultivating hatred between groups together forming the national community consequently violates its cohesion, but in its literal sense the notion of 'national cohesion' excludes foreigners from its protection. Moreover, critics reproached the Council stating that it was insufficiently established that the spectacle would cause any disturbances to public order and to have extended the traditional notion of 'public order' from 'immaterial or exterior' to 'immaterial' by linking 'public order' with 'human dignity'; then racist and Anti-Semitic expression becomes in itself a violation of public order based on its infringement of human dignity.[1365]

However, on this point, the decision appears to be in line with established case law. In a number of instances, the Council of State has attached the protection of human dignity with the protection of public order. In one instance, the Council of State validated the decision of a mayor to interdict a public spectacle, which consisted of a dwarf tossing competition 'au nom du principe de dignité composante de l'ordre public'. In 2007, the Council of State validated the decision of the chief of police in Paris to interdict the public distribution of soup containing pork, known as '*soupe au cochon*' (pig soup), with the aim of excluding people of Muslim and Jewish religions. It considered that the manifestation was discriminatory and constituted a violation of public order on the basis of the 'risques de réactions à ce qui est conçu comme une démonstration susceptible de porter atteinte à la dignité des personnes privée du secours proposé et de causer ainsi des troubles à l'ordre public'.[1366]

French jurisdictions have equally referred to the respect for human dignity in order to justify limitations to freedom of expression. For example, the Paris Court of Appeal has interdicted an advertising poster of the clothing trademark Benetton depicting a human buttock presented as a piece of meat on which the sign 'HIV' had been tattooed, because the poster used 'une symbolique de stigmatisation dégradante pour la dignité des personnes atteintes de manière implacable en leur chair et en leur être de nature à provoquer à leur détriment un phénomène de rejet

---

1365 'On s'achemine vers une jurisprudence Dieudonné' *Le Monde* 7 January 2014; Lochak, D., "*Victoire pour la République*" ou défaite de la démocratie? La decision *Dieudonné* ne mérite ni cet excès d'honneur ni cette indignité, *Légipresse* n° 315 April 2014, p. 221–230.

1366 CE 27 October 1995, Commune de Morsang-sur-Orge, Les Grands arrêts de la jurisprudence administrative, 15th edition, *Dalloz*, 25, n° 102; CE 5 January 2007, Min. d'Etat, min. Intérieur et aménagement du territoire c/ Assoc. "Solidarité des Français", n° 300311.

ou de l'accentuer'.[1367] According to Cammilleri-Subrenat, in this case, human dignity seemed to form 'un rempart contre un libéralisme sauvage'.[1368] She considers the principle of human dignity to be the best constitutional barrier against hate speech in general.[1369]

The question of the constitutionality of Article 24*bis* was raised in several legal cases. In a decision of 7 May 2010, the French Supreme Court refused to transmit a QPC concerning Article 24*bis* to the Constitutional Council filed by Le Pen and les Editions des Tuileries. They had been condemned on the basis of the article with regard to the publication of an interview in the extreme right winged, weekly *Rivarol*, in which Le Pen had stated that the German occupation of France 'n'a pas été particulairement inhumaine'. The French Supreme Court considered that the question posed lacked a serious character, because the article defined the offence of denial of crimes against humanity in a clear and precise manner and did not, therefore, violate the constitutional principles of freedom of expression and opinion. Subsequent decisions of the Court have a similar purport.[1370] The Court thus seemed to attach more importance to the question of whether the offence is precisely qualified than to the question of whether the offence criminalizes an opinion that is closely connected to a subsequent action. According to De Montalivet, the solution of the Court is not self-evident. Given the lack of consensus in legal doctrine on the matter, the constitutionality of the article is not obvious. While the opinion of the Court seems to be that the article does not violate the principle of legality of criminal offences and sanctions, its motivation notably concerns the fact that the article does not violate the constitutional principle of freedom of expression and opinion. The Court thus gives a decision based on the merits of the case and its aim seems to be to smother any 'contestation' of the constitutionality of Article 24*bis*. By answering the QPC itself, the Court shows a certain resistence against the system of the QPC. According to De Montalivet, it can, however, be expected that the Constitutional Council would adopt the approach of the ECtHR.[1371] Indeed, in the absence of a decision on the question as to the constitutionality of the offence of

---

1367 CA Paris, 28 May 1996, *D.* 1996, p.617, annotation B. Edelman.

1368 Edelman, B., *La personne en danger.* Paris: PUF collection Doctrine juridique 1999, p.525.

1369 Cammilleri-Subrenat, A., L'incitation à la haine et la Constitution, *Revue internationale de droit comparé*, Vol.54 N° 2, April-June 2002, p.541.

1370 French Supreme Court, crim.ch., 7 May 2010, n°09–80774, *published.* See also: French Supreme Court, crim.ch., 10 October 2012, n°12–81505; French Supreme Court, crim.ch., 5 December 2012, n°12–86382; French Supreme Court, crim.ch., 6 May 2014, n° 14–90010.

1371 Annotation P. de Montavilet, *Cahiers du Conseil constitutionnel* n° 29 – October 2010, at: French Supreme Court, crim.ch., 7 May 2010, n°09–80774. Vgl. Bigot, C., QPC et loi du 29 juillet 1881 – Bilan et perspectives, *Légipresse* n°292, March 2012, p.152. Cassia however strongly disagrees with Montavilet and considers 'ce n'est pas parce qu'une loi est mauvaise qu'elle est inconstitutionnelle. Cette maxime s'applique bien à la loi Gayssot.' Cassia, P., L'incidence des protections conventionnelles sur le contrôle de constitutionnalité de la liberté d'expression, *Légipresse* n°292, March 2012, p.157.

denial of crimes against humanity pursuant to Article 24*bis* by Constitutional Council, the question arises as to whether Article 24*bis* is in conformity with international provisions, notably Article 10 ECHR.

9.5. Compatibility with international law: the cases of *Garaudy* and *Faurisson*

The French Supreme Court has always considered the offence of denial of crimes against humanity in Article 24*bis* as being in conformity with Article 10 ECHR. In 1994, the Court considered that the second paragraph of Article 10 ECHR provides that the exercise of the right to freedom of expression carries duties and responsibilities and can be submitted to certain restrictions necessary in a democratic society, most notably for the protection of morals and the rights of others and 'que tel est l'objet de l'article 24*bis* de la loi du 29 juillet 1881 modifiée par la loi du 13 juillet 1990.'[1372]

The ECtHR, for its part, also considers Article 24*bis* to form an interference with freedom of expression that is legitimate and necessary in a democratic society, due to the fact that it protects the rights of others and the public order and because revisionistic and negationistic discourse run counter to the fundamental values of the Convention.[1373] In the case *Garaudy v. France*, the ECtHR evoked Article 17 in order to deprive revisionist expression from the protection of Article 10. The case concerned the publication of the book *Les mythes fondateurs de la politique israélienne* by the author Garaudy, in which he denounces the pseudo-existence of the Holocaust and imputes the State of Israel and Jews in order to take financial advantage of this situation. The French Supreme Court had rejected an appeal against the condemnation of Garaudy on the grounds of denial of crimes against humanity, racial defamation and racial provocation.[1374] The ECtHR declared Garaudy's complaint of violation of freedom of expression to be inadmissible considering: 'There can be no doubt that denying the reality of clearly established

1372 French Supreme Court, crim.ch., 20 December 1994, n°93–80267, *Bull. Crim.* 1994, n°424, p.1031.

1373 See also: ECmHR 24 June 1996, n°31159/96, *Marais/France*. The ECmHR rejected a complaint against a condemnation of the ground of *24bis* with regard to an article published in the magazine *Revision* that doubted 'les prétendus gazages' committed in the concentration camps of Struthof and more generally the use of the gas chambers in order to eliminate the Jewish community, because the expression run counter to the fundamental values of the Convention as expressed in its preamble, being justice and peace.

1374 French Supreme Court, crim.ch., 12 September 2000, n°98–88200; 98–88201; 98–88202; 98–88203; 98–88204, *unpublished*. The Court of Appeal had considered 'derrière l'utilisation permanente du qualificatif "sioniste" c'est bien le lobby juif et les communautés juives dans leur ensemble que Roger Garaudy a cherché à mettre en cause. En réalité, l' ouvrage de Monsieur Garaudy ne constitue pas un travail d' histoire mais de polémique qui visant l' ensemble de la communauté juive, en tant que coupable de cette gigantesque escroquerie, apparaît comme l'une des formes les plus forte de la diffamation raciale et de la provocation à la haine raciale.'

historical facts, such as the Holocaust, as the applicant does in his book, does not constitute historical research akin to a quest for the truth. The aim and the result of that approach are completely different, the real purpose being to rehabilitate the National-Socialist regime and, as a consequence, accuse the victims themselves of falsifying history. Denying crimes against humanity is therefore one of the most serious forms of racial defamation of Jews and of incitement to hatred of them. The denial or rewriting of this type of historical fact undermines the values on which the fight against racism and anti-Semitism are based and constitutes a serious threat to public order. Such acts are incompatible with democracy and human rights because they infringe the rights of others. Their proponents indisputably have designs that fall into the category of aims prohibited by Article 17 of the Convention.'[1375]

The HRC has ruled equally against revisionists, but takes a different approach than the ECtHR. In 1996, the HRC rejected a complaint by Faurisson who had been condemned in France on the ground of 24*bis*[1376] for having denied in an interview in the magazine *Le choc du mois* the existence of the systematic extermination of the Jews by the Nazi regime and having stated, amongst others statements, that the myth of the gas chambers is 'une gredinerie' (dirty trick). The HRC did not, like the ECtHR, emphasize the negative effects that negationistic expression can have on social cohesion, peace, justice, pluralism and tolerance and did not declare the complaint inadmissible on the ground of Article 5–1 ICCPR, which prohibits the abuse of rights.[1377] The HRC emphasized the profoundly racist and anti-Semitic nature of Faurisson's negationistic discourse that violated the rights of the Jewish community and considered that: 'Since the statements made by the author, read in their full context, were of a nature as to raise or strengthen anti-Semitic feelings, the restriction served the respect of the Jewish community to live free from fear of an atmosphere of anti-Semitism. The Committee therefore concludes that the restriction of the author's freedom of expression was permissible under article 19, paragraph 3 (a), of the Covenant.'[1378] However, in the New General Comment no. 34 on Article 19 ICCPR (GC 34), adopted in 2011,[1379] the HRC considers that 'Laws

1375 ECtHR 24 June 2003, n°65831/01, *Garaudy/France*.

1376 TGI de Paris, 18 April 1991; CA Paris, 9 December 1992, both cited in: CNCDH 1992, p.82; French Supreme Court, crim.ch., 20 December 1994, n°93–80267, *Bull. Crim.* 1994, n°424, p.1031. The Paris TGI considered that article *24bis* criminalizes 'toute contestation, même inscrite dans un discours logique et cohérent, des lors qu'elle conduit à contester, en les niant, *en des termes de mépris envers les victims*, l'existence d'un crime contre l'humanité ayant entraîné des condamnations de ce chef par le Tribunal Militaire Internationale de Nuremberg.'

1377 Cohen-Jonathan, G., Négationnisme et droits de l'homme, *RTDH* 1997, p.592.

1378 *Robert Faurisson v. France*, Communication No. 550/1993, 8 November 1996, U.N. Doc. CCPR/C/58/D/550/1993(1996).

1379 HRC, Summary Record of the 2820th meeting, 21 July 2011, CCPR/C/SR.2820, para. 86. It replaces General Comment no. 10 that dates back to 1983. See: HRC, General Comment no. 10: Freedom of Expression (art. 19), 29 June 1983, HRI/GEN/1/Rev. 9 (Vol. 1), at 181;1–2 IHRR 9 (1994).

that criminalize the expression of opinions about historical facts' are deemed incompatible with the Covenant that 'does not permit general prohibition of expressions of an erroneous opinion or an incorrect interpretation of past events'.[1380] It remains to be seen how the HRC will interpret this consideration in subsequent case law (Chapter 3, para. 5.3 *supra*).

9.6. Revisionism as an abuse of right: 'neutralization' of the conflict

French legal doctrine generally holds that the solution of an abuse of right for the purposes of Article 17 ECHR is at the basis of the Gayssot Act of 13 July 1990 against revisionism and negationism that inserted Article 24*bis* into the 1881 Press Act. The denial of crimes against humanity committed by the Nazis during the Second World War falls outside the scope of the freedom to express an opinion and authors of such expression are simply deprived of this right and cannot invoke it in their defence.[1381] The solution thus consists of what is called a 'neutralisation' or denial of the conflict between freedom of expression and the fight against racism.[1382] This approach is clearly reflected in the drafting history of the Act; during the parliamentary debates it was argued at several reprises that racism does not constitute an opinion but an offence and in support of this vision the formula of Sartre was cited according to which anti-Semitism does not form a category of expression protected by freedom of opinion (para.8.2.2 *supra*). This radical solution by the French legislator is said to be inspired by the case law of the ECtHR.[1383] According to De Gouttes, the solution is implicitly consecrated in other international provisions, such as Article 20–2 ICCPR and Article 4 ICERD, according to which the diffusion of racist ideas is not a matter of opinion, but a punishable offence and the notion of an abuse of rights was equally at the core of the draft Act of Toubon in 1996 that sought the criminalization of the diffusion of racist and xenophobic messages (para.7.1 *supra*). According to De Gouttes, one must be prudent with the criminalization of such opinions, because France has interpreted Article 4–5 ICERD as meaning that States must refrain from adopting offences that are not in conformity with freedom of opinion.[1384]

The solution thus diverges from the solution that according to French legal doctrine was at the basis of the Pleven Act of July 1972, i.e. the search for conciliation, the correct balance between two interests, freedom of expression and the fight against racism.[1385] The French Supreme Court has adopted this solution by affirming on several occasions that Article 24–8; 32–2 and 33–3 are in conformity

---

1380 General Comment no. 34, para. 49.

1381 De Gouttes, R, À propos du conflit entre le droit à la liberté d'expression et le droit à la protection contre le racisme, *GP* 25 September 2001, n°268, p.6 *et seq*; Dreyer 2003, p.19 *et seq*.

1382 De Gouttes 2001, p.6 *et seq*.

1383 Droin 2009, p.215 *et seq*.

1384 De Gouttes 2001, p.6 *et seq*.

1385 Derieux 1992, p.81 *et seq*.; De Gouttes 2001, p.6 *et seq*.

with Article 10–2 ECHR.[1386] The French Supreme Court has, however, also considered that Article 24*bis* is in conformity with Article 10–2 ECHR.

Droin highly criticizes the view that the neutralization of the conflict is the basis of Article 24*bis*. The Article evokes the sentiment of creating a délit d'opinion by referring to the Statute of Nuremberg and taking as a starting point an official reality based on the judgments of the Nuremberg tribunal, installed by the victors of the Second World War. According to Droin, as Holocaust denial consists of – false – statements concerning facts and has an undisputable anti-Semitic nature and political aim, it violates the rights of others and the public order and is closely related to the offences of racial defamation and racial provocation; in order to clarify this the offence thus must be modified.[1387]

9.7. Development of memorial laws since 1990 and proposals to modify Article 24*bis*

Since the Gayssot Act of 13 July 1990, the French legislator has adopted several other texts recognizing the existence of historical events, notably the Act of 29 January 2001 'tendant à la reconnaissance du génocide arménien de 1915',[1388] the Act of 21 May 2001 'tendant à la reconnaissance de la traite et de l'esclavage en tant que crime contre l'humanité'[1389] and the Act of 23 February 2005 'portant reconnaissance de la Nation et contribution nationale en faveur des Français rapatriés'.[1390] On 18 October 2011, a draft act 'portant transposition du droit communautaire sur la lutte contre le racisme et réprimant la contestation de l'existence du génocide arménien' was deposed on the initiative of Valerie Boyer, representative of UMP in the National Assembly.[1391] Article 1 of the Act sought – after an amendment[1392] – the insertion of a new Article 24*ter* into the 1881 Press Act that provided 'les peines prévues à l'article 24*bis* sont applicables à ceux qui ont contesté ou minimisé de façon outrancière, par un des moyens énoncés à l'article 23, l'existence d'un ou plusieurs crimes de génocide défini à l'article 211–1 du code pénal et reconnus comme tels par la loi française'.[1393] The element 'de façon

1386 De Gouttes 2001, p.6 *et seq.*

1387 Droin 2009, pp.313–314.

1388 La loi n° 2001–70 du 29 janvier 2001 relative à la reconnaissance du génocide arménien de 1915.

1389 La loi n° 2001–434 du 21 mai 2001 – dite "Loi Taubira" – tendant à la reconnaissance de la traite et de l'esclavage en tant que crime contre l'humanité.

1390 La loi n° 2005–158 du 23 février 2005 portant reconnaissance de la Nation et contribution nationale en faveur des Français rapatriés.

1391 Proposition de loi n° 3842 'portant transposition du droit communautaire sur la lutte contre le racisme et réprimant la contestation de l'existence du génocide arménien', déposée le 18 octobre 2011.

1392 Proposition de loi n° 4035 'visant à réprimer la contestation de l'existence des génocides reconnus par la loi', déposée le 7 décembre 2011.

1393 Article 211–1 reads 'Constitue un génocide le fait, en exécution d'un plan concerté tendant à la destruction totale ou partielle d'un groupe national, ethnique, racial ou religieux, ou d'un groupe

outrancière' was to ensure that scientific historical works would fall outside its scope.[1394]

After the text had been adopted by the National Assembly[1395] and the Senate[1396], the draft Act was submitted to the Constitutional Council. Contrarily, in its decision of 28 February 2012 the Council declared the Article to be unconstitutional, considering that 'une disposition législative ayant pour objet de "reconnaître" un crime de génocide ne saurait, en elle-même, être revêtue de la portée normative qui s'attache à la loi; que, toutefois, l'article 1er de la loi déférée réprime la contestation ou la minimisation de l'existence d'un ou plusieurs crimes de génocide "reconnus comme tels par la loi française"; qu'en réprimant ainsi la contestation de l'existence et de la qualification juridique de crimes qu'il aurait lui-même reconnus et qualifiés comme tels, le législateur a porté une atteinte inconstitutionnelle à l'exercice de la liberté d'expression et de communication; que, dès lors, et sans qu'il soit besoin d'examiner les autres griefs, l'article 1er de la loi déférée doit être déclaré contraire à la Constitution;'[1397] The unconstitutionality of the proposed article was thus due to the requirement that the French legislator must have recognized in French law the existence of the genocide in order for its denial to be punishable. It is exactly this requirement, which discerns the proposed article from Article 24*bis* that takes the authority – or reality – of the legal judgments by the Nuremberg tribunal as a starting point. The decision is not surprising, when placed in the context of the intense debate caused by the development of laws qualifying historical events.[1398]

It was the adoption of the Act of 23 February 2005, in which the French legislator declares in Article 4–2: 'Les programmes scolaires reconnaissent en particulier le rôle positif de la présence française outre-mer, notamment en Afrique du Nord, et accordent à l'histoire et aux sacrifices des combattants de l'armée française issus de

---

déterminé à partir de tout autre critère arbitraire, de commettre ou de faire commettre, à l'encontre de membres de ce groupe, l'un des actes suivants: atteinte volontaire à la vie; atteinte grave à l'intégrité physique ou psychique; soumission à des conditions d'existence de nature à entraîner la destruction totale ou partielle du groupe; mesures visant à entraver les naissances; transfert forcé d'enfants.'

1394 Rapport n°4035 fait au nom de la commission des lois constitutionnelles sur la proposition de loi n°3842 'portant transposition du droit communautaire sur la lutte contre le racisme et réprimant la contestation de l'existence du génocide arménien', Assemblée Nationale, 7 décembre 2011.

1395 Proposition de loi 'visant à réprimer la contestation de l'existence des génocides reconnus par la loi', texte adopté n°813, Assemblée Nationale, 22 décembre 2011.

1396 Proposition de loi 'visant à réprimer la contestation de l'existence des génocides reconnus par la loi', texte définitif n°52, Sénat, 23 janvier 2012; Rapport n°269 fait au nom de la commission des lois constitutionnelles sur la proposition de loi 'visant à réprimer la contestation de l'existence des génocides reconnus par la loi', Sénat, 18 janvier 2012.

1397 Cons. Con. 28 February 2012, n°2012–647 DC concerning 'loi visant à réprimer la contestation de l'existence des génocides reconnus par la loi', *JO* 2 March 2012, p. 3988.

1398 For a clear synthesis of the debate on the criminalization of the denial of the existence of genocides see: Pénalisation de la négation des génocides: pour ou contre?, Actes de colloque, *Légipresse* n° 293 April 2012, p. 227–242.

ces territoires la place éminente à laquelle ils ont droit.', that evoked a national debate concerning the ensemble of laws, from then on designated as 'lois mémorielles'. In 2006, Mathieu published a petition signed by sixty other legal scholars imputing memorial laws, comprising the Gayssot Act, of being unconstitutional (para.9.4 *supra*).[1399] In 2008, a parliamentary commission issued a report, in which it fundamentally reflected 'sur les questions mémorielles'.[1400]

The concern for reassurance and reconciliation of the French Republic with its past meant that the Commission did not to challenge the existing 'memorial laws', notably the aforementioned Acts of 13 July 1990; 29 January 2001; 21 May 2001; and 23 February 2005.[1401] However, according to the commission the National Assembly must renounce the creation of further laws that appreciate or qualify history. In the vision of the Commission, it is not within the competences of political majorities to give an appreciation of facts of the past. And the multiplication of laws that qualify history increases the risk of bringing into play the responsibility of historians and the creation of délits d'opinion. It considered 'que le rôle du Parlement n'est pas d'adopter des lois qualifiant ou portant une appréciation sur des faits historiques, *a fortiori* lorsque celles-ci s'accompagnent de sanctions pénales. Mais le Parlement est dans son rôle quand il édicte des normes ou des limitations destinées à défendre des principes affirmés par le Préambule de la Constitution notamment pour lutter contre le racisme et la xénophobie.'[1402]

The Commission recalled, in defence of freedom of expression, that the 1881 Press Act already permits the sanctioning of expression that questions History for racist purposes on the ground of the offence of racial provocation pursuant to Article 24–8. The Commission thought the use of this offence preferable in order to sanction the most severe expression.[1403] It cited Mallet-Poujol, who advised 'L'arsenal juridique existe, servons-nous en, quitte à le retravailler. Pour les propos les plus graves, utilisons l'arsenal pénal, les dispositions relatives à la provocation à la discrimination et à la haine raciale. Pour les propos les plus stupides, la bêtise relevant moins de la poursuite pénale que de la poursuite civile, utilisons l'arsenal civil sur le droit de la responsabilité, avec un débat intellectuel sur la fausseté des allégations.'[1404]

With regard to the Gayssot Act Mallet-Poujol declared: 'A mon sens, la loi "Gayssot" de 1990, à laquelle j'adhère sentimentalement, procède d'un grand malentendu en raison de sa formulation et de son manque de lisibilité par rapport aux logiques d'incrimination du droit de la presse, notamment par rapport à l'incrimination de la provocation: les dispositions de l'article 24*bis* auraient pu

1399 Mathieu 2006, B., p.7.

1400 Rapport d'information n°1262 de M. Bernard Accoyer fait au nom de la mission d'information sur les questions mémorielles, 18 November 2008, *Documents d'information*, Assemblée Nationale, 2008.

1401 Rapport d'information n°1262, p.93 *et seq.*

1402 Rapport d'information n°1262, p.98.

1403 Rapport d'information n°1262, p.95.

1404 Rapport d'information n°1262, p.95; p.402.

figurer à l'article 24 sur les provocations et apologies de crime. (...) Le négationnisme est un déni, c'est donc une provocation; cette assimilation est systématiquement faite par le juge, européen ou français, ainsi que par la doctrine. Mais le législateur, et c'est pourquoi je parlais de malentendu, n'a pas clairement fait ce parallèle avec la provocation: la loi "Gayssot" a dépassé une sorte de ligne blanche, d'où le malaise des juristes et des historiens; l'incrimination, peu lisible, ne met pas en valeur la faute et le préjudice, et donne l'impression de recréer un délit d'opinion.'[1405]

The commission also recalled that the 1958 Constitution and the case law of the Constitutional Council requires that the National Assembly must respect the normative character of the law and implies that laws of a mere declarative nature are unconstitutional.[1406] According to the commission, the National Assembly, instead of creating new 'memorial laws', could take recourse to the new possibility created by the Constitutional reform of 2008 to vote resolutions on matters it regards to be important, such as historical events.[1407] It stated: 'le vote des résolutions prévues par l'article 34–1 nouveau de la Constitution devrait donner au Parlement un meilleur outil d'expression sur l'histoire lorsqu'il souhaite reconnaître des évènements significatifs pour l'affirmation des valeurs de la citoyenneté républicaine.'[1408]

1405 Rapport d'information n°1262, p.402. See also: Mallet-Poujol, N., La loi de pénalisation du négationnisme: la censure constitutionnelle ou le crépuscule des lois mémorielles, *Légipresse* n° 293 April 2012, p. 219–226.

1406 It results from Article 34 of the 1958 Constitution, which determines the fields of competence of the National Assembly, that the Constitution does not permit the National Assembly to qualify historical facts. See: Rapport d'information n°1262, p.37. What is more, in a decision in 2004 (Cons. Con. 29 July 2004, n° 2004–500 DC), the Constitutional Council considered that it results from Article 6 of the 1789 Declaration, according to which 'la loi est la volonté générale', the law has the vocation to create rules and therefore must have a normative character. See: Rapport d'information n°1262, p.97. For these reasons, the so-called memorial laws can be regarded as unconstitutional.

1407 Before the constitutional reform of 2008, the vote of such resolutions was however not possible. The report regards the multiplication of memorial laws as a consequence of the limitations that the case law of the Constitutional Council has imposed on the power of the National Assembly. It results from two decisions of 1959 of the Constitutional Council (Cons. Con. 17 June 1959, n° 59–2 DC and Cons. Con. 24 June 1959, n° 59–3 DC) that the National Assembly is not allowed to adopt declarations in which it takes political stand on matters it regards to be important, such as historical events, by means of the vote of resolutions. In previous French Republics, the vote of resolutions that held the French Government responsible had been a common practice by parliamentarians, which contributed to the Republic's political instability. Deprived of an important means of democratic expression on matters it thought to be of general interest, the National Assembly has compensated this restriction by the vote of laws that are rather of a symbolic than of a normative nature. See: Rapport d'information n°1262, p.23 *et seq.*

1408 Rapport d'information n°1262, p.101. Article 34–1 reads: 'Les assemblées peuvent voter des résolutions dans les conditions fixées par la loi organique. Sont irrecevables et ne peuvent être inscrites à l'ordre du jour les propositions de résolution dont le Gouvernement estime que leur adoption ou leur rejet serait de nature à mettre en cause sa responsabilité ou qu'elles contiennent des injonctions à son égard.'

After the Constitutional Council declared the proposal to insert a new Article 24*ter* penalizing the denial of genocides into the French Press Act to be unconstitutional and in violation of freedom of expression, representative Valérie Boyer proposed a new draft Act in Parliament on 14 October 2014 'visant à réprimer la negation des genocides et des crimes contre l'humanité du XXème siècle'. In this draft Act negationism is no longer seen as a simple abuse of freedom of expression, but as an ordinary crime under the general framework penalizing genocides and all crimes against humanity. Therefore, the act proposes to insert a new Article 213–6 into the section 'Atteintes à la dignité de la personne humaine' of the French Penal Code penalizing *'La contestation systématique, la négation par principe, la banalisation, la minimisation grossière, et la tentative de justification des crimes contre l'humanité et des génocides du XXème siècle tels qu'ils sont définis par l'article 211–1 et 212–2 du code pénal et/ou par le statut du Tribunal pénal international'.* The proposal thereby aims not only to circumvent the strict procedural rules applicable to the press offences, but to anticipate the event that the Constitutional Council will declare Article 24*bis* of the French Press Act unconstitutional.[1409] However, it appears that a formal relocation of the latter article to the Penal Code does not prevent it from constituting an interference with freedom of expression.

9.8. Conclusion

In French legal doctrine, the criminalization of the denial of crimes against humanity in Article 24*bis* is highly controversial. It is notably due to the reference in the Article to the Statute of the Nuremberg tribunal and the focus on the authority of its legal judgments, or the reality of the Holocaust as established by its judges, that many legal scholars judge the offence as a délit d'opinion by appearances. However, the statutory elements of the offence can be said to be insufficient to do justice to the actual rationale and purport of the offence as it can be derived from its drafting history, the national and international case law and French legal literature; the denial of the Holocaust does not form an opinion, but the affirmation concerning facts of the history of the Second World War that have a profound racist, anti-Semitic and political aim and violate the rights of others and the public order and for this reason are dangerous for democracy and incompatible with the values of the French Republic, such as human dignity. Although the offence is generally understood in French legal doctrine to exclude a mere opinion from the scope of freedom of expression in accordance with Article 17 ECtHR and is on this account severely criticized, this thesis is contradicted by some legal scholars that understand the offence to be rather the outcome of a conciliation between freedom of expression

1409 Proposition de loi n° 2276 'visant à réprimer la negation des genocides et des crimes contre l'humanité du XXème siècle', depose le 14 octobre 2014. See also: Jouanneau, B., Répression du négationnisme: la voix dissonante, *Légipresse* n° 320, October 2014, p. 531–537.

and the rights of others and the public order. These legal scholars have suggested the modification of Article 24*bis* in order to better bring out its common characteristics with the offences of racial defamation and racial provocation.

From this perspective, the offence of denial of crimes against humanity must be distinguished from existing 'memorial laws' in *senso strictu.* Such memorial laws are unconstitutional, because they constitute declarations and appreciations concerning historical facts by the French legislator itself and lack a normative character. The criminalization of the denial of the existence of genocides as defined and qualified by French law is therefore also unconstitutional. Because of its specific nature, the question as to the unconstitutionality of the offence of denial of crimes against humanity in accordance with Article 24*bis* is not an open-and-shut case. One has to wait for the initiation of a test case in order to seize the Constitutional Council with a QPC on the matter.

III. FRATERNITÉ: A SHARED ROLE OF THE STATE AND ASSOCIATIONS IN THE FIGHT AGAINST RACISM AND DISCRIMINATION

'Il est important d'encourager toutes les associations qui tendent à resserrer les liens de fraternité entre les individus vivant dans une même société. (...) Oui, dans notre lutte antiraciste les associations sont nos alliés naturels.'

'Cela [le droit d'action pour les associations antiracistes – EHJ] permettra à des hommes, qui ne se rendent pas toujours exactement compte du sort qui leur est fait ... d'être défendus, même lorsqu'ils ne connaissent pas l'étendue de leurs droits dans notre pays de liberté et d'égalité des citoyens par des associations qui, partageant ces responsabilités avec nous, avec le Gouvernement, avec le Parlement, sachent rendre leurs droits à chacun de ces hommes, nos égaux.'

French National Assembly, *parliamentary debate of 7 June 1972 concerning the fight against racism*[1410]

10. THE ENGAGEMENT OF PUBLIC PROSECUTIONS

In France, the public prosecution of the hate speech bans can be set in motion by three different parties: the public prosecution (10.1); the affected party (10.2); and anti-racism associations – under certain conditions (10.3). The shared role of the State and associations in the prosecution of the hate speech bans contributes to their effective enforcement (10.4) and forms an integral part of the Government's national policy on the fight against racism and discrimination (10.5). The analysis results in a general conclusion about the enforcement of the hate speech bans in France (10.6).

10.1. The public prosecutor

According to general French criminal procedure, the public prosecutor has certain discretionary power in determining whether or not to prosecute. 'Le principe de l'opportunité', established in Article 40–1 CPP, equally applies in French press law and is adopted in Article 47 of the 1881 Press Act, which provides that the prosecution of the press offences of the 1881 Press Act takes place *ex officio* and at the request of the public prosecutor. However, Article 48 of the 1881 Press Act immediately sets out the limitations to this principle. It provides for a limited number of press offences, comprising in Article 48–6 the offences of defamation and insult of individuals, that the public prosecution is dependent on a prior to a

1410 Assemblée Nationale, débats parlementaires, séance du 7 Juin 1972, Lutte contre le racisme, Discussion des conclusions d'un rapport, *JO* 8 Juin 1972, p.2281.

complaint by the victim. In this case, the competence of the public prosecutor to engage a public prosecution is subordinate to a request thereto by the person targeted by the expression. The 1881 Press Act thus confers an essential role on the victim in the engagement of public prosecutions of certain press offences. In fact, the French legislator has desired that the plaintiff remains 'juge de opportunité du débat', because of the impact that media trials can have and the echo they can give to the expression.[1411] This does however not signify that the public prosecutor is obliged to give effect to the complaint; the public prosecutor preserves the opportunity to prosecute. The principle of opportunity often leads public prosecutors to remain inactive in the prosecution of insults and defamations against individuals and prefers to leave the initiative to the plaitiffs to engage a prosecution, if they consider the damages caused to be sufficiently grave (para.10.2–10.3 *infra*).[1412] The victim of a violation of a press offence does, however, have the right to question the decision of the public prosecutor not to prosecute before his superior, the prosecutor-general, who can instruct the district prosecutor to proceed with the prosecution.[1413]

With regard to the French hate speech bans, a different regime applies. In this field the public order is concerned to such an extent that the engagement of the public prosecution on the initiative of the public prosecutor has been admitted since the 1939 Decree-law 'Marchandeau'. Article 48–6 provides that the public prosecutor can engage the public prosecution in relation to the offences of defamation and insult against a group on the ground of their origin, ethnic background, nation, race or religion – and the offences of defamation and insult against a group on the ground of their sex or sexual orientation – *ex officio*, without the need for a prior complaint from the victim. This applies equally to racial defamation and insult committed against a person considered individually, if he or she has given his or her consent thereto. Public prosecutors are inclined to prosecute racial insult and defamation on their own initiative.[1414] This policy is in line with the general guidelines for criminal policy, which aim at intensifying public action against racism and discrimination, issued by the Ministry for Justice (para.10.5 *infra*). Likewise, as a result of the combination of articles 47 and 48 of the 1881 Press Act, the public prosecutor can freely engage public prosecutions of the press offences that are not mentioned in these articles, comprising the offence of denial of crimes against humanity and the offence of racial provocation.

1411 French Supreme Court, crim.ch., 11 May 1984, n°83–94501, *Bull. Crim.* 1984, n°170. Cited in: Beignier, De Lamy & Dreyer 2009, p.584.

1412 Beignier, De Lamy & Dreyer 2009, p.589.

1413 Article 40–3 CPP.

1414 *Report on the relationship between freedom of expression and freedom of religion: the issue of regulation and prosecution of blasphemy, religious insult and incitement to hatred*, European Commission for Democracy through Law, study no.406/2006, Strasbourg: Council of Europe, 23 October 2008, Annex II, pp. 37–38.

10.2. The affected party

It results from general French criminal procedure that any person who has personnally suffered damages directly caused by a violation of a felony or misdemenor can take legal action for the reparation of damages before the criminal judge, which is also called an 'action civile' and for this purpose can set in motion a public prosecution.[1415] This signifies that the affected party can initiate or 'trigger' the public prosecution by deposing a complaint and constitute as a civil party in order to provoke the designation of the investigating judge ('juge d'instruction')[1416] or by directly summoning the offender of an offence before the criminal court ('citation directe').[1417] The affected party can thus deprive the public prosecutor of any power of appreciation and can force the engagement of a public prosecution, even if the public prosecutor has decided not to prosecute. The victim is said to form a 'contre-pouvoir' against a public prosecutor who remains inactive.[1418] French legal doctrine underscores the dual nature of the civil action.[1419] However, the victim remains a civil party to the public prosecution. Unnecessarily, it is stipulated that an affected party can bring a legal action for reparation of damages before the civil judge, separately from a public prosecution.[1420] Hereunder, I will, however, focus on the civil action before the criminal court.

The 1881 Press Act likewise affords the affected party the possibility to set in motion a public prosecution, but only on the grounds of a limited number of press offences as enumerated in the last paragraph of Article 48, which comprise of the offences of defamation and insult of individuals. That same article 48 furthermore affords the affected party the possibility to set in motion the public prosecution in

---

1415 Article 1 CCP provides 'L'action publique pour l'application des peines est mise en mouvement et exercée par les magistrats ou par les fonctionnaires auxquels elle est confiée par la loi. Cette action peut aussi être mise en mouvement par la partie lésée, dans les conditions déterminées par le présent code.' Article 2 CCP provides 'L'action civile en réparation du dommage causé par un crime, un délit ou une contravention appartient à tous ceux qui ont personnellement souffert du dommage directement causé par l'infraction.'

1416 Articles 85 CCP *et seq.* Article 85 CCP provides 'Toute personne qui se prétend lésée par un crime ou un délit peut en portant plainte se constituer partie civile devant le juge d'instruction compétent en application des dispositions des articles 52, 52–1 et 706–42.'

1417 Articles 550–566 CCP and 389–392–1 CCP. Article 551 provides 'La citation est délivrée à la requête du ministère public, de la partie civile, et de toute administration qui y est légalement habilitée. L'huissier doit déférer sans délai à leur réquisition. La citation énonce le fait poursuivi et vise le texte de la loi qui le réprime.' Article 550 provides 'Les citations et significations, sauf disposition contraire des lois et règlements, sont faites par exploit d'huissier de justice.'

1418 Leroy, J., *Procédure pénale*, Paris: L.G.D.J., pp.354–355.

1419 *Ibid.*

1420 Article 4–2 CCP. With regard to the press offences, the victim has generally the choice to bring his civil action before the penal or civil judge, except for the situations provided for in Article 46 of the 1881 Press Act concerning certain determined persons protected in Articles 30 and 31 (ministers, representatives, public officials) who can bring defamation cases only before the penal judge.

case of a refusal by a medium to insert a request of reply.[1421] In these cases, by derogation of Article 47, the affected party can set in motion the public prosecution of a press offence and deprive the public prosecutor of any power of appreciation.[1422] In other words, in these cases, the affected party can force the engagement of a public prosecution of a press offence, even if the public prosecutor has decided not to prosecute. Apart from the situations enumerated in Article 48, the affected party has no such right; public prosecutions of press offences are engaged *ex officio* and are exclusively reserved for the initiative of the public prosecutor.

This, however, does not prevent the possibility for the affected party – in relation to all press offences – to constitute as a civil party by means of an intervention by joining his or her civil action to a public prosecution engaged by the public prosecution. The affected party can constitute as a civil party on any moment during the investigation and even during the court hearing.[1423]

10.3. Associations

10.3.1. Qualification: legal entitlement and an interest to act

Pursuant to articles 5 to 6 of the Act of 1 July 1901 'relative au contrat d'associations', every association can act legitimately in court on the condition that they have been regularly declared.[1424] The defence in court presupposes a qualification – that is a legal title – and an interest to act.[1425] As, according to general French criminal procedure, any person who has personnally suffered damages directly caused by a violation of a criminal offence can initiate an 'action civile' and for this purpose set in motion a public prosecution; this equally applies to groupings with legal personality. Hence, associations and other legal entities that are the victim of a racial defamation, insult or provocation can take legal action in order to request damages by invoking a direct and personal interest. An example of this can be found in a previously discussed case, in which the religious movement of the Jehovah witnesses could take legal action on the ground of the offence of religious defamation with regard to expression that equated the movement with an 'association de malfaiteurs' (para.4.3.2 *supra*).[1426] This reasoning was similarly

1421 Article 13 of the 1881 Press Act.

1422 Beignier, De lamy & Dreyer 2009, p.590.

1423 Article 87, respectively 418 CCP.

1424 Loi du 1 Juilliet 1901 relative au contrat d'associations, *JORF* du 2 juillet 1901, p. 4025. Article 5 provides 'Toute association qui voudra obtenir la capacité juridique prévue par l'article 6 devra être rendue publique par les soins de ses fondateurs. (...)'. Article 6 provides 'Toute association régulièrement déclarée peut, sans aucune autorisation spéciale, ester en justice (...)'.

1425 Mallet-Poujol, N., L'action judiciaire des associations en droit des médias, *Légipresse* n° 193, July/August 2002, p.95.

1426 French Supreme Court, civ.ch. II, 14 March 2002, n° 99–19238, *Bull.* 2002 II, n° 46, p.39.

applied in another case, which involved the imputation that the religious movement constituted 'un mouvement totalitaire destructeur'.[1427]

As a result of the general French law and established case law, associations cannot take legal action in defence of collective interests of which they have taken charge, if French law does not explicitly afford such a right. In 1954, the French Supreme Court ruled that 'les associations ne tiennent d'aucune loi le droit de poursuivre des diffamations ou des injures qui ne les atteignent pas personnellement et qui ne peuvent être poursuivies que sur la plainte de ceux qui en ont été directement victimes.'[1428] Nevertheless, French law has increasingly afforded the right to associations to take legal action in order to defend collective interests in certain fields.[1429] This equally applies to the field of press law, which is seriously mobilized by associations that frequently take the initiative to start proceedings. For a large part, these legal actions concern images or messages that hurt certain convictions and religious or moral sensibilities.[1430]

The right of legal action for associations is highly criticized as part of French legal doctrine. Guinard denounces the 'activisme moralisateur' by associations, because 'vouloir transformer en vérité officielle une morale qui n'est peut-être pas partagée par tout le monde, le risque est réel de faire de notre société une société soumise à certaines formes d'intégrisme, de nous conduire à un État ou les conduites individuelles ne seraient plus déterminées par des règles fixées par la représentation nationale, mais par des corps intermédiaires, aux intérêts certes louables, mais qui s'articulent mal avec la notion d'intérêt général'.[1431] What is more, the system of affording associations a qualification to act in court has been characterized as a 'véritable démembrement de la notion d'intérêt général, sous couvert d'un intérêt collectif, transformant lesdites associations, ainsi habilitées, en véritables auxiliares du Parquet, en sentinelles avancées de celui-ci'.[1432] According to Beignier, the civil actions of associations are not aimed at reparation of damages, instead their goal is merely to set in motion the public prosecution in order to get a criminal condemnation and civil reparation is reduced to a symbolic aspect. The civil action is not accessoire to the public action, but an action that prepares the public action. In other words 'l'action civile associative n'a pour finalité que de supprimer l'opportunité des poursuites du Ministère public dans un certain nombre de cas'.[1433] Furthermore, Beignier analyzes how the favor of the law towards the

1427 French Supreme Court, civ.ch. II, 14 March 2002, n°99–19239, *Bull.* 2002 II, n°41, p.43.

1428 French Supreme Court, crim.ch., 16 December 1954, *Bull. Crim.* 1954, n°409. Cited in: Beignier, De Lamy & Dreyer 2009, p.592.

1429 See generally: Mayer, N., Democracy in France: do associations matter?, in: *Generating social capital, civil society and institutions in comparative perspective*, Hooge, M. & Stolle, D. (ed.), New York: Palgrave MacMillen 2003.

1430 Mallet-Poujol 2002, p.95.

1431 Guinchard, S., *Les moralistes au prétoire*, Mélanges Foyer, Paris: PUF 1997, pp.477–478.

1432 Vincent, J. and Guinchard, S., *Procédure civile*, 25th edition, Paris: Dalloz 1999, n° 128.

1433 Beignier 1995, p.257.

civil action of associations had soon been translated into 'l'incrimination de délits envers des collectivités susceptible d'être blessées dans leur honneur.'[1434]

In order to prevent the existence of true censorship exercised by associations, the 1881 Press Act, however, limits the right of legal action for associations in several respects. The associations can only take legal action in the cases provided by the 1881 Press Act and their statutes; Articles 48–1 to 48–6 limitatively enumerate the associations that 1) according to their statutes defend a determined interest and 2) are regularly declared at least five years before the occurrence of the facts, that is the publication of the expression, that can take legal action on the ground of 3) determined press offences. For example, in 2011, the French Minister for Internal Affairs, Brice Hortefeux, remained unpunished in a case set in motion by an anti-racism association on the ground of racial insult with regard to his statement concerning Arabs 'Quand il y en a un ça va. C'est quand il y a beaucoup qu'il y a des problèmes'. Although the event had secretly been filmed and placed on the Internet, it had taken place during an annual youth gathering of the political party UMP. Therefore, the facts had to be requalified as a non-public racial insult (Article 624–4 of the French Criminal Code), with regard to which, the association had no capacity to act.[1435]

It was the Pleven Act of 1972 that inserted into Article 48–1 of the 1881 Press Act the right for associations, which according to their statutes fight against racism or assist victims of discrimination based on their origin, nation, ethnic background, race or religion to exercise the rights afforded to the civil affected party in case of a violation of the offences of racial defamation, insult and provocation (para.3.3.4 *supra*). By derogation of Articles 47 and 48, these associations can, even though they cannot invoke any personal and direct damages, set in motion public prosecutions and constitute as a civil party. The statutory qualification to represent a collective interest exempts an association from the burden of proving the existence of direct damages, i.e. to have personally suffered from the facts. The courts have had some difficulty in admitting this competence. In a decision of 1 December 1981, the French Supreme Court had to recall 'que les associations détiennent de par la loi le pouvoir d'exercer les droits reconnus à la partie civile pour mettre en movement l'action publique, sans autre condition.'[1436] The Act of 30 December 2004 extended this right to the discriminatory grounds of sex, sexual orientation and handicap in Articles 48–4 until 48–6 in the 1881 Press Act (para.7.2 *supra*). The Gayssot Act of 13 July 1990 inserted this right into Article 48–2 with regard to the offence of denial of crimes against humanity for associations, which according to their statutes defend the moral interests and honour of the Resistence and the deportees (para.8.2.4 *supra*).

1434 Beignier 1995, p.249.

1435 Paris Court of Appeal 15 September 2011, *Légipresse* n° 287 October 2011, 287–21, p. 531–532.

1436 French Supreme Court, crim.ch., 1 December 1981, n° 80–92810, *Bull. Crim.* 1981, n° 317. NB. The case concerned a civil action of the association MRAP on the ground of Articles 187–1 and 416 CP.

If racial defamations, insults and provocations target a group as a whole, the legal action of an association is admissible without prior consent. For example, the French Supreme Court has considered that the public prosecution on the ground of racial provocation 'ne peut être mise en mouvement que par le ministère public, sans d'ailleurs qu'une plainte préalable soit nécessaire, ou par l'une des associations habilitées.'[1437] If such expression targets an individual person, the association must obtain his or her prior consent in order for the association to be admissible in its legal action. This requirement is strictly interpreted. An example can be seen in a previously discussed case, in which AGRIF could take legal action on the ground of the offence of religious defamation with regard to expression that associated the Carmel of Auschwitz with Nazi practices without the consent of the victim(s), because the expression targeted 'non seulement la congregation religieuse d'Auschwitz, à la supposer dotée de la personalité morale, mais encore le groupe de personnes physiques membres de ladite congregation [...] ainsi que l'ensemble des religieux susceptibles d'être associés à ce comportement.' (para.4.3.2 *supra*).[1438]

Other than anti-racism associations, persons who are individually targeted by racial defamations, insults or provocations cannot set in motion public prosecutions, but can merely constitute as a civil party by means of an intervention.[1439] For example, the French Supreme Court considered that the annulment of a prosecution on the ground of racial provocation exercised based on the complaint of a victim did not violate article 6 ECHR and determined that the special rules of articles 47 and 48 do not deprive the affected party of intervening in the public prosecution engaged by the public prosecutor or engage a civil action separately from the public action.[1440]

Associations can only set in motion a public prosecution on the ground of the French hate speech bans, if they according to their statutes have the objective of fighting against racism and discrimination. Such an objective must be clearly expressed in the statutes of the association. Hence, in 2002, the French Supreme Court considered that an association that defends the rights of families could not take legal action on the ground of 24–8 with regard to expression alleged to provoke discrimination against families of foreign origin. In 2013, the French Supreme Court found that the Chamber of commerce France-Israël could not constitute as a civil party in a case concerning a video that incited the boycott of Israeli products, because its sole social objective was to fight against *commercial* discrimination and not against racism and discrimination based on national or ethnic background, race or religion.[1441] Likewise, anti-racism associations can only constitute as a civil

[1437] French Supreme Court, crim.ch., 3 March 1980, n°78–91949, *Bull. Crim.* 1980, n° 74.

[1438] French Supreme Court, crim.ch., 7 December 1993, n°90–87508, *Bull. Crim.* 1993 n°373, p.472.

[1439] Beignier, De Lamy, Dreyer 2009, p.593.

[1440] French Supreme Court, crim.ch., 5 March 2002, n°01–83777, *Bull. Crim.* 2002 n°55, p.166.

[1441] French Supreme Court, crim.ch., 17 December 2002, n°01–85650, *Bull. Crim.* 2002 n°227, p.832. French Supreme Court, crim.ch., 19 November 2013, n°12–84083, *Bull. Crim.* 2002 n°232.

party in a proceeding concerning the offence of denial of crimes against humanity, if their statutes explicitly provide in the defence of moral interests or honour of the Resistence or the deportees. This is the case for the association LICRA,[1442] but not for the association SOS Racisme.[1443]

The French Supreme Court has, however, given a broad interpretation to the notion of an anti-racism association. It was in 1993, in the previously discussed case concerning the caricature of a gonflated Christ in the journal *Fluide glacial* (para.6.5.1 *supra*), that the French Supreme Court considered that AGRIF could have directly summoned the journal before the court on the ground of the offence of religious provocation, because according to its statutes the association had the intention to fight against racism, more specifically the defence of 'des valeurs menacées de notre civilisation' and against 'le racisme antifrançais et antichrétien', which constituted a punishable form of racism and because 'le racisme (…) s'entend de toute discrimination fondée sur l'origine ou l'appartenance ou la non-appartenance soit à une race, soit à une ethnie, soit à une nation, soit à une religion, *sans restriction ni exclusion* [curs. EHJ].'[1444] For the same reasons, in 1993 the French Supreme Court found the legal actions of AGRIF based on the offence of religious defamation admissible in the previously discussed cases concerning the Carmel of Auschwitz and 'les églises catholiques de l'Est' (para.4.3.2 *supra*).[1445]

This case law of the French Supreme Court is criticized for extending the right of legal action of anti-racism associations that fight against racism and discrimination in general, to associations with the limited objective of fighting against racism and discrimination of certain groups. According to Korman, the French Supreme Court has justified an objective of an association that is in itself discriminatory of Frenchmen, as the aim of AGRIF is to protect 'les Français Chrétiens'. Korman argues that although every particular group has the right to be protected as a group an association that *a priori* aims to fight racism cannot limit this objective to one single group.[1446]

AGRIF forms a group of persons that was constituted in 1974 under the name 'Centre national de coordination des comités d'action politique et sociale'. Its original statutes did not originally comprise the fight against racism in its objectives. This objective was added in 1984 when it was transformed under its new name.[1447] For this reason, in 1986, the French Supreme Court confirmed the inadmissibility of AGRIF in its complaint grounded on the offence of racial provocation. According

1442 French Supreme Court, crim.ch., 28 September 2004, n°04–80688, *Bull. Crim.* 2004, n° 223, p.796.

1443 French Supreme Court, crim.ch., 28 November 2006, n° 06–80340, *Bull. Crim.* 2006, n° 300, p.1080.

1444 French Supreme Court, crim.ch., 7 December 1993, n°92–81.091, *Bull. Crim.* 1993 n°374, p.935.

1445 French Supreme Court, crim.ch. 7 December 1993, n°90–87508, *Bull. Crim.* 1993 n°373, p.472; French Supreme Court, crim.ch., 2 March 1993, n° 91–84653, *Bull. Crim.* 1993, n° 94, *Légipresse* n° 110, p.44.

1446 Korman 1998, p.132.

1447 Mallet-Poujol 2002, p.96.

to the French Supreme Court, AGRIF was admissible in its fight against racism five years from the date on which the social objective defined by its statutes was modified, not from the moment it was declared; the objective to 'défendre les valeurs menacées de notre civilisation, combattre les idées subversives et proposer des solutions de renouveau' did not comply with the aim assigned to Article 48–1.[1448] In the *Fluide glacial* case in 1993, the French Supreme Court found AGRIF admissible, not only because the objective to fight against racism had been added to its statutes five years before the occurrence of the facts, but also because Article 48–1 does not require that an association has 'l'unicité d'objet', one single objective.[1449]

Given the favor of the law towards the civil action of associations, the question arises as to whether the fear expressed by the legislator of 1972 has become a reality: have anti-racism associations become too powerful in initiating proceedings, because they, being specialized in their personal anti-racism campaigns, have lost sight of the general interest in the fight against racism? In the case of AGRIF, I would tend to answer this question in the affirmative. The association was, without exception, at the origin of all previously discussed cases concerning the ridiculing of the Catholic faith and at every turn its demands were denied (para.4.5.3 and 6.5.1 *supra*). The interest of freedom of expression seems to call for a de-juridization in this field.

10.3.2. Les Français Chrétiens

There has been a multiplication in the eighties and nineties of actions before the civil judge grounded on 1382 CC or 809 CCP against images or messages that hurt certain convictions and religious or moral sensibilities instituted by associations that defend religious interests (para.5.4.1 *supra*). The cases are not only criticized for introducing into French law a civil prohibition of blasphemy, but also for creating the right for religious associations to defend their religion and dogmas in court, while the French legislator has not explicitly afforded such legal entitlement.[1450]

In the *Ave Maria* case, the tribunal declared the association Saint Pie X admissible in its action, 'dès lors qu'elle endendait defendre par ses statuts, les principes et dogmes constitutant la religion et la morale catholique, et invoquer pour ce faire un intérêt moral tenu pour légitime par les règles de la vie sociale française'.[1451] Such was confirmed in appeal.[1452] In this case, the French civil judge did not only reintroduce a prohibition of blasphemy into French law, but also afforded associations that aim to protect religious principles and dogmas against

1448 French Supreme Court, crim.ch., 22 October 1986, n° 85–95307, *Bull. Crim.* 1986, n° 302, p.771.

1449 French Supreme Court, crim.ch., 7 December 1993, n°92–81.091, *Bull. Crim.* 1993 n°374, p.935.

1450 Droin 2009, pp.439–440.

1451 TGI de Paris, 23 October 1984, *GP* 1984, p.722; *D.* 1985, p.31, annotation R. Lindon.

1452 CA Paris, 26 October 1984, *JCP* 1985 II 20452, annotation Th. Hassler.

criticism that might hurt religious feelings the right to act in the interests of religious adherents before the judge, while this is reserved for the exclusive competence of the French legislator, who has not created any provision affording such a specific legal capacity.[1453]

In the *VSD* case, the tribunal found a complaint made by AGRIF admissible because of 'l'atteinte aux sentiments religieux que partagent ses membres et qu'elle s'est donnée pour objectif de protéger'. The Court of Appeal repeated the considerations from the *Ave Maria* case: 'les associations sont recevables à agir dès lors que, par les statuts ou par leur titre personnel fondé sur une croyance individuelle propre, elles agissent pour défendre par les voies de droit les principes et dogmes de la religion et invoquent un intérêt moral légitime sans que pour autant les tribunaux aient à arbitrer entre les différentes conceptions que peuvent avoir les croyants quant aux exigences de leur foi'.[1454] The Court thus, however, admitted that the objective of AGRIF that pretends to defend all Catholics against the offence of their religion and dogmas is not that general and decided on the merits that the expression constituted an offence of the religious feelings of 'certain Catholics'.[1455]

In the *Je vous salue Marie* case, the tribunal called the action of AGRIF 'au nom d'un intérêt collectif très vivement contesté'.[1456] In the case of *La dernière tentation du Christ*, the jurisdictions gave judgments without the question of admissibility even being raised.[1457] In both cases, the demands of the associations were finally rejected on the merits of the case.

In 2000, the French Supreme Court annulled the decision of the Court of Appeal that had declared AGRIF inadmissible in its action, which aimed at the prohibition of the sale of the book entitled INRI depicting on its cover a crucified naked woman, because the expression did not violate any collective interest of the association. Contrarily, according to the Supreme Court, 'il résulte des statuts de l'association que'elle avait un intérêt légitime à agir contre un publication qui, selon elle, porte atteinte aux sentiments religieux de ses membres, qu'elle s'est donné pour objet de protéger'.[1458]

In all of these cases, the courts, with regard to the question of the admissibility of the religious associations, admitted certain actions grounded on the argument of their statutory objective and thus their speciality, but at the same time leaned on the idea of a violation of the interests of their members and thus of their representativeness and function of defence. According to Mallet-Poujol, the decisions are therefore torn between two ideas. However, the diffusion of 'indecent'

1453 In the same sense: Droin 2009, p.439.

1454 TGI de Paris, 15 December 1993; CA Paris, 3 July 1995, *JCP G* 1996, II, 22601, annotation C. Duvert.

1455 Droin 2009, p.440.

1456 TGI de Paris, 28 January 1985, *D.* 1985, p.129, annotation R. Lindon.

1457 TGI de Paris, 22 September 1988; CA Paris, 27 September 1988, *D.* 1989 Somm. 301, annotation Th. Hassler; French Supreme Court, civ.ch. I, 29 October 1990, no°88–19366, *Bull.* 1990 I, n°226, p.161.

1458 French Supreme Court, civ.ch. I, 14 November 2000, n° 99–10778, *Bull.* 2000 I, n°289, p.187.

images or messages will not shock 'la Moralité' with a big M, without shocking the spectators. In press law, the interest of individual members is therefore rarely indissociable from the collectif interest that can be regarded as the sum of the interests of individual members.[1459]

Beignier criticizes the actions of religious associations in order to protect their religion, dogmas and religious feelings: 'toutes ces actions, qu'il s'agisse de préserver la foi chrétienne ou la foi islamique, ont été intentées par des personnes minoritaires dans leur confession, souvent animées de convictions 'intégristes' en totale opposition avec les valeurs unanimement respectées en France. Cela est tout particulièrement vrai pour les catholiques, certains prêtres ayant esté en justice étant à l'époque suspens a divinis, et depuis peut-être excommuniés.[1460] Likewise, Fourest and Venner analyze how the legal actions of associations of different kinds of religions have put 'la laïcité à l'épreuve des intégrismes juif, chrétien et musulman'.[1461] Boulègue describes in detail how early cases were initiatied by extreme right winged, conservative Catholic associations and supported by the Episcopat and how Islamic associations have followed their tracks of activism. What is more, the religious associations found the support of 'islamo-gauchistes'; the actions are evident of a certain convergence and solidarity between religious conservatives.[1462]

10.4. Effective enforcement

By placing the action of anti-racism associations at the core of the mechanism that sets in motion the public prosecution, the French legislator has placed the associations on seemingly equal footing with the public prosecutor. An association that sets in motion a public prosecution by a complaint and constitution as a civil party in order to provoke the designation of the investigating judge or by directly summoning the offender of a press offence before the court produces the 'initial act' of the prosecution. Like the public prosecutor in his Introductory Submission or summons, it must therefore comply with the strict procedural rules of the 1881 Press Act and use the correct legal definition of the acts, i.e. the exact qualification of the criminal act and the applicable article, under penalty of nullity (para.1.3.1 *supra*). In the case of a complaint, after its consignation, the complaint of the association and the Introductory Submission of the public prosecutor form an indivisible whole; they can neutralize each others insufficiencies and irregularities and the appreciation of the validity of the prosecution is exercised in a global manner on the basis of these two acts.[1463] In case of a direct citation before the

[1459] Mallet-Poujol 2002, pp.100–101.

[1460] Beignier 1995, p.336.

[1461] Fourest, C.; Venner, F., *Tirs croisés, La laïcité à l'épreuve des intégrismes juif, chrétien et musulman*, Paris: Le livre de Poche, Calmann-Lévy 2003.

[1462] Boulègue, J., *Le Blasphème en procès 1984–2009, l'église et la mosquée contre les libertés*, Paris: Nova Éditions 2010.

[1463] Beignier, De Lamy & Dreyer 2009, p.603.

court, the association must notify the public prosecutor of the prosecution, in order to associate him to the prosecution as a joined party.[1464]

An association that sets in motion a public prosecution thus has a relatively strong position as a civil party to the public prosecution; it chooses and indicates which exact passages within a publication are prosecuted and the exact press offence as the legal basis. This implies that an association, in its civil action before the criminal court, may or even must give an appreciation as to the constitution of the press offence and thus the punishability of the expression; a qualification supposes an argumentation. Contrarily, as an association remains a civil party, it cannot give an opinion as to the imposition of a penalty, but can only request for damages. It equally results that an association can appeal the decision of the court to reject the requested damages up until the French Supreme Court.

On the basis of empirical research, Secondi-Nix describes how anti-racism associations, by initiating public prosecutions, have contributed to the evolution of case law.[1465] According to Secondi-Nix, by their legal actions, the associations have played a determinant role in the evolution of the definition of the notion of a group. While in early decisions the courts used a quantitative criterion for the notion of a group, they have replaced this quantitative criterion by qualitative criteria, by accepting the arguments elaborated by the associations. In a decision of 3 December 1991, the French Supreme Court adopted the arguments by LICRA that the publication of an article entitled 'Les Juifs qui en font trop' in the extreme right magazine *Le choc du mois* did not only intend to criticize certain Jews that exploit the Jewish martyrdom, but the Jewish community as a whole and considered 'l'auteur étend à la collectivité juive dans son ensemble les griefs énoncés dans le texte, formulés auparavant à l'egard de certaines personnes prises individuellement.'[1466] The Court therefore rejected an appeal against the condemnation on the ground of racial defamation.

In the previously discussed decision of 16 July 1992 (para.6.2 *supra*), the French Supreme Court approved the argumentation of LICRA that, although an article reproducing two stickers with the text 'Rapport Leuchter, fini les chambres à gaz?' and 'les coupeurs de verge à la grande vergue' that imputed the Jewish community to lie about the existence of gaz chambers did not explicitly designate the Jewish community, the author, who had found the text on the stickers not to be intolerable or scandalous, he had aimed at the Jewish community as the principle victim of the Nazi concentration camps. The Court therefore confirmed the condemnation on the ground racial provocation.[1467]

In the previously discussed decision of 24 June 1997 (para.6.3 *supra*), the French Supreme Court adopted the arguments by LICRA, i.e. that an election pamphlet making a commitment to fight immigration fiercely, calling for the 'envahisseurs' to

---

1464 Article 53–2 of the 1881 Press Act. See further: Beignier, De Lamy & Dreyer 2009, p.618.

1465 Secondi-Nix, M., *Lutte contre le racisme et justice pénale, Rôle des associations*, CNRS, CESDIP, October 1996, p.116.

1466 French Supreme Court, crim.ch., 3 December 1991, n°90–83605, *unpublished*.

1467 French Supreme Court, crim.ch., 16 July 1992, n° 91–86.156, *Bull. Crim.* 1992, n° 273, p.740.

be driven out immediately and demanding the expulsion of 'des étrangers irrespectueux et nuisibles' formed a punishable racial provocation, because immigrants constitute a protected group. The Court, therefore, confirmed the condemnation and considered 'Qu'en effet, les étrangers résidant en France, lorsqu'ils sont visés *en raison de leur non-appartenance à la nation française*, forment un groupe de personnes au sens de l'article 24 alinéa 6 de la loi du 29 juillet 1881'.[1468] [curs. EHJ]

The possibility for associations to set in motion a public prosecution enables assocations to bring cases before the court concerning politically delicate subjects that the public prosecutor might be reluctant to prosecute exactly for this reason. In the case concerning the expression of politician Le Pen 'd'autant que quand je dis qu'avec 25 millions de musulmans chez nous, les français raseront les murs, des gens dans la salle me disent non sans raison: 'mais monsieur Le Pen, c'est déjà le cas maintenant', it was the association LDH that had directly cited Le Pen before the correctional tribunal. The French Supreme Court finally rejected the appeal by Le Pen who argued that he denounced the danger of an augmentation of Muslim immigrants on the ground of their general dominant attitude, not on the ground of their religion and that Islam was not a religion, but a political, sociological or philosophical ideology.[1469]

In the *Mohammed cartoons* case, it was the association *La société des habous et des lieux saints de l'Islam* that had directly cited the chief-editor of *Charlie Hebdo* before the court and was joined by several other Muslim associations.[1470] Contrarily, the associations SOS Racisme and LDH had declared its support of the publication, although the lawyer of the LDH declared that the cartoon depicting Mohammed with a bomb in its turban constituted an insult of Muslims on the ground of their religion.[1471] According to the public prosecutor, the cartoon merely denounced the use of violence by Islamic terrorists and therefore requested an acquittal.[1472]

In fact, all previously discussed cases concerning criticism of Islam, islamization and Muslim-immigration on the ground of religious provocation have been, without exception, initiated by the associations (para.6.5.2 *supra*).[1473] While the French

1468 French Supreme Court, crim.ch., 24 June 1997, n° 95–81187, *Bull. Crim.* 1997, n°253, p.864.

1469 French Supreme Court, crim.ch., 3 February 2009, n°06–83.063 08–82.402, *Bull. Crim.* 2009, n° 25.

1470 Amongst others the associations *L'Union des organisations islamiques de France* and *la Ligue islamique mondiale*.

1471 Boulègue 2010, p.179.

1472 Boulègue 2010, p.186.

1473 The associations LDH and MRAP deposed a complaint and constituted as a civil party with regard to the pamphlet 'Stop l'immigration, la France pour les Français'; LICRA and MRAP deposed a complaint and constituted as a civil party with regard to the expression 'des hordes musulmans inadmissilables'; MRAP directly cited the person responsible for the expression 'commerçants extra-européens' before the court; SOS Racisme initiated the case about the pamphlet concerning the city of Menton; l'Association de solidarité avec les travailleurs immigrés (ASTI) directly cited the person responsible for the tract 'Non à l'islamisation de Sainte Lazare' before the court; LICRA directly cited the person responsible for the pamphlet 'Pas de cathédrale à la Mecque, pas de mosquée à Strasbourg' before the court; the associations LICRA, SOS Racisme and MRAP all started multiple cases against the pamphlet 'Non à l'islamisme'.

Supreme Court in some of these cases endorsed the vision of the associations that the expression aimed at Muslims as a group on the ground of their religion, in the other cases the French Supreme Court rejected this vision and found that the expression formed free criticism of a religion, its practices and immigration policy. By their legal actions, the associations have thus played a determinant role in the development of the line in case law that demarcates free criticism of a religion that might hurt religious feelings from the disqualification in harsh terms of a determined religious group.

10.5. Government policy

The hypothesis according to which anti-racism associations form a 'contre-pouvoir' against the public prosecutor who remains inactive can be attenued by an analysis of the criminal policy of the French Ministry for Justice that is aimed at an effective response to racism, anti-Semitism and discrimination. This policy is twofold. Firstly, it establishes highly specialized officials charged with the enforcement of anti-racism and anti-discrimination laws, which includes amongst others, the magistrates of the judiciary, of the Public Prosecution, and public servants such as police officers. The circular of 11 July 2007 created the 'pôles antidiscriminations' within every Tribunal de Grande Instance, which are directed by a referent magistrate of the Public Prosecution, who is charged with taking action in the field of racism and discrimination in close connection with several associations that dispose of relevant knowledge.[1474]

Secondly, the policy establishes dense relations between these officials and civil society, amongst others anti-racism and anti-discrimination associations and representatives of religious associations in order to cooperate and consult in the joint fight against racism and discrimination. Several circulars and specific framework conventions provide for such cooperation and consultation.[1475] On 14 December 2007 the Minister for Justice signed two framework conventions with the associations LICRA and SOS Racisme that were aimed at joint action in the fight against discrimination. According to the preamble of these conventions:

> 'Le ministère de la justice, en s'appuyant d'une part sur une législation renforcée dans le domaine et d'autre part sur la mise en place de pôles anti-discriminations au sein des parquets sur l'ensemble du territoire national, comme prévu par la circulaire du 11 juillet 2007, démontre son engagement dans la lutte contre les discriminations et sa volonté d'encourager les victimes à saisir la justice.
> La lutte contre les discriminations, pour être efficace, doit s'appuyer sur un partenariat réunissant tous les acteurs institutionnels et associatifs. Dans cette perspective le ministère de la justice et l'association LICRA, décident de conclure la présente

1474 Described in: CNCDH 2009, pp. 149–150.; CNCDH 2008, pp.146–147.; CNCDH 2007, pp.173–174.; CNCDH 2006, pp.154–155.; CNCDH 2005, pp.135–136.

1475 Described in: CNCDH 2009, pp. 149–150.; CNCDH 2008, pp.146–147.; CNCDH 2007, pp.173–174.; CNCDH 2006, pp.154–155.; CNCDH 2005, pp.135–136.

> convention afin de développer des réseaux, articulés avec les poles anti-discriminations, chargés de la lutte contre les discriminations fondées sur l'origine, l'appartenance réelle ou supposée, à une ethnie, une nation, une race ou une religion.'[1476]

Article 1 stipulates the engagements of the associations to, on the one hand, develop an active partnership with the offices of the public prosecution of the Tribunaux de Grande Instance and more specifically with the pôles anti-discriminations by means of a close and regular relation with the referent magistrate charged with the direction of the pôle,[1477] and to, on the other hand, educate the staff of the judiciary, judges and clerks, and other professionals susceptible of being in contact with victims of discrimination, such as police officers, in order to create awareness about discriminations.

The circular of 8 January 2009 recalled the necessity for the offices of the public prosecution to firmly respond to facts concerning Islamic or Jewish places of worship or persons on the ground of their religion or origin. In the circular of 5 March 2009, the Minister for Justice requested the Prosecutors-General to extend the competence to all acts committed on the ground of ethnic background, nation, race or religion or sexual orientation, in order to consign the treatment of the complete body of infractions of a racist or xenophobic character to a specialized magistrate – as the specific procedural rules for several infractions demand particular expertise – and to favor the exchanges between the offices of the public prosecution, the associations and the representatives of religious communities, seen as essential for a pertinent response to acts of a racist or xenophobe character. The circular of 1 April 2009 recalls the possibility for the public prosecutors to request any association helping victims of discrimination or racism to intervene in order to support them at all stages of the procedure of complaint.

Pursuant to the policy of the Ministry of Justice, an informal collaboration between the Public Prosecutor and the associations has thus increasingly come into existence. Such collaboration dates back to 1989, when for the first time the idea was launched with the Public Prosecution to associate themselves with the actions taken by the associations by presenting them as 'privileged interlocutors'.[1478] Starting from this date, the collective action taken by private groups was regarded as complementary to the actions by the Public Prosecution. Rather than a 'contre-pouvoir', the associations are even said to have become a 'relais-citoyen', civil assistant, of the Public Prosecution before the repressive jurisdictions.[1479]

1476 The Framework conventions are available at www.justice.gouv.fr/art_pix/1_LICRA.pdf; www.justice.gouv.fr/art_pix/1_sosracisme.pdf.

1477 In particular, the associations engage amongst others to inform the judiciary about the difficulties victims of discrimination meet when filing complaint and solutions to favor the emergence of complaints by victims of discrimination; to accompany victims in their actions; to participate in the operation of testing; and to keep the offices of the public prosecution up to date about current events and case law in the field of discrimination.

1478 Secondi-Nix 1996, p.70.

1479 Secondi-Nix 1996, p.78.

In the Parisian district – where nine out of ten press cases take place given the high concentration of publishing companies – the office of the public prosecution organizes monthly consultations with anti-racism associations, where MRAP and LICRA are principally represented, in order to discuss the engagement of proceedings. The meetings facilitate the constitution as a civil party by associations in the public actions engaged by the public prosecution; a devision of roles that remains most common and preferred by the associations given the high procedural requirements for, and thus risk of invalidity of, the engagement of prosecutions. The annual reports concerning *La lutte contre le racisme, l'antisémitisme et la xénophobie* comprise the perspectives and evaluations of the activities of the anti-racism associations LDH, LICRA, MRAP and SOS Racisme. In the report on 2012, LICRA states to have been a civil party in 109 procedures throughout 2012, 61 percent of which concerned the hate speech bans.[1480]

The anti-racism associations thus play an important role in the fight against racism by the French government. Therefore, the legal services of the anti-racism associations LICRA, SOS Racisme, MRAP and LDH obtain financial support from the government in the context of the specific framework conventions. For example, on 1 December 2010, LICRA signed a convention with the Minister for Interior Affairs that aimed *inter alia* to exchange information on hate speech offences committed on the Internet. Since 2012, the partnerships of the French Government with the anti-racism and other civil society associations now form part of the broader *National Plan of Action against Racism and Anti-Semitism 2012–2014*.[1481]

10.6. Conclusion

Racism and discrimination affects the public order to such an extent that, pursuant to Articles 47 jo 48 of the 1881 Press Act, the engagement of the public prosecution of the French hate speech bans takes place *ex officio*, i.e. on the initiative of the public prosecutor without the need for a prior complaint by the victim. In addition, Article 48–1 affords anti-racism associations the right to set in motion public prosecutions on the ground of the hate speech bans by deposing a complaint and by constituting as a civil party in order to provoke the designation of the investigating judge or by directly citing the offender of a hate speech ban before the criminal court. The anti-racism associations can thus deprive the public prosecutor of any power of appreciation and can force the engagement of a public prosecution. In addition to anti-racism associations, persons who are individually targeted by racial defamations, insults or provocations cannot set in motion public prosecutions, but can merely constitute as a civil party by means of an intervention.

1480 CNCDH report 2012, p. 394.

1481 Available at: www.interieur.gouv.fr/Le-ministere/Organisation/Delegue-Interministeriel-a-la-Lutte-contre-le-Racisme-et-l-Antisemitisme/Plan-national-d-action-contre-le-racisme-et-l-antisemitisme-2012–2014.

The 1881 Press Act limits the possibility to take legal action on the ground of the hate speech bans to associations that according to their statutes have the objective of fighting against racism and are regularly declared at least five years before the publication of the expression. The French Supreme Court has, however, given a broad interpretation of the notion of an anti-racism association, comprising associations with the limited objective of fighting against racism and discrimination of certain groups. In the field of press law, associations are very active in the initiation of legal actions that for a large part concern images or messages that hurt certain convictions and religious or moral sensibilities. This moral activism is denounced for protecting collective interests, which is difficult to reconcile with the notion of – the fight against racism in – the general interest, and for being primarily aimed at obtaining criminal condemnations, not reparation of damages.

In the eighties and nineties, the civil judge afforded the right for religious associations to defend their religion and dogmas in court, on the ground of Articles 1382 CC or 809 CCP, while the French legislator has not explicitly afforded such legal entitlement, and has found religious associations admissible as much on the idea of a violation of the collective interests of their members as on their statutory objective. Given the overall favor of the law towards the legal actions of anti-racism associations, the fear of the legislator of 1972 that anti-racism associations would become too powerful in initiating proceedings might be justified.

On the other hand, the possibility for associations to bring politically delicate subjects before the judge might be regarded as an advantage. As an association that sets in motion a public prosecution produces the 'initial act' in the prosecution, it has a relatively strong position as a civil party to the public prosecution. Subsequently, anti-racism associations, by initiating public prosecutions, have contributed to the evolution of case law concerning the notion of a group, more specifically to the development of the line in case law that demarcates free criticism of a religion that might hurt religious feelings from the disqualification in harsh terms of a determined religious group.

The thesis according to which anti-racism associations form a 'contre-pouvoir' against the public prosecutor who remains inactive can be attenued by an analysis of the criminal policy of the French Ministry for Justice aimed at an effective response to racism, anti-Semitism and discrimination. Several circulars and specific framework conventions provide for a dense cooperation and consultation between specialized officials and anti-racism associations and religious associations for a joint fight against racism and discrimination. The associations are regarded as 'privileged interlocutors', whose collective actions complement the actions by the Public Prosecution. This practice fits into the vision of the French legislator of 1972, according to which associations must reinforce the fraternity between citizens, form natural allies in the fight against racism and discrimination, and share responsibility with the Government to ensure the freedom and equality of all citizens.

CHAPTER 5
THE NETHERLANDS

ABBREVIATIONS

Aant.	Comment
BW	Dutch Civil Code
CDA	Christian Democratic Party
CEDAW	UN Women's Treaty
CGB	Equal Treatment Commission
CHU	(former) Protestant Party
CU	Christian Union
Comm.	Commentary
CPH	(former) Communist Party
Crim ch.	Criminal chamber
D66	Democratic Party
diss.	dissertation
ECHR	European Convention of Human Rights
ECmHR	(former) European Commission of Human Rights
ECtHR	European Court of Human rights
ed./eds.	editor/ editors
et al.	et alii – and others
et seq.	et sequens – and the following
ICERD	International Convention on the Elimination of all forms of Racism and Discrimination
ICCPR	International Covenant on Civil and Political Rights
LJN	National jurisprudence number
NJ	Nederlandse jurisprudentie
para.	paragraph
PvdA	Labour Party
PVV	Freedom Party
SGP	Reformed Protestant Party
Sr	Dutch Criminal Code
Stb.	Staatsblad – Dutch law gazette
Sv	Dutch Code of Criminal Procedure
Trb.	Treatises gazette
VARA	Socialist Broadcasting Company
VVD	Liberal Party
WODC	Scientific Research and Documentation Centre
WRR	Scientific Council for Government Policy

INTRODUCTION

This chapter gives an in-depth examination of the relationship between freedom of expression and restrictions to hate speech in the national law of the Netherlands. The chapter analyses the content and scope of the existing Dutch hate speech bans, their underlying rationales and their relationship with freedom of expression on the basis of their drafting history, their application by the judge, their embedding in Dutch law and on the basis of primarily Dutch literature. Furthermore, particular attention is paid to the interplay between the different actors in the determination of the restrictions to hate speech: the Dutch legislator, the public prosecution, the judge, and the victims of hate speech and anti-racism and other civil society associations. The chapter provides the reference points for the comparison with the French law and the approach under the European Convention of Human Rights (ECHR) in Chapter 6 – on the basis of the four factors of the analytical framework of Chapter 2.

To a certain extent, the current chapter continues with the structure used in the previous chapter on France. That chapter was divided into three parts based on the devise of the French Republic '*Freedom, Equality, Brotherhood*' that inspires French public law and is also understood to reflect three pillars of the democratic constitutional state. The chosen structure thereby enabled the discussion of the French law on hate speech against the background of the French conception of democracy. Although the Dutch Constitution does not declare a particular device of the Dutch state and the three principles of the French device cannot simply be transposed to Dutch law, the latter may be used as a general model to frame the discussion of the Dutch law on hate speech. Moreover, continuing the structure of the previous chapter is a good way to bring to the fore not only the similarities but also the differences between French and Dutch law on hate speech.

In Dutch law *freedom* and *equality* also constitute two fundamental principles and the restrictions on hate speech are also influenced by a certain interpretation of their interrelatedness. The Dutch Constitution, however, does not define the characteristics of the Dutch Constitutional State. The Dutch State is not envisioned as a political bond of *brotherhood*, a political entity inseparable from civil society consisting of an *active participation* in civil and political rights and collective power. The fact that the Dutch legislator has afforded the public prosecution the exclusive right to prosecute criminal offences may be placed in this light. This may also explain the limited cooperation and consultation between the public prosecution and anti-racism and other civil society associations concerning the enforcement of the hate speech bans. Criminal justice is considered to be a public interest that should not to be governed by private considerations.

This has not always been the case. In 1811, when the Kingdom of the Netherlands was annexed by Napoleon's France, the first Dutch Criminal Code *Crimineel Wetboek voor het Koninkrijk Holland (1809–1811)* was replaced by the French *Code Pénal* of 1810. In that same year, the French *Code d' Instruction Criminelle* entered into force, which provided for the 'action civile', i.e. the right of the victim of a criminal offence to set in motion a public prosecution. After the Netherlands had regained its independence, the civil action was abrogated in 1838, but the French *Code Pénal* remained in force until the first version of the Dutch Criminal Code was established in 1881 and entered into force in 1886.[1482] Given this shared history, the French legal system has undeniably influenced the Dutch legal system – both in relation to its criminal and civil law.[1483] But the precise aim of the Dutch Criminal Code of 1886 was to depart from the system of the French *Code Pénal* and inspiration was drawn, amongst others, from the Belgian, German and Italian Criminal Codes.[1484] This also notably applied to the insertion of certain speech offences.

Dutch free speech doctrine also did not explicitly adopt the French traditional concept of the 'délit d'opinion'. Dutch and French criminal laws were on the other hand grounded on the same basic principles; the only punishable conduct is conduct that consciously causes direct harm to others and if it has actually caused harm to someone.[1485] Just as with the French Press Act, over time the Dutch Criminal Code has been supplemented with offences that increasingly deviate from its original principles. Certain values were considered so important that the criminalization of the violation thereof was considered to be justified. This also applied to the interests protected by the hate speech bans. However, in the Netherlands the necessity of their existence primarily results from the obligations arising from international treaties and they cannot be said to be a corollary of any basic principles or values set by the Dutch Constitution; given its sober character, the latter functions less as a compass for the organization of society including the parameters of public debate.

Against this background, *Part One* discusses the central characteristics of the protection of the free expression of opinion in Dutch law. *Part Two* discusses the hate speech bans as restrictions to the free expression of opinion in Dutch law. *Part Three* discusses the enforcement of the hate speech bans by the public prosecution in Dutch law and the position of affected parties including anti-racism associations. While the first and third part of the chapter forms an introduction, respectively a complement to the second part, the latter forms the body of the chapter and consists of several paragraphs. The paragraphs are always completed with a conclusion. This is different to the rest of the chapters as a whole as it does not culminate in a final conclusion. To avoid unnecessary repetition, chapter 6, the last chapter of this study, provides a joint further analysis and synthesis of the consistency of

---

1482 Wet van 15 April 1886, Stb 1886, 64, tot invoering van het Wetboek van Strafrecht.

1483 Cf. Asscher, B.E. & Simons, D., *Het nieuwe wetboek van strafrecht vergeleken met den code pénal*, Den Haag: Belinfante 1886.

1484 Smidt, H. J., *Geschiedenis van het Wetboek van strafrecht: volledige verzameling van regeeringsontwerpen, gewisselde stukken, gevoerde beraadslagingen, Deel 1*, Haarlem: Tjeenk Willink 1881, p. 3–4.

1485 Smidt, H.J., *Geschiedenis van het Wetboek van strafrecht: volledige verzameling van regeeringsontwerpen, gewisselde stukken, gevoerde beraadslagingen, Deel 3*, Haarlem: Tjeenk Willink 1882, p. 364.

restrictions to hate speech in French and Dutch law, followed by a comparison with the approach under the ECHR, on the basis of the four factors of the analytical framework (Chapter 6, para. 1 *infra*).

I. FREE EXPRESSION OF OPINION IN DUTCH LAW

1. HISTORY AND FUNDAMENTS: FREE EXPRESSION OF OPINION PROVIDED THE RESPONSIBILITY UNDER THE LAW

The Netherlands is known for its rich history of press freedom (1.1). In the Netherlands, the right to the free expression of an opinion is protected in the Dutch Constitution (1.2) and has both vertical and horizontal effect (1.3). Legal scholars disagree on the exact relationship of the right with the right to freedom of religion also protected in the Constitution (1.4). The restrictions to the right to freedom of expression on the basis of the content of expression are incorporated into the Dutch Criminal and Civil Codes (1.5). They are to a significant extent influenced by the large room for judicial interpretation (1.6), generally in conformity with the international law, notably the case law of the European Court of Human Rights (ECHR) (1.7). The analysis results in a general conclusion about the free expression of opinion in Dutch law (1.8).

1.1. History of freedom of the press

The Netherlands has much less of a theory on freedom of expression than France. During the drafting of the constitutional provisions protecting freedom of expression or the public speech offences that form limitations to this freedom, the Dutch legislator has not dedicated extensive considerations on the principle distinction between actions and opinions or the question as to what constitutes a 'délit d'opinion'.[1486] Subsequently, Dutch legal scholars have equally not developed such notions (para. 1.5.1 *infra*). This does not signify that the Netherlands does not have a rich history of freedom of expression – to the contrary. France has played a considerable role in the history of freedom of expression in the Netherlands., During the Republic of the Seven United Provinces (1581–1795) a relatively large press freedom existed, which attracted many foreign authors who could freely publish their works that could not be published elsewhere.[1487] No systematic censorship was exercised. Although, a licensing system for the printing press and a regime of preliminary authorization, complemented with severe sanctions had to prevent the distribution of placards of a dangerous political or religious nature. This relative freedom has been assigned to the lack of a strong central authority that

1486 For a commentary on the Dutch Constitution, see: Koekkoek, A.K. (ed.), *De Grondwet, Een systematisch en artikelsgewijs commentaar*, Derde Editie, Deventer: W.E.J. Tjeenk Willink 2000. For a commentary on the Dutch public speech offences, see: Janssens, A.L.J.; Nieuwenhuis, A.J., *Uitingsdelicten*, Derde Editie, Deventer: Kluwer 2011.

1487 De Meij, J. M., *De vrije informatiestroom in grondwettelijk perspectief*, Tweede Editie, Amsterdam: Otto Cramwinckel Uitgever 1996, p. 16.

could effectively enforce the regulation in place.[1488] Hence, French refugees of the Ancien Régime could publish their French-Dutch newspapers, such as the famous *Gazette de Leyde*, primarily destined for France but having an international readership.

At the end of the Eighteenth century the insistence for liberalization of the press increased. With the armed support of the French Republic, the revolution of the Patriots founded the Batavian Republic (1795–1806). Freedom of the press was laid down for the first time in the *Staatsregeling* – the Constitution of 1798 – that was inspired by the French 1789 Declaration.[1489] The liberal period was however brought to a definitive end, when the 'client state' was annexed by the First French Empire and Napoleon reintroduced censorship (1810–1813). After the independence in 1813, the Kingdom of the United Netherlands was created and censorship was abolished by King Willem I.[1490] The Constitution of 1814 still lacked a provision protecting freedom of the press; as in the Netherlands no censorship had existed except during the French occupation and press freedom thus existed de facto, regulation was regarded as unnecessary.[1491] However, the merging with Belgium required explicit acknowledgement. Article 227 of the Constitution of 1815 protected freedom of the press and clearly expressed the ideals of the enlightenment by referring to freedom of the press as an 'effective means to extend knowledge and progress the Enlightenment'.[1492]

Nevertheless, the following years many repressive criminal offences were introduced, amongst others by the Acts that aimed to 'curb unrest and malice'; the Act of 10 April 1815,[1493] the Decree of 20 April 1815[1494] and the regulations of 6 March 1818,[1495] for which a strict prosecution policy was pursued.[1496] The Act of

1488 Diemer, E., *Vrijheid van Drukpers*, Rotterdam-Utrecht: Libertas Drukkerijen 1937, p. 58.

1489 Article 16 of the *Bataafse Staatsregeling van 1798* reads: 'Iedere burger mag zijn gevoelens uiten en verspreiden, op zoodanige wijze, als hij goedvind, des niet strijdig met het oogmerk der Maatschappij. De vrijheid der Drukpers is heilig, mids de Geschriften met den naam van Uitgever, Drukker, of Schrijver voorzien zijn. Dezen allen zijn, ten allen tijde, aansprakelijk voor alle zoodanige bedrijven, door middel der Drukpers, ten aanzien van afzonderlijke Persoonen, of der gantsche Maatschappij, begaan, die door de Wet als misdaadig erkend zijn.'

1490 Soeverein Decreet van 24 januari 1814, *Stb.* 1814, nr. 17. Cited in: Nieuwenhuis, A.J., *Over de grens van de vrijheid van meningsuiting*, Nijmegen: Ars Aequi Libri 2011, p. 208.

1491 Colenbrander, H.T., *Ontstaan der Grondwet*, tweede deel (1815), Den Haag: Martinus Nijhoff 1909, p. 474.

1492 Article 227 reads: 'Het is aan elk geoorloofd om zijn gedachten en gevoelens door de drukpers, als zijnde een doelmatig middel tot uitbreiding van kennis en voortgang van verlichting, te openbaren, zonder eenig voorafgaand verlof daartoe noodig te hebben, blijvende nogtans elk voor hetgeen hij schrijft, drukt, uitgeeft of verspreidt, verantwoordelijk aan de maatschappij of bijzondere personen, voor zoo verre deze regten mogen zijn beleedigd.' The drafting history furthermore shows the rationales of the assurance of a democratic government system and the prevention of the creation of laws abridging press freedom. De Meij 1996, p. 22.

1493 Stb. 1815, 32.

1494 Journal Officiel, 1815 nr. 10.

1495 Stb. 1818, 11.

1496 Diemer 1937, p. 78–84.

10 April criminalized the publication of writings that showed sympathy for foreign occupation or caused dispute and distrust amongst the inhabitants with flogging, branding, imprisonment and even the death penalty. A famous application of the Acts of 1815 and 1818 formed the trial against priest J.B. Buelens, who was convicted to one year of imprisonment for publishing a poem in the magazine 'The Religion Friend'.[1497] In 1828 several authors, printers and editors were condemned mostly for criticizing the government or its members. The political resistance against the laws particularly increased in the South; the sanctions were disproportionate, considering the fact that the laws criminalized the purport of writings, not actions. What is more, prosecutions were primarily directed at discourses of Catholic priests, while they could be freely ridiculed in several magazines.[1498]

On 22 December 1828 the Government proposed a draft act to replace the laws that sought the criminalization, in particular, of the insult of the King, the Royal Family, the States-General, Colleges of State, courts, judges etc. and the insult of one of the Religions protected by the Constitution. The proposal was not agreed upon, due to the fact that it would considerably hinder freedom of criticism. Contrarily, a new draft act that aimed to curb scorn and libel against the King and the Royal Family and other offences against the public authorities and the general peace proposed by the King on 11 December 1829 was adopted, but only after the most contested and vague offence against the agitation of unrest and discord between citizens had been deleted.[1499] Subsequently, the Act of 3 November 1830 aimed to 'curb harmful tumults and practices of the evil-minded' and criminalized amongst others the incitement to revolt by means of writings.[1500] The Acts to 'curb unrest and malice' would be mirrored in Articles 112;113;117;118 and 131 of the Dutch Criminal code of 1881 (para. 1.5.1 *infra*).

According to Diemer, this period is characterized by a continuous interplay between on the one hand the countering of seditious expression by criminal offences and on the other hand the dissatisfaction on these same criminal offences expressed in a seditious manner. The Government made an effort to adopt laws that would satisfy both parties. This explains why both the adoption of laws to counter seditious expression, and greater freedom of the press were requested. Surprisingly, a possible reform of Article 227 of the 1815 Constitution did not form part of these discussions.[1501]

With the Constitutional reform of 1848, the constitutional right to freedom of the press protected by Article 8 was included in the terms that have been preserved in current Article 7 paragraph 1 of the current Dutch Constitution, which reads: 'No

1497 Diemer 1937, p. 79.

1498 Kort-van Welzen, W., *Christelijke kamerleden en de vrijheid van meningsuiting, een parlementair-historisch onderzoek* (diss.), Zwolle: W.E.J. Tjeenk Willink 1994, p. 15–16.

1499 Stb. 1830, 15. Diemer 1937, p. 78–84; Kort-van Welzen 1994, p. 19.

1500 Stb. 1830, 75.

1501 Diemer 1937, p. 84.

one shall require prior permission to publish thoughts or feelings through the press, without prejudice to the responsibility of every person under the law.'[1502] The Dutch legislator did not seek to bring any changes to the scope of the freedom afforded by Article 227 of the 1815 Constitution, but merely aimed to determine the freedom as simply and clearly as possible.[1503] The Article prohibits preventive measures and thus denounces prior censorship, which had been exercised by past regimes. Contrarily, the Article does not prohibit repressive measures. After 1848, the repressive criminal offences that date back to the reign of Willem I have, however, been abolished or less frequently applied.[1504]

After the abolishment of prior censorship, other than in France, in the Netherlands no specific limitations on the periodical press, such as the requirement of a deposit for possible violations of the law, were introduced. What did exist were the *dagblagzegel*, a special tax on periodical publications, and a tax on advertisements that impeded the development of the press. Under pressure from the liberal movement, the taxes were finally abrogated in 1869, which triggered an acceleration in the flourishing of the press.[1505] The Press, however, remained subjected to the existing criminal offences.

In the turbulent political contexts of the rise of national socialism in the thirties and the Cold War in the fifties of the twentieth century, propositions had even been made to submit the periodical press to a special regime and introduce certain prohibitions of publication in order to prevent public agitation; newspapers could have a negative influence on public opinion and undermine state authority. Upon these proposals no legislative action was however taken.[1506]

Although the text of the Constitutional provision protecting press freedom has not changed since 1848, the Dutch Supreme Court has interpreted the article in such a manner that next to the 'publication of thoughts or feelings through the press' the *distribution* of writings has certain protection as a 'connected right'.[1507] The Court has further elaborated the exact purport of this freedom to *distribute* writings in a series of case law (para. 1.2.1 *infra*).

Until the constitutional reform of 1983, the Constitution contained no reference to no other media than the printed press. Theatre, cinema and broadcasting fell outside the scope of the right to freedom of the press. The substantial control of these media was justified, because of their public nature and intrusiveness.[1508]

1502 Translation of the Constitution published by the Ministries of Foreign Affairs and the Interior in 2002, available at: www.minbzk.nl/english.

1503 De Meij 1996, p. 21.

1504 De Meij 1996, p. 23.

1505 De Meij 1996, p. 24.

1506 De Meij 1996, p. 25; 30.

1507 Dutch Supreme Court, 23 May 1961, *NJ* 1961, 427.

1508 Theatre and cinema could therefore be subjected to prior supervision and prohibitions with regard to their content and broadcasting was subjected to a licensing system based on the scarcity of frequencies.

However, the needs of modern times required that other media than the printed press were brought under the scope of freedom of the press.

1.2. Constitutional protection of the free expression of opinion

1.2.1. Article 7 of the 1983 Constitution

The 1983 Constitution extended the constitutional protection of freedom of expression provided in Article 7. The Government considered freedom of expression important for inter human contact and individual development, but also indispensable for the participation of citizens in the public cause and the free flow of information, which in its turn is indispensable for a democratic state.[1509] The first paragraph of the Article, however, preserves the formulation that has been in existence since 1848 ('No one shall require prior permission to publish thoughts or feelings through the press, without prejudice to the responsibility of every person under the law'). In this manner, the aim of the government was to preserve the series of case law concerning the distribution of writings, a doctrine that would be difficult to incorporate into Article 7.[1510] The article was supplemented with three new paragraphs, two of which inserted media other than the printed press. Other than in France, where Articles 10 and 11 of the 1789 Declaration protect the manifestation and communication of thoughts and opinions, thus the communication *process* in general, Article 7 of the Dutch Constitution rather protects the communication '*means*' and provides in a tri-partition with regard to the level of protection afforded to freedom of expression depending on the technical means used.

Article 7 paragraph 1 protects the free publication of thoughts and opinions through the *press*. The press comprises techniques of multiplication equitable with the press, readable signs and images, paintings, drawings or photos.[1511] The Internet or demonstrations, even though they may include texts, do not fall under the scope of this paragraph.[1512] 'No one shall require prior permission' signifies a prohibition on prior censorship and thus of prior supervision by the government with regard to the content of the expression that is to be published. This concerns an absolute prohibition for which no restrictions are possible.

Next to the prohibition of prior censorship, the 'publication' of thoughts and feelings forms the 'core' right of freedom of the press. Other phases in the communication process than this active side of communication, such as the receiving of thoughts and opinions, were not inserted into the article. On the one hand, the government wanted to prevent the creation of a right on government

1509 *Kamerstukken I*, 1976/77, 13872, nr. 55b, p. 49; *Kamerstukken I*, 1976/77, 13872, nr. 55b, p. 37.

1510 *Kamerstukken II*, 1975–1976, 13872, nr. 7, p. 28.

1511 Dutch Supreme Court, 24 January 1967, *NJ* 1967, 270; ARRS 17 May 1983, *AB* 1983, 514.

1512 Tekst & Commentaar Grondwet, Comm. Bunschoten Art. 7 sub 2, p. 17.

information, on the other hand the government stated that the gathering and receiving certainly partly falls under the scope of publication.[1513] Subsequently, the freedom to receive information has been elaborated in Dutch case law based on Article 10 ECHR, which is why the scope of Article 7 remains unclear in this respect (para. 1.7 *infra*).[1514] Even though pluralism of media is not explicitly guaranteed in the Constitution, the existence of a pluralistic press is regarded as a task of the government and assured by the Dutch Media Act.[1515]

The terms 'thoughts and feelings' are broadly interpreted by the constitutional legislator of 1983 and in case law.[1516] Although they give the impression that statements of fact fall outside the scope of the article, the constitutional legislator has explicitly assured that this is not the case. Newspaper articles are thus protected by Article 7. What is more, opinions would be inherent to the selection of facts.[1517] Next, Dutch case law has adopted the distinction made in the case law of the ECtHR between facts or value judgments (para. 1.7 *infra*). It results from the phrase 'without prejudice to the responsibility of every person under the law' that the publication of thoughts and feelings through the press can only be restricted by statutory laws originating from the formal legislator, that is the States-General and the Government.[1518]

Subordinate to the constitutionally protected core right to publish thoughts and feelings, the Dutch Supreme Court has developed the right to distribute printed matter. This right is generally referred to as a 'connected' or 'peripheral' right.[1519] The local government may not entirely prohibit so-called 'independent means of distribution', such as the distribution of handbills, offering of printed works, posting, or the installation of neon signs.[1520] Other than the right to publish, this right to distribute can be restricted by regulations issued by local authorities, as long as such regulations do not concern the content of the expression, or consist of an entire prohibition to distribute or a licensing system.[1521] In sum, use of a certain significance of the right to distribute must remain possible.[1522]

1513 *Kamerstukken II*, 1981–1982, 16905–16938, nr. 5, p. 14.

1514 Peters, J.A. & De Vré, I.J., *Vrijheid van meningsuiting, de betekenis van een grondrecht in tijden van spanning*, Deventer: Kluwer 2005, p. 29.

1515 Media Act of 21 April 1987, *Stb.* 249.

1516 Have been brought under the scope of 'thoughts and feelings': a billboard indicating the name of an educational institution (ARRS 24 June 1991, *AB* 1992, 26) and posters depicting artwork or entertaining posters (Dutch Supreme Court, 21 March 2000, *NJ* 2000, 482).

1517 *Kamerstukken II*, 1976–1977, 13872, nr. 7, p. 26; *Kamerstukken I*, 1976–1977, 13872, 13873, nr. 55b, p. 37–38.

1518 Dutch Supreme Court, 28 November 1950, *NJ* 1951, 137 and Dutch Supreme Court, 28 November 1950, *NJ* 1951, 138.

1519 Nieuwenhuis 2011, p. 220.

1520 Dutch Supreme Court, 27 February 1951, *NJ* 1951, 472; Dutch Supreme Court, 27 March 1953, *NJ* 1953, 389; Dutch Supreme Court, 19 September 1977, *NJ* 1978, 516; Dutch Supreme Court, 24 January 1967, *NJ* 1967, 270.

1521 Dutch Supreme Court, 28 November 1950, *NJ* 1951, 137; Dutch Supreme Court, 24 January 1967, *NJ* 1967, 270.

1522 Dutch Supreme Court, 27 March 1953, *NJ* 1953, 389.

Paragraph two of Article 7 concerns broadcasting. Contrary to the printed press, no absolute prohibition of prior permission applies to broadcasting. In the field of broadcasting, a licensing system is therefore permitted and only prior supervision with regard to the content of specific broadcasts is excluded.[1523] Paragraph three of Article 7 forms a general guarantee of freedom of expression by means other than the press or broadcast and comprises forms of expression and distribution, such as speaking in public, theatre, cinema and the distribution through new media such as the Internet that cannot be regarded as broadcast. With regard to these media, it prohibits prior approval with regard to the content of expression.[1524] The prohibition of prior censorship does, however, not apply to performances open to persons younger than sixteen years of age for which the legislator may issue regulations – even by means of delegation – in order to protect good morals. A licensing system is allowed, as long as it does not regard the content of expression. Repressive restrictions concerning the content of expression may only be determined by the formal legislator. Local authorities may issue regulations that do not concern the content of expression. However, case law has set limitations to these regulations comparable to the right to distribute thoughts and opinions through the press.[1525]

Despite its tri-partition in technical means of communication, a common characteristic of Article 7 paragraphs 1 and 3 thus forms the prohibition of prior censorship. Besides, the rule that repressive restrictions concerning the content of expression may only be determined by the formal legislator applies to both paragraphs 1 and 3 equally.

Paragraph four of Article 7 excludes commercial expression from the constitutional protection of freedom of expression.[1526] During the Constitutional reform the government stipulated the intrusive and aggressi ve nature of commercial expression that did, however, not comprise of advertisements on cultural goods. On the one hand, the government wanted to preserve the possibility of prior supervision on the content of commercial expression, on the other hand the government deemed it impossible to enumerate all restrictions on the content of commercial expression in statutory laws.[1527] The distinction between commercial expression and idealistic expression can be problematic. The Dutch Supreme Court has, however, afforded protection to commercial expression on the ground of Article 10 ECHR without

---

1523 Article 7 paragraph 2 reads: Rules concerning radio and television shall be laid down by Act of Parliament. There shall be no prior supervision of the content of a radio or television broadcast.

1524 Article 7 paragraph 3 reads: No one shall be required to submit thoughts or opinions for prior approval in order to disseminate them by means other than those mentioned in the preceding paragraphs, without prejudice to the responsibility of every person under the law. The holding of performances open to persons younger than sixteen years of age may be regulated by Act of Parliament in order to protect good morals.

1525 Tekst & Commentaar Grondwet, Comm. Bunschoten Art. 7 sub 4, p. 18.

1526 Article 7 paragraph 4 reads: 'The preceding paragraphs do not apply to commercial advertising'.

1527 *Handelingen II*, 1976/77, 2196.

reference to Article 7 paragraph 4 of the Dutch Constitution.[1528] The distinction, therefore, has considerably lost its importance.[1529]

1.2.2. Limitations

Like most fundamental rights in the Constitution, the right of freedom of the press has no absolute nature and its exercise can be limited. Between the fundamental rights protected in the Constitution no hierarchy exists. The right to freedom of the press must be balanced with other rights or interests, for example as regulated in the Dutch Constitution.[1530] The constitutional legislator has rejected the possibility of general limitations to fundamental rights that cannot be traced back to the clauses of the fundamental rights. The constitutional legislator has equally rejected the doctrine of the core of fundamental rights, according to which restrictions are possible as long as they do not violate the core of a fundamental right.[1531]

In fact, Article 7 paragraphs 1 and 3 only afford protection against prior censorship. The Article furthermore declares the formal legislator, that is the States-General and the Government, competent to determine restrictions on the content of expression, but – like Article 11 of the 1789 Declaration – it does not indicate the interests these restrictions must protect. The constitutional legislator thought that a reference to the interests that the restrictions on fundamental rights must protect would lead to a long list of policy aims that would hollow the fundamental rights.[1532] The Dutch legal system, however, lacks the possibility to review the constitutionality of statutory laws. The Dutch Constitution even prohibits such constitutional review (para. 1.6 *infra*). In France, the Constitutional Council exercises such review and as a result of its case law, freedom of communication must be conciliated with the rights of others, the public order and human dignity. Another difference with France is that the Dutch Constitution is 'non-ideological'[1533] in the sense that it does not determine any constitutional values, such as human dignity or the respect for religious beliefs, from which limitations to freedom of expression could be derived.

The rejection of general limitations to fundamental rights raises the question as to the abuse of fundamental rights. The Dutch Constitution lacks a prohibition of the abuse of rights comparable with Article 17 ECHR. The government thought that the clauses of the fundamental rights afford sufficient possibilities to counter the abuse of fundamental rights. What is more, the introduction of a prohibition of abuse of right would add a strong political component to the question as to the limitations to

[1528] Dutch Supreme Court, 13 February 1987, *NJ* 1987, 899.
[1529] Peters & De Vré 2005, p. 30.
[1530] *Kamerstukken II*, 1975/76, 13872, nr. 3, p. 11.
[1531] Kortmann, C.A.J.M., *De Grondwets-herzieningen 1983 en 1987*, Tweede Druk, Deventer: Kluwer 1987, p. 52.
[1532] Kortmann 1987, p. 51.
[1533] Kortmann 1987.

the freedoms of citizens in the exercise of fundamental rights and the general starting point of the Dutch Constitution was to avoid as much as possible the appreciation of political conflicts with regard to the exercise of fundamental rights by the judge.[1534]

Repressive restrictions to freedom of expression must merely comply with the clause in Article 7 'without prejudice (...) under the law'. As the clause does not indicate the protected interests and the Dutch constitution has no general limitations and no prohibition of abuse of right, in principle the legislator is competent to determine any restriction with regard to the content of expression, as long as control takes place after and not prior to the publication. Legal scholars have, however, emphasized that the legislator must exercise restraint in the formulation of restrictions.[1535] Criminal restrictions to freedom of expression are incorporated into the Dutch Criminal Code (Sr) and civil restrictions to freedom of expression result from the Dutch Civil Code (BW), notably the open formula of the wrongful act of Article 6:162 BW (para. 1.5.2 *infra*).

1.2.3. Proposals for reform

Since its creation in 1983, Article 7 of the Constitution has received much criticism. The criticism particularly concerns the emphasis of the article on the prohibition of censorship, on the publication of thoughts and feelings and no other phases in the communication process, on the terms 'thoughts and feelings', on the exclusion of commercial expression, on its tri-partition of technical means that causes problems with regard to the integration of new means of communication and on the lack of a reference to interests for the determination of restrictions. In several respects, Article 10 ECHR affords a broader protection to freedom of expression (para. 1.7 *infra*).

Several proposals for reform have therefore been made. In 1999 the Association of Media and Communication law issued a preliminary report concerning a new text for Articles 7 and 13 of the Constitution that protects the privacy of correspondence.[1536] Earlier, Dommering and Asscher had proposed the combination of these two articles.[1537] In 2000, the Commission Franken issued the report Fundamental rights in the Digital Age that proposed the reformulation of Article 7 by deleting the tri-partition of technical means and the exclusion of commercial expression and by inserting the right to receive and distribute expression.[1538] In

---

1534 *Kamerstukken II*, 1976–1977, 13872, nr. 7, p. 4.

1535 De Meij 1996, p. 147.

1536 Jurgens, E.C.M. *et al.*, Preadvies inzake een nieuwe tekst voor de artt. 7 en 13 van de Grondwet, bijlage bij *Mediaforum* 1999, nr. 11/12.

1537 Dommering, E.J. 'De Grondwet in de Informatiemaatschappij', in: Burkens. M.C. *et al.*, *Gelet op de Grondwet,* Deventer: Kluwer 1998, p.110–123; Asscher, L.F., *Constitutionele convergentie van pers, omroep en telecommunicatie*, Deventer: Kluwer 1999.

1538 Report *Commissie grondrechten in het digitale tijdperk*, Den Haag: Ministerie van Binnenlandse Zaken 2000. For a criticism, see: Asscher, L.F., *Communicatiegrondrechten* (diss.), Amsterdam: Otto Cramwinckel Uitgever 2002, p. 66–75.

2011, the State Commission on the Constitution equally proposed to reformulate Article 7 by extending the prohibition of censorship to all forms of expression, replacing the term 'feelings' by 'opinions', inserting the right to receive information and the respect of pluralism of media by the government.[1539, 1540]

Other than previous commissions, the latter State Commission also advised changing the system of restrictions to fundamental rights of the Constitution. It advised the insertion of a general clause declaring that restrictions to fundamental rights must be proportionate to their aims and may not impair the core of fundamental rights.[1541] Furthermore, it advised the insertion of a general provision declaring that the Netherlands is a constitutional state and that the government respects and guarantees human dignity and the fundamental rights and principles.[1542] The articulation of the core values of the constitutional state could be relevant for the promotion of integration and citizenship and function as a reflexion of the Dutch constitutional identity. The provision has a normative character in the sense that it must function as a guideline for the interpretation of (fundamental) rights. Even though the proposal of the Commission does not envision the insertion of a reference to the interests that restrictions to Article 7 must protect, it thus provides for a broader protection in the field of repressive restrictions. This particularly applies since the Commission, similar to the Commission Franken, advised the abrogation of the prohibition of constitutional review (para. 1.6 *infra*).

However, in reaction to the advice, the Government decided not to adopt these proposals, most notably due to the fact that it wanted to maintain the sober and open character of the Dutch Constitution and also because the proposals are not strictly necessary.[1543] Subsequently, the Senate adopted two motions, in which the Government was requested to nevertheless develop, next to a provision that assures the right to a fair trail,[1544] a general provision in the Constitution expressing that the Netherlands is a democratic constitutional state.[1545] The Government has

---

1539 Report *Staatscommissie Grondwet*, November 2010, *Kamerstukken II* 2010/11, 31 570, nr. 17, bijlage.

1540 Proposed Article 7 reads '1. Niemand heeft voorafgaand verlof nodig om gedachten en meningen te openbaren, behoudens ieders verantwoordelijkheid volgens de wet. 2. Het ontvangen van informatie is vrij, behoudens beperkingen bij de wet gesteld. 3. De overheid eerbiedigt de pluriformiteit van de media.'

1541 The proposed article reads '1. Beperkingen van grondrechten gaan niet verder dan het doel van de beperking vereist. 2. De kern van grondrechten wordt niet aangetast.'

1542 The proposed article reads '1. Nederland is een democratische rechtsstaat. 2. De overheid eerbiedigt en waarborgt de menselijke waardigheid, de grondrechten en de fundamentele rechtsbeginselen. 3. Openbaar gezag wordt alleen uitgeoefend krachtens de Grondwet of de wet.'

1543 The Government only adopted the proposal to amend Article 13 of the Constitution that – similar to Article 7 – rather protects a limitative enumeration of *means* of correspondence (letter, telephone and telegraph) than the privacy of the correspondence *process*, which complicates the interpretation of the article in the light of new technical developments. *Kamerstukken II*, 2011–2012, 31570, nr. 20, p. 5–8; 31570, nr. 21.

1544 *Kamerstukken I*, 2013–2014, 31570, C.

1545 *Kamerstukken I*, 2013–2014, 31570, B.

indicated that it will submit a proposal to that effect in 2014.[1546] Depending on the exact formulation (including a reference to the inviolability of the human dignity), such a general provision in the Dutch Constitution could – amongst others – serve as a compass for the legislator to set the statutory restrictions to hate speech and for the judge to interpret and apply them in individual cases. Yet, the general criticism remains that the protection of fundamental rights by the Dutch Constitution – notably of freedom of expression – has been superseded by the ECHR (para. 1.6;1.7 *infra*).

1.3. Vertical and horizontal effect

The right to freedom of expression is primarily directed against the government; against prior censorship exercised by the government, other preventive measures and also repressive measures that hinder freedom of expression. The Constitutional legislator of 1983 has explicitly recognized the horizontal effect of fundamental rights, defined as the legal force of fundamental rights in the mutual relations between citizens.[1547] As the extent of the effect of fundamental rights in relations between citizens would vary 'per article, per paragraph, and even per category of cases', the government did not make any statements with regard to the extent of horizontal effect of any fundamental right in particular. Thus, the question of horizontal effect was reduced to a question of the interpretation of the Constitution that was shifted towards the legislator and the judge.[1548]

The legislator has attached importance to freedom of expression, when determining the restrictions to freedom of expression. Likewise, the judge increasingly attaches importance to freedom of expression, not only in legal actions between citizens based on the wrongful act (6:162 BW), but also in criminal cases based on public speech offences. The question arises as to whether in these cases one can speak of horizontal effect in the strict sense; while speech offences such as insult or defamation or the civil norm of the wrongful act concern the relations between citizens, these norms originate directly from the legislator.[1549]

Indeed, in Dutch legal doctrine, the question of to how to comprehend the application of fundamental rights by the judge in relations between citizens is the object of continuous discussion. Some authors argue that fundamental rights only have horizontal effect, if they have 'full' effect in the sense that one can invoke them in the same manner against citizens as against the government.[1550] Others consider that fundamental rights such as freedom of expression play an important role in cases between citizens, because the judge attaches importance to them when

1546 *Kamerstukken I,* 2013–2014, 31570, H en K.

1547 *Kamerstukken II,* 1975–1976, 13872, nr. 3, p. 15–16.

1548 *Kamerstukken II,* 1975–1976, 13872, nr. 3, p. 15–16.

1549 Nieuwenhuis 2011, p. 211.

1550 De Graaf, F. & De Haas, M.J.O.M., Horizontale werking van grondrechten: een heilloos leerstuk, *NJB* 1984, p. 1353–1358.

interpreting civil notions such as the 'wrongful' act in Article 6:162 BW and thus 'translates' the fundamental right into a civil right.[1551] Third parties opine that fundamental rights such as freedom of expression function as general legal principles in both public and private law.[1552] De Meij considers the discussion to be a matter of legal dogmatism. In any case, freedom of expression is an interest to be weighed in relations between citizens.[1553] The criminal and the civil judge, as we will see, increasingly apply the statutory restrictions in light of freedom of expression (para. 1.5;5.8;6.4 *infra*).

1.4. The relationship to freedom of religion

Other than in France, in the Netherlands the constitutional provision protecting freedom of expression does not explicitly protect religious opinions, nor is the free exercise of religion regulated outside the Constitution in a separate act. Article 6 paragraph 1 of the Dutch Constitution protects the right of any person to freely profess his religion or belief either individually or in community with others, without prejudice to his responsibility under the law.[1554] The paragraph forms a general guarantee of the free profession of religion or belief, both inside and outside buildings and enclosed places. Paragraph 2 of Article 6 guarantees the free profession of religion or belief outside buildings and enclosed places in specific. The Article replaces a series of articles in the former Constitution[1555] that regulated freedom of religion, comprising the equal protection of denominations and the guarantee of equal civil rights of religious adherents, which nowadays falls under the scope of current Article 1.

The profession of religion or belief comprises the following components: to have, *change and not have a conviction,* the private and public religious exercise, the religious propagation in education, nurture and preaching and the establishment of organizations.[1556] These forms of religious exercise are constitutionally protected. The government did not desire to extend constitutional protection to freedom of conscience.[1557] It is plausible that the legislator did not want to unconditionally guarantee the freedom to act according to one's religion or

---

1551 Burkens, M.C., *Algemene leerstukken van grondrechten naar Nederlands constitutioneel recht,* Zwolle: W.E.J. Tjeenk Willink 1989, p. 185.

1552 Koekkoek, A.K., De betekenis van grondrechten voor het privaatrecht, *WPNR* 1985, nr. 5742, 5743 en 5744, p. 406.

1553 De Meij 1996, p. 83.

1554 Article 6 reads '1. Everyone shall have the right to profess freely his religion or belief, either individually or in community with others, without prejudice to his responsibility under the law. 2. Rules concerning the exercise of this right other than in buildings and enclosed places may be laid down by Act of Parliament for the protection of health, in the interest of traffic and to combat or prevent disorders.'

1555 Entire Chapter 8, consisting of Articles 181–187.

1556 Tekst & Commentaar Grondwet, Comm. Bunschoten Art. 6 sub 3, p. 15.

1557 *Kamerstukken II*, 1975–1976, 13872, nr. 3, p. 32.

belief.[1558] The Dutch Supreme Court has brought the freedom to act according to one's religion or belief under the scope of the article in so far as it, according to objective standards, directly gives expression to one's religion or belief.[1559]

The constitutional reform of 1983 inserted the term 'belief' into the article in order to equate the profession of a belief, which comprises the freedom to *act* according to one's belief[1560], with the profession of a religion. Freedom of belief was not guaranteed in a separate article in order to clarify that carrying out a belief differs from expressing an opinion.[1561] A belief thus apparently concerns a principle a strongly anchored conviction, comparable with a religious conviction. The government acknowledged that certain convictions are intertwined with conceptions of the social order to such an extent that the expression of the conviction could fall under the scope of freedom of expression. However, the protection of freedom of belief alongside freedom of religion would function as a guideline for interpretation.[1562] No further criteria to demarcate convictions stemming from religion or belief from political convictions or other social conceptions were given.

When does the expression of religiously motivated opinions fall under the scope of Article 6 and when does it fall under the scope of Article 7 of the Constitution? When one act falls under different fundamental rights, there is an overlap or competition between fundamental rights.[1563] In such an event, the judge can apply the fundamental right that is most appropriate to the case or the fundamental right that affords the most protection.[1564] Strictly speaking, contrary to Article 7, Article 6 does not prohibit prior censorship.[1565] On the other hand, where former Article 181 only allowed criminal restrictions to freedom of religion, current Article 6 paragraph 1, similar to Article 7 paragraph 1, refers to restrictions determined by the formal legislator.[1566] In several criminal and civil cases

1558 Kortmann 1987, p.80. See generally: Vermeulen, B.P., *De vrijheid van geweten, een fundamenteel rechtsprobleem* (diss.), Arnhem: Gouda Quint 1989.

1559 Dutch Supreme Court, 31 October 1986, *NJ* 1987, 173.

1560 *Kamerstukken II*, 1975–1976, 13872, nr. 3, p. 29.

1561 *Kamerstukken II,* 1975–1976, 13872, nr. 3, p. 29.

1562 *Kamerstukken II,* 1975–1976, 13872, nr. 3, p. 29.

1563 Such competition can notably arise between Article 6, 7 and Article 9 that protects the right of assembly and demonstration. During the drafting of the Constitution, Minister of Internal Affairs de Gaay Fortman declared not to have experienced a public gathering of the Jesus People, where he participated in the signing of Christmas carols led by the Mayor, as the exercise of a religion. However, the gathering could be considered as an assembly or a demonstration or just a form of expression of opinion. See: *Handelingen II* 1976–1988, p. 2190. The Government considered the use of banners to generally form part of a demonstration. See: *Kamerstukken II,*, 13872, nr. 7, p. 30.

1564 De Meij 1996, p. 55–56.

1565 This signifies that prior supervision with regard to the content of the exercise of religion and belief is not prohibited. However, as delegation is impossible, the cases in which and the conditions under which such prior supervision can take place must be precisely determined in statutory laws originating from the formal legislator. The creation of such laws is very unlikely.

1566 The government thought the extension of possible limitations necessary, because the consequences of the introduction of freedom of belief could not be entirely overseen.

concerning expression of religiously motivated opinions, the Dutch Supreme Court has referred to both the right to freedom of expression and to freedom of religion together. This case law gives the impression of affording opinions based on religion or belief a higher level of protection than opinions in other fields (para. 5.10 *infra*).

Dutch legal scholars disagree not only on the scope of freedom of religion or belief, but also on its separate constitutional protection *as such*.[1567] According to De Beer, Article 6 can be abrogated, because freedom of religion and belief can be sufficiently guaranteed by freedom of expression and freedom of assembly and demonstration protected in the following Articles 7 and 9. If Article 6 affords any other rights to citizens on the ground of their religion or belief that others do not have, this is contrary to the principle of equality and non-discrimination protected in Article 1.[1568] Vermeulen argues that the religious dimension of an act or claim can precisely justify a difference in treatment. Furthermore, freedom of religion comprises different actions and opinions than freedom of expression, such as religious dress and ritual slaughtering. An extensive interpretation of this latter freedom merely entails the problem of qualification. Hence, the function of freedom of religion or belief cannot be transferred to freedom of expression and freedom of assembly and demonstration; this deprives certain acts and manifestations from their protected status, which would notably affect religious minorities (para. 5.10 *infra*).[1569]

1.5. The relationship between criminal and civil law

1.5.1. Criminal responsibility and speech offences

Unlike France, the Netherlands does not have a specific press act that further regulates freedom of the press protected in Article 7 and lists all existing press offences, i.e. all public speech offences. The criminal restrictions to freedom of expression are incorporated into the Dutch criminal code. Neither does the Dutch criminal code contain a specific section that cites all speech offences. The speech offences are spread out over the entire code and incorporated into different sections. As the Dutch legislator thus does not clearly distinguish the restrictions to actions from the restrictions to opinions, it is difficult to bring the criminal restrictions to freedom of expression under a common denominator.

The former customary term ‘drukpersmisdrijven’, which signifies ‘press offences’, is outdated due to the fact that the speech offences in the criminal code

---

Kamerstukken II, 1975–1976, 13872, nr. 3, p. 30.

1567 See generally Van Ooijen, H.M.A.E., Egmond, L.F., Eijkman, Q.A.M., Olujic, F. & Vos, O.P.G. (eds.), *Godsdienstvrijheid: afschaffen of beschermen?*, Leiden: Stichting NJCM-Boekerij, 2008.

1568 Beer, P. de, Waarom vrijheid van godsdienst uit de grondwet kan., *Socialisme & Democratie* 2007 64 (10), p. 23.

1569 Vermeulen, Ben, Waarom de vrijheid van godsdienst in de grondwet moet blijven., *Socialisme & Democratie* 2008 65 (3), p. 14–26.

do not distinguish between the media used to express opinions. What is more, while most speech offences require expression to have been uttered publicly, sometimes expression is also punishable when uttered non-publicly, such as insult of an individual. Unlike French law, Dutch law thus does not strictly categorize public and non-public speech offences. The criminal code refers to 'offences committed through the press',[1570] but only to afford the publisher or printer immunity from prosecution under the condition that the publication indicates the name and residence of the publisher or printer and the author (Articles 53, 54; for liability of providers see Article 54a). The rationale of these articles was to prevent censorship by publishers and printers.[1571] The Dutch rules regarding the criminal responsibility for press offences thus seems the mirror image of the French 'responsabilité en cascade' that holds the publisher liable as a primary author. Another difference with the French Press Act is that the prosecution of the Dutch speech offences are bound by the general rules of Dutch criminal procedure.

Occasionally, criminal restrictions on freedom of expression have been referred to as 'opiniedelicten', the Dutch equivalent of 'délits d'opinion'.[1572] In this study, I will use the more common, neutral and broader term 'speech offences' defined by Janssens and Nieuwenhuis as 'offences that criminalize expressions on the ground of their content'[1573], which has been taken into use by the legislator.[1574] It is notable that as this definition – unlike the traditional French conception of a press offence – does not require that opinions support a criminal or punishable act, even the criminalization of opinions that do not produce harmful *actions*, can fall under its scope.

Unlike the French Press Act, the Dutch criminal code criminalizes the expression of opinions and the distribution of those same expressions – by third parties – in separate articles; the latter are criminalized in so-called 'verspreidingsdelicten', which means 'offences of distribution'. In accordance with these latter offences, even a distributor who might not have actual knowledge about the content of expression, but who has reasonable grounds to suspect its punishable nature can be held liable. Given their close connection with the offences penalizing

1570 The category 'offences committed through the press' is smaller than the category 'speech offences'. It concerns offences consisting of the publication of a press product that contains illegal content, thus merely offences that criminalize *public* expression destined for an *undetermined* public. The so-called offences of distribution are excluded.

1571 De Meij *et al.*, *De vrije informatiestroom in grondwettelijk perspectief*, Derde Druk, Amsterdam: Otto Cramwinckel Uitgever 2000, p. 282. They afford publishers and printers a strong position, a privilege, and protect them from prosecution even if they know the content of a punishable publication. On the other hand, they are liable for anonymous publications that do not indicate the author on the ground of Articles 418 and 419, even if they do not know the content of the publication. Furthermore, they can be liable as an accomplice of a press offence, if their intent with regard to the punishable nature of the publication can be proven.

1572 Ellian, A., Enkele overpeinzingen over opiniedelicten en vrijheid., *Strafblad*, 5 (5) 2007, p. 397–409.

1573 Janssens & Nieuwenhuis 2011, p. 3. Vgl. De Meij 2000, p. 258.

1574 *Kamerstukken II*, 1998/99, 26671, nr. 3, p. 7.

the expression of opinions, these offences of distribution can also be regarded as 'speech offences'. Contrarily, offences that criminalize certain conduct that may involve expressions but do not primarily concern expression, such as extortion or desecration, fall outside the scope of the term.

The speech offences incorporated into the criminal code include defamation of an individual (261 sub 1 and 2), slander (262), insult of an individual (266), libel (268), defamation of a deceased person (270); insult of specific persons, such as members of the royal family (111 and 112), foreign fellow heads of state or government members, government officials or bodies (118), a group of persons on specific discriminatory grounds (137c); blasphemy (147); the publication or distribution of offensive writings (240), showing audio visual material to the youth (240a), child pornography (240b); incitement to a criminal offence (131); incitement to hatred, discrimination or violence against a group of persons on specific discriminatory grounds (137d); and the accessory offences that criminalize the distribution of these same expressions.

Most speech offences predate the ratification of the ECHR by the Netherlands. The government considered that – all – national statutory laws would be consistent with the convention, because they formed the expression of 'what a democratic society requires'. The judge would therefore accept the well-considered decisions made by the legislator.[1575] Subsequently, however, the legislator has revised several speech offences in light of freedom of expression.

In the seventies, in response to the conviction with regard to the exclamations 'Johnson murderer' and 'Johnson war criminal' made during a demonstration against the American president Johnson and the American war in Vietnam on the ground of the offence of insult of a foreign fellow head of state (former 117 Sr),[1576] the legislator adapted several articles penalizing forms of insult or defamation.[1577] The insult of a foreign fellow head of state is punishable only when he is officially staying in the Netherlands (118–119). In the offence of defamation of an individual the existing justification ground 'to have acted in the general interest' was expanded to comprise a person who could have supposed in good faith that the stated facts were true (261 sub 3). In the offence of insult of an individual the justification ground 'to give an opinion on the representation of public interests' that is – put shortly – not gratuitously offensive was inserted that however was to be interpreted narrowly in the sense of political criticism (266 sub 2).[1578] The two justification grounds thus give a more robust protection to expression concerning the democratic

1575 *Kamerstukken II,* 1952/53, nr. 5.

1576 Dutch Supreme Court, 7 November 1967, *NJ* 1968, 44; Dutch Supreme Court, 5 November 1968, *NJ* 1968, 78.

1577 Janssens, A.L.J.M., *Strafbare belediging* (diss.), Amsterdam: Thela Thesis 1998, p. 56 *et seq.*

1578 *Kamerstukken II,* 1975/76, 11249, nr. 6–8.

institutions of the state system and therefore are of special social and 'public' interest.[1579]

The offence of group insult, created in 1934, was replaced in 1971 by Articles 137c and d Sr that were revised in 1991. The legislator did not insert any specific justification grounds into these articles comparable with Articles 261 sub 3 and 266 sub 2 Sr. On several occasions, the Dutch Supreme Court has considered that these specific justifications do not apply to other offences of insult, such as the offence of group insult of Article 137c Sr.[1580]

In the creation of the speech offences, the Dutch legislator has rather implicitly assumed that the speech offences are compatible with Article 10 ECHR. It has not, however, explicitly considered whether the articles satisfy the three-step test of its second paragraph.

Originally, the Dutch Supreme Court only marginally tested as to whether the speech offences were consistent with Article 10 ECHR. For example, with regard to a conviction on the ground of Article 240 Sr, the Court determined that the Article: '(...) aims to protect morals in the sense of the second paragraph of the previously mentioned convention article, this purpose apparently is still considered necessary by the Dutch legislator and does not exceed the limits of what nowadays can be regarded as necessary in a democratic society in order to protect that interest.'[1581] In another case concerning a conviction on the ground of Article 137c Sr, the Court considered that: 'the conviction (...) does not constitute a violation of Article 10 paragraph 1 ECHR, because the second paragraph of that Article 10 provides in the possibility of criminal offences as set out in Articles 137c and d Sr.'[1582] These considerations of the Dutch Supreme Court resemble the reasoning by the French Supreme Court that generally confines itself to affirm that a press offence or its application has the objective of guaranteeing one of the interests mentioned in Article 10(2) ECHR and that its necessity is therefore incontestable. Similarly to the French Supreme Court, the Dutch Supreme Court thus rather used to perform an act of conciliation *in abstracto* not *in concreto,* because it did not effectively balance the conflicting norms in every case.

In subsequent cases concerning the application of the speech offences, the Dutch Supreme Court has increasingly performed a balancing test *in concreto*.[1583] In a

---

1579 Peters, J.A. *Het primaat van de vrijheid van meningsuiting* (diss.), Nijmegen: Ars Aequi Libri 1981, p. 66 *et seq.*

1580 Dutch Supreme Court, 6 December 1983, *NJ* 1984, 601; Dutch Supreme Court, 19 April 2005, *NJ* 2006, 566.

1581 Dutch Supreme Court, 30 January 1968, *NJ* 1968, 199. For a similar test see: Dutch Supreme Court, 19 January 1962, *NJ* 1962, 107.

1582 Dutch Supreme Court, 14 March 1989, *NJ* 1990, 29. For a similar test see the older judgments – cited in: De Meij 2000, p. 263, footnote 62: Dutch Supreme Court, 16 December 1986, *NJ* 1987, 534; Dutch Supreme Court, 12 May 1987, *NJ* 1988, 299; Dutch Supreme Court, 27 October 1987, *NJ* 1988, 538.

1583 Schuijt, G.A.I., Hoge Raad niet meer bang voor de uitingsvrijheid?, *Informatierecht/AMI* 1996, p. 23–30.

series of case law, the Court has developed a 'three-step-test' in order to determine whether insulting expression is punishable in accordance with Article 137c Sr (para. 5.8 *infra*). Put simply, according to this test, the insulting character of the expression strongly depends on the direct context of the expression and the broader context of the public debate and its punishability finally depends on a proportionality-test, i.e. the question as to whether the expression is gratuitously offensive. In this test, the interest of freedom of expression is thus incorporated into the statutory elements of the offence.[1584] The test affords the possibility of accommodating the Article 10 case law of the ECtHR. Lower judges have applied a similar test with regard to other speech offences, such as Articles 261 or 137d Sr (para. 6.4 *infra*).[1585]

1.5.2. Civil responsibility and the wrongful act of Article 6:162 BW

The expression of an opinion can constitute a wrongful act under Article 6:162 BW[1586] that reads 'A person who commits an unlawful act towards another which can be imputed to him must repair the damage which the other person suffers as a consequence thereof.' Subsequently, the article cites the following unlawful acts: the violation of a right, an act or omission violating a statutory duty or a rule of unwritten law pertaining to proper social conduct. Civil responsibility for wrongful expression does not defer from civil responsibility for wrongful acts in general.[1587] The Dutch civil code lacks provisions similar to Articles 53 and 54 Sr, which afford the publisher and printer immunity from liability. The different regime can be explained, firstly, because from a social viewpoint publishers are responsible for making expression public, and secondly, because due diligence requires publishers to cooperate and take adequate measures in order to stop an unlawful situation caused by one of his authors.[1588]

In contrast to France, the Dutch speech offences do not take precedence over the general open civil norm of the wrongful act. While Article 6:162 BW forms the legal ground of civil actions, the speech offences, being statutory duties, can form a guideline for its interpretation. Furthermore, civil restrictions can be based on the

1584 Jansssens & Nieuwenhuis 2011, p. 45 *et seq.*

1585 CA Amsterdam, 7 December 2005, *LJN* AU 1916, respectively Amsterdam District Court, 23 June 2011, *Mediaforum* 2011, p. 280–282, annotation Van Noorloos; *Ars Aequi* 2012, p. 288–289, annotation Rozemond; p. 290–294, annotation Schutgens.

1586 Full Article 6:162 reads '1) A person who commits an unlawful act toward another which can be imputed to him must repair the damage which the other person suffers as a consequence thereof. 2) Except where there is a ground for justification, the following acts are deemed to be unlawful: the violation of a right, an act or omission violating a statutory duty or a rule of unwritten law pertaining to proper social conduct. 3) An unlawful act can be imputed to its author if it results from his fault or from a cause for which he is answerable according to law or common opinion.' Translation from Haanappel, P.P.C. & Mackaay, E., *New Netherlands Civil Code, Patrimonial Law*, Deventer: Kluwer 1990, p. 298.

1587 In the event of a plurality of authors, every author is severally liable and the injured party can choose which author to hold liable.

1588 De Meij 2000, p. 289.

'due-diligence'- norm of 6:162 BW. Other than in France, the criminal and civil restrictions to freedom of expression can thus differ; when expression is not punishable on the ground of the speech offences, it can nevertheless be unlawful on the ground of the due-diligence-norm of Article 6:162 BW.

In the *Sunday Times* case, the ECtHR considered that the law can result from statutory and unwritten law, but in any event must be adequately accessible and formulated with sufficient precision to enable the citizen to regulate his conduct. Some legal scholars, such as Biesheuvel, question whether the notion 'a rule of unwritten law pertaining to proper social conduct' meets this requirement.[1589, 1590] Equally in light of legal certainty, on the occasion of two convictions on the ground of 6:162 BW with regard to religiously motivated expression, commentators have advocated the 'royal path of criminal law' by referring to former Article 181 of the Dutch Constitution that protected freedom of religion (para. 5.9 *infra*).

However, in the *Het Parool/Van Gasteren* case, the ECtHR declared a complaint of a violation of Article 10 ECHR by a Dutch newspaper for being convicted on the ground of former Article 1408 – current Article 6:162 BW – as inadmissible and stated that even though the article might produce problems of interpretation this did not signify that it was too vague and insufficiently precise, given the case law of the Dutch Supreme Court.[1591] That case law can be broadly summarized as followed.

In the *Gemeenteraadslid* case in 1983, the Dutch Supreme Court ruled that the question as to whether certain expression violates a rule of unwritten law pertaining to proper social conduct in accordance with Article 6:162 BW must be answered according to a balancing test between two opposing high social interests, *in casu* the interest of individuals not to be exposed to reckless imputations in the press and the interest of preventing the persistence of abuses in society caused by a lack of awareness among the general public.[1592] In order to perform this balancing test, the Dutch Supreme Court created a 'checklist' of relevant factors.[1593] The Court has specified that the lower judge has the task of determining which of these factors are relevant in the specific circumstances of the case, which can require the inclusion of other factors, and to determine their relative weight.[1594] Next to imputations of a

1589 ECtHR, 26 April 1979, *NJ* 1980, 146 (*Sunday Times/United Kingdom*).

1590 Biesheuvel, Het Softenon drama en de vrije meningsuiting, *NJCM-Bulletin*, nr. 16/17, 1979, p. 58–63.

1591 ECmHR, 21 October 1998, *Mediaforum* 1999–1, nr. 3.

1592 Dutch Supreme Court, 24 June 1983, *NJ* 1984, 801.

1593 The checklist comprises the nature of the published imputations and the seriousness of the expected consequences for the person fallen under suspicion; the seriousness of the abuse that the publication aims to expose; the degree to which the imputations were founded in the factual evidence available at the moment of their publication; the presentation of the imputations; degree of likelihood that the pursued aim could have been reached without publication in the press by other means less harmful to the affected party; the chance that the affair would surely become public.

1594 Dutch Supreme Court, 8 March 1985, *NJ* 1985, 437.

specific fact, the Dutch Supreme Court has applied the balancing test to insulting expression.[1595]

In the *Gemeenteraadslid* case, the Dutch Supreme Court did not, however, refer to the general interest of freedom of expression and did not apply this right as a general justification ground. The Court merely referred to the interest to expose and denounce the existence of abuses. This interest is much more limited in scope and comparable to the 'legitimate interest to inform the public' that forms one of the factors to which in France a suspect, in the context of his defence, can appeal in order to demonstrate his good faith. The Court did not, therefore, attribute an independent weight to freedom of expression and did not consider whether the restriction was necessary in a democratic society for the protection of one of the interests enumerated in Article 10(2) ECHR. According to Schuijt, the Court previously rather considered whether a publication is sufficiently important to be published than – as it should have done – whether the restriction complies with the proportionality test of 10(2) ECHR.[1596]

The Supreme Court for the first time explicitly referred to the interest of freedom of expression in Article 10 ECHR in the *Rails* case concerning the admissibility of a rectification with regard to a photo documentary.[1597] In the *Het Parool/Van Gasteren* case, the Supreme Court for the first time applied the three-step-test of Article 10(2) ECHR. The case concerned the admissibility of an adjudication of a claim for damages with regard to a publication that compared an act of resistance with a 'vulgar murder with robbery'.[1598]As a result of these cases, in order to determine the unlawfulness of certain expression the judge must balance two opposing high social interests on the basis of the circumstances of the case. Subsequently, in order for the judge to determine the unlawfulness of the expression and to impose an injunction or adjudicate a claim for damages, he must decide whether this decision is necessary in a democratic society for the protection of the interests enumerated in Article 10(2) ECHR.

In subsequent cases, this proportionality test increasingly coincides with the balancing test.[1599] In the second *Van Gasteren* case, the Supreme Court determined that in the event of two conflicting fundamental rights, *in casu* the right to freedom of expression protected in Article 10 ECHR and the right of privacy protected in Article 8 ECHR, the balancing test must be performed all at once, whereby in a decision where, considering all circumstances of the case, one of the fundamental rights outweighs the other entails the compliance of the infringement of that other right to its second paragraph. The balancing test thus cannot consist of a 'double'

[1595] Schuijt, G.A.I., 'VII Aantasting eer en goede naam en andere aantasting van de persoon', in: Bloembergen, A.R. (ed.), *Onrechtmatige daad* (losbl.), aant. 26–96, Deventer: Kluwer.

[1596] Schuijt, G.A.I., Is de Hoge Raad bang voor de uitingsvrijheid?, *Informatierecht/AMI* 1990, p. 83–88.

[1597] Dutch Supreme Court, 21 October 1994, *NJ* 1996, 346.

[1598] Dutch Supreme Court, 6 January 1995, *NJ* 1995, 422, annotation Dommering.

[1599] Schuijt, G.A.I., Hoge Raad niet meer bang voor de uitingsvrijheid?, *Informatierecht/AMI* 1996, p. 23–30.

test that determines firstly, which fundamental right outweighs the other and secondly, whether the second paragraphs of the fundamental rights oppose to the outcome of this first balancing test.[1600]

It results from this established case law that the Dutch Supreme Court can review whether the restriction of freedom of expression is necessary in a democratic society, a test in which the case law of the ECtHR plays a decisive role.

1.6. The relationship between the legislator and the judge

The central characteristics of freedom of expression in Dutch law can be placed in the light of the constitutional system of the Kingdom of the Netherlands. The Dutch Constitution provides in a division – rather than in a separation – of powers between the legislature, the executive and the judiciary that constitutes a system of checks and balances.[1601] Within the division, the legislator plays an important role.[1602] In fact, according to Article 120 of the Dutch Constitution, the legislator is solely competent to determine whether its own legislation is in conformity with the Dutch Constitution, that reads: 'The constitutionality of Acts of Parliament and treaties shall not be reviewed by the courts'. Unlike France, the Dutch legal system thus lacks the possibility of judicial review by a special constitutional court. The prohibition signifies that courts cannot decide as to whether a statutory law is compatible with the Dutch Constitution. In the landmark *Harmonisatiewet* case in 1989, the Dutch Supreme Court decided that the prohibition of constitutional review also comprises general principles of law.[1603] However, as a general rule courts are empowered to review whether any provision other than statutory laws is consistent with a higher rule of law; they thus can review the constitutionality of decrees, administrative or regional regulations.

Article 120 thus suggests that by creating laws and reviewing their constitutionality the Dutch legislator solely determines and decides on major issues concerning the general interest.[1604] This primacy is grounded in the principle of legal certainty – that in relation to criminal law is assured by Article 16 of the Constitution and Article 1 Sr that assure the legality of criminal offences, which comprises the requirement of accessible and precisely formulated offences.[1605] This primacy according to constitutional theory is however mitigated by the current

---

1600 Dutch Supreme Court, 18 January 2008, *LJN* BB3210, *NJ* 2008, 274, annotation Dommering.

1601 Woltjer, A., *Wetgever, rechter en het primaat van de gelijkheid, Over primaten in het recht* (diss.), Den Haag: Boom Juridische uitgevers 2002, p. 495.

1602 The clauses of the fundamental rights of the Dutch Constitution primarily refer to an Act of Parliament.

1603 Dutch Supreme Court, 14 April 1989, *NJ* 1989, 469. Nevertheless, the Court seemingly addressed the legislator by clearly showing that it considered the Harmonization Act of 1988 in violation with the principle of legal certainty.

1604 Uzman, J., Barkhuysen, T. & Van Emmerik, M.L., The Dutch Supreme Court: A Reluctant Positive Legislator?, *EJCL*, vol.14.3 (December 2010), available at: www.ejcl.org.

1605 De Hullu, J., *Materieel strafrecht,* Deventer: Kluwer 2009, p. 92.

legal practice of the legislator and the judge. Firstly, by inserting specific justification grounds into Articles 261 and 266 Sr, the legislator explicitly gives the judge the task not only to ensure compliance with the law by their strict application, but also to determine whether expressions are in the general interest or the interest of the political debate. Explicitly making such a judicial appreciation an inherent part of determining the punishability of certain defamatory or insulting expression on the ground of the offences would not fit into the French legal system.

Furthermore, Dutch civil law has 'open norms' such as the norm of due diligence in Article 6:162 BW, precisely in order to enable the judge to 'color' the norms to the circumstances and facts of every case. This fits into the vision of the Dutch legal system as an 'open system', in which a priori defined abstract legal norms are on their own insufficient in order to ensure justice in every case.[1606] The judge must therefore not merely strictly apply, but also interpret legal norms using general principles of law. The legislator has recognized a certain 'law-making role' for the courts by the inserting current Article 81 into the Judicial Organization Act that considers it a duty of the Supreme Court 'to secure the uniformity of the law and *advance the development of the law*' [curs. EHJ].[1607] This vision diametrically opposes the French vision of the judge as 'la bouche de la loi'.

Secondly, the Netherlands has a monist system. Pursuant to Articles 93 and 94 of the Constitution, international law has direct effect in the Netherlands and courts are competent to set aside statutory laws that are in conflict with self-executing provisions of international treaties and to apply a provision of international law instead.[1608] In the Netherlands treaties thus take precedence over national law, including the Constitution, and the ECHR can be relied upon before all Dutch courts. In order to ensure compliance with the obligations of the treaties to which the Netherlands is a party, the courts may challenge the legislator, under the condition that the international provision is 'self-executing' in the sense that it provides a judicially manageable standard for review and the application of a statutory law would be in conflict with that international provision. Due to the ban on constitutional review, since the 1980s the Dutch courts have increasingly applied the ECHR as a judicially enforceable equivalent for the Dutch Constitution or a 'Bill of Rights for the Netherlands'[1609] and instead of setting statutory laws aside, it has interpreted national laws in light of the rights in the ECHR, notably the right to freedom of expression.[1610] The ban thus signifies that international treaties can afford more robust legal protection than the Dutch Constitution. It is precisely in

---

1606 See generally: Scholten, P., *Mr. C. Asser's handleiding tot de beoefening van het Nederlands burgerlijk recht. Algemeen deel.* Zwolle: W.E.J. Tjeenk Willink 1974; Slootweg, T. (ed.), *Dorsten naar Gerechtigheid / Paul Scholten*, Deventer: Kluwer 2010.

1607 Uzman, Barkhuysen & Van Emmerik 2010.

1608 Article 94 reads 'Statutory regulations in force within the Kingdom shall not be applicable if such application is in conflict with provisions of treaties or of resolutions by international institutions that are binding on all persons.'

1609 Uzman, Barkhuysen & Van Emmerik 2010.

1610 Peters 2005; Nieuwenhuis 2011; Janssens & Nieuwenhuis 2011.

order to enhance the normative character of the Constitution and to help to actualize and interpret fundamental rights that are sensible to social and technological developments, such as the newly proposed technically neutral formulated right to freedom of expression, that the State Commission, as well as the Commission Franken, has advised the abrogation of Article 120.[1611]

1.7. Influence of ECtHR case law

The beneficial influence of the ECHR on freedom of expression is apparent in several fields. Next to the previously mentioned example of the protection of commercial expression, in the field of the press, the Supreme Court has acknowledged its function of 'a public watch dog' to denounce the existence of abuses – but to observe due diligence when making accusations[1612] – and acknowledged the protection of sources.[1613] In particular, the punishability of insulting expression has been significantly curtailed under the influence of the case law of the ECtHR. Insulting expressions less frequently form the object of a prosecution and are less likely to lead to convictions. Hence, in the *Boomsma* case, the Dutch Supreme Court endorsed the acquittal by the lower courts with regard to the expression: '[t]hey were not SS men, no, even though they could certainly be compared to them on the ground of the things they did.' concerning the military intervention of the Netherlands against the Indonesian Republic, which was proclaimed after the Japanese capitulation in 1945 (1947–1949).[1614] The lower courts explicitly referred to Article 10 ECHR and considered that a conviction was not necessary in a democratic society.[1615] Furthermore, the Dutch Supreme Court has adopted the distinction made by the ECtHR between facts and value judgments made in public discussions and equally affords the latter more robust protection. Hence, in the *PDA-Grubben* case, the Supreme Court considered that a politician who himself utters opinions of an extreme right winged nature, may be referred to as a 'neo-Nazi'.[1616] The question arises as to whether the accommodation of the standards concerning the general interest of a public debate set out by the Article 10 case law of the ECtHR in the application of the speech offences has not rendered the specific justification grounds of Articles 261 sub 3 and 266 sub 2 Sr void.[1617] The Dutch Supreme Court has answered this question in the negative and decided

1611 Report *Staatscommissie Grondwet*, November 2010, *Kamerstukken II* 2010/11, 31 570, nr. 17, bijlage.

1612 Dutch Supreme Court, 6 January 1995, *NJ* 1995, 422, annotation Dommering.

1613 Dutch Supreme Court, 10 May 1996, *NJ* 1996, 578.

1614 Dommering, E.J., De Nederlandse publieke discussie en de politionele akties in Indonesië, *NJB* 1994, p. 277 *et seq.*

1615 Groningen District Court, 9 June 1994, *Mediaforum* 1994–7/8, p. 67; CA Leeuwarden, 26 January 1995, *NJ* 1995, 388.

1616 Dutch Supreme Court, 17 June 1997, *NJ* 1998, 361.

1617 Janssens & Nieuwenhuis 2011, p.164 *et seq.*

that when an appeal to Article 10 ECHR is rejected, the justification ground of Article 261 sub 3 Sr can have an independent significance.[1618]

As a possible result of the friendly attitude towards the ECHR, the Netherlands has in the past been condemned a relatively limited number of times by the ECtHR for violation of Article 10 ECHR. Between 1959–2014, the Netherlands has been condemned seven times by the ECtHR for violations of Article 10 ECHR amongst all members states, with Turkey leading with 248 violations, followed by Austria with 34 violations.[1619] It is noteworthy that these cases rather concern sanctions imposed on the press, for example, the disclosure of government information and violation of the protection of journalistic sources.[1620] With regard to the existence or the application of the Dutch speech offences, in 1979, the ECtHR declared the complaint of Glimmerveen and Hagenbeek, two Dutch politicians of the former NVU, an extreme right winged political party, inadmissible. While the applicants argued that their conviction on the ground of article 137e Sr for having distributed discriminatory expression violated Article 10 ECHR, the ECtHR deprived them of an appeal to the right to freedom of expression on the ground of Article 17 (para. 6.6 *infra*).[1621]

1.8. Conclusion

In Dutch law, freedom of expression is protected pursuant to Article 7 of the 1983 Dutch Constitution that provides a tri-partition with regard to the level of protection depending on the technical means used. The Article does not explicitly protect religious and non-religious opinions on equal footing. Religiously motivated opinions can either fall under Article 7 or Article 6 that protects freedom of religion and case law remains ambiguous as to whether an accumulation of the articles results in a higher level of protection. A general criticism of Article 7 is that it has been superseded by Article 10 ECHR that in several respects affords more robust protection of freedom of expression. Several proposals for reform have therefore been made, upon which, however, no legislative action has been undertaken.

The Dutch legislator has not further regulated the freedom of the press in a separate act and submitted it to a special regime. The Dutch legislator thus does not clearly distinguish the restrictions to actions from the restrictions to opinions. The restrictions are incorporated into the Dutch criminal code and are a result of Article 6:162 BW, which prohibits wrongful acts and legal actions on the grounds of

---

1618 Dutch Supreme Court, 14 June 2011, *LJN* BP0287, *NJ* 2011, 504, annotation Dommering.

1619 Statistics by States and table of violations accessible on: www.echr.coe.int.

1620 ECtHR, grand chamber, 14 September 2010, n° 38224/03 *(Sanoma Uitgevers BV/ the Netherlands)*; ECtHR, 22 November 2007, n° 64752/01 *(Voskuil/ the Netherlands)*; ECtHR, 30 November 2006, n° 10807/04 *(Veraart/ the Netherlands)*; ECtHR, 28 October 2003, n° 39657/98 *(Steur/ the Netherlands)*; ECtHR, 9 February 1995, n° 16616/90 *(Vereniging Weekblad Bluf!/ the Netherlands)*.

1621 ECmHR, 10 October 1979, n° 8348/78 8406/78, *(Glimmerveen and Hagenbeek/ the Netherlands)*.

these provisions and are bound by the general rules of criminal and civil liability. A general and neutral term for the criminal restrictions to freedom of expression is that of 'speech offences', which can be defined as 'offences that criminalize expressions on the ground of their content', which implies that even the criminalization of opinions that do not produce harmful actions can fall under its scope.

In order to conciliate the free expression of opinion with other rights or interests, the Dutch constitutional legislator has afforded the legislator the competence to determine any restriction with regard to the content of expression – regardless of the technical means used – as long as control takes place after, and not prior to the publication. He has not determined in the clause of Article 7 which interests the restrictions must protect. The ban of constitutional review in Article 120 of the Constitution prohibits the judge from reviewing whether these statutory restrictions are consistent with the Dutch Constitution that is moreover non-ideological in the sense that it does not determine any constitutional values from which limitations to fundamental rights could otherwise be derived.

Due to the ban on constitutional review, since the 1980s the Dutch courts, applying Articles 93 and 94 of the Constitution, have increasingly applied the ECHR as a judicially enforceable equivalent for the Dutch Constitution and – instead of setting them aside – interpreted the statutory restrictions, both the speech offences and Article 6:162 BW, in light of Article 10 ECHR. The Dutch Supreme Court has shifted from balancing the statutory restrictions *in abstracto* with freedom of expression to effectively balancing the conflicting rights to freedom of expression and rights and interests that oppose to its free exercise *in concreto* in every case. This practice has facilitated the importation or 'accommodation' by the judge of the Article 10 case law of the ECtHR that sets standards concerning the general interest of a public debate, the influence of which is undeniable. Where the courts used to merely take into account the interest to inform the public about the existence of abuses, they increasingly take into account the general interest of a public debate.

This practice might seem at odds with the primacy of the legislator in law-making or the primacy of politics in deciding on major issues concerning the general interest suggested by Article 120 and grounded in the principle of legal certainty in relation to criminal law assured by Article 16 of the Constitution and Article 1 Sr. However, it fits well into the Dutch 'open' legal system that has broadly formulated open civil norms, such as 6:162 BW, precisely in order to enable the judge to 'color' the norms to the circumstances and facts of every case using general principles of law.

II. THE DUTCH HATE SPEECH BANS

This section begins with a characterization of the Dutch notion of equality as it results from relevant Dutch law and policies (2). Next, the preservation of the offence of blasphemy in Dutch law for over eighty years and the final abolishment of the offence in 2013 is discussed (3). Against this background, the implementation of ICERD with the introduction of the main hate speech bans into Dutch law, is examined (4). Subsequently, the two following paragraphs analyse the main Dutch hate speech bans and their application by the Dutch judge, respectively the offences of 'group insult' (5); and 'incitement to hatred, discrimination or violence' (6) – also with regard to the issue of Holocaust denial. The section ends with a discussion of the modifications of the hate speech bans since their adoption (7).

2. The Dutch notion of equality

In the Netherlands, equality is a fundamental principle incorporated into the Dutch Constitution (2.1). The traditional structure of Dutch society by the system of 'pillarization' explains the recognition of minorities under Dutch law and has influenced Dutch immigration and integration policy for a long time (2.2). Pillarization can also be connected with the Dutch conception of separation of Church and State, also known as 'inclusive neutrality', that allows for the accomodation of religious practices in the public domain (2.3). The analysis results in a general conclusion about the Dutch notion of equality (2.4).

2.1. Equality in the Constitution of the Kingdom of the Netherlands

Unlike the French Constitutions of 1946 and 1958 or the 1789 Declaration, the Dutch Constitution lacks a preamble that refers to the principle of human dignity, the sovereignty of the state, its attachment to human rights and its common values on which its institutions are founded, or that in order to mark a new beginning denounces previous historic events and – under the auspices of a 'neutral' Supreme Being – enumerates its aims. Nor does the Dutch Constitution contain a general provision that defines the central characteristics of the Kingdom of the Netherlands, comparable to Article 1 of the French 1958 Constitution. The Dutch Constitution is thus 'non-ideological'[1622] and does not provide, in a general normative framework, for the interpretation of the fundamental rights listed in its first chapter. This has not always been the case. The *Staatsregeling* of 1798, strongly inspired by the 1789 Declaration, contained a preamble.[1623] However, the Dutch Constitution

[1622] Kortmann 1987.

[1623] The preamble read: 'Het Bataafsche volk zig vormende tot eenen ondeelbaren staat en bezeffende, dat het voornaame bederf van alle regeeringen gelegen is in de miskenning der

traditionally has a relatively sober, purely legal character and the Netherlands takes a rather pragmatic approach to fundamental rights. During the Constitutional reform of 1983, the reference to human dignity and certain fundamental rights[1624] were not inserted into the 1983 Constitution, because the Dutch Constitution only played a subsidiary role compared to the ECHR that already protected these rights.[1625]

However, Article 1 of the Dutch Constitution that proclaims the principle of equality can be regarded as expressing a fundamental principle that underlies Dutch law.[1626] The Constitutional reform of 1983 inserted the right of non-discrimination into the Article, which reads: 'All persons in the Netherlands shall be treated equally in equal circumstances. Discrimination on the grounds of religion, belief, political opinion, race or sex or on any other grounds whatsoever shall not be permitted.' Its insertion in Article 1 does not signify any priority of the principle over other fundamental rights. The legislator or the judge must balance the opposing rights or interests in specific cases.[1627] As the prohibition of constitutional review equally applies to Article 1, the Article, however, has a somewhat symbolic significance.[1628] The principle of equality is further specified in Article 3 of the Dutch Constitution that protects the equal eligibility for the appointment to public services and is further elaborated in concrete statutory laws.[1629] The principle primarily applies in the relationship between the government and individuals; the government must assure that rules apply equally to every individual and are not discriminatory.[1630] Besides, the principle applies to the relation between individuals; the Equal Treatment Act assures the equal treatment in the field of labour, professions and the offering of services. Compliance with the act is monitored by the Equal Treatment Commission (CGB) that judges in concrete cases (non-binding) and issues advisory opinions in social matters (para. 2.3 *infra*). Finally, the principle is of interest to the hate speech bans in Articles 137c-e Sr (para. 5–6 *infra*).

Unequal treatment is only prohibited when it constitutes discrimination. The Government has, however, not provided a fixed definition of discrimination, but has described the purport of the prohibition as: 'to interdict the distinction on the ground of people's features or characteristics that are reasonably irrelevant for the determination of entitlements and duties in certain fields of social life.'[1631]

---

natuurlyke en geheiligde regten van den mensch in maatschappy, verklaart de navolgende stellingen als de wettigen grondslag waarop het zyne staatsregeling vestigt en als zoo veele regels, waarnaar het zyne burgerlyke en staatkundige betrekkingen wil hebben gewyzigd.'

1624 The right to life, the prohibition of torture, the right to a fair trial and access to the judge.

1625 Peters 2005, p. 8.

1626 Hirsch Ballin, E.M.H., Artikel 1 van de Grondwet als fundamentele constitutionele norm, in: Maris, C.W. (ed.), *Gelijkheid en recht*, Deventer/ Zwolle: Tjeenk Willink 1988.

1627 Koekkoek 2000, p. 64.

1628 Tekst en Commentaar Grondwet, Comm. Bunschoten Art.1, aant.1, p. 7.

1629 Koekkoek 2000, p. 69.

1630 Tekst en Commentaar Grondwet, Comm. Bunschoten Art.1, aant.1, p. 7.

1631 *Kamerstukken II,* 1981/82, 16905–16938, nr. 5, p. 16.

Discrimination has a pejorative signification and suggests the making of a distinction that is offensive. Minister of Internal Affairs, De Gaay Fortman, considered that: 'discrimination is treating another person in such a manner as to make him understand that he regards him as deficient in these aspects of his human being.'[1632] It must be assumed that discrimination concerns unequal treatment on the ground of characteristics that are fundamental to one's personality.[1633] Article 1 does not, however, give a limitative list of discriminatory grounds, but its scope is extended to 'any other grounds whatsoever', which diminish the determination of the article.

Not all forms of discrimination are prohibited, only unjustified equal treatment.[1634] The Government considered that affirmative action, thus preferential treatment of subordinated minority groups, is allowed, as long as it is temporary and necessary to eliminate an actual disadvantage.[1635]

2.2. 'Pillarization' and minority policy

The Netherlands has traditionally been a country consisting of minorities and known for a large religious and cultural diversity.[1636] Contrary to France, Dutch law specifically recognizes minorities and facilitates groups defined by a common origin, religion or culture on the grounds of their common characteristics. Unlike France, the Netherlands has not made an exemption to Article 27 ICCPR that refers to minorities and has signed and ratified the European Charter for Regional or Minority Languages that recognizes the right to use a regional language both in the private and the public sphere and has designated the Friesians as a national minority.[1637]

The Dutch notion of equality and approach towards minority groups can be understood in light of the traditional structure of Dutch society by the system of 'pillarization', which dates back to 1917 (para. 2.3 *infra*).[1638] Under this structure, different religious and ideological communities (notably Protestants, Catholics and socialists) have their own political and social institutions, such as schools, hospitals, newspapers, political parties, trade unions, social support agencies and radio and

---

1632 *Handelingen II,* 1976/77, p. 2150–2151.

1633 Koekkoek 2000, p. 66.

1634 The Equal Treatment Act explicitly determines that with regard to certain professions making a distinction can be allowed, for example the distinction on the ground of political convictions with regard to administrative functions, or the distinction on the ground of religion or belief with regard to religious offices.

1635 *Handelingen I,* 1981/82, p. 392.

1636 Vermeulen, B.P., *Vrijheid, gelijkheid, burgerschap,* Den Haag: Sdu Uitgevers 2007, p. 5.

1637 Wet van 26 januari 1996 tot goedkeuring van het op 5 november 1992 te Straatsburg tot stand gekomen Europees Handvest voor streektalen of talen van minderheden (Trb. 1993, 1 en 199), *Stb.*1996, 136.

1638 See generally: Lucassen, J. & Penninx, R., *Newcomers: immigrants and their descendants in the Netherlands 1550–1995,* Amsterdam: Het Spinhuis 1997.

television broadcasting agencies. These institutions, assembled in so-called 'pillars', are largely paid for by the state that remains neutral by treating all communities in the same manner. The communities have, according to a Protestant maxim, 'sovereignty in one's own circle'[1639] or 'sphere sovereignty'[1640] which can be translated with 'living apart together', signifying that they can make their own arrangements and thereby preserve their own identity and emancipate their own members. This group-orientated system that focusses on separate facilities based on community identities can be characterized as 'institutionalized multiculturalism'.[1641]

Within this institutionalized diversity, several factors provided for unity and social cohesion. While Dutch citizens were active within their respective pillars, they normally obeyed their paternalistic leaders. National politics were left to the elite, who represented the pillars and regularly met to discuss common interests and build coalitions. They thus constituted the 'common roof' that supported the pillars and conducted a 'consociational democracy', a consensus and co-operation orientated form of democracy or politics of 'social engineering'.[1642] The Dutch population also shared the dominant existing Christian moral values across the pillars.[1643] In the 1960s, due to secularization and increased schooling of the population, pillarization, however, started to decrease in the Netherlands. Nowadays, only orthodox religious communities strictly abide by pillarization. The *concept* of pillarization was, however, for a long time maintained in the Dutch minority policy.

Until the 1970s, immigration to this 'pillarized' Netherlands – of the Molluccans in the 1950s, the so-called 'guestworkers' from the Mediterranean in the 1960s and people of Suriname in the 1970s after it had become an independent Republic in 1975 – was regarded as temporary. In order to facilitate the return of migrants to their countries of origin, a policy of 'integration with the retention of one's own identity' was pursued, which was comprised of the education of children in their mother tongue and original culture and the facilitation of own associations and consultative bodies. An exception to this policy was the 'repatriates' from the Dutch East Indies after it had become the independent Republic of Indonesia in 1945,

---

1639 Entzinger, H., 'Changing the rules while the game is on; From multiculturalism to assimilation in the Netherlands', in: Michal Bodemann, Y. & Gökçe Yurdakul (eds.), *Migration, Citizenship, Ethnos: Incorporation Regimes in Germany, Western Europe and North America*, New York: Palgrave MacMillan 2006, p. 121–144.

1640 Kennedy, J. & Valenta, M., 'Religious pluralism and the Dutch state: reflections on the future of Article 23', in: Wetenschappelijke Raad voor het Regeringsbeleid, *Geloven in het publieke domein,* Amsterdam University Press: Amsterdam 2006, p. 338.

1641 Entzinger, H., 'The Rise and Fall of Multiculturalism: The Case of the Netherlands'; in: Joppke & Morawska (eds.), *Toward Assimilation and Citizenship; Immigration in Liberal Nation-States*; London: Palgrave Macmillan 2003, p. 59–86; Entzinger 2006.

1642 Lijphart, A., *The politics of Accomodation. Pluralism and Democracy in the Netherlands*, Berkeley: University of California Press 1975.

1643 Lijphart 1975.

whose assimilation into Dutch society was encouraged. When the immigration increased and the temporality of the residence of immigrants became unclear, the government pursued a 'two-track policy' that aimed at stimulating next to re-migration, integration into Dutch society along the lines of the pillar system by means of a specific, categorical policy.[1644]

At the end of the 1970s, the economy and the social economic backlogs of immigrants had worsened. In 1979, the Scientific Council for Government Policy (WRR) issued the report *Ethnic minorities* that advised the pursual of a more coordinated policy for those migrants that were here to stay.[1645] The *Minority Policy* of 1983 introduced such a general policy for 'ethnic minorities' that focussed on the reduction of their social economic backlogs; their participation, emancipation and enjoyment of their cultural identities; and an intensified fight against their discrimination, comprising of an active prosecution policy with regard to offences penalizing discrimination, such as the hate speech bans (para. 8.1 *infra*).[1646] The government enumerated the target groups of the policy, being people from Suriname and the Caribbean, Moluccans, foreign workers, refugees, gipsies and caravan dwellers, for whom the creation of separate institutions supported by public funds in line with the pillarization continued in order to preserve and enjoy their culture. The Government thus actively promoted the multicultural society. This differential policy making on the basis of ethnicity was largely supported, but criticised by some for its possible opposite effect of 'ethnicization or minorization', signifying a further marginalization of minority groups.[1647]

This new policy could not prevent unemployment from increasing disproportionately among minority groups. In 1989, the Scientific Council for Government Policy issued the report *Foreigners Policy* that advised taking a different approach and to acknowledge that the Netherlands had *de facto* become an immigration country and therefore to focus on the actual integration of immigrants through labour, education and the schooling of adults, and to consider the preservation of their culture a private matter.[1648] The Government partly adopted this advice and connected it to its *Social Innovation Policy* of 1990 that preluded the reduction of the minority policy to a policy against social backlogs.[1649] The Government, however, did not alter its policy of accommodation of cultural identities at this time.

1644 Fermin, A.M.E., *Nederlandse politieke partijen over minderhedenbeleid 1977–1995* (diss.), Amsterdam: Thesis Publishers 1997.

1645 Wetenschappelijke Raad voor het Regeringsbeleid, *Etnische Minderheden*, Rapporten aan de Regering 17, Den Haag: Sdu 1979.

1646 Ministerie van Binnenlandse Zaken, *Minderhedennota*, Tweede Kamer 1982–1983, 16102, nr. 21.

1647 Rath, J., *Minorisering: de sociale constructie van 'ethnische minderheden'*, Amsterdam: Sua 1991.

1648 Wetenschappelijke Raad voor het Regeringsbeleid, *Allochtonenbeleid*, Rapporten aan de Regering 36, Den Haag: Sdu 1989.

1649 Ministerie van Binnenlandse Zaken, *Regeringsstandpunt ten aanzien van het rapport Allochtonenbeleid*, Tweede Kamer 1989–1990, 21472, nr. 2.

For a long time, openly pointing out existing problems related to immigration and the integration of minorities and questioning the public policy on such matters was considered to be 'politically incorrect' or even racist. The absence of a harsh and critical public and political debate on matters of public concern has been attributed to the specific Dutch pillar system, in which a fragmented media only covered news considered to be relevant to the pillar's members and where the dissemination of dissenting opinions would only disturb the 'pacification politics' of the elites.[1650] In 1991, politician and at that time leader of the Liberal Party (VVD) Frits Bolkestein, however, triggered a national debate with his statement in a national newspaper that the integration of minority groups had to be tackled with guts.[1651] In the media discussion arose as to the desirability of Islamic schools, segregation in education and crime rates among young immigrants. Subsequently in 1992, a 'public debate on the integration of minorities' was organized, comprising of the subject of the future of young immigrants in the fields of labour, education and security, which did not, however, lead to new policy measures.[1652]

The so-called *Contours Policy* of 1994, in which the Government renamed the Minority Policy 'Integration Policy', did express the vision that integration is a reciprocal process of acceptance and required efforts from all parties in society, with all the associated rights and duties.[1653] On the one hand, the criminal prosecution of discrimination was considered as an appropriate measure to clearly mark the norm of non-discrimination and to afford victims redress. The Public Prosecution therefore had to pursue an active prosecution policy with regard to expressions of racism and discrimination (para. 8.1 *infra*). Besides, the Equal Treatment Act of 1994 enabled discriminated groups to engage collective actions themselves. On the other hand, minority groups were no longer seen as 'categories of care' and the preservation of their culture was no longer seen as a task for the government, but as a private matter. A key principle formed the notion of 'citizenship' that expressed the primary aim of the policy to realize an active citizenship of members of ethnic groups. This mandatory civic integration notably comprised mandatory language courses. The statutory basis for this policy was created by the 'Newcomers' Integration Act of 1998 (WIN).[1654]

Hence, over time the focus of the minority policy shifted from multiculturalism to civic integration, from groups to individuals.[1655] The report *The Netherlands as*

1650 Van Noorloos, M., *Hate Speech Revisited, A comparative and historical perspective on hate speech law in the Netherlands and England & Wales* (diss.), Antwerpen: Intersentia 2011, p. 200–201.

1651 Bolkestein, F., Integratie van minderheden moet met lef worden aangepakt, *De Volkskrant*, 12 september 1991.

1652 De Jong, W., Drie WRR-rapporten vergeleken, *Migrantenstudies*, 2002 18 (2), p. 78–86.

1653 Ministerie van Binnenlandse Zaken, *Integratiebeleid etnische minderheden (Contourennota)*, Tweede Kamer 1993–1994, 23684, nr. 2.

1654 Wet van 9 april 1998, *Stb.* 1998, 261, houdende regels met betrekking tot de inburgering van nieuwkomers in de Nederlandse samenleving (*Wet inburgering nieuwkomers*).

1655 Fermin 1997.

immigration country of the Scientific Council for Government Policy of 1998 shifted the emphasis on the responsibility of individuals even further. It primarily focussed on a restrictive admission policy for new immigrants instead of the integration of minorities already present in Dutch society. Furthermore, it stressed the limited role for the government in the integration process, in particular existing of mandatory integration courses.[1656] The *Integration Policy of 1999–2002* adopted this approach.[1657] The government considered that an active citizenship required an active participation of migrants in society, their personal responsibility or self-reliance and the organization by local governments and civil society of the 'encountering' between migrants and the native population. In line with this focus on communication was the Media and Minorities Policy that aimed – next to increase the offering of specific programs for minority groups by the public broadcasting service – to make the public broadcasting service an accurate reflexion of the different ethnic groups in society, because of its special binding function.[1658] In the *Integration Policy* of 2011, the Government finally explicitly endorsed the criticism of the multicultural society, renounced its relativism and envisioned a strict immigration policy and compulsory integration through a generic policy based on 'citizenship, participation and self-reliance'.[1659]

The increasingly compulsory integration policy was prompted by an unprecedentedly critical and harsh public and political debate on integration and immigration.[1660] In 2000, the historian and member of the Labour Party (PvdA) Paul Scheffer published the article *The Multicultural Tragedy* in a national newspaper in which he argued that Dutch multiculturalism had failed.[1661] Subsequently, a series of events flamed an anti-immigrant and anti-Muslim discourse and paved the way for the so-called 'new politics'.[1662] After the terrorist attacks of 9/11, the populist politician Pim Fortuyn, leader of the populist party

---

1656 Wetenschappelijke Raad voor het Regeringsbeleid, *Nederland als immigratiesamenleving*, Rapporten aan de Regering 60, Den Haag: Sdu 1998.

1657 Minister voor Grote Steden- en Integratiebeleid, *Integratiebeleid 1999–2002 'Kansen krijgen, kansen pakken'*, Tweede Kamer 1998–1999, 26333, nr. 2.

1658 Bink, S., 'Media en minderheden in Nederland', in: Overdijk- Francis, J.E., Boot, J.S.M., Smeets, H.M.A.G., & Verheyden, J.A.C. (eds.), *Handboek Minderheden*, Houten: Sdu Uitgevers 2006, p. 1–57; Bink, S.,, *Bijna 25 jaar media- en minderhedenbeleid. Van exclusiviteit naar inclusiviteit*, Utrecht: Mira Media 2006.

1659 Ministerie van Binnenlandse Zaken, *Integratiebeleid*, Tweede Kamer 2010–2011, 32824, nr. 1.

1660 This has been explained as an intensive reaction to and breach with the decent and rational public debate existent during the pillarization. Van Noorloos 2011, p. 192.

1661 Scheffer, P., Het multiculturele drama., *NRC Handelsblad*, 29 januari 2000. Scheffer argued that cultural relativism and the respect for cultural differences had created a growing ethnic underclass, notably consisting of Moroccan and Turkish Muslims, that did not adhere to western values and the principles of liberal democracy and was unable and unwilling to integrate into Dutch culture and society. Only a 'civilisation offensive', consisting of a more compulsory integration policy emphasising on Dutch culture and history, could counter further segregation and preserve social cohesion and the functioning of the democratic state.

1662 Prins, B., Het lef om taboes te doorbreken. Nieuw realisme in het Nederlandse discours over multiculturalisme, *Migrantenstudies*, 2002 18 (4), p. 241–254.

Leefbaar Nederland and subsequently of the List Pim Fortuyn, voiced the general dissatisfaction of the electorate with the 'left-right' coalition, accusing it of having refused to face the socio-economic problems caused by Muslim-immigration and the threat of Islam to western liberal values.[1663] After the political assassin of Fortuyn in 2002 by an animal rights activist, populist politician Geert Wilders, leader of the populist Freedom Party (PVV) further radicalized the public and political debate about multiculturalism (para. 6.7 *infra*).

In the light of traditional Dutch institutionalized multiculturalism, the principle of non-discrimination can be understood as affording people the right to enjoy their cultural identities rather than – according to the French vision – of indifference towards their common characteristics. However, pillarization is criticized not to have generated the religious tolerance for which the Netherlands is famous, but rather the indifference of groups in society towards each other, and to have served as a means of excluding immigrants from mainstream society.[1664] Hirsch Ballin has objected to this stating that '[m]ulticulturalism is a fact, but if its acceptance results in an isolated co-existence of cultural traditions, it indeed works counterproductive.'[1665]

2.3. The separation between State and Church

The pillarization and the recognition of minorities in Dutch law can be connected with the Dutch vision on the separation of the church and the state and the accommodation by the Dutch State of religions and cults. Unlike the situation in France, the Dutch Constitution lacks a provision that explicitly proclaims the principle of the separation of church and state as a characteristic of the Dutch State. The principle forms a rule of unwritten law that is expressed through a set of provisions, notably the constitutional rights of non-discrimination in Article 1, freedom of religion in Article 6, and freedom of education in Article 23.[1666] As a result of this, the principle is not often referred to and is not further elaborated in case law. Legal scholars, therefore, fundamentally disagree on its exact purport.[1667]

Historically, religious freedom originates in the religious developments of the sixteenth and seventeenth century. The Government prevented the outbreak of

1663 Among his controversial statements were 'The Netherlands is full' and 'Islam is a backward culture' and his proposal to abrogate the prohibition of discrimination in Article 1 of the Dutch Constitution in order to allow the expression of discriminatory statements in: Pim Fortuyn op herhaling: 'De islam is een achterlijke cultuur.', Interview met Pim Fortuyn, *De Volkskrant*, 9 februari 2002.

1664 Entzinger 2006.

1665 Hirsch Ballin, E.M.H., *Burgerrechten,* oratie rede van 9 September 2011, oratie 409, Universiteit van Amsterdam, available at: www.oratiereeks.nl.

1666 Bijsterveld, S., 'Scheiding van kerk en staat: een klassieke norm in een moderne tijd', in: Wetenschappelijke Raad voor het Regeringsbeleid, *Geloven in het publieke domein,* Amsterdam University Press: Amsterdam 2006, p. 248.

1667 Diepenhorst, I.A., *De verhouding tusschen kerk en staat in Nederland*, Kemink en Zoon: Utrecht 1946.

religious civil wars by affording individual citizens the right to exercise their religion in the private sphere. One of the first constitutional acknowledgements of religious freedom was Article XIII of the Union of Utrecht of 1579, the alliance of defence between several Dutch Provinces against Spain. The scope of the freedom was, however, limited. Outside the domestic sphere the government had the competency to regulate religion, which it did by privileging the dominant Calvinist religion; the right of public religious exercise was reserved to Calvinists, who were solely eligible for public functions. The Calvinist Church was financed by the State that in its turn felt free to intervene in its internal religious affairs.[1668] Nevertheless, compared to the cruelties to which religious minorities were subjected in other countries, a practice of religious tolerance existed.[1669]

In 1795, the French formally abolished the privileged status of the Calvinist Church and afforded all religions equal status. The ties between religion and state were however not entirely cut. The Staatsregeling of 1789 underlined the importance of religion for the morals and unity of the state consisting of a shared Christian identity; public education formed an essential instrument to transmit enlightened Christen values.[1670] The State kept financing the Calvinist Church. During the nineteenth century, the privileging and paternalism of the Calvinist Church and the discrimination and repression of other religions decreased. The Act on denominations of 1853 acknowledged the freedom of denominational organizations. The Act of 7 December 1983 finally discontinued the financial ties between the State and several designated churches.[1671]

Strictly speaking, the principle of separation of state and church thus signifies that in the relationship between state and church there can be no institutional or direct substantive control on both sides. On the one hand, churches cannot have a formal position in political decision-making nor can government action be based on religious standards. On the other hand, the government cannot influence the doctrine and internal organization of churches.[1672] The freedom of religious organization is further elaborated in Article 2:2 BW and assured by the exclusion of the application of the Equal Treatment Act to churches and religious services.

Like other laws and royal Decrees, the preamble of the Criminal Code still refers to 'the Grace of God' in order to express the vision that the legislator derives its authority to create laws from God, and thus acts according to divine authority or even as a representative of God on earth.[1673] As the words express a connection between the state and God, they are at odds with the principle of the separation of state and church in the strict sense. The words, however, have no legal significance

---

1668 Koekkoek 2000, p. 93.

1669 See generally: Kaplan, B.J., *Divided by Faith: Religious Conflict and the Practice of Toleration in Early Modern Europe,* Cambridge MA: Harvard University Press 2007.

1670 Vermeulen 2007, p. 6.

1671 Koekkoek 2000, p. 94.

1672 Bijsterveld 2006, p. 248.

1673 Joosting,.J.G.C., *Bij de gratie Gods*, Leiden: Brill 1912, p. 5.

and are a recollection to the past. Subsequently, the Criminal code cites several offences that specifically protect the free – collective – exercise of a religion.[1674] Articles 147 sub 2 and 3 Sr criminalize the ridiculing of a clergyman in the lawful observation of his service, respectively the scoffing of objects devoted to a service, during the lawful practice of a service. Articles 145 and 146 Sr criminalize the impediment, respectively the disturbance of lawful public gatherings for the profession of a religion or belief or of lawful religious or philosophical ceremonies. Churches, religious servants or adherents may however not violate the – criminal – law. Article 449 of the Dutch Criminal Code, which prohibits religious marriage without a previous civil marriage, is the only article that explicitly restricts the religious exercise.[1675]

In its strict interpretation, the principle does not, however, entirely describe the relationship between the state and religion.[1676] Similar to France, the process of disentanglement of the Dutch state and religion focussed in particular on education, but had the opposite outcome of the accommodation of religion. The 'battle on education' was at the basis of the pillarization and the forming of political parties based on religious or ideological convictions.[1677] During the French occupation, education had become a state affair and public schools were directed not to lay too much emphasis on religion. The Constitution of 1848 – founded by liberal leader Thorbecke – affirmed the principle of separation of state and church and enhanced freedom of religion and education; it enabled the establishment of private denominational and confessional schools separate from the government, but only by private funding. However, most Protestants and Roman Catholics considered religious education primarily as a task for parents and wanted their schools to receive financing equal to that received by public schools, while maintaining their freedom in, for example, curriculum policy and teacher appointments. Contrarily, the liberals tried to protect the privileged financial position of public schools. The 'pacification' of 1917 equated private and public education financially. Since then, Article 23 of the Constitution assures complete state funding for denominational and confessional schools.

This right to 'special education' forms the key to the Dutch vision on state neutrality towards religions that has been characterized as 'inclusive neutrality'[1678] or 'pluralistic cooperation'.[1679] These notions signify that, contrary to France, in the

1674 Van Kempen, P.H., 'Religie in het Wetboek van Strafrecht', in: Broeksteeg, H. & Terlouw, A. (ed.), *Overheid, Recht en Religie*, Kluwer: Deventer 2011, p. 161–194.

1675 Van Kempen 2011, p. 175.

1676 Nieuwenhuis, A.J. & Zouthout, C.M. (eds.), *Rechtsstaat en religie*, Nijmegen: Wolf Legal Publishers 2008.

1677 Koekkoek 2000, p. 245 *et seq.*

1678 Van der Burg, W., *Het ideaal van de neutrale staat, inclusieve, exclusieve en compenserende visies op godsdienst en cultuur*, Erasmus Law Lectures 18, Den Haag, Boom Juridische Uitgevers 2009, p. 40.

1679 Vermeulen, B.P. & Kanne, M.J., 'Kerk en staat en de mensenrechten', in: Van Drimmelen, L.C. & Van der Ploeg, T.J. (eds.), *Kerk en recht*, Utrecht: Lemma 2004, p. 73.

Netherlands religion has a place in the private and the public sphere, including the domain of public institutions and services. In specific laws, the government guarantees equal denominational or confessional participation in the access to and the supply of public services, comprising next to education, the public broadcasting system and health care. The Act on Social Support forms an example of the cooperation between the government and religious organizations in the realization of civil and social aims.[1680]

'Inclusive neutrality' has been the subject of further interpretation since 1917. It has increasingly come under pressure in public and political debates that obviously focus on the accommodation of practices of the Islamic faith, in which the concepts of the separation of state and church and state neutrality and the scope of freedom of religion are confusingly mixed. Subsequently, a series of government reports has explored the place of religion in the public sphere and fundamental rights in a multicultural society that, however, did not advise to adopt a fundamentally different approach to possible conflicting claims concerning notably the rights of freedom of expression, religion and non-discrimination.[1681] With regard to the possibility of wearing religious dress in public, gradually the view has established – in the judgments and opinions of the CGB, the judicial decisions and politics – that a distinction must be made between the different institutions in society.

With regard to schools, in principle public schools cannot prohibit the wearing of headscarves and veils by teachers or students.[1682] Contrarily, private schools can apply specific religious dress codes and refuse teachers or students unwilling to comply with them in order to realize their religious or ideological foundations, as long as policies are carried out consistently.[1683] When educational institutions however refuse students or teachers on the ground of seemingly neutral dress codes that in practice notably target religious adherents, there must be an objective justification. Furthermore, although religious schools may set special requirements

---

1680 Wet van 29 Juni 2006 houdende nieuwe regels betreffende maatschappelijke ondersteuning (Wet maatschappelijke ondersteuning), *Stb.* 2006, 351.

1681 Nota Grondrechten in een pluriforme samenleving, *Kamerstukken II,* 2003–2004, 29614, nr. 2; Wetenschappelijke Raad voor het Regeringsbeleid, *Geloven in het publieke domein,* Amsterdam: Amsterdam University Press 2006; *Godslastering, discriminerende uitingen wegens godsdienst en haatuitingen: Een inventariserende studie*, Van Stokkum, B.A.M., Sackers, H.J.B. & Wils, J.-P., Den Haag: WODC 2006; Religie en grondrechten, *Justitiële Verkenningen*, WODC, nr. 1, 2007.

1682 CGB Advies/2003/01, 16 April 2003.

1683 As the judge uses a more flexible 'necessity-test' than the CGB, he can reach a different outcome in one case. For example, the Amsterdam Court of Appeal considered that the Catholic Bosco College had not acted inconsistently by refusing one of its Islamic students, when one day she appeared at school wearing a scarf, even though the school lacked a policy in this field, because previously none of their students had worn a headscarf. What is more, the school had the right to change its policy. CA Amsterdam, 6 September 2011, *LJN* BR6764. Contrarily, the CGB considered that the Catholic Bosco College had made it unsufficiently clear that its headscarf policy aimed to realize its Catholic foundation. The policy therefore constituted an unjustified distinction on the ground of religion. CGB 7 January 2011, Decision 2011–02.

for the function of a teacher in order to realize their religious foundations, a school may not fire a teacher on the sole ground of his homosexuality and the fact that he has a relationship or lives together with his partner.[1684]

With regard to the workplace, private companies cannot easily prohibit their employees from wearing religious symbols and dressing on the ground of representativeness.[1685] This is different for the public authorities. Public institutions and services, such as the police in the light of its specific and special task[1686] and to a lesser extent the Immigration and Naturalization Service (IND),[1687] can require such neutral representation of their officials as long as dress codes are formulated in neutral terms.[1688] In 2001 the CGB decided that the rejection by the Zwolle tribunal of an Islamic candidate soliciting to the function of interim clerk on the ground of her wearing a headscarf constituted discrimination on the ground of religion. According to the CGB, the prohibition on wearing a headscarf formed a disproportional measure and the argument of neutrality was deemed to be an insufficient justification, considering the nature of the function. However, the aim of the prohibition – the expression of the independence and impartiality of the judiciary – was legitimate and not discriminatory. The prohibition served an important interest.[1689]

Several legislative proposals aimed to introduce a general criminal prohibition to wear religious dress in public or in the exercise of public functions. In 2007, the Freedom Party initiated a draft that proposed to specifically prohibit the wearing of a burqa and niqaab in all public places on the ground of their incompatibility with Western fundamental constitutional values, the emancipation and integration of women and for security reasons.[1690] The Council of State considered that the criminal prohibition formed an absolute limitation of freedom of religion that could not be justified by security reasons. The draft did not demonstrate that the wearing of such dress constituted a danger to the constitutional state. Furthermore, the prohibition was discriminatory, because it only targeted a limited religious group.[1691] Subsequently, the Liberal Party proposed to prohibit the covering of the

1684 Den Haag District Court, 2 November 2011, *LJN* BU3104. In the same sense: CGB 29 April 1999, Decision 1999–38.

1685 CGB Advies/2004/06, 12 August 2004.

1686 CGB Advies/2007/08, November 2007.

1687 CGB Advies/2012/01, 6 April 2012.

1688 For example, the Amsterdam Court of Appeal has decided that the municipal transport service of Amsterdam could suspend a Coptic tram conductor for violation of the company dress code by wearing a golden crucifix on his chest, because the aim of the dress code to realize a neutral and more professional representation could be objectively justified. CA Amsterdam, 15 June 2010, *LJN* BM7410.

1689 CGB 22 June 2001, *AB* 2001, 308, annotation Vermeulen.

1690 *Kamerstukken II,* 2007/08, 31108, nr. 7.

1691 *Advies Raad van State*, 21 September 2007, W03.07.0219/II; *Kamerstukken II,* 2007/08, 31108, nr. 4.

face in general for security reasons,[1692] which would, however, in effect function as a prohibition of the burqa.[1693]

In 2012, a draft was submitted that proposed the prohibition of the covering of the face in public places, publicly accessible buildings, educational institutions, non-residential areas within health care institutions and public transport that was grounded this time on the protection of the *social* order by eliminating obstacles in open communication – a freedom that the government, however, had not wanted to explicitly protect in Article 7 of the Dutch Constitution (para. 1.2 *supra*) – and by ensuring full and equal participation of women in society.[1694] The Council of State considered that the criminal prohibition violated freedom of religion, because the wearing of religious dress is a personal choice and subjective feelings of insecurity cannot form a sufficient, independent justification for such a measure. The draft did not demonstrate why a general criminal prohibition provided a pressing social need and why existing specific prohibitions and competences did not suffice or could be complemented.[1695]

Another issue is that of ritual slaughtering. In 2007 the Animal Party initiated a draft that proposed the prohibition of ritual slaughtering.[1696] The Council of State considered that the absolute prohibition would have the effect of preventing Jewish and Islamic adherents from consuming religiously slaughtered meat and therefore violated freedom of religion.[1697] The draft finally perished in the Senate in 2011.

The polemic concerning Dutch multiculturalism is, however, not limited to practices of the Islamic faith, which can be illustrated by the affair of the conscience objections of civil servants and the *SGP*-case. Traditionally, Dutch municipalities afford civil servants the right to refuse to perform same-sex marriages on the ground of their conscience and religion, a right readily used in municipalities predominantly populated by orthodox Christians. In 2008, the CGB had already opined that this possibility violated the principle of equality. By offering this possibility, municipalities allowed civil servants to discriminate against a statutorily protected group.[1698] In 2012, the Democratic Party (D66) presented a draft that proposed the amendment of the appointment criteria for registrars in Article 1:16 BW in order to abolish this possibility.[1699] According to the Council of State, the proposal, however, violates the principle of equality and the right to equal eligibility in public functions, because it categorically excludes persons with religious or philosophical objections against same sex marriage from the public function of

---

1692 *Kamerstukken II*, 2007/08, 31331.

1693 *Advies Raad van State*, 6 May 2008, W03.08.0028/II.

1694 *Kamerstukken II*, 2011/1012, 33165, nrs. 1–3.

1695 *Advies Raad van State*, 28 November 2011, W04.11.0379/I; *Kamerstukken II*, 2011/1012, 33165, nr. 4.

1696 *Kamerstukken II*, 2007/2008, 31571, nr. 1–3.

1697 *Advies Raad van State*, 20 October 2008, W11.08.0398/IV; *Kamerstukken II*, 2009/2010, 31571, nr. 4.

1698 CGB Advies/2008/04, April 2008.

1699 *Kamerstukken II*, 2011–2012, 33344, nr. 2.

registrar. The Council advocated a more pragmatic approach, in which municipalities must carefully strike a balance in individual cases.[1700]

In 2010, the Dutch Supreme Court considered that the policy of the Reformed Protestant Party (SGP), whose political opinions are grounded on the bible, not to afford women full membership (including representative functions in political organs)[1701] violated Article 7 sub c of the UN Women's Treaty (CEDAW). The Article obliges the State to effectively ensure that women can fully participate in political parties and therefore also to ensure that women can stand as candidates of political parties. According to the Supreme Court, the State therefore has to take measures that ensure that the SGP actually affords women the right to stand for election, but at the same time interfere the least with the fundamental rights of the SGP.[1702] Like the Court of Appeal, the Supreme Court upheld the decision of the Council of State that the CEDAW does not require the discontinuation of the public funding of the SGP, but did not specify what exact measures are to be taken instead.

Notably, the Supreme Court considered that the SGP has the right to continue to proclaim its opinion that women should not be allowed on the election list, but cannot transpose this opinion into policy and thus put it into practice.[1703] This distinction signifies that freedom of expression or religion – of purely verbal expression – has a larger extent than the freedom to convert this opinion or religion into actions (para. 6.7 *infra*).

The SGP filed a complaint to the ECtHR arguing that the decision of the Supreme Court violated its freedom of religion, expression and association protected in Articles 9, 10 and 11 ECHR. On 10 July 2012, the ECtHR however declared the complaint inadmissible in remarkably strong terms. Firstly, only very weighty reasons would make a difference to treatment on the ground of sex compatible with the Convention. Moreover, the advancement of the equality of sexes prevents the State from supporting views of the man's role as primordial and the woman's as secondary. Finally, not only did the decision of the Supreme Court not violate Articles 9, 10 and 11 ECHR, in terms of the Convention the same conclusion flows naturally from Article 3 of Protocol no. 1 that assures free elections, together with Article 14 ECHR.[1704]

The separation of state and church equally influences the extent of the freedom to manifest and express religious convictions. Although the existence of the offence

---

1700 *Advies Raad van State*, 12 October 2012, W04.12.0331/I; *Kamerstukken II* 2012/2013, 33 344, nr. 4.

1701 For an historical overview of the ideas of the SGP on women's right to vote and the position of women in the SGP see: Post, H., *In strijd met de roeping der vrouw: de Staatkundig Gereformeerde Partij en het vrouwenkiesrecht*, Heerenveen: Groen 2009.

1702 Dutch Supreme Court, 9 April 2010, *LJN* BK4549; BK4547, *AB* 2010, 190, annotation Van Ommeren; *Gst.* 2010, 7338, nr. 63, annotation Broeksteeg; *JB* 2010, 115, annotation Schutgens; *NJ* 2010, 388, annotation Alkema; *NJCM-Bulletin* 2010, p. 485–500, annotation Nehmelman and Woltjer.

1703 Dutch Supreme Court, 9 April 2010, *LJN* BK4549; BK4547, para. 4.5.5.

1704 ECtHR, 10 July 2012, n° 58369/10, (*SGP/ the Netherlands*).

of blasphemy in Dutch law is not a feature exclusive to the Dutch 'inclusive pluralistic' State, the creation and indefinite preservation of the offence can notably be attributed to the Christian political parties that traditionally had a large backing and have often participated in the government coalitions.[1705] Unlike France, according to the Dutch legislator the repression of blasphemy does not suppose a specific conception of God by the State, it does not constitute unequal treatment by the Dutch State of religious and other philosophical convictions, nor does it violate freedom of conscience, expression and religion. To the contrary, the offence of blasphemy was established precisely to prevent abuses of freedom of expression that could impair freedom of religion. Nevertheless, the offence has been highly controversial from the outset (para. 3.1 *infra*).

2.4. Conclusion

Despite the 'non-ideological' nature of the Dutch Constitution, Article 1 of the Dutch Constitution, which proclaims the principle of equality and assures the right of non-discrimination, can be regarded as expressing a fundamental principle that underlies Dutch law. The principle primarily assures the equality of all individuals before the law. The further elaboration of the principle is indissolubly linked to the traditional structure of Dutch society by the 'pillarization' that dates back to 1917. It consists of a group-orientated system that focusses on separate publicly funded facilities based on community identities that can be characterized as 'institutionalized multiculturalism'. Dutch law therefore precisely recognizes minorities and facilitates the enjoyment of the specific identities of groups defined by a common origin, religion or culture on the ground of their common characteristics.

Due to depillarization, a persistent immigration and increased socio- economic problems, since the 1970s, the focus of the minority policy has shifted from 'multiculturalism' to 'civic integration', from groups to individuals, but comprised an active prosecution policy with regard to expressions of racism and discrimination. In the light of traditional Dutch institutionalized multiculturalism, the principle of non-discrimination can be understood to afford people the right to enjoy their cultural identities rather than – according to the French vision – of indifference towards their common characteristics.

The pillarization and the recognition of minorities in Dutch law can be connected with the Dutch vision on the principle of the separation of the church and the state and the accommodation by the Dutch State of religions and cults. The principle forms a rule of unwritten law that is notably expressed through the constitutional rights of non-discrimination in Article 1, freedom of religion in Article 6 and freedom of education in Article 23. Article 23 affords the right to 'special education' and resulted from the 'battle of education' in 1917 that formed

[1705] Kort-van Welzen 1994, p. 187 *et seq.*

the basis of the pillarization. The Article forms the key to the Dutch vision on state neutrality towards religions that has been characterized as 'inclusive neutrality'. This notion signifies that in the Netherlands religion has a place in the private and the public sphere, including the domain of public institutions and services. In specific laws, the government guarantees equal denominational or confessional participation in the access to and the supply of public services, comprising next to education, the public broadcasting system and health care.

Nowadays, the public and political debate concerning the place of religion in the public sphere is not limited to, but focuses on the accommodation of practices of the Islamic faith, notably the possibilities to wear religious symbols and dress in public. Gradually, the view has established that a distinction must be made between the different institutions in society, being schools, the workplace and public authorities. The Council of State has generally opined that legislative proposals to introduce absolute criminal prohibitions to wear religious symbols and dress in public institutions and areas violated the principle of equality and freedom of religion.

The separation of state and church equally influences the extent of the freedom to manifest and express religious convictions. Although the existence of the offence of blasphemy in Dutch law is not a feature exclusive to the Dutch State, such an offence fits into its 'inclusive neutrality' and does not – according to the Dutch legislator – violate freedom of expression or religion. The creation and indefinite preservation of the offence that has nevertheless been highly controversial from the outset can be attributed to the political influence of the Christian parties.

3. The Long Preservation and Final Abolishment of the Offence of Blasphemy – Article 147 Sr

The punishment of blasphemy dates back to the Middles Ages, but the offence of blasphemy was introduced into modern Dutch law in the early 1930s (3.1). Given the problems involved in the legal prohibition of the offence to God, the legislator has chosen a particular wording of the offence (3.2) that has been applied for the last time in the 1960s in the famous Donkey-trial against Dutch author Gerard van het Reve (3.3). Subsequently, several proposals to revive or abolish the offence have been made before it was finally abolished in 2013 (3.4). The analysis results in a general conclusion about the rise and fall of the offence of blasphemy in Dutch law (3.5).

3.1. History

In Europe throughout the Middles Ages and during the Reformation, blasphemy formed a topic of inter-confessional and intra-confessional conflicts. In practice, blasphemy was severely punished by means of the piercing or cutting of the tongue, chopping off of the hand, branding, the death penalty or expulsion. As far as the

Netherlands is concerned, the early modern discourse of religious tolerance in the 17th century did not foresee that the offence of blasphemy would exist for a long time.[1706] In 1811, during the French occupation, the French Criminal code was introduced, which lacked an offence of blasphemy. From then onwards, the offence of blasphemy did no longer form part of Dutch law.

The Dutch Criminal Code of 1881[1707] that entered into force in 1886 originally, equally did not comprise an offence of blasphemy. According to Minister for Justice Modderman, the criminal legislator had to protect the rights of society, not the rights of God, who would be indefinitely better at this job Himself.[1708] The prohibition on the impediment or disturbance of religious gatherings in Articles 145 and 146 Sr was criminalized, merely because in the mind of the nation the violation of religious gatherings was differently perceived than the disturbance of other gatherings, not because it gave offence to a religion.[1709] The criminalization of the ridiculing of a clergyman during the lawful observation of his service and the scoffing of objects devoted to a service, during the lawful practice of a service in Article 147 Sr protected the right of citizens not to be disturbed in their religious *exercise* (para. 2.3 *supra*).[1710]

Similar to other municipalities, the municipality of Wonseradeel had filled this lacuna by penalizing the public defamation of God in a scornful and libellous manner in a local regulation that became the object of a political debate in 1924.[1711] Several representatives requested the Minister for Internal Affairs to cooperate in the annulment of the regulation. The minister, however, refused to do so, because the regulation aimed to protect the public morals and therefore complied with Article 135 of the Municipality Act.[1712] Slotemaker de Bruine, representative of the Protestant Party (CHU), strongly criticized this restriction of freedom of conscience by counting the religious domain as part of the moral domain. The propaganda of atheism and materialism – against which the regulation was used – had to be countered by the moral and intellectual forces within the population, not by the government.[1713] This passionate speech did not convince the minister, who considered that the regulation did not violate freedom of opinion and expression in private, because it merely prohibited the *public* defamation of God.[1714]

During the affair, the idea of criminalizing blasphemy had hardly ever been brought to the fore. Several years later the frequent publication of anti-religious propaganda did provoke this desire among part of the population, the parliament

---

1706 Van Stokkum, Sackers & Wils 2006, p. 35–48, p. 82–90.

1707 Wet van 3 Maart 1881, *Stb.* 35.

1708 *Handelingen II,* 1880–1881, p. 102.

1709 *Handelingen II,* 1880–1881, p. 99;102.

1710 *Handelingen II,* 1880–1881, p. 100–102.

1711 *Handelingen I,* 1923–1924, p. 483 *et seq*. See more extensively: Kort-Van Welzen 1994, p. 187–190.

1712 *Handelingen I,* 1923–1924, p. 529.

1713 *Handelingen I,* 1923–1924, p. 552–555.

1714 *Handelingen I,* 1923–1924, p. 567.

and the government.[1715] In the early thirties of the twentieth century, the distribution of the pamphlet 'God is Evil' by the association *De Dageraad* arose much indignation. Furthermore, several publications in the newspaper of the Communist Party (CPH) *The Tribune* caused the Minister of Education, Arts and Sciences to remove the newspaper from the publicly funded reading rooms and to discontinue their funding if they continued to provide it. The National Railway Company decided not to sell the newspaper any longer in its bookshops. Controversial publications by *The Tribune* comprised the headline 'Eliminate Christmas', the song 'Christ to the dung heap! The Holy Virgin in the stable! The Holy Fathers to Hell! Long live the voice of the canon – the canon of the proletarian revolution!' and the cartoon depicting God as the inventor of a new poisonous gas for the destruction of the entire population of the Soviet Union. The measure led to the motion of Communist representative Wijnkoop, who accused the minister of trying to censure the Communists, which was, however, finally rejected.[1716]

On 25 April 1931, the Dutch government introduced a bill that proposed to criminalize 'public expression that is offensive to religious feelings by means of 'scornful' blasphemy' in a new Article 147 sub 1 Sr and 'the display of blasphemous expression visible from the public road' in Article 429*bis* Sr.[1717] According to the explanatory memorandum, in order not to interfere excessively with the free expression of opinion, Minister for Justice Donner had decided to merely criminalize the scornful form of expression that injured religious feelings. The criminalization of all expression hurtful to religious feelings would go too far. Cursing or swearing, thoughtless remarks or scientific expression of honest convictions fell outside the scope of the offence.[1718] The offence did not affect the contestation of a religion as such, as long as the form of the expression did not exceed a certain limit. Freedom of religion was considered as the fruit of historic development. What was to be prevented was, however, the abuse of freedom of conscience that leads to lawlessness.[1719]

The bill was discussed in great detail in the House of Representatives[1720] and the Senate.[1721] Many representatives, both proponents and opponents, objected to the ambivalent wording of the offence. The statutory elements of the offence criminalized on the one hand 'scornful blasphemy' and on the other hand 'the

1715 *Kamerstukken II*, 1930–1931, 348, nr. 3. See more extensively: Koolen, B., Het smalle pad van Jan Donner, De ontstaansgeschiedenis van de *Lex Donner* 1932, *Tijdschrift voor Religie, Recht en Beleid,* 2011 (2) 1, p. 72–84; Kort-Van Welzen 1994, p. 190–196.

1716 *Handelingen II*, 1930–1931, p. 2796.

1717 *Kamerstukken II*, 1930–1931, 348, nrs. 1–2.

1718 *Kamerstukken II*, 1930–1931, 348, nr. 3, p. 2; *Kamerstukken II*, 1931–1932, 34, nr. 1, p. 3.

1719 *Kamerstukken II*, 1930–1931, 348, nr. 3, p. 2.

1720 *Handelingen II*, 1931–1932, 26 Mei 1932; *Handelingen II*, 1931–1932, 27 Mei 1932; *Handelingen II*, 1931–1932, 31 Mei 1932; *Handelingen II*, 1931–1932, 1 Juni 1932; *Handelingen II*, 1932–1933, 3 November 1932–1933.

1721 *Handelingen I*, 1932–1933, 2 November 1932; *Handelingen I,* 1932–1933, 3 November 1932.

offence to religious feelings': what was the exact rationale and scope of the offence? While some desired the criminalization of the sin of blasphemy *as such* thus the offence to Gods Person, others desired the criminalization of the offence to religious feelings of religious adherents. Opinions diverged not only between the confessional and non-confessional parties, but also between the different confessional parties.[1722]

Several arguments were put forward against the introduction of the offence.[1723] Firstly, as anti-religious propaganda was not a new phenomenon and previous publications such as 'The Red Devil' and 'Bible amusant' had not resulted in immediate legislative action, the bill constituted ad hoc legislation – which especially in the field of criminal law was to be rejected – against publications in *The Tribune* that surely diid not have a very large impact. Secondly, the recognition of God by the State was not to lead to the unequal protection of religious and other philosophical convictions. Anti-religious propaganda was to be countered by word, by anti-religious propaganda, and not by criminal law that could not completely repress the offence to religious feelings, but rather fuel more anti-religious propaganda. In any case, religious adherents had themselves fueled the anti-religious propaganda due to the fact that many war atrocities had been defended in the name of religion and scornful expression against socialistic principles was often made from the religious side.

A first rationale of the offence formed the protection of the public order. Anti-religious expression had become a persistent problem. Proponents feared that the anti-religious propaganda from the Communist side would provoke strong reactions and reprisals on the religious side, mainly from the orthodox Christian youth, and would therefore cause problems with the public order. However, the Minister rejected the suggestion to model the offence after Article 156 of the Criminal Code of the (former) Dutch East Indies that prohibited scornful or offensive expression of feelings of hostility, hatred or disdain against one or more religious groups of the population. The situation in the Netherlands could not be compared with the large religious diversity in the Dutch East Indies. The offence of blasphemy did not regard the expression of feelings of hostility, hatred or disdain against groups, but the expression of feelings of hostility, hatred or disdain against God.[1724]

According to the Minister, the State openly acknowledged the existence of God, public authority was exercised by the grace of God and, despite the broadest recognition of freedom of religion, the State was not an 'État athée'. Hence, the State had to clear from the public sphere expression that directly defamed God.[1725] The construction of God as part of the legal order was considered by some to be a somewhat artificial attempt to justify the criminalization of the sin of blasphemy *as such*. The Minister, however, strongly opposed such an offence for the protection of God or a Religion, which belonged to God's domain and not to the domain of the

1722 For an analysis see: Kort-Van Welzen 1994, p. 197 *et seq.*
1723 For an overview see: *Kamerstukken II*, 1930–1931, 348, nr. 4.
1724 *Kamerstukken II*, 1930–1931, 348, nr. 4, p. 7; *Kamerstukken II*, 1931–1932, 34, nr. 1, p. 4.
1725 *Kamerstukken II*, 1930–1931, 348, nr. 3, p. 2.

State.[1726] A more practical argument was that such an offence would require an awareness of the true existence of God with the offender, while he who blasphemes as a general rule does not believe in God's existence.

A second rationale for the offence was the protection of the religious feelings as they existed in society. The Minister argued that the direct defamation of God in a scornful manner offends one of the most elementary and general moments of the religious feeling. A parallel could therefore be drawn with the existing prohibitions of Article 147 Sr that criminalized the ridiculing of a clergyman or the scoffing of an object only *at the location where the service is held*, in other words within another person's domain.[1727] Likewise, he who blasphemes accepts the religious representations of others and enters into their sphere or domain to subsequently commit the offence.[1728]

The minister rejected the amendment presented by Slotemaker de Bruine who proposed the criminalization of the offence to religious feelings 'in an intolerable manner', thus in more neutral terms than 'by means of scornful blasphemy'. The minister had precisely avoided the use of such general terms in order to limit the scope of the offence that could apply to the phrase 'God is Evil', but certainly not to phrases such as 'Religion is opium to the people' or 'Disbelief is a plague'. As the offence used an objective conception of God – a Supreme Being – that could be determined by the State or the judge independently from personal convictions,[1729] it did not constitute a discriminatory protection of freedom of religion of a religious majority; other religions or beliefs did not have a comparable conception that was left unprotected.[1730] The minister disputed that the offence violated freedom of expression, because Article 7 of the Dutch Constitution merely prohibited prior censorship and thus reserved the possibility to secure the public order (para. 1.2.2 *supra*). It merely required that the form of expression that contests another religion does full justice to what is sacred within that religion.[1731]

The bill was eventually adopted on 1 June 1932 by the House of Representatives with 49 against 44 votes.[1732] Subsequently, the bill was adopted by the Senate with 28 against 18 votes[1733] and published in the law gazette as the Act of 4 November 1932.[1734] The offence was included in Book II Section V of the Dutch Criminal

---

1726 *Kamerstukken II*, 1931–1932, 34, nr. 1, p. 1–4.

1727 *Kamerstukken II*, 1930–1931, 348, nr. 3, p. 2.

1728 *Ibid.*, p. 2.

1729 *Kamerstukken II*, 1931–1932, 34, nr. 3.

1730 *Kamerstukken II*, 1931–1932, 34, nr. 1, p. 1.

1731 *Handelingen I*, 1932–1933, p. 42–45.

1732 *Handelingen II*, 1931–1932, p. 2654. Among the 44 representatives who voted against the bill were 21 Social-Democrats; 8 Liberals; 7 Liberal Protestant-Democrats; 3 Reformed Protestants; 2 Communists; 1 representative of the Centre Party for City and Country and 2 of the Protestant Party (CHU).

1733 *Handelingen I*, 1932–1933, p. 49. It were the Roman-Catholics; the Anti-Revolutionists and the Protestants of the CHU, who voted in favour of the bill.

1734 *Stb.* 1932, 524.

Code concerning 'crimes against the public order', which according to its explanatory memorandum are acts that constitute a danger to social life and the natural order of society.[1735] In 1934, the Dutch Criminal Code was supplemented with Article 147a Sr that criminalizes the distribution of expression that is offensive to religious feelings by means of scornful blasphemy.

3.2. Elements of the offence

The wording of the offence of blasphemy in Article 147 sub 1 Sr has remained unchanged since its introduction in the 1930s and stated that 'any person who publicly, orally, in writing or by means of portrayal, expresses himself in a manner insulting for religious feelings by means of scornful blasphemy' was liable to an imprisonment up to three months or a fine up to € 3,800. Blasphemy signifies the insult of God's Person or the Supreme Being.[1736] Although the offence originated in the outburst of anti-Christian propaganda, its wording thus did not limit its application to the Christian religion. The offence was tailored to religions with one Supreme Being, such as the Christian (God), Jewish (JHWH) and Islamic (Allah) faith, and was therefore difficult to apply to polytheistic religions. With regard to the Christian religion, the Supreme Being comprises all persons of the Holy Trinity, i.e. Christ and even the Eucharist, but other religious figures, such as Maria, and rituals or practices were excluded.[1737] The offence thus offered a smaller scope of protection to monotheistic religions other than the Christian religion by lack of the concept of the Holy Trinity.

The offence furthermore required blasphemy to be *scornful*. The term expresses a high standard of intent that limited the scope of the offence to forms of expression that have the intention to deeply scoff, ridicule, or disparage Gods Person.[1738] The element 'in a manner insulting for religious feelings' enabled to bring under the scope of the article an offender who does not believe in God himself, but abuses the representations of God as held by others in society. However, it had no independent significance in the sense that proof of the fact that expression has actually resulted in the offence of the religious feelings of others was not required.[1739]

3.3. Application: the *Donkey* trial

The offence of blasphemy could be applied on the initiative of the public prosecution, on indication by the Minister of Justice, or in reaction to a complaint.

1735 Cleiren, C.P.M. & Nijboer, J.F., *Strafrecht, Tekst en Commentaar*, Deventer: Kluwer 2008, p. 745.

1736 Janssens & Nieuwenhuis 2011, p. 200.

1737 *Kamerstukken II*, 1931–1932, 34, nr. 1, p. 4.

1738 *Kamerstukken II*, 1930–1931, 348, nr. 3, p. 2; *Kamerstukken II*, 1931–1932, 34, nr. 1, p. 3.

1739 *Ibid.*

The prosecution of the offence thus did not depend on a prior complaint by an interested party. The application of the offence of blasphemy has been limited. Between 1932 and 1968 there have been 9 convictions and 3 dismissals on the basis of Article 147 sub 1 Sr.[1740] On certain occasions the courts have used a rather extensive interpretation of 'scornful blasphemy'; convictions comprised not only the exclamation 'A God, who has invented the bacillus of tuberculosis, is not a God, but a criminal' by a radical socialist,[1741] but also a publication that questioned the virtue of *Mary*[1742] and the mere *ridiculing* of Christ for being a 'demagogue, faith healer, Savior/gynecologist, Champion-surf-rider and amateur-ombudsman'.[1743]

The last blasphemy-case formed the famous '*Donkey trial*' in 1968.[1744] The case concerned the publication of a letter by the Dutch author Gerard Kornelis van het Reve in *Dialoog*, a magazine for homosexuality and society, and the publication of the book 'Nearer to Thee' by the same author in 1965. Both publications comprised passages that described how the author has sexual intercourse with God who has taken the form of a donkey. After representatives of the SGP had raised questions about the blasphemous nature of the publications, the Minister for Justice instructed the Public Prosecution to institute criminal proceedings.

The case revolved around the question as to whether 'scornful' blasphemy required that an offender must have had a 'subjective' intention to deeply offend God's Person, or an intention to do so according to 'objective' standards. The question resulted from Reve's defence that, being a faithful Catholic, he had merely intended to express his religious beliefs and not to offend God. The author was baptized just before the trial, which had been exhaustively reported in the media. According to Reve, the case therefore concerned 'a religious dispute that he had not intended to start, in which one conception of God was placed above the other.'[1745] The offence was indeed modeled in such a manner that it was directed against propaganda from the non-religious side; religious propaganda was not foreseen.

In literature, Reve's defence is considered to have played a weighty role in the decision by the Court of Appeal to acquit him. The Supreme Court endorsed the decision and considered that 'the term scornful comprises the subjective element,

---

1740 Conclusion Solicitor General Mr. Remmelink at: Dutch Supreme Court, crim.ch, 2 April 1968, *NJ* 1968, 373. The cases are documented in: Baelde, R., *Studiën over godsdienstdelicten* (diss.), Den Haag: Nijhoff 1935; De Roo, E.J., *Godslastering: rechtsvergelijkende studie over blasfemie en andere religiedelicten* (diss.), Deventer: Kluwer 1970, p. 129; Plooy, J., *Strafbare godslastering*, Amsterdam: Buijten en Schipperheijn 1986, p. 68–82; Van Stokkum, Sackers & Wils 2006, p. 98–109; Janssens & Nieuwenhuis 2011, p. 202–205.

1741 Dordrecht District Court, crim.ch., 15 January 1934, (unpublished).

1742 Haarlem District Court, crim.ch., 19 May 1938, (unpublished).

1743 Amsterdam District Court, crim.ch., 23 June 1965, *NJ* 1965, 282.

1744 Dutch Supreme Court, crim.ch, 2 April 1968, *NJ* 1968, 373, annotation Brinkhorst. The case is documented in: Plooy 1986; Abspoel, J.J., *Studenten, moordenaars en ander volk: kritische kanttekeningen van een officier van justitie*, Ede: Veen 1979; Fekkes, J. *De God van je tante: ofwel Het Ezel-proces van Gerard Kornelis van het Reve: een documentaire*, Amsterdam: De Arbeiderspers 1968; De Hullu, J., Strafrecht en literatuur, *Ars Aequi* 1984, p. 757–761.

1745 De Roo 1970, p. 121.

the intention of he who disparages the highest Supreme Being, presented as real; the term scornful thus does not merely have the function to describe a certain form of expression that is offensive to religious feelings; for these reasons an author is not already affected by the offence, if he has the intention to express himself in such a form that others must be offended in their religious feelings.'[1746] The Supreme Court thus set a very high standard of proof and threshold for criminal liability, which is in keeping with the aim of the legislator to limit the scope of the offence.

As the Donkey-trial took place in the early stages of the 'ECHR-era', unsurprisingly, the courts did not explicitly balance the application of the offence of blasphemy with the right to freedom of expression or religion. The case therefore leaves the question as to whether religious opinions are afforded a higher level of protection than other opinions undecided. The judges left the act of balancing between the different interests to the legislator and the Public Prosecutor. The Public Prosecutor considered that, after having balanced the interest of the community, the suspect, freedom of expression, the satisfaction of people who felt offended in their religious feelings, and of the requirement of tolerance, he wished to request no more than 100 Dutch Guilders.[1747]

The decision of the Supreme Court was criticized for making the offence of blasphemy unapplicable.[1748] This criticism has proved to be justified. After the Donkey-trial, the public prosecution has structurally dismissed complaints against blasphemous expression and courts of appeal have structurally affirmed these decisions on the ground that the author's intent could not be proven.[1749] Likewise, in 2001 the Amsterdam District Court rejected the request in summary proceedings of Hindoes that the Company Shiva Entertainment must stop bringing pornographic videos on the market under the name of the Supreme Being, because the company did not have the intention to use the name of Shiva in a scornful manner.[1750]

Complaints were notably filed by the Bond tegen Vloeken (Association against Cursing) against satirical programs of the socialist broadcasting company (VARA).[1751] In 1979–1980, the rejection of the complaint against the screening of the film *The Life of Brian* even raised questions in the House of Representatives.[1752] The Christian parties argued that the structural dismissals and rejections of appeals signified the erosion of the offence of blasphemy and demanded the Minister for Justice to undertake action. The Minister has, however, consistently held – in 1996 with regard to the display on the public road of the advertisement poster of the film

1746 Dutch Supreme Court, crim.ch, 2 April 1968, *NJ* 1968, 373, annotation Brinkhorst.

1747 Plooy 1986, p. 75.

1748 Annotation Bronkhorst at: Dutch Supreme Court, crim.ch, 2 April 1968, *NJ* 1968, 373; De Hullu 1984, p. 560; Plooy 1986, p. 77.

1749 Baelde1935; De Roo 1970, p. 112–129; Plooy 1986, p. 68–82; Van Stokkum, Sackers & Wils 2006, p. 98–108; Janssens & Nieuwenhuis 2011, p. 202–205.

1750 Amsterdam District Court, summary proceedings, 2 August 2001, *LJN* AB3067.

1751 Documented in: Van der Wilt, H., *Smalende Godslastering verboden?*, Veenendaal: Stichting Onderzoek- en Publicatiefonds Bond tegen het vloeken 2009, p. 19–29.

1752 *Aanhangsel II*, 1979–1980, 1108.

The people versus Larry Flint[1753] and in 2008 with regard to the crucifixion-act of Madonna during her *Confessions Tour*[1754] – that interference is outside of his competence.

3.4. Political developments and proposals of abolishment

In 1989 the Minister for Justice, however, took the initiative to examine whether criminal proceedings could be instituted against the publication of the Dutch translation of the novel *Satanic Verses* by Salman Rushdie on the ground of the offence of blasphemy. In a heated debate in Parliament, the Minister was criticized for giving in to the violent threat posed by Islamic fundamentalists and was accused of censorship. The Minister objected to this criticism stating that he had merely examined whether the offence afforded equal protection to adherents of Islam.[1755]

In 2004, Dutch cineaste Theo Van Gogh known for his film Submission was brutally slaughtered by Muslim fundamentalist Mohammed Bouyeri.[1756] The killing of Van Gogh triggered a countrywide series of assaults against Muslim institutions. In response to the murder, the minister for justice announced the examination of whether the offence of blasphemy was to be revived and used to channel the public debate concerning Islam in order to prevent Muslim radicalization[1757] and the intentional harm and offence of people in their beliefs or religion.[1758] Subsequently, the motion of representative of the Democratic Party (D66) Van der Laan proposed to abolish the offence of blasphemy.[1759] The motion was, however, considered to be inconvenient in light of the political tensions at the time and was therefore rejected. The minister announced the initiation of an investigation into the criminalization of blasphemy.[1760] In 2007, the Scientific Research and Documentation Centre of the Ministry of Justice (WODC) published the report 'Blasphemy, discriminatory expression on the ground of religion and hate speech'.[1761] One of its main findings was that the offence of blasphemy could not be considered to be a dead letter, but merely that it has led a dormant existence; it still had an independent function and value next to the other speech offences. However, its wording did create an inequality before the law between adherents of monotheistic religions and adherents of other beliefs.

1753 *Aanhangsel II*, 1996–1997, 929.

1754 *Aanhangsel II*, 2005–2006, 2019.

1755 *Kamerstukken II*, 21 februari 1989, p. 5099 – 5109.

1756 The film – co-produced by Liberal politician Ayaan Hirsi Ali who strongly opposed Islam – criticized the treatment of women in Islam.

1757 *Kamerstukken II*, 2004–2005, 29854, nr. 3.

1758 *Handelingen II*, 2004–2005, nr. 23, p. 1335–1342.

1759 *Kamerstukken II*, 2004–2005, 29800 VI, nr. 52.

1760 *Kamerstukken II*, 2004–2005, 29800 VI, nr. 41.

1761 *Kamerstukken II*, 2006–2007, 30800 VI, nr. 38.

The government decided to preserve the offence of blasphemy on the basis of its standard setting character[1762] and the minister for justice announced the initiation of an investigation into the possibility to broaden the scope of the offence in order to afford equal protection to all religious and philosophical beliefs.[1763] Subsequently, the Dutch Supreme Court, in its case law, gave a restrictive interpretation of Article 137c, the offence of insult of a group on the ground of their religion, in that it does not include religious offence and considered that in order to constitute punishable group insult, expression must *unmistakably* concern a group characterized by a religion (para. 5.7 *infra*). This development caused the Minister to change his position several times, which raised much criticism in Parliament.[1764] After the proposal to abolish the offence of blasphemy but to broaden the offence of group insult,[1765] the Minister finally renounced his plans altogether in 2009.[1766]

In response to the decision of the Minister to preserve the offence of blasphemy, the Motion of representative of the Democratic Party (D66) Van der Ham that proposed to abolish the offence was widely supported and adopted.[1767] In reaction to the decision of the government to prepare a bill for the abolishment, the Motion of representative of the Reformed Protestant Party (SGP) Van der Staaij proposed to preserve the offence based on its standard setting function, but the Motion was rejected.[1768] In the Motion, Van der Ham strongly emphasized the interest of freedom of expression and the importance of a profound public debate on philosophical questions. The offence of blasphemy afforded an unequal protection of monotheistic and non-monotheistic religions and constituted unequal treatment of religious and non-religious convictions. What is more, as freedom of religion formed a classically negative fundamental right, the offence to religious feelings did not constitute an interference with this freedom. Finally, the offence had primary been motivated by the protection of the public order, but its preservation was both unnecessary and undesirable, because other existing speech offences sufficed for this purpose.[1769]

The Council of State opined that a provision that affords protection to a facet of religion that does not have an equivalent in non-religious convictions cannot be considered to constitute *unequal* treatment of *equal* cases. Furthermore, the offence did not merely aim to protect the public order, but was founded on freedom of religion and the task of the government to protect 'freedom of conscience' and religious feelings. The Council of State concluded that the question of the preservation of the offence could not be answered according to strict Constitutional boundaries concerning the right to freedom of expression, freedom of religion and

---

1762 *Kamerstukken II*, 2007–2008, 31200 VI, nr. 8.
1763 *Kamerstukken II*, 2007–2008, 31200 VI, nr. 130.
1764 *Kamerstukken II*, 2008–2009, 31700 VI, nr. 104.
1765 *Kamerstukken II*, 2008–2009, 31700 VI, nr. 33.
1766 *Kamerstukken II*, 2008–2009, 31700 VI, nr. 128.
1767 *Kamerstukken II*, 2008–2009, 31700 VI, nr. 94.
1768 *Kamerstukken II*, 2008–2009, 31700 VI, nr. 99.
1769 *Kamerstukken II*, 2009–2010, 32203, nr. 2–3.

the principle of equality; this applied both to the Constitution and the ECHR. Determinent for the issue were aspects of criminal policy, public considerations and factors, and the views of other member states of the Council of Europe. The Council therefore advised the placing of the abolishment of the offence in a broader context and emphasized a number of possible –negative – legal and social consequences; the abolishment of the offence might lead to tensions in society and the loss of its preventive and normative function and the remaining speech offences might not be sufficient for an adaquate protection of religious minorities against insults of their religion.[1770]

The reservations made by the Council of State did not convince the initiators of the bill, who in essence attached more importance to the right to freedom of expression and placed the bill in the context of international developments; only eight of the 47 member states of the Council of Europe still have an offence of blasphemy and institutions of the Council of Europe have expressed their opposition to blasphemy laws. These developments can be connected to, on the one hand, the processes of secularism and secularization and, on the other hand, the increasingly diverse population. The offence is grounded on a connection between the State and God, between the public order and public morality, which can be historically explained, but is nowadays difficult to legitimize.[1771] The plurality of religions and differences between their adherents, rather calls for the criminalization of expression against religious groups than expression against God.

On 16 April 2013, the proposal to abolish the offence of blasphemy was adopted by the Parliament.[1772] All parties voted in favor of the proposal, except the three confessional parties (SGP, Christenunie, CDA). According to the initiators and the majority, the fact that the offence of blasphemy had an *independent* value (the protection of religious feelings) next to the hate speech bans of Article 137 did not signify that it also had an *added* value; the hate speech bans offered sufficient protection of all persons against insults, hatred and discrimination on the grounds of their religion or belief equally. Only this expression overstepped the limits to freedom of expression.[1773] On 3 December 2013, the proposal was adopted in the Senate with 49:21 votes. Next to the three confessional parties, seven members of the Liberal Party (VVD) voted against it. In the Senat, more emphasis was placed on the connection between the offence of blasphemy and the protection of freedom of religion. In line with the reservations put forward by the Council of State, the senators questioned whether the offence of blasphemy could have any *residual* value and whether its abolishment would not amount to an insufficient protection of

---

1770 *Kamerstukken II*, 2009–2010, 32203, nr. 4.

1771 For a discussion about the desirability of the offence see notably the contributions to: Thema Omtrent Van Gogh, *NJB* 17 December 2004, nr. 45–46; De Blois, M., Van der Poll, R. & Van Woudenberg, R. (eds.), Vloeken als een Hollander, Godslastering: religieuze, juridische en culturele aspecten, Veenendaal 2007.

1772 *Handelingen II*, 2012–2013, nr.75, item 18.

1773 *Kamerstukken II*, 2010–2011, 32203, nr. 5; *Kamerstukken II*, 2011–2012, 32203, nr. 7; *Handelingen II*, 2012–2013, nr.64, item 9.

religious minorities against insults of their religion. In fact, the debates in Parliament and the Senat had insufficiently clarified the exact relationship between the offence of blasphemy in Article 147 and the hate speech bans in Artice 137.[1774]

The Senat therefore adopted the motion by senator Schrijver that requested the government to examine the possible amendment of the hate speech bans of Article 137 of the Dutch Criminal Code 'in order to assure that this article affords a sufficient protection against a serious perceived insult of citizens through insult of a religion, without unduly restricting freedom of expression'. The report subsequently made by WODC answered in the negative, because 1) no positive obligations can be derived from international law to penalize these sort of expressions and the hate speech bans of 137 offer sufficient protection to comply with the international obligations; 2) the *subjective* conception of insult of citizens that is *experienced* as very serious through the insult of a religion, is incompatible with the *objective* conception of insult in 137c, which protects people's dignity in the eyes of others (*negative imaging*). Its penalization can conflict with the principle of legality, and does not fit with the premise that criminal law is an *ultimum remedium*; 3) the penalization of insult of religion violates Article 19 ICCPR, which sets the threshold for criminal prohibitions with the 'incitement to discrimination, hostility or violence'.[1775] According to the report, the question of when exactly insulting remarks about religious convictions and practices can amount to a punishable form of group insult or incitement to hatred, discrimination or violence on the ground of religion constitutes a highly contextual matter. In fact, as we will see later on, the consideration of the Supreme Court that expression must *unmistakably* concern a group characterized by a religion – in lower case law also applied with regard to incitement to hatred or discrimination – needs further precision (para. 5.7 *infra*).

3.5. Conclusion

Originally, the Dutch Criminal code of 1886 did not comprise of an offence of blasphemy, because the criminalization of blasphemy belonged to the domain of God. In 1932 the offence of blasphemy was, however, introduced in order to counter the outburst of anti-religious propaganda from the Communist side. The primary rationale of the offence was the protection of the public order. This notion however had a broad significance; as the State was not an 'État athée' and acknowledged the existence of God, it had the obligation to remove expression that defamed God from the public sphere. Another rationale was the protection of the religious feelings of religious adherents, because he who blasphemes enters into their domain of religious representations and thus interferes with their freedom of conscience and

1774 *Kamerstukken I*, 2012–2013, 32203, A; *Kamerstukken I*, 2013–2014, 32203, C; *Handelingen I*, 2013–2014, nr. 10, item 2; *Handelingen I*, 2013–2014, nr. 10, item 12.

1775 *Kamerstukken I*, 2013–2014, 32203, E herdruk; Noorloos, van M., Strafbaarstelling 'belediging van geloof', WODC, Den Haag: Boom Lemma Uitgevers 2014.

religion. As the offence used an objective notion of God, it was not considered as discriminatory between religions and beliefs. Nor would it violate freedom of expression, because Article 7 of the Dutch Constitution merely prohibited prior censorship and thus reserved the possibility to secure the public order.

The ambivalent wording of the offence that criminalized, on the one hand 'scornful blasphemy', and on the other hand 'the offence to religious feelings' formed the object of a heated debate not only between confessional and non-confessional parties but also between the different confessional parties. The Minister, however, limited the scope of the offence to *forms* of expression that have the intention to deeply scoff, ridicule or disparage God's Person in order not to interfere excessively with freedom of expression and has criminalized an offender who does not believe in God himself, but abuses the representations of God as held by others in society.

In the famous Donkey-trial in 1968 the Supreme Court set a high standard of proof by requiring the 'subjective' intention of the author to defame God. The offence has not been applied ever since. After the murder of Van Gogh in 2004, the minister announced his plan to use the offence to channel the excesses of the public debate concerning Islam and to prevent further Muslim radicalization. After several proposals to modify the offence, the minister finally decided to preserve the offence in its existent form. In 2009, a widely supported motion that proposed to abolish the offence was however adopted, which emphasized the interest of freedom of expression, the discriminatory character of the offence and that its preservation was unnecessary for the protection of the public order. The Council of State advised that abolishment of the offence be placed in a broader context, including the normative and preventive power of the offence. The proposal was, however, adopted in both the Parliament and the Senat. After existing in Dutch law for 80 years and being preserved due to the continued support of the confessional parties, the offence of blasphemy was finally abolished in 2013. This can be considered a welcome development; the processes of secularism and secularization and the increasing religious diversity among the population make the offence difficult to legitimize.

4. Implementation of ICERD

The Netherlands implemented the International Convention on the Elimination of all forms of Racial Discrimination (ICERD) in 1971 (4.1). Before the implementation, hate speech was regulated by several speech offences primarily aimed at the protection of the public order (4.2). With the implementation of ICERD a number of new prohibitions of forms of hate speech and discrimination were introduced that were more particularly aimed at the protection of persons against discrimination (4.3). The analysis results in a general conclusion about the background and merit of the implementation of ICERD into Dutch law (4.4).

4.1. Adhesions to ICERD

On 13 September 1968, the Dutch Government introduced a bill to adopt ICERD[1776], together with a bill to implement the convention. The bills were discussed in great detail both in the House of Representatives[1777] and in the Senate.[1778] While the former was adopted unanimously in Parliament and in the Senate, the latter was adopted unanimously in Parliament and in the Senate with 44 against 21 votes. ICERD was finally adopted by the Act of 18 February 1971[1779] and ratified on 10 December 1971.

Unlike France, the Netherlands did not make any reservations to the convention. However, similar to France, the Dutch Government was of the opinion that the significance of ICERD for the Netherlands would be limited, because racial discrimination simply did not exist: 'the Dutch public authorities and institutions neither exercised nor promoted any form of racial discrimination'.[1780] The Government thus reasoned from a rather limited conception of discrimination; only the Government or institutions and groups of comparable influence could discriminate against citizens.[1781] ICERD did not concern discrimination between citizens in private, i.e. all kind of social relations, but discrimination in *public life*. The purport of the convention closely connected to the public life existent in the Netherlands and thus there was no need for radical law reform. Besides, ICERD would not affect the institution of civil actions concerning discrimination by citizens in the private sphere based on Article 6:162 BW separate from ICERD.[1782]

The Dutch Parliament, however, stipulated that future acts of discrimination were not excluded.[1783] In the Government's vision, ICERD did not have direct effect and did not create rights for citizens and thus could not be directly relied upon before the courts. Hence, the creation of national provisions was required.[1784] According to the Minister for Justice, the legislative proposals would largely comply with the convention obligations that were however considered as quite obscure, notably Article 5 ICERD.[1785] According to Van der Neut[1786] and Swart,[1787] the adaptations of the Dutch law would certainly not have been made if ICERD had not existed.

1776 *Kamerstukken II* 1967–1968, 9724, nr. 1–2.

1777 *Handelingen II,* 1969–70, 27 August 1970, p. 4333–4354; *Handelingen II,* 2 September 1970, p. 4379; *Kamerstukken II,* 1968–69, 9724, nr. 4; 6; 7.

1778 *Kamerstukken I,* 1970–71, 9724, nr. 22; 22a.

1779 The Act of 18 February 1971, *Stb.* 1971, 96.

1780 *Kamerstukken II,* 9723 (R 663), nr. 3, p. 3; 5.

1781 *Kamerstukken II,* 9724, nr. 3, p. 5.

1782 *Kamerstukken II,* 9724, nr. 6, p. 1.

1783 *Kamerstukken II,* 9723 (R 663), nr. 4, p. 1.

1784 *Kamerstukken II,* 9724, nr. 22a, p. 3.

1785 *Handelingen II,* 27 August 1970, p. 4347–4348.

1786 Van der Neut 1986, p. 33.

1787 Swart, A.H. J., Rassendiscriminatie en de Nederlandse strafwet, *DD* 1970, 2, p. 77.

4.2. The situation before the implementation of ICERD

The original Dutch Criminal Code of 1886 did not comprise of any speech offences with a racial character. Until 1934, only the insult of an individual was criminalized. The Act of 19 July 1934 'concerning the protection of the public order' introduced an important reform to the criminalization of insult. The Act introduced four new Articles (137a-d Sr) penalizing the insult of public authority, public institutions, public bodies (137a-b) and groups of people that formed part of the Dutch population (137c-d). The Act aimed to protect public authority and the public order against the increasingly common malicious expression of extreme right and extreme left groupings that could develop into objectionable movements, considering related phenomena abroad. With articles 137c and d Sr, the Act particularly aimed to counter the excesses of anti-Semitism, such as the public anti-Semitic expression of the Dutch fascist political organization 'De Bezem' (The Broom) that had gained a certain 'epidemic character'.[1788] The existing offences were considered insufficient to counter such abuses of freedom of the press.[1789]

The offences were incorporated into Book II section V of the Dutch Criminal Code concerning the protection of the public order, because 'they are primarily destined to protect the public order, in addition to protecting the honour and reputation of institutions and groups and – only in third instance and indirectly – also protect the individual persons, who, at a certain moment more or less coincidentally form those institutions and groups.'[1790] Indeed, the offences did not protect the individual government official or individual person of a certain race or religion against insults. During the drafting, the question was raised as to whether it would be better to incorporate the offences into the section XVI of the Dutch Criminal Code concerning insult. The strong emphasis on the rationale of the public order could be relevant for civil cases concerning insult of collectivities; the civil judge could reject claims based on – current – Article 6:162 BW, if the infringed norm was not created to protect the plaintiff.[1791] According to the Minister for Justice, violation of the offences certainly constituted a wrongful act in accordance with Article 6:162 BW. However, as only institutions and groups could form an insulted party, individual persons forming part of these collectivities could never claim damages on their own account. Furthermore, the collectivities had to have legal personality and demonstrate concrete damages.[1792]

Article 137c Sr criminalized he who 'expresses himself intentionally in an insulting *form* about a *group of the population* or a group of persons that *partly*

1788 *Handelingen II,* 1933–34, 237, nr. 3, p. 2–3.
1789 Kort-van Welzen 1994, p. 214.
1790 *Kamerstukken II*, 1933–34, 237, nr. 5, p. 16.
1791 *Kamerstukken II*, 1933–34, 237, nr. 4, p. 9.
1792 *Kamerstukken II*, 1933–34, 237, nr. 5, p. 16.

belonged to the population.[1793] Article 137d Sr criminalized the dissemination of such expression.[1794] According to the Government, the denigration of certain groups in society without cause violated Christian charity and national traditions, was unethical and formed a danger to solidarity within the nation. All persons in the Kingdom of the Netherlands were entitled to the protection of their person and goods; their honour and reputation formed an integral part of their personality. Besides, insulting expression formed a direct threat to the public order. In fact, the structural offence of a part of the population had already led to disturbances of the public order at certain locations.[1795]

Article 137c Sr thus protected all groups of the population without distinction. During the parliamentary debates, the Article was, however, criticized for being primarily aimed at protecting Jews, pastors and the Roman Catholic clergy, thus racial and religious groups, while not explicitly referring to the discriminatory grounds of race or religion. And it was feared that the offence interfered with, for example, the freedom of orthodox Protestants to call the Roman-Catholic faith 'adangerous superstition'.[1796] According to the Minister for Justice, the article did not prevent all criticism of all negative characteristics of a certain group. Moreover, the category of persons was not limited to groups that could be distinguished on the grounds of a common religion, race, language, political or ideological conviction, but was extended to every category of persons brought under a common characteristic or indication by the insulting expression. This included Jews, pastors and the Roman Catholic clergy, but also 'opponents of alcohol' or 'foreigners', as expression against their person could equally endanger the public order. Furthermore, the offence was not limited to groups that were entirely located in the Netherlands, because many groups, such as 'the Jews' or 'the Roman Catholics', were international and only partly resided in the Netherlands.[1797]

The wording of Article 137c Sr confined the offence to expression that was insulting in its form. The specific chosen words and terms thus determined to an

---

1793 Article 137c Sr read: 'Hij, die zich in het openbaar, mondeling of bij geschrift of afbeelding, opzettelijk in beleedigenden vorm uitlaat over eene groep van de bevolking of over eene ten deele tot de bevolking behoorende groep van personen, wordt gestraft met gevangenisstraf van ten hoogste een jaar of geldboete van ten hoogste zeshonderd gulden.'

1794 Article 137d Sr read: 'Hij die een geschrift of afbeelding, waarin eene uitlating in beleedigenden vorm over eene groep van de bevolking of over eene ten deele tot de bevolking behoorende groep van personen voorkomt, verspreidt, openlijk ten toonstelt of aanslaat of, om verspreid, openlijk tentoongesteld of aangeslagen te worden, in voorraad heft, wordt, indien hij weet of ernstige redden heft om te vermoeden, dat in het geschrift of de afbeelding zoodanige uitlating voorkomt, gestraft met gevangenisstraf van ten hoogste zes maanden of geldboete van ten hoogste zeshonderd gulden. Met dezelfde straf wordt gestraft hij die, met gelijke wetenschap of een gelijke reden tot vermoeden, den inhoud van een zoodanig geschrift openlijk ten gehoore brengt.'

1795 *Kamerstukken II*, 1933–34, 237, nr. 3, p. 4.

1796 *Handelingen II*, 1933–34, p. 1832–1833. Eventually all representatives of the Christian parties voted in favour of the bill.

1797 *Kamerstukken II*, 1933–34, 237, nr. 5, p. 15.

important extent the punishable character of the insulting expression. According to the Government, as factual criticism did not fall under the scope of the article, it did not unnecessarily interfere with the right to freedom of expression. Expression of an insulting form was socially undesirable and could never be justified;[1798] after all it could lead to sentiments of hatred.[1799] Contrary to the former French offence of group insult, Article 137c Sr did not, however, require proof of the fact that the expression had the aim of inciting hatred or that it had actually led to such feelings among the population. Similarly to the drafting of the offence of blasphemy, the Minister rejected the suggestion to model the offence of group insult after Article 156 of the Criminal code of the (former) Dutch East Indies that prohibited scornful or offensive expression of feelings of hostility, hatred or disdain against one or more religious groups of the population. This latter offence did not only prohibit expression uttered in a certain *form*, but also constituted a far-reaching interference with the *substantive* freedom of expression, thus the *content* of expression. The existence of such an offence could be explained by the needs of a colonial society, but was certainly not to be adopted for the Netherlands.[1800]

Former Article 137c Sr thus merely criminalized the form of insulting expression. According to the Government, if the content of insulting expression was criminalized, a suspect had to be allowed to appeal to the public interest and the proof of the truth of his statements. If a suspect was prosecuted for vague rousing of public sentiment against and stigmatization of groups, he had to be allowed to prove that he merely expressed legitimate criticism. In political cases this would lead to scandalous trials that would afford smart racists a forum to utter their opinions. An appeal to a statutory free speech clause comparable to those in Articles 261 and 266 Sr was therefore excluded. However, such a limitation to express political criticism was unacceptable from a democratic perspective. The introduction of the formal insult formed a practical solution to this problem.[1801]

Given its general character, the offence has been applied to insulting expression against a wide variety of groups;[1802] religious servers;[1803] the Catholic clergy;[1804] members of the neo-Malthusian union;[1805] and even 'the planters in the Dutch East Indies', because part of this group resided in the Netherlands.[1806] In 1940, the Dutch Supreme Court decided that the reference to the international Jewry as a 'parasite on the labour market' formed a gratuitously offensive qualification and therefore constituted an expression in an insulting form for the purposes of article 137c Sr.[1807]

1798 *Kamerstukken II*, 1933–34, 237, nr. 5, p. 15.
1799 *Handelingen II*, 1933–34, 2 May 1934, p. 1852 R.
1800 *Kamerstukken II*, 1933–34, 237, nr. 5, p. 16.
1801 Rosier 1997.
1802 Janssens & Nieuwenhuis 2011, p. 195. See also: Janssens 1998; Van der Neut 1986.
1803 Dutch Supreme Court, 4 March 1940, *NJ* 1940, 830.
1804 Dutch Supreme Court, 29 April 1940, *NJ* 1940, 831.
1805 Rotterdam District Court, 16 July 1937, *NJ* 1938, 736.
1806 Dutch Supreme Court, 17 April 1939, *NJ* 1939, 927.
1807 Dutch Supreme Court, 19 February 1940, *NJ* 1940, 754.

The offence thus comprised expression that could not possibly be qualified as a term of abuse, but was nevertheless gratuisously offensive. Contrarily, in the 1950s, the prosecution of the Dutch author W.F. Hermans with regard to the statement that Catholics reproduce themselves like rabbits uttered by the protagonist in one of his novels resulted in an acquittal, precisely because the expression lacked an insulting *form*.[1808] Since this affair, the article has been scarcely applied.[1809]

4.3. The merit of the implementation of ICERD

4.3.1. The hate speech bans

Similar to France, the Dutch act implementing ICERD did not create, for the implementation of article 4 ICERD, an independent offence that criminalized the 'diffusion of ideas based on racial superiority or hatred'. In its explanatory memorandum, the Dutch Government recalled the discussion that this prohibition had raised during the drafting of Article 4 ICERD with regard to its compatibility with freedom of information, expression, and sciences on race related questions and that had led to the introduction of the clause of Article 5 ICERD. The Government assured that the amendments brought by the bill to Articles 137c-d Sr did not violate these freedoms.[1810] The bill amended the offence of 'group insult' in Article 137c Sr, created the new offence of 'incitement to discrimination, hatred and violence' in Article 137d Sr and criminalized the distribution of expression punishable in accordance with Articles 137c-d Sr in Article 137e Sr.

As the Government considered existing Articles 137c-d Sr to be insufficient for the implementation of ICERD, new Articles 137c-e Sr were broadly formulated. Although ICERD did not oblige States to criminalize the *insult* of groups on the ground of race, the Dutch Government thought this necessary to fully comply with the obligations of ICERD.[1811] The offence of 'formal insult' was changed into the offence of 'substantive insult', which signified an extension of its scope: not only the form but also the content of expression became punishable.

During the parliamentary debates, several representatives argued that this alteration constituted an undesirable extension of the scope of the offence, which conflicted with freedom of expression.[1812] Representative of the Democratic Party (D66) Goudsmit brought under discussion the translation of an English article entitled 'News from Poland', which accused Polish Jews of several political, economic and criminal offences and of neglecting their official duties. Although the expression was clearly anti-Semitic, such expression in decent language was not to

---

1808 De Hullu 1984, p. 754–755.

1809 Van der Neut 1986, p. 29.

1810 *Kamerstukken II*, 1967–68, 9724, nr. 3, p. 4.

1811 *Ibid.*

1812 *Handelingen II*, 1969–70, 27 August 1970, p. 4335; 4341.

be criminalized.[1813] The Minister for Justice twisted this line of reasoning and defended the alteration by arguing that the simple soul who resorts to nasty abusive words fell under the scope of the former offences, but the clever man who expresses himself in a neat manner but at the same time utters grave insults, was left unpunished.[1814] Moreover, the distinction between formal insults and substantive insults would be difficult to make.[1815] The Amendment of Goudsmit that proposed to preserve the formal insult was rejected.[1816]

New Article 137c Sr no longer required that at least a part of the group formed part of the Dutch population. On the other hand, new Article 137c Sr was confined to insults of *racial and religious groups*.[1817] Although some representatives supported the inclusion of other groups, it was argued that noticeably vulnerable groups that lacked the means of defence needed protection by criminal law.[1818] Groups such as 'guestworkers' would not fall under the scope of the articles.[1819] Unlike France, the Dutch provisions implementing ICERD simply refer to the term 'race' and do not adopt the entire list of discriminatory grounds of Article 1 ICERD. According to the Government, such an enumeration is more suitable for an international political document than for national provisions directed to citizens.[1820] The terms could easily be given a meaning that is not in keeping with the aim of the convention. The judge had to interpret the term 'race' according to the purport of the enumeration in Article 1 ICERD.[1821] Nationality in the sense of national citizenship did, however, not fall under the term 'national origin' used in Article 1 ICERD and therefore it neither fell under the term 'race' (para. 5.4;6.3 *infra*).[1822]

Although ICERD merely obliged States to criminalize forms of discrimination on the ground of *race*, the Dutch Government equally introduced the discriminatory ground of *religion or belief* in order to anticipate the establishment of the international convention on the elimination of all forms of religious intolerance and discrimination, which at the time was under preparation at the United Nations.[1823] The government considered it important to stress the norm of tolerance, also in the field of religion and belief, as a standard in the present philosophically and religiously differentiated Dutch society.[1824] The discriminatory ground of 'belief' afforded equal protection to adherents of non-religious, fundamental convictions,

1813 *Handelingen II*, 1969–70, 27 August 1970, p. 4341.
1814 *Ibid.*, p. 4348–4349.
1815 *Handelingen II*, 27 August 1970, p. 4353.
1816 *Kamerstukken II*, 1969–70, 9724, nr. 10.
1817 *Kamerstukken II*, 1967–68, 9724, nr. 3.
1818 *Kamerstukken II*, 1969–70, 9724, nr. 6, p. 3.
1819 *Kamerstukken II*, 9724, nr. 6, p. 3.
1820 *Kamerstukken II*, 9724, nr. 3, p. 4.
1821 *Ibid.*
1822 *Kamerstukken I*, 1970–71, 9724, nr. 22a, p. 3.
1823 *Kamerstukken II*, 1967–68, 9724, nr. 3, p. 4.
1824 *Kamerstukken I*, 1970–71, 9724, nr. 22a, p. 4.

such as atheists.[1825, 1826] Besides, as religious groups were already protected under existing Article 137c Sr, the government did not establish their protection, but did not abolish it either.

During the parliamentary debates, the discriminatory grounds of religion and belief raised more criticism than it did in France. Firstly, religious groups could not be considered as vulnerable and had sufficient means of defence. Secondly, all criticism of religion and belief would be hindered, which conflicted with freedom of expression. The Minister, however, stressed that the offences did not form a general protection of the conduct of religious or philosophical institutions or organizations in society and did not affect criticism of such institutions or organizations, even when it concerned their deepest convictions. Criticism of convictions or conduct, in whatever form, fell outside their scope. The articles criminalized the offence on points that were beyond discussion. Such protection was of fundamental value for human existence. Criticism of a religion or belief becomes punishable, 'when it degenerates into injuring the honor and good name of a group or into incitement to hatred and discrimination against it for the mere fact that its members adhere to a religion or belief. Against such expression no defence exists, no matter how strong the social position of the group is.'[1827]

But would an insulting attack on a conviction *eo ipso* constitute an attack on the people who adhere to and identify themselves with that conviction? The Minister considered that insulting qualifications of a conviction can only constitute an insult of people, if *conclusions are drawn* about those people.[1828] Subsequently, representative of the Anti-Revolutionary Party (ARP) Boertien questioned: Suppose that a theologian, after a discussion on an imaginary sect, draws the following conclusion: 'This sect is so foolish that only the mentally disturbed can be a joyful member.' Does this impair the self-esteem of that group? Is this insulting criticism? Is it punishable or not?[1829] According to the Minister for Justice, the key question was whether the theologian intended to judge that the members were idiots or that the conviction was idiotic.[1830]

Notably in this area, a reserved prosecution policy was to be pursued; such cases could easily become an advertisement for the conviction. More generally, the contribution brought by criminal law to solutions to tensions in society was considered to be restricted. Its application was to be carefully thought through, because it could even intensify conflicts.

The amendment by representative of the Labour Party (PvdA) Roethof that proposed to preserve the offence of formal insult and to only create an offence

1825 *Kamerstukken II*, 1967–68, 9724, nr. 3, p. 5.

1826 *Kamerstukken II*, 1969–70, 9724, nr. 7.

1827 *Kamerstukken I*, 1970–71, 9724, nr. 22a, p. 3; *Kamerstukken I*, 1970–71, 9724, nr. 22, p. 2; *Kamerstukken II*, 1969–70, 9724, nr. 6, p. 4.

1828 *Kamerstukken I*, 1970–71, 9724, nr. 22a, p. 4.

1829 *Handelingen II*, 1969–70, 27 August 1970, p. 4343; 4344.

1830 *Ibid.*, p. 4350.

penalizing the incitement to hatred and discrimination against a group on the ground of *race* was rejected.[1831] It was feared that the absence of the discriminatory ground of religion would leave the incitement against Jews unpunished, because an offender could argue that the incitement was aimed at the Jewish religion and not the Jewish race.[1832] Under the new Articles expression against Jews would fall under the ground of either race or religion.[1833]

The creation of Article 137d Sr penalizing the incitement to discrimination, hatred or violence raised surprisingly less criticism, in fact no criticism at all. The term discrimination had to be interpreted according to the definition in Article 90*quater* Sr (para. 4.3.3 *infra*). The Dutch legislator, however, did stress that although the rationale of Articles 137c-d Sr was the prevention of discrimination, expression punishable on the ground of these articles do not constitute acts of discrimination; 'The factual element of subordination entails that oral expression, writings and portrayals cannot contain discrimination in the sense of the definition.'[1834] The legislator thus strictly distinguished between discriminatory actions and discriminatory opinions.

Article 137e Sr criminalized the distribution of discriminatory expression that could not be considered as the provision of factual information. While articles 137c-d Sr merely criminalized discriminatory expression uttered in *public*, strictly speaking Article 137e Sr is not confined thereto.

4.3.2. Rationale

While the rationale of the existing Articles 137c-d Sr had primarily been the protection of the public order, the implementation of ICERD added more emphasis on the norm of equality and non-discrimination; after all the rationale of this convention was the elimination of all forms of racial discrimination. During the parliamentary debates, representative of the Communist Party (CPN) Bakker recalled that racial discrimination has always originated in existing social differences or attempts to establish such differences. Anti-discrimination policy concerned the realization of the social dimension of the fundamental right to equal treatment.[1835]

Articles 137c-e Sr were, however, inserted – or maintained – in Book II section V of the Dutch Criminal Code concerning offences against the public order that criminalized 'conduct that forms a danger to social life and the natural order of society'.[1836] The prohibition of incitement to violence fits perfectly into this section

---

1831 *Kamerstukken II*, 1969–70, 9724, nr. 9.

1832 *Handelingen II*, 1969–70, 27 August 1970, p. 4340.

1833 *Ibid.*, p. 4351.

1834 *Kamerstukken II*, 1969–70, 9724, nr. 6, p. 4.

1835 *Handelingen II*, 1969–70, 27 August 1970, p. 4344.

1836 Tekst & Commentaar, Wetboek van Strafrecht, Titel V, inleidende opmerkingen, Ten Voorde, Aant. 1.

and the incitement to hatred and discrimination to a lesser extent. Racial insults can be considered to prelude racial hatred, which can lead to discrimination and violence on the ground of race. The connection between the expression and a possible disturbance of the public order, however, seems to be weaker than with the incitement.

Given this categorization, more than France, the Dutch Government connected the norm of equality and non-discrimination to the protection of the public order. Noorloos concludes that the term public order did no longer merely cover the prevention of violence or disturbances of the peace, but included the 'preservation of a decent society without discrimination'.[1837] But even given this supposed coloration of the term public order by the Dutch legislator, from the categorization of Articles 137c-d Sr as offences against the public order legal scholars such as Van Kempen and Van Stokkum conclude that the *application* of Articles 137c-d Sr should be limited to those *situations* in which a real risk to the disturbance of the public order exists.[1838] Moreover, in the *Wilders* case the question even arose as to whether the existence of the risk of violent conflicts forms an *element of the offence* of incitement to hatred that had to be proven (para. 6.7 *infra*). In my opinion, the categorization of the offence should not be confused with the elements of the offence, because 'Rubrica non est lex'. The public order can nevertheless form a relevant factor in the appreciation of the expression in light of its context and all circumstances of the case, thus at a different level (para. 6.4; 6.7 *infra*).

Compared to the French drafting history, the Dutch legislator indeed placed less emphasis on the independent value of the protection of the human dignity of individual citizens and more emphasis on the protection of the public order by the prevention of disharmony between groups. This notably also follows from the fact that unlike in France, Articles 137c-e Sr do not protect next to groups, *individual persons* belonging to a racial or religious group. Another feature of 137c-e Sr connected to the rationale of the public order is that although the vulnerability of minority groups formed an important argument for their protection, racial and religious majorities are equally protected under the articles.

4.3.3. The criminalization of discrimination

The act implementing ICERD created Article 90*quater* Sr that defined discrimination as 'any form of distinction, any exclusion, restriction or preference, which has the purpose or effect of nullifying or impairing the recognition, enjoyment or exercise, on an equal footing, of human rights and fundamental freedoms in the political, economic, social, cultural or any other field of public life'. The article was thus inspired by Article 1 ICERD, but lacked a reference to *any* of the discriminatory grounds of race, colour, descent or national or ethnic origin. The

1837 Noorloos 2011, p. 211.

1838 Van Kempen 2011, p.193; Van Stokkum 2006.

definition therefore comprised any discrimination, regardless of the discriminatory ground. Considering such a broad definition to be unnecessary and too far reaching, representatives Van der Spek and Roethof proposed to insert the discriminatory ground of 'race, color, descent and national or ethnic origin'.[1839] Their amendment was, however, rejected.[1840] The Minister advocated the very general definition of discrimination that would certainly comprise Anti-Semitism, but to the question 'what is racial discrimination' he answered 'The judge can and must explain what it is.'[1841]

Article 90*quater* Sr was incorporated into section IX, which explains the terms used in the Dutch Criminal Code. The article thus did not concern a *general criminal prohibition* of discrimination in the economic, social or cultural domain, because it would be too vague for the Public Prosecutor to initiate criminal proceedings and for the judge to decide upon.[1842] Furthermore, the Minister wanted to avoid the difficult question of the third party effect on fundamental rights.[1843] Discrimination concerned the impairment of fundamental rights, although ICERD and subsequently the implementation act did not specify the rights and freedoms concerned. Article 5 ICERD therefore had to serve as a guideline.[1844] Although some representatives argued that Article 5 ICERD actually ensured the rights and freedoms it enumerated,[1845] the Minister maintained that it merely afforded protection against discrimination on racial grounds in the areas there referred to.[1846]

Two new petty offences in Articles 429*ter* and 429*quater* Sr criminalized specific forms of discrimination; the participation in or the financial or other material support of activities aimed at racial discrimination, respectively the distinction between people on the ground of their race in the professional offer of one's goods and services. These articles lacked the discriminatory ground of religion or belief; in this field the legislator did not want to anticipate the establishment of a convention on religious intolerance and discrimination.[1847] Besides, new Articles 1 of the Collective Agreement Act and 9a of the Economic Competition Act, provided that a condition in a collective agreement or a competition regulation of a discriminatory purport is null or non-binding.

Since 1971, the Dutch legislator has amended the provisions concerning discrimination several times, after the Dutch courts signaled that their scope and

---

1839 *Kamerstukken II*, 1969–70, 9724, nr. 8.
1840 *Handelingen II*, 1969–70, 2 September 1970, p. 4379.
1841 *Handelingen II*, 27 August 1970, p. 4349–4352.
1842 *Handelingen II*, 1969–70, 27 Augustus 1970, p. 4350.
1843 *Ibid.*
1844 *Kamerstukken II*, 1967–68, 9724, nr. 3.
1845 *Handelingen II*, 1969–70, 27 Augustus 1970, p. 4337.
1846 *Ibid.*, p. 4348.
1847 *Kamerstukken II*, 1967–68, 9724, nr. 3, p. 4.

purport were too limited in the light of the convention obligations.[1848] Besides, they have been supplemented with other discriminatory categories. The constitutional reform of 1983 introduced the general prohibition on discrimination in Article 1 of the Constitution (para. 2.1 *supra*). Article 429*quater* Sr was amended in several respects. It had been difficult to bring the common practice of Dutch companies to sign 'non-Jewish-declarations' under the scope of the article. This condition set by Arab countries for economic trade formed part of the larger Arab boycott of products coming from Israel. As this 'internal' economic practice did not concern 'public life', in the 1980s the scope of the article was broadened to incorporate all 'social-economic trade', which also included the labor and housing market.[1849] Furthermore, it was difficult to demonstrate that the economic boycott resulted in the actual discrimination of Jews. The term 'subordination' was therefore replaced by 'distinction'.[1850]

Although the legislator had opined that the subordination of Jews constituted a form of anti-Semitism proscribed by the term 'race', it was thought that this kind of distinction was probably rather connected to religion or belief.[1851] In the 1990s, Article 429*quater* Sr was therefore supplemented with the discriminatory grounds of religion or belief.[1852] The term distinction was replaced by 'discrimination', which expressed the pejorative element, comprised indirect forms of discrimination and was more consistent with ICERD.[1853] Furthermore, discrimination by government officials was prohibited. Finally, all criminal provisions concerning discrimination were classified as felonies. The petty offences of Articles 429*ter* and 429*quater* were classified as felonies in Articles 137f and g.[1854]

From the same strand of thought, in the 1990s in Article 90*quater* Sr the term 'public order' was replaced by 'societal order'.[1855] The definition of discrimination was no longer confined to public life, but extended to all sections in society and the relationship between citizens. However, the *public* hate speech bans were preserved, because of 'how reprehensible racist expression may be, there is no use in penalizing them, if they are strictly uttered in the private sphere.'[1856] Article 137e Sr was, on

---

1848 For a comprehensive analysis see: Woltjer 2002.

1849 *Kamerstukken II,* 1979–80, 16115, nr. 3, p. 3–4.

1850 *Kamerstukken II,* 1979–80, 16115, nr. 3, p. 3–4.

1851 Henceforth, making a distinction on the ground of religion was considered as a form of *direct* distinction and no longer a form of *indirect* distinction for which an objective justification could exist.

1852 *Kamerstukken II,* 1988–89, 20239, nr. 5, p. 20; nr. 6.

1853 *Kamerstukken II,* 1987–88, 20239, nr. 3. For a critical analysis see: Van der Neut 1986, p. 39–44. Van der Neut argues that the non-Jewish declarations constituted rather a disguised form of discrimination than indirect discrimination.

1854 With regard to Article 429*quater*, this only concerned the discriminatory ground of race. Article 429*quater* was maintained as a petty offence with regard to the other discriminatory grounds.

1855 *Kamerstukken II*, 1989–90, 20239, nr. 15, p. 3.

1856 *Kamerstukken II*, 1987–88, 20239, nr. 3, p. 3.

the other hand, extended to the unsolicited sending of expression, which is not carried out in public.[1857]

Unlike France, Dutch law does not have so called 'hate crimes', being criminal offences that stipulate a suspect's racist motive as an aggravating circumstance and element of the offence. However, the current policy of the Dutch public prosecution requires a 50–100 per cent increase in the penalty for 'generic offences' that are motivated by discrimination or hatred. It also requires that the discriminatory background of the offence be announced in the prosecutor's closing statement (para. 8.1 *infra*). Other than 'hate crimes', this policy does not *oblige* the judge to establish the racist motive of a suspect and attach importance to it in determining the penalty. Since 1 March 2010, Article 137h Sr provides that he, who commits one of the offences of 131–134, 137c-137g and 147a Sr in the exercise of his profession, can be put out of his profession. The article thus does not form an independent offence and does not merely apply to the specific anti-discrimination offences of 137c-g and 429*quater* Sr.

4.3.4. The prohibition of associations violating the public order

Complementary to the provisions prohibiting acts of discrimination, the act implementing ICERD supplemented Article 3 of the Act on Assembly and Association of 1855 with a provision that enabled the proscription by the judge at the instance of the public prosecutor of associations that engage in, preserve or promote racial discrimination.[1858] In 1976, these provisions were inserted into Book II of the Dutch Civil Code that prohibited legal persons with aims or activities that violated 'the public order or good morals'. The possibility for the Public Prosecution to request a prohibition that had existed since 1939 was thereby cancelled. Only the civil judge could pronounce the illegal character of an association on the ground of Article 2:15 BW and could subsequently dissolve the association in question on the ground of Article 2:16 BW. As the judge was not obliged to dissolve an association that he nevertheless had proscribed, a prohibited association could however continue to function and engage in activities that violated Article 4 ICERD. Moreover, the articles lacked a reference to the proscription ground of 'the engagement, preservation or promotion of racial discrimination'.

Taking action on the grounds of these articles against extreme right winged political parties such as the Dutch Popular Party (NVU) and later the Centre Party (CP'86) appeared to be rather difficult, because, although their factual activities – such as the spreading of election pamphlets that incited to racial hatred – gave rise to request their dissolution, in 1978 the Amsterdam District Court only saw reasons to prohibit the NVU and not to dissolve it; the latter would have no effect given the

[1857] *Kamerstukken II*, 1988–89, 20239, nr. 5, p. 13.
[1858] Article 3 of the Act of 22 April 1855, *Stb.*32.

existence of an adjoining foundation.[1859] The Court considered that the prohibition of the party would however certainly have legal effect in the sense that it would enable the prosecution of its members on the ground of 130 Sr that criminalized participation in a criminal organization and that it would hinder the running of the party in the elections.[1860] In 1979, the Dutch Supreme Court endorsed the rejection by the Court of Appeal of the appeal against the decision of the Amsterdam District Court, but considered that the latter did not have legal effect.[1861] The prohibition thus had a non-binding nature.

In the 1990s, the articles were therefore replaced by new Article 2:20 BW.[1862] According to the article the judge, after having concluded that the activities of an association violate the public order or good morals, must proscribe and dissolve the association in question. When the goals of an association do violate the public order or good morals, but its activities do not, the judge can dissolve the association in question, but cannot proscribe it. It is striking that unlike France, the Dutch legislator did not explicitly stress the prohibition ground of racial discrimination. The preservation of the prohibition ground of 'the public order and good morals' was criticized for being on the one hand too broad and on the other hand not directly connected to the prohibition of racial discrimination.[1863] According to the Minister, the term 'public order' was, however, not to be interpreted broadly in the sense of 'undesirable from a social perspective'; it merely comprised 'acts violating the fundaments of the legal system, the unjustified impairment of the freedom of others or human dignity, the use of violence or the threat of violence against the authorities of people and racial or other prohibited forms of discrimination.'[1864] It was assumed that consensus existed about the fact that racial discrimination violated the public order. Referring to racial discrimination separately was therefore unnecessary.[1865]

Furthermore, the proposal to prohibit associations on the grounds of their racial, national-socialistic or fascistic aspirations in a separate article was rejected.[1866] The same goes for the proposal to regulate the prohibition of political parties in a separate article, in light of their special function in a constitutional state, freedom of expression and freedom of assembly. According to the Minister, the prohibition ground of the public order had to apply equally to political parties. The

1859 For a comprehensive analysis see: Woltjer 2002, p. 408–415; 449–462; Eskes, J.A.O., *Repressie van politieke bewegingen in Nederland* (diss), Zwolle: Tjeenk Willink: 1988, p. 435–460.

1860 Amsterdam District Court, 8 March 1978, *NJ* 1978 281, annotation Maeijer.

1861 Dutch Supreme Court, 9 March 1979, *NJ* 1979, 363, annotation Maeijer. The judgment did not prevent local polling stations from refusing to registrar NVU representatives. The ECmHR declared the complaint filed by NVU that this practice violated Article 3, Protocol no. 1 to ECHR manifestly ill-founded; given the illegal character of the association, there was an abuse of rights in the sense of Article 17 ECHR. ECmHR, 11 October 1979, n°8348/840678, *NJ* 1980, 525, annotation Alkema.

1862 Act of 2 April 1991, *Stb.* 1991, 199.

1863 *Kamerstukken II*, 1982–83, 17476, nr. 4, p. 16–21.

1864 *Kamerstukken II*, 1982–83, 17476, nr. 5, p. 13.

1865 *Kamerstukken II*, 1982–83, 17476, nr. 5, p. 17; *Kamerstukken II*, 1982–83, 17476, nr. 12, p. 2.

1866 Woltjer 2002, p. 456.

interpretation of the term 'public order' would eventually become a task of the judge.[1867]

One had to wait until 1998 before CP'86 was finally prohibited and dissolved by the Amsterdam District Court. The court referred to the multiple condemnations of the party and its leaders on the ground of Articles 137c and d Sr (para. 6.6 *infra*) and considered that the prohibition ground of the public order certainly covered the repeated incitement, provocation and propagation to discrimination, even in a very strict interpretation of the term.[1868]

4.4. Conclusion

ICERD was adopted by the Act of 18 February 1971. Although the Netherlands did not make any reservations to ICERD, it did not criminalize the diffusion of ideas based on racial superiority or hatred and recalled the controversy about the compatibility of such an offence with freedom of expression. The implementation of ICERD signified a reinforcement of the laws protecting the public order that were primarily aimed at preventing disturbances of the peace, not the human dignity and the equality of all individual Dutch citizens. The norm of equality and non-discrimination was subsumed in the notion of the public order. The merit of the implementation act was threefold. Firstly, it altered the offence of formal insult into substantive insult and created the new offence of incitement to racial discrimination, hatred or violence. A leitmotiv in the drafting of the offences formed the question as to the compatibility of the prohibition of content of expression and the discriminatory ground of religion with the right to freedom of expression. The rationale of the offences was rather to prevent than to prohibit discrimination. Secondly, it prohibited acts of discrimination. The Dutch Government did not understand the prohibition of discrimination as an absolute prohibition that applies to all sections of society. While the conception of discrimination was originally confined to public life, it was however later extended to societal life. Thirdly, it prohibited associations that engage in, preserve or promote racial discrimination. This prohibition was later merged into the prohibition of associations that violate the public order and good morals. The Dutch legislator has thus rather formulated the repression of racial discrimination in terms of public order than stressed the norm of non-discrimination independently to assure the equal human dignity of all citizens.

5. Group insult – Article 137c Sr

Dutch law criminalizes insult of an individual person (5.1) and group insult (5.2) in separate offences. Group insult is characterized by a number of elements, being –

1867 *Kamerstukken II*, 1982–83, 17476, nr. 5, p. 11–12.

1868 Amsterdam District Court, 18 November 1998, *NJ* 1999, 377.

next to insult – intent thereto (5.3) and the designation of a group on the ground of race (5.4) or religion (5.6). Indirect forms of racial insult, such as Holocaust denial, can also be punishable (5.5). In principle, this does not apply to indirect insult of people via offensive speech about their religion ((5.7). The Dutch judge balances the application of the offence with the right to freedom of expression by means of a contextual review (5.8) and sometimes also with the right to freedom of religion (5.10). Civil liability for group insult may already exist with the offence to feelings (5.9). Even though a higher threshold exists for criminal liability, the criminality of group insult is controversial (5.11). The analysis results in a general conclusion about the offence of group insult in Dutch law (5.12).

5.1. The criminalization of insult to an individual person

Until the nineteenth century, Dutch cities had their own criminal codes. The regulation of punishable insults thus differed from place to place. The Criminal Code for the Kingdom of Holland of 1809 included offences of insult in Articles 164–166, but the Code remained in force for only two years.[1869] In 1811, the French Penal Code entered into force.[1870] The Code used a tri-partition in the offences of insult. Article 367 criminalized the imputation of a criminal act or a concrete fact that incites contempt and hatred (calomnie). Article 375 criminalized the imputation of a vice or a not further elaborated, non-concrete fact (expression outrageante). Articles 376 j 471 sub 11 criminalized abusive words and invectives concerning 'minor vices'. The Dutch Criminal Code of 1881 that entered into force in 1886 replaced these French provisions that were considered to be out-dated. Moreover, the regulation of insults was inconveniently arranged, because many complementary offences of specific forms of insult were spread out over the entire code. The new offences were based on the Italian Criminal Code of 1868 that distinguished defamation and libel/slander from insult.[1871] This dichotomy still exists today – in amended version (para. 1.5.1 *supra* and 5.2 *infra*).

Article 261 sub 1 Sr criminalizes as defamation 'the intentional assault of another person's honour or good name by the imputation of a specific fact, uttered with the apparent aim of publicity'.[1872] A difference with the French offence of defamation is that Article 261 Sr does not include a collectivity (corps) in its definition of a victim. Furthermore, the offence even criminalizes defamation in secret or private, provided that it is expressed with the apparent aim of publicity. Article 261 sub 2 Sr criminalizes libel, i.e. defamation in writing, as an aggravated

---

1869 Janssens 1998, p. 23.

1870 Besluit van 11 December 1813, S. 10.

1871 Janssens 1998, p. 35–36.

1872 Article 261 sanctions defamation with an imprisonment of maximum six months or a fine up to 7800, – euros.

form of defamation.[1873] Other than former Article 367 of the French Penal Code, Article 261 Sr does not attach importance to the question as to whether the posed facts are true. Furthermore, Article 262 Sr criminalizes 'he who imputes a specific fact, while knowing that it is untrue' as a qualified form of defamation/libel.[1874] In French law, an equivalent to this offence no longer exists.

Article 266 Sr criminalizes as insult 'every intentional insulting expression that does not constitute defamation or libel'.[1875] The offence does not only concern public, but also non-public expression, because publicity was not considered as the core of the offence that equally covers sent or handed letters.[1876] Other than former Article 375 of the French Penal Code and the current French offence of insult, this offence criminalizes – next to insulting opinions – insults 'by facts'. This encompasses annoying insulting *acts*, such as spitting in a person's face or kissing an honourable woman.[1877] With regard to the insult of an individual, the legislator has not thus strictly distinguished actions from opinions. Although Article 266 Sr demarcates insult from defamation, it does not actually define insult as it is for example defined in French law 'all offensive expression, terms of contempt and invectives', which however could serve as a useful guideline for the Dutch judge when qualifying expression as an insult. The Dutch Supreme Court considers expression to be insulting on the ground of Article 266 Sr 'when it has the purport to discredit another person with the public and to assault him in his honor or good name'.[1878] It falls outside the scope of this research to give a comprehensive overview of expression that has been found to constitute a punishable insult of individuals.[1879] Examples include terms of abuse, such as 'bitch' and 'bastard'[1880] or 'fascistic dogs'[1881] and vague allegations and other insinuations, such as the statement that the policy of local authorities is hypocritical and corrupt[1882] or the statement that a judge 'fits into a National-Socialistic legal system'.[1883]

In the 1970s, the desirability of the criminalization of insult of an individual was brought under discussion in the light of freedom of expression (para. 1.5.1 *supra*). The Government agreed with the Parliamentary Commission Langemeijer that had examined the criminalization of insult that the offences of insult were to be

---

1873 Article 261 sub 2 sanctions libel with an imprisonment of maximum one year or a fine up to 7800, – euros.

1874 Violation of Article 262 is sanctioned with an imprisonment of maximum two years or a fine up to 19.500, – euros.

1875 Article 266 sanctions insult with an imprisonment of maximum three months or a fine up to 3900, – euros.

1876 Janssens 1998, p. 45.

1877 Other acts could be qualified as assaults, if they are not performed 'animo iniuriandi', See: Janssens 1998, p. 46.

1878 Dutch Supreme Court, 30 October 2001, *NJ* 2002, 129.

1879 See generally: Janssens & Nieuwenhuis 2011, p. 98 *et seq.*

1880 Dutch Supreme Court, 17 November 1993, *NJ* 1993, 275.

1881 Dutch Supreme Court, 2 November 1993, *NJ* 1994, 197.

1882 Dutch Supreme Court, 30 October 2001, *NJ* 2002, 129.

1883 Dutch Supreme Court, 25 October 1994, *LJN* 97691.

preserved, not abrogated. The criminal prohibition of insult would prevent vengeance by the victim and repetition by the offender and was preferable to the time-consuming civil procedure. Preservation of the offence would prevent an undesirable hardening of political and social morals. Subsequently, a report of WODC on the criminalization of insult concluded that the offence formed a ground for police assistance and its abolishment would remove its signal function for the police with regard to other problems. The government decided to preserve the offence, because it considered the criminal sanction to be the most appropriate means for enforcement and the civil procedure to be 'too problematic'.[1884] The discussion finally resulted in the introduction of the free speech clauses of 261 sub 3, 266 sub 2 and 267 sub 3 Sr (para. 1.5.1 *supra*).

5.2. The criminalization of group insult

It is striking that in the seventies the criminalization of insult of an individual was put up for discussion, whereas at the same time one insisted on the introduction of an offence of group insult.

Article 137c Sr criminalizes 'any person who, publicly – orally, in writing or by means of portrayal – and intentionally, expresses himself in an insulting manner about a group of persons on the ground of their race, religion or belief, hetero- or homosexual orientation or physical, psychical or mental handicap' with an imprisonment of a maximum of one year or a fine up to € 7,800.[1885] Unlike in France, the article does not formulate an aggravated circumstance to the offence of insult of an individual in Article 266 Sr and does not protect – next to groups – individual persons, but forms an independent offence. Article 137c Sr thus does not form a *lex specialis* to Article 266 Sr as a *lex generalis*.[1886]

Although the offence of group insult thus requires that expression concerns a plurality of persons, it does not indicate as to whether or not a group must be explicitly named in the expression. In 1984, the Dutch Supreme Court considered expression about 'a German Jewish woman who apparently had not been gassed' to constitute the offence of 137c Sr, because 'it was clear for every normal reader that the expression was insulting to the Jewish population.'[1887] As a result, expression concerning one person in particular can be insulting to a group at the same time. However, it must be possible to connect the group characteristic used to insult an individual to the group. Otherwise, insult of an individual is punishable on the ground of Article 266 Sr.

1884 Janssens 1998, p. 58–59.

1885 Article 137c sub 2 criminalizes as an aggravating circumstance he who structurally commits the offence as a habit or in the exercise of his profession with an imprisonment of maximum two years or a fine up to 19.500 EUR.

1886 Vgl. Brants, Kool, & Rignalda 2007, p. 58.

1887 Dutch Supreme Court, crim. Ch., 26 June 1984, *NJ* 1985, 40.

The question of the insult of a group or an individual is connected with the objectivation of a suspect's intent; what was evidently his intention?[1888] In order for a racist insult to constitute the offence of 266 Sr, it must publicly violate a person's honor by referring to his race, religion etc. The difference with a group insult resides in the lack of a group connotation. A discriminatory insult of a group, in the sense of 137c Sr, thus does not imply the insult of an individual, in the sense of 266 Sr, per se. This would require that aside from the insult of a group, a connection can be made with the individual, who files a complaint as a victim of an insult against his person.[1889]

Article 137c Sr, however, does share some characteristics with Article 266 Sr. With regard to the term 'insulting', the drafting history of Article 137c Sr refers to the signification of the term in Article 266 Sr; expression about a group is insulting, if it impairs the self-esteem or honor of the group or discredits the group, because it belongs to a particular race, religion or belief.[1890] The article thus protects the group targeted by the insult against the effect that the insult has on *third parties*; after all, the honor and good name and the (dis)credit of the group exist in the eyes of others.[1891] In addition, the article can be considered to protect the group against the effect of the insulting expression on the group *itself* (self-esteem).

This latter idea is controversial among legal scholars. Rosier criticizes the tendency to equate the assault of one's honor with other forms of impairment of the person as a person. He distinguishes the insult from the mere offence to feelings. Insult concerns a particular form of impairment of one's personality; expression containing the message that another person is or may be disparaged, disregarded or despised. The criminalization of such insulting expression is primarily aimed at protecting one's honor, which can be defined as 'the special status that assures the lack of circumstances that would degrade one's respectability.'[1892] According to Janssens & Nieuwenhuis, the offences of insult protect the moral integrity to which every person in society is entitled. This moral integrity is externally perceivable in the sense that it concerns one's honor in the eyes of others. The offences cannot protect one's personal honor, self-esteem or self-respect, because such internal

[1888] Hence, the phrase 'Fucking Turks, I'm sick of your mess. You always make a mess, you make a mess of the entire Netherlands.' exclaimed against a suspect's neighbours could be understood as a group insult, because the latter sentence could only be understood as an attack of all Turks as a group. Contrarily, the phrase 'You are dirty fagots, I hate that like poison.' equally exclaimed against a suspect's neighbours could not be understood as a group insult, because the suspect later declared 'I'm not concerned about all homosexuals, I just hate thém.' See: Brants, Kool & Ringnalda 2007, p. 65–66.

[1889] Brants, Kool & Ringnalda 2007, p. 80–81.

[1890] Tekst & Commentaar, Wetboek van Strafrecht, Artikel 137c, Ten Voorde, Aant. 8c; Noyon, Langemeijer & Remmelink, Wetboek van Strafrecht, Tweede boek, Artikel 137c, Fokkens, Aant. 10.

[1891] Janssen & Nieuwenhuis 2012, p. 182.

[1892] Rosier 1997, p. 66–67.

feelings are difficult for the judge to appreciate. This distinction thus equally enables the demarcation of the offence of insult with the offence of feelings, which is not punishable.[1893] According to Van Bemmelen, Articles 137c-e Sr criminalizes certain conduct mainly because of its immorality and the moral indignation such conduct can raise; as a result people could take justice into their own hands.[1894] This vision is, however, generally rejected by other legal scholars.

Examples of expression found punishable on the ground of 137c Sr form abusive terms, such as 'dirty cancer Jews, dirty Nazi swines and dirty rotten Jews',[1895] the slogan often used by football supporters 'Hamas, Hamas, Jews to the gas',[1896] or calling Muslims 'the rat population'.[1897] It results from case law that next to abusive terms and value judgments, more factual statements can be punishable on the ground of 137c Sr. Other than for the insult and defamation of an individual person (261; 266), Dutch law does not distinguish between group insult and group defamation. Strictly speaking, Article 137c Sr does not refer to and therefore does not concern defamation for the purposes of Article 261 Sr. Unlike France, Dutch law does not have a separate offence of group defamation. However, in practice, Article 137c Sr thus functions as a broad generic offence of group insult that comprises forms of defamation and insult. Due to the lack of an offence of group defamation, unlike the situation in France, the problem of the absorption of the offence of group insult by the offence of group defamation does not exist for 137c Sr.[1898]

The question as to whether a group *qua* group is capable of having a reputation is, however, debatable. Janssens argues that the notion of reputation of Article 261 Sr is not suitable for groups of people. Reputation is connected to concrete persons, not to non-further specified groups on the ground of race. What is more, the imputation of a specific fact to a person on the ground of his or her race is difficult

---

1893 Another requirement could be that one's moral integrity is not merely 'disregarded', but 'assaulted' or 'violated'. These thresholds for punishability fit into the vision of the legislator that the offence of group insult protects the dignity of groups in society in the light of the prevention of possible subsequent disturbances of the peace. See: Janssens & Nieuwenhuis 2011, p. 43–44.

1894 Van Bemmelen, J.M., Positieve criteria voor strafbaarstelling, in: Glastra van Loon, J.F. *et al.* (eds.), Speculum Langemeijer; 31 rechtsgeleerde opstellen, Zwolle: W.E.J. Tjeenk Willink 1973, p. 13.

1895 Amsterdam District Court, Crim. Ch., 27 January 2005, *LJN* AS4126.

1896 Dutch Supreme Court, Crim. Ch., 15 September 2009, *LJN* BI4739, *NJ* 2009, 445; *NS* 2009, 344; *RvdW* 2009, 1058.

1897 Haarlem District Court, Crim. Ch., 3 May 2005, *LJN* BC6780.

1898 As insult of an individual is defined negatively in relation to defamation of an individual, it is beyond doubt that one fact cannot constitute defamation and insult of an individual at the same time. Like in France, a cumulative qualification of one fact under 261 and 266 is therefore impossible. However, if a certain text contains multiple allegations that contain both defamatory words and insulting words an accumulation of qualifications remains possible and a suspect can be declared punishable on the ground of both defamation and insult. See: Janssens & Nieuwenhuis 2011, p. 97.

to imagine, because one's reputation is not derived from certain group characteristics. Reputation on the ground of race is therefore difficult to imagine.[1899] One could, however, argue that it is precisely because groups cannot have a common group reputation, certainly not one based on their race, that defamation of a group of people on the ground of its race must be prohibited. An additional argument can therefore be that reputation concerns not only concrete persons, but also concrete facts. It is difficult to imagine that a non-further specified group can as a group commit and be held liable for one specific, concrete fact.

But if groups cannot have a common group reputation for the purposes of 261 Sr, can they have a common group honor, i.e. dignity, for the purposes of 266 Sr? According to Janssens, Article 137c Sr does not concern a specific group dignity, because this would imply that this specific group dignity is limited to the dignity connected to race etc. This would violate the idea that every person has an inherent, basic dignity and therefore deserves the acknowledgement of a full position in society, regardless of class, origin or position. The fact that the denial of that dignity has a specific reason is a different issue; with regard to Article 137c Sr the reason is connected with one of the discriminatory grounds. Janssens argues that racial insults for the purposes of 137c Sr do not, therefore, have to concern a group *per se*. An individual can be denied in his or her dignity on the ground of specific common group characteristics and therefore be insulted in accordance with Article 137c Sr.[1900]

From this perspective, Article 137c Sr protects the honor of the group to the extent that it concerns the individual members of the group. Then the signification of the term insulting in Article 137c Sr differs little from the term in Article 266 Sr. The higher penalty is grounded on the reasons to insult that are connected to specific group characteristics. In this vision, Article 137c Sr can thus be understood as a *lex specialis* to Article 266 Sr. Given this relationship with 266 Sr made by the Dutch legislator himself, the question arises as to whether the criminalization of racial insults can rather better protect – next to groups – individual persons and be categorized in Book II section XVI of the Dutch Criminal Code concerning insults, as is the case in France where racial grounds form an aggravating ground to the offence of insult of an individual. Thus the offence of group insult would lose its explicit connection with the preservation of the public order, which could be justified by the relatively remote direct effect racial insults have on the public order.

As 137c Sr however does not form such a *lex specialis* to 266 Sr, the regime of Article 137c Sr can defer from the system of Article 266 Sr in several respects. Firstly, Article 137c Sr is confined to public expression, which can be explained in the light of its rationale of the preservation of the public order. Furthermore, Article 137c Sr does not criminalize insult 'by facts'. According to the drafting

[1899] Janssens 1998, p. 392.
[1900] Janssens 1998, p. 392–393.

history, discriminatory opinions cannot constitute discriminatory actions (for the purposes of 90*quater*), by lack of a factual element (para. 4.3.1 *supra*). According to Janssens, it is plausible that the legislator assumed that the manifestation of such insulting acts would require a direct presence of the victim and the specific public character of the offence would render their criminalization difficult. Another possibility is that the legislator considered insulting acts on the ground of race to be unlikely.[1901] In 1986, the Dutch Supreme Court found that the action of the Hitler salute during a demonstration formed an 'offending gesture', but that it did not constitute a fixed 'image', such as a photographical image, a print or plate, for the purposes of Article 137c Sr.[1902] The action of the Hitler salute could however constitute a punishable insult under Article 266 Sr, if done in the presence of another person. Van der Neut argues that the aggressive use of symbols that evoke recollections of the Nazi-regime should be criminalized in a specific, separate offence.[1903]

Secondly, the free speech-clause in Article 266 sub 2 Sr does not apply to Article 137c Sr (para. 1.5.1 *supra*). The original proposal to criminalize group insult in 1971 comprised a free speech clause comparable to 266 sub 2 Sr that excluded expression aimed at giving an opinion on matters of public interest that is not gratuitously offensive. The proposal was rejected, because insults on the ground of race could not easily be considered as expression in the public interest.[1904] Hence, in balancing the principle of non-discrimination with freedom of expression, the Dutch legislator has given a certain priority to the principle of non-discrimination with regard to the discrimination ground of race.

But how does Article 137c Sr relate to Article 137d Sr? It is not required that the author of an insult has the intention to incite hatred, that an insult can have this possible effect on third parties or is actually followed by this effect. Van der Neut questions whether a specific need exists for Article 137c Sr, since in practice concurrence with Article 137d Sr would almost always exist.[1905] Sometimes, the Dutch judge indeed seems not to distinguish group insult from incitement to racial discrimination, hatred or violence very strictly. For example, the Haarlem District Court decided in a few words that a whole set of expressions – amongst others – the statements 'I agree with the prohibition to breed, which would be a good solution to exterminate Islam in our country' and 'In any case gays should not exist, it is an

1901 Janssens 1998, p. 71.

1902 Dutch Supreme Court, Crim. Ch., 11 March 1986, *NJ* 1987, 462, annotation Mulder. However, in 1988 the Dutch Supreme Court rejected an appeal against the conviction by the Court of Appeal on the ground of 137c of that same suspect with regard to his expressions 'Okay NSB', 'Away with the Jews', 'Sieg Heil' and 'Hitler' exclaimed during that same demonstration. See: Dutch Supreme Court, Crim. Ch., 22 March 1988, *Rechtspraak Rassendiscriminatie,* edition 1995, p. 297, annotation Pattipawae.

1903 Van der Neut 1986, p. 72.

1904 Janssens & Nieuwenhuis 2011, p. 208.

1905 Van der Neut 1986, p. 81–82.

illness that must be exterminated' could be qualified and were punishable under both 137c Sr and 137d Sr.[1906]

Janssens argues that both articles prohibit related conduct, but not the same conduct; incitement to hatred can under certain circumstances be insulting, but not every insult incites to hatred *per se*.[1907] This equally results from the case law. Like in France, one fact can be prosecuted at the same time on the ground of group insult and incitement to racial discrimination, hatred or violence. When expression cannot be qualified as group insult, this, however, does not hinder its qualification as an incitement to racial discrimination, hatred or violence and vice versa. For example, the Dutch Supreme Court confirmed the conviction on the ground of 137d Sr, but the acquittal on the ground of 137c Sr of a Dutch politician with regard to his statement 'As soon as we get the possibility and the power, we abolish the multicultural society.'[1908] Likewise, the Utrecht District Court considered that a poster with the drawing of a burning church with the text 'burn the' could be interpreted by third parties as an incitement to violence thus punishable on the ground of 137d Sr, but was not insulting in the sense of 137c Sr.[1909] The courts generally consider expression that denies or minimizes the Holocaust rather to constitute the offence of 137c Sr than 137d Sr (para. 5.5.3 *infra*).

Unlike the situation in France, there needs to be no fear of choosing the wrong qualification, because it is permitted that the indictment contains both cumulative and alternative qualifications with regard to all speech offences.[1910] In this manner, possible uncertainties about the application of 137c Sr or 266 Sr thus can equally be overcome.

5.3. Intent

Article 137c Sr explicitly requires that an offender must have the intention to insult. Unlike in France, an author's intention or bad faith is not presumed, but forms a constituent element of the offence that must be explicitly established. The intent can be characterized by every possible degree: even the 'voorwaardelijk opzet' applies, i.e. the situation in which an offender willingly and consciously accepted the considerable risk that his or her expression would insult a group on one of the discriminatory grounds.[1911] For example, according to the District Court Leeuwarden the intent of a person to insult for the purposes of 137c Sr with regard to his expression 'If you were Jewish, I would have killed you.' uttered during a police control out of dissatisfaction with the police action was established, because he had 'willingly and consciously accepted the considerable risk that his expression

1906 Haarlem District Court, Crim. Ch., 3 May 2005, *LJN* BC6780.

1907 Janssens 1998, p. 76.

1908 Dutch Supreme Court, Crim. Ch., 18 May 1999, *NJ* 1999, 634, annotation A.C. 't Hart.

1909 Utrecht District Court, Crim. Ch., 26 April 2010, *LJN* BM8138, *NJFS* 2010, 231.

1910 The so-called 'en/of-tenlastelegging'.

1911 Tekst & Commentaar, Wetboek van Strafrecht, Ten Voorde, Artikel 137 c, Aant. 7.

would insult people with a Jewish background.'[1912] The subjective intention of the author is irrelevant; an offender who does not have the personal aim to insult can thus still be liable on the ground of 137c Sr.[1913] For example, the Arnhem Court of Appeal found an 'Auschwitz cartoon' published by the Arabic European League (AEL) on the Internet that insinuated that the Jews exaggerated the Holocaust to constitute an insult of Jews on the ground of their race. The court notably considered the argument that the subjective intention of its author was to put into question the 'doubles standards' in the appreciation of expression against Muslims and expression by Muslims not to be decisive for its punishability.[1914]

The intention of the offender must relate not only to the insulting character of the expression, but also to its public nature and the insulted person. The Dutch judge generally objectifies the intent and derives the proof of an author's intent from the content, manner and context of the expression.[1915] The question arises as to whether on this point much difference actually exists between Dutch law and French law, where the French judge takes the intention of the author of an insult into account, not to establish its presence or absence, but to determine the actual sense and purport of the expression. Differences rather seem to follow from the French rigid versus the Dutch broad application of justifications (para. 5.8;6.4 *infra*).

5.4. Designation of a racial group

A group must be insulted – amongst others – 'on the ground of its race'. The Dutch Supreme Court uses a broad interpretation of the term 'race' based on the enumeration in Article 1 ICERD that includes national and ethnic background, skin colour and origin, but not nationality in the sense of national citizenship (para. 4.3.1 *supra*). For example, in 1976 the Dutch Supreme Court found the electoral pamphlets by the NVU comprising the phrase 'The Hague must remain white and safe. Out with the people from Suriname and the Antilles, who sponge off our labor and prosperity (...)' to constitute an insult of a group on the ground of its race. According to the Court, the indictment clearly concerned '*non-white* people from Suriname and the Antilles', thus a group on the ground of its *race*, which included *skin-colour* next to national and ethnic background and origin, and not its *nationality*.[1916] As the expression merely concerned those non-white people who came from *Suriname and the Antilles*, it equally results that, similar to France, in order for the offence of group insult to be constituted it is not a requirement that the defamatory expression be aimed at the racial group in its entirety; it will suffice if

---

1912 Leeuwarden District Court, crim. ch., 19 January 2010, *LJN* BL1747.

1913 Tekst & Commentaar, Wetboek van Strafrecht, Ten Voorde, Artikel 137 c, Aant. 7.

1914 Arnhem Court of Appeal, crim. ch., 19 August 2010, *LJN BN4204*, *NJFS* 2010, 294, para. 4.3; 4.4.

1915 Janssens & Nieuwenhuis 2011, p. 115–117.

1916 Dutch Supreme Court, crim. Ch., 24 June 1975, *NJ* 1975, 450, annotation Mulder; Dutch Supreme Court, crim. ch., 15 June 1976, *NJ* 1976, 551, annotation Van Veen.

the expression is aimed at a group of people regardless of its size on the ground of its race.

It is precisely in order to determine whether expression concerns people of either a certain nationality or a certain national or ethnic background that the Dutch Supreme Court takes into account the context of the expression. Expression about non-racial groups uttered in the context of expression about racial groups can therefore be punishable on the ground of 137c Sr. For example, in 1983 the Dutch Supreme Court considered expressions about 'guest workers, people from Suriname, Hindu, Creoles, Moroccans, Jews and Turks' insulting on the ground of race.[1917] In 1990, the Dutch Supreme Court found expression about 'foreigners, Turks, Moroccans and others from Africa' to constitute expression about groups of 'a certain ethnic background' and therefore about groups on the ground of their 'race', considering the connection and context in which it was uttered.[1918] Likewise, in 2003 the Dutch Supreme Court considered the designation of foreigners, in specific asylum seekers and refugees, as 'tyrants, thieves, murderers, severe condemned men and rapists' in the context of the entire publication to constitute an insult of asylum seekers and refugees the ground of their race.[1919]

Strictly speaking, without a 'racist context' expression about foreigners, guest workers and groups of a particular nationality, such as Moroccans and Turks, is not punishable on the ground of 137c Sr. The same holds true for caravan dwellers.[1920] Contrarily, gypsies can be considered as a 'race'.[1921] Often, on the basis of a contextual interpretation insult on the ground of nationality can be construed as an insult on the ground of race. The question arises as to whether it is desirable to supplement the discriminatory grounds of 137c-e Sr with the discriminatory ground of 'nationality'. Van der Neut argues that although it might be inevitable to make a distinction on the basis of nationality with regard to many statutory laws, *insult* grounded on nationality should be criminalized just as much as insult grounded on national descent.[1922]

Several Dutch legal scholars consider it possible that national minorities, such as the Friesians can constitute a 'race', thus a group protected against discrimination and insult. More generally, every cultural minority could fall under the term 'race'.[1923] A less far-reaching interpretation would be to include cases where a nexus exists between culture and religion or belief. A broad interpretation of the term would, however, fit into the traditional Dutch policy of accommodation of cultural identities that fundamentally differs with the French approach of indifference towards common characteristics of national communities, from which

1917 Dutch Supreme Court, crim. ch., 29 March 1983, *NJ* 1983, 532.
1918 Dutch Supreme Court, crim. ch., 14 March 1989, *NJ* 1990, 29, annotation Schalken.
1919 Dutch Supreme Court, Crim. Ch., 15 April 2003, *NJ* 2003, 334.
1920 The Hague Court of Appeal, 10 February 1984, *NJ* 1984, 445.
1921 Van der Neut 1986, p. 61–62.
1922 Van der Neut 1986, p. 59–60.
1923 Annotation Melai at: Dutch Supreme Court, 26 June 1984, *NJ* 1985, 531; Woltjer 2001, p. 393–394; Brants, Kool & Ringnalda 2007, p. 67. For criticism, see: Van der Neut 1986, p. 56.

it results that Corsicans and Harkis do not constitute a group on the ground of their national or ethnic background protected by the offences of group defamation and insult.

Compared to the French Supreme Court, with regard to the offence of group insult the Dutch Supreme Court has thus given a broader interpretation of the discriminatory ground of race. Furthermore, the Dutch Supreme Court uses a less restrictive requirement of the designation of a group on the ground of its race. This is a result of the fact that the Court has brought several forms of indirect insult on the ground of race under its scope.

5.5. Indirect insult on the ground of race

5.5.1. Nazi propaganda

On several occasions the Dutch Supreme Court has found Nazi propaganda by using swastikas and other Nazi symbols to constitute a punishable insult of Jews on the ground of their race in accordance with Article 137c or e Sr. In 2010, the Dutch Supreme Court rejected an appeal against a condemnation by the Court of Appeal on the ground of Article 137e Sr of a suspect for hanging a flag depicting the swastika in his house in such a manner that it was clearly visible from the public road.[1924] The flag constituted an insult to people of the Jewish race or religion, because it injured the honor and dignity of this group and showed a lack of respect for them and their history connected to their race/religion. Furthermore the flag had a character that shocked the legal order and caused feelings of social unrest in society.[1925]

In 1995, the Dutch Supreme Court rejected an appeal against a conviction by the Court of Appeal on the ground of Article 137c Sr of a member of a neo fascistic group for having publicly worn a swastika on a red armlet during a demonstration.[1926] According to the Court, the overall majority of the Dutch population interpreted the wearing of a black swastika in public as a propagation of the ideas of National Socialism. It was a 'generally known fact' that the national socialistic ideology is pre-eminently characterized by racial doctrine and anti-Semitism. The same applied to the fact that in the Second World War, on the ground of that ideology, the Jews in Europe had been prosecuted and murdered on large scale. Hence, publicly wearing the swastika was insulting to Jews on the ground of their race.[1927] In order for the expression to be punishable, it was unnecessary that the swastika was accompanied by an explicit reference to Jews.

1924 Dutch Supreme Court, Crim. Ch., 21 September 2010, *LJN BM2483.*

1925 Amsterdam Court of Appeal, Crim.Ch., 16 July 2008, *LJN BO1540.*

1926 Dutch Supreme Court, Crim. Ch., 21 February 1995, *Rechtspraak Rassendiscriminatie,* edition 1995–2000, p. 43–46, annotation Schalken.

1927 Dutch Supreme Court, Crim. Ch., 21 February 1995, *Rechtspraak Rassendiscriminatie,* edition 1995–2000, p. 43–46, annotation Schalken.

In his annotation, Schalken concludes that the use of the swastika forms an indirect form of discrimination because of its 'association' with the Nazi ideology. The connection between the swastika and the Nazi regime is so compelling that the true intentions of its user are crystal clear. A suspect's defence that symbolic expression is multi interpretable is therefore generally rejected.[1928] However, the question arises as to whether the use of a swastika can be regarded as a group insult per se and whether the use of Nazi symbols in general can be exclusively reduced to the aspect of the prosecution of Jews and be regarded as an expression of racial discrimination per se.[1929] According to Schalken, the punishability of expression must always be determined in the light of its context and the circumstances of the case. When the power of the imagination can activate criminal liability, this is generally not without risk when it comes to political preferences.[1930] As a result of a decision of the Dutch Supreme Court in 2011, it cannot be assumed as 'a generally known fact' that the symbol 'ACAB' signifies 'All Cops Are Bastards'.[1931]

The Dutch Supreme Court has generally held the distribution of Mein Kampf by Adolf Hitler punishable on the ground of Article 137e Sr, even if the suspect did not have the subjective intention of propagating the Nazi ideology. In 1987, the Dutch Supreme Court considered with regard to the sale of a Dutch translation of Mein Kampf in the window of a second-hand shop that 'to commit the fact as described in Article 137e Sr, (…) it is not necessary that the object (…) is offered in a provocative or offensive manner or that it has been found that the offender had any political or discriminatory motive.'[1932] In his annotation, Melai argues that a bookseller who aims to sell a copy of Mein Kampf to a person for his or her historical or political interest is already liable.[1933] Indeed, two market vendors, who had offered Mein Kampf for sale at their a market stalls, one of which concerned historical literature about the Second World War, have subsequently been convicted on the ground of Article 137e Sr.[1934]

1928 Conclusion Jörg, para.17–21 at: Dutch Supreme Court, Crim. Ch., 5 November 2002, *LJN AE8821*.

1929 If the swastika is used in the broader context of expression about for example Turks or Moroccans, it can hardly constitute an insult of *Jews* on the ground of their race. Moreover, the association with the massive extermination in the Second World War seems in principle to be absent with regard to *Turks* and *Moroccans*.

1930 Annotation Schalken at: Dutch Supreme Court, Crim. Ch., 21 February 1995, *Rechtspraak Rassendiscriminatie*, edition 1995–2000, p. 43–46.

1931 Dutch Supreme Court, crim. ch., 11 January 2011, *LJN BP0291*, *NJ* 2011, 116, annotation Mevis.

1932 Dutch Supreme Court, Crim. Ch., 12 May 1987, *Rechtspraak Rassendiscriminatie*, edition 1995, p. 223–225, *NJ* 1988, 299, annotation Melai, para. 5.2.

1933 Annotation Melai at: Dutch Supreme Court, Crim. Ch., 12 May 1987, *Rechtspraak Rassendiscriminatie*, edition 1995, p. 223–225, *NJ* 1988, 299.

1934 Amsterdam District Court, Crim. Ch. 18 November 1998, *Rechtspraak Rassendiscriminatie*, edition 1995–2000, pp.389–391, annotation Schoep; District Court Dordrecht, Crim. Ch., 9 November 1999, *Rechtspraak Rassendiscriminatie*, edition 1995–2000, p. 473–475.

5.5.2. *Political criticism of the State of Israel*

In 1983, the Dutch Supreme Court upheld a conviction by the The Hague Court of Appeal on the ground of Article 137e Sr with regard to the political action of the Palestina-Committee to spread pamphlets that depicted angry solders wearing helmets with the caption 'Israel' and the sign of a swastika. According to the Court of Appeal, the image constituted an insult of Jews on the ground of their race, because it strongly criticized the foreign politics of the State of Israel with regard to the Palestinians and associated it with the extermination of the Jews in the Second World War and a strong connection existed between the Jews and the State of Israel.[1935] The Attorney General agreed before the Supreme Court with the decision of the Court of Appeal that the identification of the Jews with a system that is hostile to them (the Nazi-system) constitutes an insult to Jews on the ground of their race. Such a comparison was not only gross, but also repugnant towards Jews in general. This form of criticism of the State of Israel therefore was and could be felt by Jews as insulting against their person and was not protected by the right to freedom of expression.[1936] The Supreme Court finally rejected the appeal on formal grounds.

In his annotation, Mulder agrees with the decision and considers the image to be an annoying example of anti-Semitism. According to Mulder, the term Israel is used as a collective name for all descendants of Israel, i.e. patriarch Jacob, together and thus for the nation, the people, the community of Israelites. The term Israel has not lost these significations because of the creation of the *State* of Israel. The identification of Israel with SS is therefore insulting to Jews 'on the ground of their national or ethnic origin'. The possible political purport of the image does not alter this.[1937]

Contrarily, many legal scholars have criticized the decision. Van der Neut complains that the condemnation resounds the aftermath of the once widespread idea that he, who criticizes Israel or does not unconditionally support its politics, is automatically anti-Semitic. At worst, the image constitutes an insult of the State of Israel or its residents with an Israeli *nationality*, but not of Jews *on the ground of their race*. The latter would only be the case, if – quod non – in the image a direct connection would be made between the violent practices of the Israeli army and the fact that the authors of these atrocities are Jewish. Articles 137c-e Sr should not criminalize over-simplified criticism of a country, of which an important amount of inhabitants share a common race, religion or belief, because such expression does not automatically constitute an insult *on the ground of* race, religion or belief.[1938] Likewise, Janssens argues that severe criticism of the State of Israel, for example, with regard to the treatment of the Palestinians, can offend Israeli citizens, sympathizers or Jews in the Diaspora, in their personal feelings of honour. This

1935 The Hague Court of Appeal, 22 September 1982, *NJ* 1984, 600.

1936 Dutch Supreme Court, crim. ch., 6 December 1983, *NJ* 1984, 601, annotation Mulder.

1937 Annotation Mulder, para. 4–5, at: Dutch Supreme Court, crim. ch., 6 December 1983, *NJ* 1984, 601.

1938 Van der Neut 1986, p. 69–70. In the same sense: Janssens & Nieuwenhuis 2011, p. 209.

does not signify that the criticism constitutes an expression of the inferiority of group members on the ground of their race.[1939] Indeed, nowadays expression about the politics of Israel, however gross it may be, is not punishable, unless it equally constitutes discriminatory expression about Jews.[1940]

In the French case law, several cases can be found concerning similar criticism of the State of Israel. It is striking that the expressions were, however, found punishable on the ground of the offence of incitement to hatred, discrimination or violence, not on the ground of the offences of group defamation or group insult. This can be explained by the fact that in French case law it is generally not required that the group being the victim of a racial provocation is identified with the same precision that is required with regard to the offences of racial defamation and racial insult.

5.5.3. Holocaust denial as a subset of group insult

Unlike France, Dutch law does not have a specific offence that criminalizes Holocaust denial. In the absence of such a specific offence, revisionist expression, i.e. expression that puts up for discussion the history of the Second World War and tends to deny or minimize the genocide of the Jews by the Nazis, can only be prosecuted on the grounds of the hate speech bans of Articles 137c-e Sr. Predominantly, the Dutch courts have found the ridiculing, denial or minimization of the Second World War and the Holocaust to constitute an indirect form of punishable group insult of Jews on the ground of their race or religion for the purposes of 137c or e Sr. Although in the wording of the expression the Jews were not always explicitly designated as a group, the expression was nevertheless insulting to them, because the expression concerned a topic with which the group identified itself or because the expression brought to mind certain associations with the Nazi-ideology. Such insulting expression was found punishable, notably because it 'offended the feelings of the group'.

On several occasions, the Dutch Supreme Court has upheld a conviction by the Court of Appeal with regard to expression that denied the Holocaust. In 1985, the Dutch Supreme Court upheld a conviction of the notorious 'widow Rost van Tonningen'[1941] on the ground of 137e Sr for having in stock the publication 'Sechs Millionen Juden vergast-verbrannt?' that denied the fact that millions of Jews have

[1939] Janssens 1998, p. 394–395.

[1940] LECD, *Cijfers in beeld: Discriminatiecijfers 2010, Overzicht discriminatiecijfers Openbaar Ministerie 2006–2010*, December 2011, p. 23.

[1941] Florrie Rost van Tonningen, alias 'the Black Widow', was the widow of Meinoud Rost van Tonningen, an infamous Dutch leader of National Socialism during the Second World War. After the Second World War, Rost van Tonningen has defended the Nazi-ideology of her husband uncompromisingly in the media. In 1986, the fact that she received a surviving relatives' pension by the Dutch State, because her husband had been a member of parliament, caused a public debate. However, the Government continued to pay the pension until her death in 2007.

been murdered in concentration camps during the Second World War. Its punishable character was as a result of the specific words used.[1942] Solicitor-General Meijers argued that the element in the offence of Article 137e Sr that exempts from punishability expression 'for the purpose of objective reporting' is connected to the *distribution or stocking* of the expression. The defence used by Van Tonningen, i.e. that his aim was to enter into a free scientific historical debate cannot be considered to form an appeal to this exemption, because this defence concerns an appeal to a justifying ground connected to the content of expression.[1943] In his annotation, Veen agreed on this point: the content of Rost van Tonningen's expression however missed the scientific character.[1944] In 1997, the Dutch Supreme Court upheld a conviction of Verbeke, a notorious Belgian revisionist, on the ground of Articles 137c and e Sr for the spreading of pamphlets, in which the Holocaust was denied and Jews were accused of maintaining this 'myth' for their own financial gain, and for similar expression uttered in court during a civil law suit.[1945]

Although in these cases the Dutch Supreme Court itself did not decide on the punishability of the expression, the cases are generally interpreted in such a way that the Supreme Court has implicitly recognized the punishable character of Holocaust denial.[1946] However, the Supreme Court has not yet decided on the question as to whether the *sole denial* of Holocaust is punishable as such. It results from the case law by lower courts that the denial of the Holocaust generally constitutes an insult to Jews on the ground of their race or religion, because it is uttered in the broader context of anti-Semitic expression, the proclamation of racial doctrines or the support of the Nazi-ideology.[1947] The fact that cases often concern the distribution or stocking of multiple expressions might reinforce the gratuitously offensive character of the denial of the Holocaust to Jews.[1948] In 2002, the Dutch Supreme Court upheld the decision of a District Court to allow a request for extradition by Germany of a suspect, who was under suspicion for having in stock fifteen CD's comprising the song 'Wir wollen Beweise', in which the Holocaust was denied, and CD covers, books and sheets showing Nazi flags and swastikas. The suspect had also participated in a demonstration in Berlin against the memorial of the Holocaust, with his head decorated with a tattoo of a SS-skull.[1949]

1942 Dutch Supreme Court, crim. ch., 27 October 1985, *NJ* 1988, 538, annotation Van Veen.

1943 Conclusion Solicitors General Meijers, para. 15–20, at: Dutch Supreme Court, crim. ch., 27 October 1985, *NJ* 1988, 538, annotation Van Veen.

1944 Annotation Van Veen, para. 3, at: Dutch Supreme Court, crim. ch., 27 October 1985, *NJ* 1988, 538.

1945 Dutch Supreme Court, crim. ch., 25 November 1997, *NJ* 1998, 261.

1946 Korteweg, D., Strafbaarstelling negationisme: geschiedschrijving via het recht?, *Mediaforum* 2010–3, p.81.

1947 For example: Amsterdam Court of Appeal, Crim. Ch., 20 May 1994, *Rechtspraak Rassendiscriminatie*, edition 1995, pp. 773–775; 's-Hertogenbosch District Court, crim. ch., 21 December 2004, *LJN AR7891*.

1948 's-Hertogenbosch District Court, Crim. Ch., 21 December 2004, *LJN AR7891*.

1949 Dutch Supreme Court, crim. ch., 5 November 2002, *LJN AE8821*.

The minimization of the Holocaust can however also constitute a punishable group insult of Jews on the ground of their race or religion, when such expression does not – aim to – propagate the Nazi-ideology. Hence, in 1988 the Dutch Supreme Court annulled the acquittal on the ground of Article 137e Sr by the Court of Appeal of Mr and Mrs Goeree with regard to publications in an evangelist magazine 'Evan'. In these publications the evangelist couple claimed that the Jews have themselves to blame for all that had happened to them since 33 AD, especially the prosecution and assassination of 6 million Jews by the Nazi regime, because of the choice of the Jewish people, at the time of the trial of Jesus, to release Barrabas and to crucify Jesus. The publications also comprised images of concentration camps.[1950] According to the Court of Appeal, the intentions of the Goeree couple were unmistakably pure and in the light of the entire articles it was not self-evident that the writings had an insulting purport characterized by anti-Semitism or racism. Besides, for the suspects the verb 'to blame' referred to the rejection by the Jews of Jesus as Messias, a fundamental aspect in their religious convictions, not to an ethnic or social ground of being a Jew.

The Supreme Court rejected this focus on the subjective intention of the authors, the animus injurandi, considering that the insulting character of the expression depended on its nature and not on the intent of the suspect. Punishability under Article 137e Sr had to be determined independently from the reasons as to why a suspect is of the opinion that 'it is all their [the Jews'] own fault'. In his annotation, Mulder describes the dilemma of the case as the polarity *within* the right to freedom of religion: on the one hand the unhindered experience and exercise of one's own religion and on the other hand the freedom to propagate personal religious convictions and challenge those of others. *If* done with respect for the convictions and feelings of others, such religious propaganda must not be restricted.[1951]

Furthermore, the mere ridiculing of the Holocaust can constitute a punishable group insult of Jews on the ground of their race for the purposes of Article 137c or e Sr. In 1990, the Dutch Supreme Court rejected an appeal against a conviction on the ground of 137c Sr by the Court of Appeal of cineaste Van Gogh with regard to a column, in which he ridiculed the practice of gas chambers and the diary of Anne Frank during the Second World War. The column was comprised of comments about 'an animation film about two copulating yellow stars in a gas chamber' and the phrase 'It smells like Caramel here. Today, they only burn the diabetic Jews.' The Court rejected the defence that the column was intended as a 'literary insult' of another filmmaker who had used his Jewish identity to promote his film and thus had 'advertised with 6 million deceased people'. The passages did not lose their insulting character in the alleged artistic context of the column. The Court did not have to express an opinion on the question as to whether the column had to be regarded as art.[1952] However, in a subsequent case, Van Gogh was acquitted with

1950 Dutch Supreme Court, crim. ch., 18 October 1989, *NJ* 1989, 476, annotation Mulder.

1951 Dutch Supreme Court, crim. ch., 18 October 1989, *NJ* 1989, 476, annotation Mulder.

1952 Dutch Supreme Court, crim. ch., 11 December 1990, *NJ* 1991, 313, annotation 't Hart.

regard to the same 'sick jokes', this time published in a book, because the judge had to use restraint when deciding on the question as to whether expression is 'unmistakably entirely unnecessary and gratuitously offensive.'[1953]

Contrarily, in 2012 the Dutch Supreme Court endorsed the conviction on the ground of Articles 137c and e Sr by the Court of Appeal with regard to the publication of an 'Auschwitz cartoon' by the AEL on the Internet.[1954] The cartoon depicted two Jewish men examining corpses under a notice 'Auschwitz'. The one says 'I don't think they are Jews'. The other responds 'We have to get to the 6.000.000 somehow.' The Court of Appeal considered that the Holocaust is a pitch-black page in the history of human kind. The suggestion that it would be made up or exaggerated, nota bene by the victims, is extremely offending to the victims and their relatives. The subjective intention of the suspect to raise a public debate about the double standards with regard to Articles 137c-e Sr that were applied to sensitive issues in the secular western society such as the Holocaust, but not applied to sensitive issues for Muslims such as cartoons about Mohammed, was not decisive. This aim could have been reached in another way.[1955]

Rosier highly criticizes the extension in case law of the scope of the offence of group insult to opinions on sensitive issues, such as the Holocaust, in order to protect the feelings of a particular group: 'And so a special group with a special history obtained a special protection.'[1956] According to Peters, notably the application of vague criteria such as the 'gratuitously offensive' character of expression would disregard the essence of freedom of expression.[1957] Likewise, Janssens & Nieuwenhuis argue that in the light of the requirement of legality of criminal offences in Article 1 Sr, the denial or minimization of the Holocaust can only be punishable on the ground of Article 137c Sr, if the expression constitutes an *insult*.[1958] The question arises as to whether it is desirable to create a separate offence that criminalizes the *sole denial* of the Holocaust.

Janssens considers the creation of such an offence undesirable for four reasons. Firstly, the *sole denial* of the Holocaust causes insufficient harm, because it merely offends the personal inner feelings of surviving relatives or causes moral indignation by others. It does not constitute an insult, because it does not deny the honour or dignity or constitutes an outward show of disrespect of Jews. Moreover, in the Dutch context, it is unlikely that a large amount of revisionist literature will be produced that could violate the public order. Secondly, as a principle freedom of

---

1953 For a detailed analysis of the cases, see: Beekman, K., Grüttemeier, R., *De wet van de letter Literatuur en rechtspraak,* Athenaeum – Polak & Van Gennep: Amsterdam 2005, p. 104 *et seq.*

1954 Dutch Supreme Court, crim. ch.,27 March 2012, *NJ* 2012, 220.

1955 Arnhem Court of Appeal, crim. ch., 19 August 2010, *LJN BN4204; NJFS* 2010, 294. In first instance, the suspect had been acquitted: Utrecht District Court, crim. ch., 22 April 2010, *LJN BM1987,* annotation Nieuwenhuis in: *Mediaforum* 2010–5, p. 179–181.

1956 Rosier 1997, p. 54–56.

1957 Peters 1981, p. 214–215; 220–221.

1958 Janssens & Nieuwenhuis 2011, p. 237.

expression protects expression regardless of content; nonsense or lies must be falsified in public debate. Thirdly, criminalization is ineffective, because it will not convince revisionists to change opinion, and counter-productive, because it will create martyrdom and generate attention for revisionist ideas. Fourthly, criminalization paves the way to the comparison of suffering with surviving relatives of other genocides, which is immoral.[1959] And yet, in 2006 a bill was introduced that proposed the criminalization of the denial of genocides, notably the Holocaust, in a separate offence.

5.5.4. Proposal to create an offence penalizing the denial of genocides

On 1 June 2006, a draft act was proposed on the initiative of Huizinga-Heringa, representative of the Christian Union in Parliament that proposed to criminalize 'negationism'.[1960] Article 1 of the Act sought – after an amendment[1961] made in reaction to the advice of the Council of State[1962] – the insertion into the Dutch Criminal Code right after existing Article 137d Sr of a new Article 137da Sr that sanctioned, he, who publicly – orally, in writing or by portrayal – denies or minimizes, approves or justifies genocides in a gross manner, either with the malicious intent to incite to hatred, discrimination or violence against persons or property on the ground of their race, religion or belief, gender or homosexual orientation or physical, psychical or mental handicap (137da sub 1), or with the knowledge or reasonable suspicion that he thereby insults a group of people on those same discriminatory grounds (137da sub 2), with an imprisonment of maximum one year or a fine of up to € 7,800.[1963] Article 137da sub 4 Sr declared Article 137e Sr applicable to these offences.[1964]

The deposer of the draft rejected the use of the term 'revisionism', because this would include legal scientific historical research that aims to revise history on the basis of new facts and more precise information. The term 'negationism' on the other hand was more suitable, because it concerned expression that aims to promote extreme opinions as an acceptable political movement and thus can create a climate in which discrimination becomes a negotiable option. The term encompassed the denial of the crimes of the Nazi-regime, but also of genocide and crimes against humanity in general. These crimes had been committed against persons on the basis of their race. Subsequently, the denial of these crimes was therefore deeply

---

1959 Janssens, A.L.J., De loochenaars van Auschwitz; de ongewenstheid van strafbaarstelling, *Ontmoetingen: Voordrachtenreeks van het Lutje Psychiatrisch-Juridisch Gezelschap,* 1999, nr. 5.

1960 *Kamerstukken II*, 2005–2006, 30579, nr. 2.

1961 *Kamerstukken II*, 2008–2009, 30579, nr. 6.

1962 *Kamerstukken II*, 2008–2009, 30579, nr. 5.

1963 *Kamerstukken II*, 2008–2009, 30579, nr. 6.

1964 Furthermore Article 137da sub 3 elevated the sanctions to these facts, if committed by a person who makes a profession or habit out of it or by two or more organized persons to an imprisonment of maximum two years or a fine of up to 19.500 euros.

offensive to the victims of these crimes or their relatives. Negationist expression was reprehensible, precisely because the denial is uttered intentionally, while knowing exactly that the crimes in question have taken place, thus with the aim to dismiss, insult, discriminate, or marginalize the victims of these crimes or their relatives. This obvious discriminatory aim made negationist expression punishable as a matter of principle.[1965]

In short, according to the explanatory memorandum, the explicit criminalization of negationism was thus necessary, because persons and groups deserved to be protected against such punishable facts. A democracy had to take a firm position against negationism. The explicit criminalization of such expression formed a powerful signal to potential victims and offenders. Besides, many European countries had comparable offences. Moreover, the Protocol concerning the criminalization of racist and xenophobic acts via computer systems comprised the possibility of such an explicit criminalization in national law, which had to be interpreted as an incentive to do so.[1966]

Although the Dutch Criminal Code did not provide the criminalization of negationism, as a result of the case law Holocaust denial can be punishable under certain circumstances. In principle, Dutch law therefore sufficiently complied with the international treaties comprising norms concerning the criminalization of racist and xenophobic acts.[1967] However, the norm existent in jurisprudence had to be codified, because an explicit statutory foundation was preferable. The aim of the draft was to explicitly and separately criminalize negationism in the light of an effective fight against racist and xenophobic acts and thereby to contribute to a clear and consistent regulation in this field.[1968] The draft thus constituted an addition to the existing speech offences, but was not to be considered as an extension of the existing law.[1969]

Although Huizinga-Heringa and her successor Voordewind received high praise for their thorough preparatory work, the bill was severely criticized by the Council of State and in Parliament. In fact, no parliamentary party, except for the Christian Union and to a lesser extent the SGP, supported the bill and during the Parliamentary debates most parties declared in advance to vote against it.[1970] Firstly, the Council of State doubted the necessity of the explicit criminalization of negationism. As a result of the case law of Articles 137c and d Sr, these articles already sufficed for the purposes of the proposed Article 137da Sr; as this latter offence required that an offender must have the malicious intent to incite to hatred, discrimination or violence or that a suspicion exists that the expression is insulting, the scope of the draft seemed to fall entirely under the existing Articles 137c and d

1965 *Kamerstukken II*, 2005–2006, 30579, nr. 3, p. 1–3.
1966 *Kamerstukken II*, 2005–2006, 30579, nr. 3, p. 6.
1967 *Kamerstukken II*, 2005–2006, 30579, nr. 3, p. 11.
1968 *Kamerstukken II*, 2005–2006, 30579, nr. 3, p. 1–3.
1969 *Kamerstukken II*, 2008–2009, 30579, nr. 7, p. 4.
1970 *Handelingen II*, 13 September 2011, 105–15, p. 52–64.

Sr. Codification of the case law concerning Holocaust denial seemed unnecessary, because it was based on sufficiently clear and broad offences that provided sufficient legal foundation. Moreover, the explanatory memorandum did not give any example of punishable expression that would fall under new Article 137da Sr, but could not fall under the scope of Articles 137c or d Sr.[1971] The parliamentary parties therefore opined that the draft would merely have a symbolic value.[1972]

The reaction in Parliament is in keeping with the vision of the Dutch legal system as an 'open system' with 'open norms' in order to enable the judge to 'colour' the norms to the circumstances and facts of every case. During the debates, the socialist group stated: 'the strength of current Articles 137c-e Sr lies precisely in the fact that these form open norms that must be further interpreted by judges. Indeed, it would be practically impossible to precisely describe every act or punishable expression. Does this [new Article 137da] not entail the risk that the more specific actions or opinions are determined, the more is 'forgotten'? If the denial of genocides is determined so specifically and with such precision, does the fact that another expression deserving of punishment is not specified in the code not form a signal that it is not punishable? In other words, having open norms has advantages, it is impossible to specify every conduct or expression in such a manner that it captures every conduct or expression worthy of punishment.'[1973] Likewise, the social democrats stated that '[i]n the Netherlands, we have a generic, general criminalization of insult. To arbitrarily single out one form of insult in a specific criminal provision is not only unnecessary, but also incorrect in light of the system of the law.'[1974]

Secondly, much doubt was raised as to whether the draft would actually reach its aim to establish a clear legal norm that would enhance legal certainty. It was anticipated that several statutory elements of Article 137da Sr would be difficult to prove. The Council of State anticipated that the requirement that an offender must have the malicious intent to incite to hatred, discrimination or violence would be difficult to prove, which is why prosecutors would exercise restraint in their prosecutions.[1975] Several members of parliament supported this view, referring to the offence of blasphemy that led a dormant existence since the Dutch Supreme Court had required the malicious intent to deeply offend God's Person.[1976] It is recalled that in French law the former offence of racial defamation and insult of persons with the aim to incite to hatred between citizens was abrogated in 1972, precisely because it appeared to be impossible to prove the author's malicious intent to incite to hatred.

1971 *Kamerstukken II*, 2008–2009, 30579, nr. 5, p. 2.
1972 *Kamerstukken II*, 2009–2010, 30579, nr. 8, p.10.
1973 *Kamerstukken II*, 2009–2010, 30579, nr. 8, p. 11–12.
1974 *Handelingen II*, 13 September 2011, 105–15, p. 52.
1975 *Kamerstukken II*, 2008–2009, 30579, nr. 5, p. 4.
1976 *Handelingen II*, 13 September 2011, 105–15, p. 64.

Furthermore, the proposed Article 137da Sr originally criminalized the denial of both genocides and crimes against humanity 'as defined in Articles 6 and 7 of the Statute of Rome concerning the International Court of Justice'.[1977] This signified that in the absence of case law by the ICJ or other relevant tribunals, the Dutch judge had to decide on the question as to whether certain acts constituted genocides or crimes against humanities. In order to prevent this, the Council of State had proposed to limit the scope of the offence to those genocides or crimes against humanities that have been acknowledged as such by a final decision of an acknowledged international tribunal – which would be more comparable to the French offence of Holocaust denial.[1978]

The drafter however rejected this limitation, considering it inopportune to exclude historical events that never had been or could not have been brought before the court. Instead, the elements 'crimes against humanity' and 'as defined in Articles 6 and 7 of the Statute of Rome concerning the International Court of Justice' were deleted. Article 137da Sr was thus amended so that it simply criminalized the denial of 'genocides'. Other than the denial of genocides, the denial of crimes against humanities would not always have a negationist, i.e. racist, purport. Furthermore, for the interpretation of whether an event constituted a 'genocide' now the Dutch judge could be inspired not only by Article 6 of the Statute of Rome, but also the case law of the ICJ or institutions, such as the tribunal of Neurenberg, Tokyo, Rwanda and Yugoslavia, and even the 'communis opinio' on the subject as it results from authoritative scientific publications or declarations from national parliaments or the European Parliament.[1979]

Most parties highly criticized this vague circumscription of the offence that entailed a possibly boundless scope. The Social Democrats cynically recalled a page in Dutch history: '[c]an the denial of the massacre in 1621 of almost the entire population of the Banda-Islands on the orders of Jan Pieters-zoon Coen, Governer-General of The Dutch East India Company (VOC), be punishable under the offence, because of its offensive character for the current inhabitants of those Islands?'[1980] According to the drafter, the event could indeed be qualified as genocide pursuant to the article, but the expression would most likely lack the malicious intent to offend or discriminate.[1981] The Christian Democrats were highly opposed to the possibility for a Dutch judge to base his decision on the acknowledgement of certain genocides by national parliaments or the European Parliament: '(...) Parliaments are political institutions par excellence. History is not a matter of absolute truths. A particular genocide can be acknowledged by one parliament, but at the same time denied by another parliament. It is undesirable that the denial of a particular genocide is punishable in one country, when precisely its acknowledgement is

1977 *Kamerstukken II*, 2005–2006, 30579, nr. 2.
1978 *Kamerstukken II*, 2008–2009, 30579, nr. 5, p. 5.
1979 *Kamerstukken II*, 2008–2009, 30579, nr. 7, p. 7–8.
1980 *Kamerstukken II*, 2009–2010, 30579, nr. 8, p. 3.
1981 *Kamerstukken II*, 2010–2011, 30579, nr. 9, p. 3.

punishable in another country.'[1982] This vision is in line with the decision of the French Constitutional Council, in which it found the offence of the denial of genocides unconstitutional, precisely because it referred to a declaration from the French National Assembly, which violated the separation of powers.

Thirdly, most parliamentary parties considered the criminalization of the denial of genocides undesirable on principled grounds. The Green Left Party made a fundamental distinction between discriminatory actions and discriminatory opinions and the consequences connected to them. The basic assumption of the Dutch Criminal Code of 1886 had been to merely criminalize those acts that intentionally cause concrete harm to others. Since its creation, the Code had, however, been supplemented with offences that are remote from this principle. This development could be explained as a clear political signal of the Dutch legislator that some values are so precious that their violation deserves to be sanctioned. A fundamental objection to this trend was, however, that Dutch law gradually shifts towards the criminalization of thoughts, a state of mind or a motive, not concrete consequences. Contrarily, Dutch law was to adopt the American approach and thus return to its own principles of the Nineteenth century; only situations that form a clear and present danger to others had to be punishable. The defence of the historic truth was a task for education, not criminal law. Negationism was sickening, but did not constitute a clear and present danger as physical discrimination and incitement to hatred and violence did.[1983] The SGP was, however, strongly opposed to such a strict distinction between physical discrimination and opinions, considering: '[c]an words not be more offensive and far-reaching than certain acts?'[1984]

The drafter of the proposal feared that in the absence of a specific offence in the future Holocaust denial would no longer be punishable on the ground of the current case law, because with the passing of time no surviving victims and their relatives would remain. However, in the eyes of the drafter, negationist expression aimed to offend the entire Jewish population.[1985] The criticism of the opponents of the draft nevertheless seemed to be a result of its apparent emphasis to protect the surviving victims and their relatives of the Holocaust against offence to their feelings. The Democrats considered the criteria of offence too subjective. This triggered a comparison of the proposed offence of the denial of genocides with the offence of blasphemy; the preservation of the latter for the protection of certain religious feelings against offence was equally considered to be untenable.[1986] Precisely because Holocaust denial served a political aim, the socialist group considered that these opinions had to be countered in the political arena.[1987]

1982 *Handelingen II*, 13 September 2011, 105–15, p. 64.
1983 *Handelingen II*, 13 September 2011, 105–15, p. 56.
1984 *Handelingen II*, 13 September 2011, 105–15, p. 57.
1985 *Kamerstukken II*, 2010–2011, 30579, nr. 9, p. 12.
1986 *Handelingen II*, 13 September 2011, 105–15, p. 58 *et seq.*
1987 *Handelingen II*, 13 September 2011, 105–15, p. 64.

5.6. Designation of a religious group

In order to be punishable, an insult concerning a religious group must be made against a group 'on the ground of its religion or belief'. The discriminatory ground of 'religion or belief' has a core demarcation similar to the discriminatory ground of race. A line is crossed when expression explicitly targets a determined, designated group exclusively on the ground of its religion. In order to determine whether this is the case, the Dutch judge takes into account the context of the entire publication. As a result, expression about a group of a particular nationality can, in a broader context, be punishable as expression about a religious group. It equally results that in order for the offence of group insult to be constituted it is not required that the defamatory expression is aimed at the religious group in its entirety; it suffices that the expression is aimed at a group of people regardless of its size on the ground of its religion or belief. The insulting expression does not explicitly and with so many words have to attribute the – negative – qualities to the group on the basis of its religion; this follows from the designation of the religious group itself.

A good illustration of an application of these criteria is a decision of 26 June 2012 of the Dutch Supreme Court.[1988] The Court rejected an appeal against a conviction by the Court of Appeal with regard to several publications on a website in which Muslims, Turks and immigrants were compared with 'berber-monkeys, cockroaches, rats and rapists', were said to have been treated as worthy guests '[a]t least, until they started to rape our blonds.' and were urged to 'stay in your desert and go have it off once again with one of your camels.' According to the Court of Appeal, the expressions, regarded both in isolation and in the context of the articles, were unmistakably insulting about groups on the ground of their race or religion. Although certain paragraphs merely spoke of 'radicals, terrorists, racists and extremists', it was obvious that every time Muslims (and Turks) were addressed as a collectivity. This could notably be derived from the fact that the publications indicated the amount of Muslims in the Netherlands (one million). The expression, as the suspect must have known, denied the dignity of the group in question.[1989] According to the Supreme Court, the court could have considered that the expression concerned 'persons of non-western origin who adhere to Islam' and was insulting to Muslims on the ground of their religion or to immigrants on the ground of their race.[1990]

1988 Dutch Supreme Court, crim. Ch., 26 June 2012, *NJ* 2012, 415.

1989 Amsterdam Court of Appeal, Crim. Ch., 11 October 2010, *LJN* BO0041. Contrarily, the Haarlem District Court had acquitted the suspect on the ground of 137c. See: Haarlem District Court, Crim. Ch., 7 April 2009, *LJN* BI0374.

1990 The Supreme Court rejected the argument that Muslims could neither be offended by the epithets because these did not concern their religion nor be offended on the ground of their race and that immigrants could not be regarded as a collectivity of a particular race or religion. See: Dutch Supreme Court, 26 June 2012, *NJ* 2012, 415.

5.7. Indirect insult on the ground of religion: the *Cancer called Islam* case

On several occasions, the Dutch Supreme Court has demarcated the punishable insult of a religious group from the free opinion concerning religious convictions or practices that might hurt religious feelings. In 1986, the Dutch Supreme Court rejected an appeal against the acquittal on the ground of 137e Sr by the Court of Appeal of an editor with regard to a critical publication on Israel in the weekly 'Bazuin' which included the passage: 'It shows that closed religious communities, 'chosen people' are characterized by the fact that religion is turned into legislation and regulations and that the outside world is almost automatically wished and helped to hell. Such a 'religion' deserves to be abolished.' According to the court, the editors' intent to insult could not be proven.[1991] In his annotation, Mulder disagrees with the decision, arguing that the expression constituted an insult to Jews on the ground of their religion, precisely because it concerned their religion. If their religion had to be abolished, then what had to be done with their 'religious community'?[1992]

Twenty-three years later, the Dutch Supreme Court, however, made a fundamental distinction between expression about a religion and expression about a group on the ground of its religion. In a decision of 10 March 2009, the Supreme Court considered that, given the fact that the Dutch legislator had foreseen a limited scope of Article 137c Sr, in order to be punishable an expression must *unmistakably* concern *a group of people* that is characterized by their *religion*.[1993] The case concerned a poster placed behind a window of a house facing the public road with the text: 'Stop the cancer called Islam (…)'.[1994] The poster depicted no Muslims at all. Nevertheless, both the District Court and the Court of Appeal considered the poster to be insulting to adherents of Islam, 'considering the connection between Islam and its adherents', and convicted the suspect. Contrarily, the Dutch Supreme Court acquitted the suspect, because 'the mere fact that offensive expression concerning a religion equally offends its adherents formed an insufficient ground to equate it to expression about the adherents, thus about a group of people on the ground of their religion.'[1995] The Supreme Court explicitly left open the question as to whether the distinction between criticism of a religion and criticism of religious adherents would equally apply to the discriminatory ground of race (para. 6.5 *infra*).

1991 Dutch Supreme Court, Crim. Ch., 16 December 1986, *NJ* 1987, 534, annotation Mulder.

1992 Dutch Supreme Court, Crim. Ch., 16 December 1986, *NJ* 1987, 534, annotation Mulder.

1993 's-Hertogenbosch District Court, Crim. Ch., 19 July 2005, *LJN* AT9494; 's-Hertogenbosch Court of Appeal, Crim. Ch., 10 November 2006, *LJN* BH3383; Dutch Supreme Court, Crim. Ch., 10 March 2009, *LJN* BF0655; *NJ* 2010, 19, annotation Mevis; *NS* 2009, 139; *RvdW* 2009, 414.

1994 The text continues: '*Theo died for us, who will be next? Resist NOW! National Alliance, we do not bow to Allah. Join us! N.A. P.O Box (001) (place). www.nationalealliantie.com.*'

1995 Dutch Supreme Court, Crim. Ch., 10 March 2009, *LJN* BF0655, *NJ* 2010, 19 annotation Mevis; *NS* 2009, 139; *RvdW* 2009, 414, para. 2.5.1–2.5.2.

In essence, the Dutch Supreme Court confirmed the vision of the Dutch legislator that criticism of religious convictions or practices that offend religious feelings do not fall under the scope of Article 137c Sr (para. 4.3.1 *supra*). The ratio of the offence to religious feelings merely applies to the offence of blasphemy in Article 147 Sr and is limited to the category of expressions that deeply disparage God's Person. Hence, the Dutch Supreme Court has notably demarcated the offence of group insult from the offence of blasphemy. After this decision by the Supreme Court, the Minister for Justice renounced his plan to 'clarify' the scope of the offence of group insult by inserting the words 'direct and indirect' insult and at the same time abolish the much criticized offence of blasphemy that had, since the '*Donkey trial*', led a dormant existence and merely had a symbolic function (para. 3.4 *supra*).[1996] The plan thus apparently aimed to create the possibility to criminalize expression about a religion that offends religious feelings under Article 137c Sr and thus to 'transfer' the function of Article 147 Sr to 137c Sr. However, the decision of the Supreme Court in 2009 left no room for this transfer.[1997]

Several Dutch legal scholars have criticized the above decision of the Supreme Court. Vermeulen argues that the distinction between a religion and its adherents made by the Supreme Court presupposes a secularized vision on mankind, according to which people's religion forms a very limited part of their identity; criticism on a religion would therefore say little about their appreciation as a person. This vision (secularization) however does insufficient justice to people who deeply believe and often concern vulnerable orthodox religious minorities.[1998] One can object that even the offence of the feelings of adherents of orthodox religions cannot form an independent ground for liability under Articles 137c-e Sr. After all, this can result in the protection of personal religious convictions of certain religions against – harsh – criticism, which is contrary to freedom of expression, freedom of religion and the principle of equality. The distinction made by the Supreme Court thus does spring from a vision on the – neutral – position of the state towards religions and the inter-relationship between these latter fundamental rights (secularism).

The criterion that expression must 'unmistakably' concern a group on the ground of its religion cannot in so many words be traced back in the drafting history. It was acknowledged that hybrid expressions existed for which it was necessary to determine whether the author aimed to target and draw conclusions about a religion or its adherents (para. 4.3.1 *supra*). Precisely because of the possible amalgam of a religion and its adherents, the consideration of the Dutch legislator and the Supreme Court that criticism of religious convictions and practices is not

---

[1996] *Kamerstukken II*, 2008–2009, 31700 VI, nr. 33.

[1997] *Kamerstukken II*, 2008–2009, 31700 VI, nr. 128.

[1998] Vermeulen, B., 'Strafbare belediging van God, godsdienst, godsdienstigen', in: P.H.P.H.M.C. van Kempen e.a. (red.), Levend strafrecht, strafrechtelijke vernieuwingen in een maatschappelijke context, Liber amicorum Ybo Buruma, Deventer: Kluwer 2011, p. 662–663.

2011, p. 653–666.

punishable needs further explanation. After all, if all criticism on the behaviour of a group attributed to it on account of its religion would be free, the discriminatory ground of religion would lose its signification. A workable method could be to determine whether behaviour and practices can reasonably be connected to a religion.

According to the drafting history, the key criterion is whether expression concerns 'points that are beyond discussion' (para. 4.3.1 *supra*). Does this concern generally known factual behaviour, or drawing a possible connection between a religion and antisocial behaviour? Eventually, of overriding importance is the question of whether expression constitutes an insulting value judgment or is simply untrue. For example, in this manner a distinction can be made between permissible criticism on ritual slaughtering or religious circumcision by Muslims and the impermissible attribution of an inherent criminal nature to Muslims.

In his annotation, Mevis criticizes the decision for treating the question as to whether expression 'unmistakably concerns a group on the ground of its religion' as a preliminary question. The Supreme Court has dictated a new sequence in the determination by the judge as to whether the elements of the offence of 137c Sr are established. As a result, the focus shifts from the core question of whether the expression has an insulting character to the question of whether it concerns a group on the ground of its religion. If the answer to the latter question is negative, the former question needs no further examination. Mevis questions as to whether the boundary between permissible and impermissible expression is correctly drawn; a clever man can escape liability by formulating his words in such a manner that they do not unmistakably concern a group on the ground of its religion at first sight.[1999]

From a same strand of thought, Veraart argues that this new sequence can result in a very abstract test on the basis of the literal wording of the expression, whereby this text is not placed in its specific textual and social context. The Supreme Court did not take this context into account. The Solicitor-General did, but endorsed the defence of the suspect that the poster constituted a political opinion on the increasing influence of Islam in the Netherlands and a call to the people to become a member of a political movement. Veraart objects that it concerned an expression of an extreme right winged movement uttered in a time of increasing acts of discrimination and violence against Muslims in Dutch society. This formed a relevant context that had to be taken into account.[2000]

The approach of the Supreme Court has subsequently been applied in case law.[2001] For example in the *Wilders* case, the District Court found that Wilders' equations of

1999 Annotation Mevis at: Dutch Supreme Court, Crim. Ch., 10 March 2009, *LJN* BF0655, *NJ* 2010, 19.

2000 Veraart, W., 'Beledigen kan alleen in context, Kanttekeningen bij het "belediging islam"-arrest van 10 maart 2009', *NJB* 26 March 2010, p. 724–730.

2001 For example: Utrecht District Court, Crim. Ch., 26 April 2010, *LJN* BM8138, *NJFS* 2010, 231. The Utrecht District Court acquitted a suspect on the ground of Article 137c in relation to

Islam with Nazism did not unmistakably concern Muslims, but concerned Islam.[2002] With regard to Fitna, one could object that although the expression charged only concerned 'islamization', the rest of the film did depict and gave a negative image of Muslims. The criticism on the *Cancer called Islam* case seems justified; a strict application of the distinction between a religion and its adherents can result in a very abstract test based on the literal text. Then the precise charge by the prosecution becomes very important (para. 6.7;8.2.2 *infra*).

When the 'unmistakably' criterion is strictly applied, only direct insults by means of degrading disqualifications or terms of abuse against explicitly designated religious groups seem to be punishable on the ground of 137c Sr. It is submitted that this can be undesirable; more disguised forms of the rousing of public sentiment against and the stigmatizing of a religious group, such as the depiction of Islam as a criminal religion, are not punishable under 137c Sr, while they can equally discredit Muslims on the basis of their religion. Even though such expression discredits people, it equally cannot constitute a punishable insult of an individual in the sense of Article 266 Sr, because the expression does not aim at one particular person.

Hence, in order to better determine whether expression about a religion violates the honour and good name of a group on the basis of its religion for the purposes of 137c Sr, it must firstly be clarified whether religious practices and behaviour can reasonably be connected to a religion and secondly, whether expression constitutes an insulting value judgment or is simply untrue. To this end, the expression must be interpreted in its specific textual and social context.

5.8. Contextual review

For the determination of the punishability of expression under Article 137c Sr, the judge begins by placing the expression in its direct textual context. The judge can attach importance to a suspect's freedom of expression by setting strict requirements to the elements of the offence of 137c Sr – as is the case for the designation of a religious group (para. 5.7 *supra*). If expression can be qualified as a group insult for the purposes of 137c Sr, the judge subsequently balances the application of the speech offence with the right of freedom of expression. It is notably at this stage that the judge attaches importance to freedom of expression;

several posters he had placed behind the window of his house facing the public road, depicting a Christian cross, the equal-sign and a swastika; a burning church with the text 'burn the'; and a Christian cross covered by a prohibition sign with the text 'Bad Religion', because these symbols and texts did not concern Christian adherents, but exclusively concerned the Christian religion.

2002 The public prosecution charged Wilders with three expressions in a newspaper article 'Enough is enough: prohibit the Islam.', in which Wilders compared Islam with Nazism and the Quran with Mein Kampf, and one expression in the film Fitna: 'Islam wants to predominate and subject and aims to destroy our civilization. In 1945 Europe conquered Nazism. In 1989 Europe conquered Communism. Now, the Islamic ideology must be conquered. Stop the islamization. Defend our freedom.' See: Closing speech Public Prosecution 25 May 2011, p. 31.

thus when the judge determines whether the application of 137c Sr is proportional. To this purpose, in three decisions in 2001 and 2003, the Dutch Supreme Court has developed a method of contextual review consisting of a 'three-step-test'. The cases all concerned the question of whether expression about homosexuals based on a religious conviction uttered in public debate constituted a punishable group insult. The first step of the test concerns the question of whether expression taken in isolation and its direct textual context, thus according to its nature and purport, is insulting. The second step concerns the question of whether the broader context – being to enter into a public debate by proclaiming a religious conviction – can remove the punishable insulting character of the expression. The third step concerns the question of whether the expression, despite its broader context of proclaiming a religious conviction in a public debate, is gratuitously offensive and therefore nevertheless punishable.[2003]

In the first case in 2001, the Supreme Court rejected an appeal against the acquittal by the Court of Appeal on the ground of 137c and e Sr of clergyman and politician Van Dijke with regard to his statement during an interview published in a Dutch magazine 'Yes, why would a practicing homosexual be better than a thief?' The Court of Appeal had firstly considered that this equation of practicing homosexuals with criminal offenders violated the dignity of homosexuals; as the homosexual practice is strongly connected to their identity, the rejection thereof implied the rejection of their particular identity. However, the court continued that 'the expression in question was no more than an illustration that clarified a religious conviction.' and this rhetorical question therefore 'did not impair the dignity of practicing homosexuals'. According to the Supreme Court, the court had interpreted the term insulting correctly by considering that the expression was 'evidently directly connected to the suspect's religious conviction and as such was of importance to him in the public debate.'[2004] In the second case in 2001, on similar grounds the Supreme Court rejected an appeal against the acquittal by the Court of Appeal on the ground of 137c Sr of a police officer with regard to similar statements[2005] made in a (public) policy magazine in reaction to the plan of the government to open marriage to homosexuals.[2006]

In the third case in 2003, the Dutch Supreme Court confirmed these two decisions by rejecting an appeal against the acquittal by the Court of Appeal on the ground of 137c Sr of Reverend Herbig for having called homosexuality a 'filthy and vile sin' in a letter published in a regional newspaper. The Supreme Court considered again that the court had interpreted the term insulting correctly by

2003 Dutch Supreme Court, crim. ch., 9 January 2001, *NJ* 2001, 203; Dutch Supreme Court, crim. ch., 9 January 2001, *NJ* 2001, 204, annotation De Hullu; Dutch Supreme Court, crim. ch., 14 January 2003, *NJ* 2003, 261, annotation Mevis.

2004 Dutch Supreme Court, Crim. Ch., 9 January 2001, *NJ* 2001, 203, annotation De Hullu.

2005 The police officer stated 'Homosexuality is equated with heterosexuality. That is much the same as equating theft with gift tax or assault with nursing.'

2006 Dutch Supreme Court, Crim. Ch., 9 January 2001, *NJ* 2001, 204, annotation De Hullu.

deciding that 'the expression, regarded in its context, is evidently directly connected to the suspect's religious conviction and his intent to warn humankind is clear, which is why for the suspect the expression is of importance to a public debate.' and that the terminology used was not gratuitously offensive, because 'in the Bible homophilia is regarded as an 'atrocity' or a 'horrible sin'.[2007]

This three-step-test equally applies to the situation in which a suspect expresses an opinion in a public debate that is not based on a religious conviction. This results from another case before the Dutch Supreme Court in 2003. The Supreme Court rejected an appeal against the conviction by the Court of Appeal on the ground of 137c Sr with regard to a letter published in a regional newspaper in which asylum seekers and refugees were called 'tyrants, thieves, murderers, criminals and rapists'. Even in the context of a public debate on a never resolved murder-case and the unrest this case had caused in society, the use of such terms was gratuitously offensive.[2008]

Even though lower courts of law on occasion deviate from this three-step-test,[2009] they often explicitly refer to the *Herbig* case and apply it as their general framework.[2010] The judge merges the second and third step into one step, when he considers that the context of a public debate does *not* remove the insulting character of the expression and that it is gratuitously offensive.[2011] Generally, the context of a public debate, however, seems to rather easily remove the insulting character of expression that taken in isolation is insulting. As Mevis points out in his annotation of the *Herbig* case, the context of a public debate forms a very easily 'exculpating factor' to expression that taken in isolation is insulting. Expression uttered in the context of a public debate must be very heated and fierce before it is gratuitously offensive and therefore nevertheless punishable. What is more, the approach seems to prevent the possibility of setting any requirement to contributions to public debate, for example, to have a certain level of serenity.[2012] It is not required that an expression forms an *actual substantial contribution* to a public debate.[2013] An expression must on the other hand have a *function* in a public debate.[2014] This does

2007 Dutch Supreme Court, Crim. Ch., 14 January 2003, *NJ* 2003, 261, annotation Mevis.

2008 Dutch Supreme Court, crim. ch., 15 April 2003, *NJ* 2003, 334.

2009 For example, the judge did not apply the second and third step in: *Havana*, Amsterdam District Court, Crim. Ch., 2 June 2008, *LJN* BD2957. The case concerned the acquittal on the ground of Article 137c with regard to a column in a university magazine containing aggressive criticism of Jews. The Amsterdam Court of Appeal upheld that judgment in: Amsterdam Court of Appeal, 17 February 2010, *LJN* BL4528.

2010 For example in the case: Arnhem Court of Appeal, Crim. Ch., 19 August 2010, *LJN* BN4204; *NJFS* 2010, 294, para. 4.1.

2011 An example forms: Amsterdam Court of Appeal, Crim. Ch., 11 October 2010, *LJN* BO0041.

2012 Annotation Mevis at: Dutch Supreme Court, Crim. Ch., 14 January 2003, *NJ* 2003, 261.

2013 Conclusion Solicitor-General Machielse, para. 3.10, at: Dutch Supreme Court, Crim. Ch., 10 March 2009, *NJ* 2010, 19, annotation Mevis.

2014 Amsterdam Court of Appeal, 23 November 2009, *LJN* BK4139, *Mediaforum* 2010–1, p. 24, annotation Nieuwenhuis.

not signify that a suspect could have formulated his expression in another manner. An expression must merely not be more offensive than can be justified by the suspect's aim.[2015]

This method of a contextual review by means of a three-step-test thus ensures that the judge does not determine *in abstracto*, but *in concreto* as to whether expression can be qualified as a group insult in the sense of 137c Sr. The judge explicitly balances the application of the offence with a suspect's right to freedom of expression in the light of all circumstances of the case. However, no objective criteria exist for striking the right balance between 137c Sr and freedom of expression. The judge must, to a certain degree, seek a connection with what the group concerned can reasonably experience as insulting. Wortel discerns three manners, in which the judge could attach importance to a suspect's right to freedom of expression: by the establishment of a suspect's *intent* to insult, by the determination of the insulting *character* of the expression, or by applying it as an unwritten free speech clause or justifying fact (mitigating circumstances), after and independent from establishing liability under 137c Sr.[2016]

As a result of the previously discussed case law, freedom of expression generally forms a factor to be weighed in the determination of the insulting character of the expression. This approach has the advantage that the success of a suspect's appeal to his right to freedom of expression always depends on the nature and content of the expression itself. A suspect of gratuitously offensive expression that can reasonably be considered as insulting cannot object that by using provocative language he has intended to contribute to a public debate. However, courts sometimes rather attach importance to a suspect's motive, which can result in a very 'subjective' explanation of a suspect's expression (para. 6.7 *infra*). Treating freedom of expression as an unwritten justifying fact has the disadvantage that the motivation on the punishable character of the expression by the judge can become incomprehensible. For example, in the *Polinco* case, the District Court firstly considered that the designation of immigrants as 'rats' and Jews as 'riffraff, scum and paranoid schizophrenics' on an Internet website was evidently punishable under 137c Sr, but finally concluded that it was not punishable on the ground of an abstract, separate consideration on the basis of Article 10 ECHR.[2017]

The contextual review ensures that the interest of freedom of expression is incorporated into the statutory elements of the offence.[2018] The three-step-test

2015 Arnhem Court of Appeal, Crim. Ch., 19 August 2010, *LJN* BN4204, *NJFS* 2010, 294.

2016 Conclusion Solicitor-General Wortel, para.15 *et seq.* at: Dutch Supreme Court, Crim. Ch., 15 April 2003, *NJ* 2003, 334.

2017 Amsterdam District Court, 2 June 2008, *LJN* BD2977. However the suspect was convicted in appeal. See: Amsterdam Court of Appeal, 23 November 2009, *LJN* BK4139, *Mediaforum* 2010–1, p. 22–24, annotation Nieuwenhuis.

2018 Jansssens & Nieuwenhuis 2011, p. 45 *et seq.*

affords the possibility for the judge to accommodate the Article 10 case law of the ECtHR that has developed norms concerning the permissibility of restrictions to a free political and public debate[2019] and of gratuitously offensive expression.[2020] As Article 120 of the Dutch Constitution prohibits constitutional review, the judge does not test Article 137c Sr against Article 7 of the Constitution, but applies it in light of the Article 10 ECHR, thus 'in conformity with the treaty' (para. 1.6 *supra*).[2021]

This is precisely where Dutch law differs from French law. In France, the press offences in the 1881 Press Act are generally thought to, in themselves, strike the right balance between freedom of expression and other rights and interests. French courts do not explicitly balance the press offences with the right to freedom of expression *in concreto* in every case. They rather strictly apply them *in abstracto* and only implicitly attach importance to freedom of expression when establishing whether the elements of the offence are met. Other than in France, the Dutch judge precisely colours the statutory norms to the circumstances of the case, but has not developed in case law a detailed closed national system of specific justifications connected to specific speech offences that complicates the accommodation of the Article 10 case law of the ECtHR.

Dutch legal scholars notably criticize the application of the criterion that expression must not be gratuitously offensive, because it concerns an opinion on the proportionality of the expression. The ECtHR uses the term, but in order to determine the proportionality of a restriction of freedom of expression. Determining the proportionality of expression would on the other hand have a chilling effect on freedom of expression (para. 1.5.2 *infra*). One must however keep in mind that, before the judge determines the gratuitously offensive character of expression, he first determines whether expression constitutes an insult in the sense of 137c Sr, thus whether its discredits a group and violates its moral integrity. Consistently determining the gratuitously offensive character of expression as a final objective subsidiarity test is important, because otherwise the punishable insulting character of expression can be simply cancelled out by the – suspect's – interest – to contribute – to a public debate. The gratuitously offensive character of expression can reside in both the content and the form of the expression, but seems to notably depend on the intemperance of the terms used.[2022]

Next to the context of a public debate, the religious context (para. 5.10 *infra*) or artistic context of an expression can also be important for the determination of

2019 For example in: Dutch Supreme Court, Crim. Ch., 18 May 1999, *NJ* 1999, 634, annotation 't Hart; Utrecht District Court, Crim. Ch., 26 April 2010, *LJN* BM8138; *NJFS* 2010, 231.

2020 For example in: Arnhem Court of Appeal, Crim. Ch., 19 August 2010, *LJN* BN4204; *NJFS* 2010, 294.

2021 Rotterdam District Court, Crim. Ch., 8 April 2002, *NJCM-Bulletin*, jrg.27 (2002) nr.8, p. 1019, annotation De Haseth, Starreveld & Loof.

2022 Amsterdam Court of Appeal, 23 November 2009, *LJN* BK4139, *Mediaforum* 2010–1, p. 24, annotation Nieuwenhuis; Amsterdam Court of Appeal, Crim. Ch., 11 October 2010, *LJN* BO0041.

liability under 137c Sr. In 2001, the Dutch Supreme Court endorsed the acquittal by the Court of Appeal on the ground of 137c Sr of the author of the novel 'Dancing lessons' with regard to the criticism made by a fictional character in the novel on the city council of the Dutch city of Zandvoort that notably concerned the Jewish mayor: 'Well, what do you want, with a Jew in command?'. According to the Supreme Court, an author must not abuse his artistic freedom in order to utter insults. The fact that expression is uttered by a novel character does not signify that the author cannot be liable under Article 137c Sr. However, the question as to whether a 'literary insult' concerns an actual, real person or official must be answered objectively and does not depend on whether that person or official can identify him or herself. The nature and purport of the passages were hilarious and not based on reality; in the context of the entire novel the expression was not insulting.[2023] In his annotation, De Hullu argues that the Supreme Court has given the signal that cases concerning artistic expression should not to be settled through criminal law.[2024] This latter vision can equally be derived from several decisions by lower courts of law. In 1951, the Dutch author W.F. Hermans was acquitted on the ground of 137c Sr with regard to the statement made by a novel character in his novel that 'Catholics reproduce like rabbits'. In 1995, the Dutch author Holman was acquitted on the ground of 137c Sr with regard to the use of the term 'Christian dogs' in a column.[2025] However, the previously discussed *Van Gogh* case in 1991 shows that freedom of humoristic or artistic expression is not unlimited (para. 5.5.3 *supra*).

5.9. The special case of the protection of feelings in civil cases

The two civil *Goeree* cases in 1987 and 1991 concerned the rejection by the Supreme Court of an appeal against the prohibition by the Court of Appeal for Mr and Mrs Goeree, an evangelist couple, to disseminate two publications of an evangelist magazine 'Evan'. These publications claimed that the Jews have themselves to blame for the Holocaust, that the existence of AIDS was caused by homosexuals and that their death as a consequence of homosexual praxis served them right. The Court of Appeal considered these expressions to be gratuitously offensive to the feelings of Jews, respectively homosexuals and therefore violated the rule of unwritten law pertaining to proper social conduct for the purposes of Article 6:162 BW. In both cases neither the Supreme Court nor the Court of Appeal referred to any violation of a speech offence and the restrictions to the proclamation of a religious conviction were entirely justified by the offence of the feelings of a

2023 Dutch Supreme Court, Crim. Ch., 9 October 2001, *NJ* 2002, 76, annotation De Hullu.

2024 Annotation De Hullu para. 3 at: Dutch Supreme Court, Crim. Ch., 9 October 2001, *NJ* 2002, 76.

2025 The cases are described in: Beekman, K. & Grüttemeier, R., *De wet van de letter Literatuur en rechtspraak,* Athenaeum – Polak & Van Gennep: Amsterdam 2005. See further: De Hullu, J., Strafrecht en literatuur, *Ars Aequi* 1984, p. 757–761.

particular group.[2026] In a criminal case in 1988, the Dutch Supreme Court annulled the acquittal on the ground of Article 137e Sr by the Court of Appeal of the Goeree couple with regard to the same publication concerning Jews and the Holocaust (para. 5.5.3 *supra*). Expression on the sensitive issue of the Holocaust that offends the feelings of Jews can thus be prohibited according to both criminal and civil law.

Vermeulen argues that in these civil cases the Supreme Court should not have accepted without reserve that the norm of due diligence can set restrictions to the free proclamation of religious convictions. Only in highly exceptional cases the proclamation of one's faith must be declared impermissible towards third parties on account of its content and therefore prohibited. It is the legislator, not the judge, who has the task to judge such complex, philosophical and often politically sensitive questions. The restrictive legislation by the formal legislator must therefore be sufficiently precise, otherwise the judge has too much margin of appreciation to impose prohibitions.[2027]

According to Vermeulen, the norm of due diligence of Article 6:162 BW does not meet this criteria. To the contrary, it constitutes the most general, open, civil norm that must be concretised by the judge. In this process of judicial interpretation, freedom of expression or religion is reduced to a 'factor to be weighted'. The proclamation of religious convictions must therefore only be unlawful on the basis of its content, if it violates a norm of criminal law, i.e. a speech offence. The Goeree couple however could have been convicted on the ground of 6:162 BW by reference to Article 137c Sr.[2028]

Indeed, the speech offences form limitations to the content of expression and therefore form direct limitations to freedom of expression or religion that interfere with their core. There is a democratic thought behind the principle that restrictions to the content of expression require an explicit expression of the will of the formal legislator.[2029] The speech offences can express this will more precisely than the open norm of Article 6:162 BW. The vision that insulting, offensive and discriminatory expression can only be unlawful if it violates a criminal speech offence fits in with the situation in France, where the press offences take priority over the general civil norm of the wrongful act of 1382 CC and form the legal grounds in civil cases, which can be explained in the light of the French emphasis on legal certainty and the separation of powers.

2026 Dutch Supreme Court, civ. ch., 5 June 1987, *NJ* 1988, 702, annotation Alkema; Dutch Supreme Court, civ. ch., 2 February 1990, *NJ* 1991, 289. Although, in the second case the Court of Appeal specified that Article 6:162 BW afforded protection against 'insulting, offensive and discriminatory expression', which formed a permissible restriction of fundamental rights.

2027 Koekkoek 2000, p. 107–108.

2028 Koekkoek 2000, p. 108.

2029 This does not apply to restrictions to the form in which religious convictions are proclaimed. For example Article 6 of the Constitution allows for the delegation of the regulation of religious manifestations such as processions and Article 7 of the Constitution allows for the delegation of the regulation of the distribution of expression (para. 1.2.1 *supra*).

In his annotation, Alkema argues that a reference to criminal law would have provided for a certain objectification; now the restriction to religious freedom is notably justified by the feelings of certain persons and groups. Moreover, by choosing the 'royal path of criminal law' one avoids the 'trouble of horizontal effect', to which both the plaintiff (prohibition of discrimination) and the defendant (freedom of expression) could appeal. On the other hand, it just might not be as awful that in civil cases conflicting fundamental rights require an explicit judicial balancing.[2030] The question arises as to whether the requirement that in order to be unlawful pursuant to 6:162 BW, the expression must violate a speech offence will not provide for a better framework in civil cases. After all, in this framework nowadays – other than in France – not only the speech offence, but also the method of contextual review as established by the Supreme Court will apply in civil cases. This could precisely ensure that the civil judge will explicitly balance conflicting fundamental rights (one of the specified norms of non-discrimination in Articles 137c-e Sr with the right to freedom of expression in 10 ECHR) and that the notion of 'gratuitously offensiveness' remains a final subsidiarity-test. Within this contextual review, due diligence considerations can equally play a role.

In the Netherlands, in theory the criteria for civil liability under the due-diligence norm of 6:162 BW can thus be less strict than the criteria for criminal liability under 137c-e Sr. However, just as expression on the sensitive issue of the Holocaust that offends the feelings of Jews is prohibited according to both criminal and civil law, the mere offence to *religious* feelings forms an insufficient ground for liability under 6:162 BW just as under 137c-e Sr.

In 2005, the summary judge found several strong opinions about Islam made by Hirsi Ali and the film entitled *Submission* made by her and Van Gogh, not to be unlawful and rejected the request to prohibit them. The judge determined the case in the light of Article 10–2 ECHR and considered that Hirsi Ali had not overstepped the boundaries of the acceptable and the requirements of proportionality and subsidiarity. In his annotation Schuijt nevertheless criticizes the reasoning of the judge for having a chilling effect on freedom of expression; it is the restriction that must be proportionate, not the expression itself.[2031] In two following cases, the judge explicitly considered that the fact that citizens experience certain opinions as shocking or offensive does not in itself make that expression unlawful. In 2006, the civil judge, therefore, considered the phrase: 'In the thirties, the elite looked way from the rise of the Nazis, now the same happens with islamization' uttered by the political leader of EenNL, a former nationalist political party, during an election broadcast, not to be unlawful.[2032] Likewise, in 2008 the civil judge considered several expressions by politician Geert Wilders, in which he compared the Quran

2030 Annotation Alkema at: Dutch Supreme Court, civ. ch., 5 June 1987, *NJ* 1988, 702.

2031 The Hague District Court, summary judgment, 15 March 2005, *Mediaforum* 2005–4, p. 178–180, annotation Schuijt.

2032 Rotterdam District Court, summary judgment, 21 November 2006, *LJN* AZ3031.

with Mein Kampf, called it fascist and called Mohammed a barbarian, not to be unlawful. Later on, the criminal prosecution of Wilders on the ground of 137c-e Sr with regard to similar expression equally failed (para. 6.7 *infra*).[2033]

In these cases, the judge notably attached importance to the fact that the expression did not explicitly designate adherents of Islam, but concerned 'islamization' as a social phenomenon. Although in the above cases the civil judge did not refer to Article 137c Sr, his motivation nevertheless seemed to be inspired by the norms established in the criminal case law based on 137c Sr. In practice, no fundamental differences seem to exist between the restrictions to offensive expression as set out in criminal and civil case law.

5.10. Concurrence between freedom of religion and freedom of expression

In the Netherlands, religiously motivated opinions can either fall under freedom of expression protected in Article 7 of the Dutch Constitution or freedom of religion protected in Article 6 of the Dutch Constitution (para. 1.4 *supra*). As both fundamental rights have the same system of repressive restrictions, at first sight it seems irrelevant whether the judge determines the permissibility of religiously motivated opinions in the light of freedom of expression or freedom of religion. However, the judge can attach importance to a suspect's religious motivation and weigh it as a factor when applying the method of contextual review.

As a result of the case law, the judge does not make a conscious motivated choice between the two fundamental rights in the event that they overlap. In the two civil *Goeree* cases, it remained ambiguous as to whether the Goeree couple's freedom of expression or religion was at stake.[2034] In the three criminal cases concerning expression about homosexuals based on a religious conviction uttered in public debate in 2001 and 2003, the Supreme Court considered both the suspects' freedom of religion and freedom of expression an important factor for the determination of liability under 137c Sr.[2035] Explicitly referring to the cases of 2001, in 2002 the Rotterdam District Court and the Hague Court of Appeal acquitted imam El Moumni on the ground of 137c and d Sr with regard to the statement he made during a Dutch television program that homosexuality is a contagious disease and harmful to society, because it formed a direct expression of religious convictions that are protected by freedom of religion.[2036]

2033 The Hague District Court, summary judgment, 7 April 2008, *LJN* BC8732.

2034 Dutch Supreme Court, civ. ch., 5 June 1987, *NJ* 1988, 702, annotation Alkema; Dutch Supreme Court, civ. ch., 2 February 1990, *NJ* 1991, 289.

2035 Dutch Supreme Court, crim. ch., 9 January 2001, *NJ* 2001, 203; Dutch Supreme Court, crim. ch., 9 January 2001, *NJ* 2001, 204, annotation De Hullu; Dutch Supreme Court, crim. ch., 14 January 2003, *NJ* 2003, 261, annotation Mevis.

2036 Rotterdam District Court, Crim. Ch., 8 April 2002, *NJCM-Bulletin*, jrg.27 (2002) nr.8, p. 1016–1019, annotation De Haseth, Starreveld & Loof.; The Hague Court of Appeal, Crim. Ch., 18 November 2002, *LJN* AF0667, *NJ* 2003, 24.

Vlemminx criticizes the approach because it would afford a higher level of protection to religiously motivated expression than to secular expression.[2037] Contrarily, De Haseth, Starreveld and Loof argue that in this case law the suspect's religious conviction only partly colors the context, but forms no independent justification. This is only different, if expression is not aimed at the participation in a public debate, but at the contribution to a theological debate in a somewhat private circle.[2038]

Likewise, according to Nieuwenhuis, the case law of the Supreme Court might seem to afford a higher level of protection to religiously motivated expression than to secular expression on the ground of a suspects' freedom of religion, but because of the Supreme Court's emphasis on the public debate, the entire justifying fact forms 'a suspect's religious conviction in the context of (his contribution to) a public debate'.[2039] Mevis objects that such a subjective interpretation of the insulting character of expression very easily accommodates religious convictions, but on the other hand reduces the role of criminal law to the benefit of reactions in public debate and, in the event of a criminal prosecution, prevents the judge from having to decide upon the correctness of a religious conviction.[2040] Vermeulen argues that a higher level of protection for the proclamation of religious convictions than expression in other fields can be justified by the sincerity or innocence of a suspect's motive.[2041] Such a special protection for religiously motivated expression would fit in with the Dutch tradition of the accommodation of people's specific religious identities.

Dutch scholars thus disagree on the question of whether this case law affords religiously motivated opinions a higher level of protection than secular opinions per se. In certain decisions the judge, however, tends to rather equate the regime of religious and political convictions. In 2003, the Dutch Supreme Court applied the method of contextual review to a situation in which a suspect expressed an opinion in a public debate that was not based on a religious conviction (para. 5.8 *supra*). In 2012, the Amsterdam District Court explicitly applied the Supreme Court's three-step-test to the political opinions on Islam uttered by politician Geert Wilders (however in relation to Article 137d Sr – para. 6.7 *infra*). The court acquitted the politician, because in Wilders' perspective his expressions were necessary to expose social problems.[2042] The court thus equated the regime of religious and

---

2037 Vlemminx, F.M.C., 'Mogen sympathieen zwaarder wegen dan constitutionele zuiverheid?', *NJB* 2002, p. 1696–1699.

2038 Annotation De Haseth, Starreveld & Loof at: Rotterdam District Court, Crim. Ch., 8 April 2002, *NJCM-Bulletin*, jrg.27 (2002) nr.8, p. 1016–1019.

2039 Nieuwenhuis, A.J., Godsdienstvrijheid en bijdragen aan het maatschappelijk debat, *NJCM-Bulletin,* jrg.29 (2004) nr.2, p. 154–166.

2040 Dutch Supreme Court, Crim. Ch., 14 January 2003, *NJ* 2003, 261, annotation Mevis.

2041 Vermeulen, B.P., 'De Goerees en de kardinaal, ofwel: vrijheid van godsdienst versus discriminatieverbod', in: L. Heyde e.a. (red.), *Begrensde vrijheid*, Zwolle: Tjeenk Willink 1989; Koekkoek 1992, p. 127–128 and p. 131–133.

2042 Amsterdam District Court, 23 June 2011, *Mediaforum* 2011, p. 280–282, annotation Van Noorloos; *Ars Aequi* 2012, p. 288–289, annotation Rozemond; p. 290–294, annotation Schutgens.

political convictions. This fits in with the situation in France, where Articles 10 j 11 of the 1789 Declaration protect religious and non-religious opinions on equal footing, which can be understood in the light of the French notions of equality and laïcité. The equation seems justified, because it is incomprehensible why religious convictions uttered in public debate must be afforded a higher level of protection than political opinions.[2043]

5.11. Desirability of the criminalization of group insult

The desirability of the criminalization of group insult is an idea not shared by all Dutch legal scholars. Legal scholars disagree with 1) the creation of the offence as such; 2) the broadening of the scope of the offence by the insertion of new discriminatory grounds since its creation; or 3) its alleged broad application in case law. These objections will be discussed in this order.

Van der Neut states that racial group insults are annoying for the persons concerned yet are not harmful per se. He questions whether a specific need exists for Article 137c Sr, since in practice concurrence with Article 137d Sr would almost always exist. A broad interpretation of Articles 137c-e Sr by the courts is notably undesirable. If Article 137c Sr would be abrogated and Articles 137d-e Sr maintained and Dutch law would still comply with ICERD.[2044] Peters goes even further. Inspired by American free speech doctrine, he advocates a preferred position of the freedom of public debate with regard to other rights and interests and thus a hierarchy between fundamental rights.[2045] Because of the importance of freedom of expression, the concurring interests must be very important. The legislator must indicate the importance of other interests and the judge must balance them *in concreto*. This signifies that the judge must start from the presumption of the unconstitutionality of offences that constitute direct limitations to freedom of expression. The judge has an active role in the appreciation of restrictions, because he has the task of preserving the channels of democratic decision-making. According to Peters, the Dutch legislator has acknowledged the preferred position of a free public debate by the insertion of a free speech clause in Articles 266 and 267 Sr. Contrarily, the criminalization of discriminatory expression in Articles 137c-e Sr does not fit into this more consequent acceptance of the primacy

---

Previously, in its review of the decision by the public prosecution not to prosecute Wilders, the Amsterdam Court of Appeal had considered that the three-step test concerned religious convictions and could not be applied by analogy to political opinions. See: Amsterdam Court of Appeal, 21 January 2009, *NJ* 2009, 191, annotation Buruma, *Strafblad* 2009, p. 198–208, annotation Fennema, *Mediaforum* 2009, 8, annotation Nieuwenhuis.

2043 In the same sense: Nieuwenhuis, A.J., Godsdienstvrijheid en bijdragen aan het maatschappelijk debat', *NJCM-Bulletin* 2004, p. 154–166.

2044 Van der Neut 1986, p. 81–82; 137.

2045 For this purpose, Peters distinguishes 'public speech', which forms part of a public discussion on matters of public concern, from 'private speech', such as commercial advertising.

of a free public debate, which is why the offences should be abrogated. The preferred position of a free public debate should only yield to incitement to violence that constitutes a clear and present danger.[2046]

In the vision of Peters, discriminatory expression is thus only punishable, if it constitutes defamation or insult of an individual person or an incitement to violence or criminal offences for the purposes of 261, 266 and 131 Sr. In my opinion, this vision disregards the fact that discriminatory expression precisely often does not aim to target one concrete designated person in particular, but any person or all persons belonging to a group characterized by a common race or religion (para. 7.3 *infra*). On the other hand, discriminatory expression could still be unlawful under 6:162 BW. But if Articles 137c-e Sr are abrogated, then what will the guideline for determining the (un)lawfulness of expression be? It should certainly not only be the 'vague criterion of its gratuitously offensive character' (para. 5.5.3 *supra*).

Sackers argues that the Dutch legislator, with the creation of 137c Sr, originally aimed to counter anti-Semitism, but by the insertion of new discriminatory grounds has turned the offence into a 'container concept'.[2047] We therefore have lost sight of the rationale of the offence; the protection against the risks of disturbances of the public order.[2048] Likewise, Van Stokkum considers the protection of the public order to be the primary rationale of the offence.[2049] Van Kempen concludes that the scope of Articles 137c-d Sr should be limited to those situations in which a real risk to the disturbance of the public order exists.[2050]

Rosier and Janssens criticize the very broad application of 137c Sr by the judge to opinions on sensitive issues such as the Holocaust or religious convictions in order to protect the feelings of a particular group, but both authors see the value of Article 137c Sr. Rosier argues that to publicly discredit groups on the ground of their race, their negative imaging by insults, causes harm; their loss of status and the denial of their equal dignity as individuals. Insult of minority groups hinders their healthy social functioning. Moreover, insults can lead to the casting out of minority groups and even to genocide. The criminalization of group insult contributes to the preservation of the moral climate of the society.[2051] Janssens argues that Article 137c Sr rightly criminalizes group insult, because racial insults evidently cause harm to minority groups, who must be protected by criminal law because of their vulnerable position in society.[2052] Rosier draws a parallel between

---

2046 Peters 1981, p. 214–215; 220–221. See also Peters' contribution to: Stelling 'De woorden 'godsdienst of levensovertuiging' in artikel 137c Wetboek van Strafrecht dienen geschrapt te worden', *NJB* 2003–16, 18 April 2003, p.832.

2047 Sackers, H., 'De opmerkelijke geschiedenis van artikel 137c Sr', in: Ellian, A., Molier, G. & Zwart, T. (eds.), Mag ik dit zeggen? Beschouwingen over de vrijheid van meningsuitingen, Den Haag: Boom Juridische Uitgevers 2011, p. 309–327.

2048 Van der Neut 1986, p. 327.

2049 Van Stokkum, Sackers & Wils 2006.

2050 Van Kempen 2011, p.193.

2051 Rosier 1997, p. 286; 295; 308.

2052 Janssens 1998, p. 76; 400–401.

the offence of group insult and the offences of defamation, libel and insult of an individual.[2053, 2054] These latter offences do not prohibit opinions on sensitive issues in order to protect the feelings of an individual. They protect citizens against the effects of *misleading* expression about *individuals*. They assure that citizens can in a good environment shape their personal convictions about another individual free from the rousing of public sentiment against his person. Likewise, the offence of racial group insult protects citizens against undesirable effects of racist expression. It assures that citizens can, in a good climate, shape an adequate impression of the status or peculiarities of an attacked group free from the rousing of public sentiment against it.[2055]

Rosier suggests limiting the scope of the offence to attacks on the human dignity of groups on the ground of their race. This not only comprises direct declarations of inferiority of particular designated groups, but every expression that unambiguously expresses the opinion that others on account of their race do not deserve the care and respect people are entitled to. The insertion of the discriminatory ground of religion would, however, be unnecessary, because in the Netherlands religious groups are not under a systematic attack by insults at their address.[2056] Since 9/11 Muslims have, however, increasingly become the victim of negative imaging in public debate.

The Dutch Supreme Court has met this criticism in the broad application and interpretation of 137c Sr, firstly by nowadays actively balancing the application of Article 137c Sr *in concreto* with the interest of a free public debate through the method of a contextual review and second by a restrictive interpretation of the discriminatory ground of religion and belief. This accommodating case law that increasingly attaches importance to the interest of freedom of expression is connected to the social developments of the past decennia. It appears to be a reaction to the climate of political correctness of the eighties and nineties, in which harsh criticism of ethnic and religious minorities and the multi-cultural society easily amounted to social and criminal convictions. After events such as 9/11 and the assassinations of Fortuyn and Van Gogh, people increasingly wear their heart on their sleeves. Criticism on social problems related to immigration, integration of minorities and the multi-cultural society less frequently amounted to social and criminal convictions (para. 2.2 *supra*/ para. 6.7 *infra*). This shift in case law, which is nevertheless based on precisely the same offences, has caused uncertainty about their interpretation and application.

In legal literature, no consensus exists on the 'sense and nonsense' of the speech offences.[2057] This uncertainty also notably exists in cases concerning the religion of

---

2053 Rosier 1997, p. 295.

2054 See also: Janssens 1998, p. 392–393.

2055 Rosier 1997, p. 295.

2056 Rosier 1997, p. 288. See also: Rosier, T. E., 'Discriminerende Belediging', *Recht & Kritiek* 1996, p. 305–334;.Rosier, T.E., Tolerantie en religie. Over de zaak Van Dijke en de visie van het EHRM inzake godslastering, *RM Themis 2000/1*, p. 3–14.

2057 See notably the contributions to: Thema Uitingsdelicten en discriminatie, *Strafblad* 2007, p. 363–409; Thema Het publiek debat, *Strafblad* 2009–3, 19 June 2009, jrg.7; Ellian, A., Molier,

a particular group. Mixed reactions followed the proposition to simply abrogate the discriminatory ground of religion and belief in Article 137c Sr.[2058] The legislator could meet the objections to the discriminatory ground of religion or belief by the insertion in Article 137c Sr of a free speech clause clarifying that expression that evidently solely aims to criticize convictions and practices that can reasonably be connected to a religion (para. 7.2 *infra*). The question however remains as to whether such a specification would fit in with the Dutch system of 'open norms' in general that precisely enables further judicial interpretation and balancing in concrete cases and in the system of hate speech bans in specific; other discriminatory grounds, such as sexual preference, might equally qualify for similar specifications (para. 7.1 *infra*).

The legislative proposals to modify Articles 137c-e Sr were rather aimed at the entire abrogation of Article 137c Sr or the insertion of a free speech clause that exempts from liability under 137c-d Sr the contributor to a public debate, which could partly meet Peter's 'preferred position' of 'public expression' (para. 7.3 *infra*).

5.12. Conclusion

Article 137c Sr concerns a generic offence of group defamation/insult and criminalizes he who willingly and consciously accepts the considerable risk that his expression may impair the self-esteem or honor of a group or discredit a group, because it belongs to a particular race, religion or belief etc. With regard to Article 137c Sr, the Dutch legislator has not made a distinction between facts and value judgments. Both the insulting character of the expression and a suspect's intent to insult must be proven and can be derived from the nature, purport and context of the expression. The discriminatory ground of race is broadly interpreted; national minorities, such as the Frisians, can form a group in the sense of Article 137c Sr. Moreover, in certain contexts expression about foreigners and persons of a particular nationality can be understood as expression about persons on the ground of their race. A racial group does not have to be precisely designated; Nazi propaganda and the denial, minimization or ridiculing of the Holocaust can constitute a punishable insult of Jews on the ground of their race, even though such expression does not explicitly designate Jews. Associations with the Nazi ideology have as a 'generally known fact' an 'evidently' racist purport. Under certain circumstances, criticism of the State of Israel can equally constitute a punishable racial insult about Jews. Even expression about a mere part of a group in accordance with 137c Sr can be punishable. In Dutch legal doctrine, the criminalization of group insult is highly controversial, notably because of its broad interpretation by

G. & Zwart, T. (eds.), Mag ik dit zeggen? Beschouwingen over de vrijheid van meningsuitingen, Den Haag: Boom Juridische Uitgevers 2011.

2058 See the contributions to: Stelling 'De woorden 'godsdienst of levensovertuiging' in artikel 137c Wetboek van Strafrecht dienen geschrapt te worden', *NJB* 2003–16, 18 April 2003, p. 829–834.

the judge of opinions on sensitive issues such as the Holocaust or religious convictions in order to protect the feelings of a particular group. In order to demarcate the punishable insult of a religious group from the free opinion concerning religious convictions or practices that might hurt religious feelings, the Dutch Supreme Court has however required that expression must *unmistakably* concern *a group of people* that is characterized by their *religion.*

If expression can be qualified as a group insult for the purposes of 137c Sr, the judge subsequently balances the application of the speech offence with the right of freedom of expression by means of the method of contextual review consisting of a 'three-step-test' in order to determine as to whether expression that in the context of a public debate has lost its insulting character nevertheless is gratuitously offensive. Next to the context of a public debate, the religious or artistic context can remove the insulting character of expression. This method of a contextual review ensures that the interest is incorporated into the elements of the offence and the judge determines *in concreto* as to whether expression can be qualified as a group insult for the purposes of 137c Sr. The method equally affords the possibility for the judge to accommodate the Article 10 case law of the ECtHR that has developed norms concerning a free public debate. Although the judge can attach special importance to a suspect's religious motivation and weigh it as a factor when applying the method of contextual review, in case law the regime of religious and political convictions tends to be equated. In theory the criteria for civil liability under the due-diligence norm of 6:162 BW can be less strict than the criteria for criminal liability pursuant to 137c-e Sr, but in practice no fundamental differences seem to exist between the restrictions to offensive expression set in criminal and civil case law.

6. Incitement to hatred, discrimination or violence – Article 137d Sr

The offence of racial provocation is characterized by a number of elements, being provocation and intent thereto (6.1), discrimination, hatred or violence (6.2) and the designation of persons (6.3). In the application of the offence of incitement, the Dutch judge also attaches importance to the right to freedom of expression and exercises a contextual review (6.4). The Dutch Supreme Court has, to a certain extent, clarified the limits to Nazi-propaganda (6.5) and the public debate on the immigration and integration of foreigners (6.6) and, in the famous case against Dutch politician Geert Wilders, the judge has set a number of criteria for the limits to the public debate on the immigration and integration of Muslims (6.7). The analysis results in a general conclusion about the offence of incitement to hatred, discrimination or violence in Dutch law (6.8).

6.1. Incitement and intent

Article 137d Sr criminalizes 'any person who, publicly – orally, in writing or by means of portrayal – incites to hatred against or discrimination of persons or violence against persons or property on the ground of their race, religion or belief, gender, hetero- or homosexual orientation or physical, psychical or mental handicap' with an imprisonment of maximum one year or a fine up to € 7,800.[2059] The Article does not give a definition of 'incitement'. The drafting history neither clarifies how one incites third parties to discrimination, hatred or violence. It is assumed that 'to incite' signifies 'to urge' someone to do something.[2060] Incitement is broader than to 'provoke' in the sense of to 'abet' an act, because one can incite a person for the purposes of 137d Sr, if he himself has already taken the initiative to act in the desired manner.[2061] In other words, one can add fuel to the fire. It results from the case law on 137d Sr of the Dutch Supreme Court that expression that does not constitute an explicit call to act, but more implicitly incites others to discrimination, hatred or violence can equally constitute an 'incitement' in accordance with 137d Sr, because of the 'associations' such expression can evoke with a racist ideology (para. 6.5 *infra*).

Article 137d Sr is to a certain level akin to Article 131 Sr that criminalizes the incitement to criminal offences, but cannot be equated with it. Contrary to 131 Sr, the statutory elements of 137d Sr do not require that a suspect incites others to commit a determined, punishable act under Dutch law. Similar to 131 Sr, 137d Sr, however, merely criminalizes the utterance of expression and does not require that the incitement is followed by effect. The question as to whether the intended effect of the expression has subsequently set in, is irrelevant. The term 'incitement' contains the author's intent.[2062] Similar to Article 137c Sr, even the Dutch 'voorwaardelijk opzet' can apply, which in the context of 137d Sr consists of willingly and consciously accepting the considerable risk that expression incites third parties to discrimination, hatred or violence.[2063] Hence, strictly speaking the determination of the link between expression and the consequence of the existence of discrimination, hatred or violence is not a question of causality.

In the *Wilders* case, the question however arose as to whether expression must be merely likely, sensible, capable or suitable to incite to discrimination, or to actually be aimed at having that effect. According to the public prosecution, the Dutch 'voorwaardelijk opzet' should not apply, because a speaker does not have to

2059 Article 137d sub 2 criminalizes as an aggravating circumstance he who structurally commits the offence as a habit or in the exercise of his profession with an imprisonment of maximum two years or a fine up to 19.500 EUR.

2060 Noyon, Langemeijer & Remmelink, Wetboek van Strafrecht, Fokkens, Article 131, Aant. 1.

2061 Noyon, Langemeijer & Remmelink, Wetboek van Strafrecht, Fokkens, Artikel 137d, Aant. 2; Dutch Supreme Court, 18 March 1895, W. 6636.

2062 Tekst & Commentaar, Wetboek van Strafrecht, Ten Voorde, Artikel 137 d, Aant. 7.

2063 Utrecht District Court, Crim. Ch., 26 April 2010, *LJN* BM8138, *NJFS* 2010, 231.

take into account 'how the frustrated, the prejudiced and buttheads could be expected to interpret his expression'. Expression must be actually *aimed at* factual discrimination.[2064]

Likewise, the Amsterdam District Court considered, for example, with regard to Wilders' film Fitna concerning the bad influence of Islam in Dutch society that neither the entire film, nor any expression or image in it, was *aimed at* evoking the idea that third parties should discriminate against Muslims.[2065] The prosecution and the court thus used a stricter level of intent.

6.2. Hatred, discrimination or violence

Article 137c Sr criminalizes the violation of an interest: people's honor and good name. Article 137d Sr on the other hand criminalizes – and indicates – the threat of the violation of an interest: hatred, discrimination and violence. Where 137c Sr thus directly protects the interest in non-discrimination in the sense of insult, Article 137d Sr thus prevents discrimination in the sense of factual subordination in the exercise of fundamental rights.[2066]

The term hatred is derived from ICERD. However, strictly speaking, Article 4a ICERD does not oblige states to criminalize the 'incitement to hatred', but the 'dissemination of ideas based on hatred'. This obligation was incorporated in ICERD, because it was thought that the existence of racial hatred can prelude racial discrimination and racial violence.[2067] The term hatred is neither defined nor criminalized in Dutch law. This is understandable, because hatred forms rather a feeling than an act. In common parlance, hatred signifies 'a feeling of profound aversion against someone and the desire to see him decline, whether with the desire to harm him or not.'[2068] In literature, incitement to hatred has been defined as 'agitation by means of the public expression of hostility or gross contempt'.[2069] A legal definition of incitement to hatred can be found in Dutch case law. In 2002, the Dutch Supreme Court rejected an appeal against the conviction of a town councilor of Dordrecht with regard to a speech held in the town hall. The speech depicted the 'average citizen' as an ignorant victim of the government policy on the acceptance of immigrants in the Netherlands that would lead to the predomination of foreigners of a certain ethnic descent, notably Muslims. The 'average citizen' had to fear not

---

2064 Closing speech Public Prosecution 25 May 2011, p. 57–58; p. 66–68. The public prosecution here cites Rosier, who critically analyzes Dutch free speech doctrine in the light of a comparison with American free speech doctrine. See: Rosier 1997, p. 105. As the prosecution used Rosier's dissertation as a primary source. one could argue that its closing speech was inspired by (a comparison with) American free speech doctrine.

2065 Amsterdam District Court, 23 June 2011, *LJN* BQ9001, para. 4.2.

2066 Tekst & Commentaar, Wetboek van Strafrecht, Ten Voorde, Artikel 137 d, Aant. 1.

2067 Lerner, N., *The U.N. Convention on the Elimination of All Forms of Racial Discrimination*, Alphen aan den Rijn: Sijthoff & Noordhoff 1980, p. 52.

2068 Van Dale Groot Woordenboek van de Nederlandse Taal, 14e Editie, Utrecht: Van Dale 2010.

2069 Van Stokkum, Sackers & Wils 2006, p. 76.

only for his chances on the labor market and the curtailing of his fundamental rights, but also for his safety and prosperity. According to the Court, these words set a group against 'the average, native citizen', thus the rest of the population in order to discredit it and to incite to hatred against it, which leads to an 'intrinsic conflicting dichotomy' in society'.[2070]

The question arises as to whether the criterion that expression must set groups against each other and incite to an 'intrinsic conflicting dichotomy' in society signifies that the incitement to *feelings* of hatred is punishable in itself, or only if the hatred is aimed at the exclusion of a group from society by the consequence of *acts* of discrimination or violence against it as a result of that hatred. Requiring such a link between the incitement to racial hatred and the consequence of the existence of racial discrimination and violence seems to be in line with the rationale of ICERD that the existence of racial hatred can prelude racial discrimination and racial violence.[2071] More generally, the question concerns the interpretation of Article 137d Sr as a prohibition of the broader 'spreading of ideas based on hatred and discrimination', or of the more narrow 'incitement to hatred or discrimination'.

This latter issue seems to be the assumption in the *Wilders* case, where the District Court set high requirements for incitement to hatred. It somewhat equated 'incitement' to hatred in accordance with 137d Sr to incitement in accordance with 131 Sr and required that expression must comprise a seditious, *'reinforcing element'*. Only two expressions met this requirement: the statement 'There is a battle going on and we need to defend ourselves.' had such seditious character, partly due to its strong terms. The film Fitna equally had a seditious form, because it showed images of the Netherlands as a country increasingly populated by Muslims in combination with threatening music. The mere incitement to *intolerance* of certain religious groups in society thus cannot be considered to be punishable under 137d Sr. Other than the prosecution, the District Court did not also require *as an element of the offence* that the hatred, i.e. dichotomy, to which the expression incites, can lead to severe and violent conflicts. By requiring the existence of such a threat of the disturbance of the public order, the prosecution limited the *scope* of the offence in a manner that would not comply with ICERD.[2072]

Article 137d Sr furthermore criminalizes incitement to discrimination. The term discrimination must be interpreted according to the definition in Article 90*quater* Sr. Article 90*quater* Sr does not concern all forms of distinction, but only distinctions that are unjustified.[2073] This broad definition supposes a further act of balancing in more concrete cases. It is therefore understandable that the Dutch Criminal Code does not criminalize discrimination in general, but only specific

---

2070 Dutch Supreme Court, Crim. Ch., 2 April 2002, *LJN* AD8693, *NJ* 2002, 421, annotation Mevis, para. 3.4.

2071 Janssens & Nieuwenhuis 2011, p. 219.

2072 Closing speech Public Prosecution 25 May 2011, p. 54.

2073 *Kamerstukken I*, 1990–1991, 20239, 76a, p. 2.

discriminatory acts (para. 4.3.3 *supra*). Incitement to these acts certainly falls under the scope of 137d Sr. However given the broad definition of discrimination, discussion about the signification of incitement to discrimination is possible, just as with incitement to hatred. In 1996, the Dutch Supreme Court, however, rejected an appeal against a conviction of the extreme right winged political party Centre Democrats (CD) on the ground of 137c-d Sr considering that Articles 137c *et seq.* Sr are formulated with sufficient precision in order for the citizen to attune his behavior.[2074]

In light of the rationale of ICERD, it is obvious that 137d Sr would comprise of not only expression that directly incites third parties to commit concrete described discriminatory acts against a designated group, but also expression that in more general terms incites to the adoption – by the legislator – of discriminatory laws or that propagates an ideology grounded on racial discrimination. After all, ICERD precisely aimed to counter the dissemination of racist political opinions in light of the elimination of all forms of racial discrimination. Hence, in several cases in the 1970–90s against the extreme right winged political parties NVU, CP'86, CD and/or its leaders, the Dutch Supreme Court upheld a conviction on the ground of 137d Sr with regard to their political pamphlets and statements that solicited to the voters' favor by criticizing the government policy on immigration and expressing the intention to expel guest workers or to abolish the multicultural society after gaining political power (para. 6.6 *infra*).

However, in relation to the Dutch Constitution, Article 137d Sr does not necessarily prohibit the incitement to law reform that – if implemented and enforced – would constitute a prohibited form of discrimination for the purposes of Article 1 of the Constitution. As a matter of fact, contrary to the French Constitution, the Dutch Constitution is 'non-ideological' and does not determine the fundamental principles or values of the Dutch Constitutional State. Nor does it have a provision that prohibits the abuse of rights, because this would burden the judge with political matters, which was considered as undesirable with regard to legal certainty (para. 1.2.2 *supra*). In other words, the Constitution does not afford any protection against anti-democratic tendencies and laws; it does not provide for a 'lock' on acquired, constitutional rights. Political proposals to change the Constitution, such as the proposal to abrogate Article 1 of the Dutch Constitution, or to adopt discriminatory laws are not punishable per se.

The lack of any constitutional guidance, however, precisely seems to afford the judge a broad margin for the interpretation of 137d Sr and to notably, in political issues, render its application questionable. After the political correctness was cast off in the public debate on immigration, integration of minorities and the multicultural society since 9/11, in the *Wilders* case, the District Court required that the advocating of political proposals in order to be punishable under 137d Sr more or less directly and explicitly incite to discrimination against Muslims on account of

2074 Dutch Supreme Court, Crim. Ch., 16 April 1996, *NJ* 1996, 527, para. 7.5.

their religion (para. 6.7 *infra*). Therefore, only expression that incited to concrete described measures and acts of discrimination against Muslims could qualify as incitement to discrimination for the purposes of 137d Sr, such as 'Everybody assimilates to our dominant culture. Whoever refuses to do so, will not be here in twenty years. He will be expelled.' and 'We have plenty ideas. The borders closed, no more Muslims to the Netherlands, many Muslims out of the Netherlands, denaturalization of Islamic criminals (...).'[2075] This strict interpretation of 137d certainly deviates from the broad interpretation of 137d Sr in certain previous cases against NVU, CP'86 and CD in the 1970–90s (para. 6.6 *infra*).

Finally, Article 137d Sr criminalizes incitement to violence against persons or property. Compared with the incitement to hatred or discrimination, the connection with the disturbance of the public order is most obvious with the incitement to violence. Incitement to violence is therefore equally most akin to the offence of incitement to criminal offences or violence against the public authorities in Article 131 Sr. Incitement to violence in accordance with 137d Sr criminalizes the incitement to all kinds of violent behaviour that – if effectuated – could constitute a criminal offence. Incitement to violence in accordance with 137d Sr will therefore most likely also constitute incitement to a criminal offence for the purposes of 131 Sr. Article 131 Sr is broader in the sense that it criminalizes the incitement to all criminal offences and 137d Sr prohibits only the incitement to violence on the ground of race etc. On the other hand, Article 131 Sr is limited to the incitement to violence against the public authorities.

Although the incitement to a criminal offence for the purposes of 131 Sr concerns the incitement to a specific criminal act, in order to be punishable under 131 Sr, the expression does not in so many words have to describe that offence; it must be derived from the circumstances of the case whether it is sufficiently clear that the incited facts would constitute a criminal offence.[2076] Hence more implicit forms of incitement to criminal acts can constitute the offence of 131 Sr. This does not comprise of mere criticism on public institutions and authorities or the propagation to alter the form of government as such. In 2006, in Parliament the question was raised as to whether the scope of Article 131 Sr should be broadened in order to criminalize the incitement against the democratic constitutional state, but the Minister replied that 131 Sr constituted an offence against the public order, which is why importance must be attached to the public character of expression.[2077]

In 2010, the Utrecht District Court convicted a suspect on the ground of 137d Sr with regard to several posters placed behind the windows of a house facing the public road. The posters depicted a drawing of a Christian cross, followed by the

[2075] Amsterdam District Court, 23 June 2011, *LJN* BQ9001.

[2076] Tekst & Commentaar, Wetboek van Strafrecht, Ten Voorde, Artikel 131, Aant. 9d.

[2077] *Kamerstukken II* 2006/07, 30 449, nr. 5, p. 28; *Kamerstukken II* 2009/10, 32 123 XVIII, nr. 57, p. 3; Tekst & Commentaar, Wetboek van Strafrecht, Ten Voorde, Artikel 131, Aant. 1.

so-called 'equal-sign' (=) and a swastika; a drawing of a burning church with the text 'burn the'; and two images of a Christian cross covered by a prohibition sign with the text 'Bad Religion'. The court considered that the suspect had consciously accepted the considerable risk that others could interpret the images as an actual incitement to burn a Church; the suspect had stated that he was aware of the fact that in other countries Satanists had burned churches. The court therefore rejected the defence that the posters formed symbolic expression that merely criticized the church as an institution.[2078]

The *Hofstadgroep* case concerned a group of Muslim fundamentalists that were accused of constituting a terrorist cell that propagated the violent jihad during meetings and distributed radical fundamentalist writings, mostly written by group member Mohammed Bouyeri – the murderer of Van Gogh. In 2006, the members were prosecuted for participation in a criminal organization (140–140a Sr) that – amongst others – had the aim to incite to criminal offences and violence against the public authorities for the purposes of 131–132 Sr and to incite to hatred and violence against disbelievers pursuant to 137d Sr.[2079]

In 2008, The Hague Court of Appeal considered that adhering to a radical fundamentalist ideology does not necessarily lead to the use of violence. One is free to proclaim the opinion that only God should be acknowledged as the sovereign power, democracy is incompatible with Islam and must therefore be rejected and replaced by a system founded on the Sharia.[2080] It therefore found that the writings that pointed out the obligation to hate disbelievers and to show hostility towards them or the obligation of true Muslims to distance themselves from them were not punishable. Contrarily, the writings that glorified or incited to the jihad were punishable under 137d or 131 Sr.[2081] The Hague Court thus strictly distinguished lawful opinions that reject the constitutional state and democracy, but do not contain a threat of violence, from the punishable advocacy of a violent subversion of the constitutional state and democracy that constitutes a real risk.[2082]

According to the Supreme Court, The Hague Court had wrongly considered that 'disbelievers' did not constitute a protected group under 137d Sr (para. 6.3 *infra*).[2083] After referral, the Amsterdam Court therefore considered that pointing out the obligation to show hostility towards disbelievers, to loathe and dislike them and to

---

2078 Utrecht District Court, Crim. Ch., 26 April 2010, *LJN* BM8138, *NJFS* 2010, 231.

2079 The case started before the Rotterdam District Court: Rotterdam District Court, Crim. Ch., 10 March 2006, *LJN* AV5108, 10/000322–04;10/000328–04;10/000396–04;10/000393–04;10000325–04;10/000323–04;10/000395–04.

2080 The Hague Court of Appeal, Crim. Ch., 23 January 2008, *LJN* BC2576 / 4129, p. 12; 19.

2081 The Hague Court of Appeal, Crim. Ch., 23 January 2008, *LJN* BC2576 / 4129, p. 21–23.

2082 For a thorough analysis of the decision of The Hague Court of Appeal, see: Van Noorloos, M., De 'Hofstadgroep' voor het Haagse hof: over de vrijheid van radicale uitingen in het publieke debat, *DD* 2008, 34, p. 475–498; Noorloos 2011, p. 244–246.

2083 Dutch Supreme Court, Crim. Ch., 2 February 2010, BK5172/ 5174 / 5175 / 5182 / 5189 / 5193 / 5196.

fight them, dead or alive, equally constituted an incitement to hatred and violence against disbelievers punishable under 137d Sr.[2084]

6.3. Designation of persons

Article 137d Sr criminalizes incitement to hatred or discrimination against 'people' or to violence against 'persons' or their goods. Unlike Article 137c Sr, 137d Sr thus does not refer to a 'group'. The question arises as to whether Article 137d, similar to 137c Sr, only protects groups or also individual persons, who belong to a particular group characterized by a common race, religion etc. Noyon, Langemeijer & Remmelink argue that the term 'persons' signifies the plural and not also the singular, because of the connection of Article 137d Sr with previous Article 137c Sr. In other words, if the expression aims at one person in particular, Article 137d Sr does not apply, except when 'the hatred or discrimination reflect on the group to which the individual belongs'.[2085] Likewise, Janssens & Nieuwenhuis argue that if expression names and is directed against one person in particular, it cannot be punishable under 137d Sr, but can be punishable under Article 131 or 285 Sr. But if such expression has the purport to incite to hatred, discrimination and violence against several persons, Article 137d Sr applies.[2086] Contrarily, Mevis emphasizes the different characteristics of 137c and d Sr. If expression is not 'about a group', it is not punishable under 137c Sr. Other than with 137c Sr, 137d Sr concerns the possible effect of the incitement on *individual persons* and not to the effect (of insult) on a group *qua group*. The plural in 137d Sr is therefore irrelevant. The incitement must precisely threaten people individually, not collectively, even though the incitement must origin in negative feelings with regard to the characteristics that unite these people (race, religion etc.).[2087] This latter vision fits in with the situation in France, where the French equivalent of 137d Sr criminalizes incitement to hatred, discrimination or violence against 'a person or a group', similar to the French offences of racial defamation and insult.

Expression must incite to hatred, discrimination or violence against a group – amongst others – 'on the ground of its race'. With regard to 137d Sr, the judge uses the same broad interpretation of the term 'race' as with 137c Sr, which comprises national and ethnic background, skin colour and origin, but not nationality in the sense of national citizenship. Again, the discriminatory ground

2084 Amsterdam Court of Appeal 17 December 2010, *LJN* BO07690 / 8032 / 9014 / 9015 / 9016 / 9017 / 9018. The conviction of the Amsterdam Court became final after the Dutch Supreme Court rejected an appeal against it in 2012. See:Dutch Supreme Court, crim. Ch., 3 July 2012, *LJN* BW5121/ 5132 / 5136 / 5161 / 5178, *NS* 2012, 296, *RvdW* 2012, 1021.

2085 Noyon, Langemeijer & Remmelink, Wetboek van Strafrecht, Fokkens, Artikel 137d, Aant. 6.; Brants, Kool & Ringnalda 2007, p. 72–73.

2086 Janssens & Nieuwenhuis 2011, p. 217.

2087 Annotation Mevis, para. 15 at: Amsterdam District Court, 23 June 2011, *LJN* BQ9001, *NJ* 2012, 370.

of race is broadly interpreted; national minorities, such as the Friesians, and cultural minorities can form a group in the sense of Article 137d Sr. Moreover, in certain contexts expression about foreigners and persons of a particular nationality can be understood as expression about persons on the ground of their race. Unlike in France, the Dutch Supreme Court does not as a principle use different criteria for the identification of a racial group being the victim of 137d or 137c Sr. Similar to 137c Sr, a racial group does not have to be precisely designated and even expression about part of a group in the sense of 137d Sr can be punishable.

Other than for 137c Sr, with regard to 137d Sr the Dutch Supreme Court has not decided that in order to be punishable an expression must *unmistakably* concern *a group of people* characterized by their *religion*. This question was raised in the *Wilders* case. The District Court applied the distinction made by the Supreme Court between a religion and its adherents with regard to 137c Sr to 137d Sr and found that most of Wilders' expression concerned Islam and not Muslims.[2088] However, the court interpreted the scope of the discriminatory ground very restrictively, because even the attribution of the fact that one out of five Moroccan youngsters are registered as a suspect by the police to their religion and culture, because Islam is a violent religion and the problems thus originate in the community itself, constituted pure criticism of Islam.

One could object that this expression according to its wording clearly concerns the group of Moroccans on the basis of their religion. Even if it might be true that Moroccans are overrepresented in crime rates, a problem that must be possible to freely discuss, the imputation of an *inherent* criminal nature to them *on the basis of their religion* constitutes the drawing of negative conclusions about them *on the basis of their religion*; this is precisely what 137c-d Sr according to the drafting history prohibits. Does such a negative value judgment need the demonstration of a sufficient factual basis? It seems that Article 137c Sr must be distinguished from 137d Sr; such a defence seems relevant with regard to insult or defamation of a group rather than with regard to incitement to hatred, discrimination and violence against persons. Moreover, proving 'the true tenets of a religion' for this purpose seems to be impossible (para. 6.7 *infra*). In previous cases, courts had convicted suspects on the ground of 137d Sr with regard to similar expression, in which Muslims were depicted as criminal, such as '[i]f the Muslims had not come here, or in any event would not reproduce themselves as much as they do, the Netherlands would not be what it is now: a criminal mess.'[2089]

2088 Closing speech Public Prosecution 25 May 2011, p. 38–39.

2089 Amsterdam Court of Appeal, 11 September 2003, *LJN* AK8302. See for a similar expression concerning race: The Hague District Court, 12 May 2011, *LJN* BQ4301, concerning the phrase 'If you look at it objectively, Moroccans and people from the Antilles cause most of the trouble. These are the most criminal races.'

In his annotation to the *Wilders* case, Mevis argues that the distinction made by the Supreme Court between a religion and its adherents with regard to 137c Sr does not apply to 137d Sr, because 137d Sr concerns incitements that are threatening *to* individual persons that share a common race or religion – comprising of indirect incitements via expression about a religion – and does not concern insults *about* a group *qua group*.[2090] Likewise, Vermeulen argues that the distinction made by the Supreme Court between a religion and its adherents with regard to 137c Sr should not be applied with regard to 137d/e Sr. While in principle insulting criticism about a religion can at the same time respect the dignity of its adherents, this does not apply to the incitement to hatred and discrimination against persons. As a result of the nature of the matter, incitement to hatred, discrimination or violence against the tenets of a religion also targets its adherents, precisely because they will be the victims of the effectuation of such incitements.[2091]

In my opinion, in principle a distinction can be made between, on the one hand expression that pictures religious convictions and practices as entirely reprehensible and hateful, and on the other hand expression about persons. It would be odd, if the Supreme Court decided that the legislator had intended for 137c Sr to leave sufficient room for harsh criticism, but that such criticism could fall under the scope of 137d Sr.[2092] However, it must still be further clarified when practices and behaviour of a religious group can fall under the discriminatory ground of religion. Eventually the determinant factor is the question of whether the expression incites to hatred or discrimination.

Another question is whether Article 137d Sr merely protects *minorities* or also *majorities* of a particular race or religion against incitement to hatred, discrimination or violence. This question arose in the *Hofstadgroep* case. According to the Hague Court of Appeal, Article 137d Sr merely protects certain minority groups on the ground of religion or belief, because of their vulnerability. 'Disbelievers' could hardly be considered as a vulnerable group.[2093] The Supreme Court annulled this decision, because it neither resulted from the wording of the offence nor its drafting history that Article 137d Sr was confined to protect vulnerable minorities.[2094] Indeed, the provision protects, for example, heterosexuals next to homosexuals. *Religious majorities* such as disbelievers can thus also constitute a group for the purposes of 137d Sr.[2095]

2090 Annotation Mevis, para. 15 at: Amsterdam District Court, 23 June 2011, *LJN* BQ9001, *NJ* 2012, 370.

2091 Likewise, incitement to hatred against and fight God or Allah could therefore be interpreted as incitement to its believers and 137d could take over the function of the offence of blasphemy in 147. Vermeulen 2011, p. 663–664.

2092 Janssen & Nieuwenhuis 2012, p. 188.

2093 The Hague Court of Appeal, Crim. Ch., 23 January 2008, *LJN* BC2576, p. 37–38.

2094 Dutch Supreme Court, Crim. Ch., 2 February 2010, *LJN* BK5193, para. 5.3.

2095 Amsterdam Court of Appeal 17 December 2010, *LJN* BO8032, para. 3.2.2.

6.4. Contextual review

Similarly to 137c Sr, for the determination of the punishability of expression under Article 137d Sr, the context and circumstances in which expression is uttered is of importance. This naturally applies to its direct context. Expression that in itself is not punishable can nevertheless be qualified as incitement to discrimination. For example, in 1999 the Dutch Supreme Court endorsed the condemnation on the ground of 137d Sr of Dutch politician Janmaat, leader of the former extreme right winged party Centre Democrats (CD), with regard to expression that was not punishable in itselfbut in the context of expressions of others nevertheless incited to discrimination (para. 6.6 *infra*).[2096] Contrarily, the direct context of expression can also remove its punishable character. For example, in the *Wilders* case, the court considered that although one statement by Wilder together with his film *Fitna* that criticized Islam and gave a negative image of Muslims constituted an incitement to hatred regarded in isolation. These expressions were nevertheless not punishable because Wilders had repeatedly stated that Islam should be rejected and not Muslims.[2097]

With regard to 137d Sr, the judge can attach importance to a suspect's freedom of expression by setting strict requirements to the elements of the offence of 137d Sr. If expression can be qualified as an incitement for the purposes of 137d Sr, can the judge subsequently balance the application of the speech offence with the right of freedom of expression? Can the context of a public or political debate remove the punishable character of expression that incites to hatred, discrimination or violence in the sense of 137d Sr? In other words, can the method of contextual review established by the Supreme Court for 137c Sr be applied to 137d Sr by analogy?

Although the Dutch Supreme Court with regard to 137d Sr attaches importance to the context of expression, the Court has not explicitly developed a similar three-step-test. The introduction of such a test for 137d Sr is not self-evident. It is recalled that in 1971 the Dutch Government thought that it would go against the spirit of ICERD to introduce a clause that excluded from liability under 137c-d Sr expression aimed at giving an opinion on matters of public interest that is not gratuitously offensive.[2098] It is difficult to imagine that once expression has been found to incite to hatred, discrimination or violence, the context of a public debate can nevertheless justify such a threat. Notably, it is difficult to imagine that the incitement to violence must be tolerated as a side effect of a public debate.[2099] This applies to a lesser extent to the incitement to hatred or discrimination. Furthermore, the criterion that expression should not be gratuitously offensive seems unsuitable with regard to 137d Sr, because 137d Sr does not criminalize racial insults that are offensive but prevents the existence of factual discrimination and violence. The weight due to

2096 Dutch Supreme Court, Crim. Ch., 18 May 1999, *NJ* 1999, 634, annotation 't Hart.
2097 Amsterdam District Court, 23 June 2011, *LJN* BQ9001, para. 4.3.1.
2098 Janssens & Nieuwenhuis 2011, p. 208.
2099 Nieuwenhuis & Janssen 2011, p. 100.

freedom of expression thus can depend on whether expression incites to either hatred, or discrimination or violence.

It is striking that the method of contextual review was explicitly applied in the *Hofstadgroep* case by the Hague Court of Appeal with regard to fundamentalist writings that incited to violence and criminal offences. However, the Hague Court considered that the suspect had explicitly stated that he did *not* have the intention to contribute to or to start any public debate, which is why 'the expression was not of importance for the suspect of a public debate.'[2100] Subsequently, the Court nevertheless applied the criteria the ECtHR had set in the *Gündüz* case with regard to similar expression against the democratic order uttered in public debate (requirement that the expression incited to violence and contained an actual risk of violence).

In the *Wilders* case, the District Court for the first time explicitly applied the method of contextual review to 137d Sr with regard to incitement to discrimination.[2101] The four expressions that in first instance qualified as incitement to discrimination all lost their punishable character, because they were uttered in the context of the free political and public debate concerning the multicultural society, immigration and Islam. Subsequently, the court introduced a new term comparable to the term 'gratuitously offensive' for 137c Sr: despite its broader context of a public debate, expression is nevertheless punishable under 137d Sr, if it is 'exceeding'. The court, however, did not apply this final proportionality test to all expressions and did not clarify why Wilders' expressions were finally not 'exceeding' nor did it provide any further explanation of the term. It rather seemed to trade off the discriminatory character of Wilders' expression with the interest of freedom of expression.

6.5. Nazi propaganda: the *Combat 18* case

In a set of established case law, the Dutch Supreme Court has not only consistently ruled that the propagation of racist ideologies through the distribution of Nazi-symbols constitutes a punishable insult of Jews for the purposes of Article 137c/e Sr (para. 5.5.1 *supra*), but also that it constitutes a punishable form of incitement to hatred and discrimination against Jews on the ground of their race in accordance with 137d/e Sr.[2102] Such expression did not more or less *directly* incite third parties to a well-circumscribed act or feeling unmistakably aimed at the Jewish population, but the expression did incite to hatred against that group because of the *associations* it evoked with Nazism, the Second World War and the Holocaust. Here, it was the

---

2100 The Hague Court of Appeal, Crim. Ch., 23 January 2008, *LJN* BC2576. For a criticism of this reasoning, see: Noorloos 2008, p. 489.

2101 Amsterdam District Court, 23 June 2011, *LJN* BQ9001, para. 3.2.1.

2102 Dutch Supreme Court, 6 December 1983, *NJ* 1984, 601, annotation Mulder; Dutch Supreme Court, 11 March 1986, *NJ* 1987, 462, annotation Mulder; Dutch Supreme Court, 22 March1988, *RR* 1995, p. 297, annotation Pattipawae; Dutch Supreme Court, 21 February 1995, *RR* 1995–2000, p. 43–46, annotation Schalken; Dutch Supreme Court, 21 September 2010, *LJN* BM2483, *NJ* 2010, 518.

historical context that influenced the punishable character of expression; the context of Nazism does not remove but rather attributes a punishable character to expression that might not evidently have a racist purport.

The *Combat 18* case of 2010 fits with this line of case law. The case revolved around the question of whether several t-shirts with the text 'Combat 18', 'whatever it takes' and 'support' were punishable under 137e Sr. Combat 18 is the name of a racist movement in England that originates from the extreme right winged group Blood & Honour. The numbers refer to the first and eighth letter of the alphabet, A and H, the initials of Adolf Hitler. The Hague Court of Appeal acquitted the suspect because the expression regarded 'in isolation' could not be considered as an incitement to hatred and discrimination. The Supreme Court annulled the acquittal of the Hague Court, because the meaning of the expression had to be determined 'in the light of the circumstances of the case and the possible associations it evokes'.[2103]

The question arises as to how the *Combat 18* case, according to which 'associative expression' can be punishable, relates to the *Cancer called Islam* case, according to which expression must 'unmistakably concern a particular group'. In my opinion, the difference between the two cases resides in the discriminatory ground of race and religion respectively. Suggestive criticism of a religion should not be too easily equated with racist propaganda that evokes associations with Nazism, the Second World War or the Holocaust. In principle, expression about Islam and islamization lacks an association with such a racist ideology. When such associations are too easily attributed to expression, this has a chilling effect on freedom of expression.

More generally, the question arises as to which differences exist between the discriminatory grounds of race and religion. It is understandable that ICERD obliges the criminalization of the spreading of ideas based on racial superiority; expression about a particular race per definition constitutes expression about the persons belonging to that race to the extent that a speaker considers race an unalterable characteristic. The spreading of ideas based on the superiority of a particular religion should on the other hand fall under the scope of freedom of religion; such expression can have the aim of converting adherents to another religion. More generally, one can abandon one's religion.[2104]

6.6. The political discussion about immigration: the cases against the *NVU*, *CP'86* and *CD*

On several occasions, the Dutch Supreme Court has upheld a conviction on the ground of 137d/e Sr (and/or 137c) with regard to criticism on the government policy on immigration and on foreigners uttered by political parties and/or its leaders. In

[2103] Dutch Supreme Court, crim. ch., 23 November 2010, *LJN* BM9135.

[2104] Janssen & Nieuwenhuis 2012, p. 197. See also: Vermeulen 2011, p. 661–662.

several cases the question brought before the Supreme Court concerned the question of whether expression about foreigners and non-Dutch residents referred to their nationality in the sense of citizenship and therefore could not be punishable under 137c-e Sr or to their national or ethnic descent and therefore could be punishable under 137c-e Sr (para. 5.4 *supra*).[2105] In 1995, the Dutch Supreme Court upheld a conviction for group insult and incitement to racial hatred or discrimination on the ground of 137e Sr with regard to 154 folders by CP'86 about a 'multiracial hotchpot'. According to the Court, the term 'multiracial hotchpot' regarded in the context of the other words used in the folders such as 'illegal foreigners', 'asylum frauds' and 'uncontrollable crime rates' was aimed at the group of ethnic minorities residing in the Netherlands.[2106] Likewise, in 1996, the Dutch Supreme Court annulled an acquittal for group insult and incitement to racial hatred or discrimination on the ground of 137c-d Sr with regard to several statements made by the leader and members of the CD during television shows that had the following purport: the Dutch society and population had to be protected against the youth gangs of, mixed race marriages with and affirmative action to the benefit of 'foreigners, minorities and asylum seekers'. According to the Court, liability under 137c-e Sr does not depend on the question of whether the expression about these latter groups explicitly refers to their race, but on the nature and context of the expression.[2107]

In other cases the central question brought before the Supreme Court concerned the question of whether 137d Sr is comprised of only direct incitements of third parties to hate or discriminate a particular group, or whether it also encompasses attempts to gain votes in order to create discriminatory laws. In 1978, the Dutch Supreme Court endorsed a conviction for incitement to discrimination on the ground of 137e Sr with regard to electoral pamphlets by the NVU comprising the phrase 'As soon as the NVU has obtained the political power in our country, it will restore order, starting by expelling all people from Suriname and Turkey and other so-called guest workers from the Netherlands.' The Court rejected the plea made by the NVU that the party only wanted to realize the desired distinction, if that was possible in a lawful manner and therefore did not incite to discrimination for the purposes of 137e and 90*quater* Sr.[2108]

Likewise, in 1999, the Dutch Supreme Court confirmed the conviction on the ground of 137d Sr of politician Janmaat, leader of the CD with regard to his statement 'As soon as we get the possibility and the power, we abolish the multicultural society.' uttered during a demonstration. According to the Court of Appeal, a 'multicultural society' consists of different communities, amongst others ethnic minorities'. The expression thus concerned ethnic, thus racial groups, even

2105 Woltjer considers this a question of whether a *direct distinction* on the ground of *nationality* can at the same time constitute an *indirect distinction* on the ground of *race*. See: Woltjer 2002, p. 389.

2106 Dutch Supreme Court, crim. Ch., 2 May 1995, *NJ* 1995, 621, para. 5.3.

2107 Dutch Supreme Court, crim. ch., 16 April 1996, *NJ* 1996, 527, para. 6.4.

2108 Dutch Supreme Court, crim. ch., 14 March 1978, *LJN* AC3463, *NJ* 1978, 664.

though it did not explicitly refer to them. The expression was not punishable in itself, but had to be interpreted in the context of exclamations by other participants in the demonstration, such as 'The Netherlands for the Dutch', 'Our people first' and 'Full is full'. In this context, Janmaat's statement could be not be considered in any other way than aiming to remove ethnic minorities from the Dutch society. The expressions taken as a whole had the purport to incite to hatred and discrimination of ethnic minorities. In casu, Janmaat had not addressed himself to the legislator and simply criticized the government. Janmaat had no parliamentary immunity, because this only applied to expression made in Parliament. He had to act with reserve and caution, because of the influence of public opinion and the bad language generally connected with demonstrations. Co-citizens are entitled to protection against the rousing of public sentiment that impairs their human dignity on the ground of Articles 137c-e Sr.[2109]

In his annotation, Hart objects that multiculturalism is often defined as the co-existence of multiple value systems that are based on multiple ethnic and religious traditions. The fight against such diversity on a normative level therefore does not necessarily form a fight against the existence of ethnic minorities in a society.[2110] Indeed, it seems unlikely that nowadays advocating the abolishment of the multicultural society as such will be punishable under one of the offences of 137c-e Sr. What is more, the present minority policy of the government appears to be precisely aimed at realizing this (para. 2.2 *supra*). This does not signify that the *Janmaat* case of 1999 could be revised, because 'at that time the Court of Appeal was unaware of the fact that the expressed desire was shared by many classes of society.' In 2003, the Dutch Supreme Court therefore rejected this request by the widow of Janmaat.[2111]

6.7. The *Wilders* case: a controversial acquittal for hate speech uttered in the context of a political and public debate about Islam, 'islamization' and Muslim-immigration

It results from the previous paragraphs that in the *Wilders* case many central questions about the interpretation and application of 137d Sr were raised and on several points the decision of the District Court deviated from previous case law. The *Wilders* case encompassed around five years (2007–2011) and formed a significant media-event.[2112] The case concerned several expressions concerning

---

2109 Dutch Supreme Court, Crim. Ch., 18 May 1999, *NJ* 1999, 634, annotation 't Hart.

2110 Annotation 't Hart at: Dutch Supreme Court, Crim. Ch., 18 May 1999, *NJ* 1999, 634.

2111 Dutch Supreme Court, crim. ch., 6 May 2003, *LJN* AF7895.

2112 Most of the case files were published on the Internet and the audiences before the court were broadcasted live on national television. The case proceeded turbulently, was extensively reported in the media and the following public discussion notably focussed on the (im)partiality of the judge in a 'political trial' and the proof concerning 'the truth about Islam'. The public discussion focussed on a diner, during which a judge of the Amsterdam Court of Appeal that

Islam, islamization and Muslims uttered by politician Geert Wilders, leader of the popular nationalist Freedom Party (PVV), in interviews and writings in the media and his film Fitna, which was published on the Internet.

After receiving many complaints about Wilders' expression starting 2007, the public prosecution dismissed the case in 2008, because in the vision of the public prosecution Wilders' expression was not punishable.[2113] Eight affected parties appealed this decision before the Amsterdam Court of Appeal in a so-called Article 12 Sv-procedure (para. 8.2.1 *infra*). In 2009, the Amsterdam Court ordered the public prosecution to prosecute Wilders after all for incitement to hatred and discrimination and group insult.[2114] The public prosecution however persisted in its view that Wilders could not be held liable under 137c-d Sr and requested a complete acquittal.[2115] The affected parties, comprising of many anti-racism, Muslim and other minority associations, constituted as a civil party. Their position in the trial will be discussed in a following paragraph (para. 8.2.2 *infra*). Finally, the Amsterdam District Court acquitted Wilders with regard to all facts charged and rejected the civil claims in 2011.[2116]

The different instances strongly disagreed on the exact rationale of 137c-d Sr and the values that these offences aim to protect. According to the public prosecution, the legislator of 1971 aimed to prevent negative imaging of certain groups with *third parties*, because these third parties could put ideas into action and start to discriminate and neglect those groups. 137c-d Sr was inserted into the section concerning offences against the public order not without reason: they aimed to protect 'first the *public order*, second the honour and good name of certain groups and third – and only indirect – the individual persons forming part of these groups'.[2117] In fact, here the public prosecution fell back on a consideration that originated in the drafting history of the former offences of insult of the public authorities, institutions and groups of the population (137a-d), which were indeed primarily introduced in the 1930s to prevent the disturbance of the peace.

---

had ordered Wilders' prosecution had justified this court order before an expert witness on Islam on the side of the defence, who was equally present at the diner. The Amsterdam District Court had instructed the investigating judge to hear this expert in the Wilders-case about the core tenets of Islam; in this manner Wilders tried to prove his innocence.

2113 Letter of dismissal of the complaints against Wilders, 28 June 2008, Public Prosecution, unpublished.

2114 Amsterdam Court of Appeal 21 January 2009, *LJN* BH0496, *NJ* 2009, 191, annotation Buruma, *Strafblad* 2009, p. 198–208, annotation Fennema, *Mediaforum* 2009, 8, annotation Nieuwenhuis.

2115 Closing speeches of 12 and 15 October 2010, Wilders-case, no. 13/425046–09, Public Prosecutors P. Velleman and B. van Roessel; Closing speech 25 May 2011, Wilders-case, no. 13/425046–09, Public Prosecutors P. Velleman and B. van Roessel.

2116 Amsterdam District Court, 23 June 2011, *Mediaforum* 2011, p. 280–282, annotation Van Noorloos; *Ars Aequi* 2012, p. 288–289, annotation Rozemond; p. 290–294, annotation Schutgens; *NJ* 2012, 370, annotation Mevis.

2117 Closing speech Public Prosecution 25 May 2011, p. 15–18; 34–36.

Contrarily, in the eyes of the Amsterdam Court of Appeal, the offences were precisely aimed at preventing the existence of discriminatory expression in itself because of its negative effect on the *individual persons* forming part of the group targeted in the expression, not on third parties. Wilders' expression raised such a barrier in the public debate that in effect Muslims were excluded from participating in that debate, solely due to their religion. He who excludes another person from the public debate also places him outside the democratic constitutional order.[2118] Hence, while the prosecution opined that opinions are solely punishable on account of their close *consecutive* connection with possible subsequent actions as an effectuation of those opinions, because only these subsequent actions could violate the public order, The Amsterdam Court of Appeal considered certain expression uttered in public debate thus *qualitate qua* as an actual disturbance of the public order.

The different interpretation by the instances of 137d Sr as a prohibition of the more narrow notion of 'incitement to hatred and discrimination' or of the broader notion of 'spreading hatred and discrimination' clearly shows from the discussion about extent to which the different expressions by Wilders must be regarded in their interrelationship in order to determine liability under 137d Sr. The Court of Appeal had considered that Wilders' expressions uttered on different data, regarded in their interrelationship, together were suitable to spread hatred and incite to discrimination.[2119] The prosecution objected that it was principally incorrect to lift certain expression from its direct textual context in order to construe a connection with expression from another publication. The juridical relevant context of one expression was confined to one book, interview or gathering: the mere repetition of an expression that does not incite to hatred or discrimination in this context cannot render it punishable after all.[2120] The Amsterdam District Court chose a middle ground and considered the context of all expression by Wilders included in the case files partly relevant to the question whether Wilders' separate expressions incite to hatred and discrimination.[2121] Wilders' expressions thus had to be interpreted in the light of his political discourse on Islam and Muslim-immigration.

The Amsterdam Court of Appeal had found that Wilders' expressions constituted a punishable form of incitement to hatred, not only on the basis of their content, but also because of their presentation in a peremptory, militant style, characterized by biased and strongly generalizing formulations with a radical purport, a constant repetition and increasing fervour. They thus did not lack a seditious element. In Fitna, the selection of images and information contained the barely concealed suggestion that Islam must be equated with Muslim extremism and that a

2118 Amsterdam Court of Appeal 21 January 2009, *LJN* BH0496, para. 13.2.
2119 Amsterdam Court of Appeal, 21 January 2009, *LJN* BH0496, para. 12.1.2.
2120 Closing speech Public Prosecution 25 May 2011, p. 43–45; 48–49.
2121 Amsterdam District Court, 23 June 2011, *LJN* BQ9001, para. 4.3.1.

connection existed between the growing number of Muslims in the Netherlands and the increasing crime rates in general.[2122]

As discussed in previous paragraphs, the District Court on the other hand, on the whole following the analysis by the prosecution, set strict requirements to the elements of 137d Sr. It required that expression must unmistakably concern a group on the basis of its religion and thus strictly distinguished criticism of Islam from criticism of Muslims. With regard to incitement to hatred it required that expression must include a seditious, *'reinforcing element'* and thereby brought 137d Sr close to 131 Sr. With regard to incitement to discrimination it required that expression more or less directly and explicitly incite to concrete forms of discrimination. Most of Wilders' expressions did not meet these requirements and their punishablility failed for not meeting the *elements of the offence*. This equally applied to the phrase 'We must stop the tsunami of the islamization.' The fact that it was preceded by 'I'm talking about what comes to the Netherlands and breeds here. If you look at the statistics and its development (...) Muslims will migrate from cities to the countryside.' did not alter this.

Subsequently, with regard to expression that did qualify as incitement to discrimination for the purposes of 137d Sr, the District Court applied the method of contextual review and placed Wilders' expression in the broader context of the public debate on Islam, immigration and the multicultural society.[2123] At this stage the court thus reviewed the *proportional application of the offence* in the light of freedom of expression and the circumstances of the case. Following the example of the 'context-decisions' of the Supreme Court, the court gave a very 'subjective interpretation' of Wilders' expression and attached much importance to the perspective of Wilders, who considers his expression necessary to expose social problems. The question arises of whether this manner of attaching importance to freedom of expression does not amount to the requirement of a very high standard for a speaker's intent.

The Court considered Wilders' expression as criticism of government policy or as political proposals that he hopes to realize after he has gained political power in a democratic manner. Concrete political measures that – if effectuated – could violate a statutory prohibition of discrimination are thus not punishable per se. On this point, the decision of the court is difficult to reconcile with previous case law. In her annotation, Noorloos argues that the court, in its interpretation of incitement to discrimination, abandoned the 'militant democracy' idea that would spring from this previous case law.[2124] Finally, the court introduced a new term comparable to the term 'gratuitously offensive' for 137c Sr: despite its broader context of a public debate, expression is nevertheless punishable under 137d Sr, if it is 'exceeding'.

2122 Amsterdam Court of Appeal, 21 January 2009, *LJN* BH0496, para. 12.1.2.
2123 Amsterdam District Court, 23 June 2011, *LJN* BQ9001, para. 3.2.1.
2124 Annotation Noorloos at: Amsterdam District Court, 23 June 2011, *Mediaforum* 2011, p. 282.

Likewise, the prosecution – in my opinion wrongly (para. 6.2 *supra*) – argued that the term discrimination in Article 137d Sr comprised justified forms of making a distinction; incitement to justified distinctions should however not be punishable. In order to correct this, the judge had to make a further balance with the freedom of expression. However, according to the prosecution, the judge did not have to determine whether the proposed measures – if effectuated – would constitute a prohibited form of discrimination, but only whether they were not 'excessive' in relation to the underlying social problem.[2125]

Both the prosecution and the court thus seemed reluctant to give any appreciation of the discriminatory content of the expression. But what is the standard for determining whether expression is 'exceeding' or 'excessive'? One could think of the possible disturbance of the public order or the risk of violent conflicts. In my opinion, this would signify a shift from giving an appreciation of the discriminatory content of the expression to a kind of 'clear-and-present-danger-test'. This would require to not only – as the court and the prosecution did – taking into account the direct textual context and the context of a public debate, but also to take into account the broader social context, in which discrimination and violence against a particular group exists to a greater or lesser extent.

In his annotation, Mevis remarks that the District Court first found the elements 'incitement' against 'people' a useful handle to attribute a specific signification to Article 137d Sr, but subsequently softened these criteria with the review in the context of the public debate. However, as this review did not draw a clear line between lawful and unlawful expression, the court should have better determined punishability under 137d Sr on the basis of the element of 'incitement' that forms the core of 137d Sr and a useful handle for its interpretation. This would also clearly distinguish the group insult of 137c Sr from the incitement to hatred, discrimination or violence of 137d Sr, a distinction to which the Supreme Court had hinted in its *Cancer called Islam* decision.[2126] From this perspective it results that incitements to hatred, discrimination or violence – other than group insults – cannot be tolerated even in the context of a public debate.

Another difference between 137c and d Sr concerns the demonstration of the existence of a sufficient factual basis for negative value judgments. At Wilders' request, the District Court had instructed the examining judge to hear certain expert-witnesses about the 'true core of Islam'.[2127] In this manner, Wilders tried to prove his innocence. It is striking that the District Court did not finally include Wilders' furnishing of proof by means of testimonies about Islam in its motivation. Other than for insult and defamation of a group for the purposes of 137c Sr, in principle the proof of the truth of certain statements does not seem to be a legitimate justification in the field of incitement to hatred, discrimination or violence against persons in the sense of 137d Sr. What matters is whether or not expression

2125 Closing speech Public Prosecution 25 May 2011, p. 61–63.

2126 Annotation Mevis, para. 23–24, at: Amsterdam District Court, 23 June 2011, *LJN* BQ9001.

2127 Amsterdam District Court, 3 February 2010, *LJN* BL1868.

constitutes an 'incitement'. Moreover, proving 'the true tenets of a religion' seems to be simply impossible.

The instances strongly disagreed on the question whether Wilders' expression, notably Fitna, could be qualified as 'associative expression' in relation to – amongst others – the *Combat 18* case. The Amsterdam Court of Appeal had found that the association in Wilders' expression of Islam with Muslims made it not only expression about Muslims, but also a punishable disguised form of incitement to hatred and discrimination. Contrarily, the public prosecution held that 'associative expression' must refer to something that exists outside the expression and the term should not apply to suggestive (visual) language within expression. The *Combat 18* case therefore did not apply to Wilders' expression.[2128] However, the District Court considered that Wilders' expression must not be regarded in isolation and that the associations it evoked formed a relevant context with regard to the question of whether it incited to hatred.[2129]

In my opinion, this case law concerning racist propaganda by means of Nazi symbols that evoke associations with Nazism, the Second World War or the Holocaust should undoubtedly not be applicable to the *Wilders* case that for a large part concerned suggestive criticism of a religion. In principle, Wilders' expression about Islam and islamization lacks an association with such a racist ideology, or at least has a different character. Nazi symbols evoke associations with a racist ideology that forms an actual threat to Jews. In racist propaganda, by means of Nazi symbols Jews are perceived from a Nazi-perspective. Wilders on the other hand compares two books, the Quran and Mein Kampf, and thereby suggests the existence of a resemblance between Muslims and Nazis. This association of Islam with Nazism does not contain an inherent threat to Muslims, because they are not perceived from a Nazi-perspective.

The District Court limited its reference to the Article 10-case law of the ECtHR to the consideration that freedom of expression equally applies to opinions that 'offend, shock or disturb'. It did not delve into the question – central in recent European case law – of whether a politician has a special responsibility to prevent his expression from inciting to religious intolerance and religious hatred and discrimination. This raises surprise, because disregarding the European case law deviates from the general friendly attitude of Dutch law to the ECHR and the judicial interpretation of the speech offences in the light of Article 10 ECHR in specific.

2128 Closing speech Public Prosecution 25 May 2011, p. 46–49.

2129 Unfortunately, the District Court subsequently omitted to take this context into account in its motivation of its appreciation of the expressions, which is why the exact significance of the reference by the court to the *Combat 18*-case remains unclear. See: Amsterdam District Court, 23 June 2011, *LJN* BQ9001, para. 4.3.1.

Moreover, the interpretation of the case law of the ECtHR on so-called 'hate speech' and its application to the *Wilders* case formed a central controversy in the case. In its advice to the public prosecution, Lawson concluded from international law and the case law of ECtHR that Wilders had to be prosecuted. According to cases such as *Soulas, Féret* and *Le Pen*, a politician would have a special responsibility that obliges him to exercise more restraint in public debate.[2130] The Amsterdam Court of Appeal had explicitly considered that Wilders' appeal to freedom of expression constituted an abuse of right in the light of the case law of the ECtHR.[2131] Contrarily, the prosecution and the District Court found the case law of the ECtHR of mere secondary importance and emphasized the special freedom of a politician, but did not specify whether this concerned the political debate in general or the position of the politician within this debate.[2132] The District Court did not refer to the concept of abuse of right, although the proportionality test that expression must not be 'exceeding' might be interpretable as such.[2133]

The strict interpretation of 137d Sr by the District Court in the *Wilders* case thus resulted in a limited scope. Not all expression that the ECtHR describes as hate speech against which limitations are justified fall under this scope. Other than the District Court, in the previously mentioned cases the ECtHR did not require the existence of a strong link between discriminatory opinions and subsequent discriminatory actions in order to justify limitations on freedom of expression. In the application of 137d Sr, the case law of the ECtHR unmistakably influences the 'context of the public debate'. However, even the previously mentioned European case law on hate speech does not determine which limitations are prescribed but only whether limitations are in conformity with Article 10 ECHR or not. In this respect, it is a pity that the ECtHR found the complaint by the As-Soennah mosque in Rotterdam of a violation of Article 9 with regard to Wilders' acquittal inadmissible.[2134] The case could have further clarified the positive obligations to

---

2130 The purport of the advice is published in: Lawson, R. A.'WILD, WILDER, WILDST. Over de ruimte die het EVRM laat voor de vervolging van kwetsende politici', *NJCM-bulletin* 2008, p. 469–484.

2131 Amsterdam Court of Appeal, 21 January 2009, *LJN* BH0496, para. 12.2.2.

2132 Closing speech Public Prosecution 12 October 2010 Part 1, p. 13–19.

2133 Janssen & Nieuwenhuis 2012, p. 202. Generally, in applying 137d the Dutch judge does not establish whether expression constitutes an abuse of rights, which is understandable since the Dutch Constitution lacks this concept (para. 1.2.2 *supra*).

2134 The complaint was denied by letter of 11 October 2012 sent to the applicant (unpublished). The applicant, the As-Soennah mosque in Rotterdam, however argued that Wilders' offensive statements about *Islam* and the *Koran* affected the 'peaceful enjoyment' by its members of their freedom of religion. The mosque might have had more success, if it had argued that Wilders' political proposals were discriminatory towards Muslims and formed an actual threat to the equal exercise of their religion or that Wilders' attribution of an inherent criminal nature to Muslims on account of their religion and culture formed 'a negative stereotyping of the group, capable of impacting on the group's sense of identity and the feelings of self-worth and self-confidence of members of the group, thus affecting the private life of members of the group' (cf. the Aksu-case).

prevent hate speech on the basis of religion on the ground of Articles 8 and or 9 ECHR (Chapter 3, para. 1.6, ftn. 513).

Furthermore, a group of Dutch-Moroccan Muslims have filed a complaint of violation of Article 20(2) ICCPR with regard to Wilders' acquittal before the HRC.[2135] Firstly, it is not certain that the HRC will decide that individuals may invoke Article 20 under the Optional Protocol, but if so, it might for the first time directly deal with a case on the merits on the ground of Article 20(2). Even if the HRC decides that this is the case, on the basis of the strict requirements recently developed for 'incitement' under Article 20(2) ICCPR, it is not certain that the HRC will decide that the acquittal in the Wilders case amounts to a violation of that article. This does not signify that, if Wilders would have been convicted and had filed a complaint of a violation of freedom of expression, his conviction could not be considered permissible under Article 19(3) ICCPR (Chapter 3, para. 5.3, ftn. 633).

One could question whether the success rate of a complaint about Wilders' acquittal might be higher before CERD, even though ICERD is strictly speaking limited to racial discrimination and hate speech. After all, CERD considers itself as competent to deal with cases in which an 'intersectionality between race and religion' exists, i.e. when an utterance treats the religious beliefs of members of a group as the hallmark of their racial and ethnic identity. Wilders' statements that the violent nature of non-western immigrants and Morroccans is a result of their religion and culture may precisely form a pre-eminent case of such an 'intersectionality between race and religion'; inherent negative qualities are attributed to a designated group of a particular national and ethnic background and associated with their religion and culture. This question was underexposed in the *Wilders* case, because the public prosecution and the District Court strictly separated Wilders' prosecution for hate speech on the basis of race and hate speech on the basis of religion and simply found that Wilders' criticism on Moroccans and non-western immigrants did not concern their race.[2136]

Moreover, ICERD is the only treaty among the three that actually obliges its member states to *criminalize* incitement to hatred and discrimination and to effectively enforce such an offence. In fact, the national offences, on the basis of which Wilders was prosecuted, were introduced in order to implement ICERD into Dutch law. Finally, under ICERD the required degree of probability that the speech would succeed in inciting actual action against the target group is in principle less strict than under 20 ICCPR and CERD has recommended the criminalization of several categories of expression when it amounts to 'incitement'. Therefore, the threshold for criminal liability for hate speech under ICERD may be reached earlier (Chapter 3, para. 6.4, ftn. 676).

2135 Communication of 15 November 2011, available at: www.prakkendoliveira.nl/user/file/complaint-ep-geanonimiseerde-s60bw-111111712190.pdf.

2136 Amsterdam District Court, 23 June 2011, *LJN* BQ9001, para. 4.4.

A decision of an international institution about the compatibility of Wilders' acquittal with international law seems important. Although the *Wilders* case did not reach the Dutch Supreme Court, as a notorious public and principled trial, it can have a special signification or even be regarded as preluding a shift in the limits to freedom of expression in the Netherlands. After Wilders' acquittal, in 2011 the Hague Court acquitted a suspect on the ground of 137c-e Sr with regard to several expressions and emails, in which he called Muslims liars and a danger to our Western freedoms. The court obliquely remarked that the expressions did not have a more insulting or hateful character than those of Wilders uttered in the same period.[2137] In 2012 (and 2014), Wilders' Freedom Party initiated a bill proposing the entire abrogation of 137c-d Sr, except for incitement to violence (para. 7.3 *infra*). However, on 18 December 2014, the public prosecution has announced that they will prosecute Wilders for group insult on the basis of race and incitement to hatred and discrimination, following the thousands of complaints filed against him, for promising that he would arrange for there to be 'fewer Moroccans' in the Netherlands to his chanting supporters ('fewer, fewer fewer!') in a café during a local election night and to a TV reporter during a campaign on a market in The Hague. The public prosecution thus apparently viewed these utterances clearly directed against a designated racial group (Morroccans) differently from Wilders' previous statements on Islam as a religion. The case may shed further light on the ambiguous relationship between the special freedoms and responsibilities of a politician with regard to statements made in the context of a public or political debate.

In fact, on 16 December 2014, the Dutch Supreme Court further delineated the freedom of expression of a politician. The Court annulled the decision of the Amsterdam Court of Appeal, in which a politician had been acquitted from the charges of group insult and incitement to discrimination with regard to homophobic expression uttered during a television interview after a local election debate in Amsterdam. The Court of Appeal considered that the politician had not overstepped the limits to free public debate, because his expression was neither threatening nor intimidating, nor did it constitute incitement to hatred or violence. The Supreme Court found, however, that a politician has a responsibility in public debate not to express views that are contrary to the law and the principles of the democratic state. This does not exclusively concern expression that incites hatred, discrimination or violence, but also includes expression that incites intolerance. The Court thereby explicitly referred to the case law of the ECtHR (Dutch Supreme Court, crim. ch. 16 December 2014, *NJB* 2015/160). The decision may form an important compass for the second *Wilders* case.

6.8. Conclusion

In order for expression to constitute the offence of incitement to hatred, discrimination or violence in 137d Sr, it does not have to constitute an explicit call

[2137] The Hague District Court, 11 November 2011, *LJN* BU3944.

to commit a precise determined fact that is punishable under Dutch law. As a result of the case law of the Supreme Court, more implicit incitements to discrimination, hatred or violence can equally constitute the offence of 137d Sr. Theexpression must be likely or sensible to incite others to discrimination, hatred or violence. Hence, 'associations' with a racist ideology and political pamphlets that do not with so many words incite third parties to discriminate themselves, but rather aim to obtain political power in order to install discriminatory laws can be punishable.

With regard to 137d Sr, the Supreme Court uses the same broad interpretation of the discriminatory ground of race and the same criteria for the identification of a racial group as with 137c Sr. In a 'racist context' expression about immigrants or a group of a non-Dutch nationality can be punishable. Similar to137c Sr, 137d Sr comprises expression about part of a racial group, but does not protect individual persons as such. Other than for 137c Sr, with regard to 137d Sr the Supreme Court has not strictly distinguished criticism of a religion from criticism of its adherents and has not established that expression must unmistakably concern a group on the ground of its religion. Neither has the Supreme Court developed a method of contextual review comparable to 137c Sr, in which the context of a public debate can remove liability under 137d Sr.

In several respects the *Wilders* case does not fit into this established case law of the Supreme Court. The court applied the distinction between expression about a religion and expression about its adherents to 137d Sr so restrictively that most criticism of islamization and Muslim-immigration formed lawful criticism of Islam. The court required that expression more or less literally, direct and in strong terms incites to hatred or concrete described acts of discrimination against a religious group. Subsequently, the court applied the contextual review of 137c Sr to 137d Sr by analogy. As a result, Wilders' political proposals on measures against Muslims uttered in the context of the public debate on Muslim-immigration and the multicultural society were not per definition 'exceeding' even though they might constitute a prohibited form of discrimination.

7. Modifications of 137c-d Sr

After their introduction into Dutch law in 1971, the hate speech bans have successfully been extended to the discriminatory grounds of sex, sexual preference and handicap (7.1). Given the increasing importance attached to the free public debate, the question arises whether is would be desirable to insert a free-speech clause into the hate speech offences (7.2). Several draft proposals to limits the scope of the offences have, however, remained without effect (7.3). The analysis results in a general conclusion about the evolution of the criminalization of hate speech in Dutch law (7.4).

7.1. Extension of the scope of 137c-e Sr to the discriminatory grounds of sex, sexual preference and handicap

In 1991, the scope of Articles 137c-e Sr was extended to the discriminatory grounds of sex and hetero- or homosexual orientation.[2138] In 2005 the scope of Articles 137c-e Sr was extended to the discriminatory ground of handicap.[2139] The extension of 1991 formed part of the larger development of the anti-discrimination policy: both insulting expression and expression inciting to hatred and discrimination could lead to negative imaging of a particular group which could lead to their discrimination and subordination.[2140] However the government subsequently did distinguish between the offences of 137c and d Sr.

Unlike in France, the government thought that the insertion of the discriminatory ground of sex into the offence of group insult was unnecessary, because discrimination against women would not originate in insults against women, but in existing opinions about the 'natural' role of women in society. As the criminalization of anti-women insults would not contribute to a better position of women in society, in this field freedom of expression therefore prevailed.[2141] This non-falsified hypothesis is disputable and the question arises as to why this argument would not also apply to racial or religious insults.[2142] An amendment to insert the discriminatory ground of sex into the offence of group insult in order to counter forms of pornography was rejected.[2143] Contrarily, Article 137d Sr was broadened to incitement to hatred, discrimination or violence against people on the ground of hetero- or homosexual orientation *and* sex. The government thought that here the insertion of the discriminatory ground of sex was desirable to prevent actual discrimination and aggression against women.[2144]

The insertion of the discriminatory ground of hetero- or homosexual orientation in both 137c and d Sr was desirable, because discrimination of homosexuals, other than of women, was often the result of repeated public insults and Articles 137c-d Sr would both prevent aggression against homosexuals.[2145] Several Christian political parties that rejected the homosexual practice for constituting a sin feared that the insertion of the discriminatory ground of hetero- or homosexual orientation would render the expression of traditional Christian convictions about the homosexual practice punishable. Therefore, they desired to limit the discriminatory ground of sexuality in 137c-d Sr to sexual inclination. During the parliamentary debates this was rejected: sexual orientation comprised both sexual preference and

2138 Act of 14 November 1991, Stb. 623.

2139 Act of 10 March 2005, Stb. 111.

2140 *Kamerstukken II*, 20239, 1988–1989, nr. 3, p. 4, nr. 8, p. 1.

2141 *Kamerstukken II*, 20239, 1988–1989, nr. 3, p. 4.

2142 For a criticism see: Rosier 1997, p. 91 *et seq.*

2143 *Kamerstukken II*, 20239, 1988–1989, nr. 3, p. 4, nr. 5, p. 5–6.

2144 *Kamerstukken II*, 20239, 1988–1989, nr. 3, p. 2.

2145 *Kamerstukken II*, 20239, 1988–1989, nr. 3, p. 4–5.

its manifestation (thus sexual practice), because such conduct of adults among themselves cannot form a ground to hinder people in their social functioning.[2146] Sexual preference comprises hetero-, homo- and bisexuality, but not transsexuality.[2147] In my opinion, paedophilia should also be omitted because people should only be protected in their lawful conduct.

Unlike in France, the Dutch legislator attempted to meet the objections raised against the ground of hetero- or homosexual orientation, not by limiting the *scope* of 137d Sr to incitement to *certain forms of discrimination criminalized in the Dutch Criminal Code*, but by introducing a *justifying ground*. In the original draft a new Article 137f Sr was inserted, which exempted from liability under Articles 137 c-e Sr expression that has the purport to give an opinion on the protection of public interests that is not gratuitously offensive. It was feared that the extension of the scope of Articles 137c-e Sr to the discriminatory grounds of sex, and hetero- or homosexual preference would seriously interfere with freedom of expression. Expression of an innocent character, such as honest commentary on matters of public concern, should not be punishable. However, it was thought that once an expression would fall under *137d Sr*, it could not nevertheless constitute honest commentary on matters of public concern that were not gratuitously offensive. The proposed Article 137f Sr would therefore notably be applicable to insulting expression for the purposes of *137c Sr* and would scarcely be applied to insults about groups on the basis of their *race or religion*. Finally the insertion of this due regard-clause was however rejected, because it was feared that the proposed Article 137f Sr would violate ICERD. Besides, the Christian Parties had argued that the clause was too selective in its justifying ground; Articles 137c-e Sr not only threatened the free expression of political opinions but also the free proclamation of religious convictions, thus freedom of religion.[2148]

ICERD, however, also required that the principles of the Universal Declaration of Human Rights were taken into account and with regard to Article 4 ICERD freedom of expression in particular. But the ICERD-Committee that was established by the Convention opined that the convention already struck the right balance with freedom of expression. The Committee therefore rejected the insertion by the Member States of extra elements to the offences, such as the requirement of the disturbance of the public order or the risk of violence.[2149] Likewise, the Dutch legislator of the 1970s seemed to opine that his formulation of Articles 137c-e Sr equally precisely struck the right balance, because he did not insert a free speech clause in 137c-d Sr. He thereby deviated from the system of Articles 266 and 261 and seemed to afford a certain priority to the protection of *racial* groups against discrimination over the interest of freedom of expression.

2146 *Kamerstukken II*, 20239, 1988–1989, nr. 5, p. 19.

2147 Leeuwarden Court of Appeal, 13 January 1995, *NJ* 1995, 243.

2148 *Kamerstukken II*, 20239, 1988–1989, nr. 5, p. 2–3.

2149 Mahalic & Mahalic 1987, p. 98.

In the 1990s, with the insertion of the new discriminatory grounds the question as to how to balance the criminalizations in Articles 137c-e Sr with freedom of expression became weightier. However, it was nevertheless feared that proposed Article 137f Sr would undermine the functioning of Articles 137c-e Sr. Finally, it was thought that when applying Articles 137c-e Sr judges would attach importance to freedom of expression even without the existence of proposed Article 137f Sr. According to the Minister for Justice, the rejection of proposed Article 137f Sr did not mean that an appeal to freedom of expression could no longer be made, but that there was no reason to give a detailed description of the situations, in which an appeal to freedom of expression could be made.[2150]

7.2. Desirability of a free speech clause

Indeed, even without the existence of proposed Article 137f Sr, since the 1990s the judge has increasingly attached importance to freedom of expression through the method of contextual review. It is not surprising that the method of contextual review was first developed with regard to expression concerning homosexuals, such as rejection of the homosexual practice or same sex marriage, thus with regard to the discriminatory ground of sexual orientation, before it was subsequently also applied to expression concerning Jews or Muslims, such as denial of the holocaust or criticism of Muslim-immigration, thus with regard the discriminatory ground of race and religion. Although the free public debate on matters of public concern has generally gained importance over time, the specific weight of freedom of expression in one case however remains dependent on the issue concerned and the specific discriminatory ground. This is understandable, because proposals that oppose same sex marriage are not punishable to the same extent as proposals that oppose interracial marriage and pleas for an immigration policy based on race are not punishable to the same extent as pleas to abolish Dutch 'institutionalized multiculturalism'.[2151]

The criteria that the Supreme Court and lower courts have developed for the application of 137c and d Sr raised many questions[2152] and might give reason for the current legislator to give a more detailed description of the situations in which an appeal to freedom of expression could be made after all. In my opinion, there are notably three ways in which the legislator could incorporate the interest of freedom of expression into Articles 137c-d Sr. Firstly, he could insert extra elements to the

---

2150 *Kamerstukken I*, 1990–1991, 20239, nr. 76a, p. 5.

2151 Nieuwenhuis & Janssen 2011, p. 100.

2152 The questions that raised from cases such as *Herbig, Janmaat, Cancer called Islam, Combat 18, Hofstadgroep* and *Wilders* were: must the criterion that expression unmistakably concerns a group apply to all discriminatory grounds? Must it apply both with regard to 137c and d? Must the contextual review apply to both 137c and d? Which associations can partly determine the signification of expression? How to distinguish between legitimate and illegitimate criticism on behavior of a religious group?

offence that limit the scope of the offences and elevate the threshold for punishability, such as defining what constitutes insult or incites or by specifying that expression must constitute a 'direct insult' or 'direct incitement'.[2153] Such specifications would, however, not fit in with the Dutch system of open statutory norms that accommodate judicial interpretation and balancing in concrete cases. The same holds true for the creation of more specific offences next to 137c and d Sr, such as a separate offence of holocaust denial. This would open up a Pandora's box in relation to the creation of more and more specific speech offences depending on the development of ideas on punishability of expression.

Finally, the legislator could insert a free speech clause that exempts from liability expression uttered in public debate on a matter of public concern that is not gratuitously offensive or excessive after all. As such a clause would merely consolidate an existing judicial practice, the question arises as to what would be its exact added value? In my opinion, it would oblige the judge in each case to explicitly take into account freedom of expression and force him to use in his motivation a specific method or order that could safeguard that the different stages of the balancing-test are not merged into one single test.[2154] Furthermore, the clause could sharply distinguish between the discriminatory grounds of race and religion in order to allow relative far-reaching limitations to expression concerning race but to allow free severe criticism on religious convictions and practices that can reasonably be connected with a religion. Finally, the clause could sharply distinguish between 137c and 137d Sr and determine that the context of a public debate can only remove the punishable character of group insults in the sense of 137c Sr, provided that the expression is not gratuitously offensive.

It is difficult to imagine that once expression has been found to incite to hatred, discrimination or violence, the context of a public debate can nevertheless justify such a threat. However, further clarification is needed in relation to the limitations to expression that incites to discrimination pursuant to Article 137d Sr. In my opinion, 137d Sr criminalizes incitement of third parties to make unjustified distinctions based on race or religion etc., thus prohibited forms of discrimination. This signifies that the judge must give an appreciation of the (un)lawfulness of the discriminatory content of the expression and cannot shift the threshold for punishability to expression that contains the risk of a disturbance of the public order or of violent conflicts. Being a normative term, 'unjustified distinction' already entails a balance by the judge. Strictly speaking, the insertion of a free speech clause is therefore unnecessary. However, in order to give sufficient room to

---

2153 Nieuwenhuis proposes the limitation of group insult to slander/libel and terms of abuse or the entire abrogation of 137c Sr and the abrogation of the vague 'incitement to hatred' in 137d Sr. See: Nieuwenhuis, A.J., Na de zaak Wilders. Is de wetgever nu aan zet?, *Ars Aequi*, December 2011, p. 869.

2154 For example connecting freedom of expression with the insulting or inciting character of expression rather than a suspects' intent or requiring that the gratuitously offensive or excessive character of expression remains a final proportionality test.

political proposals that do not directly incite third parties to discriminate, but – merely – aim to reform the law, the legislator could insert a free speech clause determining that the context of a political or public debate can remove the punishable character of incitement to discrimination in the sense of 137d Sr, provided that the expression does not violate people's human dignity by aiming at the destruction of their fundamental rights. Another possibility would be to adopt the proposal of the State Commission to insert a general provision into the Dutch Constitution declaring that the Netherlands is a constitutional state that respects and guarantees human dignity. Such a provision can partly function as a guideline for the interpretation of Articles 137c-e Sr (para. 1.2.3 *supra*). Thus the principle of human dignity becomes a final constitutional barrier against 'hate speech'.[2155]

7.3. Draft proposals to modify 137c-e Sr in the light of freedom of expression

While in France several draft proposals have been made that proposed to *broaden* the scope of the French hate speech bans in order to more effectively fight the diffusion of racist propaganda and xenophobe ideas, in the Netherlands several draft proposals have been made that proposed to *limit* the scope of the Dutch hate speech bans in the light of freedom of expression. In May 2009, the Liberal Party launched a plan to modify the offences that to a certain extent corresponds with American free speech doctrine.[2156] The plan suggested two methods to broaden the scope of freedom of expression in the Netherlands. The first method was to maintain the offence of incitement to violence, but to abrogate the offences of blasphemy, group insult and incitement to hatred, to abrogate incitement to discrimination or limit it to direct incitement to discrimination and to define discrimination restrictively. The second method was to introduce a clause that exempts a person that participates in public debate from liability under group insult, incitement to hatred and if desired incitement to discrimination.

Peters has welcomed the plan, because it affords a preferred position to expression that contributes to the public debate and therefore fits in with his plea to follow the American free speech doctrine on this point (para. 5.11 *supra*).[2157] The plan, however, faded under severe criticism on the statement of the leader of the Liberal Party Rutte that holocaust denial should be allowed, which is a pity due to the fact that the plan could have induced a profound debate on the necessity of further specification of the hate speech bans.

After Wilders' acquittal, in September 2012 Driessen, representative of Wilders' Freedom Party, initiated a bill that revived the issue but remained without effect, because Driessen subsequently left the party. On 10 October 2014 another

[2155] If the prohibition of constitutional review of Article 120 of the Constitution would be abrogated.

[2156] 'Opzet wijziging wetboek Vrijheid van Meningsuiting', 27 May 2009, *Elsevier* op: http://tinyurl.com/ycpbbcb.

[2157] Peters, J. A., 'Rutte en de vrijheid van meningsuiting', *Mediaforum* 2009–6, p. 237.

representative of the Freedom Party, Van Klaveren, proposed a new but identical bill. In its critical advice of 5 December 2014, the Council of State concluded that the bill is contrary to the Netherlands' obligations under international law (EU Council Framework; Additional Protocol to the Convention on Cybercrime; ICERD; and ICCPR).[2158] Indeed, the bill is very far-reaching, because it proposes the entire abrogation of 137c-d Sr, except for incitement to violence. According to the explanatory memorandum to the bill, the bill primarily aims to restore the '*lex certa* principle'. In the eyes of the initiator, Articles 137c-d Sr are too vague and for this reason must be abrogated.[2159] However, from this perspective it is surprising that the initiator subsequently argues that the bill does not prevent any civil action based on Article 6:162 BW, one of the most open statutory norms in Dutch law.[2160]

Furthermore, the initiator argues that the interests and values protected in 137c-d Sr are already sufficiently protected by the offences of defamation and insult of an individual, incitement to violence, incitement to criminal offences, threatening and factual discrimination.[2161] This argument disregards the fact that 137c-d Sr form independent offences that protect groups and do not formulate racist motives as an aggravating circumstance to generic offences that protect individuals as 'hate crimes' do and thus are not *leges speciales* to 261, 266, 131, 285 or 90 quater and 429*quater* Sr as *leges generales*. Hence, if 137c-d Sr would be abrogated, these generic offences cannot simply take over their function; there will be a – either desired or not – gap in the protection of non-further specified racial or religious groups against insults or incitement to hatred or discrimination that do not refer to any person in particular. Subsequently, the initiator argues that the generic offences would already comply with the obligations of international treaties, such as ICERD, the Additional Protocol to the Convention on Cybercrime and the EU Framework Decision for combating Racism and Xenophobia. One could object that the rationale of these treaties is precisely to oblige the state to explicitly criminalize certain expression *with a racist purport*. Moreover, the fact that the offences of defamation and insult of an individual can only be prosecuted on complaint of the victim does not fit in with the general rationale of these treaties that the state has the positive obligation to actively fight racism and discrimination.

Finally, the initiator argues that the obligations of the international treaties would conflict with the 'consensus in the case law of the ECtHR on the preferred position of political opinions regardless of their content.' The bill aims 'to contribute to this consensus by abrogating 137c-d Sr'.[2162] However, as previously mentioned, the European case law on hate speech does not determine which limitations are prescribed but only whether limitations are in conformity with 10 ECHR or not.

[2158] *Kamerstukken II*, 33369, nr. 1–2. *Kamerstukken II*, 34051, nr. 1–2. *Kamerstukken II*, 34051, nr. 4–5.

[2159] *Kamerstukken II*, 34051, nr. 3, p. 3–4.

[2160] *Kamerstukken II*, 34051, nr. 3, p. 8.

[2161] *Kamerstukken II*, 34051, nr. 3, p. 4; 7.

[2162] *Kamerstukken II*, 34051, nr. 3, p. 4–8.

The difference between the French and Dutch proposals for law reform clearly shows the different underlying characteristics of French and Dutch law. In French legal doctrine, the preservation of specific hate speech bans is justified, because specific legislation ensures legal certainty and effectiveness in the protection of the value of (individual) human dignity as part of the public order. The decriminalization of defamation and insult of an individual person is on the other hand justified, because these offences protect mere personal interests.

Contrarily, in Dutch legal doctrine, the abrogation of the hate speech bans is justified with the preservation of the generic offences of defamation, insult and incitement to criminal offences. Such open norms enable further judicial interpretation and balancing in concrete cases. However, in my opinion such open norms can neither effectively ensure freedom of expression nor non-discrimination, if there is no legal certainty about which discriminatory expression they cover. I doubt whether these generic offences could function as a sufficient criminal safety net, an *ultimum remedium*, for discriminatory expression that targets not one particular identifiable individual person but larger groupings.

7.4. Conclusion

In 1991 and 2005, the scope of Articles 137c-e Sr was extended to the discriminatory grounds of sex and hetero- or homosexual orientation, respectively handicap. The Dutch legislator of 1991 attempted to meet the objections raised against the ground of hetero- or homosexual orientation, not by limiting the *scope* of 137d Sr to incitement to *certain forms of discrimination criminalized in the Dutch Criminal Code*, but by introducing a free speech clause in new Article 137f Sr. Article 137f Sr was finally rejected, because it was feared that it would undermine the functioning of Articles 137c-e Sr. Nevertheless, the judge has increasingly attached importance to freedom of expression through the method of contextual review, starting with regard to expression concerning homosexuals and subsequently with regard to criticism of immigration policies or the multi-cultural or multi-religious society.

The fact that the criteria that the Supreme Court and lower courts have developed for the application of 137c and d Sr raise many questions might be a reason for the legislator to give a more detailed description of the situations in which an appeal to freedom of expression could be made after all. There have been several plans to modify Articles 137c-e Sr in the light of a more robust freedom of expression that sought to entirely abrogate the offences, limit the scope of the offences by specifying the existing elements of the offences or adding new elements to the offences, or insert a free speech clause, which might fit best in the Dutch system of open norms that accommodates judicial interpretation and balancing.

III. THE GOVERNMENT AS THE SOLE GUARDIAN OF THE PUBLIC ORDER

8. THE ENGAGEMENT OF PROSECUTIONS

In the Netherlands, the public prosecution has the exclusive right to engage in the public prosecution on the ground of the hate speech bans (8.1). However, civil parties can appeal the decision of the public prosecution not to prosecute a particular fact on the ground of the hate speech bans before the Court of Appeal. Only complaints by 'interested parties' are admissible. If the Court of Appeal orders the public prosecution to prosecute, they have no special position in the criminal case on the merits as joint civil parties, which can be well illustrated by the *Wilders* case (8.2). The analysis results in a general conclusion about the enforcement of the hate speech bans in the Netherlands (8.3).

8.1. The engagement of prosecutions by the public prosecutor

In the Netherlands, the public prosecution is charged with the prosecution of criminal offences pursuant to Article 124 of the Judicial System Act (Wet RO). Pursuant to the principle of opportunity in Article 167 j 242 of the Dutch Code of Criminal Procedure (Sv) the public prosecution has a discretionary power in relation to whether to prosecute or not. Under the principle of opportunity the decision to prosecute depends not only on the feasibility of the prosecution but also on the public interest in the prosecution.[2163]

The exclusive right of the Dutch public prosecution to engage public prosecutions of criminal offences prevents criminal prosecutions from being dependant on the personal views of the injured parties.[2164] Unlike in France, a person who has personally suffered damages directly caused by a violation of a felony or misdemeanor cannot therefore set in motion a public prosecution in order to obtain reparation of damages as a joint party. This has not always been the case. When the Kingdom of the Netherlands was annexed by Napoleon's France in 1811, the French *Code d'Instruction Criminelle* entered into force that provided in this 'action civile'. The civil action was abrogated by the Code of Criminal Procedure in 1838 and this decision was maintained in the current code that dates back to

---

2163 Article 167 Sv. reads: '1) Indien naar aanleiding van het ingestelde opsporingsonderzoek het openbaar ministerie van oordeel is dat vervolging moet plaats hebben, door het uitvaardigen van een strafbeschikking of anderszins, gaat het daartoe zoo spoedig mogelijk over; 2) Van vervolging kan worden afgezien op gronden aan het algemeen belang ontleend. Het openbaar ministerie kan, onder het stellen van bepaalde voorwaarden, de beslissing of vervolging plaats moet hebben voor een daarbij te bepalen termijn uitstellen.'

2164 Tekst & Commentaar, Wetboek van Strafvordering, Artikel 167, Valkenburg, para. 1a.

1926.[2165] Criminal justice was (and is) considered to be a *public* interest and could not be governed by personal feelings of revenge. Affording a right of prosecution to affected parties was undesirable, because it would cause an increase in minor cases.[2166]

This does not signify that criminal law does not take into account the interests of victims in a prosecution. The prosecution of the offences of defamation or insult of an individual person of Articles 261 and 266 Sr depends on a prior complaint filed by an injured party.[2167] Contrary to France, this equally applies to defamation or insult of an individual person *on the ground of his race or religion etc.*, because such expression falls under these generic offences (para. 5.2 *supra*). The prosecution of the hate speech bans of Articles 137c-e Sr on the other hand does not depend on a prior complaint filed by an injured party. The decision to prosecute discriminatory expression under Articles 137c-e Sr is regulated by the principle of opportunity of the public prosecution.

The principle of opportunity is, however, curtailed by the Discrimination Directive of the College of the Attorneys General that determines the prosecution policy with regard to discrimination.[2168] The first Discrimination Directive was drafted in 1999 in order to more effectively and coherently enforce the anti-racism and discrimination laws.[2169] The directive was renewed in 2003 and 2007 and still remains in force.[2170] It more specifically concerns the prosecution of Articles 137c-g and Article 429*quater* Sr and generic offences 'with a discriminatory aspect', including defamation or insult of an individual person if motivated by discrimination or hatred.[2171] It establishes, as a general rule, that if the violation of these offences can be proven and the suspect is liable to punishment, in principle the suspect must be prosecuted, given the negative effect of insufficient enforcement and the preventive effect of prosecution. Hence, in cases concerning discrimination, opportunity is assumed in advance. The decision to dismiss a case for policy reasons must be taken with restraint; opportunity considerations can only lead to a dismissal in exceptional cases. Under no circumstances, the potential martyrdom of a suspect or the potential exploitation by the suspect of the forum that a public

2165 De Lange, A. De beklagprocedure en criminele politiek, *Strafblad* 2009, p. 480.

2166 *Bijlagen II*, 1913–14, nr. 3, p. 55.

2167 Tekst & Commentaar, Wetboek van Strafrecht, Inleidende opmerkingen bij Titel XVI, Van Maurik/Janssens, aant. 10.

2168 Discrimination Directive, 2007A010, *Stb.* 2007, 233.

2169 Discrimination Directive, 1999A008.

2170 Discrimination Directive, 2003A005; Discrimination Directive, 2007A010, *Stb.* 2007, 233.

2171 Other than France, Dutch law does not have so called 'hate crimes', being criminal offences that stipulate a suspect's racist motive as an aggravating circumstance and element of the offence. However, the Discrimination Instruction requires a 50–100 percentage increase in the penalty for generic offences that are motivated by discrimination or hatred. The directive also requires that the discriminatory background of the offence be announced in the prosecutor's closing statement.

prosecution would afford him to expound his ideas can form a ground to dismiss a case.[2172]

In the past, this latter argument often formed a ground for the public prosecution not to prosecute discriminatory expression uttered by extreme right-winged politicians. For example, in the 1980s the public prosecution prosecuted a suspect for having distributed discriminatory pamphlets during a manifestation of the extreme right winged political party Centrumpartij, but refrained from prosecuting politician Janmaat, the leader of the party, even though he was primarily responsible for the content of the pamphlets, had confessed his guilt and had asked for the acquittal of the other distributors. The public prosecution did not contradict the thesis that it had aimed to prevent Janmaat from becoming a martyr and having potential electoral advantage from a trial. According to the Court of Appeal, the prosecution thereby aimed to influence the results of the elections, which did not form a public interest that prevailed over the interest in prosecution.[2173] In his annotation, 't Hart criticizes the Court of Appeal for twisting things around; the prosecution aimed to prevent a politician from abusing the administration of criminal justice as an instrument for his own electoral advantage. The prevention of such manipulation did form a public interest.[2174, 2175]

Pursuant to the Discrimination Directive, the prosecution can only dismiss a case for reasons of feasibility, thus on technical grounds – except for exceptional cases. In my opinion, determining liability under 137c-d Sr does not, however, entail an ordinary appreciation of the proof of the facts like in any other case. The question of whether a suspect has committed the charged facts requires an interpretation and the attribution of a certain meaning to expression and a balancing test with the interest of a suspect's freedom of expression that is incorporated into the statutory elements of the offence (para. 5.8;6.4 *supra*). These factors make it difficult to anticipate the decision by the judge.

Moreover, technical and policy arguments seem to easily merge into one another.[2176] In 2008, the prosecution dismissed the complaints in the *Wilders* case,

2172 Discrimination Directive, 2007A010, *Stb.* 2007, 233, para. 2–3; 5.

2173 Dutch Supreme Court, crim. Ch., 21 June 1988, *NJ* 1988, 1021, annotation 't Hart.

2174 Annotation 't Hart para. 6 at: Dutch Supreme Court, crim. Ch., 21 June 1988, *NJ* 1988, 1021. While the District Court had convicted the suspect, the Court of Appeal found the decision to prosecute the suspect but not Janmaat arbitrary and declared the prosecution inadmissible. The Supreme Court finally annulled the decision of the Court of Appeal for being insufficiently motivated, because it was limited to the decision not to prosecute Janmaat and did not take into account the decision to prosecute the suspect.

2175 Courts generally reject a suspects' defence that his expression is prosecuted for a political purpose. The prosecution of political opinions uttered in public debate does not necessarily constitute a political trial. See: Dutch Supreme Court, Crim. Ch., 18 May 1999, *NJ* 1999, 634, annotation 't Hart; Dutch Supreme Court, Crim. Ch., 16 April 1996, *NJ* 1996, 527; 's-Hertogenbosch Court of Appeal, Crim. Ch., 10 November 2006, *LJN* BH3383.

2176 An undisputable technical dismissal formed the decision in 2010 not to prosecute Prime Minister Rutte with regard to his statements on dual citizenship during a parliamentary debate, because

because it considered Wilders' criticism of Islam, islamization and Muslims not to be punishable.[2177] Dommering criticizes the prosecution for having resorted to technical grounds, while in fact the dismissal constituted a policy decision.[2178] Indeed, the idea that a criminal prosecution of Wilders would inevitably result in his acquittal seems untenable, considering the different appreciations of the case by legal scholars, the legal advisors of the prosecution and the court order of the Amsterdam Court of Appeal (para. 6.7 *supra*). This raises the question about the tenability of the directive itself.

In the last decade the prosecution has dismissed more complaints against severe criticism of Islam and Muslims.[2179] In 2003, the prosecution dismissed the complaints against politician Hirsi Ali for calling Islam 'backward' and prophet Mohammed a 'pedophile' in a national newspaper. In 2009, the prosecution found the distribution of the Danish cartoons by Wilders on his website and by a national television program not punishable under 137c and d Sr, because they did not concern Muslims as a group, but Islam as a religion. In 2010, the prosecution finally dropped charges against Dutch cartoonist Gregorius Nekschot with regard to several cartoons critical of Islam and Muslims. Although it found the cartoons punishable under 137c and d Sr, Nekschot had been arrested and put in pretrial detention in 2008, which caused much public and political debate.[2180] Since then, the cartoons were no longer online, a considerable period of time had passed and no new complaints were filed.

The prosecution has been criticized by Dommering for applying double standards with regard to Articles 137c-e Sr that it applied to sensitive issues in the secular western society such as the Holocaust and not to sensitive issues for Muslims such as the Mohammed-cartoons.[2181] In 2009, although the prosecution found the Auschwitz cartoon punishable under 137c Sr, it dismissed the case under

---

nationality does not form a protected ground and the Prime Minister enjoyed parliamentary immunity on the ground of Article 71 Dutch Constitution. More questionable formed the dismissal in 2010 with regard to the statement 'Intifada, intifada, free Palestine' uttered by a socialist politician during a demonstration against the invasion by the Israeli army of the Gaza Strip, while other participants exclaimed 'Hamas, hamas, Jews to the gas'. According to the prosecution, the politician was not responsible for expressions of others and his statement constituted mere criticism of the State of Israel that incited to non-violent resistance. The press releases by the public prosecution with regard to the dismissals are accessible at: www.om.nl.

2177 Letter of dismissal of the complaints against Wilders, 28 June 2008, Public Prosecution, *unpublished.*

2178 Dommering, E. J., 'Zwijgen is zilver, wraken is goud. De tunnelvisie van het OM in het Wilders-proces' (essay), *De Groene Amsterdammer* 4 November 2010.

2179 The press releases by the public prosecution with regard to the dismissals are accessible at: www.om.nl.

2180 *Handelingen II*, 20 May 2008, 2007–2008, 85, p. 6010–6037; *Handelingen II*, 16 June 2008, 2007–2008, 85, p. 6989–6992.

2181 Dommering, E.J., 'De dubbele moraal van het groepsbeledigen in cartoons: Een fictieve redevoering ter gelegenheid van het niet op 30 september gevierde vijfjarige jubileum van de Deense cartoonrellen' (9/30), *NJB* 2010, p. 2264–2268.

the condition that the cartoon would be removed. Initially, the AEL met this condition, but the dismissal in the Danish cartoon-case brought the AEL to replace its cartoon on its website. The prosecution thus nevertheless pressed charges and finally the Supreme Court confirmed that the cartoon constituted an insult to Jews, because it insinuated that Jews deliberately invented the Holocaust.

In the *AEL* case, the status of the Discrimination Directive was explicitly under discussion. Although the directive does not constitute a general mandatory regulation, pursuant to principles of due process the instruction binds the public prosecution and suspects can therefore directly appeal to it in court and argue that the prosecution has acted contrary to it.[2182] The Court of Appeal, however, rejected the suspect's defence that the directive requires expression to be 'unmistakably punishable', which could not be said of the cartoon in question; it would be undesirable, if the prosecution could not bring a doubtful case to court in order to get a decision by the judge.[2183] In my opinion, the latter can equally form a valid argument to prosecute certain forms of harsh criticism of Islam and Muslims; the somewhat structural dismissals in this field have cost legal uncertainty by a lack of case law and social unrest by a lack of a judicial decision in concrete cases.

This social unrest might be partly explained by the little involvement in the Dutch prosecution policy of victims or civil society in general. Certainly, the aim of the Discrimination Directive is to provide an effective response to racism and discrimination through a close cooperation between specialized referent magistrates of the public prosecution charged with the enforcement of anti-racism and discrimination laws, local authorities, the police and regional anti-discrimination services.[2184] But other than in France, the Dutch policy does however not establish dense relations between these officials and civil society for collaboration in a joint fight against racism and discrimination by means of so-called framework conventions with anti-racism associations or monthly consultations with such associations organized by the Parisian offices of the prosecution in order to discuss the engagement of prosecutions.

Moreover, pursuant to Article 167 sub 3 Sv, 51a Sv and the Discrimination Directive, the prosecution must give a written motivated notification of his final decision to prosecute, dismiss or settle a case to the complainants about a violation of an offence, but the law does not prescribe that the prosecution hears complainants in the decision-process. In principle, victims and other affected parties thus have no part in the decision making process of the public prosecution. It is therefore good that affected parties can appeal a dismissal in court.

2182 It nevertheless constitutes written law subject to interpretation by the Supreme Court in the sense of Article 79 of the Judicial System Act. The Supreme Court established this general rule applicable to all instructions by the College of Attorneys General in: Dutch Supreme Court, Crim. Ch., 19 June 1990, *NJ* 1991, 119. See: Tekst & Commentaar, Wetboek van Strafvordering, Artikel 167, Valkenburg, para. 5b.

2183 Arnhem Court of Appeal, Crim. Ch., 19 August 2010, *LJN* BN4204, *NJFS* 2010, 294, para. 3.1.1.3.

2184 Discrimination Directive, 2007A010, *Stb.* 2007, 233.

8.2. Appealing the dismissal of the prosecution

8.2.1. Complaint procedure of Article 12 Sv

The monopoly and opportunity of the public prosecution, said to be quite unique from a comparative perspective,[2185] affords the government much power that calls for control. In order to prevent possible arbitrariness of the public prosecution, the Dutch legislator of 1926 created Article 12 Sv,[2186] according to which an interested party can appeal the decision of the prosecution (not to prosecute, not to further prosecute or to settle a case) before the Court of Appeal.[2187] The court can review whether prosecution must take place and order the prosecution to nevertheless prosecute with regard to specific criminal facts (offences) or refuse to do so in the public interest.[2188] Against the decision of the court no appeal in cassation is possible. Although in the field of discrimination appeals against dismissals have often been rejected,[2189, 2190] certain appeals that were allowed finally resulted in landmark decisions by the Supreme Court or a lower court, such as the cases against

---

2185 De Lange 2009, p. 477.

2186 Corstens, G.J.M., *Het Nederlandse Strafprocesrecht,* Deventer: Kluwer 2008, p. 545.

2187 Article 12 sub 1 reads: 'Wordt een strafbaar feit niet vervolgd, de vervolging niet voortgezet, of vindt de vervolging plaats door het uitvaardigen van een strafbeschikking, dan kan de rechtstreeks belanghebbende daarover schriftelijk beklag doen bij het gerechtshof, binnen het rechtsgebied waarvan de beslissing tot niet vervolging of niet verdere vervolging is genomen, dan wel de strafbeschikking is uitgevaardigd. Indien de beslissing is genomen door een officier van justitie bij het landelijk parket of bij het functioneel parket, is het gerechtshof te 's-Gravenhage bevoegd.'

2188 Article 12i reads: '1) Indien het beklag tot de kennisneming van het gerechtshof behoort, de klager ontvankelijk is en het gerechtshof van oordeel is dat vervolging of verdere vervolging had moeten plaats hebben, beveelt het gerechtshof dat de vervolging zal worden ingesteld of voortgezet ter zake van het feit waarop het beklag betrekking heeft. Tenzij het gerechtshof anders bepaalt, kan de vervolging niet worden ingesteld of voortgezet door het uitvaardigen van een strafbeschikking; 2. Het gerechtshof kan het geven van zodanig bevel ook weigeren op gronden aan het algemeen belang ontleend.' See further: Tekst & Commentaar Wetboek van Strafvordering, Artikel 12i, Valkenburg, para. 5.

2189 Van Gend, S.J.A.M.; Visser, G.J., *Artikel 12 tussen recht en onrecht. Een scala van zaken,* Nijmegen 2004: Ars Aequi, para. 4, p. 138 *et seq.*, available at: www.arsaequi.nl.

2190 In 2000, the Court of Appeal rejected a complaint against the dismissal with regard to the remark 'bomb that country' made by columnist Blokker in a national newspaper in reaction to a demonstration of Iraqi in The Hague; the expression did not concern the race, religion or belief of the Iraqi nor incited to discrimination. See: Amsterdam Court of Appeal, Crim. Ch., 20 February 2000, *R 99/158.* In 2001, the Court of Appeal rejected a complaint against the dismissal with regard to an article by cineaste Van Gogh critical of Islam comprising phrases such as 'that goat fucker from Mekka' and 'potential murderers'; although the expression was gross, in the light of the discussion in the article, did not overstep the limits of journalistic freedom. See: Amsterdam Court of Appeal, Crim. Ch., 9 April 2001, Art.1 nr. *2039*; Amsterdam Court of Appeal, Crim. Ch., 29 March 2001, R 97/083, Art. 1 nr. *1976.* Available at: www.art1.nl.

the religiously motivated anti-gay expression of Mr and Mrs Goeree[2191] and Reverend Van Dijke[2192], or the anti-Islam expression of Wilders.

The court reviews both the feasibility and opportunity of the prosecution and does not have to take the Discrimination Directive into account.[2193] The courts' review is not limited to a marginal test, but can consist of an integral review. Hence, the court can step into the shoes of the public prosecution.[2194] The review could be regarded as a 'shift in the separation of powers' that would not fit into the French legal system. Indeed, it implies that the court can interfere with the prosecution policy that falls under the political responsibility of the Ministry for Justice. Several scholars argue that the review in fact violates the principle of the separation of powers and must therefore be limited to a marginal review.[2195] Moreover, the decision of the prosecution to prosecute is also marginally reviewed in the case on the merits. De Lange objects that the complaints procedure should not be limited to a marginal review, because this would benefit the suspect and affect the equal position that the suspect and the victim have in the complaints procedure – other than in a case on the merits.[2196] In any event, the court must proceed with caution: although it must decide on the punishability of a suspect's expression (feasibility), it cannot step into the shoes of the judge on the merits and decide on the liability of the suspect.[2197]

Kaptein strictly holds on to the principle according to which the public prosecution of criminal offences serves the public interest and the interests of victims in prosecutions are marginal side issues. In the Article 12 procedure, the judge should therefore only take into account the interest in the prosecution and not also the interests violated by criminal offences. These are only indirectly relevant for the possibility of obtaining damages in criminal proceedings.[2198] Several legal scholars, however, opine that the legislator let the power of the prosecution as the 'sole guardian of the public order' go too far and therefore suggest a reorientation of the Article 12 procedure in order to reinforce the position of the victim.[2199]

2191 Arnhem Court of Appeal, Crim. Ch., 21 January 1991, Art.1 nr. *0725*.

2192 Annotation de Hullu, para.3 at: Dutch Supreme Court, Crim. Ch., 9 January 2001, *NJ* 2001, 203; 204.

2193 Tekst & Commentaar, Wetboek van Strafvordering, Artikel 12i, Valkenburg, para. 2.

2194 Corstens, G.J.M., *Het Nederlandse Strafprocesrecht,* Deventer: Kluwer 2008, p. 551; Melai, Wetboek van Strafvordering, Artikel 12i, para. 5.

2195 Van der Leij, J.B.J., Het slachtoffer in de beklagprocedure van artikel 12 Sv, *Strafblad* 2009, p. 467.

2196 De Lange 2009, p. 490–491.

2197 Corstens 2008, p. 551; Melai, Wetboek van Strafvordering, Artikel 12i, para. 5.

2198 Kaptein, H., Slachtoffers van Wilders' vervolging op klacht, in: Ellan, Molier & Zwart 2011, p. 150.

2199 Groenhuijsen and Kwakman argue that a more active involvement of victims in prosecution decisions would prevent unnecessary annulments of dismissals in appeal and propose – amongst others- that a victim before lodging an appeal is required to turn to the prosecution that must review its decision in the light of the interests of the victim. The Minister of Justice however opposed the introduction of a requirement that a victim must be heard by the public prosecution

De Lange argues that while the opportunity of the prosecution is tested against the criterion of the 'public interest', this vague criterion does not actually exist, but forms an abstraction of a balanced plurality of special interests. This focus on the public interest has caused a loss of sight of the concrete values and interests that criminal offences aim to protect. Criminal offences consist of different layers and protect next to the legal and the public order, specific underlying values. With regard to 137c-d Sr, these would be the honour of a group or the non-existence of hatred, discrimination and violence against a group. These underlying values form the core of criminal offences and should partly determine the opportunity of the prosecution. In other words, 'criminal politics should get content'.[2200] To achieve this, the prosecution would benefit from a more active participation of affected parties. After all, the individual person who is entitled to, for example, the respect to his honour has most knowledge about the gravity of the criminal act and an opinion about its morality. This information is valuable for the decision to prosecute and the opinion of the victim matters, because *his* interest is violated. This equally applies to representatives of collective interests, such as anti-racism associations, precisely because it is difficult to indicate the individual rights holders of impartible values or interests.[2201]

However, even when adapted, the Dutch system of the complaints procedure does not afford an interested party a relatively strong position as a joint civil party in the case on the merits comparable to the French civil action. Firstly, although the interested party can obtain a court order that commands the prosecution to prosecute with regard to specific criminal facts, the interested party does not produce the initial act of the prosecution. He cannot exactly qualify the criminal act and thus choose and indicate which exact passages within a publication are prosecuted and the exact speech offence as the legal basis. This signifies that as a joint civil party he may not give any appreciation as to the constitution of the speech offence and the punishability of the expression. Indeed, strictly speaking a joint civil party is only allowed to demonstrate damages and subsequently prove the causal link with the violation of the speech offence.

However, although the prosecution is bound by and must execute the court's order to prosecute, the prosecution can freely determine its own sentence. Thus,

before taking the decision to dismiss a case (*Kamerstukken II*, 26436, nr. 12). This is understandable considering the work load that would burden the prosecution. Van der Leij therefore advocates a less obligatory criterion and proposes that the prosecution must, after having reached its decision, invite victims to hear both sides of the argument and give further explanation, which would equally reduce appeals.
Groenhuijsen, M.S. & Kwakman, N.J.M., Het slachtoffer in het vooronderzoek, in: Groenhuijsen & Kwakman (eds.), *Dwangmiddelen en rechtsmiddelen, Derde interimrapport onderzoeksproject Strafvordering 2001*, Deventer: Kluwer 2002, p. 933–935; Van der Leij 2009, p. 466–467. See generally: Thema Artikel 12 Sv, *Strafblad* 2009, 29 October 2009, jrg. 7, nr. 5.

2200 De Lange 2009, p. 479.

2201 Hence, De Lange proposes that in the complaint-procedure victims should always be heard and even be allowed to put forward supporting evidence, because the victim must demonstrate that the dismissal was incorrect. De Lange 2009, p. 482–488.

despite the court's order to prosecute, the prosecution can persist in its vision that a suspect's expression is not punishable under 137c-e Sr, motivate this vision in its closing speech and request an acquittal of the suspect with regard to the entire charge. If the prosecution decides to do so, the case on the merits runs the risk of lacking the character of an adversarial prosecution. After all, the suspect will not contradict the requested acquittal and the joint civil parties are prohibited from contradicting the prosecution and expressing the reasons why, in their vision, the suspect's expression is punishable.

In my opinion, in the specific event that the prosecution persists in its vision and requests an acquittal, the joint civil parties should be allowed to express their vision on what the concrete values and interests protected by the speech offences are and why a suspect's expression violates these values and interests and is punishable on this account. The participation of the joint civil parties preserves the character of an adversarial prosecution that assures that all pros and cons and evidence are brought before the judge, who must decide on the basis of the case files. This is particularly true with regard to the speech offences, because punishability of expression notably depends on interpretation and the attribution of a certain meaning. In France, the civil actions of the anti-racism association contributed to the development of the case law concerning the notion of a group, more specifically to the development of the line in case law that demarcates free criticism of a religion that might hurt religious feelings from the disqualification in harsh terms of a determined religious group.

Secondly, another difference with the French system is that the joint civil party cannot appeal the decision of the court to reject the requested damages up until the Dutch Supreme Court. A joint civil party can, on the other hand, subsequently initiate a separate civil case based on Article 6:162 BW. Unlike in France, when expression is not punishable on the ground of the speech offences, it can nevertheless be unlawful on the ground of the due-diligence-norm of Article 6:162 BW. It is, however, doubtful whether such a civil case will succeed, given the fact that the criminal and civil restrictions to freedom of expression appear to differ little and due-diligence considerations may already be included in the contextual review of 137c-d Sr (para. 5.9 *supra*). Nevertheless, unlike in France, the initiation of such a civil case seems indispensable in order to be able to finally file a complaint with the ECtHR for violating a possible positive obligation to protect citizens against 'hate speech', because in order to be admissible before the ECtHR all national remedies must be exhausted.

The position of the affected parties in the prosecution of the speech offences is well illustrated in the *Wilders* case.

8.2.2. The position of the affected parties in the Wilders case

In the *Wilders* case, before the Amsterdam District Court amongst others the foundations Nederland Bekent Kleur (The Netherlands' True Colors – NBK),

Landelijk Beraad Marokkanen (National Counsel of Moroccans – LBM), Movimentu Antiano i Arubano por Promové Participashon (MAAPP), the association Arbeiders uit Turkije in Nederland (Workers from Turkey in the Netherlands – HTIB) and two Islamic Dutchmen of Moroccan origin joined as civil parties. The case first and foremost highlighted the disagreement between the prosecution and the affected parties about which underlying values Articles 137c-d Sr aim to protect. The interpretation of the offences by the prosecution was notably colored by their categorization as 'public order-offences' (para. 4.3.2 *supra*). Before the District Court, the joint civil parties argued that Article 137d Sr had to be colored by the norms arising from international law that are grounded on the value of *human dignity*. Therefore, 137d Sr was not merely an offence against the public order that prohibits the threat of the violation of an interest; it protects the intrinsic worth of the right to live in a society that is free from intolerant, hateful and discriminatory expression. He, who utters offensive expression, does not merely pass a message or express an opinion: he commits a harmful act.[2202]

According to the civil parties, the combination in Fitna of images of 9/11 with ordinary Muslims in the street and flats with satellite dishes was so suggestive that all Muslims were depicted as terrorists and a threat to society. Wilders was guilty of *'framing'* a technique, in which a speaker uses specific words to bend the debate to his will: the term 'islamization' evoked the association with 'criminalization', thus with people; what was presented as criticism of Islam, actually concerned Muslims.[2203] Wilders' suggestive use of language that connects islamization and Muslim-immigration with increased crime rates was punishable, because the existence of such expression can form a breeding ground for discrimination.

Like the Amsterdam Court of Appeal, the civil parties thus saw a certain overlap between actions and opinions. The *constructive* force of language turns the simple expression of an opinion into a 'speech-act' that *qualitate qua* constitutes an actual disturbance of the public order. Moreover, Wilders' framing and associations already violated the human dignity and position of Muslims in society. In its court order, the Amsterdam Court of Appeal had thus largely taken the victims' interests into account. Its comprehensive motivation to order the prosecution of Wilders was criticized precisely for leaving the judge little room to independently decide on the merits (para. 6.7 *supra*).[2204] In my opinion, the court rightly integrally reviewed the decision by the prosecution.[2205] For the determination of the public interest in the prosecution, the Court explicitly included the interest of a judicial decision on the merits of the case, in the light of legal certainty and the direction of future public debate.[2206]

2202 Motivation of the claims by the civil parties 27 May 2011, p. 15; 21–22.

2203 Motivation of the claims by the civil parties 18 October 2010, p. 7; Motivation of the claims by the civil parties 27 May 2011, p. 9.

2204 Amsterdam Court of Appeal, Crim. Ch., 21 January 2009, *LJN* BH0496.

2205 See also: Schalken, T., 'Over volle of marginale toetsing van OM-beleid in 12-Sv-zaken: haalbaarheid, opportuniteit of opportunisme?' in: Van Kempen *et al.* 2011, p. 481–490.

2206 Amsterdam Court of Appeal, Crim. Ch., 21 January 2009, *LJN* BH0496, para. 13.2.

Before the District Court, the closing speech and request for Wilders' acquittal of the prosecution was naturally not contradicted by Wilders, but even won the prosecution the highest praise of the defence.[2207] Both the prosecution and the defence objected to the plea of the civil parties as to why Wilders' expression was punishable under 137d Sr, whereupon the court prohibited them from continuing to do so. The civil parties, however, persisted stating that as the unlawfulness of Wilders' expression under 6:162 BW resulted from the liability pursuant to 137d Sr, they had to be able to discuss which underlying values Article 137d Sr aimed to protect. This question was not only relevant for the interpretation of the scope of the article, but also to contradict the vision of the prosecution that the civil parties did not suffer direct damages. After all, direct damages emerge if a person is harmed in an interest protected by the violated criminal offence. The civil parties claimed to suffer from the poisoned atmosphere created in the Netherlands by Wilders' expression.[2208]

The District Court seemed to have disregarded the reasoning of the civil parties and to have followed the analysis of the prosecution for the most part of its decision (para. 6.7 *supra*). Neither the prosecution nor the defence appealed the decision of the District Court and the Prosecutor General at the Supreme Court has refrained from filing an appeal in cassation in the interest of the law. On behalf of one of the civil parties, a complaint has been brought before the ECtHR for violation of Article 9 ECHR that could have contributed to the development of the European case law concerning 'hate speech' (para. 6.7 *supra*).[2209] However, on 11 October 2012 the ECtHR declared the complaint to be inadmissible without motivation.[2210] On behalf of the other civil parties a complaint has been brought before the HRC for violation of Article 20 sub 2 ICCPR, which explicitly provides that states should protect citizens against hate speech.[2211]

The *Wilders* case furthermore showed the disagreement between the prosecution and the affected parties about the concrete execution of the court order of the Court of Appeal by the prosecution. The Court of Appeal had partly rejected the complaints of the affected parties and ordered the prosecution of Wilders with regard to specific criminal facts, i.e. incitement to hatred and discrimination and – with regard to Wilders' comparisons of Islam with Nazism – group insult, and not

---

2207 Wilders did argue that the prosecution was inadmissible on account of the alleged condemnatory nature of the court order of the Amsterdam Court of Appeal, but the District Court rejected this preliminary defence. See: Amsterdam District Court, 23 May 2011, *LJN* BQ5561.

2208 Motivation of the claims by the civil parties 27 May 2011, p. 4; 23.

2209 In my opinion, admissibility on the ground of 8 or 9 j 14 ECHR was not entirely unimaginable, since Wilders' expression comprises very negative qualifications of Muslims. In the same sense: Rosier, Th., 'Kunnen de klagers in de Wilders-zaak een beroep doen op artikel 8 EVRM?', *NTM/NJCM-bull.* 2011, p. 725–737.

2210 Decision unpublished (by letter sent to the complaining party).

2211 The complaint is accessible at: www.prakkendoliveira.nl/user/file/complaint-ep-geanonimiseerde-s60bw-111111712190.pdf.

with regard to specific expressions.[2212] The prosecution subsequently converted the order into a concrete charge that filled in the specific criminal facts with concrete expressions of Wilders.

The civil parties, unsatisfied with the charge of the prosecution, requested in summary proceedings the replacement of the attending public prosecutors, the supplementation of the summons with more expressions of Wilders[2213] and a different substantial preparation by the prosecution. All requests of the civil parties were denied.[2214] This is not surprising, because any uncertainties about the court order to prosecute Wilders must be clarified by the Court of Appeal itself. Moreover, the prosecution's request for Wilders' acquittal did not bind the judge.[2215]

However, in my opinion, as the prosecution persisted in its vision and requested Wilders' acquittal, the District Court should have taken into account the reasoning of the joint civil parties in relation to what the concrete values and interests protected by 137d Sr are and why Wilders' expression violated these concrete values and interests and was punishable on this basis. This could have preserved the character of the *Wilders* case as an adversarial prosecution and could have prevented the after taste of it constituting a one-sided judgment strongly relying on the analysis of the prosecution (para. 6.7 *supra*).

In his annotation, Mevis concludes that the *Wilders* case can be considered as the 'fitna' of the Dutch system of criminal justice. Despite Wilders' acquittal, the discussion the case raised about the scope of the hate speech bans seems sufficiently important to continue to bring similar cases before the judge in the future. If the prosecution fails to prosecute, then interested parties can persist in appealing to Article 12 Sv.[2216]

8.2.3. Interested parties

In order to be admissible in his complaint against a dismissal by the prosecution, a complainant must have a direct interest in the prosecution in order to prevent any third party from having the power to confront the person of whose prosecution he desires with the threat of prosecution.[2217] According to the drafting history of Article 12 Sv, an interested party must have a 'reasonable interest' in the prosecution. This stands midway between the too narrow 'aggrieved party' and the too broad 'interested party' or 'any person'.[2218] Although the right of complaint does not merely serve the interest of the complainant but also the public interest, the

2212 Amsterdam Court of Appeal, Crim. Ch., 21 January 2009, *LJN* BH0496, para. 14.

2213 It concerned several expressions uttered by Wilders since 2004 about for example expelling dozens of Muslims, a ban on wearing the headscarf and the introduction of a 'tax on Head Rags'.

2214 The Hague District Court, summary proceedings, 26 November 2010, *LJN* BO5107.

2215 Annotation Mevis, para. 4–6 at: Amsterdam District Court, 23 June 2011, *NJ* 2012, 370.

2216 *Ibid.*, para. 25.

2217 Corstens 2008, p. 547–548.

2218 *Kamerstukken II* 1917/18, 77, nr. 1, p. 23; 45.

term interested party should not be interpreted broadly; the argument that any person has an interest in a fair criminal justice would lead to the 'actio popularis'.[2219]

Hence, in 1973, the Dutch Supreme Court further specified the term interested party as 'a person who is affected by the dismissal in an interest of his particular concern.' The Supreme Court rejected the vision of the Court of Appeal that had considered a complainant admissible on account of his status as 'a Dutchman, father and concerned intellectual' with regard to the decision not to prosecute the performance of the alleged obscene musical 'Oh Calcutta'. According to the Court of Appeal, the term interested party had to be broadly interpreted in relation to 'criminal offences that affect the legal order to such an extent that possibly any person can be considered as an interested party.'[2220] Furthermore, as a result of the case law, a complainant must have a personal interest that can be objectively determined.[2221] An interested party must be personally affected by the criminal offence, either materially or immaterially, and must be aggrieved by the dismissal.[2222]

Pursuant to Article 12 sub 2 Sv, legal persons, such as foundations and associations that according to their statutes and factual activities protect an idealistic interest or collective interests, can equally form a direct interested party.[2223] The Article aimed to afford a right of compliant to associations because it was considered a loss that interests that concern every person could not be represented and defended by any one.[2224] The article applies only with regard to the situation in which an association defends an idealistic or collective interest, not to the situation in which an association acts in another capacity; then Article 12 sub 1 Sv can apply.[2225] According to the drafting history, the article does not afford a right of complaint to groups lacking any legal personality or 'ad hoc groups'. The interests that an association aims to represent must be sufficiently described in its statutes. The requirement of factual activities assures that associations actually

---

2219 Melai, Wetboek van Strafvordering, Artikel 12, aant. 10.

2220 Dutch Supreme Court, crim. ch., 7 March 1972, *NJ* 1973, 35; Arhnem Court of Appeal, 10 January 1963, *NJ* 1963, 404.

2221 Melai, Wetboek van Strafvordering, Artikel 12, aant. 11.

2222 Tekst & Commentaar, Wetboek van Strafvordering, Artikel 12, Valkenburg, para. 6; Corstens 2008, p. 547–548.

2223 Article 12 Sv sub 2 reads: 'Onder rechtstreeks belanghebbende wordt mede verstaan een rechtspersoon die krachtens zijn doelstelling en blijkens zijn feitelijke werkzaamheden een belang behartigt dat door de beslissing tot niet vervolging of niet verdere vervolging rechtstreeks wordt getroffen.'

2224 Melai, Wetboek van Strafvordering, Artikel 12, aant. 19.

2225 The right of collective action origins and is guaranteed in Article 3:305 sub a and b BW. Associations and foundations with legal personality can exercise this right and protect similar interests of other persons. The legislator has determined that in collective action individual files cannot be used without prior permission of the parties involved. Furthermore, associations must first try to reach an agreement before taking legal action. Moreover, a legal demand cannot be aimed at obtaining damages.

exist and are not only on paper and prevents 'ad hoc advocating'.[2226] The admissibility furthermore depends on the protected interest of the criminal offence concerned: the interests that an association according to its statutes protects must correspond to the interests protected by the criminal offence. However, the statutes of an association do not have to specify that the association aims to realize its objectives by means of criminal proceedings.[2227]

An interesting case is the appeal against the decision not to prosecute Fortuyn's political opponents on the ground of 137d Sr with regard to their expressions against Fortuyn's controversial political ideas. The complaint was filed by the representatives of the deceased Fortuyn, his surviving relatives and his political party, List Pim Fortuyn. In their view, the 'hate speech' of Fortuyn's opponents had led to his assassination. In 2003, the Hague Court of Appeal declared all complainants inadmissible. The late Fortuyn had lost his personal interest in a prosecution by dying. His surviving relatives were only indirectly affected by the violation of the name and memory of Fortuyn. His political party did not, according to its statutes, specifically aim to protect the interests protected by 137d Sr. Moreover, in principle political parties could not be considered to represent special, partial interests. Perhaps unnecessarily, the Court recalled that in any event Article 137d Sr would not be applicable to the case, because it does not protect persons against incitement to hatred on the basis of their *political ideas* that must be distinguished from a religion or belief.[2228]

According to the Minister for Justice, associations such as the Anne Frank Foundation and the Dutch Centre for Foreigners would in principle be admissible in their complaints with regard to concrete cases of discrimination.[2229] Indeed, anti-racism and discrimination associations, such as the Anne Frank Foundation, CIDI (Centre Information and Documentation Israel) and regional ADV's (Anti-Discrimination Services) are generally admissible in their complaints against dismissals with regard to racist and other discriminatory expression and acts of discrimination.[2230]

In the *Wilders* case, the Court of Appeal seemed to use a very different criterion to determine the admissibility of the nine complainants against the dismissal with regard to Wilders' expression about Islam and Muslims. The complainants consisted of a motley crew of individuals, associations and legal professionals, comprising of a concerned Dutch student, the board of the As Soennah Mosque in The Hague, Dutch politician and attorney Lucas in private capacity, Dutch pastor Ipenburg in private capacity and on behalf of several Dutch University professors, the chairmen

2226 Melai, Wetboek van Strafvordering, Artikel 12, aant. 18.

2227 Amsterdam Court of Appeal, 9 April 2008, *NJ* 2005, 599, annotation Legemaate.

2228 The Hague Court of Appeal, Crim. Ch., 19 May 2003, *LJN* AF8921, *NJ* 2003, 382.

2229 *Handelingen II* 1983/84, p. 4342.

2230 Decisions by Courts of Appeal in complaint procedures ex. Article 12 Sv are accessible at: www.Art.1.nl.

of the Elfath Mosque in Maastricht, the Islamic Student Association in Maastricht, Mad-Der, an Association of Alevites in Maastricht and the Islamic Council of Limburg.

According to the Court, on the one hand the requirement to belong or have a certain connection to the Muslim community was difficult to use because it was impossible to verify. On the other hand, the criterion of the abstract desire of the enforcement of the law was too broad. The right criterion consisted of the fear of social unrest that can arise from an actual disturbance of the functioning of the democratic order caused by disorder. Individual citizens had a concrete interest in the aversion of a dangerous disturbance of social life and public debate. The Court declared all complainants admissible, because their complaints specifically concerned the offences of group insult and incitement to hatred, thus offences against public order; and every person had a verifiable and personal interest in the preservation of the public order.[2231]

In my opinion, the Court of Appeal wrongly based the admissibility on the preservation of the public order. Although this does form a legitimate ground to partly motivate the order of Wilders' prosecution, it does not constitute an interest of the particular concern of the complainants.[2232] As every person has an interest in the preservation of the public order, the Court thus left the door slightly open to the 'actio popularis' in the field of the hate speech bans. This is a pity, because the collective action should not be confused with the 'actio popularis' and criticized on this basis. In the context of the Article 12 Sv procedure, the actions of anti-racism associations could precisely complement the 'sole guardian of the public order' in the protection of the underlying values or interests of 137c-d Sr.

In the broader context of criminal, civil and administrative law and the CGB, Van Stokkum and Rodrigues observe that in the Netherlands, collective action is underexposed as a means of fighting discrimination.[2233] However, an individual can refrain from action out of fear of reprisals, i.e. 'victimization'. It can be easier to take action as an organization. Furthermore, the collective action compensates the existing inequalities between the parties to the case and decreases the thresholds (time, money, effort, knowledge) to a lawsuit. Finally, an economic argument for the right to collective action is to avoid separate individual cases. It thus signifies an efficient, effective and economic use of the law.[2234]

2231 Amsterdam Court of Appeal, Crim. Ch., 21 January 2009, *LJN* BH0496, para. 7.4.

2232 In the same sense: Kaptein 2011, p. 154.

2233 Rodrigues, P.R., Collective acties als structureel instrument tegen discriminatie, in: Jongbloed, A.W. (ed.), *Samen sterk, over optreden in rechte door groeperingen*, Den Haag: Boom Juridische Uitgevers 2002, p. 91–103; Van Stokkum, Sackers & Wils 2006, p. 212–214.

2234 Rodrigues, P.R., Eén voor allen: gelijke behandeling en collectieve acties, in: Forder, C. (ed.) *Gelijke behandeling: oordelen en commentaar 2010*, Nijmegen: Wolf Legal Publishers 2011, p. 309–324.

Hence, in the fight against discrimination, the right of collective action can form an important instrument. This notably applies to forms of structural discrimination, such as continuous hate speech on the Internet that has an international dimension. For example, in the 1990s, the Dutch National Anti-racism Service (LBR), CIDI and the Anne Frank Foundation successfully undertook collective action against the distribution of Holocaust denial by a Belgian association and Verbeke (para. 5.5.3 *supra*). The Dutch judge imposed an injunction prohibiting the further distribution of the material in the Netherlands. When Verbeke continued to distribute his material, it took two and a half years of lobbying to convince the prosecution to start criminal proceedings that resulted in a fine of 6000 florins.[2235] Interestingly, De Boer argues that the standards for civil actions should approximate criminal standards and the same importance must be attached to freedom of expression as in the event that the government would have initiated action. If a criminal action has failed, it would be strange if a legal person or individual would succeed in getting a publication removed on the basis of 6:162 BW.[2236]

In 2005, in the context of the discussion about the preservation of 'fundamental rights in a pluralistic society' and countering 'radicalization and radicalism', in Parliament the idea was even launched to create a commission comparable to the CGB for an adequate and easily accessible approach to counter hate speech that, on the request of complainants, can judge in concrete cases. The Minister, however, did not support the idea of creating such an alternative form of dispute settlement.[2237]

8.3. Conclusion

The Dutch public prosecution has the exclusive right to engage public prosecutions with regard to discriminatory expression on the ground of Articles 137c-e Sr. The prosecution of discriminatory expression against one person in particular on the ground of 261 or 266 Sr depends on a prior complaint by the victim. The opportunity of the public prosecution is curtailed by the Discrimination Directive, which concerns the enforcement of – amongst others – Articles 137c-e Sr. The Directive establishes, as a general rule, that a suspect must be prosecuted if the violation of the offence can be proven and he is liable for punishment. Given the difficulties in determining liability under 137c-d Sr, the tenability of the directive is questionable with regard to these offences. Several legal scholars opine that the legislator let the power of the prosecution go too far. In the last decade the prosecution dismissed several complaints against severe criticism of Islam and Muslims. Affected parties can appeal such dismissals in the so-called

2235 The case can be compared to the famous French *Yahoo*-case started by French anti-racism associations against Yahoo for facilitating the auctioning of Nazi-collector items on the Internet.

2236 De Boer, J., De collectieve actie in verband met discriminatie van een collectiviteit, *NJB* 27 June 1987, nr. 26, p. 818.

2237 *Handelingen II*, 22 February 2005, 503259; 24 February 2005, 523370.

Article 12-procedure before the Court of Appeal that can order the prosecution of a suspect with regard to specific criminal facts. Compared with the French civil action, this procedure, however, provides an interested party with a less strong position as a joint civil party in the case on the merits.

This can be illustrated by the *Wilders* case that did not constitute an adversarial prosecution, because the acquittal requested by the prosecution was not contradicted by Wilders while the joint civil parties were not allowed to give their opinion in relation to which concrete values and interests Article 137d Sr protects. However, the participation of victims and other affected parties such as anti-racism associations could complement the 'sole guardian of the public order' in the protection of the underlying values or interests of 137c-d Sr. However, in the *Wilders* case, the Court of Appeal wrongly based the admissibility of complainants against the dismissal by the prosecution on the preservation of the public order and threatening character of Wilders' expression, because this does not constitute an interest of their particular concern; it thereby opened the door to the 'actio popularis'. The right of collective action can, however, form an important instrument to counter structural forms of hate speech and discrimination.

Chapter 6
Analysis and Conclusion

Introduction

Against the background of the problem defined in chapter 1 and the analytical framework established in chapter 2, chapter 3 described the international and European obligations with regard to restrictions to hate speech. From this chapter it can be seen that a substantial balancing act must be made between the right to freedom of expression and the interests served with the restriction of hate speech on the basis of religion. Subsequently, chapters 4 and 5 described what the restrictions to hate speech – on the basis of religion – are in France and the Netherlands respectively. The analysis shows that the restrictions to hate speech and the way in which they are drawn differ between the different legal systems. The aim of the present and final chapter is to combine the findings and further analyze them in order to provide a synthesis on France, the Netherlands and the European Convention on Human Rights (ECHR) (para. 1) and to discuss some concluding observations (para. 2).

To that end, paragraph 1 of this chapter further analyzes how the four factors[2238] elaborated in chapter 2 influence the determination of restrictions to hate speech in the examined legal systems. Paragraph 1 will then conclude to which extent the restrictions in the systems are drawn in a consistent manner. Subsequently, paragraph 2 advances, on the basis of the entire research, a number of considerations that could form an inspiration for the making of certain fundamental choices in the determination of restrictions to hate speech. It is not intended to create one particular, conclusive model to develop a universal, uniform approach to hate speech. Its modest intention is rather to provide certain tools for enhancing consistency *within* existing approaches to hate speech, thus answering the central research question of this study.

1. Synthesis France, the Netherlands and the ECHR

This paragraph starts by sketching a number of differences and similarities in the French and Dutch approaches to freedom of expression and the regulation of hate speech against the background of the characteristics of the constitutional state and the national legal culture in general (1.1). Attention is paid to the interrelationship between different actors. There then follows a comparison with the approach under the ECHR (1.2). Thereafter follows a more elaborated comparison of the restrictions to hate speech in the three legal systems as far as the four factors are concerned (1.3–1.7).

2238 Being: *actions* versus *opinions*; *public debate* versus *other* types of expression; *facts* versus *value judgments*; and *race* versus *religion*.

1.1. France versus the Netherlands

Both France and the Netherlands have prohibited certain forms of hate speech. A striking difference between France and the Netherlands is the number of hate speech bans. France has four different hate speech bans; the offences of 'racial defamation', 'racial insult' and 'racial provocation', as well as the offence of 'Holocaust denial'. The Netherlands has only two different hate speech bans; the offences of 'group insult' and 'incitement to hatred, discrimination or violence'. The offence of blasphemy has existed for a long time in the Netherlands and has only recently been abolished in 2013. The distinction in the number of hate speech bans can be explained by the fact that French law is very legalistic – the French legislator must create precisely circumscribed norms that the French judge must strictly apply –, while Dutch law is characterized by more open norms that can be further 'coloured' by the Dutch judge in concrete cases. Hence, in the Netherlands defamatory statements about a group fall under the prohibition of group insult and Holocaust denial can, under certain circumstances, amount to a prohibited form of group insult or incitement to hatred. The number of hate speech bans thus gives an indication but does not in itself determine the exact restrictions on hate speech. One must also look at their application by the judge (*infra*).

Unlike the Dutch hate speech bans, the French hate speech bans are imbedded into the – values of the – French Constitution. In both France and the Netherlands, freedom of expression is protected in the Constitution. A striking similarity is that the limitation clause of both the French and Dutch provisions indicate that the formal legislator is competent to determine the substantive restrictions to freedom of expression, but does not indicate the interests these restrictions must protect. More than the Dutch Constitution, the French 'Constitutional bloc' can form guidance for the determination of the restrictions to freedom of expression by the legislator and the judge.

In fact, the constitutionality of restrictions can be reviewed by the French Constitutional Council either in the context of the legislative process or an individual case at the request of the French Supreme Court (Question Prioritaire de Constitutionalité/ QPC). The French hate speech bans have, however, not been subjected to such a constitutional review. The offences of racial defamation, racial insult and racial provocation were adopted unanimously in 1972. Contrarily, the adoption of the offence of Holocaust denial in 1990 was controversial and it is argued that a review of its constitutionality was bypassed for political reasons.

The French Supreme Court, for its part, has up to this date refused to transmit a QPC about the offences of racial provocation and Holocaust denial that it considers to be sufficiently formulated and in conformity with the right to freedom of expression in the Constitution and Article 10(2) ECHR. A tension thus appears to be possible between the fields of competence of the Supreme Court and the Constitutional Council. The Constitutional Council has, however, decided in general that restrictions to freedom of expression must protect either the rights of others or human dignity or the public order. Furthermore, freedom of expression and the restriction thereof is bound by the harm-principle in the French Declaration (individual freedom finds its limits in the harm to others and the enjoyment of their rights and the law can only prohibit harmful actions).

The Netherlands does not have a Constitutional Council. The Dutch Constitution even prohibits the constitutional review of statutory laws. The legislator must himself preserve the constitutionality of his laws. However, the Dutch Constitution does not contain a reference to values such as human dignity or an abuse of rights clause that can form a guideline in the determination of restrictions. The Dutch Supreme Court has established that the Dutch hate speech bans are in conformity with Article 10(2) ECHR.

The French hate speech bans are incorporated into the French Press Act of 1881 that originally has a criminal law nature and forms a 'closed legal world'; it not only cites the specific press offences, but also creates, in the context of a suspect's defence, specific justifications in relation to each press offence – such as the excuse of provocation for the offence of insult and the exception of truth for the offence of defamation –, and very strict procedural rules for the prosecution of the press offences. The French legalism and fear of free judicial interpretation explains why the 1881 Press Act has developed into a hybrid act that also applies in civil cases. How paradoxical it may seem, precisely criminal law is regarded as the appropriate means to assure freedom of expression by precisely determining its limitations. The press offences therefore form the legal basis in both criminal and civil cases; when an utterance cannot be qualified under a specific hate speech ban, it cannot nevertheless constitute a wrongful act under Article 1382 of the French Civil Code (CC). In principle the criminal and civil restrictions to hate speech are thus the same. The French Press Act appears to provide precise and clear norms concerning the prosecution of hate speech, which at first sight can be assumed to benefit the consistency of the restrictions to hate speech.

The question does arise as to whether the 1881 Press Act with its specific press offences and procedural law meets its objective to strike a fine balance between freedom of the press and the rights of victims of defamations, insults and provocations. More generally put, whether the very legalistic French legal system meets its objective to assure legal certainty in order to protect and guarantee the effective enjoyment of – fundamental – rights of citizens. From the perspective of the defence, the 1881 Press Act poses problems by establishing a regime of criminal responsibility disconnected from an author's intention (through the presumption of bad faith) and the existence of actual prejudice. From the perspective of the prosecuting party, the very strict procedural rules of the 1881 Press Act form actual obstacles in the prosecution. The protection of freedom of expression by means of higher procedural thresholds can jeopardize effective access to the judge. The formalism of the 'closed legal world' of the 1881 Press Act cannot be intended to complicate access to justice.

The Dutch hate speech bans are incorporated into the Dutch Criminal Code and their prosecution is subjected to the general rules of criminal procedure. Unlike in France, prosecutions on the ground of double – either cumulative or alternative – qualifications and requalification by the judge are generally permitted. The Dutch Criminal Code does not determine specific justifications for a suspect's defence in relation to the hate speech bans. The Dutch system appears to provide more open norms concerning the prosecution of hate speech, which at first sight can be assumed to complicate the consistency of the restrictions to hate speech. The hate speech bans do form a primary guideline for the determination of unlawfulness of expression under Article 6:162 of the Dutch Civil Code (DCC – wrongful act). When an utterance cannot be qualified under a specific hate speech ban, it can nevertheless constitute a wrongful act on the basis of due diligence norms.

In principle, the Dutch criminal and civil restrictions to hate speech can thus differ. From the (French) perspective of legal certainty, one could argue that an utterance may only be unlawful when it is punishable under a specific hate speech ban and that the French 'hybrid' approach could therefore form an inspiration for the Dutch judge. In practice, the Dutch criminal and civil restrictions do not, however, necessarily have to differ much; both the criminal and civil judge, when applying the statutory norm, make a further balancing act with the right to freedom of expression. Possible distinctions between criminal restrictions ('intent') and civil restrictions ('due diligence') are to some extent already discounted in this balancing act or 'contextual review'. The French uniform approach appears to be notably more efficient; hate speech cases are often joint criminal and civil cases brought before and decided by the same judge, while in the Netherlands after such a joint case civil parties can still initiate a separate civil case.

Given the fact that French law does not recognize the existence of minorities (*infra*), it appears quite paradoxical that in France the public prosecutor and anti-racism associations representing minority interests have a shared role in the enforcement of hate speech bans. In fact, anti-racism associations have the right to set in motion public prosecutions on the ground of the hate speech bans and constitute as a civil party. The activism of the anti-racism associations has led to an extensive case law concerning hate speech. On the one hand, one could argue that this right of legal action for associations has led to a far-reaching juridification of public debate, which may have a chilling effect on freedom of expression. The legal actions can indeed be criticized for sometimes being aimed at protecting religious or moral interests rather than the fight against racism in the general interest and for being aimed at obtaining criminal condemnations rather than the reparation of damages. Furthermore, there is a risk of over – and under – representation of certain groups (Some groups, such as the Roma's, may not be so well organized as others). Moreover, as the anti-racism associations have had a role in the drafting of the hate speech bans and their right to legal action, the question is whether they are not too influential in the restriction of hate speech; who in the French system will speak for freedom of expression?

On the other hand, the right to legal action does afford associations the possibility to bring politically delicate subjects, such as harsh criticism on Islam and immigration, in which the public prosecutor remains inactive, before the judge and assure effective access to justice. Generally, however, a dense cooperation and consultation between the public prosecution and anti-racism associations exists. The anti-racism associations can form the checks and balances *within* the strict separation of powers by continuously renewing the discussion with the legislature, the executive (i.e. the public prosecutor) and the judiciary on the creation, application and interpretation of the hate speech bans. They can falsify the premises that shape the relationship between freedom of expression and discrimination in new cases, new circumstances. Their direct invocation of the hate speech bans before the judge submits the norms to a constant adaptation to the needs and state of society. Such activism seems to fit perfectly into the goal of the French social contract: the indefinite promotion of individual rights.

In the Netherlands, the fact that the law precisely assumes the existence of minorities and generally accommodates groups in the enjoyment of their cultural and ethnic identities, does not also lead to a dense cooperation between the public prosecutor and minority associations in the enforcement of hate speech bans. The public prosecutor has the exclusive right to engage public prosecutions on the basis of the hate speech bans. Affected parties can obtain a court order demanding the prosecution that initially dismissed a case to prosecute a particular publication on the basis of the hate speech bans after all. However, the Wilders case showed that joint civil parties do not then have a strong position in the case on the merits, which is notably objectionable when the prosecution requests an acquittal. A better cooperation and consultation between the public prosecution and anti-racism associations with regard to the prosecution of hate speech could prevent such non-adversarial prosecutions.

1.2. The approach under the ECHR

The European Court of Human Rights (ECtHR) uses a broad and autonomous notion of hate speech that includes 'all forms of expression which spread, incite, promote or justify hatred based on intolerance (including religious intolerance)'. According to the ECtHR, the prohibition on hate speech thus described under the ECHR is primarily informed by its underlying values of equal human dignity and non-discrimination. It results from the ECtHR's case law that the existence of national prohibitions of incitement to hatred, discrimination or violence, Holocaust denial, group defamation and even of blasphemy are not per definition incompatible with the Convention. The ECtHR has on several occasions reviewed the compatibility of national convictions for hate speech on the basis of such provisions with the right to freedom of expression.

If the statements did not fall into the category of abuse of rights for the purposes of Article 17 ECHR, the ECtHR examined the restriction in question in the light of Article 10(2) ECHR. The ECtHR then balances the interest of a particular restriction with the interest of freedom of expression in the specific context of the case, thereby affording the state a certain margin to determine the restrictions to hate speech. With regard to hate speech, this margin is often quite broad. Subsequently, the ECtHR has generally found restrictions to hate speech to have the legitimate aim of protecting the rights of others and/or the public order and has found them to be necessary in a democratic society. The ECtHR does not principally favor the use of civil law to counter hate speech. Based on the ECtHR's case law concerning hate speech one could argue that national convictions for utterances that amount to hate speech will normally not constitute a violation of Article 10 ECHR as long as criminal sanctions remain proportionate and for example do not consist of long prison sentences.

This does not signify that the refusal to prosecute or acquittals in comparable hate speech cases necessarily amount to a violation of the Convention. This can be illustrated by a comparison between the two admissibility decisions in the cases Le Pen and Wilders. It is stipulated that the ECtHR does not oblige states to prohibit and prosecute particular forms of hate speech, but merely leaves this possibility open for states. After all, the ECtHR does not determine which restrictions are prescribed, but only which restrictions are in violation of the right of freedom of expression as protected in Article 10 ECHR and which are not. The ECHR also does not include a general right to have criminal proceedings instituted against a third person on the basis of existing national offences. Furthermore, the ECtHR appears to be quite reluctant to derive any *positive obligations* from the right to privacy (reputation) or freedom of religion in Article 8 and 9 ECHR respectively, for states to prosecute and convict utterances that amount to hate speech on account of race, ethnicity or religion, thus to restrict and sanction such use of freedom of expression. The broad margin afforded by the ECtHR with regard to the setting of restrictions to hate speech thus limits the impact of the ECtHR's case law concerning hate speech on national law (*infra*).

1.3. Actions versus Opinions

French free speech doctrine makes a fundamental distinction between the performance of physical actions and the expression of opinions. According to the traditional French concept of the 'délit d'opinion', as articulated by Constant, French law cannot criminalize – the expression of – a mere opinion, but only of an opinion that supports a criminal act. This concept presupposes that for the criminality of an opinion there is a requirement of a close link with a following action. The 'délit d'opinion' can furthermore be defined as an offence that 1) does not form the object of a precise qualification by the legislator, 2) does not determine the specific rights and interests with which it interferes and 3) its arbitrary prosecution and sanction constitutes a danger to freedom of expression. Strictly speaking, the French hate speech bans display some of these features and are therefore inconsistent with the traditional French free speech doctrine.

In fact, the French law on hate speech starts precisely from the premise as articulated by Sartre, 'racism is not an opinion, but a criminal offence'. Racist discourse violates the core values of the French Republic, because it denies the equal human dignity of French citizens and forms an aggression against both the members of the target group and the indivisible French Republic as a whole. Racist expression therefore lacks the protection of freedom of expression. At stake is not so much the preservation of the French public order through the prevention of subsequent actions causing disorder and violence, but rather the preservation of the French social order created by 'le pacte républicain' through the prevention of the existence of intolerant, inhuman racist opinions. The value of human dignity is at the basis of the change in thought about the criminality of opinions; from opinions that prepare reprehensible actions to opinions that form reprehensible actions. The French vision of what constitutes a 'délit d'opinion' has thus changed. Therefore, the particular liberal aims of the 1881 Press Act have also been adjusted.

As the hate speech bans were created precisely to intervene in racist discourse in an earlier stage, they require a relatively weak link between the expression of an opinion and a subsequent criminal act. The Decree law Marchandeau of 1939 still prohibited defamation and insult of a *group* with the aim to incite *hatred* between citizens and thus was primarily aimed at preventing disharmony between groups that violated the public order, even though the prohibitions were categorized as 'misdemeanors against persons'. In 1972, the prohibitions were adapted to protect the members of a group and the requirement of the aim to incite hatred was abrogated. Since then, the prohibitions thus primarily protect individual persons belonging to a group against violations of their reputation, thus their estimation in the eyes of others, or dignity rather than to prevent the effects defamations and insults may have on the actions of third parties and public order.

The French offence of provocation to discrimination, hatred or violence specifically protects members of the target group against possible effects of expression on third parties who may, as a result of an utterance, proceed to discriminatory or violent actions against their person. Its scope is not limited to expression that directly, literally and with so many words provokes third parties to commit precisely defined punishable acts, but encompasses more disguised forms of racial provocation that can form a breeding ground for such acts and is likely to lead to future discrimination and violence. This comprises a large variety of utterances that according to its purport could set groups against each other. Although the French legislator has thus not precisely qualified the offence of racial provocation, it is not seriously contested because it clearly determines the interests it aims to protect; the right of others not to be discriminated or exposed to hatred or violence.

To the contrary, the offence of Holocaust denial cannot be criticized for lacking a precise qualification by the legislator. A legitimate and common objection is, however, that the offence does not clearly determine the right or interest it protects and with which it interferes. Its actual rationale is to protect the Jewish community and other victims of the war crimes committed during the Second World War against defamatory and provocative statements of a clearly profound racist and anti-Semitic nature and to prevent the rehabilitation of national socialism, thus equally to protect the dignity and rights of others and the French political order. However, the offence forms a 'délit d'opinion' by appearances, because – contrary to the other hate speech bans – according to its statutory elements it seemingly prohibits mere opinions on the history of the Holocaust regardless of whether they are harmful to *persons*. To the extent that the offence protects the 'human dignity', the latter notion then rather functions as a public moral.

Dutch free speech doctrine has less fundamental principles about the distinction between actions and opinions and lacks a concept comparable to the 'délit d'opinion'. The Dutch hate speech bans can therefore not be said to be inconsistent with any traditional Dutch free speech doctrine. To a certain extent they share some characteristics with their French equivalents; the offence of group insult does not require that an utterance has the aim of inciting hatred and the offence of incitement to hatred, discrimination or violence has a similar wording as the French provision. In 1971, these hate speech bans replaced the offences of group insult of 1934 that – just as in France – were still primarily aimed to prevent disturbances of the public peace as a result of public insults of sectors of the population. Although the rationale of the new hate speech bans was to prevent discrimination of groups in society, the offences were categorized as 'offences against the public order'. The significance of 'public order' thus became more substantive and shifted from disturbances of the peace to a society free from discrimination.

The subsumption of the norm of equality and non-discrimination under the term of public order, however, makes the hate speech bans susceptible to an inconsistent application and interpretation. With the creation of the hate speech bans, the legislator precisely aimed to prohibit utterances that according to their content violated the independent value of the equal human dignity of citizens, even though it laid less emphasis thereon. The fact that such utterances may affect the public order rather formed a reason for their criminalization than an extra requirement for the criminality of expression. Hence, negative utterances about immigration, the multicultural society and foreigners used to easily amount to prohibited forms of group insult or incitement to hatred or discrimination, because such expression violates the dignity of minorities by targeting their position in society and can form a breeding ground for and is likely to lead to future discrimination and violence.

Conceptions about the criminality of utterances and the importance of freedom of expression have however changed; nowadays, one is less willing to prohibit expression on the basis of its content. Therefore, in case law and scholarship the scope of the offence of incitement is sometimes limited to expression that directly, literally and with so many words incites third parties to commit precisely defined acts of discrimination and violence and its application is sometimes limited to those situations where there is a direct threat to public order or actual risk of violent conflicts. The question is whether the Dutch legislator must more specifically determine the scope and rationale of the Dutch hate speech bans, precisely because a broader constitutional framework that compels or constrains to an unambiguous interpretation by the judge is absent.

Although it results from the case law of the ECtHR that expression that amounts to 'hate speech' may be prohibited, the term is not evidently clear and does not in itself form a solution to the disagreement within the Court about its exact criteria, which notably came to the fore in the *Féret* case (Chapter 3, para. 1.3). According to a majority, expression may be prohibited as hate speech for the reason that it is insulting, ridiculing or defamatory of a group and violates their dignity and security and because it can lead to intolerance and feelings of distrust, rejection or hatred towards foreigners or other groups. The negative influence of hatred based on prejudices on the political stability and serene social climate is sufficient in order to justify a restriction.

For the ECtHR, reasons for the suppression of hate speech thus form both the harm it causes to the members of the target group and its possible harmful – long-term – effects on society at large. This latter criterion has been compared with the American 'bad tendency test' and criticized on this account: the nature of the act – incitement – and the intention of the author are deduced from the 'tendency' of the words to persuade others to adopt hateful or discriminatory attitudes. The minority within the ECtHR requires a stricter connection between the content of expression (actual incitement) and subsequent concrete forms of discrimination and violence by others in order to justify a restriction and incidentally refers to the American 'clear- and-present-danger-test'. The different approaches can, to a certain extent, also be found in the opinions of the majority and minority in other cases, such as in the *Gündüz* case (Chapter 3, para. 1.1).

An important factor is whether the ECtHR considers expression that seems primarily directed against the – form of or the policy of the – government to at the same time constitute an unacceptable attack on groups in society. Possible inconsistencies in the ECtHR's case law might notably flow from its interpretation of expression. The distinction is important, because the ECtHR's approach to hate speech deviates from its approach to the incitement to violence against the authorities (Chapter 3, para. 1.2). With regard to the latter, the Court sets relatively clear and strict criteria for 'incitement', the intention of the author to stigmatize the other side to the conflict, and the likelihood of its impact and affords the state a large margin only for the assessment of the national security situation. Contrarily, with regard to hate speech, the Court leaves states a large margin not only to assess the possible impact of expression and the sensitivity of the situation given the specific national context, but also to bring a large variety of expressions, on the basis of its content, under this broad notion.

This does *not* signify that the ECtHR's approach to hate speech is in itself inconsistent. For hate speech, the ECtHR has simply not developed clear standards and precise criteria of review comparable with incitement to violence, such as the expression of actual 'incitement', the intention of the speaker to stigmatize others and the likelihood of subsequent violent action as a probable effect of the expression. Nor does the ECtHR principally distinguish between group defamation and incitement to hatred, discrimination or violence and between the harm of hate speech to its target group and its harm to society at large, although it does mention both. Nor does the ECtHR require any demonstration of *how* hate speech consisting of group defamation affects the dignity or security of the target group, for example by reference to its psychological effects.

This *does* signify that the ECtHR leaves national authorities a certain margin to interpret and apply its national provisions prohibiting specific forms of hate speech. These need not necessarily cover all expressions that the ECtHR describes as hate speech and for which the ECtHR considers measures justified. In general, national courts need to ensure that hate speech bans are not applied in contravention of Article 10 ECHR. On the other hand, they are at liberty to place a narrow interpretation on those provisions ('imminence'), even if a broader interpretation ('likelihood') would not be inconsistent with the ECtHR's case law. This would only be different, if clearly defined obligations to make the act in question a criminal offence followed from this case law, and at the moment this is not the case, even in relation to the abuse of rights (Chapter 3, para. 1.6).

1.4. Public Debate versus Other Types of Expression

France has the particular concept of the state as a distributor of rights, which results in a somewhat paternalistic conception of freedom of expression; freedom of expression therefore notably exists within the contours of the state. This also applies to the free public and political debate. Furthermore, pursuant to the French strict separation of powers, the legislator primarily determines the public interest by voting on precisely circumscribed laws and the judge may not reconsider the balance struck *a priori* by the legislator. Therefore, when an utterance constitutes a prohibited form of hate speech, the French judge cannot further balance the interest in upholding the norm with the interest of a free public debate. In other words, freedom of expression cannot form a general justification for expression that is punishable on the ground of the hate speech bans (Chapter 4, para. 6.4). The French legislator and judge thus work in unison.

On the one hand, the legalistic French legal system provides for a 'lock' on acquired rights, in the Constitution and in relation to the principles of the French Republic. The courts cannot nullify, expand or create laws. Under no circumstances is it permitted to incite to hatred, discrimination or violence, defame or insult racial or religious groups: un point c'est tout. In principle, the context of a public or political debate about immigration or integration cannot remove the criminality of expression that depicts a particular minority group as criminal and thus dangerous exclusively on the basis of its race or religion or of political proposals that violate a binding prohibition of discrimination, such as the proposal to deport foreign nationals from the country (Chapter 4, para. 6.2). Furthermore, it results from the French notion of equality that all citizens participating in public debate have equal freedom of expression; this also applies to politicians, including elected representatives (Chapter 4, para. 6.5.2).

On the other hand, this leads to a very rigid and abstract application of the hate speech bans, in which there is little room for attaching importance to the general interest of free public debate in the light of the concrete circumstances of the case. The French judge, however, sometimes gives weight to the interest of freedom of expression in the question whether an utterance meets all the statutory elements of the offence. This implies that the judge does a bit more than strictly applying the hate speech bans and in fact implicitly attaches importance to freedom of expression. This results in certain inconsistencies in French case law in relation to the distinction between the imputation of specific facts and free value judgments (Chapter 4, para. 4.5) and the requirement that an utterance must designate a particular group (Chapter 5, para. 5.2), depending on whether the judge desires the preservation of a free debate on a specific topic (*infra*).

If the French judge could and would more explicitly and structurally attach importance to freedom of expression as a justifying ground, he could make his motivation more transparent and consistent. Although the case law increasingly refers to and takes into account the interest of a free public debate, neither the French Supreme Court nor the lower courts have developed a specific 'balancing-test' as a standard for judicial review in all hate speech cases. This again leads to certain inconsistencies in case law. It is in itself incomprehensible why the French judge finds the qualification of Roma's as particularly criminal and thus dangerous permissible because the expression is uttered in the context of a public debate about their integration, but in the case of North Africans finds the same qualification a punishable form of hate speech even though it is uttered in a similar context (Chapter 4, para. 6.2). The French courts originally introduced the reference to the general interest of a public debate in defamation cases, because the traditional notion of the good faith developed in French case law as a suspect's means of defence proved not to meet the standards of the Article 10 case law of the ECtHR (Chapter 4, para. 4.4.3). This has created confusion as to the interrelationship between the two notions and questions about the subjectivity of the judge.

Strictly speaking, it is not clear why the French judge could not develop further standards about the interest of public debate, if he can develop standards about a suspect's good faith as a justifying ground (Chapter 4, para. 4.4.2). Yet French legalism appears to oppose not only to the judicial balancing involved therein but also the accommodation or 'importation' of European free speech standards. As far as the latter is concerned, the ECtHR, however, has always decided that the French convictions for *hate speech* fall within the margin it uses to review restrictions to hate speech (Chapter 3, para. 1.3). With regard to the former, a judicial balancing act does not necessarily amount to a reconsideration of the balance struck by the legislator, but can also form a method to determine why, in the particular circumstances of the case, negative remarks about a particular group, although uttered in public debate, nevertheless violate the values or rights protected by the hate speech bans.

In the Netherlands, free public and political debate is not only allowed by the authority of the Dutch State but is also legitimizing it. Although this perspective leads in itself to wider boundaries in public debate, it does not prevent the existence of certain paternalistic prohibitions protecting authorities, morals and religion, such as the offence of lese majesty and the former offence of blasphemy, as the outcome of the political process. Dutch law is, however, less legalistic than French law and is characterized by more open norms that can be further 'colored' by the Dutch judge in concrete cases. In general, these may not be interpreted extensively, given the principle of legality. The Dutch Supreme Court has developed a 'three-step-test' as a standard for judicial review of the criminality of utterances under the offence of group insult and in the Wilders case the District court applied a similar test with regard to the offence of incitement to discrimination that, however, has not been endorsed by the Supreme Court – yet.

Pursuant to this test, when an utterance according to its purport and direct textual context constitutes a punishable insult, the fact that it is uttered in the context of a public or political debate on a matter of public interest can nevertheless remove its punishable character, provided that it is not gratuitously offensive. Likewise, the context of a public or political debate on a matter of public interest can remove the punishable character of an utterance that according to its purport and direct textual context constitutes a punishable incitement to discrimination, provided that it is not exceeding. Hence, when an utterance constitutes a prohibited form of hate speech, the Dutch judge can further balance the interest in upholding the norm with the interest of a free public debate. In other words, freedom of expression can form a general justification for expression that is punishable on the ground of the hate speech bans. The Dutch Constitution protects freedom of religion and freedom of expression in separate provisions. It is unclear from the case law of the Dutch Supreme Court whether in the Netherlands – unlike in France – a concurrence of these rights can result in a higher protection of religiously motivated opinions uttered in public debate than non-religiously motivated opinions *per se*. In certain decisions lower courts tend to equate the regime of religious and political convictions.

On the one hand, a further balancing act in the light of the concrete circumstances of the case appears desirable, because the hate speech bans restrict utterances on the basis of their content and therefore interfere with the core of the right to freedom of expression. This method of judicial review, then, results in a more proportional application of the hate speech bans and leaves room to discuss certain taboos in public debate; negative utterances about immigrants and foreigners in the context of a debate on the problems related to their integration and the multicultural society do not always amount to a prohibited form of hate speech but can be justified to expose social problems. Furthermore, it results from the Wilders-case that other than the direct incitement of third parties to proceed to particular acts of discrimination or violence against a particular group, political proposals to take concrete measures against a particular group, such as the proposal to refuse Muslims access to the country, that – if implemented – could violate a binding prohibition of discrimination are not by definition punishable. It remains undecided as to whether within these broad contours of public debate all citizens have equal freedom of expression or whether politicians are afforded an even larger freedom. In any event, in the Netherlands there can be a wide scope to plead for discriminatory legislation as a political solution to immigration problems and criticism of the government's immigration policy.

On the other hand, this method of judicial review can interfere with the aim of the legislator in relation to the introduction of the hate speech bans and can entirely deprive the hate speech bans of the protection they aim to assure as grounded in international law. One could even wonder whether the judge, instead of making a substantial balancing act, does not afford the right to freedom of expression such weight that competing rights or interests necessarily pale into insignificance. In fact, in certain cases the judge does not apply this test consistently and in a reasoned fashion; he seems to be inclined to simply cancel out the insulting or discrimination-inciting nature of statements with reference to the interests of freedom of expression, omitting to review whether the statements were 'gratuitously offensive' or 'exceeding'. At first sight it might appear inconsistent, when the legislator has decided to only criminalize insults and incitements that violate the reputation or dignity of the target groups and threaten their right to non-discrimination, but the judge subsequently determines the criminality of utterances on the ground of whether they are 'gratuitously offensive' or 'exceeding'. These criteria must therefore only be applied as a final proportionality-test, otherwise the judge would alter the rationale and scope of the hate speech bans as intended by the legislator. The exact significance of the criterion that discriminatory political proposals may not be 'exceeding', however, remains unclear. The latter term is open to different interpretations and is thus sensitive to an inconsistent application; it could refer both to the risk of a breach of public order in the form of violent conflict and to the aim of the destruction of the fundamental rights of others. Therefore the term must be further clarified.

The legislative history points to the latter interpretation. The Constitutional legislator of 1983 found it unnecessary to insert an abuse of rights clause into the Dutch Constitution; the hate speech bans would suffice for the protection of democracy. The function of the hate speech bans is thus notably to guarantee the fundamental rights as they exist in society without distinction on account of race and so on. The same follows from the background of the hate speech bans; the aim of the ICERD is to eliminate all forms of racial discrimination that impairs the equal enjoyment of fundamental rights. Its drafting history precisely opposes the requirement of a breach of public order or a risk of violence for the criminality of hate speech. Such a requirement resembles the 'imminent lawless action test', of which the underlying premise is, however, that the state must be entirely neutral with regard to the – discriminatory – content of expression. The hate speech bans, on the other hand, prohibit expression precisely on the basis of its discriminatory content and the effect it may have on fundamental rights. Hence, even if discriminatory political proposals are only considered punishable when they are 'exceeding', then it must still be determined whether, according to their purport and aim, they overstep the outer limits of the constitutional state, i.e. the rule of law.

If the Dutch legislator does not more specifically determine the scope and rationale of the Dutch hate speech bans, it is incumbent on the judge to crystallize further standards. The current standards in case law are, however, unclear and inconsistent. Contrary to the Wilders decision, the results of earlier case law of the Dutch Supreme Court is that the fact that a discriminatory statement forms an unspecific political proposal that the speaker hopes to put into practice once he has come to power democratically does *not* divest it of its criminality. Furthermore, the case law is also not clear in relation to which extent the interest in a free public debate can remove the punishable character of utterances that incite to hatred or violence. This appears less likely the case than with racist insults. Given the ambiguity in case law, a more ideological Constitution could nevertheless form a useful guideline for the application and interpretation of the hate speech bans. Alternatively, the judge, for the determination of the outer boundaries of public debate, could refer to Article 17 ECHR, which prohibits the abuse of rights.

The ECtHR has found complaints about a violation of the right to freedom of expression inadmissible by reference to Article 17 ECHR, which prohibits the abuse of rights. The ECtHR has applied Article 17 ECHR in this *direct* manner with regard to Nazi- and other racist propaganda, Holocaust denial, anti-Semitic and Islamophobic expression and has excluded these categories of expression from the protection of Article 10(1) ECHR on account of their content without reviewing the restriction under Article 10(2) ECHR. The ECtHR however increasingly applies Article 17 ECHR in an *indirect* manner, as an interpretative tool, when it examines the necessity of a restriction on expression in a democratic society under Article 10(2) ECHR in the case on the merits (Chapter 3, para. 1.1).

The ECtHR generally affords a high level of protection to contributions to public and political debate compared to other types of expression (Chapter 3, para. 1.1). It results from the case law that hate speech can concern, or can in itself be, a topic of general interest. Furthermore, in principle hate speech can also be aimed at contributing to a public debate. However, the Court often leaves states a large margin of appreciation to determine the necessity of restrictions to hate speech, most notably for the reason that the expression addressed problems related to the immigration and integration of foreigners or other groups. According to the Court, states are entitled to set the boundaries to the public and political debate concerning immigration and integration differently, because the extent of these problems and the measures to solve them may differ from country to country (Chapter 3, para. 1.3). This approach appears to be inconsistent with the Court's general approach towards political expression.

Firstly, immigration and integration are highly political, European issues and the ECtHR generally exercises a stringent review of restrictions on political speech, regardless of its specific topic. The fact that member states may adopt different solutions to counter political problems does not generally alter this. Secondly, the exercise of a stringent review of restrictions on political speech need not necessarily result in the conclusion that Article 10 ECHR has been violated. The two should not be equated. The ECtHR could also arrive at the conclusion that a measure is justified because a particular form of hate speech is not acceptable in political debate. The ECtHR however essentially seems reluctant to set criteria for hate speech in the politically sensitive context of immigration and integration.

Furthermore, it results from the case law that politicians in particular and more specifically parliamentarians – of the opposition – must have a large freedom to contribute to public debate and to criticize the government (Chapter 3, para. 1.1). At the same time, a majority within the ECtHR stresses the special responsibility of politicians thereby not to incite hatred and intolerance against a part of the population. The public must be protected against such irrational 'dangerous discourse'. Politicians must be aware of the effects of their words, precisely because they aim for political support, and must respect the principles of democracy, precisely because they strive to obtain political power (Chapter 3, para. 1.3). The relationship between the special freedom and the special responsibilities of politicians is thus diffuse.

The ECtHR seems to ascribe an exemplary role to politicians, whose words inevitably have a larger impact on society. To a certain extent, the duties and responsibilities of politicians can therefore be compared with those of teachers, who, according to the ECtHR, form a symbol of authority for their students and therefore must act with reserve and tolerance, even in their activities outside the school. In both cases, awareness of their special position seems to partly color the authors' intent. Moreover, one is inclined to conclude that expression of politicians may qualify as an abuse of rights sooner than expression of any other citizen. On the other hand, although the ECtHR has gradually extended the scope of Article 17 ECHR to many forms of speech deemed contrary to the 'spirit of the Convention', the ECtHR nowadays appears to exercise restraint in recurring to Article 17 ECHR – except for Holocaust denial and revisionist theories –, also with regard to speech by politicians.

The manner in which Article 17 ECHR is applied by the ECtHR appears to be inconsistent and is considered as undesirable by some because all limitations to freedom of expression should be reviewed under Article 10(2) ECHR that would be sufficient to achieve the goal of Article 17 ECHR to protect the democratic system and human rights. Furthermore, the ECtHR has been criticized for affording political parties a larger freedom to contribute to public and political debate than individual politicians have, while anti-democratic ideas expounded by political parties form a greater threat to democracy the more they reach the centre of power. In fact, the ECtHR found the dissolution of the Turkish Welfare Party justified, because its long-term political policy to set up a regime based on the Sharia was contrary to the concept of a democratic society and its leaders did not exclude the recourse to violence to force the implementation of this policy; 'the risk to democracy' was proven to be 'sufficiently imminent' (Chapter 3, para. 1.1). Indeed, this test forms a higher threshold than the standards used in hate speech cases, but actually it is tailored to the far-reaching measure of the *prohibition* and *dissolution* of a political party.

The added value of Article 17 ECHR appears to be that it can form a helpful tool for the ECtHR in determining the outer boundaries of free public and political debate. First, Article 17 ECHR can justify such far-reaching measures that otherwise might not easily pass the test of Article 10(2) / 11(2) ECHR. Secondly, the prohibition on the abuse of rights can play a role in the development of positive obligations; it seems reasonable that expression that can be qualified as an abuse of rights must at least be prohibited by law or even criminalized and prosecuted by the state. This in principle does not just apply to political parties, but also to individual politicians or citizens.

1.5. Allegation of Facts versus Value judgments

French law distinguishes between the imputation of facts and the expression of value judgments in a number of ways. The concept of the 'délit d'opinion' assumes that the expression of an opinion is only punishable, if it supports a criminal act. This principle thus does not apply to the expression of a – false – factual statement. The French legislator has, however, criminalized both defamation and insult of an individual person as an offence; he thus has found it necessary to protect persons not only against the harm 'imputations of a specific fact' inflict on their reputation, but also against the harm insults consisting of 'outrageous expression, terms of contempt or invectives' cause to their dignity. The distinction between the two offences is notably relevant, because the law sanctions defamation more severely than insult and affords a suspect the possibility to prove the truth of his defamatory statements, but not of his insulting opinions; the latter are not susceptible of proof.

French law also criminalizes defamation and insult of a person or group on the basis of his/their race, religion and so on as two separate offences and sanctions the former more severely than the latter. The distinction between racial defamation and racial insult appears, however, somewhat artificial. With regard to racial defamation, the possibility for a suspect to prove the truth of his imputations is excluded just as with regard to racial insult (Chapter 4, para. 4.4.1). The premise thus is that factual accusations against persons on the basis of their race or religion are also not susceptible of truth. Furthermore, in cases of racial defamation and racial insult, a suspect's bad faith is always presumed and his appeal on his good faith as a justifying ground is generally rejected, respectively not permitted (Chapter 4, para. 4.4.2).

On the one hand, in this practice utterances appear likely to be interpreted to the disadvantage of the suspect, as having a racist or discriminatory purport, and the burden of proof is shifted towards the suspect, who in practice has few means of defence at his disposal. Criticism of relatively high crime rates among a particular group of the population is generally interpreted as an allegation that criminality is inherent in and an immutable characteristic of that group and is thus considered punishable (Chapter 4, para. 4.3.1). However, if such criticism does not explicitly draw this conclusion, it does not necessarily have a racist or discriminatory purport, but can also have the aim of discussing problems existing within a particular group in society that might just as well be caused by socio-economic circumstances. Although to require or allow the demonstration of the factual proof that a particular group possesses certain inherent discrediting characteristics would run counter to the essence of anti-discrimination laws, the question is whether the French judge should more explicitly take into account whether or not such criticism contains any truth or a sufficient factual basis in the context of a suspect's appeal to his good faith or a free public debate on a matter of public interest. In France, such assertions are, however, in any event difficult to sustain, given the prohibition of collecting data on the behaviour of groups categorized on the basis of their race, ethnicity or religion (Chapter 4, para. 2.2). Although this prohibition has the laudable aim to prevent statistics from being misused, which may lead to racism and discrimination, it appears to complicate an informed and open public debate on and valuation of social problems.

On the other hand, the French judge discounts the interest of freedom of expression in relation to the question of whether an utterance constitutes an imputation of a specific fact or a value judgment. As a result of the case law, there is a high threshold in relation to the imputation of 'a specific fact' as the offence of racial defamation is not easily met, because hate speech often consists of generalizations about a group. This results, however, in certain inconsistencies in French case law about this distinction, depending on whether the judge desires to preserve a free debate on a specific topic. Although the imputation of the Jews to humiliate, despise and persecute the Palestinians appears just as precise as the imputation of North Africans to live off social security benefits, the judge only considered the former sufficiently precise to constitute punishable defamation (Chapter 4, para. 4.3.1; 4.5.1). Without further motivation, these different outcomes are incomprehensible and inconsistent. Such inconsistency is notably objectionable, because prosecutions on the ground of double – either cumulative or alternative – qualifications (defamation/insult) and requalification by the judge is not permitted.

Dutch law less explicitly discerns imputations of a specific fact from the expression of value judgments. While the law criminalizes defamation and insult of an individual person separately, the offence of group insult comprises both defamatory and insulting statements about a group on the basis of its race, religion and so on and in principle does not sanction them differently. Furthermore, with regard to the offence of group insult, neither the legislator nor the judge has crystalized a suspect's means of defence. The same applies to the offence of incitement to hatred, discrimination or violence. Therefore, it is unclear to which extent it is relevant that an utterance constitutes the imputation of a specific fact or a negative value judgment about a particular group and to which extent a suspect is allowed to demonstrate that his assertions contain any truth or have a sufficient factual basis.

The latter criteria do appear to be implicitly relevant for the question of whether the context of a public debate on a matter of public interest can divest an utterance from its criminality under the hate speech bans. Where the French judge thus discounts the interest of freedom of expression in relation to the question of whether all elements of the offence are met (a false fact or an insulting opinion), the Dutch judge appears to discount the distinction between facts or value judgments in the question whether the statement in question forms part of public debate. However, as the judge omits to give a more explicit motivation as to whether assertions contain any truth or have a sufficient factual basis, the case law appears to be inconsistent. In certain cases, the judge considered the depiction of Moroccans and Muslims as inherently criminal in the context of a public debate on their immigration and integration punishable. Contrarily, in the Wilders case, the judge found the conclusion from the relatively high crime rates among Moroccans and Muslims that criminality is inherent in their religion and culture permissible in the context of a public debate on problems related to immigration and integration. The judge thus sometimes appears to accept statistical correlations as a sufficient basis for the making of causal connections. However, such a negative conclusion about the inherent nature of all members of a group on the basis of its religion or ethnic background has more of a racist purport than the aim to discuss social problems and thus runs counter to the essence of the hate speech bans.

For the determination of the criminality of utterances about the Holocaust under the offence of group insult, the judge does not explicitly distinguish between facts and value judgments. The flat denial of the fact that the Holocaust has taken place, the imputation of the fact that Jews have invented the Holocaust, the minimization of the Holocaust or the making of gross jokes can all, under certain circumstances, constitute an insult that is 'gratuitously offensive' and thus punishable. The first two assertions can, however, be qualified as pertinent untrue factual statements, the aim and value of which appears likely to be more questionable than that of the latter two provocative opinions that – contrary to untrue facts – form a matter of degree; the term 'gratuitously offensive' therefore also appears to be more applicable to negative value judgments than to untrue factual statements.

The ECtHR generally strictly distinguishes between facts and value judgments in its case law concerning defamation of individual persons (Chapter 3, para. 1.1). As a result of the case law, other than for untrue factual statements, the state may not require any proof of truth with regard to negative value judgments, which in principle one is free to express, although strong negative opinions may require a sufficient factual basis and may not be 'gratuitously offensive'. These principles have notably had a strong impact on the national law in the Netherlands and also, albeit to a lesser extent, in France. It is striking that, in cases concerning hate speech, the ECtHR refers little or not at all to this distinction, while the utterances in question mainly consisted of imputations, allegations and negative opinions about a particular group. Nevertheless, the distinction appears to be implicitly relevant in the considerations of the Court. For example, the ECtHR found the restrictions to the accusation against Jews of plotting against Russia and the linking of the entire group of Muslims with the terrorist attacks of 9/11 acceptable, because these statements constituted a prohibited 'general and vehement attack on a group' (Chapter 3, para. 1.3); the underlying premise appears to be that these utterances constitute 'false factual allegations or strong negative value judgments that lacked a sufficient factual basis'.

If the ECtHR would more explicitly refer to these principles, it would make its reasoning more transparent. In its hate speech case law, however, the distinction often seems to fade, because of the broad notion of hate speech used by the ECtHR and the large margin afforded to states in determining the restrictions to the immigration and the integration debate. An exception to this is the *Le Pen* case, in which the ECtHR explicitly rejected the news facts to which Le Pen referred in his defence as a 'sufficient factual basis' for his negative value judgments about Muslims (Chapter 3, para. 1.3). However, the ECtHR neither discussed the content of these news facts nor did it give further reasoning for its decision on this point. Therefore, the decision does not shed much light on the requirement of a 'sufficient factual basis' for allegations in hate speech cases. The distinction between facts and value judgments is more structurally apparent in the ECtHR's case law concerning religious group defamation and Holocaust denial. Here it functions as a helpful tool in order to discern strong but free critical opinions about religious dogmas, institutions or officials that might hurt religious feelings but are not 'gratuitously offensive' from the prohibited actual defamation of religious groups (Chapter 3, para. 1.4) and the prohibited negation of 'the category of clearly established historical facts' which amount to the racial defamation of Jews, Nazi-propaganda and glorification from the free research, interpretation and debate on historical events (Chapter 3, para. 1.5).

By referring to the distinction between facts and value judgments in a more structural manner, the ECtHR could develop further standards to consistently distinguish between free critical remarks and hate speech. For example, the accusation that Jews are responsible for 80 percent of all murders in the Netherlands is evidently untrue and the depiction of Muslims as animals constitutes a strong value judgment that lacks any factual basis and can in any event be considered to be 'gratuitously offensive'. Such statements therefore appear unjustifiable in any public debate. More difficulties arise with the category of expression that lies in between such pertinent untrue statements and terms of abuse and merely intolerant and offensive remarks. Criticism of relatively high crime rates among a particular group of the population must be allowed. The fact that such high crime rates exist among a particular group can, however, not justify the negative conclusion that the criminality is caused by their belonging to a particular race or religion and therefore forms an inherent characteristic of that group. The proposal is thus not to introduce the proof of truth or a sufficient factual basis as a means of defence that justifies such racist conclusions; the distinction is precisely aimed at discerning such racist expression that actually affects the dignity of members of the target group from critical contributions to subjects of public debate.

The distinction between facts and value judgments does not apply to the direct and literal incitement of others to hatred, discrimination or violence against a particular group. After all, such utterances may be grounded in factual claims and opinions about a group. They do not express them but instead primarily urge others to discriminatory or violent action. Contrarily, it can be of relevance for the valuation of more indirect and disguised forms of spreading hatred and creating a breeding ground for discrimination or violence. Such expression also falls under the ECtHR's broad notion of hate speech and can consist of pertinent falsehoods, value judgments that affect people's basic dignity or mere intolerance. Generally put, the ECtHR could differentiate more between different utterances in order to better evaluate their purport in the specific context of the case. This could contribute to the development of clear and consistent standards for restrictions to hate speech. The ECtHR can only differentiate between (different levels of protection for) different forms of hate speech, if it starts using a stricter review in hate speech cases as well as in highly sensitive political discussion.

1.6. Race versus Religion

A particularity of the French law is that it does not recognize the existence of national minorities, defined by a common race, ethnic origin or religion. The French Republic only recognizes individual and equal citizens that have the right of indifference to their specific characteristics (strict equality). Against this background, the hate speech bans can be understood as a means of social integration; French citizens are not to be addressed on the basis of their specific characteristics. On the one hand, this notion of strict equality results in a more limited protection under the hate speech bans. Certain national minorities, such as the Corsicans, are not considered to constitute a group protected by the hate speech bans, even though they do form the target of defamatory and insulting remarks (Chapter 4, para. 4.3.1).

On the other hand, for those minority groups that are protected by the hate speech bans, the French strict equality results in a more robust protection of their individual members against hate speech, because the offences of racial insult, defamation and provocation explicitly protect both individuals and groups. The offences of racial defamation and insult thus protect the individual members belonging to the group on the basis of their basic, civic reputation or dignity and not a group *qua* group on the basis of a common group reputation or dignity. They protect individuals when defamatory or insulting statements are associated with shared characteristics such as race or religion. Hence, in order for an utterance to fall under the hate speech bans it does not have to target a particular group in its entirety (quantitative criterion), but a member or certain members of the group limited to a geographical area as a sum of individuals each entitled to protection (qualitative criterion) (Chapter 4, para. 4.3.1).

The hate speech bans do require that an utterance targets *persons* and, as hate speech often consists of statements about groups, the case law requires that in order for an utterance to be punishable under the hate speech bans, the group must be 'precisely designated'. The French judge does not, however, apply the latter criterion in a consistent manner. In some cases this criterion seems to signify that an utterance must explicitly name a particular target group; the judge found the enouncement of 'the inequality of races' or the denouncement of 'the mixing of races' permissible, precisely because these remarks did not refer to a particular group. Contrarily, the judge has found associations with the Nazi-ideology that did not in so many words refer to the Jewish community punishable because such expression has an inherent racist and anti-Semitic purport (Chapter 4, para. 5.2.1). Nevertheless, draft proposals to criminalize racist propaganda or the diffusion of racist and xenophobic ideas have all failed, precisely because they no longer required that the expression must directly address a person or group.

In other cases, the criterion that a group must be precisely designated seems to be more substantive and signify that, in order to qualify for protection under the hate speech bans, a group must, on the basis of its common characteristic, be sufficiently demarcated. Foreigners, immigrants and 'Harkis', i.e. North Africans who served in the French army during the Algerian wars and their descendants, do not form sufficiently designated groups to qualify for protection under the offences of racial defamation and insult (Chapter 4, para. 4.3.1; 5.2.1). On the one hand, the judge thus does require a sufficient commonality of a group in order for defamatory and insulting remarks to affect the individual reputation or dignity of its members. On the other hand, the exclusion of these groups from protection seems to be inspired by the desire to preserve a free public debate on certain topics. The degree of strictness of the 'designation'criterion, then, conceals a judicial balancing act between different interests that not necessarily always turns in favour of freedom of expression, but can differ per hate speech ban. Given the different protected interests by the different hate speech bans, then, this is not inconsistent *per se*. In fact, foreigners, immigrants and 'Harkis' are protected against incitement to hatred, discrimination or violence (Chapter 4, para. 6.3). It is likely that this also applies to Corsicans. The incitement of others to commit harmful acts against persons on whatever ground is simply not permitted in public debate.

In France, utterances concerning race and utterances concerning religion are valued differently. Unlike with race, it is not only permitted to express negative value judgments about religion in general, but also about one religion in particular, its religious figures, tenets, dogmas, institutions and practices. In fact, in 1881 the French legislator abolished the offence of blasphemy and other prohibitions of religious offence, because in his vision such offences protect religious feelings based on personal religious convictions, which requires the recognition of a religion by the State. This is contrary to the laic principle of the French Republic, which has been elaborated since 1905 and affirmed in the French Constitution since 1946. This is also contrary to the French principle of equality, according to which the State respects all beliefs equally. Since 1789, Articles 10 and 11 DDHC indeed explicitly protect the expression of religiously and non-religiously motivated opinions on equal footing.

Since the 1930s, the French hate speech bans, however, do criminalize forms of hate speech both on the basis of race and religion. Not only racial groups, but also religious groups are thus protected against hate speech. Religious and conservative associations often take legal action against vehement criticism on their religion. For the determination of the criminality of utterances about people's religion under the hate speech bans the French judge uses a number of distinct methods. First of all, the judge points to the laic character of the French State and the absence in French law of the offence of blasphemy as a reference point for the fact that opinions about the tenets, dogmas and practices of a particular religion do not fall under the scope of the hate speech bans (Chapter 4, para. 5.4; 6.5.2). Hence the ridiculing of the Catholic faith or the denouncement of the 'islamization' of French society and of the accommodation by the French State of Islamic practices, such as the wearing of the garb or the burqa, ritual slaughtering, the financing of mosques, how offensive it may be to personal religious convictions, are permitted.

Furthermore, the judge rejects any civil responsibility on the ground of Article 1382 CC that prohibits the wrongful act for utterances that merely offend religious feelings by referring to the application of the hate speech bans in civil cases and their primacy over the latter article (Chapter 4, para. 5.4.2). Subsequently, the judge interprets the hate speech bans strictly and requires utterances concerning people's religion to constitute an imputation or a 'personal and direct attack' against a 'designated' group. On the one hand, the criterion of the 'designation' of a group has proved a helpful tool for the judge to demarcate free criticism of religion from punishable hate speech against people on account of their religion. The explicit depiction of Muslims as harmful, criminal or dangerous exclusively on the ground of their religion is punishable, also in the context of a debate on immigration, integration, the 'islamization' of society and religion-state relationships (Chapter 4, para. 6.5.2; 6.5.3).

On the other hand, the application of the designation-criterion appears to be particularly delicate with regard to *religious* groups. For example, in the Mohammed cartoons case, the judge found the cartoons permissible, because they did not target 'the entire group of Muslims as a whole', but formed part of the public debate about the criminal acts committed by fundamentalists in the name of Islam (Chapter 4, para. 5.4.4). The judge thus returned to the 'old' quantitative criterion that in order to be prohibited an expression must designate the entire group. However, the criticism was eventually considered to be permissable, not because of the 'demarcation' of the group as such, but because the criticism was founded on a sufficient factual basis. Without a further elaboration on this point, however, the case law is inconsistent. The judge thus must further clarify whether the criterion that a group must be perfectly designated signifies that an utterance explicitly names a particular group, a group meets a certain degree of homogeneity or that a discrediting characteristic or behaviour is considered inherent to all members of the group. For the determination of whether an utterance about such a designated group has either a racist purport or enters into a public debate, it is inevitable that the judge will consider whether it contains any truth or has a sufficient factual basis.

In the Netherlands, the law precisely recognizes the existence of minorities and *accommodates* the enjoyment of people's ethnic identities and their cultural rights (institutionalized multiculturalism). Unlike in France, this minority approach does not raise any problems in relation to the protection of different minority groups under the hate speech bans. Strictly speaking, this focus on groups does, however, result in *less strong protection* of individuals belonging to a minority group under the hate speech bans. In fact, the offence of group insult explicitly only protects groups and not individual persons against insults on the basis of their race, religion and so on. Insults about an individual person on the basis of his race, religion and so on can only amount to group insult, when according to its purport it concerns the entire group. In practice, references to a person's race or religion are, however, likely to be interpreted as such. Otherwise, such expression can be punishable under the offences of defamation or insult of an individual person, but then the judge is not obliged to weigh the racist purport of an utterance when imposing a penalty. This technical and theoretical distinction might notably become important, if the offence of group insult would be abrogated on the ground that such expression should only be prohibited by civil law. Strictly speaking, the offences of defamation or insult of an individual cannot form a guideline for its unlawfulness under Article 6:162 DCC, because defamatory and insulting remarks about larger groupings do not identify particular persons.

Just as in France, the Dutch hate speech bans criminalize since the 1930s forms of hate speech both on the basis of race and religion. It results from the drafting history and the case law that 'criticism of religious convictions and practices' must be free and that offended religious feelings is not a criterion for criminality under the hate speech bans. The mere fact that offensive statements about a religion also offend the adherents of that religion is not sufficient for those statements to be equated with statements about those adherents. The Dutch Supreme Court has therefore ruled that in order to constitute a punishable group insult a statement must *unmistakably* refer to a particular group of people characterized by their religion. The Court has thereby demarcated the offence of group insult from the at the time 'dormant' offence of blasphemy that precisely criminalizes statements that denigrate the concept of God by 'scornful' blasphemy, i.e. in a manner that is offensive to religious feelings. This *unmistakably* criterion, then, forms the Dutch equivalent of the French requirement that a group must be 'precisely designated'. In Dutch case law, it seems to notably signify that an utterance must explicitly name the target group ('Muslims'). On the one hand, a strict application of this criterion appears to be a helpful tool for the determination of the criminality of utterances about people's religion under the hate speech bans; it has the advantage of simplicity and thus serves legal certainty. On the other hand, a strict application of this criterion appears inconsistent with the drafting history, according to which in 'hybrid' cases the criminality of an utterance about a particular religion/its adherents depends on whether the speaker intended to pass judgment on the adherents or the beliefs. Eventually the judge must determine whether such a judgment constitutes a punishable form of insult.

Another question is whether certain statements about a religion can be so vicious and aggressive that they should be regarded as a punishable form of inciting hatred or discrimination against believers. In the Wilders case, the court considered that a statement must also *unmistakably* refer to a particular religious group in order to constitute a punishable incitement to hatred and discrimination. On the one hand, it logically follows that making associations and links between the 'islamization' of immigration to the Netherlands and higher crime rates in the Netherlands in the abstract without naming a particular group is not punishable. On the other hand, it appears to be inconsistent that in that case the offence did not even cover the attribution of the fact that one in five Moroccans are registered with the police as suspects to their religion and culture, because Islam is a violent religion and the problems therefore lie in the community itself. After all, the statement, by the way it is worded, clearly refers to the group of Moroccans in connection with their religion. Furthermore, it also appears inconsistent that in that same case statements that explicitly name Muslims are initially regarded as incitements to discrimination against them on the basis of their religion, but are later divested of their criminality by the argument of the need for free public debate on Islam *without any further motivation* (*supra*).

This illustrates that the fact that an utterance explicitly names a religious group does not in itself say anything about whether it has a punishable purport and that the view of the legislators and the Supreme Court that criticism of 'religious practices' is not a criminal offence is in need of clarification. Does this effectively refer to facts of common knowledge? Does it refer to establishing a – potential – connection between religion and antisocial behaviour? Must all the members of the group display particular behaviour, or is it sufficient for there to be a statistical relationship? Is it merely about gauging particular risks? Hence, just as in France, the Dutch judge must thus further clarify the criterion that an utterance must 'unmistakably' refer to a particular group of people characterized by their religion and, for the determination of whether an utterance has either a racist purport or enters into a public debate, must consider whether it contains any truth or has a sufficient factual basis.

Also in the Netherlands utterances concerning race and utterances concerning religion are valued differently. The criterion that an utterance must 'unmistakably' refer to a particular group does not apply to hate speech on the basis of race. The Supreme Court accepts the propagation of racist ideologies through the dissemination of Nazi symbols as a punishable form of incitement to hatred and discrimination against the Jewish population. Such statements do not explicitly name the Jewish population, but do spread hatred against that group because of the associations they awaken with Nazism, the Second World War and the Holocaust. The Court also accepts the ridiculing, denial or trivialization of the Second World War and the Holocaust as a punishable form of group insult to the Jewish population. Such insulting statements are also not worded so as to refer directly to the Jewish population, but because of the sensitivity of the subject with which the group identifies these statements 'offend the feelings of the group'.

On the one hand, the rejection of the associative power of utterances about Islam and islamization but the acceptance of such power of racist ideologies and symbols is not in itself inconsistent, because the association is of a different nature. The association with Nazism can be regarded as a substantial threat to the Jewish population, as it involves behaving towards them from a Nazi point of view. Contrarily, the association by Wilders between Islam and Nazism through a comparison between the Koran and *Mein Kampf* suggests a similarity between Muslims and the Nazis, but this does not imply a Nazi-type threat. However, it does appear that the question of whether, in the context of a public debate on the immigration and integration of foreigners, Islam as a religion is not treated as the hallmark of people's racial and ethnic identity is somewhat overlooked in the case law. When an attack on Islam may, on the basis of its context, actually be considered to be an attack on immigrants or Arabs, at least the judge should explain why it is not regarded and treated as such.

On the other hand, the case law does appear to be inconsistent in that Holocaust denial can constitute a punishable form of group insult on the ground that such expression deeply offends the sensitivities and feelings of the victims of the Holocaust or their relatives. This creates a special protection for a specific group; why would the law not also protect the feelings of other groups of the population against offence through statements about other atrocities? Moreover, why then would the law not also protect the feelings of Muslims or other religious adherents against offence through statements about Islam or another religion? Hence, it must be clearly explained why an utterance about the Holocaust or Islam constitutes a defamatory or insulting statement *about* Jews, respectively Muslims that violate their dignity or constitutes an incitement against them.

It follows from the ECtHR's broad notion of hate speech that the Court does not principally distinguish between hate speech on the basis of religion and hate speech on the basis of race. The case law does suggest that racist expression that refers to the superiority or inferiority of a race, the attribution of inherited biological characteristics to a racial group and Anti-Semitism qualifies sooner as an abuse of rights. A majority within the ECtHR however also considers restrictions to discourses that incite to hatred founded religious, ethnic or cultural prejudices acceptable under Article 10(2). This equally applies to hate speech on the basis of sexual orientation. The ECtHR implies that such religious prejudice and hatred based on sexual orientation is just as serious as racist hate speech (Chapter 3, para. 1.3).

A minority within the ECtHR makes a stricter distinction between 'classic racist hate speech' and other forms of intolerant speech that, in the vision of the minority, do not have a racist purport. The strict distinction between hate speech on the basis of race and hate speech on the basis of religion seems untenable. Most cases concerning hate speech on the basis of religion before the ECtHR concerned the attribution of negative qualities or behavior to immigrants, foreigners, or a particular ethnic group on the basis of their religion, as it were their inherited biological characteristics. If the ECtHR found the restrictions to religious prejudice in these cases acceptable, because a religion was in fact treated as the hallmark of people's racial and ethnic identity, it had better explicitly explain this.

The ECtHR has, however, also accepted restrictions to hate speech against a group purely on the basis of its religion. The ECtHR increasingly distinguishes between unprotected gratuitously offensive attacks on *persons* on the basis of their religion from protected criticism on a religion, its religious dogmas, institutions or officials (Chapter 3, para. 1.4). However, unlike in the Dutch and French courts, the ECtHR does not require that an utterance must 'unmistakably' concern a particular group or that a group must be precisely designated. The Court leaves open the possibility that criticism on religious dogmas and institutions expressed in a provocative manner and insulting tone can constitute an improper attack on a religion and thereby be indirectly gratuitously offensive or defamatory to its adherents. Moreover, the ECtHR does not principally reject the criminalization of blasphemy as such. Finally, the ECtHR has also not explicitly abandoned its conception of the issue of blasphemy and religious offence as a direct conflict between freedom of expression and freedom of religion that – in the vision of the Court – includes the right of respect of religious feelings of others.

The reference by the ECtHR to Article 9 appears to be quite inconsistent. In fact, other than in cases concerning blasphemy, in cases of hate speech on the basis of religion such reference was absent, while religious rights appear notably at stake in cases of actual incitement to hatred against a particular religious group. However, when the ECtHR accepts restrictions to religiously offensive expression for constituting a violation of Article 9, the Court should explain in which manner such speech actually affected or threatened to affect the free exercise of the religion by its adherents, the onus of which is on the state. The ECtHR has, however, rejected any positive duty for the state to prosecute expression that amounts to blasphemy and religious offence under Article 9 (Chapter 3, para. 1.6). This is not in itself inconsistent, because affording states the *possibility* to criminalize such speech under the ECHR does not necessarily entail the *obligation* to prosecute it. To date, under the ECHR, this also applies to hate speech against people on the basis of their religion.

1.7. In sum

It results from the above synthesis that the approaches to hate speech in the examined legal systems each have their own (dis)advantages and score differently with regard to the four factors. As far as the ECHR is concerned, it is briefly stipulated that the development of clearer standards for the restriction of hate speech on the grounds of religion and religiously offensive speech, is principally blocked by the ECtHR's broad margin of appreciation. The ECtHR could notably make a clearer distinction between utterances about people's race and utterances about people's religion and better explain when and why restrictions to the latter are permissible.

As for France, on the whole, one could say that the French legalism cannot prevent the appearance of inconsistencies in the case law on hate speech. To the contrary, the strict and abstract application of the French hate speech bans by the judge dissimulates the importance that is sometimes implicitly attached to freedom of expression. In France, the interest of a free public debate could be taken into account in a more explicit and structural manner. The Dutch approach, then, could form an inspiration for France in that the Dutch judge more explicitly balances the less crystallized hate speech bans with the right to freedom of expression. This generally leads to a more transparent judicial reasoning.

However, the Dutch case law must also provide clear standards that are structurally applied. It appears that the Dutch approach is also not without inconsistencies. Dutch law precisely scores low on the distinction between actions and opinions. The Dutch norms could better clarify the exact values and interests they aim to protect and the required connection between an utterance and subsequent acts of discrimination and violence by third parties against members of the target group. The French approach, then, could form an inspiration for the Netherlands in that the principles and values of the French Constitution function more as a compass for the application of the hate speech bans and the determination of the outer limits to public and political debate.

Finally, it appears that all examined legal systems could more accurately differentiate between different types of hate speech. One can distinguish, on the one hand, between pertinent untrue factual claims, strong value judgment that lack any factual basis and are 'gratuitously offensive'; and direct and literal incitements for which the proof of truth or a sufficient factual basis can be no means of defence and, on the other hand, value judgments that have a sufficient factual basis or are not gratuitously offensive and mere intolerant and offensive remarks. The former qualify sooner for restriction than the latter. By referring to the distinction between facts and value judgments in a more structural manner, further standards could be developed to consistently distinguish between free critical remarks and hate speech.

2. Towards greater consistency

The previous paragraph analysed the law of the examined legal systems. Each system scored differently as far as the four factors of the analytic framework are concerned. This paragraph advances, on the basis of the entire research, a number of considerations that could contribute to the determination of restrictions to hate speech – on account of religion – in a consistent manner. Ten bullet points are formulated and further elaborated in smaller font. Here the four factors selected for the analysis (being actions versus opinions; public debate versus other types of expression; facts versus value judgments; and race versus religion) and the actors in the determination of restrictions to hate speech (being the legislator, the judge, the public prosecution and victims, and anti-racism and minority associations) are being interlinked. No further detailed reference to the law of the examined systems is made; these have precisely been excluded in order to make recommendations of a more general application.

- The French concept of the 'délit d'opinion' can form an inspiration for the thought that a consistent norm directed against a particular form of hate speech must as precisely as possible determine which types of utterances it prohibits and reflect which rights and interests it wants to protect. More generally, given the principle of legality, restrictions to hate speech must be strictly construed and not be 'overbroad'.

  It is, in principle, the legislator who *a priori* and *in abstracto* determines the restrictions to hate speech by creating specific hate speech offences. Hate speech bans, by their very nature, prohibit utterances that target persons or groups defined by a common characteristic. It is desirable that this is unambiguously reflected in the statutory wording of the offences. Offences criminalizing defamation or insult of groups or incitement to hatred, discrimination or violence against persons comply with this criterion. Contrarily, blasphemy and Holocaust denial laws may not be regarded as proper hate speech bans, because, according to their statutory wording, they prohibit utterances that target religious figures or a historical truth. This does not signify that utterances about a particular religion or the Holocaust under certain circumstances, thus *in concreto*, cannot amount to hate speech against a particular group and constitute a prohibited form of group defamation or 'incitement'. The judge then must clearly explain why this is the case. Furthermore, the legislator must, one way or another, clarify what interests the hate speech bans protect. It is preferable that these can unmistakably be derived from the hate speech bans themselves. In any event, the categorization of the hate speech bans in the law must, as much as possible, fit in with the protected interests. As hate speech bans, by their very nature, can be assumed to primarily protect persons, they in principle belong to the category of offences against persons. This applies in any event to group defamations and insults. To the extent that the legislator with the creation of the offence of incitement – as well as group defamation and insult – has aimed to protect the public order, he must at least clarify what the notion of public order in this particular context signifies. In fact, the judge must, in the application of the hate speech bans, take the aims of the legislator into account.

– Hate speech bans can prohibit expression on the basis of a certain degree of probability that the expression will succeed in inciting to discrimination and violence by others against the target group. Such causation can be more or less direct, varying from likelihood to capability to imminence. A consistent norm must mark a spot somewhere on this gradual scale.

The offence of incitement to hatred, discrimination or violence requires the 'activation of a triangular relationship between the object and subject of the speech as well as the audience', i.e. a speaker can induce third parties to act in a certain manner towards the target group of the speech. It is precisely this triangular relationship that may, next to harming persons, also affect public order. This does not signify that any proven effect on the public order necessarily forms a requirement of criminality on the basis of 'incitement'. Nor does the incitement have to be followed by effect; it is by definition an 'inchoate crime'. The triangular relationship does signify that criminal law can be regarded as the proper means to counter incitements to hatred, discrimination or violence. 'Hatred' is, however, a vague term that refers to an emotion or an attitude towards others and not to particular actions against them. However, the importance of the prevention of discrimination and violence may precisely justify the countering of racist discourse at an early stage. In principle, the offence, according to its statutory wording, can include both utterances that have an imminent connection with subsequent actions of discrimination or violence and whose harmful effect are rather direct and utterances that do not have such an imminent connection with subsequent actions, but still are likely to contribute to future discrimination and violence and can be harmful in the mid- and long term. The legislator must therefore clearly choose the required degree of probability that expression will succeed in inciting to discrimination and violence in order for it to be punishable. In the application of the offence in concrete cases, the judge then must clearly determine whether or not an utterance complies with this required degree of probability. One could question whether it is desirable for the legislator to prohibit *a priori* and *in abstracto* a category of expression, such as the 'dissemination of ideas based on racial hatred' or 'racist propaganda', without explaining that such expression is harmful because it can lead to discrimination or violence or is per definition harmful to human dignity. After all, such an offence would, according to its statutory wording, just as with Holocaust denial and blasphemy, prohibit 'opinions' without indicating the interests (object) it aims to protect. It might then be considered preferable if the judge would only under certain circumstances, given the contextual factors, thus *in concreto*, qualify such racist opinions as a prohibited form of 'incitement'.

- Hate speech bans can also prohibit expression, because it violates human dignity. Then, a consistent norm must clearly indicate when expression actually *affects* the equal basic dignity of members of the target group.

The prohibition of group defamation or insult by the legislator without the requirement that such expression is uttered with the aim to incite hatred or that it in fact constitutes an incitement is controversial; it directly protects members of the target group against a violation of their reputation or dignity not against subsequent actions by third parties. The prohibition of group defamation and insult without the requirement that expression is aimed at 'inciting' hatred is therefore not required by international law, let alone its criminalization. However, with Waldron and French Republicanism, it can be presumed that every citizen has the right to respect for his equal basic dignity and that the reciprocal respect between citizens thereof forms a public good. In the context of hate speech this signifies that group vilifications and insults that violate people's equal basic dignity can be prohibited as a form of aggression in and of itself. A consistent norm must then clarify that such expression is prohibited not because it violates human dignity as a public moral, but because it actually *affects* the equal basic dignity of its victims because of the consecutive effects it has on them (psychic harm) or the public at large (discriminatory views or practices). Then human dignity takes on a different meaning and assault on human dignity becomes a concrete problem for victims of hate speech. The legislator can clarify this by explicitly referring to the impairment of the equal basic dignity of the target group as an element of the offence. This does not only afford legal certainty, it also demarcates the scope of the offence; offensive and intolerant opinions will not meet this threshold. The public interest to counter expression that affects people's equal basic dignity separate from any aim or likelihood that such expression leads to acts of discrimination or violence, its effect on the public order and the harm to the target group caused by such expression may, however, be considered too little to justify its criminal repression. Then, group defamation and insult that actually violate people's equal basic dignity can at least be considered unlawful. Such expression may not identify one particular person and harm its personal reputation, it is directed against a large number of people, thought of as a group, and can harm the equal basic dignity of all persons of that kind.

- For a consistent demarcation of – prohibited forms of hate speech against – persons adhering to a particular religion from – permissible criticism of – the convictions and practices of religion as such, a first starting point can be to consider whether expression clearly designates a particular religious group.

  In principle, one can distinguish criticism of a particular religion from utterances about its religious adherents. After all, religion generally consists of a coherent set of convictions and prescriptions. Those convictions and prescriptions can also form the basis for opinions on social and political issues and for behaviour and practices of religious adherents. Criticism thereof can be aimed at a religion as well as its followers as a group. In order to consistently demarcate permissible criticism of religious convictions and practices from prohibited hate speech against persons on the basis of religion, the criterion that an utterance must 'unmistakably' concern a group on the basis of its religion or that a group must be 'perfectly designated' in principle forms a helpful and simple tool. A consistent norm, then, must clarify whether this signifies that utterances, in order to constitute hate speech, must always explicitly name a group, whether a group must have a certain degree of homogeneity or whether a negative quality or characteristic is in fact attributed to all members of the group. The criterion that, in order to be punishable, an utterance must clearly designate a religious group is most applicable to the offences of defamation and insult that according to their nature prohibit utterances *about* a group. With regard to the offence of incitement to hatred, discrimination or violence, in principle a distinction can also be made between statements that present certain religious convictions and practices as totally reprehensible and hateful on the one hand and statements about persons on the other. On the other hand, situations are conceivable where statements about a religion are so vicious that they can be punishable as incitements to hatred. The judge then must clearly explain why this is the case. In fact, statements on the 'islamization' of society that do not explicitly refer to Muslims as a group can also be interpreted as criticism on existing state – religious relationships and the place of religion in the public domain. In the end, the criminality of an utterance does not, however, merely depend on whether it clearly designates a particular group; the judge must clearly explain where the defamatory, insulting or threatening character of expression resides.

- Another criterion for demarcating speech about religious adherents from speech about a religion as such can be whether an 'intersectionality between race and religion' exists, i.e. whether an utterance treats the religious beliefs of members of a group as the hallmark of their racial and ethnic identity.

Another criterion for demarcating speech about religious adherents from speech about a religion as such can be whether an 'intersectionality between race and religion' exists. In principle, a distinction can be made between utterances about a particular religion and utterances about a particular race. Unlike religion, race is supposed to be an immutable characteristic that people cannot change. The rejection of a particular race implies that the people belonging to that race must also be rejected. This is different to religion. It is likely that utterances about a particular race will sooner exceed the limits of the law than utterances about a particular religion. However, cases can arise where hate speech discourse is careful to avoid direct racial or ethnic insults or incitements and may have 'switched' its language from the racial/ethnic to the religious in relation to the same targeted community. For example, an attack on Islam may, on the basis of its context, actually be an attack on immigrants or Arabs. When the public prosecution demonstrates that such an 'insectionality between race and religion' exists, then the judge should at least motivate why he does not regard and treat an utterance as such. Given the problematic character of the discriminatory ground of religion, some argue in favour of confining the hate speech bans to the discriminatory ground of race. Even then, hate speech bans must at least include cases where an 'intersectionality between race and religion' exists. Such a broad interpretation of the discriminatory ground of race by the judge appears, however, not to be beneficial to the clarity of the prohibitions. Another solution can be that the legislator gives a better description of the scope of the discriminatory ground of religion, for example by inserting a clause that exempts criticism of religious convictions and practices. In principle such criticism must be allowed, even when it can have all kinds of associations and connotations. This is different with utterances that contain 'associations' with certain racist ideologies such as Nazism that is per definition harmful to human dignity. In the end, the criminality of an utterance does not merely depend on whether, according to the context, an 'intersectionality between race and religion' exists; the judge must always clearly explain where the defamatory, insulting or threatening character of expression resides.

- In order to consistently distinguish between free critical remarks and prohibited hate speech on the basis of religion, a norm must accurately differentiate between factual statements and value judgments. Pertinent untrue factual statements about a particular group and strong value judgments that lack a sufficient factual basis or are 'gratuitously offensive' are in principle unjustifiable; this is also the case when uttered in the context of a public debate.

A consistent norm must clearly distinguish between different types of hate speech. Restrictions to pertinent untrue factual statements and strong value judgments about a particular group that lack a sufficient factual basis or are 'gratuitously offensive', such as strong racist epithets, invectives and terms of abuse, are in principle justifiable, precisely because such statements violate people's equal basic dignity. This also applies when such expression is uttered in the context of a public debate. It is difficult to sustain that such statements enter into a public debate on a matter of public concern. More difficulties arise with the category of expression that lies in between such pertinent untrue statements and negative value judgments that are gratuitously offensive and merely intolerant and offensive remarks, such as vague allegations and generalizations. It is beyond discussion that serious scientific research into the role of people's religion in certain tendencies and conduct must be permitted. Furthermore, criticism of relatively high crime rates among a particular group of the population uttered in the context of a public debate on the issue of immigration and integration must also be allowed. Such criticism can, however, amount to prohibited hate speech when it refers to high crime rates among a particular group as being per definition caused by their belonging to a particular race or religion, especially if it is presented as a ground to discriminate the members of the group and deny them an equal enjoyment of fundamental rights. Then the statement violates the equal basic dignity of members of the target group. In order to consistently distinguish between free critical remarks and prohibited hate speech, a consistent norm must clarify to which extent an utterance that makes a connection between certain actual or supposed behaviour or practices and people's race or religion can/must be substantiated by a factual basis. This primarily is a task for the judge when applying offences of group defamation/insult *in concreto*. From the perspective of both freedom of expression and legal certainty, the legislator could, however, also more clearly demarcate the scope of the offence of group defamation/insult, by limiting its statutory wording to pertinent untrue factual accusations and strong epithets, invectives and terms of abuse. Another possibility that would afford the judge more leeway is if the legislator introduces a clause exempting contributions to public debate provided that they are not 'gratuitously offensive'. The latter term is, however, more applicable to negative value judgments than to untrue facts; other than facts, value judgments can be viewed as a matter of degree. The distinction between facts and value judgments does not apply to the direct and literal incitement of others to hatred, discrimination or violence against a particular group. After all, such utterances may be grounded on factual claims and opinions about a group, they do not express them but primarily urge others to discriminatory or violent action. Contrarily, the distinction can be of relevance for the valuation of more indirect and disguised forms of spreading hatred and creating a breeding ground for discrimination or violence through vague allegations. Therefore, in such cases the judge can also take into account the distinction between facts and value judgments for the application of the offence of incitement to hatred, discrimination or violence.

- In order to consistently distinguish between harsh criticism of the government and hate speech against particular minorities, a norm must clarify when contributions to public debate overstep the outer limits of the democratic constitutional state. This is in any event the case when speech aims at the destruction of the fundamental rights of others. It can be argued that at least a positive obligation for the state exists to criminalize and prosecute against such forms of hate speech.

A consistent norm directed at expression uttered in public debate must clearly distinguish harsh criticism of government authorities, officials and policies from hate speech against particular minorities. It is not obvious that the context of a public debate can remove the punishable character of an utterance that incites to hatred, hostility or violence against sectors of the population. With regard to 'incitement' to 'discrimination', a consistent norm must more specifically distinguish between the persuasion of others to adopt discriminatory thoughts or visions; the calling into question of constitutional principles of human dignity, equality and non-discrimination in the abstract; the urging of fellow citizens to proceed to specific acts of discrimination; and concrete legislative proposals that discriminate on account of race or religion. Only the latter two may be characterized as hate speech, because they target the position of particular groups within the state in such a manner that it can affect their fundamental rights. Incitement to 'discrimination' precisely refers to such prohibited and unjustified forms of unequal treatment. The law then must clarify whether both types of utterences are punishable. It can be argued that the judge, for the determination of the criminality of an utterance, must always explicitly take into account the importance of a public debate; this can structure a robust motivation on the proportional application of the offence given the specific circumstances of the case. For those legal systems where the judge is only permitted to strictly apply statutory law as created by the legislator, the question arises whether the latter had better facilitate such robust motivation by introducing a clause exempting contributions to public debate provided that they do not exceed the outer limits of the democratic state. For those legal systems where the judge is permitted to interpret statutory law and balance the upholding of a norm with the right to freedom of expression, the introduction of such a clause can also be useful, especially when a broader constitutional framework that compels or constrains an unambiguous interpretation of the offence by the judge is absent. A more fundamental approach would be, if the Constitution would define the characteristics of the democratic state or refer to the inviolability of the human dignity, which can function as a compass for a consistent determination of restrictions to hate speech by both the legislator and the judge.

- A consistent norm must also clarify whether citizens, who participate in public and political debate, all have the same degree of freedom of expression or whether certain functions or positions bring either special freedoms or special responsibilities. The position or function of a politician can in any event form a contextual factor that influences the valuation of his intent or the qualification of his expression as an abuse of rights.

It is in principle logical that in a democracy, citizens must have an equal degree of freedom to express their opinions in public and political debate. It can be argued that the principle of equality is opposed to affording certain citizens per definition special freedoms or special responsibilities on the basis of their particular functions or positions. However, this does not signify that a speaker's position or function cannot form a contextual factor that influences the valuation of his intent or the qualification of his expression as a prohibited form of hate speech. For example, politicians and notably members of the opposition in Parliament must have ample room to criticize the government, for example with regard to its immigration policy. Harsh criticism of the government's immigration policy often goes along with harsh criticism of a particular minority group and political proposals for improvement, which include measures that can affect the fundamental rights of the group concerned. Then an inherent tension exists between the freedom and responsibilities of a politician. In fact, politicians strive to obtain the support of citizens for their ideas and their words inevitably have a larger impact on society. This is precisely why politicians may be aware of the effect of their speech. This awareness can partly color their intent. Furthermore, politicians may be considered to take into account the principles of a democracy, precisely because they strive to obtain political power. It can be contended that expression of politicians may qualify as an abuse of rights sooner than expression of any other citizen.

- While the legislator must set restrictions to hate speech *a priori* and *in abstracto*, the judge must apply the hate speech bans created by the legislator *in concreto* thereby explicitly taking into account certain contextual factors and the right to freedom of expression. The legislator must define the speech offences in such a way that facilitates consistent judicial adjudication and compels the judge to give a structural robust motivation of his decisions.

Restrictions to hate speech are determined by the interplay of different actors. It is primarily the legislator who has the task of determining the substantive restrictions to freedom of expression by setting them out in statutory laws. The legislator must interpret the extent of freedom of expression in the light of the broader constitutional framework that may to a stronger or lesser extent have an ideological nature. When constitutional principles are absent, the legislator has to rely on his own considerations; this does not make it impossible for the legislator to create consistent legislation, but a changing policy increases the chance of inconsistency. It can be reasoned that the less clear the broader constitutional framework compels an unambiguous application of a hate speech ban by the judge, the more precise the norm must arise from the offence itself. The judge, in the application of the norm as defined, is confronted with a series of complicated questions related to the four previously discussed factors, being actions/opinions; public debate/other expression; facts/value judgments; race/religion. The legislator must provide a legislative framework that not only facilitates consistent judicial adjudication but also compels the judge to give a structural robust motivation of his decisions. This applies both to those legal systems where the judge is only permitted to strictly apply statutory law as created by the legislator and to those legal systems where the judge is permitted to interpret statutory law and balance the upholding of a norm with the right to freedom of expression. This research has brought to the fore a number of suggestions for law reform that can form the basis for further discussion. The legislator is, amongst others, faced with the choice of the creation of specific criminal speech offences and/or restrictions in civil law. A rationale behind the criminalization of hate speech can be – next to the public interest in countering such speech – that in a constitutional state based on the separation of powers, a primary task of the legislator is to assure legal certainty for its citizens by creating clearly defined, demarcated norms. Creating specific criminal offences is a means of clearly demarcating such substantive restrictions and thereby, paradoxically, guaranteeing freedom of expression. Criminal speech offences may function as a guideline or even a basis for determining civil liability for hate speech. As a result, the criminal and civil restrictions to freedom of expression do not necessarily defer much or can even coincide. In fact, from the perspective of legal certainty, it can be argued that hate speech may only be considered unlawful when it violates a particular hate speech ban.

- Existing hate speech bans must be effectively enforced. The public prosecution must carry out a clear prosecution policy, the consistency of which he must be able to explain to civil society. As regards the explanation of this policy to the victims of hate speech, anti-racism associations and other interest groups could play a role. One could even go further and afford the latter a role in the decision to prosecute in cases of hate speech.

Existing hate speech bans must be effectively enforced. A clear legislative framework facilitates a clear prosecution policy of the public prosecution. The appreciation of the criminality of utterances is, however, not an evaluation of the evidence like any other; it requires an interpretation of an utterance within its context and a balancing act with freedom of expression. The line between opportunity, evaluation of the evidence and sitting on the seat of the judge seems particularly vague. Furthermore, in politically sensitive cases, the public prosecution may refrain from prosecuting out of fear of creating 'free speech martyrs'. The public prosecution must, however, be able to explain the consistency of its prosecution policy to civil society. One can go even further and afford anti-racism associations and other interest groups a role in the decision to prosecute. One option is to establish a structural cooperation and consultation between the prosecution and anti-racism associations and other interest groups in the process of deciding on the prosecution of cases of hate speech. A more far reaching option is that the law affords anti-racism associations and other interest groups the possibility to set in motion criminal prosecutions on the ground of the hate speech bans. The participation of civil society in the enforcement of the hate speech bans can contribute to their effective enforcement, – clarifying – developments in case law and can afford victims of hate speech, who nowadays also notably include Muslims as a religious group, effective access to justice. It must be ensured, however, that such participation does not have a chilling effect on freedom of expression and does not amount to an unduly juridification of public debate.

These findings hopefully answer the central research question of this study, being to which extent restrictions to hate speech on the basis of religion can be determined in a consistent manner. The modest intention of this study has been to draw lessons from a comparative analysis of the consistency of restrictions to hate speech in French, Dutch and – selected instruments of – international and European law on the basis of a limited number of factors. The study identified those areas where the determination of restrictions to hate speech on the basis of religion may be improved. The intention has not been to offer single ready-made solutions. The findings of this study can, however, form a starting point for further research, for example, about the role of anti-racism, minority and other civil society associations in the effective countering of hate speech and providing victims of hate speech with effective access to justice. Hopefully, this study can give an impetus to scientific, political and public discussion about the regulation of hate speech.

Bibliography

Chapter 1 General Introduction

Books, contributions to collective works and scientific articles

Borgetto 1997
Borgetto, M., *La devise "Liberté, Égalité, Fraternité"*, Que sais-je?, n° 3196, Paris: Presses Universitaires de France 1997.

Dommering 2008
Dommering, E.J., De Teddybeer Mohammed, gesluierde homo's en het lawaai van Wilders: Over de stand van de vrijheid van meningsuiting anno 2008, *Nederlands Juristenblad*, 2008–7, p. 376–382.

Gonthier 2000
Gonthier, C.D., Liberty, Equality, Fraternity: The Forgotten Leg of the Trilogy, or Fraternity: The Unspoken Third Pillar of Democracy, *Mc Gill Law Journal* 2000, vol. 45, p. 567–589.

Hare & Weinstein 2009
Hare, I. & Weinstein, J. (Eds.), *Extreme Speech and Democracy*, Oxford: Oxford University Press 2009.

Hennebel & Hochmann 2011
Hennebel, L. & Hochmann, T. (eds.), *Genocide denials and the law*, Oxford: Oxford University Press 2011.

Herz & Molnar 2012
Herz, M., & Molnar, P. (Eds.), *The Content and Context of Hate Speech: Rethinking Regulation and Responses*, Cambridge: Cambridge University Press 2012.

Janssen 2014
E.H. Janssen, Wilders, waardigheid en de grenzen van het politiek debat, *Nederlands Juristenblad* 2014–24, p. 1814–1820.

Maitra & McGowan 2012
Maitra, I., & McGowan, M. K., *Speech & Harm: Controversies over Free Speech*, Oxford: Oxford University Press 2012.

McGonagle 2011
McGonagle, T.E., *Minority rights, freedom of expression and of the media: dynamics and dilemmas*, Cambridge: Intersentia 2011.

McGonagle 2013
McGonagle, T., *The Council of Europe against online hate speech: Conundrums and challenges*, Expert paper, doc.no. MCM 2013(005), the Council of Europe Conference of Ministers responsible for Media and Information Society, 'Freedom of Expression and Democracy in the Digital Age: Opportunities, Rights, Responsibilities', Belgrade, 7–8 November 2013.

Molnar & Post 2012
Molnar, P & Post, R., Interview with Robert Post, in: Herz & Molnar 2012, p. 11–36.

Nieuwenhuis 2011
Nieuwenhuis, A.J., *Over de grens van de vrijheid van meningsuiting*, Nijmegen: Ars Aequi Libri 2011.

Parekh 2012
Parekh, B., Is There a Case for Banning Hate Speech?, in: Herz & Molnar 2012, p. 37–56.

Peters 1981
Peters, J.A. *Het primaat van de vrijheid van meningsuiting* (diss.), Nijmegen: Ars Aequi Libri 1981.

Rosier 1998
Rosier, T.E., *Vrijheid van meningsuiting en discriminatie in Nederland en Amerika* (diss.), Nijmegen: Ars Aequi 1998.

Van Noorloos 2011
Van Noorloos, M., *Hate Speech Revisited, A comparative and historical perspective on hate speech law in the Netherlands and England & Wales* (diss.), Antwerpen: Intersentia 2011.

Waldron 2012
Waldron, J., *The Harm in Hate Speech*, Cambridge: Harvard University Press 2012.

Weber 2009
Weber, A., *Manual on hate speech,* Council of Europe, Leiden: Martinus Nijhoff Publishers 2009.

Weinstein & Hare 2009
Weinstein, J. & Hare, I., General introduction: free speech, democracy, and the suppression of extreme speech past and present, in: Hare & Weinstein 2009, p. 1–7.

Reports and documents

Committee of Ministers, *Recommendation No. R (97)20 to Member States on 'hate speech'*, adopted on 30 October 1997.

European Commission against Racism and Intolerance, *Report on France (fourth monitoring cycle)*, adopted 29 April 2010.

European Commission against Racism and Intolerance, *Report on The Netherlands (fourth monitoring cycle)*, adopted 20 June 2013.

Case law

ECtHR 16 July 2009, no. 15615/07 (Féret v. Belgium).
ECtHR 20 April 2010, no. 18788/09 (Le Pen v. France).

French Supreme Court, crim. Ch., 3 February 2009, n°06–83063 08–82402, *Bull. Crim.* 2009, n°25 (*LePen*).

Amsterdam District Court 23 May 2011, *LJN* BQ5561 (*Wilders*).

Newspaper articles

'Marine Le Pen compare les 'prières de rue' des musulmans à une 'occupation', *Le Monde* 11 December 2010.

''Incitation à la haine raciale': que risque vraiment Marine Le Pen?', *Le Monde* 2 July 2013.

'Marine Le Pen wil Wilders helpen bij campagne Europese verkiezingen', *NRC Handelsblad* 14 September 2013.

'*Minute*: la justice ouvre une enquête pour injure publique à caractère racial', *Le Figaro online* 12 November 2013.

Chapter 2 Analytic Framework

Books, contributions to collective works and scientific articles

Alexander 1993
Alexander, L., Liberalism, Religion, and the Unity of Epistemology, *San Diego law review*, 1993, vol. 30, no. 4, p. 763–798.

Alexander 2005
Alexander, L., *Is there a right of freedom of expression?*, Cambridge: Cambridge University Press 2005.

Audi 1997
Audi, R., *Religion in the public square, the place of religious convictions in political debate*, Lanham, MD: Rowman & Littlefield 1997.

Austin 1976
Austin, J.L., *How to do things with words*, Oxford: Oxford University Press 1976.

Baker 1989
Baker, C.E., *Human Liberty and Freedom of Speech,* New York: Oxford University Press 1989.

Baker 2012
Baker, C. E., Hate Speech, in: Herz & Molnar 2012, p. 57–80.

Barendt 2005
Barendt, E., *Freedom of Speech*, 2nd ed., Oxford: Oxford University Press 2005.

Barendt 2007
Barendt, E., Free Speech and Religion: Secular and Religious Perspectives on Truth, in: Sajó 2007, p. 23–40.

Berlin 1958
Berlin, I., *Two concepts of liberty*, Oxford: Clarendon Press 1958.

Bermann 2008
Bermann, G. A. & Picard, E. (eds.), *Introduction to French law*, Alphen aan den Rijn: Kluwer Law International 2008.

Bollinger 1986
Bollinger, L.C., *The tolerant society,* New York: Oxford University Press 1986.

Bollinger 1990
Bollinger, L.C., 'The tolerant society': a response to critics, *Columbia Law Review* 1990, vol. 90, no. 4, p. 979–1003.

Bollinger 1995
Bollinger, L.C., Rethinking Group Libel, in: Freedman & Freedman 1995, p. 243–251.

Bollinger & Stone 2002
Bollinger, L.C. & Stone, G. R. (Eds.), *Eternally vigilant, Free Speech in the Modern Era*, Chicago: The University of Chicago Press 2002.

Bromme 1985
Bromme, J.S., Group Defamation, *Texas Law Review,* 1985, vol. 64, p. 591–624.

Butler 1997
Butler, J., *Excitable speech a politics of the performative*, New York, NY: Routledge 1997.

Casanova 2001
Casanova, J., Articles – 2000 Presidential Address – Religion, the New Millennium and Globalization, *Sociology of religion: a quarterly review*, 2001, vol. 62, no. 4, p. 415–441.

Chafee 1948
Chafee, Z., *Government and Mass Communications*, Cambridge: Cambridge University Press 1948.

Colliver 1992
Colliver, S. (ed.), *Striking a Balance: Hate Speech, Freedom of Expression and Non-Discrimination,* Colchester, UK: Human Rights Centre, University of Essex 1992.

Delgado & Stefancic 2004
Delgado, R. & Stefancic, J., *Understanding words that wound*, Boulder, CO: Westview Press 2004.

Douglas 1995
Douglas, L., The Force of Words: Fish, Matsuda, MacKinnon, and the Theory of Discursive Violence, *Law & society review* 1995, vol. 29, no. 1, p. 169–190.

Dworkin 1979
Dworkin, R.M., *Taking rights seriously*, Cambridge, MA: Harvard University Press 1979.

Dworkin 2009
Dworkin, R.M., Foreword, in: Hare & Weinstein 2009, vii.

Dworkin 2012
Dworkin, R., Reply to Jeremy Waldron, in: Herz & Molnar 2012, p. 341–344.

Evans 2001
Evans, C., *Freedom of religion under the European Convention on Human Rights*, Oxford: Oxford University Press 2001.

Feinberg 1984
Feinberg, J., *The moral limits of the criminal law, vol. 1 Harm to Others*, New York: Oxford University Press 1984.

Feinberg 1985
Feinberg, J., *The moral limits of the criminal law, vol. 2 Offense to Others*, New York: Oxford University Press 1985.

Feinberg 1990
Feinberg, J., *The moral limits of the criminal law, vol. 4 Harmless wrongdoing*, New York: Oxford University Press 1990.

Feldman 1999
Feldman, D., Human Dignity as a legal value: Part 1, *Public Law* 1999, Winter, p. 682–702.

Feldman 2000
Feldman, D., Human Dignity as a legal value: Part 2, *Public Law* 2000, Spring, p. 61–76.

Finan 1988
Finan, E., The fact-opinion determination in defamation, *Columbia Law Review*, 1988, vol. 88, p. 809–840.

Fish & Olson 1994
Fish, S. & Olson, G.A., *There's no such thing as free speech and it's a good thing, too*, New York: Oxford University Press 1994.

Freedman & Freedman 1995
Freedman, M.H., & Freedman, E.M. (Eds.), *Group Defamation and Freedom of Speech, the relationship between language and violence*, Westport, CT: Greenwood Press 1995.

Galenkamp 1998
Galenkamp, E.M., Individualism versus collectivism, the concept of collective rights, Arnhem: Gouda Quint 1998.

Gray & Smiths 1991
Gray, J. & Smiths, G.W. (Eds.), *J.S. Mill 'On Liberty' in focus*, London: Routledge 1991.

Greenawalt 1984
Greenawalt, K., Religion as a concept in constitutional law, *California law review*, 1984, vol. 72, no. 5, p. 753–815.

Greenawalt 2002
Greenawalt, K., 'Clear and Present Danger' and Criminal Speech, in: Bollinger & Stone 2002, p. 96–119.

Greene 2012
Greene, J., Hate Speech and the Demos, in: Herz & Molnar 2012, p. 92–115.

Grimm 2009
Grimm, D., The Holocaust Denial Decision of the Federal Constitutional Court of Germany, in: Hare & Weinstein 2009, p. 557–561.

Gunn 2003
Gunn, T.J., The Complexity of Religion and the Definition of 'Religion' in International Law, *Harvard Human Rights Journal*, 2003, vol. 16, p.189–215.

Haarscher 2009
Haarscher, G., Are religious sensitivities above the Constitution? Reflections on the collective defamation of religious people, in: Sajó 2009.

Habermas & Rehg 1996
Habermas, J. & Rehg, W., *Between facts and norms, contributions to a discourse theory of law and democracy*, Cambridge, Mass.: The MIT Press 1996.

Habermas 2006
Habermas, J., Religion in the public sphere, *European journal of philosophy*, 2006, vol. 14, no. 1, p. 1–25.

Haney Lopez 1994
Haney Lopez, I.F., The Social Construction of Race, *Harvard Civil Rights – Civil Liberties Law Review*, 1994, vol. 29, p. 1–62.

Hansen 1993
Hansen, M.F., Fact, Opinion and Consensus: The Verifiability of Allegedly Defamatory Speech, *The George Washington Law Review*, 1993, vol. 62, p. 43–99.

Hare & Weinstein 2009
Hare, I. & Weinstein, J. (Eds.), *Extreme Speech and Democracy*, Oxford: Oxford University Press 2009.

Heinze 2006
Heinze, E., Cumulative Jurisprudence and Hate Speech: Sexual Orientation and Analogies to Disability, Age and Obesity, in: Hare & Weinstein 2006, p. 265–285.

Herz & Molnar 2012
Herz, M., & Molnar, P. (Eds.), *The Content and Context of Hate Speech: Rethinking Regulation and Responses*, Cambridge: Cambridge University Press 2012.

Heyman 2008
Heyman, S., *Free Speech and Human Dignity*, New Haven, CT: Yale University Press 2008.

Heyman 2009
Heyman, S., Hate Speech, Public Discourse and the First Amendment, in: Hare & Weinstein 2009, p. 158–181.

Hennebel & Hochmann 2011
Hennebel, L. & Hochmann, T., *Genocide Denials and the Law*, Oxford: Oxford University Press 2011.

Huntington 1996
Huntington, S.P., *The clash of civilizations and the remaking of world order*, New York: Simon & Schuster 1996.

Jones 1999
Jones, P., Human Rights, Group Rights and Peoples' Rights, *Human Rights Quarterly: a comparative and international journal of the social sciences, philosophy and law*, 1999, vol. 21, no. 1, p. 80–107.

Keane 2006
Keane, D., Addressing the aggravated meeting point of race and religion, *University of Maryland Law Journal of Race, Religion, Gender & Class* 2006, p. 367–406.

Kyriakides, Virdee & Modood 2009
Kyriakides, C., Virdee, S. & Modood, T., Racism, Muslims and the National Imagination, *Journal of Ethnic and Migration Studies*, 2009, Vol. 35, no. 2, p. 289–308.

Laclau & Mouffe 2001
Laclau, E. & Mouffe, C., *Hegemony and Socialist Strategy, Towards a Radical Democratic Politics*, 2nd ed., London: Verso 2001.

Langton 1993
Langton, R., Speech Acts and Unspeakable Acts, *Philosophy & public affairs* 1993, vol. 22, no. 4, p. 293–330.

Langton 1998
Langton, R., Subordination, Silence, and Pornography's Authority, in: Post (ed.) 1998, p. 261–283.

Lerner 1987
Lerner, N., Group Libel Revisited, *Israel Yearbook on Human Rights* 1987, 17, p. 189–196.

Lerner 2000
Lerner, N., The Nature and Minimum Standards of Freedom of Religion or Belief, *Brigham Young University Law Review* 2000, p. 905–932.

Lewis 2009
Lewis, A., *Freedom for the Thought We Hate: A Biography of the First Amendment*, New York: Basic Books 2009.

Lindgren Alves 2008
Lindgren Alves, J.A., Race and Religion in the United Nations Committee on the Elimination of Racial Discrimination, *University of San Francisco Law Review* 2008, vol. 42, p. 941–982.

Loewenstein 1937-I
Loewenstein, K., Militant Democracy and Fundamental rights I, *The American Political Science Review*, 1937, Vol. 31, No. 3, p. 417–432.

Loewenstein 1937-II
Loewenstein, K., Militant Democracy and Fundamental rights II, *The American Political Science Review*, 1937, Vol. 31, No. 4, p. 638–658.

Mahlmann 2007
Mahlmann, M., Free Speech and the Rights of Religion, in: Sajó 2007, p. 41–69.

Maitra & McGowan 2012
Maitra, I., & McGowan, M. K. (Eds.), *Speech & Harm: Controversies over Free Speech*, Oxford: Oxford University Press 2012.

Marcus 1983
Marcus, E.T., Group defamation and Individual Actions: A New Look at an Old Rule, *California Law Review*, 1983, vol. 71, no. 5, p. 1532–1556.

Matsuda 1989
Matsuda, M., Public Responses to racist Speech: Considering the Victim's Story, *Michigan Law Review*, 1989, vol. 87, p. 2320–2381.

Matsuda 1993
Matsuda, M. *et al.* (Eds.), *Words That Wound: Critical Race Theory, Assaultive Speech, and the First Amendment*, Boulder, CO: Westview Press 1993.

Mbongo 2009
Mbongo, B., Hate speech, extreme speech and collective defamation in French law, in: Hare & Weinstein 2009, p. 221–236.

McCrudden 2008
McCrudden, C., Human Dignity and Judicial Interpretation of Human Rights, *EJIL* 2008, vol. 19, no. 4, p. 655–724.

McDonald 1991
McDonald, M., Should communities have rights? Reflections on liberal individualism, *Canadian Journal of Law and Jurisprudence*, 1991, Vol. 4, no. 2, p. 217–217.

McGeever & Ashe 2011
McGeever, B.F. & Ashe, S.D., Marxism, racism and the construction of 'race' as a social and political relation: an interview with professor Robert Miles, *Ethnic and Racial Studies*, 2011, Vol. 34, no. 12, p. 2009–2026.

McGonagle 2011
McGonagle, T.E., *Minority rights, freedom of expression and of the media: dynamics and dilemmas*, Cambridge: Intersentia 2011.

Meiklejohn 1979
Meiklejohn, A., *Political freedom the constitutional powers of the people,* Westport, Conn.: Greenwood Press 1979.

Mill 1936
Mill, J.S., *On Liberty,* Fourth ed., London: Watts & Co. Ltd., 1936.

Milo 2008
Milo, D., *Defamation and freedom of speech*, Oxford: Oxford University Press 2008.

Milton 1999
Milton, J., *Areopagitica and other political writings of John Milton*, Indianapolis: Liberty Fund 1999.

Molnar 2009
Molnar, P., Towards an improved law and policy on 'Hate Speech' – The clear and present danger test in Hungary, in: Hare & Weinstein 2009, p. 237–264.

Molnar 2012
Molnar, P., Responding to 'Hate Speech' with Art, Education, and the Imminent Danger Test, in: Herz & Molnar 2012, p. 193–195.

Molnar & Malik 2012
Molnar, P., & Malik, K., Interview with Kenan Malik, in: Herz & Molnar 2012, p. 81–91.

Molnar & Post 2012
Molnar, P., & Post, R., Interview with Robert Post. in: Herz & Molnar 2012, p. 11–36.

Molnar & Strossen 2012
Molnar, P., & Strossen, N., Interview with Nadine Strossen, in: Herz & Molnar 2012, p. 378–398.

Muller 2008
Muller, J.Z., Us and them: the enduring power of ethnic nationalism, *Foreign Affairs*, March-April, 2008, Vol. 87, no. 2, p. 18 – 35.

Nagel 1987
Nagel, T., Moral Conflict and Political Legitimacy, *Philosophy & public affairs*, 1987, vol. 16, no. 3, p. 213–240.

Nieuwenhuis 2011
Nieuwenhuis, A.J., *Over de grens van de vrijheid van meningsuiting*, Nijmegen: Ars Aequi Libri 2011.

Ott 1990
Ott, R.W., Fact and opinion in defamation: recognizing the formative power of context, *Fordham Law Review*, 1990, vol. 58, p. 761–794.

Parekh 2012
Parekh, B., Is There a Case for Banning Hate Speech?, in: Herz & Molnar 2012, p. 37–56.

Pech 2011
Pech, L., The Law of Holocaust Denial in Europe, in: Hennebel & Hochmann 2011, p. 185–234.

Polelle 2003
Polelle, M.J., Racial and ethnic group defamation: a speech-friendly proposal, *Boston College Third World Law Journal* 2003, vol.23, p. 213–273.

Post 1986
Post, R.C., The Social Foundations of Defamation law: Reputation and the Constitution, *California Law Review* 1986, vol. 74, p. 691–742.

Post 1988
Post, R., Cultural Heterogeneity and Law: Pornography, Blasphemy and the First Amendment, *California Law Review*, 1988, vol. 76, no. 2, p. 297–335.

Post 1990
Post, R., The Constitutional Concept of Public Discourse: Outrageous Opinion, Democratic Deliberation, and Hustler Magazine v. Falwell, *Harvard Law Review*, 1990, vol. 103, no. 3, p. 601–686.

Post 1998
Post, R.C., *Censorship and silencing, practices of cultural regulation*, Los Angeles: Getty Research Institute for the History of Art and the Humanities 1998.

Post 2007
Post, R., Religion and Freedom of Speech, Portraits of Muhammed, *Constellations: an international journal of critical and democratic theory*, 2007, vol. 14, no. 1, p. 72–90.

Rao 2011
Rao, N., Three concepts of dignity in constitutional law, *Notre Dame Law Review* 2011, vol. 86, p. 183–271.

Rawls 1993
Rawls, J., *Political liberalism*, New York: Colombia University Press 1993.

Raz 1988
Raz, J., *The morality of freedom*, Oxford: Clarendon Press 1988.

Rosenfeld 2012
Rosenfeld, M., Hate Speech in Constitutional Jurisprudence, A Comparative Analysis, in: Herz & Molnar 2012, p. 242–289.

Rosier 1997
Rosier, T., *Vrijheid van meningsuiting en discriminatie in Nederland en Amerika*, Nijmegen: Ars Aequi Libri 1997.

Sadurski 1989
Sadurski, W., On Legal Definitions of Religion, *The Australian law journal*, 1989, vol. 63, p. 834–843.

Sadurski 1996
Sadurski, W., 'On seeing speech through an equality lens': a critique of egalitarian arguments for suppression of hate speech and pornography, *Oxford journal of legal studies* 1996, vol. 16, no. 4, p. 713–724.

Sadurski 1999
Sadurski, W., *Freedom of Speech and its Limits*, Dordrecht: Kluwer Academic Publishers 1999.

Sajó 2004
Sajó, A. (ed.), *Militant democracy*, Utrecht: Eleven International Publishing 2004.

Sajó & Uitz 2005
Sajó, A. & Uitz, R., (eds.), *The constitution in private relations: expanding constitutionalism*, The Hague: Eleven International Publishing 2005.

Sajó 2007
Sajó, A. (Ed.), *Censorial sensitivities: free speech and religion in a fundamentalist world*, Utrecht: Eleven International Publishing 2007.

Sajó 2009
Sajó, A. (Ed.), *Is there something above/behind the Constitution?*, Kluwer 2009.

Scanlon 1972
Scanlon, T., A Theory of Freedom of Expression, *Philosophy & public affairs* 1972, vol. 1, no. 2, p. 204–226.

Scanlon 1979
Scanlon, T., Freedom of expression and categories of expression, *University of Pittsburg Law Review* 1979, vol. 40, no. 3, p. 519–550.

Schauer 1982
Schauer, F., *Free speech a philosophical enquiry*, Cambridge: Cambridge University Press 1982.

Schauer 1985
Schauer, F., Slippery Slopes, *Harvard Law Review,* 1985, vol. 99, p. 361–383.

Schauer 2004
Schauer, F., Media Law, Media Content, and American Exceptionalism, in: IRIS *Special*, Political Debate and the Role of the Media, the Fragility of Free Speech, European Audiovisual Observatory, Strasbourg 2004, p. 61–70.

Schauer 2005
Schauer, F., The Exceptional First Amendment, in: Ignatieff, M. (Ed.), *American Exceptionalism and Human Rights*, Princeton: Princeton University Press 2005, p. 29–56.

Schauer 2012
Schauer, F., Social Epistemology, Holocaust Denial, and the Post-Millian Calculus, in: Herz & Molnar 2012, p. 129–143.

Searle 1969
Searle, J., *Speech Acts: An Essay in the Philosophy of Language,* Cambridge: Cambridge University Press 1969.

Smedley & Smedley 2005
Smedley, A. & Smedley, B.D., Race as biology is fiction, racism as a social problem is real: anthropological and historical perspectives on the social construction of race, *The American Psychologist*, 2005, Vol. 60, no. 1), p.16 – 26.

Stern 2008
Stern, N., The certainty principle as justification for the group defamation rule, *Arizona State Law Journal*, 2008, vol. 40, p. 951–1001.

Stone 2009
Stone, G.R., Free Speech in the Twenty-First Century: Ten Lessons from the Twentieth Century, *Pepperdine Law Review* 2009, vol.36, p. 273–300.

Suk 2012
Suk, J. C., Holocaust Denial and the Free-Speech Theory of the State, in: Herz & Molnar 2012, p. 144–63.

'Symposium: An Ocean Apart – Freedom of Expression in Europe and the United States', *Indiana Law Journal* 2009, vol. 84, no. 3, p. 809 *et seq.*

Thiel 2009
Thiel, M. (ed.), *The 'Militant Democracy' Principle in Modern Democracies*, Farnham, Surrey: Ashgate 2009.

Thomas 1986
Thomas, J.E., Statements of Fact, Statements of Opinion, and the First Amendment, *California Law Review*, 1986, vol. 74, p. 1001–1056.

Troper 2005
Troper. M., Who needs a third party effect doctrine? – The case of France, in: Sajó & Uitz 2005, p. 115–128.

Troper 2008
Troper, M., Constitutional Law, in: Bermann & Picard 2008, p. 1–34.

Tsesis 2009
Tsesis, A., Dignity and Speech: The Regulation of Hate Speech in a Democracy, *Wake Forest Law Review*, 2009, vol. 44, p. 497–532.

Van Noorloos 2011
Van Noorloos, M., *Hate Speech Revisited, A comparative and historical perspective on hate speech law in the Netherlands and England & Wales*, Cambridge: Intersentia 2011.

Vermeulen 2011
Vermeulen, B., 'Strafbare belediging van God, godsdienst, godsdienstigen', in: P.H.P.H.M.C. van Kempen e.a. (red.), *Levend strafrecht, strafrechtelijke vernieuwingen in een maatschappelijke context, Liber amicorum Ybo Buruma*, Deventer: Kluwer 2011, p. 663–664.

Vrielink 2010
Vrielink, J., *Van haat gesproken? Een rechtsantropologisch onderzoek naar de bestrijding van rasgerelateerde uitingsdelicten in België*, Antwerpen-Apeldoorn: Maklu 2010.

Waldron 2008
Waldron, J., The Dignity of Groups, in: Barnard-Naudé, J. *et al.* (Eds.), *Acta Juridica 2008: Dignity, Freedom and the Post-Apartheid Legal Order*, South Africa, Juta Law 2008, p. 66–90.

Waldron 2012-I
Waldron, J., *The Harm in Hate Speech*, Cambridge: Harvard University Press 2012.

Waldron 2012-II
Waldron, J., Hate Speech and Political Legitimacy, in: Herz & Molnar 2012, p. 329–340.

Weil 2009
Weil, P., The politics of Memory: Bans and Commemorations', in: Hare & Weinstein 2009, p. 562–579.

Weinstein 2009
Weinstein, J., Extreme Speech, Public Order, and Democracy: Lessons from *The Masses*, in: Hare & Weinstein 2009, p. 23–61.

Weinstein 2012
Weinstein, J., Overlapping Consensus or Marketplace of Religions? Rawls and Smith, *Philosophia*, 2012, Vol. 40, no. 2, p. 223–236.

Judgments by the U.S. Supreme Court

Schenck v. United States, 249 *U.S.* 47 (*1919*).
Abrams v. US, 250 U.S. 616 (1919).
Chaplinsky v. New Hampshire, 315 U.S. 568 (1942).
Terminiello v. Chicago, 337 U.S. 1 (1949).
Beauharnais v. Illinois, 343 U.S. 250 (1952).
Brandenburg v. Ohio, 395 U.S. 444, 447 (1969).
Street v. New York, 394 U.S. 576 (1969).
Cohen v. California, 403 U.S. 15 (1971).
Gooding v. Wilson, 405 U.S. 518 (1972).
Lewis v. City of New Orleans, 408 U.S. 913 (1972).
Gertz v. Robert Welch, Inc., 418 U.S. 323 (1974).
Ollman v. Evans, 750 F.2d 970 (D.C. Cir. 1984) (en banc), *cert. denied,* 471 U.S. 1127 (1985).
National Socialist Party of America v. Village of Skokie, 432 U.S. 43 (1977).
R.A.V. v. City of St. Paul, 505 U.S. 377 (1992).
Virginia v. Black, 538 U.S. 343 (2003).

Websites

www.article19.org/
www.merriam-webster.com/
http://oxforddictionaries.com/

Chapter 3 International and European law

Books, contributions to collective works and scientific articles

Belavusau 2010
Belavusau, U., A *Dernier Cri* from Strasbourg: an ever formidable challenge of hate speech (*Soulas & Others v. France, Leroy v. France, Balsyte-Lideikiene v. Lithuania), European Public Law*, 2010, vol. 16, no. 3, p. 373–389.

Berry 2011
Berry, S.E., Bringing Muslim Minorities within the International Convention on the Elimination of All Forms of Racial Discrimination – Square Peg in a Round Hole?, *Human Rights Law Review* 2011, vol. 11, no. 3, p. 431–450.

Bossuyt 1987
Bossuyt, M.J., *Guide to the 'Travaux Préparatoires' of the International Covenant on Civil and Political Rights*, Dordrecht: Martinus Nijhoff Publishers 1987.

Buyse 2014
Buyse, A., Contested Contours, the limits of freedom of expression from an abuse of rights perspective – Article 10 and 17 ECHR, in: Brems, E., & Gerards, J. (eds.), *Shaping Rights in the ECHR, the Role of the European Court of Human Rights in Determining the Scope of Human Rights,* Cambridge: Cambridge University Press 2014, p. 183–208.

Cannie & Voorhoof 2011
Cannie, H. & Voorhoof, D., The abuse clause and freedom of expression in the European human rights convention: an added value for democracy and human rights protection?, *Netherlands Quarterly of Human Rights*, 2011, vol. 29, no. 1, p. 54–83.

Chelini-Pont 2010
Chelini-Pont, B., La mobilisation de l'Organisation de la Conférence Islamique Mondiale contre la diffamation de l'Islam (1999–2009) et ses conséquences en Europe, *Droit et Religions* 2009–2010, vol. 4, p. 525–552.

Evans 2009
Evans, M., The Freedom of Religion or Belief and the Freedom of Expression, *Religion and Human Rights*, Vol. 4, No. 2–3, September 2009, p. 197–235.

Fenwick & Philipson 2006
Fenwick, H. & Phillipson, G., *Media Freedom under the Human Rights Act*, Oxford: Oxford University Press 2006.

Gerards 2010
Gerards, J.H., Pluralism, Deference and the Margin of Appreciation Doctrine, *European Law Journal* 2010, vol.17, issue 1., p. 80–120.

Gerards 2014

Gerards, J.H., Diverging Fundamental Rights Standards and the Role of the European Court of Human Rights, To be published in: M. Claes and M. De Visser (eds), *Constructing European Constitutional Law*, Oxford: Hart 2014.

Haarscher 2010

Haarscher, G., Are Religious Sensitivities above the Constitution? Reflections on the Collective Defamation of Religious People, in: Sajo, A, & Uitz, R., *Constitutional Topography: Values and Constitutions*, Issues in Constitutional law, no. 6, The Hague: Eleven Publishing 2010, p. 367–384.

Harris, O'Boyle & Warbrick 2009

Harris, D.J., O'Boyle, M. & Warbrick, C., Law of the European Convention on Human Rights, Oxford: Oxford University Press 2009.

Keane 2006

Keane, D., Addressing the aggravated meeting point of race and religion, *University of Maryland Law Journal of Race, Religion, Gender & Class* 2006, p. 367–406.

Keane 2007

Keane, D., Attacking hate speech under Article 17 of the European convention on human rights, *Netherlands Quarterly of Human Rights,* 2007, vol. 25, no. 4, p. 641–663.

Lawson 2010

Lawson, R.A., Schuifelend langs de muur, Het Hof markeert de grenzen van de vrijheid van meningsuiting voor politici, *NTM/NJCM-bulletin* 2010, vol. 35 no. 5, p. 539–540.

Leigh 2011

Leigh, I., Damned if they do, Damned if they don't: the European Court of Human Rights and the Protection of Religion from Attack, *Res Publica,* 2011, vol. 17, p. 55–73.

Lerner 1980

Lerner, N., *The U.N. Convention on the Elimination of all Forms of Racial Discrimination*, Alphen aan den Rijn: Sijthoff & Noordhoff 1980.

Lerner 2000

Lerner, N., The Nature and Minimum Standards of Freedom of Religion or Belief, *Brigham Young University Law Review* 2000, p. 905–932.

Lindgren Alves 2008

Lindgren Alves, J.A., Race and Religion in the United Nations Committee on the Elimination of Racial Discrimination, *University of San Francisco Law Review* 2008, vol. 42, p. 941–982.

Mahalic & Mahalic 1987

Mahalic, D. & Mahalic, J., The Limitation Provisions of the ICERD, *Human Rights Quarterly* 1987, p. 74–101.

McGonagle 2012
McGonagle, T., A Survey and Critical Analysis of Council of Europe Strategies for Countering 'Hate Speech', in: Herz & Molnar 2012, p. 456–498.

Mendel 2012
Mendel, T., Does International Law Provide for Consistent Rules on Hate Speech?, Herz & Molnar 2012, p. 417–429.

Meron 1985
Meron, T., The Meaning and Reach of the ICERD, *The American Journal of International Law* 1985, vol. 79, no. 2, p. 296–298.

Nowak 2005
Nowak, M., *U.N. Covenant on Civil and Political Rights: CCPR commentary*, Kehl: N.P. Engel 2005.

Oetheimer 2009
Oetheimer, M., Protecting freedom of expression: the challenge of hate speech in the European court of human rights case law, *Cardozo Journal of International and Comparative Law*, 2009, vol. 17, p. 427–443.

O'Flaherty 2012
O'Flaherty, M., Freedom of Expression: Article 19 of the International Covenant on Civil and Political Rights and the Human Rights Committee's General Comment No 34, *Human Rights Law Review* 2012, vol. 12, no. 4, p. 627–654.

Partsch 1992
Partsch, K.J., Racial speech and human rights: Article 4 of the Convention on the Elimination of All Forms of Racial Discrimination, in: Coliver, S., (ed.), *Striking a Balance: Hate Speech, Freedom of Expression and Non-Discrimination*, London: Article 19 1992, p. 21–28.

Randall 2006
Randall, M.H., Commercial Speech under the European Convention on Human Rights: Subordinate or Equal?, *Human Rights Law Review*, 2006, vol. 6, no. 1, p. 53–86.

Schwelb 1966
Schwelb, E., The International Convention on the Elimination of All Forms of Racial Discrimination, *The International and Comparative Law Quarterly* 1966, vol. 15, no. 4, p. 996–1068.

Schokkenbroek 1996
Schokkenbroek, J.G.C., *Toetsing aan de vrijheidsrechten van het Europees Verdrag tot bescherming van de rechten van de mens: een onderzoek naar de toetsing aan de beperkingsclausules bij de Europese vrijheidsrechten in de Europese en in de Nederlandse rechtspraak*, Zwolle: W.E.J. Tjeenk Willink 1996.

Sottiaux 2003

Sottiaux, S., The 'Clear and Present Danger' Test in the Case Law of the European Court of Human Rights, *Zeitschrift für ausländisches öffentliches Recht und Völkerrecht*, 2003, vol. 64, no. 3, p. 653–681.

Sottiaux 2011

Sottiaux, S., 'Bad Tendencies' in the ECtHR's 'Hate Speech' Jurisprudence, *European Constitutional Law Review*, 2011, vol. 7, no. 1, p. 40–63.

Sottiaux & Rummens

Sottiaux, S. & Rummens, S., Concentric democracy: Resolving the incoherence in the European Court of Human Rights' case law on freedom of expression and freedom of association, *International Journal of Constitutional Law*, 2012, vol. 10, no. 1, p.106–126.

Special issue on Advocacy of religious hatred Religion & Human Rights, Martinus Nijhoff Publishers, Brill, Leiden, Volume 5, no. 2–3, 2010.

Sullivan 1988

Sullivan, D.J., Advancing the Freedom of Religion or Belief Through the UN Declaration on the Elimination of Religious Intolerance and discrimination, *The American Journal of International Law* 1988, vol. 82, no. 3, p. 487–520.

Temperman 2008

Temperman, J., Blasphemy, Defamation of Religions and Human Rights Law, *Netherlands Quarterly of Human Rights* 2008, 26/4, p. 517–545.

Temperman 2011

Temperman, J., Freedom of expression and religious sensitivities in pluralist societies: facing the challenge of extreme speech, *Brigham Young University Law Review* 2011, p. 729–757.

Thornberry 2010

Thornberry, P., Forms of Hate Speech and the Convention on the Elimination of all Forms of Racial Discrimination (ICERD), *Religion & Human Rights* 2010, vol. 5, p. 97–117.

Tulkens 2012

Tulkens, F., When to say is to do, Freedom of expression and hate speech in the case law of the European Court of Human Rights, in: *Freedom of Expression, Essays in honour of Nicolas Bratza, President of the European Court of Human Rights*, Oisterwijk: Wolf Legal Publishers 2012, p. 279–297.

Van Dijk *et al* 2006

Van Dijk, P., Van Hoof, F., Van Rijn, A. & Zwaak, L., Theory and Practice of the European Convention on Human Rights, Antwerpen: Intersentia 2006.

Vande Lanotte & Haeck 2004

Vande Lanotte, J. & Haeck, Y., *Handboek EVRM*, Antwerpen: Intersentia 2004.

Vandenhole 2005
Vandenhole, W., *Non-Discrimination and Equality in the View of the UN Human Rights Treaty Bodies*, Antwerpen: Intersentia 2005.

Voorhoof 1999
Voorhoof, D. 'Het Europese First Amendment'. De Straatsburgse jurisprudentie over artikel 10 EVRM (1996-juli 1999), *Mediaforum* 1999, no. 10, p. 264–271.

Weber 2009
Weber, A., *Manual on Hate Speech*, Strasbourg: Council of Europe Publishing 2009.

Case law

ECmHR / ECtHR

ECmHR 20 July 1957, no. 250/57 (Kommunistische Partei Deuthschlands v. Germany).
ECmHR 11 October 1979, no. 8348/78 8406/78 (Glimmerveen and Hagenbeek v. the Netherlands).
ECmHR 12 May 1988, no. 12194/86 (Kuhnen v. Germany).
ECmHR 5 March 1991, no. 17439/90 (Choudhury v. United Kingdom).
ECmHR 6 September 1995, no. 25096/94 (Otto E.F.A. Remer v. Germany).
ECmHR 18 October 1995, no. 25062/94 (Honsik v. Austria).
ECmHR 24 June 1996, no. 31159/96 (Marais v. France).
ECmHR 18 April 1997, no. 33490/96 (Dubowska and Skup v. Poland).

ECtHR 1 July 1961, no. 332/57 (Lawless v. Ireland no. 3).
ECtHR 7 December 1976, no. 5095/71 5920/72 5926/72 (Kjeldsen, Busk Madsen and Pedersen v. Denmark).
ECtHR 7 December 1976, no. 5493/72 (Handyside v. United Kingdom).
ECtHR 26 April 1979, no. 6538/74 (Sunday Times v. The United Kingdom).
ECtHR 13 August 1981, no. 7601/76 7806/77 (Young, James and Webster v. the United Kingdom).
ECtHR 24 May 1985, no. 10737/84 (Muller v. Switzerland).
ECtHR 8 July 1986, no. 9815/82 (Lingens v. Austria).
ECtHR 24 May 1988, no. 10737/84 (Muller and Others v. Switzerland).
ECtHR 22 May 1990, no. 12726/87 (Autronic v. Switzerland).
ECtHR 23 May 1991, no. 11662/85 (Oberschlick v. Austria).
ECtHR 26 November 1991, no. 13166/87 (Sunday Times 2 v. The United Kingdom).
ECtHR 23 April 1992, no. 11798/85 (Castells v. Spain).
ECtHR 28 August 1992, no. 13704/88 (Schwabe v. Austria).
ECtHR 16 December 1992, no. 12945/87 (Hadjianastassiou v. Greece).
ECtHR 24 January 1993, no. 13914/88 15041/89 15717/89 15779/89 17207/90 (Lentia and Others v. Austria).
ECtHR 20 September 1994, no. 13470/87 (Otto Preminger Institute v. Austria).

ECtHR (Grand Chamber) 23 September 1994, no. 15890/89 (Jersild v. Denmark).
ECtHR (Grand Chamber) 23 March 1995, no. 15318/89 (Loizidou v. Turkey).
ECtHR 13 July 1995, no. 18139/91 (Tolstoy Miloslavsky v. The United Kingdom).
ECtHR (Grand Chamber) 26 September 1995, no. 17851/91 (Vogt v. Germany).
ECtHR 25 November 1996, no. 17419/90 (Wingrove v. The United Kingdom).
ECtHR 24 February 1997, no. 19983/92 (De Haes and Gijsels v. Belgium).
ECtHR 1 July 1997, no. 20834/92 (Oberschlick v. Austria no. 2).
ECtHR (Grand Chamber) 25 November 1997, no. 18954/91 (Zana v. Turkey).
ECtHR (Grand Chamber) 30 January 1998, no. 19392/92 (United Communist Party of Turkey and Others v. Turkey).
ECtHR (Grand Chamber) 19 February 1998, no. 24839/94 (Bowman v. The United Kingdom).
ECtHR (Grand Chamber) 9 June 1998, no. 22678/93 (Incal v. Turkey).
ECtHR 23 September 1998, no. 24662/94 (Lehideux and Isorni v. France).
ECtHR 23 September 1998, no. 24838/94 (Steel and Others v. The United Kingdom).
ECtHR 20 April 1999, no. 41448/98, (Witschz v. Germany).
ECtHR (Grand Chamber) 29 April 1999, no. 25088/94 28331/95 28443/95 (Chassagnou v. France).
ECtHR (Grand Chamber) 20 May 1999, no. 21980/93 (Bladet Tromsø and Stensaas v. Norway).
ECtHR 20 May 1999, no. 25390/94 (Rekvényi v. Hungary).
ECtHR 8 July 1999, no. 23168/94 (Karakaş v. Turkey).
ECtHR (Grand Chamber) 8 July 1999, no. 23536/94 24408/94 (Başkaya and Okçuoğlu v. Turkey).
ECtHR (Grand Chamber) 8 July 1999, no. 23556/94 (Ceylan v. Turkey).
ECtHR (Grand Chamber) 8 July 1999, no. 23927/94 24277/94 (Sürek and Özdemir v. Turkey).
ECtHR (Grand Chamber) 8 July 1999, no. 25067/94 25068/94 (Erdoğdu and İnce v. Turkey).
ECtHR (Grand Chamber) 8 July 1999, no. 26682/95 (Sürek no. 1 v. Turkey).
ECtHR 28 September 1999, no. 22479/93 (Öztürk v. Turkey).
ECtHR 16 March 2000, no. 23144/93 (Özgür Gündem v. Turkey).
ECtHR 7 November 2000, no. 44802/98 (United Christian Broadcasters Ltd. v. The United Kingdom).
ECtHR 27 February 2001, no. 26958/95 (Jerusalem v. Austria).
ECtHR 19 April 2001, no. 32686/96 (Maronek v. Slovakia).
ECtHR 8 June 2001, no. 24699/94 (VGT Verein gegen Tierfabriken v. Switzerland).
ECtHR 12 July 2001, no. 29032/95 (Feldek v. Slovakia).
ECtHR 2 October 2001, no. 29221/95 29225/95 (Stankov and the United Macedonian Organization Ilinden v. Bulgaria).
ECtHR 26 February 2002, no. 28525/95 (Unabhängige Initiative Informationsvielfalt v. Austria).
ECtHR 25 June 2002, no. 51279/99 (Colombani and others v. France).
ECtHR 17 December 2002, no. 35373/97 (A. v. The United Kingdom).

ECtHR (Grand Chamber), 13 February 2003, no. 41340/98 41342/98 41343/98 41344/98 (Refah Partisi and others v. Turkey).
ECtHR (Grand Chamber) 6 May 2003, no. 48898/99 (Perna v. Italy).
ECtHR 24 June 2003, no. 12194/86 (Garaudy v. France).
ECtHR 10 July 2003, no. 44179/98 (Murphy v. Ireland).
ECtHR 4 December 2003, no. 35071/97 (Gündüz v. Turkey).
ECtHR 30 March 2004, no. 53984/00 (Radio France and Others v. France).
ECtHR 18 May 2004, no. 57383/00 (Seurot v. France).
ECtHR 18 May 2004, no. 58148/00 (Plon v. France).
ECtHR 24 June 2004, no. 59320/00 (Hannover v. Germany).
ECtHR 2 September 2004, no. 42264/98 (W.P. and Others v. Poland).
ECtHR 29 September 2004, no. 64915/01 (Chauvy v. France).
ECtHR 16 November 2004, no. 23131/03 (Norwood v. The United Kingdom).
ECtHR (Grand Chamber) 17 December 2004, no. 33348/96 (Cumpana v. Romania).
ECtHR (Grand Chamber) 17 December 2004, no. 49017/99 (Pedersen and Baadsgaard v. Denmark.
ECtHR 15 February 2005 no. 68416/01, (Steel and Morris v. The United Kingdom).
ECtHR 29 March 2005, no. 40287/98 (Alinak v. Turkey).
ECtHR 13 September 2005, no. 42571/98 (I.A. v. Turkey).
ECtHR 18 October 2005, no. 5446/03 (Perrin v. The United Kingdom).
ECtHR (Grand Chamber) 10 November 2005, no. 44774/98 (Leyla Sahin v. Turkey).
ECtHR 17 November 2005, no. 56720/00 (Metzger v. Germany).
ECtHR 24 November 2005, no. 27574/02 (Otto v. Germany).
ECtHR 22 December 2005, no. 54968/00 (Paturel v. France).
ECtHR 19 January 2006, no. 46389/99 (Albert-Engelmann-Gesellschaft MBH v Austria).
ECtHR 31 January 2006, no. 64016/00 (Giniewski v. France).
ECtHR 26 May 2006, no. 50692/99 (Aydin Tatlav v. Turkey).
ECtHR 29 June 2006, no. 76900/01 (Őllinger v. Austria).
ECtHR 6 July 2006, no. 59405/00 (Erbakan v. Turkey).
ECtHR 31 October 2006, no. 72208/01 (Klein v. Slovakia).
ECtHR 14 November 2006, no. 32842/02 (Medya FM Reha Radyo ve İletişim Hizmetleri A.Ş. v. Turkey).
ECtHR 11 December 2006, no. 5853/06 (Ben El Mahi and others v. Denmark).
ECtHR 21 December 2006, no. 73604/01 (Monnat v. Switzerland).
ECtHR 25 January 2007, no. 68354/01 (Vereinigung Bildender Künstler v. Austria).
ECtHR 20 February 2007, no. 35222/04 (Ivanov v. Russia).
ECtHR 24 April 2007, no. 7333/06 (Lombardo v. Malta).
ECtHR 3 May 2007, no. 71156/01 (97 members of the Gldani congregation of Jehovah's witnesses and 4 others v. Georgia).
ECtHR (Grand Chamber) 22 October 2007, no. 21279/02 36448/02 (Lindon, Otchakovsky-Laurens and July v. France).
ECtHR 8 July 2008, no. 33629/06 (Vajnai v. Hungary).
ECtHR 10 July 2008, no. 15948/03 (Soulas and others v. France).

ECtHR 2 October 2008, no. 36109/03 (Le Roy v. France).
ECtHR 14 October 2008, no. 78060/01 (Petrina v. Romania).
ECtHR 4 November 2008, no. 72596/01 (Balsyte-Lideikiene v. Lithuania).
ECtHR 10 March 2009, no. 3002/03 23676/03 (Times Newspapers LTD v. United Kingdom no. 1 and 2).
ECtHR 14 April 2009, no. 37374/05 (Társaság a Szabadságjogokért v. Hungary).
ECtHR 16 July 2009, no. 10883/05 (Willem v. France).
ECtHR 16 July 2009, no. 15615/07 (Féret v. Belgium).
ECtHR 16 February 2010, no. 41056/04 (Akdas v. Turkey).
ECtHR 30 March 2010, no. 20928/05 (Petrenco v. Moldova).
ECtHR 20 April 2010, no. 18788/09 (Le Pen v. France).
ECtHR 7 June 2011, no. 48135/08 (Gollnisch v. France).
ECtHR 9 February 2012, no. 1813/07 (Vejdeland and Others v. Sweden).
ECtHR (Grand Chamber) 15 March 2012, nos. 4149/04 and 41029/04 (Aksu v. Turkey).
ECtHR (Grand Chamber) 3 April 2012, no. 41723/06 (Gillberg v. Sweden).
ECtHR 12 June 2012, no. 31098/08 (Hizb Ut-Tahrir v. Germany).
ECtHR 10 July 2012, no. 46443/09 (Björk Eiðsdóttir v. Iceland).
ECtHR 24 July 2012, no. 40721/08 (Fáber v. Hungary).
ECtHR 9 July 2013, no. 35943/10 (Vona v. Hungary).

Human Rights Committee

Herzberg v. Finland, (61/1979), CCPR/C/15/D/61/1979 (1982).
J.R.T. and the W.G. Party v. Canada, (104/1981), CCPR/C/OP/2 (1984).
John Ballantyne, Davidson and McIntyre v. Canada, (359/1989) and (385/1989) CCPR/C/47/D/359/1989 and 385/1989/Rev.1 (1993).
Faurisson v. France, (550/1993), CCPR/C/58/D/550/1993.
Ross v. Canada, (736/1997), CCPR/C/70/D/736/1997.
Vassilari et al. v. Greece, (1570/2007), CCPR/C/95/D/1570/2007 (2009).

CERD Committee

Communication No. 134 B/1981, CERD/C/107/Add.4 (1984).
P.S.N. v. Denmark, Communication No. 36/2006, A/62/18.
A.W.R.A.P. v. Denmark, Communication No. 37/2006, A/62/18.

Documents of international institutions

Council of Europe

Committee of Ministers, *Recommendation No. R (97)20 to Member States on 'hate speech'*, adopted on 30 October 1997.

Committee of Ministers, *Recommendation No. R (97)21 to Member States on 'the media and the promotion of a culture of tolerance'*, adopted on 30 October 1997.

Committee of Ministers, *Additional Protocol to the Convention on cybercrime, CETS No. 185, concerning the criminalization of acts of a racist and xenophobic nature committed through computer systems*, adopted on 8 November 2001.

European Commission against Racism and Intolerance, *General Policy Recommendation No. 7 on National legislation to combat racism and racial discrimination*, adopted on 13 December 2002.

European Commission for Democracy through Law (Venice Commission), *Report on the relationship between freedom of expression and freedom of religion: the issue of regulation and prosecution of blasphemy, religious insult and incitement to religious hatred*, Study no. 406 2006, Strasbourg, 23 October 2008, CDL-AD(2008)026.

European Commission for Democracy through Law (Venice Commission), *Blasphemy, insult and hatred, Finding answers in a democratic society*, Science and technique of democracy, No. 47, Strasbourg: Council of Europe Publishing 2010.

European Commission of Human Rights, *Preparatory work on Article 10 of the European Convention on Human Rights*, 17 August 1956, DH (56) 15.

European Commission of Human Rights, *Preparatory work on Article 17 of the European Convention on Human Rights*, 23 April 1957, DH (57) 4, CDH (75) 7.

Parliamentary Assembly, *Resolution 1510 (2006) on Freedom of expression and respect for religious beliefs*, adopted on 28 June 2006.

Parliamentary Assembly, *Recommendation 1805 (2007) on Blasphemy, religious insults and hate speech against persons on grounds of their religion*, adopted on 29 June 2007.

Vienna Declaration and Plan of Action on combating racism, xenophobia, anti-Semitism and intolerance, adopted at the Vienna Summit of Heads of State and Government of the Council of Europe Member States, 9 October 1993.

European Union

Council of the European Union, Council Framework Decision 2008/913/JHA of 28 November 2008 *on combating certain forms and expressions of racism and xenophobia by means of criminal law*, OJ L 328/55, 6 December 2008.

Council of the European Union, Council Joint Action 96/443/JHA of 15 July 1996 *concerning action to combat racism and xenophobia*, OJ L 185, 24 July 1996.

Commission of the European Communities, *Proposal for a Council Framework Decision on combating racism and xenophobia*, 28 November 2001, COM(2001) 664 final, Explanatory Memorandum.

United Nations

CERD Committee, General Recommendation no. 15, *Measures to eradicate incitement to or acts of discrimination* (Art. 4), 23 March 1993, CERD/A/48/18.

CERD Committee, General Recommendation no. 32, *The meaning and scope of special measures in the International Convention on the Elimination of Racial Discrimination*, 6 October 2009, CERD/C/GC/32.

CERD Committee, General Recommendation no. 35, *Combating racist hate speech*, 26 September 2013, CERD/C/GC/35.

CERD Committee, *Concluding Observations regarding The Netherlands*, 1 April 2010, CERD/C/NLD/CO/17–18.

Human Rights Committee, CCPR General Comment no. 10: *Freedom of Opinion and Expression* (Art. 19), 29 June 1983, HRI/GEN/1/Rev. 9 (Vol. 1), p. 181.

Human Rights Committee, CCPR General Comment No. 11: *Prohibition of Propaganda for War and Inciting National, Racial, or Religious Hatred* (Art. 20), 29 July 1983, HRI/GEN/1/Rev.9 (Vol. I), p. 182.

Human Rights Committee, CCPR General Comment no. 34: *Freedom of Opinion and Expression* (Art. 19), 21 July 2011, CCPR/C/GC/34.

Human Rights Council, *Report on the study by the five experts on the content and scope of substantive gaps in the existing international instruments to combat racism, racial discrimination, xenophobia and related intolerance*, 27 August 2007, A/HRC/4/WG.3/6.

Human Rights Council, *Complementary International Standards, Compilation of Conclusions and Recommendations of the Study by the five experts on the content and scope of substantive gaps in the existing international instruments to combat racism, racial discrimination, xenophobia and related intolerance*, 18 February 2008, A/HRC/AC.1/1/CRP.4.

Rabat Plan of Action on the prohibition of advocacy of national, racial or religious hatred that constitutes incitement to discrimination, hostility or violence, Conclusions and recommendations emanating from the four regional expert workshops organised by OHCHR, in 2011, and adopted by experts in Rabat, Morocco on 5 October 2012.

Websites

www.echr.coe.int/
www.venice.coe.int/
https://wcd.coe.int/
http://eur-lex.europa.eu/

www.ohchr.org/EN/HRBodies/CCPR/Pages/CCPRIndex.aspx
www.ohchr.org/en/hrbodies/cerd/pages/cerdindex.aspx
www.article19.org/

Chapter 4 France

Books and dissertations

Antoine 1981
Antoine, G., *Liberté, Égalité, Fraternité ou les fluctuations d'une devise*, Paris: Presses Universitaires de France 1981.

Barthélemy 2002
Barthélemy, M., *Associations: un nouvel âge de la participation?*, Paris: Presses de Sciences Po 2002.

Baubérot 2000
Baubérot, J., *Histoire de la laïcité en France*, Que sais-je?, Paris: Presses Universitaires de France (PUF) 2000.

Baubérot 2006
Baubérot, J., *L'intégrisme républicain contre la laïcité*, Paris: Aube ed. 2006.

Baubérot 2008
Baubérot, J., *La laïcité expliquée à Nicolas Sarkozy et à ceux qui écrivent ses discours*, Paris: Albin Michel 2008.

Beignier 1995
Beignier, B., *L'honneur et le droit*, (diss.) Paris: L.G.D.J. 1995.

Beignier, De Lamy & Dreyer 2009
Beignier, B., De Lamy, B., Dreyer, E., *Traité de droit de la presse et des médias*, Paris: LexisNexis SA Litec 2009.

Bigot 2004
Bigot, C., *Connaître la loi de 1881 sur la presse*, Guide Légipresse, Paris: Victoires-Éditions 2004.

Bergeal 2009
Bergeal, C. red., Diffamation, injure, outrage… Comment se défendre?, *CJFI*, June 2009, Paris: La Documentation Française 2009.

Bermann & Picard 2008
Bermann, G.A. & Picard, E., *Introduction to French law*, Alphen aan den Rijn: Kluwer Law International 2008.

Blin, Chavanne & Drago 1969
Blin, H. Chavanne, A. & Drago, R., *Traité du droit de la presse*, Paris: Librairies techniques 1969.

Brubaker 1992
Brubaker, B., *Citizenship and nationhood in France and Germany*, London: Harvard University Press 1992.

Borgetto 1993
Borgetto, M., *La notion de fraternité en droit public français*, Titre II La solidarité comme principe inspirateur du droit public actuel, Paris: L.G.D.J. 1993.

Borgetto 1997
Borgetto, M., *La devise "Liberté, Égalité, Fraternité"*, Que sais-je?, n° 3196, Paris: Presses Universitaires de France 1997.

Boulègue 2010
Boulègue, J., *Le Blasphème en procès 1984–2009, l'église et la mosquée contre les libertés*, Paris: Nova Éditions 2010.

Bouloc 2010
Bouloc, B., *Procédure pénal*, Paris: Éditions Dalloz 2010.

Code de la communication commenté 2009
Code de la communication commenté, 4th edition, Paris: Éditions Dalloz 2009.

Code constitutionnel commenté 2012
Code constitutionnel et des droits fondamentaux commenté, 1re édition, Paris: Éditions Dalloz 2012.

Cohen 2003
Cohen, F., *La difficile insertion de la legislation pénale sur la lutte contre le racisme dans la loi sur la presse*, (diss.) Paris I 2003.

De Bellescize & Francescini 2005
De Bellescize, D.; Francescini, L., *Droit de la communication*, Paris: PUF 2005.

De Lamy 2000
De Lamy, B. de, *La liberté d'opinion et le droit penal*, (diss.) Paris: L.G.D.J. 2000.

Decaux (ed.) 1999
Decaux, E. (ed.), *Le droit face au racisme*, Paris: Éditions A. Pedone 1999.

Derieux & Granchet 2010
Derieux, E. & Granchet, A., *Droit des médias, droit français, européen et international*, Paris: L.G.D.J. 2010.

Desmons & Paveau 2008
Desmons, E.; Paveau, A.-M., *Outrages, insultes, blasphemes et injures: violences du langage et polices du discourse,* Paris: l'Harmattan 2008.

Dreyer 2002
Dreyer, E., *Droit de l'information, responsabilité pénale des médias*, Paris: Litec 2002.

Dreyer 2008
Dreyer, E., *Responsabilité civile et pénale des medias*, Paris: Litec 2008.

Dreyer 2011
Dreyer, E., *Responsabilités civile et pénale des médias*, Paris: LexisNexis 2011.

Droin 2009
Droin, N., *Les limitations à la liberté d'expression dans la loi sur la presse du 29 juillet 1881, Disparition, permanence et résurgence du délit d'opinion*, (diss.) Paris: L.G.D.J. 2009.

Duverger & Ménard 2003
Duverger, E.; Ménard, R., *La censure des bien-pensants*, Paris: Editions Albin Michel S.A. 2003.

Edelman 1999
Edelman, B., *La personne en danger.* Paris: PUF collection Doctrine juridique 1999.

Fauvel 1912
Fauvel, L, *Le délit de tendance et le délit d'opinion dans les lois sur la presse,* (diss.) Paris: Librairie nouvelle de droit et de jurisprudence 1912.

Favoreau & Philip 1999
Favoreau, L. & Philip, L., *Les grandes décisions du Conseil constitutionnel*, Dalloz, 10thedition, 1999.

Fenet & Soulier 1989
Fenet, A.; Soulier, G. (ed.), *Les minorités et leur droits depuis 1789*, Paris: L'Harmattan 1989.

Fetzer & Soper 2005
Fetzer, J.S. & Soper, J.C., *Muslims and the State in Britain, France and Germany,* New York: Cambridge University Press 2005.

Fourest & Venner 2003
Fourest, C.; Venner, F., *Tirs croisés, La laïcité à l'épreuve des intégrismes juif, chrétien et musulman*, Paris: Le livre de Poche, Calmann-Lévy 2003.

Goudemare & Pierrat 2003
Goudemare, S,; Pierrat, E., *L'Édition en procès*, Paris: Éditions Léo Scheer 2003.

Guinchard 1997
Guinchard, S., *Les moralistes au prétoire*, Mélanges Foyer, Paris: PUF 1997.

Hauriou 1929
Hauriou, M., *Précis de droit constitutionnel*, Paris: Sirey 1929.

Heringa & Kiiver 2009
Heringa, A.W.; Kiiver, P., *Constitutions Compared, An Introduction to Comparative Constitutional Law*, Antwerp: Intersentia 2009.

Hofmann, E. (ed.) 1980
Hofmann, E. (ed.), *Constant, B., Principes de politique applicables à tous les gouvernements,* Genève: Librairie Droz S.A. 1980.

Hoffmann 2003
Hofmann, E. (ed.), O'keeffe, D. (trans.), *Constant, B., Principles of politics applicable to all governments*, Indianapolis, Indiana: Liberty Fund 2003.

Kepel 1987
Kepel, G., *Les banlieues de l'Islam: Naissance d'une religion en France*, Paris: Éditions du Seuil 1987.

Kepel 2012
Kepel, G., *La diversité de l'islam en France – Quatre vingt treize*, Paris: Gallimard 2012.

Lamont 2000
Lamont, M., *The Dignity of Working Men: Morality and the Boundaries of Race, Class, and Immigration,* Cambridge MA: Harvard University Press 2000.

Laske & Valdiguié 2008
Laske, K.; Valdiguié, L., *Le vrai Canard, Les dessous du Canard enchaîné*, Paris: Éditions Stock 2008.

Larousse 2007
Le Petit Larousse illustré, dictionnaire encyclopédique, édition 1997, Paris: Larousse 1997.

Lécuyer 2006
Lécuyer, G., *Liberté d'expression et responsabilité, Étude de droit privé*, (diss.) Paris: Dalloz 2006.

Leroy 2009
Leroy, J., *Procédure pénal*, Paris: L.G.D.J. 2009.

Mély 2004
Mély, B., *De la séparation des Eglises et de l'Ecole. Mise en perspective historique. Allemagne, France, Grande-Bretagne, Italie,* (diss.) Lausanne: Editions Page deux, collection 'Cahiers libres', 2004.

Morange 2009
Morange, J., *La Liberté d'expression*, Brussels: Bruylant 2009.

Netz 1997
Netz, R., *Histoire de la censure dans l'édition*, Que sais-je?, Paris: Presses universitaires de France 1997.

Pech 2003
Pech, L., *La liberté d' expression et sa limitation: les enseignements de l'expériences européennes (Allemagne, France et Convention européenne des droits de l' homme),* diss., Clermont-Ferrand: Presses Universitaires de la Faculté de droit de Clermont-Ferrand 2003.

Pierrat 2000
Pierrat, E., *Le Droit de l'Édition Appliqué*, Paris: Éditions du cercle de la librairie 2000.

Pierrat 2002
Pierrat, E., *Le Droit de l'Édition Appliqué, Tome 2*, Paris: Éditions du cercle de la librairie 2002.

Pierrat 2005
Pierrat, E., *Le droit du livre*, Paris: Éditions du cercle de la librairie 2005.

Pierrat 2008
Pierrat, E. ed., *Le livre noir de la censure*, Paris: Éditions du Seuil 2008.

Rivero 2003
Rivero, J., *Libertés publiques,* Tome 2, 7th edition, Paris: Presses universitaires de France 2003.

Robitaille-Froidure 2011
Robitaille-Froidure, A., *La liberté d'expression face au racisme*, Paris: L'Harmattan 2011.

Rousseau 1755
Rousseau, J.-J., *Discours sur l'economie politique* (1755).

Rousseau 1762
Rousseau, J.-J., *Du contrat social* (1762).

Roy 2005
Roy, O., *La laïcité face à l'islam*, Paris: Editions Stock 2005.

Sartre 1954
Sartre, J.P., *Réflexions sur la question juive*, Paris: Gallimard 1954.

Schain 2012
Schain, M.A., *The politics of immigration in France, Britain and the United States, a comparative study*, 2nd edition, New York: Palgrave Macmillan 2012.

Shields 2007
Shields, J.G., *The Extreme Right in France: from Pétain to Le Pen*, London: Routledge 2007.

Van Ooijen 2012
Van Ooijen, H., *Religious Symbols in Public Functions, A comparative analysis of Dutch, English and French justifications for limiting the freedom of public officials to display religious symbols*, Antwerpen: Intersentia 2012.

Vincent & Guinchard 1999
Vincent, J. and Guinchard, S., *Procédure civile*, 25th edition, Paris: Dalloz 1999.

Weil 2008
Weil, P., *How to be French, Nationality in the Making since 1789,* London: Duke University Press 2008.

Scientific articles and contributions to collective works

Ader 2002
Ader, B., Retour sur un an de jurisprudence en droit de la presse, *Légipresse* n°192, June 2002, p. 65–76.

Ader 2007
Ader, B., La procédure de presse, Novembre 2005- janvier 2007, *Légipresse* n° 240, May 2007, p. 43–47.

Ader 2009
Ader, B., La procédure de presse, janvier – décembre 2008, *Légipresse* n° 260, April 2009, p. 41–45.

Ader 2010-I
Ader, B., La procédure de presse, janvier – décembre 2009, *Légipresse* n° 270, March 2010, p. 48–52.

Ader 2010-II
Ader, B., Quelle nouvelle procédure pénale pour la presse? Présentation des incidnces de l'avant-projet de nouveau code de procédure pénale, *Légipresse* n°271, April 2010, p. 57–58.

Ader 2011
Ader, B., La procédure de presse, janvier 2010- décembre 2010, *Légipresse* n° 280, February 2011, p. 129–132.

Ader 2012-I
Ader, B., L'état de la jurisprudence sur la notion de négation depuis la loi Gayssot, *Légipresse* n° 293, April 2012, p. 236.

Ader 2012-II
Ader, B., Quelles limites à la polémique politique?, *Légipresse* n° 294 May 2012, p. 292–296.

Agostinelli 2003
Agostinelli, X., Provocation à la discrimination, diffamation et injure raciales, *Légicom* 2002/3, n°28, p. 47–60.

Beignier 1998
Beignier, B., "De la langue perfide, délivre moi...", Réflexions sur la loi du 13 juillet 1990 dite "Loi Gayssot", in: *Pouvoir et Liberté, Études offertes à Jacques Mourgeon*, Brussels: Bruylant 1998, p. 497–533.

Bigot 2008
Bigot, C., Contentieux de la presse: les errements de la commission Guinchard, *Légipresse*, September 2008, n°254, I, p. 109–110.

Bigot 2012-I
Bigot, C., La portée de la rénovation de la théorie de la bonne foi sous l'emprise de l'intérêt general, *Légipresse* n°290, January 2012, p. 29–30.

Bigot 2012-II
Bigot, C., QPC et loi du 29 juillet 1881 – Bilan et perspectives, *Légipresse* n°292, March 2012, p.152.

Body-Gandrot 2007
Body-Gandrot, S., Urban 'Riots' or Urban Violence in France?, *Policing* 2007, 1 (4), p. 416–427.

Bonnal 2010
Bonnal, N., Les règles processuelles de la loi de 1881 sont-elles toujours applicables devant le juge civil?, *Légipresse* n°272, May 2010, p. 19–25.

Burgorgue-Larsen 2011
Burgorgue-Larsen, L., The impact of European fundamental rights on the French Constitutional Court, in: Patricia Popelier, P., Van de Heyning, C. & Van Nuffel, P. (Eds.), *Human Rights Protection in the European Legal Order: the Interaction between the European and the National Courts*, Cambridge: Intersentia 2011, p. 211–236.

Cammilleri-Subrenat 2007
Cammilleri-Subrenat, A., L'incitation à la haine et la Constitution, *Revue internationale de droit comparé*, Vol.54 N° 2, April-June 2002, p. 513–548.

Carbonnier 1951
Carbonnier, J., Le silence et la gloire, *D.* 1951, chron., p.119.

Carcassonne 2012
Carcassonne, G., Les interdits et la liberté d'expression, in: *Les Nouveaux Cahiers du Conseil Consitutionnel, Dossier La liberté d'expression et de communication, Dalloz* n°36–2012, p. 55–65.

Cassia 2012
Cassia, P., L'incidence des protections conventionnelles sur le contrôle de constitutionnalité de la liberté d'expression, *Légipresse* n°292, March 2012, p.157.

Charrière-Bournazel 2014
Charrière-Bournazel, C., La liberté d'opinion, le racisme et l'histoire, Les neuf mois ferme de Cayenne, *Légipresse* n°319, September 2014, p. 451–452.

Chelini-Pont 2009
Chelini-Pont, B., La mobilisation de l'Organisation de la Conférence Islamique Mondiale contre la diffamation de l'Islam (1999–2009) et ses conséquences en Europe, *Droit et Religions*, 2009–2010, 2009–4, p. 525–552.

Cohen-Jonathan 1997
Cohen-Jonathan, G., Négationnisme et droits de l'homme, *RTDH* 1997, p. 571–597.

De Bellescize 2005
De Bellescize, D., La France et l'article 10 de la convention européenne de sauvegarde des droits de l'homme, *RTDH* 61–2005, p. 225–264.

De Bellescize 2006
De Bellescize, D., Délits d'opinion et liberté d'expression, *D* 2006, p. 1476.

De Gouttes 2001
De Gouttes, R, À propos du conflit entre le droit à la liberté d'expression et le droit à la protection contre le racisme, *GP* 25 September 2001, n°268, p. 6 *et seq.*

De la Pradelle 1999
De la Pradelle, G., Moyens juridiques et moyens politiques de la lutte contre le racisme, Table ronde, in: *Le droit face au racisme*, Decaux, E. (ed.), Paris: Éditions A. Pedone 1999, p. 49–63.

De Lamy 2008
De Lamy, B., Vers une dépénalisation de la diffamation et de l'injure, *JCP G* 2008, I, p. 209.

De Lamy 2012
De Lamy, B., La Constitution et la liberté de la presse, in: *Les Nouveaux Cahiers du Conseil Consitutionnel, Dossier La liberté d'expression et de communication, Dalloz* n°36–2012, p. 19–29.

Derieux 1990
Derieux, E., Répression du racisme de l'antisémitisme et de la xénophobie. Commentaire de la loi du 13 juillet 1990, *Légipresse* n°75, October 1990, p. 56–58.

Derieux 1992
Derieux, E., Lutte contre le racisme et liberte d'expression, *Légipresse* n° 94, September 1992, p. 81–90.

Derieux 1996
Derieux, E., Lutte contre le racisme, *Légipresse* n°135, October 1996, p. 121–122.

Derieux 1998
Derieux, E., Justice pénale et droit des médias, *Justices* n°10, April-June 1998, p. 133–149.

Derieux 2003
Derieux, E., La "censure" en droit français, Censures, Actes du colloque du 16 mai 2003, *Auteurs & Medias* 2003, p. 155–175.

Derieux 2005
Derieux, E., L'État de la jurisprudence nationale, *Annuaire Droit et Religions*, Volume 1, 2005, p. 105–126.

Derieux 2007
Derieux, D., L'affaire des "Caricatures de Mahomet": liberté de caricature et respect des croyances, *JCP, G,* n° 19, 9 May 2007, II 10079.

Derieux 2009
Derieux, E., Respect des croyances et liberté d'expression, Droit français et européen – Actualité jurisprudentielle (2007–2008), *Annuaire Droit et Religions*, Volume 4, 2009–2010, p. 619–648.

Derieux 2009-I
Derieux, E., Diffamation et injure envers les Harkis: une infraction non réprimée, *JCP G*, n°16, 15 April 2009, act.207.

Derieux 2011
Derieux, E., *Dépénalisation de la diffamation. Contribution à la réflexion, in: Philosophie juridique du journalisme, La liberté d'expression journalistique en Europe et en Amérique du Nord*, Mbongo, P. (ed.), Paris: Éditions Mare & Martin, 2011, p. 73–90.

Derieux 2013
Derieux, B., Des incidences de la suppression du mot "*race*" sur l'efficacité de la legislation reprimant les comportements racistes, *Légipresse* n°306 June 2013, p. 327.

Derieux 2014
Derieux, E., Lutte contre le terrorisme et droit de la communication, *Légipresse* n° 322, December 2014, p. 686–691.

Dreyer, E., *Voies de recours. Contrôle exercé par la Cour de cassation: JCL. Communication*, Fasc. 3100, n°59.

Dreyer 2003
Dreyer, E., Le fondement de la prohibition des discours racistes en France, *Légipresse* n°199, March 2003, p. 19–25.

Dreyer 2007
Dreyer, E., Les infractions de presse, Septembre 2005- novembre 2006, *Légipresse* n° 239, March 2007, p. 32–36.

Dreyer 2008
Dreyer, E., Les infractions de presse, janvier – décembre 2007, *Légipresse* n° 249, March 2008, p. 40–59.

Dreyer 2009
Dreyer, E., Les infractions de presse, janvier – décembre 2008, *Légipresse* n° 259, March 2009, p. 19–28.

Dreyer 2010
Dreyer, E., Les infractions de presse, janvier – décembre 2009, *Légipresse* n° 269, February 2010, p. 29–36.

Dreyer 2012
Dreyer, E., L'accès au juge civil en matière de presse, *Légipresse* n°291, February 2012, p. 83–89.

Duvert 2007
Duvert, C., Le contrôle judiciaire du traitement médiatique des symbols religieux: du numéro d'équilibriste à la boîte de Pandore, *Légipresse* n°242, June 2007, p. 76–78.

Flauss 2002
Flauss, J-F., La diffamation religieuse, in: *La protection internationale de la liberté religieuse*, Flaus, J-F. (ed.), Brussels: Bruylant 2002, p. 273–300.

Flauss 2002
Flauss, J-F., La diffamation religieuse en droit international, *LPA*, 23 July 2002, n° 146, p. 5.

Foulon-Piganiol 1970-I
Foulon-Piganiol, J., Réflexions sur la diffamation raciale, Eléments constitutifs du délit et imperfections du texte actuel, *D* 1970, Chronique XXIX, p. 133–136.

Foulon-Piganiol 1970-II
Foulon-Piganiol, J., Nouvelles réflexions sur la diffamation raciale, Critique des propositions de loi en instance devant le Parlement, *D* 1970, Chronique XXXV, p. 163–166.

Foulon-Piganiol 1972
Foulon-Piganiol, J., La lutte contre le racisme, Commentaire de la loi du 1er juillet 1972, *D* 1972, Chronique XL, p. 261 *et seq.*

Garay 2005
Garay, A., Diffamations, injures et conviction en proces: Mise en perspective, *Annuaire Droit et Religions*, Volume 1, 2005, p. 91–103.

Garay *et al.* 2005
Garay, A.; Chélini-Pont, B.; Tawil, E.; Anseur, Z., The permissible scope of legal limitations on the freedom of religion or belief in France, *Emory Int'l L. l. Rev.* 2005, 19, p. 785–840.

Gonthier 2000
Gonthier, C.D., Liberty, Equality, Fraternity: The Forgotten Leg of the Trilogy, or Fraternity: The Unspoken Third Pillar of Democracy, *Mc Gill Law Journal* 2000, vol. 45, p. 567 *et seq.*

Granchet 2005
Granchet, A., Le droit de la presse: une spécialité légitime ou dépassée? Compte rendu du Forum Légipresse, *Légipresse* n° 226, p. 121–127.

Guerder 2011
Guerder, P., Les infractions de presse, Décembre 2009- décembre 2010, *Légipresse* n° 281, March 2011, p. 187–196.

Jouanneau 2009
Jouanneau, B., A propos de la dépénalisation de la diffamation, *Légipresse*, January-February 2009, n°258, I, p. 2.

Jouanneau 2013
Jouanneau, B., Oui, on peut supprimer le mot "*race*" de la loi, sans dommage!, *Légipresse* n°307 July/August 2013, p. 387.

Jouanneau 2014
Jouanneau, B., Répression du négationnisme: la voix dissonante, *Légipresse* n° 320, October 2014, p. 531–537.

Kastoryano 2006
Kastoryano, R., French secularism and the headscarf affair, in: Modood, T., Triandafyllidou, A., Zapata-Barrero, R. (eds), *Multiculturalism, Muslims and Citizenship, A European Approach*, London: Routledge 2006.

Korman 1989
Korman, C., Le délit de diffusion d'idées racistes, *JCP, G,* 1989, n° 30, I, 3404.

Korman 1998
Korman, C., La situation française en matière de législation antiraciste, *Légipresse* n° 156, November 1998, p. 130–133.

Korman 2001
Korman, C., La repression des discourse racistes en France, *RTDH* 2001, p. 385–401.

Koubi 1993
Koubi, G., Droit, droit à la difference, droit à l'indifference, en France, *RTDH* 1993, p. 243–262.

Lacabarats 1997
Lacabarats, Le juge et la laïcité: le droit du respect des croyances, *LPA*, 3 October 1997, p. 4.

Latil 2014
Latil, A., Les fautes d'expression, Ou la renaissance de l'article 1382 du Code civil en matière de liberté d'expression, *Légipresse* n° 318, July-August 2014, p. 409–412.

Lazerges 2014
Lazerges, C., La lute contre le terrorisme peut-elle mettre en danger la liberté d'expression, *Légipresse* n° 321, November 2014, p. 579–581.

Léger 2005
Léger, J-M., La pub nous fera-t-elle perdre foi en la justice? L'exploitation publicitaire des croyances, *Légipresse* n°221, May 2005, p. 55–60.

Lepage 2007
Lepage, A., Protection du sentiment religieux et injure publique envers un groupe de personnes à raison de leur appartenance à une religion déterminée, *CCE,* n° 5, May 2007, comm. 74.

L.F. 2006
L.F., Liberté d'expression et convictions religieuses dans la jurisprudence européenne, *Légipresse* n° 235 October 2006, p. 109–117.

Lochak 1989
Lochak, D., 'Les minorités et le droit public français: du refus des différences à la gestion des différences', in: Fenet, A. and Soulier, G. (ed.), *Les minorités et leur droits depuis 1789*, Paris: L'Harmattan 1989, p. 125–128.

Lochak 1999
Lochak, D., Les références à la "race" dans le droit français, in: *Le droit face au racisme*, Decaux, E. (ed.), Paris: Éditions A. Pedone 1999, p. 27–40.

Lochak 2014
Lochak, D., "*Victoire pour la République*" ou défaite de la démocratie? La decision *Dieudonné* ne mérite ni cet excès d'honneur ni cette indignité, *Légipresse* n° 315 April 2014, p. 221–230.

Malaurie 2008
Malaurie, P., Ne dépénalisons pas la diffamation et l'injure. – Contre la proposition n°12, alinéa 1 du rapport Guinchard, *JCP G* n°39, 24 September 2008, act.566.

Mallet-Poujol 2002
Mallet-Poujol, N., L'action judiciaire des associations en droit des medias, *Légipresse* n°193, July/August 2002, p. 95–101.

Mallet-Poujol 2005
Mallet-Poujol, N., Le juge et l'idéologie dans les procès en diffamation, *Légipresse* n°218, January/February 2005, p. 1–8.

Mallet-Poujol 2006-I
Mallet-Poujol, N., De la liberté de la caricature, *Légipresse* n°229, March 2006, p. 37–38.

Mallet-Poujol 2006-II
Mallet-Poujol, N., De la "cohabitation" entre la loi du 29 juillet 1881 sur la liberté de la presse et l'article 1382 du Code civil, *Légipresse* n°234, September 2006, p. 93–100.

Mallet-Poujol 2012
Mallet-Poujol, N., La loi de pénalisation du négationnisme: la censure constitutionnelle ou le crépuscule des lois mémorielles, *Légipresse* n° 293 April 2012, p. 219–226.

Mallet-Poujol 2013
Mallet-Poujol, N., Diffamation et amnistie: l'étrange sacrifice du filter de la bonne foi, *Légipresse* n° 309 October 2013, p. 531–537.

Martin-Valente 2003-I
Martin-Valente, S., *La place de l'article 1382 du code civil en matière de presse depuis les arrêts de l'Assemblée plénière du 12 juillet 2000, Approche critique (1re partie)*, *Légipresse* n°202, June 2003, p. 71–77.

Martin-Valente 2003-II
Martin-Valente, S., *La place de l'article 1382 du code civil en matière de presse depuis les arrêts de l'Assemblée plénière du 12 juillet 2000, Approche critique (2e partie)*, *Légipresse* n°203, July/August 2003, p. 89–94.

Massias 1993
Massias, F., La liberté d'expression et le discours raciste ou révisionniste, *RTDH* 1993, n° 13, p. 183–210.

Massias 2001
Massias, F., Faut-il pénaliser le racisme?, *RTDH* 2001, n° 16, p. 601–623.

Massis 1992
Massis, Th., La liberté de conscience, le sentiment religieux et le droit pénal, *D* 1992, Chronique XXII, p. 113–116.

Massis 1996
Massis, Th., Convictions, respect des croyances et liberté d'expression à travers la presse et les medias, *Légipresse* 131, May 1996, p. 43–47.

Massis 2002
Massis, Th., Respect des croyances, dignité et loi du 29 juillet 1881, *Légipresse* 197, December 2002, p. 172–174.

Mathieu 2006
Mathieu, B., Les lois mémorielles ou la violation de la constitution par consensus, *D* 2006, p.3001, *LPA* 15 December 2006, n°250, p. 7.

Mathieu 2007-I
Mathieu, B., La liberté d'expression en France: de la protection constitutionnelle aux menaces legislatives, *RDP* 2007, p. 321 *et seq.*

Mathieu 2007-II
Mathieu, B., *Cahiers du Conseil constitutionnel* n° 21 (Dossier: la normativité) – January 2007.

Mayer 2003
Mayer, N., Democracy in France: do associations matter?, in: *Generating social capital, civil society and institutions in comparative perspective*, Hooge, M. & Stolle, D. (ed.), New York: Palgrave MacMillen 2003.

Mbongo 2007-I
Mbongo, P., Les caricatures de Mahomet et la liberté d'expression, *Revue Esprit*, May 2007, p. 145.

Mbongo 2007-II
Mbongo, P., Le traitement juridictionnel des offenses aux convictions religieuses, in: *Mélanges en l'honneur de Jean-François Lachaume*, Paris: Dalloz 2007.

Mbongo 2009
Mbongo, P., Hate Speech, Extreme Speech, and Collective Defamation in French Law, in: Hare, I.; Weinstein, J. (ed.), *Extreme Speech and Democracy*, New York: Oxford University Press 2009, p. 221–236.

Mbongo 2011
Mbongo, P., Droit des medias et question prioritaire de constitutionnalité, *Légipresse* n°283, May 2011, p. 281–286.

Mémeteau 1976
Mémeteau, G., L'incitation illicite à des faits licites ou: les remords du legislateur, *JCP, G,* 1976, I, 2781.

Mény 1986
Mény, Y., 'La légitimation des groupes d'intérêts par l'administration Française', *Revue Française de l'Administration Publique*, 1986, 39, p. 483–94.

Michalak & Saeed 2002
Michalak, L. and Saeed, A., The Continental Divide: Islam and Muslim Identities in France, in: AlSayyad & Castells 2002, p. 151–152.

Monfort 2005
Monfort, J-Y, Les nouvelles incriminations de la loi du 30 décembre 2004 au regard de la liberté d'expression et des droits de l'homme, *GP* 17 December 2005, n° 351, p. 2 *et seq.*

Monfort 2012
Monfort, J.-Y., L'apparition en jurisprudence du critère du '*débat d'intérêt général*' dans le droit de la diffamation, *Légipresse* n°290 January 2012, p. 21.

Morange 2008
Morange, J., *La conception française de la liberté d'expression*, in: Zoller, E. (ed.) *La liberté d'expression aux Etats-Unis et en Europe*, Paris: Dalloz 2008.

Padova 2005
Padova, Y., Liberté d'expression versus repression du sexisme et de l' homophobie, À propos de la loi du 30 décembre 2004, *GP* 17 March 2005, n° 76, p. 2 *et seq.*

Pénalisation de la négation des génocides: pour ou contre?, Actes de colloque, *Légipresse* n° 293 April 2012, p. 227–242.

Prélot 2011

Prélot, P-H., Religious symbols and the law of 1905: reflections on the prohibition of the full veil in light of the French law on religious practices, *Société, Droit et Religion* n°2, 2011.

Rolland 1998

Rolland, P., Du délit d'opinion dans la démocratie française, in: *Pouvoir et Liberté, Études offertes à Jacques Mourgeon*, Brussels: Bruylant 1998, p. 645–670.

Rolland 2004

Rolland, P., Existe-il un droit au respect des convictions religeiuses dans les medias? Sur une jurisprudence récente de la Cour européenne des droits de l'homme, *RFDA* September-October 2004, n°5, p. 1001–1008.

Saurugger 2007

Saurugger, S., Democratic 'Misfit'? Conceptions of Civil Society Participation in France and the European Union, *Political Studies,* 2007, vol. 55, p. 390.

Taguieff 1990

Taguieff, P.-A., Mobilisation national-populiste en France. Vote xénophobe et nouvel antisémitisme politique, *Lignes* n°9, March 1990, annex.

Teyssier 2006

Teyssier, J.-P., Medias et religion: jusqu'ou le respect?, *GP* 2006 31 May – 1 June, p. 3.

Théron 1998

Théron, J-P, Dignité et libertés, Propos sur une jurisprudence contestable, in: *Pouvoir et Liberté, Études offertes à Jacques Mourgeon*, Brussels: Bruylant 1998, p. 295–306.

Tricoire 2002

Tricoire, A., L'art, la censure et les droits de l'homme, *Légipresse* n° 196, November 2002, p. 148–157.

Troper 1999

Troper, M., Droit et négationnisme: la loi Gayssot et la Constitution, *Annales Histoire Sciences Sociales* 1999, n°6, p.1239 *et seq.*

Troper 2005

Troper, M., Who Needs a Third Party Effect Doctrine? – The Case of France, in: Sajó, A. & Uitz, R. (Eds.), *The Constitution in Private Relations: Expanding Constitutionalism*, The Hague: Eleven International Publishing 2005, p. 115–128.

Valat 2007

Valat, J-P., De quelques particularités de l'instruction des infractions prévues par la loi du 29 juillet 1881, *Légipresse* n°241, May 2007, p. 49–55.

Véron 1990

Véron, M., Le renforcement du dispositif répressif contre la discrimination et le racisme. Présentation des lois des 12 et 13 juillet 1990, *Dr. pénal* October 1990, p. 1–3.

Wachsmann 2001
Wachsmann, P., Liberté d'expression et négationnisme, *RTDH* 2001, p. 585–599.

Wachsmann 2003
Wachsmann, P., Le délit d'offense envers un chef d'Etat étranger à l'épreuve de la Convention européenne des droits de l'homme, *RTDH* 2003, n°55, p. 996.

Wachsmann 2008
Wachsmann, P.: *JCl. Libertés, V° Liberté d'expression*, Fasc. 800, n°89, 2008.

Wallon 1999
Wallon, E., Entre globe et le groupe: le paradoxe français, in: *Le droit face au racisme*, Decaux, E. (ed.), Paris: Éditions A. Pedone 1999, p. 17–23.

Wieviorka 2002
Wieviorka, M., Race, Culture and Society: The French Experience with Muslims, in: AlSayyad, N. and Castells, M. (eds.), *Muslim Europe or Euro-Islam, Politics, Culture and Citizenship in the Age of Globalization*, Lanham: Lexington Books 2002.

Wihtol de Wenden 2006
Wihtol de Wenden, C., Urban riots in France, *SAIS Review* 2006, 26.2, p. 47–53.

Case law

HRC

Faurisson v. France, (550/1993), CCPR/C/58/D/550/1993.

ECmHR/ ECtHR

ECmHR 24 June 1996, n°31159/96 (Marais/France).
ECtHR 24 February 1997, n°19983/92 (De Haes and Gijsels v. Belgium).
ECtHR 29 March 2001, n°38432/97 (Thoma v. Luxembourg).
ECtHR 17 July 2001, n°39288/98 (Association Ekin/France).
ECtHR 25 June 2002, n°51279/99 (Colombani and others/France).
ECtHR 24 June 2003, n°65831/01 (Garaudy/France).
ECtHR 30 March 2004, n°53984/00 (Radio France/France).
ECtHR 22 December 2005, n°54968/00 (Paturel/France).
ECtHR 31 January 2006, n°64016/00 (Giniewski/France).
ECtHR 7 November 2006, n°12697/03 (Mamère/France).
ECtHR 14 February 2008, n°20893/03 (July/France).
ECtHR 7 June 2011, no. 48135/08 (Gollnisch v. France).
ECtHR 14 March 2013, n°26118/10 (Eon v. France).

Constitutional Council

Cons. Con. 17 June 1959, n°59–2 DC.
Cons. Con. 24 June 1959, n°59–3 DC.
Cons. Con. 23 November 1977, n°77–87 DC.
Cons. Con. 27 July 1982, n°82–141 DC.
Cons. Con. 9 May 1991, n°91–290 DC.
Cons. Con. 27 July 1994, n°94–343/344 DC.
Cons. Con. 15 June 1999, n°99–412 DC.
Cons. Con. 26 March 2003 n° 2003–469 DC.
Cons. Con. 29 July 2004, n°2004–500 DC.
Cons. Con. 15 November 2007, n°2007–557 DC.
Cons. Con. 20 May 2011, n°2011–131 QPC.
Cons. Con. 28 February 2012, n°2012–647 DC.
Cons. Con. 12 April 2013, n°2013–302 QPC.
Cons. Con. 17 May 2013, n°2013–311 QPC.
Cons. Con. 17 May 2013, n°2013–669 DC.
Cons. Con. 7 June 2013 n° 2013–319, QPC.

Council of State

CE 27 October 1995, *Dalloz*, 25, n°102.
CE 5 January 2007, n° 300311.

CE Ordonnance of 9 January 2014, n°374508.
CE Ordonnance of 9 January 2014, n°374508.
CE Ordonnance of 10 January 2014, n°374528.
CE Ordonnance of 11 January 2014, n°374552.

French Supreme Court

French Supreme Court plenary assembly

French Supreme Court, plenary assembly, 12 July 2000, n°98–10160, *Bull.* 2000 A. P., n°8, p. 13.
French Supreme Court, plenary assembly, 16 February 2007, n°06–81785, *Bull. Crim.* 2007, n°1, p. 1.
French Supreme Court, Plenary Assembly, 15 February 2013, n°11–14637, *Bull.* 2013, n°606.

French Supreme Court mixed chamber

French Supreme Court, mixed ch., 24 November 2000, n°97–81554, *Bull. Ch. M.* 2000, n°4, p. 5.

French Supreme Court criminal chambers

French Supreme Court, 5 January 1883, *DP* 1883, jp. p. 95.
French Supreme Court, crim.ch., 30 June 1893, *DP* 1897, I, 341.
French Supreme Court, 31 May 1949, *D.* 1949, I, p. 348–349.
French Supreme Court, crim.ch., 23 February 1950, *Bull. Crim.* 1950, n°69.
French Supreme Court, crim.ch., 26 June 1952, *D.* 1952, J, 641.
French Supreme Court, crim.ch., 11 February 1954, *Bull. Crim.* 1954, n°71.
French Supreme Court, crim.ch., 25 February 1954, *Bull. Crim.,* 1954, n°89.
French Supreme Court, crim.ch., 18 May 1954, *Bull Crim.* 1954, n°186.
French Supreme Court, crim.ch., 16 December 1954, *Bull. Crim.* 1954, n°410.
French Supreme Court, crim.ch., 12 January 1956, *Bull. Crim.* 1956, n°52.
French Supreme Court, crim.ch., 22 February 1966, n°65–90518, *Bull. Crim.* 1966, n°62.
French Supreme Court, crim.ch., 8 February 1972, n°71–91102, *Bull. Crim.* 1972, n°48.
French Supreme Court, crim.ch., 11 July 1972, n°70–93211, *Bull. Crim.* 1972, n°236, p. 618.
French Supreme Court, crim.ch., 2 July 1975, n°74–91717, *Bull. Crim.* 1975, n°174.
French Supreme Court, crim.ch., 12 April 1976, n°74–92515, *Bull. Crim.*1976, n°112, p. 273.
French Supreme Court, crim.ch., 2 January 1980, n°78–92224, *Bull. Crim.* 1980, n°3.
French Supreme Court, crim.ch., 3 March 1980, n°78–91949, *Bull. Crim.* 1980, n°74.
French Supreme Court, crim.ch., 17 February 1981, n°79–92748, *Bull. Crim.* 1981, n°64.
French Supreme Court, crim.ch., 1 December 1981, n°80–92810, *Bull. Crim.* 1981, n°317.
French Supreme Court, crim.ch., 15 March 1983, n°82–90533, *Bull. Crim.*1983, n°82.
French Supreme Court, crim.ch., 28 June 1983, *Bull. Crim.* 1983, n°202.
French Supreme Court, crim.ch., 11 May 1984, n°83–94501, *Bull. Crim.* 1984, n°170.
French Supreme Court, crim.ch., 16 April 1985, n°83–94866, *Bull. Crim.* 1985, n°140.
French Supreme Court, crim.ch., 6 May 1986, *Bull. Crim.* 1986, n°153.
French Supreme Court, crim.ch., 22 October 1986, n°85–95307, *Bull. Crim.* 1986, n°302, p. 771.
French Supreme Court, crim.ch., 30 January 1990, n°88–86.549, *unpublished.*
French Supreme Court, crim.ch., 8 October 1991, n°90–83336, *Bull. Crim.* 1991, n°334.
French Supreme Court, crim.ch., 3 December 1991, n°90–83605, *unpublished.*
French Supreme Court, crim.ch., 28 January 1992, n°91–81778, *Dr. pén.* 1992, 223.
French Supreme Court, crim.ch., 16 July 1992, n°91–86.156, *Bull. Crim.* 1992, n°273, p. 740.
French Supreme Court, crim.ch., 20 October 1992, n°91–84253, *Bull. Crim.* 1992, n°329.
French Supreme Court, crim.ch., 2 March 1993, n°91–84653, *Bull. Crim.* 1993, n°94.
French Supreme Court, crim.ch., 16 March 1993, *Bull. Crim.*1993, n°115.
French Supreme Court, crim.ch., 7 December 1993, n°90–87508, *Bull. Crim.* 1993 n°373, p. 472.
French Supreme Court, crim.ch., 7 December 1993, n°92–81094, *Bull. Crim.* 1993, n°373, p. 931.
French Supreme Court, crim.ch., 7 December 1993, n°92–84439, *Bull. Crim.*1993 n°374, p. 935.
French Supreme Court, crim.ch., 18 January 1994, n°91–86228, *unpublished.*

French Supreme Court, crim.ch., 17 May 1994, n°91–82129, *Dr. pén.* 1994, 258.
French Supreme Court, crim.ch., 20 December 1994, n°93–80267, *Bull. Crim.* 1994, n°424, p. 1031.
French Supreme Court, crim.ch., 24 January 1995, n°93–84701, *Bull. Crim.* 1995, n°33.
French Supreme Court, crim.ch., 13 June 1995, n°93–82144, *Bull. Crim.* 1995, n°217, p.591; *JCP*, 1995, IV, 2350.
French Supreme Court, crim.ch., 7 September 1995, *Dr. pén.* 1995, 280.
French Supreme Court, crim.ch., 24 October 1995, n°94–83666, *unpublished.*
French Supreme Court, crim.ch., 21 May 1996, n°94–83365, *Bull. Crim.* 1996, n° 210, p. 593.
French Supreme Court, crim.ch., 17 June 1997, n°94–85126, *Bull. Crim.* 1997, n°236 p.786, *D.* 1998, p. 51.
French Supreme Court, crim.ch., 24 June 1997, n°95–81187, *Bull. Crim.* 1997, n°253, p. 864.
French Supreme Court, crim.ch., 4 November 1997, n°96–84338, *Dr. pén.,* 1998.
French Supreme Court, crim.ch., 29 January 1998, n°95–83763, *unpublished.*
French Supreme Court, crim.ch., 29 January 1998, n°96–82731, *GP* 24/26 May 1998, p. 32.
French Supreme Court, crim.ch., 29 January 1998, n°96–84851, *GP* 1998, I, p. 75.
French Supreme Court, crim.ch., 28 April 1998, n°96–81655, *unpublished.*
French Supreme Court, crim.ch., 13 April 1999, n°98–81625, *Bull. Crim.* 1999, n°77.
French Supreme Court, crim.ch., 8 June 1999, n°98–83461, *unpublished.*
French Supreme Court, crim.ch., 7 September 1999, n°98–85.177, *unpublished.*
French Supreme Court, crim.ch., 14 December 1999, n°98–87529, *Bull. Crim.* 1999, n°305, p. 943.
French Supreme Court, crim.ch., 25 January 2000, n°98–87278, *unpublished.*
French Supreme Court, crim.ch., 26 April 2000, n°98–87633, *Bull. Crim.* 2000, n°167, p. 486.
French Supreme Court, crim.ch., 14 June 2000, n°99–80043, *unpublished.*
French Supreme Court, crim.ch., 12 September 2000, n°98–88201, *unpublished.*
French Supreme Court, crim.ch., 12 September 2000, n°99–82281, *unpublished.*
French Supreme Court, crim.ch., 27 February 2001, n°00–82557, *unpublished.*
French Supreme Court, crim.ch., 13 March 2001, n°00–85102, *unpublished.*
French Supreme Court, crim.ch., 19 June 2001, n°00–86167, *unpublished.*
French Supreme Court, crim.ch., 13 November 2001, n°01–80510, *unpublished.*
French Supreme Court, crim.ch., 5 March 2002, n°01–83777, *Bull. Crim.* 2002 n°55, p. 166.
French Supreme Court, crim.ch., 14 May 2002, n°01–85482, *unpublished.*
French Supreme Court, crim.ch., 5 November 2002, n°01–88461, *Bull. Crim.* 2002, n°200, p. 745.
French Supreme Court, crim.ch., 3 December 2002, n°01–86088, *Bull. Crim.* 2002, n°218.
French Supreme Court, crim.ch., 17 December 2002, n°01–85650, *Bull. Crim.* 2002 n°227, p. 832.
French Supreme Court, crim.ch., 6 January 2004, n°02–87803, *unpublished.*
French Supreme Court, crim.ch., 2 March 2004, n°03–82549, *unpublished.*
French Supreme Court, crim.ch., 28 September 2004, n°03–87450, *unpublished.*

French Supreme Court, crim.ch., 28 September 2004, n°04–80688, *Bull. Crim.* 2004, n°223, p. 796.
French Supreme Court, crim.ch., 15 March 2005, n°04–84463, *Bull. Crim.* 2005, n°90, p. 321.
French Supreme Court, crim.ch., 30 March 2005, n°04–85709, *Bull. Crim.* 2005, n°110.
French Supreme Court, crim.ch., 14 February 2006, n°05–82475, *Bull. Crim.* 2006, n°40.
French Supreme Court, crim.ch., 14 February 2006, n°05–81932, *Bull. Crim.* 2006, n°42, p. 165.
French Supreme Court, crim.ch., 10 May 2006, n°05–82971, *unpublished.*
French Supreme Court, crim.ch., 20 June 2006, n°05–86690, *Bull. Crim.* 2006, n°187, p. 667.
French Supreme Court, crim.ch., 28 November 2006, n°06–80340, *Bull. Crim.* 2006, n°300, p. 1080.
French Supreme Court, crim.ch., 2 May 2007, n°06–84710, *Bull. Crim.* 2007, n°115.
French Supreme Court, crim.ch., 30 May 2007, n°06–84.328, *Bull. Crim.* 2007 n°140.
French Supreme Court, crim.ch., 11 September 2007, n°07–80.783, *unpublished.*
French Supreme Court, crim.ch., 29 January 2008, n°07–83695, *Bull. Crim.* 2008, n°25, p. 98.
French Supreme Court, crim.ch., 11 March 2008, *Dr. pén.* 2008/4, p. 871.
French Supreme Court, crim.ch., 12 November 2008, n°07–83398, *Bull. Crim.* 2008, n°229.
French Supreme Court, crim.ch., 3 February 2009, n°06–83063 08–82402, *Bull. Crim.* 2009, n°25.
French Supreme Court, crim.ch., 3 February 2009, n°08–85220, *unpublished.*
French Supreme Court, crim.ch., 31 March 2009, n°07–86.892, n°07–88.021, *Bull. Crim.* 2009, n°61, n°62.
French Supreme Court, crim. Ch., 23 June 2009, *Légipresse* n° 269, February 2010, III 269–19, p. 38.
French Supreme Court, crim.ch., 24 November 2009, n°09–83256, *Bull. Crim.* 2009, n°193.
French Supreme Court, crim.ch., 19 March 2010, *Légipresse,* n°272, May 2010, p. 46–47.
French Supreme Court, crim.ch., 7 May 2010, n°09–80774, *published.*
French Supreme Court, crim.ch., 22 June 2010, n°10–82337, *unpublished.*
French Supreme Court, crim.ch., 15 March 2011, n°10–82.809, *unpublished.*
French Supreme Court, crim.ch., 7 June 2011, n°10–85179, *Légipresse,* n°287, October 2011, p. 550–554.
French Supreme Court, crim.ch., 7 June 2011, n°10–88315, *Crim. Bull.* 2011, *published.*
French Supreme Court, crim.ch., 10 October 2012, n°12–81505.
French Supreme Court, crim.ch., 5 December 2012, n°12–86382.
French Supreme Court, crim. ch., 16 April 2013, n° 13–90008/ 13–90010, *Légipresse* n° 306 June 2013, p. 337–338.

French Supreme Court, crim.ch., 19 November 2013, n°12–84083, *Bull. Crim.* 2002 n° 232.
French Supreme Court, crim.ch., 6 May 2014, n° 14–90010.

French Supreme Court civil chambers

French Supreme Court, civ.ch. I, 10 January 1990, n°88–14235, *Bull.* 1990 I, n°11, p. 9.
French Supreme Court, civ.ch. I, 29 October 1990, n°88–19366, *Bull.* 1990 I, n°226, p. 161.
French Supreme Court, civ.ch. II, 18 December 1995, n°91–14785, *Bull.* 1995 II, n°314, p. 184.
French Supreme Court, civ.ch. I, 14 November 2000, n°99–10778, *Bull.* 2000 I, n°289, p. 187.
French Supreme Court, civ.ch. II, 8 March 2001, n°98–17.574, *Bull.* 2001 II n°47, p. 32.
French Supreme Court, civ.ch. II, 29 March 2001, n°99–10332, *Bull.* 2001 II, n°67 p. 44.
French Supreme Court, civ.ch. II, 26 April 2001, n°99–10490, *Légipresse,* 2001, n°183–35.
French Supreme Court, civ.ch. II, 14 March 2002, n°99–19239, *Bull.* 2002 II, n°41, p. 43.
French Supreme Court, civ.ch. II, 14 March 2002, n°99–19238, *Bull.* 2002 II, n°46, p. 39.
French Supreme Court, civ.ch. II, 10 March 2004, n°00–16934, *Bull.* 2004 II, n°114, p. 94.
French Supreme Court, civ.ch. I, 27 September 2005, n°03–13622, *Bull.* 2005 I, n°348, p. 289.
French Supreme Court, civ.ch. I, 29 November 2005, n°04–16.508, *Bull.* 2005 I, n°453, p. 380.
French Supreme Court, civ.ch. I, 16 July 2006, n°05–17704, *Bull.* 2006 I, n°395, p. 340.
French Supreme Court, civ.ch. I, 14 November 2006, n°05–15822 05–16001, *Bull.* 2006 I, n°485, p. 417.
French Supreme Court, civ.ch. I, 30 October 2008, n°07–19223, *Bull.* 2008 I, n°244.
French Supreme Court, civ.ch. I, 19 March 2009, n°07–19667, *Légipresse* 2009, n°262–1, p. 83.
French Supreme Court, civ.ch. I, 6 May 2010, n°09–67.624, *Bull.* 2010 I, n°103.
French Supreme Court, civ.ch. I, 6 October 2011, n°10–18142, *Bull.* 2011 I.
French Supreme Court, civ. Ch., 10 April 2013, n°12–10177, *Bull.* 2013, I, n° 67.

Courts of Appeal

CA Paris 9 April 1951, *GP* 1951, I, 417.
CA Paris, 26 March 1952, *D.* 1953, J, 342.
CA Paris, 11 July 1979, *GP* 1979 (Mein Kampf).
CA Paris, 26 October 1984, *JCP* 1985 II 20452.
CA Paris, 13 May 1985, *GP* 1985, p. 344.
CA Paris, 27 September 1988, *D.* 1989 Somm. 301.
CA Paris, 30 January 1991, *JCP* 1991, IV, p. 207.
CA Paris, 9 December 1992.
CA Paris, 3 July 1995, *JCP G* 1996, II, 22601.
CA Paris, 28 September 1995, final judgment, *Légipresse* 1995, n°129, p. 19.
CA Paris, 9 November 1995.
CA Paris, 28 May 1996, *D.* 1996, p. 617.
CA Orléans, 14 December 1998.

CA Paris, 16 December 1998, *Légipresse* 1999, n°159-III, p. 30.
CA Paris, 30 June 2004.
CA Toulouse, 12 January 2005, *Légipresse* 2005 n°222–1, p. 17.
CA Paris, 8 April 2005, *D.* n° 20 2005, pp.1327–1328; *Légipresse* n°223 July/August, p. 145.
CA Versailles, 30 June 2005, *Légipresse* n°228, January/February 2006.
CA Paris, 9 February 2006.
CA Douai 25 January 2007, *Légipresse* 2007, n°242-III, p. 139.
CA Paris, 12 March 2008, *Légipresse* n° 252 – June 2008, p. 107–110.
CA Paris, 17 March 2011, annotation D. Lefranc, *Légipresse* n°285, July/August 2011, p. 430.
CA Paris, 15 September 2011, *Légipresse* n° 287 October 2011, 287–21, p. 531–532.
CA Paris, 28 November 2013, *Légipresse* n°315 April 2014, p. 204–205.

Tribunals of First Instance criminal case law

Tribunal corr. de la Seine, 7 February 1857, *La Gazette des tribunaux*, 9 February 1857.
Tribunal corr. de la Seine, 20 August 1857, *La Gazette des tribunaux*, 21 August 1857.
Tribunal corr. de la Seine, 2 June 1858, *La Gazette des tribunaux*, 5 June 1858.
Trib. corr. de Nîmes, 28 February 2013, *Légipresse* n° 305 May 2013, p. 270.

TGI Grenoble 18 December 1973, *D.* 1975, p. 489.
TGI de Paris, 17 June 1974, *D.* 1975.J.468.
TGI de Paris, 12 July 1989, *Légipresse,* 1989, n°66-I, p. 69.
TGI de Paris, 18 April 1991.
TGI de Paris, 8 March 1995.
TGI de Paris, 15 October 2002, *Légipresse* n°197, I, p. 155.
TGI de Paris, 22 October 2002, *unpublished.*
TGI de Paris, 22 March 2007, *Légipresse* n°242, June 2007, p. 123.
TGI de Paris, 12 February 2014, *Légipresse* n° 314 March 2014, 314–18, p. 140–141.
TGI de Paris, 18 February 2011, *Légipresse* n°282, April 2011, p. 240.
TGI de Nanterre, 5 April 2011, *Légipresse* n°286, September 2011, p. 465.
TGI de Paris, 10 April 2014, *Légipresse* n° 318, July-August 2014, p. 398–399.
TGI de Paris, 8 July 2014, *Légipresse* n° 319 September 2014, p. 461.
TGI de Paris, 19 September 2014, *Légipresse* n° 320 October 2014, p. 526.
TGI de Paris, 26 September 2014, *Légipresse* n° 321 November 2014, p. 591–592.
TGI de Paris, 30 October 2014, *Légipresse* n° 321 – November 2014, p. 588.

Tribunals of First Instance civil case law

TGI de Paris, 23 October 1984, *GP* 1984, p.722; *D.* 1985, p. 31.
TGI de Paris, 28 January 1985, *D.* 1985, p. 129.
TGI de Paris, 22 September 1988, *D.* 1989 Somm. 301.
TGI de Paris, 29 July 1989.

TGI de Paris, 15 December 1993, *JCP G* 1996, II, 22601.
TGI de Paris, 20 February 1997, *Légipresse* April 1997, p. 50–51.
TGI de Paris, 21 February 2002, *JCP G* n°17 – 23 April 2003; *Légipresse* n°192 June 2002, p. 105–106.
TGI de Paris, 15 October 2002, *Légipresse* n°197, I, p.155.
TGI de Paris, 10 March 2005, *D.* n°20 2005, p. 1326–1327.
TGI de Bobigny (ord. réf.), 13 November 2013, LICRA c/ Alain Soral, *Légipresse* n° 313, February 2014, p. 107–114, annotation Ader.

Annotations (selection)

Ader, B., *Des propos trop généraux ne sont pas susceptibles d'être diffamatoires*, annotation French Supreme Court, plenary assembly, 25 June 2010 *(Bourokba and de Buretel de Chassey), Légipresse* n°275, September 2010, p. 240–241.

De Lamy, B., *La cour de cassation et les marchands du temple: publicité et injure aux sentiments religieux*, annotation French Supreme Court, civ.ch., 14 November 2006, *Société GIP vs Association croyances et libertés et al*, *Légipresse* n° 239, March 2007, p. 41–47.

Derieux, E., *Contestation de la doctrine catholique et bonne foi,* annotation ECtHR 31 January 2006, *Giniewski vs France*, *Légipresse* n° 230, April 2006, p. 43–49.

Derieux, E., *Cassation d'une condamnation pour contestation de crimes contre l'humanité,* annotation French Supreme Court, crim.ch., 23 June 2009, *Légipresse* n°269, February 2010, p. 32–38.

Derieux, E., *Affaire Zemmour: distinction entre diffamation et provocation à la discrimination raciales*, annotation TGI Paris 18 February 2011, *Légipresse* n°282 April 2011, p. 243.

Dreyer, E., *Les pièges de la lutte antiraciste: la qualification précipitée d'un propos*, annotation French Supreme Court, crim.ch., 29 January 2008, *Légipresse* n°253, July/ August 2008, p. 135–138.

Hassler, T., *Droit de réponse et digressions relatives aux caricatures de Mahomet*, annotation French Supreme Court, civ.ch., 29 November 2005, *Sté nationale de television France 2, M. Tessier vs Mme Durand dite Bessey, Légipresse* n°229, p. 34–37.

Francillon, J., *Liberté d'expression et respect des convictions religieuses*, annotation French Supreme Court, crim. ch., 14 February 2006, *RSC* 2006, p. 625.

Gautron, A., *L'exploitation publicitaire des symbols religieux et le juge: À la recherche d'un équilibre entre liberté d'expression et droit au respect des convictions intimes*, annotation TGI Paris (ord.réf.) 10 March 2005/ CA Paris 8 April 2005, *RLDI* July/ August 2005, n°7, p. 28–32.

Guerder, P., *L'article 53 de la loi de 1881 soumis au verdict de l'Assemblée plénière?*, annotation CA Paris, 15 February 2011, *Légipresse* n°283, May 2011, p. 292–296.

Leclerc, H., *Vinci et le code*, annotation CA Paris, 8 April 2005, *Légipresse* n°223 July/ August, p. 143–149.

Leclerc, H. *Caricatures, blasphème et défi*, annotation TGI Paris, 22 March 2007, *Légipresse* n° 242 – June 2007, p. 123–128.

Leclerc, H., *Les caricatures de Mahomet, suite*, annotation CA Paris, 12 March 2008, *Légipresse* n° 252 – June 2008, p. 107–110.

Lefranc, D., *Dieudonné ou la subversion par l'ambiguïté,* annotation CA Paris 17 March 2011, *Légipresse* n°285, July/August 2011, p. 429–433.

Louvet, M-N., *Liberté d'expression et respect des croyances*, annotation TGI Paris, 20 February 1997, *AGRIF vs Colombia Tristar Films*, *Légipresse* April 1997, p. 49–53.

Lécuyer, G., *Responsabilité civile et droit de la presse: le tumulte permanent*, annotation at: French Supreme Court, civ.ch. I, 6 October 2011, n°10–18142, *Bull.* 2011 I, *Légipresse* n°290, January 2012, p.31.

Massis, Th., *De la libre critique à l'injure: tant va la cruche à l'eau...*, annotation French Supreme Court, plenary assembly, 16 February 2007, *RLDI* 2007, n°27.

Moritz, P.; Capitani, A., *Les caricatures de Mahomet face au juge correctionnel ou le délit d'injure entre droit penal et droit européen*, annotation TGI Paris, 22 March 2007, *RLDI* June 2007, n°28, p. 46–51.

Pendu, M., *Caricatures de Mahomet, liberté d'expression et respect des croyances religieuses*, annotation TGI Paris, 22 March 2007, *RLDI* July 2007, n°29, p. 44–45.

Rolland, P., *La critique, l'outrage et le blasphéme*, annotation TGI Paris (ord.réf.) 10 March 2005 and CA Paris (14e ch. B) 8 April 2005, *D* n° 20 2005, p. 1326–1331.

Tillement, G., *Diffamation raciale et critique de la politique israélienne,* annotation French Supreme Court, civ.ch., 12 July 2006, *Légipresse* n°237, December 2006, p. 223–228.

Tricoire, A., *Interprétation du sens de l'affiche d'un film par le juge*, annotation TGI Paris, 21 February 2002, *Légipresse* n°192 June 2002, p. 105.

Tricoire, A., *La nonne et le preservative*, annotation French Supreme Court, crim. ch., 14 February 2006, *M. Diouf and N. Vallade vs AGRIF*, *Légipresse* n°232, June 2006, p. 117–120.

Tricoire, A., *Quand la fiction exclut le délit, ou la reconnaissance de l'autonomie de la liberté de créer,* annotation TGI Paris, 16 November 2006, *Légipresse* n°240, April 2007, p. 74–79.

Drafting histories

Drafting history of the Act of 29 July 1881 on freedom of the press

Report of Eugène Lisbonne of 5 July 1880, *JO* 18 July 1880, French national assembly, annex n°2865.

Parliamentary debates, *JO* 25 January 1881, French national assembly, p. 33 *et seq.*

Parliamentary debates, *JO* 26 January 1881, French national assembly, p. 49 *et seq.*

Parliamentary debates, *JO* 28 January 1881, French national assembly, p. 65 *et seq.*

Parliamentary debates, *JO* 30 January 1881, French national assembly, p. 81 *et seq.*

Parliamentary debates, *JO* 1 February 1881, French national assembly, p. 96 *et seq.*

Parliamentary debates, *JO* 2 February 1881, French national assembly, p. 116 *et seq.*

Parliamentary debates, *JO* 15 February 1881, French national assembly, p. 235 *et seq.*

Parliamentary debates, *JO* 16 February 1881, French national assembly, p. 257 *et seq.*

Parliamentary debates, *JO* 22 July 1881, French national assembly, p. 1719 *et seq.*

Report of Eugène Pelletan of 18 June 1881, *JO* 5 July 1881, French Senate, annex n°334.

Parliamentary debates, *JO* 10 July 1881, French Senate, p. 1090 *et seq.*

Parliamentary debates, *JO* 12 July 1881, French Senate, p. 1106 *et seq.*

Parliamentary debates, *JO* 16 July 1881, French Senate, p. 1152 *et seq.*

Parliamentary debates, *JO* 17 July 1881, French Senate, p. 1168 *et seq.*

Drafting history of the Act of 1 July 1972 on the fight against racism

Parliamentary debates, *JO* 16 April 1971, French national assembly, p. 1115 *et seq.*

Parliamentary debates, *JO* 8 June 1972, French national assembly, p. 2280 *et seq.*

Parliamentary debates, *JO* 23 June 1972, French Senate, p. 1172 *et seq.*

Drafting history of the Act of 13 July 1990 on the repression of all acts of a racist, anti-Semitic or xenophobic nature

Parliamentary debates, *JO* 2 May 1990, French national assembly, p. 886 *et seq.*

Parliamentary debates, *JO* 28 June 1990, French national assembly, p. 3103 *et seq.*

Parliamentary debates, *JO* 11 June 1990, French Senate, p. 1445 *et seq.*

Documents of national institutions

Centre Nationale de la Recherche Scientifique, Secondi-Nix, M., *Lutte contre le racisme et justice pénale, Rôle des associations*, CNRS, CESDIP, October 1996.

Commission de réflexion sur l'application du principe de laïcité dans la république, *'la Commission Stasi', Rapport au président de la République*, 11 décembre 2003, Paris: La Documentation Française 2003.

Commission nationale consultative des droits de l'homme, *La lutte contre le racisme, l'antisémitisme et la xénophobie, annual reports 2009–2012*, CNCDH, Paris: La documentation française.

Commission nationale consultative des droits de l'homme, *Avis concernant un avant-projet de loi relative à la 'lutte contre la diffusion d'idées racistes ou xénophobes'*, CNCDH, 3 November 1994.

Commission nationale consultative des droits de l'homme, *Avis portant sur un projet de loi renforcant la repression de la diffusion de messages racistes ou xenophobes*, CNCDH, 26 September 1996.

Commission nationale consultative des droits de l'homme, *Avis sur le projet de loi relative à la lutte contre les propos discriminatoires à caractère sexiste ou homophobe*, CNCDH, 18 November 2004.

Commission nationale consultative des droits de l'homme, *Avis sur les statistiques 'ethniques'*, CNCDH, 22 March 2012.

Commission des lois constitutionnelles, Rapport n°4035 *sur la proposition de loi n°3842 'portant transposition du droit communautaire sur la lutte contre le racisme et réprimant la contestation de l'existence du génocide arménien'*, Assemblée Nationale, 7 décembre 2011.

Commission des lois constitutionnelles, Rapport n°269 *sur la proposition de loi 'visant à réprimer la contestation de l'existence des génocides reconnus par la loi'*, Sénat, 18 janvier 2012.

Commission des lois constitutionnelles, Rapport n°989 *sur la proposition de loi n°218 'tendant à la suppression du mot 'race' de notre législation*', Assemblée Nationale, 24 avril 2013.

Commission sur la répartition des contentieux, Serge Guinchard, *Report L'ambition raisonnée d'une justice apaisée, Proposal n°12–1,* Paris: La documentation française, coll. 'Rapports officiels' 2008.

Conseil d'État, *Un siècle de laïcité – Rapport public 2004*, Paris: La Documentation Française 2004.

Haut Conseil de l'Intégration, *L'islam dans la République*, Paris: La Documentation Française 2000.

Haute Conseil à l'Intégration, *Le bilan de la politique d'intégration 2002–2005*, Paris: La Documentation Française 2005.

Haute Conseil à l'Intégration, *La France sait-elle encore intégrer les immigrés? Les élus issus de l'immigration dans les conseils régionaux (2004–2010)*, Paris: la Documentation Française 2011.

Haut Conseil à l'Intégration, *Investir dans les associations pour réussir l'intégration*, Paris: La Documentation Française 2012.

Ministère de la Justice, Convention Cadre LICRA, 14 Décembre 2007.

Ministère de la Justice, Convention Cadre SOS Racisme, 14 Décembre 2007.

Ministère de l' Intérieur, *Plan national d'action contre le racisme et l' anti-Semitisme 2012–2014*, 15 Février 2012.

Mission d'information sur les questions mémorielles, M. Bernard Accoyer, *Rapport d'information n°1262*, Assemblée Nationale, 18 Novembre 2008.

Documents of international institutions

CERD Committee, *Annual report*, 15 February 1990, A/44/18.

CERD Committee, *Annual report*, 19 September 1994, A/49/18 (SUPP).

CERD Committee, *Annual report*, 17 October 2000, A/55/18 (SUPP).

CERD Committee, *Annual report*, 3 October 2005, A/60/18 (SUPP).

CERD Committee, *Annual report*, 31 October 2010, A/65/18.

CERD Committee, *Eight periodic report of France*, CERD/C/148/Add.3.

CERD Committee, *Ninth, tenth, and eleventh periodic report of France*, CERD/C/225/Add.2.

CERD Committee, *Twelfth, thirteenth, and fourteenth periodic report of France*, CERD/C/337/Add.5.

CERD Committee, *Fifteenth and sixteenth periodic report of France*, CERD/C/430/Add.4.

CERD Committee, *Seventeenth, eighteenth and nineteenth periodic report of France*, CERD/C/FRA/17–19.

European Commission against Racism and Intolerance, *First report on France*, 15 June 1998, CRI(98)47.

European Commission against Racism and Intolerance, *Second report on France*, 27 June 2000, CRI (2000)31.

European Commission against Racism and Intolerance, *Third report on France*, 15 February 2005, CRI(2005)3.

European Commission against Racism and Intolerance, *Fourth report on France*, 15 June 2010, CRI(2010)16.

European Commission against Racism and Intolerance, *Legal measures to combat racism and intolerance in the member States of the Council of Europe, France*, December 2001, CRI(98)80 Rev.2.

European Commission for Democracy through Law (Venice Commission), *Report on the relationship between freedom of expression and freedom of religion: the issue of regulation and prosecution of blasphemy, religious insult and incitement to religious hatred*, Study no. 406 2006, Strasbourg, 23 October 2008, CDL-AD(2008)026, Annex II, CDL(2008)090add2, p. 37–38.

Human Rights Committee, *Consideration of Reports Submitted by States Parties Under Article 40 of the Covenant: France,* 10 May 1982, CCPR/C/22/Add.2 (1982).

Human Rights Committee, *Consideration of Reports Submitted by States Parties Under Article 40 of the Covenant: France,* 26 August 1987, 540, CCPR/C/46/Add.2 (1987).

Newspaper articles (selection)

'Grandes affaires criminelles 28 – 1990. La profanation de Carpentras. Des tombes juives vandalisées', *Le Monde* 11 August 2006.

Larcher, L., Heurs et malheurs de l'islam cathodique.; Dossier. Quel dialogue avec l'Islam?; Dans les journaux, les magazines ou les fictions, le regard porté sur l'islam est varié. Selon les observateurs et les musulmans, ce traitement va de la caricature à l'autisme, *La Croix* 15 November 2008.

Interview Guéant: 'Les prières dans la rue doivent cesser', *Le Figaro* 14 September 2011.

Le gouvernement déterminé à faire cesser les prières de rue, *Agence France Presse,* 16 September 2011.

'On s'achemine vers une jurisprudence Dieudonné' *Le Monde* 7 January 2014.

'Dieudonné: le Conseil d'Etat maintient l'interdiction du spectacle à Nantes' *Le Monde* 9 January 2014.

Websites

www.lagrif.fr/
http://blog.dalloz.fr/blogdalloz/2008/10/la-lacit-un-fti.html
www.cesdip.fr/
www.coe.int
www.conseil-constitutionnel.fr/
www.conseil-etat.fr/
www.courdecassation.fr/
www.cncdh.fr/
www.droitdesreligions.net
http://jeanbauberotlaicite.blogspirit.com/
www.ladocumentationfrancaise.fr/
www.ldh-france.org/

www.legifrance.org/
www.legifrance.gouv.fr/
www.licra.org/
www.mrap.fr/
www.sos-racisme.org/
www.venice.coe.int/
www2.ohchr.org

Chapter 5 The Netherlands

Books and dissertations

Abspoel 1979
Abspoel, J.J., *Studenten, moordenaars en ander volk: kritische kanttekeningen van een officier van justitie*, Ede: Veen 1979.

Asscher & Simons 1886
Asscher, B.E. & Simons, D., *Het nieuwe wetboek van strafrecht vergeleken met den code pénal*, Den Haag: Belinfante 1886.

Asscher 1999
Asscher, L.F., *Constitutionele convergentie van pers, omroep en telecommunicatie*, Deventer: Kluwer 1999.

Asscher 2002
Asscher, L.F., *Communicatiegrondrechten* (diss.), Amsterdam: Otto Cramwinckel Uitgever 2002.

Baelde 1935
Baelde, R., *Studiën over godsdienstdelicten* (diss.), Den Haag: Nijhoff 1935.

Beekman & Grüttemeier 2005
Beekman, K., Grüttemeier, R., *De wet van de letter Literatuur en rechtspraak,* Athenaeum – Polak & Van Gennep: Amsterdam 2005.

Bink 2006
Bink, S., *Bijna 25 jaar media- en minderhedenbeleid. Van exclusiviteit naar inclusiviteit,* Utrecht: Mira Media 2006.

Bovent'Eert 2009
Bovent'Eert, P.P.T. *et al.*, *Grondwet, Tekst & Commentaar,* Deventer: Kluwer 2009.

Burkens 1989
Burkens, M.C., *Algemene leerstukken van grondrechten naar Nederlands constitutioneel recht,* Zwolle: W.E.J. Tjeenk Willink 1989.

Burkens 1998
Burkens. M.C. *et al.*, *Gelet op de Grondwet,* Deventer: Kluwer 1998.

Cleiren & Nijboer 2008
Cleiren, C.P.M. & Nijboer, J.F., *Strafrecht, Tekst en Commentaar*, Deventer: Kluwer 2008.

Cliteur 2004
Cliteur, P. B., *De neutrale staat, het bijzonder onderwijs en de multiculturele samenleving*, oratie rede 28 May 2004, Universiteit Leiden.

Colenbrander 1909
Colenbrander, H.T., *Ontstaan der Grondwet*, tweede deel (1815), Den Haag: Martinus Nijhoff 1909.

Corstens 2008
Corstens, G.J.M., *Het Nederlandse Strafprocesrecht,* Deventer: Kluwer 2008.

De Blois, Van der Poll & Van Woudenberg 2007
De Blois, M., Van der Poll, R. & Van Woudenberg, R. (eds.), *Vloeken als een Hollander, Godslastering: religieuze, juridische en culturele aspecten,* Veenendaal 2007.

De Hullu 2009
De Hullu, J., *Materieel strafrecht,* Deventer: Kluwer 2009.

De Meij 1996
De Meij, J. M., *De vrije informatiestroom in grondwettelijk perspectief*, Tweede Editie, Amsterdam: Otto Cramwinckel Uitgever 1996.

De Meij 2000
De Meij *et al.*, *De vrije informatiestroom in grondwettelijk perspectief*, Derde Druk, Amsterdam: Otto Cramwinckel Uitgever 2000.

De Roo 1970
De Roo, E.J., *Godslastering: rechtsvergelijkende studie over blasfemie en andere religiedelicten* (diss.), Deventer: Kluwer 1970.

Diemer 1937
Diemer, E., *Vrijheid van Drukpers*, Rotterdam-Utrecht: Libertas Drukkerijen 1937.

Diepenhorst 1946
Diepenhorst, I.A., *De verhouding tusschen kerk en staat in Nederland*, Kemink en Zoon: Utrecht 1946.

Ellian, Molier & Zwart 2011
Ellian, A., Molier, G. & Zwart, T. (eds.), *Mag ik dit zeggen? Beschouwingen over de vrijheid van meningsuitingen*, Den Haag: Boom Juridische Uitgevers 2011.

Fekkes 1968
Fekkes, J. *De God van je tante: ofwel Het Ezel-proces van Gerard Kornelis van het Reve: een documentaire*, Amsterdam: De Arbeiderspers 1968.

Fermin 1997
Fermin, A.M.E., *Nederlandse politieke partijen over minderhedenbeleid 1977–1995* (diss.), Amsterdam: Thesis Publishers 1997.

Haanappel & Mackaay 1990
Haanappel, P.P.C. & Mackaay, E., *New Netherlands Civil Code, Patrimonial Law*, Deventer: Kluwer 1990.

Hirsch Ballin 2011
Hirsch Ballin, E.M.H., *Burgerrechten,* oratie rede van 9 September 2011, oratie 409, Universiteit van Amsterdam.

Janssens 1998
Janssens, A.L.J.M., *Strafbare belediging* (diss.), Amsterdam: Thela Thesis 1998.

Janssens & Nieuwenhuis 2011
Janssens, A.L.J.; Nieuwenhuis, A.J., *Uitingsdelicten*, Derde Editie, Deventer: Kluwer 2011.

Joosting 1912
Joosting,.J.G.C., *Bij de gratie Gods*, Leiden: Brill 1912.

Kaplan 2007
Kaplan, B.J., *Divided by Faith: Religious Conflict and the Practice of Toleration in Early Modern Europe,* Cambridge MA: Harvard University Press 2007.

Koekkoek 2000
Koekkoek, A.K. (ed.), *De Grondwet, Een systematisch en artikelsgewijs commentaar*, Derde Editie, Deventer: W.E.J. Tjeenk Willink 2000.

Kortmann 1987
Kortmann, C.A.J.M., *De Grondwets-herzieningen 1983 en 1987,* Tweede Druk, Deventer: Kluwer 1987.

Kort-van Welzen 1994
Kort-van Welzen, W., *Christelijke kamerleden en de vrijheid van meningsuiting, een parlementair-historisch onderzoek* (diss.), Zwolle: W.E.J. Tjeenk Willink 1994.

Lerner 1980
Lerner, N., *The U.N. Convention on the Elimination of All Forms of Racial Discrimination,* Alphen aan den Rijn: Sijthoff & Noordhoff 1980.

Lijphart 1975
Lijphart, A., *The politics of Accomodation. Pluralism and Democracy in the Netherlands,* Berkeley: University of California Press 1975.

Lucassen & Penninx 1997
Lucassen, J. & Penninx, R., *Newcomers: immigrants and their descendants in the Netherlands 1550–1995*, Amsterdam: Het Spinhuis 1997.

Nieuwenhuis & Zouthout 2008
Nieuwenhuis, A.J. & Zouthout, C.M. (eds.), *Rechtsstaat en religie*, Nijmegen: Wolf Legal Publishers 2008.

Nieuwenhuis 2011
Nieuwenhuis, A.J., *Over de grens van de vrijheid van meningsuiting*, Nijmegen: Ars Aequi Libri 2011.

Noyon, Langemeijer & Remmelink, Wetboek van Strafrecht.

Peters 1981
Peters, J.A., *Het primaat van de vrijheid van meningsuiting* (diss.), Nijmegen: Ars Aequi Libri 1981.

Peters & De Vré 2005
Peters, J.A. & De Vré, I.J., *Vrijheid van meningsuiting, de betekenis van een grondrecht in tijden van spanning*, Deventer: Kluwer 2005.

Plooy 1986
Plooy, J., *Strafbare godslastering*, Amsterdam: Buijten en Schipperheijn 1986.

Post 2009
Post, H., *In strijd met de roeping der vrouw: de Staatkundig Gereformeerde Partij en het vrouwenkiesrecht*: Heerenveen: Groen 2009.

Rath 1991
Rath, J., *Minorisering: de sociale constructie van 'ethnische minderheden'*, Amsterdam: Sua 1991.

Smidt 1881
Smidt, H. J., *Geschiedenis van het Wetboek van strafrecht: volledige verzameling van regeeringsontwerpen, gewisselde stukken, gevoerde beraadslagingen, Deel 1*, Haarlem: Tjeenk Willink 1881.

Smidt 1882
Smidt, H.J., *Geschiedenis van het Wetboek van strafrecht: volledige verzameling van regeeringsontwerpen, gewisselde stukken, gevoerde beraadslagingen, Deel 3*, Haarlem: Tjeenk Willink 1882.

Scholten 1974
Scholten, P., *Mr. C. Asser's handleiding tot de beoefening van het Nederlands burgerlijk recht. Algemeen deel.* Zwolle: W.E.J. Tjeenk Willink 1974.

Slootweg 2010
Slootweg, T. (ed.), *Dorsten naar Gerechtigheid / Paul Scholten*, Deventer: Kluwer 2010.

Tekst & Commentaar Grondwet.

Tekst & Commentaar, Wetboek van Strafrecht.

Tekst & Commentaar, Wetboek van Strafvordering.

Van der Burg 2009
Van der Burg, W., *Het ideaal van de neutrale staat, inclusieve, exclusieve en compenserende visies op godsdienst en cultuur*, Erasmus Law Lectures 18, Den Haag, Boom Juridische Uitgevers 2009.

Van der Neut 1986
Van der Neut, J.L., Discriminatie en strafrecht, Arnhem: Gouda Quint 1986.

Van der Wilt 2009
Van der Wilt, H., *Smalende Godslastering verboden?*, Veenendaal: Stichting Onderzoek- en Publicatiefonds Bond tegen het vloeken 2009.

Van Gend & Visser 2004
Van Gend, S.J.A.M.; Visser, G.J., *Artikel 12 tussen recht en onrecht. Een scala van zaken*, Nijmegen: Ars Aequi 2004.

Van Noorloos 2011
Van Noorloos, M., *Hate Speech Revisited, A comparative and historical perspective on hate speech law in the Netherlands and England & Wales* (diss.), Antwerpen: Intersentia 2011.
Vermeulen 1989
Vermeulen, B.P., *De vrijheid van geweten, een fundamenteel rechtsprobleem* (diss.), Arnhem: Gouda Quint 1989.

Vermeulen 2007
Vermeulen, B.P., *Vrijheid, gelijkheid, burgerschap,* Den Haag: Sdu Uitgevers 2007.

Woltjer 2002
Woltjer, A., *Wetgever, rechter en het primaat van de gelijkheid, Over primaten in het recht* (diss.), Den Haag: Boom Juridische uitgevers 2002.

Scientific articles and contributions to collective works

Biesheuvel 1979
Biesheuvel, Het Softenon drama en de vrije meningsuiting, *NJCM-Bulletin,* nr. 16/17, 1979, p.58–63.

Bijsterveld 2006
Bijsterveld, S., 'Scheiding van kerk en staat: een klassieke norm in een moderne tijd', in: Wetenschappelijke Raad voor het Regeringsbeleid, *Geloven in het publieke domein,* Amsterdam University Press: Amsterdam 2006, p. 227–259.

Bink 2006
Bink, S., 'Media en minderheden in Nederland', in: Overdijk- Francis, J.E., Boot, J.S.M., Smeets, H.M.A.G., & Verheyden, J.A.C. (eds.), *Handboek Minderheden*, Houten: Sdu Uitgevers 2006, p. 1–57.

De Beer 2007

De Beer, P., Waarom vrijheid van godsdienst uit de grondwet kan., *Socialisme & Democratie* 2007 64 (10), p. 18–24.

De Boer 1987

De Boer, J., De collectieve actie in verband met discriminatie van een collectiviteit, *NJB* 27 June 1987, nr. 26, p. 818.

De Graaf & De Haas 1984

De Graaf, F. & De Haas, M.J.O.M., Horizontale werking van grondrechten: een heilloos leerstuk, *NJB* 1984, p. 1353–1358.

De Hullu 1984

De *Hullu*, J., *Strafrecht* en literatuur, Ars Aequi 1984, p. 757–761.

De Jong 2002

De Jong, W., Drie WRR-rapporten vergeleken, *Migrantenstudies*, 2002 18(2), p. 78–86.

De Lange 2009

De Lange, A. De beklagprocedure en criminele politiek, *Strafblad* 2009, p. 480.

Dommering 1994

Dommering, E.J., De Nederlandse publieke discussie en de politionele akties in Indonesië, *NJB* 1994, p. 277 *et seq.*

Dommering 1998

Dommering, E.J. 'De Grondwet in de Informatiemaatschappij', in: Burkens. M.C. *et al.*, *Gelet op de Grondwet,* Deventer: Kluwer 1998, p.110–123.

Dommering 2010-I

Dommering, E.J., 'De dubbele moraal van het groepsbeledigen in cartoons: Een fictieve redevoering ter gelegenheid van het niet op 30 september gevierde vijfjarige jubileum van de Deense cartoonrellen' (9/30), *NJB* 2010, p. 2264–2268.

Dommering 2010-II

Dommering, E. J., 'Zwijgen is zilver, wraken is goud. De tunnelvisie van het OM in het Wilders-proces' (essay), *De Groene Amsterdammer* 4 November 2010.

Ellian 2007

Ellian, A., Enkele overpeinzingen over opiniedelicten en vrijheid., *Strafblad*, 5 (5) 2007, p. 397–409.

Entzinger 2003

Entzinger, H., 'The Rise and Fall of Multiculturalism: The Case of the Netherlands'; in: Joppke & Morawska (eds.), *Toward Assimilation and Citizenship; Immigration in Liberal Nation-States*; London: Palgrave Macmillan 2003, p. 59–86.

Entzinger 2006

Entzinger, H., 'Changing the rules while the game is on; From multiculturalism to assimilation in the Netherlands', in: Michal Bodemann, Y. & Gökçe Yurdakul (eds.), *Migration, Citizenship, Ethnos: Incorporation Regimes in Germany, Western Europe and North America*, New York: Palgrave MacMillan 2006, p. 121–144.

Hirsch Ballin 1988

Hirsch Ballin, E.M.H., 'Artikel 1 van de Grondwet als fundamentele constitutionele norm', in: Maris, C.W. (ed.), *Gelijkheid en recht*, Deventer/ Zwolle: Tjeenk Willink 1988.

Groenhuijsen & Kwakman 2002

Groenhuijsen, M.S. & Kwakman, N.J.M., Het slachtoffer in het vooronderzoek, in: Groenhuijsen & Kwakman (eds.), *Dwangmiddelen en rechtsmiddelen, Derde interimrapport onderzoeksproject Strafvordering 2001*, Deventer: Kluwer 2002, p. 933–935.

Janssens 1999

Janssens, A.L.J., De loochenaars van Auschwitz; de ongewenstheid van strafbaarstelling, *Ontmoetingen: Voordrachtenreeks van het Lutje Psychiatrisch-Juridisch Gezelschap*, 1999, nr. 5.

Jurgens 1999

Jurgens, E.C.M. *et al.*, Preadvies inzake een nieuwe tekst voor de artt. 7 en 13 van de Grondwet, bijlage bij *Mediaforum* 1999, nr. 11/12.

Kaptein 2011

Kaptein, H., Slachtoffers van Wilders' vervolging op klacht, in: Ellian, Molier & Zwart 2011, p. 150.

Kennedy & Valenta 2006

Kennedy, J. & Valenta, M., 'Religious pluralism and the Dutch state: reflections on the future of Article 23', in: Wetenschappelijke Raad voor het Regeringsbeleid, *Geloven in het publieke domein,* Amsterdam University Press: Amsterdam 2006, p. 337–351.

Koekkoek 1985

Koekkoek, A.K., De betekenis van grondrechten voor het privaatrecht, *WPNR* 1985, nr. 5742, 5743 en 5744, p.406.

Koolen 2011

Koolen, B., Het smalle pad van Jan Donner, De ontstaansgeschiedenis van de *Lex Donner* 1932, *Tijdschrift voor Religie, Recht en Beleid,* 2011(2) 1, p. 72–84.

Korteweg 2010

Korteweg, D., Strafbaarstelling negationisme: geschiedschrijving via het recht?, *Mediaforum* 2010–3, p.81.

Peters 2009

Peters, J. A., 'Rutte en de vrijheid van meningsuiting', *Mediaforum* 2009–6, p. 237.

Prins 2002
Prins, B., Het lef om taboes te doorbreken. Nieuw realisme in het Nederlandse discours over multiculturalisme, *Migrantenstudies*, 2002 18 (4), p. 241–254.

Nieuwenhuis 2004
Nieuwenhuis, A.J., Godsdienstvrijheid en bijdragen aan het maatschappelijk debat, *NJCM-Bulletin,* jrg.29 (2004) nr.2, p. 154–166.

Nieuwenhuis 2011
Nieuwenhuis, A.J., Na de zaak Wilders. Is de wetgever nu aan zet?, *Ars Aequi*, December 2011, p. 869.

Sackers 2011
Sackers, H., 'De opmerkelijke geschiedenis van artikel 137c Sr', in: Ellian, A., Molier, G. & Zwart, T. (eds.), Mag ik dit zeggen? Beschouwingen over de vrijheid van meningsuitingen, Den Haag: Boom Juridische Uitgevers 2011, p. 309–327.

Rodrigues 2002
Rodrigues, P.R., Collective acties als structureel instrument tegen discriminatie, in: Jongbloed, A.W. (ed.), *Samen sterk, over optreden in rechte door groeperingen*, Den Haag: Boom Juridische Uitgevers 2002, p. 91–103.

Rodrigues 2011
Rodrigues, P.R., Eén voor allen: gelijke behandeling en collectieve acties, in: Forder, C. (ed.) *Gelijke behandeling: oordelen en commentaar 2010*, Nijmegen: Wolf Legal Publishers 2011, p. 309–324.

Rosier 1996
Rosier, T. E., 'Discriminerende Belediging', *Recht & Kritiek* 1996, p. 305–334.

Rosier 2000
Rosier, T.E., Tolerantie en religie. Over de zaak Van Dijke en de visie van het EHRM inzake godslastering, *RM Themis 2000/1*, p. 3–14.

Rosier 2011
Rosier, Th., 'Kunnen de klagers in de Wilders-zaak een beroep doen op artikel 8 EVRM?', *NTM/NJCM-bull.* 2011, p. 725–737.

Schalken 2011
Schalken, T., 'Over volle of marginale toetsing van OM-beleid in 12-Sv-zaken: haalbaarheid, opportuniteit of opportunisme?' in: Van Kempen *et al.* 2011, p. 481–490.

Schuijt, G.A.I., 'VII Aantasting eer en goede naam en andere aantasting van de persoon', in: Bloembergen, A.R. (ed.), *Onrechtmatige daad* (losbl.), aant. 26–96, Deventer: Kluwer.

Schuijt 1990
Schuijt, G.A.I., Is de Hoge Raad bang voor de uitingsvrijheid?, *Informatierecht/AMI* 1990, p. 83–88.

Schuijt 1996
Schuijt, G.A.I., Hoge Raad niet meer bang voor de uitingsvrijheid?, *Informatierecht/AMI* 1996, p. 23–30.

Stelling 'De woorden 'godsdienst of levensovertuiging' in artikel 137c Wetboek van Strafrecht dienen geschrapt te worden', *NJB* 2003–16, 18 April 2003, p. 829–834.

Swart 1970
Swart, A.H. J., Rassendiscriminatie en de Nederlandse strafwet, *DD* 1970, 2, p. 77.

Thema Artikel 12 Sv, *Strafblad* 2009, 29 October 2009, jrg. 7, nr. 5.

Thema Het publiek debat, *Strafblad* 2009–3, 19 June 2009, jrg.7.

Thema Omtrent Van Gogh, *NJB* 17 December 2004, nr. 45–46.

Thema Uitingsdelicten en discriminatie, *Strafblad* 2007, p. 363–409.

Uzman, Barkhuysen & Van Emmerik 2010
Uzman, J., Barkhuysen, T. & Van Emmerik, M.L., The Dutch Supreme Court: A Reluctant Positive Legislator?, *EJCL*, vol.14.3 (December 2010).

Van Bemmelen 1973
Van Bemmelen, J.M., Positieve criteria voor strafbaarstelling, in: Glastra van Loon, J.F. *et al.* (eds.), Speculum Langemeijer; 31 rechtsgeleerde opstellen, Zwolle: W.E.J. Tjeenk Willink 1973.

Van der Leij 2009
Van der Leij, J.B.J., Het slachtoffer in de beklagprocedure van artikel 12 Sv, *Strafblad* 2009, p. 467.

Van Kempen 2011
Van Kempen, P.H., 'Religie in het Wetboek van Strafrecht', in: Broeksteeg, H. & Terlouw, A. (ed.), *Overheid, Recht en Religie*, Kluwer: Deventer 2011, p. 161–194.

Van Ooijen, Egmond, Eijkman, Olujic & Vos 2008
Van Ooijen, H.M.A.E., Egmond, L.F., Eijkman, Q.A.M., Olujic, F. & Vos, O.P.G. (eds.), *Godsdienstvrijheid: afschaffen of beschermen?*, Leiden: Stichting NJCM-Boekerij, 2008.

Veraart 2010
Veraart, W., 'Beledigen kan alleen in context, Kanttekeningen bij het "belediging islam"-arrest van 10 maart 2009', *NJB* 26 March 2010, p. 724–730.

Vermeulen 1989
Vermeulen, B.P., 'De Goerees en de kardinaal, ofwel: vrijheid van godsdienst versus discriminatieverbod', in: L. Heyde e.a. (red.), *Begrensde vrijheid*, Zwolle: Tjeenk Willink 1989; Koekkoek 1992, p. 127–128 and p. 131–133.

Vermeulen & Kanne 2004
Vermeulen, B.P. & Kanne, M.J., 'Kerk en staat en de mensenrechten', in: Van Drimmelen, L.C. & Van der Ploeg, T.J. (eds.), *Kerk en recht*, Utrecht: Lemma 2004.

Vermeulen 2008
Vermeulen, Ben, Waarom de vrijheid van godsdienst in de grondwet moet blijven., *Socialisme & Democratie* 2008 65(3), p. 14–26.

Vermeulen 2011
Vermeulen, B., 'Strafbare belediging van God, godsdienst, godsdienstigen', in: P.H.P.H.M.C. van Kempen e.a. (red.), *Levend strafrecht, strafrechtelijke vernieuwingen in een maatschappelijke context, Liber amicorum Ybo Buruma*, Deventer: Kluwer 2011, p. 653–666.

Vlemminx 2002
Vlemminx, F.M.C., 'Mogen sympathieën zwaarder wegen dan constitutionele zuiverheid?', *NJB* 2002, p. 1696–1699.

Drafting histories

Drafting history of the offence of blasphemy

Handelingen II, 1880–1881, p. 99 *et seq.*
Kamerstukken II, 1930–1931, 348.
Handelingen II, 1930–1931, p. 2796.
Kamerstukken II, 1931–1932, 34.
Handelingen II, 1931–1932, 26 Mei 1932.
Handelingen II, 1931–1932, 27 Mei 1932.
Handelingen II, 1931–1932, 31 Mei 1932.
Handelingen II, 1931–1932, 1 Juni 1932.
Handelingen II, 1932–1933, 3 November 1933.
Aanhangsel II, 1979–1980, 1108.
Kamerstukken II, 21 februari 1989, p. 5099 – 5109.
Aanhangsel II, 1996–1997, 929.
Kamerstukken II, 2004–2005, 29854.
Handelingen II, 2004–2005, nr. 23, p. 1335–1342.
Kamerstukken II, 2004–2005, 29800 VI.
Aanhangsel II, 2005–2006, 2019.
Kamerstukken II, 2006–2007, 30800 VI.
Kamerstukken II, 2007–2008, 31200 VI.
Kamerstukken II, 2008–2009, 31700 VI.
Kamerstukken II, 2009–2010, 32203.
Kamerstukken II, 2010–2011, 32203.
Kamerstukken II, 2011–2012, 32203.

Handelingen II, 2012–2013, nr.64, item 9.

Handelingen I, 1923–1924, p. 483 *et seq.*
Handelingen I, 1932–1933, 2 November 1932.
Handelingen I, 1932–1933, 3 November 1932.
Kamerstukken I, 2012–2013, 32203, A-C, E herdruk.
Handelingen I, 2013–2014, nr.10, item 2.
Handelingen I, 2013–2014, nr.10, item 12.

Drafting history of the implementation of ICERD

Kamerstukken II, 9723 (R 663).
Kamerstukken II 1967–1968, 9724.
Handelingen II, 1969–70, 27 August 1970, p. 4333–4354.
Handelingen II, 2 September 1970, p. 4379.

Kamerstukken I, 1970–71, 9724.

(Proposals for) modifications of the hate speech bans: extension to the discriminatory grounds of sex, sexual preference and handicap; proposal to introduce a free speech clause; and an offence penalizing the denial of genocides

Kamerstukken II, 1988–1989, 20239.
Kamerstukken II, 2005–2006, 30579.
Kamerstukken II, 2008–2009, 30579.
Kamerstukken II, 2009–2010, 30579.
Kamerstukken II, 2010–2011, 30579.
Handelingen II, 13 September 2011, 105–15, p. 52–64.
Kamerstukken II, 2012–2013, 33369.
Kamerstukken II, 2014–2015, 34051.

Kamerstukken I, 1990–1991, 20239, nr. 76a.

Case law

ECmHR/ ECtHR

ECmHR, 10 October 1979, n°8348/78 8406/78, (Glimmerveen and Hagenbeek/ the Netherlands).
ECmHR, 21 October 1998, Mediaforum 1999–1, nr. 3.

ECtHR, 26 April 1979, NJ 1980, 146 (Sunday Times/United Kingdom).
ECtHR, 9 February 1995, n°16616/90 (Vereniging Weekblad Bluf!/ the Netherlands).

ECtHR, 28 October 2003, n°39657/98 (Steur/ the Netherlands).
ECtHR, 30 November 2006, n°10807/04 (Veraart/ the Netherlands).
ECtHR, 22 November 2007, n°64752/01 (Voskuil/ the Netherlands).
ECtHR, grand chamber, 14 September 2010, n°38224/03 (Sanoma Uitgevers BV/ the Netherlands).
ECtHR, 10 July 2012, n°58369/10, (SGP/ the Netherlands).

Dutch Supreme Court

Dutch Supreme Court, 17 April 1939, *NJ* 1939, 927.
Dutch Supreme Court, 19 February 1940, *NJ* 1940, 754.
Dutch Supreme Court, 4 March 1940, *NJ* 1940, 830.
Dutch Supreme Court, 29 April 1940, *NJ* 1940, 831.
Dutch Supreme Court, 28 November 1950, *NJ* 1951, 137.
Dutch Supreme Court, 28 November 1950, *NJ* 1951, 138.
Dutch Supreme Court, 27 February 1951, *NJ* 1951, 472.
Dutch Supreme Court, 27 March 1953, *NJ* 1953, 389.
Dutch Supreme Court, 23 May 1961, *NJ* 1961, 427.
Dutch Supreme Court, 19 January 1962, *NJ* 1962, 107.
Dutch Supreme Court, 24 January 1967, *NJ* 1967, 270.
Dutch Supreme Court, 7 November 1967, *NJ* 1968, 44.
Dutch Supreme Court, 30 January 1968, *NJ* 1968, 199.
Dutch Supreme Court, crim.ch, 2 April 1968, *NJ* 1968, 373, annotation Brinkhorst.
Dutch Supreme Court, 5 November 1968, *NJ* 1968, 78.
Dutch Supreme Court, crim. ch., 7 March 1972, *NJ* 1973, 35.
Dutch Supreme Court, crim. Ch., 24 June 1975, *NJ* 1975, 450, annotation Mulder.
Dutch Supreme Court, crim. ch., 15 June 1976, *NJ* 1976, 551, annotation Van Veen.
Dutch Supreme Court, 19 September 1977, *NJ* 1978, 516.
Dutch Supreme Court, crim. ch., 14 March 1978, *LJN* AC3463, *NJ* 1978, 664.
Dutch Supreme Court, 9 March 1979, *NJ* 1979, 363, annotation Maeijer.
Dutch Supreme Court, crim. ch., 29 March 1983, *NJ* 1983, 532.
Dutch Supreme Court, 24 June 1983, *NJ* 1984, 801.
Dutch Supreme Court, 6 December 1983, *NJ* 1984, 601.
Dutch Supreme Court, crim. Ch., 26 June 1984, *NJ* 1985, 40.
Dutch Supreme Court, 8 March 1985, *NJ* 1985, 437.
Dutch Supreme Court, crim. ch., 27 October 1985, *NJ* 1988, 538, annotation Van Veen.
Dutch Supreme Court, Crim. Ch., 11 March 1986, *NJ* 1987, 462, annotation Mulder.
Dutch Supreme Court, 31 October 1986, *NJ* 1987, 173.
Dutch Supreme Court, 16 December 1986, *NJ* 1987, 534.
Dutch Supreme Court, 13 February 1987, *NJ* 1987, 899.
Dutch Supreme Court, 12 May 1987, *NJ* 1988, 299.
Dutch Supreme Court, civ. ch., 5 June 1987, *NJ* 1988, 702, annotation Alkema.
Dutch Supreme Court, 27 October 1987, *NJ* 1988, 538.

Dutch Supreme Court, Crim. Ch., 22 March 1988, *Rechtspraak Rassendiscriminatie*, edition 1995, p. 297, annotation Pattipawae.
Dutch Supreme Court, crim. Ch., 21 June 1988, *NJ* 1988, 1021, annotation 't Hart.
Dutch Supreme Court, 14 March 1989, *NJ* 1990, 29.
Dutch Supreme Court, 14 April 1989, *NJ* 1989, 469.
Dutch Supreme Court, crim. ch., 18 October 1989, *NJ* 1989, 476, annotation Mulder.
Dutch Supreme Court, civ. ch., 2 February 1990, *NJ* 1991, 289.
Dutch Supreme Court, Crim. Ch., 19 June 1990, *NJ* 1991, 119.
Dutch Supreme Court, crim. ch., 11 December 1990, *NJ* 1991, 313, annotation 't Hart.
Dutch Supreme Court, 2 November 1993, *NJ* 1994, 197.
Dutch Supreme Court, 17 November 1993, *NJ* 1993, 275.
Dutch Supreme Court, 21 October 1994, *NJ* 1996, 346.
Dutch Supreme Court, 25 October 1994, *LJN* 97691.
Dutch Supreme Court, 6 January 1995, *NJ* 1995, 422, annotation Dommering.
Dutch Supreme Court, Crim. Ch., 21 February 1995, *Rechtspraak Rassendiscriminatie*, edition 1995–2000, p. 43–46, annotation Schalken.
Dutch Supreme Court, crim. Ch., 2 May 1995, *NJ* 1995, 621.
Dutch Supreme Court, Crim. Ch., 16 April 1996, *NJ* 1996, 527.
Dutch Supreme Court, 10 May 1996, *NJ* 1996, 578.
Dutch Supreme Court, 17 June 1997, *NJ* 1998, 361.
Dutch Supreme Court, crim. ch., 25 November 1997, *NJ* 1998, 261.
Dutch Supreme Court, Crim. Ch., 18 May 1999, *NJ* 1999, 634, annotation A.C. 't Hart.
Dutch Supreme Court, 21 March 2000, *NJ* 2000, 482.
Dutch Supreme Court, crim. ch., 9 January 2001, *NJ* 2001, 203.
Dutch Supreme Court, crim. ch., 9 January 2001, *NJ* 2001, 204, annotation De Hullu.
Dutch Supreme Court, 30 October 2001, *NJ* 2002, 129.
Dutch Supreme Court, Crim. Ch., 2 April 2002, *LJN* AD8693, *NJ* 2002, 421, annotation Mevis.
Dutch Supreme Court, Crim. Ch., 5 November 2002, *LJN AE8821*.
Dutch Supreme Court, crim. ch., 14 January 2003, *NJ* 2003, 261, annotation Mevis.
Dutch Supreme Court, Crim. Ch., 15 April 2003, *NJ* 2003, 334.
Dutch Supreme Court, crim. ch., 6 May 2003, *LJN* AF7895.
Dutch Supreme Court, 19 April 2005, *NJ* 2006, 566.
Dutch Supreme Court, 18 January 2008, *LJN* BB3210, *NJ* 2008, 274, annotation Dommering.
Dutch Supreme Court, Crim. Ch., 10 March 2009, *LJN* BF0655; *NJ* 2010, 19, annotation Mevis; *NS* 2009, 139; *RvdW* 2009, 414.
Dutch Supreme Court, Crim. Ch., 15 September 2009, *LJN* BI4739, *NJ* 2009, 445; *NS* 2009, 344; *RvdW* 2009, 1058.
Dutch Supreme Court, Crim. Ch., 2 February 2010, BK5172/ 5174 / 5175 / 5182 / 5189 / 5193 / 5196.
Dutch Supreme Court, 9 April 2010, *LJN* BK4549; BK4547, *AB* 2010, 190, annotation Van Ommeren; *Gst.* 2010, 7338, nr. 63, annotation Broeksteeg; *JB* 2010, 115, annotation

Schutgens; *NJ* 2010, 388, annotation Alkema; *NJCM-Bulletin* 2010, p. 485–500, annotation Nehmelman and Woltjer.
Dutch Supreme Court, Crim. Ch., 21 September 2010, *LJN BM2483.*
Dutch Supreme Court, crim. ch., 23 November 2010, *LJN* BM9135.
Dutch Supreme Court, crim. ch., 11 January 2011, *LJN BP0291*, *NJ* 2011, 116, annotation Mevis.
Dutch Supreme Court, 14 June 2011, *LJN* BP0287, *NJ* 2011, 504, annotation Dommering.
Dutch Supreme Court, crim. ch., 27 March 2012, *NJ* 2012, 220.
Dutch Supreme Court, crim. Ch., 26 June 2012, *NJ* 2012, 415.
Dutch Supreme Court, crim. Ch., 3 July 2012, *LJN* BW5121/ 5132 / 5136 / 5161 / 5178, *NS* 2012, 296, *RvdW* 2012, 1021.
Dutch Supreme Court, crim. ch. 16 December 2014, *NJB* 2015/160.

Courts of Appeal

CA Arhnem, 10 January 1963, *NJ* 1963, 404.
CA The Hague, 22 September 1982, *NJ* 1984, 600.
CA The Hague, 10 February 1984, *NJ* 1984, 445.
CA Arnhem, Crim. Ch., 21 January 1991, Art.1 nr. *0725.*
CA Amsterdam, 20 May 1994, *Rechtspraak Rassendiscriminatie*, edition 1995, p. 773–775.
CA Leeuwarden, 13 January 1995, *NJ* 1995, 243.
CA Leeuwarden, 26 January 1995, *NJ* 1995, 388.
CA Amsterdam, Crim. Ch., 20 February 2000, *R 99/158.*
CA Amsterdam, Crim. Ch., 29 March 2001, R 97/083, Art. 1 nr. *1976.*
CA Amsterdam, Crim. Ch., 9 April 2001, Art.1 nr. *2039.*
CA The Hague, 18 November 2002, *LJN* AF0667*, NJ* 2003, 24.
CA The Hague, Crim. Ch., 19 May 2003, *LJN* AF8921, *NJ* 2003, 382.
CA Amsterdam, 11 September 2003, *LJN* AK8302.
CA Amsterdam, 7 December 2005, *LJN* AU 1916.
CA 's-Hertogenbosch, 10 November 2006*, LJN* BH3383.
CA The Hague, Crim. Ch., 23 January 2008, *LJN* BC2576 / 4129.
CA Amsterdam, 9 April 2008, *NJ* 2005, 599, annotation Legemaate.
CA Amsterdam, 16 July 2008, *LJN BO1540.*
CA Amsterdam, 21 January 2009, *NJ* 2009, 191, annotation Buruma, *Strafblad* 2009, p. 198–208, annotation Fennema, *Mediaforum* 2009, 8, annotation Nieuwenhuis.
CA Amsterdam, 23 November 2009, *LJN* BK4139, *Mediaforum* 2010–1, p. 24, annotation Nieuwenhuis.
CA Amsterdam, 17 February 2010, *LJN* BL4528.
CA Amsterdam, 15 June 2010, *LJN* BM7410.
CA Arnhem, 19 August 2010, *LJN BN4204*, *NJFS* 2010, 294.
CA Amsterdam, 11 October 2010, *LJN* BO0041.
CA Amsterdam, 17 December 2010, *LJN* BO07690 / 8032 / 9014 / 9015 / 9016 / 9017 / 9018.
CA Amsterdam, 6 September 2011, *LJN* BR6764.

District Courts

Dordrecht District Court, crim.ch., 15 January 1934, (unpublished).
Rotterdam District Court, 16 July 1937, *NJ* 1938, 736.
Haarlem District Court, crim.ch., 19 May 1938, (unpublished).
Amsterdam District Court, crim.ch., 23 June 1965, *NJ* 1965, 282.
Amsterdam District Court, 8 March 1978, *NJ* 1978 281, annotation Maeijer.
Groningen District Court, 9 June 1994, *Mediaforum* 1994–7/8, p. 67.
Amsterdam District Court, 18 November 1998, *NJ* 1999, 377.
Dordrecht District Court, Crim. Ch., 9 November 1999, *Rechtspraak Rassendiscriminatie,* edition 1995–2000, p. 473–475.
Amsterdam District Court, summary judgment, 2 August 2001, *LJN* AB3067.
Rotterdam District Court, Crim. Ch., 8 April 2002, *NJCM-Bulletin*, jrg.27 (2002) nr.8, p. 1019, annotation De Haseth, Starreveld & Loof.
'’s-Hertogenbosch District Court, crim. ch., 21 December 2004, *LJN* AR7891.
Amsterdam District Court, Crim. Ch., 27 January 2005, *LJN* AS4126.
The Hague District Court, summary judgment, 15 March 2005, Mediaforum 2005–4, p. 178–180, annotation Schuijt.
Haarlem District Court, Crim. Ch., 3 May 2005, *LJN* BC6780.
’s-Hertogenbosch District Court, Crim. Ch., 19 July 2005, *LJN* AT9494.
Rotterdam District Court, Crim. Ch., 10 March 2006, *LJN* AV5108, 10/000322–04;10/000328–04;10/000396–04;10/000393–04;10000325–04;10/000323–04;10/000395–04.
Rotterdam District Court, summary judgment, 21 November 2006, *LJN* AZ3031.
The Hague District Court, summary judgment, 7 April 2008, *LJN* BC8732.
Amsterdam District Court, Crim. Ch., 2 June 2008, *LJN* BD2957.
Haarlem District Court, Crim. Ch., 7 April 2009, *LJN* BI0374.
Amsterdam District Court, 3 February 2010, *LJN* BL1868.
Utrecht District Court, crim. ch., 22 April 2010, *LJN BM1987*, annotation Nieuwenhuis in: *Mediaforum* 2010–5, p. 179–181.
Utrecht District Court, Crim. Ch., 26 April 2010, *LJN* BM8138, *NJFS* 2010, 231.
The Hague District Court, summary proceedings, 26 November 2010, *LJN* BO5107.
The Hague District Court, 12 May 2011, *LJN* BQ4301.
Amsterdam District Court, 23 May 2011, *LJN* BQ5561.
Amsterdam District Court, 23 June 2011, *Mediaforum* 2011, p. 280–282, annotation Van Noorloos; *Ars Aequi* 2012, p. 288–289, annotation Rozemond; p. 290–294, annotation Schutgens.
Den Haag District Court, 2 November 2011, *LJN* BU3104.
The Hague District Court, 11 November 2011, *LJN* BU3944.

CGB – decisions and advisory opinions

CGB 29 April 1999, Decision 1999–38.
CGB 22 June 2001, *AB* 2001, 308, annotation Vermeulen.
CGB 7 January 2011, Decision 2011–02.

CGB Advies/2003/01, 16 April 2003.
CGB Advies/2004/06, 12 August 2004.
CGB Advies/2007/08, November 2007.
CGB Advies/2008/04, April 2008.
CGB Advies/2012/01, 6 April 2012.

Council of State – advisory opinions

Advies Raad van State, 21 September 2007, W03.07.0219/II; *Kamerstukken II,* 2007/08, 31108, nr. 4.

Advies Raad van State, 6 May 2008, W03.08.0028/II.

Advies Raad van State, 20 October 2008, W11.08.0398/IV; *Kamerstukken II,* 2009/2010, 31571, nr. 4.

Advies Raad van State, 28 November 2011, W04.11.0379/I; *Kamerstukken II,* 2011/1012, 33165, nr. 4.

Advies Raad van State, 12 October 2012, W04.12.0331/I; *Kamerstukken II* 2012/2013, 33344, nr. 4.

Advies Raad van State, 5 December 2014, W03.14.0376/II, *Kamerstukken II* 2014/2015, 34051, nr. 4.

Documents of national institutions

Commissie grondrechten in het digitale tijdperk, *Rapport 2000*, Den Haag: Ministerie van Binnenlandse Zaken 2000.

Discrimination Directive, 1999A008.

Discrimination Directive, 2003A005.

Discrimination Directive, 2007A010, *Stb.* 2007, 233.

Landelijk Expertise Centrum Discriminatie, LECD, *Cijfers in beeld: Discriminatiecijfers 2010, Overzicht discriminatiecijfers Openbaar Ministerie 2006–2010*, December 2011.

Ministerie van Binnenlandse Zaken, *Minderhedennota*, Tweede Kamer 1982–1983, 16102, nr. 21.

Ministerie van Binnenlandse Zaken, *Regeringsstandpunt ten aanzien van het rapport Allochtonenbeleid*, Tweede Kamer 1989–1990, 21472, nr. 2.

Ministerie van Binnenlandse Zaken, *Integratiebeleid etnische minderheden (Contourennota)*, Tweede Kamer 1993–1994, 23684, nr. 2.

Ministerie van Binnenlandse Zaken, *Nota Grondrechten in een pluriforme samenleving*, Tweede Kamer 2003–2004, 29614, nr. 2.

Ministerie van Binnenlandse Zaken, *Integratiebeleid*, Tweede Kamer 2010–2011, 32824, nr. 1.

Minister voor Grote Steden- en Integratiebeleid, *Integratiebeleid 1999–2002 'Kansen krijgen,*
kansen pakken', Tweede Kamer 1998–1999, 26333, nr. 2.

Staatscommissie Grondwet, *Rapport November 2010*, *Kamerstukken II* 2010/11, 31 570, nr. 17, bijlage.

Wetenschappelijk Onderzoek- en Documentatiecentrum, WODC, Van Stokkum, B.A.M., Sackers, H.J.B. & Wils, J.-P., *Godslastering, discriminerende uitingen wegens godsdienst en haatuitingen: Een inventariserende studie*, Den Haag: WODC 2006.

Wetenschappelijk Onderzoek- en Documentatiecentrum, WODC, *Religie en grondrechten, Justitiële Verkenningen*, WODC, nr. 1, 2007.

Wetenschappelijk Onderzoek- en Documentatiecentrum, WODC, Van Noorloos, M., *Strafbaarstelling 'belediging van geloof'*, Den Haag: Boom Lemma Uitgevers 2014.

Wetenschappelijke Raad voor het Regeringsbeleid, WRR, *Etnische Minderheden*, Rapporten aan de Regering 17, Den Haag: Sdu 1979.

Wetenschappelijke Raad voor het Regeringsbeleid, WRR, *Allochtonenbeleid*, Rapporten aan de
Regering 36, Den Haag: Sdu 1989.

Wetenschappelijke Raad voor het Regeringsbeleid, WRR, *Nederland als immigratiesamenleving*, Rapporten aan de Regering 60, Den Haag: Sdu 1998.

Wetenschappelijke Raad voor het Regeringsbeleid, WRR, *Geloven in het publieke domein*, Amsterdam: Amsterdam University Press 2006.

Newspaper articles

Bolkestein, F., Integratie van minderheden moet met lef worden aangepakt, *De Volkskrant*, 12 september 1991.

Scheffer, P., Het multiculturele drama., *NRC Handelsblad*, 29 januari 2000.

Pim Fortuyn op herhaling: 'De islam is een achterlijke cultuur.', Interview met Pim Fortuyn, *De Volkskrant*, 9 februari 2002.

Websites

http://overheid.nl/
https://www.officielebekendmakingen.nl/
www.raadvanstate.nl/
http://wrr.nl/
https://www.wodc.nl/
www.om.nl/
www.rechtspraak.nl/Pages/default.aspx
www.art1.nl/
www.mensenrechten.nl/
www.annefrank.org/nl/Educatie/Discriminatie-in-Nederland/
www.nederlandbekentkleur.nl/
www.prakkendoliveira.nl/
www.pvv.nl/

Samenvatting

Geloof in het publieke debat betreft een onderzoek naar de verhouding tussen vrijheid van meningsuiting en 'hate speech' op grond van religie en ras. De studie bespreekt de vragen die spelen bij het stellen van grenzen aan hate speech, met name op grond van religie en geuit in de context van een publiek debat. Er bestaat groot verschil van mening en veel onduidelijkheid over de interpretatie en toepassing van 'hate speech bans'. Vanuit het oogpunt van rechtszekerheid is het echter belangrijk dat het recht een duidelijke grens trekt aan hate speech geuit in het publiek debat.

Dit onderzoek stelt de centrale vraag: 'In hoeverre kunnen grenzen aan 'hate speech' op grond van religie op consistente wijze worden bepaald?'. Ter beantwoording van deze vraag presenteert deze studie eerst een analytisch kader (hoofdstuk 2). Op basis daarvan wordt vervolgens het relevante internationale en Europese recht geëvalueerd (hoofdstuk 3). Dan volgt een bespreking van het recht in Frankrijk (hoofdstuk 4) en in Nederland (hoofdstuk 5). Dat wordt samen met het EVRM, op basis van het analytisch kader, geëvalueerd, waarna aanbevelingen worden gedaan (hoofdstuk 6). Deze hoofdstukken worden hieronder samengevat.

Hoofdstuk 2 onderzoekt de wetenschappelijke discussie over vrijheid van meningsuiting en hate speech op grond van religie aan de hand van vier factoren-koppels: *handelingen* versus *meningsuitingen*; *publiek debat* versus *overige uitlatingen*; *feitelijke uitspraken* versus *waardeoordelen*; en *ras* versus *religie*. De deelparagrafen leiden steeds tot een definitie van de factoren ten behoeve van de verdere analyse in deze studie. De aldus gedefinieerde factoren vormen samen een analytisch kader dat identificeert welke problemen er spelen bij het op consistente wijze bepalen van de grenzen aan hate speech op grond van religie geuit in het publiek debat. Het analytisch kader kan als volgt worden samengevat.

Hate speech bestaat uit allerlei uitlatingen die een bepaalde groep in de samenleving stigmatiseren: letterlijke aansporingen van anderen tot concrete handelingen; discriminerende politieke voorstellen; racistische invectieven en scheldwoorden; vage aantijgingen en generalisaties die bepaald werkelijk of verondersteld gedrag of praktijken van personen associëren met hun ras of religie, die worden gepresenteerd als een grond om een bepaalde groep te discrimineren. Dergelijke uitlatingen produceren misschien niet onmiddellijk gewelddadige en onrechtmatige handelingen die direct fysieke schade veroorzaken en de openbare orde aantasten, maar zij schaden wel de waardigheid van leden van hun target groep, leiden tot discriminatie van hen en tasten het sociale klimaat aan.

Allereerst moet dus duidelijk zijn welke belangen beperkingen van hate speech beogen te beschermen; een norm, die niet duidelijk maakt welke gevolgen van hate speech de grond vormen voor haar verbod, kan moeilijk consistent worden toegepast. Vervolgens dienen die belangen vertaald te worden naar concrete juridische vereisten van 'hate speech bans'; helder gedefinieerde delicten dienen rechtszekerheid te bieden over de rechten en belangen die zij beschermen en over de reikwijdte van de uitingsvrijheid. Tot slot moet duidelijk zijn hoe 'hate speech bans' moeten worden toegepast in concrete gevallen, i.e. hoe uitlatingen onder de delicten moeten worden gekwalificeerd en welk gewicht daarbij toekomt aan het belang van het publiek debat.

Hate speech mag verboden worden op de grond dat haar racistische boodschap kan leiden tot haat tegen en discriminatie van leden van haar target groep op de middellange en lange termijn. Een consistente norm dient dan wel een punt te markeren op deze glijdende schaal. Hate speech mag ook verboden worden op de grond dat haar racistische boodschap de waardigheid van leden van haar target groep aantast. Een consistente norm dient dan wel duidelijk te maken dat 'waardigheid' niet begrepen moet worden als een 'publieke moraal' die losstaat van de schade aan personen. Hate speech die de menselijke waardigheid schendt wordt dan verboden, niet omdat het bepaalde standaarden van 'moraliteit, beschaafdheid of respect' overschrijdt, maar omdat de aanval op de waardigheid van de leden van haar target groep een concreet probleem voor hen wordt (psychologische schade, waardevermindering in de ogen van anderen etc.). Gegeven het publiek belang in het voorkomen van discriminatie en de bescherming van de gelijke menselijke waardigheid, kan een staat zowel 'aanzetten tot haat, discriminatie of geweld' als 'groepsbelediging' op grond van ras, religie etc. strafbaar stellen.

Of zulke hate speech bans ook moeten worden toegepast op bijdragen aan het publiek debat hangt af van het gehanteerde schadebegrip in het licht van het belang dat wordt gehecht aan dat debat ter legitimatie van de democratie. Een vrij, levendig en inclusief publiek discours is van fundamenteel belang voor het goed functioneren van een democratie; daartoe kunnen daarom ook behoren extreme of onpopulaire politieke opvattingen over een bepaalde religie in het licht van staat-religie verhoudingen of immigratie- en integratieproblematiek. Dergelijke discussies kunnen echter culmineren in hate speech tegen een religieuze groep. Juist omdat het politiek debat niet gericht is op universele waarheidsvinding maar op machtsvorming en de wetten van de staat, nemen bijdragen die neerkomen op hate speech tegen een bepaalde groep in de samenleving een bijzondere positie in en mogen zij worden verboden. Men kan echter menen dat het vrije publiek debat van dermate groot belang is dat de schadelijke effecten van hate speech, i.e. schade aan de waardigheid en het ontstaan van discriminatie, voor lief moeten worden genomen en dat het belang van de bescherming van het publiek debat zwaarder weegt. Dan moet nog steeds duidelijk zijn wanneer hate speech de uiterste grens van dat debat overschrijdt. Een norm die niet duidelijk maakt waarin de excessiviteit van de uitlating schuilt kan moeilijk consistent worden toegepast.

Om op consistente wijze een onderscheid te maken tussen vrije kritische bijdragen aan het publiek debat en verboden vormen van hate speech, dient men nauwkeurig te differentiëren tussen verschillende typen uitlatingen, i.e. tussen feitelijke uitlatingen en waardeoordelen. Een probleem bij de afbakening van vrije kritische opmerkingen met racistische uitlatingen is namelijk dat inconsistente argumentaties worden gebruikt die niet duidelijk maken in hoeverre negatieve uitlatingen over een bepaalde groep gestoeld dienen te zijn op een voldoende feitelijke basis. De grens van het vrije publiek debat kan zijn bereikt wanneer hate speech de waardigheid van mensen aantast omdat het bestaat uit pertinent onjuiste uitspraken of waardeoordelen die voldoende feitelijke basis missen en onnodig grievend zijn.

Dit zal eerder het geval zijn bij kritiek op een bepaald ras dan kritiek op een bepaalde religie. Anders dan bij ras, kunnen bepaald gedrag en bepaalde praktijken van personen daadwerkelijk gegrond zijn in religieuze voorschriften of drijfveren, welke vrijelijk bediscussieerd moeten kunnen worden. Dit kan leiden tot inconsistente argumentaties die niet duidelijk maken hoe 'een religieuze groep afgebakend dient te worden' in de context van hate speech. Een aspect is dat in acht moet worden genomen of een religie niet wordt behandeld als een centrale component van de etnische of nationale afkomst en identiteit van een groep.

Een norm dient ook een helder onderscheid te maken tussen kritiek op overheidsbeleid en politieke voorstellen die de grondrechten van bepaalde minderheden aantasten. Dan kan hate speech misbruik van het recht op vrijheid van meningsuiting vormen, omdat het gericht is op de vernietiging van de gelijke grondrechten van die minderheden. Dergelijke uitlatingen brengen de 'openbare orde' in gevaar in die zin dat zij het belang in gevaar brengen van een ordelijke democratische samenleving vrij van discriminatie. Dat betreft een ander waardeconflict en een ander schadebegrip dan het belang van het voorkomen van wanorde door gewelddadige en onrechtmatige acties. Tegen de achtergrond van dit analytisch kader wordt vervolgens het positieve recht geanalyseerd.

Hoofdstuk 3 analyseert welke staatsverplichtingen met betrekking tot de beperking van hate speech er voortvloeien uit vijf geselecteerde instrumenten van internationaal en Europees recht: het Europees Verdrag van de Rechten van de Mens (EVRM); het Internationaal Verdrag inzake Burgerrechten en Politieke Rechten (IVBPR); het Internationaal Verdrag inzake de Uitbanning van alle vormen van Rassendiscriminatie (IVURD); het EU Kaderbesluit betreffende de bestrijding van racisme en vreemdelingenhaat door middel van het strafrecht; een selectie resoluties en aanbevelingen van instituties van de Raad van Europa; en een Aanvullend Protocol bij het Verdrag inzake de bestrijding van strafbare feiten verbonden met elektronische netwerken, betreffende de strafbaarstelling van handelingen van racistische en xenofobische aard verricht via computersystemen.

Deze instrumenten vormen een lappendeken aan standaarden betreffende de beperking van hate speech. Zij gebruiken niet alleen verschillende noties van hate speech, zij hebben ook verschillende maten van doorwerking in het nationaal recht. Daarom alleen al kunnen zij nauwelijks fungeren als een coherent en consistent framework voor het stellen van grenzen aan hate speech. Verder zijn verplichtingen voor de staat om specifieke vormen van hate speech bij wet te verbieden bindend voor wat betreft het te behalen resultaat, maar zij schrijven niet de implementatie van exacte, uniforme bepalingen voor. Bovendien wordt staten een zekere marge gelaten om de bepalingen in te bedden in de principes van hun nationale juridische systemen. Dit geldt zelfs voor instrumenten die gericht zijn op Europese harmonisatie van het strafrecht. Die marge heeft gevolgen voor de doorwerking van het internationale recht in de nationale rechtsorde.

Complete consensus lijkt slechts te bestaan over een wettelijk verbod van aanzetten tot haat en geweld. Dit vereist 'de activering van een triangulaire relatie tussen het object en het subject van de uitlating alsmede de toehoorders'. Artikel 20(2) IVBPR verplicht lidstaten 'het propageren van op nationale afkomst, ras of godsdienst gebaseerde haatgevoelens die aanzetten tot discriminatie, vijandigheid of geweld bij de wet te verbieden', maar het artikel eist niet per se een strafrechtelijk verbod. Artikel 4a IVUR eist van lidstaten juist *strafbaar* bij wet te verklaren niet alleen 'aanzetting tot rassendiscriminatie, zomede alle daden van geweld of aanzetting daartoe' maar ook het veel bredere 'verspreiden, op welke wijze ook, van denkbeelden die zijn gegrond op rassensuperioriteit of rassenhaat'. Dit laatste verbod behelst een keur aan racistische meningsuitingen die wellicht niet aan de standaarden van 20(2) IVBPR voldoen ('aanzetten' en 'opzet' daartoe) maar die wel weer onder de brede definitie van hate speech gebruikt door het EHRM vallen en waartegen het EHRM strafrechtelijk optreden gerechtvaardigd acht.

Geen enkel bindend instrument verplicht staten echter om racistische meningsuitingen bij wet te verbieden, laat staan door middel van het strafrecht, op grond van hun directe negatieve effecten op de leden van de targetgroep (psychische schade, aanstoot, schade aan hun waardigheid door scheldwoorden of negatieve beeldvorming) los van hun mogelijke effecten op derden en de openbare orde. Dat betekent niet dat dergelijke uitlatingen niet beperkt mogen worden. Anders dan het EHRM, acht het VN-Mensenrechtencomité de strafbaarstelling van blasfemie en Holocaustontkenning of andere meningen over historische feiten *in abstracto* zonder het vereiste van 'aanzetten' echter in strijd met het IVBPR. Het EU Kaderbesluit en het Aanvullend Protocol bij de Cybercrime Conventie gebieden lidstaten verschillende categorieën delicten te creëren, zoals belediging of smaad van groepen en ontkenning van grove misdaden, maar staan daarbij steeds toevoeging van vergelijkbare vereisten toe; opzet tot of waarschijnlijkheid dat uitingen 'aanzetten' tot haat en geweld.

Uit deze categorieën en ook uit de interpretatie van artikel 20(2) IVBPR en 4a IVUR volgt wel hoe veelvormig het verbod op hate speech onder Europees en internationaal recht is. Het verbod richt zich primair op hate speech op grond van ras, maar daaronder dient ook te worden begrepen vormen van hate speech waarin sprake is van een 'intersectionaliteit van ras en religie' of waarin 'religie wordt gebruikt als voorwendsel voor de factoren ras, huidskleur en nationale of etnische afkomst'. De 6 stappen test ontwikkeld in het Rabat Actie Plan voor het bepalen van strafbaarheid van uitingen onder 20(2) IVBPR (context; spreker; opzet; inhoud en vorm; bereik van de uiting; gevolg) en de mede daarop geïnspireerde aanbevelingen van het IVUR-comité voor het bepalen van strafbaarheid van uitingen onder 4a IVUR kunnen zich ontwikkelen tot een leidraad voor een meer consistente interpretatie en toepassing door rechters van nationale strafbepalingen op vormen van hate speech. Bij het bepalen of uitlatingen naar internationaal recht onder het verbod van hate speech vallen kan daarnaast het onderscheid tussen feitelijke aantijgingen en waardeoordelen een rol spelen juist omdat dat veelvormig verbod zich niet beperkt tot letterlijke aansporingen van derden tot concrete handelingen tegen de target groep.

Hoofdstuk 3 geeft een uitgebreidere analyse van de hate speech jurisprudentie van het EHRM die in hoofdstuk 6, op basis van het analytisch kader, wordt geëvalueerd. Het EHRM omschrijft hate speech ruim als 'alle typen uitlatingen die haat gebaseerd op intolerantie (waaronder religieuze intolerantie) verspreiden, daartoe aanzetten, bevorderen of rechtvaardigen'. Het verbod van hate speech aldus omschreven onder het EVRM is primair ingegeven door haar onderliggende waarden van gelijke menselijke waardigheid en non-discriminatie. Op grond van de jurisprudentie van het EHRM mogen uitlatingen als hate speech worden verboden, omdat zij een groep beledigen, ridiculiseren of smaden, hun waardigheid en veiligheid aantasten en leiden tot intolerantie en gevoelens van wantrouwen, afwijzing of haat jegens buitenlanders of andere groepen.

De slechte invloed die haat gebaseerd op vooroordelen heeft op de politieke stabiliteit en een sereen sociaal klimaat is voldoende om een beperking te rechtvaardigen. Het EHRM heeft dan ook geen heldere standaarden en precieze criteria gecreeerd voor de toetsing van beperkingen van hate speech zoals het EHRM dat wel heeft gedaan met betrekking tot beperkingen van uitlatingen die aanzetten tot geweld, i.e. daadwerkelijk 'aanzetten', het opzet van de spreker om anderen te stigmatiseren en de waarschijnlijkheid van gewelddadige acties als mogelijk effect van de uitlating. Het EHRM vereist evenmin enig bewijs van hoe smadelijke of beledigende uitlatingen de waardigheid of veiligheid van leden van hun target groep aantasten, bijvoorbeeld door verwijzing naar hun psychologische effecten. In principe maakt het EHRM geen onderscheid tussen verschillende typen van hate speech.

Het EHRM lijkt beperkingen van uitspraken over een bepaalde groep in verband met hun religie echter vaak impliciet gerechtvaardigd te achten, omdat 'de algemene aanval op de groep' bestaat uit onjuiste feitelijke aantijgingen of sterke negatieve waardeoordelen die een voldoende feitelijke basis missen. Een belangrijke factor lijkt daarbij te zijn dat een religie in feite wordt behandeld als een centraal kenmerk van de raciale of etnische identiteit van een groep. Het EHRM verwijst echter niet expliciet naar deze principes. Belangrijke overwegingen – over de schadelijke effecten van de uitlating in kwestie afgewogen tegen het belang van het publiek debat en de rol daarin van het onderscheid tussen feitelijke uitspraken en waardeoordelen en tussen uitlatingen over ras en over religie – vallen vaak weg doordat het EHRM zo'n brede definitie van hate speech hanteert en staten vervolgens een ruime beoordelingsvrijheid verleent om de grenzen te stellen aan het immigratie- en integratiedebat onder Artikel 10(2) EVRM. Dat laatste lijkt inconsistent met de strikte toetsing die het EHRM over het algemeen hanteert voor beperkingen van politieke uitlatingen.

Wanneer het EHRM de beperkingen van het zo gevoelige immigratiedebat strikter zou toetsen, zou het EHRM meer kunnen differentiëren tussen verschillende typen hate speech en heldere en consistente standaarden kunnen creëren voor beperkingen daarvan en voor het onderscheid tussen vrije kritische bijdragen aan het publiek debat en verboden hate speech. Uiteindelijk laat het EHRM nationale autoriteiten een bepaalde marge om hun nationale hate speech bepalingen te interpreteren en toe te passen. Dit heeft consequenties voor de doorwerking van de EHRM jurisprudentie in nationaal recht. Dat zou alleen dan anders zijn als uit de jurisprudentie heldere verplichtingen voor strafbaarstelling zouden voortvloeien, maar dat is tot op heden niet het geval, zelfs niet voor misbruik van recht. Het EHRM past Artikel 17 EVRM ook inconsistent toe. Het EHRM zou juist verstrekkende maatregelen tegen uitlatingen die een onmiddellijke bedreiging van de democratie vormen onder 10(2) /11(2) EVRM kunnen rechtvaardigen met expliciete verwijzing naar Artikel 17. Bovendien kan Artikel 17 een rol spelen voor de ontwikkeling van positieve verplichtingen voor de staat om vormen van hate speech die als misbruik van recht kunnen worden gekwalificeerd strafbaar te stellen en te vervolgen.

Uit hoofdstuk 3 volgt dat het internationale en Europese recht dus brede kaders zet, waar binnen nationale staten de optie hebben om een variëteit aan beperkingen aan hate speech te stellen. Hoe dergelijke grenzen in een staat precies worden getrokken wordt daarom nog steeds eerst en vooral bepaald door nationaal recht; die grenzen kunnen het best worden begrepen tegen de achtergrond van de constitutionele tradities van de nationale juridische systemen. Hoofdstukken 4 en 5 geven een uitgebreide beschrijving van het recht op vrijheid van meningsuiting en de beperking van hate speech in Frankrijk, respectievelijk Nederland. Hoofdstuk 4 doet dat aan de hand van het Franse devies 'Vrijheid, Gelijkheid, Broederschap' dat het Franse publiekrecht inspireert en ook wel wordt begrepen als drie pijlers van de democratische rechtsstaat. Die structuur wordt in hoofdstuk 5 doorgetrokken. Het Franse en Nederlandse recht wordt, op basis van het analytisch kader, geëvalueerd in hoofdstuk 6 en kan als volgt worden samengevat.

In Frankrijk heeft de vrijheid van meningsuiting grondwettelijke bescherming. De beperkingsclausule van de bepaling somt geen beperkingsgronden van de uitingsvrijheid op. Maar de Franse Constitutionele Raad heeft vastgesteld dat de uitingsvrijheid beperkt kan worden om de rechten van anderen, de menselijke waardigheid of de openbare orde te beschermen. De Franse wet kent vervolgens vier 'hate speech bans': raciale smaad; raciale belediging; raciale provocatie; en Holocaustontkenning. De eerste drie delicten zijn in 1972 ingevoerd ter implementatie van het IVUR en beogen dus de menselijke waardigheid te beschermen en discriminatie te voorkomen. Het vierde delict kent eenzelfde ratio en is in 1990 ingevoerd ter bestrijding van oplaaiend Antisemitisme. Deze delicten zijn niet onderworpen aan enige constitutionele toetsing, noch gedurende het wetgevingsproces noch op verzoek van de Hoge

Raad in een individuele zaak. Toch vormt het Franse 'Constitutionele Blok' een kompas voor het bepalen van beperkingen van de uitingsvrijheid door de wetgever en de rechter en kunnen de delicten beschouwd worden te zijn ingebed in de principes en waarden van de Franse Constitutie.

Het Franse recht kent een abstract gelijkheidsideaal wat inhoudt dat het recht het bestaan van nationale minderheden, gedefinieerd door een bepaald ras of bepaalde etniciteit, niet erkent ten aanzien van de wetten van de Republiek. De hate speech bans kunnen beschouwd worden als een uitwerking van dit ideaal; gelijke burgers dienen niet aangesproken te worden op grond van hun specifieke karakteristieken. Er is evenwel voorgesteld om het begrip 'ras' geheel uit de Franse wet te schrappen en te vervangen door 'om racistische redenen'. Frans recht gaat uit van de premisse, zoals gearticuleerd door Sartre: 'racisme is geen mening, maar een misdrijf'. Een racistisch discours schendt de kernwaarden van de Franse Republiek, omdat het de gelijke waardigheid van Franse burgers ontkent en een agressie vormt tegen zowel de leden van de target groep als de ondeelbare Franse Republiek in haar geheel. Op het spel staat niet het bewaren van de Franse openbare orde door het voorkomen van wanordelijkheden, maar het bewaren van de Franse sociale orde gecreëerd door 'het Republikeinse pact' door het voorkomen van het bestaan van intolerante, inhumane, racistische meningsuitingen die de menselijke waardigheid schenden en tot discriminatie kunnen leiden. Dergelijke uitlatingen ontberen dan ook de bescherming van de uitingsvrijheid.

Strikt genomen voldoen de hate speech bans niet aan de uitgangspunten van de traditionele Franse uitingsvrijheid doctrine die het 'délit d'opinion', het 'opiniedelict' verbiedt. Volgens dit negentiende-eeuwse concept, zoals gearticuleerd door Benjamin Constant, kan het Franse recht slechts een meningsuiting strafbaar stellen indien zij een strafbaar handelen ondersteunt, i.e. in direct verband staat tot daaropvolgende strafbare feiten. In de literatuur wordt het opiniedelict verder gedefinieerd als een delict dat 1) niet precies door de wetgever is gekwalificeerd; 2) niet de specifieke rechten en belangen bepaalt waarmee het interfereert; en 3) door zijn arbitraire vervolging en bestraffing een gevaar voor de uitingsvrijheid vormt. De strafbaarstelling van blasfemie wordt gezien als een opiniedelict par excellence dat tevens indruist tegen het laïque karakter van de Franse staat en is om die reden al in 1881 afgeschaft.

Raciale smaad en belediging vormen daarentegen 'delicten tegen personen' en 'provocatie tot haat, discriminatie en geweld' en 'Holocaustontkenning' zijn gecategoriseerd als 'provocaties'. Provocatie tot haat, discriminatie en geweld wordt beschouwd als een 'indirecte provocatie' en is dan ook niet beperkt tot letterlijke aansporingen van derden tot directe concrete strafbare handelingen, maar omvat een keur aan uitlatingen die wegens hun racistische strekking haat kunnen zaaien tegen een bepaalde groep. In de literatuur wordt het Holocaustontkenning delict echter veelal beschouwd als een opiniedelict; anders dan de overige hate speech bans verbiedt het delict naar de letter bepaalde meningen over de geschiedenis van de Holocaust ongeacht of die uitlatingen ook *personen* schaden. Uit de achtergrond van de bepaling en de jurisprudentie volgt wel dat het delict slechts strafbaar stelt smadelijke en provocatieve uitspraken die wegens hun racistische en Antisemitische strekking de 'menselijke waardigheid' schenden. Maar die laatste notie functioneert ogenschijnlijk meer als een publieke moraal.

Frankrijk kent inderdaad een enigszins paternalistische opvatting van de uitingsvrijheid, hetgeen voortkomt uit de bijzondere opvatting van de staat als een 'distributeur van rechten'; vrijheid van meningsuiting bestaat daarom vooral binnen de contouren van de staat. Dit geldt ook voor het publiek debat. Ingevolge de strikte machtenscheiding wordt het publiek belang primair bepaald door de wetgever die precies omschreven wetten aanneemt die de rechter strikt moet toepassen. De rechter mag de afweging gemaakt door de wetgever niet heroverwegen. Wanneer een uitlating een verboden vorm van hate speech vormt kan de Franse rechter het belang van de handhaving van die norm niet verder afwegen tegen het belang van een vrij publiek debat. Vrijheid van meningsuiting kan dus geen algemene rechtvaardiging vormen voor uitlatingen die strafbaar zijn op grond van de hate speech bans. De Franse wetgever en rechter werken dus samen.

Het Franse legisme voorziet in een 'slot' op verkregen rechten, de Constitutie en de principes van de Franse Republiek. Uit het Franse gelijkheidsideaal vloeit ook voort dat alle burgers die aan het publiek debat deelnemen een gelijke mate van uitingsvrijheid hebben. Dit geldt ook voor politici. Wanneer een bepaalde groep als crimineel wordt afgeschilderd of voorstellen worden gedaan om bepaalde minderheden het land uit te zetten blijft dit strafbaar ook wanneer dergelijke uitspraken worden geuit in de context van het immigratie- en integratiedebat. Negatieve feitelijke beweringen over een bepaalde groep zijn ook moeilijk te schragen, want als uitvloeisel van het strikte gelijkheidsideaal mag de overheid in principe geen statistische gegevens over burgers verzamelen op basis van hun ras etniciteit of religie. Dit verbod heeft het lofwaardige doel om te voorkomen dat statistieken worden misbruikt en tot racisme en discriminatie leiden, maar het lijkt een open en onderlegd debat en de evaluatie van sociale problemen wel te compliceren. Het Franse legisme leidt ook tot een wel erg rigide en abstracte toepassing van de hate speech bans met weinig oog voor het belang van het vrije publiek debat. De Franse rechter verdisconteert het belang van de uitingsvrijheid echter soms in de vraag of een uitlating aan alle elementen van de delictsomschrijving voldoet. Dit impliceert dat de rechter wel iets meer doet dan de hate speech bans strikt toe te passen en toch impliciet belang aan de uitingsvrijheid hecht.

Deze praktijk leidt tot enige inconsistenties in de Franse hate speech jurisprudentie, afhankelijk van of de rechter een vrij publiek debat wil bewaren over een bepaald onderwerp. Dit betreft allereerst het onderscheid tussen feitelijke aantijgingen en waardeoordelen. Generaliserende uitspraken over een bepaalde groep zijn niet gauw strafbaar wegens 'raciale smaad', gegeven het strikte vereiste dat het moet gaan om de aantijging van een 'specifiek feit'. De Franse rechter achtte de betichting van Joden dat zij de Palestijnen vernederen en vervolgen wel maar de betichting van Noord-Afrikanen dat zij op sociale uitkeringen leven niet 'voldoende precies' om strafbare smaad op te leveren. Dit verschil in uitkomst is echter, zonder nadere motivering, onbegrijpelijk en inconsistent. De rechter past ook het vereiste dat een uitlating 'helder een bepaalde groep moet aanduiden' inconsistent toe. Het vereiste vormt een handige tool voor de rechter om vrije religie kritiek te scheiden van hate speech tegen een religieuze groep. Maar op basis van de jurisprudentie is onduidelijk of dit criterium nu betekent dat een uiting om strafbaar te zijn expliciet een bepaalde groep moet noemen, of de betreffende groep een bepaalde mate van homogeniteit moet hebben of dat een negatief kenmerk of gedrag wordt toegedicht aan alle groepsleden. Impliciet lijkt toch steeds een rol te spelen of kritiek gestoeld is op een voldoende feitelijke basis en daarom in een publiek debat treedt.

Wanneer de Franse rechter in de motivering van zijn beslissingen explicieter en op structurele wijze belang zou hechten aan de uitingsvrijheid, i.e. het publiek debat, als rechtvaardigingsgrond, zou de Franse hate speech jurisprudentie winnen aan transparantie en consistentie. Maar het Franse legisme verzet zich niet alleen tegen de belangenafweging die de rechter daarvoor dient te maken maar ook tegen het accommoderen of het 'importeren' van Europese standaarden over de uitingsvrijheid en het publiek debat. Het EHRM heeft echter steeds geoordeeld dat Franse veroordelingen voor hate speech binnen de beoordelingsvrijheid vallen die de staat heeft om hate speech te beperken. Bovendien vormt het maken van een belangenafweging door de rechter slechts een methode om te motiveren waarom, in de specifieke omstandigheden van het geval, negatieve uitspraken over een groep, hoewel gedaan in de context van een publiek debat, desalniettemin strafbaar zijn omdat zij de waarden of rechten schenden die de hate speech bans beschermen.

De hate speech bans staan opgenomen in de Franse perswet van 1881 die een gesloten juridisch systeem vormt: de wet somt niet alleen de uitingsdelicten op maar ook hun specifieke rechtvaardigingsgronden en kent zeer strikte procesrechtelijke regels. De Perswet is van origine van strafrechtelijke aard maar heeft zich ontwikkeld tot een hybride wet die ook van toepassing is in civiele zaken. Hoe paradoxaal het ook moge lijken, juist het strafrecht wordt gezien als het geschikte middel om de uitingsvrijheid te garanderen door precies haar grenzen te bepalen. Daarom vormen de uitingsdelicten de juridische basis in zowel strafzaken als civiele zaken. Wanneer een uiting niet gekwalificeerd kan worden onder een specifieke hate speech ban, kan het niet alsnog een onrechtmatige daad op grond van artikel 1382 van het Frans Burgerlijk Wetboek opleveren. De Franse rechter heeft een civielrechtelijk recht op respect op religieuze gevoelens op grond van 1382 CC afgewezen. In principe zijn de strafrechtelijke en civielrechtelijke grenzen aan hate speech dus hetzelfde.

De Perswet voorziet in precieze, heldere normen ten aanzien van de vervolging van hate speech; men kan aannemen dat zij in eerste instantie de consistentie van de grenzen aan hate speech ten goede komen. De vraag komt echter op of de Perswet wel de juiste balans opmaakt tussen de persvrijheid en de rechten van slachtoffers van smaad, beledigingen en provocaties. Vanuit het perspectief van de verdediging is een probleem van de Perswet dat het een regime van strafrechtelijke aansprakelijkheid vestigt losgekoppeld van het oogmerk van de spreker (via de presumptie van de kwade trouw) en van het bestaan van daadwerkelijke schade. Vanuit het perspectief van de vervolgende partij, vormt het zeer strikte procesrecht van de Perswet een daadwerkelijk obstakel in de vervolging. De bescherming van de uitingsvrijheid door middel van hoge procesrechtelijke drempels kan een effectieve toegang tot de rechter in gevaar brengen. Het formalisme van het gesloten juridische systeem van de Perswet kan niet bedoeld zijn om toegang tot recht te compliceren.

Vanuit de solidariteitsgedachte gebaseerd op de idee van de staat als politieke broederschap hebben het openbaar ministerie en antiracismeorganisaties echter een gedeelde rol in de handhaving van de hate speech bans. De Perswet verleent antiracismeorganisaties het recht om strafzaken op grond van de hate speech bans in gang te zetten en zich te voegen als civiele partij. In een dergelijke 'action civile' zijn het de antiracismeorganisaties die de rechtszaak inhoudelijk voeren en adviseert het openbaar ministerie als het ware over de strafbaarheid. Men kan stellen dat het activisme van de antiracismeorganisaties heeft geleid tot een vergaande juridisering van het publiek debat, hetgeen een chilling effect kan hebben op de uitingsvrijheid. De juridische acties van sommige organisaties lijken eerder gericht te zijn op de bescherming van religieuze of morele belangen dan op de strijd tegen racisme in het algemeen belang en eerder gericht te zijn op het verkrijgen van strafrechtelijke veroordelingen dan op schadevergoeding. Verder bestaat het risico van over- en ondervertegenwoordiging van bepaalde groepen. Bovendien komt de vraag op of de antiracismeorganisaties, die een rol hebben gehad in de totstandkoming van de hate speech bans en hun recht om strafzaken in gang te zetten, niet te invloedrijk zijn in de beperking van hate speech; wie in het Franse systeem spreekt voor de uitingsvrijheid?

Aan de andere kant geeft het recht om strafzaken in gang te zetten de organisaties de mogelijkheid om politiek gevoelige zaken, zoals felle kritiek op Islam en immigratie, die het openbaar ministerie seponeert toch aan de rechter voor te leggen. Het verzekert aldus een effectieve toegang tot recht. Over het algemeen bestaat er juist een nauwe samenwerking en nauw overleg tussen het openbaar ministerie en de antiracismeorganisaties. De organisaties kunnen dus de checks and balances vormen binnen de strikte machtenscheiding door continu de discussie met de wetgevende, uitvoerende (openbaar ministerie) en rechtsprekende macht te vernieuwen over het bestaan, de toepassing en de interpretatie van de hate speech bans. Zij kunnen de premissen die de verhouding tussen vrijheid van meningsuiting en discriminatie vormgeven falsifiëren in nieuwe zaken, nieuwe omstandigheden. Hun directe beroep op de hate speech bans voor de rechter onderwerpt de norm aan een constante aanpassing aan de behoeften en stand van de maatschappij. Een dergelijk activisme lijkt perfect te passen in het doel van het Franse sociale contract; de oneindige bevordering van individuele rechten.

Hoofdstuk 5 geeft vervolgens een uitgebreide beschrijving van het recht op vrijheid van meningsuiting en de beperking van hate speech in Nederland. Ook in Nederland heeft de vrijheid van meningsuiting grondwettelijke bescherming. De beperkingsclausule van de grondwetbepaling somt geen beperkingsgronden van de uitingsvrijheid op. De Nederlandse rechter mag de grondwettelijkheid van de wettelijke beperkingen van de uitingsvrijheid niet toetsen, maar over het algemeen interpreteert en past de rechter de uitingsdelicten toe in het licht van Artikel 10 EVRM dat de grondwetsbepaling grotendeels heeft overschaduwd. De Nederlandse grondwet heeft minder normatieve kracht en de uitingsdelicten zijn daarom minder ingebed in de principes en waarden van de grondwet. Nederlands recht wordt juist gekenmerkt door meer open normen die door de rechter verder kunnen worden 'ingekleurd' in concrete gevallen. De Nederlandse wet kent slechts twee 'hate speech bans': groepsbelediging; en aanzetten tot haat, discriminatie of geweld. Het aantal hate speech bans geeft wel een indicatie over maar bepaalt op zichzelf nog niet de precieze grenzen aan hate speech. Uit de jurisprudentie blijkt dat onder de bepalingen onder andere ook kunnen vallen feitelijke aantijgingen die een groep smaden en vormen van Holocaustontkenning.

De achtergrond van de hate speech bans vormt het IVUR en de bepalingen beogen dus de menselijke waardigheid te beschermen en discriminatie te voorkomen. De delicten zijn in de strafwet gecategoriseerd als 'delicten tegen de openbare orde' en de betekenis van het openbare orde begrip is daarmee uitgebreid van 'de publieke vrede' naar 'een samenleving vrij van discriminatie'. Het feit dat haatzaaiende uitingen de openbare orde raken vormde eerder een reden voor *strafbaarstelling* van dergelijke uitingen dan dat de openbare orde als een extra vereiste voor strafbaarheid gold. Maar de subsumptie van de norm van gelijkheid en non-discriminatie onder het openbare orde begrip maakt de hate speech bans gevoelig voor een inconsistente interpretatie en toepassing. Zo wordt in de literatuur en in jurisprudentie het haatzaaidelict soms beperkt tot uitingen die een directe dreiging voor de openbare orde vormen of een risico op gewelddadige conflicten in zich dragen en daarom tot letterlijke aansporingen tot precies omschreven discriminerende handelingen en geweld tegen een groep.

De inconsistenties lijken met name ingegeven door veranderende perspectieven over het belang van het bestaan van een vrij publiek debat. De Nederlandse Hoge Raad heeft een drie-stappen-toets ontwikkeld om de strafbaarheid van uitingen wegens groepsbelediging te toetsen ('contextuele toetsing'). De toets houdt in: wanneer een uitlating volgens zijn strekking en directe tekstuele context een strafbare belediging vormt (1), kan het feit dat de uiting is gedaan in de context van een publiek debat zijn strafbaar karakter ontnemen (2), mits de uiting niet onnodig grievend is (3). De lagere rechter heeft ook wel een vergelijkbare toets gebruikt om de strafbaarheid van uitingen wegens 'aanzetten tot discriminatie' te toetsen, die echter (nog) niet door de Hoge Raad is onderschreven. Volgens die toets kan de context van het publiek debat het strafbaar karakter ontnemen (2) van een uitlating die volgens zijn strekking en direct tekstuele context aanzet tot discriminatie (1), mits de uiting niet 'grensoverschrijdend' is (3). Wanneer een uitlating een verboden vorm van hate speech vormt weegt de Nederlandse rechter het belang van de handhaving van die norm verder af tegen het belang van een vrij publiek debat. Vrijheid van meningsuiting kan dus een algemene rechtvaardiging vormen voor uitlatingen die strafbaar zijn op grond van de hate speech bans.

Deze nadere belangenafweging door de rechter is wenselijk, omdat de hate speech bans uitlatingen op grond van hun inhoud verbieden en de uitingsvrijheid dus in haar kern beperken. Deze methode resulteert dan in een proportionele toepassing van de hate speech bans met meer oog voor de specifieke omstandigheden van het geval. Het laat ruimte voor het bespreken van taboes; negatieve kritische opmerkingen over immigranten zullen al gauw beledigend en provocatief zijn, maar kunnen gerechtvaardigd zijn om sociale problemen bloot te leggen in een discussie over integratievraagstukken en de multiculturele samenleving. Aan de andere kant kan deze methode interfereren met de bedoelingen van de wetgever en de hate speech bans geheel hun beschermende functie ontnemen zoals die is gegrond in het internationale recht. In sommige zaken voert de rechter deze toets namelijk niet consequent uit, maar streept hij het beledigende of haatzaaiende karakter van een uiting simpel weg tegen het belang van de uitingsvrijheid zonder ook de laatste proportionaliteitstoets of de uitlating niet 'onnodig grievend' of 'grensoverschrijdend' is toe te passen. Men kan zich afvragen of de rechter dan, in plaats van een belangenafweging te maken, de uitingsvrijheid niet een zodanig gewicht geeft dat tegengestelde door de hate speech bans beschermde belangen noodzakelijkerwijs verbleken.

Voor de nadere inkleuring van de belangenafweging lijkt de jurisprudentie van het EHRM waaruit blijkt welke uitlatingen verboden mógen worden om de menselijke waardigheid te beschermen en discriminatie te voorkomen, maar weinig gewicht te hebben. De exacte betekenis van de criteria in de jurisprudentie dat bijdragen aan het publiek debat uiteindelijk niet 'onnodig grievend' of 'grensoverschrijdend' mogen zijn is onduidelijk. Wat betreft grove generaliseringen over een groep lijkt de mate waarin een bewering een voldoende feitelijke basis heeft impliciet een rol te spelen. Waar de Franse rechter het belang van de uitingsvrijheid verdisconteert in de vraag of een uiting voldoet aan alle elementen van het delict (betichting van 'een specifiek feit'), lijkt de Nederlandse rechter het 'gewicht' van onjuiste feitelijke aantijgingen of negatieve waardeoordelen te verdisconteren in de vraag of een uiting onderdeel vormt van het publiek debat. Maar bij gebrek aan enige expliciete motivering op dit punt lijkt de jurisprudentie inconsistent. Zo heeft de rechter verschillende malen het afschilderen van Marokkanen en Moslims als van nature crimineel in de context van het debat over de Islam en integratie strafbaar geacht, maar achtte de rechter het trekken van deze conclusie in dezelfde context onder verwijzing naar hoge criminaliteitscijfers onder deze groepen toelaatbaar. Kennelijk accepteert de rechter statistische correlaties soms als een voldoende basis voor het leggen van causale verbanden. Maar dergelijke conclusies hebben eerder een racistische strekking dan dat zij sociale problemen adresseren.

Uit lagere rechtspraak blijkt dat het vervolgens doen van politieke voorstellen tot het nemen van maatregelen tegen een bepaalde groep in de samenleving die, wanneer zij worden uitgevoerd, een bindend verbod van discriminatie schenden ('Alle Moslims het land uit') niet per definitie 'grensoverschrijdend' en dus strafbaar is. Dit laatste criterium is (nog) niet door de Hoge Raad bevestigd, maar de jurisprudentie lijkt hierin opgeschoven te zijn. Het is onduidelijk of binnen de aldus breder gestelde contouren van het politiek debat een politicus nu een grotere mate van uitingsvrijheid heeft dan gewone burgers. In ieder geval lijkt er grote ruimte te bestaan om te pleiten voor discriminatoire maatregelen als oplossing voor de immigratieproblematiek en kritiek op het overheidsbeleid. Het is echter onduidelijk wanneer dergelijke voorstellen wél 'grensoverschrijdend' dus strafbaar zijn. De term kan zowel verwijzen naar het vereiste van een dreigende verstoring van de openbare orde of een risico op geweld als naar het doel om de grondrechten van anderen te vernietigen, i.e. misbruik van recht in de zin van Artikel 17 EVRM. De achtergrond en wetsgeschiedenis van het haatzaaidelict wijzen in die laatste richting.

De vraag komt op of de wetgever de ratio en omvang van de hate speech bans en het gewicht van het publiek debat nu preciezer moet bepalen juist omdat een breder grondwettelijk kader dat dwingt tot een eenduidige interpretatie en toepassing van de delicten door de rechter ontbreekt. Wanneer de wetgever de ratio en omvang van de hate speech bans niet nader omschrijft dan dient de rechter nadere standaarden te formuleren. Het kabinet heeft zich voorgenomen een algemene bepaling in de grondwet op te nemen, die luidt: 'De grondwet waarborgt de democratie, de rechtsstaat en de grondrechten'. Een dergelijke bepaling kan in de toekomst als kompas en referentiepunt fungeren voor het stellen van heldere, goed gemotiveerde grenzen aan haatzaaiende uitlatingen in het publiek debat door wetgever en rechter binnen een en hetzelfde waardeconflict.

Waar het de strafbaarheid van beledigende uitspraken met betrekking tot een bepaalde religie betreft is het door de Hoge Raad gestelde vereiste dat een uitlating 'onmiskenbaar over een bepaalde groep mensen op grond van hun religie' moet gaan omdat 'kritiek op religieuze overtuigingen en praktijken' niet strafbaar is onduidelijk en dient nader uitgewerkt te worden. Het criterium, dat ook wel is toegepast op het haatzaaidelict, bakende in ieder geval de groepsbelediging af van het blasfemiedelict, dat vervolgens in 2013 is afgeschaft. Maar voor zover het criterium betekent dat een uitlating expliciet een religieuze groep bij naam moet noemen is het inconsistent met de wetsgeschiedenis waaruit blijkt dat in 'hybride' gevallen de strafbaarheid van uitingen over een religie bepaald dient te worden aan de hand van de vraag of een spreker heeft bedoeld een oordeel te vellen over het geloof of zijn aanhangers.

Bovendien lijkt het dan inconsistent dat de rechter soms uitlatingen die expliciet 'Marokkanen' of 'Moslims' als groep crimineel noemen op grond van hun Islamitisch geloof in eerste instantie als een strafbaar aanzetten tot discriminatie kwalificeert, maar vervolgens toch niet strafbaar acht onder verwijzing naar de noodzaak van een vrij publiek over Islam. Die conclusie is zonder enige nadere motivering onbegrijpelijk. Gaat het nu om feitelijke gedragingen van algemene bekendheid? Gaat het om het leggen van een mogelijk verband te bestaan tussen een religie en asociaal gedrag? Dienen alle leden dan bepaald gedrag te vertonen? Of gaat het alleen om het inschatten van bepaalde risico's? De vraag of dergelijke uitingen over Islam niet strafbaar zijn omdat een religie daarin wordt behandeld als een centraal kenmerk van de raciale of etnische identiteit van een groep lijkt in de Nederlandse jurisprudentie enigszins over het hoofd te worden gezien.

Het vereiste dat een uitlating 'onmiskenbaar over een groep' moet gaan geldt niet voor uitingen met betrekking tot ras. Dat is niet per definitie inconsistent. Nazipropaganda vormt een strafbare vorm van haatzaaien tegen Joden ook al verwijst het niet expliciet naar de Joodse bevolkingsgroep; associaties met het Nazidom kunnen als wezenlijk bedreigend voor Joden worden beschouwd omdat zij vanuit Nazi-perspectief worden bejegend. Maar de jurisprudentie lijkt wel inconsistent op het punt dat de ridiculisering, ontkenning of trivialisering van de Holocaust een strafbare groepsbelediging van Joden kan vormen omdat dergelijke uitlatingen 'de gevoelens van de groep kwetsen'. Waarom zou de wet dan niet ook de gevoelens van Moslims beschermen tegen kwetsende uitlatingen over de Islam? De rechter zal steeds de strafbaarheid van een uiting over de Holocaust of Islam aldus dienen te motiveren dat het de waardigheid van mensen aantast omdat het bestaat uit pertinent onjuiste uitspraken of waardeoordelen die voldoende feitelijke basis missen en onnodig grievend zijn.

Deze bijzondere bescherming van 'gekwetste gevoelens van een groep' is ontstaan in het civiel recht. De hate speech bans vormen wel een primaire leidraad voor het bepalen van civielrechtelijke aansprakelijkheid voor hate speech op grond van het onrechtmatige daad Artikel van 6:162 BW. Maar wanneer een uitlating niet onder een specifieke hate speech ban gekwalificeerd kan worden, kan die uiting toch onrechtmatig zijn in de zin van 6:162 BW op grond van 'zorgvuldigheidsnormen'. In principe kunnen de criteria voor strafrechtelijke en civielrechtelijke aansprakelijkheid voor hate speech dus verschillen en zullen uitlatingen eerder onrechtmatig dan strafbaar zijn. Maar in de praktijk verschillen de strafrechtelijke en civielrechtelijke grenzen aan hate speech niet veel. Zowel de strafrechter als de civiele rechter maakt, bij de toepassing van de wettelijke norm, een nadere belangenafweging met de uitingsvrijheid. Mogelijke verschillen tussen strafrecht ('opzet') en civiel recht ('zorgvuldigheid') worden tot op zekere mate verdisconteerd in deze belangenafweging of 'contextuele toetsing'. Vanuit het Franse perspectief van rechtszekerheid kan men echter stellen dat een uitlating alleen onrechtmatig mag zijn wanneer die uiting strafbaar is onder een specifiek uitingsdelict.

De Franse 'hybride' benadering kan ook een inspiratie vormen op het punt van de handhaving van de hate speech bans. In Nederland fungeert de overheid als enige bewaker van de openbare orde en heeft het Openbaar Ministerie het exclusieve recht om vervolgingen in te stellen op grond van de hate speech bans. In het geval het Openbaar Ministerie een zaak seponeert kunnen slachtoffers van hate speech wel een gerechtelijk bevel tot vervolging verkrijgen maar het Openbaar Ministerie kan vervolgens alsnog tot vrijspraak rekwireren. Een betere samenwerking en beter overleg tussen Openbaar Ministerie en antiracismeorganisaties ten aanzien van de vervolging van gevallen van hate speech zou dergelijke rechtszaken zonder tegenspraak kunnen voorkomen. In gevallen waarin het Openbaar Ministerie toch tot vrijspraak rekwireert dienen gevoegde civiele partijen de mogelijkheid te hebben zich uit te spreken over de interpretatie van de hate speech bans en hun toepassing op de uitlatingen in kwestie juist omdat diens onrechtmatigheid is gegeven met de strafbaarheid.

Uit de analyse van de juridische systemen blijkt dat elke systeem verschillend 'scoort' waar het de factoren van het analytisch kader betreft. Zo zou de Franse rechter bij de toepassing van de hate speech bans op concrete uitlatingen explicieter en op structurele wijze belang kunnen hechten aan het belang van het publiek debat. De Nederlandse wetgever zou juist de beschermde belangen en de reikwijdte van de hate speech bans kunnen expliciteren door ze beter in te bedden in de waarden van de constitutie. De jurisprudentie van het EHRM zou weer helderder onderscheid kunnen maken tussen de toetsing van beperkingen van racistische hate speech en van kritiek op een religie. Voor alle juridische systemen geldt dat voor de afbakening van vrije kritische opmerkingen met verboden hate speech meer onderscheid gemaakt kan worden tussen verschillende typen uitlatingen, i.e. feitelijke aantijgingen en waardeoordelen.

Op basis van het gehele onderzoek worden tot slot de volgende algemene aanbevelingen gedaan voor de bepaling van grenzen aan hate speech op grond van religie op consistente wijze:

- Het Franse concept van het 'délit d'opinion' kan een inspiratie vormen voor de idee dat een consistente norm gericht tegen een bepaalde vorm van hate speech zo precies mogelijk dient te bepalen welk typen uitlatingen het verbiedt en dient te reflecteren welke rechten en belangen het beoogt te beschermen. Op grond van het legaliteitsprincipe dienen beperkingen van hate speech strikt te worden uitgelegd en niet 'overbroad' te zijn.
- Hate speech bans kunnen uitlatingen verbieden op grond van een bepaalde mate van waarschijnlijkheid dat de uiting zal slagen in het aanzetten van anderen tot discriminatie en geweld tegen de target groep. Een dergelijk oorzakelijk verband kan meer of minder direct zijn, variërend van 'waarschijnlijk' tot 'geschikt' tot 'onmiddellijk'. Een consistente norm dient een punt te markeren ergens op deze glijdende schaal.
- Hate speech bans kunnen ook uitlatingen verbieden op de grond dat zij indruisen tegen de menselijke waardigheid. Dan dient een consistente norm duidelijk aan te geven wanneer een uiting de gelijke waardigheid van leden van de target groep daadwerkelijk *aantast*.
- Voor een consistente afbakening van – verboden vormen van hate speech tegen – personen die een bepaalde religie aanhangen met – toegestane kritiek op – religieuze overtuigingen en praktijken als zodanig, kan een eerste uitgangspunt zijn of een uiting helder een religieuze groep aanduidt.
- Een ander criterium om uitlatingen over personen die een religie aanhangen af te bakenen van uitlatingen over een religie als zodanig kan zijn of er sprake is van een 'intersectionaliteit tussen ras en religie', i.e. als een uiting de religieuze over-

tuigingen van leden van een groep behandelt als een centraal kenmerk van hun raciale of etnische identiteit.

- Om op consistente wijze een onderscheid te maken tussen vrije kritische uitlatingen en verboden hate speech op grond van religie, dient een norm nauwkeurig te differentiëren tussen feitelijke uitspraken en waardeoordelen. Pertinent onjuiste feitelijke aantijgingen tegen een bepaalde groep en sterk negatieve waardeoordelen, die een voldoende feitelijke basis missen of onnodig grieven zijn in principe niet te rechtvaardigen, ook indien zij worden geuit in het publiek debat.
- Om op consistente wijze een onderscheid te maken tussen stevige kritiek op de overheid en hate speech tegen bepaalde minderheden, dient een norm duidelijk te maken wanneer bijdragen aan het publiek debat de uiterste grenzen van de democratische rechtsstaat overschrijden. Hiervan is in ieder geval sprake wanneer een uiting gericht is op de vernietiging van de grondrechten van anderen. Gesteld kan worden dat ten minste een positieve verplichting voor de staat bestaat om dergelijke vormen van hate speech strafbaar te stellen en te vervolgen.
- Een consistente norm dient ook duidelijk te maken of burgers, die deelnemen aan het publiek en politiek debat, allen dezelfde mate van uitingsvrijheid hebben of dat bepaalde functies of posities speciale vrijheden of verantwoordelijkheden met zich meebrengen. De positie of functie van een politicus kan in ieder geval een contextuele factor vormen die de waardering van zijn opzet of de kwalificatie van zijn uiting als misbruik van recht beïnvloedt.
- Waar de wetgever beperkingen van hate speech *a priori* en *in abstracto* dient vast te stellen, dient de rechter de hate speech bans zoals door de wetgever gecreëerd *in concreto* toe te passen en daarbij expliciet rekening te houden met een aantal contextuele factoren en het recht op vrijheid van meningsuiting. De wetgever dient de uitingsdelicten zodanig te definiëren dat zij een consistente rechtspraak bevorderen en de rechter dwingen tot een robuuste motivering van haar beslissingen.
- Bestaande hate speech bans dienen effectief te worden gehandhaafd. Het openbaar ministerie dient een helder vervolgingsbeleid te voeren en de consistentie daarvan te kunnen uitleggen aan civil society. Waar het de uitleg van dit beleid aan slachtoffers van hate speech betreft, zouden antiracismeorganisaties en andere belangengroepen een rol kunnen spelen. Men zou zelfs een stap verder kunnen gaan en dergelijke organisaties een rol kunnen geven in de beslissing om gevallen van hate speech te vervolgen.

School of Human Rights Research Series

The School of Human Rights Research is a joint effort by human rights researchers in the Netherlands. Its central research theme is the nature and meaning of international standards in the field of human rights, their application and promotion in the national legal order, their interplay with national standards, and the international supervision of such application. The School of Human Rights Research Series only includes English titles that contribute to a better understanding of the different aspects of human rights.

For previous volumes in the series, please visit http://shr.intersentia.com.

Published titles within the Series:

62. Ramona Biholar, *Transforming Discriminatory Sex Roles and Gender Stereotyping: The implementation of Article 5(a) CEDAW for the realisation of women's right to be free from gender-based violence in Jamaica*
    ISBN 978-1-78068-167-2
63. Jasper Krommendijk,*The Domestic Impact and Effectiveness of the Process of State Reporting under UN Human Rights Treaties in the Netherlands, New Zealand and Finland. Paper-pushing or policy prompting?*
    ISBN 978-1-78068-244-0
64. Jennifer Anna Sellin, *Access to Medicines. The Interface between Patents and Human Rights. Does one size fit all?*
    ISBN 978-1-78068-247-1
65. Gustavo Arosemena Solorzano, *Rights, Scarcity, and Justice. An Analytical Inquiry into the Adjudication of the Welfare Aspects of Human Rights*
    ISBN 978-1-78068-275-4
66. Etienne Ruvebana, *Prevention of Genocide under International Law. An analysis of the obligations of states and the United Nations to prevent genocide at the primary, secondary and tertiary levels*
    ISBN 978-1-78068-273-0
67. Evgeni Moyakine, *The Privatized Art of War. Private Military and Security Companies and State Responsibility for Their Unlawful Conduct in Conflict Areas*
    ISBN 978-1-78068-281-5